MW01255835

Abnormal Psychology:

A Scientist-Practioner Approach

FOURTH EDITION

Deborah C. Beidel
University of Central Florida

Cynthia M. Bulik
University of North Carolina at Chapel Hill
Karolinska Institutet, Stockholm, Sweden

Melinda A. Stanley
Baylor College of Medicine

330 Hudson Street, NY, NY 10013

To our parents

Anthony and Jean Casamassa

Frank and Marie Bulik

Pat and Bob Stanley

Thank you for teaching us the value of education and for providing the love and encouragement that allow us to achieve our dreams.

Portfolio Manager: Amber Chow
Content Producer: Cecilia Turner
Content Developer: Thomas Finn
Portfolio Manager Assistant: Stephany Harrington
Product Marketer: Lindsey Prudhomme Gill
Content Producer Manager: Amber Mackey
Content Development Manager: Sharon Greary
Content Developer, Learning Tools: Christopher Fegan
Art/Designer: Blair Brown
Digital Producer: Pam Weldin/Lindsay Verge
Full-Service Project Manager: Gina Linko/Integra
Compositor: Integra
Printer/Binder: LSC Communications
Cover Printer: LSC Communications
Cover Design: Lumina Datamatics

Acknowledgments of third party content appear pages 640, which constitutes an extension of this copyright page.

Library of Congress Cataloging-in-Publication Data

Names: Beidel, Deborah C., author. | Bulik, Cynthia M., author. | Stanley, M. A. (Melinda Anne) author.
Title: Abnormal psychology / Deborah C. Beidel, University of Central Florida, Cynthia M. Bulik, University of North Carolina at Chapel Hill, Melinda A. Stanley, Baylor College of Medicine.
Description: 4th edition. | Hoboken, NJ: Pearson, [2016] | Includes bibliographical references and indexes.
Identifiers: LCCN 2016025559 | ISBN 9780134238944 (alk. paper) | ISBN 013423894X
Subjects: LCSH: Psychology, Pathological.
Classification: LCC RC454 .B428 2016 | DDC 616.89—dc23
LC record available at https://lccn.loc.gov/2016025559

1 2019

Student Edition
ISBN-10: 0-13-423894-X
ISBN-13: 978-0-13-423894-4

Books à la Carte
ISBN-10: 0-13-423888-5
ISBN-13: 978-0-13-423888-3

Brief Contents

Contents

Preface

As we prepare the fourth edition of this textbook, we reflect on the positive response to the previous editions, and we are pleased to find that our scientist–practitioner approach still resonates with both students and professors. Abnormal psychology remains one of the most popular courses among undergraduate students as national and world events impel us to advance our understanding of human behavior and the forces that influence it. What drives someone to take a gun and shoot a member of the U.S. Congress? How could a celebrity, who seemingly has everything—wealth, family, fame—shoplift a $50 jewelry item? There are no easy answers to these questions, and in fact, simplistic answers based on fraudulent science, such as "the measles vaccine causes autism," are harmful both to the public who believes in and acts on the false information and the scientists who spend their time carefully seeking empirically based answers.

The fourth edition of this textbook is another opportunity for students to see science in action. Based on the diagnostic schemas of the *Diagnostic and Statistical Manual of Mental Disorders*, Fifth Edition (DSM-5), students are exposed to the evolving nature of our catalog of psychological disorders, as research sheds new light on syndromes and forces scientists and clinicians to grapple with disparate data sets and to work together to produce a scientifically accurate and clinically meaningful system for understanding and communicating about abnormal behavior. Because the DSM-5 is still relatively new, there are some areas of abnormal behavior where the research has not yet caught up to the new diagnostic criteria. This is particularly relevant in chapters where revisions to the diagnoses were extensive. The new criteria have been adopted; however, the epidemiological data for the new disorders are not available—researchers simply have not had time to conduct studies using the new criteria. In those instances, we rely on the published data based on the DSM-IV categories, while giving appropriate caveats to help bridge the transition to the DSM-5 criteria.

Although our diagnostic criteria evolve, understanding human behavior requires integration of brain *and* behavior and includes data from scientists *and* insights from clinicians and patients. As in the first three editions, a scientist–practitioner approach integrates biological data with research from social and behavioral sciences to foster the perspective that abnormal behavior is complex and subject to many different forces. Furthermore, these variables often interact reciprocally. Psychotherapy was built in part on the assumption that behavior could be changed by changing the environment, but science has revealed that environmental factors can also change the brain. Scientific advances in molecular genetics have expanded our understanding of how genes influence behavior. Virtual reality treatment systems have provided new insights, raised new questions, and unlocked new areas of exploration. As this fourth edition illustrates, we remain firm in our conviction that the integration of leading-edge biological and behavioral research, known as the *translational approach*, or *from cell to society*, is needed to advance the study of abnormal psychology. As in previous editions, we reach beyond the old clichés of nature or nurture, clinician or scientist, genes or environment, and challenge the next generation of psychologists and students to embrace the complexity inherent in replacing these historical "ors" with contemporary "ands."

What's New in the Fourth Edition

- **A completely new chapter on obsessive-compulsive and impulse control disorders:** Integrating attention disorders characterized by repetitive behaviors, including obsessive-compulsive disorder (OCD), OC related disorders (trichotillomania, body dysmorphic disorder, hoarding disorder, excoriation disorder) and impuslve control disorders (pyromania, kleptomania).
- **Coverage of disorders expanded to include the following, based on their inclusion in DSM-5:** premenstrual dysphoric disorder, binge-eating disorder, illness anxiety disorder, gender dysphoria, autism spectrum disorder, substance use disorder, compulsive gambling added to addiction and related disorders, and others.
- **New and updated content throughout, including new topics for these special features:** "Real People, Real Disorders," "Examining the Evidence," "Research Hot Topic," and "Real Science: Real Life."
- **Current research:** Hundreds of new research citations throughout reflect the ever-advancing field of abnormal psychology.
- **Additional emphasis and in-depth analysis of ethics and responsibility** in the Revel version of this text.
- **New videos** including coverage of OCD and trichotillomania.

The Scientist–Practitioner Approach

We subtitled this book *A Scientist–Practitioner Approach* because understanding abnormal psychology rests on knowledge generated through scientific studies and clinical practice. Many psychologists are trained in the scientist–practitioner model and adhere to it to some degree in their professional work. We live and breathe this model. In addition to our roles as teachers at the undergraduate, graduate, and postdoctoral levels, we are all active clinical researchers and clinical practitioners. However, the scientist–practitioner model means more than just having multiple roles; it is a philosophy that guides all of the psychologist's activities. Those who are familiar with the model know this quote well: "Scientist-practitioners embody a research orientation in their practice and a practice relevance in their research" (Belar & Perry, 1992). This philosophy reflects our guiding principles, and we wrote this text to emphasize this rich blend of science and practice. Because we are scientist–practitioners, all of the cases described throughout this text are drawn from our own practices with the exception of a few quotations and newspaper stories designed to highlight a specific point. We have endeavored to "bring to life" the nature of these conditions by providing vivid clinical descriptions. In addition to the clinical material that opens each chapter and the short clinical descriptions that are used liberally throughout each chapter, a fully integrated case study drawn from one of our practices is presented at the end of each chapter, again illustrating the interplay of biological, psychosocial, and emotional factors. Of course, details have been changed and some cases may represent composites in order to protect the privacy of those who have shared their life stories with us throughout our careers.

The goal of our textbook is to avoid a dense review of the scientific literature but to maintain a strong scientific focus. Similarly, we wanted to avoid "pop" psychology, an overly popularized approach that we believe presents easy answers that do not truly reflect the essence of psychological disorders. Having now used the book with our own undergraduate classes, we find that students respond positively to material and features that make these conditions more understandable and vivid. Our goal is to "put a face" on these sometimes perplexing and unfamiliar conditions by using rich clinical material such as vignettes, case histories, personal accounts, and the feature "Real People, Real Disorders." We hope that these illustrations will entice students to learn more about abnormal psychology while acquiring the important concepts. Thus, although the book represents leading-edge science, our ultimate goal is to portray the human face of these conditions.

A Developmental Trajectory

It has become increasingly clear that many types of abnormal behaviors either begin in childhood or have childhood precursors. Similarly, without treatment, most disorders do not merely disappear with advancing age, and in fact, new disorders may emerge. Quite simply, as we grow, mature, and age, our physical and cognitive capacities affect how symptoms are expressed. Without this developmental perspective, it is easy to overlook behaviors that indicate the presence of a specific disorder at a particular phase of life. We are proud that we embraced a developmental perspective before its introduction in the DSM-5. Now that DSM-5 has shifted to a developmental focus, students and instructors will find that certain disorders are not in the same chapters as in previous editions. In each chapter where we discuss psychological disorders, we also include a section called "Developmental Considerations," which highlights what is known about the developmental trajectory of each condition. Failure to understand the various manifestations of a disorder means that theories of etiology may be incorrect or incomplete and that interventions may be inappropriately applied.

Sex, Race, and Ethnicity

In each chapter, we describe the current literature regarding the effect of sex, race, or ethnicity on a disorder's clinical presentation, etiology, and treatment. We carefully considered the terms used in the text to refer to these concepts. Indeed, the terms used to refer to sex, gender, race, and ethnicity are continually evolving, and the words that we use vary throughout the text. When we describe a particular study, we retain the labels that were used in the publication (e.g., Afro-Caribbean, Caucasian, Pacific Islander). To create some consistency throughout the text, when we discuss general issues regarding race and ethnicity, we use standard terms (e.g., *whites, African Americans, Hispanics*). Although we are admittedly uncomfortable with calling groups by any labels, whether they refer to race, ethnicity, or diagnosis (e.g., *blacks, whites, schizophrenics*), for clarity of presentation and parsimony in the case of race and ethnicity, we opted for these categorical labels rather than the more cumbersome "individuals of European-American ancestry" approach. Throughout the book, however, we have not labeled individuals who have psychological disorders by their diagnosis because people are far more rich and complex than any diagnostic label could ever capture. Moreover, referring to a patient or patient group by a diagnostic label (e.g., *bulimics, depressives, schizophrenics*) is fundamentally disrespectful. People have disorders, but their disorders do not define them.

Ethics and Responsibility

We continue our feature titled "Ethics and Responsibility," with additional in-depth ethical situations and analysis in Revel. The discussion of ethics and responsibility varies with respect to the individual chapter, but in each case, we have attempted to select a topic that is timely and illustrates how psychologists consider the impact of their behavior on those with whom they work and on society in general. We hope that this feature will generate class discussion and impress on students the impact of one's behavior upon others.

Clinical Features

Consistent with our belief that the clinical richness of this text will bring the subject matter to life, each chapter begins with a clinical vignette that introduces and illustrates the topic of the chapter. These descriptions are not extensive case studies but provide the reader a global "feel" for each disorder. Additionally, short case vignettes are used liberally throughout the text to illustrate specific clinical elements. Another important clinical element is the "Dimensions of Behavior: From Adaptive to Maladaptive," in which we illustrate the dimensionality of human emotions (such as elation or mania). We include these descriptions in each chapter devoted to an area of abnormal behavior to emphasize that psychological disorders are not simply the presence of emotions or specific behaviors but whether the emotions or behaviors create distress or impair daily functioning.

Each chapter discussion concludes with a case study titled "Real Science, Real Life," a clinical presentation, assessment, and treatment of a patient with a particular disorder, again drawn from our own clinical files. Each concluding case study illustrates much of the material covered in the chapter and uses the scientist–practitioner approach to understanding, assessing, and treating the disorder. Furthermore, this concluding case study demonstrates how the clinician considers biological, psychological, environmental, and cultural factors to understand the patient's clinical presentation. Finally, we describe the treatment program and outcome, highlighting how all of the factors are addressed in treatment. In Revel, we take this engagement even further with interactive journal prompts for student participation. Through this process, the case study allows the student to view firsthand the scientist–practitioner approach to abnormal behavior, dispelling myths often propagated through the media about how psychologists think, work, and act.

Special Features

We draw the reader's attention to three specific features that appear in each chapter. The first, "Examining the Evidence," presents a current controversy related to one of the disorders in the chapter. However, we do not simply present the material; rather, to be consistent with the scientist–practitioner focus, we present both sides of the controversy and lead students through the data, allowing them to draw their own conclusions. Thus, "Examining the Evidence" features do not just present material but also foster critical thinking skills about issues in abnormal psychology. By considering both sides of the issues, students will become savvy consumers of scientific literature.

The second feature is "Research Hot Topic," which presents topical, leading-edge research at the time of publication. Consistent with the focus of this text, the "Research Hot Topic" features illustrate how science informs our understanding of human behavior in a manner that is engaging to students (e.g., "Virtual Reality Therapy for the Treatment of Anxiety Disorders"). As teachers and researchers who open our clinical research centers to undergraduate students, we have seen their excitement as they participate in the research enterprise.

The third feature, "Real People, Real Disorders," presents a popular figure who has suffered from a condition discussed in the chapter. Many people, including undergraduate students, suffer from these disorders, and they often feel that they are alone or "weird." We break down the stereotypes that many undergraduate students have about people with psychological disorders. Using well-known figures to humanize these conditions allows students to connect with the material on an emotional as well as an intellectual level.

Learning Objective Summaries and Critical Thinking Questions

Finally, we would like to draw the reader's attention to the "Learning Objective Summaries" and "Critical Thinking Questions" that are found throughout the chapter. The "Learning Objective Summaries" provide quick reviews at the end of chapter sections, allowing students to be sure that they have mastered the material before proceeding to the next section. Instructors can use the "Learning Objective Summaries" and "Critical Thinking Questions" to challenge students to think "outside the box" and critically examine the material presented within that section.

Learning Tools

REVEL™

Experience Designed for the Way Today's Students Read, Think, and Learn

When students are engaged deeply, they learn more effectively and perform better in their courses. This simple fact inspired the creation of REVEL: an immersive learning experience designed for the way today's students read, think, and learn. Built in collaboration with educators and students nationwide, REVEL is the newest, fully digital way to deliver respected Pearson content.

REVEL enlivens course content with media interactives and assessments—integrated directly within the authors' narrative—that provide opportunities for students to read about and practice course material in tandem. This immersive experience boosts student engagement, which leads to better understanding of concepts and improved performance throughout the course.

Learn more about REVEL

http://www.pearsonhighered.com/revel/

The REVEL Edition (ISBN: 0134320387) includes integrated videos and media content throughout, allowing students to explore topics more deeply at the point of relevancy.

Watch

Revel also offers the ability for students to assess their content mastery by taking multiple-choice quizzes that offer instant feedback and by participating in a variety of writing assignments such as peer-reviewed questions and auto-graded assignments.

MyPsychLab for Abnormal Psychology

MyPsychLab is an online homework, tutorial, and assessment program that truly engages students in learning. It helps students better prepare for class, quizzes, and exams—resulting in better performance in the course. It provides educators a dynamic set of tools for gauging individual and class performance. To order the fourth edition with MyPsychLab, use ISBN 0134624297.

Supplemental Teaching Materials

Speaking Out: Interviews with People Who Struggle with Psychological Disorders. This set of video segments allows students to see firsthand accounts of patients with various disorders. The interviews were conducted by licensed clinicians and range in length from 8 to 25 minutes. Disorders include major depressive disorder, obsessive-compulsive disorder, anorexia nervosa, PTSD, alcoholism, schizophrenia, autism, ADHD, bipolar disorder, social phobia, hypochondriasis, borderline personality disorder, and adjustment to physical illness. These video segments are available on DVD or through MyPsychLab.

Volume 1: ISBN 0-13-193332-9
Volume 2: ISBN 0-13-600303-6
Volume 3: ISBN 0-13-230891-6

Instructor's Manual (ISBN: 013455695X). A comprehensive tool for class preparation and management, each chapter includes a chapter-at-a-glance overview; key terms; teaching objectives; a detailed chapter outline including lecture starters, demonstrations and activities, and handouts; a list of references, films and videos, and web resources; and a sample syllabus. Available for download on the Instructor's Resource Center at www.pearsonhighered.com.

Test Bank (ISBN: 0134556968). The Test Bank has been rigorously developed, reviewed, and checked for accuracy to ensure the quality of both the questions and the answers. It includes fully referenced multiple-choice, true/false, and concise essay questions. Each question is accompanied by a page reference, difficulty level, skill type (factual, conceptual, or applied), topic, and a correct answer. Available for download on the Instructor's Resource Center at www.pearsonhighered.com.

MyTest (ISBN: 0134556976). A powerful assessment-generation program that helps instructors easily create and print quizzes and exams. Questions and tests can be authored online, allowing instructors ultimate flexibility and the ability to efficiently manage assessments anytime, anywhere. Instructors can easily access existing questions and edit, create, and store questions using a simple drag-and drop technique and Word-like controls. Data on each question provide information on difficulty level and the page number of corresponding text discussion. For more information, go to www.PearsonMyTest.com.

Lecture PowerPoint Slides (ISBN: 0134556844). The PowerPoint slides provide an active format for presenting concepts from each chapter and feature relevant figures and tables from the text. Available for download on the Instructor's Resource Center at www.pearsonhighered.com.

Enhanced Lecture PowerPoint Slides with Embedded Videos (ISBN: 0134631935). The lecture PowerPoint slides have been embedded with video, enabling instructors to show videos within the context of their lecture. No Internet connection is required to play videos. Available for download on the Instructor's Resource Center at www.pearsonhighered.com.

PowerPoint Slides for Photos, Figures, and Tables (ISBN: 0134631927). These slides contain only the photos, figures, and line art from the textbook. Available for download on the Instructor's Resource Center at www.pearsonhighered.com.

Acknowledgments

As we wrote in the first edition, this book began with the vision of our mentor and friend, Samuel M. Turner, Ph.D. He was the one who believed that the book could be written, convinced us to write it with him, and contributed substantially to the initial book prospectus. The success of the first edition surprised us, but we often felt that Sam would have just looked at us and said, "I told you so." We hope this edition continues to honor him and his lasting influence on us.

We met Sam and each other more than 30 years ago when the three of us were in various stages of graduate training under his tutelage at Western Psychiatric Institute and Clinic (WPIC), University of Pittsburgh School of Medicine. We want to thank David Kupfer, M.D., who was Director of Research at WPIC at that time, for creating the cross-disciplinary and fertile research environment that allowed us to learn and grow. We are also grateful to the other scientist–practitioners who mentored us at various stages of our undergraduate and graduate careers: Alan Bellack, Bob D'Agostino, John Harvey, Michel Hersen, Stephen Hinshaw, Alan Kazdin, and Sheldon Korchin.

Second, we want to thank our editor, Amber Chow, for her enthusiasm, support, and good humor. Her understanding of all of our other time commitments kept this revision on time and (almost) stress free. We thank Thomas Finn, our developmental editor, who helped make our ideas and vision "work" within the confines of the world of publishing, and Gina Linko for her copyediting assistance.

Third, a big thank you goes to our students, colleagues, and friends who listened endlessly, smiled supportively, and waited patiently as we said once again "next month will be easier."

Fourth, we thank our patients and their families whose life journeys or bumps along life's road we have shared. Good psychologists never stop learning. Each new clinical experience adds to our knowledge and understanding of the illnesses we seek to treat. We thank our patients and families for sharing their struggles and their successes with us and for the unique opportunity to learn from their experience. It is an honor and a privilege to have worked with each of you.

Fifth, our thanks go to our spouses, Ed Beidel, Patrick Sullivan, and Bill Ehrenstrom, children (Brendan, Emily, Natalie, Brendan, and Jacob), and families who celebrate the publication of each edition with us and smile understandingly when we tell them we have to start on the next edition.

Sixth, special thanks to Emily Bulik-Sullivan, Jose Cortes, Susan Kleiman, Diane Mentrikoski, Anette Ovalle, and Belinda Pennington for assistance with updating the fourth edition and creative content.

As authors, each of us feels enormous gratitude to our coauthors for their tireless work, unending support and friendship, and dedication to this project. Abnormal psychology is a broad topic, requiring ever-increasing specialization. Having colleagues who share an orientation but possess distinct areas of expertise represents a rare and joyful collaborative experience.

Finally, we hope the students and instructors who used the previous three editions and who will use this new text experience the joy and wonder that comes with learning about the challenging and intriguing topic of abnormal psychology. We are passionate about our science and compassionate with our patients. We are also dedicated educators. As such, we encourage you to contact us with comments, questions, or suggestions on how to improve this book. No textbook is perfect, but with your help, we will continue to strive for that goal.

Text and Content Reviewers

We would like to thank the following colleagues who reviewed this text at various stages and gave us a great many helpful suggestions: Bethann Bierer, Metropolitan State College of Denver; James Clopton, Texas Technical University; Bryan Cochran, University of Montana; Andrew Corso, University of Pennsylvania; Joseph Davis, California State University System; Diane Gooding, University of Wisconsin, Madison; Claudine Harris, Los Angeles Mission College; Gregory Harris, Polk State College; Jim Haugh, Rowan University; Jeffrey Helms, Kennesaw State University; Zoe Heyman, Shasta College; Rob Hoff, Mercyhurst College; Robert Intrieri, Western Illinois University; Steve Jenkins, Wagner College; Jennifer Katz, SUNY College at Geneseo; Lynne Kemen, Hunter College; Jennifer Langhinrichsen-Rohling, University of South Alabama; Robert Lawyer, Delgado Community College; Marvin Lee, Tennessee State University; Barbara Lewis, University of West Florida; Freda Liu, Arizona State University; Joseph Lowman, University of North Carolina at Chapel Hill; Kristelle Miller, University of Minnesota Duluth; Michelle Moon, California State University, Channel Islands; Anny Mueller, Southwestern Oregon Community College; Tess Neal, Arizona State University; Edward O'Brien, Marywood University; Jason Parker, Old Dominion University; Lauren Polvere, Concordia University (full time) and Clinton Community College (adjunct); Karen Rhines, Northampton Community College; Grace Ribaudo, Brooklyn College; Rachel Schmale, North Park University; Marianne Shablousky, Community College of Allegheny County; Mary Shelton, Tennessee State University; Nancy Simpson, Trident Technical College; George Spilich, Washington College; Mary Starke, Ramapo College of NJ; David Steitz, Nazareth College; Lynda Szymanski, St. Catherine University; Melissa Terlecki, Cabrini College; David Topor, Harvard Medical School.

Focus Group Participants

Thank you to the following professors for participating in a focus group: David Crystal, Georgetown University; Victoria Lee, Howard University; Jeffrey J. Pedroza, Santa Ana College; Grace Ribaudo, Brooklyn College; Brendan Rich, Catholic University of America; Alan Roberts, Indiana University; David Rollock, Purdue University; David Topor, Harvard Medical School.

About the Authors

DEBORAH C. BEIDEL received her B.A. from the Pennsylvania State University and her M.S. and Ph.D. from the University of Pittsburgh, completing her predoctoral internship and postdoctoral fellowship at Western Psychiatric Institute and Clinic. At the University of Central Florida, she is Trustee Chair and Pegasus Professor of Psychology and Medical Education, Associate Chair for Research, and the Director of UCF RESTORES, a clinical research center dedicated to the study of anxiety and posttraumatic stress disorders through research, treatment and education. Previously, she was on the faculty at the University of Pittsburgh, Medical University of South Carolina, University of Maryland-College Park, and Penn State College of Medicine-Hershey Medical Center. Currently, she holds American Board of Professional Psychology (ABPP) Diplomates in Clinical Psychology and Behavioral Psychology and is a Fellow of the American Psychological Association, the American Psychopathological Association, and the Association for Psychological Science. She is past Chair of the Council for University Directors in Clinical Psychology (CUDCP), a past Chair of the American Psychological Association's Committee on Accreditation, the 1990 recipient of the Association for Advancement of Behavior Therapy's New Researcher Award, and the 2007 recipient of the Samuel M. Turner Clinical Researcher Award from the American Psychological Association. While at the University of Pittsburgh, Dr. Beidel was twice awarded the "Apple for the Teacher Citation" by her students for outstanding classroom teaching. In 1995, she was the recipient of the Distinguished Educator Award from the Association of Medical School Psychologists. She was editor in chief of the *Journal of Anxiety Disorders* and author of more than 250 scientific publications, including journal articles, book chapters, and books, including *Childhood Anxiety Disorders: A Guide to Research and Treatment* and *Shy Children, Phobic Adults: The Nature and Treatment of Social Anxiety Disorder*. Her academic, research, and clinical interests focus on child, adolescent, and adult anxiety disorders, including their etiology, psychopathology, and behavioral interventions. Her research is characterized by a developmental focus and includes high-risk and longitudinal designs, psychophysiological assessment, treatment development, and treatment outcome. She is the recipient of numerous grants from the Department of Defense, the National Institute of Mental Health, and the Autism Speaks Foundation. At the University of Central Florida, she teaches abnormal psychology at both the undergraduate and graduate level and is currently establishing a new multidisciplinary center devoted to using technology to enhance and disseminate empirically supported treatments for anxiety and stress- and trauma-related disorders. She is also a wife, an active participant in community service organizations, and a rescuer/adopter of shelter cats and dogs.

CYNTHIA M. BULIK is the Distinguished Professor of Eating Disorders in the Department of Psychiatry in the School of Medicine at the University of North Carolina at Chapel Hill, where she is also Professor of Nutrition in the Gillings School of Global Public Health, Founding Director of the UNC Center of Excellence for Eating Disorders, and Co-Director of the UNC Center for Psychiatric Genomics. She is also Professor of Medical Epidemiology and Biostatistics at Karolinska Institutet in Stockholm, Sweden, where she directs the Center for Eating Disorders Innovation. A clinical psychologist by training, Dr. Bulik has been conducting research and treating individuals with eating disorders since 1982. She received her B.A. from the University of Notre Dame and her M.A. and Ph.D. from the University of California, Berkeley. She completed internships and postdoctoral fellowships at the Western Psychiatric Institute and Clinic in Pittsburgh, Pennsylvania. She developed outpatient, partial hospitalization, and inpatient services for eating disorders both in New Zealand and the United States. Her research has included treatment, basic science, epidemiological, twin, and molecular genetic studies of eating disorders and body weight regulation. She is the Director of the first NIMH-sponsored Post-Doctoral Training Program in Eating Disorders. She has active research collaborations in 21 countries around the world. Dr. Bulik has written more than 500 scientific papers and chapters on eating disorders and is author of the books *Eating Disorders: Detection and Treatment* (Dunmore), *Runaway Eating: The 8 Point Plan to Conquer Adult Food and Weight Obsessions* (Rodale), *Crave: Why You Binge Eat and How to Stop, The Woman in the Mirror: How to Stop Confusing What You Look Like with Who You Are, Midlife Eating Disorders: Your Journey to Recovery* (Walker), and *Binge Control: A Compact Recovery Guide.* She is a recipient of the Eating Disorders Coalition Research Award, the Hulka Innovators Award, the Academy for Eating Disorders Leadership Award for Research, the Price Family National Eating Disorders Association Research Award, the Carolina Women's Center Women's Advocacy Award, the Women's Leadership Council Faculty-to-Faculty Mentorship Award, and the Academy for Eating Disorders Meehan-Hartley Advocacy Award. She is a past President of the Academy for Eating Disorders, past

Vice-President of the Eating Disorders Coalition, and past Associate Editor of the *International Journal of Eating Disorders*. Dr. Bulik holds the first endowed professorship in eating disorders in the United States. She balances her academic life by being happily married, a mother of three, and a competitive ice dancer and ballroom dancer.

MELINDA A. STANLEY is Professor and Head of the Division of Psychology in the Menninger Department of Psychiatry and Behavioral Sciences at Baylor College of Medicine. She holds the McIngvale Family Chair in Obsessive Compulsive Disorder Research and a secondary appointment as Professor in the Department of Medicine. Dr. Stanley is a clinical psychologist and senior mental health services researcher within the Health Services Research and Development Center of Innovation, Michael E. DeBakey Veterans Affairs Medical Center, Houston, and an affiliate investigator for the South Central Mental Illness Research, Education, and Clinical Center (MIRECC). Before joining the faculty at Baylor, she was Professor of Psychiatry at the University of Texas Health Science Center at Houston, where she served as Director of the Psychology Internship program. Dr. Stanley completed an internship and postdoctoral fellowship at Western Psychiatric Institute and Clinic, University of Pittsburgh School of Medicine. She received a Ph.D. from Texas Tech University, an M.A. from Princeton University, and a B.A. from Gettysburg College, where she was a Phi Beta Kappa and summa cum laude graduate. Dr. Stanley's research interests involve the identification and treatment of anxiety and depressive disorders in older adults. Her current focus is on expanding the reach of services for older people into primary care and underserved communities where mental health needs of older people often remain unrecognized and undertreated. In these settings, the content and delivery of care require modifications to meet cultural, cognitive, sensory, and logistic barriers. Some of Dr. Stanley's work in this domain includes the integration of religion and spirituality into therapy to enhance engagement in care for traditionally underserved groups. Dr. Stanley and her colleagues have been awarded continuous funding from the National Institute of Mental Health (NIMH) for 19 years to support her research in late-life anxiety. In 2008, Dr. Stanley received the Excellence in Research Award from the South Central MIRECC. In 2009, she received the MIRECC Excellence in Research Education Award. She has received numerous teaching awards and has served as mentor for nine junior faculty career development awards. Dr. Stanley is a Fellow of the American Psychological Association, and she has served as a regular reviewer of NIMH grants. She is the author of more than 200 scientific publications, including journal articles, book chapters, and books. Dr. Stanley's other roles in life include wife, mother, dog rescue volunteer, and Sunday School teacher.

Chapter 1

Abnormal Psychology: Historical and Modern Perspectives

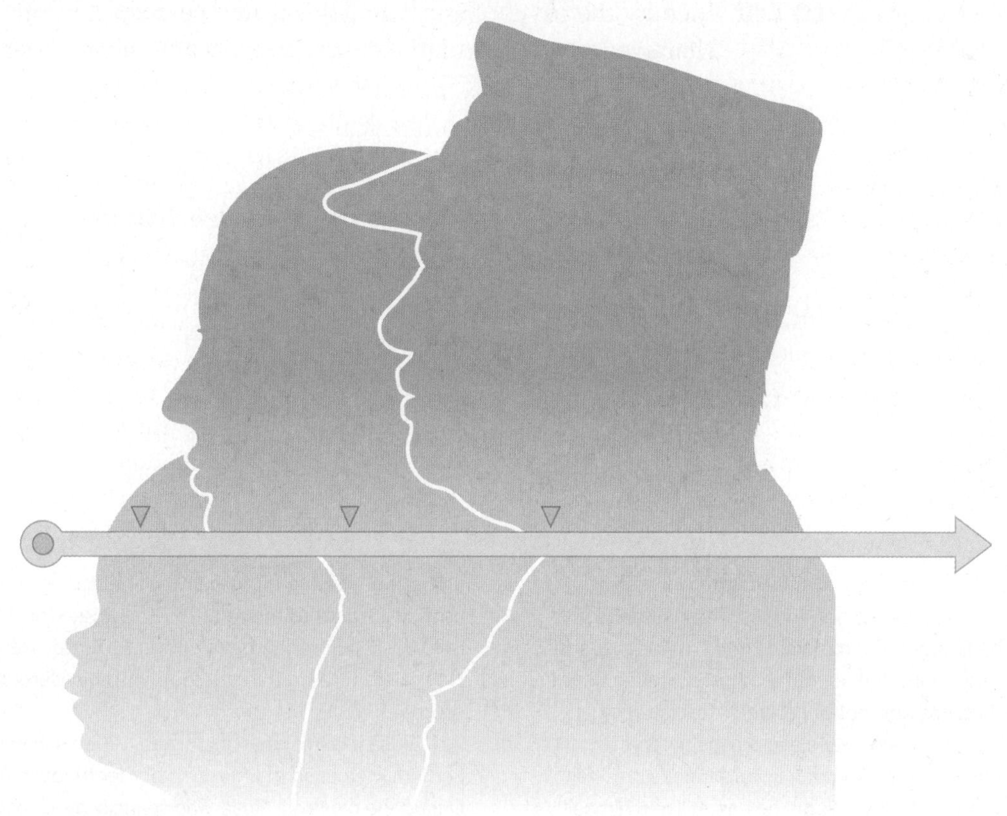

Chapter Learning Objectives

Normal vs. Abnormal Behavior	**LO 1.1**	Understand why simply being different does not mean abnormality.
	LO 1.2	Understand why simply behaving differently is not the same as behaving abnormally.
	LO 1.3	Understand why simply behaving dangerously does not always equal abnormality.
	LO 1.4	Explain the difference between behaviors that are different, deviant, dangerous, and dysfunctional.
	LO 1.5	Identify at least two factors that need to be considered when determining whether a behavior is abnormal.
The History of Abnormal Behavior and Its Treatment	**LO 1.6**	Discuss ancient spiritual and biological theories of the origins of abnormal behavior.

LO 1.7 Discuss spiritual, biological, and environmental theories of the origins of abnormal behavior in classical Greek and Roman periods.

LO 1.8 Discuss the spiritual, biological, and environmental theories of the origins of abnormal behavior from the Middle Ages to the Renaissance.

LO 1.9 Discuss the spiritual, biological, psychological, and sociocultural theories of the origins of abnormal behavior in the nineteenth century.

LO 1.10 Identify the psychological, biological, and sociocultural models that characterize the twentieth-century models of abnormal behavior.

Current Views of Abnormal Behavior and Treatment

LO 1.11 Identify at least two biological mechanisms that are considered to play a role in the onset of abnormal behavior.

LO 1.12 Identify at least two psychological models that may account for the development of abnormal behavior.

LO 1.13 Explain the sociocultural mode of behavior and how it differs from the biological and psychological models.

LO 1.14 Explain how the biopsychosocial model accounts for the limitations in the three unidimensional models (biological, psychological, sociocultural).

Steve was a member of the U.S. Marine Corps who served during the Vietnam War. One night, the Viet Cong attacked his squad. During the firefight, the marine next to him lost his arm. Steve got his buddy to the medic, but the horrific image never left him. He felt helpless and out of control. After returning from Vietnam, Steve had difficulty sleeping, lost interest in his hobbies, isolated himself from family and friends, and felt helpless and sad. Even 45 years later, he can still see himself in the rice paddy, watching in horror as the grenade hits his friend, amputating his arm. Every night he wakes in yet another cold sweat and with a racing heart—unable to breathe as the nightmare occurs again.

Malcom is 9 years old. He lived in New Orleans with his family. One day Hurricane Katrina ripped through town. Malcom's family thought they were safe—the floodwalls would protect them. But they were wrong. Trapped in their house, they escaped to the attic. Luckily, his father grabbed an axe and cut a hole through the roof. After 8 hours, soaking wet and hungry, they were rescued by a helicopter. They now live in another state. But Malcom has had difficulties adjusting. He has nightmares about being trapped on the roof. He wants to move to "Iowa—they don't have hurricanes in Iowa." His grades have slipped; he refuses to go to school. He insists that he has to sleep with his parents or his older brother.

Rosa is a freshman in college. When she was 6 years old, her family crossed the Mexican border to reach the United States. During the crossing, Rosa was sexually molested by the *coyote*—the man who helped the family navigate the border crossing. Her family settled in New York, but a year later, both parents, who were working as janitorial staff inside the World Trade Center, were killed in the 9/11 attack. Rosa went to live with her aunt, who assisted her in obtaining U.S. citizenship. Rosa grew up as a shy and very intelligent person. Her transition to college was difficult. It was hard to be separated from her aunt. She has difficulty concentrating and has started to miss classes when feeling depressed and anxious. She has trouble getting out of bed. Rosa gets panicky feelings and has premonitions that something bad might happen to her aunt. At times, she abruptly runs out of classes to check on her.

The physical, cognitive, and behavioral symptoms that Steve, Malcom, and Rosa displayed represent common mental health problems. These behaviors are considered abnormal because most people do not run out of class to check on someone, and they sleep more than 4 hours a night. Most children do not cry when they hear a helicopter. Although often unrecognized, psychological disorders exist in substantial numbers of people across all ages, races, ethnic groups, and cultures and in both sexes. Furthermore, they cause great suffering and impair academic, occupational, and social functioning.

Defining abnormality is challenging because behaviors must be considered in context. For example:

> Donna and Matthew were very much in love. They had been married for 25 years and often remarked that they were not just husband and wife but also best friends. Then Matthew died suddenly, and Donna felt overwhelming sadness. She was unable to eat, cried uncontrollably at times, and started to isolate herself from others. Her usually vivacious personality disappeared.

When a loved one dies, feelings of grief and sadness are common, even expected. Donna's reaction at her husband's death would not be considered abnormal; rather, its *absence* at such a time might be considered abnormal. A theme throughout this book is that *abnormal behavior must always be considered in context.*

Normal vs. Abnormal Behavior

Sometimes it is fairly easy to identify behavior as abnormal, as when someone is still deeply troubled by events that happened 45 years ago or is feeling so hopeless that he or she cannot get out of bed. But sometimes identifying behavior as abnormal is not clear-cut. Put simply, *abnormal* means "away from normal," but that is a circular definition. By this standard, normal becomes the statistical average and any deviation becomes "abnormal." For example, if the average weight for a woman living in the United States is 140 pounds, then women who weigh less than 100 pounds or more than 250 pounds deviate significantly from the average. Their weight would be considered abnormally low or high. For abnormal psychology, defining abnormal behavior as merely being away from normal assumes that deviations on both sides of average are negative and in need of alteration or intervention. This assumption is often incorrect. Specifically, we must first ask whether simply being different is abnormal.

Is Being Different Abnormal?

LO 1.1 Understand why simply being different does not mean abnormality.

Many people deviate from the average in some way. LeBron James is 6 feet 8 inches tall and weighs 262 pounds—far above average in both height and weight. However, his deviant stature does not affect him negatively. To the contrary, he is a successful basketball player in the National Basketball Association. Mariah Carey has an abnormal vocal range—she is one of a few singers whose voice spans five octaves. Because of her different ability, she has sold millions of songs. Professor Stephen Hawking, one of the world's most brilliant scientists, has an intellectual capacity that exceeds that of virtually everyone else, yet he writes best-selling and popular works about theoretical physics and the universe and appears on popular television shows like *The Big Bang Theory*. He does this despite suffering from amyotrophic lateral sclerosis (ALS, also known as *Lou Gehrig's disease*), a debilitating and progressive neurological disease. Each of these individuals has abilities that distinguish him or her from the general public; that is, they are away from normal. However, their "abnormalities" (unusual abilities) are not negative; rather, they result in positive contributions to society. Furthermore, their unusual abilities do not cause distress or appear to impair their daily functioning (as appears to be the case for Steve, Malcom, and Rosa). In summary, being different is not the same as being psychologically abnormal.

Is Behaving Deviantly (Differently) Abnormal?

LO 1.2 Understand why simply behaving differently is not the same as behaving abnormally

When the definition of abnormal behavior broadens from simply *being* different to *behaving* differently, we often use the term *deviance*. Deviant behaviors differ from prevailing societal standards.

LeBron James, Mariah Carey, and Stephen Hawking differ from most people (in height, vocal range, and intelligence, respectively). However, these differences are not abnormalities and have resulted in positive contributions to society.

> On February 9, 1964, four young men from Liverpool, England, appeared on *The Ed Sullivan Show* and created quite a stir. Their hair was "long," their boots had "high (Cuban) heels," and their "music" was loud. Young people loved them, but their parents were appalled.

The Beatles looked, behaved, and sounded deviant in the context of the prevailing cultural norms. In 1964, they were considered outrageous. Today, their music, dress, and behavior appear rather tame. Was their behavior abnormal? They looked different and acted differently, but their looks and behavior did no harm to themselves or others. The same behavior, outrageous and different in 1964 but tame by today's standards, illustrates an important point: *deviant behavior* violates societal and cultural norms, but those norms are always changing.

> Derek is 7 years old. From the time he was an infant, he was always "on the go." He has a hard time paying attention and has boundless energy. His parents compensate for his high level of energy by involving him in lots of physical activities (soccer, Tiger Cub Scouts, karate). Derek had an understanding first-grade teacher. Because he could not sit still, the teacher accommodated him with "workstations" so that he could move around the classroom. But now Derek is in second grade, and the new teacher does not allow workstations. She believes that he must learn to sit like all the other children. He visits the principal's office often for "out-of-seat behavior."

Understanding behavior within a specific context is known as **goodness of fit** (Chess & Thomas, 1991). Simply put, a behavior can be problematic or not problematic depending on the environment in which it occurs. Some people change an environment to accommodate a behavior in the same way that buildings are modified to ensure accessibility by everyone. Derek's situation illustrates the goodness-of-fit concept. At home and in first grade, his parents and teacher changed the environment to meet his high activity level. They did not see his activity as a problem but simply as behavior that needed to be accommodated. In contrast, his second-grade teacher expected Derek to fit into a nonadaptable environment. In first grade, Derek was considered "lively," but in second grade, his behavior was considered abnormal. When we attempt to understand behavior, it is critical to consider the context in which the behavior occurs.

GROUP EXPECTATIONS The expectations of family, friends, neighborhood, and culture are consistent and pervasive influences on why people act the way they do.

Sometimes the standards of one group are at odds with those of another group. Adolescents, for example, often deliberately behave very differently than their parents do (they violate expected standards or norms) as a result of their need to *individuate* (separate) from their parents and be part of their peer group. In this instance, deviation from the norms of one group involves conformity to those of another group. Like family norms, cultural traditions and practices also affect behavior in many ways. For example, holiday celebrations usually include family and cultural traditions. As young people mature and leave their family of origin, new traditions from extended family, marriage, or friendships often blend into former customs and traditions, creating a new context for holiday celebrations.

Often, these different cultural traditions are unremarkable, but sometimes they can cause misunderstanding:

> Maleah is 12 years old. Her family recently moved to the United States from the Philippines. Her teacher insisted that Maleah's mother take her to see a psychologist because of "separation anxiety." The teacher was concerned because Maleah told the teacher that she had always slept in a bed with her grandmother. However, a psychological evaluation revealed that Maleah did not have any separation fears. Rather, children sleeping with parents and/or grandparents is what people normally do (what psychologists call normative) in Philippine culture.

Culture refers to shared behavioral patterns and lifestyles that differentiate one group of people from another. Culture affects an individual's behavior but also is reciprocally changed by the behaviors of its members (Tseng, 2003). We often behave in ways that reflect the values of the culture in which we were raised. For example, in some cultures, children are expected to be "seen and not heard," whereas in other cultures, children are encouraged to freely express themselves. **Culture-bound syndrome** is a term that originally described abnormal behaviors that were specific to a particular location or group (Yap, 1967); however, we now know that some of these behavioral patterns extend across ethnic groups and geographic areas. How culture influences behavior will be a recurring theme throughout this book. Maleah's behavior is just one example of how a single behavior can be viewed differently in two different cultures.

DEVELOPMENT AND MATURITY Another important context that must be taken into account when considering behavioral abnormality is age. As a child matures (physically, mentally, and emotionally), behaviors previously considered developmentally appropriate and therefore normal can become abnormal.

> Nick is 4 years old and insists on using a night-light to keep the monsters away.

At age 4, children do not have the *cognitive*, or mental, capacity to understand fully that monsters are not real. However, at age 12, a child should understand the difference between imagination and reality. Therefore, if at age 12 Nick still needs a night-light to keep the monsters away, his behavior would be considered abnormal and perhaps in need of treatment. Similarly, very young children do not have the ability to control their bladder; bed-wetting is common in toddlerhood. However, after the child achieves a certain level of physical and cognitive maturity, bed-wetting becomes an abnormal behavior and is given the diagnostic label of *enuresis* (see Chapter 13).

Eccentricity What about the millionaire who wills his entire estate to his dog? This behavior violates cultural norms, but it is often labeled eccentric rather than abnormal. Eccentric behavior may violate societal norms but is not always negative or harmful to others. Yet sometimes behaviors that initially appear eccentric cross the line into dangerousness (see "Real People, Real Disorders: James Eagan Holmes").

REAL People REAL Disorders

James Eagan Holmes

On July 20, 2012, James Eagan Holmes walked into a Colorado movie theater and bought a ticket to the midnight showing of the Batman movie *The Dark Knight Rises*. After the movie began, he left the theater through an emergency exit, came back, and set off gas/smoke canisters and opened fire on the audience, killing 12 people and wounding 58 others. He was quickly arrested, and he warned the police not to go to his apartment. They did but found that he had booby-trapped it before leaving for the theater. At his first legal hearing, he appeared in court with his hair dyed orange, appearing dazed and confused, looking bug-eyed, and spitting on the officers who were escorting him. He called himself The Joker. In August 2015, Holmes was sentenced for his crimes, receiving 12 life sentences plus 3,318 years.

Holmes graduated from the University of California, Berkeley, in the top 1% of his class, with a 3.94 GPA and a degree in neuroscience. Described by some as socially inept and uncommunicative, he described himself as quiet and easygoing on an apartment rental application. He applied to graduate school at the University of Illinois at Urbana-Champaign, and the application included a picture of himself with a llama. The choice of such a picture on something as important as a graduate school application certainly could qualify as eccentric behavior, but does that mean that he was psychologically disturbed?

In 2011, Holmes enrolled as a Ph.D. student in neuroscience at the University of Colorado Anschutz Medical Campus in Aurora. In 2012, his grades declined and he failed his comprehensive examination. Although the university did not plan to dismiss him, he started the process to withdraw from the university. At the same time, he purchased large quantities of guns and more than 6,000 rounds of ammunition. Is this irrational behavior? Is it potentially dangerous behavior?

He asked someone if he or she had ever heard of a disorder called dysphoric mania and told a graduate student to stay away from him because he was "bad news." His answering machine recording was described as "freaky, guttural sounding, incoherent, and rambling." He dyed his hair orange, called himself The Joker, and went to the movie theater. Does this behavior prove that Holmes had a psychological disorder?

From all accounts, Holmes evolved from being a brilliant if socially awkward neuroscience student to a mass murderer. Whatever label is applied, he evolved from behaving differently to behaving dangerously (perhaps as a result of disordered thinking). In this instance, his behavior was extremely harmful to others and could no longer be considered merely eccentric. It is also important to point out that most people who have psychological disorders are not dangerous and do not commit crimes or attempt to harm other people.

Is Behaving Dangerously Abnormal?

LO 1.3 Understand why simply behaving dangerously does not always equal abnormality

The police arrive at the emergency room of a psychiatric hospital with a man and a woman in handcuffs. Jon is 23 years old. He identifies himself as the chauffeur for Melissa, who is age 35 and also in handcuffs. They are both dressed in tight leather pants and shirts, have unusual "spiked" haircuts, and wear leather "dog collars" with many silver spikes. Jon and Melissa live in the suburbs but spent a day in the city buying clothes and getting their hair cut. As they were leaving the parking garage to return home, Melissa began to criticize Jon's hair. Jon became angry and ran the car (which belonged to Melissa) into the wall of the parking garage—several times. When a clinician asked the police officer why they were brought to the psychiatric emergency room, the officer replied, "Well, would a sane person keep ramming a car into the wall of a parking garage?" Neither Jon nor Melissa had any previous history of psychological disorders. An interview revealed that Jon's behavior was the result of a lover's quarrel, and although their relationship was often volatile, they denied any incidents of physical aggression toward each other or anyone else.

Certainly, repeatedly ramming a car into the wall of a parking garage is dangerous, is outside of societal norms, and could be labeled abnormal. Dangerous behavior can result from intense emotional states, and in Jon's case, the behavior was directed outwardly (toward another person or an inanimate object). In other cases, dangerous behavior such as suicidal thoughts may be directed toward oneself. However, it is important to understand that most people with psychological disorders do not engage in dangerous behavior (Linaker, 2000;

Monahan, 2001). Individuals with seriously disordered thinking rarely present any danger to society even though their behaviors may appear dangerous to others. Therefore, behavior that is dangerous may signal the presence of a psychological disorder, but dangerous behavior alone is not necessary or sufficient for the label of abnormality to be assigned.

Is Behaving Dysfunctionally Abnormal?

LO 1.4 Explain the difference between behaviors that are different, deviant, dangerous, and dysfunctional.

Thus far, simply being different, behaving differently, or behaving dangerously clearly does not constitute abnormal behavior. A final consideration when attempting to define abnormal behavior is whether that behavior causes *distress* or *dysfunction* for the individual or others. Consider the examples of Robert and Stan (see "Side-by-Side Case Studies").

Both Robert and Stan engage in checking behaviors, but Robert's behavior falls into the category of what is called "normal checking" (Rachman & Hodgson, 1980). Stan's routine of checking the house before he leaves for work or goes to bed is *different* from the way in which most people lock up their house before going to work, so his behavior *deviates* from the norm. Even though simple deviance is not abnormal, Stan's behavior differs from Robert's in another way: Stan's checking occurs more frequently. Frequency alone does not mean a behavior is maladaptive, but frequency can lead to two other conditions: distress and dysfunction. Specifically, Stan's worries are so frequent and pervasive that they cause him to feel anxious and lose sleep at night. In this case, maladaptive behavior results in *distress*; Stan's worries result in a negative mood (anxiety) and cause him to lose sleep. Frequently, they also cause him to arrive late for work or for social engagements. Thus, his behaviors create occupational and social *dysfunction*. When one of these conditions is evident, the presence of a psychological disorder must be considered.

A Definition of Abnormal Behavior

LO 1.5 Identify at least two factors that need to be considered when determining whether a behavior is abnormal.

To summarize, to define abnormal behavior, we need to consider several factors. Merely being different or behaving differently is not enough, although the latter certainly might

SIDE by SIDE Case Studies

Dimensions of Behavior: From Adaptive to Maladaptive

Adaptive Behavior Case Study

Example A

Robert is a very cautious person. He does not like to make mistakes and believes that the behavior standards that he sets for himself are high but fair. He is concerned about safety and worried that other people might take advantage of him if he makes a mistake. Before leaving his house or going to sleep, he walks through the house, checking to make sure that every door and window is locked and the oven and stove are turned off. This usually takes about 5 minutes.

Maladaptive Behavior Case Study

Example B

Stan also is cautious and very concerned. When away from home, he worries that he forgot to lock a door and that his house has been robbed. Often he returns home to check that the house is locked. But even after he checks, he remains doubtful and spends hours each day checking and rechecking. He has an elaborate system of checking the locks, the doors, the garage door, and the burglar alarm system. He checks the stove seven times to make sure that the oven and the burners are off. Thoughts of a burglar in his house or his house burning down cause him great distress, sometimes interfering with his sleep. He is often late for work or for social engagements because he needs to go back to the house to check and recheck.

be a signal that something is wrong. Some abnormal behaviors are dangerous, but dangerousness is not necessary for a definition of abnormality. In this book, we define **abnormal behavior** as behavior that is inconsistent with the individual's developmental, cultural, and societal norms and creates emotional distress or interferes with daily functioning.

The following chapters will examine many different types of abnormal behavior. As a guide, the behaviors are considered using the *Diagnostic and Statistical Manual of Mental Disorders*, Fifth Edition (American Psychiatric Association, 2013), commonly known as the *DSM-5*. This diagnostic system uses an approach that focuses on symptoms and the scientific basis for the disorders, including their *clinical presentation* (what specific symptoms cluster together?), *etiology* (what causes the disorder?), *developmental stage* (does the disorder look different in children than it does in adults?), and *functional impairment* (what are the immediate and long-term consequences of having the disorder?). The DSM system uses a *categorical approach* to defining abnormal behavior. A categorical approach assumes that a person either has a disorder or does not, just as one is pregnant or not pregnant. Although this method is somewhat controversial (see "Research Hot Topic: Categorical vs. Dimensional Approaches to Abnormal Behavior"), it remains the most widely accepted diagnostic system in the United States.

ABNORMAL BEHAVIOR IN THE GENERAL POPULATION Psychological disorders are common in the general population. Approximately 47% of adults in the United States have suffered from a psychological disorder at some time in their lives (Kessler, Berglund, Demler, Jin, et al., 2005). The most commonly reported disorders in the United States are anxiety disorders and depressive disorders (see Figure 1.1). More than 20% of adults will suffer from major depression, and more than 14% will struggle with alcohol dependence at some point in their lives. Anxiety disorders are also common, affecting more than 28% of adults during their lifetimes. What most people do not know is that mental disorders rank as one of the most substantial causes of death (Walker et al., 2015). People with mental disorders have a mortality rate that is 2.2 times higher than people without mental disorders, and the median years of potential life loss is 10 years. Clearly, many people suffer from serious psychological disorders; this emphasizes the need for more understanding of these conditions and the development of effective treatments.

Figure 1.1 Lifetime Prevalence of Various DSM-IV Psychiatric Disorders at Different Ages in Adulthood.

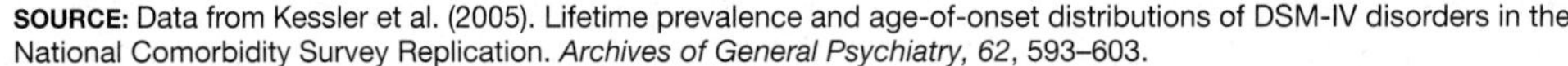

SOURCE: Data from Kessler et al. (2005). Lifetime prevalence and age-of-onset distributions of DSM-IV disorders in the National Comorbidity Survey Replication. *Archives of General Psychiatry*, *62*, 593–603.

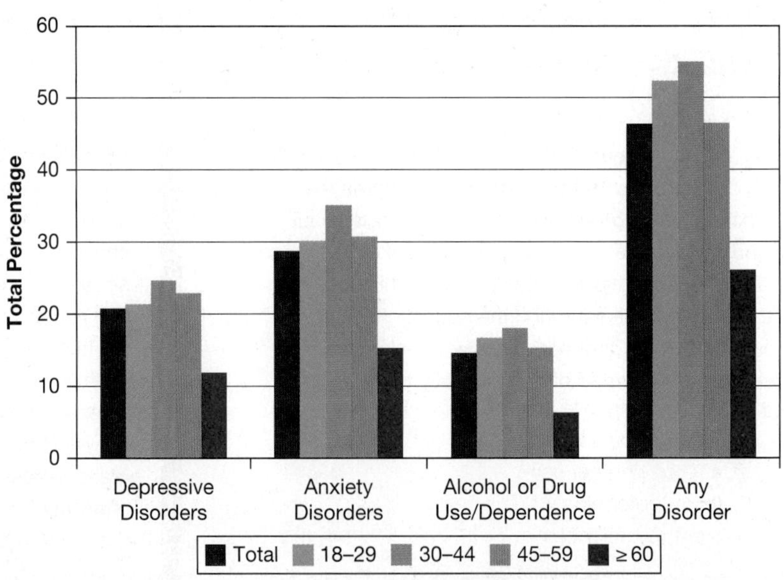

FACTORS INFLUENCING THE EXPRESSION OF ABNORMAL BEHAVIORS Contextual factors play an important role when considering if and when abnormal behaviors may develop. Some factors include personal characteristics such as sex and race or ethnicity. For example, women are more likely to suffer from anxiety disorders (see Chapter 4) and mood disorders (see Chapter 7), and men are more likely to suffer from alcohol and drug abuse (see Chapter 10; Kessler et al., 2005a). With respect to race and ethnicity, whites and African Americans suffer equally from most types of psychological disorders. Hispanics are more likely to have mood disorders such as depression than are non-Hispanic whites. In addition, as we shall see throughout this book, culture may influence how symptoms are expressed.

Socioeconomic status (SES), defined by family income and educational achievement, is another important factor that affects the prevalence of psychological disorders in the general population. Except for drug and alcohol abuse, which occurs more often among people with the middle education level (a high school graduate but no college degree), psychological disorders occur most frequently among those with the lowest incomes and the least education. A continuing debate is whether psychological disorders are the result of lower SES. Do more education and higher income serve to protect someone against psychological disorders by providing more supportive resources? An alternative hypothesis is that the impairment that *results* from a psychological disorder (inability to sleep, addiction to alcohol) leads to job loss or limited educational achievement, a phenomenon known as *downward drift*. Another alternative is that a third factor, such as genetic predisposition, contributes both to the onset of a psychiatric disorder and to the inability to achieve academically or occupationally.

Few studies address the relationship of SES to psychological disorders specifically, but one study of the development of psychological disorders in children does help us understand this relationship. In this study, children were interviewed at yearly intervals, in some cases for 9 consecutive years. During that time, children from all SES groups *developed*

Research HOT Topic

Categorical vs. Dimensional Approaches to Abnormal Behavior

The current diagnostic system, the *Diagnostic and Statistical Manual of Mental Disorders* (DSM-5), presents a primarily *categorical* approach to understanding psychological disorders. The DSM assumes that a person either has a disorder or does not, just as one is pregnant or not pregnant. The current DSM is superior to previous diagnostic systems, which were tied to theory but not necessarily to data. However, two issues continue to present problems for a categorical approach: (1) symptoms rarely fall neatly into just one category and (2) symptoms often are not of sufficient severity to determine that they represent a psychological disorder despite distress and impairment.

In fact, people in psychological distress rarely have only one psychological disorder (Nathan & Langenbucher, 1999). A woman struggling with an eating disorder often feels depressed as well. Does she have two distinct disorders, or is her depression merely part of her abnormal eating pattern? Making these distinctions is more than just an academic exercise—it affects whether someone receives treatment. It may, for example, determine whether a psychologist decides to refer a depressed patient for medication treatment or just monitors her sadness to see whether it disappears when the eating disorder is successfully treated.

The second issue—deciding when one has "enough" of a symptom to have a diagnosis—can be illustrated through the following example. Shyness and sadness are two behaviors that may be personality dimensions rather than a distinct category. When is one "sad enough" or "shy enough" to be diagnosed with a psychological disorder? Is shyness a personality feature or a psychological disorder? Currently, one is considered to have a psychological disorder when the distress is severe enough or when functional impairment results. However, in many instances, this is an artificial distinction and may deny people with moderate distress the opportunity to seek services. Scientifically, a **dimensional approach** would allow an understanding of how abnormal behavior varies in severity over time, perhaps increasing and decreasing, or how behaviors change from one disorder to another.

Researchers continue to investigate the most accurate way to describe abnormal behavior. The DSM-5 emphasizes the need to consider not just the presence of symptoms but also whether those symptoms affect functioning when attempting to understand abnormal behavior.

Figure 1.2 Cumulative Prevalence of Psychiatric Disorders by Age 16.

SOURCE: Data from Costello et al. (2003). Prevalence and development of psychiatric disorders in childhood and adolescence. *Archives of General Psychiatry, 60*, 837–844 /Pearson Education, Inc.

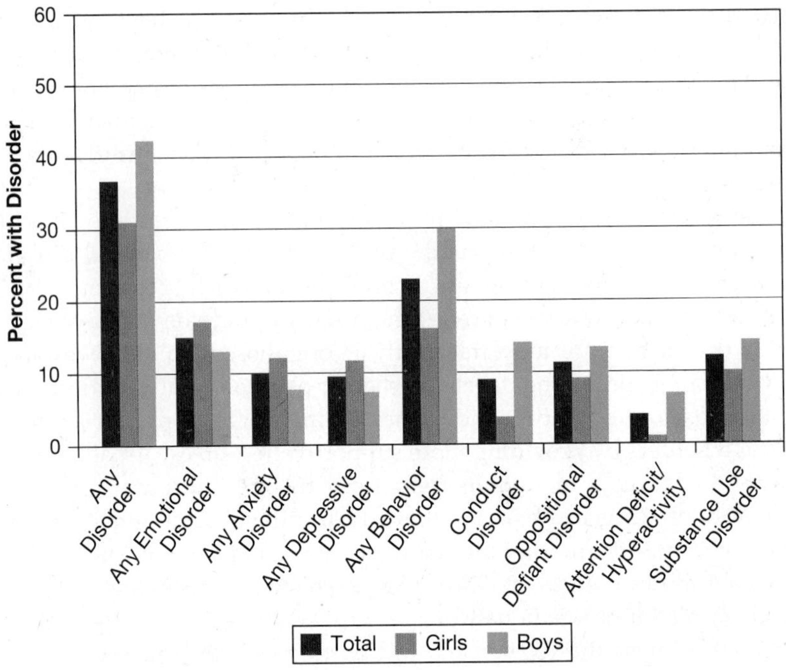

psychological disorders at the same rate (Wadsworth & Achenbach, 2005). However, once the disorder was present, children from the lower SES category were less likely to *overcome* or recover from their disorder. Lower income usually means fewer economic resources and less access to treatment. Over time, reduced recovery resulted in more children from the lower SES group having more psychological disorders.

As the preceding example illustrates, children as well as adults suffer from psychological disorders, and we know that age and developmental stage are important factors affecting abnormal behaviors. The Great Smoky Mountains Study examined the presence of psychological disorders in children who were assessed yearly, in some cases for up to 7 consecutive years (Costello et al., 2003). Figure 1.2 illustrates the prevalence of psychological disorders in children and adolescents.

It may be quite surprising that by age 16, one of three children and adolescents (36%) has suffered from a psychological disorder. As illustrated in Figure 1.3, the prevalence of disorders is highest among 9- to 10-year-old children, lower at age 12, and higher again in adolescence. Psychologists know that developmental maturity affects when and how symptoms develop, what types of symptoms develop, and even what kinds of disorders occur. The idea that the common symptoms of a disorder vary according to a person's age is known as the **developmental trajectory** (a *trajectory* is a path or progression). For example, compared with children who are diagnosed with depression, adolescents with depression are more likely to feel hopelessness/helplessness, to lack energy or feel tired, to sleep too much, and to commit serious suicidal acts (Yorbik et al., 2004). Therefore, the symptoms of depression may change as a child matures. Even among adults, age also plays a role in the frequency of specific depressive symptoms. As adults mature, they are less likely to report feelings of sadness or negative thoughts about themselves or others (Goldberg et al., 2003). Therefore, even an emotion as common as sadness can appear differently at different ages.

Inattention to developmental differences may result in inaccurate detection of psychological disorders. For example, social anxiety disorder is characterized by a behavioral pattern of pervasive social timidity (see Chapter 4). Adults with social anxiety disorder report extreme fear when asked to give a speech. Young children rarely have to give a speech, and because they have no experience in the situation, they deny fear of giving speeches. However, a similar childhood activity would be reading aloud in front of the

Figure 1.3 Prevalence of DSM-IV Psychological Disorders in Children by Age and Sex.
For boys, the prevalence of disorders peaks around age 9 or 10; for girls, prevalence peaks around age 16.

SOURCE: Data from Costello et al. (2003). Prevalence and development of psychiatric disorders in childhood and adolescence. *Archives of General Psychiatry, 60,* 837–844 /Pearson Education, Inc.

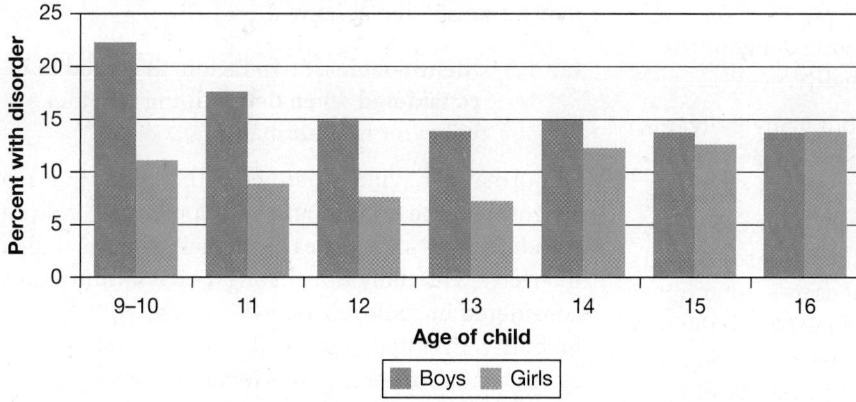

class. Children with social anxiety disorder often report great fear when asked to read aloud. Therefore, accurately diagnosing social anxiety disorder depends on understanding not only the disorder but also how the disorder appears at different ages. As noted above, older adults with depression are less likely to report feelings of sadness and negative thoughts, but all adults (regardless of age) report physical symptoms of depression (inability to sleep or eat or being easily tired). Therefore, a clinician who assesses depression only by asking about sadness may overlook depression in older adults. Throughout this book, we often will return to this issue of developmental psychopathology and how the same disorder may appear differently across the life span.

This developmental perspective also illustrates why the prevalence of psychological disorders varies by age (see Figure 1.3). Certain disorders that are common in childhood (separation anxiety disorder, attention deficit/hyperactivity disorder; see Chapters 4 and 13) become less common as children mature physically, cognitively, and emotionally. During adolescence, other disorders begin to emerge (depression, alcohol and drug use, eating disorders, panic disorder, and generalized anxiety disorder; see Chapters 4, 7, 8, and 10). The emergence of some disorders has practical and societal components (e.g., older adolescents are more likely to have access to alcohol, which is a prerequisite to developing substance abuse). The emergence of other disorders coincides with cognitive maturity. Generalized anxiety disorder is defined, in part, by worry about future events (American Psychiatric Association, 2013). This requires the ability to understand the concept of "future," a cognitive skill that usually emerges around age 12 (see Alfano et al., 2002). Therefore, although it is possible for younger children to suffer from generalized anxiety disorder, many more cases occur later as cognitive maturity is achieved. Finally, biological changes also influence the emergence of psychological disorders. Hormonal changes associated with puberty may increase the likelihood of the emergence of eating disorders (anorexia and bulimia nervosa) in those who are at high risk for the development of these disorders.

Learning Objective Summaries

LO 1.1 Understand why simply being different does not mean abnormality.

Abnormal behavior is sometimes difficult to define. It is not just behavior that is different because differences can sometimes be positive for the individual and perhaps for society. Being different does not necessarily mean that a person is suffering from a psychological disorder. In some cases, being different can create significant advantages or opportunities for someone.

LO 1.2 Understand why simply behaving differently is not the same as behaving abnormally.

Behaving differently also does not mean that one is suffering from a psychological disorder. Behavior that is deviant may be different but not necessarily abnormal. New trends often start as deviant but then become accepted by mainstream society. Determining the presence of abnormal behavior requires evaluation of the behavior in terms of its developmental, cultural, and societal contexts.

LO 1.3 Understand why simply behaving dangerously does not always equal abnormality.

Dangerous behavior may be abnormal, but many individuals who have psychological disorders do not engage in dangerous behavior. In some instances, people who are suffering from psychological disorders may behave in dangerous ways, such as James Eagan Holmes. However, not all people who behave in a dangerous fashion or commit crimes suffer from mental disorders, and the vast majority of people who suffer from mental disorders do not commit crimes. Behaving dangerously is not always the result of a psychological disorder.

LO 1.4 Explain the difference between behaviors that are different, deviant, dangerous, and dysfunctional.

Two primary considerations for determining whether a behavior is abnormal are whether it creates dysfunction (interferes with daily activities) and/or emotional distress. When behavior interferes with the ability to achieve goals, hold down a job, or socialize with others, the behavior is referred to as dysfunctional. If one's emotional or cognitive state results in dysfunctional behavior, then the behavior may be considered abnormal.

LO 1.5 Identify at least two factors that need to be considered when determining whether a behavior is abnormal.

Abnormal behavior is defined as behavior that is inconsistent with the individual's developmental, cultural, and societal norms and creates significant emotional distress or interferes with daily functioning. Behavior must always be considered in context. Context includes culture as defined by both individual and social spheres of influence as well as cultural traditions. It also includes consideration of developmental age, physical and emotional maturity, and SES. What might be considered abnormal in adults may not be considered abnormal in children.

Critical Thinking Question

At different ages, the same disorder may appear with very different symptoms. Young children are still developing in many ways. How might immature physical and cognitive development affect the emotional expression of psychological disorders?

The History of Abnormal Behavior and Its Treatment

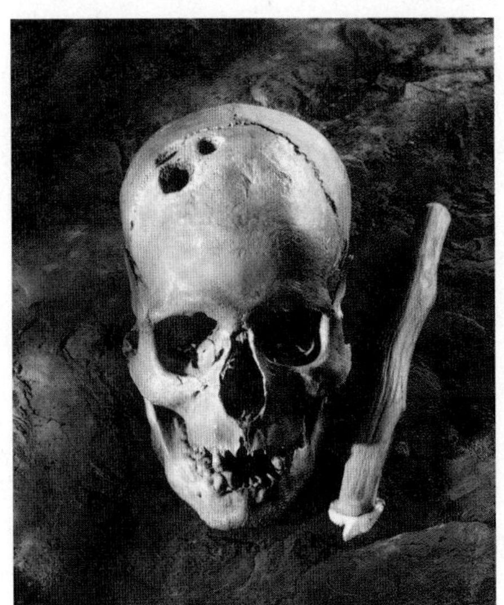

Trephination involved making a hole in the skull. It may have been a way that ancient peoples tried to release evil spirits from the body of an afflicted person.

Throughout history, certain behaviors have been recognized as abnormal—often the same ones we recognize today. However, the explanations for these abnormal behaviors have evolved, ranging from an imbalance of bodily fluids to possession by demons, genetic abnormalities, and traumatic learning experiences. Today, new technologies allow us to watch the brain as it processes sights, smells, and sounds; solves problems; and experiences emotions. As this knowledge has increased, some of the earlier ideas about abnormal behavior seem outlandish or quaint. Here, we review those theories and show how scientific advances have changed our understanding of abnormal behavior.

Ancient Theories

LO 1.6 Discuss ancient spiritual and biological theories of the origins of abnormal behavior.

Much of what we know about ancient theories of abnormal behavior is based on available archeological evidence and ancient texts. Ancient Egyptians believed that spirits controlled much of the environment as well as aspects of a person's behavior. Even before the Egyptians, some cultures engaged in a practice called **trephination**, using a circular instrument to cut away sections of the skull. One interpretation of trephination is that it was a treatment for abnormal behaviors. Opening up the skull, it may have been thought, released the evil spirits that had assumed control of the person (Selling, 1940). This is only an assumption. Trephination might simply have been used to treat head wounds received in battles (Maher & Maher, 1985). Even today, we are not sure why ancient peoples practiced it.

Classical Greek and Roman Periods

LO 1.7 Discuss spiritual, biological, and environmental theories of the origins of abnormal behavior in classical Greek and Roman periods.

The ancient Greeks believed that the gods controlled abnormal behavior and that defiance of the deities could result in mental illness. Around the thirteenth century BC, the physician Melampus of Pilus introduced an organic model of illness to explain psychological symptoms and provided treatment using plants and other natural substances. He prescribed root extract for "agitated uterine melancholia" and iron powder for "traumatic impotence" (Roccatagliata, 1997). Asclepius, best known as a Greek god, is now believed to have been a historical figure whose healing abilities were so widely respected that he was elevated to the status of a god (http://www.nlm.nih.gov/hmd/greek/greek_asclepius.html). Many temples were established throughout Greece to honor Asclepius, one of which was the first known sanctuary for mental disorders, offering biological (mandrake root and opium), physical (music, massage, drama), and psychological treatments (dream interpretation; Roccatagliata, 1997). During this period, mental illnesses were considered to result from either traumatic experiences or an imbalance in fluids (such as blood) found within the body. These fluids were called *humors*.

Often considered the father of medicine, Hippocrates (460–377 BC) was the most famous Greek physician. He produced both a diagnostic classification system and a model by which to explain abnormal behavior. Hippocrates identified common psychological symptoms such as *hallucinations* (hearing or seeing things not evident to others), *delusions* (beliefs with no basis in reality), *melancholia* (severe sadness), and *mania* (heightened states of arousal that can result in frenzied activity). All of these symptoms are still recognized today. He also introduced the term *hysteria*, now called *conversion disorder* (see Chapter 6). See Table 1.1 for a brief summary. The term *hysteria* was used to describe patients who appeared to have blindness or paralysis for which there was no organic cause. Hippocrates, assuming incorrectly that the condition occurred only in women, attributed it to an empty uterus wandering throughout the body searching for conception. The external symptoms indicated where the uterus was lodged internally. He believed that the cure for hysteria was an environmental one: marriage or pregnancy. Of course, with advanced understanding of human anatomy and physiology, the "wandering uterus" theory was discarded. But even in very recent times, the term *hysteria* continued to describe an intense, dramatic pattern of behavior once associated with women.

Hippocrates, the ancient Greek physician, believed that abnormal behaviors were caused by an imbalance in four bodily humors.

Hippocrates believed that other abnormal behaviors resulted when environmental factors (changes of seasons) and/or physical factors (fever, epilepsy, and shock) created an imbalance in four bodily humors. In his model, the four humors were yellow bile, black bile, blood, and phlegm. Blood was associated with a courageous and hopeful outlook on life, and phlegm was associated with a calm and unemotional attitude. Excessive yellow bile caused mania, and excessive black bile caused melancholia, which was treated with a vegetable diet, a tranquil existence, celibacy, exercise, and sometimes bleeding (controlled removal of some of the patient's blood). Hippocrates advocated the removal of patients from their families as an element of treatment, foreshadowing the practice of humane treatment and institutionalization.

Table 1.1 The Diagnostic Criteria of Hippocrates

Psychological Symptom	Description
Hallucinations	hearing or seeing things not evident to others
Delusions	beliefs with no basis in reality
Melancholia	severe sadness
Hysteria	blindness or paralysis with no organic cause

Another very influential Greek physician was Galen, the personal physician of the Roman emperor Marcus Aurelius. Although the terms we use today differ from those used in ancient times, Galen's writings (which still survive) indicate that his areas of expertise included many fields of medicine: neurophysiology and neuroanatomy, neurology, pharmacology, psychiatry, and philosophy (Roccatagliata, 1997; http://www.nlm.nih.gov/hmd/greek/greek_galen.html). An important distinction can be made between Hippocrates's and Galen's descriptions of hysteria. Because Galen had studied human anatomy, he discounted the "wandering uterus" theory. Galen attributed hysteria to a psychological cause, believing it to be a symptom of unhappiness in women who had lost interest in and enjoyment of sexual activity.

After the fall of the Roman Empire, demonology again dominated theories of mental illness in Europe, but the enlightened thinking of Hippocrates and Galen remained influential in Islamic countries. There, Avicenna (AD 980–1037; Namanzi, 2001), known as the "prince and chief of physicians" and "the second teacher after Aristotle," wrote approximately 450 works, including the *Canon of Medicine*, considered the most influential textbook ever written. Avicenna considered depression to result from a mix of humors, and he believed that certain physical diseases were caused by emotional distress. He stressed the beneficial effects of music on emotional disturbance. His approach to mental illness foreshadowed what would take an additional 600 years to appear in Europe—humane treatment of the mentally ill.

The Middle Ages Through the Renaissance

LO 1.8 Discuss the spiritual, biological, and environmental theories of the origins of abnormal behavior from the Middle Ages to the Renaissance.

The Islamic philosopher and physician Avicenna wrote an influential medical text that recognized the interconnections between emotional distress and physical illness.

In medieval Europe, demons were considered to be the source of all evil, preying on the "captive and outwitted minds of men" (Tertullian, in Sagan, 1996). There were many challenges (wars, plagues, social oppression, famine) to survival during the Middle Ages, and people often sought reasons for these events. Church officials interpreted negative behavior as the work of the devil or as witchcraft, even when other, less dramatic, explanations existed. As a result of the church's powerful influence, witchcraft became a prominent theory to explain abnormal behavior. Over a 300-year period (1400s to 1700s), at least 200,000 people in Europe were accused of witchcraft and 100,000 were put to death, approximately 80 to 85% of whom were women (Clark, 1997). In fact, many of those accused probably suffered from psychological disorders (Zilboorg, 1939, cited in Clark, 1997). Once accused of being a witch, the person was tried and always found guilty. Thankfully, the Renaissance period brought new attitudes toward science and the church that challenged the reality of witches. Accusations of witchcraft were not limited to European countries. "Witches" were also executed in Massachusetts in the seventeenth century. However, as illustrated by today's stories of alien abductions, beliefs in the supernatural/paranormal still exist in our modern world.

During the Middle Ages, episodes of **mass hysteria** would sweep through large groups of people. People affected were convinced that they were afflicted or possessed by a demonic spirit (again, similar to beliefs regarding alien abduction). One of the first recorded cases (originating in Italy in the early thirteenth century) is known as *tarantism*, caused by the belief that the bite of a wolf spider (also known as a tarantula) would cause death unless a person engaged in joyous, frenetic dancing. Another form of the legend was that the spider's bite would cause frenetic dancing, jumping, or convulsing (Sigerist, 1943). In fact, the spider's bite was harmless, and people's responses were fueled by mass hysteria. Another form of mass madness was *lycanthropy*, in which individuals believed that they were possessed by wolves. The belief was so strong that those affected would act like a wolf, even to the point of believing that their bodies were covered in fur.

There is a scientific basis for mass hysteria. Group **emotional contagion** is defined as the sharing and transferring of moods among the members of a group (Barsade, 2002). When these overt behaviors converge, emotions come together as well. These mimicking behaviors are not under voluntary control but nevertheless serve to influence behavior. Although many people may no longer believe that wolves or spider bites are responsible for abnormal behaviors, the process of emotional contagion remains a powerful influence on behavior (see "Examining the Evidence: Modern-Day Mass Hysteria").

The Renaissance period (fourteenth to seventeenth century) marked a second time of enlightenment in the treatment of mental illnesses in Europe. Much of this transformation can be traced back to the Dutch physician Johann Weyer (1515–1588) and the Swiss physician Paracelsus (1493–1541). Weyer was the first physician to specialize in the treatment of mental illness, and Paracelsus refuted the idea that abnormal behaviors were linked to demonic possession. Paracelsus believed that mental disorders could be hereditary and that some physical illnesses had a psychological origin (Tan & Yeow, 2003).

These changing views toward mental illness altered treatment approaches as well. A movement that was genuinely concerned with providing help arose, and its goal was to separate those with mental illness from those who engaged in criminal behavior (Sussman, 1998). Beginning in the sixteenth century, people with mental illness were housed in asylums—separate facilities designed to isolate them from the general public. Although the concept of asylums was based on good intentions, the asylums quickly filled to capacity (and overcapacity). The lack of effective treatments turned the facilities into warehouses, often called *madhouses*. One of the most famous was St. Mary of Bethlehem in London. Treatment consisted of confinement (chains, shackles, isolation in dark cells), torturous practices (ice-cold baths, spinning in chairs, severely restricted diets), and "medical" treatments (emetics, purgatives, and bloodletting). For a small price, people in London could visit the asylum to view the inmates (Tan & Yeow, 2004). They called the place *Bedlam* (a contraction of "Bethlehem"), a word that came to describe chaotic and uncontrollable situations. Similar conditions existed in other parts of Europe as well as eventually in North America.

The Nineteenth Century and the Beginning of Modern Thought

LO 1.9 Discuss the spiritual, biological, psychological, and sociocultural theories of the origins of abnormal behavior in the nineteenth century.

A turning point for the medical treatment of mental illness occurred during the late eighteenth century when the French physician Philippe Pinel (1745–1826) and the English Quaker William Tuke (1732–1822) radically changed the approach to treating mental illness. In 1793, Pinel was the director of Bicêtre, an asylum for men. In his *Memoir on Madness*, he proposed that mental illness was often curable and that to apply appropriate treatment, the physician must listen to the patient and observe his behavior. Both would help the physician to understand the natural history of the disease and the events that led to its development. Pinel advocated calm and order within the asylum (Tan & Yeow, 2004). He removed the chains from the patients, both at Bicêtre and at the women's asylum known as Salpêtrière. Instead of using restraints, Pinel advocated daytime activities such as work or occupational therapy to allow for restful sleep at night.

At the same time, across the English Channel, William Tuke established the York Retreat (Edginton, 1997), a small country house deliberately designed to allow people with mental

Philippe Pinel, a French physician, released mental patients from their chains and advocated a more humane form of treatment.

illnesses to live, work, and relax in a compassionate and religious environment. Instead of bars on the windows, Tuke used iron dividers to separate the glass windowpanes and even had the dividers painted to look like wood. The Retreat was built on a hill, and although it contained a hidden ditch and a wall to ensure confinement, the barriers could not be seen from the buildings; this gave the illusion of a home rather than an institution (Scull, 2004). The work of both Pinel and Tuke heralded *moral treatment*, "summed up in two words, kindness and occupation" (W. A. F. Browne, 1837, cited in Geller & Morrissey, 2004). Moral treatment was quite comprehensive. In the United States, it included removal of the patient from the home and former associates as well as respectful and kind treatment that included "manual labor, religious services on Sunday, the establishment of regular habits and of self-control, and diversion of the mind from morbid trains of thought" (Brigham, 1847, p. 1, cited in Luchins, 2001).

Moral treatment in the United States is most commonly associated with Benjamin Rush (1745–1813) and Dorothea Dix (1802–1887). Rush was a well-known physician at Pennsylvania Hospital and a signer of the Declaration of Independence. He limited his practice to mental illness, which he believed had its causes in the blood vessels of the brain

Examining the EVIDENCE

Modern-Day Mass Hysteria

- **The Facts** Although we tend to think of mass hysteria as occurring in an unenlightened era, episodes of emotional contagion still occur today.
- **The Evidence** In 2012, a high school cheerleader in Le Roy, New York, awoke from a nap to find that something was wrong. Her chin was jutting forward, and her face had spasms. A few weeks later, her best friend, the captain of the cheerleading squad, awoke from a nap stuttering and twitching, her arms and legs flailing. Soon other cheerleaders had similar symptoms. Eventually, 18 teenage girls in a school of 600 students had uncontrollable twitches, spasms, and vocal outbursts. Despite an exhaustive search for environmental toxins, no medical or environmental reason was identified. Mass psychogenic illness was suggested to be the cause.
- **Let's Examine the Evidence** Evidence that emotional contagion and mass psychogenic illness may have been the basis for the symptom reports includes the following:
  1. Initial symptom onset occurred in the same dramatic manner among the first girls who developed the illness—upon awakening from a nap. If environmental toxins were the cause, there is no reason why the toxin would repeatedly activate only upon awakening from a nap.
  2. The town began to receive a lot of media coverage, including a visit from Erin Brockovitch. The girls were interviewed on TV. All of the girls began to get better once the media coverage disappeared and the YouTube videos were removed from the Internet.
  3. A physician suggested that the girls might be suffering from a rare viral infection. Half the girls took antibiotics (which does not work on viral infections) and anti-inflammatory drugs. The girls seemed to be recovering at the same rate whether or not they were taking the drugs.
  4. Those who reported illness were more likely to be female, were of high social status within the school (i.e., cheerleaders), had more often observed another person who became ill, or knew a classmate was ill. All of these factors have been repeatedly associated with onset of mass psychogenic illness.
- **Conclusion** It is important to note that the individuals experienced the symptoms they reported; it is incorrect to deny that the symptoms occurred. What is at issue, however, is the cause of the symptoms. In this case, after exhausting all possible environmental alternatives, the most likely explanation for the large outbreak of illness was emotional contagion, producing mass psychogenic illness (Laub, 2012; National Public Radio, 2012).

(Farr, 1994). Although this theory was later disproved, Rush believed that the human mind was the most important area of study, and he became known as the father of American psychiatry (Haas, 1993).

In the United States, perhaps no name is more closely associated with humane care than that of Dorothea Dix, the Boston schoolteacher who devoted her life to the plight of the mentally ill and the need for treatment reform. Through her efforts, 32 institutions that included programs in psychiatric treatment, research, and education were established (Gold, 2005). Dix believed that asylums, correctly designed and operated, would allow for treatment and perhaps even cure. Although Dix brought the plight of the mentally ill to public attention, moral treatment alone did not cure most forms of mental illness. In fact, mental hospitals became associated with permanent institutionalization, custodial care, isolation, and very little hope.

During the late 1700s in Europe, the treatment of mental disorders went beyond providing rest and humane care. The German physician Franz Anton Mesmer (1734–1815) hardly followed the conventional medical establishment. His academic thesis explored the clinical implications of astrology (McNally, 1999). Mesmer proposed that the body was a magnet and that using the physician's body as a second magnet could achieve a cure for mental illness (Crabtree, 2000). Mesmer believed that a substance called **animal magnetism** existed within the body. When it flowed freely, the body was in a healthy state; however, when the flow of this energy force was impeded, disease resulted. The cure involved "magnetic passes" of the physician's hands over the body (McNally, 1999). Mesmerism was roundly criticized by a committee of scientists and physicians that included Benjamin Franklin and the noted French chemist Antoine Lavoisier.

Nonetheless, Mesmer's experiments constitute an important chapter in psychology. Although his theory of animal magnetism and his flamboyant cures (including a cape, music, magic poles used to touch various parts of the body, and magnetized water) were ultimately debunked, they illustrate the power of the **placebo effect** in which symptoms are diminished or eliminated not because of any specific treatment but because the patient believes that a treatment is effective. A placebo can be in the form of pills with inert ingredients such as cornstarch. It can also be in the form of a therapist or physician who displays an attitude of caring about the patient. However, it is important to add that although placebos may change how patients feel, the effect is usually temporary. Placebos are not the same as actual treatment.

A significant event for establishing a biological basis for some psychological disorders occurred in the latter part of the nineteenth century. Scientists discovered that syphilis (a sexually transmitted disease caused by a bacterium) led to the chronic condition called *general paresis* manifested as physical paralysis and mental illness and eventually death. The discovery that a physical disease could cause a psychological disorder was a significant advance in understanding abnormal behavior, but we now know that bacteria are not the cause of most psychological disorders, even though in some cases psychological symptoms may have a medical basis.

The work of the German psychiatrist Emil Kraepelin (1856–1926) was another important chapter in the history of abnormal behavior. During medical school, Kraepelin attended lectures in the laboratory of Wilhelm Wundt, the founder of modern scientific psychology (Decker, 2004). He applied Wundt's scientific methods to measure behavioral deviations, hoping to provide the theoretical foundations that he considered to be lacking in psychiatry (compared with general medicine and psychology). On Wundt's advice, Kraepelin began to study "the abnormal" (Boyle, 2000). In 1899, after observing hundreds of patients, he introduced two diagnostic categories based not just on symptom differentiation but also on the *etiology* (cause) and *prognosis* (progression and outcome) of the disease. **Dementia praecox**, now called **schizophrenia** (see Chapter 11), was Kraepelin's term for a type of mental illness characterized by mental deterioration. *Manic-depressive insanity* was defined as a separate disorder with a more favorable outcome. Kraepelin was best known for his studies of dementia praecox, which he believed resulted from *autointoxication*, the self-poisoning of

Dorothea Dix of Massachusetts was a tireless reformer who brought the poor treatment of the mentally ill to public attention.

brain cells as a result of abnormal body metabolism. With new studies documenting the contribution of genetic and biological factors to the onset of schizophrenia, Kraepelin's contributions, in terms of both a classification system and a description of schizophrenia, cannot be overstated.

Another physician interested in the brain was Jean-Martin Charcot (1825–1893), who established a school of neurology at La Salpêtrière in Paris (Haas, 2001). Charcot was interested in hysteria, and he believed that it was caused by degenerative brain changes. However, at the same time, other researchers, Ambrose August Liébeault (1823–1904) and Hippolyte Bernheim (1840–1919) in Nancy, France, were conducting experiments to determine whether hysteria was a form of self-hypnosis. Debate raged between Charcot and the physicians collectively called the *Nancy School*. Eventually, most scientific data supported the views of the Nancy School. To his credit as a scientist, once the data were established, Charcot became a strong proponent of this view.

At about the same time, the Viennese physician Josef Breuer (1842–1925) was studying the effect of hypnotism. Breuer used hypnosis to treat patients with hysteria, including a young woman named Anna O., who had cared for her ailing father until his death. Shortly thereafter, she developed blurry vision, trouble speaking, and difficulty moving her right arm and both her legs. Breuer discovered that when under hypnosis, Anna O. would discuss events and experiences that she was unable to recall otherwise. Furthermore, after discussing these distressing events, her symptoms disappeared. Breuer called his treatment the **talking cure**, laying the foundation for a new approach to mental disorders.

The Twentieth Century

LO 1.10 Identify the psychological, biological, and sociocultural models that characterize the twentieth-century models of abnormal behavior.

Although biological theories were still influential, two psychological models of abnormal behavior dominated the early part of the twentieth century: psychoanalytic theory and behaviorism. In this section, we examine the roots of these theories and how they set the stage for modern-day approaches to understanding abnormal behavior.

PSYCHOANALYSIS Sigmund Freud (1856–1939) was trained as a neurologist. His career in psychiatry began in France, where he worked with Charcot. After settling in Vienna, Freud published *Studies in Hysteria* in 1895 with Josef Breuer. He introduced **psychoanalysis**, a comprehensive theory that attempts to explain both normal and abnormal behavior. Freud believed that the roots of abnormal behavior were established in the first 5 years of life. Because they happened so early, he believed that the person would retain no conscious memory of them—yet the unconscious memories would exert a lifelong influence on behavior. Psychoanalytic theory has three important aspects: the structure of the mind, the strategies used to deal with threats to the stability of the mind, and the stages of psychosocial development crucial for the development of normal (or abnormal) behavior.

Sigmund Freud introduced psychoanalysis, a theory that attempts to explain abnormal behavior as driven by unconscious biological and sexual urges.

In psychoanalytic theory, the mind consists of three regions: the id, ego, and superego. Basic instinctual drives and the source of psychic energy, called *libido*, are found in the *id*. Always seeking pleasure, the id is totally unconscious, so its urges and activities are outside our awareness. Think of the id as a professional athlete—"I want a big salary; I want a signing bonus." The *ego* develops when the id comes in contact with reality. Think of the ego as a sports agent who mediates between the id's impulses (the athlete's desires) and the demands and restrictions of reality (the owner's contract offer). Rather than always seeking pleasure, the ego copes with reality or, as Freud put it, the ego obeys the reality principle. The ego has both conscious and unconscious components, so we are often aware of its actions. The third region of the mind is the *superego*. Similar to a conscience, the superego imposes moral restraint on the id's impulses (particularly those of a sexual or an aggressive nature). Think of the superego as the team owner or the league commissioner who doles out monetary fines for breaking team or league rules. When moral rules are violated, the superego punishes with guilt feelings. Like the ego, the superego is partly conscious and partly unconscious and tries to manage or inhibit the id's impulses. Because these three intrapsychic forces are constantly competing, there is ever-changing conflict, creating a dynamic, in this case, a *psychodynamic* system.

Freud proposed that through the use of *defense mechanisms*, the mind's negative or distressing thoughts and feelings were disguised to emerge to consciousness in a more acceptable form. Some defense mechanisms prevented the onset of abnormal behavior. Other defense mechanisms (such as regression) may result in abnormal or age-inappropriate behaviors. Some of the defense mechanisms identified by Freud are presented in Table 1.2.

Almost as well known as the id, ego, and superego are Freud's stages of psychosexual development. According to the theory, each person passes through these stages between infancy and 5 years of age. How a child copes with each stage has important effects on psychological development. The *oral phase* occurs during the first 1½ years of life. Sucking and chewing are pleasurable experiences; aggressive impulses emerge after the development of teeth. The *anal phase* (from age 1½ to 3 years) coincides with toilet training. During this time, parents emphasize discipline and control issues, and power struggles develop. Aggressive impulses on the part of the child could lead to personality traits of negativism and stubbornness as well as the emergence of hostile, destructive, or sadistic behaviors. During the *phallic phase* (ages 3 to 5), psychosexual energy centers on the genital area and children derive pleasure from touching or rubbing the genitals. During this phase, children may develop romantic fantasies or attachments toward their opposite-sex parent. The two additional stages, the latency phase (the formant stage of psychosexual development when children are disinterested in the opposite sex) and the genital phase (the mature stage of psychosexual development), are considered to play a more limited role in abnormal behavior.

Table 1.2 Defense Mechanisms and Their Function

Defense	Function	Example
Denial	Dealing with an anxiety-provoking stimulus by acting as if it doesn't exist	Rejecting a physician's cancer diagnosis
Displacement	Taking out impulses on a less-threatening target	Slamming a door instead of hitting someone
Intellectualization	Avoiding unacceptable emotions by focusing on the intellectual aspects of an event	Focusing on a funeral's details rather than the sadness of the situation
Projection	Attributing your own unacceptable impulses to someone else	Making a mistake at work but, instead of admitting it, blaming it on a coworker whom you call "incompetent"
Rationalization	Supplying a plausible but incorrect explanation for a behavior rather than the real reason	Saying you drink three martinis every night because it lowers your blood pressure
Reaction formation	Taking the opposite belief because the true belief causes anxiety	Overtly embracing a particular race to the extreme by someone who is racially prejudiced
Regression	Under threat, returning to a previous stage of development	Not getting a desired outcome results in a temper tantrum
Repression	Burying unwanted thoughts out of conscious thought	Forgetting aspects of a traumatic event (such as sexual assault)
Sublimation	Acting out unacceptable impulses in a socially acceptable way	Acting out aggressive tendencies by becoming a boxer
Suppression	Pushing unwanted thoughts into the unconscious	Actively trying to forget something that causes anxiety
Undoing	Attempting to take back unacceptable behavior or thoughts	Insulting someone and then excessively praising him or her

Based on *Psychology 101, Freud's Ego Defense Mechanism*. http://allpsych.com/psychology101/defenses.html. Copyright © 1999–2003, AllPsych and Heffner Media Group, Inc. /Pearson Education, Inc.

In psychoanalytic theory, anxiety and depression are caused by negative experiences. Depending on the age at which the experience occurs, individuals become *fixated* (stalled) at a stage of psychosexual development. This leaves a psychological mark on the unconscious. For example, harsh parenting during toilet training results in a toddler who withholds his feces as a reaction. As an adult, this person will be stingy with money or gifts. In psychoanalytic theory, even though the individual is unaware of the early experience, it still influences daily functioning. In short, the individual behaves psychologically at the stage of development when the fixation occurred.

The goals of psychoanalysis, the treatment Freud developed, include *insight*, bringing the troubling material to consciousness, and *catharsis*, releasing psychic energy. Several techniques are used to achieve these goals. In *free association*, the person minimizes conscious control and, without selection or censorship, tells the analyst everything that comes to mind, allowing the analyst to draw out information regarding unconscious conflicts. In *dream analysis*, individuals are encouraged to recall and recount their dreams, which are discussed in the analytic sessions. Freud called dreams the *royal road to the unconscious*. He believed that dream content included many symbolic images that revealed the meaning of unconscious conflict. Another technique is *interpretation*. In psychoanalytic treatment, the analyst's silence encourages the patient's free association. The analyst offers interpretations about these associations to uncover the patient's resistance to treatment, to discuss the patient's transference feelings, or to confront the patient with inconsistencies. Interpretations may focus on present issues or draw connections between the patient's past and the present. The patient's dreams and fantasies are also sources of material for interpretation.

Freud's ideas were very controversial. His belief that much of human behavior was controlled by unconscious, innate biological and sexual urges that existed from infancy outraged Viennese Victorian society. Freud believed that the first 5 years of life were very important and events that occurred during that time could even influence adult behavior. He was one of the first theoreticians to highlight the role of environmental factors in abnormal behavior, but he considered the early environment to consist almost exclusively of one's mother and father. This belief sometimes led to detrimental and undeserved blaming of parents as the cause of abnormal behavior. For Freud, the key therapeutic ingredient was the achievement of *insight*. Overcoming psychological difficulties meant understanding their causes and meaning. Unlike Breuer, Freud did not view hypnosis as necessary to achieve insight, but he did believe in the talking cure, a lengthy relationship between therapist and patient.

BEHAVIORISM In 1904, Ivan Pavlov (1849–1936) received the Nobel Prize for his research on the physiology of dog digestion, which in turn led to his discovery of conditioned responses. A landmark moment for psychology was Pavlov's discovery of **classical conditioning**, in which an *unconditioned stimulus* (UCS) produces an *unconditioned response* (UCR). For example, you touch a hot stove (UCS) and immediately withdraw your hand (UCR). A *conditioned stimulus* (CS) is something neutral that does not naturally produce the UCR. In the classical conditioning paradigm, the UCS is repeatedly paired with a CS, resulting in the UCR. After sufficient pairings, the CS, presented alone, becomes capable of eliciting a *conditioned response* (CR), which is similar in form and content to the UCR. In Pavlov's paradigm, food powder was the UCS that produced salivation (UCR) in his dogs. Pavlov paired a neutral stimulus, a ringing bell (CS), with the food powder. After a sufficient number of pairings, the CS (the bell alone) produced salivation (CR) (see Figure 1.4).

This paradigm seems simple, but it is both powerful and more complex than it first appears. We will return to the conditioning theory of emotional disorders later in the chapter.

Figure 1.4 Classical Conditioning.

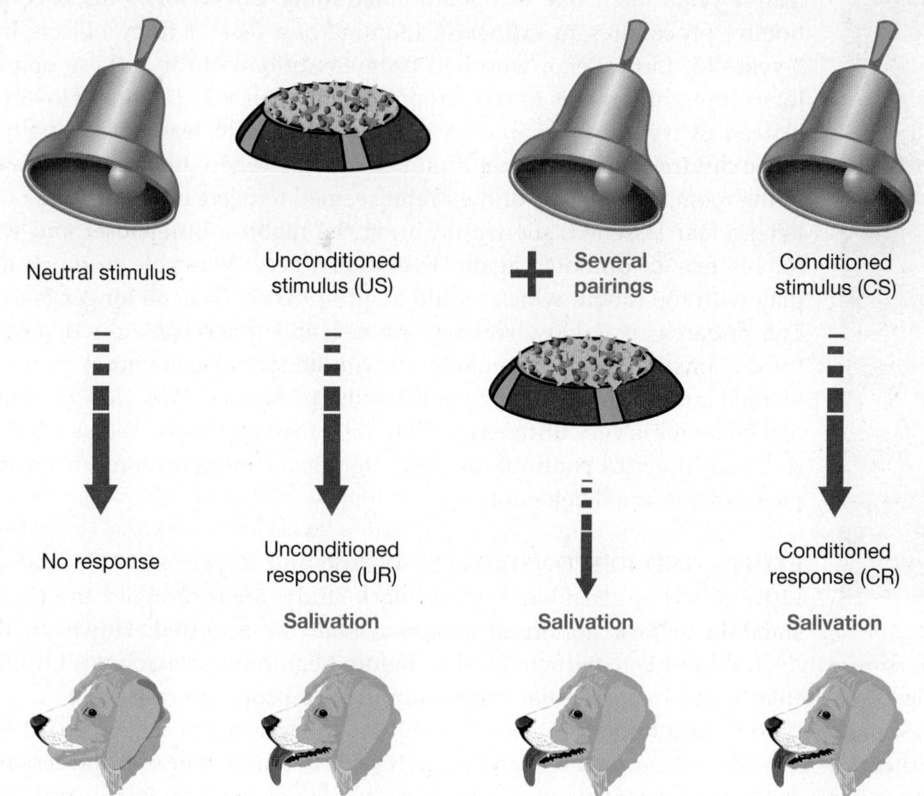

In 1908, John B. Watson (1878–1958), a well-known animal psychologist, joined the faculty of Johns Hopkins University. Watson believed that the only appropriate objects of scientific study were observable *behaviors*, not inner thoughts or feelings. This view, known as **behaviorism**, is based on principles that consider all behavior (normal or abnormal) to be *learned* as a result of experiences or interactions with the environment. Watson is most famous for his work with his student Rosalie Rayner. In 1920, they published the case of Little Albert, which demonstrated that emotional responses such as fear could be acquired through classical conditioning. In this case, Little Albert's fear of a white rat was established by pairing the white rat with a loud, aversive noise (Watson & Rayner, 1920). In addition, not only was an extreme emotional response established, but it generalized to other objects that, like the rat, were white and furry (a rabbit, a Santa Claus beard).

Ivan Pavlov's pioneering experiments with dogs led him to discover classical conditioning, a process that underlies much normal and abnormal behavior.

Unfortunately, Little Albert and his mother left Johns Hopkins soon after the experiments were completed, and for many years, psychologists were unsure about his fate. We now know that Little Albert's real name was Douglas Merritte, and he died at age 6 from congenital hydrocephalus, the condition in which the cavities of the brain have an excess of cerebrospinal fluid. Although initial reports suggested that Douglas's hydrocephalus was acquired later in his life as a result of a disease such as encephalitis or meningitis or the development of a brain tumor (Beck et al., 2009), it is now believed that Douglas was born with this brain condition (Fridlund et al., 2012).

John Watson introduced behaviorism, which in its strictest form asserts that all behavior is learned. With his student Rosalie Rayner, he studied infants' emotional responses, showing that emotions could be acquired by classical conditioning.

Although Watson never attempted to eliminate Albert/Douglas's fear, 4 years later, one of his students, Mary Cover Jones, used conditioning procedures to *extinguish* (eliminate) a fear of furry objects in a 2-year-old, Little Peter, who had been conditioned to fear these objects. Jones brought a rabbit into the room where Peter was playing. However, instead of trying to associate a neutral object with fear, she brought in other children who were not afraid of rabbits. When other children were in the room, Peter's fear of the rabbit seemed to decrease. Every time that Peter's fear lessened, she would bring the rabbit a little closer and wait for his fear to diminish again. Eventually, Peter was able to touch and play with the rabbit, which would suggest that he was no longer fearful. The research of Pavlov, Watson, Rayner, and Jones constituted powerful demonstrations that behaviors (even abnormal behaviors) could be learned and unlearned using conditioning principles. This view of abnormal behavior is very different from psychoanalytic theory. Yet, as we shall see, both theories continue to exert significant influence on our current views of abnormal behavior.

ETHICS AND RESPONSIBILITY Watson and Rayner's (1920) study of Little Albert is considered a landmark study, for it changed the understanding of how abnormal behavior could be acquired. However, this type of research could not be conducted today. Before beginning research with human subjects, particularly children, scientists must submit their proposed research to a committee usually known as a human subjects committee or institutional review board (see Chapter 15). This committee reviews the research plan to make sure that the research will not harm the potential participants. Research studies designed to demonstrate that a scientist can create a psychological disorder in someone, particularly a child, would not be permitted today. Scientists must now be more creative in their research designs and in many instances use less direct methods to examine how disorders might develop. Although less direct methods sometimes cannot produce the same data as Watson and Rayner produced, protecting research participants from harm is the most important consideration.

Explore ETHICS AND RESPONSIBILITY

Interactive

Learning Objective Summaries

LO 1.6 Discuss ancient spiritual and biological theories of the origins of abnormal behavior.

Historically, spirit possession was among the first proposed causes of abnormal behavior. Ancient theories held that spirits controlled aspects of human behavior and that the biological seat of abnormal behavior was the brain.

LO 1.7 Discuss spiritual, biological, and environmental theories of the origins of abnormal behavior in classical Greek and Roman periods.

As early as the classical Greek and Roman periods, biological and environmental explanations were given for some of the major psychiatric disorders (depression, schizophrenia). We know from writings from the classical Greek and Roman period that many psychological disorders that exist today were also present then. Hippocrates proposed that abnormal behavior resulted from an imbalance of bodily humors, indicating a biological cause. Other physicians, such as Galen and Avicenna, proposed that psychological factors also played a role.

LO 1.8 Discuss the spiritual, biological, and environmental theories of the origins of abnormal behavior from the Middle Ages to the Renaissance.

Such theories fell out of favor in Western Europe shortly afterward, although they continued to flourish in the Middle East. During medieval times, there was a return to theories of spirit possession, and charges of witchcraft were common. This was also the time when people with psychological disorders were locked up in institutional settings with little or no access to care. During the Renaissance period, theories based on biology and environmental factors re-emerged in Europe.

LO 1.9 Discuss the spiritual, biological, psychological and sociocultural theories of the origins of abnormal behavior in the nineteenth century.

The nineteenth century marked the beginning of humane treatment advanced by leaders such as Pinel, Tuke, Rush, and Dix. During this time, Kraepelin also introduced a system for the classification of mental disorders, and Charcot introduced psychological treatments.

LO 1.10 Identify the psychological, biological, and sociocultural models that characterize the twentieth-century models of abnormal behavior.

During the twentieth century, biological theories still looked to abnormalities in the mind or brain as the basis for abnormal behavior. Psychological theories predominated, particularly psychoanalysis and behaviorism. Sociocultural models remind us that behavior exists within a context. Behaviors that are considered problematic or abnormal in one culture may not be viewed that way in a different culture.

Critical Thinking Question

Central figures in abnormal psychology during the twentieth century were Freud, Pavlov, and Watson. How does Freud's theory of the development of abnormal behavior differ from those of Pavlov and Watson?

Current Views of Abnormal Behavior and Treatment

This journey through the history of theories and treatments of abnormal behavior leads us to several conclusions. First, scientific advances lead to new and more sophisticated approaches to understanding human behavior. Research findings allow unsupported theories to be discarded and provide new hypotheses to be tested and evaluated. This is the core of a scientific approach to abnormal behavior. Scientists form hypotheses and conduct controlled experiments to determine whether their hypotheses are supported. If empirical evidence supports the hypotheses, then those theories continue. If the evidence does not provide support, the theory is discarded or changed, and the process begins again.

Second, scientific discoveries in areas other than psychology may later provide insight into abnormal behavior. For example, the Human Genome Project officially completed in 2003 sequenced the entire human genome, although analyses will continue for many years. As our understanding of this map develops, new techniques (see Chapter 2) allow us to examine genetic abnormalities that may be associated with specific psychological disorders, such as schizophrenia and autism spectrum disorder. Similarly, new technologies such as magnetic resonance imaging (see Chapter 2) lead us to examine the brain in ways never before possible. Although not developed to study abnormal behavior, these technologies help us to identify brain areas that we now know are involved in specific emotions such as sadness or fear. These examples illustrate how, as science advances, newer insights replace older theories such as demonology. Furthermore, as scientifically advanced as our current theories appear, they too will be replaced as new discoveries emerge.

For the past 70 years, psychologists who study abnormal behavior have been trained in the **scientist–practitioner model**, meaning that when providing treatment, psychologists rely on the findings of research. In turn, when conducting research, the psychologist investigates topics that help to guide and improve psychological care. Psychologists who utilize this perspective have a unique advantage because their scientific training allows them to differentiate fact from opinion when evaluating new theories, new treatments, and new research findings. This perspective also allows psychologists to apply research findings in many different areas to develop more comprehensive models of abnormal behavior. Critically applying a scientific perspective to theories of etiology and examining the evidence behind proposed theories prevent us from adopting explanations that are without a firm scientific basis (such as witchcraft and demonology). "Treatments" based on such nonscientific ideas could have quite negative results and in some cases might even be deadly. As you read through this book, keep the scientist–practitioner model in mind.

For undergraduates, one of the most frustrating aspects of studying abnormal behavior is that psychologists often cannot provide a simple explanation for why a behavior occurs. What causes people to become so depressed that they commit suicide? Society often wants answers to these questions, but the answers are not simple. Unlike medical illness, abnormal behavior cannot be explained by bacteria or viruses that infect the body. Clinical descriptions and research findings have identified many different, and sometimes conflicting, factors. The different findings have given rise to perspectives, known as *models*, which try to weave coherent explanations from the available clinical observations and research findings. These models consist of basic assumptions that provide a framework for organizing information and a set of procedures and tools that can be used to test aspects of that framework (Kuhn, 1962).

In this chapter, we introduce some of the different models that try to explain abnormal behavior. You might wonder why so many different models exist. The answer is that abnormal behavior is very complex, and no one model appears capable of providing a comprehensive explanation. Using a scientific approach, researchers develop, examine, and discard models as new facts emerge. Next we examine some of the currently accepted models of abnormal behavior.

Biological Models

LO 1.11 Identify at least two biological mechanisms that are considered to play a role in the onset of abnormal behavior.

The biological model assumes that abnormal behavior results from biological processes of the body, particularly the brain. Although long suspected to be the seat of abnormal behavior, only in the past 20 or 30 years have scientific advances allowed us to observe brain mechanisms directly. One area of scientific breakthrough has been in our understanding of genetics. As already noted, through genetic mapping, we are beginning to understand whether psychological disorders such as schizophrenia or manic-depressive disorder have a genetic basis and, if so, how that understanding might lead to better intervention and prevention efforts. Technology breakthroughs such as computerized axial tomography (CAT) scans, magnetic resonance imaging (MRI), and functional MRI (fMRI) allow direct examination of brain structure and activity. With this direct observation, we now have a much greater understanding of the role of the brain in abnormal behavior.

THE BRAIN'S MESSAGING SYSTEM Although we often refer to the brain as if it were a single entity, it is a very complex organ. In fact, about 100 billion **neurons** (brain cells) make up the brain. Between the neurons are spaces known as **synapses**. Neurons (see Figure 1.5) communicate when **neurotransmitters** (chemical substances) are released into the synapse (i.e., the neuron fires) and land on a receptor site of the next neuron. That neuron then fires, sending an electrical impulse down the axon, releasing neurotransmitters into the next synapse, and so the process begins again. Neurotransmitter activity is the basis for brain activity (thinking, feeling, and motor activity) and is related to many physical and mental disorders. Until recently, the activity of neurotransmitters in the brain had to be assessed indirectly from their presence in other parts of the body (blood or spinal fluid). However, it was always unclear how accurately chemicals in blood or spinal fluid really reflected neurotransmitter activity in the brain. Through advances in **neuroscience**, we now rely less on assumptions and indirect measures to understand the structure and function of the nervous system and its interaction with behavior. We can now directly observe many aspects of the brain's functioning, just as we do external behavior.

Watch HOW NEURONS WORK

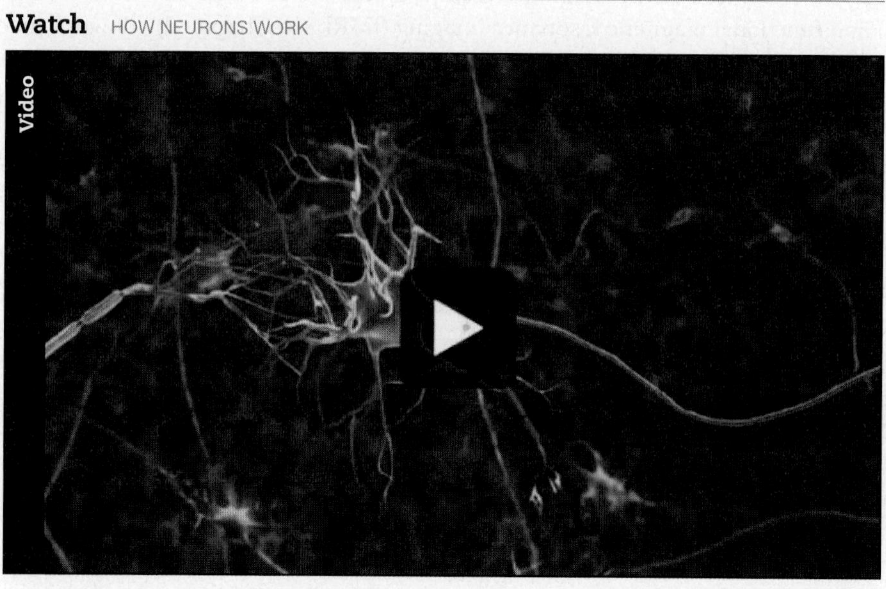

Figure 1.5 The Neuron Fires, Sending an Impulse to the Next Neuron.

Each individual neuron transmits information that is vital for virtually every aspect of our functioning.

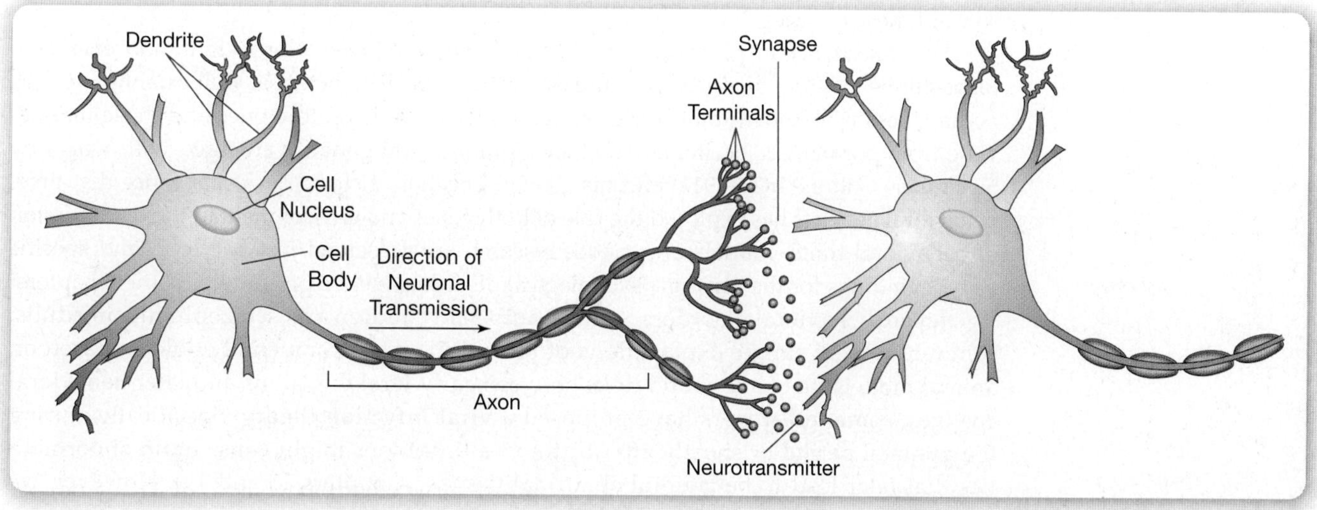

THE BRAIN'S STRUCTURE Imaging tests such as the CAT scan and MRI examine the *morphology* (structure) of the brain and are used to determine whether parts of the brain are structurally different in those with and without psychological disorders. For example, the brains of patients with Alzheimer's disease have two structural abnormalities, *plaques* and *tangles*, which exist in greater number than among older people without Alzheimer's disease (see Chapter 14). For other psychological disorders, the evidence is less definitive. In disorders such as depression, the biological, psychological, and cognitive changes may be the result of, not the cause of, the disorder (Wichers et al., 2010). In other words, years of living with the disorder cause changes in the brain, a process sometimes known as **biological scarring**. In other instances, when compared to people with no disorder, the brains of people with schizophrenia show structural brain abnormalities that could have occurred before birth (Malla & Payne, 2002; Sallet et al., 2003; see Chapter 11). Although we do not know for certain how these structural abnormalities may influence behavior, they illustrate how our understanding of the brain and abnormal behavior has changed as a result of new technologies.

THE BRAIN'S FUNCTIONS Although some abnormal behaviors may be related to structural abnormalities, studies of brain *functioning* appear to be a more promising avenue of research. Advanced neuroimaging techniques such as positron emission tomography (PET) and functional magnetic resonance imaging (fMRI; see Chapter 2) allow for mapping various areas of the brain and identifying brain areas that might be associated with various disorders. Differences in brain functioning have been reported for adults with schizophrenia and depression (A. J. Holmes et al., 2005; Milak et al., 2005), adults and children with anxiety disorders (Baxter, 1992; Bellis, 2004), eating disorders (van Kuyck et al., 2009), and many other psychiatric disorders. These studies are numerous and will be reviewed throughout this book.

POTENTIAL CAUSES OF ABNORMAL BRAIN STRUCTURE OR FUNCTION Although neuroscience data provide exciting new avenues for further research, it is still too soon to conclude that brain abnormalities cause psychological disorders. First, not all studies that compare people with and without a disorder find differences in brain structure or function. Furthermore, even when differences are detected, the abnormalities are not always found in a second trial, meaning that the abnormalities are not consistent. Second, to date, when differences exist, they are sometimes found in several different disorders. This means that whatever difference exists probably does not *cause* a specific disorder. Just like a fever that may be associated with many different physical illnesses, abnormal brain functioning may indicate that *something* is wrong, but not specifically what is wrong. Third, in most instances, few data indicate that these structural or functional abnormalities existed *before* the disorder occurred (schizophrenia and autism may be exceptions). It is just as likely that some disorders, such as PTSD, may cause changes in brain functioning, if not necessarily brain structure. Over the next decade, continued research in these areas coupled with the development of even more sophisticated assessment devices and strategies may help clarify some of these issues.

The inheritance of physical traits such as hair color, eye color, height, and even predispositions to some diseases (e.g., breast cancer, type 1 diabetes) is well established. It is perhaps less well known that some behavioral traits, both healthy ones and those that deviate from normal, are heritable. The field of **behavioral genetics** emerged with works by Sir Francis Galton (1822–1911) and his 1869 publication, *Hereditary Genius*. Since that time, behavioral genetics has explored the role of both genes and environment in the transmission of behavioral traits. Models of genetics research are presented in Chapter 2, and specific genetic findings for the various psychological disorders will be presented in other chapters.

Severe behavioral disorders, such as autism in children and schizophrenia in adults, continue to defy simple explanations of biological or environmental etiology. Based on animal models that have found links between early viral infections and later behavioral changes, some researchers have proposed a **viral infection theory**. Specifically, during the prenatal period or shortly after birth, viral infections might cause brain abnormalities that later lead to behavioral abnormalities (see Chapters 11 and 13). However, we cannot yet say that this is a definitive cause, for the results of one study sometimes directly contradict those of another. Such contradictory findings are not unusual for psychology or any other science. As research continues, disparate findings are either reconciled or the theory is revised or discarded.

Even if future research confirms a relationship between viral infection and the onset of psychological disorders, there are still several different pathways that may produce this relationship. First, the virus may act *directly* by infecting the central nervous system (CNS). Similarly, infection elsewhere in the body could trigger the onset of a CNS disease. Second, viruses may act *indirectly* by changing the immune system of the mother or the fetus, thereby making one or both more susceptible to other biological or environmental factors. Third, both mechanisms may be involved (Libbey et al., 2005). Although some animal models suggest a possible relation between certain viruses and changes in the brain, evidence that the virus *triggers* the onset of a disorder has proved elusive. The etiology of most psychological disorders is likely to be complex—not traceable to a single genetic, biological, or environmental factor. Other variables, yet to be discovered, may be responsible for triggering or modifying the course of illness.

Psychological Models

LO 1.12 Identify at least two psychological models that may account for the development of abnormal behavior.

The biological model seeks the causes of abnormal behavior in the workings of the brain or body. In contrast, psychological approaches emphasize how environmental factors such as family and cultural factors may influence the development and maintenance of abnormal behavior. In actuality, parental influence may be biological or psychological. Parents pass on their genes, but their influence is much broader. Parents can affect their children's behavior in at least four ways:

- direct interaction
- responses to a child's behavior
- modeling certain behaviors
- giving instructions

Of course, a child's environment extends far beyond parents or even immediate family. The impact of other environmental factors, such as SES, was illustrated earlier in the chapter. To provide another example, environmental events such as separation from biological parents increase the likelihood of depression in adolescents (Cuffe et al., 2005). Furthermore, in some cases, environmental and cultural influences may produce behavior that is considered abnormal in one culture but not in another, as in the earlier case of Maleah, in which intergenerational bed sharing was a commonly accepted practice in the Philippines. Cultural influences such as these are addressed subsequently (see "Sociocultural Models").

MODERN PSYCHOANALYTIC MODELS Modern psychoanalysts no longer discuss the id or fixation at the phallic stage. They do, however, still agree that much of mental life is unconscious and that personality patterns begin to form in childhood. They propose that mental representations (views) of the self and others guide our interactions and may lead to psychological symptoms. Finally, they believe that personality development involves not only learning to regulate sexual and aggressive feelings but also having mature interpersonal relationships with others (Westen, 1998).

Freud's ideas have influenced a number of other theorists. Initially, he named Carl Gustav Jung (1875–1961) as his successor. However, they disagreed over several key theoretical components, and Jung broke away to develop *analytic therapy*. Unlike Freud, Jung believed that behavioral motivators were psychological and spiritual (not sexual) and that future goals rather than past events motivated behavior. Another former colleague, Alfred

Adler (1870–1937), also broke with Freud to develop his own psychoanalytic school called *individual psychology*. Less comprehensive than Freud, Adler introduced several concepts that are part of everyday language and are associated with abnormal behavior: *sibling rivalry*, the importance of *birth order*, and the *inferiority complex*, by which real or perceived inferiority leads to efforts to compensate for the deficiency.

More contemporary models of psychoanalysis, such as **ego psychology**, deviate from Freud by their increased focus on conscious motivations and healthy forms of human functioning. *Object relations theory*, for example, addresses people's emotional relations with important *objects* (in this sense, people or things to which the person is attached). This theory emphasizes that people have a basic drive for social interactions and that motivations for social contact are more than simply to satisfy sexual and aggressive instincts. Therapy uses the patient's relationship with the therapist to examine and build other relationships in their lives.

BEHAVIORAL MODELS Unlike the psychodynamic perspective, where internal mental elements exert an influence on behavior, learning theory stresses the importance of external events in the onset of abnormal behaviors. According to learning theory, *behavior* is the product of an individual's learning history. Abnormal behavior is therefore the result of maladaptive learning experiences. Behavioral theories do not ignore biological factors; instead, they acknowledge that biology interacts with the environment to influence behavior. Strict behaviorists focus on observable and measurable behavior and do not examine inner psychic causes. They believe that abnormal behavior results from environmental events that shape future behavior, such as the conditioning events that led to Little Albert's fear. In contrast to psychoanalytic theory's emphasis on the first 5 years of life, according to behavioral theory, significant experiences can occur at any point in life.

Despite the pioneering work of Pavlov, Watson, Rayner, and Jones, behavior therapy remained in its infancy until the 1950s. Then a South African psychiatrist, Joseph Wolpe (1915–1997), dissatisfied with psychoanalysis, began to study experimental *neurosis* (anxiety) in animals. Using a classical conditioning paradigm, a dog learned that food followed the presentation of a circle but not an ellipse. Then Wolpe altered the shape of the circle and the ellipse so that *discrimination* (and, therefore, the signal for food) became increasingly difficult (is it a circle? is it an ellipse?). The dog struggled, became agitated, barked violently, and attacked the equipment, behaviors that would indicate the presence of negative emotions. Once Wolpe demonstrated how classical conditioning principles could account for the development of anxiety, he applied the same principles to eliminate fear. In his landmark book *Psychotherapy by Reciprocal Inhibition* (Wolpe, 1958), he proposed that a stimulus will not elicit anxiety if an *incompatible behavior* (such as feeling relaxed) occurs at the same time. In other words, it is not possible to feel anxious and relaxed (or anxious and happy) at the same time; they are incompatible emotions. Mary Cover Jones treated Peter by selecting a situation that she thought would promote relaxation (other children playing in the room). In contrast, Wolpe specifically taught his patient how to relax. Then he deliberately paired relaxation (the incompatible response) with the fear-producing event. With repeated pairings, he eliminated anxiety.

Just as Jones began treatment of Little Peter by placing the rabbit at the opposite corner of the room and then moving it progressively closer, Wolpe used a *hierarchy*, in which elements of the anxiety-producing object are presented in a gradual fashion. For someone who fears flying, the hierarchy might include going to the airport, sitting in the boarding area, getting on the plane, taking off, and so on. Relaxation is paired with each step in the hierarchy. This therapy, called *systematic desensitization*, is very effective for a range of anxiety problems. Although used less frequently today than 30 to 40 years ago, systematic desensitization still forms the foundation for many current behavior therapy procedures.

"The more often I tell him to sit down, the more he stands up." This line, which could have been spoken by Derek's second-grade teacher, illustrates the powerful effect of attention. Sometimes yelling at a child for bad behavior actually increases it. To understand

B. F. Skinner explained how behaviors could be acquired or changed by reinforcement, a process called *operant conditioning.*

why, it is necessary to first understand the work of B. F. Skinner (1904–1990). He observed that many behaviors occurred without *first* being elicited by a UCS. Using animal models, Skinner demonstrated that behavior could be acquired or changed by the events that happened *afterward*. Known as **operant conditioning**, these principles are relevant to the behaviors of individuals, groups, and entire societies.

The basic principle behind operant theory is **reinforcement**, which is defined as a contingent event that strengthens the behavior that precedes it. In its simplest form, a reinforcer may be considered to be a reward—a child does household chores and the reward is a weekly allowance. If the allowance is contingent upon (occurs only after) the completion of the chores, it is likely that the child will do chores again. The allowance is a *reinforcer* because it functions to increase behavior. Skinner identified several principles of reinforcement. First, reinforcers are always individual: What is a reinforcer for one person is not necessarily a reinforcer for another person (chocolate is not a reinforcer for everyone). Second, there are primary and secondary reinforcers. *Primary reinforcers* are objects such as food, water, or even attention. They have their own intrinsic value (i.e., they satisfy basic needs of life or make one feel good). *Secondary reinforcers* are objects that have acquired value because they become associated with primary reinforcers. Money is a secondary reinforcer because it symbolizes the ability to acquire other reinforcers (heat in cold weather, a cold drink when thirsty). Much of Skinner's work was devoted to *schedules of reinforcement*, which established the "when" and "how" of reinforcement and set forth conditions under which behavior was more likely to be acquired or less likely to be extinguished. Skinner's work has applications for parenting, education, psychology, and many other aspects of behavior. How does this work apply to Derek? For children, adult attention is a powerful reinforcer. If every time Derek stands up, the teacher calls out his name (gives him attention) and asks him to sit down (or, even worse, calls him aside and spends time asking him why he keeps standing up), this positive attention could be reinforcing, increasing the likelihood that when Derek wants attention, he will stand up again.

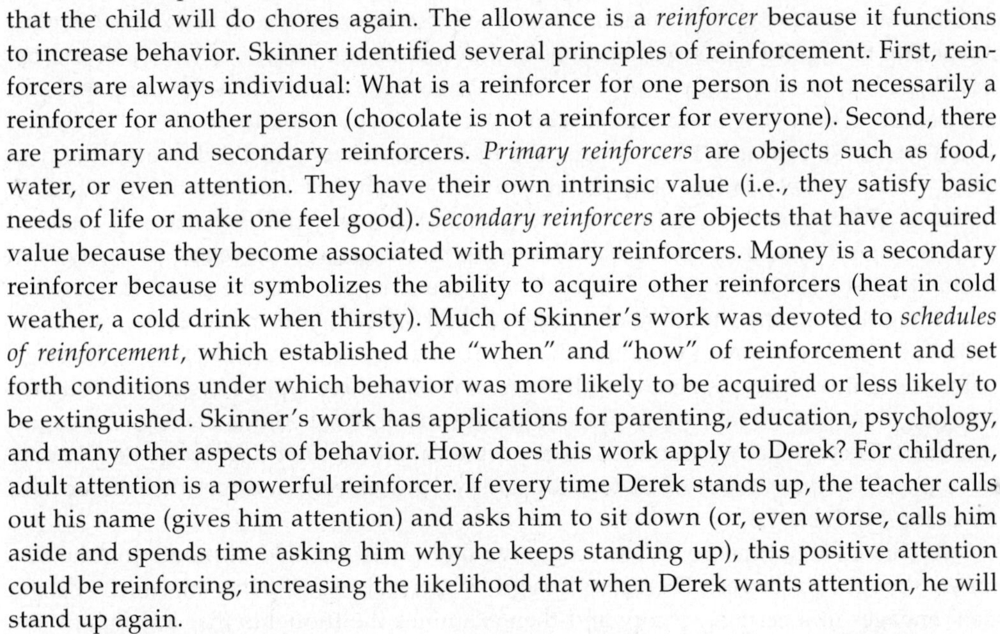

Whereas reinforcement serves to increase the frequency of a behavior, **punishment** has the opposite effect: It decreases or eliminates a behavior. Punishment can be the application of something painful (spanking) or the removal of something positive (no television). Sometimes punishment is necessary to quickly eliminate a very dangerous behavior, for example, a child with severe mental retardation engages in self-mutilating behaviors. The withdrawal of something positive, such as in a *time-out* (having a child sit in a corner for a few minutes), is often effective for behaviors such as tantrumming. Skinner advocated the use of reinforcement rather than punishment. Punishment suppresses a behavior, but if an alternative, substitute behavior is not acquired, the punished behavior reemerges. Therefore, when punishment is used to suppress a behavior, reinforcement of an alternative, positive behavior must also occur.

How do the dolphins in captivity learn to leap into the air, spin around three times, and then slide on a ramp to receive the applause of a human audience? The trainers use a procedure called *shaping*, a process whereby closer steps, or successive approximations, to a final goal are rewarded. Dolphin trainers begin by reinforcing (with food) any initial attempt or slight movement that resembles a turn. Gradually, the trainer requires a larger turn before providing reinforcement until finally the dolphin must completely spin around before receiving reinforcement. Shaping is an effective procedure for the acquisition of new behaviors in children and adults and will be discussed in several other chapters in this book.

We have reviewed two types of learning so far: classical conditioning and operant conditioning. A third type of learning was described by Albert Bandura (1925–) and his colleagues at Stanford University during the early 1960s. **Vicarious conditioning** is characterized by *no trial learning*—the person need not actually do the behavior in order to learn it. Learning occurs when the person watches a model, that is, someone who demonstrates a behavior. Observation of another person can have a disinhibiting or inhibiting effect on current behaviors or can teach new behaviors. This kind of *social learning* can explain the acquisition of abnormal behaviors such as aggression.

Behavior therapists focus therapy on the elimination of abnormal behaviors and on the acquisition of new behaviors and skills. Treatment targets the patient's current symptoms. Although the past is considered important in understanding the present and the patient's current psychological distress, behavior therapy does not focus specifically on the early years of life. Furthermore, achieving insight is not considered sufficient to produce behavior change. Rather, behavior therapists focus directly on helping patients change their behavior in order to alleviate their psychological problems.

THE COGNITIVE MODEL The cognitive model proposes that abnormal behavior is a result of distorted cognitive (mental) processes, not internal forces or external events. According to cognitive theory, situations and events do not affect our emotions and behavior; rather, the way we perceive or think about those events does. Imagine that you fail the first test in your abnormal psychology class. If you think to yourself, "Well, that was a hard test, but now I know what the instructor wants and I'll do better the next time," you are likely to feel okay about yourself and study harder for the next test. If, however, after you fail the test, you think, "I'm an idiot; why did I ever think I could be a psychologist?" you may feel sad and lose your enthusiasm for the class. You may even decide that you should drop out. In each case, the situation was the same. It was what you thought about the situation, and yourself, that affected your mood and your future behavior. That is the core of cognitive theory. According to Aaron Beck (1921–), the originator of cognitive therapy, people with depression have three types of negative thoughts: a negative view of the self, the world, and the future. Beck called this the negative cognitive triad. These negative assumptions are often called *cognitive distortions*. People may have many different types of distorted cognitive processes that affect their mood and behavior (see Table 1.3).

To change abnormal behaviors, cognitive therapy is directed at modifying the distorted thought processes. Therapists assign behavioral experiments in which the patient engages in a certain activity and then examines the thoughts that accompany the activity. With therapist assistance, the patient learns to challenge negative thoughts, to assess the situation more realistically, and to generate alternative, more positive thoughts. Cognitive therapy and behavior therapy share many similarities, but there are some differences. First, cognitive therapy is based on the assumption that internal cognitive processes must be the target of therapy, whereas behavior therapy assumes that changing behavior will lead to a change in cognitions. Second, cognitive therapy relies more on the use of traditional talk psychotherapy and insight than does traditional behavior therapy. Despite some theoretical differences, comparisons of behavior therapy and cognitive therapy suggest that they are equally effective treatments for most psychological disorders. In many cases, treatment procedures originally developed under one model or the other are now used together, thus the term *cognitive–behavior therapy*.

Children often learn behaviors by watching a model perform them, a process called *vicarious conditioning*.

Table 1.3 Common Cognitive Distortions

Type	Example
All-or-nothing thinking	If I don't go to an Ivy League school, I'll be a bum.
Overgeneralizing	Everything I do is wrong.
Mental filtering	The instructor said the paper was good, but he criticized my example on page 6. He really hated the paper.
Disqualifying the positive	Sure, I got an A, but that was pure luck. I'm not that smart.
Jumping to conclusions	The bank teller barely looked at me. She really hates me.
Magnifying or minimizing	I mispronounced that word in my speech. I really screwed up.
OR	I can dance well, but that's not really important—being smart is what's important, and I'm not smart.
Catastrophizing	I failed this quiz. I'll never graduate from college.
Reasoning emotionally	I feel hopeless, so this situation must be hopeless.
Making "should" statements	I should get an A in this class even though it is really hard.
Mislabeling	I failed this quiz. I'm a complete and total idiot.
Personalizing	We did not get that big account at work. It's all my fault.

Based on Burns, D. D. (1989). *The feeling good handbook.* New York: William Morrow and Company /Pearson Education, Inc.

THE HUMANISTIC MODEL Based on **phenomenology**, a school of thought that holds that one's subjective perception of the world is more important than the actual world, humanists believe that people are basically good and are motivated to *self-actualize* (develop their full potential). Abnormal behaviors occur when there is a failure in the process of self-actualization, usually as a result of people's failure to recognize their weaknesses and establish processes and strategies to fulfill their potential for positive growth.

The psychologist most closely associated with humanistic psychology is Carl Rogers (1902–1987). His theory of abnormal behavior begins with the assumption that psychopathology is associated with psychological incongruence, or a discrepancy between one's self-image and one's actual self. The greater the discrepancy, the more emotional and real-world problems one experiences. Incongruence results from the experience of *conditional* positive regard—a person is treated with respect and caring only when meeting the standards set by others (i.e., conditionally). The person comes to believe that he or she is worthy only when meeting those standards. Because this is an inaccurate, overly demanding image, emotional or behavioral problems result.

The goal of Rogers' psychotherapy, called *client-centered therapy*, is to release the individual's existing capacity to self-actualize (reach full potential) through interactions with the therapist. Therapy is based on three components. *Genuineness* means that the therapist relates to the person in an open, honest way and does not hide behind a professional mask. *Empathic understanding* means that the therapist understands the client's world as the client sees it. Finally, the therapist expresses *unconditional positive regard* by genuinely accepting the client with full understanding, trusting the client's resources for self-understanding and positive change. Whereas psychoanalytic therapy focuses on understanding the patient's past experiences, client-centered therapy focuses on present experiences, believing that the reestablishment of awareness and trust in that experience will lead to positive change.

Sociocultural Models

LO 1.13 Explain the sociocultural mode of behavior and how it differs from the biological and psychological models.

All of the models of abnormal behavior discussed so far begin with the assumption that abnormality lies within the individual. Instead, **sociocultural models** propose that abnormal behavior must be understood within the context of social and cultural forces, such as gender roles, social class, and interpersonal resources. From this perspective, abnormal behavior does not simply result from biological or psychological factors but also reflects the social and cultural environment in which a person lives. Many social and cultural forces may influence behavior; we discuss only a few here.

One well-studied social factor is *gender role,* defined as the cultural expectations regarding accepted behaviors for men and women, boys and girls. These differing role expectancies often exert a powerful influence on the expression of abnormal behavior. Consider the fact that girls (and women) are much more likely than boys (or men) to admit to having a phobia. Could gender role expectations, rather than biology, explain this difference? In Western cultures, girls are allowed to express emotions openly, whereas society discourages such behavior among boys—consider the phrases "boys don't cry" or "take it like a man." The implication is that showing emotion is not appropriate behavior for males and therefore not accepted in Western society. So boys learn to hide or deny emotions, such as fear. Other disorders possibly influenced by gender role are eating disorders, which are more common in girls and may be triggered in some cases by pervasive sociocultural pressures on females to be thin (see Chapter 8).

In addition to gender role, other social factors such as hunger, work, and domestic violence may make women more vulnerable to psychological distress (Lòpez & Guarnaccia, 2000). More than 60% of women in developing countries do not have adequate food. In both developed and developing countries, women do not receive equal pay even when they are performing dangerous, labor-intensive jobs, and more often than men, they are victims of domestic violence. These factors, perhaps in combination with others, are perceived to play a significant role in the development of psychological disorders, perhaps placing women at higher risk, not because of their biology but because of the social context in which they live.

Gender role expectations affect behavior. In Western cultures, showing emotion openly is more acceptable among females than among males.

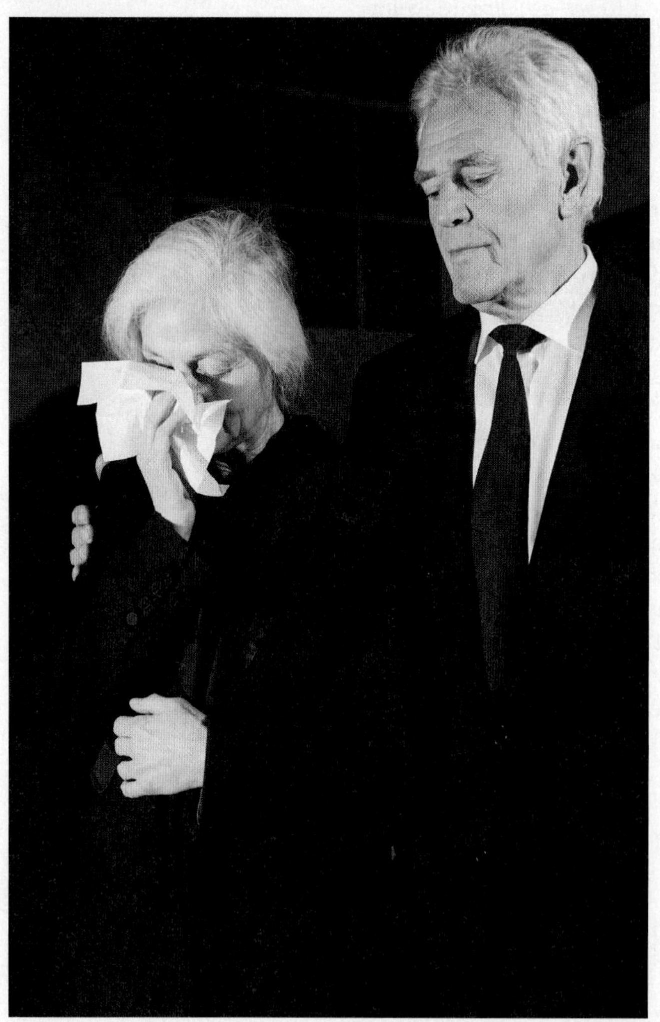

SES is another social factor that may affect the development of psychological disorders. After Hurricane Andrew, rates of one type of psychological disorder, PTSD, were higher among African American and Hispanic children than among white children (LaGreca et al., 1996). On first glance, this difference might be attributed to race or ethnicity, but another important factor might be SES. Why might SES be important? People from the lowest income bracket are more likely to live in housing that is easily damaged by strong winds and therefore are more likely to be homeless after a storm. In 2005, Hurricane Katrina hit the city of New Orleans. Although all areas of New Orleans were affected by the storm, the areas of the city that were closest to the floodplain housed some of the city's poorest families. Coupled with the limited economic resources that existed before the storm, residents faced continuing economic hardship and slow recovery (Meyers, 2008). With few social or economic resources, the likelihood of emotional distress and psychological disorders increases.

Interpersonal support is another social factor that helps people during times of emotional distress. Although many of the people most affected by Hurricane Katrina had little money, they had deep neighborhood roots. Now, even years later, many remain displaced from their homes and their former social support systems, leading to the development of psychological disorders such as depression, anxiety, and PTSD. As is obvious from this brief review, many different social factors can affect the onset of psychological distress, and throughout this volume, we return to these issues as we attempt to understand abnormal behavior.

Although Hurricane Sandy affected many residents of New York and New Jersey, people pulled together to help one another, creating a social network that could prevent or lessen the hurricane's impact.

Along with social factors, the sociocultural model also includes cultural influences such as race and ethnicity. Historically, these variables were used unfairly to stereotype groups. In the early nineteenth century, for example, the brains of Africans, Native Americans, and Asians were considered to be simple and crude, leading to lower rates of insanity (Raimundo Oda et al., 2005). Insanity was believed to result from having to cope with the stressful Western civilized life and to require sophisticated cognitive abilities. Today, that explanation has been discarded, but context and culture are still important influences on behavior, including abnormal behavior.

Cultural factors may affect symptom expression and diagnosis. With respect to symptom expression, several different variables are important. First, behaviors that are considered abnormal in one culture may be considered normal in other cultures. In Puerto Rico, *dissociation* (a feeling of being detached from one's body—sometimes called an *out-of-body experience*) is considered a normal part of spiritual and religious experiences, but it would be regarded as abnormal in other Western cultures (Lewis-Fernandez, 1998; Tsai et al., 2001). Similarly, behaviors that suggest extreme suspiciousness and mistrust of others may justifiably be labeled paranoia in some patients. Among other cultures and groups, however, suspiciousness may simply be an adaptive response from people who have been marginalized because of sociodemographic factors or who have been the victims of stereotype or racial discrimination (Whaley, 1998).

Researchers with a sociocultural perspective examine how psychological disorders may express themselves differently in different cultures. Certain conditions that are specific to a culture are known as *culture-bound syndromes* (Lòpez & Guarnaccia, 2007; Miranda & Fraser, 2002). One such disorder, *koro,* occurs among people of South and East Asia and consists of intense anxiety that the penis (or vulva and nipples in women) will disappear or cause one's death (American Psychiatric Association, 2013).

As researchers gain a better understanding of the important roles that social and cultural factors play in the onset, expression, and treatment of psychological disorders, they are developing culturally sensitive treatments for many different disorders. These treatment approaches incorporate cultural values and expressions that may enhance the therapeutic process by increasing the number of people who seek and benefit from these enhanced interventions. Consider the cultural context that surrounds suicide. U.S.-born Latino adolescents are twice as likely to attempt suicide as foreign-born Latino youth (CDC, 2006). Although many factors are involved in the decision to attempt suicide, familismo may be one important factor. *Familismo* (or *familism*), a concept common in Latino cultures, emphasizes the centrality of and obligation to family over self or peers (Lugo Steidel & Contreras, 2003). This orientation differs from that of mainstream U.S. teen culture, which emphasizes peer relationships, individualism, and moving away from the family (Goldston et al., 2008). It is possible that Latino teens born in the United States experience weakening of familism values when constantly exposed to the mainstream U.S. culture of individualism. Less emphasis on familial obligation may be a factor that leads to higher rates of suicide among U.S.-born Latino youth. Familism may also be an important factor when providing treatment to Hispanic families. Currently, several interventions developed for depressed adolescents have been modified by

Among Hispanic families, "familism" may buffer people against stressful environments and events. Here a family participates in a cultural tradition. Quinceañera, a coming of age ceremony and celebration that occurs on a girl's 15th birthday, dates back to ancient native cultures of Central and South America and Mexico.

including more direct involvement of parents in the treatment program. Although much more research is needed, culturally sensitive interventions are likely to increase the acceptance of, and therefore the effectiveness of, psychological interventions for psychological disorders.

The Biopsychosocial Model

LO 1.14 Explain how the biopsychosocial model accounts for the limitations in the three unidimensional models (biological, psychological, sociocultural).

In this chapter, we have examined biological, psychological, social, and cultural factors that affect the development and expression of abnormal behaviors. One reason there are so many different models is that no one perspective is able to explain all aspects of behavior and certainly not all cases of abnormal behavior.

Current approaches to physical medicine assume that all illnesses are based on biological processes that can be reduced to a biological cause even if the specific physical process has not yet been determined. For example, we know that cancer occurs when abnormal cells develop and attack the body's systems even though we do not know yet what physical processes caused these cells to develop. In contrast, in the case of mental disorders, there is no single model of abnormal behavior even though scientists continue to search for such single explanations (Lake, 2007). Instead, there are as many different models, and often the training backgrounds of mental health professionals result in different perspectives being emphasized. Modern scientists now recognize that (1) abnormal behavior is complex, (2) abnormal behavior cannot be understood using a single theoretical explanation, and (3) understanding abnormal behavior will advance only if we embrace and integrate the various conceptual models (Kendler, 2005). A significant challenge to understanding abnormal behavior is to understand how the mind and the brain interact and how to combine these very different perspectives to create a coherent theory of psychological disorders. In fact, modern scientists have moved past trying to reduce all behavior to one singular explanation. It is clear that causality can begin in the brain *or* the mind and can set off a chain of events that ultimately affects both components, leading to the onset of abnormal behavior (Kendler, 2005). Other researchers (Lake, 2007) have argued that integrating the perspectives of biomedicine, human consciousness, and neuroscience will lead to significant advances in understanding and treating psychological disorders.

Currently, most mental health clinicians subscribe to a **biopsychosocial perspective**, which acknowledges that many different factors probably contribute to the development of abnormal behavior and that different factors may be important for different people. This perspective utilizes a **diathesis-stress model of abnormal behavior**, which begins with the assumption that psychological disorders may have a preexisting vulnerability (see Figure 1.6). The presence of a biological or psychological predisposition to a disease or disorder is called a *diathesis*. However, just having a *predisposition* for a disorder does not mean that a person will actually *develop* it. Rather, the predisposition is assumed to lie dormant (as if it does not exist) until stressful environmental factors create significant distress for the individual. People react differently to stressful events. The combination of a biological or psychological predisposition and the presence of environmental stress creates psychological disorders. The diathesis-stress model integrates biological, psychological, and sociocultural systems to provide explanations that are consistent with what we know are complex human behaviors. We will return to this biopsychosocial model and the diathesis-stress model many times throughout this volume.

Figure 1.6 The Diathesis-Stress Model.

In this model, a diathesis, or vulnerability, interacts with individual stressors to produce a psychological disorder. The biopsychosocial model uses the concept of diathesis-stress to acknowledge that many different factors (biological, psychological, and social) may contribute to the development of a disorder.

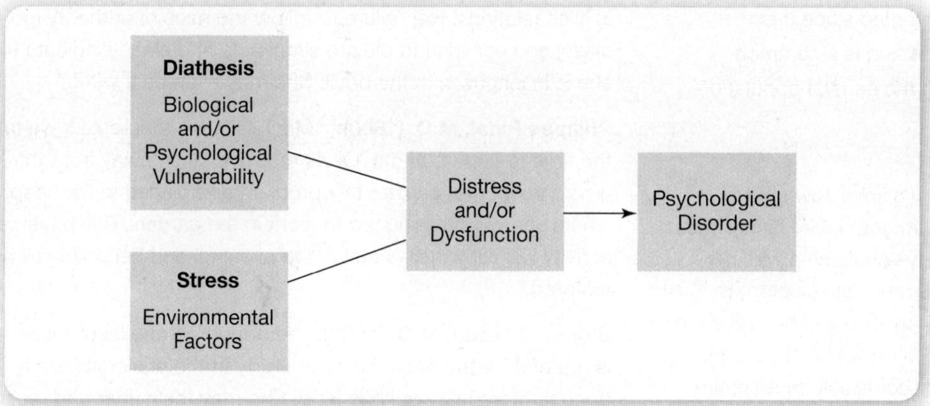

Learning Objective Summaries

LO 1.11 Identify at least two biological mechanisms that are considered to play a role in the onset of abnormal behavior.

The biological model of abnormal behavior assumes that abnormal behavior is rooted in a person's biology. The basis may be a genetic abnormality, abnormal brain structures, or abnormal brain functioning.

LO 1.12 Identify at least two psychological models that may account for the development of abnormal behavior.

Within the psychological model are several distinctive approaches, including modern psychoanalytic, behavioral, and cognitive models. Rather than looking to biology as the basis for psychological disorders, these models assume that environmental events and the way we interpret and react to them play a causal role in the onset of abnormal behavior.

LO 1.13 Explain the sociocultural mode of behavior and how it differs from the biological and psychological models.

Sociocultural models are based on a broader perspective, proposing that broad social and cultural forces (not individual or unique environmental events) contribute to the onset of psychological disorders.

LO 1.14 Explain how the biopsychosocial model accounts for the limitations in the three unidimensional models (biological, psychological, sociocultural).

The biopsychosocial perspective incorporates a diathesis-stress model, in which biology is thought to lay the foundation for the onset of the disorder through the presence of biological abnormalities. However, biology alone is insufficient; environmental, social, and cultural factors are always part of the equation that leads to the onset of psychological disorders. Today biological, psychological, sociocultural, and biopsychosocial explanations dominate the explanations for the development of abnormal behavior. Each of the etiological theories has strengths and weaknesses, and each alone is inadequate to fully explain the presence of abnormal behavior. Determining abnormal behavior is complex, and it is likely that a combination of factors is responsible for any specific psychological disorder. There are many competing theories, and as science progresses, new theories will be developed and others will be discarded.

Critical Thinking Question

Using a biopsychosocial perspective, what factors might influence the development of a psychological disorder in a member of the military who served in Operation Iraqi Freedom?

Real SCIENCE Real LIFE

Olivia—How One Disorder Might Have Been Understood and Treated Throughout the Ages

Feelings of depression have been documented since the beginning of recorded history, and depression is a common psychological disorder, affecting 17% of the general population.

THE PATIENT

Olivia just started college. She grew up in a small town but enrolled in a major state university far from home. Her family has few financial resources, and the university scholarship was her only opportunity for a college education. She was reluctant to leave home, but her family and teachers encouraged her because it was a tremendous opportunity. When Olivia was a child, she went to camp one summer and was very homesick for an entire week. Now Olivia is having those same feelings again as she tries to adjust to college life in a new town. She is very sad, cries for no reason, and has stopped attending classes. She believes that she is a failure for being unable to adjust and is afraid to tell her parents how she feels. She barely talks to her roommate, who is very concerned about the change in her behavior. Olivia no longer takes a shower, sometimes does not get out of bed, and will go for several days without eating. She talks about being "better off dead."

Depression can be conceptualized from various perspectives, each of which would provide a unique approach toward treatment. If we were to convene a panel of experts to discuss various approaches to Olivia's treatment, we might hear a number of perspectives over time.

ASSESSING THE SITUATION

How would the following people think about and treat Olivia?

- Hippocrates
- A Roman Catholic Priest from the Middle Ages
- Phillippe Pinel, M.D.
- Sigmund Freud, M.D.
- B. F. Skinner, Ph.D.
- A Cognitive Psychologist in 2005
- A Biological Psychiatrist in 2006
- A Biopsychosocial Psychologist in 2016

THE TREATMENT

Hippocrates (380 BC): "It is obvious that the patient is suffering from an excess of black bile, which causes feelings of melancholia. To restore the humors to a balanced state, she needs to eat a vegetable diet and engage in physical activity. She also needs a tranquil existence, which would include a period of celibacy."

Roman Catholic Priest (1596): "Her symptoms are a direct result of possession by a demon with whom she has engaged in illicit relations. Her failure to follow the rules of authority (go to class) and her wish to die are sinful acts and clearly indicate that she is in league with the devil. She may even be a witch."

Philippe Pinel, M.D. (1800): "Mental illness is curable if we take the time to understand it. Olivia must be taken away from the environment that caused this problem and placed in the hospital, where she will be assigned to work in the garden. This physical activity will allow her to rest in the evening, and her spirit will be restored."

Sigmund Freud, M.D. (1920): "Although on one level, Olivia is grateful for the opportunity to study at the university, on a deeper, more unconscious level, she may feel anger and resentment toward her parents for not having the resources to allow her to study at a more prestigious school that was closer to home. This anger was particularly scary because her mother was suffering from breast cancer. Her superego, whose job it is to keep these unacceptable emotions in check, turned the anger she felt toward her parents back onto herself, resulting in depression, which especially because of her mother's condition, is a more socially acceptable emotion."

B. F. Skinner, Ph.D. (1965): "Olivia has learned depressive behaviors through a series of reinforcing experiences. She probably receives significant attention from her family every time that she calls home and tells them she is homesick. She may feel sad, but the way to change emotion is to change behavior and the contingencies that control it. I suggest that all those who interact with her provide positive reinforcement for 'nondepressive' behaviors (e.g., engaging in social activities, completing assignments) and extinguish, or ignore, depressive behaviors (e.g., not going to class, staying in her dorm room)."

Cognitive Psychologist, Ph.D. (2005): "Olivia's depression is the result of her negative perspective regarding herself and the world. Many college students have trouble adjusting to new environments. However, Olivia's cognitive schema has falsely interpreted this adjustment difficulty as a sign of personal weakness and failure. In therapy, we will examine these dysfunctional beliefs and help Olivia develop a more positive, functional perspective."

Biological Psychiatrist, M.D. (2006): "This patient meets diagnostic criteria for major depressive disorder, single episode. She has no history of mania. Her family history is positive for depression (mother, maternal aunt, possibly grandmother), and her paternal grandfather committed suicide. Because her mother had a positive response to a selective serotonin reuptake inhibitor, I recommend a course of fluoxetine (Prozac) 20 mg/day as an initial dose."

Biopsychosocial Psychologist (2016): "Olivia's depression clearly shows how numerous factors combine to create her distress. Her family history indicates the presence of a genetic predisposition, leaving her vulnerable to the development of depression. However, she did not have any difficulties until she went to college, and the stress from (1) moving far away from home for the first time and (2) needing to keep her grades high so that she could maintain her scholarship are most likely environmental and social factors that triggered the actual onset of the negative mood. Medication may be useful in the short term, but Olivia needs to learn how to cope with stress so that she has the tools to counteract her biological predisposition and prevent future episodes because she will face stressors throughout her lifetime."

Key Terms

abnormal behavior, p. 8
animal magnetism, p. 17
behavioral genetics, p. 26
behaviorism, p. 21
biological scarring, p. 26
biopsychosocial perspective, p. 34
classical conditioning, p. 20
culture, p. 5
culture-bound syndrome, p. 5
dementia praecox, p. 17
developmental trajectory, p. 10
diathesis-stress model of abnormal behavior, p. 34
dimensional approach, p. 9
ego psychology, p. 28
emotional contagion, p. 15
goodness of fit, p. 4
mass hysteria, p. 14
neuron, p. 25
neuroscience, p. 25
neurotransmitter, p. 25
operant conditioning, p. 29
phenomenology, p. 31
placebo effect, p. 17
psychoanalysis, p. 18
punishment, p. 29
reinforcement, p. 29
schizophrenia, p. 17
scientist–practitioner model, p. 24
sociocultural model, p. 31
synapse, p. 25
talking cure, p. 18
trephination, p. 13
vicarious conditioning, p. 30
viral infection theory, p. 26

Chapter 2

Research Methods in Abnormal Psychology

Chapter Learning Objectives

Ethics and Responsibility in Research	**LO 2.1**	Describe three core principles of ethics in the scientific study of abnormal behavior.
	LO 2.2	Understand important features of informed consent.
Research in Abnormal Psychology at the Cellular Level	**LO 2.3**	Identify the two main parts of the nervous system and brain/body components of each.
	LO 2.4	Explain the role of neurotransmitters as they relate to abnormal behavior.
	LO 2.5	Recognize new techniques used to study abnormal psychology at the cellular or neuroanatomical level.

	LO 2.6	Understand the differences between family, adoption, and twin studies (which do not study genes directly) and molecular genetics research (which does directly study genes) and the strengths and limitations of each approach.
Research in Abnormal Psychology at the Individual Level	**LO 2.7**	Describe the strengths and limitations of case studies.
	LO 2.8	Identify two types of single-case designs and the strengths and limitations of each.
Research in Abnormal Psychology at the Group Level	**LO 2.9**	Understand the principles of correlational research and their application to the study of abnormal behavior.
	LO 2.10	Describe the factors that influence outcomes of randomized controlled trials.
	LO 2.11	Understand the importance of diversity in group-based research in abnormal psychology.
	LO 2.12	Explain the difference between cross-sectional and longitudinal cohorts and the strengths and limitations of each.
Research in Abnormal Psychology at the Population Level	**LO 2.13**	Differentiate incidence and prevalence as these terms relate to understanding abnormal behavior.
	LO 2.14	Recognize the types of epidemiological research as they relate to understanding abnormal behavior.

I was taking introductory psychology, and we had the option of participating in research to get extra credit. There was an information board in the department where we could read about studies and sign up. There were lots of studies to choose from. I saw one that caught my interest and signed up.

I read the information sheet and signed the consent form. On the first day of the study, I met with a researcher who asked me all sorts of questions about my family history of alcohol use and about my own drinking patterns. I also had to fill out several questionnaires—mostly about alcohol and drug use.

She then scheduled me to come back the next day, and I was told not to eat for 1.5 hours before I came in and also not to smoke or brush my teeth!

On the second day I had to taste 10 different sweet solutions. She told me to sip the solution, swish it around in my mouth, and spit it out. Then I had to rate the solution, rinse my mouth with distilled water, and proceed to the next solution. For each solution, I had to rate how sweet and how pleasurable the taste was.

That was pretty much it. Afterward, the researcher told me that she was studying the association between a family history of alcoholism and sweet taste preference.

A few years later, I was checking around on the Internet to see if anything ever came of the study, and I typed in the researcher's name. To my surprise, she published a paper on the study and concluded that people with a family history of alcoholism actually do prefer sweeter tastes! The theory is that sweet taste preference is associated with risk of developing alcohol-related problems. It was pretty incredible to have been a participant in a study that actually got published.

Kampov-Polevoy, A., Garbutt, J., & Khalitov, E. Family history of alcoholism and response to sweets. *Alcoholism, Clinical and Experimental Research, 11*, 1743–1749. Copyright © 2003. /Wiley-Blackwell Publishing Ltd.

In introductory classes, psychology is often described as the scientific study of behavior and mental processes. To understand human behavior, psychologists require research volunteers such as the participant described above. Much of what we know about abnormal behavior is based on studies conducted using college students. Although there are biases inherent in such research (i.e., college students are not representative of the entire population), such studies do provide important starting points for further research. In much of psychological research, investigators are looking at individuals' observable behaviors.

However, for abnormal psychology, a scientific approach requires research of human behavior at all levels (genes, biological indices such as heart rate, internal events such as thoughts and feelings, observable behaviors such as interacting with another person, and population trends). The National Institutes of Health (NIH) emphasize the critical importance of understanding health and disease by conducting research at every level—from a single cell to society. **Translational research** is a scientific approach that focuses on communication between basic science and applied clinical research. The NIH states:

> To improve human health, scientific discoveries must be translated into practical applications. Such discoveries typically begin at "the bench" with basic research—in which scientists study disease at a molecular or cellular level—then progress to the clinical level, or the patient's "bedside." The translational approach is really a two-way street. Basic scientists provide new tools for use with patients, and clinical researchers make novel observations about the nature and progression of disease that often stimulate basic investigations. Translational research has proven to be a powerful process that drives the clinical research engine.

Our introductory case illustrates one type of basic research—understanding how taste mechanisms may be related to alcoholism. This case illustrates another important point as well. The goal of most research is to publish the results so that other investigators can use the data to generate new hypotheses and further our understanding of abnormal behavior. The public—those who do not do research—also needs to be aware of research findings that have implications for their lives.

Consistent with a translational approach, this chapter begins with research strategies that focus on factors at the cellular and neuroanatomical level and that affect behavior in the entire organism. We then examine research at the individual and group level, where most scientific inquiry in the area of abnormal psychology occurs. Finally, we turn to studies examining behavior at the population level. Each approach provides a unique perspective on mental illness. Combined, they allow us to understand broadly the biological, psychological, and societal aspects of mental illness.

Ethics and Responsibility in Research

Core Principles of Ethics in Research

LO 2.1 Describe three core principles of ethics in the scientific study of abnormal behavior.

Our research participant read an information sheet before deciding to participate in the study and signing a consent form. One of the core principles in the scientific study of abnormal behavior is that the research must be conducted in an ethical manner in accord with the principles outlined in the Belmont Report (see Chapter 15 for details). The report covers three fundamental ethical principles. First is *respect for persons*. That means that individuals participating in a study must be capable of making decisions about themselves. Anyone lacking that ability is entitled to protection: A parent or guardian must give consent for that person to participate. Second is the principle of **beneficence**. This means that researchers not only must respect participants' decisions and protect them from harm but also must attempt to secure their well-being. This obligates the researcher to do no harm and to maximize possible benefits and minimize possible harms. The third ethical principle, *justice*, emphasizes "fairness in distribution" or "what is deserved." An injustice occurs when a benefit to which a person is entitled is denied without good reason or when an unnecessary burden is imposed. It would be unjust, for example, for a person who is qualified and willing to participate in a study to be excluded.

The Informed Consent Process

LO 2.2 Understand important features of informed consent.

A researcher who designs a study and develops the consent form makes sure that all potential participants can easily understand the informed consent document and clarifies that participation in the research project is voluntary. The researcher also takes time to consider all foreseeable risks and benefits of participating in the project. Risks may include side effects of medication or discomfort in answering questions about sensitive topics. Finally, the researcher must ensure that participants are selected through a fair process. An institutional review board (IRB), also known as an *independent ethics committee* (IEC) or *ethical review board* (ERB), must review and approve all research conducted on humans. In turn, in the United States, the Office for Human Research Protections (OHRP) within the Department of Health and Human Services governs these boards and committees. Separate committees exist to oversee the ethics of laboratory animal research. The Institutional Animal Care and Use Committee (IACUC) is a separate committee established by institutions that use laboratory animals for research or instructional purposes. These committees oversee and evaluate all aspects of the institution's animal care and use program. These bodies both approve and oversee all research to ensure that researchers adhere to all mandated ethical principles.

Explore ETHICS AND RESPONSIBILITY

Learning Objective Summaries

LO 2.1 Describe three core principles of ethics in the scientific study of abnormal behavior.

One core ethical principle is respect for persons, which means that individuals participating in a study must be capable of making decisions about themselves. A second principle is beneficence, which means that researchers must respect participants' decisions, protect them from harm, and attempt to secure their well-being. The third ethical principle, justice, emphasizes "fairness in distribution" or "what is deserved."

LO 2.2 Understand important features of informed consent.

All potential participants must be able to understand the informed consent document and recognize that participation is voluntary. The researcher also needs to consider risks and benefits of participating in the project and ensure that participants are selected fairly. An IRB must review and approve all research conducted on humans.

Critical Thinking Question

You are serving as a member of the IRB at your college. One of the professors submitted a request to conduct a study of children who have separation anxiety. She is hoping to measure the children's psychological responses when their parents leave them in a playroom alone. Considering the three core principles of ethics reviewed here, what questions do you have for this professor?

Research in Abnormal Psychology at the Cellular Level

Research at the cellular level is an exciting and rapidly advancing area of study for abnormal psychology and intersects with the field of neuroscience. Although the idea that the brain is the site of abnormal behavior dates back to ancient times, only recently have we had the tools to study the brain and the nervous system accurately. Before discussing these new research findings, we will review the workings of the nervous system and the other parts of the body that influence behavior.

Neuroanatomy

LO 2.3 Identify the two main parts of the nervous system and brain/body components of each.

The two main parts of the human nervous system are the **central nervous system** (CNS) and the **peripheral nervous system** (PNS). The CNS consists of the brain and the spinal cord. As noted in Chapter 1, the brain contains approximately 100 billion nerve cells, or neurons. Each neuron extends along distinct and specific pathways, creating a complex but ordered web of neural circuitry. Typical neurons are composed of the *soma*, or the cell body, which contains the nucleus. The *dendrites* are fingerlike projections that extend from the soma. Dendrites branch out and receive information from other neurons. The fiber through which a cell transports information to another cell is called the *axon*. *Axon terminals* are the branched features at the end of the axon that form *synapses*, or points of communication with dendrites or cell bodies of other neurons (see Figure 2.1).

Watch ANATOMY OF A NEURON

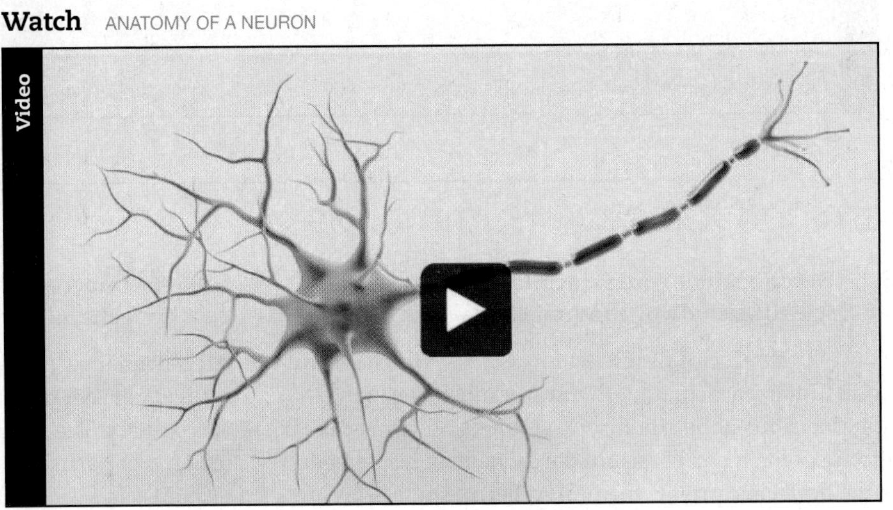

Having a general understanding of the structure of the brain is important because as we discuss the various psychological disorders, you will see that we are starting to understand the relationship between specific parts of the brain and specific disorders. An evolutionary perspective helps us to understand which parts of the brain appeared earliest in the course of human evolution and govern the most basic aspects of our functioning.

Starting with the oldest parts of the brain, at its base is the **brain stem**, which controls most of the fundamental biological functions associated with living, such as breathing. The brain stem has several sections with separate functions (see Figure 2.2). At its base is the *hindbrain*, consisting of the *medulla*, *pons*, and *cerebellum*. These structures regulate breathing, heartbeat, and motor control: activities required for life that occur

Figure 2.1 The Neuron.

The cell body contains the nucleus and has projections called *dendrites*, which branch out and receive information from other neurons. Nerve impulses pass down the neuron. The gap between the axon terminals and the dendrites of the next neuron is called the *synapse*. Chemicals called *neurotransmitters* enable the nerve impulse to cross the gap to the receptors of the next neuron.

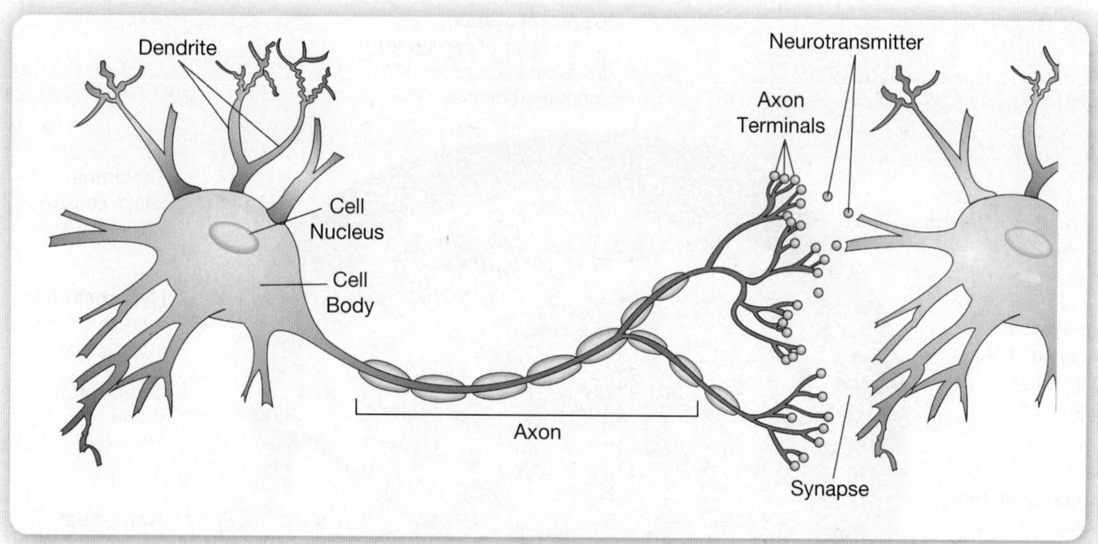

automatically. You do not need to think about breathing or making your heart beat in order for those processes to occur. The term *lesion* refers to an area of damage or abnormality. We can tell a lot about the function of a particular brain structure by observing what happens to people when a specific structure is lesioned. For example, the cerebellum is critical for motor coordination. When lesions occur in the cerebellum, they result in disorders of fine movement, balance, and motor learning.

The **midbrain** portion of the brain stem has two important functions. First, it is a coordinating center that brings together sensory information with movement. It also houses the *reticular activating system*, which regulates our sleep and arousal systems.

Figure 2.2 The Brain Stem.

The oldest part of the brain, located at its base, controls most basic biological functions, such as breathing.

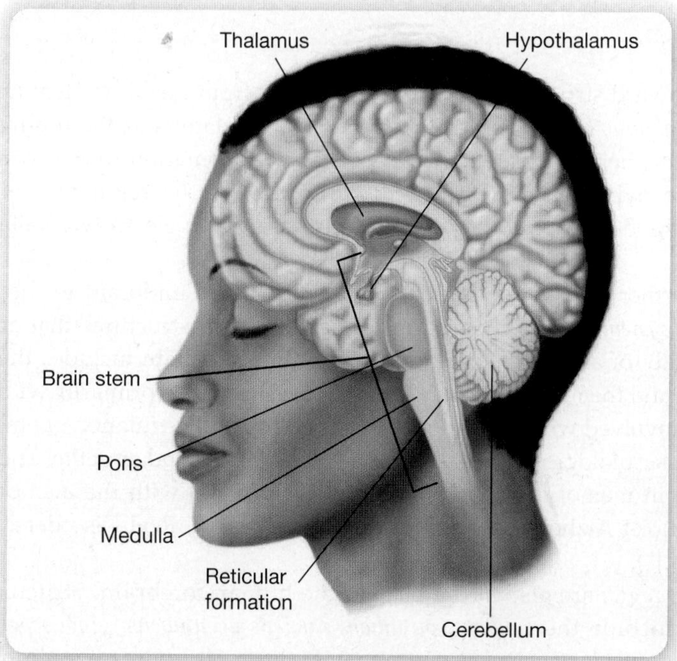

Figure 2.3 The Thalamus, Hypothalamus, and Limbic System.

The thalamus is the brain's relay system, directing sensory information to the cortex; the hypothalamus regulates bodily functions; and the limbic system is a major center for human emotion.

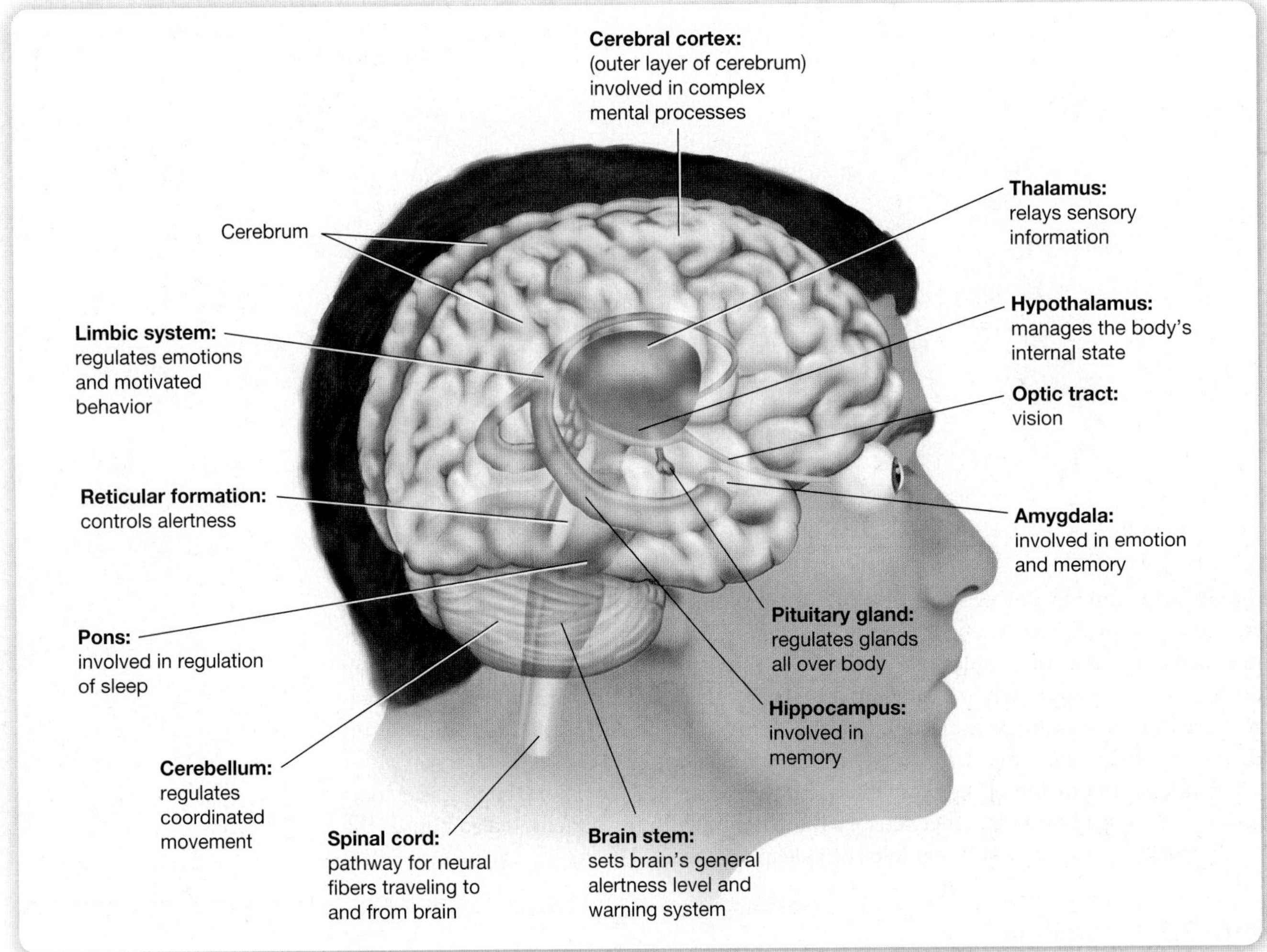

Moving upward structurally and evolutionarily from the brain stem are the *thalamus* and the *hypothalamus* (see Figure 2.3). Think of the thalamus as the brain's relay station because it directs nerve signals that carry sensory information to the cortex. A primary function of the hypothalamus is *homeostasis,* which is the regulation of bodily functions such as blood pressure, body temperature, fluid and electrolyte balance, and body weight.

Moving further up the evolutionary ladder from the midbrain to the **forebrain**, we find the *limbic system,* an umbrella term for several brain structures that are very important for the study of abnormal psychology. The **limbic system** includes the *amygdala,* the *cingulate gyrus,* and the **hippocampus**. The limbic system deals primarily with emotions and impulses. It is involved with the experience of emotion, the regulation of emotional expression, and the basic biological drives such as aggression, sex, and appetite. The hippocampus also has a role in memory formation and has been linked with the memory deficits that are characteristic of Alzheimer's disease (see "Real People, Real Disorders: Henry Gustav Molaison [H.M.]").

The *basal ganglia* are also at the base of the human forebrain. Structures within the basal ganglia include the *caudate, putamen, nucleus accumbens, globus pallidus, substantia nigra,* and *subthalamic nucleus.* In general, these structures are thought to inhibit movement. Diseases that affect the basal ganglia are characterized by abnormal movements; these include Parkinson's disease (rigidity and tremor), bradykinesia (slow movements), and Huntington's disease (uncontrollable dancelike movements of the face and limbs).

Watch PARTS OF THE BRAIN

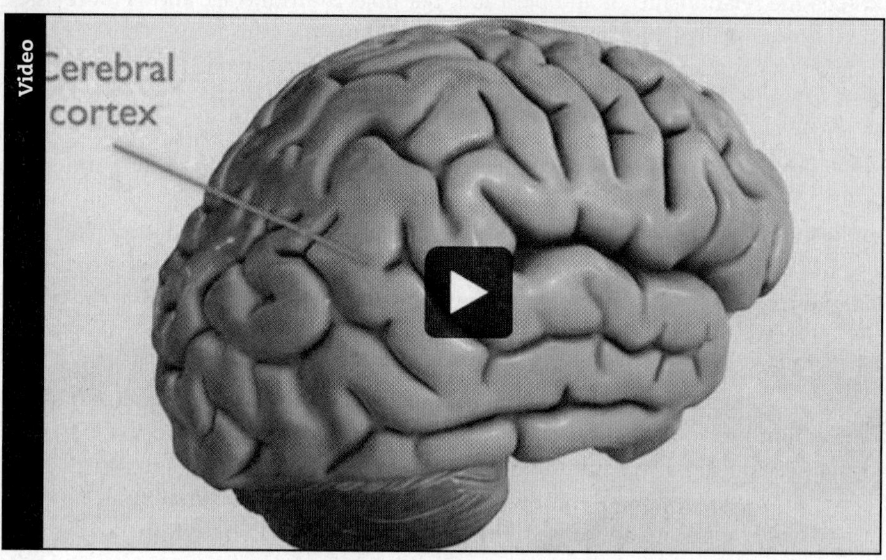

Moving even further up the evolutionary ladder, we encounter the largest part of the forebrain, the **cerebral cortex**. Here we find the structures that contribute to the abilities that make us uniquely human, such as reasoning, abstract thought, perception of time, and creativity. The cerebral cortex is divided into two hemispheres, known as the left and right. Popular psychology commonly refers to people as "left brained" or "right brained," but brain functioning is more complicated than that simple distinction. Although the two

REAL People, REAL Disorders

Henry Gustav Molaison (H.M.)

The brain of Henry Gustav Molaison (H.M.) from Thibodaux, Louisiana, has been studied more than that of any person in history. For reasons of confidentiality, he was known to psychologists only as "H.M." until his death. Born in 1926 and raised in Connecticut, H.M. was an ordinary bicycle-riding, ice-skating boy. At age 9, he banged his head hard after being hit by a bicycle rider in his neighborhood. At approximately age 16, he developed epilepsy and experienced many *grand mal* (severe) seizures. In 1953, he underwent major surgery in which parts of his medial temporal lobe were removed on both sides of his brain. His doctor, William Scoville, wanted to remove this part of the brain because it was where the seizures originated.

Two thirds of H.M.'s hippocampus was removed; leading neurologists assumed that this part of the brain was entirely nonfunctional. After the surgery, however, H.M. suffered from a form of amnesia in which he could not save new experiences as long-term memories. Much to the joy of his doctors, H.M. was able to complete tasks that required recall from his short-term memory (Corkin, 1968). He was also able to recall long-term memories of events that occurred before his operation. But he could not recall events that occurred after the operation.

Henry Molaison died on December 2, 2008, of respiratory failure in a nursing home in Connecticut. Although he was unsure of exactly how old he was, had to be reintroduced to his doctors every day, and repeatedly grieved when he heard about the death of his mother, he had a positive outlook on life. He was quoted as saying that he hoped his medical condition would help others and allow researchers to learn more about memory.

Scientific research has benefited greatly from H.M.'s experience. It has resulted in two key findings: short-term memories do not depend on a functioning hippocampus, but long-term memories must go through the hippocampus in order to be permanently stored (Kolb & Whishaw, 1996). These findings have forever changed the way scientists view the formation, retention, and recall of short- and long-term memory.

hemispheres look structurally similar, they appear to oversee different processes. Indeed, some people tend to favor one type of processing over the other.

The **left hemisphere** is primarily responsible for language and cognitive functions and tends to process information in a more linear and logical manner. The left hemisphere processes information in parts, sequentially, and uses both language and symbols (including numbers). The **right hemisphere** processes the world in a more holistic manner, a spatial context (i.e., the relationship of an object to other objects around it), and is more associated with creativity, imagery, and intuition. Considerable communication occurs between the hemispheres, and, in some cases, they can also compensate for each other by taking over some of the functions of the damaged area.

Each hemisphere consists of four lobes: temporal, parietal, occipital, and frontal (see Figure 2.4). The **temporal lobe** is associated with processing and therefore understanding auditory and visual information, and it plays a role in the naming or labeling of objects and verbal memory. The **parietal lobe** integrates sensory information from various sources and may also be involved with visuospatial processing (e.g., when you imagine rotating a three-dimensional object in space). The **occipital lobe**, located at the back of the skull, is the center of visual processing. The **frontal lobe** is the seat of reasoning and plays a critical role in impulse control, judgment, language, memory, motor function, problem solving, and sexual and social behavior. Frontal lobes are instrumental in planning, coordinating, inhibiting, and executing behavior. The *corpus callosum* connects the two sides of the brain, allowing them to communicate. A severed corpus callosum is not entirely incapacitating, but it can lead to an inability to integrate certain brain functions. For example, if an image of a key is flashed in the right field of vision, a person whose corpus callosum has been severed might *recognize* the image but not be able to correctly *name* it. A flash in the opposite field of vision could yield the correct *label*, but the person would not be able to discuss its *function*.

Beyond the brain and the spinal cord, the other major division of the human nervous system is the PNS. It is subdivided into the sensory-somatic nervous system and the autonomic nervous system. The *sensory-somatic nervous system* consists of the cranial nerves,

Figure 2.4 The Cerebrum.

The four lobes of the cerebrum (temporal, parietal, occipital, and frontal) control sensory, motor, speech, and reasoning functions. The outer ("gray matter") layer of the cerebrum is known as the cerebral cortex.

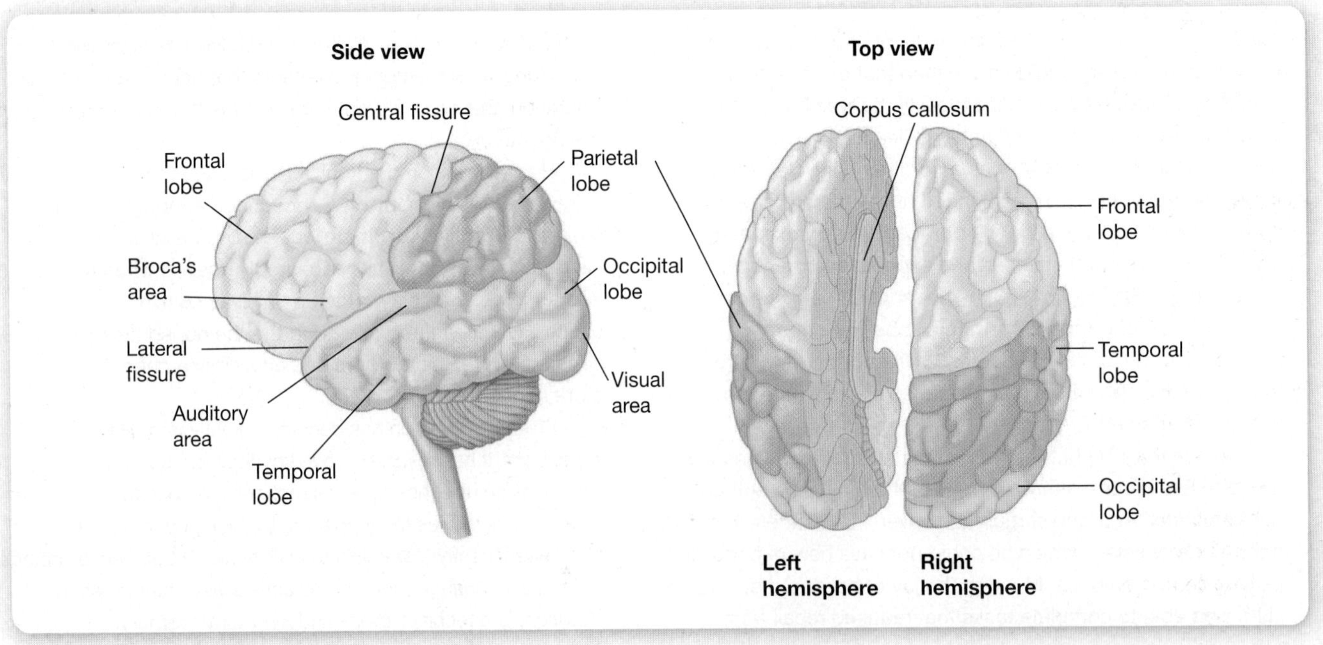

which control sensation and muscle movement. The *autonomic nervous system* includes the sympathetic and parasympathetic nervous systems. The *sympathetic nervous system* (SNS) primarily controls involuntary movements. It serves to activate the body, creating a state of physical readiness. The SNS stimulates heartbeat; raises blood pressure; dilates the pupils; diverts blood away from the skin and inner organs to the skeletal muscles, brain, and heart; and inhibits digestion and peristalsis in the gastrointestinal tract, creating a bodily state of arousal that could indicate the presence of stress or anxiety (see Chapter 4). In contrast, the *parasympathetic nervous system* returns the body functions to resting levels after the SNS has activated them.

Finally, the body's **endocrine system** regulates bodily functions but uses hormones rather than nerve impulses to do so (see Figure 2.5). Endocrine glands produce **hormones**, which are chemical messengers released directly into the bloodstream and act on target organs. The pituitary gland, located at the base of the brain, is known as the "master gland." It controls many endocrine functions including those central to the female menstrual cycle, pregnancy, birth, and lactation. (Another gland, the hypothalamus, regulates the pituitary gland.) The adrenal glands (located on top of the kidneys) release epinephrine (adrenaline) in response to external and internal stressors such as fright, anger, caffeine, or low blood sugar. Thyroid hormones regulate metabolism including body temperature and weight. The pancreas includes a gland (islets of Langerhans) that secretes insulin and glucagon to regulate blood sugar level. A number of studies have demonstrated that certain hormones (e.g., cortisol, prolactin) are elevated in people with depression, anxiety, and other psychological symptoms.

Figure 2.5 The Endocrine System.

This system includes glands, such as the thyroid, gonads, adrenal, and pituitary, and the hormones they produce, such as thyroxin, estrogen, testosterone, and adrenaline. Hormones are chemical messengers that transmit information and instructions throughout the bloodstream, targeting cells that are genetically programmed to receive and respond to specific messages.

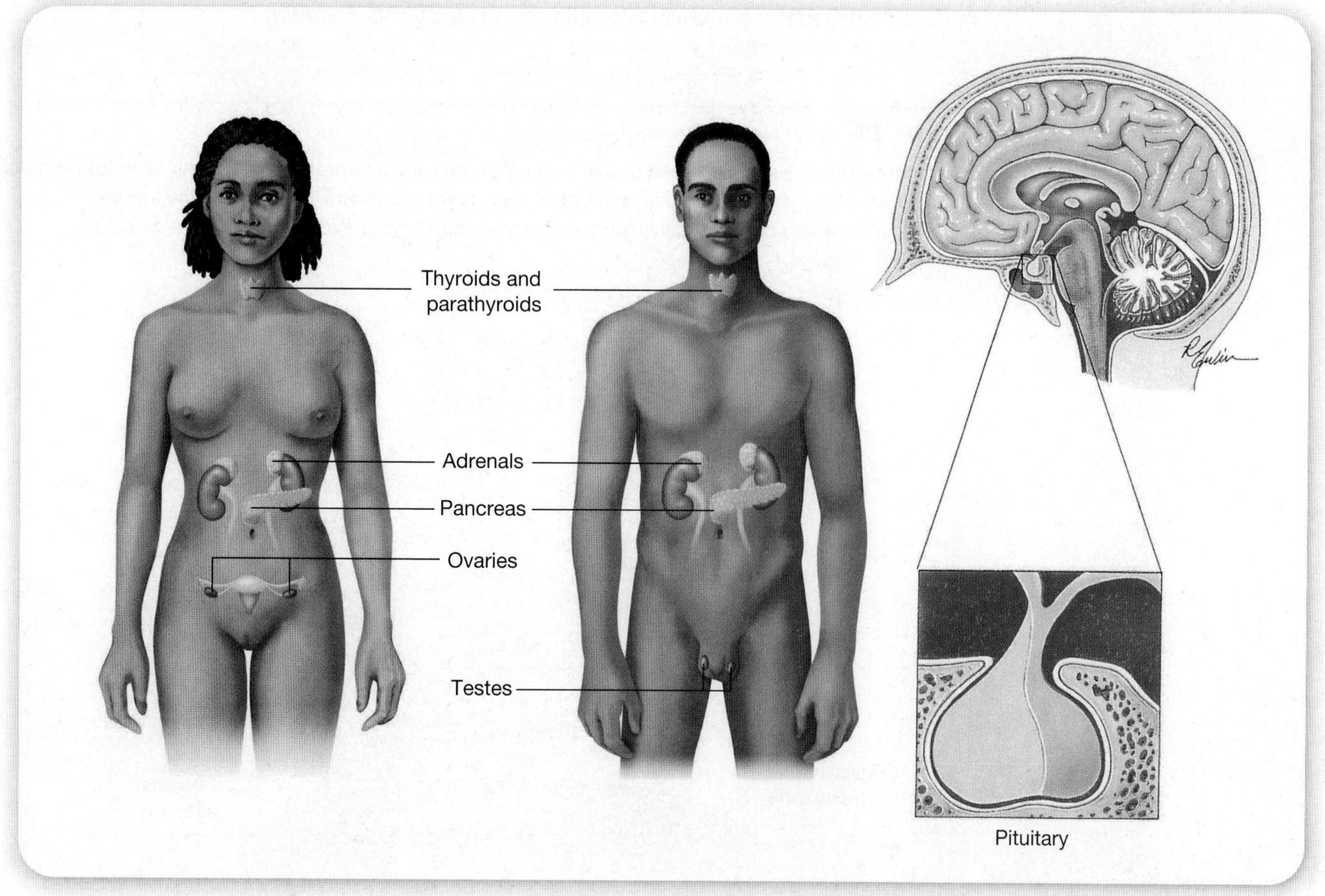

Neurotransmitters

LO 2.4 Explain the role of neurotransmitters as they relate to abnormal behavior.

Clearly, many different minisystems exist within the overall nervous system. To understand human emotions, we need to know how these various systems operate and cooperate. Communication in the nervous system is both electrical and chemical. Neurons do not actually touch each other, but chemicals called **neurotransmitters** relay the electrical signals from one neuron to the next (see Figure 2.6). When the electrical signal reaches the axon terminal, the neurotransmitters are released. They travel across the space between the neurons (called the *synapse*) and land on the surface of the neighboring neuron, at which point they trigger the second neuron to "fire," releasing the electrical impulse. Research on neurotransmitters has revolutionized psychiatry because most drug treatments affect one or more of the core neurotransmitters by influencing their availability and/or their action in the brain. This highly active field of research is constantly identifying new substances that function as neurotransmitters. Specific neurotransmitter systems have been widely studied and will be discussed in the chapters on specific disorders.

Understanding the basics of the nervous system, we are ready to begin the journey from the individual cell to the level of society. Throughout this journey, we will examine the many different procedures that psychologists use to study human behavior at each of these levels. The brief case description that follows provides a context for those strategies.

> Monica is 26 years old. She has been feeling sad, helpless, and hopeless and crying for no reason. She has thought about taking her life. She has trouble falling asleep at night, and when she finally does, she wakes up several times. She has lost 20 pounds in 2 months because she does not feel like eating. Her primary care physician sent her to a psychologist who diagnosed her with depression.

We will look closely at depressive disorders in Chapter 7, but here we will explore the methodologies that researchers typically use to study this disorder.

Figure 2.6 How Neurotransmitters Work.

The electrical signal reaches the end of the first neuron, causing it to fire and release the neurotransmitters from their vesicles at the presynaptic membrane. The neurotransmitters travel across the synapse and land on receptors on the postsynaptic membrane. This initiates a signal in the second neuron, relaying the message.

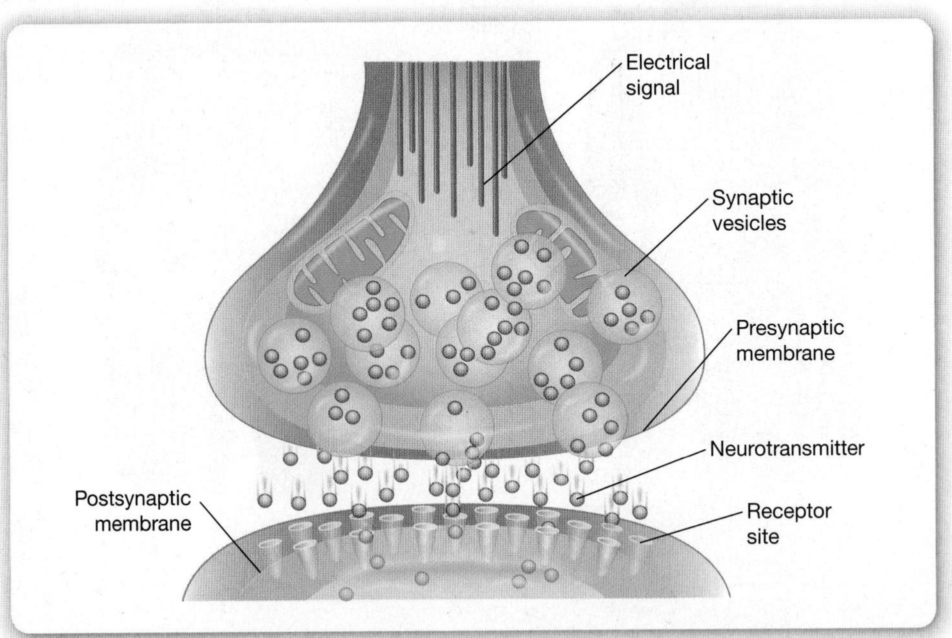

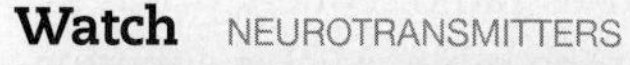

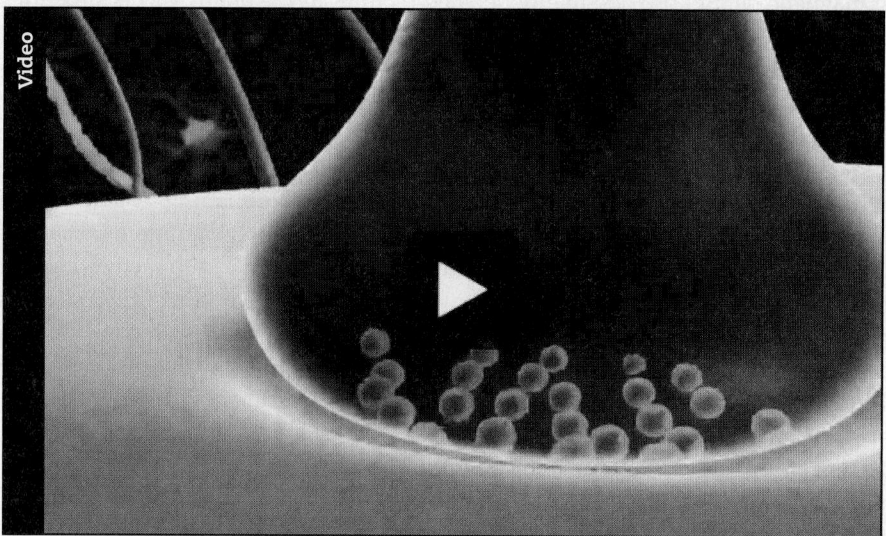

Neuroimaging

LO 2.5 Recognize new techniques used to study abnormal psychology at the cellular or neuroanatomical level.

You may wonder how scientists know how the brain functions and which of its structures are responsible for human abilities and activities. Much of our early information came from unique cases such as accident victims or survivors of surgery (like H.M.) that allowed us to understand what functions were lost if a certain part of the brain was damaged or removed. More recently, understanding the structure and the function of the brain has been facilitated by advances in **neuroimaging** technology, which creates detailed images of the brain. Tests such as *CT* or *CAT* (computerized axial tomography) scans and *MRI* (magnetic resonance imaging) provide static images like snapshots. With such images, clinicians can detect lesions or damaged areas in the brain. For a CAT scan, the patient is injected with a radioactive dye, and specialized X-ray equipment photographs the brain from different angles. The computerized

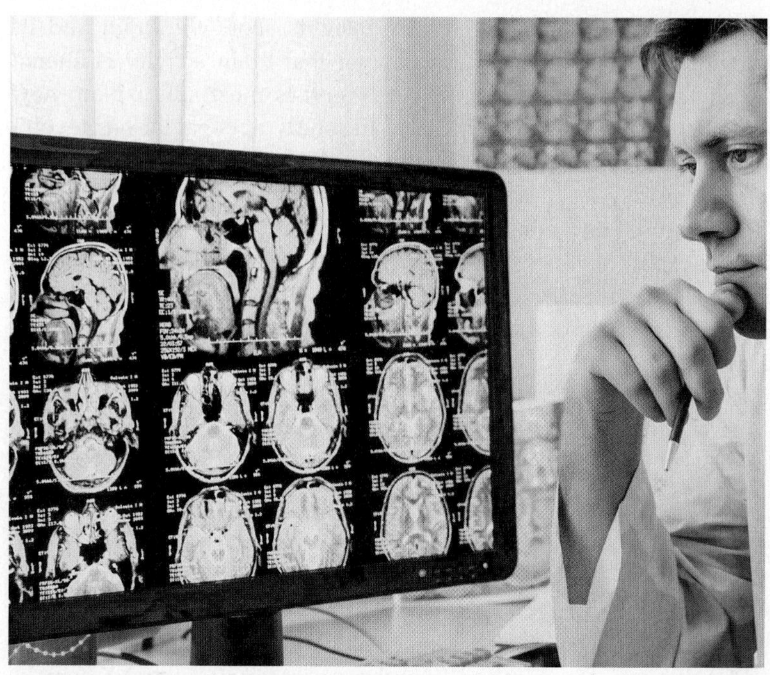

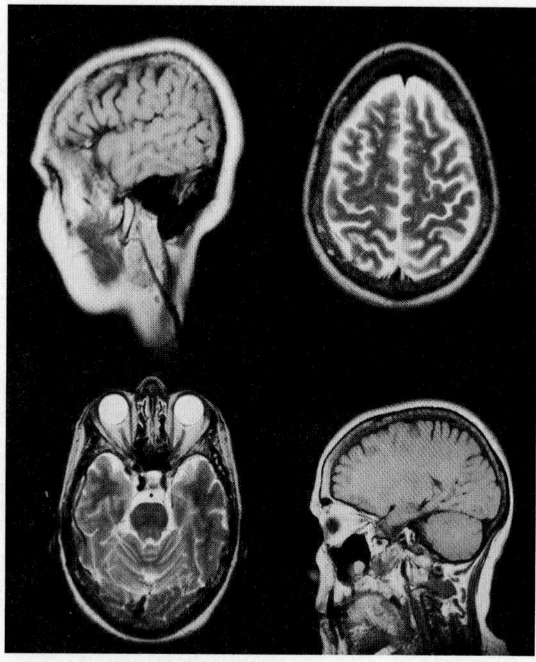

CAT (left) and MRI (right) scans, in which X-ray or radio waves scan the brain, produce images that reveal brain anatomy.

images create a cross-sectional picture of the brain. MRI uses radiofrequency waves and a strong magnetic field to provide highly detailed pictures of the brain. MRI is superior to CT technology because it does not require the use of radiation. Instead, radiofrequency waves are directed at protons in a strong magnetic field. The protons are first "excited" and then "relaxed," emitting radio signals that can be computer processed to form an image.

CAT and MRI technology explore **neuroanatomy** (brain structure). These tests are sometimes referred to as **structural neuroimaging** procedures. Other tests are used to detect brain function, usually referred to as **functional neuroimaging**. A *positron emission tomography* (PET) scan creates images based on the detection of radiation from the emission of positrons. Before the scan occurs, the patient is given a radioactive biochemical substance. As the radioactive isotope in the substance decays, it emits tiny particles that can be measured. PET brain imaging enables scientists to trace neurotransmitter pathways in the brain and from these data to determine which brain structures and pathways are involved in specific aspects of human behavior. *Functional MRI* (fMRI) identifies increases in blood flow that are associated with increases in neural activity in various parts of the brain. This technique allows not only a map of brain anatomy but also a map of brain function. fMRI allows the researcher to isolate specific brain activity in response to an event or stimulus (e.g., flashing an image of a spider to someone with a fear of spiders or examining the brain activity of someone experiencing auditory hallucinations, or "hearing voices").

Neuroimaging is an elegant, sophisticated, and expensive research tool. In typical clinical practice, neuroimaging is not needed to diagnose depression.

However, Monica and all those with psychological disorders are benefiting greatly from neuroimaging studies that help mental health professionals understand which brain structures and functions appear to be affected when someone is depressed. In turn, understanding altered brain functioning has helped with the development of interventions that target specific brain areas and functions.

Genetics

LO 2.6 Understand the differences between family, adoption, and twin studies (which do not study genes directly) and molecular genetics research (which does directly study genes) and the strengths and limitations of each approach.

Studies of brain structure and function provide many insights about the brain and its relationship to psychological disorders. However, knowing that brain activity is altered does not fully explain why abnormal behavior occurs. Scientists must still explain how and why brain abnormalities exist. Applying genetics to the study of behavior has revolutionized abnormal psychology, and research on genetic factors now reaches from the cell to the population level. *Behavioral genetics* approaches include family, twin, and adoption studies and allow critical glimpses into whether certain behavioral traits or mental disorders run in families and the extent to which these familial patterns are due to genetics (are heritable) or environment. Modern *molecular genetic* approaches including genome-wide methods of examining genetic associations have allowed scientists to discover genetic *loci* (specific places on specific chromosomes) that are associated with many complex traits. We now know that single genes rarely cause behavioral traits and mental disorders. Instead, research suggests that many genes and environmental factors that exert small to moderate effects influence most behavioral traits (known as *complex traits*) and disorders.

GENETICS BASICS Recall from your high school biology class that the "building block of life" is *deoxyribonucleic acid* (DNA). The collection of DNA that exists in humans is called the human *genome*. Thanks to the *Human Genome Project*, we know that approximately 20,000 to 25,000 genes make up each person. Each gene is a section of DNA, and together, genes make an organism unique. In humans, the genes are contained on 23 pairs of chromosomes—22 somatic (bodily) chromosome pairs and 1 sex chromosome pair, either XX (female) or XY (male) (see Figure 2.7). The mother always contributes an X chromosome to the sex

Figure 2.7 Human Chromosomes.

A typical human being has 46 chromosomes—23 derived from each parent. Sex is determined by X and Y chromosomes; males are XY, and females are XX. Is this the DNA of a male or female?

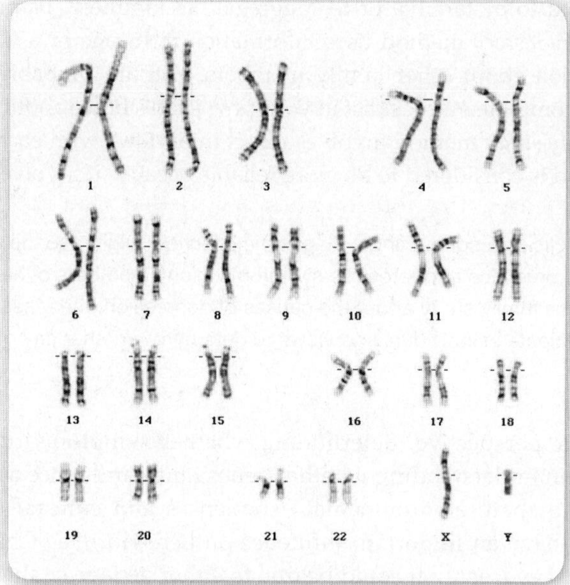

chromosome pair. If the father's contribution is also an X chromosome, then the baby is a girl. If he contributes a Y chromosome, then the baby is a boy. Genes can exist in several different forms, called *alleles*, and specific alleles create variation in species (e.g., height, hair color, eye color, personality, disease risk).

Genes follow several laws. Gregor Mendel (1822–1884), a Czech monk, working with the common garden pea, discovered two genetic laws of heredity. The *law of segregation* states that an individual receives one of two elements from each parent. One of the elements could be *dominant* (in which case the trait would be expressed in offspring), or the element could be *recessive* (genetically present but usually not expressed in offspring). If a child receives two recessive elements—one from each parent—then the recessive element or trait is expressed. In the case of eye color, brown is a dominant trait and blue is a recessive trait. So, a person with blue eyes must have inherited two recessive elements, one from each parent.

Mendel's second law, the *law of independent assortment*, states that the alleles (variations) of one gene assort independently from the alleles of other genes. For example, the alleles for height and eye color do not always travel together. Not every short person has blue eyes. Short people may have brown eyes or hazel eyes. Similarly, people with blue eyes can be short, average, or tall. In short, genes for eye color and height assort independently.

Although Mendel laid the foundation for our understanding of genetics, his work was criticized by later scientists (Fisher, 1936), who suggested that Mendel's results were too good to be true. Others scientists supported Fisher's observations. Nevertheless, Mendel's laws provided an important first step toward understanding the basic principles of genetics.

Although the influence of genes on characteristics such as height, eye color, and various diseases has been known for generations, more recently, behavior geneticists have studied genetic effects on personality, attitudes, and abnormal behavior such as extraversion, depression, and schizophrenia.

With so many genes in the human genome, how do we even begin the search for genes that may increase the risk for developing certain psychological conditions? This is the province of scientists in the field of *behavioral genetics*, which refers to the study of the relationship between genetics and environment in determining individual differences in behavior. Approaches in this category include family, twin, and adoption studies. Basically, these studies focus on whether traits and disorders run in families and, if so, why.

FAMILY STUDIES Do psychological disorders "run in families"? **Familial aggregation** studies examine whether the family members of someone with a particular disorder (called the **proband**) are more likely to have that disorder than are family members of people without the disorder. If the disorder is more commonly found among the proband's family, the disorder is considered to be familial or to "aggregate in families." Family studies can take two forms. The *family history* method uses information from one or a few family members to provide information about other family members. You are probably familiar with this method if you have completed a checklist in your physician's office about your family's medical history. The *family study* method involves direct interviews with each consenting family member. This method is considered to be more reliable because it involves direct interviews.

In Monica's case, a clinician conducting a diagnostic interview might use the family history method to ask her about the presence of depressive symptoms in any members of her family. If Monica were participating in a family study about the causes of depression, the researchers might invite her relatives to participate in individual interviews to determine whether any of them ever suffered from depression.

From a scientific perspective, determining whether symptoms run in families is an important first step in understanding whether genes might influence a disorder. However, family members also share environmental experiences and cultural contexts, including families, which can have an important influence on behavior (see Chapter 1). Therefore, any observed familial aggregation could be due to either genetic *or* **shared environmental factors** (environmental factors that family members share) or most likely some combination of these influences. Large family studies can be used to explore the extent to which genes or environment contribute to liability to a disorder or trait; however, the relative contributions of genetic and environmental factors can be best determined by adoption and twin study designs (see Figure 2.8).

ADOPTION STUDIES Adoption creates a unique situation in which genetically related individuals live in separate families and, therefore, do not share a common family environment. In such cases, similarities between biological parents and their adopted-away

Figure 2.8 Family Pedigree of Disorders.

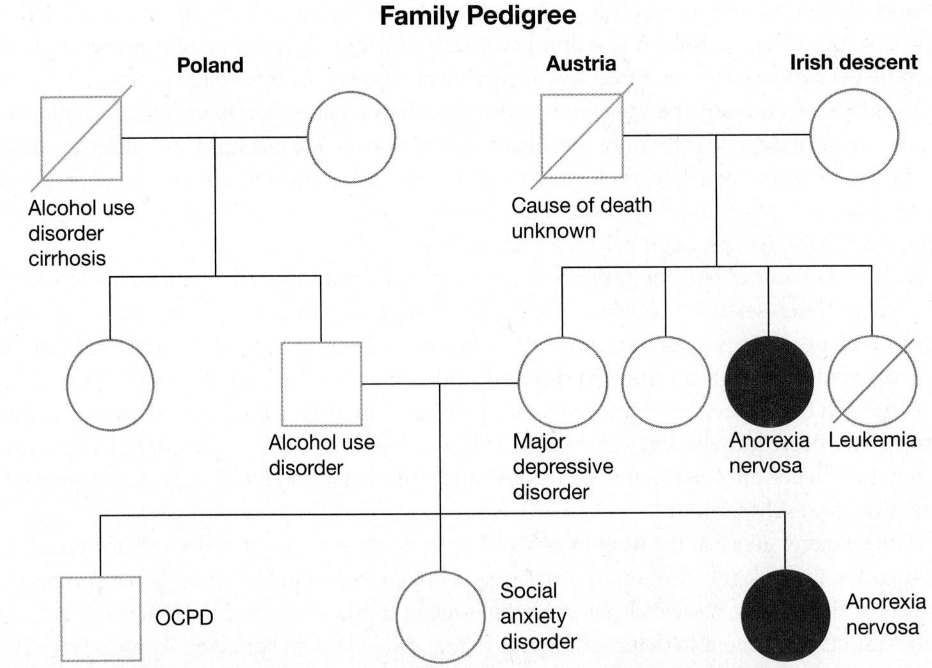

This pedigree shows how psychopathology tracks through the family. This three-generation depiction shows the transmission of substance related disorders, major depressive disorder, anxiety disorders, personality disorders, and eating disorders.

offspring are assumed to represent the *genetic* contribution to a given trait or behavior. By contrast, similarities between the adopted child and his or her adoptive parents measure the *environmental* contribution to parent–child similarity.

Adoption studies represent a middle ground when it comes to examining behavioral genetic models: they are more able to separate genetic from environmental effects than family studies, but they have their pitfalls and biases as well. One bias is that adoption placement is not always random. Often adoption is selective, meaning that babies are placed with adoptive families who resemble their own biological parents on a number of dimensions such as race, religion, and socioeconomic status. As international adoptions become increasingly popular, additional issues arise including what conditions the adoptee faced before placement. Many of these conditions, such as placement in orphanages and lack of early attachment experiences, can lead to serious developmental consequences that can confound the interpretation of adoption studies.

TWIN STUDIES The scientific study of twins was another important step in understanding the contribution of genes and environment to abnormal behavior (Cederlöf et al., 1982; Kendler, 2001; Martin et al., 1997). These studies revolutionized our understanding of several major psychiatric conditions and modernized approaches to treatment (Polderman et al., 2015). For example, three decades ago, it was widely believed that autism and schizophrenia resulted solely from environmental trauma or parental deficits. However, based on a body of scientific evidence (Folstein & Rosen-Sheidley, 2001; Polderman et al., 2015; Sullivan, 2008), we now know that these disorders have critically important genetic components.

Twin studies examine the similarities and differences between *monozygotic* (MZ, or identical) and *dizygotic* (DZ, or fraternal) twin pairs to identify genetic and environmental contributions to psychological disorders. MZ twins start out as a single embryo (fertilized egg). At some stage in the first 2 weeks after conception, the zygote (fertilized egg) separates and yields two embryos that are, for most intents and purposes, genetically identical. Therefore, behavioral differences between MZ twins, who essentially share all of their genes, allow examination of the role of *environmental influences* (Plomin et al., 1994). By contrast, DZ twinning results from the fertilization of two eggs by different spermatozoa. DZ twins are no more similar genetically than other siblings and share, on average, one half of their genes. Thus, behavioral differences between DZ twins can result from genetic and/or environmental effects.

The most rigorous twin research design uses MZ twins who were separated in infancy and reared apart (i.e., in different environments). In this case, genes and familial environment are

Identical (MZ) twins separated at birth and raised apart have been found to show strong similarities in adulthood.

distinctly separated, and studies can examine **nonshared environmental factors** (environmental factors not shared between twins). Two large studies of MZ twins reared apart in Minnesota (Bouchard et al., 1990) and Sweden (Pedersen et al., 1985) were critical in demonstrating the strength of genetic factors in determining IQ. In addition, reunited MZ twins have discovered similarities on dimensions not usually considered to be under genetic control including where they have moles on their body, the age they started balding, their occupation, their choice of cars and motorcycles, and even their favorite beer.

MOLECULAR GENETICS Whereas twin and adoption studies can tell us whether genes are involved in a particular trait or disorder, they do not tell us which of the 20,000 to 25,000 identified genes might be related to the presence of the disorder. To actually identify risk genes, research needs to drill down to the molecular level. **Molecular genetics** uses three primary methods: genome-wide linkage analyses, candidate gene association studies, and genome-wide association studies (Slagboom & Meulenbelt, 2002; Wang et al., 2005). **Genome-wide linkage analysis** allows researchers to narrow the search for genes from the entire genome to specific areas on specific chromosomes. To conduct a linkage analysis, researchers need large families in which many individuals have a particular disorder *or* large samples of "affected relative pairs." These are pairs of relatives who both have the illness under study. Researchers then look for regions of the genome that the affected relatives share. Then they can narrow their search for genes on these areas of increased sharing.

In a **candidate gene association study**, scientists compare specific genes in a large group of individuals who have a specific trait or disorder with a well-matched group of individuals who do not have that trait or disorder. In this approach, the researcher chooses one or several genes in advance based on some knowledge of the biology of the trait or the function of the gene. For example, we know that serotonin may be involved in depression, so a candidate gene study might compare one or a few serotonergic genes in a large sample of people with the disorder (called *cases*) versus people who do not have the disorder but are similar to the cases in other ways (called *controls*). If scientists find that one variant of the gene is more common in the ill group, there is evidence that this gene might be associated with the illness. By and large, candidate gene studies tend to be initially very exciting when they emerge in the literature, but often other groups fail to replicate (repeat) the findings. For this reason the single-gene candidate gene approach is falling out of favor for more comprehensive and powerful approaches discussed next.

A **genome-wide association study** (GWAS) also uses large samples of cases and well-matched controls. Given that most genes implicated in psychiatric disorders are of small effect, tens and even hundreds of thousands of cases and controls are needed to achieve adequately powered sample sizes. Unlike the candidate gene studies in which only one or a few genes are studied at one time, in GWAS, hundreds of thousands of possible genetic variants scattered across the genome are tested for association in the same study. This is a key advantage of GWAS. In the candidate gene studies, a researcher must choose a gene or genes based on some prior knowledge of biology. GWAS does not require any such choice and yields a relatively unbiased search of the genome that can discover new genetic associations. Given that so many comparisons are made, rigorous controls must be implemented to ensure that significant results are truly significant and not just chance occurrences. The conventional significance level for GWAS is 5×10^{-8} as illustrated by the red line in the fictional Manhattan plot (Figure 2.9). Loci above that strict threshold are considered to be "associated" with the disorder or trait under investigation and are targeted for further study related to their function and impact on biology. For many diseases, including psychiatric disorders, GWAS has unlocked new biological pathways that had not been considered in the past (O'Donovan, 2015; Sullivan, 2012).

Studying Monica's genes would not be part of the usual clinical assessment to determine the diagnosis of depression. However, certain researchers (usually working in medical school settings) may be conducting a study on genetics and depression, and someone with symptoms like Monica's might be asked to participate by giving a sample of her blood or providing a saliva sample—both of which contain DNA.

Figure 2.9 Manhattan Plot.

The red-dotted line represents the significance level of 5×10^{-8}. Loci on chromosomes 5, 6, 8, 12, and 19 are significantly associated with the condition under study.

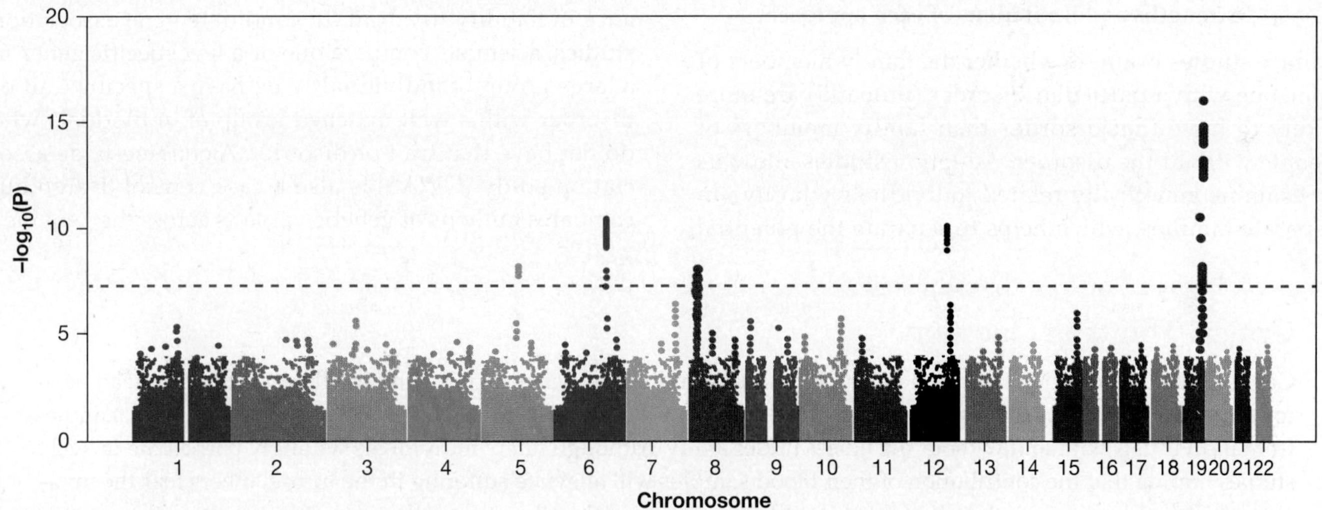

Epigenetics focuses on heritable changes in the expression of genes, which are not caused by changes in actual DNA sequence but rather by environmental exposures (Petronis, 2010). Unlike your actual genetic sequence, the epigenome has the ability to react and adapt to a rapidly changing environment. What this means is that the environment has the ability to influence which genes are activated and which are silenced. Intriguingly, these changes may actually be passed down to succeeding generations.

Psychiatric genomics have truly revolutionized our perspectives on abnormal psychology and have spawned further more granular investigations on every level of biological functioning representing the palette of "-omics" inquiries. These approaches include, but are not limited to, genomics (the study of genes and their function), transcriptomics (RNA transcripts that are produced by the genome), proteomics (the study of proteins), metabolomics (the study of molecules involved in cellular metabolism), and a host of other "-omic" approaches representing collective technologies used to explore the roles, relationships, and actions of the various types of molecules that make up the cells of an organism. As research in these areas advances at lightning pace, researchers are challenged to translate observations on the cellular level to understanding the expression of abnormal behaviors at the individual level. These processes are complex, but the tools we have to answer these questions make this an exciting time for scientific discovery in this field (Kendler, 2013).

Learning Objective Summaries

LO 2.3 **Identify the two main parts of the nervous system and brain/body components of each.**

The two main parts of the nervous system are the central nervous system (CNS) and the peripheral nervous system (PNS). The CNS consists of the brain and the spinal cord. The PNS includes the sensory-somatic and autonomic nervous systems. The autonomic nervous system includes the sympathetic and parasympathetic systems.

LO 2.4 **Explain the role of neurotransmitters as they relate to abnormal behavior.**

Neurotransmitters are chemicals that relay electrical signals from one neuron to the next. They travel across the synapse from one neuron to another, triggering the second neuron to release an electrical impulse. Most drug treatments for abnormal behavior affect one or more of the core neurotransmitters.

LO 2.5 **Recognize new techniques used to study abnormal psychology at the cellular or neuroanatomical level.**

Neuroimaging technology allows us to create detailed images of the brain. Tests such as the CAT (computerized axial tomography) and MRI (magnetic resonance imaging) provide snapshot images of brain structure (structural neuroimaging). PET (positron emission tomography) and fMRI (functional MRI) allow us to see neurotransmitter pathways and changes in blood flow (functional neuroimaging).

LO 2.6 Understand the differences between family, adoption, and twin studies (which do not study genes directly) and molecular genetics research (which does directly study genes) and the strengths and limitations of each approach.

Family studies examine whether the family members of someone with a particular disorder (proband) are more likely to have that disorder than family members of people without the disorder. Adoption studies allow us to examine genetically related individuals who live in separate families, which helps to separate the potential effects of genetic and environmental factors. Twin studies compare concordance rates between monozygotic (MZ, or identical) and dizygotic (DZ, or fraternal) twin pairs to quantify genetic and environmental contributions to variance in liability to a trait. In candidate gene association studies, scientists compare one or a few specific genes in a large group of individuals who have a specific trait or disorder with a well-matched group of individuals who do not have that trait or disorder. A genome-wide association study (GWAS) is also a case-control design but compares millions of genetic variants across the genome.

Critical Thinking Question

Genome-wide association studies, a key tool in understanding the genetics of psychiatric illness, require researchers to study the DNA of thousands of individuals. The only way they can achieve this is by collecting biological samples from individuals with and without the illness under study. Although many individuals willingly participate in such studies hoping that the contribution of their blood samples will alleviate suffering in the future, others fear the invasion of personal privacy that such research could entail. Discuss the ethical complications of human genetic research into psychiatric disorders.

Research in Abnormal Psychology at the Individual Level

Studies of brain structure and function and genetics are sophisticated research tools, but they are time-consuming and not always cost-effective. Most research in abnormal psychology has been based on comparing groups of people who have different characteristics, are tested in different ways, or receive different treatments. Conclusions are drawn based on the average responses for the group. Research at the individual level also helps identify general principles about abnormal behavior and its treatment. In fact, the practice of clinical psychology is generally directed toward the individual. Valuable information can be learned from intensive study of individual people, families, or small groups of people who can be considered a single unit. This research complements large group-based studies by allowing for richer examination of details and the development of hypotheses and theories that can later be tested in group designs. At the individual level, the two main methods of study are case studies and single-case designs.

The Case Study

LO 2.7 Describe the strengths and limitations of case studies.

The brief description of H.M. presented earlier in the chapter is drawn from a **case study**, a comprehensive description of an individual (or group of individuals) using clinical data typically drawn from a clinician's practical experience. The case study provides a detailed narrative of abnormal behavior and/or its treatment. It is sometimes accompanied by a quantitative measurement (such as measuring the frequency of a problematic behavior), but it does not allow us to draw conclusions about causes of behavior. In the case study, nothing is manipulated by the observer. The individual's story is simply recounted. Nevertheless, case studies are useful for the study of abnormal behavior.

BENEFITS OF CASE STUDIES As the case of H.M. illustrates, case studies allow the examination of rare phenomena, when group-based research would be nearly impossible simply because an inadequate number of cases are available (Kazdin, 2003). In her memoir, *The Center Cannot Hold*, author Elyn Saks provides another example of a case study approach. Saks's chronology of the development of schizophrenia and the vivid descriptions of its symptoms allowed millions to experience the psychological descent into schizophrenia firsthand. Her story is one of triumph—despite the presence of this disease, she is a law professor at the University of Southern California.

Case studies also can generate hypotheses for group studies. In the true spirit of the scientist–practitioner model, clinical observations can lead to the development of testable theories and/or treatment using group designs. For example, John B. Watson's detailed study of Little Albert and Mary Cover Jones's report of Little Peter (see Chapter 1) served as the basis for the development of treatments for anxiety disorders that have been tested scientifically and are still used today.

Finally, case studies illustrate important clinical issues that are not readily apparent in a group-based report. An example is a case report of five patients who had both anxiety/depression and chronic obstructive pulmonary disease, a lung disorder (Stanley et al., 2005), and participated in a large treatment trial. The case report provided more details about their specific clinical symptoms and their specific responses to treatment than was possible in the full clinical report (Kunik et al., 2008). This increased detail can be useful for clinicians who seek to use empirically supported treatments.

Case studies are detailed descriptions of a single person that may help us understand a particularly rare behavior. A case study of the serial killer Theodore (Ted) Bundy, for example, could shed light on the reasons that a person might engage in multiple murders.

VARIATIONS AND LIMITATIONS OF CASE STUDIES The amount and type of data included in case studies vary considerably. Some of them simply provide case descriptions. Others illustrate clinical points using standardized measures of behaviors or symptoms, allowing comparisons with other larger studies.

> Monica's symptoms of depression are more severe than those of patients included in most large studies of depression treatments.

Scientifically rigorous case reports also attempt to standardize (keep consistent) the types of assessment and treatment procedures reported. Such reports enable other researchers or clinicians to attempt to replicate the same findings with another patient. Standardizing procedures for assessment or treatment also makes it possible to combine results from a small group of patients into a single report. In addition, standardized procedures make comparing symptoms or the amount of change over time easier than what might be observed in studies of large groups of patients.

> Through the course of Monica's work with her therapist, she regularly answered a set of questions that helped the therapist evaluate how severe her symptoms were. Over time, as Monica tried different medications and non-medication treatments, her scores gradually decreased, showing that her symptoms were improving.

With all their advantages, however, the ability of case studies to help us understand abnormal behavior is limited. Most importantly, although case studies allow us to develop hypotheses about what might have caused certain symptoms or what type of treatment might be helpful, they do not allow us to make any firm conclusions about the cause(s) of symptoms or change following treatment. For example, improvement in a patient's symptoms could result from the specific treatment or from other factors that are unrelated to that treatment. These factors could include the simple passage of time, attention from a therapist, or subjective biases on the part of the patient or clinician. To draw conclusions about the causes of symptoms or change, an *experimental control* condition is needed. At the individual level of research, experimental control is provided by the single-case design.

Single-Case Designs

LO 2.8 Identify two types of single-case designs and the strengths and limitations of each.

Single-case designs are experimental studies conducted at the individual level (i.e., with a single person). This approach uses quantitative measurement and incorporates control conditions that allow clearer demonstration of causal relationships in a single individual. *Single-case designs* control for alternative hypotheses (i.e., that something other than the treatment caused the change), and unlike case histories, they can lead to causal inferences. They require fewer resources than group-based research (see "Research in Abnormal Psychology at the Group Level") and allow more detailed attention to individual patterns of change. In the single-case design, each person is a complete experiment, at various times participating in both the treatment and the comparison (or control) condition. The goal of the experiment is to examine whether behavior changes systematically, depending on whether the participant is in the treatment or the comparison phase.

Single-case design research begins with a baseline assessment that measures the behavior targeted for change (e.g., how often a child has a tantrum, how frequently panic attacks occur) before implementing any experimental or control condition. An interesting challenge for this type of research is that sometimes merely asking a person to *monitor* a behavior may change how often or how long the behavior occurs. For example, asking a smoker to count the number of cigarettes smoked per day often results in decreased smoking. Why? Simply becoming aware of how many cigarettes one smokes each day can motivate a person to decrease his or her smoking. Behavior change that results from *self-monitoring*, however, is only temporary. Therefore, baseline monitoring (i.e., assessment that occurs before beginning treatment) continues until the behavior pattern is stable. Next, a treatment is applied and withdrawn with *continuous assessment* of the target behavior. If the target behavior decreases with treatment and then returns to baseline when the treatment is withdrawn, the researcher can conclude that the treatment may have been effective (provided alternative explanations can be ruled out). If other researchers do similar research with the same results, the finding is *replicated* and confidence in it increases. Providing sufficient details about the patient, therapist, setting, and nature of the intervention aids in the replication of findings, which reinforces the study's conclusions. Regardless of the number of replications, however, the focus remains on describing individual patterns of behavior for one person, not aggregate data from multiple patients.

DESIGN STRATEGIES The most common single-case design is known as the ***ABAB*, or reversal**, design in which A represents a baseline phase and B represents a treatment phase. In this model, the two phases are alternated to examine their impact on behavior. Behavior is first evaluated at baseline until stability is demonstrated (A). The treatment is then applied (B), and assessment continues until behavior stability is achieved. Next the treatment is withdrawn (A). Behavior that returns to baseline during the second A phase is evidence that the treatment was the cause of the behavior change. Even more evidence for the power of the treatment is obtained when the intervention is applied again (another phase B) and another behavior change takes place. Each AB sequence is considered a replication, and each time the B phase has the same effect provides additional evidence that the treatment is the agent of change (Kazdin, 2003). The ABAB design can be used with patients of all ages, but it often is a particularly useful strategy to test the effects of behavioral treatments for children.

Caitlin is 3 years old. Since she was 15 months old, she has pulled out the hair on her head. Her pediatrician diagnosed her with trichotillomania, a disorder characterized by repetitive hair pulling (see Chapter 5). He referred Caitlin and her family to a psychologist who worked with them to develop a behavioral treatment plan using a single-case design to try to stop this behavior.

Because most of Caitlin's hair pulling occurred at night, the psychologist directed her mother to collect the hair from her pillow each morning, put it in a plastic bag, and label it by the day of

Figure 2.10 ABAB Research Design.

Number of hairs pulled by Caitlin during baseline (A) and intervention (B) phases of behavioral treatment for hair pulling.

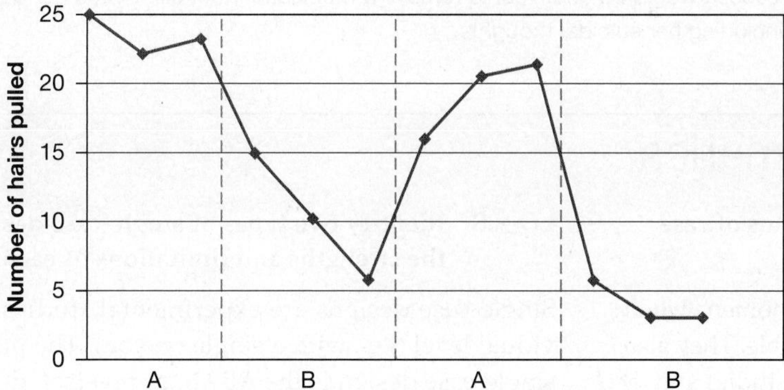

the week. The number of hairs pulled each night would be used to determine whether treatment was effective. The treatment plan was as follows:

Caitlin had a pair of pink mittens that she liked to wear, and her favorite food was cherry jam. If Caitlin wore her mittens all night (which would prevent her from pulling her hair) and they were still on her hands in the morning, she could have cherry jam for breakfast.

Using an ABAB design, the effectiveness of the treatment was evaluated (see Figure 2.10). The A phase was the baseline phase (no pink mittens or cherry jam). The B phase was the actual treatment (cherry jam for breakfast if Caitlin was wearing her mittens in the morning). Her mother continued to collect the hair each morning and recorded the average number of hairs pulled per night. See Figure 2.10 for the number of hairs on Caitlin's pillow each morning (averaged over the week) during the treatment program. Each phase was 3 weeks in length. As Caitlin's hair began to return, the treatment program was gradually withdrawn. Six months later, she had a full head of hair.

Some interventions produce learning that cannot easily be reversed. For example, relaxation training to reduce the frequency of panic attacks may produce changes in physical state (lower blood pressure) that do not quickly revert to baseline levels. Moreover, once a person has learned to use a particular coping skill, the skill cannot be "removed." When a behavior cannot be reversed, a *multiple baseline design* may be used (Morgan & Morgan, 2001). This design applies only one AB sequence, but the sequence is repeated across individuals, settings, or behaviors. When the *multiple baseline design* is conducted *across individuals,* the treatment is introduced at a different time for each person. This is often done by varying the length of the baseline assessment for each participant so that the cause of any improvement cannot be attributed to the duration of any standard baseline period. As in the ABAB design, repeating the AB sequence across people increases confidence in the conclusions.

Multiple baseline studies can also be conducted *with a single individual* as the intervention is applied independently *across behaviors* (e.g., first smoking, then overeating) or *settings* (e.g., first home, then school, then on the playground). If the B phase consistently produces the same behavior change (or is replicated), this is evidence that the intervention is effective.

LIMITATIONS OF SINGLE-CASE DESIGNS Single-case designs allow clinicians working in full-time practice to use experimental strategies to determine whether a treatment is efficacious (reduces psychological symptoms) for a particular patient. These strategies are also useful for situations in which it is unethical to withhold treatment completely but testing the causal relationship between the treatment and a person's behavior is needed. Single-case designs do not allow researchers to generalize the results to heterogeneous groups of people, however. Furthermore, they do not address the impact of individual differences (related to age, sex, ethnicity), which may be very important in determining treatment response. Group-based research, discussed in the next section, is best suited to address these types of questions.

ETHICS AND RESPONSIBILITY In some cases, reversing a treatment is unethical or impractical. For example, it would be unethical to remove a treatment that reduces self-injurious behavior, such as head banging in children with developmental disabilities.

> In Monica's case, it would be unethical to remove a medication that eliminated her depressive symptoms, including her suicidal thoughts.

Learning Objective Summaries

LO 2.7 Describe the strengths and limitations of case studies.

Case studies allow the examination of rare phenomena when group-based research would be nearly impossible. They also can be used to generate hypotheses for group studies and illustrate important clinical issues that are not readily apparent in a group-based report. Case studies vary with regard to the amount and type of data included, but they do not allow us to determine causes of symptoms or change following treatment.

LO 2.8 Identify two types of single-case designs and the strengths and limitations of each.

Single-case designs are experimental studies at the individual level (i.e., with a single person). The most common single-case design is the ABAB, or reversal, design. In this design, two phases (A and B) are alternated such that treatment occurs only during the B phase. If behavior changes occur only during B phases, we can conclude that the treatment was effective. This design, however, cannot be used if learning during the B phase cannot be reversed. In these cases, multiple baseline designs may be used to examine separate AB sequences across individuals, settings, or behaviors.

Critical Thinking Question

Paul does not like school and throws a temper tantrum every day when it is time to walk to the school bus. If you were a therapist in private practice, how would you set up an experimental test to determine whether a treatment program you designed for Paul's parents was working to decrease the tantrums?

Research in Abnormal Psychology at the Group Level

Studies based on groups of people are the most common types of research used in abnormal psychology. Using groups allows researchers to draw conclusions based on the average performance across all participants. For example, an investigator recruits a large number of patients with depression for a study of a new treatment. The investigator measures depressive symptoms before and after treatment. After the experiment, depression decreases by 50%, suggesting that, on average, patients who participated improved to that degree. The results do not mean, however, that each patient improved by 50%. Some patients benefited less from the treatment and others more. Because the results of the study are based on the average score of the group, they do not allow us to predict the behavior of any single individual. However, this type of research allows us to develop conclusions about important outcomes such as the impact of different treatments on different people and the prevalence of various disorders in different groups of people. Group-based studies may be correlational or controlled in nature.

Correlational Methods

LO 2.9 Understand the principles of correlational research and their application to the study of abnormal behavior.

Many important questions in abnormal psychology use **correlations**, or relationships, between different variables or conditions to understand aspects of behavior. Perhaps

Figure 2.11 Examples of Correlational Relations.

When data are graphed as points, the shape of the distribution reveals the correlation (or lack of correlation).

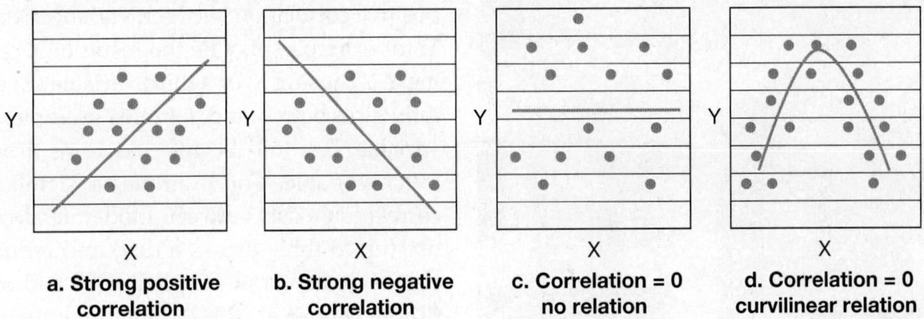

an investigator wants to know whether the severity of depressive symptoms increases with age. To examine this relationship, the investigator can graphically plot subjects' ages and scores on a depression symptom inventory with age on one axis (perhaps the *X* axis) and depression scores on the other (*Y*) axis. Then, using mathematical calculations, the investigator fits a line to the points to determine the degree of association (see Figure 2.11). A statistical concept known as a **correlation coefficient** indicates the *direction* and *strength* of the relationship. The direction of the relationship is considered positive or negative. When a *positive correlation* exists, an increase in one variable is associated with an increase in another variable (e.g., increased use of caffeine is associated with increased depression in children/adolescents; Benko et al., 2011). In contrast, a *negative correlation* means that an increase in one variable is associated with a decrease in another variable (e.g., increased levels of cognitive engagement such as reading, playing card games, and doing crossword puzzles are associated with decreased risk for Alzheimer's disease; Morris, 2005). The strength of a relationship is determined by the value of the correlation coefficient, which ranges from –1.0 to 1.0. Values close to those end points at 1.0 and –1.0 indicate a stronger relationship. A correlation of 0.0 indicates no linear relationship (see Figure 2.11). It is important to note that a strong relationship can be *either* positive or negative.

Interpreting the significance of a correlation depends on different factors. The first factor involves the size and heterogeneity of the study sample. If the sample of people studied is not sufficiently diverse with regard to the variables of scientific interest, the data may lead to inaccurate conclusions. For example, the relationship between age and memory would appear very different if data were collected from a sample of people between the ages of 18 and 85 compared to a sample of people between the ages of 60 and 70. In the latter group, the restricted age range would lead to correlations that did not represent the true relation between these two variables for the population as a whole.

Another factor important in interpreting correlational data is the way participants are selected. If study participants are chosen because they have a certain psychiatric disorder or because they come from a particular ethnic group, results will generalize only to that subset of people. The study findings may not be relevant for other diagnostic groups or other ethnicities.

Sometimes the relationship between two variables does not appear as a straight line, that is, it is not linear in nature. For example, a popular theory about the association between stress and performance proposes an *inverted-U* relationship. For testing situations or athletic performances, moderate levels of stress are associated with optimal performance. Much higher and lower levels of stress create poor performance (Muse et al., 2003). This is known as a *curvilinear* relationship. Plotting a straight line through an inverted-U shape would yield a linear correlation coefficient near 0 (see Figure 2.11d). This would lead to a false conclusion that no relation exists between the two variables.

CORRELATION IS NOT CAUSATION Often correlations are inaccurately interpreted to imply a causal relationship. Correlations explain only the degree to which a change in one

Correlation is not causation. Looking at these pictures, you might conclude that larger fires are caused by the presence of more fire trucks. Why would this be an incorrect assumption?

variable is *associated* with a change in the other; they do not allow you to conclude that one variable *causes* the second. A strong positive correlation between variables X and Y, for example, may be the result of X causing Y, Y causing X, or a third variable (Z) that influences both X and Y. In this example, the variable Z would be referred to as a *moderator* variable. For example, a significant correlation exists between moderate alcohol use (up to three drinks a day) and reduced risk of dementia in people age 55 and over (Ruitenberg et al., 2002). Often inaccurately reported in the media as causal (e.g., drinking moderately can prevent dementia), the data merely suggest that these two phenomena are related. In fact, moderate alcohol use may have a *direct* impact on cognitive functioning through the release of a neurotransmitter (acetylcholine, or ACTH) in the hippocampus (a center for learning and memory). Alcohol use might also influence cognitive status *indirectly* through its effects on cardiovascular risk factors, decreasing the possibility of high blood pressure or stroke, both of which in turn could affect cognitive functioning. Other explanations might implicate different variables that could influence both alcohol use and the development of dementia (e.g., exercise level, education, genetic predispositions, type of dementia). Any of these alternatives could be the moderator variable (Z) that affects the relationship between alcohol and dementia.

It is even more tempting to assume a causal relationship when a significant correlation occurs between two variables that are measured at different points in time (e.g., SAT scores and college grades). In these cases, terms such as *risk factor* or *predictor* are used to describe this temporal relationship. For example, it is generally well known that cigarette smoking and lack of exercise are *risk factors* for elevated cholesterol and heart disease. However, other intervening factors may affect the relationship (e.g., nutrition). Because it would be unethical to conduct an experiment in which people were assigned to smoke a certain number of cigarettes per day, we can understand these relationships only through the use of correlational data.

Similarly, the severity of a disorder before treatment is often interpreted to *predict* treatment response. In most cases, more severe symptoms are associated with less positive treatment response, but it is not always clear that more severe symptoms *cause* the less positive response. This is an important point to understand because although *predict* may imply causality in everyday language, in psychology it simply indicates that certain levels of Variable X, assessed at Time 1, are significantly associated with certain levels of Variable Y assessed at Time 2. *Predict* in this sense does not mean *cause*.

In treatment-focused research, correlational analyses can be very useful. By investigating the relationship between patient characteristics (e.g., demographics, clinical severity, social support resources) and improvement as a result of treatment, investigators find correlational analyses useful both theoretically and practically. For example, identifying groups of patients who do not respond to a treatment may lead to the development of alternative treatments. Although correlational designs may yield important information, these studies can measure only covariation between predictors and outcomes. To draw conclusions about *causality*, controlled group designs must be used.

Controlled Group Designs

LO 2.10 Describe the factors that influence outcomes of randomized controlled trials.

Most research in psychology uses **controlled group designs** that expose groups of participants to different conditions that the investigator manipulates and controls. In these designs, participants in at least one **experimental group** are typically compared with at least one **control group**. These groups are usually designed to be highly similar with regard to as many variables as possible (e.g., age, sex, education) and to vary only on the **independent variable** (IV) that the experimenter controls. For example, one group of depressed patients (*the experimental group*) receives a treatment and the other group (*the control group*) does not, but in all other ways the groups are similar. The impact of the IV on some **dependent variable** (DV), or outcome measure, is then assessed. Statistical analyses examine whether group differences on the DV occur more often than chance. If so, and if the groups differed only on the IV, one can conclude that the IV is likely to have caused the differences. The strongest inferences about causality come from randomized controlled designs.

RANDOMIZED CONTROLLED DESIGNS The most critical feature of this design is the **random assignment** of participants to groups. When assignment is truly random, each participant has an equal probability of being assigned to either group. In addition to random assignment, other features of randomized controlled designs can affect the study's conclusions. These include *participant selection procedures, internal and external validity*, and *assessment strategies*. When deciding how to select participants, an important consideration is whether to recruit an *analogue* or a *clinical* sample. *Analogue samples* (just like an analogy) are people who have the characteristics of interest and resemble treatment-seeking populations but are not seeking clinical services. Researchers interested in social anxiety, for example, may recruit an analogue sample by placing an ad in the paper seeking people with public speaking anxiety. Analogue samples are most often recruited from college campuses or community groups. In contrast, *clinical samples* are people who are seeking services for a specific problem. A researcher in an anxiety disorders clinic may approach patients in the clinic to ask them to participate in a treatment study.

A research study is examining whether therapy is better than no therapy for the treatment of depression. Why would the internal validity of the study be threatened if some participants in the no therapy group started taking an antidepressant drug?

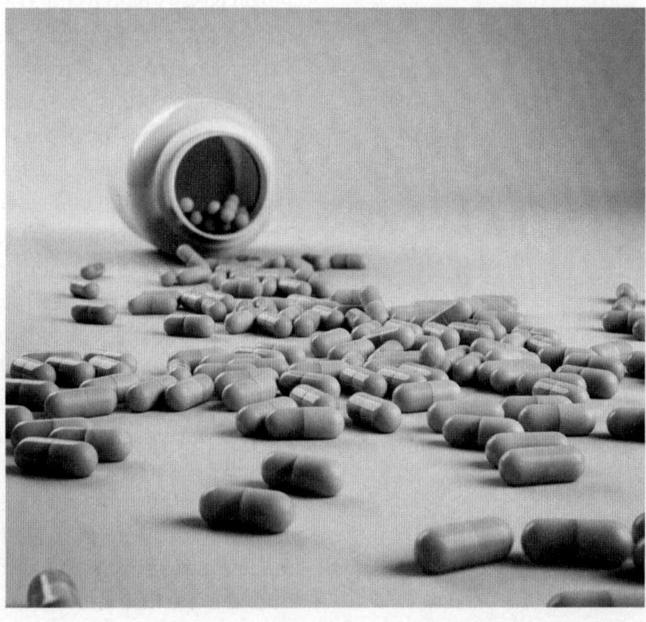

The decision to recruit an analogue or clinical sample is based on both theoretical and practical issues (e.g., what question will be addressed and what resources are available), but the decision has significant implications for the study's conclusions. Consider, for example, an investigator who wishes to examine the efficacy of a treatment for depression in young adults. Conclusions may be dramatically different if the sample is recruited from a general college population (who may have a wide range of feelings of sadness) or from the student counseling center, where higher levels of depression may be more common (because the students are motivated to seek treatment). Results based on one sample simply may not *generalize* (be relevant) to the other.

The diversity and representativeness of the recruited sample also affect whether study findings can be generalized. For instance, many studies fail to include a sufficient number of participants representing underrepresented minority groups; findings therefore may not be relevant for large segments of the population. Guidelines from the NIH, in fact, have emphasized the importance of including diverse groups of participants in clinical research to represent the population adequately in terms of age, sex, and ethnicity.

Another issue of critical importance when examining the data from any study is the concept of validity. **Internal validity** is the extent to which the study design allows conclusions that the IV (intervention) caused changes in the DV (outcome). To increase *internal validity*, the researcher tries to control (keep constant) all variables except the one being tested (the IV). Limiting a study sample to women only, for example, increases internal validity and our ability to draw causal conclusions because potential differences in response based on sex need not be considered. To increase internal validity in a treatment study, a researcher would want to make sure that both subgroups of participants (those getting treatment and those not getting treatment) have exactly the same experiences over the course of the study with the exception of the actual treatment being tested. For example, to increase internal validity in a study of depression treatment, it would be important to ensure that participants in both groups receive no additional services or experiences that might reduce depression (e.g., support groups at church, medication from a primary care doctor) during the study period.

When internal validity increases, however, **external validity**, or the ability to generalize study findings to situations and people outside the experimental setting, often decreases because study conditions that are well controlled often fail to represent the "real world." For example, results of a study based only on women participants may be relevant only to women but not to men, and studies of depression treatment that restrict participants' activities outside of the experimental treatment may not represent what happens in real life.

A major challenge for researchers is to strike an adequate balance between internal and external validity. Researchers want to be able to draw adequate conclusions about causal relationships, yet they also want results that are relevant to real-life phenomena. In treatment outcome research, internal and external validity are differentially emphasized in **efficacy** versus **effectiveness research** (Roy-Byrne et al., 2003). **Efficacy research** attempts to maximize internal validity, allowing the researcher to feel confident in identifying causal relationships. Patients are carefully selected to represent a *homogeneous group* (i.e., to have only the disorder the investigators want to study and no other conditions); specialized providers use a highly structured intervention; and comparison groups are chosen carefully to control for key elements of the treatment approach. These well-controlled studies allow the researcher to draw solid conclusions about the impact of the specific treatment, but sometimes the research procedures do not reflect real-world patients and clinics. In effectiveness research, which focuses more on external validity than efficacy research, patients are more heterogeneous and more similar to the types of patients treated in routine care. Treatment is often provided in typical health care settings (e.g., primary care) by clinicians who work in those settings; control conditions more often consist of the type of care typically offered in that clinic; and more emphasis is given to the cost–benefit ratio of treatment. These studies are sometimes less well controlled with respect to research design, but the results are more representative of what might happen when treatments are used in the real world. Efficacy and effectiveness designs are best viewed as complementary approaches to treatment research.

Conclusions from randomized controlled designs also depend on the assessment strategies researchers use. First and foremost, assessment instruments must be *reliable* (measure a particular variable consistently over time and across patients) and *valid* (measure a variable accurately) (see Chapter 3 for more detailed information about reliability and validity). Using more than one assessment method is also important. For example, some measures of depression emphasize physical symptoms, such as sleep, whereas others emphasize difficulties in thinking, such as concentration and memory problems. Depression can be evaluated using self-report (typically through standardized questionnaires or surveys), global ratings by expert evaluators, direct observations of behavior, and psychobiological measures. Choosing measures that represent different methods of assessment also increases the confidence and generalizability of study findings.

Two other important issues related to our ability to draw conclusions from controlled research studies include the use of **placebo control** conditions and the consideration of *blinded* assessment. Even in controlled research, the expectations or biases of the researcher and the participants can affect study findings (participants who think they are getting a good treatment may get better just because they expect to do so). A placebo control group is one in which an inactive treatment is provided; all aspects of this treatment are like those of the experimental condition but without the active ingredients of the treatment. For example, in medication studies, the placebo control group receives a pill that looks exactly like the real medication but in fact has no real medication (i.e., is like a "sugar pill"). Because a significant proportion of patients get better with a placebo treatment (called *placebo response*), this type of control condition allows the researcher to estimate what percent of improvement is actually due to the medication. Only if the experimental treatment produces greater response than the placebo can we say that the active ingredients of the treatment are important. In placebo-controlled studies, it is important for patients and any people who rate the degree of improvement to remain blinded to (unaware of) the condition to which the patient has been assigned.

For example, what if Monica agreed to participate in a research treatment study for depression, but she and the researchers knew that she had been assigned to the "placebo group"? How would Monica evaluate her improvement if she knew that she was not receiving active treatment?

To reduce bias that may influence study findings, it is important to keep research participants and evaluators blinded, or uninformed, about study goals and hypotheses as well as their assigned treatment condition (active treatment, placebo, or no treatment control). Completely blind assessment is not always feasible, but this assessment strategy is helpful for enhancing study validity because it reduces bias regarding treatment outcome.

CLINICAL VS. STATISTICAL SIGNIFICANCE Another important consideration when evaluating clinical research is clinical versus statistical significance.

Suppose that after treatment, people in the treatment condition report that it now takes only 2 hours to fall asleep compared with 2.2 hours for people in the control group.

Statistical significance refers to the mathematical probability that after treatment, changes that occurred in the treatment group did not occur by chance but were actually due to the treatment. Statistically significant findings show that the treatment changed the target behavior. But an equally important question is whether the significant findings have any practical or clinical value. Sometimes statistical significance indicates the presence of important clinical changes but not always. In some studies, particularly those with large samples, statistically significant differences may actually be quite small (as in the sleep example just mentioned) and have no real implications for patient care.

By contrast, *clinical significance* examines whether significant findings have practical or clinical value. For example, do treatments that reduce symptom severity have a meaningful impact on patients' lives?

Does a patient such as Monica, who was so depressed that she could not get out of bed before treatment, now not only feel less depressed but also feel well enough to be able to return to work?

Clinical significance addresses whether the patient's functioning is improved as a result of treatment and the patient no longer has symptoms of a disorder. When statistically significant change occurs without major impact on patients' functioning, its clinical value is questionable. From a statistical perspective, various measures of the magnitude of the treatment effect are known as *effect sizes*. The larger the effect size, the greater the difference between the active treatment and the control group.

A psychologist needs to consider both clinical and statistical significance in the study and treatment of abnormal behavior.

Improvement of Diversity in Group-Based Research

LO 2.11 Understand the importance of diversity in group-based research in abnormal psychology.

As noted earlier, one major limitation of group-based research in abnormal psychology is the failure to include sufficiently diverse samples with regard to race, ethnicity, and culture. For many years, samples were also restricted with regard to sex and age. Much medical and clinical research conducted well into the 1980s, for example, excluded women. There are several reasons for this exclusion. One was the difficulty inherent in controlling for biological differences between the sexes, increasing the complexity and costs of any research design. Another concern, especially with medication trials, is the unknown effect of many new medications on the developing fetus and the difficulties inherent in ensuring that women participating in a clinical trial do not become pregnant during the course of the trial. Third, phase of the menstrual cycle can influence response to many interventions and is another variable that needs to be either incorporated into the study design or controlled. Although many of these reasons for exclusion are practical and defensible from a legal and ethical perspective, they have resulted in our knowing less about the efficacy of some medications in women. Older adults were often excluded from research as well because of the complex medical, psychological, and social changes that accompany aging. Such exclusion criteria made it impossible to draw conclusions relevant to diverse groups of people. Similarly, the overabundance of research in abnormal psychology that has been conducted with white individuals (often those attending college) may have little relevance for understanding abnormal behavior in people of other races, ethnicities, and cultures.

A growing body of research has begun to document differences in the expression, prevalence, and treatment response of mental health symptoms across different racial and ethnic groups, but recruiting adequate samples is still a challenge. As a result of a series of unethical practices that occurred during the first half of the twentieth century (see Chapter 15), lack of trust and fear of stigmatization make some participants from ethnically diverse backgrounds reluctant to participate in research (Shavers et al., 2002). In addition, recruitment strategies often are inadequate for engaging minority participants (Sheikh, 2006). To encourage sex, age, racial, and ethnic diversity in research samples, the NIH and other agencies that fund research now require all grant applications to include specific recruitment plans targeting traditionally underrepresented groups. Some agencies also focus solely on funding research that addresses diversity (e.g., National Institute of Minority Health and Health Disparities). Increasing diversity in research samples will enhance our ability to generalize study findings to more people. Furthermore, using a diverse sample provides a context for evaluating cultural differences that may affect assessment and treatment. Including diverse participants in research may require increased recruitment resources to target underrepresented groups. It also requires cultural sensitivity to explain the purpose of the research and ensure that assessment instruments are available for persons who speak different languages and come from different educational backgrounds. Recent research that focuses on the development of partnerships between academic researchers and community agencies (e.g., primary care clinics, social service agencies, community centers) is one key way to increase diversity and address issues of primary concern to minority groups (Jameson et al., 2012).

NIH and other agencies that fund research now require all grant applications to include specific recruitment plans targeting traditionally underrepresented groups.

Cross-Sectional and Longitudinal Cohorts

LO 2.12 Explain the difference between cross-sectional and longitudinal cohorts and the strengths and limitations of each.

One question that has long fascinated researchers who conduct group-based research is how mental illness has changed in the population over time. It appears that some disorders are more common today than they once were, but how do we know this for sure? A related question is whether disorders occur only in one phase of life, such as childhood, or continue to be present once they appear. Specific types of group-based studies, often called **cohort studies**, can be used to answer such questions.

WHAT IS A COHORT? A **cohort** is a group of people who share a common characteristic and move forward in time as a unit. Examples include a *birth cohort* (e.g., all individuals born in a certain geographic area in a given year), an *inception cohort* (e.g., all individuals enrolled in a study at a given point in time based on a unifying factor such as place of work or school of attendance), and an *exposure cohort* (e.g., individuals sampled based on a common exposure such as witnessing the traumatic events of 9/11 [2001] in New York City or exposure to lead paint in childhood). Cohort designs are used to study **incidence** (onset of new cases, see "Epidemiology"), causes, and prognosis (outcome). Because they measure events in chronological order, they can help us to distinguish more clearly between cause and effect. For example, if we observe that experience of a traumatic event precedes the onset of posttraumatic stress disorder (PTSD), we can be more confident that the traumatic events might play a causal role in the development of the disorder than if we had no information on which came first—the trauma or the symptoms. Cohort designs can include longitudinal studies to measure outcomes over time. Longitudinal designs measure the same cohort of individuals on several occasions (see "Longitudinal Design").

CROSS-SECTIONAL DESIGN A **cross-sectional design** provides a snapshot in time. In a cross-sectional design's most basic form, participants are assessed once for the specific variable under investigation. This design is efficient and can sample large numbers of individuals; however, cause and effect can rarely be determined. Expanding the design to include several cohorts of different ages who are assessed at the same point in time (e.g., all children enrolled in classes in a specific school district) provides a more complex picture of the variable of interest. The Centers for Disease Control and Prevention (CDC) collects data about suicide rates per year. See Figure 2.12 for the percentages of individuals who

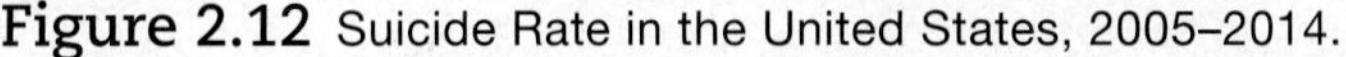

Figure 2.12 Suicide Rate in the United States, 2005–2014.

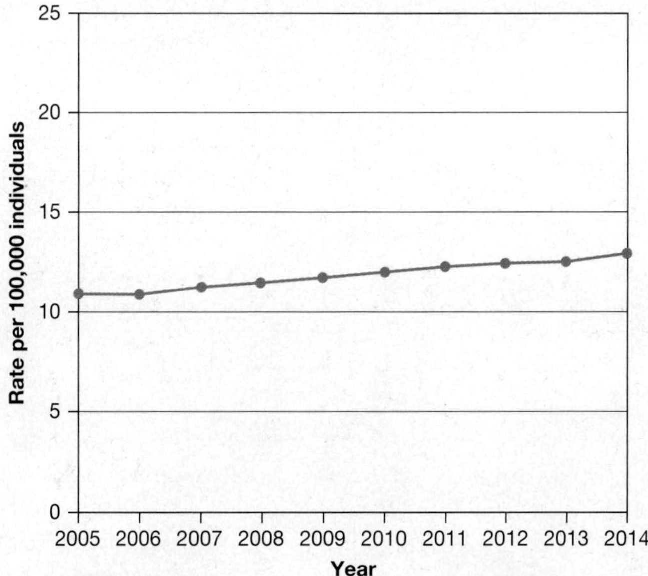

committed suicide between 2005 and 2014. This research design provides a cross-sectional landscape of people over a period of 9 years, but it does not follow the same people over this period of time. This design does not identify changes that might occur across years.

LONGITUDINAL DESIGN A **longitudinal design** is a study that takes place over time. This design includes at least two and often more measurement periods with the same individuals at different times. Many longitudinal studies have provided valuable data about the development of mental illness across the life span. Longitudinal cohorts can be assessed over the years by using age-appropriate measures at each measurement interval. A longitudinal birth cohort might sample all babies born during a certain month in a given area and follow those babies well into adulthood. Early assessments will be based on parental observations of the child, and later assessments will include age-appropriate assessments that the children complete themselves—as well as reports from parents and teachers. Outcomes measured in a longitudinal study may include incidence rates of disease, descriptions of the natural course of a variable of interest, and observations of risk factors. For example, in the birth cohort just mentioned, we could observe the incidence of autism spectrum disorder (or the number of newly diagnosed cases during the observation period), the natural course of autism spectrum disorder (how symptoms develop over the course of the 20-year observation period), and factors that were measured before the onset of the illness that are associated with those individuals who develop autism spectrum disorder (e.g., older parents). Although longitudinal studies are slow and expensive to complete, their findings are valuable because they show us what happens to the same people over a long period of time.

In a longitudinal study of data from the Swedish Adoption/Twin Study of Aging (SATSA), statistical analyses examined the different contributions of genetic and environmental variables on the experience of anxiety symptoms in older adulthood (Petkus et al.,

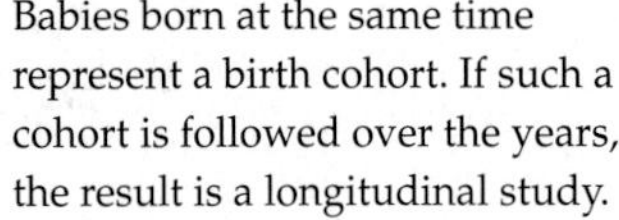

Babies born at the same time represent a birth cohort. If such a cohort is followed over the years, the result is a longitudinal study.

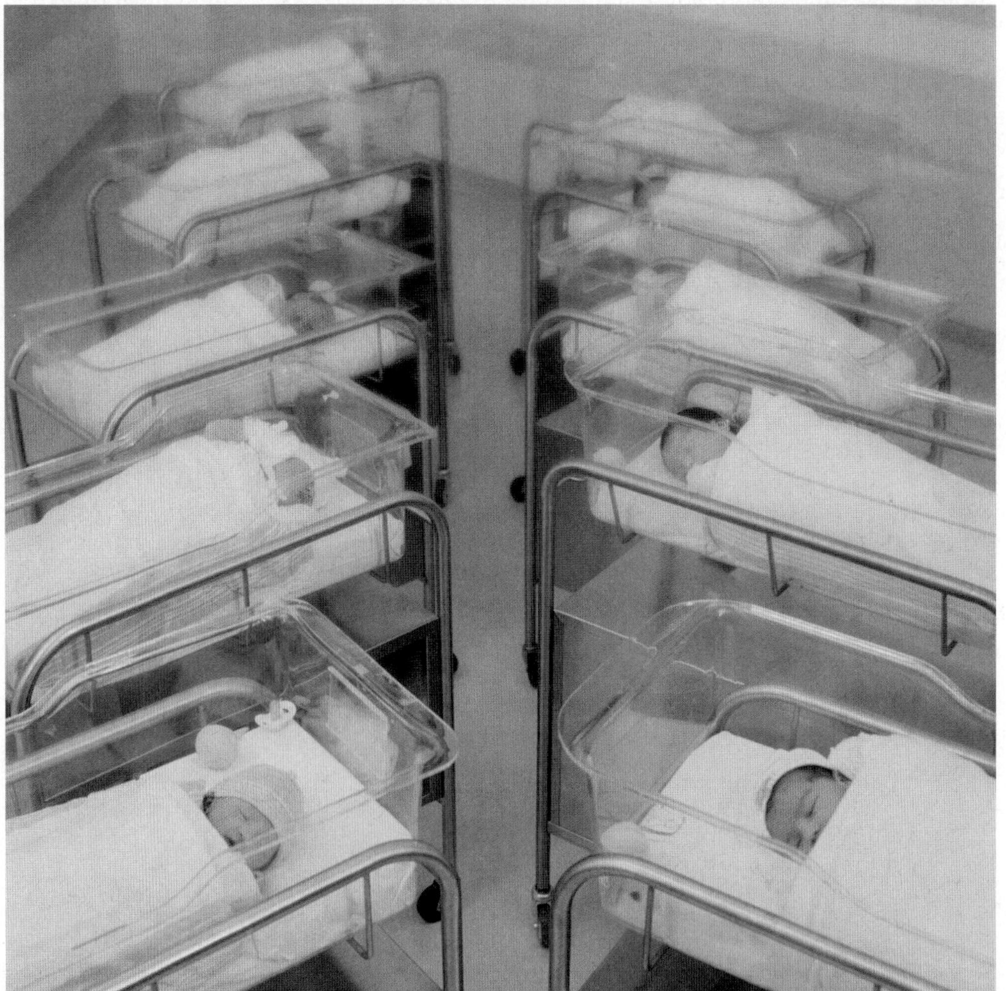

2015). The study sample included same-sex twin pairs who were born in Sweden between 1886 and 1958. The twins were interviewed between the years of 1984 and 2010 at which time they were 50 to 85 years old. Some of the twins grew up in the same home, whereas others were raised in different homes, allowing the researchers to look at potential separate genetic and environmental causes. Results suggested that genetic and environmental contributions to anxiety may change over time. An increase in the role of genetic factors seemed to occur between the ages of 60 and 64 years as well as between ages 70 and 75 years. New contributions of environmental factors also were apparent for adults in their 70s. Interestingly, as has been found in other genetic research, environmental contributions to the experience of anxiety were not due to the home environments where the twins were raised. This kind of longitudinal study allows us to learn about not only potential causes of anxiety in older people but also changes that might occur in these causal factors over time.

Learning Objective Summaries

LO 2.9 Understand the principles of correlational research and their application to the study of abnormal behavior.

Correlational research helps us understand abnormal behavior by examining relations between variables or conditions. A correlation coefficient is a statistic that tells us whether the relation between two variables is positive or negative and how strong the relation is. Correlational research, however, tells us nothing about whether one variable causes the other.

LO 2.10 Describe the factors that influence outcomes of randomized controlled trials.

The outcomes of randomized controlled trials are influenced by how participants are selected, the internal validity and external validity of the study (how well controlled the variables are and how representative conditions are to the real world), and assessment strategies (most importantly, whether they are blinded).

LO 2.11 Understand the importance of diversity in group-based research in abnormal psychology.

Generalizability of findings from group-based research is influenced by how diverse the study sample is. For many years, studies of abnormal behavior excluded women, older people, and racial and ethnic minorities. To encourage improved diversity research, the NIH and other funding agencies now require studies to include specific recruitment plans for traditionally underrepresented groups.

LO 2.12 Explain the difference between cross-sectional and longitudinal cohorts and the strengths and limitations of each.

Cross-sectional research allows us to compare groups of people (cohorts) who are assessed at the same point in time. Longitudinal research examines changes in a single group of people over time. Cross-sectional research is efficient and cost-effective, whereas longitudinal designs allow us to examine changes in people over time.

Critical Thinking Question

In a new study, the investigators examine the impact of cognitive behavior therapy (CBT) for depression in a group of children ages 7 to 17 years. Half of the children will receive CBT, and the other half will get "supportive treatment" (i.e., they will spend time talking to the therapist about whatever they want). The investigators are interested in how well the treatment affects depressive symptoms and quality of life. What are the independent and dependent variables in this investigation?

Research in Abnormal Psychology at the Population Level

When a researcher's goal is to understand abnormal psychology at the broadest possible level, the "group" of interest can become the general population. To achieve this bird's-eye view, we use the research tools associated with epidemiological research, which examines abnormal behavior at its most global level, that of entire populations.

Epidemiology

LO 2.13 Differentiate incidence and prevalence as these terms relate to understanding abnormal behavior.

Epidemiology focuses on disease patterns in human populations and factors that influence those patterns (Lilienfeld & Lilienfeld, 1980). As applied to abnormal psychology, epidemiology focuses on the occurrence of psychological disorders by time, place, and persons. Several concepts are key to understanding epidemiological research. The first is **prevalence**, which is the total number of cases of a disorder in a given population at a designated time. *Point prevalence* refers to the number of individuals with a disorder at a specified point in time. *Lifetime prevalence* refers to the total number of individuals in a population known to have had a particular disorder at some point during their lifetimes. For example, the lifetime prevalence for major depression is the number of people in the United States who have had an episode of major depressive disorder at any point in their lives.

In contrast, *incidence* refers to the number of new cases that emerge in a given population during a specified period of time. An example of incidence could be the number of new cases of anorexia nervosa reported by pediatricians in the United States over the period of 1 year. Both incidence and prevalence are valuable in understanding patterns of occurrence of psychological disorders across time and across populations, and we will refer to these concepts throughout this book.

Epidemiological Research Designs

LO 2.14 Recognize the types of epidemiological research as they relate to understanding abnormal behavior.

Researchers studying the epidemiology of a disorder typically ask questions including these: How often do certain disorders occur in the population? Are certain characteristics of people or places more likely to be associated with certain kinds of disorders? Can we do anything to change certain patterns of prevalence and incidence? These research designs can be observational (the researcher simply observes what is happening) or experimental (the researcher tries to change something and examine the effects).

OBSERVATIONAL EPIDEMIOLOGY The most basic form of epidemiological research is *observational epidemiology*, which documents the presence of physical or psychological disorders in human populations. For psychological disorders, the most common method of documentation is to conduct diagnostic interviews using a structured interview format in which all people interviewed are asked the same questions. Using randomly selected segments of the population, this design allows researchers to determine the point or lifetime prevalence of various psychological disorders. Quite simply, it answers these questions: How many people suffer from a disorder (e.g., depression)? Are certain subsets of the population (e.g., women) more likely than others to suffer from the disorder? Data from epidemiological studies were presented in Chapter 1 in the discussion of rates of psychological disorders in the United States.

Research HOT Topic

National Comorbidity Survey Replication (NCS-R)

How prevalent are mental illnesses in the United States? At what point do persons suffering from these disorders seek treatment? In 2005, four articles published in the *Archives of General Psychiatry* (Kessler, Birnbaum, et al., 2005) reported on a breakthrough national investigation of mental illness in the United States. The study is an extension of the 1990 National Comorbidity Survey, a landmark study that estimated the prevalence of mental disorders in a large nationally representative sample.

A large sample size is one of the strengths of the NCS-R study: the researchers surveyed and collected data on 9,282 individuals living in the United States. To be considered for the study, participants had to be at least 18 years old, belong to a U.S. household, and speak English. Researchers used the International World Health Organization—Composite International Diagnostic Interview to determine which respondents met the criteria for psychological diagnoses. Four categories of disorders were assessed: anxiety, mood, impulse control, and substance use disorders. Researchers also collected information on treatment use, barriers to treatment, and satisfaction with treatment.

Results indicated that mental illnesses are common in the United States: 26% of respondents met diagnostic criteria for a mental disorder within the past year. **Comorbidity** is the term used to describe the presence of at least two mental disorders affecting an individual. The NCS-R found that 45% of people with one mental disorder also met criteria for at least one other disorder. Unfortunately, the study revealed that long time intervals often occur between the time a person's mental disorder begins and his or her first attempt to seek treatment. Even more startling was the finding that only 41.1% of people with symptoms characteristic of a mental illness diagnosis received treatment. Untreated mental disorders were associated with problems in school, teenage pregnancy and unstable marriages, and unemployment later in life. Long-term effects of mental illness include reduced educational attainment, lower employment, and increased suicide-related outcomes (Borges et al., 2007; Mojtabai et al., 2015).

The findings in this study make it clear that although mental illnesses are common in U.S. households, prompt and ongoing treatment is not. The NCS-R was conducted with a large representative sample and indicated that mental illnesses are highly comorbid; it also revealed that for most people, symptoms of mental disorders begin appearing early in life. Because of the chronic nature and high prevalence of mental illness, it is imperative to expand and improve treatment for all persons in the United States who need it.

One highly informative study funded by the NIH, the National Comorbidity Survey (1990–1992), was a nationally representative mental health survey in the United States that used a standard set of questions to assess the prevalence and associated characteristics of psychological disorders. The cohort was first interviewed in 1990–1992 and then re-interviewed in 2001–2002 (NCS-2) to study patterns and predictors of the course of mental disorders. The study also evaluated whether certain primary mental disorders predicted the onset and course of secondary disorders (e.g., whether people with depression developed alcohol abuse). One of the subsequent studies was the NCS-R in which diagnostic interviews were conducted on a new sample of 10,000 respondents focusing on areas not covered in the original study [see

Examining the EVIDENCE
Can Obesity Be Prevented in Children?

- **The Facts** The Girls health Enrichment Multi-site Studies (GEMS) was aimed at preventing the onset of obesity in African American girls (Ebbeling & Ludwig, 2010; Klesges et al., 2010; Robinson et al., 2010).
- **The Evidence** At one site (Memphis), girls ages 8 to 10 years were randomly assigned to either a group that used group behavioral counseling to promote healthy eating and increased physical activity (obesity prevention program) or a self-esteem and social efficacy group (control group). At the second site (Stanford), girls ages 8 to 10 years and their families were randomly assigned to either after-school hip-hop, African, or step dance classes and programs to reduce screen media use (obesity prevention program) or information-based health education (control group). Girls participated in the programs for 2 years. Despite the carefully controlled investigations, culturally appropriate interventions, inclusion of families, and many community and government resources, changes in body mass index (the primary outcome variable that is calculated as weight in kilograms divided by height in meters squared (kg/m^2) were the same for the prevention and control groups, indicating that treatment had no effect. What went wrong?
- **Examining the Evidence** First, this was a trial to prevent obesity, but a number of the girls were already obese (40.6% in Memphis; 33.0% in Stanford). The results may have been different if obese children had not been included in the sample. Second, although the study focused on healthy eating and exercise, many of the girls lived in low-income communities where fresh foods were not available, school lunches were not always nutritious, fast food was common, and neighborhoods were not necessarily safe places for children to play outdoors. These negative environmental factors may have been more powerful than the positive effects of the intervention. Third, the diet and exercise programs may have been too complicated for 8- to 10-year-old girls to understand.
- **Conclusion** It would be easy to conclude from this study that obesity cannot be prevented, but that would be incorrect. Although it did not produce the expected results, the research provided a number of important clues that researchers can use to develop potentially more effective prevention trials.

"Research Hot Topic: National Comorbidity Survey Replication (NCS-R)"]. In the NCS-A (adolescent) study, researchers interviewed 10,000 adolescents to determine the prevalence and correlates of mental disorders in youth. The NCS series has provided invaluable information for clinicians and policy makers by establishing the magnitude of the public health burden of mental disorders and documenting the need to plan services accordingly.

EXPERIMENTAL EPIDEMIOLOGY In **experimental epidemiology**, the scientist manipulates exposure to either causal or preventive factors. A scientist might want to assess whether various environmental manipulations would be effective in producing weight loss (see "Examining the Evidence: Can Obesity Be Prevented in Children?"). The focus in this instance is on weight loss for a community as a whole, not for any one individual person. Ten geographically separated communities could be randomly assigned to a community-based weight control program focusing on increasing walking to school, decreasing fast-food consumption, and decreasing video game and TV time. The active intervention communities could be saturated with billboards, newspaper ads, local television commercials, and direct mailings, all promoting healthy approaches to weight control. The control communities would receive no intervention. Population-level outcomes would include the extent to which people were reached by the intervention and the extent to which the intervention was effective in producing both behavior and weight change.

Learning Objective Summaries

LO 2.13 Differentiate incidence and prevalence as these terms relate to the understanding of abnormal behavior.

Incidence refers to the number of new cases that emerge in a given population during a specified period of time (e.g., the number of new cases of depression over the past year). Prevalence is the total number of cases of a disorder in a given population at a designated time (e.g., the number of people with depression at any specified point in time or over their lifetime).

LO 2.14 Recognize the types of epidemiological research as they relate to understanding abnormal behavior.

Observational epidemiology documents the presence of psychological disorders in human populations usually by administration of diagnostic interviews. Experimental epidemiology involves documenting the presence of psychological disorders after the researcher manipulates exposure to causal or preventative factors.

Critical Thinking Question

A researcher wants to design a study to determine how frequently anxiety occurs in adults and whether the frequencies change as people get older. What type of study would be best to conduct, and how might you design it?

Real SCIENCE Real LIFE

Susan—A Participant in a Randomized Controlled Trial

Susan had been having episodes of depression and finally went to see her primary care doctor for advice. She gave Susan brochures about a therapy trial for depression at a nearby university and suggested that she call for more information. The following describes Susan's experience as a participant in the clinical psychotherapy trial.

SCREENING CALL

Today I called the research coordinator for information. She told me that the study was for women between 20 and 40 and was designed to compare two different psychotherapies for depression. She described the two treatments to me—one was based on something called cognitive-behavioral therapy, and the other one was based on interpersonal psychotherapy. She explained that I would not be able to choose which treatment I received, but it would be decided by a procedure that was like a flip of a coin [randomization]. She asked me a bunch of questions on the phone about my mood; how long I had been feeling this way; my sleep, appetite, energy levels; whether I was suicidal; and whether I was on any medications. Then, based on my answers to those questions, she said we could set up an appointment for an initial evaluation.

INITIAL EVALUATION

I got to the clinic and was greeted by the research coordinator. She spent a lot of time explaining the study to me and gave me an information sheet. I read it, and she asked if I had any questions. Then came all of the forms! First I filled out a **consent form** agreeing to the terms of the study and indicating that I understand my rights as a participant. I was assured that I could withdraw from the study at any time. Then I had to sign a **HIPAA** form, which was all about the privacy of my records and who could have access to them. This worried me a little bit because I certainly did not want my boyfriend to find out, so I talked with the research coordinator about it. She explained that HIPAA stood for the Health Insurance Portability and Accountability Act and that I could be completely assured that my boyfriend would not be able to have access to my records. Just when I thought I was finished filling out forms, she gave me a packet of questionnaires that asked all sorts of questions—not only about my mood but also about anxiety, eating, my family, and all sorts of questions about what sort of person I am. Some of them were really hard to answer, but I had to choose yes or no. That took about an hour and a half.

Then I had a little break, and the coordinator explained that the next step would be a comprehensive evaluation by a psychiatrist. The psychiatrist, she explained, would not be the person who would be seeing me for therapy but would conduct interviews with me throughout the study to see how I was progressing. The psychiatrist would not know which treatment I was receiving. In the evaluation, the psychiatrist asked a lot of the same questions that were on the questionnaires. This was a little irritating, but I guess the psychiatrist went into more depth than the questionnaires. She even asked about the first time I ever felt depressed when I was very young. She also asked questions about whether I heard voices or saw things that other people did not see, asked about my drug and alcohol use (I was honest with her about almost everything—I just couldn't bring myself to tell her about that one experience with Ecstasy, though—I barely know the woman and it was kind of embarrassing). She also asked all sorts of questions about my health and medications.

I met with the research coordinator again, she invited me into the study, and then she got an envelope that had my participant number on it, opened it, and told me I was randomized to cognitive-behavioral therapy.

BASELINE WEEK

At the end of the evaluation day, the research coordinator instructed me on how to "self-monitor" my mood for the baseline week. She gave me a special personal digital assistant (PDA) into which I was supposed to type in how depressed I felt every time it prompted me. I thought that was kind of cool—but worried about whether it would wake me up at night. She explained that the PDA was programmed for 8 a.m. to 10 p.m. and that I would not be bothered by prompts any other time. So off I went with my PDA for a week of recording before my first appointment. I also left with the card of my therapist, Dr. McIntosh, whom I would see the following Thursday. For a week I dutifully responded every time it pinged me. It was kind of interesting. I noticed that my mood ratings always seemed to be worse in the afternoon.

COURSE OF THERAPY

I went to the clinic, and Dr. McIntosh greeted me. The first session went well. I liked her. She had a positive attitude and seemed like she really believed that the therapy had the potential to help. She took her time and explained everything clearly. She also told me that I needed to continue responding to the PDA throughout the study. For the first 2 weeks we met twice a week. She gave me a workbook and we worked through it step by step. Every session she started off reviewing how things had gone since the last session and whether I had done all of my self-monitoring and homework. It felt a little bit like school, but she really seemed to care about how I was feeling. She helped me start to recognize how negative my thinking was, and she challenged me to start doing some of those fun things that I had lost interest in recently. I never realized how much I catastrophized from the smallest of things or, as Dr. McIntosh said, really made mountains out of molehills. I also had not realized how much my mood improved when I did some of the things on my fun list (even if I had to really push myself to do them in the first place). After the eighth session, I met with the psychiatrist again for another assessment. She went over many of the same questions as in the beginning, and I had to fill out MORE questionnaires. After eight sessions, I felt as if my mood was getting better. I still had some bad days, but it did not feel like the same oppressive cloud that had been there before. I had eight more sessions—first once a week and then once every 2 weeks. Dr. McIntosh and I spent a lot of time working on strategies for what to do if I feel like my mood was slipping again—like identifying early warning signs and taking immediate action. By the end I really felt like I understood how much my own thinking patterns contributed to my staying depressed.

FOLLOW-UP

At the end of treatment I met with the psychiatrist again for an interview and I filled out more questionnaires. The research coordinator also asked me lots of questions about how I liked the treatment and whether I would have it again or recommend it to others. I came back at 6 months and 1 year for follow-up appointments when I met with the psychiatrist again and filled out more papers. Each time, the research coordinator checked in with me to see how things were going and to update my contact information. The second time, I ran into Dr. McIntosh. It was great to see her and to report that I was still feeling really well. When I look back on the whole experience of being in the study, honestly, I had been a little worried about being a "guinea pig," but truth be told, I felt really taken care of. So many people seemed to care about my well-being, and they were all involved with my treatment. It was an amazing experience.

Key Terms

ABAB, or reversal, p. 58
beneficence, p. 40
brain stem, p. 42
candidate gene association study, p. 54
case study, p. 56
central nervous system, p. 42
cerebral cortex, p. 45
cohort, p. 67
cohort studies, p. 67
comorbidity, p. 71
consent form, p. 73
control group, p. 63
controlled group design, p. 63
correlation, p. 60
correlation coefficient, p. 61
cross-sectional design, p. 67
dependent variable, p. 63
effectiveness, p. 64
efficacy, p. 64
endocrine system, p. 47
epidemiology, p. 70
epigenetics, p. 55
experimental epidemiology, p. 72
experimental group, p. 63
external validity, p. 64
familial aggregation, p. 52
forebrain, p. 44
frontal lobe, p. 46
functional neuroimaging, p. 50
genome-wide association study, p. 54
genome-wide linkage analysis, p. 54
HIPAA, p. 73
hippocampus, p. 44
hormones, p. 47
incidence, p. 67
independent variable, p. 63
internal validity, p. 64
left hemisphere, p. 46
limbic system, p. 44
longitudinal design, p. 68
midbrain, p. 43
molecular genetics, p. 54
neuroanatomy, p. 50
neuroimaging, p. 49
neurotransmitters, p. 48
nonshared environmental factors, p. 54
occipital lobe, p. 46
parietal lobe, p. 46
peripheral nervous system, p. 42
placebo control, p. 64
prevalence, p. 70
proband, p. 52
random assignment, p. 63
right hemisphere, p. 46
shared environmental factors, p. 52
single-case design, p. 58
structural neuroimaging, p. 50
temporal lobe, p. 46
translational research, p. 40

Chapter 3
Assessment and Diagnosis

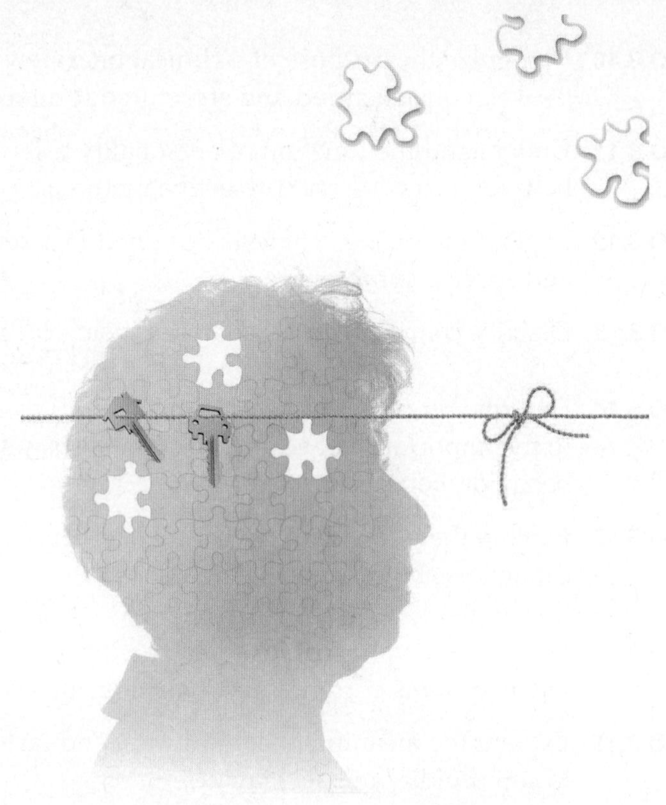

Chapter Learning Objectives

Goals of Assessment	**LO 3.1**	Understand the steps in a clinical assessment.
	LO 3.2	Identify the purpose of a screening assessment and define what is meant by sensitivity and specificity.
	LO 3.3	Describe the purpose of a diagnostic assessment and how it is different from screening.
	LO 3.4	Explain how clinical assessments can be used to evaluate a person's progress during treatment.
Properties of Assessment Instruments	**LO 3.5**	Explain the importance of standardization to the interpretation of assessment results and the difference between normative and self-referent comparisons.
	LO 3.6	Describe how reliability is important for understanding results of a clinical assessment.

	LO 3.7	Explain how validity of a measure affects a psychologist's ability to predict behavior.
	LO 3.8	Understand how a person's age, developmental status, and culture affect the clinical assessment process.
	LO 3.9	Describe at least two ethical issues that a psychologist needs to consider before conducting an assessment.
Assessment Instruments	**LO 3.10**	Recognize the purpose of a clinical interview and the difference between unstructured and structured formats.
	LO 3.11	Understand the function of personality tests and the difference between objective and projective methods.
	LO 3.12	Explain the purpose of tests designed to assess general functioning and specific symptoms.
	LO 3.13	Describe commonly used neuropsychological and intelligence tests.
Behavioral and Physiological Assessments	**LO 3.14**	Describe procedures used in a behavioral assessment with attention to the importance of a functional analysis, self-monitoring, and behavioral observation.
	LO 3.15	Explain the purpose of psychophysiological assessment and what it can tell us about abnormal behavior.
Diagnosis and Classification	**LO 3.16**	Describe the value of classifying abnormal behavior and the two major systems currently used for this purpose.
	LO 3.17	Explain the meaning of comorbidity and factors that may contribute to comorbidity in psychiatry.
	LO 3.18	Recognize the importance of developmental and cultural variables that affect the experience and classification of abnormal behavior.
	LO 3.19	Describe some of the limitations and drawbacks of a diagnostic classification system.
	LO 3.20	Discuss the potential benefits of dimensional models for understanding abnormal behavior as alternatives to more traditional classification systems.

Pauline was 75 years old and functioned well for her age. She saw Dr. McGuire, a psychologist, every couple of weeks to help her manage anxiety and depression. Pauline had experienced anxiety and depression much of her life, and the coping skills she had learned in treatment were helping. She was active at church and with volunteer groups, traveled, and had many friends. Dr. McGuire, however, had recently started talking with her about the possibility of increasing memory problems. He had noticed that she was starting to repeat herself during their meetings and that she sometimes forgot major topics of their conversations from one session to the next. Pauline's daughter had also mentioned to her the possibility of memory problems, but Pauline didn't think her memory was that bad. Sure, she misplaced things—and people told her that she repeated herself—but at her age, who didn't? As long as she could stay active and involved, it didn't bother her that she might be having some minor memory problems.

One day before a scheduled appointment, Pauline called Dr. McGuire to say that she was in the hospital. She had suffered a bad fall the day before while walking in a shopping mall, and the doctors were running a series of tests. Dr. McGuire requested Pauline's permission to speak to her doctor and learned that there was some concern that Pauline might have had a minor stroke. The doctor would conduct additional tests before she could be discharged.

When Pauline was released from the hospital, she went home with her daughter and followed up with her internist. She had not suffered a stroke, but the doctor was monitoring her symptoms because her blood pressure was high. She was more unstable on her feet and was using a cane. She was not allowed to drive. When Pauline came to her next therapy appointment with Dr. McGuire, her daughter came along. At this session, Pauline was quite confused. She could not recall many details about her hospitalization, and she repeated herself many times. She reported that she was taking pain medication as prescribed and that she would be seeing her internist the following day.

In the weeks that followed, Pauline began to regain some of her prior abilities, but her memory problems got worse, and she was more depressed and anxious. She was more lethargic than usual and worried more about the future and what might happen to her. Dr. McGuire became increasingly concerned about Pauline's ability to live independently and talked with Pauline and her daughter about the need for a more formal clinical assessment. There was a need to differentiate any medical, cognitive, and psychological reasons for Pauline's overall decline in functioning.

For Pauline and Dr. McGuire, many questions arose at this point. Did the fall result from some undiscovered medical problem? Was her pain medication creating more memory problems and depression? Might Pauline's fall and its consequences, such as losing independence, have produced increased worry and depression? Could Pauline's decreased functioning be the result of a progressive, deteriorating cognitive disease such as a neurocognitive disorder (see Chapter 14)? These questions, posed by Pauline, her therapist, and her family members, suggested the need for a clinical assessment to determine the nature and cause of her increasing difficulties as well as to help guide future treatment. In this chapter, we review the nature and goals of clinical assessment as well as the most commonly used assessment instruments and procedures. We also discuss the pros and cons of diagnostic classification, which is often a primary outcome of a clinical assessment.

Goals of Assessment

What Is a Clinical Assessment?

LO 3.1 Understand the steps in a clinical assessment.

The **clinical assessment** of any psychological problem involves a series of steps designed to gather information (or *data*) about a person and his or her environment in order to make decisions about the nature, status, and treatment of psychological problems. Typically, clinical assessment begins with a set of *referral questions* developed in response to a request for help. Usually, the request comes from the patient or someone closely connected to that person, such as a family member, teacher, or other health care professional. These initial questions help determine the goals of the assessment and the selection of appropriate psychological tests or measurements. As in Pauline's case, referral questions sometimes suggest the need for a thorough medical evaluation in addition to a psychological assessment.

As part of the assessment process, the psychologist decides which assessment procedures to use. These might include measures of biological function, cognition, emotion, behavior, and personality style. The patient's age, medical condition, and description of his or her symptoms strongly influence the tools selected for assessment, but the psychologist's theoretical perspective also affects the nature of the assessment (see Chapter 1). When evaluating a patient who is significantly depressed and anxious, for example, a behavioral psychologist focuses on measuring the environmental cues that produce the low moods and the thoughts, behaviors, and consequences associated with them. A psychoanalytic psychologist would direct more effort toward assessing the patient's early childhood experiences and typical patterns of interpersonal functioning.

Once an assessment has been completed and all data have been collected, the psychologist integrates the findings to develop preliminary answers to the initial questions. Typically, the psychologist shares those findings with the patient and family members involved in the assessment. Other health care providers who were part of the referral or assessment process also may receive the results of the assessment but only with the patient's permission. Although it is not the purpose of patient evaluation, the process of assessment sometimes has a therapeutic effect (Finn & Martin, 2010). As people begin to understand their emotions, their behaviors, and the links between them, their symptoms tend to improve, at least

Figure 3.1 Primary Goals of Assesment

The primary goals of a clinical assessment are screening, diagnosis and treatment planning, and outcome evaluation.

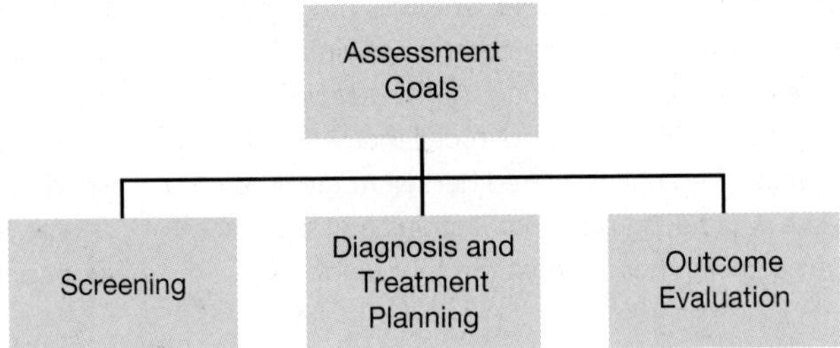

temporarily. For example, if you start to monitor the number of calories you consume each day, you might discover that the number is far more than originally estimated. In some cases, this assessment serves as feedback, and you decrease the number of calories that you eat as a result.

A clinical assessment actually can be useful even before a referral is provided as well as during the process of treatment. Three primary goals of assessment include *screening, diagnosis and treatment planning,* and *outcome evaluation* (see Figure 3.1). We will discuss each of these goals in detail through the remainder of this module.

Screening

LO 3.2 Identify the purpose of a screening assessment and define what is meant by sensitivity and specificity.

Screenings can help identify people who have problems but who may not be aware of them or may be reluctant to mention them as well as people who may need further evaluation. **Screening** assessments identify potential psychological problems or predict the risk of future problems if someone is not referred for further assessment or treatment. In a screening assessment, all members of a group (e.g., a community group, patients in a medical practice) are given a brief measure for which some identified cutoff score indicates the possibility of significant problems. For example, the Center for Epidemiologic Studies—Depression Scale (CES-D) (Radloff, 1977) is a 20-item scale used in many community studies to screen people for depression and to estimate its prevalence. A score of 16 or higher on the CES-D indicates the possibility of significant depression and suggests the need for further evaluation (Derogatis & Lynn, 1999). Other screening instruments are more broad based, covering many different psychological symptoms including depression, anxiety, and social problems (e.g., the General Health Questionnaire [GHQ]; Goldberg & Hillier, 1979, see General Tests of Psychological Functioning). In most cases, when individuals score above a certain cutoff score on a screening instrument, a more thorough evaluation can determine the nature and extent of their difficulties.

Because many people with psychological problems are more likely to see their physician than a mental health professional, brief methods for screening patients in medical settings have been developed. In fact, very simple two-item screening instruments have been used to identify medical patients with depression (Unützer et al., 2002) or anxiety (Roy-Byrne et al., 2005) who might benefit from psychological or psychiatric

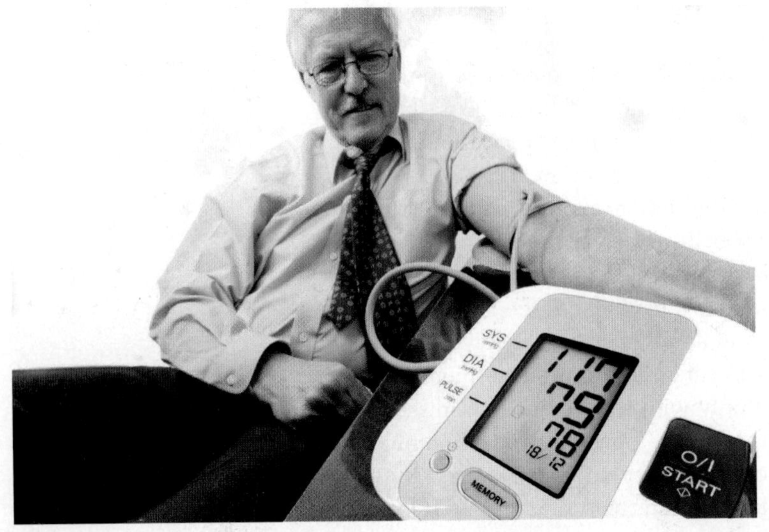

A quick blood pressure screening may be the first step in identifying serious medical problems. Similarly, mental health screenings may be key in the identification of psychological disorders.

Table 3.1 Screening Questions

Depression Screening Questions	Anxiety Screening Questions
• During the past month, have you often been bothered by feeling down, depressed, or hopeless? • During the past month, have you often been bothered by little interest or pleasure in doing things you normally enjoy?	During the past 2 weeks, how often have you been bothered by the following symptoms? • Feeling nervous, anxious, or on edge • Not being able to stop or control worrying

treatment (see Table 3.1). An affirmative answer to any of these questions suggests the need for further evaluation.

Asking questions such as these takes just a few minutes in a busy medical practice. Similarly, a 10-item screen can quickly identify substance abuse problems (e.g., Alcohol Use Disorders Identification Test [AUDIT]; Barbor et al., 2001). Sample questions from the AUDIT include:

- How often do you have a drink containing alcohol?
- How often do you have six or more drinks on one occasion?
- How often during the last year have you been unable to remember what happened the night before because you had been drinking?

To evaluate the usefulness of any particular screening measure, psychologists look for instruments that have strong sensitivity and specificity. *Sensitivity* describes the ability of the screener (or the instrument) to identify a problem that actually exists (e.g., the screener identifies depression and the person is actually depressed). *Specificity* indicates the percent of the time that the screener accurately identifies the absence of a problem (e.g., the cutoff score suggests no depression, and the patient truly is not depressed). *False positives* occur when the screening instrument indicates a problem when no problem exists (e.g., the patient's score exceeds the cutoff, but subsequent evaluation confirms the absence of depression). *False negatives* refer to instances in which the screening tool suggests that there is no depression when the patient actually is depressed. Good screening tools have high specificity and sensitivity but low false positive and false negative rates (see Figure 3.2).

Figure 3.2 Evaluating a Screening Tool for Depression.

A good screening tool is sensitive and specific: it identifies problems that do exist and does not indicate problems when none exist. The quality of the screening instrument is determined by the numbers in these cells.

		Screening Results (Does the score on a depression measure indicate depression is present?)	
		Positive (Score suggests depression is present)	Negative (Score suggests depression is absent)
Actual Problem (Does the person have depression?)	Depression is present	Sensitivity (Test accurately identifies depression)	False Negative (Test suggests there is no depression, but patient is depressed)
	Depression is absent	False Positive (Test suggests patient is depressed, but patient is not depressed)	Specificity (Test accurately suggests depression is absent)

Diagnosis and Treatment Planning

LO 3.3 Describe the purpose of a diagnostic assessment and how it is different from screening.

One of the major goals of assessment is to determine an individual's diagnosis. **Diagnosis** refers to the identification of an illness. In some branches of medicine, diagnosis can be made on the basis of laboratory tests. In psychology, making a diagnosis is more complicated; it requires the presence of a cluster of symptoms. Typically, a diagnosis is made after a clinical interview with the patient. Clinicians use the term **differential diagnosis** when they attempt to determine which diagnosis most clearly describes the patient's symptoms. Patients often have sets of symptoms that require more than one diagnosis. Using different assessment instruments, the clinician gathers data from the patient and often other sources (partner, parents, and teachers) to make the diagnosis or diagnoses that fit the patient best. Diagnosis also facilitates communication across clinicians and researchers. Diagnostic assessments are more extensive than screens and are designed to provide a more thorough understanding of a person's psychological status.

Accurate diagnoses are critical for appropriate treatment planning (see "Real People, Real Disorders: Cases of Misdiagnosis"). In addition, a diagnosis is often needed for insurance companies to reimburse a psychologist or other health care provider.

A clinical assessment that leads to a diagnosis usually includes the evaluation of symptom and disorder severity, patterns of symptoms over time (e.g., number, frequency, and duration of episodes), and the patient's strengths and weaknesses (Maruish, 1999). The assessment may also include the results from personality tests, neuropsychological tests, and/or a behavioral assessment. You will learn more about these assessment tools later in this chapter.

Outcome Evaluation

LO 3.4 Explain how clinical assessments can be used to evaluate a person's progress during treatment.

Clinical assessments can be repeated at regular intervals during treatment to evaluate a patient's progress. This kind of **outcome evaluation** is a key component of clinical psychology as practiced from a scientist–practitioner perspective. Outcome evaluations help us know whether patients are getting better, when treatment is "finished," or when it is necessary to modify an approach that is not achieving its aims. Outcome assessment may include evaluating patient satisfaction and providing data to support the marketing of treatment programs.

For outcome assessments to be useful, the same measures must be administered regularly over the course of treatment. The individual measures included in the assessment should represent a range of outcomes (e.g., symptom severity, treatment satisfaction, ability to function, and quality of life). There is a strong movement centered in the Patient-Centered Outcomes Research Institute (PCORI) (Frank et al., 2014) to consider the outcomes of treatment that are meaningful to patients and caregivers. PCORI values the critical perspective of the core mental health stakeholders (patients, caregivers, physicians, therapists) when deciding on critical outcomes. Clinically, when possible, assessment of treatment outcome should extend beyond the patient's viewpoint to include the therapist's perspective and perhaps that of family members or others close to the patient (Lambert & Lambert, 1999). To be useful, the assessment measures must also be reliable and valid (see "Properties of Assessment Instruments"). To evaluate whether treatments have the desired effect, both the degree of change and the patient's actual level of functioning after treatment must be assessed. For example, imagine that you are very sick and have a fever of 104°F. You take some medicine, your fever goes down to 101°F, and you feel better. The drop in your fever from 104 to 101°F is the degree of change from the medicine. But you still have a fever of 101, and so you are still sick—this is your actual level of functioning. In evaluating the outcome of psychological disorders, the goal may be to reduce symptoms and/or to eliminate the disorder.

The degree of change (how much a patient's symptoms have been reduced) is generally considered in terms of **clinical significance** (see Chapter 2). Clinically significant change means that meaningful improvement in symptoms has occurred (e.g., social anxiety improves to the

REAL People REAL Disorders

Cases of Misdiagnosis

In some cases, insufficient assessment and inaccurate diagnosis can lead to inadequate or inappropriate treatment and disastrous consequences. The importance of careful assessment and diagnosis is illustrated in these real cases.

- **Deafness, not Intellectual Disability** Kathy Buckley, comedienne and inspirational speaker (pictured at right), has received numerous awards and accolades for her comic abilities and advocacy for persons with disabilities. Her own poor academic performance in the second grade led to a diagnosis of mental retardation and placement in a school for mentally and physically impaired children. It took professionals a year to determine that Kathy's academic difficulties were due to hearing loss, not mental incapacitation (http://www.kathybuckley.com/).
- **Epilepsy, not Schizophrenia** A 46-year-old woman was hospitalized in a university-affiliated facility with depressive symptoms and hallucinations that had urged her to commit suicide (Swartz, 2001). Laboratory tests (e.g., electroencephalogram, or EEG) revealed that she was having seizures characteristic of complex partial epilepsy, which can also have symptoms such as depression and hallucinations. A review of the patient's clinic records revealed that she had been treated for schizophrenia and schizoaffective disorder (see Chapter 10) for 10 years without an alleviation of her symptoms. Subsequently, she was put on an antiseizure medication, and her symptoms disappeared.
- **Medication Reaction, not Depression** A 77-year-old woman developed symptoms of depression (e.g., fatigue, weight loss, motor slowing, and social withdrawal) 1 month after starting the medication digoxin for congestive heart failure. She took antidepressant medication for 7 months, but her symptoms did not improve. When she was admitted to a hospital for further evaluation, medical tests revealed a very high level of digoxin. The medication was discontinued, and symptoms of depression decreased rapidly (Song et al., 2001).
- **Brain Tumor, not Anorexia Nervosa** A 19-year-old girl was admitted to the hospital with symptoms of anorexia nervosa (e.g., rapid weight loss of 16.5 pounds, dissatisfaction with her body, and occasional binge eating). Doctors started her on nasogastric feeding to increase her caloric intake, and she was given antidepressant medication to help control her anxiety. After the patient was discovered unconscious on the bathroom floor with symptoms consistent with a seizure, a brain scan revealed a brain tumor. Following its surgical removal, the patient's fear of weight gain and her distorted views of her body decreased, and 2 years later, she no longer showed any residual signs of an eating disorder (Houy et al., 2007).

extent that the college student can now take courses that require oral presentations). A measure known as the Reliable Change Index (RCI) (Jacobson & Truax, 1991) is now frequently used to determine whether the degree of change from beginning to end of treatment is meaningful. For example, was the change more than we would expect based on normal changes that occur over time (see "Reliability")? Patients' scores on various measures after treatment are sometimes compared with scores of people without the disorder who have also completed the assessment to evaluate whether symptoms and functioning have moved into the normal range.

Learning Objective Summaries

LO 3.1 Understand the steps in a clinical assessment.

A clinical assessment usually begins with a referral question that establishes the assessment goals and influences the selection of instruments and procedures. The patient's age, medical condition, and description of symptoms also affect the measures chosen, as does the psychologist's theoretical perspective. Once the assessment is completed, the psychologist develops preliminary answers to the referral question(s) and shares the findings with the patient and others (family members, health care providers) involved in the assessment.

LO 3.2 Identify the purpose of a screening assessment and define what is meant by sensitivity and specificity.

Screening assessments are used to identify potential psychological problems that require further assessment. Sensitivity describes the ability of the screening assessment or tool to identify a problem that actually exists. Specificity indicates the percent of time that the screener accurately identifies the absence of a problem.

LO 3.3 Describe the purpose of a diagnostic assessment and how it is different from screening.

A diagnostic assessment usually involves a clinical interview to determine which diagnosis or diagnoses best describe a person's symptoms. Diagnostic assessments are more extensive than screenings and are designed to provide a more thorough understanding of a person's psychological status. Accurate diagnosis is critical for treatment planning.

LO 3.4 Explain how clinical assessments can be used to evaluate a person's progress during treatment.

Clinical assessments can be repeated at regular intervals during treatment to evaluate whether change in symptoms is occurring. To be useful, the same measures must be administered consistently. It also is important to consider both the degree of change in symptoms over time and whether this change is associated with meaningful improvement in functioning.

Critical Thinking Question

When Jennifer visited her family doctor because she was losing weight and having trouble sleeping, he was sufficiently concerned to refer her to a psychologist for an evaluation. What types of assessments might the psychologist do to determine whether the symptoms Jennifer described were related to depression or anxiety?

Properties of Assessment Instruments

The potential value of an assessment instrument rests in part on its various **psychometric properties**, which describe how well the instrument works and affect how confident we can be in the testing results. We need to know, for example, how well the instrument measures the features or concepts it is intended to measure. How well does a test for depression actually measure depressive symptoms? An instrument's *psychometric properties* include *standardization, reliability*, and *validity*.

Standardization

LO 3.5 Explain the importance of standardization to the interpretation of assessment results and the difference between normative and self-referent comparisons.

To understand the results of clinical assessments, the score must be put in context. Think back to the concept of a fever. A temperature of 104°F creates concern because it is so much higher than the body's normal temperature of 98.6°F. In the same way, to understand the results of a psychological assessment, we must put test results in context. Does a particular score indicate the existence of a problem, its severity, or its improvement over time? **Standardization**, which involves standard ways of evaluating scores, can involve normative or self-referent comparisons (or both). **Normative comparisons** require comparing a person's score with the scores of a sample of people who are representative of the entire population (with regard to characteristics such as age, sex, ethnicity, education, and geographic region) or with the scores of a subgroup who are similar to the person being assessed. If we took the temperature of 100 adults, the average (mean) temperature would be 98.6 degrees, which is the normative body temperature for humans. If a person's score falls too far outside the range of the normative group, we can assume that a problem exists. To decide whether a score is too far outside the range of the normal group, we use a statistic called the *standard deviation* (SD) (see Figure 3.3). SD is a measure that tells us how far away from the mean (average) a particular score is. According to statistical principles, a score that is more than 2 SDs away from the mean is found in only 5% of the population and is considered meaningfully different from what is normal. In comparing scores with normative groups, however, we must always consider the characteristics of both the person and the group.

Figure 3.3 The Normal Curve.

Numbers indicate standard deviations (SDs). A score more than 2 standard deviations away from the mean (the center point, 0) is considered meaningfully different from normal.

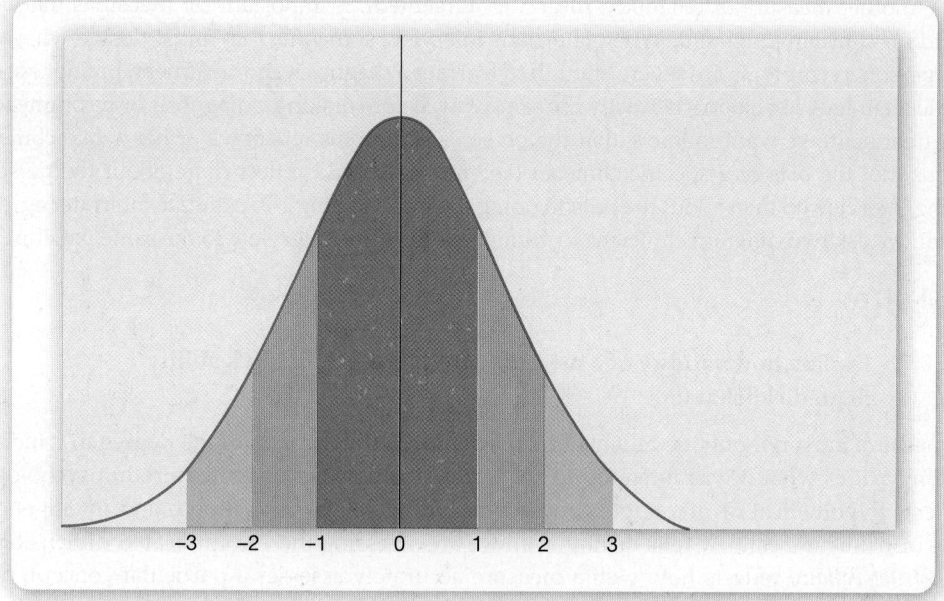

If Pauline's scores on the memory tests are low relative to those of the average older adult but are the same as the scores of other people who are her age and education level, we would not be concerned about the presence of cognitive impairment. If, however, her scores are very low relative to people who are the same as Pauline in terms of age and education, we can conclude that she is experiencing significant cognitive difficulties.

Self-referent comparisons are those that equate responses on various instruments with the person's own prior performance, and they are used most often to examine the course of symptoms over time. In the example of the fever, not everyone has a standard body temperature of 98.6. Some people may have a usual body temperature of 99.2 degrees. In a self-referent comparison, we would compare the temperature of 104 to the person's usual body temperature of 99.2 degrees.

If Pauline's scores on measures of cognitive functioning turn out to be very low compared with how she performed 6 months ago, we would be concerned about a potentially deteriorating course of symptoms.

Self-referent comparisons are also used to evaluate treatment outcome. Over the course of treatment, we would hope to see self-referent comparisons that indicate improvement of symptoms and quality of life.

Reliability

LO 3.6 Describe how reliability is important for understanding results of a clinical assessment.

The **reliability** of an instrument is its consistency, or how well the measure produces the same result each time it is used (Compas & Gotlib, 2002). Thermometers that measure your body temperature are generally quite reliable: They produce similar readings if you take your temperature now and again in 10 minutes. Psychological measures must also be reliable. If they do not produce consistent results, they are of no use. Reliability is assessed in many ways. **Test-retest reliability** addresses the consistency of scores across time. To estimate test-retest reliability, we administer the same instrument twice to the same people over some consistent interval, such as 2 weeks or 1 month. We then calculate a *correlation coefficient* (see Chapter 2) to estimate the similarity between the scores. Correlations of .80 or higher indicate that a measure is highly reliable over time.

Another measure of reliability, **interrater agreement**, is important for measures that depend on clinician judgment. When clinicians interview someone, they must decide whether the person's symptoms are severe enough to warrant a diagnosis and treatment, but not every clinician judges a behavior in exactly the same way. Before making a diagnosis or recommending treatment, we want to know that the person's symptoms reflect his or her actual clinical status, not the bias of a specific clinician (i.e., ratings should reflect more about the person being interviewed than about the person doing the interviewing). To estimate interrater agreement, we ask two different clinicians to administer the same interview to the same patients.

Validity

LO 3.7 Explain how validity of a measure affects a psychologist's ability to predict behavior.

A measure must not only be reliable but also valid. **Validity** refers to the degree to which a test measures what it was intended to measure. Much of what we measure in psychology reflects hypothetical or intangible concepts including self-esteem, mood, and intelligence. The instrument's validity tells us how well we are assessing these complicated dimensions. *Construct validity* reflects how well a measure accurately assesses a particular concept, not other concepts that may be related. For example, a valid measure of shyness should reflect the components of that problem (including worrying about being liked by other people, feeling sweaty and blushing when interacting with others, and avoiding situations that require social interaction) but should not reflect other types of fears (such as the fear of snakes) or depressive symptoms, even if those symptoms often occur along with shyness.

Criterion validity is another form of validity. It assesses how well a measure correlates with other measures that assess the same or similar constructs. One type of criterion validity, *concurrent validity*, assesses the relationship between two measures that are given at the same time, such as the Scholastic Aptitude Test (SAT) and the American College Testing Program (ACT). *Predictive validity* refers to the ability of a measure to predict performance at a future date, such as the ability of the SAT to predict performance in college and scores on graduate school admissions tests. A good measure of depressive symptoms, for example, should correlate well (have good concurrent validity) with a clinician's diagnosis of depression made at the same time. A good measure of intelligence also should correlate well with a person's subsequent academic performance (predictive validity).

Predictive validity refers to the ability of a measure to predict performance at a future date, such as the ability of the SAT to predict performance in college.

Another issue related to validity is the accuracy of a psychologist's predictions or conclusions at the end of the assessment process. After all the assessment data have been collected, a clinician is often asked to make a judgment: Does this person have panic disorder? Will a sex offender re-offend? What type of treatment might be best for this person at this time? Is this student a good match for this academic program? To reach their answers, clinicians can make predictions based on statistical data or clinical observations. *Clinical prediction* relies on a clinician's judgment. Many people believe that psychologists are able to predict dangerous behavior in people with psychological disorders. An example of a clinical prediction would be a psychologist's interview of a patient and, on the basis of that interview, prediction that the person would commit a violent act in the near future (see Chapter 15 for a discussion on the accuracy of clinical predictions of dangerousness).

Statistical prediction results when a clinician uses data from large groups of people to make a judgment about a specific individual. Insurance companies, for example, decide how to price their policies using data from large studies that determine the probability of death or accidents based on certain identified risk factors, such as age, smoking history, and alcohol use (Compas & Gotlib, 2002). People with more risk factors pay more for their insurance. In general, results of predictions based on the same patient data can be very different when clinical and statistical strategies are used (Grove, 2005), but data from more than 136 studies support the conclusion that statistical predictions are more accurate than clinically based predictions (Grove et al., 2000). Statistical prediction is used in the practice of evidence-based medicine when data are available to predict who will benefit from which treatments. Clinical judgment, however, is useful when relevant statistical data do not exist and when new hypotheses need to be developed. Clinician judgment also plays a role in the use of the structured interview procedures discussed in "Clinical Interviews."

Developmental and Cultural Considerations

LO 3.8 Understand how a person's age, developmental status, and culture affect the clinical assessment process.

Many factors affect a clinician's choice of assessment techniques and instruments, but probably one of the most important factors is the patient's age and developmental status. The nature of the tests chosen, the normative values against which patient scores are compared, the people involved in the testing process, and the testing environment can vary significantly depending on whether the person to be assessed is a child, an adolescent, an adult, or an older person. The assessment of cognitive abilities in children who are too young to read, for example, requires different tests than those used with educated adults (Anastasi & Urbina, 1997).

The abilities of older adults with significant cognitive impairment must also be assessed with unique instruments that capture more specific symptoms of problems such as dementia (e.g., Mattis Dementia Rating Scale 2 [DRS-2]; Mattis, 2001). Measures of psychological symptoms vary across age as well. Tests of psychological distress designed specifically for children, such as the Social Phobia and Anxiety Inventory for Children (SPAI-C) (Beidel et al., 1995) and the Children's Depression Inventory (CDI) (Kovacs, 1992), typically have different questions, fewer response choices, and simpler wording than adult measures because of children's limited (still developing) cognitive abilities. Unique measures of psychological symptoms such as the Geriatric Depression Scale (GDS) also exist for older adults (Sheikh & Yesavage, 1986); they have content and response choices that better match the experience and cognitive skill of older people than tests not specific for them.

Psychological assessment of children requires instruments that match their still-developing cognitive abilities.

The assessment process itself may also vary depending on the patient's age. For example, different people may be involved in the assessment process if the patient is a child, an adult, or an older person with major neurocognitive disorder. When assessing children, input from parents and teachers is essential. For older adults with cognitive limitations, obtaining input from another adult who spends time with the patient is helpful. Children who are unable to read and older people with limited vision may also need help completing self-report measures. Young children with limited attention capacity and older adults with cognitive and/or physical limitations may also need short testing sessions with additional breaks.

The assessment process should also consider cultural factors. Many measures used routinely in psychological evaluations were originally developed within the majority culture of the United States. Administering these measures to people with more diverse cultural backgrounds may produce biased results due to differences in educational backgrounds, language use, and cultural beliefs and values (Anastasi & Urbina, 1997). To address these issues, researchers have worked to develop "culture fair" assessments that take into account variables that may affect test performance. Many measures of psychological variables have been translated into other languages, and data from different minority groups have been collected (Novy et al., 2001). Simply translating measures into new languages, however, may not be sufficient to reflect other cultural influences. Thus, some measures of psychological performance have been developed that rely more on nonverbal skills. For example, the Leiter International Performance Scale—Revised (Roid & Miller, 1997) is a nonverbal test of intelligence that requires no speaking or writing by either the examiner or the test taker. Some of the tasks on the test include categorizing objects or geometric designs, matching response cards to easel pictures, and remembering and repeating sequences of objects in the correct order. Measures like this help to increase the cross-cultural utility of psychological assessments.

Ethics and Responsibility

LO 3.9 Describe at least two ethical issues that a psychologist needs to consider before conducting an assessment.

Psychologists who administer psychological assessments must adhere to the American Psychological Association Code of Ethics (American Psychological Association, 2010; see Chapter 15). Section 9 of that code requires that psychologists only use tests on which they have received training. Psychologists must only use instruments that have good reliability and validity and are appropriate for the purpose of the examination. For example, it would be unethical for a psychologist to give a test if (1) he or she had not been trained to give the test, (2) the test had poor reliability and validity, or (3) the test was designed for adults but the psychologist used it to test a teenager. Furthermore, psychologists should not use outdated instruments, and they must obtain informed consent from the person whom they want to test (or, in the case of a child, the parent). *Informed consent* indicates that the person to be tested understands the test's purpose, its related fees, and who will see the results. In some cases, test results will be shared with employers or other health care professionals, so people need to be aware of confidentiality limits before the assessment begins. Testing data should remain confidential and be stored in a secure location, even when assessments occur via the Internet.

Explore ETHICS AND RESPONSIBILITY

Learning Objective Summaries

LO 3.5 Explain the importance of standardization to the interpretation of assessment results and the difference between normative and self-referent comparisons.

Standardization helps us to interpret the results of clinical assessments by comparing a person's score either with the scores of a large sample of people who are representative of the population (normative comparison) or with the person's own prior scores (self-referent comparison).

LO 3.6 Describe how reliability is important for understanding results of a clinical assessment.

Reliability of an assessment instrument indicates how consistently the measure produces the same results each time it is used. Test-retest reliability addresses the consistency of scores over time. Interrater agreement estimates the similarity of conclusions drawn by two clinicians who administer the same measure. Measures with strong reliability increase our confidence in the meaning of assessment results.

LO 3.7 Explain how validity of a measure affects a psychologist's ability to predict behavior.

Validity refers to the degree to which a test measures what it was intended to measure. Because psychologists often measure intangible concepts such as self-esteem, mood, and intelligence, validity is often assessed by evaluating correlations between measures of similar or different constructs and by examining how well assessment scores predict behavior. Measures with strong validity improve a psychologist's ability to predict behavior.

LO 3.8 Understand how a person's age, developmental status, and culture affect the clinical assessment process.

Different tests need to be used for children, adolescents, adults, and older people. The assessment process also may involve different people depending on the age and functional status of the person being assessed. Cultural factors such as educational background, language use, and beliefs/values may affect test performance.

LO 3.9 Describe at least two ethical issues that a psychologist needs to consider before conducting an assessment.

A psychologist should have adequate training in any assessment instrument he/she chooses to use. The psychologist also should use only measures with adequate reliability and validity. Measures that are outdated should not be used, and informed consent must be obtained before a clinical assessment is initiated.

Critical Thinking Question

What are some of the ways that psychological tests might produce biased or inaccurate results? What are some ways this could be avoided?

Assessment Instruments

Psychologists can select from a wide range of assessment instruments when planning an evaluation. The variety of available tests allows a psychologist to assess a patient's difficulties thoroughly and from many different perspectives. Failing to conduct a thorough assessment can have disastrous consequences (see "Real People, Real Disorders: Cases of Misdiagnosis"). Choosing the best set of instruments depends on the goals of the assessment, the properties of the instruments, and the nature of the patient's difficulties. Some instruments ask patients to evaluate their own symptoms (*self-report measures*); others require a clinician to rate the symptoms (*clinician-rated measures*). Some instruments assess *subjective responses* (what the patient perceives) and others *objective responses* (what can be observed). Some measures are *structured* (each patient receives the same set of questions), and others are *unstructured* (the questions vary across patients). When a number of tests are given together, the group of tests is referred to as a *test battery*. We turn now to the major categories of assessment instruments including clinical interviews, personality tests, tests of general functioning and specific symptoms, and cognitive assessment.

Clinical Interviews

LO 3.10 Recognize the purpose of a clinical interview and the difference between unstructured and structured formats.

Clinical interviews consist of a conversation between an interviewer and a patient, the purpose of which is to gather information and make judgments related to the assessment goals. Interviews can serve any of the major purposes of assessment including screening, diagnosis, treatment planning, or outcome evaluation. They also can be conducted in either an unstructured or structured fashion.

UNSTRUCTURED INTERVIEWS In an **unstructured interview**, the clinician decides what questions to ask and how to ask them. Typically, the *initial interview* is unstructured, which allows the clinician to get to know the patient and helps the clinician determine what other types of assessments might be useful. Another purpose of the initial interview is for the clinician and patient to begin getting to know each other and develop a working relationship.

At the start of an initial interview, the clinician usually provides some education about the assessment process and then asks a series of questions about the patient's difficulties. These questions can be *open ended*, allowing the patient flexibility to decide what information to provide (e.g., "Tell me about what brings you here today."), or *close ended*, allowing the clinician to ask for specific information about a topic (e.g., "Have you been having crying spells?"). Both the *presenting problem* (the identified reason for the evaluation) and the clinician's theoretical perspective guide the content and style of the questions. A psychodynamic clinician, for example, might spend more time in an initial interview asking about the patient's early history, whereas a behavioral clinician might ask more questions about the sequence of events surrounding current symptoms. At the end of an initial interview, the clinician typically summarizes what has been learned and offers some guidelines about what will happen next.

The primary benefit of an unstructured interview is its flexibility: it allows the clinician to move in whatever directions seem most appropriate, following up on the patient's comments. The major limitation is its potential unreliability. It is quite possible, for example, that two different interviewers could come to very different conclusions about the same patient if their interviews did not include the same topics or ask the same questions. For instance, if the interviewer does not ask questions about alcohol use and a patient is reluctant to bring up this topic, the interviewer may erroneously conclude that some other difficulty (e.g., depression) is the major cause of the presenting problem when in fact the patient is drinking heavily, missing work, and feeling depressed because of the likelihood of losing her or his job. Structured interviews help to minimize such problems.

STRUCTURED INTERVIEWS In a **structured interview**, the clinician asks each patient the same standard set of questions, usually with the goal of establishing a diagnosis. In the case of *semistructured interviews*, after the standard question, the clinician uses less structured supplemental questions to gather additional information as needed. Structured or semistructured interviews are used frequently in scientifically based clinical practice and in clinical research (Summerfeldt & Antony, 2002), and they increase the reliability of the interview process (see Figure 3.4). Although a patient's scores still rely on clinician judgment, the consistency in content and the order of questions increases the likelihood of agreement across interviewers.

Many structured and semistructured interviews are available to help clinicians make diagnoses. Choosing one depends on the goal of the assessment, the clinician's knowledge of and training with the particular interview, and the properties of the interview itself (length, content focus, reliability, etc.). Some structured interviews are designed to be used with adults; others are intended for use with children. In some cases, structured interviews provide a broad overview of many diagnostic categories while others are more focused on particular sets of diagnoses (e.g., anxiety, depression). Frequently, a more focused interview is used after an unstructured screening interview indicates that certain diagnoses may be appropriate. Focused interviews can be useful in research

Figure 3.4 Sample of Structured Interview.

MODULE 1 – Depression

	YES	NO
1a. Have you been consistently depressed or down, most of the day, **NEARLY EVERY DAY**, for the past two weeks?	O	O
→ IS QUESTION **1a.** CODED **YES**? IF **YES** CONTINUE WITH ITEM **2.** IF **NO** CONTINUE WITH ITEM **1b**, directly below.		
1b. Have you been consistently depressed or down, most of the day, **MORE THAN HALF THE DAYS**, for the past two weeks?	O	O
2. In the past two weeks, have you been much less interested or lost pleasure in most things?	O	O
→ IF QUESTION 1 **OR** 2 IS CODED **YES** CONTINUE TO THE ITEMS BELOW. IF **NO** SKIP TO MODULE 2 ON THE NEXT PAGE.	O	O

Over the past two weeks, when you felt depressed or uninterested:	YES	NO	If NO, "More than half the Days?" YES	NO
3. Was your appetite decreased or increased nearly every day?	O	O	O	O
4. Did you have difficulty sleeping nearly every night, such as difficulty falling asleep, waking up in the middle of the night, early morning wakening or sleeping excessively?	O	O	O	O
5. Did you talk or move more slowly than normal or were you fidgety, restless or having trouble sitting still almost every day?	O	O	O	O
6. Did you feel tired or without energy almost every day?	O	O	O	O
7. Did you feel worthless or guilty almost every day?	O	O	O	O
8. Did you have difficulty concentrating or making decisions almost every day?	O	O	O	O
			If NO, "Occasionally?" YES	NO
9. Did you <u>repeatedly</u> consider hurting your self, feel suicidal, or wish that you were dead?	O	O	O	O

ADDITIONAL QUESTIONS FOR BACKGROUND INFORMATION:	YES	NO	If NO, "Somewhat?"
- Did the symptoms of depression cause you significant distress or impair your ability to function at work, socially, or in some other important way?	O	O	O
- During your lifetime, did you have other periods of two weeks or more when you felt depressed or uninterested in most things, and had most of the problems we just talked about?	O	O	
→ ARE **5** OR MORE ANSWERS (**1-9**) CODED **YES (on either scale)**? IF **YES** CONTINUE TO THE ITEMS BELOW. IF **NO** SKIP TO MODULE 2 ON THE NEXT PAGE.	O	O	

→ DETERMINE TYPE OF FOLLOW-UP REQUIRED BELOW (ASSESS INTENSITY OF PROBLEM):

O FOLLOW-UP NOT NECESSARY, REASON ____________________

O STANDARD FOLLOW-UP

O IMMEDIATE FOLLOW-UP

(continued)

Figure 3.4 Continued

MODULE 3 - PTSD

	NO	YES
A. Have you **EVER** experienced or witnessed or had to deal with an extremely traumatic event, (for example, actual or threatened death or serious injury to you or to someone else)?	O	O
→ IF **NO** SKIP TO MODULE 4 ON THE NEXT PAGE. IF **YES** CONTINUE TO THE ITEMS BELOW AND ASK ALL QUESTIONS.		
B. Did you respond with intense fear, helplessness, or horror?	O	O
In the past month, have you re-experienced the event in a distressing way, such as:	**NO**	**YES**
1. Intense recollections? (e.g., images or thoughts of the event)	O	O
2. Dreams?	O	O
3. Flashbacks? (e.g., acting or feeling as if the event were happening again)	O	O
4. Intense distress in reaction to something that reminds you of the event?	O	O
5. Physical reactions? (e.g., increased heart rate)	O	O
In the past month:	**NO**	**YES**
6. Have you avoided thinking about the event?	O	O
7. Have you avoided things that remind you of the event?	O	O
8. Have you had trouble recalling some important part of what happened?	O	O
9. Have you become less interested in being with your friends?	O	O
10. Have you felt detached or estranged from others?	O	O
11. Have you noticed that your feelings are numbed? (e.g., that you have less ability to feel emotions?)	O	O
12. Have you felt that your life will be shortened or that you will die sooner than other people?	O	O
In the past month:	**NO**	**YES**
13. Have you had more difficulty sleeping?	O	O
14. Were you especially irritable or did you have outbursts of anger?	O	O
15. Have you had difficulty concentrating?	O	O
16. Were you nervous or constantly on your guard?	O	O
17. Were you easily startled?	O	O
During the past month, have these problems significantly interfered with your work or social activities, or caused significant distress?	**NO** O	**YES** O
→ ARE 6 OR MORE ANSWERS **(1-17)** CODED **YES**? IF YES, CONTINUE TO THE ITEMS BELOW. IF **NO** SKIP TO MODULE **4**. DETERMINE TYPE OF FOLLOW-UP REQUIRED BELOW (ASSESS INTENSITY OF PROBLEM).	**NO** O	**YES** O

O FOLLOW-UP NOT NECESSARY, REASON______________________________

O STANDARD FOLLOW-UP

O IMMEDIATE FOLLOW-UP

settings in which it is often important to make sure that all patients in a study have similar diagnoses. These interviews are also important in clinical practice so that a provider has sufficient details about a diagnosis to design an appropriate treatment plan. The drawback of structured interviews is that the interviewer has less flexibility with regard to questioning.

Personality Tests

LO 3.11 Understand the function of personality tests and the difference between objective and projective methods.

The choice of a **personality test**, which measures personality characteristics, depends on its purpose and on whether one is assessing a healthy population or a clinical sample, although many personality tests measure overlapping concepts. Perhaps the best-known personality test is the *Minnesota Multiphasic Personality Inventory* (MMPI), developed in 1943 by Starke Hathaway and J. Charnley McKinley, a psychologist and psychiatrist, respectively, from the University of Minnesota (Graham, 2000). To develop the pencil-and-paper test, they used a then-innovative technique that overcame some of the subjectivity of earlier scoring approaches. Using a method known as *empirical keying*, they developed statistical analyses to identify items and patterns of scores that differentiated various groups (e.g., patients with and without depression). Only items that differentiated the groups were retained. The MMPI also includes statistical scales to evaluate a number of test-taking behaviors. For example, a *Lie scale* identifies people who may not wish to describe themselves accurately. Other scales determine whether someone is "faking good" (describing oneself as more psychologically healthy than one is) or "faking bad" (presenting oneself as more psychologically distressed than is actually true); many clinical scales assess specific psychological characteristics.

A revised version of the MMPI, the MMPI-2, has 567 items and includes 9 validity scales and 10 clinical subscales: hypochondriasis, depression, hysteria, psychopathic deviance, masculinity-femininity, paranoia, psychasthenia (anxiety), schizophrenia, hypomania, and social introversion. Nine restructured clinical subscales were also designed to improve validity and relate more directly to newer theories of personality: demoralization, somatic complaints, low positive emotions, cynicism, antisocial behavior, ideas of persecution, dysfunctional negative emotions, aberrant experiences, and hypomanic activation. The MMPI-2 is scored by a computer program that creates a profile that the testing psychologist can then interpret (see Figure 3.5). Another version of the test, the MMPI-A, was developed for use with adolescents ages 14 to 18. Concerns exist regarding the use of the MMPI with ethnic minority samples because the test was originally standardized on white samples (Butcher et al., 1989), although the normative sample for the MMPI-2 was more diverse.

The Millon Clinical Multiaxial Inventory (MCMI) is a 175-item true-false inventory that corresponds to eight basic personality styles (schizoid, avoidant, dependent, histrionic, narcissistic, antisocial, compulsive, passive-aggressive; see Chapter 11), three pathological personality syndromes (schizotypal, borderline, paranoid), and nine symptom disorders scales (anxiety, somatoform, hypomanic, dysthymia, alcohol abuse, drug abuse, psychotic thinking, psychotic depression, psychotic delusions). The MCMI has adequate reliability and validity, and clinicians sometimes prefer it to the MMPI because it requires less time to complete. There also are concerns, however, that the MCMI does not map onto the categories of disorders as they are described in the DSM system and that the test is culturally biased.

Unlike the MMPI and the MCMI, which are considered objective personality tests, projective testing is a type of personality testing that emerged from psychoanalytic theory. Two widely used **projective tests** are the *Rorschach Inkblot Test* and the *Thematic Apperception Test.* The Rorschach, first published in 1921, was developed by a Swiss psychiatrist, Hermann Rorschach. The patient taking this test is presented increasingly complex and ambiguous inkblots (see Figure 3.6). The first blots are rather simple black and white images, and the later blots are more complex and colorful. The test's rationale is that when given such ambiguous stimuli, the patient "projects" a unique interpretation onto them that reflects his or her underlying unconscious processes and conflicts. Holding the Rorschach to our standards

Figure 3.5 Sample MMPI Profile.

The MMPI yields scores on several clinical subscales. It is scored by a computer that produces a personality profile.

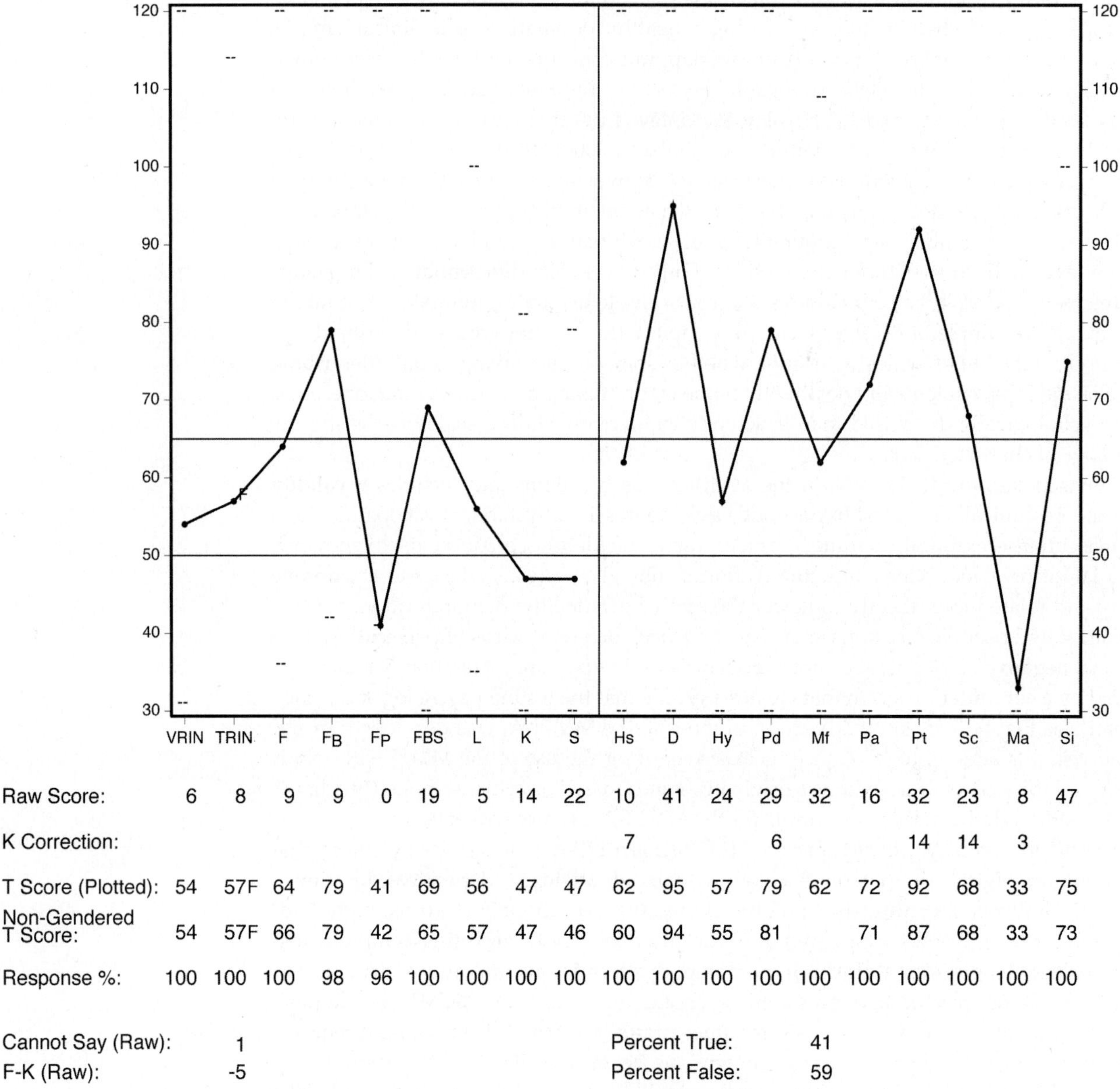

of reliability and validity would be a considerable task. Although Rorschach died before he could develop a reliable scoring system, clinical psychologist John Exner constructed a rigorous system for standardized administration and scoring of the test known as the *Comprehensive System* (CS). The CS is a multivolume work that breaks the inkblot test into a complex matrix of variables. These variables are interpreted and scored to form a Structural Summary, which the clinician can use to understand the person's personality traits and psychological functioning (Exner & Erdberg, 2005). Despite these valiant attempts to impose structure on the Rorschach, many criticisms remain, and its usefulness is questionable and highly controversial (see "Examining the Evidence: The Rorschach Inkblot Test").

Researchers at the Harvard Psychological Clinic developed another popular projective test, the *Thematic Apperception Test* (TAT), in 1935. There are a total of 31 cards, but for each individual, 20 cards are used for the test, depending upon the person's age and sex. The test

Figure 3.6 An Inkblot Similar to Those in the Rorschach Inkblot Test.

What does this look like to you?

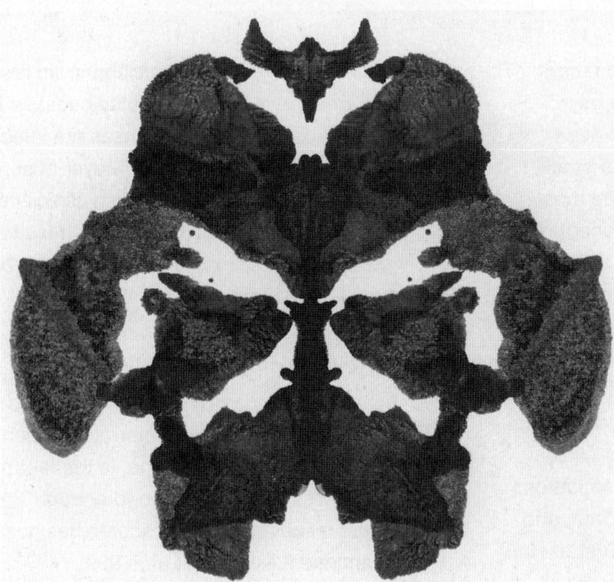

taker is asked to make up a story about the black and white images on the cards. The examiner interprets each story without a formalized scoring system and is free to evaluate the response from within his or her own theoretical orientation. As with the Rorschach, many clinicians believe that the test taker's descriptions of the images provide insight into the person's psychological and unconscious processes. Given the qualitative nature of the test data and the absence of rigorous scoring and interpretation methods, the TAT remains a subjective test.

Despite their weaknesses, projective tests remain popular in some circles. Even when the tests are not used as part of an actual diagnostic battery, many clinicians use them at the start of therapy to "get the patient talking." For patients who have difficulty discussing their emotions, such tests may help them get in touch with what they are feeling.

Tests of General Psychological Functioning and Specific Symptoms

LO 3.12 Explain the purpose of tests designed to assess general functioning and specific symptoms.

GENERAL TESTS OF PSYCHOLOGICAL FUNCTIONING These assessments gather general information about mental functioning without a focus on one specific symptom area, such as depression or anxiety. Instead, these tests give a broad overview of how well a person is doing psychologically. The tests can also be used to compare behavior across groups or populations or to test people before and after a specific event or intervention.

The *Global Assessment of Functioning Scale* (GAF) (see Figure 3.7) was a rating assigned by a clinician to describe a patient's overall well-being. The clinician made a rating between 0 to 100 intended to capture both symptom severity and level of impairment in social relationships and job or school performance. The GAF was dropped from DSM-5 due to a lack of conceptual clarity.

Another commonly used brief questionnaire is the 12-item *General Health Questionnaire* (GHQ) (Goldberg & Hillier, 1979). The GHQ gives a snapshot of mental health status over the previous weeks and can provide a meaningful change score. Each item is rated on a 4-point scale indicating degree of deviation from the individual's usual experience. These are some example questions: Have you recently:...Been able to concentrate on what you're doing? Lost much sleep over worry? Been able to enjoy your normal day-to-day activities? Been feeling reasonably happy, all things considered?

Examining the EVIDENCE
The Rorschach Inkblot Test

- **The Facts** Despite some declining popularity in recent years, the Rorschach remains a frequently used psychological test that graduate students in clinical psychology are often trained to administer (Lilienfeld et al., 2000). Exner's Comprehensive System (CS) is the most commonly taught administrative and scoring procedure. Using this system produces approximately 70 scores referred to as *CS scores* (Mihura et al., 2013). However, the utility of the measure is a hotly contested issue in the psychological community with many scientific articles either praising or criticizing the test. Its proponents contend that it elicits a type of information that other psychological measures do not obtain and that is important for clinical decision making. Its critics point to three major limitations: the test's reliability, the adequacy of normative data, and the validity of scores. Is the Rorschach Inkblot Test useful? Let's examine the evidence.

The Evidence

1. As evidence of reliability, proponents note that 75% of CS scores have adequate interrater agreement (Wood et al., 2006), and the reliability of summary CS scores (based on sums of individual scores) is higher than the reliability of individual items (Hibbard, 2003).
2. Original normative data published by Exner and his colleagues were collected during the 1970s and 1980s and were not consistently scored according to the most recently established procedures. Comparison with these scores leads to overdiagnosis of individuals as having significant mental health problems when, in fact, they do not (Garb et al., 2005). Proponents of the test, however, have argued that patterns of overdiagnosis are explained by the healthier nature of the normative samples, changes in scoring procedures since the original normative data were collected, increased psychopathology in society over time, and/or inadequate scoring in subsequent studies (Hibbard, 2003). More recently, normative data from 21 samples of adults across 17 countries have suggested a reasonable degree of cross-sample and cross-national similarity using currently recommended scoring procedures (Meyer et al., 2007). Similar consistency is not evident for children.
3. A recent meta-analysis examined validity data for 65 of the main CS scores (Mihura et al., 2013). This report concluded that 13 CS scores (20%) had excellent validity, 17 (26%) had good validity, 10 (15%) had modest validity, 13 (20%) had little validity, and 12 (19%) had no evidence of validity. Scores with the highest validity assessed cognitive and perceptual processes. Those with the least support reflected rare responses or more recently developed scales. Proponents have sometimes argued that validity coefficients from research studies may underestimate the test's utility because the Rorschach is most useful when responses are integrated into an individualized assessment (Meyer et al., 2001). In other words, validity increases when clinicians use their clinical judgment to integrate Rorschach results with other assessment scores. This process may be too complex to be validated (Meyer et al., 2001).

Let's Examine the Evidence

1. What does it mean if 25% of CS scores do not meet traditional standards of interrater agreement (Wood et al., 2006)? In a test of this type, is the fact that only 75% of the scores are reliable "good enough"? Furthermore, test-retest reliability for most scores has not been adequately examined (Lilienfeld et al., 2000).
2. Normative data from the original studies by Exner should not be used to interpret patient responses. New international reference data suggest norms that should be used for score interpretation for adults, but adequate normative data do not yet exist for children (Meyer et al., 2007).
3. Critics of the Rorschach agree that CS scores reflecting cognitive ability and thought disorder have sufficient validity (Wood et al., 2015). However, they question the validity of CS scores that measure noncognitive aspects of personality and abnormal functioning. Moreover, even proponents of the test have documented validity (good to excellent) for less than half of the CS scores (Mihura et al., 2013). The two camps continue to challenge each other with regard to the methods used to demonstrate validity (Mihura et al., 2015).

- **Conclusions** Critics and advocates of the Rorschach agree that empirical data support the utility of some CS scores. They also agree that many CS scores have not yet demonstrated adequate validity. Differences of opinion beyond these areas of agreement largely reflect the degree to which psychologists rely on empirical data versus clinician judgment in the assessment process (Wood et al., 2006). Scientifically based psychologists oppose the use of assessment tools that are not empirically validated, and therefore they do not support using unvalidated CS scores in the context of psychological decision making. People in this camp also point to the lack of evidence that clinical judgment improves predictions (see the discussion of clinical versus statistical prediction in this chapter). Yet proponents of the Rorschach, many of whom define themselves as scientist–practitioners, continue to argue for the clinical utility of patient responses even when relevant empirical data are not available. Still others hang inkblots on their walls as artistic mementos of psychology's past.

Figure 3.7 DSM-IV Global Assessment of Functioning.

SOURCE: Reprinted with permission from the Diagnostic and Statistical Manual of Mental Disorders (4th ed., text rev.). Copyright © 2000, American Psychiatric Association.

91–100	Superior functioning in a wide range of activities, life's problems never seem to get out of hand, is sought out by others because of his or her many positive qualities. No symptoms.
81–90	Absent or minimal symptoms (e.g., mild anxiety before an exam), good functioning in all areas, interested and involved in a wide range of activities, socially effective, generally satisfied with life, no more than everyday problems or concerns (e.g., an occasional argument with family members).
71–80	If symptoms are present, they are transient and expectable reactions to psychosocial stressors (e.g., difficulty concentrating after family argument); no more than slight impairment in social occupational, or school functioning (e.g., temporarily falling behind in schoolwork).
61–70	Some mild symptoms (e.g., depressed mood and mild insomnia) OR some difficulty in social occupational, or school functioning (e.g., occasional truancy or theft within the household), but generally functioning pretty well, has some meaningful interpersonal relationships.
51–60	Moderate symptoms (e.g., flat affect and circumstantial speech, occasional panic attacks) OR moderate difficulty in social, occupational, or school functioning (e.g., few friends, conflicts with peers or co-workers).
41–50	Severe symptoms (e.g., suicidal ideation, severe obsessional rituals, frequent shoplifting) OR any serious impairment in social, occupational or school functioning (e.g., no friends, unable to keep a job).
31–40	Some impairment in reality testing or communication (e.g., speech is at times illogical, obscure, or irrelevant) OR major impairment in several areas, such as work or school, family relations, judgment, thinking, or mood (e.g., depressed man avoids friends, neglects family, and is unable to work; child frequently beats up younger children, is defiant at home, and is failing at school).
21–30	Behavior is considerably influenced by delusions or hallucinations OR serious impairment in communication or judgment (e.g., sometimes incoherent, acts grossly inappropriately, suicidal preoccupation) OR inability to function in almost all areas (e.g., stays in bed all day, no job, home, or friends).
11–20	Some danger of hurting self or others (e.g., suicidal attempts without clear expectation of death; frequently violent; manic excitement) OR occasionally fails to maintain minimal personal hygiene (e.g., smears feces) OR gross impairment in communication (e.g., largely incoherent or mute).
1–10	Persistent danger of severely hurting self or others (e.g., recurrent violence) OR persistent inability to maintain minimal personal hygiene OR serious suicidal act with clear expectation of death.
0	Inadequate information.

TESTS FOR SPECIFIC SYMPTOMS In addition to tests of general psychological functioning, we also need assessment tools that provide reliable and valid measures of specific types of symptoms, such as depression and anxiety. When testing treatments, we want to know how well certain treatments reduce symptoms of a particular disorder (e.g., which of two treatments better reduces the specific symptoms of depression). A therapist treating someone for a particular problem, such as test anxiety, may administer a questionnaire that measures severity of test anxiety over the course of treatment to see how well the intervention is working. Many scales have been developed for just this purpose. Some are clinician-administered assessments and others are self-report.

The *Brief Psychiatric Rating Scale* (BPRS) (Overall & Gorham, 1988) is a clinician-administered scale that assesses many different psychological symptoms including bodily concerns, anxiety, emotional withdrawal, guilt feelings, tension, mannerisms and posturing, depressed mood, hostility, suspiciousness, hallucinations, motor retardation, uncooperativeness, unusual thought content, reduced emotional response, excitement, and disorientation. Other tests are more limited in scope, assessing the symptoms of one particular disorder.

These disorder-specific scales exist for virtually every psychiatric disorder. Depressive symptoms, for example, are commonly assessed by the *Beck Depression Inventory–II* (BDI–II) (Beck et al., 1996a), a 21-item self-report questionnaire. The *Beck Anxiety Inventory* (BAI) (Beck & Steer, 1993) is a 21-item self-report measure of anxiety that focuses on the severity of anxiety symptoms. The use of such specific scales by different researchers has the added advantage of allowing comparisons of treatment effects across different studies and patient groups. Clinicians who use these measures are also better able to evaluate their patients' progress during treatment.

Assessment of Cognitive Functioning

LO 3.13 Describe commonly used neuropsychological and intelligence tests.

Assessment of cognitive functioning can serve a range of purposes, including evaluation of functioning following a medical event (e.g., brain injury or stroke), developmental disabilities, progressive cognitive decline associated with neuropsychiatric diseases (e.g., Parkinson's or Alzheimer's disease), or intellectual functioning. Common types of cognitive assessment include neuropsychological and intelligence testing.

NEUROPSYCHOLOGICAL TESTING Neuropsychological tests detect impairment in cognitive functioning using both simple and complex tasks to measure language, memory, attention and concentration, motor skills, perception, abstraction, and learning abilities. Performance on these tasks provides insight into the functioning of the brain.

The *Halstead-Reitan Neuropsychological Battery* (Reitan & Davidson, 1974) is widely used to evaluate the presence of brain damage. The battery differentiates healthy individuals from those with cortical damage and includes 10 measures of memory, abstract thought, language, sensory-motor integration, perceptions, and motor dexterity.

Another commonly used neuropsychological assessment is the *Wisconsin Card Sorting Test* (WCST), which measures *set shifting*, or the ability to think flexibly as the goal of the task changes (see Figure 3.8). The test taker looks at four stimulus cards that display figures representing three stimulus parameters (color, form, and number). Then the test taker is given additional cards and asked to match each to the original four stimulus cards. The examiner does not explain *how* to match the cards but states whether the match is correct based on a specific rule known only to the examiner. The rule is then changed based on the success of the test taker, and the test continues for 128 trials or until all rule changes, or "achieved categories," have been completed (Psychological Assessment Resources, 2003). Completion of the card test requires attention, working memory, and visual processing. The WCST is considered a frontal lobe test because individuals with frontal lobe lesions do poorly on it. Because it discriminates between frontal and nonfrontal lesions, it is useful for testing patients with schizophrenia, brain injuries, and neurodegenerative diseases such as dementia or Parkinson's disease, who often have brain damage in these areas.

Other commonly used neuropsychological assessments include the *Bender Visual Motor Gestalt Test* (see Figure 3.9), a simple screening tool often used to detect problems in visual-motor development in children and general brain damage and neurological impairment (Piotrowski, 1995), and the *Luria-Nebraska Neuropsychological Battery* (Golden et al., 1980). The Luria-Nebraska is similar to the Halstead-Reitan test but is a more precise measure of organic brain damage. In contrast to many batteries, the Luria-Nebraska uses an unstructured qualitative method, generating 14 scores including motor, rhythm, tactile, expressive speech, writing, reading, arithmetic, memory, intellectual processes, and left and right hemispheric function. Clinicians are trained to administer neuropsychological batteries to ensure a standardized approach to administering the tests. In this way, we know that scores are comparable across testers.

INTELLIGENCE TESTS Although their results are often misinterpreted, **intelligence tests** are some of the most frequently used tests among psychologists. Created to predict success in school, these tests were designed to produce an **intelligence quotient**, or IQ, score. Children were tested on a series of questions that reflected cognitive abilities at

Figure 3.8 The Wisconsin Card Sorting Test.

This test measures set shifting, the ability to display flexibility in thinking. It is used to test patients with brain disorders.

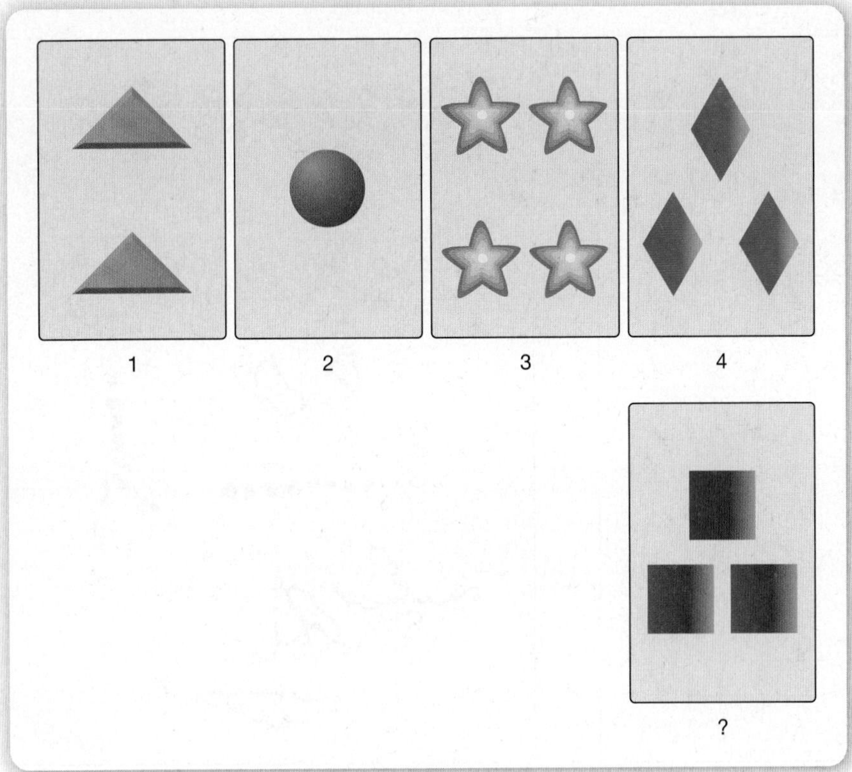

different ages. Performance on the test yielded a score known as the child's *mental age.* This number was then divided by his or her chronological age, and the resulting number was the child's IQ. Today, scoring focuses on an individual's performance relative to his or her age-matched peers. IQ scores are standardized so that the mean is 100 and the standard deviation is 15. This means that a person with an IQ of 130 is two standard deviations above the mean and has performed quite well on the test relative to the rest of the population. IQ scores generally predict academic performance in traditional learning environments, but there is always individual variation. IQ scores do not represent the broader concept of intelligence, which is considered by some theorists to include creativity, artistic and athletic abilities, and other behaviors.

The origin of the IQ test began in France at the turn of the twentieth century with psychologist Alfred Binet and his colleague Theodore Simon, who were commissioned by the French government to create a test to predict academic success. In 1916, Lewis Terman at Stanford University translated a revised edition of Binet's instrument for use in English, which was subsequently named the *Stanford–Binet Intelligence Scale.*

Since its conception, the Stanford–Binet has gone through many revisions and is currently in its fifth edition. Subtests within the Stanford–Binet assess both verbal and nonverbal skills. The most recent version was standardized on 4,800 people, and the test items were evaluated for any kind of bias based on the demographic characteristics of the test takers (whether responses to any items would be biased for anyone based on sex, ethnicity, age, etc.). The test's validity was evaluated against other well-validated intelligence tests including the previous editions of the *Stanford–Binet Intelligence Scale* and the *Wechsler Adult Intelligence Scale,* another widely used intelligence test. Extensive research suggests that the Stanford–Binet is appropriate for measuring intelligence among people with low intellectual functioning as well as among those at the highly gifted end of the continuum.

Figure 3.9 The Bender Visual Motor Gestalt Test.

This neuropsychological test is often used to detect brain damage or neurological impairment. The patient's attempts to copy the figures (A) show whether damage or impairment is present (B).

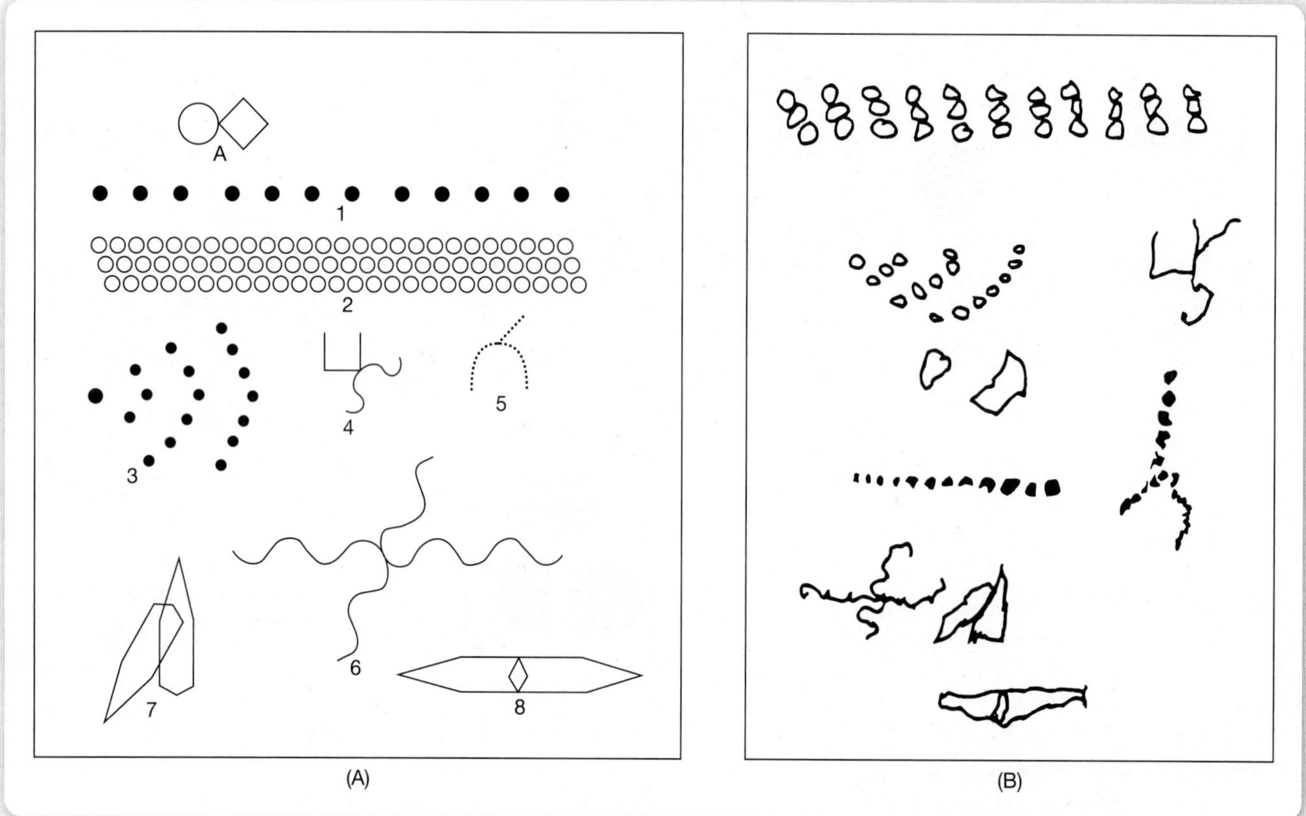

First published by David Wechsler in 1955 and currently in its fourth edition, the *Wechsler Adult Intelligence Scale* (WAIS-IV) (Wechsler, 2008) is one of the most commonly used general tests of intelligence to evaluate patients, students, employees, criminals, and other population subgroups. Initially adapted from the intelligence tests used by the Army, the test was based on Wechsler's definition of intelligence as "the aggregate or global capacity of the individual to act purposefully, to think rationally, and to deal effectively with his [sic] environment" (Wechsler, 1939, p. 229).

The WAIS-IV produces four index scores: Verbal Comprehension Index (VCI), Working Memory Index (WMI), Perceptual Reasoning Index (PRI), and Processing Speed Index (PSI). The combination of these four index scores creates a composite Full Scale IQ (FSIQ) score. Each of the four index scores reflects a person's performance on a group of subtests that measure similar intellectual skills. VCI subtests measure verbal reasoning (e.g., the ability to describe how two objects are alike), general fund of knowledge, the ability to define words, and understanding of social expressions (e.g., "killing two birds with one stone"). WMI subtests assess attention, concentration, and memory by asking people to recall sequences of digits forward and backward, perform mental math problems, and remember sequences of letters and numbers. PRI and PSI subtests all require the test taker to perform certain tasks as quickly as possible. PRI subtests measure skills such as attention to detail (e.g., what is missing from a certain picture), nonverbal reasoning (putting puzzles together), and spatial perception (arranging blocks to match a printed design). PSI subtests assess visual-motor coordination and visual perception by asking test takers to determine whether a target symbol is in an array of symbols and to copy numbers that correspond with symbols into a grid. For these tasks, speed and accuracy are considered.

Taking a little more than 60 minutes to administer, the WAIS-IV (Wechsler, 2008) assesses cognitive functioning in people ages 16 to 90 matched to the 2005 U.S. Census data with respect to sex, socioeconomic status, ethnicity, educational attainment, and geographical location. For children under age 16, the Wechsler Intelligence Scale for Children (WISC-V, 6 to 16 years) and the Wechsler Preschool and Primary Scale of Intelligence (WPPSI-IV 2 to 7 years) are used.

Critics of intelligence tests say that because they were originally standardized on white populations they are inappropriate measures of intelligence for ethnic minorities and non-English-speaking students.

The measurement of intelligence has always been controversial. This is one area in which the roles of nature and nurture have been hotly debated. In addition to questions about how these factors influence intelligence, our conceptualization of intelligence has changed over time. In contrast to Wechsler's early approach to measuring cognitive function, current tests of intelligence recognize and assess various subtleties and components of intelligence. Even more intriguing are advances in neuroscience that give us glimpses into the brain and the nature of brain activity associated with various tasks that reflect different aspects of intelligence.

Another controversy involves the bias of intelligence measures along the dimensions of sex, socioeconomic status, and racial, ethnic, and cultural background (Shuttleworth-Edwards et al., 2004). Many argue that because intelligence tests were originally standardized primarily on white male populations, they are inappropriate for women, ethnic minorities, non-English speakers, and people who are physically challenged (Suzuki et al., 2001). Research is ongoing to develop tests that are free of such potential biases.

Intelligence tests have additional pitfalls. Most importantly, they do not and cannot reflect all types of intelligence. Intelligence is a multifaceted and complex concept, and many believe that its measurement should not be limited to testing attention, perception, memory, reasoning, and verbal comprehension (Gardner, 2011). The IQ tests currently in use do not capture other facets of intelligence such as Tom Brady's skills on the football field or Claude Monet's extraordinary talent as a painter. However, provided that an IQ score is not used as a measure of the broad concept of intelligence, it has useful applications, most notably the prediction of academic success and the assessment of performance deficits and inequalities, cognitive impairment, and mental retardation.

Learning Objective Summaries

LO 3.10 Recognize the purpose of a clinical interview and the difference between unstructured and structured formats.

Clinical interviews involve a conversation between an interviewer and a patient, the purpose of which is to gather information and make judgments related to assessment goals. In an unstructured interview, the clinician decides what questions to ask and how to ask them. In a structured interview, the clinician asks the same standard set of questions to each patient.

LO 3.11 Understand the function of personality tests and the difference between objective and projective methods.

Personality tests measure personality characteristics. Objective personality tests are self-report and ask the person being tested to answer a series of standardized questions. Projective personality tests require the person being tested to respond in an unstructured way to a series of images.

LO 3.12 Explain the purpose of tests designed to assess general functioning and specific symptoms.

Assessments of general functioning give a broad overview of how well a person is doing psychologically without attention to specific symptoms. Tests of specific symptoms also are important, with attention to constructs like depression and anxiety. Both general and specific assessments can be useful to compare a person's functioning to a normative group and/or to evaluate change as a result of treatment.

LO 3.13 Describe commonly used neuropsychological and intelligence tests.

Commonly used neuropsychological tests include the Wisconsin Card Sorting Test, which measures a person's ability to think flexibly, and the Bender Visual Motor Gestalt Test, which detects problems in visual-motor development in children and general brain damage. The most commonly used intelligence tests are the Stanford–Binet and Wechsler Adult Intelligence Scales. Different versions of the Wechsler scale are available for children.

Critical Thinking Question

You are the psychologist who was asked to conduct a clinical assessment for Pauline. What types of assessment instruments would you choose and why?

Behavioral and Physiological Assessment

Behavioral Assessment

LO 3.14 Describe procedures used in a behavioral assessment with attention to the importance of a functional analysis, self-monitoring, and behavioral observation.

Carly had no idea when she first visited a behavior therapist to talk about her panic attacks that she would have "homework." Actually, the therapist assigned some at the end of the very first session! When their session was close to ending, he handed her some forms that he called practice records. He asked Carly to use these forms to record every panic attack she had during the next week and every time she avoided doing something that she thought might lead to a panic attack (e.g., going to grocery stores or movie theaters, driving on the freeway). The therapist also told Carly that he would be going with her to some of the frightening places that seemed to produce the panic so that he could learn more about her symptoms. That was a little scary, but she was glad that someone was finally going to help her figure out what was going on.

Many of the assessment instruments discussed so far measure internal, enduring states such as intelligence and personality that may underlie psychological problems. Behavioral assessment is different. This approach relies on applying the principles of learning to understand behavior, and its ultimate goal is a functional analysis (Haynes & O'Brien, 2003). When conducting a **functional analysis** (also known as *behavioral analysis* or *functional assessment*), the clinician attempts to identify causal (or functional) links between problem behaviors and contextual variables (e.g., environmental and internal variables that affect the problem behavior). Recalling the principles of classical and operant conditioning (see Chapter 1), we know that events that precede or follow certain symptoms or behaviors can have powerful effects in causing or maintaining those symptoms. Thus, to identify causal links, we need to look at both *antecedents* and *consequences* of the behavior.

To identify antecedents and consequences of behavior, a behavioral assessment often starts with a behavioral interview. The interviewer asks very specific questions to discover the full sequence of events and behaviors surrounding the patient's primary problems. In Carly's case, the therapist might ask her to describe in detail her most recent panic attack—where she was, who else was there, and what she was doing or thinking when she noticed the first symptoms. After those first symptoms, what did she think, feel, and do? What happened to the panic as a result of what she was thinking, feeling, and doing? What did other people do and when? All of these details might reveal that Carly was in the grocery store alone worrying about having a panic attack and monitoring her body when she noticed her heart rate increasing. She then pushed the cart to the side of the aisle and raced to the front door. After leaving the store so suddenly, she felt embarrassed but also completely relieved that the symptoms of panic were subsiding. When she got home and told her husband, he felt sorry for her and gave her a big hug.

Learning about the specific sequence of events can help a clinician identify important functional relationships. In Carly's case, thoughts and expectations about panic may lead her to monitor her body for signs, perhaps noticing symptoms that are normal but that nonetheless frighten her because they have become a cue for panic. Noticing potential panic symptoms leads her to escape from the situation (leave the store), which reduces the panic symptoms and reinforces her need to escape in order to control the symptoms. Her husband's comforting hug further reinforces her fear of panic. A good behavioral interview can uncover many different potential relationships. Other assessment tools that behavior therapists use include self-monitoring and behavioral observation.

SELF-MONITORING Carly's homework assignment to record her episodes of panic is an example of **self-monitoring**, a process in which a patient observes and records his or her own behavior as it happens (Compas & Gotlib, 2002). Psychological questionnaires are *retrospective*; that is, they ask about symptoms the patient may have had over the past week or past month. In contrast, self-monitoring requires patients to record their symptoms when they occur, allowing real-time information about the frequency, duration, and nature of the symptoms. Self-monitoring can contribute to a functional analysis if patients record contextual variables (aspects of the environment in which the behavior takes place) and sequences of events and behaviors (see Figure 3.10). Self-monitoring now incorporates technology such that people are asked to record mood and behaviors using mobile phones and Web-based applications (Agarwal & Lau, 2010; Mouton-Odum et al., 2006; Sinadinovic et al., 2010).

Self-monitoring can also create a record of how often problem behaviors are occurring before treatment begins and how symptoms change over time. For example, before treatment begins, a woman who is monitoring her weight might record every food or drink item that she consumed that day and be surprised to find that she has six "snacks" per day. As treatment progresses, the number of snacks she eats may decline to four, then to two, and finally to one snack per day. Self-monitoring is an important component of treatment because the act of recording symptoms by itself may increase patients' awareness of a problem behavior and reduce its frequency.

BEHAVIORAL OBSERVATION **Behavioral observation** also involves measuring behavior as it occurs, but in this approach someone other than the patient monitors the frequency, duration, and nature of behavior. The first step is to define the behavior in a way that allows it to be clearly observed and reliably monitored. For a child with attention problems, particular problem behaviors must be specified, such as leaving one's seat, speaking out of

Figure 3.10 Awareness Practice Form.

Patients use such forms to monitor and record their own behavior.

What situation created stress today? ____________________

How did you feel?

[ ] anxious
[ ] worried, nervous
[ ] embarrassed
[ ] other: ________
[ ] fearful
[ ] angry
[ ] sad

What physical signs did you have?

[ ] muscle tension
[ ] rapid pulse
[ ] shortness of breath
[ ] butterflies in stomach
[ ] shaking
[ ] sweating
[ ] other: ________

What thoughts/worries did you have? ____________________

What actions did you take to reduce anxiety? ____________________

turn, and fidgeting (Compas & Gotlib, 2002). Simply asking raters to measure a global concept such as "inattentiveness" would lead to poor reliability across time and across raters.

Next, it is important to decide how to observe the behaviors of interest. *Event recording* involves monitoring each episode of the identified behavior, such as counting the number of times a child gets out of his or her seat, speaks out of turn, or fidgets during the school day (Compas & Gotlib, 2002; Tyron, 1998). Using *interval recording*, the behavioral assessor measures the number of times the identified behavior occurs during a particular interval of time (e.g., counting the number of times a child gets out of the seat during each 15-minute interval of a class period). Sometimes behavior can be observed in a *natural environment*. An assessor could go to a child's classroom to observe behavior, or a therapist could accompany a patient to the scene of a problem behavior. In other cases, behavior must be observed in an *analogue* fashion. In these instances, the assessor creates a situation similar to those in which the problem occurs to allow direct observation. For example, a patient with speech anxiety may be asked to stand up behind a desk or podium and give a speech. The therapist can count the number of times the patient stutters, the duration of silences in the speech, the amount of eye contact the patient makes, and the like.

Actigraphy is a noninvasive way to measure activity level. The actigraph unit looks like a wristwatch and is typically on the wrist of the nondominant arm (a right-handed person wears the actigraph on the left wrist). The unit records vibrations associated with movement, allowing the researcher to detect different patterns of activity (sitting, running, sleeping). Actigraphy has been used often to assess sleep patterns and circadian rhythms, daytime sleepiness, insomnia, and effects of sleep interventions (Troxel et al., 2010; Westermeyer et al., 2010) as well as movement in children with attention deficit hyperactivity disorder (Uebel et al., 2010).

Behavioral avoidance tests are often used to assess phobias and avoidance behavior by asking a patient to approach a feared situation as closely as possible (Compas & Gotlib, 2002). A patient with a height phobia might be asked to climb an outdoor set of stairs as high as possible. The observer measures how close the person can approach the feared situation. As with self-monitoring, behavioral observation strategies can be used to evaluate the severity of symptoms at baseline (before treatment begins) and to assess the degree of change after treatment.

Psychophysiological Assessment

LO 3.15 Explain the purpose of psychophysiological assessment and what it can tell us about abnormal behavior.

Psychophysiological assessment measures brain structure, brain function, and nervous system activity. This type of assessment measures physiological changes in the nervous system that reflect emotional or psychological events. Different types of measurements assess a range of biochemical alterations in the brain or physiological changes in other parts of the body.

One of the oldest, most common, and least invasive types of psychophysiological measurements is *electroencephalography* (EEG). Researchers first measured and recorded brain waves in dogs in 1912, and by the 1950s, this method was used regularly throughout the United States (Niedermeyer, 1999). Electrodes are placed on the scalp, or, in unusual circumstances, in the cerebral cortex, to measure differences in electric voltage between various parts of the brain (Eisen, 1999). Electrode locations and names are standardized to ensure consistency across laboratories and clinical facilities.

The EEG is a useful research tool because it is noninvasive and requires little effort from the participant. In some instances, the brain activity is recorded when the participant is engaged in cognitive processing related to the presentation of a simple, evoked stimulus, called an *event-related potential* (ERP). Changes in brain activity are recorded together with a time-stamped presentation of the stimulus, which can take many forms including auditory (sounds), visual (flashes of light or images), olfactory (smells), and more cognitive stimuli that can engage memory, pattern recognition, or emotional responses, for example.

EEG patterns include both rhythmic activity and nonrhythmic patterns, and different wave frequencies signal relaxation, sleep, or comatose states. Nonrhythmic patterns may represent seizure activity. EEGs are useful tools for monitoring and diagnosing certain clinical conditions, such as a coma state and brain death, and for monitoring brain function while under anesthesia (Fein & Calloway, 1993).

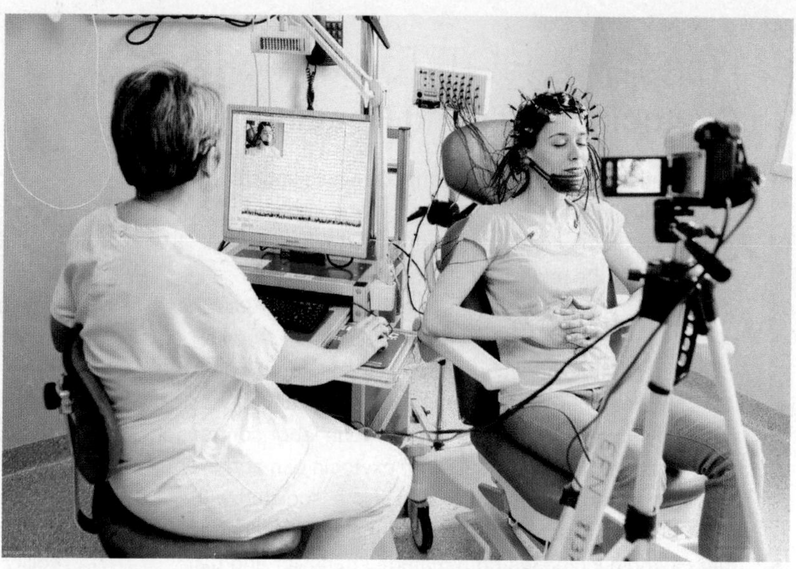

The EEG is one of the oldest psychophysiological assessments, often used in research because it is noninvasive. It records changes in brain activity.

Most people have heard about rapid eye movement (REM) sleep, but the second broad sleep stage is non-REM sleep when the eyes are at rest. Stages of sleep and wakefulness are divided into the following categories: Stage W (wakefulness), Stage N1 (NREM 1 sleep), Stage N2 (NREM 2 sleep), Stage N3 (NREM 3 sleep), and Stage R (REM sleep) (Silber et al., 2007). During Stage W, beta waves dominate our brain activity. As we relax or begin to fall asleep, alpha waves dominate. The sleeper next moves through stage N1, which is marked by even slower theta waves and is experienced as drowsy sleep, then N2 when muscular activity decreases and the sleeper becomes consciously unaware of the external environment, and then N3 when slower *delta waves* predominate. This is the deepest sleep stage. When awakened from the N3 stage, we are likely to feel disoriented and groggy. Also during this stage, sleepwalking (*somnambulism*) and sleeptalking (*somniloquy*) occur as well as night terrors and nocturnal enuresis.

The EEG has several advantages as a tool for exploring brain activity. It allows the assessment of very fast responses—measured at the level of a millisecond rather than the second and minute level of other techniques. Moreover, EEG is the only measure that directly assesses electrical activity in the brain. However, an EEG cannot determine functioning in a specific brain region (Ebersole, 2002). Accordingly, recent research has combined EEG with functional brain imaging techniques (Koessler et al., 2007).

Another type of psychophysiological assessment measure is *electrodermal activity* (EDA), formerly called *galvanic skin response* (GSR). This measurement capitalizes on the fact that the sweat glands on the palms of the hands are controlled by the peripheral nervous system and thus react to emotional states. If you have ever experienced sweaty palms, you know this feeling. EDA measures the changes in electrical conductance produced by increased or decreased sweat gland activity. EDA is a window into the presence of stress or anxiety.

A common type of psychophysical assessment incorporating EEG or EDA strategies is **biofeedback** (see Chapter 14). The term *biofeedback* was first coined in the late 1960s. *Biofeedback* refers to the use of electronic devices to help people learn to control body functions that are typically outside of conscious awareness, such as heart rate or respiratory rate. Biofeedback can be used to promote relaxation and to relieve pain. The goal of this assessment is to train patients to recognize and modify physiological signals by bringing them under conscious control. You probably use a form of biofeedback in your daily life. If you feel yourself getting anxious and your heart rate is increasing, you might start taking some deep breaths to calm yourself. You recognized that your heart was beating fast, and you did something to try to reduce your arousal.

Clinical biofeedback uses the same process but more sophisticated equipment to detect and record physiological reactions and responses with great sensitivity. For example, a patient's biosignals, such as heart rate, blood pressure, or muscle tension, can be recorded and converted into a detectable signal, such as a lightbulb that flashes every time heart rate exceeds 90 beats per minute. The patient responds to this visual signal by trying to relax tense muscles or slow heart rate. Then the light flashes less often, signaling the patient's success. Clinical biofeedback is used to treat various psychological conditions including anxiety, panic, and attention deficit hyperactivity disorder. In addition to pain, other medical conditions for which biofeedback can be helpful include

Research HOT Topic

Oxytocin and "Mind Reading"

Assessment can take many forms. One fascinating advance is our ability to understand the association between underlying biology and observed social behaviors. Is it possible that the release of a hormone in the brain can affect our ability to form close relationships, to trust other people, and even to read minds? Researchers studying oxytocin, a naturally occurring substance in our bodies, have found that such a link may exist. For years, oxytocin was known only as a hormone involved in labor contractions and lactation. Now it appears that oxytocin can act as a neurotransmitter in the brain where it is associated with many complex social behaviors. Animal studies have shown that oxytocin increases both maternal behavior and pair bonding (Carter, 1998; Young & Wang, 2004). A preliminary and intriguing study in humans found that after people took oxytocin, they were more likely to trust another person with their money (Kosfeld et al., 2005). This initial glimpse into the possible role of oxytocin led researchers to wonder whether an increased ability to "read" people was part of the mechanism responsible for the reduction in social stress and apprehension and increased attachment behavior associated with oxytocin.

The ability to detect another's thoughts and emotions purely through external observation, such as noticing facial expression, is integral to human social interaction. Referred to as *mind reading*, this practice of analyzing another's emotional state based on external cues alone is critical not only in conversation but also in the establishment and maintenance of trust.

Researchers (Domes et al., 2007) examined the effect of oxytocin on people's ability to "read minds." When asked to describe someone's thoughts or feelings based on a picture of their eyes alone, participants who had been given oxytocin performed better than those not given any hormone. This ability to sense another's emotional state may facilitate social attachment and trusting behavior. Although the results must be viewed as preliminary, they provide an intriguing window into how our biology may influence our social functioning.

This information may also be useful in the future to researchers studying and treating patients with severe social impairments, especially autism (see Chapter 13). People with autism spectrum disorders have been shown to have a significant impairment in "mind reading" as well as low plasma oxytocin levels.

migraine headaches (Nestoriuc & Martin, 2007), Raynaud's disease (a circulatory disorder; Karavidas et al., 2006), temporomandibular joint (TMJ) dysfunction (Crider et al., 2005), fibromyalgia (Kayiran et al., 2010) epilepsy, incontinence, digestive system disorders, high and low blood pressure, cardiac arrhythmias, and paralysis). Biofeedback is a vivid illustration of how feelings and emotions affect bodily functions and how changing emotional states can directly affect physical functioning.

In an exciting new area of research, scientists are studying how biological compounds (such as the medication oxytocin) may enhance perceptual abilities, such as being better able to understand the emotions of others (see "Research Hot Topic: Oxytocin and 'Mind Reading'").

Learning Objective Summaries

LO 3.14 Describe procedures used in a behavioral assessment, with attention to the importance of a functional analysis, self-monitoring, and behavioral observation.

Behavioral assessment relies on applying principles of learning to understand behavior. A functional analysis allows the clinician to identify causal links between problem behaviors and contextual variables that include internal and environmental antecedents and consequences of the behavior. Self-monitoring allows real-time assessment of symptoms and contextual cues. Behavioral observation also involves measuring behavior as it occurs, but measures are taken by someone other than the person with the symptoms.

LO 3.15 Explain the purpose of psychophysiological assessment and what it can tell us about abnormal behavior.

Psychophysiological assessment measures brain structure, brain function, and nervous system activity as it changes in response to emotions or psychological events. One of the oldest, most common, and least invasive of these measures is the EEG, which measures differences in electric voltage between various parts of the brain. Measuring changes in the sweat glands of the skin (EDA) can tell us about a person's emotional reactions. Biofeedback uses these types of measures to help people control body functions that promote relaxation and reduce pain.

> **Critical Thinking Question**
>
> How might you use behavioral and psychophysiological assessments to evaluate a person who is having severe headaches, anxiety, and trouble sleeping?

Diagnosis and Classification

The use of a common language to describe observed clinical phenomena is critical to both clinical practice and research. The following discharge summary illustrates the use of such a common language as one clinician communicates to another clinician in a distant city as the patient is about to be transferred to that location.

> Between 2012 and 2013, I treated Madison intermittently for recurrent major depression together with her primary care physician, who managed medication. In that interval, Madison experienced three episodes of major depression lasting between 4 weeks and 4 months. Each time, she experienced marked low mood, anhedonia, agitation, early morning awakening, and problems with concentration. She reported frequent passive suicidal ideation but no active suicidal intent or plan. She was prescribed 40 mg fluoxetine/day and remained on the medication throughout this interval. After her initial course of cognitive-behavioral therapy, we contracted that she would contact me for booster sessions each time she identified a lowering of her mood.

These common terms for symptoms and categories allow the new clinician to develop a relatively accurate picture of the patient. Using diagnostic labels to describe sets of symptoms helps clinicians and researchers communicate about their patients. Deciding which diagnosis best fits a patient's pattern of symptoms also helps the clinician develop an appropriate treatment plan. The way clinicians refer to mental disorders has changed over the years as our understanding of these disorders continues to evolve.

History of Classification of Abnormal Behaviors

LO 3.16 Describe the value of classifying abnormal behavior and the two major systems currently used for this purpose.

In 1952, the American Psychiatric Association (APA) adopted a classification system—the **Diagnostic and Statistical Manual of Mental Disorders (DSM-I)** (1952)—from an earlier system developed in 1918 to provide the Bureau of the Census with uniform statistics about psychiatric hospitals. The 1952 DSM manual contained 106 categories of mental disorders (Grob, 1994). From that point forward, the DSM expanded to a maximum of 297 categories in

Figure 3.11 Comparison of the Number of Psychiatric Diagnoses Included in the Diagnostic and Statistical Manual of Mental Disorders.

DSM Revision	Year Published	Number of Disorders
DSM-I	1952	106
DSM-II	1968	182
DSM-III	1980	265
DSM-III-R	1987	292
DSM-IV	1994	297
DSM-5	2013	237

1994 (see Figure 3.11). Published in 1968, the DSM-II (American Psychiatric Association, 1968) listed 182 disorders in 134 pages and reflected the dominant psychodynamic perspective of the time. Symptoms were described as reflections of broad underlying conflicts or maladaptive reactions to life problems rather than in observable behavioral terms (Wilson, 1993). In 1974, the task force working to revise the DSM emphasized the importance of establishing more specific diagnostic criteria. The intention was to facilitate mental health research and to establish classifications that would reflect current scientific knowledge.

In the DSM-III (American Psychiatric Association, 1980), categorization was based on description rather than assumptions about the causes of the disorder, and a more biomedical approach replaced the psychodynamic perspective (Wilson, 1993). The DSM-III, published in 1980, was more than three times the size of the earlier DSM and described twice as many diagnostic categories (265). The controversial expansion included many new diagnostic categories. For example, the former category of anxiety neurosis was divided into several different and distinct categories including generalized anxiety disorder, panic disorder, and social phobia. All subsequent revisions have maintained the structure of the DSM-III and have attempted to refine or improve this version rather than to overhaul the diagnostic system entirely. The next version, the DSM-III-R (American Psychiatric Association, 1987), included not only revisions but also renaming, reorganization, and replacement of several disorders, which yielded 292 diagnoses (Mayes & Horwitz, 2005). In 1994, the DSM-IV listed 297 disorders. This revision emerged from the work of a steering committee, consisting of work groups of experts who (1) conducted an extensive literature review of the diagnoses, (2) obtained data from researchers to determine which criteria to change, and (3) conducted multicenter clinical trials (Shaffer, 1996). The DSM-IV-TR (American Psychiatric Association, 2000), a "text" revision, was published in 2000 with most diagnostic criteria unaltered. The DSM-5, published in 2013, includes 237 diagnoses, a reduction from prior editions, and uses a developmental approach to abnormal behavior. Also, the DSM-5 emphasizes the role of culture and gender in the expression of psychiatric disorders and, in comparison to previous editions, uses more dimensional ratings to classify symptom severity.

Although many valid criticisms have arisen as a reaction to the DSM system, which we discuss later in this section, at its most useful, it provides a framework and common language for clinicians and researchers. The DSM system helps clinicians examine presenting problems and associated features and to identify appropriate assessments and treatments. Moreover, accurate classification of mental disorders is a critical element of rigorous research. Ideally, as research in neuroscience and genetics progresses, we will see an increased reflection of underlying biology in the classification of mental disorders.

Most of the information presented in subsequent chapters of this book will cover the major clinical syndromes—what are known in everyday language as *mental disorders*. The material will be organized mostly around disorders as they are defined in DSM-5. Beyond listing diagnoses, however, the authors of the DSM wanted to devise a system that would offer more information about patients than a simple clinical diagnosis (e.g., depression). After determining if a person is suffering from a psychiatric disorder and, if so, which one, clinicians should also include observations that help explain to the patient and other health care workers characteristics of the disorder that might be unique to that person. For example, the clinician will note the presence of any psychosocial or environmental factors that might play a role in the onset or maintenance of the disorder. Additionally the clinician should indicate how the disorder affects the person's academic, social, or occupational functioning.

An alternative to the DSM classification system is the **International Classification of Diseases and Related Health Problems (ICD)**. Published by the World Health Organization (WHO, 1992), the ICD uses a code-based classification system for physical diseases and a broad array of psychological symptoms and syndromes. The ICD system for diagnosing mental disorders was developed in Europe at approximately the same time that the original DSM was being developed in the United States, shortly after World War II. The first set of mental disorders was included in the ICD in 1948. The APA and WHO have worked to coordinate the DSM and the relevant sections of ICD, although some differences remain. Like the DSM system, the ICD is regularly revised; it is currently in its 10th edition, and work on ICD-11 is under way.

The ICD has become the international standard diagnostic classification system for epidemiology and many health management purposes. Beyond its use in classifying diseases and other health problems, the ICD is used for morbidity and mortality statistics for the WHO and for third-party payers and insurance companies (WHO, 2007).

Comorbidity

LO 3.17 Explain the meaning of comorbidity and factors that may contribute to comorbidity in psychiatry.

Comorbidity refers to the presence of more than one disorder (see Chapter 2). Often a patient's symptoms cannot be fully characterized or diagnosed using a single category. For example, a patient with depression may also experience anxiety (panic) attacks and an eating disorder. When more than one disorder is diagnosed, the disorders are said to be *comorbid*. Almost half of people who have one mental disorder have symptoms that meet the criteria for at least one other disorder (Kessler, Berglund, Demler et al., 2005).

The term *comorbidity* may be misleading because it is unclear whether the co-occurring diagnoses truly reflect the presence of distinct clinical disorders or whether they may actually be different manifestations of a single clinical disorder (Maj, 2005). However, the frequent co-occurrence of multiple psychiatric diagnoses cannot be ignored. Rates of comorbidity are high. Although some of the comorbidity may be accounted for by the nature of our diagnostic system, alternative evidence is mounting that underlying genetic factors may be shared across disorders increasing the likelihood of expression of more than one specific syndrome (Bulik-Sullivan et al., 2015).

How Do Developmental and Cultural Factors Affect Diagnosis?

LO 3.18 Recognize the importance of developmental and cultural variables that affect the experience and classification of abnormal behavior.

Understanding developmental and cultural variables is important when diagnosing disorders. A major departure for the DSM-5 is the use of a developmental perspective by which to understand psychological disorders. As we noted in Chapter 1, children and adults differ on basic aspects of physical, cognitive, and emotional development, and for any specific disorder, the manner in which the symptoms are expressed also may differ by age. Therefore, when evaluating the presence of a specific disorder, such as depression, it is necessary to understand how specific symptoms may vary by age. Young children, for example, do not really understand the concept of "the future." Therefore, it would be unlikely for a young child with depression to endorse "feeling helpless about the future." DSM-5 acknowledges the existence of developmentally appropriate symptoms for a number of diagnoses.

Diagnostic criteria established for adults may not capture the experience of older people very well. They may have different symptoms or describe the symptoms differently than a younger person does.

Clinicians have also found that the prevalence of psychological disorders varies by sex. Women, for example, are more often diagnosed with depression and anxiety, whereas men are more often diagnosed with substance abuse. Men and women may actually develop different disorders at different rates, perhaps with different genetic risk factors for certain syndromes. It is also possible that in some cases, a similar underlying difficulty, such as stress, may be expressed differently for men and women.

Symptoms and disorders may also be influenced by race and ethnicity. *Culture-bound syndromes* are defined as sets of symptoms that occur together uniquely in certain ethnic or racial groups. *Ataque de nervios*, for example, is an anxiety syndrome that occurs uniquely among Latinos. In general, classification systems should consider the developmental, demographic, and cultural variables that affect the experience and description of abnormal behavior. Some symptoms are universally applicable, but others are not.

When Is a Diagnostic System Harmful?

LO 3.19 Describe some of the limitations and drawbacks of a diagnostic classification system.

Despite their benefits for diagnosing and treating mental disorders, a diagnostic system has significant limitations. First, because many diagnostic categories require that a person have a specified number of symptoms from a longer list (e.g., four of six symptoms listed might be required for a diagnosis), not all people with the same diagnosis experience the same symptoms. In addition, most diagnostic classifications do not require that the symptoms be connected to a particular etiology (cause); therefore, different patients with the same disorder may have developed the symptoms in different ways. Finally, two people who have the same diagnosis do not necessarily respond to the same treatments.

Diagnostic categories also can encourage stereotyped conceptions of specific disorders. For example, imagine that a young woman has a grandfather who was diagnosed with bipolar disorder (see Chapter 6). He had a flagrant case marked by excessive spending, sexual indiscretions, and grandiosity (an inflated sense of one's own importance), leading to several hospitalizations and therapy. Although his granddaughter is beginning to experience less extreme signs and symptoms, she might hesitate to believe that she has the same disorder. In her mind, her symptoms don't fit the stereotype associated with the label of bipolar disorder or the behavior that she saw in her grandfather. Stereotyping by diagnosis can also lead a clinician to premature or inaccurate assumptions about a patient that prevent a thorough evaluation and comprehensive treatment plan. For example, a patient diagnosed with depression may be prescribed an antidepressant without sufficient evaluation of the need for treatments to manage life problems without the use of medication. Similarly, labeling a patient with a diagnosis can lead to *self-fulfilling prophecies* (e.g., I have bulimia so I'll never be able to eat normally again.) and create *stigmas* that affect the person's ability to function well at work or in social relationships (e.g., who wants to date a woman with an eating disorder?).

Another criticism of the DSM system is that its categories can reflect the beliefs or limited knowledge of an era. A good example was the inclusion of homosexuality as a mental illness before 1974. Because it was classified as a mental disorder, homosexuality was intrinsically defined as something that caused distress and impairment and that should be treated. The classification contributed substantially to the stigmatization of homosexuality, to homosexual persons' beliefs that there was something wrong with them psychiatrically, and to many ill-conceived attempts to change their sexual orientation. Once research began to address homosexuality openly, empirical evidence did not support the claim that homosexuality was a form of mental illness or was inherently associated with psychopathology. After a majority vote, the APA replaced the diagnosis of *Homosexuality* with *Ego-Dystonic Homosexuality* in the DSM-III (American Psychiatric Association, 1980), referring to sexual orientation inconsistent with one's fundamental beliefs and personality. However, mental health professionals criticized this new diagnostic category as a political compromise designed to appease psychiatrists who still considered homosexuality pathological (American Psychiatric Association, 2006). In 1986, the diagnosis was removed entirely from the DSM. In the DSM-5 (American Psychiatric

Association, 2013), the only mention of homosexuality is found in the category *Sexual Disorders Not Otherwise Specified*. This category includes homosexuality that is marked by persistent and marked distress about one's sexual orientation, a category that may still reflect continued stigma. In 1974, the APA released the following statement:

> "Whereas homosexuality per se implies no impairment in judgment, stability, reliability, or general social or vocational capabilities, the American Psychiatric Association calls on all international health organizations and individual psychiatrists in other countries to urge the repeal in their own country of legislation that penalizes homosexual acts by consenting adults in private. And further the APA calls on these organizations and individuals to do all that is possible to decrease the stigma related to homosexuality wherever and whenever it may occur."
>
> **SOURCE:** American Psychiatric Association, "Position Statement on Homosexuality and Civil Rights", in: American Journal of Psychiatry, Vol. 131 (1974), No. 4, p. 497 (Official Actions).

Homosexuality was once considered pathological. Having shed that categorization decades ago, the gay community continues to struggle for full and equal rights.

A final criticism of the DSM is that it simply includes too many disorders and that normal variations in human behavior have been overmedicalized by giving them diagnostic labels. Overall, although diagnostic systems that rely on classifying symptoms into disorders provide substantial benefits for patients, clinicians, and researchers, the limitations of these systems need to be considered. Alternative systems for discussing psychological problems that rely on dimensional models rather than categorical classification have been developed.

Dimensional Systems as an Alternative to DSM Classification

LO 3.20 Discuss the potential benefits of dimensional models for understanding abnormal behavior as alternatives to more traditional classification systems.

The DSM and ICD are both primarily based on categorical systems that classify sets of symptoms into disorders. One alternative to such categorical diagnostic systems is a dimensional classification of abnormal behavior (see Chapter 1), which suggests that people with disorders are not qualitatively distinct from people without disorders. Rather, a dimensional model for understanding abnormal behavior suggests that symptoms of what are now called *disorders* are simply extreme variations of normal experience. Proponents of this model suggest that psychiatric illness is best conceptualized along dimensions of functioning rather than as discrete clinical conditions (Widiger & Samuel, 2005). Two features of mental illness that support the value of dimensional approaches are the high frequency of comorbidity and within-category variability (e.g., multiple people with the same diagnosis can have very different sets of symptoms and experiences). The DSM-5 approach allows for the diagnosis of comorbid conditions, an important feature because 45% of those with any mental disorder meet the criteria for two or more disorders (Kessler, Berglund, Demler et al., 2005). Proponents of a dimensional model suggest that this alternative approach would allow for a richer description of patient difficulties across multiple areas of dysfunction. In a dimensional model, for example, a patient's functioning would be rated on a range of dimensions or traits (e.g., introversion, neuroticism, openness, conscientiousness) rather than simply on the presence or absence of a set of symptoms. This type of system also would lead to better understanding of a patient whose symptoms did not fall squarely into any existing category. In many cases, patients report many symptoms of a particular disorder but not enough of them to actually meet diagnostic criteria.

Figure 3.12 Categorical vs. Dimensional Diagnostic Criteria.

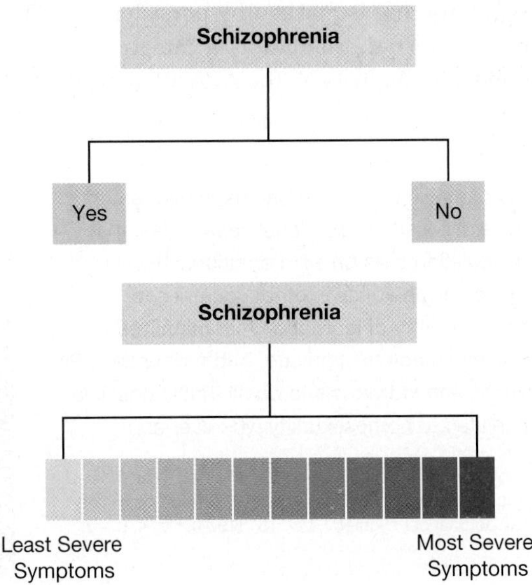

In a categorical system, these people are often considered to have *subthreshold* syndromes. A dimensional approach would allow us to describe all symptoms regardless of whether they actually met specified cutoffs or criteria (see Figure 3.12).

The dimensional approach would also allow clinicians to deal somewhat differently with the issue of multiple symptoms within diagnostic categories, known as *heterogeneity*. Despite the DSM's goal of creating relatively homogeneous diagnostic categories that would allow a "common language" of classification, individuals diagnosed with the same disorder actually may share few common features. For example, two people diagnosed with depression may have very different clinical presentations. While one may have depressed mood, crying, difficulty sleeping, fatigue, and difficulty concentrating, another may have loss of interest in things that used to bring pleasure, decreased appetite and weight loss, slowed motor behaviors, feelings of worthlessness, and recurrent thoughts of death. Both sets of symptoms would meet DSM criteria for major depression, but the primary complaints and targets for treatment would be quite different. Overall, this type of heterogeneity within diagnostic categories can adversely affect both clinical practice and research (Krueger et al., 2005). Dimensional proponents believe that their approach lends itself to an increased amount of relevant clinical information, which can have both clinical and research advantages (Watson, 2005).

Arguments against the dimensional model often focus on clinical utility. The categorical system offers a simple approach with a clear diagnostic label that provides an efficient way to share information. Dimensional models are innately more complex. For example, it is much simpler to explain to a patient that she has depression than to discuss with her where her symptoms lie along many dimensions of traits experienced by all people. A simple, easily communicated categorical system also facilitates the nature of clinical decision making (e.g., whether to hospitalize, which medication to use, whether to provide insurance coverage). The complexity of sharing information that is organized along multiple dimensions would make communication with patients extremely difficult; communication across researchers and clinicians trying to share information about common clinical syndromes would also become more difficult. Furthermore, because no single, accepted dimensional theory of psychopathology exists, achieving consensus on the type and number of dimensions required to capture the entire spectrum of mental illness could be quite difficult (Blashfield & Livesley, 1999). Proponents of categorical approaches do concede that boundaries between most diagnoses remain imprecise, and they also acknowledge that psychiatric classification needs further precision (Blashfield & Livesley, 1999).

Learning Objective Summaries

LO 3.16 Describe the value of classifying abnormal behavior and the two major systems currently used for this purpose.

Classification of abnormal behavior provides a common language to facilitate clinical practice and research. Using diagnostic labels to describe sets of symptoms helps clinicians and researchers communicate about their patients. Deciding on a diagnosis also helps a clinician determine the best course of treatment, and accurate categorization of symptoms is important for clinical research. The two major systems for diagnosing abnormal behavior are the Diagnostic and Statistical Manual of Mental Disorders (DSM) and the International Classification of Disease and Related Health Problems (ICD).

LO 3.17 Explain the meaning of comorbidity and factors that may contribute to comorbidity in psychiatry.

Comorbidity refers to the presence of more than one disorder. Shared genetic factors across psychiatric disorders may provide a biological explanation for why individuals may present with more than one disorder.

LO 3.18 Recognize the importance of developmental and cultural variables that affect the experience and classification of abnormal behavior.

Children, adults, and older people experience and express symptoms in different ways. Young children, for example, do not understand the concept of "the future," so they are unlikely to endorse a feeling of hopelessness about the future. Older adults experience cognitive changes that may affect the way they experience and describe symptoms. Gender and cultural variables also have an impact on the expression of abnormal behavior. Women are more likely to have diagnoses of anxiety and depression, whereas men are more likely to be diagnosed with substance abuse. Culture-bound syndromes occur uniquely in certain ethnic or racial groups.

LO 3.19 Describe some of the limitations and drawbacks of a diagnostic classification system.

In our current diagnostic system, not all people with the same diagnosis experience the same symptoms, nor have they necessarily developed them in the same way. Different people with the same disorder also may not respond to the same treatments. Stereotyping by diagnosis also can lead to stigma and inadequate treatment. Finally, our current diagnostic systems may include too many disorders that overmedicalize normal variations in human behavior.

LO 3.20 Discuss the potential benefits of dimensional models for understanding abnormal behavior as alternatives to more traditional classification systems.

A dimensional model for understanding abnormal behavior suggests that normal and abnormal behavior lie on a continuum and that what are now called disorders are simply extreme variations of normal experience. High rates of comorbidity and variability within a diagnostic category support the utility of a dimensional model. This kind of system allows for better understanding of behaviors that do not fall neatly into any diagnostic category, with functioning rated on a range of dimensions or traits rather than on the presence or absence of a set of symptoms.

Critical Thinking Question

What are some of the pros and cons of the diagnostic classification systems currently used to describe abnormal behavior? Explain what alternative you might choose, if any, and why.

Real SCIENCE Real LIFE

Amber—Assessment in a Clinical Research Study

In this case study, we present the experience of Amber, a young woman with bulimia nervosa, an eating disorder that involves binge eating and purging (usually vomiting) (see Chapter 7). Amber is participating in a clinical trial that compares treatment based on medication (Prozac) to cognitive-behavioral therapy. The case is presented from the perspective of the participant with commentary from the investigator about the purpose of each assessment.

Amber: *I saw an advertisement on a local bus for free treatment for bulimia nervosa. I had been suffering for years but had never had the funds to pay for treatment. All I was ever able to get was six sessions of counseling when I was an* *undergraduate. So I called the number for the study coordinator. She was a very nice woman, and she described the study to me. The first thing she did was ask me some questions on the phone—what was my age, current weight, lowest and highest past weight, and how often did I binge and purge.*

Researcher: This was the telephone screening. These questions were to determine preliminary eligibility for the study. We were looking for people with current bulimia nervosa who had been binge eating and purging at least twice per week for the past 3 months.

Amber: *The study coordinator set me up with an appointment for the following week and said she would send me a packet of information, a consent form, and some questionnaires in the mail. Three days later I received all of the information. The information sheet pretty much repeated what she had told me about the study—that there would be a randomization procedure (a flip of the coin) and I would receive either medication or group psychotherapy for bulimia. I didn't really care what group I was in. I just wanted to get some proper treatment for this illness. I read through the consent form and signed on to participate in the study. Then I opened up the packet of questionnaires. I must have answered hundreds of questions. It took me over 2 hours. They asked about things ranging from eating behavior, to how I felt about my body shape and size, to how depressed and anxious I was, and to how much I drank alcohol, smoked cigarettes, and used drugs. There was also a bunch of questions about what kind of a person I was and another questionnaire that asked about the events that had happened in my life in the last year.*

Researcher: The questionnaire battery included the Eating Disorders Examination Questionnaire to measure current eating symptoms, the Beck Depression and Anxiety Inventories to measure negative mood states that often accompany bulimia, the Fagerstrom Nicotine Tolerance Questionnaire to assess smoking and nicotine dependence, and measures of alcohol and drug use. The Life Events Schedule asks about significant environmental events that may have happened to the person in the last year. For an accurate diagnosis, it is important to understand whether any significant stressors (such as financial difficulties) or important events (such as the death of a loved one) could be influencing the person's thoughts or feelings. These were our baseline measures, many of which would be repeated at various times throughout the study.

Amber: *When I arrived for my appointment, the researcher checked my consent form and checked through to make sure I had answered all of the questions. I then had a rather extensive interview in which the psychiatrist went into real depth about the history of the problems I have had with eating, depression, and anxiety. He also asked a lot about alcohol and drugs, but eventually he seemed to catch on that I was never into those things.*

Researcher: We administered the baseline Structured Clinical Interview for DSM-IV to Amber to establish her baseline diagnosis and the Eating Disorders Examination Interview to get in-depth information about the nature of her eating disorder. According to our scoring, she met the diagnostic criteria for bulimia nervosa, major depression, and panic disorder. She was appropriate for inclusion into the study and was invited to participate.

Amber: *The researchers welcomed me into the study. They then taught me how to self-monitor how often I binged and purged, which I had to do for a full week before starting therapy. I got randomized into the group cognitive-behavior therapy condition.*

Researcher: For the next 12 weeks, Amber took part in cognitive-behavioral group treatment for bulimia nervosa. She continued to self-monitor her symptoms throughout the treatment. We could see from the text messages of her self-monitoring that her binge eating and purging behaviors were improving by Week 4.

Amber: *I kept going to group and found the homework they gave me to be really helpful in starting to get a handle on my binge eating. It was also reassuring to share my experience with the other patients in the group. I had no idea that so many people faced the same hurdles that I did in keeping my bulimia under control. After 12 weeks of therapy, I was finally starting to feel like there was a light at the end of the tunnel.*

Researcher: At the end of the 12 weeks, we asked Amber to fill out the same questionnaires she had at baseline to see how things had changed. We also re-administered the Eating Disorders Examination Interview to get specific information about progress with her eating disorder. The psychiatrist who did the interview was unaware of her treatment group assignment. The interview revealed that she had been abstinent from binge eating for the past 4 weeks and had purged only once. This corresponded nicely with her self-monitoring data.

ASSESSING THE SITUATION

In extended studies, participants, for a variety of reasons, might drop out. Why is this a problem for researchers? And how can researchers help retain participants during the course of an extended study?

Amber: *After the last interview, I set up my follow-up appointments. I was expected to return 3 months and 6 months after treatment. We had learned that relapse is common in bulimia and the best way to tell whether a treatment works is to make sure that the changes we make actually stick. I was happy to return for the evaluations—especially because they assured me they would pay for parking and give me $50 for each session I attended!*

Researcher: It is very important for us to make sure that the positive changes that we see persist. The only way to do this is by having scheduled follow-up assessments. Because many people do not return for their follow-ups, we have found that an excellent incentive to bring them back is to reimburse them for parking and provide a reasonable monetary incentive for their time. This is also an excellent opportunity for us to refer them for additional treatment if they are not doing well.

Amber: *When I returned for my follow-up visits, the psychiatrist (who still didn't know which treatment I was in) asked me many of* *the same questions that he had at the start of the study. Thinking back to my first assessment, I could even tell how different my answers were. At this point, I had been basically binge and purge free for the past 6 months with one exception. I went through a bad patch when I broke up with my boyfriend and I purged a couple of times, but I used the skills I had learned in therapy to get that behavior right back under control. Overall, I think being involved in a clinical trial was an interesting experience. I got great treatment, and the close follow-up helped me keep my symptoms under control.*

Key Terms

behavioral avoidance test, p. 102
behavioral observation, p. 101
biofeedback, p. 103
clinical assessment, p. 77
clinical interviews, p. 88
clinical significance, p. 80
comorbidity, p. 107
diagnosis, p. 80
Diagnostic and Statistical Manual of Mental Disorders (DSM), p. 105
differential diagnosis, p. 80
functional analysis, p. 100
intelligence quotient, p. 96
intelligence test, p. 96
International Classification of Diseases and Related Health Problems (ICD), p. 106
interrater agreement, p. 84
normative comparison, p. 82
outcome evaluation, p. 80
personality test, p. 91
projective test, p. 91
psychometric properties, p. 82
psychophysiological assessment, p. 102
reliability, p. 83
screening, p. 78
self-monitoring, p. 101
self-referent comparisons, p. 83
standardization, p. 82
structured interview, p. 88
test-retest reliability, p. 83
unstructured interview, p. 88
validity, p. 84

Chapter 4

Anxiety, Trauma- and Stressor-Related Disorders

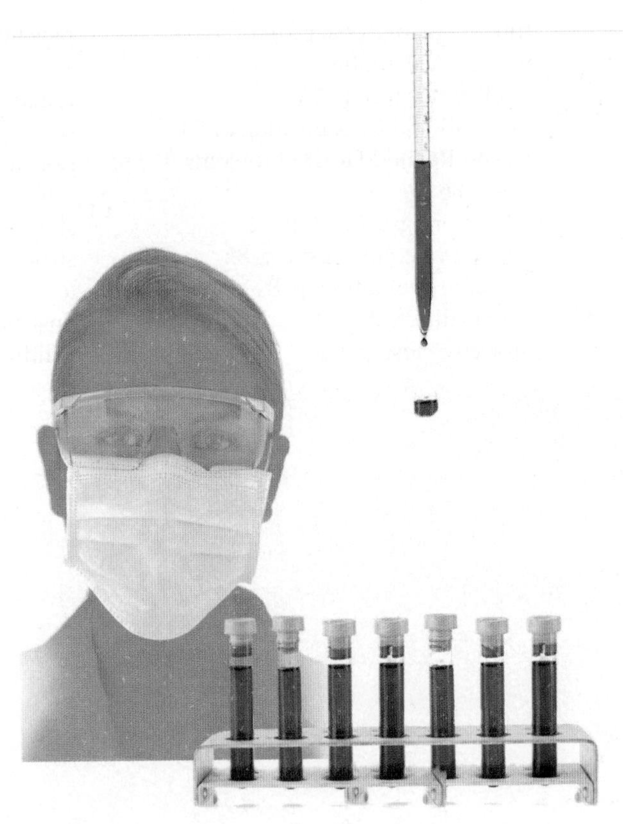

Chapter Learning Objectives

What Is Anxiety?	**LO 4.1**	Describe the fight-or-flight response including the contributions of the sympathetic and parasympathetic nervous systems.
	LO 4.2	Identify the three components of anxiety.
	LO 4.3	Recognize how functional impairment, sex, race/ethnicity, and developmental and sociocultural factors affect the expression of anxiety and contribute to anxiety disorders.
What Are the Anxiety Disorders?	**LO 4.4**	Identify the symptoms of a panic attack.
	LO 4.5	Describe how panic disorder differs from a panic attack.
	LO 4.6	Recognize the symptoms of agoraphobia and how it relates to panic disorder.

LO 4.7 Describe the relationship of worry to generalized anxiety disorder.

LO 4.8 Recognize the symptoms of social anxiety disorder and its relationship to public speaking anxiety.

LO 4.9 Explain the relationship between selective mutism and social anxiety disorder using a developmental perspective.

LO 4.10 List the subtypes of specific phobias and the unique physiological response of blood-injection-injury phobias.

LO 4.11 Identify the symptoms of separation anxiety disorder and its relationship to panic disorder.

What Are the Trauma- and Stressor-Related Disorders?

LO 4.12 Recognize the symptoms of posttraumatic stress disorder and discuss how it is different from anxiety disorders.

The Etiology of Anxiety and Trauma- and Stressor-Related Disorders

LO 4.13 Describe the biological factors that may contribute to the onset of anxiety and posttraumatic stress disorders including family and genetic influences, neuroanatomy, temperament, and behavioral inhibition.

LO 4.14 Contrast the psychodynamic, behavioral, and cognitive theories of the onset of anxiety and posttraumatic stress disorders.

The Treatment of Anxiety and Trauma- and Stressor-Related Disorders

LO 4.15 Identify efficacious pharmacological treatments for anxiety and posttraumatic stress disorders.

LO 4.16 Identify efficacious psychological treatments for anxiety and posttraumatic stress disorders.

LO 4.17 Discuss the ethical issues that need to be considered when deciding to treat someone immediately after a traumatic event.

Delores is 22 years old, lives with her parents, and has a bachelor's degree in medical technology. She is extremely fearful when in enclosed spaces and when she has to be in front of an audience. Her fear of enclosed spaces began at age 10 when her older brother locked her in a closet and would not let her out. Her fears worsened 4 years ago when she entered college and began living in a tiny dorm room. Delores feels trapped and confined in many different places such as driving through a car wash, having a dental examination, riding on a roller coaster or in certain elevators, or having her blood drawn. She is also fearful in situations in which her head and neck are partly or completely covered, such as wearing a motorcycle helmet, a plastic face shield used by dental hygienists, or even a life jacket. When in these circumstances, her heart races, she feels short of breath and dizzy, and she worries that she might die. Delores also has fears in public situations, such as public speaking, being asked to speak at a meeting, and interviewing for a job. She worries that other people can see her anxiety, that she might make a mistake, or that others will think that she is a failure.

Her fears affect her life in many ways. She cannot work as a medical technologist because she has to wear a face shield in the laboratory, and when she puts it on, she panics and cannot breathe. She accepted jobs at several different hospitals, but each one required her to wear a face shield when working with highly contagious blood specimens. So now her job history is a series of short-term positions, making it appear as if she has a problem keeping a job. She cannot work in her chosen field, and the only job she can find is cleaning houses.

Delores took out loans to pay for college, and now her income is so low that she cannot make her loan payments. Worrying about her financial situation is keeping her up at night. She lies awake for 2 hours before falling asleep. Her boyfriend is often angry at her because she will not ride roller coasters or on the back of his motorcycle. Once she took a vacation with her parents, but they had to return home immediately after arriving at the hotel. The hotel was spectacular, but all of the elevators were made of glass. Delores could not ride up to her room. They lost their hotel deposit and did not have enough money to find another hotel with a room on the ground floor.

Her social fears are also interfering with her life. She dropped out of several different colleges until she found one that did not require any oral presentations for graduation. Delores has a beautiful voice, and she would love to sing in church, but she is too anxious to join the choir. Although Delores's boyfriend does not understand her fears, her mother and grandmother do. They both have significant fears; her mother will not put her head under water, and her grandmother eloped rather than walk down the aisle as a bride with all eyes looking at her.

You can probably relate to aspects of Delores's distress. You may have had similar feelings on your first date, when you had to speak in public, or when you interviewed for a job. You worried about whether you would do well. Your heart raced, you felt tense, or perhaps your palms sweated. Maybe you had trouble sleeping the night before the event. All of these behaviors are typical of **anxiety**, a common emotion that is characterized by physical symptoms (faster heartbeat, feelings of tension) and thoughts or worries that something bad will happen.

What Is Anxiety?

Anxiety is a future-oriented response ("What if I mess up this speech? What if she does not like me?") and often occurs when people encounter a new situation or anticipate a life-changing event (starting college, getting married). In most instances, the anxiety that occurs in these situations is time limited and goes away when the event is over. In some cases, however, anxiety spirals out of proportion to the actual situation and can lead to anxiety, and trauma- or stressor-related disorders. Before examining each of these disorders, it is first necessary to understand the nature of anxiety and a closely related emotion, fear.

The Fight-or-Flight Response

LO 4.1 **Describe the fight-or-flight response including the contributions of the sympathetic and parasympathetic nervous systems.**

Suppose that you are walking in the park enjoying the solitude. You come upon two vicious-looking dogs that are fighting. You start to back away, but the dogs stop and come toward you. You know that you need to get out of there *fast*. Luckily, evolution has prepared you for this moment. Your *hypothalamus* (the part of your brain that is responsible for recognizing threatening situations and coordinating your response) sends a message to your *adrenal glands* to release the hormone *adrenaline*. You suddenly find yourself running faster and jumping higher than you ever thought possible. You did not even know that you could climb a tree, but you are doing it! Fortunately, the dogs soon get bored waiting for you to come down and they leave. Your body's response, called **fight-or-flight**, was a general discharge of your **sympathetic nervous system** (SNS) (Cannon, 1929). The fight-or-flight response has been part of human behavior since prehistoric times (see Figure 4.1).

Your body's nervous system consists of two parts: the *central nervous system*, which includes your brain and your spinal cord, and the *peripheral nervous system*, which consists of all the other nerves in your body. The peripheral nervous system is further broken down into two parts: the *somatic sensory system*, which contains sensory and voluntary motor functions, and the *autonomic nervous system*, which controls involuntary movements. Finally, the autonomic nervous system also has two elements, the *sympathetic nervous system* and *the parasympathetic nervous system*. When activated by stress or fear, the SNS goes into overdrive. Your heart beats faster than normal, supplying more blood to power the muscles. Your respiration rate increases, allowing more oxygen to get to your blood and brain. Whether it was prehistoric man trying to outrun a wooly mammoth or modern-day woman doing some fancy driving on an icy road to avoid careening off a bridge, this fight-or-flight response allows an optimal level of physical functioning in the face of threat.

Figure 4.1 The sympathetic nervous system works to produce the fight-or-flight response after which the parasympathetic nervous system returns the body to a normal resting state. Adapted from Lilienfeld et al. *Psychology: From Inquiry to Understanding* (p. 21). Copyright © 2009, Pearson/Allyn and Bacon. Reprinted by permission of Pearson Education.

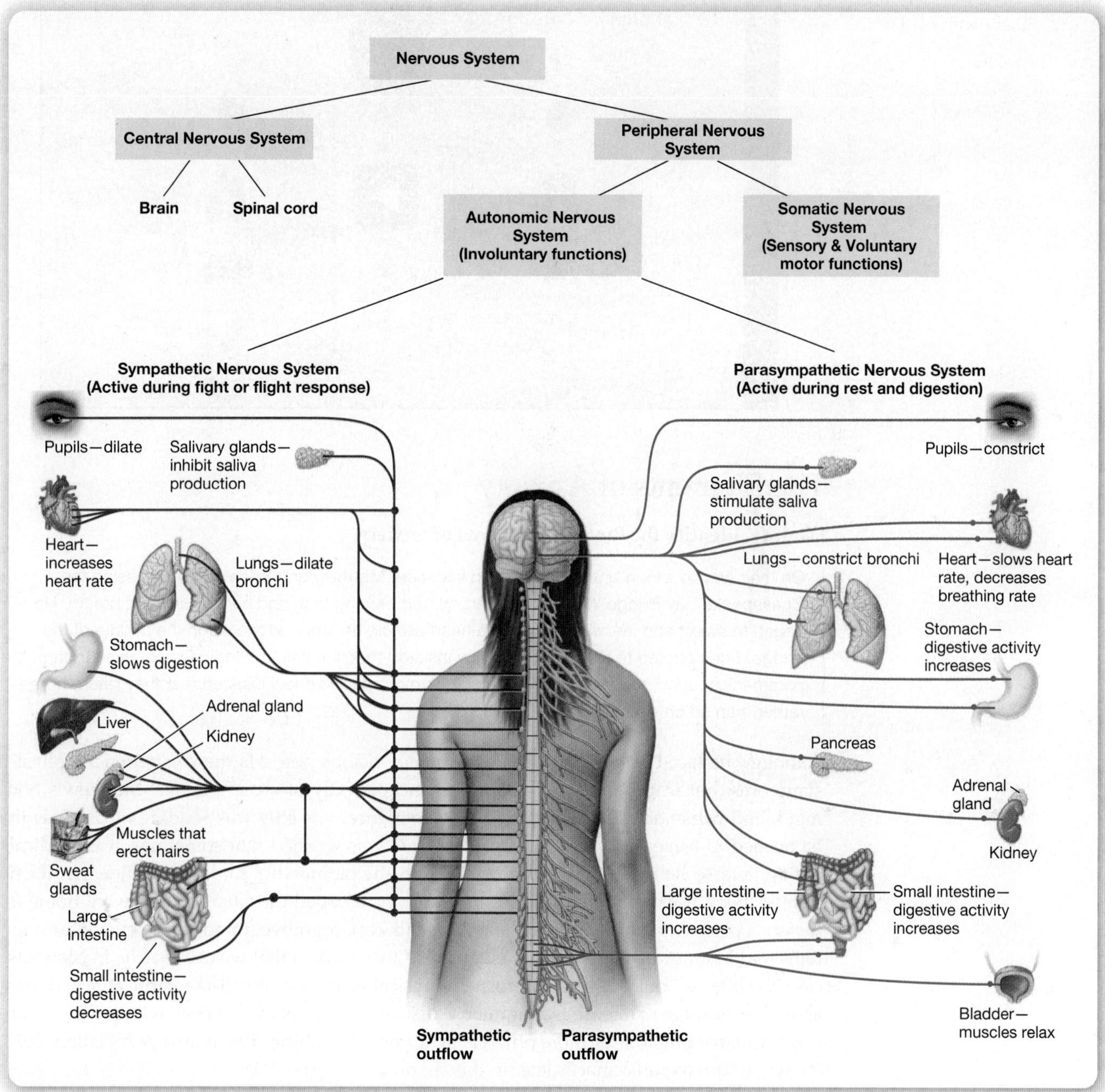

Of course, such superhuman abilities are time limited. After the SNS has been activated, the **parasympathetic nervous system** (PNS) returns your body to its normal resting state by decreasing your heart rate, blood pressure, and respiration. The fight-or-flight response is usually associated with the emotion that we call *fear*, a reaction to an existing or threatening event. The motivating power of fight-or-flight allows you to use all available resources to escape from a threatening situation. Some researchers have described this fight-or-flight reaction as an *alarm* to a present danger (Barlow, 2002).

In contrast, anxiety, as we have already noted, is a future-oriented response and sometimes consists of decreased levels of physical reactivity rather than the fight-or-flight response. Anxiety is also characterized by a thought pattern that is sometimes described as imagining the worst possible outcome. Anxiety is often present even when there is no real danger. In the next section, we examine the various components of anxiety.

Watch DIVISIONS OF THE NERVOUS SYSTEM

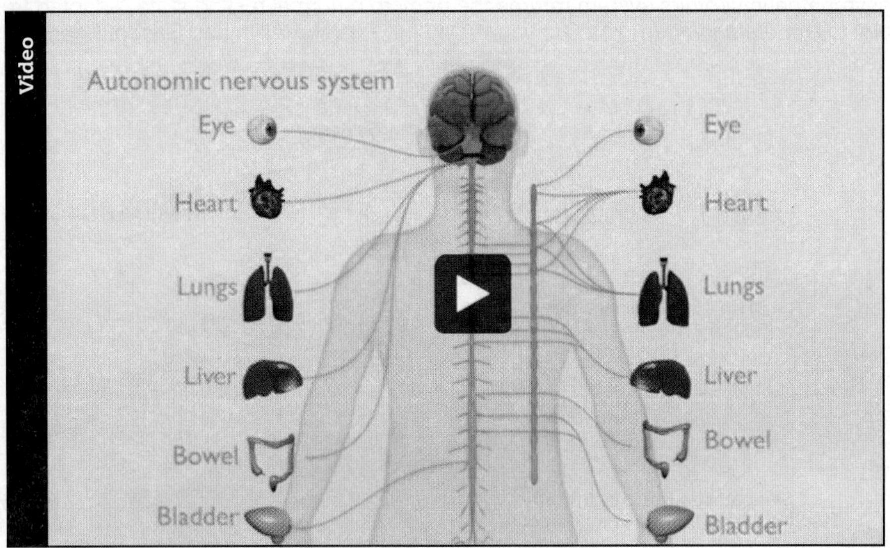

The Elements of Anxiety

LO 4.2 Identify the three components of anxiety.

> On their way to a long-anticipated beach vacation, Matthew and Eden started crossing the Chesapeake Bay Bridge. Matthew's heart started beating fast, and he was short of breath. He began to sweat and feel dizzy. Fearing a heart attack, he stopped the car in the middle of the bridge. Eden offered to drive, but Matthew insisted that she call for medical help. Even though the paramedics found no medical reason for his symptoms, Matthew insisted that they return home rather than go on vacation.

Although he faced no obvious threat, such as a vicious dog, Matthew experienced physical symptoms, but in this case, they occurred unexpectedly or *out of the blue*. Matthew's body, mind, and behavior were affected by this experience. His *body* was sending out signals that he needed to leave (flee) the situation. His *mind* was worried that something was medically wrong, and so he called for help. Even though the paramedics said he was fine, he did not believe them. Because he felt so uncomfortable, he escaped the situation and went home (*behavior*), a place where he felt safe. The physical (body), cognitive (mind), and behavioral symptoms that Matthew experienced are elements of the emotion that we call *anxiety*. In Matthew's case, the intense "burst" of anxiety-related physical symptoms is called a **panic attack**, defined as an abrupt surge of intense fear or intense discomfort that reaches a peak within minutes and is accompanied by four or more physical symptoms (American Psychiatric Association, 2013). We will return to panic attacks later in this chapter.

Emotions such as anxiety and fear have three distinct components (see Figure 4.2): physiological response, cognitive symptoms or subjective distress, and avoidance or escape. A panic attack such as Matthew's is a dramatic physical manifestation of anxiety, but it is not the only one. Other physical symptoms include blushing, buzzing or ringing in the ears, muscle tension, irritability, fatigue, gastrointestinal distress (indigestion, nausea, constipation, diarrhea), or urinary urgency and frequency. Among children, headaches and stomachaches (or butterflies in the stomach) are common complaints, although older children are more likely than younger children to report physical distress.

In addition to physical responses, anxiety includes subjective distress (also called *cognitive symptoms*). One type of cognitive symptom includes specific thoughts, ideas, images, or impulses. In some instances, the thoughts occur when the person affected sees a feared object or event, such as when someone who is afraid of spiders suddenly sees a spider ("What if that big hairy spider bites me?"). In other instances, the thoughts occur spontaneously ("What if I ran over a child when I was driving my car yesterday?"). A different type of cognitive

Figure 4.2 Anxiety is considered to have three elements: physical symptoms, negative cognitions or subjective distress, and behaviors such as escape or avoidance.

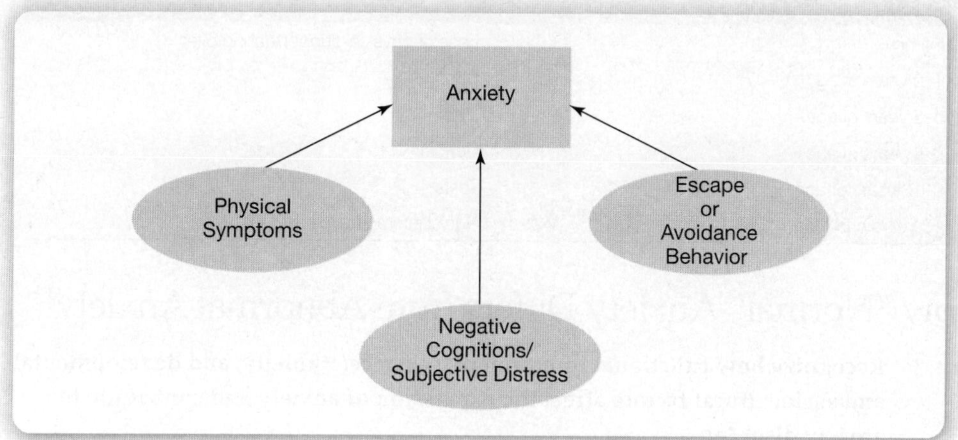

symptom is **worry**, which may be defined as apprehensive (negative) expectations about the future that are considered to be unreasonable in light of the actual situation. Worry exists among adults, adolescents, and some children. However, preadolescent children do not always report the thoughts and worries that are common among anxious adults (Alfano et al., 2006), perhaps reflecting their overall cognitive immaturity. Developmentally, young children do not yet have the ability to "think about thinking" (Flavell et al., 2001), a skill known as *metacognition*. Because of this difference, the cognitive symptom of worry is often absent in very young children. It appears later, when children mature sufficiently to allow them to recognize and report their own thoughts.

The most common behavioral symptom of anxiety is escape from or avoidance of the feared object, event, or situation. A person who is afraid of elevators walks up the stairs. After the incident on the bridge, Matthew avoided driving. Avoidance can also take the form of overdoing certain behaviors. For example, fears of contamination may result in excessive behaviors, such as washing or cleaning, designed to eliminate the feeling of contamination. Among children, unusual behaviors may be the first sign that a child is fearful. When it is time to go to school, children may play sick, cry, cling to a parent, or throw a tantrum. Some children are disobedient, refusing to follow instructions that involve contact with a feared event or object, even to the point of refusing to go to school.

Escape or avoidance behaviors bring temporary relief from distress, but they also reinforce behavioral avoidance through the process of negative reinforcement. Imagine that you are afraid of spiders. You see one in your bathroom and you run outside. You feel relieved because you are no longer in the same room as the spider. By running away, you removed a negative feeling of fear and you felt better. The feeling of relief that follows the removal of something negative is reinforcing; that is, this feeling increases the likelihood that the next time you see a spider, you will run away again. Therefore, eliminating distress by avoiding or escaping the situation can actually make the anxiety worse (see Figure 4.3). A primary goal of psychological treatment for anxiety is to reverse this pattern of negative reinforcement and eliminate avoidance of the feared situations.

Figure 4.3 Negative Reinforcement Increases Avoidance Behavior and Anxiety.
How feeling better can make your anxiety worse.

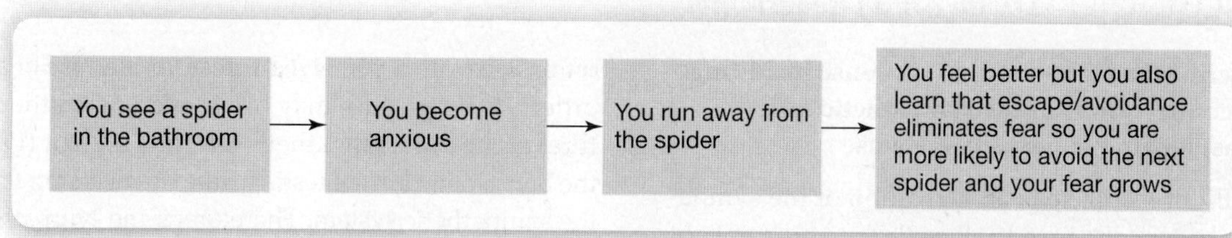

Table 4.1 Common Fears at Various Developmental Ages

Age	Fears
Infancy	Loss of physical support/falling over
1–2 years of age	Strangers
3–5 years of age	Dark
6–9 years of age	School
9–12 years of age	Tests
13 years and older	Social interaction/peers

How "Normal" Anxiety Differs from Abnormal Anxiety

LO 4.3 Recognize how functional impairment, sex, race/ethnicity, and developmental and sociocultural factors affect the expression of anxiety and contribute to anxiety disorders.

As we noted, it is normal to feel anxious from time to time, but when does *anxiety* become a *disorder?* The first factor to consider in making this decision is *functional impairment*. Remember Robert and Stan from Chapter 1? Before leaving home, Robert and Stan walk through their respective houses, checking to make sure that every door and window is locked and the oven is turned off. Robert does a quick 5-minute check, but Stan needs several hours to finish checking and as a result is sometimes late for work. Because his checking impairs his ability to get to work on time, Stan's behavior would meet the criteria for an anxiety disorder.

A second factor that differentiates normal from abnormal anxiety is developmental age. Among children, fears are common, and they follow a developmental trajectory (Ollendick, Grills, & Alexander, 2014). Two important aspects of the developmental model include the number and types of fears. The total number of fears declines as age increases. For infants and toddlers, so much of the world is new and initially scary that they are likely to have more fears than when they are older. As illustrated in Table 4.1, different fears are also common at different ages. As children mature physically and cognitively, they stop fearing loud noises (such as vacuum cleaners). They begin to understand that noisy things are not necessarily harmful. This *developmental hierarchy of fear* is not simply a matter of chronological age but also involves cognitive development. When children are cognitively challenged (i.e., they may be 7 to 9 years old but have the cognitive ability of children ages 4 to 6), their fears usually reflect their *cognitive development*, not their chronological (actual) age (Vandenberg, 1993).

Sociodemographic factors (sex, race/ethnicity, and socioeconomic status) are a third consideration when differentiating normal from abnormal fears. In the general population, anxiety disorders are more common among females than males, sometimes at a ratio of three females to one male for any particular anxiety disorder. Why females report more fear than males is unclear, but it may reflect cultural and/or gender role expectations. Social acceptability may allow girls and women to *report* more fears, but they may not necessarily *have* more fears. For example, girls report more test anxiety than boys, but when physical symptoms (blood pressure and heart rate) are measured during an actual test, test-anxious boys and girls show equal increases (Beidel & Turner, 1998). Even though in the general population more women than men report fears, the sex distribution is more equal among people who seek treatment. Therefore, when fears are severe, men and women are equally represented.

Learning Objective Summaries

LO 4.1 Describe the fight-or-flight response including the contributions of the sympathetic and parasympathetic nervous systems.

The fight-or-flight response is an activation of the sympathetic nervous system designed to allow the organism to fight off or flee from a perceived threat. In the case of anxiety disorders, this response may occur even when there is no real threat. The parasympathetic nervous system (PNS) returns the body to its normal resting state by reversing the actions of the sympathetic system. Therefore, if the sympathetic system increases heart rate, blood pressure, and respiration, the parasympathetic nervous system will decrease these responses.

LO 4.2 Identify the three components of anxiety.

Anxiety is usually considered to have three components: physiological reactivity (body), subjective distress/negative thoughts (mind), and escape or avoidance (behavior).

LO 4.3 Recognize how functional impairment, sex, race/ethnicity, developmental, and sociocultural factors affect the expression of anxiety and contribute to anxiety disorders.

Because fears are so common in the general population, people are not considered to have an anxiety disorder unless their fear is so severe that it creates substantial distress for that person or prevents the person from doing something that he or she wants to do, a concept called functional impairment. Anxiety disorders are common among different races and ethnicities. They are somewhat more common in women than men. In children, fears exist along a developmental hierarchy. At certain ages, fears are considered common and a normal part of development. At other ages, they are considered abnormal and in need of treatment.

Critical Thinking Question

Girls and women report more fears and anxiety disorders than do men and boys. However, when placed in anxiety-producing situations, both sexes show equal physiological reactions. What societal factors might explain this difference?

What Are the Anxiety Disorders?

Anxiety disorders have in common the physical, cognitive, and behavioral symptoms described earlier. For each disorder, the anxiety is expressed in a different way or is the result of a different object or situation. Some people are anxious about public speaking, others do not like to travel on airplanes, and still others fear separation from other people. Of course, some people are anxious in more than one type of situation, and in some cases they may have more than one anxiety disorder. The co-occurrence of two or more disorders existing in the same person (either at the same time or at some point in the lifetime) is called *comorbidity*. About 57% of people who are diagnosed with an anxiety disorder are comorbid for another anxiety disorder or depression (Brown et al., 2001). Therefore, although in the following sections we discuss these disorders as distinct conditions, remember that often people who have one disorder may have additional disorders as well.

In the United States, 31.2% of adults suffer from one of these disorders at some time in their lives (Kessler, Berglund, Demler, Jin et al., 2005), making them one of the most common types of psychological disorders among adults. Anxiety disorders are also common among children and adolescents, both in the United States and around the world. The prevalence of anxiety disorders among youth ranges from 8.6 to 15.7% (Costello et al., 2003; Essau et al, 2000). Most anxiety disorders develop early in life. The average age of onset is 11 years, one of the earliest for any psychiatric disorder (Kessler, Berglund, Demler, Jin et al., 2005). However, these disorders may also occur for the first time later in adulthood. Late-life onset of generalized anxiety disorder (GAD) is associated with physical health challenges and the presence of other mental disorders as well as a childhood history of poverty and parental loss/separation (Zhang et al., 2015). When agoraphobia first occurs after age 65, it is much less likely to be accompanied by panic attacks and much more likely to be accompanied by depression, general anxiety, and cognitive impairment (Ritchie et al., 2013).

Anxiety disorders occur with equal frequency across the three largest ethnic groups within the United States (Hispanics, non-Hispanic blacks, and non-Hispanic whites; Breslau et al., 2005). In addition to personal suffering, anxiety disorders compromise quality of life and social functioning (Mendlowicz & Stein, 2000), affect educational attainment (Kessler et al., 1995), and increase professional help seeking and medication use (Acarturk et al., 2009; Wittchen et al., 1994). In addition to their serious and pervasive effect on the individual, anxiety disorders exert a substantial cost on society (Acarturk et al., 2009). They produce a significant economic burden, costing the United States approximately $42.3 billion annually (Greenberg et al., 1999). Next we examine the clinical picture of the various anxiety disorders.

Panic Attacks

LO 4.4 Identify the symptoms of a panic attack.

Remember when Matthew was driving across the bridge? He had a *panic attack*—a discrete period of intense fear and physical arousal. Panic attacks develop abruptly, and symptoms reach peak intensity within minutes (American Psychiatric Association, 2013). Somatic and cognitive symptoms of a panic attack may include heart palpitations (pounding heart or accelerated heart rate), sweating, trembling, shortness of breath, choking, chest pain, nausea or abdominal distress, dizziness, derealization or depersonalization (feeling of being detached from one's body or surroundings), fear of losing control or going crazy, fear of dying, paresthesias (tingling in the hands or feet), and chills or heat sensations. Heart palpitations and dizziness are the most commonly reported symptoms, whereas paresthesias and choking are the least common (Craske et al., 2010). As many as 28.3% of adults have had a panic attack during their lifetime (Kessler et al., 2006), but just having a panic attack does not mean that the person has a panic disorder or any other anxiety disorder. Although 28.3% of adults report having had a panic attack, only about 4.7% have panic disorder. Remember that in an anxiety disorder, the anxiety symptoms must cause distress or some form of functional impairment. Many people who have had a panic attack have had only one or a few and are not distressed or impaired by their rare occurrences.

When panic attacks are not isolated events, they may be a symptom of any of the anxiety disorders. Even though only one of the anxiety disorders actually has the word *panic* in the title, panic attacks may be a symptom of other anxiety disorders and occur when a person is facing a frightening situation that is not a real threat to his or her physical well-being. People who are afraid of snakes, for example, might have a panic attack if they see a snake in a glass container at the zoo. In other cases, the anxiety reaction may be out of proportion to the object or situation. For example, suppose that you are flying and the airplane encounters mild turbulence, but you become very anxious and believe that you are going to die.

Panic attacks may be one of two types. *Expected panic attacks* are attacks that occur in response to a situational cue or trigger, such as when your friend who fears heights is suddenly confronted with the need to use a glass elevator. Expected attacks may also occur in anticipation of a feared situation as when someone with fears of public speaking has a panic attack a week before the speech. In other cases (such as Matthew's), the attack occurs unexpectedly, for no particular reason. People often say the attack came *out of the blue*. This represents the second type of panic attack, called *unexpected attacks*. These unexpected attacks are considered a *false alarm* (Barlow, 2002) because no object, event, or situation appears to precipitate the attack. Many times people misinterpret a panic attack as a heart attack and go to the hospital, which suggests just how frightening these symptoms can be. Yet it is clear that panic

People often mistake a panic attack for a heart attack and go to the hospital, which suggests how frightening and severe the symptoms may be.

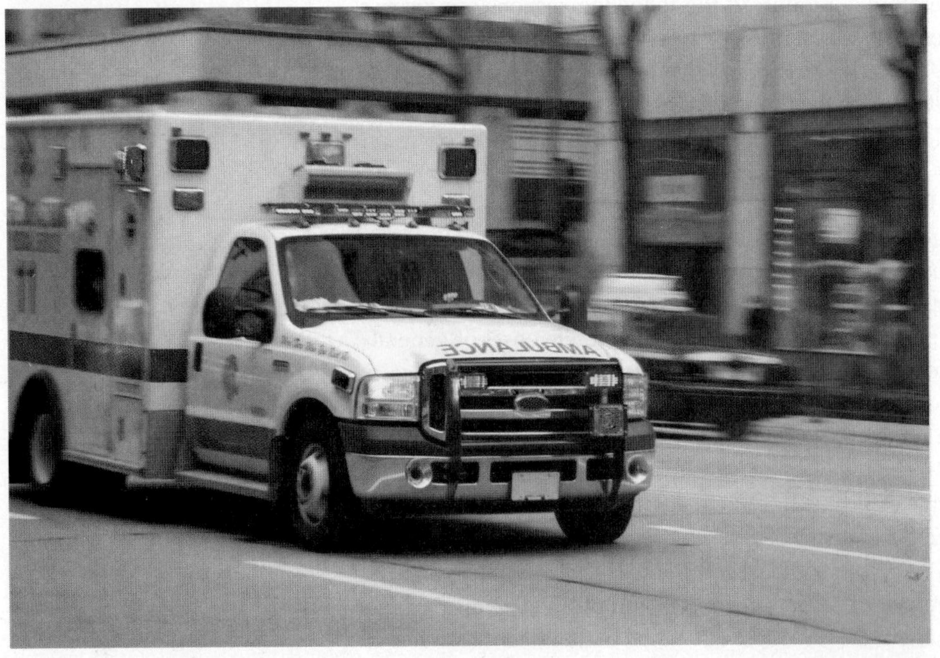

attacks are common, occurring in people with various anxiety disorders and sometimes even in people who do not have an anxiety disorder.

Panic Disorder

LO 4.5 Describe how panic disorder differs from a panic attack.

> Lena is 24 years old. She recently moved to the United States from El Salvador. Her family has a history of cardiac disease, and several relatives died when they were in their early forties. Lena is very worried that she will develop high blood pressure, which she considers the first sign of cardiac disease. Her physician referred her to an anxiety disorders clinic because she checked her blood pressure at least 20 times per day (but it was always normal). In the course of the diagnostic interview, Lena revealed that her physician in El Salvador told her she had "hypertensive crises" when for no reason her heart would race, she would get dizzy, she would feel very hot, and her hands would tingle. These "hypertensive crises" happened several times per month. When the therapist explained to Lena that these were panic attacks, she began to cry with relief—she was not suffering from cardiac disease after all.

Panic attacks are the defining feature of panic disorder (see "DSM-5: Panic Disorder"). In **panic disorder**, a person has had at least one panic attack and worries about having more attacks. The person also might worry about what a panic attack *means* ("Am I developing a heart condition?" "Am I losing my mind?") and may behave differently in response to the attacks, such as calling the doctor after every attack. Not everyone who is diagnosed with panic disorder changes their behavior or avoids situations (driving, shopping, getting on a bus) because of the fear that a panic attack might occur, but some people do.

Agoraphobia

LO 4.6 Recognize the symptoms of agoraphobia and how it relates to panic disorder.

Agoraphobia (literally meaning "fear of the marketplace") is a marked or intense fear or anxiety that occurs upon exposure to or in anticipation of a broad range of situations (see "DSM-5: Agoraphobia"). The fear or anxiety must occur in at least two out of five situations including public transportation, open spaces, enclosed places, standing in line or being in a crowd, or being outside the home alone. Sometimes people with agoraphobia are able to enter these situations but only with a trusted companion or by carrying certain items (such as a bottle of water) in case a panic attack occurs. In addition to panic symptoms, people with agoraphobia may fear the occurrence of extremely embarrassing physical symptoms such as dizziness or falling, losing control of the bowels or bladder, or, in children, a sense of disorientation or getting lost (American Psychiatric Association, 2013). Many people develop agoraphobia after they have developed panic disorder. The fear that a panic attack may occur and they may be in a situation or place where they might not be able to get help often leads to a pattern of behavioral avoidance. Not all individuals with agoraphobia, however, have panic attacks.

Although it is more common in adults, about 2.3% of adolescents (ages 13 to 18; Merikangas et al., 2011) and 0.4% of children and adolescents (ages 8 to 15; Merikangas et al., 2010) also suffer from panic disorder. In the general adult population, 3.7% have panic disorder alone, 1.4% have agoraphobia alone, and about 1% have both panic disorder and agoraphobia (Kessler, Berglund, Demler, Jin et al., 2005). Among adults age 55 and older, 1.2% suffer from panic disorder at any specific time (Chou, 2009). Another age-related difference is that whereas younger adults use the word *fear* when describing the emotion accompanying their physical symptoms, older adults use the word *discomfort* (Craske et al., 2010). It is important for clinicians to remember this distinction when interviewing older adults. If the clinicians ask only whether the person feels fearful, they may fail to diagnose panic disorder in an older adult, preventing the person from receiving appropriate treatment. Adults with panic disorder often rush to an emergency room because they believe are having a heart attack, and chest pain also is sometimes a complaint among children and adolescents with panic disorder (Achiam-Montal et al., 2013). More than 94% of people with

DSM-5

Criteria for Panic Disorder

A. Recurrent unexpected panic attacks. A panic attack is an abrupt surge of intense fear or intense discomfort that reaches a peak within minutes, and during which time four (or more) of the following symptoms occur:

Note: The abrupt surge can occur from a calm state or an anxious state.

1. Palpitations, pounding heart, or accelerated heart rate.
2. Sweating.
3. Trembling or shaking.
4. Sensations of shortness of breath or smothering.
5. Feelings of choking.
6. Chest pain or discomfort.
7. Nausea or abdominal distress.
8. Feeling dizzy, unsteady, light-headed, or faint.
9. Chills or heat sensations.
10. Paresthesias (numbness or tingling sensations).
11. Derealization (feelings of unreality) or depersonalization (being detached from oneself).
12. Fear of losing control or "going crazy."
13. Fear of dying.

Note: Culture-specific symptoms (e.g., tinnitus, neck soreness, headache, uncontrollable screaming or crying) may be seen. Such symptoms should not count as one of the four required symptoms.

B. At least one of the attacks has been followed by 1 month (or more) of one or both of the following:

1. Persistent concern or worry about additional panic attacks or their consequences (e.g., losing control, having a heart attack, "going crazy").
2. A significant maladaptive change in behavior related to the attacks (e.g., behaviors designed to avoid having panic attacks, such as avoidance of exercise or unfamiliar situations).

C. The disturbance is not attributable to the physiological effects of a substance (e.g., a drug of abuse, a medication) or another medical condition (e.g., hyperthyroidism, cardiopulmonary disorders).

D. The disturbance is not better explained by another mental disorder (e.g., the panic attacks do not occur only in response to feared social situations, as in social anxiety disorder; in response to circumscribed phobic objects or situations, as in specific phobia; in response to obsessions, as in obsessive-compulsive disorder; in response to reminders of traumatic events, as in posttraumatic stress disorder; or in response to separation from attachment figures, as in separation anxiety disorder).

panic disorder and/or agoraphobia seek treatment (Kessler et al., 2006). Without treatment, symptom-free periods are rare (Batelaan et al., 2010).

Women are more likely to experience panic attacks and panic disorder than men, and symptom variation exists across cultural groups. *Ataque de nervios*, found primarily among Latino people from the Caribbean, is one example of a disorder that might be a cultural variant of panic disorder. Some symptoms of *ataque* (heart palpitations, trembling) are similar to typical panic symptoms, whereas other symptoms (screaming uncontrollably, becoming physically aggressive) are specific to *ataque*. Whereas panic attacks typically occur out of the blue, *ataque de nervios* commonly occurs after social disruptions such as a change in family status (Guarnaccia et al., 2010). Among the Cambodian people, the cultural syndrome of *Khyâl* (wind attacks) is characterized by typical panic attack symptoms such as dizziness and culture-specific symptoms such as ringing in the ears and neck soreness (Craske et al., 2010). In Vietnam, these wind attacks are called *trung gio*. Thus, panic attacks exist across many different populations even though the specific symptom pattern may differ based on one's specific cultural background.

DSM-5

Criteria for Agoraphobia

A. Marked fear or anxiety about two (or more) of the following five situations:

1. Using public transportation (e.g., automobiles, buses, trains, ships, planes).
2. Being in open spaces (e.g., parking lots, marketplaces, bridges).
3. Being in enclosed places (e.g., shops, theaters, cinemas).
4. Standing in line or being in a crowd.
5. Being outside of the home alone.

B. The individual fears or avoids these situations because of thoughts that escape might be difficult or help might not be available in the event of developing panic-like symptoms or other incapacitating or embarrassing symptoms (e.g., fear of falling in the elderly; fear of incontinence).

C. The agoraphobic situations almost always provoke fear or anxiety.

D. The agoraphobic situations are actively avoided, require the presence of a companion, or are endured with intense fear or anxiety.

E. The fear or anxiety is out of proportion to the actual danger posed by the agoraphobic situations and to the sociocultural context.

F. The fear, anxiety, or avoidance is persistent, typically lasting for 6 months or more.

G. The fear, anxiety, or avoidance causes clinically significant distress or impairment in social, occupational, or other important areas of functioning.

H. If another medical condition (e.g., inflammatory bowel disease, Parkinson's disease) is present, the fear, anxiety, or avoidance is clearly excessive.

I. The fear, anxiety, or avoidance is not better explained by the symptoms of another mental disorder—for example, the symptoms are not confined to specific phobia, situational type; do not involve only social situations (as in social anxiety disorder); and are not related exclusively to obsessions (as in obsessive-compulsive disorder), perceived defects or flaws in physical appearance (as in body dysmorphic disorder), reminders of traumatic events (as in posttraumatic stress disorder), or fear of separation (as in separation anxiety disorder).

Note: Agoraphobia is diagnosed irrespective of the presence of panic disorder. If an individual's presentation meets criteria for panic disorder and agoraphobia, both diagnoses should be assigned.

In addition to anxiety, people with panic disorder or agoraphobia often feel sad and depressed in part because their anxiety limits their daily functioning (Stein et al., 2005) including the ability to work (Mojtabai et al., 2015). People with panic disorder and secondary (additional) disorders such as depression, eating disorders, and personality disorders may have suicidal thoughts or attempt suicide (Khan et al., 2002; Warshaw et al., 2000). Most researchers believe that the presence of the additional disorder increases the likelihood of suicidal behavior.

Generalized Anxiety Disorder

LO 4.7 Describe the relationship of worry to generalized anxiety disorder.

Medical school was extremely tough and very competitive, and Greg was worried that he would not do well enough to compete successfully for a residency. Now that he was going to be in the hospital clinic treating patients, Greg was having even more trouble sleeping. Most nights, he had difficulty falling asleep, and he was sometimes awake for a few hours in the middle of the night, thinking about what he needed to do the next day. He noticed other worries popping up more often. He worried about his father, who was adjusting to a new job, and his younger sister, who was starting college and spending too much time socializing. He became more concerned about what his classmates thought of him. He began to have trouble concentrating. Perhaps because of his sleep problems, he was not paying attention in class, and he found himself needing to reread sections of his textbooks to make sure he understood the material. He also noticed that his neck and shoulders were tight—even painful at times—after long hours of hunching over books and worrying about grades.

Watch CHRISTY: GENERALIZED ANXIETY DISORDER WITH INSOMNIA

The key feature of **generalized anxiety disorder** (GAD) is excessive anxiety and worry occurring more days than not and lasting at least 6 months. People with GAD worry about external dangers (e.g., future events, past transgressions, financial matters, and their own health and that of loved ones) (American Psychiatric Association, 2013). It is important to note that for a diagnosis of GAD, the likelihood that these events will actually occur is considered very low and the outcomes are perceived as catastrophic (Bandelow et al., 2013). Children may worry about their abilities or the quality of their academic performance. In addition to being out of proportion to the actual situation, the worry is described as uncontrollable and is accompanied by physical symptoms that include muscle tension, restlessness or feeling keyed up or on edge, being easily fatigued, difficulty concentrating, sleep disturbance, and irritability (see "DSM-5: Generalized Anxiety Disorder"). Cognitive symptoms include an inability to tolerate uncertainty (Ladouceur et al., 2000), and people with GAD attempt to control their worries by trying to distract themselves from the thoughts, by avoiding places that bring on the worrisome thoughts, by seeking reassurance from others, and by engaging in "safety behaviors" such as having a plan in case their worry comes true (Beesdo-Baum et al., 2012). People with GAD often say, "I always find something to worry about," and they often have at least one other psychological disorder (Andrews et al., 2010; Bruce et al., 2001), usually another anxiety disorder or major depression. However, the worries of people with GAD are more severe; they complain more frequently of muscle tension, feeling restless, and feeling keyed up or on edge (Andrews et al., 2010). These factors often help clinicians decide whether someone has GAD or a different anxiety disorder.

More adults than children have GAD (Bandelow et al., 2013), and the disorder most commonly starts in the late teens through the late twenties (Kessler et al., 2004). GAD begins gradually and is usually a chronic condition (Bjornsson et al., 2014). The course of the disorder is described as "chronic and fluctuating" (Newman et al., 2013); although the intensity of the symptoms may vary across time, spontaneous recovery is rare. Furthermore, GAD results in significant functional impairment, with 56.3% of people described as severely disabled (Kessler et al., 2009), and impact on physical health by increasing the risk of cardiac problems such as cardiovascular death and nonfatal myocardial infarction (i.e., "heart attacks"; Newman et al., 2013) and inflammatory bowel disease (Fuller-Thomson et al., 2005), for example. Many people with GAD seek treatment from primary care physicians. In fact, up to 12% of people who seek treatment from their primary care physicians do so because of GAD symptoms (Wittchen & Hoyer, 2001).

SIDE by SIDE case studies

Dimensions of Behavior: From Adaptive to Maladaptive

Adaptive Behavior Case Study

A Scary Event

Last month, Jamal was driving in a snowstorm. The road was icy, and he regretted his decision to drive in the storm. But he wanted to get home to his wife and young son. As he was driving down the highway, his car hit a patch of ice and he began to skid off the road—sideways at first and then in a circle. It was a terrifying few moments, and images of his son and wife flashed before Jamal's eyes. The car landed in a ditch. Jamal was banged up but otherwise safe. That night, after he got home, he was unable to sleep—he kept going in to see his son sleeping in his crib. The next morning, his heart was pounding when he started his car, and for a few weeks afterward, he felt tense every time he drove past that ditch.

Maladaptive Behavior Case Study

Posttraumatic Stress Disorder

In 1968, Jerry was drafted into the army. In Vietnam, after a daylong firefight, he was shot. His injuries were severe, and although he does not remember much of what happened after the bullet shattered his thigh bone, he does remember feeling extremely cold when he received a blood transfusion. Upon returning home, he was in the grocery store and walked down the frozen food aisle. The cold from the freezers precipitated a flashback, and Jerry thought that he was in Vietnam again. Now Jerry avoids the grocery store at all costs. Every time he hears a helicopter, he "hits the ground." Jerry has not been able to work since he came home from Vietnam.

such as a dark alley similar to the one where an assault occurred, the person may suffer an intense psychological and physiological reaction.

Watch BONNIE: POSTTRAUMATIC STRESS DISORDER

Although not necessary for the diagnostic criteria, people with PTSD report the presence of emotions such as fear, helplessness, or horror, and other emotions such as guilt and shame are also commonly reported by people with this disorder. A classic symptom of PTSD is *intrusion (reexperiencing),* through recurrent and intrusive memories, thoughts, or dreams about the trauma that occur repeatedly despite attempts to suppress them (see "DSM-5: Posttraumatic Stress Disorder"). The person suddenly acts or feels as if the event were occurring again. An interesting phenomenon in PTSD is that even though the memories can be intrusive (such as the intrusive quality of obsessions), people sometimes cannot recall specific or important details of the traumatic event.

Another unique symptom of PTSD is *negative alterations in cognitions and mood,* which is the inability to feel emotions such as joy, surprise, or even sadness. People report a

After a life-threatening or traumatic event such as the Boston Marathon bombing, some people may develop posttraumatic stress disorder.

loss of interest in formerly enjoyable activities and a feeling of detachment from other people and the environment. Another common symptom is an overactive sympathetic nervous system, which creates a state of general and persistent arousal known as *hyperarousal.* This overarousal results in difficulty sleeping and concentrating and creates emotional responses such as irritability or anger. In addition, people with PTSD report *hypervigilance* (a sense of being "on watch") and an *exaggerated startle response* (being easily startled) as well as avoidance of activities, situations, or events that remind them of the traumatic event. Finally, the fourth group of symptoms is the *persistent avoidance of situations or objects* associated with the trauma.

Up to 92% of people with PTSD may have a comorbid psychological disorder, most commonly depression, other anxiety disorders, or substance abuse (Bowe & Rosenheck, 2015; Brunello et al., 2001; Perkonigg et al., 2000). Because PTSD is such a complex disorder with so many different symptoms, determining whether the sad mood or generalized anxiety is just part of the overall disorder or whether it represents a separate diagnosis is sometimes difficult. In either case, PTSD is one of the most difficult disorders to treat.

DSM-5

Criteria for Posttraumatic Stress Disorder

Note: The following criteria apply to adults, adolescents, and children older than 6 years. For children 6 years and younger, see corresponding criteria below.

A. Exposure to actual or threatened death, serious injury, or sexual violence in one (or more) of the following ways:

1. Directly experiencing the traumatic event(s).
2. Witnessing, in person, the event(s) as it occurred to others.
3. Learning that the traumatic event(s) occurred to a close family member or close friend. In cases of actual or threatened death of a family member or friend, the event(s) must have been violent or accidental.
4. Experiencing repeated or extreme exposure to aversive details of the traumatic event(s) (e.g., first responders collecting human remains; police officers repeatedly exposed to details of child abuse).

   Note: Criterion A4 does not apply to exposure through electronic media, television, movies, or pictures, unless this exposure is work related.

B. Presence of one (or more) of the following intrusion symptoms associated with the traumatic event(s), beginning after the traumatic event(s) occurred:

1. Recurrent, involuntary, and intrusive distressing memories of the traumatic event(s).

   Note: In children older than 6 years, repetitive play may occur in which themes or aspects of the traumatic event(s) are expressed.

2. Recurrent distressing dreams in which the content and/or affect of the dream are related to the traumatic event(s).

   Note: In children, there may be frightening dreams without recognizable content.

3. Dissociative reactions (e.g., flashbacks) in which the individual feels or acts as if the traumatic event(s) were recurring. (Such reactions may occur on a continuum, with the most extreme expression being a complete loss of awareness of present surroundings.)

   Note: In children, trauma-specific reenactment may occur in play.

4. Intense or prolonged psychological distress at exposure to internal or external cues that symbolize or resemble an aspect of the traumatic event(s).
5. Marked physiological reactions to internal or external cues that symbolize or resemble an aspect of the traumatic event(s).

C. Persistent avoidance of stimuli associated with the traumatic event(s), beginning after the traumatic event(s) occurred, as evidenced by one or both of the following:

1. Avoidance of or efforts to avoid distressing memories, thoughts, or feelings about or closely associated with the traumatic event(s).
2. Avoidance of or efforts to avoid external reminders (people, places, conversations, activities, objects, situations) that arouse distressing memories, thoughts, or feelings about or closely associated with the traumatic event(s).

D. Negative alterations in cognitions and mood associated with the traumatic event(s), beginning or worsening after the traumatic event(s) occurred, as evidenced by two (or more) of the following:

1. Inability to remember an important aspect of the traumatic event(s) (typically due to dissociative amnesia and not to other factors such as head injury, alcohol, or drugs).
2. Persistent and exaggerated negative beliefs or expectations about oneself, others, or the world (e.g., "I am bad," "No one can be trusted," "The world is completely dangerous," "My whole nervous system is permanently ruined").
3. Persistent, distorted cognitions about the cause or consequences of the traumatic event(s) that lead the individual to blame himself/herself or others.
4. Persistent negative emotional state (e.g., fear, horror, anger, guilt, or shame).
5. Markedly diminished interest or participation in significant activities.
6. Feelings of detachment or estrangement from others.
7. Persistent inability to experience positive emotions (e.g., inability to experience happiness, satisfaction, or loving feelings).

E. Marked alterations in arousal and reactivity associated with the traumatic event(s), beginning or worsening after the traumatic event(s) occurred, as evidenced by two (or more) of the following:

1. Irritable behavior and angry outbursts (with little or no provocation) typically expressed as verbal or physical aggression toward people or objects.
2. Reckless or self-destructive behavior.
3. Hypervigilance.
4. Exaggerated startle response.
5. Problems with concentration.
6. Sleep disturbance (e.g., difficulty falling or staying asleep or restless sleep).

F. Duration of the disturbance (Criteria B, C, D, and E) is more than 1 month.

G. The disturbance causes clinically significant distress or impairment in social, occupational, or other important areas of functioning.

H. The disturbance is not attributable to the physiological effects of a substance (e.g., medication, alcohol) or another medical condition.

Posttraumatic Stress Disorder for Children 6 Years and Younger

A. In children 6 years and younger, exposure to actual or threatened death, serious injury, or sexual violence in one (or more) of the following ways:

1. Directly experiencing the traumatic event(s).
2. Witnessing, in person, the event(s) as it occurred to others, especially primary caregivers.

   Note: Witnessing does not include events that are witnessed only in electronic media, television, movies, or pictures.

3. Learning that the traumatic event(s) occurred to a parent or caregiving figure.

B. Presence of one (or more) of the following intrusion symptoms associated with the traumatic event(s), beginning after the traumatic event(s) occurred:

1. Recurrent, involuntary, and intrusive distressing memories of the traumatic event(s).

   Note: Spontaneous and intrusive memories may not necessarily appear distressing and may be expressed as play reenactment.

2. Recurrent distressing dreams in which the content and/or affect of the dream are related to the traumatic event(s).

   Note: It may not be possible to ascertain that the frightening content is related to the traumatic event.

3. Dissociative reactions (e.g., flashbacks) in which the child feels or acts as if the traumatic event(s) were recurring. (Such reactions may occur on a continuum, with the most extreme expression being a complete loss of awareness of present surroundings.) Such trauma-specific reenactment may occur in play.
4. Intense or prolonged psychological distress at exposure to internal or external cues that symbolize or resemble an aspect of the traumatic event(s).
5. Marked physiological reactions to reminders of the traumatic event(s).

(continued)

C. One (or more) of the following symptoms, representing either persistent avoidance of stimuli associated with the traumatic event(s) or negative alterations in cognitions and mood associated with the traumatic event(s), must be present, beginning after the event(s) or worsening after the event(s):

Persistent Avoidance of Stimuli

1. Avoidance of or efforts to avoid activities, places, or physical reminders that arouse recollections of the traumatic event(s).
2. Avoidance of or efforts to avoid people, conversations, or interpersonal situations that arouse recollections of the traumatic event(s).

Negative Alterations in Cognitions

3. Substantially increased frequency of negative emotional states (e.g., fear, guilt, sadness, shame, confusion).
4. Markedly diminished interest or participation in significant activities, including constriction of play.
5. Socially withdrawn behavior.
6. Persistent reduction in expression of positive emotions.

D. Alterations in arousal and reactivity associated with the traumatic event(s), beginning or worsening after the traumatic event(s) occurred, as evidenced by two (or more) of the following:

1. Irritable behavior and angry outbursts (with little or no provocation) typically expressed as verbal or physical aggression toward people or objects (including extreme temper tantrums).
2. Hypervigilance.
3. Exaggerated startle response.
4. Problems with concentration.
5. Sleep disturbance (e.g., difficulty falling or staying asleep or restless sleep).

E. The duration of the disturbance is more than 1 month.

F. The disturbance causes clinically significant distress or impairment in relationships with parents, siblings, peers, or other caregivers or with school behavior.

G. The disturbance is not attributable to the physiological effects of a substance (e.g., medication or alcohol) or another medical condition.

PTSD begins with the occurrence of a traumatic event and can occur at any age (McNally, 2001). Among adults, the disorder is usually categorized as either civilian PTSD or combat-related PTSD, depending on the event. Combat-related PTSD is usually more severe and less likely to respond to treatment. PTSD results in significant work impairment with work productivity loss exceeding $3 billion per year (Brunello et al., 2001). It may also lead to reduced educational attainment, increased risk of bearing a child as a teenager, and an increase in unstable marriages (Brunello et al., 2001). Individuals with PTSD also have higher rates of health care utilization (Klassen et al., 2013). Approximately 6.8% of the U.S. adult population suffers from civilian PTSD (Kessler, 2005a). The prevalence of combat-related PTSD is higher; the most common estimates range from 6 to 9%, but some have been as high as 18.5% in some samples (Hoge et al., 2007; Magruder et al., 2005; Seal et al., 2007; Tanielian & Jaycox, 2008).

Historically, the onset of PTSD followed a life event defined as "out of the range of normal human experience" (combat, concentration camp imprisonment, natural disasters, assault, or rape). More recent diagnostic criteria have expanded the list of "eligible" events to include many more human experiences, some of which are common (unexpected death of a loved one, serious illness such as cancer in oneself). The person may have experienced the traumatic event directly (such as being in a combat situation), watched the event occur to someone else (being a bystander as a crime was committed), or simply heard about or seen the event via television or the Internet. This expansion in the manner of contact with the traumatic event known as *conceptual bracket creep* (McNally, 2009) has been at least partly responsible for the increased prevalence in the number of people who are considered to have experienced a traumatic event. Using these expanded criteria, one epidemiological survey reported that 89.6% of adults (92.2% of males and 87.1% of females) experienced a potentially traumatic event (Breslau & Kessler, 2001). However, despite almost universal exposure to a traumatic event, only 11.1% of the sample had PTSD. These different percentages illustrate a very important point: exposure to trauma alone does not automatically lead to PTSD (Lukaschek et al., 2013). Events such as automobile accidents or the death of a loved one may result in temporary stress reactions (Keppel-Benson et al., 2002; Yehuda, 2002), but the typical response to a traumatic event is resilience, not PTSD (see "Research Hot Topic: Trauma, Grief, and Resilience").

After a trauma, children may engage in traumatic play, such as building a tower and knocking it down. However, engaging in this type of activity does not mean that a child was the victim of a trauma.

Among children in the United States, the prevalence of PTSD is unknown because there have been no controlled community investigations. Among German teens and young adults, 1% of males and 2.2% of females have PTSD (Essau et al., 2000). Among children actually exposed to a singular traumatic event (sniper shootings at school, earthquakes, boating accidents), estimates of PTSD range from 5.2 to 100% of people exposed (see Beidel & Turner, 2005). Prevalence estimates may vary because different investigators use different procedures (direct interviews of children versus parent report, for example) to make the diagnoses. In addition, the emergence of PTSD depends on proximity to the event. The closer you are to the event, the more likely you are to develop PTSD. After an earthquake in Armenia, for example, more children living at the earthquake's epicenter developed PTSD than did children living 50 miles away. One hopeful fact is that for many civilian traumas, PTSD symptoms decline with time (Yule et al., 2000).

Like the anxiety disorders, symptoms of PTSD are different in children than in adults (see "DSM-5: Posttraumatic Stress Disorder"). Among children, intrusion may take the form of *traumatic play* in which the child reenacts relevant aspects of the traumatic event. However, it is important to avoid misinterpreting any behavior as indicating the presence of trauma or PTSD. Consider the following example. After the Oklahoma City bombing (1995), some children in the city built and destroyed buildings made of blocks (Gurwitch et al., 2002). Were all of these children suffering from PTSD? Developmentally, many children who have never been victims of bombings build block buildings or sandcastles and then delight in knocking them down. Without knowledge of typical children's play, developmentally appropriate behaviors could be misinterpreted as indicating the presence of PTSD.

In addition to developmental differences in reexperiencing, other aspects of PTSD may differ by developmental age. Under age 6, bed-wetting, thumb-sucking, fear of the dark, and increased difficulties separating from parents may be symptoms of PTSD, but they also occur in many children who have not been exposed to trauma (Fremont, 2004). Attentional problems, impaired school performance, school avoidance, health complaints, irrational fears, sleep problems, nightmares, irritability, and anger outbursts are common in children with PTSD, but they also occur in children with other disorders and sometimes in children with no disorder. Adolescents report symptoms more commonly found among adults: intrusive thoughts, hypervigilance, emotional numbing (a DSM-IV criterion replaced by negative alterations of cognition and mood), nightmares, sleep disturbances, and avoidance. When a diagnosis of PTSD is a possibility, developmental factors must be considered.

Until very recently, PTSD among female military veterans was primarily the result of sexual assault or sexual harassment (Butterfield et al., 2000). However, the changing role of women in the military is changing the sex distribution of wartime combat exposure (Fontana et al., 2010), and approximately 20% of female veterans who served in the Iraq and Afghanistan conflicts have been diagnosed with PTSD (http://www.ptsd.va.gov/professional/trauma/war/traumatic_stress_in_female_veterans.asp), although the published figures do not describe whether the PTSD was as a result of combat trauma. Among civilian populations, some samples find that more females than males suffer from PTSD (Brunello et al., 2001), whereas others do not. Overall, among women who endure a traumatic event and later report PTSD, about 50% of the precipitating events follow a sexual assault (Brunello et al., 2001; Perkonigg et al., 2000).

Sociocultural factors are also important to consider when examining the prevalence of PTSD across racial/ethnic groups. After Hurricane Andrew devastated parts of Florida in

Research HOT Topic

Trauma, Grief, and Resilience

On October 2, 2006, Charles Carl Roberts entered a one-room schoolhouse in the Amish community of Nickel Mines, Pennsylvania. He lined up 10 young girls and shot them each at point blank range. Then he killed himself. Five girls died, and five were seriously wounded. That night, women from the Amish community went to the house of his widow bringing food and comfort. That weekend, more that 50% of those at Mr. Robert's funeral were from the Amish community he had wounded. When asked how they managed to forgive, they replied, "With God's help."

As currently defined, many stressors qualify as traumatic events and could result in a diagnosis of PTSD. Stabbings, shootings, and murder are common occurrences for inner-city adolescents (e.g., Jenkins & Bell, 1994). Natural disasters such as hurricanes, floods, and tornadoes also occur frequently and increase stress. However, merely experiencing a potentially stressful event does not mean that you will develop PTSD.

As research on loss and trauma illustrates, up to 90% of Americans report exposure to a traumatic event during their lifetime, but only 5 to 11% develop PTSD (Breslau & Kessler, 2001; Ozer et al., 2003). Although witnessing a traumatic event may result in brief PTSD or significant stress (think about your own response to a trauma in your life), for most individuals, these reactions disappear after a few months. Only a relatively small percentage of people exposed to a trauma actually develop PTSD. In the face of traumatic events such as the September 11, 2001, terrorist attacks, the Sandy Hook Elementary School shooting, or the Boston Marathon bombing, *recovery* (threshold or subthreshold psychopathology for a few months followed by a return to pretrauma levels) or *resilience* (maintaining a stable equilibrium in the face of the traumatic event) rather than PTSD was the predominant response (Bonanno, 2004). Researchers are now examining factors that predict (1) who will not recover, (2) what treatments are most likely to promote recovery, and (3) when those treatments should be applied.

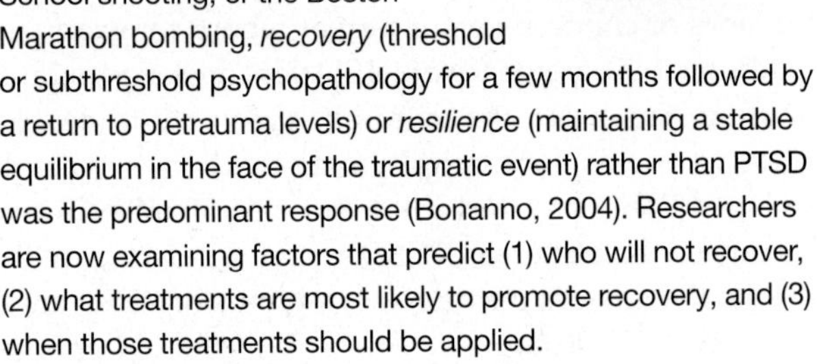

What factors would you identify as important in the development of PTSD?

1992, African American and Hispanic children reported more traumatic distress than did white children (LaGreca et al., 1996). However, as with many such differences, the important sociocultural factor may be socioeconomic status. After Hurricane Hugo in 1989, more African American than non–African American children reported fears, but the African American children also lived closer to the place where the storm came ashore. When demographic and proximity factors were controlled, the incidence of PTSD was not different (6.3 versus 5.1%; Shannon et al., 1994). This highlights the importance of controlling for socioeconomic and other environmental factors when investigating potential racial/ethnic differences in psychopathology. In many instances, it may not be the event itself but the ability to recover from the event that creates distress and precipitates the onset of PTSD. After a major hurricane, people with limited incomes have less ability to pay for needed repairs to homes and fewer personal resources to be able to start over. They are also more likely to work in minimum-wage jobs in businesses less likely to rebuild quickly after the storm. Therefore, group differences that appear to be based on racial or ethnic minority status may really reflect socioeconomic status.

Learning Objective Summary

LO 4.12 Recognize the symptoms of posttraumatic stress disorder and discuss how it is different from anxiety disorders.

Posttraumatic stress disorder (PTSD) begins with a traumatic event. Later, when confronting events or situations that symbolize or resemble part of the trauma, such as a dark alley similar to the one where an assault occurred, the person may suffer an intense psychological and physiological reaction. There are four categories of PTSD symptoms: intrusion, avoidance, negative alterations in cognition and mood, and alterations in arousal and reactivity. PTSD can occur at any age. The difference between PTSD and anxiety disorders is that in PTSD, the disorder always follows a traumatic event. For anxiety disorders, in many instances, a traumatic event has not occurred— many people fear that a future event *will* occur.

Critical Thinking Question

Historically, the onset of PTSD followed a life event defined as "out of the range of normal human experience" (combat, concentration camp imprisonment, natural disasters, assault, or rape). More recent diagnostic criteria have expanded the list of "eligible" events to include many more human experiences, some of which are common (unexpected death of a loved one, serious illness such as cancer in oneself). This expansion in the manner of contact with the traumatic event is known as *conceptual bracket creep*. Should events that will occur to everyone—death of a loved one, serious illness—be considered a traumatic event or just part of life? What are the implications for suggesting that life itself can create PTSD?

The Etiology of Anxiety and Trauma- and Stressor-Related Disorders

How do these disorders develop? As discussed in Chapter 1, Little Albert acquired the fear of a white rat after a series of conditioning trials in which the rat was paired with loud noises. This psychological model is very useful for understanding PTSD, which develops after a conditioning experience. However, not every anxiety disorder can be traced back to a traumatic event, and not everyone who experiences a negative event develops an anxiety disorder. Just as people may fear many different objects or situations, anxiety disorders may develop in a number of different ways. In some instances, the cause is unknown. Biological and psychological causes have been identified, and the same disorder can develop in very different ways in different people. As will be evident at the end of this section, the biopsychosocial model may be the most comprehensive model of the etiology of the anxiety disorders.

Biological Perspective

LO 4.13 Describe the biological factors that may contribute to the onset of anxiety and posttraumatic stress disorders including family and genetic influences, neuroanatomy, temperament, and behavioral inhibition.

Biological perspectives on abnormal behavior include investigations in genetics, family history, neuroanatomy, and neurobiology. Even when biological factors cannot fully explain the development of these disorders, they may produce the vulnerability that "sets the stage" for other biological or psychological influences that can lead to the disorder's onset.

FAMILY AND GENETIC STUDIES Are these disorders inherited? Anxiety disorders run in families. Compared with relatives of people without a disorder, relatives (parents, brothers, sisters, aunts, and uncles) of someone with an anxiety disorder are also more likely to have an anxiety disorder (e.g., Czajkowski et al., 2010; Hanna, 2000; Isomura et al., 2015; Low et al., 2008; Pauls et al., 1995). The same relationship exists between parents and children. When a parent has an anxiety disorder, the child is more likely to have one, too (Beidel & Turner, 1997; Lieb et al., 2000). However, not every child in the family will develop anxiety; genetics may play a role but do not act alone.

Twin studies also illustrate the role of genetics in the development of anxiety disorders. The concordance rate (see Chapter 2) for anxiety disorders among monozygotic (MZ) twins is twice as high as that of dizygotic (DZ) twins (34 versus 17%, respectively; Andrews et al., 1990; Torgersen, 1983). Another twin study metric to examine genetic contribution is through the concept of **heritability**, which is the proportion of variance in liability to the disorder accounted for by genetic factors. Heritability estimates have been reported for GAD (32%; Hettema et al., 2001), panic disorder (43%; Hettema et al., 2001), social anxiety disorder (13% to 42%; Kendler et al., 2001; Nelson et al., 2000; Scaini et al., 2014), and specific phobia [animal (22 to 44%), situational (0 to 33%), blood-injection-injury (28 to 63%); Van Houtem et al., 2013). A study of anxiety symptoms in adolescent twins produced heritability estimates of 65% for boys and 74% for girls (Ask et al., 2014). One study of more than 5,000 twins (Hettema et al., 2005) revealed that one common genetic factor appears to influence GAD, panic disorder, and agoraphobia. A second genetic factor influences animal phobias and situational phobias. Social anxiety disorder appears to be influenced by both genetic factors. However, all available genetic data indicate that genes do not tell the whole story. Because none of the heritability estimates was 100%, environmental factors clearly also are important in the development of anxiety disorders.

Studies of molecular genetics, using both human and animal models, brought us closer to understanding which specific genes may influence vulnerability to anxiety disorders. In mice, genetic influences for fear and anxiety have been found on 15 different chromosomes (e.g., Einat et al., 2005; Flint, 2002). In humans, studies identified chromosomal *regions* that may be important but without identifying specific *genes* (Kim et al., 2005; Martinez-Barrondo et al., 2005; Oleseon et al., 2005; Politi et al., 2006).

Genetic association studies of several candidate genes have also been conducted. Although a rat model showed significant association of the gene CTNND2 with anxious behavior, these results did not carry forward to humans (1,714 cases with GAD, panic disorder, social phobia, or agoraphobia; 4,125 controls). SNPs in CTNND2 showed increase signals, but the results did not stand up to correction for multiple testing (Nivard et al., 2014). In a study of 744 cases with panic disorder and 1,418 controls, researchers found a significant association with panic disorder for HLA-DRB1*13:02 and suggestive evidence for other genes involved in immune-regulated pathways (Shimada-Sugimoto et al., 2015). Associations have also been found between panic disorder and the serotonin transporter gene SLC6A4 (Strug et al., 2010) as well as between both panic disorder and social anxiety disorder and the α-endomannosidase gene (MANEA) (Jensen et al., 2014).

Genome-wide association studies (GWAS) are the next step in identifying specific genes that increase risk for anxiety disorders. A recent GWAS in samples of Europeans (757 cases, 940 controls) and African Americans (324 cases, 273 controls) with cases meeting criteria for a range of anxiety disorders [GAD (18.4%), panic attacks (2.1%), agoraphobia (6.5%), social phobia (14.3%), and specific phobia (11.7%)] did not find any SNPs that reached genome-wide significance. However, a meta-analysis of both samples using phenotypic factor scores found significant associations for three genes: MFAP3L, NDUFAB1, and PALB2 (Otowa et al., 2014). Similarly, in a study of anxiety-related behaviors in 2,810 children from the Twins Early Development Study, no SNPs reached genome-wide significance despite heritability estimates exceeding 50% (Trzaskowski et al., 2013). In both cases the sample sizes were too small to detect genes of small effect. Several small GWAS with up to 578 cases of PTSD have been published, with a few genome-wide significant loci implicating pathways and processes related to neuroprotection, actin polymerization, neuronal function, and immune function (Logue et al., 2015). In a larger study of U.S. veterans of the wars in Iraq and Afghanistan, which included non-Hispanic black (385 cases, 564 controls) and non-Hispanic white (325 cases, 434 controls) participants, no SNPs reached genome-wide significance (Ashley-Koch et al., 2015). However, the Psychiatric Genomics Consortium (PGC) working group on PTSD (PGC-PTSD), founded in 2013, aims to publish the first large-scale GWAS of PTSD with at least 10,000 cases and 30,000 trauma-exposed controls (Logue et al., 2015).

Based on the currently available data, what appears to be inherited is a *general vulnerability factor*, known as **trait anxiety** or *anxiety proneness* (Hettema et al., 2001). Because these types of personality traits exist along a dimension, people can have different degrees of anxiety proneness. Those high on this dimension are more "reactive" to stressful events and therefore more likely in the right circumstances to develop a disorder.

> Malika and five of her friends were flying home from spring break. The plane flew through a thunderstorm, and wind shear caused the plane to drop suddenly and tilt at a 90-degree angle for approximately 10 seconds until the pilot regained control. The plane landed safely. Several months later, Malika's friends wanted to fly to the Caribbean, but she declined. She was terrified to get on a plane. Despite their pleadings, Malika refused to go. Based on that one experience, she had developed a specific phobia of flying.

Malika's case illustrates how anxiety proneness might foster the development of fear. Even though all six women experienced the same environmental event, only Malika acquired a phobia. Perhaps Malika had an increased genetic vulnerability for the development of anxiety disorders.

NEUROANATOMY Anxiety proneness is a theoretical construct that is very useful in understanding the development of anxiety disorders. A *construct* is not something tangible; it provides only a frame of reference, such as the construct known as *free will*. Saying that someone is anxiety prone does not explain what the abnormality is or where it is located. However, newly emerging CT, MRI, fMRI, and PET imaging data indicate that several areas of the midbrain are involved in anxious emotion. When someone is stressed, certain areas of the brain—including the amygdala (Brühl et al., 2014; Kim et al., 2012; Strawn et al., 2012) as well as the limbic and paralimbic systems (Stein & Hugo, 2004)—become more active. Areas of the prefrontal cortex may become activated as well (Mochcovitch et al., 2014; Strawn et al., 2012), and there is evidence of reduced connectivity between certain areas of the brain, such as the limbic system and the prefrontal cortex (Brühl et al., 2014). Because these neuroanatomical structures are important in processing emotion, they may also be involved in the development of fear and anxiety. For example, the amygdala (see Figure 4.6) and the insula, areas that are associated with anxiety, become activated when adults with social anxiety disorder viewed faces depicting negative emotion (Shah et al., 2009). These same areas were not activated when people without social anxiety disorder viewed the same faces.

Overall, there do appear to be differences in brain *functioning* between individuals with some types of anxiety disorders and those with no disorder. However, comparative studies examining brain *structures*, such as the size of the amygdala, do not reveal differences between people with anxiety disorders and healthy controls. Therefore, anatomical differences would not appear to be a factor in the development of anxiety disorders. In some cases, PTSD may cause changes in brain function that then affect brain anatomy. In animals, exposure to chronic stress can reduce the size of the hippocampus (Sapolsky et al., 1990), and early studies reported that, when compared with groups of people who did not have PTSD, combat veterans with PTSD and children who were sexually abused had smaller hippocampal volumes (Bremner et al., 1995, 1997; Gurvits et al., 1996; Stein et al.,

Figure 4.6 View of the amygdala

The amygdala is a part of the brain associated with anxiety.

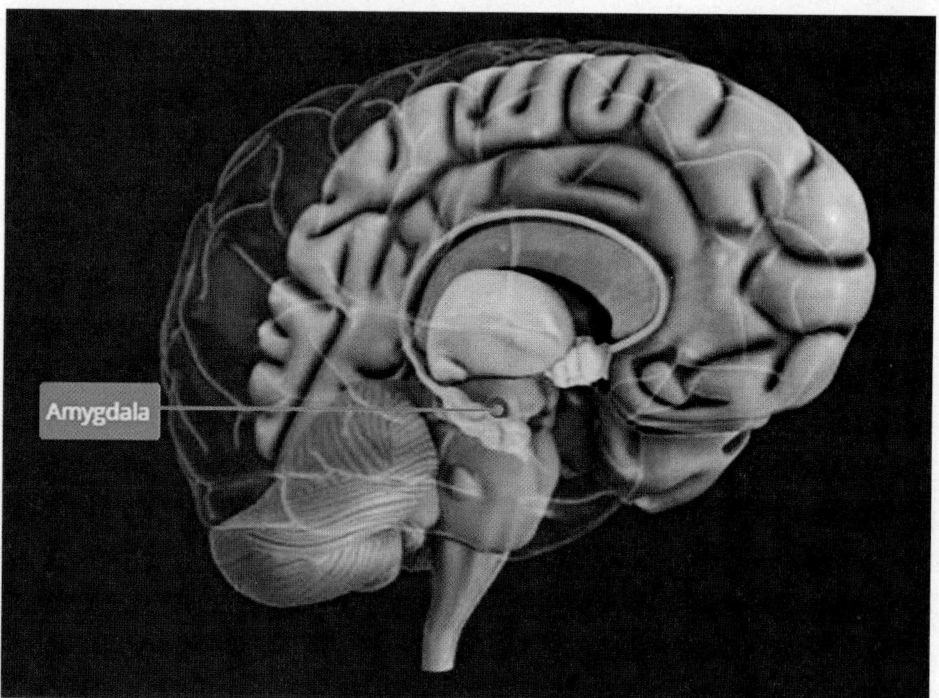

1997). These findings initially suggested that chronic stress may result in neurochemical changes (brain functioning) that over time may change neuroanatomy (brain structure). However, a more recent MRI study with more rigorous control groups examined this issue in more detail (Gilbertson et al., 2002). To better control for individual differences in hippocampal size and to control for experiencing a traumatic event but not developing PTSD, this study examined two sets of monozygotic twins, one set where one twin was exposed to trauma and the other was not and a second set where one twin was exposed to trauma and had PTSD and the other twin had no trauma exposure. The results indicated that including these controls groups provided important information. Specifically, among pairs of monozygotic twins in which only one had PTSD, even the twin unaffected by PTSD had a hippocampal volume that was as small as the twin with PTSD and smaller than people exposed to trauma but without PTSD (Gilbertson et al., 2002). These findings suggest that the smaller hippocampal volumes found in both twins was a preexisting condition and not a result of the stressor. These studies show how conclusions regarding research may change when proper control groups (such as identical twins and people who experienced the same trauma but did not have PTSD) are included in the study.

Neurons in the brain use neurotransmitters—chemicals that exist throughout the nervous system—to carry messages from one neuron to another. Different neurotransmitters are primarily responsible for regulating different brain functions, such as movement, learning, memory, and emotion. The most consistently studied neurotransmitter is serotonin: it regulates mood, thoughts, and behavior and is considered to play a key role in anxiety disorders. Low serotonin levels in the cerebral cortex will prevent the transmission of signals from one neuron to the next, inhibiting the ability of the brain to effectively regulate mood, thoughts, and behavior.

What data support the hypothesis that serotonin is important? First, compared with individuals with no psychological disorder, the cerebrospinal fluid (CSF) of people with GAD, panic disorder, and PTSD shows reduced levels of serotonin and its by-products. Although neurotransmitter levels in the spinal cord and the brain are not perfectly correlated, lower levels in the CSF suggest that these deficiencies may also exist in brain synapses (Stein & Hugo, 2004). Second, using a *biochemical challenge*, researchers give study participants a substance that alters their level of serotonin and analyze how the biochemical change is related to increases or decreases in feelings of anxiety. Challenge studies help us understand how decreased serotonin levels may increase feelings of anxiety, but the results are not always consistent (Uhde & Singareddy, 2002). Third, medications known as *selective serotonin reuptake inhibitors* (SSRIs) *increase* serotonin in the neural synapses; people who are prescribed these medications report that their feelings of anxiety *decrease*. Working backward, you might then conclude that less serotonin is related to increased anxiety. Together, all of these studies suggest that decreased serotonin at certain neural synapses is related to feelings of anxiety. However, many of the participants in these studies already had anxiety disorders, and that limits the conclusions that we can make. To conclude that low serotonin levels are a definitive cause of, rather than the result of, anxiety disorders, the studies would need to begin with people who did not have anxiety disorders and would have to manipulate the levels of serotonin in their bodies. Of course, it would not be ethical to conduct this type of study, which could deliberately create anxiety disorders in people.

Another neurotransmitter, gamma aminobutryic acid (GABA), inhibits *postsynaptic activity*, the reaction of the "receiver neuron" when a message is sent from one neuron to another. Reducing this postsynaptic activity inhibits anxious emotion. Thus, medications that allow GABA to inhibit postsynaptic activity effectively are useful for the treatment of anxiety disorders (see "The Treatment of Anxiety Disorders").

A substance called *corticotrophin-releasing factor* (CRF) also may be important for the development of anxiety disorders. CRF neurons are present in areas of the brain that regulate stress and process emotions (Bremner, 2006). These brain areas release CRF, which stimulates production of chemical substances called *adrenocorticotropic hormone* (ACTH) and *beta-endorphins*. We know that when these chemicals are injected into the brains of mice, the animals behave in ways that suggest the presence of depression and anxiety. Similarly, when animals are placed in stressful conditions such as separation and loss, abuse or neglect, and

Figure 4.7 Stress may affect brain functioning.

Early adverse experiences can alter brain functioning, which may in turn increase the likelihood of developing an anxiety disorder.

Adapted from Heim, C., & Nemeroff, C. The impact of early adverse experiences on brain systems involved in the pathophysiology of anxiety and affective disorders. *Biological Psychiatry, 46*, 1509–1522. Copyright © 1999 by the Society of Biological Psychiatry with permission from Elsevier Science Inc.

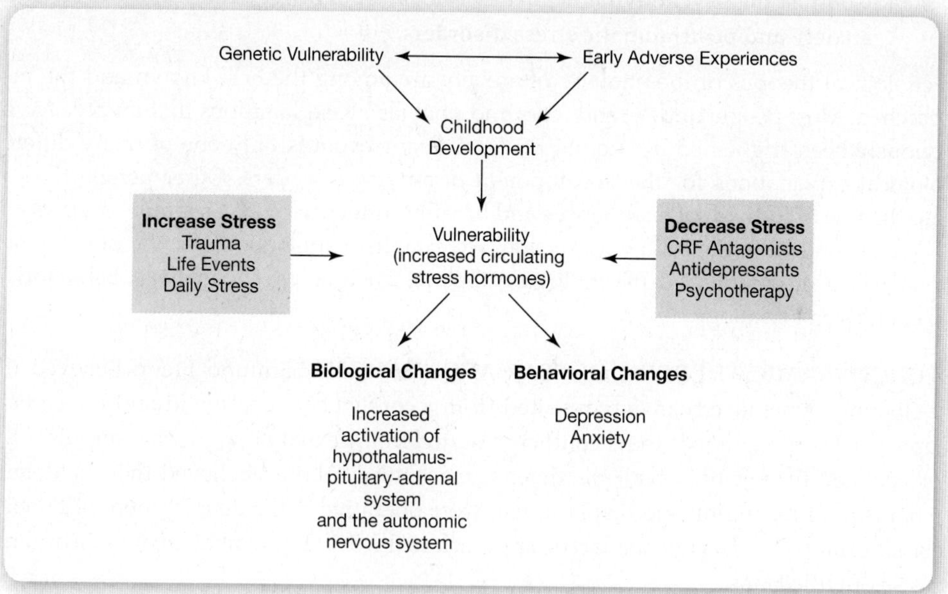

social deprivation, they respond with heightened and persistent CRF activity in the hypothalamus and the amygdala (Sanchez et al., 2001). These data suggest that early life experiences such as loss, separation, or abuse (environmental events) may change brain activity, making someone biologically vulnerable in the same way that genes produce vulnerability. In turn, when this chemical persists, overactivity (a biological contribution) persists, and the person is at risk for later developing emotional disorders such as anxiety and perhaps depression, depending on other biological or environmental contributors (see Figure 4.7).

Neuroscience offers exciting new ways to understand anxiety disorders. However, many challenges remain. Translating these neuroimaging findings into specific recommendations regarding diagnostic tests or treatment recommendations for any one person remains difficult (Savitz et al., 2013). In addition, many studies compare people with anxiety disorders only to people with no disorder. This means that we can conclude only that healthy controls differ from those of people with an anxiety disorder. We cannot conclude that a particular brain abnormality is found only in people with anxiety disorders. To draw that conclusion, we would have to examine the brain activity of people with other types of disorders and determine whether people with other disorders (such as depression or eating disorders) did or did not have the same abnormality.

TEMPERAMENT AND BEHAVIORAL INHIBITION *Temperament* describes individual behavioral differences that are present at a very early age, perhaps even at birth. **Behavioral inhibition**, a concept first proposed by Jerome Kagan (1982), is a temperamental feature that exists in approximately 20% of children. Children with behavioral inhibition withdraw from (or fail to approach) novel people, objects, or situations. They do not speak spontaneously in the presence of strangers, and they cry and cling to their mothers rather than approach other children to play. Children with behavioral inhibition are more likely to show anxiety reactions and to have childhood anxiety disorders, in particular, phobias (Gladstone et al., 2005; Hayward et al., 1998). Behavioral inhibition, identifiable at 4 months of age, may be a unique risk factor for the later development of social anxiety disorder (Clauss & Blackford, 2012). However, this relationship is not absolute; not every infant with behavioral inhibition develops social anxiety disorder. Furthermore, not every person with social anxiety disorder was a behaviorally inhibited infant. Therefore, although behavioral inhibition may increase the likelihood of developing social anxiety disorder, it does not account for every single case of the disorder.

Psychological Perspective

LO 4.14 Contrast the psychodynamic, behavioral, and cognitive theories of the onset of anxiety and posttraumatic stress disorders.

Psychological theories of the etiology of anxiety are among the best known and the most researched. Most people understand fears and phobias by explanations that involve having previously been frightened by the object. A traumatic event is only one of many different etiological explanations for the development of anxiety disorders. Other perspectives include the role of individual experiences and broader influences such as family environment and social context. In the following section, we examine explanations for the development of fear based on established psychological theories such as psychoanalysis, behaviorism, and cognitive psychology.

PSYCHODYNAMIC THEORIES OF FEAR ACQUISITION Sigmund Freud believed that free-floating (generalized) anxiety resulted from a conflict between the id and the ego (see Chapter 1). He thought that these conflicts resulted from sexual or aggressive impulses that overwhelmed the person's available defense mechanisms. Freud believed that the defense mechanisms of repression and displacement were operative in the development of phobias. A classic example of the psychoanalytic approach to the development of anxiety disorders is the case of Little Hans.

> Hans was a 5-year-old boy born in nineteenth-century Victorian Europe. After watching a carriage horse fall down and after playing horses with a friend who fell down, Hans developed a fear that a horse might fall down or bite him. This fear later extended to any horse-drawn vehicle, which he avoided at all cost. Hans refused to leave home when these vehicles might be present. He also was very concerned about his genitalia, fearing that his penis was not sufficiently large. His mother once told him not to touch his "widdler" or she would call a doctor to cut it off. Hans's father asked Freud for assistance. Using detailed information from conversations between Hans and his father (provided mostly by the father), Freud decided that Hans's fear and fixation on his genitalia represented his sexual feelings toward his mother, feelings that Freud called the Oedipus complex. Freud also noted that Hans was particularly afraid of horses with a black bit in their mouths, which Freud interpreted as a symbolic representation of his father's mustache. The horse, like Hans's father, was an object both admired and feared and was obviously a rival for the affection of Hans's mother. Because he could not deal with them directly, Hans displaced all of these feelings onto horses, resulting in fear and avoidance.

Although many alternative theories explain Hans's fears (e.g., classical conditioning, social learning theory; see Chapter 1), this case was extremely influential in the development of psychoanalytic theory in the early part of the twentieth century. Today, its overall influence has decreased markedly.

BEHAVIORAL THEORIES OF FEAR ACQUISITION Conditioning theory has a prominent role in explaining fear acquisition even though no single behavioral theory adequately accounts for the etiology of all anxiety disorders. Current behavioral theories are much more complicated than the story of Little Albert, the boy who learned to fear a white rat when it was paired with an aversive stimulus (see Chapter 1). The acquisition of fears through classical conditioning remains a primary explanation for the onset of anxiety disorders and PTSD. However, classical conditioning theories cannot provide an explanation for all anxiety disorders, and thus there are other behavioral explanations.

In addition to direct conditioning theory, people sometimes acquire fears through other forms of learning known as *vicarious learning theory* (see Chapter 1) and *information transmission* (Rachman, 1977). Consider the following example.

Lindsay and Lisa are twins. Lindsay was selected to sing a solo ("Jingle Bell Rock") at the annual Winter Holiday Pageant. She was nervous about the solo but also excited about the opportunity to perform in public. When she went on stage, she opened her mouth, but she was nervous and the words would not come out. The audience thought it was part of the act, and they laughed out loud. Lindsay was very embarrassed and ran off stage crying. Lisa, who was in the audience, saw everyone laughing at her sister. Now Lisa refuses to perform in front of an audience, and this week, she failed her English class because she refused to get up and give a speech.

Although in the past Lisa would get a little nervous when she had to speak in front of the class, after watching Lindsay's traumatic event, Lisa acquired a fear of performing in front of others, indicating that she had developed social anxiety disorder. This process is known as *observational learning* or *vicarious conditioning*. Encouragingly, not everyone who experiences a traumatic event develops a disorder via direct conditioning. Remember Malika? She developed a fear of flying, but her friends did not, although they had the same experience on the plane. How does conditioning theory account for this difference? One explanation is that previous positive experiences with the same situation may protect against the later effects of a traumatic event. Positive experiences may provide immunity against the development of anxiety or traumatic disorders in the same way that a vaccination prevents children from acquiring the measles. Rhesus monkeys, for example, can be "immunized" against a fear of toy snakes (Mineka & Cook, 1986) by first observing other monkeys who were not afraid of a toy snake. When they later saw monkeys who behaved fearfully in the presence of snakes, these "immunized" monkeys did not acquire the fear.

A third method by which anxiety disorders can develop is through information transfer, which means that a person instructs someone that a situation or object should be feared. Parents must instruct children about the dangers of crossing a busy street or the need to refrain from inserting objects (such as a knife) into an electrical outlet. When asked to report how their fears developed, a subset of children (39%) identified information transfer as the mechanism as compared to direct conditioning (37%) and modeling (56%) (Ollendick & King, 1991).

Current theories about the etiology of anxiety acknowledge that biological and psychological-environmental factors are both important elements. Contemporary models of learning theory acknowledge biological factors (genetics and temperament), environmental vulnerabilities (conditioning and social/cultural learning history), and stress factors (controllability and predictability of stressful events, conditioning experiences). All of these elements affect the quality and intensity of the conditioning event and therefore the anxiety and fear that develop as a result of the conditioning experience (Mineka & Zinbarg, 2006; see Figure 4.8).

COGNITIVE THEORIES OF FEAR ACQUISITION As is the case with behavioral theories, there is no one cognitive approach to anxiety. However, all approaches assume that anxiety disorders result from inaccurate interpretations of internal events ("My heart is racing, so I must be having a heart attack") or external events ("Here I am giving a speech and my boss is yawning—I must be really boring"). Cognitive theories propose that people with anxiety disorders process information differently and this leads to the development of anxiety (McNally, 1995). Aaron Beck, perhaps the most dominant cognitive theorist, suggested that anxiety results from maladaptive thoughts that automatically interpret an ambiguous situation (e.g., "I am short of breath") in a negative fashion (e.g., "I must be having a heart attack"; Beck & Emery, 1985). From a cognitive perspective, anxiety disorders develop because people misinterpret ambiguous situations as dangerous, resulting in physiological and cognitive distress. Because they never attempt to determine whether their beliefs are true, these negative thoughts maintain the presence of the disorder.

A second cognitive theory, and one relevant for panic disorder, is the *fear of fear* model (Goldstein & Chambless, 1978). This theory proposes that after the first panic attack, the person becomes sensitive to any bodily symptom and interprets any change in physiological state (e.g., a sudden heart flutter) as the signal of an impending panic attack (see

Figure 4.8 A contemporary theory of fear acquisition.

Although early theories of learning did not adequately account for fear acquisition, revised models take into account the presence of biological and psychological vulnerabilities as well as environmental stressors that may be present before, during, or after the traumatic (conditioning) event.

Adapted from Mineka, S., & Zinbarg, R. A contemporary learning theory perspective on the etiology of anxiety disorders: It's not what you thought it was. *The American Psychologist, 61*, 10 26. Copyright © 2006 by the American Psychological Association.

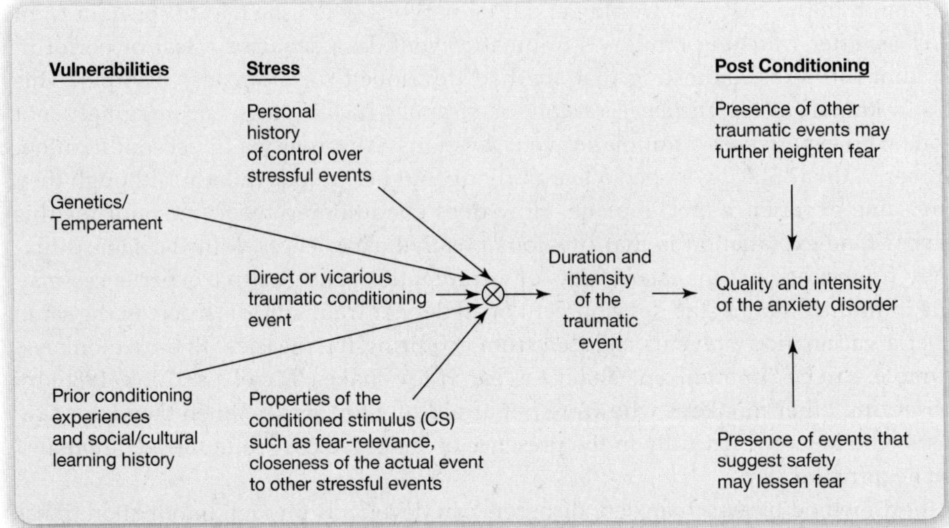

Figure 4.9). This leads to a vicious cycle of worry, which then increases the likelihood of a panic attack and further increases worry. A third cognitive model is *anxiety sensitivity*, which is a belief that anxiety symptoms will result in negative consequences such as illness, embarrassment, or more anxiety (Taylor, 1995). Anxiety sensitivity is hypothesized to result from several factors, including previous panic attacks, biological vulnerability to panic, and personality needs (to avoid embarrassment or illness or to maintain control). In this model, we see again how biology and learning interact to produce thoughts that lead to the inaccurate interpretation of future events.

Figure 4.9 The fear of fear model.

After a panic attack, a person often worries about having another. This worry can create both physical and emotional arousal, which can result in overattention to normal physical symptoms. When these occur, they are overinterpreted as a signal of another panic attack.

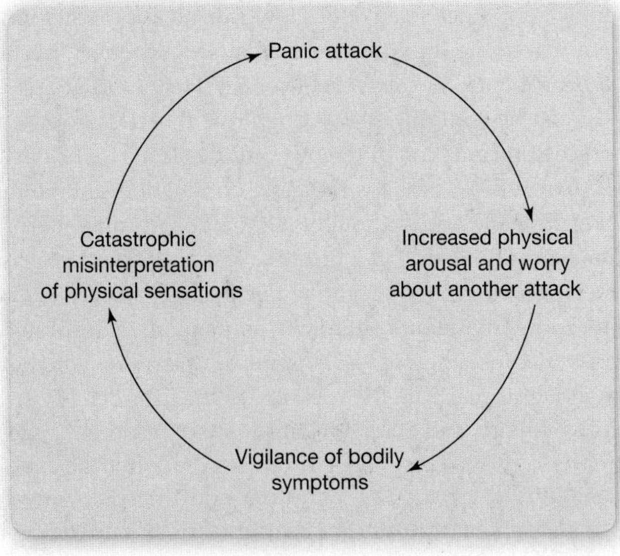

Cognitive theories have evolved since their introduction 20 years ago, and most researchers now postulate that negative and/or distorted cognitions are important in the *maintenance* of anxiety disorders. There is less evidence that cognitions are the primary mechanism by which disorders initially develop. Models of panic disorder (fear of fear and anxiety sensitivity), for example, propose that an anxiety disorder develops when a person misinterprets the physical symptoms of a panic attack. However, these theories often do not adequately explain how those cognitive biases first came to exist. The specific contribution of cognitions to etiology is actually difficult to identify without longitudinal studies that follow people before they develop the disorder. Studies of people at high risk for developing an anxiety disorder (e.g., children of parents with anxiety disorders) may be necessary in order to understand the role of cognition in the etiology of anxiety.

To summarize, both biological and psychological/environmental factors appear to be important for the development of anxiety and trauma- and stressor-related disorders. Biological influences include genetic contributions as well as potential neurotransmitter and hormonal abnormalities. On the psychological/environmental side, conditioning experiences explain the acquisition of some, but not all, anxiety disorders. Family factors may be important in modeling or reinforcing anxiety responses, and environmental stressors may affect not only emotional functioning but also neuroanatomy. Although much remains to be learned, it is clear that the etiology of anxiety disorders defies a simple explanation.

Learning Objective Summaries

LO 4.13 Describe the biological factors that may contribute to the onset of anxiety and posttraumatic stress disorders including family and genetic influences, neuroanatomy, temperament, and behavioral inhibition.

Biochemical theories regarding the etiology of anxiety disorders have investigated the role of many different neurotransmitters, but the strongest evidence exists for the neurotransmitter serotonin, which has an important role in the regulation of emotion. The amygdala and the limbic system are neuroanatomical structures in the brain that are important in the processing of emotional states such as fear. Twin and family studies support the role of genetics in the etiology of anxiety, OCD, and trauma- and stressor-related disorders, although at the current time, the evidence suggests that an anxious temperament, not a specific anxiety disorder, is most likely inherited.

LO 4.14 Contrast the psychodynamic, behavioral, and cognitive theories of the onset of anxiety and posttraumatic stress disorders.

Strict psychoanalytic interpretations regarding the etiology of anxiety disorders have fallen out of favor. From a behavioral perspective, anxiety disorders may develop as a result of direct conditioning, observational learning, or information transfer. From a cognitive perspective, anxiety results from maladaptive thoughts that automatically interpret an ambiguous situation in a negative fashion, resulting in physiological and cognitive distress.

Critical Thinking Question

How do cognitive theories of the etiology of anxiety disorder differ from traditional behavioral theories?

The Treatment of Anxiety and Trauma- and Stressor-Related Disorders

It is important to note that because the DSM-5 criteria are so new, studies of treatment outcome have not been conducted on individuals who meet the new diagnostic criteria. Therefore, in this section, we discuss the literature based on study samples diagnosed using DSM-IV-TR.

The treatment of these disorders uses several different approaches including biological, behavioral and cognitive-behavioral, and psychodynamic interventions. Psychodynamic theory is commonly applied in clinical settings but has not been the subject of much empirical research. In contrast, biological and behavioral or cognitive-behavioral approaches have substantial empirical support. All appear to be efficacious, resulting in remission rates of about 70% among people who are treated. In some instances, participants in research studies have a less complicated symptom pattern and do not have the comorbid disorders that are commonly seen in patients in nonresearch outpatient clinics. Because researchers are now only beginning to study how to implement the empirically supported treatments in traditional outpatient clinics, we do not know whether these treatments are as successful when administered to people who have anxiety disorders together with other disorders, such as substance abuse.

Biological Treatments

LO 4.15 Identify efficacious pharmacological treatments for anxiety and posttraumatic stress disorders.

Today biological treatments usually come in the form of medication, but, as we shall see, other treatments for anxiety disorders including neurosurgery exist. Historically, somatic treatments consisted of bed rest, exercise, and work at simple tasks. Today somatic treatments are based on modern knowledge of neuroanatomy and neurochemistry, allowing these interventions to target the brain directly.

MEDICATION As we noted in the section on etiology, several disorders (panic disorder, GAD, and PTSD) are associated with the depletion of serotonin in the neural synapses, which in turn prevents the neurons from functioning properly. At the end of the presynaptic neuron are terminals that release serotonin into the synapse and other terminals that take the serotonin back up into the presynaptic neuron in a process called *reuptake* (see Figure 4.10). When the postsynaptic neuron receives enough serotonin, the neuron fires, and the process continues. Without enough serotonin in the synapse, the signal does not pass to the next neuron as it should. One way to increase brain serotonin is to stimulate the neuron to release more of the neurotransmitter. An alternative is to block its reuptake, allowing the serotonin to remain in the synapse longer. Medications known as **selective serotonin reuptake inhibitors** (SSRIs) are thought to correct serotonin imbalances in this manner by increasing the time that serotonin remains in the synapse.

Watch YOUR BRAIN ON DRUGS

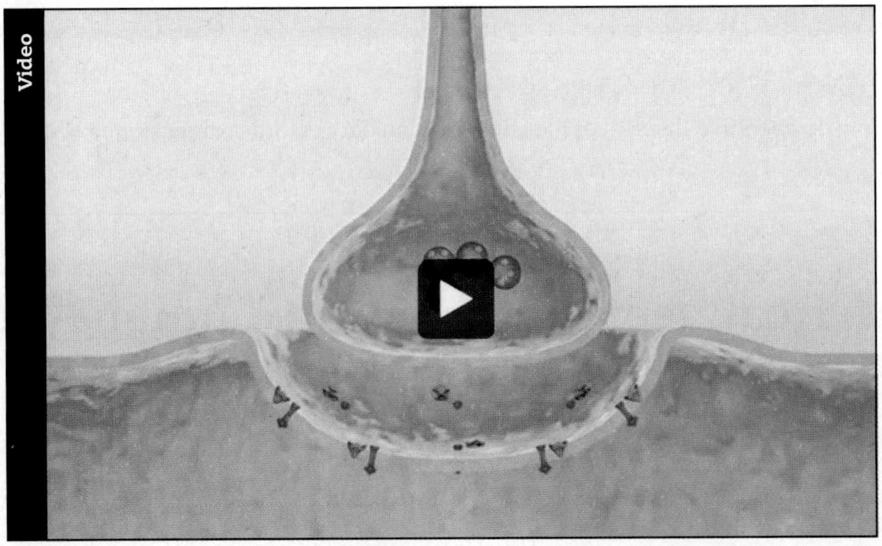

Video

Figure 4.10 How SSRIs work.

SSRIs block the neuron's normal reuptake mechanism, allowing serotonin to remain in the synapse and increasing the likelihood that it will land on the next neuron's receptor.

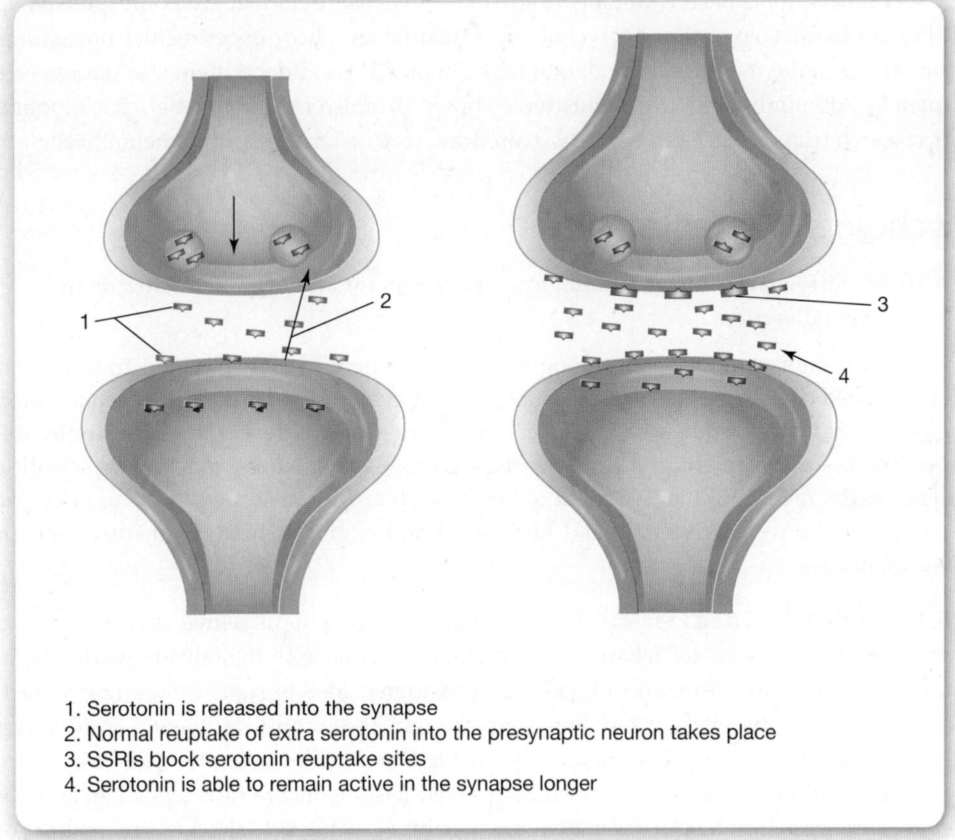

SSRIs, such as Prozac, Luvox, and Zoloft, are now the biological treatment of choice for the anxiety disorders; at least 40 studies demonstrate their efficacy compared with pill placebo. Positive treatment outcome has been demonstrated for panic disorder with or without agoraphobia (e.g., Andriasano et al., 2013; Freire et al., 2014), social anxiety disorder (e.g., Davis et al., 2014), GAD (Bandelow et al., 2013), and PTSD (Ipser & Stein, 2012; Steckler & Risbrough, 2012). The only exception is for specific phobia, for which there are no controlled studies (Antony & Barlow, 2002). Although the medications work better than placebos, they are not efficacious for everyone. Many people need to remain on these medications for an extended period of time and perhaps indefinitely because relapse is common when the medication is withdrawn. Using these medications with children and adolescents requires extra caution. The Food and Drug Administration issued a warning regarding the possibility that among children, adolescents, and young adults with depression, SSRIs may increase the risk of suicidal thinking. Although no such increase has been reported in patients with anxiety disorders, children and adolescents should be monitored closely for the presence of any suicidal thoughts or plans.

GABA is another neurotransmitter that may be associated with anxiety disorders (Stein & Hugo, 2004), although the evidence is weaker for GABA than for serotonin. Drugs known as *benzodiazepines* (tranquilizers such as Valium and Xanax) allow GABA to transmit nerve signals more effectively, which in turn reduces anxiety. Benzodiazepines have efficacy for panic disorder with or without agoraphobia (Freire et al., 2014), GAD (Bandelow et al., 2013), and social anxiety disorder (Davidson, 2004). In the 1970s and 1980s, benzodiazepines were the treatment of choice for anxiety disorders, and they were prescribed quite freely. However, the drugs may cause physical and psychological dependence if they are used for a long period of time. These medications must always be withdrawn under a doctor's supervision because seizures may occur if the withdrawal is not done properly.

Therefore, though efficacious, these medications are not considered the first choice for the treatment of anxiety disorders.

OTHER SOMATIC THERAPIES In addition to psychosurgery, new and potentially exciting interventions have been developed to treat anxiety disorders that are nonresponsive to traditional pharmacological and psychological treatments. These experimental procedures include transcranial magnetic stimulation (see Chapter 11) and deep brain stimulation (see Chapter 7). Although these treatments have shown promise (Mashour et al., 2005), many more research trials are needed before we can draw conclusions regarding their efficacy.

Psychological Treatments

LO 4.16 Identify efficacious psychological treatments for anxiety and posttraumatic stress disorders.

Psychological interventions were among the first treatments for anxiety and trauma- and stressor-related disorders. Interventions are usually developed for adults and then adapted for children. However, in the case of anxiety disorders, some of the earliest case studies described successful treatment of children with phobias. Even so, today much more scientific evidence exists regarding the treatment of adults with anxiety disorders than for children. We next describe psychodynamic and behavioral and cognitive-behavioral treatment for people of all ages.

PSYCHODYNAMIC TREATMENT Psychodynamic treatment uses free association and dream interpretation as a reflection of the patient's experience in the outside world. As in the case of Little Hans, fears and phobias are considered merely signs of internal conflict. Treatment involves discovering and "working through" these conflicts. Some therapists still use psychoanalysis and psychodynamically oriented treatments to treat anxiety disorders. Modern adaptations of psychodynamically oriented treatments are now available, and because they are briefer in length, they are more suitable for clinical trials. A recent analysis of 14 studies examining the efficacy of psychodynamic therapies for anxiety disorders found them to be more efficacious than control conditions and equally efficacious to other psychological treatments (Keefe et al., 2014). One form of psychodynamically oriented treatment is interpersonal psychotherapy (IPT; Klerman et al., 1984), which targets interpersonal disputes and conflicts, interpersonal role transitions, and complicated grief reactions. IPT has been tested in social anxiety disorder (Lipsitz et al., 1999; Dagöö et al., 2014) and PTSD (Bleiberg & Markowitz, 2005; Markowitz et al., 2015) with encouraging results. Larger controlled clinical trials are required before IPT can be recommended as a primary treatment for anxiety disorders.

BEHAVIORAL AND COGNITIVE-BEHAVIORAL TREATMENT After 40 years of study, compelling empirical data indicate that behavioral therapy (BT) and cognitive-behavioral therapy (CBT) interventions are the psychosocial treatments of choice for adults, adolescents, and children with anxiety, and trauma- and stressor-related disorders. The many different forms of BT and CBT all incorporate a procedure known as **exposure** (i.e., facing your fears to get over them). For example, a person who fears dogs must have contact with a dog. Therapists use many different methods to provide exposure opportunities. For some fears, such as those of dogs or heights, exposure can occur through real-life experiences (called *in vivo exposure*). For other fears, such as being in a plane crash or becoming seriously ill from touching germs, conducting exposure involves instructing the person to imagine the feared event (*imaginal exposure*). To treat panic disorder, exposure therapy uses various exercises (e.g., running up and down the stairs) to create the physical symptoms of panic, such as shortness of breath and racing heart in the patient. In this way, the person is exposed to what he or she fears—physical symptoms associated with panic. Despite the seemingly simple nature of this treatment, determining exactly what the exposure situation should be, how long and how often it should occur, and who should conduct the sessions are all-important factors that contribute to its success. There is now a large body of empirical literature indicating that BT and CBT are efficacious treatments for anxiety disorders (Cuijpers et al., 2014; Gould et al., 2012; Reinholt & Krogh, 2014). When it is done correctly, 70% of people with anxiety disorders show improvement (80% for specific phobia; Barlow, 2002; Compton et al., 2004). Similar rates of improvement are found with exposure therapy or cognitive processing therapy (which combines exposure and cognitive therapy) for veterans with PTSD (Haagen et al., 2015; Steenkamp et al., 2015), although even after treatment, 60 to 72% of veterans still retain their diagnosis (Steenkamp et al., 2015). This means that although their symptoms are less severe, they are still present to a significant degree.

One challenge for therapists who wish to use exposure therapy is finding or developing appropriate exposure situations. New technologies such as virtual reality now allow therapists to expose people to commonly feared situations without having to leave their office (see "Research Hot Topic: Virtual Reality Therapy"). Virtual reality/virtual environments are being used with people with social anxiety disorder (Anderson et al., 2013; Wong et al., 2014; Yuen et al., 2013) and veterans with PTSD (Gonçalves et al., 2012; Rothbaum et al., 2014). With the burgeoning technologies now available, therapist are beginning to use the Internet (Alaoui et al., 2015; Ljótsson et al., 2013; Mewton et al., 2012; Neubauer et al., 2013) and phone/tablet apps (Bunnell & Beidel, 2013; Kuhn et al., 2014) in order to deliver these efficacious treatments to people who otherwise would not be able to receive them.

Sometimes the combination of exposure and other treatments enhances the efficacy of treatment. Because people with social anxiety disorder avoid social interactions, they often do not have the basic skills needed for social communication (when it is a good time to talk to someone, how to be assertive without being aggressive). In this instance, social skills training (SST) is combined with exposure. SST teaches skills, usually conducted in a group setting, allowing for members to observe the therapist, who models the skill, and then practice in the group, which provides opportunities to rehearse skills in a safe, supportive setting. Combining SST with exposure therapy produces positive treatment outcomes for children, adolescents, and adults with social anxiety disorder (Beidel et al., 2007, 2014; Herbert et al., 2009).

CBT combines exposure with cognitive restructuring in an attempt to change negative cognitions. In cognitive restructuring, a therapist asks the person to face an

Research HOT Topic

Virtual Reality Therapy

The most efficacious treatment for specific phobias is behavior therapy whose key component is exposure to the feared object, situation, or event. A person afraid of heights can be taken to a high place and can learn to lose this fear by using operant conditioning strategies. However, when the specific feared event is a plane crash, this event cannot be re-created. Therefore, therapists need an alternative means of exposure. Virtual reality is becoming a common tool for the treatment of certain specific phobias (heights, flying). The patient is fitted with a head-mounted display that has screens for each eye, earphones, and a device that tracks head, hand, and/or foot movements. When used to treat fear of flying (Rothbaum et al., 2002), scenarios consist of sitting in a passenger airline compartment during takeoff, flying in both calm and stormy weather, and landing. Noise such as voices of flight attendants and engine noises and vibrations such as the sensations caused by weather are added. Virtual reality therapy appears to be as effective as standard exposure treatments for phobias of heights and flying (see Rothbaum et al., 2002), and emerging evidence suggests its use for treating social anxiety disorder and PTSD. With respect to the treatment of PTSD, virtual reality therapy is now being used to treat veterans returning from the conflicts in Iraq and Afghanistan.

anxiety-producing event (e.g., making a formal speech) and to reflect on any negative thoughts that occur. For example, the thought might be "I'm going to mispronounce a word and make a fool of myself, and everyone will think I'm an idiot." The therapist then asks the person to enter the situation and see whether this "worst thing" actually happens. Of course, it does not happen. The therapist may also ask the patient to generate alternative positive or "coping" cognitions to counteract the negative thoughts; for example, "The audience knows that anyone can make a mistake—they will not see me as a complete fool." Over a series of exposure assignments, the patient's anxiety decreases and negative thoughts become less frequent.

Although BT and CBT treatments are efficacious, they do not work for everyone. While retaining many behavioral principles and procedures, some researchers have developed newer interventions and strategies such as **mindfulness** (being aware of one's experience "in the moment" and doing so in a nonjudgmental fashion) and **acceptance and commitment therapy** (ACT) (teaching mindfulness skills that allows one to accept and deal with distressing thoughts and feelings, clarifying one's values, and then using those values to change behavior) (http://www.actmindfully.com.au/acceptance_&_commitment_therapy). A core feature of ACT is experiential avoidance, which is the "unwillingness to remain in contact with particular private experiences (e.g., bodily sensations, emotions, thoughts, memories, behavioral predispositions) and takes steps to alter the form or frequency of these events and the contexts that occasion them" (Hayes et al., 1996, 1154). The rationale behind ACT fits very well with the goals of CBT and BT, and randomized controlled trials indicate efficacy for the ACT approach for the treatment of social anxiety disorder (Craske et al., 2014; Kocovski et al., 2013) and GAD (Hoge et al., 2013; Millstein et al., 2015).

Ethics and Responsibility

LO 4.17 Discuss the ethical issues that need to be considered when deciding to treat someone immediately after a traumatic event.

Critical Incident Stress Debriefing (CISD) is designed to prevent the development of PTSD by intervening very quickly after a traumatic event has occurred. Lasting 3 to 4 hours, CISD is typically a one-session treatment that is provided in a group session within 24 to 48 hours of the event (Lohr et al., 2007). During the session, group members are (1) encouraged to discuss and process the event, (2) told the PTSD symptoms that they are likely to experience, and (3) discouraged from leaving the meeting once the session has begun (Lilienfeld, 2007). Despite the goals of this rapid intervention technique, empirical data suggest that CISD may actually do more harm than good. Randomized controlled trials indicate that CISD not only is ineffective (Litz et al., 2002) but also in several instances has actually been harmful with patients assigned to CISD exhibiting more PTSD or other anxiety symptoms at follow-up than the control groups do (Bisson et al., 1997; Mayou et al., 2000; Sijbrandij et al., 2006). Interestingly, people who participate in CISD report that subjectively they feel better even when objective measurement indicates the opposite. This contradiction can be explained by the concept of *resilience* (Lilienfeld, 2007; see "Research Hot Topic: Trauma Grief, and Resilience"). Most people exposed to a trauma do *not* develop PTSD. Therefore, most people assigned to CISD would not have developed PTSD even without any intervention. Furthermore, the fact that they did worse than the control group suggests that CISD may be interfering with the natural resilience process. Another intervention that was used in the past to treat children with PTSD was "rebirthing" therapy (see Chapter 15). No empirical evidence supports the use of this procedure, and its use has led to severe injury or death; rebirthing is not endorsed by mental health professionals who work with children (American Academy of Child and Adolescent Psychiatry, 2010). When therapists develop or provide interventions, it is crucial that the treatments work or at least not harm (or have the potential to harm) their patients. If the choice is between providing a potentially harmful treatment or doing nothing, psychologists should follow the words of the Hippocratic oath and "First, do no harm."

Explore ETHICS AND RESPONSIBILITY

Learning Objective Summaries

LO 4.15 Identify efficacious pharmacological treatments for anxiety and posttraumatic stress disorders.

Several different classes of medications are used for the treatment of anxiety disorders and trauma- and stress-related disorders, but the first choice is the class known as the *selective serotonin reuptake inhibitors* (SSRIs). Another class of medications, *benzodiazepines,* though efficacious, is not considered the first choice for the treatment of anxiety disorders because of the medications' potential for physical and psychological addiction.

LO 4.16 Identify efficacious psychological treatments for anxiety and posttraumatic stress disorders.

Various psychological interventions are efficacious for anxiety and posttraumatic stress disorders. Newer psychodynamic treatments, such as interpersonal psychotherapy, are efficacious when compared to control conditions. By far, the most empirical data are in support of behavioral and cognitive-behavioral treatments. *Exposure therapy* is the most supported treatment for all of these disorders and particularly for PTSD. Newer interventions such as mindfulness therapy appear to be efficacious when compared with no treatment control groups, but they do not as yet have a database of evidence as substantial as what exists for the behavioral and cognitive-behavioral therapies.

LO 4.17 Discuss the ethical issues that need to be considered when deciding to treat someone immediately after a traumatic event.

As noted in this chapter, traumatic events are common in the general population and the most common response to these events is resilience or recovery; symptoms may be present for a few days to weeks, but then they will dissipate. Intervening in the treatment of trauma too early may actually worsen the symptoms and prevent recovery. An ethical approach to treatment is to monitor symptoms for several weeks and offer treatment only if there is no indication that the symptoms will remit on their own.

Critical Thinking Question

What is the common—and crucial—ingredient for behavioral and cognitive-behavioral therapy for anxiety disorders?

Real SCIENCE Real LIFE

Ricky: Treatment of a Severe Specific Phobia

THE PATIENT

Ricky is a 32-year-old auto mechanic. He was referred to a psychologist by his physician because he had lost a substantial amount of weight (40 pounds in the past three months) and vomited after every meal because of the "texture" of the food. He complained of being hungry all the time and had sharp stomach pains. Ricky had restricted his food and drink intake in order to deal with the vomiting. His refusal to eat meals prepared by his wife caused strain on their marriage.

THE PROBLEM

Ricky dated the onset of his "eating problem" to several months ago. He was at a football game with some friends. Ricky was eating a steak sandwich when he bit into something that tasted strange. When he spit it out, he discovered that he had eaten half of a large roach, which was in the steak sandwich. Since that night, Ricky began to restrict his food intake. First, it was just crumbly "meaty" things like hamburger, as that was the texture that reminded him of the event. However, he reported constant feelings of revulsion and anxiety regarding the eating of an insect. He worried that everything he put in his mouth could have roach parts (or insect parts) mixed into it during the production process. This worry led to vomiting uncontrollably after each meal. By the time he met with the psychologist, his diet was restricted to crème-filled chocolate cupcakes and milk.

ASSESSING THE SITUATION

First, what would you say is the etiology of this disorder? How did it develop? Second, how would you treat it? Design a plan to help Ricky get over his phobia.

THE TREATMENT

After a thorough evaluation, the psychologist diagnosed Ricky with specific phobia, other type. The treatment plan consisted of two parts: imaginal exposure and in vivo exposure. Imaginal exposure was directed at the original conditioning event, exposing him to the images of himself at the football game and biting into the roach, including reimagining the texture of the roach in his mouth, the bitter taste, the acrid smell, and the feelings of horror and revulsion as he realizes that he is eating an insect. In the initial sessions, Ricky became very upset, and during the second session, he vomited into the therapist's trash can. By session 10, he was saying that he could imagine the scene and imagine the taste, but it was no longer creating anxiety and only minimal revulsion. In vivo exposure was then introduced. Together with the therapist, Ricky created a hierarchy of foods, beginning with those that were least anxiety producing to those that were most anxiety producing (a hamburger). Ricky moved through the eight-step hierarchy and did not move to the next step until he was not feeling any distress when eating the lower-hierarchy food (i.e., he did not move to step 4 until he did not feel distress eating the food in step 3).

THE TREATMENT OUTCOME

Treatment lasted 4 months at which time Ricky was not restricting from eating any foods (except steak sandwiches). Six months later, he reported that he had gained back 25 pounds and was happy with his weight, as was his physician. Although his marital relationship had improved, he and his wife decided to enter marital therapy to deal with long-standing issues that preceded the onset of his specific phobia.

Key Terms

acceptance and commitment therapy (ACT), p. 158
agoraphobia, p. 123
anxiety, p. 116
anxiety disorders, p. 121
behavioral inhibition, p. 149
exposure, p. 158
fight-or-flight, p. 116
generalized anxiety disorder, p. 126
heritability, p. 145
mindfulness, p. 158
panic attack, p. 118
panic disorder, p. 123
parasympathetic nervous system, p. 117
posttraumatic stress disorder, p. 138
selective serotonin reuptake inhibitors, p. 154
separation anxiety disorder, p. 135
social anxiety disorder, p. 128
specific phobias, p. 132
sympathetic nervous system, p. 116
trait anxiety, p. 146
vasovagal syncope, p. 134
worry, p. 119

Chapter 5

Obsessive-Compulsive and Impulse Control Disorders

Chapter Learning Objectives

What Is Obsessive-Compulsive Disorder (OCD)?	**LO 5.1**	Recognize the symptoms of OCD and differentiate obsessions from compulsions.
	LO 5.2	Describe the prevalence of OCD, considering factors such as sex, race, and ethnicity.
	LO 5.3	Explain how the symptoms of OCD vary with age.
What Are Obsessive-Compulsive Related Disorders (OCRDs)?	**LO 5.4**	Recognize the features of body dysmorphic disorder (BDD) and areas of overlap and dissimilarity with OCD.
	LO 5.5	Define the characteristics of hoarding disorder that differentiate it from OCD.

LO 5.6 Describe the symptoms of trichotillomania (TTM) and how they are similar to and different from OCD.

LO 5.7 Explain the features of excoriation disorder as they overlap or diverge from the symptoms of OCD and TTM.

What Are Impulse Control Disorders?

LO 5.8 Describe the diagnostic criteria and clinical features of pyromania.

LO 5.9 Recognize the diagnostic criteria and clinical features of kleptomania.

Etiology of Obsessive-Compulsive and Impulse Control Disorders

LO 5.10 Describe the biological factors that may contribute to the onset of OCD.

LO 5.11 Utilize the psychological theories of anxiety acquisition to explain the etiology of OCD.

LO 5.12 Understand the possible genetic and neuroanatomical factors that may contribute to onset of OCRDs, comparing and contrasting across these disorders and with OCD.

LO 5.13 Explain the possible psychological causes for OCRDs with a primary focus on cognitive and behavioral factors.

LO 5.14 Describe possible biological and psychological causes of pyromania and kleptomania.

Treatment of Obsessive-Compulsive and Impulse Control Disorders

LO 5.15 Identify biological treatments, including medication and psychosurgery, that research shows are effective for treating OCD.

LO 5.16 Describe the components typically included in psychological treatment for OCD.

LO 5.17 Understand what research tells us about the use of biological treatment (medication) for OCRDs.

LO 5.18 Describe psychological treatments for OCRDs with attention to cognitive-behavioral approaches.

LO 5.19 Identify biological and psychological treatments that may be effective for pyromania and kleptomania.

Jace is a freshman in college. He decided to attend the university in his hometown so that he could live at home and continue to receive help from his parents. He knew his behavior was unusual, but he just couldn't change the way he did things. He would only make it through college if his parents were nearby.

Even as a young child, Jace worried about getting things right; he never wanted to make any mistakes or forget anything. He checked in with his parents or teachers to make sure he was doing things correctly, and he always checked his schoolwork carefully, sometimes more than once, to be sure everything was properly completed. For many years, Jace's parents and teachers thought his concern about correctness was just a sign of his conscientiousness. He earned good grades and was a well-behaved student.

When Jace entered high school, however, the work got harder and his worries grew stronger. He couldn't get the thought of making a mistake or losing something out of his head. He started to check his work more often and for longer amounts of time. He also began asking his parents the same questions over and over to reassure himself that he hadn't made a mistake. To reduce his fears, he started taking more notes; he wrote down things he heard on podcasts or saw on the Internet. He copied over his class notes multiple times. Jace's room began to fill up with pages and scraps of paper with notes scribbled on them. When he learned to drive, he had trouble leaving his car without checking the door multiple times to be sure it was locked. He was afraid of what might happen if he made a mistake. Jace's parents tried to help him; they were worriers themselves, so they understood his concerns and wanted to help him in any way possible. His mother, in particular, tried to help by checking Jace's homework and reassuring him that he had done things correctly.

Now, in college, things were only getting worse. The flexibility of college life made it even harder for Jace to get his work done, and he began to check more things. He was spending hours and hours taking and copying notes, reviewing his class assignments, and checking locks in his car and at home. When he got out of his seat in class, he spent 10 to 15 minutes checking the desk and floor to be sure he hadn't dropped anything. His parents still tried to help, reviewing his homework and answering his repeated questions, but the problems were getting too big. Jace was at risk of failing freshman year.

You may be able to relate to Jace's worries about doing well in school, and you may sometimes check in with a friend, family member, or professor to be sure you remember something you heard correctly. In Jace's case, however, what started as potentially *normal* worry and careful attention to completing tasks gradually grew into thoughts, fears, and behaviors that consumed his days and kept him from being able to function at a level that matched his capabilities. As we'll see later, Jace's parents also tried to help him in ways that actually made things worse. Jace has *obsessive-compulsive disorder (OCD)*, which falls under the DSM-5 category of *obsessive-compulsive and related disorders.*

For the DSM-5, OCD was removed from the anxiety disorders category and placed as the "centerpiece" for a group of disorders thought to have significant overlap with OCD in terms of clinical features, family/genetic risk factors, neuroanatomical abnormalities, behavioral mechanisms for symptom onset, and treatment response. The disorders now classified as *obsessive-compulsive related disorders* (OCRDs) include body dysmorphic disorder (BDD), hoarding disorder, trichotillomania (TTM; hair-pulling disorder), and excoriation (skin-picking) disorder. These disorders have varying degrees of overlap with OCD, and some controversy still exists about how the disorders should be best classified. In the DSM-5, the impulse control disorders, including pyromania and kleptomania, are classified separately from OCD and related disorders, but we discuss them here based on the similarity of their symptoms; that is, a key feature of all of the disorders is repetitive thoughts or behaviors. As you read through this chapter, think about how you might consider classifying these disorders if you were on the committee to develop DSM-6.

What Is Obsessive-Compulsive Disorder?

Obsessive-Compulsive Disorder

LO 5.1 Recognize the symptoms of OCD and differentiate obsessions from compulsions.

Obsessive-compulsive disorder (OCD) consists of **obsessions** (recurrent, persistent, intrusive thoughts) often combined with **compulsions** (repetitive behaviors or mental acts) that are extensive, time-consuming, and distressful (see "DSM-5: Obsessive-Compulsive Disorder"). Obsessions are usually specific thoughts (e.g., "If a glass breaks near me, tiny fragments will get in my mouth"), but they may also be urges (e.g., to jump off a high place) or images (e.g., having sexual interactions with strangers). Defined as recurrent and persistent, obsessions are also unwanted, intrusive, and often abhorrent, and they create substantial anxiety or distress, as was true for Jace. People with OCD try to ignore or suppress obsessions, and they recognize that their obsessions are the product of their own minds and not imposed upon them by someone else (as may occur in schizophrenia; see Chapter 11). Common obsessions include thoughts about dirt and germs (e.g., contracting cancer or another disease, contamination from bodily fluids or household chemicals); aggression (acting on impulse to harm a loved one); failing to perform a behavior adequately, thereby putting someone at risk for harm (leaving the stove on or a door unlocked); sex (inappropriate sexual thoughts about children); and religion (thinking blasphemous thoughts).

Compulsions are the second part of OCD. They consist of repetitive behaviors that the person feels driven to do in response to obsessions or according to rigid rules (American

Psychiatric Association, 2013). Compulsions can be observable behaviors, such as repeatedly washing one's hands or checking an appliance. They can also be unobservable mental activities, such as silent counting or ritualistic praying. By completing the ritual, people with OCD feel that they can prevent their obsessions from becoming reality: "If I wash my hands for an hour, I won't get cancer." Compulsions are maintained by negative reinforcement, a process wherein a response or behavior is strengthened by stopping, removing, or avoiding a negative outcome or aversive stimulus. In OCD, it works this way: if you are afraid of contamination by "cancer germs," sanitizing your hands temporarily decreases the fear of contamination. For Jace, taking notes and checking his work reduced his anxiety for a short time. **Family accommodation**, which occurs when loved ones (like Jace's parents) perform rituals for a person with OCD (e.g., provide repeated reassurance, check for the person with OCD), also provides short-term relief and reduced anxiety (Strauss et al., 2015). The relief, however, is not long-lasting and only increases the likelihood that the next time you feel contaminated or think you may have left a door unlocked, you will sanitize your hands or check the door again. In addition to hand washing and checking, common compulsions include excessive bathing or cleaning, counting, repeating, and ordering. Often people with OCD are reluctant to discuss their obsessions and compulsions, even with members of their family. When families are aware, however, family accommodation is associated with increased OCD severity (Strauss et al., 2015).

OCD is a chronic and severe condition that rarely remits without treatment. When the disorder is severe, the compulsions can dictate all of the person's activities. In addition, more than half of people with OCD have comorbid disorders such as depression, social anxiety disorder, specific phobia, GAD, and panic disorder (Stein et al., 2010). Substance abuse may also coexist with OCD. Even when a comorbid disorder is present, the symptoms of OCD usually are most prominent and troubling. OCD is also often accompanied by a personality disorder (see Chapter 12), and in these cases, positive treatment outcome is less likely (Steketee & Barlow, 2002). Recent research also has shown an increased risk of suicidal ideation and suicide attempts in adults with OCD (Angelakis et al., 2015).

In addition to Jace's obsessions and compulsions, he experienced severe social anxiety. He was an introverted child, but as he reached adolescence, Jace became more and more afraid of what other people might think of him. He was reluctant to talk to new people and afraid to speak up in class. His escalating OCD symptoms heightened his concerns about negative evaluation from others, and he became more and more avoidant of social situations. Jace had a comorbid diagnosis of social anxiety disorder.

Watch OBSESSIVE-COMPULSIVE DISORDER

DSM-5

Criteria for Obsessive-Compulsive Disorder

A. Presence of obsessions, compulsions, or both.

Obsessions are defined by (1) and (2):

1. Recurrent and persistent thoughts, urges, or images that are experienced, at some time during the disturbance, as intrusive and unwanted, and that in most individuals cause marked anxiety or distress.
2. The individual attempts to ignore or suppress such thoughts, urges, or images, or to neutralize them with some other thought or action (i.e., by performing a compulsion).

Compulsions are defined by (1) and (2):

1. Repetitive behaviors (e.g., hand washing, ordering, checking) or mental acts (e.g., praying, counting, repeating words silently) that the individual feels driven to perform in response to an obsession or according to rules that must be applied rigidly.
2. The behaviors or mental acts are aimed at preventing or reducing anxiety or distress, or preventing some dreaded event or situation; however, these behaviors or mental acts are not connected in a realistic way with what they are designed to neutralize or prevent, or are clearly excessive.

Note: Young children may not be able to articulate the aims of these behaviors or mental acts.

B. The obsessions or compulsions are time-consuming (e.g., take more than 1 hour per day) or cause clinically significant distress or impairment in social, occupational, or other important areas of functioning.

C. The obsessive-compulsive symptoms are not attributable to the physiological effects of a substance (e.g., a drug of abuse, a medication) or another medical condition.

D. The disturbance is not better explained by the symptoms of another mental disorder (e.g., excessive worries, as in generalized anxiety disorder; preoccupation with appearance, as in body dysmorphic disorder; difficulty discarding or parting with possessions, as in hoarding disorder; hair pulling, as in trichotillomania [hair-pulling disorder]; skin picking, as in excoriation [skin-picking] disorder; stereotypies, as in stereotypic movement disorder; ritualized eating behavior, as in eating disorders; preoccupation with substances or gambling, as in substance-related and addictive disorders; preoccupation with having an illness, as in illness anxiety disorder; sexual urges or fantasies, as in paraphilic disorders; impulses, as in disruptive, impulse-control, and conduct disorders; guilty ruminations, as in major depressive disorder; thought insertion or delusional preoccupations, as in schizophrenia spectrum and other psychotic disorders; or repetitive patterns of behavior, as in autism spectrum disorder).

Epidemiology, Sex, Race, and Ethnicity

LO 5.2 Describe the prevalence of OCD, considering factors such as sex, race, and ethnicity.

The lifetime prevalence of OCD is 1.6 to 2.7% in the United States (Kessler, Berglund, Demler et al., 2005; Kessler et al., 2012) and other countries (Mohammadi et al., 2004; Subramaniam et al., 2012). The disorder occurs less often among older adults, with prevalence estimates ranging from 0.1 to 1.5% (Grenier et al., 2009; Pulular et al., 2013; Wolitzky-Taylor et al., 2010). Among children and adolescents, prevalence estimates range from 0.25 to 4% (Krebs & Heyman, 2015) and are consistent across world populations.

OCD usually begins in late adolescence or early adulthood (Stein et al., 2010), although it can also begin in very early childhood (before 10 years; Pauls et al., 2014) or in later life (Grenier et al., 2009). Sometimes significant life events accompany the onset of OCD, including early adversity and trauma (Didie et al., 2006; Lochner et al., 2002) and pregnancy and childbirth (Guglielmi et al., 2014). Even when OCD begins in early or later adulthood, the person can often look back and see that elements of the disorder were present at an earlier age (like Jace). When symptoms are present during childhood, OCD is more severe and results in greater impairment in daily functioning (Rosario-Campos et al., 2001; Sobin et al., 2000).

Younger and older adult men and women are equally likely to suffer from OCD (Grenier et al., 2009), whereas among children, more boys than girls have the disorder.

Sometimes significant life events accompany the onset of OCD, such as pregnancy and childbirth.

In addition, boys develop OCD at a younger age and more often have another family member with the disorder (March et al., 2004; Tükel et al., 2005). The symptoms of OCD are generally similar across cultures, although the content of obsessions is sometimes culture specific (e.g., fear of leprosy among those who live in Africa; Steketee & Barlow, 2002). Within the United States, the prevalence across racial and ethnic groups is comparable, but the nature of symptoms may differ. For example, African Americans and Asian Americans report more contamination-related obsessions than European Americans (Wheaton et al., 2013). In addition, greater barriers to treatment exist for minorities with OCD. African Americans, for example, report a range of barriers including cost of treatment, stigma, fears of therapy, and treatment logistics (Williams et al., 2012). These and other barriers may explain why African American patients have more severe symptoms when they are finally referred for psychological treatment (Chambless & Williams, 1995).

Developmental Factors

LO 5.3 Explain how the symptoms of OCD vary with age.

Most adults with OCD have both obsessions and compulsions, but rituals alone are common among young children. Although adults generally understand that their rituals are responses to their obsessions, younger children usually do not know why they perform the rituals and sometimes do not view the rituals as senseless (American Psychiatric Association, 2013).

> Sophia was a 6-year-old Latina girl who repeatedly washed her hands, particularly when she touched something "sticky." Because most everything felt sticky to her and she believed that washing her hands over and over was the way to get them clean, she didn't think she washed her hands too often even though they were rough and red.

For children, it is important to view behavior through a developmental lens. As discussed earlier, ritualistic behaviors alone do not automatically indicate that OCD is present, and this is particularly true for children. As with fears in general, repetitive behaviors appear to have a developmental trajectory. Toddlers have many ritualistic behaviors (e.g., preparing for bedtime using a certain routine, eating food and arranging stuffed animals in a particular way, collecting or storing objects; Zohar & Felz, 2001). Over time, most children stop these behaviors because they lose interest in them. Only in certain instances do ritualistic and repetitive behaviors persist. As noted in Chapter 1, distress and functional impairment are important explanatory concepts for differentiating compulsions from "normal rituals." In comparison to children's normal ritualistic behaviors, compulsions develop at a later age, frequently persist into adulthood, are incapacitating and distressing, and interfere with normal development (Storch et al., 2008).

Very little research has been conducted with older adults who have OCD, but symptom severity seems to be comparable for older and younger people with this disorder. Older people, however, have fewer concerns about symmetry, greater fear of having sinned, fewer counting rituals, and more hand washing than younger adults with OCD (Kohn et al., 1997).

SIDE by SIDE Case Studies

Dimensions of Behavior: From Adaptive to Maladaptive

Adaptive Behavior Case Study

Cleanliness Is a Virtue

Maria learned from a very young age that it was important to keep herself and her home clean. Her mother, grandmother, and aunts all had immaculate homes and emphasized the importance of cleanliness for good health and positive perceptions of the family. When Maria moved into her own apartment after college, she settled into a routine that involved cleaning every Saturday morning. If she made any kind of a mess during the week (e.g., spilled her coffee, tracked in leaves from the sidewalk), she immediately cleaned it up. Maria made sure to wash her hands thoroughly before eating and after using the bathroom. She also kept hand sanitizer in her office to use any time she shook hands with people at work or noticed that a coworker had coughed or sneezed around her. Her friends knew that Maria valued cleanliness more than most, and they sometimes teased her and called her "obsessive," but she took the teasing good-naturedly and remained confident that her behaviors would help to keep her healthy and maintain the values she was taught by her family.

Maladaptive Behavior Case Study

Obsessive-Compulsive Disorder

Shannon was deathly afraid of contamination from food products that came into her home from public places. She worried that the food carried unseen germs that would make her family sick. To help Shannon manage this fear, her husband did all the grocery shopping. When he came home from the store, however, he had to put all the groceries in the garage by the kitchen door, then remove his clothing and go immediately to take a shower in the basement. Shannon then put on gloves, put her husband's clothing in the laundry, and removed one item at a time from the grocery bags, wiping each thoroughly with a paper towel before she brought it into the house. Each paper towel went immediately into the garbage can before the next item was handled. This whole process took hours, so the family tried to minimize the number of trips to the store. While Shannon was moving groceries into her home, her 4-year-old daughter either had to be at her grandmother's house or in the basement with her father. Shannon was afraid that the germs would travel to her daughter and make her sick and it would be Shannon's fault because she hadn't cleaned things thoroughly enough. When Shannon finished unloading the groceries, she immediately went to the shower herself where she spent at least an hour washing her hair and body to remove any germs that might have slipped from the groceries onto her skin.

Learning Objective Summaries

LO 5.1 Recognize the symptoms of OCD and differentiate obsessions from compulsions.

OCD consists of obsessions (recurrent, intrusive thoughts, urges, or images) often combined with compulsions (repetitive behaviors or mental acts) that are time-consuming and distressful. Obsessions are unwanted and often abhorrent, and they create substantial anxiety. Compulsions temporarily reduce anxiety associated with obsessions.

LO 5.2 Describe the prevalence of OCD, considering factors such as sex, race, and ethnicity.

The lifetime prevalence of OCD among adults is 1.6 to 2.7%. The disorder occurs less often among older people (0.1 to 1.5%), and prevalence among children ranges as high as 4%. Men and women are equally likely to suffer from OCD, although among children, more boys than girls have the disorder. The prevalence and symptoms of OCD are generally similar across cultures, although the content of obsessions may be culture specific.

LO 5.3 Explain how the symptoms of OCD vary with age.

Most adults with OCD have both obsessions and compulsions, although rituals alone are common among young children. Ritualistic behavior can be normal among toddlers, but these behaviors resolve over time when OCD is not present. Symptom severity is comparable for older and younger adults with OCD, although some data suggest different symptom content may exist in these two groups.

Critical Thinking Question

OCD is less common in older than younger adults. What might be some reasons for this difference, and how would you design a study to identify them?

What Are Obsessive-Compulsive Related Disorders (OCRDs)?

Obsessive-compulsive related disorders (OCRDs) include body dysmorphic disorder (BDD), which previously was considered a somatoform disorder (see Chapter 6); hoarding disorder, a new disorder that in the past was thought to be a variant of OCD; and trichotillomania (TTM; hair-pulling disorder) and excoriation (skin-picking) disorder, both previously categorized as impulse control disorders. As you read about each of these disorders, think about how each is related to OCD and whether you agree with the new DSM-5 classifications.

Body Dysmorphic Disorder

LO 5.4 Recognize the features of BDD and areas of overlap and dissimilarity with OCD.

Body dysmorphic disorder (BDD) is defined by an excessive preoccupation with perceived defects or flaws in physical appearance, which individuals believe make them look unattractive, ugly, or deformed (see "DSM-5: Body Dysmorphic Disorder"). Usually, if the concern is even minimally based in reality, it is an extreme exaggeration of a very minor flaw (e.g., a very small acne scar is described as a "huge crater on my face"). These exaggerated "perceptions of ugliness" are much like obsessions in that they are repetitive, intrusive, and anxiety producing (Abramowitz & Jacoby, 2015). However, unlike most individuals with OCD, many people with BDD have very poor insight about their thoughts. They are often convinced that the ugliness they perceive is real and that other people notice their physical defects. These more fixed and intense beliefs are considered *delusional* (e.g., fixed but false beliefs that cannot be reasoned or argued away; see Chapter 11). Delusional beliefs occur for approximately 50% of adults and 63% of adolescents with BDD (Fang et al., 2014; Phillips et al., 2006).

Similar to OCD, obsessive thoughts about appearance in BDD often lead to repetitive, ritualistic behaviors or mental acts that temporarily reduce anxiety (Abramowitz & Jacoby, 2015). For example, people with BDD frequently check their appearance in mirrors, and they expend significant effort to hide or camouflage their defects (e.g., with clothing or makeup). They also try to avoid people or places where they think their defects will be noticed. Beliefs about perceived ugliness and the associated ritualistic and avoidance behaviors lead to occupational, social, and academic impairment.

Amie is a 26-year-old Asian American woman who is convinced that her chin juts out terribly from the rest of her face. Actually an attractive young woman, Amie sees nothing but her chin when she looks in the mirror. She obsesses about how awful she looks—and what she believes others are saying behind her back. She is so distressed about her appearance that she refuses to go outside except to the store or the doctor. When she goes out, she covers her chin with her hand and a tissue, actually making herself more noticeable to others. When at home, she checks herself in the mirror constantly. Each time, she hopes to see a different image staring back at her. But every time, all she sees is a huge chin, making her the ugliest person on earth.

Although any area of the body may cause concern, patients with BDD most commonly worry about their skin, hair, nose, and face (e.g., size or symmetry of facial features, presence of wrinkles). Women with BDD are more likely to be preoccupied with their skin, hips, weight, and excessive body hair, whereas men are more likely to worry about thinning hair, be preoccupied with their genitals, and have *muscle* dysmorphia, a preoccupation that the body is not muscular even when others view them as being of normal weight or muscular (Fang et al., 2014; Phillips et al., 2010). Men with muscle dysmorphia may follow a rigorous diet and exercise schedule that can physically damage the body (Phillips et al., 2010).

A person with BDD is convinced that some part of the body is ugly or misshapen. Worry about the "ugly" body part may become so intense that it approaches the point of a delusion.

People with BDD, especially those with delusional beliefs, are at high risk for suicide. In one sample, 78% considered suicide at some point during their illness, and 27.5% had a history of suicide attempts (Phillips et al., 2005). These rates are at least six times higher than those in the general population and higher than rates reported for people with OCD, schizophrenia, or major depression. When followed prospectively for 1 year, 2.6% of people with BDD attempted suicide and 0.3% committed suicide (Phillips & Menard, 2006). People with the most severe symptoms and the most severe impairment are most likely to attempt suicide.

The general prevalence of BDD ranges from 1.7 to 2.4%, with comparable estimates in men and women (Fang et al., 2014). The disorder may be more common in college students (3.5%) than in the general population, both in the United States and Germany (Bohne, Keuthen, et al., 2002; Bohne, Wilhelm, et al., 2002). The prevalence and characteristics of BDD have not yet been examined among older adults.

People with BDD are familiar patients in primary care, dermatology, and plastic surgery clinics. Up to 12% of dermatology patients and 16% of cosmetic surgery patients meet diagnostic criteria for BDD (Bellino et al., 2006; Thompson & Durrani, 2007). Even after undergoing dermatological and surgical treatment, they are rarely satisfied with the outcome (Phillips & Dufresne, 2002). In some instances, they focus on another "ugly" body part and begin the process all over again.

BDD appears to be particularly impairing for adolescents. They suffer significant distress, are highly likely to experience suicidal ideation (80.6%) and attempt suicide (44.5%), and have impaired academic, social, and occupational functioning (Phillips et al., 2006).

DSM-5

Criteria for Body Dysmorphic Disorder

A. Preoccupation with one or more perceived defects or flaws in physical appearance that are not observable or appear slight to others.

B. At some point during the course of the disorder, the individual has performed repetitive behaviors (e.g., mirror checking, excessive grooming, skin picking, reassurance seeking) or mental acts (e.g., comparing his or her appearance with that of others) in response to the appearance concerns.

C. The preoccupation causes clinically significant distress or impairment in social, occupational, or other important areas of functioning.

D. The appearance preoccupation is not better explained by concerns with body fat or weight in an individual whose symptoms meet diagnostic criteria for an eating disorder.

Like adults, adolescents with BDD are equally likely to be male or female, and body areas of concern vary by gender.

Among one sample of people with BDD, only 41% revealed their symptoms to their prescribing physician; instead, many were being treated for a secondary disorder such as anxiety or depression. Because many patients with BDD see their problem as solely physical, they often seek and receive treatment from dermatological or surgical clinics. Often they are displeased with the surgical outcome and may become angry and threatening toward the physician (Honigman et al., 2004).

Hoarding Disorder

LO 5.5 Define the characteristics of hoarding disorder that differentiate it from OCD.

Hoarding disorder (see "DSM-5: Hoarding Disorder") is a new disorder in DSM-5 that is characterized by a persistent difficulty discarding or parting with possessions regardless of their actual value. This behavior is more than simply collecting coins or stamps or similar hobbies. In *hoarding disorder*, the inability to discard possessions creates excessive clutter that impedes the ability to use living spaces. People with hoarding disorder may not be able to use their living rooms, kitchens, or bedrooms. Large amounts of clutter also can pose a danger to the person and the community due to associated safety and fire hazards. And though the formal diagnosis has just recently been acknowledged in the DSM, such maladaptive behavior has been witnessed for far longer, as illustrated by the story of the Collyer brothers in "Real People, Real Disorders."

People with hoarding disorder report difficulties with discarding possessions due to strong sentimental attachments to the items and/or their potential usefulness or value as well as the desire to avoid being wasteful (Mataix-Cols, 2014). In addition to an inability to discard things, 85% of people with hoarding disorder also have an excessive need to acquire new possessions (Frost et al., 2009).

> Asim was a well-respected accountant with hoarding disorder who felt the need to accumulate paper and pens. He could not pass by the recycle bin at work without reaching in to take out pieces of paper that had words printed only on one side. Certainly, the blank side of the paper would be useful at some point. Asim also traveled frequently for his work, and he always kept any pens that were offered at meetings, hotels, and restaurants. He knew that he or someone would make good use of them. When he began working with a counselor, his home office and car were completely full of paper, and he had two brief cases full of pens.

REAL People REAL Disorders

The Collyer Brothers: Partners in Hoarding

On March 21, 1947, an anonymous caller telephoned the 122nd police precinct in Harlem, New York, to report a dead body in a three-story brownstone on Fifth Avenue (Steketee & Frost, 2010). When the police broke into the home, they found behind each door a wall of newspapers, boxes, and junk too dense to penetrate. When they finally entered the home through a second-story window, they found more newspapers, magazines, books, pipes, tin cans, car parts, and antique buggies that reached almost to the ceiling and lined a series of tunnels and passageways, some of which were booby-trapped to protect against intruders (Steketee & Frost, 2010).

After hours of searching through the massive piles on the second floor, the officers found the body of 65-year-old Homer Collyer (1881–1947). Police originally thought his 61-year-old brother, Langley Collyer (1885–1947), had escaped, and an elaborate search ensued. But after another 3 weeks of cleaning through the Collyer mansion, Langley's body was found in the house. He had been crushed by an accidental tripping of a booby trap and suffocated 3 weeks before Homer died. By this time, 120 tons of debris had been removed from the house, including multiple grand pianos, an automobile chassis, and a human skeleton (http://www.nydailynews.com/new-york/collyer-brothers-brownstone-gallery-1.1187698?pm).

The Collyer brothers were raised in a well-established, wealthy family in New York. Their father was a respected obstetrician-gynecologist, and they both graduated from Columbia University. Homer was a Phi Beta Kappa student who received several law degrees. Langley received a degree in engineering but ultimately became a concert pianist (Steketee & Frost, 2010). Both brothers remained single and never lived away from their family home. Neighbors knew them as eccentric, and over the years after their mother died, they became increasingly reclusive and continued to amass mounds of items that they thought would allow them to be self-sufficient. They failed to pay their mortgage, taxes, and utility bills, resulting in numerous interactions with the court and a life that they thought was "simpler" without electricity, gas, or telephone (Frost & Steketee, 2010) (https://news.google.com/newspapers?nid=1499&dat=19420807&id=jzMdAAAAIBAJ&sjid=7CIEAAAAIBAJ&pg=3589,2129693&hl=en).

Previous editions of the DSM considered hoarding a symptom of OCD, but the creation of a new disorder in DSM-5 reflects growing evidence that hoarding is characterized by a set of unique symptoms. For example, recurring thoughts related to acquiring and saving are not intrusive, unwanted, or fear-provoking as is the case for obsessions in OCD (Abramowitz & Jacoby, 2015). Moreover, acquiring and saving items does not serve to reduce anxiety in the same ways that rituals do for people with OCD, and distress associated with having to discard items is more often associated with grief and anger than anxiety (Pertusa et al., 2010).

Because hoarding disorder is a new diagnosis in DSM-5, little research about hoarding is based on the new criteria. Nevertheless, the prevalence of hoarding is estimated to be between 2 and 6% of adults and 2% of adolescents (Mataix-Cols, 2014). The prevalence is higher among older adults (6.2%; Samuels et al., 2008), and symptom severity increases

People with hoarding disorder have large amounts of clutter and garbage that create safety and fire hazards.

with age (Ayers et al., 2013). Hoarding is particularly common among older adults with dementia (see Chapter 14).

When DSM-5 diagnostic criteria were used in a recent study, prevalence was equivalent in men and women (Nordsletten et al., 2013), although some studies have shown increased hoarding symptoms in men (Iervolino et al., 2009; Mathews et al., 2014). The gender ratio for children and adolescents is less clear with some studies suggesting that hoarding is more common among girls and others suggesting greater frequency in boys (Morris et al., in press).

Hoarding typically begins in childhood or adolescence, although as is true for rituals, some collecting and saving behaviors are developmentally appropriate in young children (Morris et al., in press). Severity increases with age, likely as a result of increasing independence and control over one's own level of possessions from adolescence to adulthood. Hoarding causes increased problems for older adults who are at higher risk for negative health consequences such as fire hazards, falls, and food contamination, particularly when they are living alone.

Trichotillomania (Hair-Pulling Disorder)

LO 5.6 Describe the symptoms of trichotillomania and how they are similar to and different from OCD.

Trichotillomania (TTM) is a disorder characterized by repetitive hair pulling that results in hair loss (see "DSM-5: Trichotillomania"). People with this disorder want to stop pulling and repeatedly try to do so, but they feel powerless to stop. Although these criteria sound very straightforward, TTM actually is a complex and highly individualized disorder with significant variation in symptoms across people (Mansueto, 2013; Woods & Houghton, 2014). For example, although the most common site of pulling is the scalp, people with TTM may also pull from eyebrows/eyelashes, arms/legs, underarms, and the pubic area. Sometimes, pulling occurs without focused awareness (i.e., without paying attention to what they are doing), although in other cases, individuals with TTM are consciously aware of when they are pulling and may even seek certain types of hairs (e.g., those that are thick, rough, gray, etc.). Pulling typically is accomplished with one's fingers, but tweezers and other cosmetic devices may also be used. Sedentary behaviors are commonly associated with pulling (e.g., watching television, reading, talking on the phone), and a range of motor behaviors may precede pulling (e.g., stroking the hair, visually searching for a particular type of hair). Pulling occurs

DSM-5

Criteria for Hoarding Disorder

A. Persistent difficulty discarding or parting with possessions, regardless of their actual value.

B. This difficulty is due to a perceived need to save the items and to distress associated with discarding them.

C. The difficulty discarding possessions results in the accumulation of possessions that congest and clutter active living areas and substantially compromises their intended use. If living areas are uncluttered, it is only because of the interventions of third parties (e.g., family members, cleaners, authorities).

D. The hoarding causes clinically significant distress or impairment in social, occupational, or other important areas of functioning (including maintaining a safe environment for self and others).

E. The hoarding is not attributable to another medical condition (e.g., brain injury, cerebrovascular disease, Prader-Willi syndrome).

F. The hoarding is not better explained by the symptoms of another mental disorder (e.g., obsessions in obsessive-compulsive disorder, decreased energy in major depressive disorder, delusions in schizophrenia or another psychotic disorder, cognitive deficits in major neurocognitive disorder, restricted interests in autism spectrum disorder).

in response to a range of emotional experiences (e.g., boredom, tension, anger, depression), and significant variability exists in post-pulling behavior. Sometimes the hair is simply discarded, but at other times, the individual may inspect the hair, play with it, or eat it. Ingesting hair can cause serious gastrointestinal problems.

Watch TRICHOTILLOMANIA

> Sylvia is a veteran of the Afghanistan conflict (Operation Enduring Freedom). She began pulling her hair from the crown of her head at the age of 12, but she stopped pulling when she entered the Army at age 18. After she left the military, the symptoms started all over again. When she finally went to see a counselor, Sylvia was pulling every day for up to a couple of hours. She pulled only when she was alone and often when she was bored, working on the computer, or in bed. She was embarrassed to admit it, but she liked the tingling feeling that occurred when she pulled, and she enjoyed running the pulled hair along her bottom lip. Because she couldn't risk letting anyone know about this odd behavior, Sylvia spent most of her time away from work by herself. She really wanted more friends, and she hoped one day to get married, but she had to get this behavior under control first.

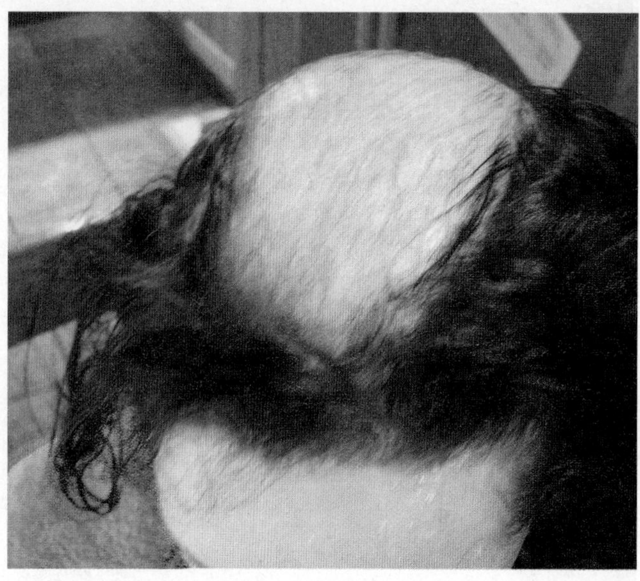

Scalp hair loss in trichotillomania

People with TTM feel significant shame about their symptoms, and they frequently avoid social activities and relationships in order to keep their behavior a secret. Other ways of camouflaging the hair loss include wearing wigs, scarves, or false eyelashes.

In previous versions of the DSM, TTM was classified as an impulse control disorder, mostly due to the feelings of pleasure, gratification, or relief associated with pulling. More recently, TTM also was considered a **body-focused repetitive behavior** (BFRB), a category that includes skin picking, nail biting, and thumb sucking (Grant & Stein, 2014). Although TTM is now classified as an OCRD, questions remain about whether this is the category that best reflects the nature of the disorder (see "Examining the Evidence").

DSM-5

Criteria for Trichotillomania

A. Recurrent pulling out of one's hair, resulting in hair loss.

B. Repeated attempts to decrease or stop hair pulling.

C. The hair pulling causes clinically significant distress or impairment in social, occupational, or other important areas of functioning.

D. The hair pulling or hair loss is not attributable to another medical condition (e.g., a dermatological condition).

E. The hair pulling is not better explained by the symptoms of another mental disorder (e.g., attempts to improve a perceived defect or flaw in appearance in body dysmorphic disorder).

Examining the EVIDENCE

Is Trichotillomania (Hair-Pulling Disorder) Adequately Categorized as an OCRD?

- **The Facts** TTM has been classified as an impulse control disorder, as a body-focused repetitive disorder, and now as an OCRD. Is TTM similar enough to OCD to place it in this category?

- **Let's Examine the Evidence** First, TTM and OCD have a number of common features (Abramowitz & Jacoby, 2015; Grant & Stein, 2014; Mansueto, 2013; Woods & Houghton, 2014):

  1. Both are characterized by repetitive behavior over which people feel a lack of control.
  2. Hair pulling sometimes decreases anxiety, as is the case for compulsions.
  3. Some people with TTM have obsessive thoughts or urges about hair pulling, wanting hair to be symmetrical or free of aberrant hairs (that are too coarse, too short, or too wiry).
  4. Both TTM and OCD are associated with high rates of coexisting anxiety and depressive disorders.
  5. Rates of OCD in families of people with TTM are higher than rates of OCD in the general population.
  6. One antidepressant (clomipramine) and behavioral treatment are effective for TTM and OCD.

  Second, TTM and OCD are different in many ways (Abramowitz & Jacoby, 2015; Grant & Stein, 2014; Mansueto, 2013; Woods & Houghton, 2014):

  1. Intrusive, anxiety-provoking obsessions do not occur for most people with TTM.
  2. Repetitive hair pulling sometimes produces pleasure, whereas OCD-related compulsions do not.
  3. Hair pulling occurs in response to a wide range of negative moods (e.g., anger, boredom, sadness, frustration, indecision), not just in response to obsessional fears.
  4. Family members of people with OCD are more likely to have OCD than are family members of people with TTM.
  5. TTM is associated with less severe OC symptoms and less anxiety and depression than occurs in OCD.
  6. Serotonergic medications effective for the treatment of OCD do not work well for TTM.
  7. Methods of behavioral treatment are quite different for TTM and OCD.

- **Conclusion** TTM and OCD have some important common features, and there may be a subtype of TTM that is very much like OCD, with hair pulling occurring in response to obsessive thoughts about hair. However, most studies suggest important differences in the clinical symptoms, associated features, and treatment procedures and responses for people with these two disorders. TTM may, in fact, have more overlap with another DSM-5 disorder, excoriation (skin-picking) disorder. Should TTM remain in its current category for future editions of the DSM? Would it be useful in future editions to include a category (or subcategory, as proposed for the ICD-11) of body-focused repetitive behaviors, possibly also known as grooming disorders, that would include TTM and excoriation disorder? Think about how these categories are useful for both research and clinical practice.

TTM occurs in up to 4.4% of adults, although the prevalence of hair-pulling behaviors that are below the threshold for the diagnostic criteria for TTM is even higher among college students (11%; Mansueto, 2013). Early childhood hair pulling (in children as young as 18 months) is often a benign habit that resolves over time without intervention (Park et al., 2012). Onset of TTM that persists into adulthood is generally between the ages of 10 and 13 (Grant & Stein, 2014), and the disorder typically is more common among women than men (Mansueto, 2013). The prevalence of TTM among adults is similar across cultures (Grant & Stein, 2014), although minorities in the United States (African American and Latinos) report less pulling from the eyebrows and eyelashes, less frequent tension before pulling, and less use of treatment (Neal-Barnett et al., 2010). Nothing is known about TTM in older adults.

Excoriation (Skin-Picking) Disorder

LO 5.7 Explain the features of excoriation disorder as they overlap or diverge from the symptoms of OCD and TTM.

Excoriation (skin-picking) disorder is defined by recurrent skin picking resulting in skin lesions (see "DSM-5: Excoriation Disorder"). Associated skin damage may include infection, ulcerations, or disfiguring scars. As is the case with TTM, people with *excoriation disorder* try to stop their behavior but are unable to do so. Also as in TTM, considerable variability occurs in skin picking symptoms. For example, picking may be directed at normal skin or may focus on skin with minor blemishes, pimples, scabs, or insect bites (Hayes et al., 2009; Tucker et al., 2011). Typical sites for picking include the face, scalp, arms, legs, and chest, although any area of the body may be a picking target. Picking sometimes occurs in BDD, in which case the focus of picking is to correct an imagined defect. In other cases, skin picking may be in response to a range of negative emotional states, and the behavior results in pleasure or gratification (like TTM).

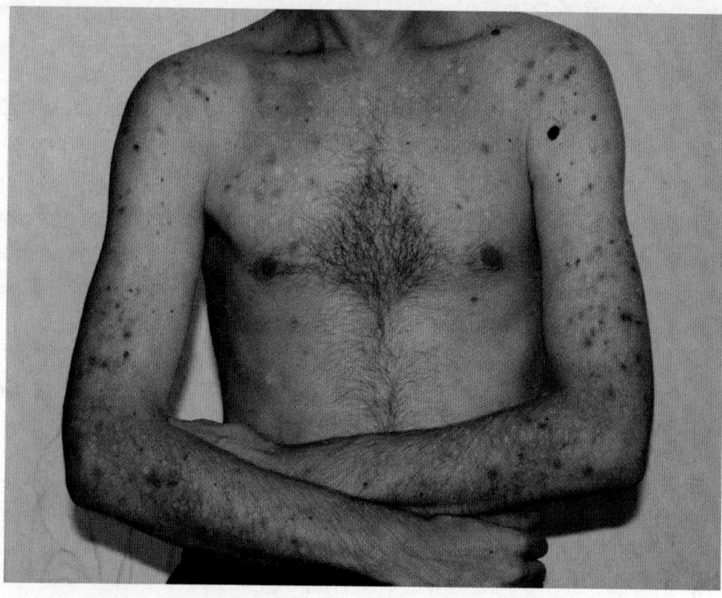

Typical sites for skin picking include the face, scalp, arms, legs, and chest.

> Each morning before school, 16-year-old Tamisha inspected her face in her makeup mirror. Although each day she hoped to see a face free of blemishes, she always saw spots—pimples or areas of dry skin—that she needed to remove. Her tweezers were always nearby, and she didn't stop picking until the pus was out of every pimple and the dry patches of skin were picked off. Then, in order to hide what she had done, she worked hard to cover the damage with makeup. Her efforts to hide the effects of her actions were not always successful; her classmates all knew she had acne, but she made it worse every time she tried to make it better. Tamisha was almost always late for the bus because all of this inspecting and picking took so long, and she had very few friends because she was afraid someone would look at her too closely and ask embarrassing questions.

People who pick typically use their fingers, but they also may use tweezers, pins, and teeth (Tucker et al., 2011). Because picking, like hair pulling, is associated with significant shame, efforts to conceal damaged skin are sometimes extensive and include use of clothing or makeup and social avoidance.

Excoriation disorder was introduced in DSM-5 as a result of research suggesting that the symptoms reflect a syndrome that is prevalent and has significant negative impact on functioning. The estimated prevalence of excoriation disorder among adults is as high as 5.4% (Hayes et al., 2009), although large-scale studies of the disorder have not yet been conducted. Significant skin picking and associated distress or impairment occur more often in women than in men, and the symptoms are reported by Caucasian and racial/ethnic minorities (Hayes et al., 2009; Tucker et al., 2011). To date, little is known about differences in the nature and prevalence of symptoms across the developmental spectrum.

DSM-5

Criteria for Excoriation (Skin-Picking) Disorder

A. Recurrent skin picking resulting in skin lesions.

B. Repeated attempts to decrease or stop skin picking.

C. The skin picking causes clinically significant distress or impairment in social, occupational, or other important areas of functioning.

D. The skin picking is not attributable to the physiological effects of a substance (e.g., cocaine) or another medical condition (e.g., scabies).

E. The skin picking is not better explained by symptoms of another mental disorder (e.g., delusions or tactile hallucinations in a psychotic disorder, attempts to improve a perceived defect or flaw in appearance in body dysmorphic disorder, stereotypies in stereotypic movement disorder, or intention to harm oneself in nonsuicidal self-injury).

Learning Objective Summaries

LO 5.4 Recognize the features of BDD and areas of overlap and dissimilarity with OCD.

BDD is characterized by an excessive preoccupation with perceived defects or flaws in physical appearance, which individuals believe make them look unattractive, ugly, or deformed. These thoughts are much like obsessions in that they are repetitive, intrusive, and anxiety-producing. Unlike OCD, however, the thoughts are often fixed beliefs that can be considered delusional. Preoccupation with appearance in BDD often leads to repetitive, ritualistic behaviors or mental acts that temporarily reduce anxiety, as in OCD. Both OCD and BDD are associated with suicidal thoughts, but these are more common in BDD.

LO 5.5 Define the characteristics of hoarding disorder that differentiate it from OCD.

People with hoarding disorder have thoughts about acquiring and saving items, but these thoughts are not intrusive, unwanted, or fear-provoking as are obsessions in OCD. Acquiring and saving items also does not serve to reduce anxiety in the same ways that rituals do for people with OCD, and distress associated with discarding items is more often associated with grief and anger than anxiety.

LO 5.6 Describe the symptoms of trichotillomania and how they are similar to and different from OCD.

TTM is defined by repetitive hair pulling that results in hair loss. As with OCD, people with TTM want to stop their repetitive behavior but are unable to do so. Although hair pulling sometimes functions to reduce anxiety as do rituals, repetitive pulling occurs in response to a wider range of emotions including boredom, tension, anger, and depression. The behavior also results in pleasure, which is not the case for rituals in OCD. Some people with TTM have obsessive thoughts about hair or urges to pull, but in many cases people pull without conscious awareness.

LO 5.7 Explain the features of excoriation disorder as they overlap or diverge from the symptoms of OCD and TTM.

Excoriation disorder is defined by recurrent skin picking resulting in skin damage that can include lesions, infection, ulcerations, or scars. This disorder has characteristics similar to TTM, and both have been classified as body-focused repetitive disorders. As with TTM, skin picking can occur in response to a range of emotions, and the behavior often produces feelings of pleasure or gratification.

Critical Thinking Question

Some of the disorders classified as OCRDs are more similar to OCD than others. Choose two disorders that you think are the most and least like OCD and justify your decision using evidence. What do you think are the benefits and drawbacks of combining all of these disorders into a single category? Would you recommend retaining this category in DSM-6? Why or why not?

What Are Impulse Control Disorders?

The **impulse control disorders** are grouped in DSM-5 with disruptive and conduct disorders (see Chapter 13) given that these disorders all reflect problems with self-control of behavior that violates the rights of others or puts the individual in conflict with societal norms or authority figures (American Psychiatric Association, 2013). The impulse control disorders reviewed here, pyromania and kleptomania, share features with OCD and OCRDs given the prominence of repetitive behaviors over which the individual feels a lack of control. Different from OCD and most OCRDs, however, is the pleasure experienced during performance of the behavior. Pyromania and kleptomania also have been considered **addictive behaviors** given overlap in clinical features with substance abuse and gambling disorder, including strong urges to perform the behavior, sometimes hedonic pleasure during the behavior, and persistence of the behavior despite adverse consequences (Grant et al., 2006).

Pyromania

LO 5.8 Describe the diagnostic criteria and clinical features of pyromania.

Pyromania is defined by deliberate and intentional setting of fires for pleasure (see "DSM-5: Pyromania). Although DSM-5 criteria require feelings of tension or arousal before the behavior,

DSM-5

Criteria for Pyromania

A. Deliberate and purposeful fire setting on more than one occasion.

B. Tension or affective arousal before the act.

C. Fascination with, interest in, curiosity about, or attraction to fire and its situational contexts (e.g., paraphernalia, uses, consequences).

D. Pleasure, gratification, or relief when setting fires or when witnessing or participating in their aftermath.

E. The fire setting is not done for monetary gain, as an expression of sociopolitical ideology, to conceal criminal activity, to express anger or vengeance, to improve one's living circumstances, in response to a delusion or hallucination, or as a result of impaired judgment (e.g., in major neurocognitive disorder, intellectual disability [intellectual developmental disorder], substance intoxication).

F. The fire setting is not better explained by conduct disorder, a manic disorder, or antisocial personality disorder.

people diagnosed with pyromania report a range of triggers including stress, boredom, inadequacy, and interpersonal conflict (Grant & Kim, 2007). They also report a fascination with fire and associated events, sometimes traveling to fires when they hear a siren and frequently serving as volunteer firefighters. Fire setting associated with a diagnosis of pyromania is not for monetary gain (e.g., to collect insurance), to conceal a crime, or to seek vengeance. People with pyromania routinely report a "rush" when watching or setting fires, but they also often experience significant distress after the behavior and sometimes consider suicide as a way of controlling their behavior (Grant & Kim, 2007).

Pyromania occurs in 1% of college students, 2.4 to 3.5% of children, and 2.8 to 3.4% of psychiatric patients (Dell'Osso et al., 2006; Grant et al., 2013). Differentiating pyromania from other types of fire setting is important, particularly among young children, as fascination with fire is normal at this developmental stage. The prevalence of pyromania among adults living in the community is unknown. Research addressing the disorder is quite limited, partially due to low prevalence but also because the behavior is illegal and people are reluctant to disclose related symptoms (Burton et al., 2012).

Pyromania is thought to begin in adolescence and is more common in males than females for both adolescents and adults (Dell'Osso et al., 2006). Comorbid substance abuse, mood and anxiety disorders, and other impulse control disorders are common. Fire setting has been associated with aggression and antisocial behavior as well as shyness and peer rejection (Dell'Osso et al., 2006).

Kleptomania

LO 5.9 Recognize the diagnostic criteria and clinical features of kleptomania.

The key symptom of **kleptomania** is a failure to resist urges to steal items that are not needed for personal use or monetary value (see "DSM-5: Kleptomania). Stealing in kleptomania is different from ordinary theft or shoplifting that is motivated by a desire to obtain an object or reflects an act of rebellion. Like pyromania, the stealing is preceded by feelings of tension, and during the act, people experience pleasure, gratification, or relief. Later, feelings of shame and guilt may lead the person to give away or return the stolen items (Grant et al., 2013).

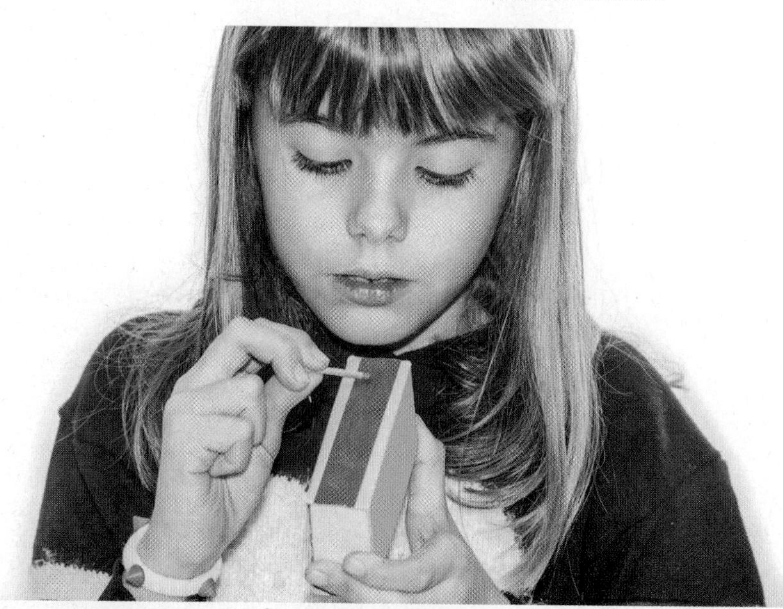

Young children have a normal fascination with fire.

DSM-5

Criteria for Kleptomania

A. Recurrent failure to resist impulses to steal objects that are not needed for personal use or for their monetary value.

B. Increasing sense of tension immediately before committing the theft.

C. Pleasure, gratification, or relief at the time of committing the theft.

D. The stealing is not committed to express anger or vengeance and is not in response to a delusion or hallucination.

E. The stealing is not better explained by conduct disorder, a manic disorder, or antisocial personality disorder.

The objects also may be hoarded or discarded. Most people with kleptomania have been arrested at some time due to their stealing, but only 5% of shoplifting in the United States is due to kleptomania (Dell'Osso et al., 2006; Grant et al., 2013).

Amanda was a 16-year-old girl from a wealthy family who was diagnosed with bulimia nervosa (see Chapter 8). At first, she only stole food for binge eating, but she soon realized that she got quite a rush from the act of stealing itself. Amanda then moved on to stealing makeup—lipstick, blush, whatever she could find—and she gave away the items she stole to try to make friends at school. Her friends didn't question where the makeup came from because everyone knew that Amanda was rich and could afford anything she wanted. When stealing makeup became too easy, Amanda moved on to clothes, which she would then return for a refund, claiming she had lost the receipt. She got an extra rush out of making money from returning stolen goods. When she finally got caught, her parents were appalled and confused because their financial resources would have made it easy for Amanda to buy all the items she stole.

Kleptomania is a rare disorder, with estimated prevalence of 0.4 to 0.6% (Dell'Osso et al., 2006; Grant et al., 2013). As with pyromania, prevalence may be underestimated due to a lack of willingness to report illegal behavior. The disorder is thought to begin in adolescence or early adulthood, but cases also have been reported in young children and older adults (Grant, 2006). Women with kleptomania outnumber men 3:1, and comorbid mood, anxiety, and substance use disorders are common, as are suicidal thoughts and behaviors (Grant et al., 2013). Women with the disorder are more likely to be married, have a later age of onset, and more often steal household items and hoard stolen items than men (Grant et al., 2008). Men are more likely to steal electronic goods (see Table 5.1).

Table 5.1 Gender Differences with Kleptomania

Numbers in bold indicate significant differences between men and women.

	Total Sample (n=95)	Women (n=68)	Men (n=27)
Places Stolen From			
Clothing Store	51 (53.7)	41 (60.3)	10 (37.0)
Household goods store	40 (42.1)	**39 (57.4)**	**1 (3.7)**
Grocery Store	35 (36.8)	26 (38.2)	9 (33.3)
Electronic goods store	18 (18.9)	**5 (7.4)**	**13 (48.1)**
Friends' homes	15 (15.8)	9 (13.2)	6 (22.2)
Work	14 (14.7)	8 (11.8)	6 (22.2)
Relatives' homes	7 (7.4)	4 (5.9)	3 (4.4)
Gift Shops	4 (4.2)	3 (4.4)	1 (3.7)
Disposition of Items			
Kept	74 (77.9)	56 (82.4)	18 (66.7)
Hoarded	40 (42.1)	**34 (50.0)**	**6 (22.2)**
Given away	29 (30.5)	18 (26.5)	11 (40.7)
Returned	16 (16.8)	14 (20.6)	2 (7.4)
Discarded	11 (11.6)	6 (8.8)	5 (18.5)

SOURCE: http://www.ncbi.nlm.nih.gov/pmc/articles/PMC3676680

Learning Objective Summaries

LO 5.8 Describe the diagnostic criteria and clinical features of pyromania.

Pyromania is characterized by deliberate and intentional setting of fires preceded by feelings of tension or arousal and associated with feelings of pleasure, gratification, or relief. People with pyromania have a fascination with fire and associated events. Their fire setting is not for monetary gain, to conceal a crime, or to seek vengeance.

LO 5.9 Recognize the diagnostic criteria and clinical features of kleptomania.

Kleptomania is defined by a failure to resist urges to steal items that are not needed for personal use or monetary value. Like pyromania, the stealing is preceded by feelings of tension, but during the act, people experience pleasure, gratification, or relief. People may hoard, discard, give away, or return the stolen items.

Critical Thinking Question

Pyromania appears to be more common in males, but kleptomania occurs more often in females. What factors do you think might account for these gender differences, and how would you design a study to test your hypothesis?

Etiology of Obsessive-Compulsive and Impulse Control Disorders

As with most psychiatric disorders, both biological and psychological factors seem to have roles in the onset of OCD, OCRDs, and impulse control disorders. Here we review evidence separately from both of these perspectives, although as in the case of other disorders you already have read about (e.g., anxiety disorders), onset of the disorders discussed here likely best fits an integrated biopsychosocial model (see Chapter 1).

OCD: Biological Perspective

LO 5.10 Describe the biological factors that may contribute to the onset of OCD.

FAMILY AND GENETIC STUDIES Family studies reveal that the prevalence of OCD in first-degree relatives of adults and children/adolescents with OCD (10 to 20%) is higher than in the general community (Browne et al. 2014), suggesting that the disorder aggregates in families. The familial transmission of OCD may be stronger for childhood-onset OCD, suggesting the possibility that different **subtypes** of OCD have different causes (Pauls et al., 2014). Differences in gender distribution for OCD that begins in childhood versus adulthood also support a hypothesis of different subtypes.

Because family studies cannot rule out the influence of environmental factors, twin studies help determine the extent to which genetic factors contribute to the familial pattern. A review of 11 twin studies, with sample sizes ranging from 14 to more than 16,000 twin pairs, demonstrated consistently higher *concordance rates* (see Chapter 2) for OCD among monozygotic than dizygotic twins (Browne et al., 2014). In the largest of these studies, *heritability* estimates for OCD (the proportion of variance in liability for the disorder accounted for by genetic factors; see Chapter 4) ranged from 45 to 58%. A **meta-analysis** (a method of data analysis that pools findings across multiple independent studies addressing a similar question) of twin studies also showed that in addition to genetic risk, *nonshared environmental factors* (environmental factors not shared between twins) contributed to the presence of OCD and may have a greater role in later onset of OCD (Taylor, 2011).

Several candidate genes have been explored for their relevance to OCD including the neuronal glutamate transporter gene *SLC1A1*, the serotonin transporter promoter variant (*5-HTTLPR*) L_a vs. ($L_g + S$) alleles, the serotonin 2A receptor *HTR2A*, and the *COMT*

Met/Val (Browne et al., 2014), although none has been uniquely associated with OCD. Two *genome-wide association studies* (GWAS; see Chapter 2) for OCD have been conducted (Mattheisen et al., 2015; Stewart et al., 2013). Although no single nucleotide polymorphism (SNP) yet meets the standard genome-wide threshold for significance (Browne et al., 2014), samples sizes are still too small to expect significant results, as has been the case for other psychiatric disorders (bipolar disorder, schizophrenia; see Chapters 7 and 11). However, we expect that hundreds if not thousands of genes alone and in combination will likely contribute to an increased risk of having OCD (Pauls et al., 2014), and genetic risk may differ across OCD subtypes (Mak et al., 2015). Moreover, twin studies suggest that genes do not act alone and that environmental factors also play a role underscoring the importance of exploring not only genetic but environmental risk factors. Genes may determine how susceptible a person is to environmental factors that then may lead to behaviors and emotions associated with changes in brain function or gene expression.

NEUROANATOMY *Structural and functional neuroimaging studies* of OCD have produced some of the most consistent findings across all the psychiatric literature (Pauls et al., 2014). Neuoroimaging studies of brain structure point to a key role for the cortico-striato-thalamo-cortical (CSTC) circuit, with reductions in gray matter and white matter volume of the orbitofrontal cortex (OFC), medial frontal gyrus, and anterior cingulate cortex (ACC) and increased volume of the ventral putamen (Barahona-Correa et al., 2015; Pauls et al., 2014).

Functional neuroimaging studies also point to a corticostriatal (or frontostriatal) model for OCD defined by increased activity in the OCF, caudate nucleus, and ACC for adults and children with OCD relative to controls. The proposed model suggests that for people with OCD there is an imbalance in two cortico-subcortical pathways, one that is excitatory and direct and another that is inhibitory and indirect. For people with OCD, the excitatory pathway is overactive, resulting in persistent experience of uncontrollable thoughts and behaviors that are not suppressed by the inhibitory, indirect pathway (Barahona-Correa et al., 2015; Pauls et al., 2014). In fact, violent or sexual thoughts or impulses (often reported by people with OCD) appear to originate in the orbital prefrontal cortex. From there, the neuronal signals travel to the caudate nucleus where normally they are filtered out. If they are not filtered out, the signals for these thoughts and impulses arrive at the thalamus, causing the person to experience a drive to focus on the thoughts and perhaps to act on them.

Psychological challenge studies have been used to test this model. In these studies, people confront objects or situations while neuroimaging procedures are used to scan suspected areas of the brain for enhanced activity. In early studies, people with OCD and healthy controls were *challenged* by asking them to touch "contaminated" objects. These studies demonstrated enhanced brain activity for people with OCD in the OFC, ACC, striatum, and thalamus areas (Trivedi, 1996). In other words, people with OCD showed different brain activity when they touched these objects than did people without OCD. More recent studies have used virtual challenges (see Figure 5.1) and begun to examine whether different patterns of brain activity are associated with different OCD symptom subtypes (e.g., patients with primarily washing symptoms; Jhung et al., 2014). These studies have suggested subtype-specific patterns of brain activity (Pauls et al., 2014), but sample sizes are typically small given the complexity and expense of the procedures, making it difficult to confirm findings for a disorder as complex as OCD.

Even more important in evaluating the results of challenge studies is the fact that selected participants already have OCD, making it impossible to know whether this enhanced brain activity originally caused the disorder. Perhaps this activation exists only if the disorder is already present. Fully answering the question of etiology would require a longitudinal design in which we identify individuals at risk for OCD (perhaps a group that reacted with brain activation in a challenge study but had no other OCD symptoms) and follow them on a regular basis for a few years to determine whether they later developed OCD. Current studies already suggest that patterns of brain activity (when the person with OCD is and is not in a challenge situation) change after successful treatment with psychotherapy or medication (Thorsen et al., 2015). Thus, brain activity is influenced by behavior and the presence of OC symptoms and may vary over time.

Figure 5.1 Augmented Reality Virtual Dirty Stimuli-Presenting System.

A participant can see his or her body and the superimposed animation of dirty stimuli on both hands through a head-mounted display (HMD).

SOURCE: Jhung, K., Ku, J., et al. (2014). Distinct functional connectivity of limbic network in the washing type of obsessive compulsive disorder. *Progress in Neuro-Psychopharmacology & Biological Psychiatry, 53*, 149–155.

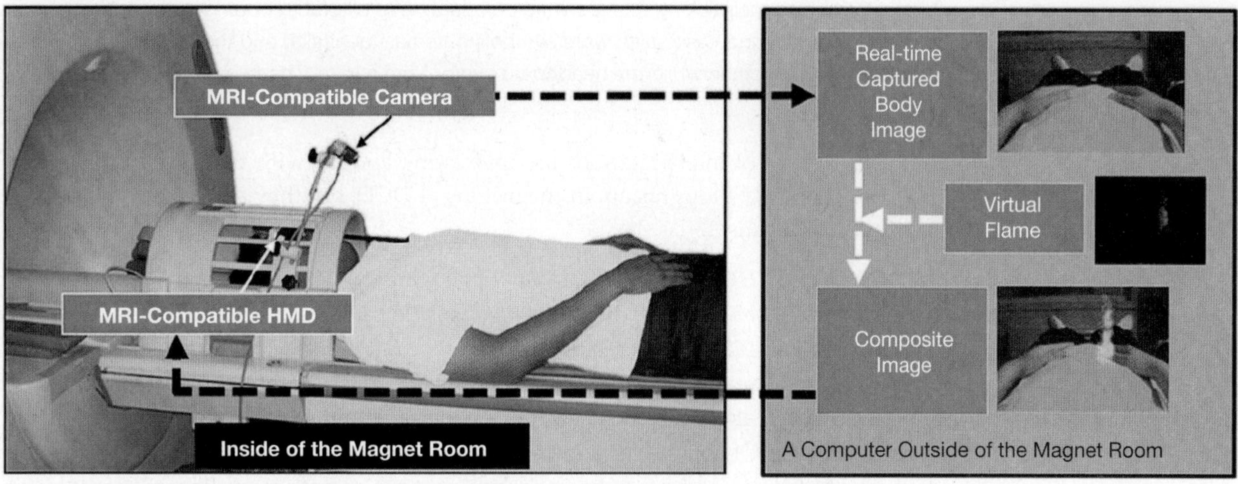

Treatment studies that document the positive effects of serotonergic medications for OCD (see "Treatment of OCD") suggest a role of this neurotransmitter in the etiology of OCD, but evidence for a causal link between serotonin and OCD is weak (Abramowitz & Jacoby, 2014; Barahona-Correa et al., 2015). As you learned in Chapter 4, we cannot conclude that a causal connection exists when a particular treatment improves symptoms. In addition, although some **biological marker studies** (studies that compare biological variables across groups) and **biological challenge studies** (studies in which a biological agent is given to trigger symptoms) suggest decreased serotonin receptivity for people with OCD, findings are inconsistent and results are correlational, not causal (Abramowitz & Jacoby, 2014). Evidence to support a role of dopamine in OCD also is inconsistent, although recent studies have documented what appears to be a link between OCD and levels of glutamate in the OFC, ACC, and striatum (Naaijen et al., 2015). Fewer studies of the receptor gamma-aminobutyric acid (GABA) have been conducted with OCD, but some evidence suggests decreased levels of GABA in prefrontal cortical areas.

OCD: Psychological Perspective

LO 5.11 Utilize the psychological theories of anxiety acquisition to explain the etiology of OCD.

As you review the psychological theories of OCD presented here, remember that in previous versions of the DSM, OCD was grouped with the anxiety disorders. Because anxiety plays such a central role in the clinical picture of OCD, many psychological theories of OCD onset are similar to those used to explain the etiology of anxiety (see Chapter 4).

PSYCHODYNAMIC THEORIES As with the anxiety disorders, Freud looked to early conflicts between the id and ego, particularly those resulting from sexual and aggressive thoughts and impulses, to explain the onset of OCD symptoms, then called **obsessional neurosis**. In a lecture he gave in 1916–17, he described a 19-year-old female patient with extensive obsessions and compulsions related to bedtime and sleep (Freud, 1963):

> The patient was obsessed with the need for complete quiet in order to go to sleep and had developed a 1- to 2-hour ritualistic routine at bedtime. To ensure that all would be quiet so that she could sleep, she stopped the big clock in her room and removed other small clocks and watches. She also put all vases and flowerpots on her writing table so that they would not fall

over during the night and make noise. Before she could go to sleep, all items on her bed had to be arranged correctly. The pillow at the top of the bed could not be touching the headboard. The bed cover had to be fully shaken out before being laid on the bed so that the bottom end was thicker than the top end. Freud's interpretation of these symptoms surrounded the patient's fears of sexual arousal and interactions. The clocks were symbols of female genitals given their periodic regularity, and their ticking sounds were comparable to clitoral throbbing during sexual arousal. The flowerpots and vases also were symbols of female genitalia, and the large pillow on the bed symbolized a woman while the headboard symbolized a man. The two could not touch.

These types of interpretations are interesting and, as with the anxiety disorders, were influential in early thoughts about the origins of OCD, but they are infrequently used today to explain OCD onset.

BEHAVIORAL THEORIES The original behavioral model used to explain OCD etiology was Mowrer's two-factor theory of fear acquisition (Mowrer, 1960). This model suggested that obsessional fears are acquired through *classical conditioning* and maintained via *operant conditioning* (see Chapter 1). Initial pairings between obsessive thoughts and fear were thought to come about as a result of prior experiences that linked, for example, germ exposure and illness. Of course these initial fears also could be learned through *vicarious learning* (a child sees his parent repeatedly checking the stove and other appliances before leaving the house) or *information transmission* (your mother repeatedly warns you of the possibility of contracting an illness from shaking hands) (see Chapter 4). OCD also is thought to "grow" as a result of classical or other conditioning models as additional thoughts and environmental stimuli are paired with existing fears (e.g., an obsessive thought about germs occurs when you sit in the passenger seat of your best friend's car, which then becomes associated with obsessional fears of disease) or as additional fears are learned through observing or receiving information from others.

Once fears are in place, operant conditioning sets in to maintain them given the *negative reinforcement* (see Chapter 1) that occurs following performance of a ritual. As you learned earlier in this chapter, rituals provide short-term relief of fear and, as such, increase the longer-term chances that the ritual will be performed again to reduce anxiety, thereby maintaining both the fear and the excessive behaviors. Mowrer's theory was the impetus for the development of a highly effective behavioral treatment for OCD, *exposure and response prevention*, explained later in this chapter. However, at least the first phase of the model is limited in its utility to explain OCD onset given that not all people with the disorder are able to remember an early conditioning experience. The second phase of the model is more regularly used to explain maintenance of the disorder.

COGNITIVE THEORIES Multiple cognitive theories of OCD have been developed with a focus on the roles of misinterpretations and erroneous thought processes. Cognitive models suggest that intrusive thoughts common in OCD may also occur for people

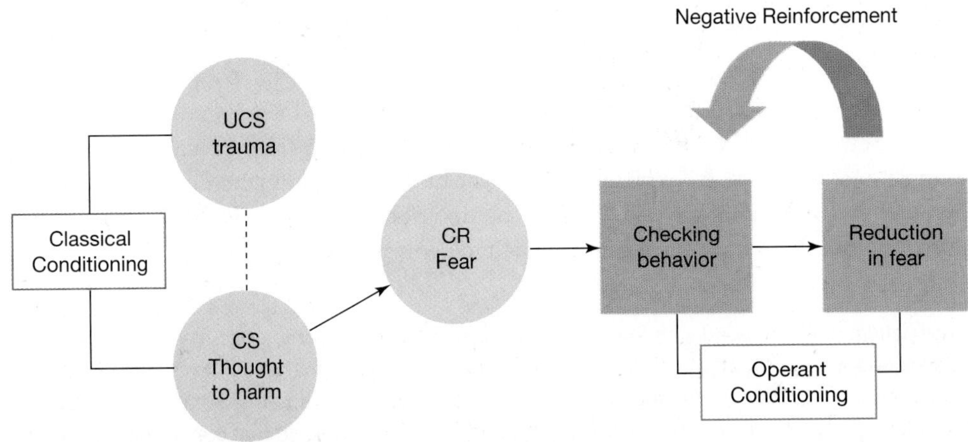

Figure 5.2 Mowrer's Two Factor Theory of Fear Acquisition

Mowrer's theory has been used to explain the onset and maintenance of OCD and was the impetus for an effective treatment for this disorder called exposure and response prevention.

Table 5.2 Domains Related to Obsessive-Compulsive Behavior

Domain	Example of Thought
Inflated personal responsibility	If you get sick, it will be my fault because I wasn't careful enough about getting and sharing germs.
Overimportance of thoughts (thought-action fusion)	Having a thought about sex with a stranger is as bad as actually engaging in the act.
Beliefs about the importance of controlling one's thoughts	I am completely responsible for all thoughts that come into my head.
Overestimation of threat	Touching that chair will certainly result in disaster.
Intolerance for uncertainty	I need to know with 100% confidence that I will not get germs from touching the chair.
Perfectionism	The only way I will be respected by my colleagues is if I never make a mistake and all of my projects are flawless.

without the disorder, but more important to the development or maintenance of OCD is the person's reaction to his or her own thoughts. For example, while sitting in an airport, you may have a sudden, unexpected sexual thought about a stranger walking by. People without OCD likely react to that thought by recognizing it as normal and transient, then directly move back to texting with friends. A person with OCD, however, might see the thought as abhorrent, feel responsible and "dirty" for having the thought, and believe that God will punish him or her for being evil. In cognitive models, the reaction to the intrusive thought is more important than the nature of the thought itself. These maladaptive perceptions of thoughts produce a drive to complete a ritual to reduce anxiety. Most cognitive models also view rituals as important to maintenance of the disorder through a process of negative reinforcement.

In the late 1990s, an Obsessive Compulsive Cognitions Working Group (CCWG, 1997) suggested key roles for six belief domains that are proposed to be important to the development and maintenance of obsessions: inflated personal responsibility, overimportance of thoughts (or **thought-action fusion**), beliefs about the importance of controlling one's thoughts, overestimation of threat, intolerance for uncertainty, and perfectionism. See Table 5.2 for examples of each.

A large number of studies have documented that these types of beliefs indeed are common for people with OCD (Hezel & McNally, 2015), and some treatments for OCD have incorporated cognitive therapy (see "OCD: Psychological Treatments"). However, as with the anxiety disorders, no research has strongly supported an etiological role for cognitions in OCD (i.e., we don't know if these beliefs are present before OCD develops), and common erroneous thoughts are instead considered more important for maintenance of the disorder.

OCRDs: Biological Perspective

LO 5.12 Understand the possible genetic and neuroanatomical factors that may contribute to onset of OCRDs, comparing and contrasting across these disorders and with OCD.

When we consider potential biological causes of OCRDs, we are interested in both the etiology of these disorders themselves and any evidence that might suggest causal overlap with OCD. Actually, very few studies have examined the potential biological causes of OCRDs, and most of these have focused on BDD and TTM given that hoarding disorder and excoriation disorder are new diagnostic categories. Although the available studies address interesting questions, conclusions are limited because the studies are correlational rather than causal (i.e., they compare characteristics across groups of people rather than manipulating any variable to determine its effect; see Chapter 2), sample sizes are small, and participants generally are recruited from clinics rather than the population as a whole, meaning that the findings may generalize only to those people who seek treatment rather than all people with a particular disorder.

With consideration of these limitations, however, family studies have suggested increased rates of hair pulling in families of people with TTM (Keuthen et al., 2014) and higher rates of hoarding among relatives of people with clinically significant hoarding behavior (Steketee et al., 2015). Although we need to remember that these patterns do not necessarily reflect a biological cause, they do suggest increased chances of having an OCRD when you have a relative with one of these disorders.

Family studies also suggest associations between OCD and OCRDs given that the prevalence of OCRDs in first-degree relatives of people with OCD is higher than general prevalence estimates (6% BDD, 4% TTM, and 17% skin picking; Browne et al., 2014). OCD also occurs more often among relatives of people with BDD and TTM than in the general community. However, these estimates are not as high as they are for relatives of people with OCD, suggesting the possibility of different genetic risk factors for these disorders (see "Examining the Evidence"). Also of interest when we consider how best to classify OCD and related disorders is the fact that anxiety disorders actually occur more often than OCRDs among family members of people with OCD (Abramowitz & Jacoby, 2015), and it is not yet clear whether prevalence of OCRDs is also high for family members of people with anxiety or trauma-related disorders.

A handful of twin studies have shown higher concordance for monozygotic than dizygotic twins within categories of OCRDs, with heritability estimates of 43% for BDD, 45 to 49% for hoarding symptoms (difficulty discarding and excessive acquisition), 32 to 76% for TTM, and 40 to 47% for skin picking (Browne et al., 2015). Twin studies of hoarding behavior suggest differences in heritability across gender and age. In a sample of adult twins, genetic factors appeared to be present for women but not men (Iervolino et al., 2009), but among adolescent twins, genetics seemed to play a stronger role for boys than girls (Morris et al., in press). Twin studies also show a significant effect of nonshared environmental factors for hoarding (Iervolino et al., 2009, Mathews et al., 2014). Whereas there appear to be some shared genetic factors between BDD and OCD (Frías et al., 2015), genetic factors for hoarding and OCD appear to be independent (Mathews et al., 2014).

A few small studies have shown a possible role of the *5HT2A* t103c variant for hair pulling and the gene encoding SAP90/PSD95-associated protein 3 (Sapap3) for hair pulling and skin picking (Flessner et al., 2012; Snorrason et al., 2012). However, results are inconsistent across studies, sample sizes are small, and there are no direct comparisons of genetic risk factors for OCD and OCRDs. Genome-wide association studies are currently underway for OCRDs.

Neuroimaging studies have suggested abnormalities in the OFC, ACC, and caudate nucleus for people with BDD that may be similar to patterns observed for people with OCD (Fang et al., 2014). These same regions have been studied in people with TTM, but results are inconsistent, with some studies showing abnormalities in frontal and striatal regions and others failing to detect any associated brain abnormalities (Flessner et al., 2012; Snorrason et al., 2012). Different findings across studies may be the result of small samples and differences in methodology (e.g., how scans are completed, how participants are selected and treated). Future larger studies will need to include people with OCD and different OCRDs to examine similarities and differences in brain structure and function across groups (Abramowitz & Jacoby, 2014).

OCRDs: Psychological Perspective

LO 5.13 Explain the possible psychological causes for OCRDs with a primary focus on cognitive and behavioral factors.

As with OCD, psychodynamic theories are not often currently used to explain the onset of OCRDs. Interesting hypotheses, however, include the potential roles of unconscious conflicts about sexuality (e.g., an adolescent girl's perceptions of her breasts being too large may result from a fear of growing up and developing into a woman; Horowitz et al., 2002), inability to progress adequately through stages of psychosexual development (e.g., hoarding as a result of overly strict toilet training), and expressions of unconscious aggressive impulses (e.g., hair pulling as a reflection of anger at a loss of power or self-punishment for sexual feelings).

Psychological perspectives of the OCRDs instead are more often rooted in social learning, behavioral, and cognitive theories. *Sociocultural factors* are thought to play a role in the onset and maintenance of BDD given the high value many societies place on appearance. Although hoarding is sometimes thought to reflect a biologically based instinct for survival (i.e., much like animals who gather and store food for sustenance during winter months), sociocultural values that emphasize "saving for a rainy day" may have an impact on the development of hoarding. More often, though, general behavioral and cognitive factors are thought to influence onset and maintenance of the OCRDs.

Given the significant role of anxiety producing, obsessive-like thoughts and associated ritualistic behaviors in BDD, behavioral models for this disorder include attention to the role of operant conditioning as an explanation for maintenance of symptoms. As you learned earlier, people with BDD often repetitively check their appearance and make repeated efforts to hide their perceived physical defects to reduce anxiety. The resultant temporary relief from these behaviors negatively reinforces both the fear and the repetitive behaviors (i.e., increases the chances that they will happen again). Operant learning also may play a role in the onset of BDD when physical appearance is reinforced in early life (e.g., "Oh, my, you are the cutest thing in that little dress."), and classical conditioning may be influential when early repeated teasing produces an association between anxiety and some body part (e.g., a girl whose breasts develop early is teased by her peers and develops anxiety that becomes associated with any situation in which people may notice her breasts). Cognitive theories of BDD focus on the erroneous beliefs about appearance (e.g., "My face is full of ugly, gross pimples.") but also on more general maladaptive beliefs about the importance of appearance (e.g., "No one likes ugly people.") and the relevance of appearance for a person's self-worth (e.g., "I am such a loser because my muscles are so small.").

Cognitive and behavioral theories of hoarding focus on beliefs about and emotional attachment to possessions. Beliefs about possessions may provide emotional comfort (e.g., "This pile of papers from my mother's desk makes me feel closer to her."), prevent fears of losing or forgetting something important (e.g., "These items from my past are part of me and keep me from forgetting important people and events."), and prepare for future needs (e.g., "Who knows when we might need these cardboard boxes?"). Saving and acquiring behaviors can be considered a form of avoidance given that these behaviors prevent negative feelings (loss, grief, anger, anxiety) associated with thoughts about discarding possessions and are therefore negatively reinforcing.

A comprehensive behavioral model for TTM (Mansueto, 2013) addresses the nature and function of hair pulling but also may be used to understand cognitive and behavioral factors associated with other body-focused repetitive behaviors (BFRBs) such as skin picking and nail biting. In this model, hair pulling (or another BFRB) is viewed as a **grooming behavior** (a behavior observed across species that serves social and hygienic roles) that becomes associated through classical and operant conditioning with various cues that trigger and maintain pulling behavior. These cues can be remembered with the acronym *SCAMP* (see Figure 5.3), where *S* stands for *sensory cues* (feeling of the hair before or after pulling), *C* for *cognitive cues* (eyebrows need to be symmetrical), *A* for *affective or emotional cues* (boredom, frustration), *M* for *motoric cues* (moving your hand to your face), and *P* for *place or environmental cues* (watching television, reading). An individual analysis of how these cues are associated with pulling (or other BFRB) then serves as the basis for developing an individual behavioral treatment plan.

> Whenever Sandra is reading (P), her left hand goes to her head (M). As she touches her hair (S), she finds hairs that feel out of place and need to be pulled (C). After she pulls, she runs the hair along her bottom lip (S), enjoying the sensation (A) while she continues to read (P).

Pyromania and Kleptomania

LO 5.14 Describe possible biological and psychological causes of pyromania and kleptomania.

Little is known about the possible causes of pyromania and kleptomania. Family studies suggest increased risk of OCD and substance use disorders among relatives of people with

Figure 5.3 Mansueto's Comprehensive Behavioral Model for TTM

The Comprehensive Behavioral Model focuses on 5 types of cues represented by the acronym SCAMP (S – sensory; C – cognitive; A – affective; M – motoric; P – place or environment)

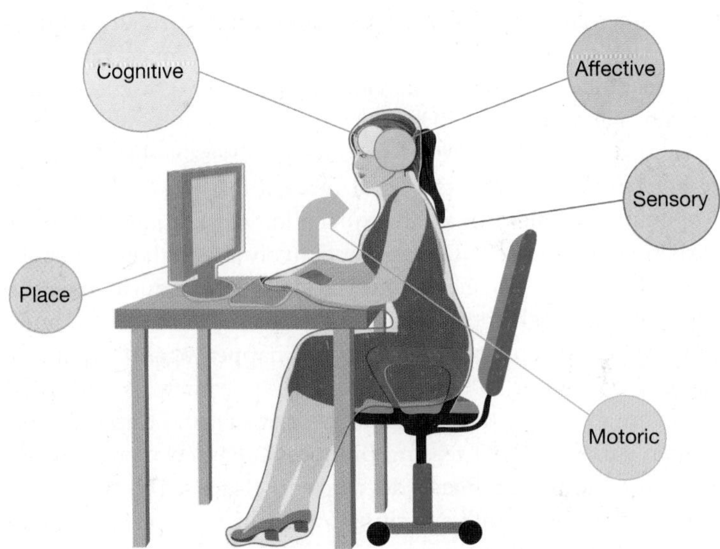

Comprehensive Behavioral (ComB) Model

kleptomania (American Psychiatric Association, 2013), but no large-scale twin studies yet have been conducted. Given that these disorders are sometimes considered behavioral addictions, a possible role for dopamine has been suggested due to the feelings of pleasure associated with release of this neurotransmitter (Grant et al., 2006). A role for dopamine is supported by research showing development of impulse control disorders among people with Parkinson's disease who are treated with medication that stimulates dopamine D3 receptors (Seeman, 2015). However, large-scale studies have not been conducted to address dopamine function among people with pyromania and kleptomania, likely due in part to the low prevalence rates of these disorders. Neuroimaging suggests abnormal white matter microstructure in the inferior frontal regions in kleptomania, as has been found in people with cocaine dependence (Grant et al., 2006).

Psychoanalytic theories of pyromania and kleptomania focus on aberrant psychosexual development (Burton et al., 2012). Behavioral theories about the reinforcing effects of addictive behaviors (see Chapter 10) also may apply to kleptomania and pyromania. For people with these disorders, stealing or setting a fire produces pleasurable feelings that reinforce the behavior and increase the likelihood that it will be repeated (positive reinforcement). Reductions in feelings of tension or craving that accompany stealing or fire setting also may serve as negative reinforcement. Additionally, as is the case for addictive disorders, environmental cues (being in a particular store, seeing a news report about a fire) may become associated with urges to perform the behavior through a process of classical conditioning. Other psychological risk factors may include family dysfunction (e.g., higher parental stress, poorer-quality parent relationships, increased marital violence, or parental substance use), childhood abuse, poor social skills, and peer rejection (Lambie & Randell, 2011).

Learning Objective Summaries

LO 5.10 Describe the biological factors that may contribute to the onset of OCD.

Family and twin studies suggest the importance of both biological (genetic) and environmental factors in the onset of OCD. Structural and functional neuroimaging studies point to a central role for the cortico-striato-thalamo-cortical circuit, although different patterns of brain activity may be associated with different subtypes of OCD. Treatment studies suggest a role of serotonin in OCD onset, but biological marker and challenge studies have produced inconsistent results.

LO 5.11 Utilize the psychological theories of anxiety acquisition to explain the etiology of OCD.

Mowrer's two-factor theory of fear acquisition has been used to explain the onset and maintenance of OCD. This model suggests that obsessional fears develop as a result of classical conditioning and are maintained via operant conditioning (negative reinforcement). This theory was the impetus for development of exposure and response prevention, an effective behavioral treatment for OCD. Cognitive theories suggest central roles for erroneous thoughts and thought processes in the onset and maintenance of OCD.

LO 5.12 Understand the possible genetic and neuroanatomical factors that may contribute to onset of OCRDs, comparing and contrasting across these disorders and with OCD.

TTM and hoarding disorder run in families, as do OCD and OCRDs. Elevated prevalence of anxiety disorders among families of people with OCD suggests a possible genetic link between these types of disorders. Twin studies suggest that all of the OCRDs are heritable but that environmental factors also play a role. Neuroimaging studies suggest common abnormalities for OCD and BDD.

LO 5.13 Explain the possible psychological causes for OCRDs with a primary focus on cognitive and behavioral factors.

Sociocultural factors may play a role in the onset of BDD and hoarding disorder. Classical and operant conditioning, as well as erroneous beliefs about appearance, likely contribute to the onset and maintenance of BDD. Cognitive and behavioral theories of hoarding focus on beliefs about and emotional attachment to possessions, and saving/acquiring can be considered a form of avoidance that negatively reinforces hoarding beliefs and behaviors. A comprehensive behavioral model for TTM focuses on the roles of sensory, cognitive, affective (emotional), motoric, and environmental cues as triggers and reinforcers for hair pulling. This model also may apply to other body-focused repetitive behaviors such as skin picking.

LO 5.14 Describe possible biological and psychological causes of pyromania and kleptomania.

Family studies suggest a possible association between kleptomania and OCD and substance use disorders. A possible role of dopamine also has been suggested, and neuroimaging suggests overlap in brain structure between kleptomania and cocaine dependence. Psychoanalytic theories of pyromania and kleptomania focus on aberrant psychosexual development. Behavioral theories about the reinforcing effects of addictive behaviors also may apply to kleptomania and pyromania.

Critical Thinking Question

Given what is known and unknown about the biological and psychological causes of OCD, OCRDs, and impulse control disorders, what do you think is the most important next question for researchers to address? Explain why and describe a study that could address this question.

Treatment of Obsessive-Compulsive and Impulse Control Disorders

The two primary treatment modalities supported by research for OCD and related disorders are biological and behavioral/cognitive-behavioral. In most cases, biological treatment involves medication, although other approaches are available for **treatment refractory** cases. The behavioral treatment of choice for OCD is **exposure and response prevention** (ERP), although other types of cognitive-behavioral treatments also are sometimes used. ERP is not an appropriate treatment for all OCRDs or impulse control disorders, and other cognitive-behavioral approaches are generally recommended. As you will see, much more research has addressed the treatment of OCD than the OC-related and impulse control disorders.

OCD: Biological Treatments

LO 5.15 Identify biological treatments, including medication and psychosurgery, that research shows are effective for treating OCD.

MEDICATION As with the anxiety disorders, the *selective serotonergic reuptake inhibitors* (SSRIs; Prozac, Luvox, Zoloft) are one of the most well-studied classes of medication treatment for OCD. More than 20 clinical trials have documented positive effects of these medications, although a positive treatment response for people with OCD generally requires higher doses of SSRIs than are needed for people with anxiety disorders or depression (Goodman et al., 2014; Pittenger & Bloch, 2014). Response rates for SSRIs are equivalent to or less than for ERP (Romanelli et al., 2014), and a significant percentage of people with OCD do not have a favorable response to SSRIs. Continued medication treatment for these individuals generally involves *pharmacological augmentation*, which means adding another medication. Augmentation studies suggest the potential benefit of adding neuroleptics (Pittenger & Bloch, 2014), which are generally used to treat disorders with psychotic symptoms (see Chapter 11). However, side effects of these medications are potentially dangerous, and a more effective strategy seems to be augmentation with behavioral treatment (Simpson et al., 2013).

SSRIs are beneficial for some children with OCD (Bloch & Storch, 2015), although behavioral treatment is generally recommended as a first-line approach (Krebs & Heyman, 2015). No clinical trials yet have examined the effects of SSRIs for older adults with OCD. Medications that target glutamate receptors (e.g., N-methyl-d-aspartate [NMDA]) show some promise for improving OCD in adults and children, but studies are small and often not controlled (Pittenger & Bloch, 2014). A popular recent approach has investigated the impact of d-cycloserine, which also affects the glutamatergic system, as an *augmentation strategy* for behavioral treatment, but a recent meta-analysis showed no effects of this medication over augmentation with placebo (Ori et al., 2015).

PSYCHOSURGERY Before SSRIs and behavior therapy, OCD was considered to be resistant to treatment. As a last resort, surgery provided some relief of symptoms. In the past, surgery was imprecise, and the side effects included unresponsiveness, decreased attention, restricted or inappropriate affect, and/or disinhibition (inability to control emotion or behavior) (Mashour et al., 2005). Today with the use of MRIs and the ability to destroy tissue with radiation (rather than needing to rely on surgery), many fewer side effects occur (although certainly no surgical procedure is without risk).

Cingulotomy and *capsulotomy* are types of neurosurgery currently used to treat OCD. *Cingulotomy* is more common and involves inserting thin probes through the top of the skull into a portion of the brain called the *cingulate bundle* (see Figure 5.4). The probes burn selective portions of the brain tissue (Clinical Research News, 2004). In *capsulotomy, gamma knife surgery* (a form of radiation treatment) makes precise lesions in brain tissue without the need for opening the skull. These surgeries are guided by the use of neuroimaging procedures such as MRI, allowing for surgical precision. Among people with *treatment refractory* OCD who underwent neurosurgery, 41% had a positive response following cingulotomy and 54% responded positively following capsulotomy (Browne et al., 2015). However, neurosurgery is considered only if the person with OCD has failed to benefit from medication and behavior therapy. Candidates for this surgery are always carefully screened because there are risks, such as memory problems and personality changes. These negative outcomes occur less often than they did in the past because we now have more sophisticated neuroimaging and neurosurgery procedures (Dougherty et al., 2002).

OCD: Psychological Treatments

LO 5.16 Describe the components typically included in psychological treatment for OCD.

The behavioral treatment of choice for OCD is ERP, which includes two primary components: (1) *exposure*, a core procedure in many behavioral and cognitive treatments for

Figure 5.4 Cingulotomy and capsulotomy

Cingultology is a neurosurgical technique used for treatment-refractory OCD

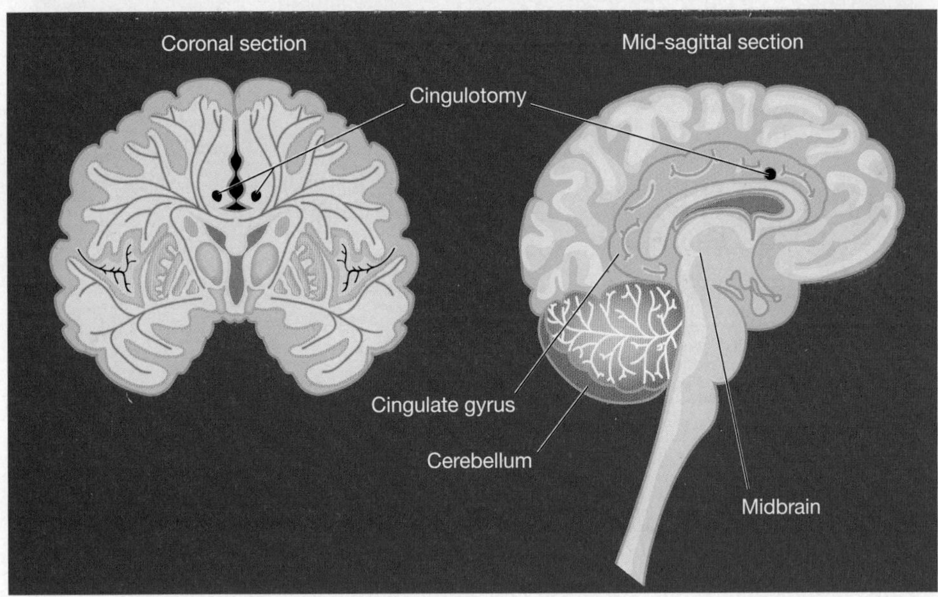

anxiety disorders (see Chapter 4), and (2) *response prevention*, which involves preventing the rituals (including mental acts) and avoidance behaviors that serve to reduce anxiety associated with obsessions. Preventing these anxiety-reducing behaviors allows people to stay in contact with obsessions and fears for long enough that the anxiety begins to dissipate, a process sometimes referred to as **habituation** (see "Real Science, Real Life: Tyler—The Psychopathology and Treatment of Obsessive-Compulsive Disorder"). As is true when exposure is used to treat anxiety disorders, selecting appropriate *in vivo* and/or *imaginal* exposure exercises is key, and often ERP involves creating a hierarchy of feared situations that allows people to begin by exposing themselves to situations that create mild or moderate anxiety and then gradually moving to face increasingly difficult situations.

Remember Jace? Table 5.3 shows a sample hierarchy of ERP tasks that his therapist might have used to help reduce the frequency and intensity of his obsessions and fears about making a mistake and the associated rituals.

This hierarchical approach is reflected in a self-help, online program called *OCD Challenge* that is sometimes used as an adjunct to treatment with a therapist or when no therapist with expertise in ERP is available.

Table 5.3 Sample ERP Hierarchy

Exposure Exercise	Response Prevention	Anticipated Anxiety Level (0 · none; 10 · worst ever)
Leave your home; close and lock the front door; walk to your car and imagine what might happen if you actually forgot to lock the door.	Continue walking to your car; don't turn around to check the lock either visually or with your hands.	3
Listen to a podcast and imagine what might happen if you forgot a detail.	Do not take any notes or repeat any information to yourself.	5
Get in your car and turn the ignition on and then off; get out of the car, lock the door once, and walk away; imagine what might happen if you didn't lock the door correctly.	Don't go back to the car to check the lock either visually or with your hands. Go inside your home, and don't turn around or look out the window to check your car.	7
Complete a class assignment.	Check your work only once; don't ask your parents for assistance.	9

Watch OCD CHALLENGE

More than 35 clinical trials have examined the effects of ERP, with results suggesting significant benefit of this approach (Ost et al., 2015). The effects of ERP are equivalent to or greater than SSRIs, and outcomes are similar when ERP is delivered with or without medication (Romanelli et al., 2014). As is true for many other disorders, ERP is now being delivered in a variety of ways, including by telephone, videoconferencing, Internet-administered programs that may or may not include contact with a therapist, and **bibliotherapy**, again with or without therapist assistance. These more *remote* delivery options also lead to positive outcomes, although treatment is more effective when a therapist is involved (Wootton, 2016).

Cognitive therapy is also used to treat OCD, sometimes in combination with ERP and sometimes alone. However, behavioral *experiments* typically used by patients in cognitive therapy to test their obsessive beliefs can certainly be considered exposure activities. Meta-analysis of clinical trials suggests that cognitive therapy for OCD produces outcomes similar to ERP (Ost et al., 2015).

> Jose discussed with his therapist his obsessions and fears about coming into contact with bird droppings. He was afraid that whenever he walked outside or sat on an outdoor chair or bench, he would come into contact with bird droppings—even when he couldn't see them. This contamination then would spread to his clothing and his hands. As a result, Jose feared that he would get sick and transfer germs to others, making him responsible for terrible outcomes. Jose's therapist asked him to write down his thoughts and think about the actual probability of coming into contact with bird droppings as well as the degree of responsibility he had for illnesses that others experienced. As part of their work together, the therapist asked Jose to spend more time outside, walking on sidewalks and sitting on benches, while he evaluated the reality of his thoughts and tested alternative explanations.

ERP is effective for children (Franklin et al., 2015; Krebs & Heyman, 2015), although treatment for children often incorporates cognitive therapy and a family component (see "Research Hot Topic"). Similarly, family involvement and cognitive approaches, as well as consideration of comorbid medical conditions, influence the delivery of treatment for OCD in older adults (Carmin & Weigartz, 2000), although no clinical trials yet have been conducted in this age group.

ETHICS AND RESPONSIBILITY ERP can seem "cruel" as it requires asking people to face their fears and experience increased anxiety, which means they have to feel worse before they feel better (Olatunji et al., 2009). The American Psychological Association (APA) ethics code states that psychologists should "do no harm" (2010), and we usually think of therapy making people feel better instead of worse. However, the increased

Research HOT Topic

Family Treatment for Children with OCD

Because children exist in families, family factors are important to consider in understanding how to best treat children with OCD. Several family variables affect outcomes following ERP for children, including *family accommodation*, parents diagnosed with OCD, and family conflict, blame, and cohesion (Peris & Piacentini, 2013). As such, recent treatment models for children that are anchored in ERP have begun to incorporate enhanced family-based components.

One recent study of family-based cognitive-behavioral treatment (FB-CBT) for young children (ages 5 to 8) tested an intervention that added a number of components to traditional ERP for children (Freeman et al., 2014). The first phase in this treatment involved psychoeducation for both children and parents (e.g., what is OCD and how does the treatment work). Parents were then involved in ERP, first by watching the therapist conduct exposure sessions and later by taking over the therapist role. Additionally, ERP was supplemented with a set of parent "tools" that included teaching parents to use reinforcement (i.e., attention, ignoring, and rewards) to encourage non-OCD behavior and to model appropriate behavior in stressful situations (Anderson et al., 2015). Parents were also encouraged to *disengage* from their child's OCD behaviors as a way of decreasing family accommodation. FB-CBT was more effective in reducing OCD symptoms than a comparison family intervention that combined education and relaxation training (Freeman et al., 2014).

Another innovative treatment for children with OCD supplements standard ERP with positive family interaction therapy (PFIT; Peris & Piacentini, 2013). In this approach, the family participates in weekly family therapy sessions that occur separately from ERP sessions, with a focus on improving family supportiveness and cohesion, learning to regulate emotions, and gaining experience in family problem solving. Preliminary data suggest that this approach improves outcomes over standard ERP (Peris & Piacentini, 2013).

anxiety produced during ERP sessions is temporary, and the treatment is supported by a large body of research that demonstrates its efficacy. ERP sessions also typically continue until the patient's anxiety has returned to baseline levels, and only psychologists who have had appropriate training in ERP should use this treatment (American Psychological Association, 2010; Olatunji et al., 2009).

As with the anxiety disorders, *mindfulness* and *acceptance and commitment therapy* (ACT) have recently been considered as possible effective treatments for OCD (Twohig et al., 2015). In many ways, this approach aligns with an ERP model in that people are asked to experience obsessional thoughts without attempting to *neutralize* or *change* them. In a similar way, the dissipation of anxiety following ERP allows people to *accept* obsessive thoughts as natural events that do not need to be feared.

Explore ETHICS AND RESPONSIBILITY

OCRDs: Biological Treatments

LO 5.17 Understand what research tells us about the use of biological treatment (medication) for OCRDs.

In general, SSRIs are less effective for the treatment of OCRDs than they are for OCD. The most positive response to these medications occurs for patients with BDD, the symptoms of which seem to have more overlap with OCD than other OCRDs. Approximately 50 to 70% of people with BDD have a positive response to SSRIs, and surprisingly, the presence of delusional beliefs does not reduce the effects of these medications (Fang et al., 2014). SSRIs are not effective for the treatment of TTM, although some evidence suggests the benefit of treatment with N-acetylcysteine (NAC), which stimulates glutamate receptors, and augmentation of SSRIs with antipsychotic medication (Rothbart & Stein, 2014). No clinical trials yet have examined the effectiveness of SSRIs specifically for hoarding disorder, but data from studies of people with OCD suggest that response to treatment is 50% less likely for those with hoarding symptoms (Abramowitz & Jacoby, 2014). Only a handful of studies have examined the effects of medication treatment for skin picking, and the results of these are inconsistent likely due to very small sample sizes (Gelinas & Gagnon, 2013). With the inclusion of excoriation disorder in DSM-5, it is likely that more clinical trials will be conducted with larger groups of subjects.

OCRDs: Psychological Treatments

LO 5.18 Describe psychological treatments for OCRDs with attention to cognitive-behavioral approaches.

As with OCD, although other types of psychological treatments are sometimes used to treat OCRDs (e.g., psychoanalytic therapy), most research has focused on cognitive and behavioral treatments. Given that BDD includes obsessive-like thoughts and ritualistic behaviors, cognitive-behavioral treatment for this disorder typically includes ERP (e.g., exposure to perceptions of ugliness and prevention of behaviors like mirror checking and social avoidance). However, because people with BDD also have inaccurate and sometimes delusional beliefs about their appearance, cognitive restructuring is generally included to help people change these beliefs (e.g., how accurate is the thought "My acne has created huge craters on my face that everyone will notice.") Another technique incorporated into cognitive-behavioral treatment for BDD is *mirror retraining*, which involves learning to describe one's appearance in the mirror in more objective, nonjudgmental ways. Research has shown that cognitive-behavioral treatment is effective for BDD (Ipser et al., 2009).

Cognitive-behavioral treatment for hoarding disorder also includes ERP and cognitive restructuring to change beliefs about possessions (Steketee et al., 2010). For hoarding disorder, ERP involves exercises designed to help people discard saved items and prevent acquisition. Other treatment components include teaching skills for organizing, making decisions, and solving problems. A randomized controlled trial of this broad type of cognitive-behavioral treatment for hoarding disorder showed significant improvement relative to a wait-list control condition for adults with hoarding disorder (Steketee et al., 2010). This same treatment, however, is not effective for older adults (Ayers et al., 2011). Given that older adults with hoarding disorder have a greater risk of cognitive deficits than younger adults, a modified cognitive-behavioral treatment for older adults has been developed to include elements of *cognitive rehabilitation* (improving memory by using calendars, to-do lists, and prioritizing). A recent open trial of this intervention was effective for a small group of older adults with hoarding disorder (Ayers et al., 2014), but larger randomized trials are needed.

The most well-studied psychological treatment for TTM and skin picking is *habit reversal training* (HRT; Azrin & Nunn, 1977), a behavioral treatment that involves two primary steps: (1) becoming more aware of the cues associated with hair pulling or skin picking and (2) using what is known as a *competing response* to physically prevent the behavior from occurring. For example, when a person notices that pulling (or picking) has started or is about to start, he or she might be asked to make a fist, fold his or her arms, or clench a steering wheel until the urge

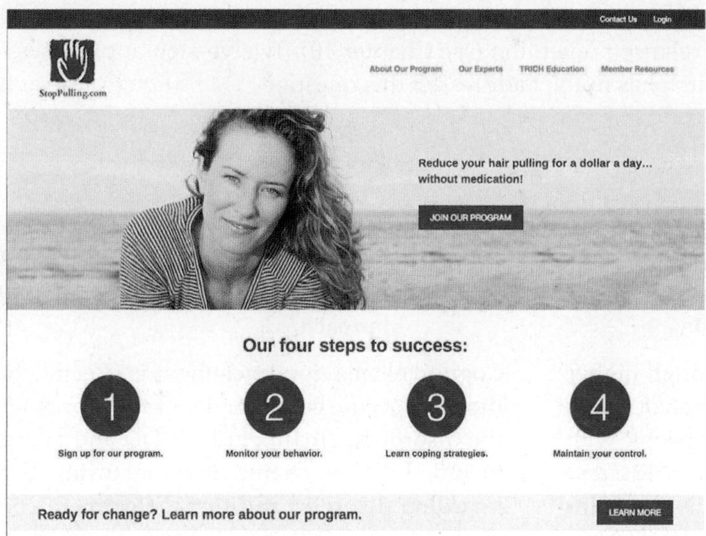

Online programs like StopPulling.com allow people to record a range of cues (place, thoughts, emotions, motor behaviors) associated with episodes of hair pulling that are then matched with associated coping skills.

to pull or pick dissipates. Research has demonstrated that HRT is an effective treatment for TTM (McGuire et al., 2014) and skin picking (Teng et al., 2006). Recent versions of psychological treatment for these disorders have added techniques from mindfulness and ACT into HRT to help people manage the negative emotions that trigger these behaviors. These integrated approaches also are effective (Flessner et al., 2008; Gelinas & Gagnon, 2013; Woods & Houghton, 2014).

Another promising treatment for TTM and excoriation disorder is based on a comprehensive behavioral treatment model (Mansueto, 2013) that utilizes a variety of cognitive and behavioral treatment techniques to address the unique patterns of cues that trigger and maintain hair pulling or skin picking for each individual. For example, a person who pulls in response to stress might be taught relaxation training, time management, or how to engage in more pleasurable activities. Someone who enjoys the feeling of a hair in their fingers after pulling might rub their fingers instead with a soft brush. This treatment approach has been incorporated into online self-help programs for hair pulling, StopPulling.com (see photo), and skin picking, StopPicking.com. Preliminary data suggest that these programs are effective (Flessner et al., 2009; Mouton-Odum et al., 2006).

Behavioral treatments also are effective for children with TTM and excoriation disorder (Woods & Hougton, 2015). These treatments include a combination of HRT, **stimulus control** (placing barriers to pulling in high-risk situations, such as wearing gloves or reducing time spent in high-risk situations), and reinforcement programs that provide praise or rewards for reduced pulling.

Pyromania and Kleptomania

LO 5.19 Identify biological and psychological treatments that may be effective for pyromania and kleptomania.

Antidepressants, including the SSRIs, have been used to treat pyromania and kleptomania, as have mood stabilizers (e.g., lithium) and opioid agonists, which affect the dopaminergic mesolimbic pathway (Grant et al., 2013). Although case studies and open trials have suggested the potential benefits of these medications, only two randomized clinical trials have been conducted for kleptomania, one showing no response to escitalopram (SSRI; Koran et al., 2007) and another demonstrating a positive response to naltrexone (opioid agonist; Grant et al., 2009). No controlled trials of medication have been conducted with pyromania.

Likewise, no randomized trials yet have addressed the effects of psychological treatments for pyromania or kleptomania, although case reports suggest the potential value of cognitive-behavioral treatment (Grant et al., 2013). **Imaginal desensitization**, which involves imagining details of stealing along with an ability to resist the urge, has some promise. Other cognitive-behavioral approaches used for treatment of addiction also may be beneficial, including avoidance of situations that trigger urges, coping skills training, and relapse prevention (see Chapter 10). Twelve-step approaches may be effective, but research has not yet addressed this question.

Learning Objective Summaries

LO 5.15 Identify biological treatments, including medication and psychosurgery, that research shows are effective for treating OCD.

SSRIs are effective for adults with OCD, although higher doses are generally needed than for people with anxiety disorders or depression. A significant percentage of people with OCD, however, do not respond to treatment with SSRIs, and continued medication treatment for these individuals involves pharmacological augmentation. SSRIs are also effective for children with OCD, but behavioral treatment is generally preferred as a first step. Cingulotomy and capsulotomy may be beneficial for people with treatment refractory OCD.

LO 5.16 Describe the components typically included in psychological treatment for OCD.

ERP is an effective treatment for adults and children with OCD. Exposure to fear-producing obsessions and prevention of rituals facilitate habituation and fear reduction. The effects of ERP are equivalent to or greater than SSRIs. When ERP is used with children, cognitive therapy and a family component are usually included.

LO 5.17 Understand what research tells us about the use of biological treatment (medication) for OCRDs.

SSRIs are effective for BDD, but these medications are not consistently effective for other OCRDs. N-acetylcysteine may be effective for TTM.

LO 5.18 Describe psychological treatments for OCRDs with attention to cognitive-behavioral approaches.

Cognitive-behavioral treatment is effective for OCRDs, although specific components of this approach vary across the disorders. Treatment for BDD and hoarding disorder include ERP and cognitive restructuring. For people with hoarding disorder, additional treatment components include teaching skills for organizing, making decisions, and solving problems. Habit reversal training is effective for TTM and skin picking, although newer models of treatment for these disorders are broader and address a wider range of triggers and outcomes of the behaviors.

LO 5.19 Identify biological and psychological treatments that may be effective for pyromania and kleptomania.

Case studies and open trials suggest potential benefits of antidepressants, mood stabilizers, and opioid agonists for pyromania and kleptomania. One clinical trial showed no response to an SSRI for kleptomania, and another demonstrated a positive response to an opioid agonist. No trials have been conducted with pyromania. Likewise, case reports suggest the potential value of cognitive-behavioral treatment for these disorders, but no clinical trials have been conducted.

Critical Thinking Question

Compare and contrast the biological and psychological treatments that have been tested for OCD, OCRDs, and pyromania/kleptomania, describing specific areas of overlapping and non-overlapping approaches. What does this research tell us, if anything, about overlap among these disorders?

Real SCIENCE, Real LIFE

Tyler—The Psychopathology and Treatment of Obsessive-Compulsive Disorder

THE PATIENT

Tyler, age 20, was a full-time college student who lived in a campus apartment. He was a Christian who valued highly his religious beliefs and affiliations.

THE PROBLEM

Tyler had repetitive and intrusive "bad" thoughts and images about sex and religion. He reported having thoughts that associated God's name with dirt and the devil ("God is dirty";

"Jesus is the Devil") and images of Jesus as a naked man having sexual relations. Tyler sometimes imagined himself having sex with relatives and strangers, and curse words repeatedly popped into his head. He felt highly distressed by these thoughts and images, believing that God expected him to control them but he could not. He was afraid that if he did not get a handle on the thoughts, God would reject him, and he would spend eternity in hell. To reduce the anxiety produced by the obsessions, Tyler repeated any behavior that he was doing when a repetitive thought or image came into his mind. For example, if he had a "bad" thought while going through a doorway, he went back and forth through the door multiple times until he could do so with a "good" thought in his mind. Similar ritualistic patterns occurred when he was sitting down in a chair, getting in or out of bed, and changing his clothes. He needed to replace "bad" thoughts with "good" ones in order to atone for his sins. Tyler also tried to control the thoughts by avoiding contact with religious symbols. For instance, if he knew his route on the freeway would take him by a church, he drove a longer distance to avoid passing it. He also kept his Bible and his favorite cross in a drawer.

Although Tyler was able to maintain adequate grades in college despite these thoughts and behaviors, he sometimes spent many hours each day repeating behaviors. He tried hard to perform his rituals when no one was watching him, and he avoided developing close friendships as that would make it harder to keep his behaviors a secret. Tyler also was depressed. He felt so guilty about his horrible thoughts, and although he sometimes thought that killing himself would be a possible solution, he knew that suicide was a sin and would therefore ensure him a place in hell.

Tyler's parents were also anxious. They did not have OCD, but they worried significantly about how and what Tyler and his sister were doing, and they tried hard to teach their children religious values. The family attended church regularly, and they said prayers together at home. Somehow, Tyler's younger sister avoided developing anxiety; she was a free spirit who hardly ever worried about anything. Tyler was the one who worried as a child and adolescent, and even then, he had special ways of doing things that he felt helped him be a better person (e.g., repeating prayers, confessing to his parents when he said a bad word). The intrusive sexual and religious thoughts, however, didn't start until he left home for college. He sought treatment at the college counseling center, but weekly "talk therapy" wasn't helping him. He knew he needed something more, so he reached out to his parents to help him find other resources.

ASSESSING THE SITUATION

Based on what you've read about Tyler's case as well as what you've learned in this chapter, what treatment would you recommend for Tyler, and what would be your rationale for choosing this course of therapy?

TREATMENT

Tyler's treatment involved three major components: (1) a trial of medication, (2) behavior therapy to target obsessions and rituals, and (3) behavioral treatment to improve his mood and social relationships. He began treatment with a 3-month trial of an SSRI, which improved his mood and reduced the frequency of obsessions and time spent doing daily rituals. The symptoms were still getting in the way of his ability to function well, however, so he also began a course of exposure and response prevention. Tyler and his therapist together created a hierarchy of "bad" thoughts and images. At the bottom (lowest anxiety) were thoughts that included repeating curse words; at the top (highest anxiety) were images of Jesus having sexual interactions. During the first session they went to the back of the building, and Tyler was asked to think (even say aloud) curse words as he went through the back door. He then was not allowed to return through the doorway (response prevention), and his therapist asked him to continue walking along the sidewalk, thinking the curse words and imagining the punishment he might receive from God for having such horrible thoughts. Over the next hour, Tyler began to feel less anxious even as he continued to think about his possible ultimate fate. For homework, Tyler was asked to do the same kind of exposure exercise at his home at least three times during the subsequent week and to begin to reduce his repeating behaviors as much as possible.

At the start of each subsequent session, Tyler reported to his therapist how his home practice assignments had gone. Sometimes it was easier to prevent himself from repeating behaviors than others, but overall, he felt a little less anxious each time he practiced. During sessions, as he was ready, Tyler and his therapist created new scenes that represented higher steps on his hierarchy. They also began to address his avoidance. Tyler was asked to get his Bible out of the drawer and put it on his bureau. Eventually, he was wearing his favorite cross necklace, driving past churches, and deliberately imagining Jesus as a naked man having sexual relations. The goal of this work, he learned, was to recognize the thoughts as just that—only thoughts that could be experienced without fear. As he exposed himself to feared thoughts, prevented his rituals, and began to face avoided situations, his fears decreased and the thoughts occurred less often.

As Tyler began to have fewer symptoms, he had more time to work on developing friendships. He and his therapist talked about activities that he might enjoy adding into his schedule. For a start, he joined a workout club at the college gym and began exercising 3 days a week. At first, he had to push himself to go, but the more he went, the more energy he had for going again as the exercise was helping him feel better. Tyler also met a few nice people at the gym and started planning exercise "dates."

THE TREATMENT OUTCOME

After 3 months of treatment, Tyler was feeling much better. He had fewer obsessions than he'd had since he started college, and he was feeling optimistic about his ability to manage these symptoms over the coming months and years. He was socializing a bit more and thinking about asking a girl he met at the gym out for coffee. He knew he would need to continue doing exposure practice, particularly during stressful times in his life when obsessive thoughts would be more likely, but he was up to the challenge.

Key Terms

addictive behavior, p. 176
bibliotherapy, p. 190
biological challenge studies, p. 181
biological marker studies, p. 181
body dysmorphic disorder, p. 168
body-focused repetitive behavior, p. 173
compulsions, p. 163
excoriation (skin-picking) disorder, p. 174
exposure and response prevention, p. 187
family accommodation, p. 164
grooming behavior, p. 185
habituation, p. 189
hoarding disorder, p. 170
imaginal desensitization, p. 193
impulse control disorders, p. 176
kleptomania, p. 177
meta-analysis, p. 179
obsessional neurosis, p. 181
obsessions, p. 163
obsessive-compulsive and related disorders, p. 168
obsessive-compulsive disorder, p. 163
psychological challenge studies, p. 180
pyromania, p. 176
stimulus control, p. 193
subtype, p. 179
thought-action fusion, p. 183
treatment refractory, p. 187
trichotillomania, p. 172

Chapter 6

Somatic Symptom and Dissociative Disorders

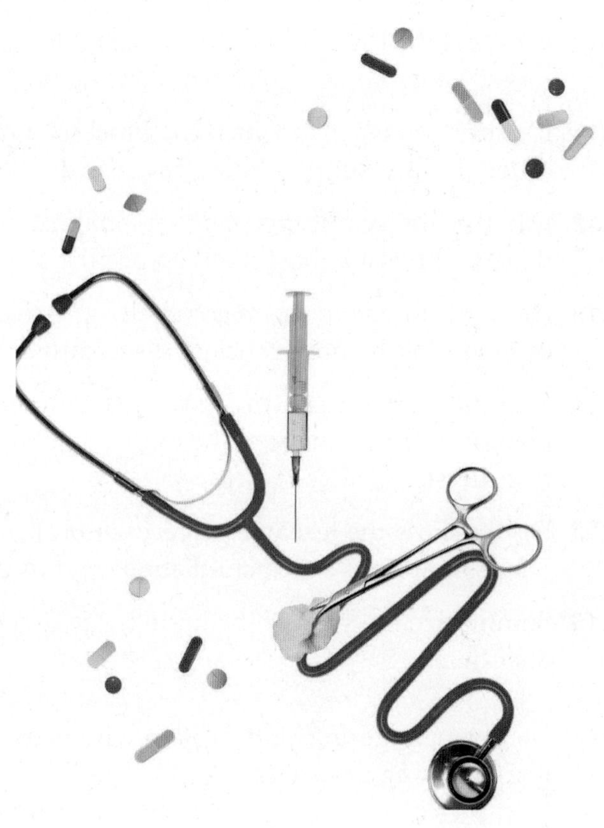

Chapter Learning Objectives

Somatic Symptom and Related Disorders	**LO 6.1**	Understand how normal physical sensations can create abnormal concerns about somatic functioning.
	LO 6.2	Identify two ways in which conversion disorder differs from somatic symptom disorder.
	LO 6.3	Describe how illness anxiety disorder differs from somatic symptom disorder.
	LO 6.4	Identify at least two characteristics of factitious disorder that make it different from other somatic symptom and related disorders.

	LO 6.5	Describe how these disorders affect the individual, community, and society.
	LO 6.6	Explain the responsibilities of mental health professionals when faced with an incident of factitious disorder imposed on another.
	LO 6.7	Discuss how these disorders are affected by demographic and sociocultural factors.
	LO 6.8	Identify the contributions of biological, psychological, and environmental factors to somatic symptom and related disorders.
	LO 6.9	Identify the challenges to successful psychological treatment for somatic symptom and related disorders.
Dissociative Disorders	**LO 6.10**	Discuss how dissociative amnesia is different from momentary forgetting or amnesia as a result of medical conditions.
	LO 6.11	Identify two ways in which the process of the diagnosis of DID differs from other psychological disorders.
	LO 6.12	Describe the symptoms of depersonalization/derealization and when those feelings are most likely to occur.
	LO 6.13	Understand one of the major challenges to establishing accurate estimates of the prevalence of dissociative disorders, including DID.
	LO 6.14	Describe how the controversy surrounding repressed/recovered memories has influenced the etiological theories of dissociative disorders.
	LO 6.15	Discuss how the research on recovered/false memories may affect our assumptions about child abuse and its aftermath.
	LO 6.16	Summarize the state of the knowledge on how to treat dissociative disorders.
Malingering	**LO 6.17**	Define malingering, and explain why it creates issues for clinicians in diagnosing disorders.

Lucy, who is married and age 40, feels awful. None of her doctors has helped her. About 12 years ago, she hurt her back while cleaning her house, and everything has gone downhill since. She has constant lower back pain and periodic neck pain despite operations to fuse together parts of her spine. Her left arm aches. She has numerous prescriptions for pain, including the powerful drug oxycontin. She complains of blood in her urine and pain during sexual intercourse.

Although her physician did not think it necessary, Lucy had a hysterectomy to reduce excessive menstrual bleeding. Now she believes that she has severe asthma and allergies. She has been taken by ambulance to the hospital emergency room for breathing treatments and regularly uses two inhalers and three asthma medications. Yet allergy testing has revealed only moderate allergic reactions to pollen and dust mites. Several years ago, Lucy had extreme gastrointestinal pain. She complained of nausea, particularly after eating, and diarrhea. She sought out several physicians, but none could find anything wrong. After hearing that a friend had similar symptoms and had gall bladder surgery, Lucy convinced a physician that she too needed the surgery.

At the time of the psychological evaluation, Lucy had numbness in both legs. Her balance was affected, and she had difficulty walking. Last year, a niece was diagnosed with amyotrophic lateral sclerosis. Three physicians have told Lucy that she does not have amyotrophic lateral sclerosis, but she insisted on yet another MRI. Upon questioning by the psychologist, Lucy revealed contentious relationships with all of her family—her symptoms were always worse when she was fighting with her husband or her children.

Lucy's case is extreme, but we all have occasional aches and pains. In fact, 85 to 95% of the general population has at least one physical symptom every 2 to 4 weeks, and some people have unexplained symptoms as often as every 5 to 7 days (Katon & Walker, 1998). Common physical complaints include chest pain, abdominal pain, dizziness, headache, back pain, and fatigue, yet an organic cause is identified only 10 to 15% of the time. Clearly, many people have physical complaints for which there is no identified medical basis. Usually, physician reassurance that "everything is fine" allows people to resume their normal activities.

A few people like Lucy resist physician reassurance. Her case poses a challenge for health care professionals. How does one determine when physical symptoms result from psychological distress rather than organic illness? The answer is complex and requires consideration of three interrelated factors (Kirmayer & Looper, 2007). First, when are physical symptoms medically unexplained? Second, when is worry or distress about physical symptoms excessive? Third, when is physical distress considered to be caused primarily by psychological factors?

To answer the first question, physical complaints are considered to be medically unexplained when physical examination and diagnostic testing cannot determine any biological or physical cause. In Lucy's case, three different physicians could not diagnose her balance problems even when using the most sophisticated medical tests. Therefore, her symptoms were medically unexplained. To answer the second question, worry about physical health is excessive when it results in functional impairment or leads to medically unnecessary procedures (such as Lucy's gall bladder surgery). The answer to the third question—When does physical distress result from psychological factors rather than physical illness?—is much more complicated. Its answer is the focus of this chapter. In fact, the interplay of physical symptoms, environmental stress, and emotional distress can create different types of psychological impairments known as *somatic symptom and related disorders,* and *dissociative disorders.* We begin with the category of somatic symptom and related disorders.

Somatic Symptom and Related Disorders

Somatic symptom and related disorders are characterized by excessive thoughts, feelings, and behaviors related to somatic symptoms. People who suffer from these disorders experience real physical symptoms, but their physical pain cannot be fully explained by an established medical condition. The somatic symptom category is a confusing diagnostic category because the individual disorders do not share an underlying emotion or a common etiology. Instead, people with somatic symptom and related disorders express thoughts, feelings, or behaviors in relation to the physical symptoms that seem out of proportion to the symptoms themselves. The specific disorders include somatic symptom disorder, illness anxiety disorder, conversion disorder, and factitious disorder. Each is described in this section.

Somatic Symptom Disorder

LO 6.1 Understand how normal physical sensations can create abnormal concerns about somatic functioning.

In 1859, the French physician Pierre Briquet (1796–1881) wrote an influential paper describing psychiatric patients with many somatic complaints that seemed to lack a physical cause. These patients were also likely to be depressed, and he noted that stressful life events could be particularly important in the onset and maintenance of their distress. This constellation of symptoms was once called *hysteria* or *Briquet's syndrome,* but these terms are no longer used because they carry negative connotations. Now known as **somatic symptom disorder**, the condition is defined as the presence of one or more somatic symptoms plus abnormal/excessive thoughts, feelings, and behaviors regarding the symptoms. It is important to note that the thoughts, feelings, and behaviors must be considered excessive or disproportionate to the symptoms. As Lucy illustrates, these physical complaints result in excessive health concerns and persistently high anxiety about one's health (see "DSM-5: Somatic Symptom Disorder"). Although any one symptom does not need to be consistently present, the presence of a symptomatic state is necessary.

There are no specific physical symptoms that are needed for the diagnosis of somatic symptom disorder, and some experts have suggested that the diagnostic criteria are so broad that 15% of patients with cancer and heart disease as well as 25% of patients with irritable bowel syndrome would meet criteria for somatic symptom disorder (Frances, 2013). This finding raises the question of whether the reactions of people with documented (and, in some cases, life-threatening medical disorders) should ever be considered so dysfunctional as to meet criteria for a psychological disorder (Dimsdale & Levenson, 2013). Also, even if some people with documented medical disorders meet the diagnostic criteria for somatic symptom disorder, the vast majority will not and the small percentage that do may benefit from therapies designed to lessen their worry or distress (Dimsdale et al., 2013). The utility of such a diagnosis will only be answered with time, as more data on the characteristics of people who meet the diagnostic criteria for this disorder emerge (Dimesdale & Levenson, 2013), but some of the more common complaints include pain and gastrointestinal distress. Common pain complaints include back pain, chest pain, and headaches. Much less common but more dramatic are the *pseudoneurological* symptoms such as **pseudoseizures**, which are sudden changes in behavior that mimic epileptic seizures but have no organic basis (see "Real Science, Real Life: Nancy—A Case of Somatic Symptom Disorder").

Conversion Disorder (Functional Neurological Symptom Disorder)

LO 6.2 Identify two ways in which conversion disorder differs from somatic symptom disorder.

Somatic symptom disorder is defined by the presence of different physical symptoms including pseudoneurological complaints. A different disorder, **conversion disorder**, consists of symptoms of altered motor or sensory dysfunction (see "DSM-5: Conversion Disorder"). Symptoms of conversion disorder can be quite dramatic, such as sudden paralysis or blindness. They are not intentionally produced and cannot be fully explained by the presence of any medical condition. Before this diagnosis is assigned, a careful medical evaluation is necessary because about 10 to 15% of people originally diagnosed with conversion disorder will later be found to have a diagnosable medical condition (Binzer & Kullgren, 1998; Hurwitz & Prichard, 2006). However, there is no way to determine which symptoms indicate a true neurological disorder. Therefore, therapists must strike a balance between excluding possible medical conditions and overdiagnosing and thereby reinforcing the behavior.

The French physician Pierre Briquet was first to identify a condition in which patients had many physical complaints without an obvious medical cause. This problem, once called Briquet's syndrome, is now called somatic symptom disorder.

Symptoms of conversion disorder consist of various types. The most common group includes *motor symptoms or deficits*, such as impaired coordination or balance, paralysis or weakness, tremor, gait abnormality, and abnormal limb posturing (American Psychiatric Association, 2013). Within this group, muscle weaknesses, particularly in the legs, are most frequent (Krem, 2004). An unusual symptom is *globus*, which may include aphonia, sensations of choking, difficulty swallowing, shortness of breath, or feelings of suffocation (Finkenbine & Miele, 2004).

> Hannah was a 28-year-old clerk at a car dealership. She had always been the "nervous" type and was very shy as a young girl. Sometimes when customers came in angry, complaining about their service, she started to feel a lump in her throat. She would put her hand up to her throat like she was choking, and when people asked if she was okay, she would gasp and say she couldn't get her breath. She would get more and more upset and was afraid she would suffocate. Sometimes the sensations would go away. At other times, Hannah would panic and call her doctor.

In many instances, globus lasts only for a short period of time. However, if left untreated, it can lead to abnormal eating patterns or food avoidance.

DSM-5

Criteria for Somatic Symptom Disorder

A. One or more somatic symptoms that are distressing or result in significant disruption of daily life.

B. Excessive thoughts, feelings, or behaviors related to the somatic symptoms or associated health concerns as manifested by at least one of the following:

1. Disproportionate and persistent thoughts about the seriousness of one's symptoms.
2. Persistently high level of anxiety about health or symptoms.
3. Excessive time and energy devoted to these symptoms or health concerns.

C. Although any one somatic symptom may not be continuously present, the state of being symptomatic is persistent (typically more than 6 months).

Gina is 6 years old and has a history of fearful and inhibited behavior. She was referred by her pediatrician because she developed a fear of choking on food. Several weeks ago she was in a crowd of people and told her mother that she was choking. She was not, but her mother could only calm her down by taking her out of the crowd. Since that time, Gina has complained of a sore throat and an inability to eat solid foods. Gina's pediatrician ruled out any medical cause. This past week, her entire food intake consisted of milk, milkshakes, mashed potatoes, and yogurt.

Sensory deficits, a less common symptom group, include loss of touch or pain sensations, double vision or blindness, deafness, and hallucinations (American Psychiatric Association, 2013). Movies sometimes portray people as having "hysterical blindness," but this condition rarely occurs in real life. Also rare is a third symptom group, which consists of behaviors such as *psychogenic or non-seizures* and *convulsions*.

Symptoms of conversion disorder do not follow known neurological patterns of the human body, a factor that is often important in differentiating between a psychological and a physical disorder. For example, a patient may complain of loss of sensitivity in the hand and

SIDE by SIDE Case Studies

Dimensions of Behavior: From Adaptive to Maladaptive

Adaptive Behavior Case Study

Amy was diagnosed with breast cancer. She had surgery, radiation, and chemotherapy. About 6 months after she finished treatment, she felt a nagging pain in her upper back. It was not a sharp pain but a dull ache that would not go away. No matter what she did, the ache was there. Amy remembered that her mother, who had died from breast cancer, had pain in her back too. It turned out that her mother's cancer had metastasized to her bones. Amy was worried, and the doctor ordered a bone scan. The results indicated that she did not have bone cancer. The doctor thought that the pain was the result of a muscle strain or injury. Amy felt better after she heard the results. Although the pain was still there and at times kept her from sleeping, she no longer worried about it. After a few months, the pain disappeared.

Maladaptive Behavior Case Study

Angela married right out of high school and did not have any special vocational skills. She recently divorced and had to take a job in a hospital cafeteria, and she hated it. On some days, she worked on the serving line—it was hot, and her feet hurt from standing. On other days, she delivered food trays to patients—it was hard work, and the patients did not seem appreciative. At work one day, she slipped and fell. Although the physician cleared her to return to work, Angela reported severe and chronic pain in her lower back and sometimes pain in her abdomen. An extensive diagnostic battery did not reveal any medical reason for her pain, yet it was so persistent that Angela applied for disability. Her financial status was so negatively affected that she had to move in with one of her children.

DSM-5

Criteria for Conversion Disorder

A. One or more symptoms of altered voluntary motor or sensory function.

B. Clinical findings provide evidence of incompatibility between the symptom and recognized neurological or medical conditions.

C. The symptom or deficit is not better explained by another medical or mental disorder.

D. The symptom or deficit causes clinically significant distress or impairment in social, occupational, or other important areas of functioning or warrants medical evaluation.

wrist, a condition sometimes called *glove anesthesia* (see Figure 6.1). However, the nerves in the hand (median, ulnar, and radial nerves) do not suddenly end at the wrist. These nerves continue, uninterrupted, throughout the arm. Therefore, if one (or all) of the nerves were damaged, the loss of sensation would not stop at the wrist; the numbness would continue up through the arm. In other words, physical anatomy cannot explain the symptom pattern of glove anesthesia. The lack of a medical reason for this phenomenon suggests that the symptoms could have a psychological basis.

The classic description of conversion disorder includes a symptom called *la belle indifference* (beautiful indifference) defined as substantial emotional indifference to the presence of these dramatic physical symptoms. Even when unable to walk or move their arms, some people appear undisturbed by their paralysis. They deny emotional distress from their unusual symptoms and behave as if nothing is wrong. However, some people with conversion disorder are distressed by their symptoms (Kirmayer & Looper, 2007); thus la belle indifference, though often present, is not a necessary symptom of conversion disorder.

The label *conversion disorder* may seem to be an unusual term for a psychological disorder. If you recall the case of Anna O. (see Chapter 1), you will remember that she had many symptoms of this disorder. Psychodynamic theorists, such as Freud and Breuer, theorized that Anna O. was not directly expressing her psychological distress (the stress of taking care of her invalid father and his subsequent death). Instead, it was expressed indirectly through physical complaints. Simply stated, they thought that her psychological distress was *converted* into physical symptoms. Although there is no strong empirical support for this theory, the term *conversion disorder* is still used to describe the presence of these symptoms.

Illness Anxiety Disorder

LO 6.3 Describe how illness anxiety disorder differs from somatic symptom disorder.

Have you ever read about an illness and then worried that you might have it? You may have mentioned your worry to someone who reassured you that you were fine, and so your worry

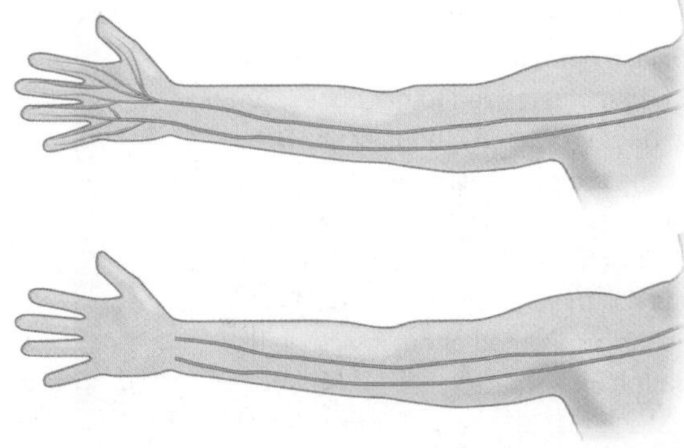

Figure 6.1 Glove Anesthesia.

A person with conversion disorder might describe numbness in the entire hand or wrist, as shown here. However, the nerves that transmit pain signals do not stop at the wrist—they continue up the arm. Numbness that stops at the wrist is not anatomically possible.

disappeared. However, when fears or concerns about having an illness persist despite medical reassurance, the problem may be **illness anxiety disorder** (American Psychiatric Association, 2013). People with this disorder have a high level of worry about health and easily become alarmed about the possibility of having an illness (see "DSM-5: Illness Anxiety Disorder"). They are preoccupied with the possibility of having or developing a physical illness and often elicit negative reactions from physicians because they cannot be reassured that they are well. Their behaviors are similar to the rituals found in obsessive-compulsive disorder (see Chapter 5). Some people with illness anxiety disorder constantly seek reassurance from physicians and monitor their own physical status (e.g., take their blood pressure). Other people with this disorder avoid situations associated with their fear (Taylor & Asmundson, 2004), such as refusing to go to a hospital for fear of catching an illness. In the past, people with these behaviors were said to have "hypochondriasis," and sometimes the person was called a "hypochondriac." However, because of the presence of these phobia-like behaviors, the disorder has been renamed *illness anxiety disorder* (e.g., Abramowitz & Moore, 2007).

Not all worries about illness warrant a diagnosis of illness anxiety disorder. Some people suffer from *transient hypochondriasis*, which may result from contracting an actual acute illness or a life-threatening illness or even from caring for someone with a medical condition (Barsky et al., 1990; Robbins & Kirmayer, 1996). Someone recovering from a heart attack may be reluctant to engage in physical activities even though a physician has approved the activity. In contrast, people with traditional hypochondriasis (the previous term for illness anxiety disorder) have persistent fears of contracting an illness and are much more likely to have additional psychological diagnoses such as major depressive disorder or an anxiety disorder. The high rate of comorbid anxiety and depressive disorders (perhaps as high as 78%) led some clinicians and researchers to question whether hypochondriasis (or illness anxiety disorder) exists as a separate disorder (Robbins & Kirmayer, 1996). If the disorder does exist alone, it does so in only approximately 23% of people with hypochondriasis.

Factitious Disorder

LO 6.4 Identify at least two characteristics of factitious disorder that make it different from other somatic symptom and related disorders.

Factitious disorder differs from other somatic symptom disorders in one very important way: physical or psychological signs or symptoms of illness are intentionally produced in what appears to be a desire to assume a sick role. Unlike **malingering**, in which a person intentionally produces physical symptoms to avoid military service, criminal prosecution, or

DSM-5

Criteria for Illness Anxiety Disorder

A. Preoccupation with having or acquiring a serious illness.

B. Somatic symptoms are not present or, if present, are only mild in intensity. If another medical condition is present or there is a high risk for developing a medical condition (e.g., strong family history is present), the preoccupation is clearly excessive or disproportionate.

C. There is a high level of anxiety about health, and the individual is easily alarmed about personal health status.

D. The individual performs excessive health-related behaviors (e.g., repeatedly checks his or her body for signs of illness) or exhibits maladaptive avoidance (e.g., avoids doctor appointments and hospitals).

E. Illness preoccupation has been present for at least 6 months, but the specific illness that is feared may change over that period of time.

F. The illness-related preoccupation is not better explained by another mental disorder, such as somatic symptom disorder, panic disorder, generalized anxiety disorder, body dysmorphic disorder, obsessive-compulsive disorder, or delusional disorder, somatic type.

work or to obtain financial compensation or drugs, symptom production in factitious disorders is not associated with any external incentives. People are aware that they are producing the symptoms and making themselves ill but appear to be unaware of *why* they do it. People with factitious disorder (see "DSM-5: Factitious Disorder") may produce primarily physical symptoms, primarily psychological symptoms, or both.

First described in 1951, factitious disorder was originally called *Munchausen syndrome,* named after Baron Karl Friedrich Hieronymus von Munchausen, an eighteenth-century German nobleman known for telling tall (and mostly false) tales. There are two types of factitious disorder. The first is **factitious disorder imposed on self**. People with factitious disorder imposed on self engage in deceptive practices to produce signs of illness. These behaviors include faking elevated body temperature, putting blood in urine to simulate kidney/urinary tract infections, or taking blood-thinning medications to produce symptoms of hemophilia. In addition, people with factitious disorder imposed on self deliberately and convincingly fake chest pain or abdominal pain. They will go through numerous invasive and dangerous diagnostic and therapeutic procedures. To convince physicians that they are physically ill, they manipulate laboratory results to substantiate their illness claims. Many of these manipulations are quite sophisticated, but Table 6.1 lists some of the simple things that patients do to convince health personnel that they are truly ill. Although they seek and often beg for medical intervention, they never reveal the fact that they are creating their own physical distress.

People with factitious disorder imposed on self often go to emergency rooms during evenings and weekends when they are more likely to be evaluated by junior clinical staff (Ford, 2005). Furthermore, they sometimes invent false demographic information, including aliases and false information about their past (they may claim to be a Medal

Table 6.1 Laboratory Results for Patients with Factitious Disorder

Presenting Complaint	Laboratory Evidence
Hematuria (blood in urine)	Red candy in urine sample
Nonhealing wound	Mouthwash found in wound
Diarrhea	Excessive ingestion of castor oil or laxatives
Pain from "kidney stones"	Glass fragments in urine
Anemia	"Self-induced" blood draws with substantial blood loss
Vomiting	Ipecac abuse

From Krahn, L. E., Li, H., & O'Connor, M. K. (2003). Patients who strive to be ill: Factitious disorder with physical symptoms. *American Journal of Psychiatry, 160*, 1163–1168; and Wallach, J. (1994). Laboratory diagnosis of factitious disorders. *Archives of Internal Medicine, 154*, 1690–1696.

DSM-5

Criteria for Factitious Disorder

Factitious Disorder Imposed on Self

A. Falsification of physical or psychological signs or symptoms, or induction of injury or disease, associated with identified deception.

B. The individual presents himself or herself to others as ill, impaired, or injured.

C. The deceptive behavior is evident even in the absence of obvious external rewards.

D. The behavior is not better explained by another mental disorder, such as delusional disorder or another psychotic disorder.

Factitious Disorder Imposed on Another (Previously Factitious Disorder by Proxy)

A. Falsification of physical or psychological signs or symptoms, or induction of injury or disease, in another, associated with identified deception.

B. The individual presents another individual (victim) to others as ill, impaired, or injured.

C. The deceptive behavior is evident even in the absence of obvious external rewards.

D. The behavior is not better explained by another mental disorder, such as delusional disorder or another psychotic disorder.

Note: The perpetrator, not the victim, receives the diagnosis.

of Honor winner or a former professional football player). If hospital staff become suspicious, they sometimes get angry, threaten to sue the hospital, and leave.

Although most people with this disorder fabricate physical symptoms, some patients may fabricate psychological symptoms (see "Real People, Real Disorders: The Piano Man—Dissociative Disorder, Factitious Disorder, or Malingering?"). Common psychological symptoms include grief and depression over the recent death of a relative, such as a spouse or a child. Later, the "dead" person turns out to be alive or has been dead for a very long time (Ford, 2005). People may also fake other psychological disorders, including multiple personality disorder (see "Real People, Real Disorders: Kenneth Bianchi, Patty Hearst, and Dr. Martin Orne" in Chapter 15), substance dependence, dissociative and conversion disorders, memory loss, and posttraumatic stress disorder.

> The physicians were puzzled by 6-year-old Jenny's illnesses. The pieces just did not seem to fit together. Her mother had brought her to the emergency room at least once a month for the past year. Jenny complained of constant nausea, but there did not seem to be a medical reason. She had a multitude of gastrointestinal procedures—upper GI series, lower GI series, CT scans, and endoscopy. Her mother had taken her to seven different hospitals in the same state, and she insisted on the same tests at each hospital. Jenny saw numerous specialists, and on many occasions, her mother insisted that Jenny be hospitalized. The medical staff became suspicious when Jenny's nausea disappeared upon hospitalization. Their first thought was that there was conflict between Jenny and her mother and Jenny was experiencing severe anxiety. In children, stomachaches are a common symptom of anxiety. Jenny's mother became angry at the suggestion. She would not consider the possibility that Jenny's distress was psychological. On the latest visit to the emergency room, her mother brought in Jenny's bloody stool sample. The medical staff was informed by the lab that there was definitely blood in the stool—but it was not Jenny's blood type.

When one person induces illness symptoms in someone else, the disorder is known as **factitious disorder imposed on another**. In most instances, a mother produces physical symptoms in the child, as in Jenny's case. After inducing the symptoms, the mother brings the child to the hospital and gives permission for or sometimes insists that the child undergo invasive and dangerous diagnostic procedures. There are few data describing the child victims of this disorder, but what exist indicate that children range in age from infancy through the teenage years and can have many different symptoms, including apnea (the child stops breathing), anorexia/feeding problems, diarrhea, seizures, cyanosis (turning blue from lack of oxygen), behavior problems, asthma, allergy, fevers, and pain (Sheridan, 2003). Child victims average 3.25 medical problems, ranging as high as 19 illnesses in a single child. Factitious disorder imposed on another, when proved, is considered a form of child abuse, and the parent can be prosecuted. Occasionally, this disorder also occurs in nursing homes, where health care personnel inflict these physical symptoms on adult residents.

Functional Impairment

LO 6.5 Describe how these disorders affect the individual, community, and society.

This group of disorders produce significant functional impairment. Approximately 10 to 15% of adults in the United States report work disability as a result of chronic back pain (Von Korff et al., 1990). Among patients with conversion disorder, only 33% maintained full-time employment (Crimlisk et al., 1998). Similarly, people with symptoms very similar to what we now call somatic symptom disorder worked fewer days per month (an average of 7.8 days) than people with no disorder (Gureje et al., 1997). These disorders also increase the likelihood of physical disability, occupational impairment, and overutilization of health services (Aigner et al., 2003; Gureje et al., 1997; Sharma & Manjula, 2013). Figure 6.2 illustrates some of the economic costs associated with these disorders.

In addition to causing functional impairment, these disorders have a complex and chronic course (Creed & Barsky, 2004; olde Hartman et al., 2009). Remission rates are likewise controversial. Early studies reported that less than 10% of people recover (Swartz et al., 1990), but more recent investigations report that between 30 and 50% of individuals recover 1 year later (Arnold et al., 2006; Creed & Barsky, 2004; olde Hartman et. al, 2009). Conversion disorder may be a more acute condition with between 33 and 90% of patients remitted or significantly improved 2 to 5 years later (Binzer & Kullgren, 1998; Crimlisk et al., 1998; Kent et al., 1995). Of course, the more chronic cases are associated with increased functional impairment (Krem, 2004).

Although many physical complaints lack an organic basis, they still have an enormous impact on our medical system. Patients with medically unexplained physical symptoms

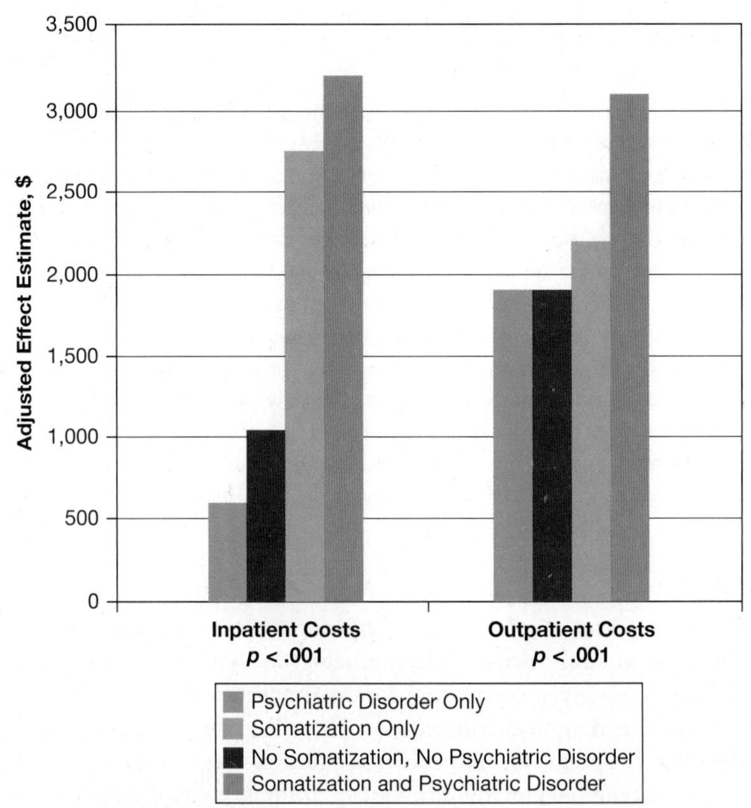

Figure 6.2 Somatization Increases Medical Use

As shown here, people with somatization disorder (DSM-IV term but similar to somatic symptom disorder) use more medical resources and therefore have higher medical costs than people with no disorders or people with psychiatric disorders (in this case, depression) alone. People with both mood disorders and somatization disorder have slightly higher costs than people with somatization alone.

Based on Barsky, A.J.,et al. (2005), Somatization increases medical utilization and costs independent of psychiatric and medical comorbidity *Archives of General Psychiatry*, *62*(8), 903–910.

constitute 15 to 30% of all primary care physician appointments (Kirmayer et al., 2004), and sometimes several different physicians evaluate the same patient complaint. People with physical symptoms often "doctor-shop" to find a physician who will provide a medical explanation, and in many instances, they receive different diagnoses from different medical specialists (Kirmayer & Looper, 2007). Some people remain unwilling to accept a psychological diagnosis; this leads to physician frustration, patient demoralization, and a continuing search for a physical explanation.

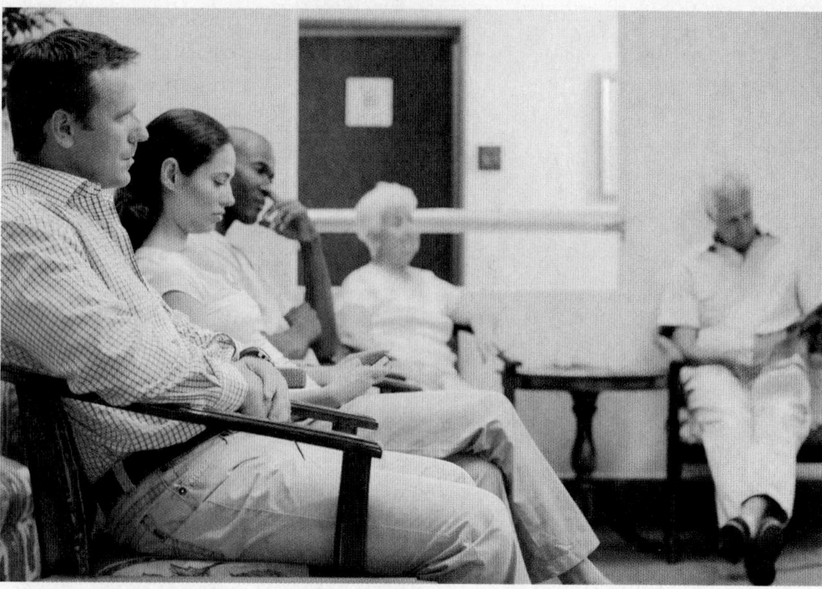

Patients with unexplained physical complaints are often seen in doctors' offices. They may even "doctor-shop" if they are told that their complaints have no medical cause.

Doctor-shopping is just one example of how these disorders increase medical utilization and costs. Over a 1-year period, people with somatoform disorders average significantly more primary care visits, more specialty care visits, more emergency room visits, and more hospital admissions as well as higher inpatient and outpatient care costs than the general population (Barsky et al., 2005; Robbins & Kirmayer, 1996). Determining a physical basis for these symptoms is quite costly (see "Research Hot Topic: The Challenge of Chronic Fatigue Syndrome"). In one sample, an average of $7,778 was spent to rule out physical causes for headache and $7,263 for back pain (Kroenke & Mangelsdorff, 1989). In all, treatment for somatoform disorders accounts for approximately 20% of all medical care expenses in the United States (Verma & Gallagher, 2000). Interestingly and consistent with patients' belief that their physical ailment has a medical explanation, mental health care was the only form of health care that was not significantly higher in people with these disorders.

People with factitious disorder often have numerous hospitalizations and can develop medical conditions as a result of their self-administered injuries. For example, scar tissue may develop as a result of numerous surgical operations or self-injections. Sometimes a phenomenon known as *peregrination* occurs in which the patient seeks treatment at different hospitals and sometimes travels from state to state or even country to country using false names. Factitious disorders are considered chronic, and although data from controlled trials are not available, it would appear that this disorder would affect social and occupational functioning.

Among child victims of factitious disorder imposed on another, 6 to 22% die as a result of the medical illnesses inflicted upon them, as do a percentage of their siblings. The most common cause of death is suffocation or apnea (Ayoub et al., 2002; Sheridan, 2003). In one investigation, 7.3% of the child victims had long-term or permanent injuries (Sheridan, 2003).

Ethics and Responsibility

LO 6.6 Explain the responsibilities of mental health professionals when faced with an incident of factitious disorder imposed on another.

Because factitious disorder imposed on another may result in serious injury or death, psychologists have a responsibility to act in the best interest of the child. In these cases, a report to the state child protection agency is the first step. The investigation requires collaboration among child protection officials, medical personnel, and psychological professionals (Day & Moseley, 2010). The child must be evaluated by a medical specialist to ensure that there is no medical reason for the child's symptoms. This can often be difficult as parents often use different physicians and hospitals in order to avoid detection. Sometimes a child is hospitalized in order to observe symptom patterns, as symptoms often disappear when parents can no longer have unfettered access to their children. In other instances, video observation of parent and child interactions in the hospital may reveal the parent engaging in behaviors designed to produce symptoms. Whereas medical professionals and child protection personnel may be most involved in determining whether the child has a legitimate medical disorder or is a victim of factitious disorder imposed on another, mental health personnel are the professionals who attempt to treat the offending parent.

Explore ETHICS AND RESPONSIBILITY

Interactive

Research HOT Topic

The Challenge of Chronic Fatigue Syndrome

Chronic fatigue syndrome (CFS) is a seriously disabling disorder that affects between 836,000 and 2.5 million Americans (Ganiats, 2015). CFS, sometimes called myalgic encephalopathy, has puzzled the medical community for many years. The original medical diagnosis published in 1988 lacked validity because it did not differentiate CFS from other types of unexplained fatigue, leading health professionals to call it a somatoform disorder. Revisions to the diagnostic criteria now yield a more reliable and valid diagnostic condition, requiring (1) severe chronic fatigue for at least 6 months with no known medical condition and (2) four or more of the following symptoms: substantial impairment in short-term memory or concentration; sore throat; tender lymph nodes; muscle pain; multi-joint pain without swelling or redness; headaches of a new type, pattern, or severity; unrefreshing sleep; and postexercise tiredness lasting more than 24 hours (Holgate et al., 2011).

CFS exerts a significant economic impact on the United States. The Centers for Disease Control and Prevention estimate that CFS leads to a total annual loss of $9.1 billion—$2.3 billion from lost household productivity and $6.8 billion from lost labor force productivity (Reynolds et al., 2004).

CFS can sometimes occur in response to a stressor or challenge such as a serious automobile accident. Increased rates of CFS in Gulf War veterans and relapses of CFS also were reported after Hurricane Andrew (www.cdc.gov/CFS/news). Despite the increasing recognition of the disorder, some people with CFS cannot convince others that they suffer from a real medical condition; many people still consider it a psychosomatic illness. The cause of CFS remains unknown despite intensive research efforts. Many potential causes, including viruses, immunological dysfunction, cortisol dysregulation, autonomic nervous system dysfunction, and nutritional deficiencies, have been investigated and ruled out.

Researchers continue to focus on a viral etiology because typical findings on blood tests suggest the presence of a viral infection. Recently, one investigative group reported that about 10% of people who contract the Ross River virus will develop CFS. Of course, this means that 90% of those with the virus will not. Other researchers have found similar results with Epstein-Barr virus, GB virus, human retroviruses, human herpes virus 6, enteroviruses, rubella, and *Candida albicans*. In each case, a few individuals with CFS may have the virus, but the relationship is small and not statistically significant, as was recently demonstrated for xenotropic murine leukemia virus (Switzer et al., 2010).

Researchers are continuing to pursue possible etiological factors, and they now believe that CFS may not have a single cause but may represent the final outcome of multiple precipitating somatic and/or psychological factors that act in combination, including viral infections, psychological stress, and toxins.

Epidemiology

LO 6.7 Discuss how these disorders are affected by demographic and sociocultural factors.

About 14 to 20% of the general population reports worrisome physical symptoms that have no organic basis (Faravelli et al., 1997; Grabe et al., 2003). However, even though many people have these symptoms, few meet strict diagnostic criteria for these disorders. There are no known epidemiological data on the prevalence of factitious disorders in the general population. Among patients referred to one psychiatric consultation liaison service over a 20-year period, 0.8% of referrals had factitious disorder (Sutherland & Rodin, 1990). At children's hospitals, the annual incidence was 2/100,000 or 0.002% (McClure et al., 1996).

SEX, RACE, AND ETHNICITY Because these disorders are rare, we have very limited data on their interplay with variables such as sex, race, and ethnicity. We do know that women endorse the presence of somatic symptom disorder more frequently than men (Kroenke & Spitzer, 1998). The disorders appear to occur equally across racial and ethnic groups (Swartz et al., 1990), but in Asian countries, similar conditions often are given different diagnostic labels such as *shenjing shuairus* (China), *shinkei suijaku* (Japan), *or Dhat syndrome* (India) (Grover & Ghosh, 2014).

Although few data are available, factitious disorder is more likely to occur in women. Compared with men with the disorder, women in one sample were younger and more likely to have had health care training or health care jobs (Krahn et al., 2003). By contrast, those with the most severe forms of the disorder, including symptoms of peregrination and the adoption of aliases, are more likely to be male. Among people with factitious disorder imposed on another, 77 to 98% are women, typically the child's biological mother, although fathers and foster mothers are also occasional perpetrators (Ayoub et al., 2006). There are no data available on race or ethnicity.

As we noted earlier, people with these disorders often reject psychological explanations for their symptoms. They believe that professionals are denying their real pain. Outside the United States, medical systems are more likely to use a sociocultural rather than a psychological explanation. Physicians discuss patients' physical distress in terms of family and community problems. When a sociocultural explanation is offered, people are more likely to acknowledge that stress, social conditions, and emotions can affect their physical status (Kirmayer et al., 2004).

DEVELOPMENTAL FACTORS Diagnostic criteria for these disorders are the same in children and adolescents as in adults, but somatic symptom and related disorders are rare before adulthood (Finkenbine & Miele, 2004; Kozlowska et al., 2007). As in adults, voluntary motor dysfunction was most common complaint in children followed by sensory dysfunction and pseudoseizures (Kozlowska et al., 2007). Factitious disorder imposed on self is most common in adults, but it does exist among children and adolescents as well. In one sample (Libow, 2000), children with the disorder ranged in age from 8 to 18, and 70% were female. Children most commonly produce symptoms such as fever (heating the thermometer to fake a fever), diabetic insulin insufficiency (deliberately manipulating their insulin levels), bruises, and infections.

Etiology

LO 6.8 Identify the contributions of biological, psychological, and environmental factors to somatic symptom and related disorders.

How these disorders develop is poorly understood. Biological factors would seem to play a role, particularly when distorted perceptual processes exist. Yet few controlled trials have examined biological causes. At this time, the body of etiological evidence lies in the realm of psychological factors, as reviewed in the following section. Again, because the DSM-5 diagnostic categories are so new, the data below are based on the similar DSM-IV category of somatoform disorders.

PSYCHOSOCIAL FACTORS Psychodynamic explanations propose that these disorders result from intrapsychic conflict, personality, and defense mechanisms. From a psychodynamic

Examining the EVIDENCE

Is Childhood Sexual Abuse Associated with Somatic Symptom Disorders?

- **The Evidence** Somatic symptom and related disorders (called somatoform disorders in DSM-IV) have been linked to physical and sexual abuse early in life (e.g., Bowman & Markand, 1996; Brown et al., 2005). Some theorists have used these observations to propose a causal relationship between abuse and these disorders. What is the validity of this relationship?
- **Let's Examine the Evidence**
- **What Types of Research Designs Were Used in These Investigations?** The idea that physical and sexual trauma might lead to the development of somatic symptom and related disorders is based on studies of patients who already have the disorder. Only rarely is a control group of people with no disorder or another disorder included in the research design. Another consideration is that these studies use correlational designs, and the data derived from them cannot support causality. In fact, two large prospective (longitudinal) studies challenge the association between these disorders and sexual/physical abuse (Linton, 2002; Raphael et al., 2001). First, among adults with no history of back pain, self-reported history of physical abuse (not sexual abuse) predicted the development of back pain 1 year later. However, no relationship existed between physical or sexual abuse and the emergence of new pain when the person had back pain at baseline (Linton, 2002). In a second study, children who had documented histories of early childhood abuse or neglect (*n* = 676) were compared with controls with no history of abuse (*n* = 520; Raphael et al., 2001). When assessed as adults, physically and sexually abused and neglected individuals were not at risk for increased pain symptoms compared with controls. These prospective studies suggest that the previous correlational relationship between sexual and/or physical abuse and somatic symptom and related disorders may be simply a result of biased self-report based on retrospective data.
- **What Other Factors Might Explain the Correlational Relationship?** In many instances, abusive acts occur in family environments that have high levels of conflict, hostility, and aggression as well as parent–child interactions that are cold, rejecting, and/or neglectful of children (Repetti et al., 2002). We know that these chronic stressors are related to abnormal neuroendocrine responses in the hypothalamic-pituitary-adrenal (HPA) axis (see Chapter 4), and this dysregulation may result in multiple somatic complaints (Heim et al., 2000).
- **What Evidence for This Relationship Exists?** A carefully designed study not only examined the presence of physical and sexual abuse among people with these disorders but also measured hostile and rejecting family environments. The study did not find a relationship between abuse and somatic symptoms but did document an association between hostility/rejection by fathers and somatic symptom and related disorders in the children (Lackner et al., 2004).
- **Conclusion** Family environments characterized by high conflict, hostility, and rejection may lead to a dysregulation of the neuroendocrine system that mediates stressful responses in the body. How could a chronic negative environment (in which abusive acts are more likely to occur) lay the foundation for the potential development of somatic symptom and related disorders?

perspective, Anna O. (Chapter 1) most likely had conversion disorder. She was probably emotionally stressed and possibly resentful because of the need to care for her father and because of his subsequent death. Anna O.'s psychological distress was unacceptable to her superego, and therefore her negative feelings were repressed and converted into physical symptoms—hence, use of the term *conversion disorder* to describe this condition. Modern-day researchers do not invoke psychodynamic constructs, but empirical data do support the hypothesis that children and adults who complained of physical aches and pains had more negative emotions. More importantly, these children and adults were also more likely to have poor self-awareness of the presence of these emotions and were less able to regulate (change) their emotional state (Gilleland et al., 2009). Perhaps these children and adults were less psychologically minded and did not understand the relation between emotional stress and its effects on physical functioning (for more on this relation, see Chapter 14). Not recognizing the impact of stress, they worried that their somatic symptoms had a medical cause.

Behavioral principles of modeling and reinforcement may also contribute to the development of illness behavior. Compared with healthy mothers, mothers with somatic symptom disorder paid more attention to their children when they played with a medical kit than when they played with a tea set or ate a snack (Craig et al., 2004). This increased attention may lead to an increase in medical concerns, medical tests, or medical procedures in their children. Similarly, the more often adolescent girls were reinforced for expressing complaints about menstrual illness, the more often they had menstrual symptoms and disability days as adults. Also, childhood reinforcement of cold illness behavior significantly predicted cold symptoms and disability days for adults (Whitehead et al., 1994). In summary, strong support exists for the theory that reinforcing somatizing behaviors may increase the future likelihood of somatic complaints.

Other environmental factors also are associated with physical symptoms, distress, and somatic symptom disorders. Among adults, stress was temporally associated with 72% of these disorders. In contrast, a history of sexual abuse was present in 28% of the cases (Singh & Lee, 1997). Among children (Kozlowska et al., 2007), family separation/loss was associated with the onset of the disorder in 34% of the cases. Family conflict/violence was associated in 20% of the cases, and sexual assault correlated in only 4%. The relationship between these disorders and childhood sexual abuse is controversial (Alper et al., 1993; Coryell & Norten, 1981; see "Examining the Evidence: Is Childhood Sexual Abuse Associated with Somatic Symptom Disorders?").

Despite much speculation about the etiology of factitious disorders, few empirical data exist. Nonspecific neuroanatomical abnormalities have been reported in isolated cases, but in addition to the absence of studies that include experimental controls, the findings are not consistent (Eisendrath & Young, 2005). Among the psychological theories, psychodynamic models explain factitious disorder as (1) an attempt to gain mastery or control that was formerly elusive, (2) a form of masochism (where pleasure occurs as a result of physical or psychological pain inflicted by oneself or another person), (3) the result of a deprived childhood in which a child did not receive attention or care, or (4) an attempt to master trauma that was experienced as a result of physical or sexual abuse with the physician unknowingly assuming the symbolic role of the abuser (Eisendrath & Young, 2005).

From a behavioral perspective, factitious behaviors are maintained because other people positively reinforce the person's illness behaviors or expressions. The attention garnered from these illnesses is a powerful reinforcer. From a cognitive perspective, people with factitious disorders, through biased cognitive processes, misinterpret normal physical processes as indicators of physical illness; this cognitive perspective is similar to the hypotheses put forth to explain the etiology of these disorders.

Distorted cognitions may also play a role in the development of these disorders, perhaps from a cognitive process called *somatic amplification* (Barsky & Klerman, 1983), a tendency to perceive bodily sensations as intense, noxious, and disturbing. How this amplification occurs is unclear. This theory suggests that some people have heightened sensory, perceptual, and/or cognitive-evaluative processes that make them more sensitive to the presence of physical symptoms. This is an interesting theory, but few studies have assessed exactly how these perceptual processes contribute to the onset of somatoform disorders.

Other cognitive theories propose that somatic symptom and related disorders develop from inaccurate beliefs about the (1) prevalence and contagiousness of illnesses, (2) meaning of bodily symptoms, and (3) course and treatment of illnesses (Salkovskis, 1989). For example, someone with anxiety about contracting breast cancer may hold inaccurate beliefs about the illness such as

- so many women get breast cancer, it must be some type of unidentified virus,
- a pain in my chest is a signal that I may have breast cancer, and
- I have had this pain for some time.
- The cancer is probably throughout my body and no treatment will help me.

These beliefs may be activated by hearing or reading about breast cancer or after perceiving vague bodily sensations. As a result, the person becomes hypervigilant and worried about having, and perhaps dying from, the illness (Rode et al., 2001). Cognitive theories propose that it is not the symptoms but how the symptoms are interpreted that leads to the development of these disorders. Although it is not clear how a person acquires these beliefs, they may result from the reinforcement and modeling theories discussed previously.

AN INTEGRATIVE MODEL Understanding the interplay between psychological and somatic factors can be quite complicated. As we noted at the beginning of this chapter, transient aches and pains and bodily disturbances occur every day: You get a headache, a fleeting pain, or an upset stomach. The reason is not necessarily clear—perhaps you are unknowingly allergic to a certain food. Whatever the reason, your symptoms exist. Whether you pay attention to your symptoms depends on their intensity and your learning history, including learning to interpret bodily symptoms as signs of a serious illness. The smallest sensation or change in your physical state may cause you to focus more intently on your body, looking for confirmation that something is wrong. Perhaps sensations such as ringing in your ears cause you to worry. If the ringing continues for some time, you may begin to worry intensely that something is wrong ("What if I have a brain tumor?"). This is normal illness behavior, and you may decide to see a physician.

A crucial factor is whether the physician's response reassured you ("There is no brain tumor") or whether you continue to worry, even though medical tests and physicians cannot find a reason for your distress. If you do continue to worry, your distress may become so severe that you change your lifestyle. Depending on your own cognitive schemas and learning history, your friends and family may support your "sick role" behavior, or they may suggest that you are a hypochondriac. The medical profession may also influence whether or how much you worry. If the physician conducts excessive and/or invasive testing, this may reinforce your belief that something is seriously wrong with you. When treating people with somatic symptom and related disorders, health care professionals must carefully convey their understanding of the physical distress yet help the patient understand the role of psychological stress in creating physical symptoms. Doing this successfully is the first step in the treatment of these disorders.

Treatment

LO 6.9 Identify the challenges to successful psychological treatment for somatic symptom and related disorders.

The first challenge in obtaining treatment is the reluctance of people with somatic symptom disorders to reveal their worries to a professional, and establishing a good therapeutic relationship is a necessary first step in treatment (Starcevic, 2015). As noted earlier, a major challenge to successful treatment is the belief of many sufferers that they do not have a psychological disorder. They emphasize their physical symptoms and often resist a psychological intervention (Arnold et al., 2006).

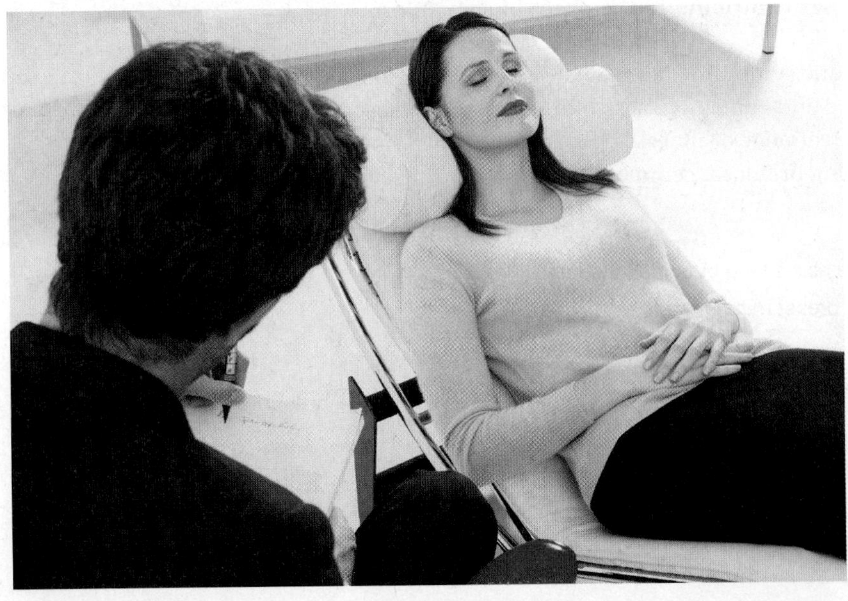

A patient undergoes relaxation training as part of cognitive-behavioral therapy. Relaxation helps the patient cope with troubling thoughts about the body and its symptoms.

In some cases, basic education about the interplay of physical and emotional factors may reduce the symptoms and distress associated with these disorders. There are few randomized placebo controlled trials of pharmacological treatments for somatic symptom disorders due in part to the difficulty with the diagnostic issues we noted earlier. However, among the few randomized trials that do exist, there is some evidence that antidepressants and antipsychotic medications are superior to placebo on measures of pain, health concerns, and depression (Somashekar et al., 2013) after short-term treatment. There are no long-term follow-up data to suggest that these medications produce long-lasting effects.

Symptom-focused cognitive-behavioral therapy (CBT) also may be helpful. As we noted earlier, people resist the notion that psychological factors play an important role in symptom onset or maintenance. Therefore, treatment focuses on teaching patients to cope with their symptoms by emphasizing how current psychological and social factors affect their symptoms without forcing people to accept a psychological basis for their disorder.

CBT includes engaging in relaxation training, diverting attention away from the physical symptoms, and correction of automatic thoughts. Similarly, because these disorders are considered to result, at least in part, from environmental and personal stressors, teaching patients strategies to reduce stress may lessen their distress and lower the costs associated with their health care. There is now substantial evidence that health anxiety (hypochondriasis/illness anxiety disorder) can be effectively treated with exposure therapy alone or CBT (Olatunji et al., 2014; Weck et al., 2014, 2015a) and that exposure therapy (without any specific cognitive therapy) changes negative thoughts about physical symptoms just as well as more formalized cognitive treatments (Weck, Neng, Schwind et al., 2015) and patients remained improved 1 year later (Weck, Neng, Richtberg et al., 2015).

To date, no controlled trials of CBT for conversion disorder have been published, but a three-pronged approach is recommended: withdrawal of medical and social attention directed at the abnormality, physical and occupational therapy to retrain normal gait and movements, and psychotherapy to help the patient cope with stress (Krem, 2004). Similar behavioral approaches have been used to treat globus hystericus (Donohue et al., 1997).

Relaxation apps on a phone or tablet allows a patient to practice these skills and decrease their stress anytime.

Learning Objective Summaries

LO 6.1 Understand how normal physical sensations can create abnormal concerns about somatic functioning.

Physical complaints are common and in many instances do not indicate the presence of a medical disorder. When normal physical sensations/complaints (regardless of the presence of a medical diagnosis) create abnormal distress or functional impairment, a diagnosis of somatic symptom disorder may be appropriate.

LO 6.2 Identify two ways in which conversion disorder differs from somatic symptom disorder.

In conversion disorder, the primary concern is not worry about the presence of a symptom but rather the presence of altered motor or sensory functioning. The altered functioning may be motoric (e.g., paralysis), sensory (e.g., blindness), or non-seizure convulsions. The symptoms do not follow known neurological patterns, and many individuals are indifferent to (rather than distressed by) their functional incapacity.

LO 6.3 Describe how illness anxiety disorder differs from somatic symptom disorder.

If someone is persistently worried about having an illness despite medical reassurance to the contrary, that person may be suffering from illness anxiety disorder. In the past, people with these behaviors were said to have "hypochondriasis," and sometimes the person was called a "hypochondriac."

LO 6.4 Identify at least two characteristics of factitious disorder that make it different from other somatic symptom and related disorders.

When physical symptoms are produced voluntarily in order for someone to assume a sick role, the person may be suffering from factitious disorder. The symptoms may be produced in oneself or in another person. People with this disorder seek medical care but do not tell the physician that they are intentionally producing the symptoms.

LO 6.5 Describe how these disorders affect the individual, community, and society.

In addition to the emotional toll that that these disorders take on the individual, people with somatic symptom and related disorders utilize medical care at a higher rate than people without these disorders. They are also significantly less likely to work and more likely to be disabled, thus increasing the costs of this disorder to society.

LO 6.6 Explain the responsibilities of mental health professionals when faced with an incident of factitious disorder imposed on another.

Factitious disorder imposed on another person may also be considered a form of physical abuse. When mental health professionals suspect that someone is deliberately producing illness in a child or elderly person, the appropriate legal authorities should be notified.

LO 6.7 Discuss how these disorders are affected by demographic and sociocultural factors.

The prevalence of somatic symptom and related disorders is unknown. Many people have physical complaints, but it becomes harder to determine when their distress or impairment is out of proportion to their illness. Furthermore, many people do not accept the idea that they might be suffering from an emotional or psychological disorder. Their symptoms are real, and they are looking for a physical cause. Somatic symptom and related disorders are more likely to occur in women than men. There do not appear to be any differences in the rates of the disorders based on race or ethnicity. These disorders are more likely to occur in adults than children. It is important to remember that in factitious disorder imposed on another person, the person with the symptoms may be a child, but it is an adult who caused the symptoms to occur.

LO 6.8 Identify the contributions of biological, psychological, and environmental factors to somatic symptom and related disorders.

How and why these disorders develop is unclear. Despite our limited understanding, we do know that the development of these disorders is quite complex and includes physical, psychological, and environmental factors.

LO 6.9 Identify the challenges to successful psychological treatment for somatic symptom and related disorders.

The biggest challenge in treating people with somatic symptom and related disorders is convincing them that at least part of their physical symptoms may be related to their emotions or stress level. Although there is some evidence that medications may be efficacious for these disorders, there is more evidence for CBT, including follow-up studies indicating that treatment gains are maintained at least 1 year later.

Critical Thinking Question

How could paying more attention to a toddler playing with a medical kit and ignoring play at other times contribute to the development of a somatic symptom disorder? How could you reverse it?

Dissociative Disorders

Perhaps no more controversial diagnostic group exists than the dissociative disorders. Mental health professionals cannot agree on the validity or even the existence of these conditions; 97% of a sample of psychologists who work in U.S. Veterans Administration hospitals believe that dissociative disorders exist (Dunn et al., 1994), but only 55% of Australian psychologists do (Leonard et al., 2005). In contrast, only 25% of American psychiatrists and 14% of Canadian psychiatrists believed that strong scientific evidence supported the diagnosis (Lalonde et al., 2001; Pope et al., 1999). These different percentages may reflect where mental health professionals work or the specific way in which the question is asked. However, as you will see, the issues run much deeper and have generated many interesting and heated debates.

In general, **dissociative disorders** involve "a disruption in the usually integrated functions of consciousness, memory, identity, emotion, perception, body representation, motor control, and behavior" (American Psychiatric Association, 2013, p. 291). But what does this mean? Have you ever been so engrossed in reading something that you suddenly looked up and were startled to see your friend standing right in front of you? You were concentrating so hard that you were briefly unaware of your surroundings, a situation similar to a dissociative experience.

Actually five types of dissociative experiences exist (Gleaves et al., 2001; Steinberg et al., 1993). *Depersonalization* is a feeling of detachment from one's body—experiencing the self as strange or unreal. Some people describe this feeling as if they were floating above their own body, watching themselves behave. *Derealization* is a feeling of unfamiliarity or unreality about one's physical or interpersonal environment. People describe feeling as if they were in a dream. *Amnesia* is the inability to remember personal information or significant periods of time. It is more than simply forgetting a name, where you put your keys, or what you had for dinner last Thursday night. *Identity confusion* describes being unclear or conflicted about one's personal identity. Finally, *identity alteration* describes overt behaviors indicating that one has assumed an alternate identity (Steinberg et al., 1993).

Isolated episodes of dissociation do not always indicate the presence of a dissociative disorder (e.g., Holmes et al., 2005). Your engrossment in your work is known as *absorption*, defined as fully engaging all your perceptual resources on one item so that you are no longer attending to other aspects of the environment. Experiences such as absorption are common, and 46 to 74% of people without psychological disorders experience occasional episodes of derealization and depersonalization (Hunter et al., 2005). Furthermore, dissociative symptoms may occur in people with panic disorder, obsessive-compulsive disorder, agoraphobia, posttraumatic stress disorder, depressive disorder, bipolar disorder, and eating disorders (Holmes et al., 2005). When dissociative experiences are temporary, such as your momentary period of absorption, they create minimal, if any, distress. However, when they develop into chronic conditions, they are called *dissociative disorders* (see "DSM-5: Dissociative Disorders").

Dissociative Amnesia

LO 6.10 Discuss how dissociative amnesia is different from momentary forgetting or amnesia as a result of medical conditions.

Have you ever awakened in the morning and for a moment been unable to recognize your surroundings? Or have you ever found yourself driving and for a moment could not remember passing familiar landmarks? Your momentary forgetting/distraction may help you understand the concept of **amnesia**. This condition has many causes, including head injuries, epilepsy, alcoholic "blackouts," and low blood sugar. A temporary state of amnesia may also occur after a stroke or seizure, after electroconvulsive therapy (ECT) for depression, or as a result of drug toxicity or global dementia. Therefore, a medical evaluation must always be the first step in the diagnostic process.

Dissociative amnesia is an inability to recall important information, usually of a personal nature (see "DSM-5: Dissociative Disorders"). When it occurs following a stressful or traumatic event, its cause is considered psychological, not biological. Several types of dissociative amnesia can occur. Failure to recall events that occur during a certain period of time is known as *localized amnesia*, whereas *generalized amnesia* is a total inability to recall any aspect of one's life. A third type of amnesia is *selective amnesia* in which the person forgets some elements of a traumatic experience. Dissociative amnesia is considered a reversible condition, and in many instances, people can later recall events, or parts of events, that they could not previously describe.

Watch SHARON

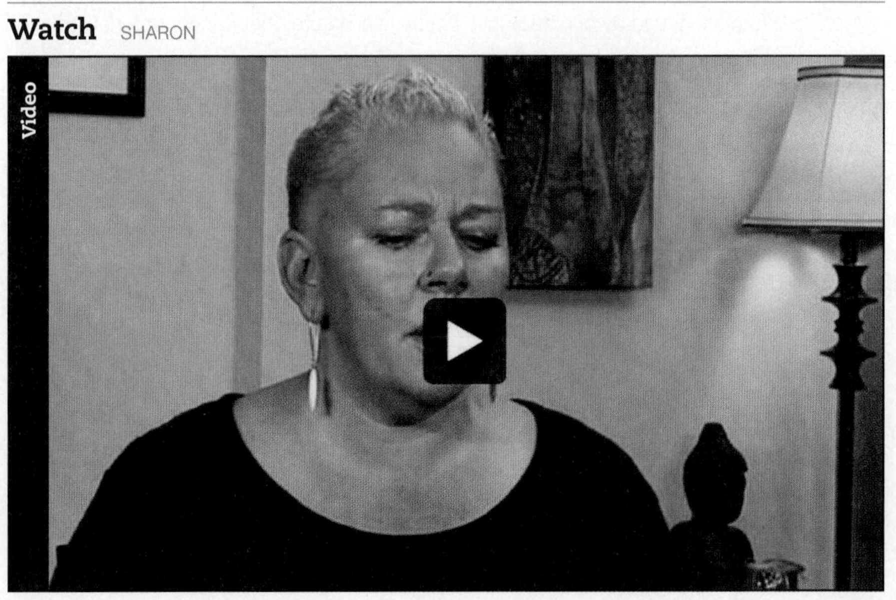

Christine Costner-Sizemore, the real "Eve" portrayed in the famous film *The Three Faces of Eve*.

In some instances, dissociative amnesia is accompanied by **dissociative fugue**, which is defined as apparently purposeful travel or bewildered wandering that is associated with identity amnesia (American Psychiatric Association, 2013). People with this disorder are found in a physical location away from their usual residence. *Fugue* means "flight." Fugue states may be associated with physical or mental traumas, depression, or legal problems (Kihlstrom, 2001). Patients in a fugue state may seek treatment if they become aware of their loss of personal identity and memory or if they come to the attention of the police.

Dissociative Identity Disorder

LO 6.11 Identify two ways in which the process of the diagnosis of DID differs from other psychological disorders.

In 1957, Hollywood released the film *The Three Faces of Eve* based on a nonfiction book of the same name. In the book and movie, Eve White is a housewife and mother, but when she is hypnotized as part of her psychotherapy, her psychiatrist discovers an alternate personality, Eve Black, who is outgoing and socially engaging, exactly the opposite of Eve White. Later, a third personality, Jane, emerges. Although the book and movie contain a number of factual inaccuracies, the real Eve, Christine Costner-Sizemore, was able to integrate her personalities. *The Three Faces of Eve* introduced the term *multiple personality disorder*, now called **dissociative identity disorder** (DID). Another example of DID is found in *Sybil*, the book published in 1976 and the movie based on it that chronicled the treatment of a young woman who seeks therapy for blackouts and nervous breakdowns. In therapy, the psychiatrist discovers that Sybil has 16 different personalities (also known as *alternative personalities*, or *alters*). The psychiatrist hypothesizes that these alters are the result of extreme physical and sexual abuse, what most people would describe as torture, by her mother, who suffered from schizophrenia. Christine Costner-Sizemore and Sybil are the two most familiar examples of DID.

DSM-5

Criteria for Dissociative Disorders

Dissociative Amnesia

A. An inability to recall important autobiographical information, usually of a traumatic or stressful nature, that is inconsistent with ordinary forgetting.

Note: Dissociative amnesia most often consists of localized or selective amnesia for a specific event or events; or generalized amnesia for identity and life history.

B. The symptoms cause clinically significant distress or impairment in social, occupational, or other important areas of functioning.

C. The disturbance is not attributable to the physiological effects of a substance (e.g., alcohol or other drug of abuse, a medication) or a neurological or other medical condition (e.g., partial complex seizures, transient global amnesia, sequelae of a closed head injury/traumatic brain injury, other neurological condition).

D. The disturbance is not better explained by dissociative identity disorder, posttraumatic stress disorder, acute stress disorder, somatic symptom disorder, or major or mild neurocognitive disorder.

Dissociative Identity Disorder

A. Disruption of identity characterized by two or more distinct personality states, which may be described in some cultures as an experience of possession. The disruption in identity involves marked discontinuity in sense of self and sense of agency, accompanied by related alterations in affect, behavior, consciousness, memory, perception, cognition, and/or sensory-motor functioning. These signs and symptoms may be observed by others or reported by the individual.

B. Recurrent gaps in the recall of everyday events, important personal information, and/or traumatic events that are inconsistent with ordinary forgetting.

C. The symptoms cause clinically significant distress or impairment in social, occupational, or other important areas of functioning.

D. The disturbance is not a normal part of a broadly accepted cultural or religious practice.

Note: In children, the symptoms are not better explained by imaginary playmates or other fantasy play.

E. The symptoms are not attributable to the physiological effects of a substance (e.g., blackouts or chaotic behavior during alcohol intoxication) or another medical condition (e.g., complex partial seizures).

Depersonalization/Derealization Disorder

A. The presence of persistent or recurrent experiences of depersonalization, derealization, or both:

1. **Depersonalization**: Experiences of unreality, detachment, or being an outside observer with respect to one's thoughts, feelings, sensations, body, or actions (e.g., perceptual alterations, distorted sense of time, unreal or absent self, emotional and/or physical numbing).
2. **Derealization**: Experiences of unreality or detachment with respect to surroundings (e.g., individuals or objects are experienced as unreal, dreamlike, foggy, lifeless, or visually distorted).

B. During the depersonalization or derealization experiences, reality testing remains intact.

C. The symptoms cause clinically significant distress or impairment in social, occupational, or other important areas of functioning.

D. The disturbance is not attributable to the physiological effects of a substance (e.g., a drug of abuse, medication) or another medical condition (e.g., seizures).

E. The disturbance is not better explained by another mental disorder, such as schizophrenia, panic disorder, major depressive disorder, acute stress disorder, posttraumatic stress disorder, or another dissociative disorder.

A graduate student in clinical psychology was conducting a study on bulimia nervosa (an eating disorder; see Chapter 8). Participant number 006 was a 32-year-old female with a 10-year history of bulimia nervosa. She had a tumultuous family history including sexual abuse, physical abuse, and neglect. She binged multiple times per day and purged up to 10 times per day. She also abused laxatives and had comorbid alcohol and drug abuse. She felt that her disorder resulted from trauma inflicted by her parents, and she saw her eating disorder as a result of living in such an abusive family. She was angry, bitter, and deeply pessimistic about her future.

Later, another volunteer, number 026, contacted the graduate student. The telephone number was the same as that of another participant, but the graduate student assumed that they were roommates. When participant 026 arrived, the graduate student was astonished to see participant 006 enter her office! Oddly, the participant did not seem to recognize her surroundings. She got lost on her way to the office and showed no recognition when she met the researcher. Although the student was sure that this was participant 006, the woman's personal and family history was completely different. The patient claimed that she had been bulimic for 4 years and before that had been overweight since childhood. She recalled her childhood as relatively happy and her parents as nurturing. Their only fault was that they frequently used food as a reward. Her first binge episode occurred after a breakup with a boyfriend, and she denied any history of anorexia nervosa, substance abuse, alcohol abuse, drug abuse, or physical or sexual abuse by her parents.

Curious about these two presentations, the researcher asked subject number 026 if she had ever been involved in research on bulimia nervosa. Astonishingly, she claimed that not only had she never been in a study but that this was the first time she had ever told anyone that she had bulimia. To cover all her bases, the researcher asked subject 026 whether she had any siblings or if she had a twin. Subject 026 responded that she was an only child. Further inquiry into the patient's medical records and medical history revealed that this patient was known in the community to have DID and possessed several alters. Needless to say, the researcher did not include this/these participant(s) in her final research sample.

DID is a fascinating topic that intrigues most abnormal psychology students. During the 1980s and early 1990s, some mental health therapists began to discuss DID with their patients and the media. An interesting phenomenon occurred. As the media attention increased, so did the number of people reported to be suffering from DID. However, even as therapists seemed to find case after case, the very existence of the disorder was called into question. Why? One of the primary criticisms surrounding DID is that, despite many published descriptions of the disorder, few quantitative studies and even fewer that constitute experimental research exist (Boysen & VanBergen, 2013; Kihlstrom, 2001; Paris, 2012). In other words, the scientific status of DID as a diagnostic category is not well established. For example, whether DID can be reliably diagnosed is unclear, although more recent studies are using accepted diagnostic strategies (Boysen & VanBergen, 2013; Dorahy et al., 2014), such as structured clinical interviews. According to its proponents, its signs are intermittent, and most DID patients do not recognize the existence of their alters before they begin therapy (see Piper & Mersky, 2004b). Therefore, unlike other disorders for which people seek treatment because they are sad or anxious, the existence of alternate personalities is discovered only after the person is in therapy.

Another challenge for DID is that the terms used to describe the symptoms are difficult to define in a way that can be studied (Paris, 2012). Neither *alter* nor *distinct personality state* has a clear definition. Furthermore, the number of alters seems to be increasing exponentially since the publication of the studies of Eve and Sybil. One descriptive study (Putnam et al., 1986) indicated that among 100 adults with DID, the average number of alternate personalities was 13.3, ranging from 1 to 60. Some therapists reported that their patients had too many alters to count. The most common alter was a child age 12 years or less. About half of the alters were of the sex opposite of the person seeking treatment, and most reported that the alter first made an appearance before age 12 although the patient was unaware of its presence.

Similarly, no agreement exists on what defines "taking control of the person's behavior." As a result, each therapist can use *idiosyncratic* definitions. How does an alter take control? Does the alter simply have to speak to the therapist to be legitimate, or must the behavior be more complicated? Proponents of DID describe alters who engage in "doing schoolwork, selling illicit drugs, dancing in strip clubs, cleaning bathtubs" (Piper & Mersky, 2004a, p. 679). It is obvious that these questions have no clear answers. In the sections that follow, we examine further the validity of DID.

Depersonalization/Derealization Disorder

LO 6.12 Describe the symptoms of depersonalization/derealization and when those feelings are most likely to occur.

During times of heightened emotionality or stress (e.g., panic disorder, posttraumatic stress disorder, depression, or near-death experiences) or altered physical states such as substance abuse or head injury, many people report feelings of being detached from their mind, body, or behavior. Others report feeling as if the world around them were unreal (Baker et al., 2003; Kihlstrom, 2001). In one group of people who reported these experiences, 62% had a documented medical condition, and 50% had a previous psychiatric diagnosis; most had depression and/or panic disorder (Baker et al., 2003). In some people, these experiences occur with great frequency and not necessarily in the context of emotional stress or physical illness. Similar to what is seen in some anxiety disorders, when presented with ambiguous physical symptoms (e.g., "sometimes things seem unreal"), people with depersonalization disorder are more likely to generate a catastrophic reason for the symptom (e.g., "something is really wrong with me"), whereas people with no psychiatric disorder are more likely to generate a benign reason (e.g., "I woke up in the middle of a dream"), suggesting that how one interprets ambiguous information may play a role in the onset or maintenance of this disorder (Hunter et al., 2014).

> Lucinda described multiple periods of time when the world suddenly felt unreal. Once, when she was with her friends, she felt as if they were in a movie and she was sitting in the audience, watching the others perform on the screen in front of her. Another time, she was walking and suddenly felt as if she were floating above the surface of the sidewalk.

When periods of dissociation are frequent and severe, the person may be suffering from **depersonalization/derealization disorder**, described as feelings of being detached from one's body, behavior, or mind or unreality or detachment with respect to one's surroundings. It is described as a state of feeling as if one is an external observer of one's own behavior. The changes occur suddenly and are perceived as unreal and inconsistent with a person's prior experiences. People can experience symptoms of either depersonalization (being detached from one's body, mind, or behavior) or derealization (a feeling of unfamiliarity or unreality about one's physical or interpersonal environment). Most people with this disorder have symptoms of both types of dissociation (Baker et al., 2003).

Epidemiology

LO 6.13 Understand one of the major challenges to establishing accurate estimates of the prevalence of dissociative disorders, including DID.

The reported prevalence of dissociative disorders varies greatly depending on the characteristics of the sample (community sample or clinic sample) or the degree to which the interviewer believes in the diagnosis. In one epidemiological sample, 0.8% had depersonalization disorder, 1.8% had dissociative amnesia, and 1.5% had DID (Johnson, Cohen, Kase et al., 2006). One challenge in determining the epidemiology of these disorders is that the standardized diagnostic interview schedule most often used to determine the presence of psychological disorders in community samples does not include questions about dissociative disorders (Şar & Ross, 2006). Among inpatient samples, dissociative disorders affect from 4 to 21% of all psychiatric inpatients (Foote et al., 2006), and settings specifically established to treat these disorders report higher rates. Data from outpatient samples are very limited. Among one clinic sample of inner-city outpatients, 29% had a dissociative disorder. These patients also had many other disorders, including depression, posttraumatic stress disorder, and anxiety disorders, and it is possible that depersonalization experiences were the result of one of those disorders. The issue of whether dissociative symptoms represent a primary disorder or are secondary to another disorder may seem to be simply an intellectual exercise. However, it is important for determining mental health policy, reimbursement for services, and approaches to treatment.

SEX, RACE, AND ETHNICITY. Both men and women suffer from dissociative disorders (e.g., Simeon et al., 2003). Worldwide prevalence estimates range from 18.5% of women in the general population of Turkey (Şar et al., 2007) to 8% of women in an inpatient sample in the Netherlands (Friedl & Draijer, 2000). These estimates are higher than those in the United States, suggesting that some of these disorders may represent culture-bound syndromes. Dissociative symptoms, such as trance-like states, are commonly part of religious experiences throughout the world. In Uganda, dissociative amnesia and depersonalization are defined as psychological disorders much as they are in the United States (Van Duijl et al., 2005).

In depersonalization/derealization disorder, a person feels detached from body or mind, as if observing his or her behavior from the outside, or the person may feel that the external environment is unreal.

> Mary was born in Malaysia but moved to the United States when she was in her thirties. Shortly after she arrived, she received word that her mother, still in Malaysia, had died suddenly. Mary was filled with grief. About 4 weeks after she received the news, she was waiting for the subway when someone suddenly bumped her on the platform. Mary became dissociated, alternating between talking incoherently and using foul language, pointing at what she said was a "snake." After about 5 minutes (during which time the police arrived), she became quiet and contemplative. She claimed amnesia regarding the event.

When Mary's husband arrived, he informed police that she had a long history of *latah*, a condition in which a person, after being startled by a sound or touch, suddenly falls into an altered state of consciousness during which he or she behaves as Mary did. The disorder occurs primarily among women from Malaysia, and those who are "latah" have numerous episodes, almost always precipitated by a sudden external event (Tseng, 2003). As this case shows, sociocultural factors may play a significant role in the experience of dissociative disorders.

One challenge in determining prevalence of these disorders around the world is that DSM criteria are used primarily in the United States and Canada. Most other countries use the International Classification of Diseases (ICD) to determine the presence of a psychological disorder, and the ICD does not have a specific category called DID (Dorahy et al., 2014). DID is listed with other disorders under the "other dissociative disorders" category in the ICD. The lack of a specific diagnostic label would certainly affect estimates of the existence of the disorder. The issue of prevalence across cultures is an important one when determining the impact of sociocultural factors in DID (see "Examining the Evidence: Can Therapy Cause Dissociative Identity Disorder?"). In fact, the distribution of cases of DID around the world plays a role in determining the validity of DID as a response to horrific traumatic events (most commonly childhood sexual abuse). Proponents of DID as a unique diagnostic category point out that in addition to Western countries, cases of DID have been reported in Japan, Taiwan, Turkey, China, and the Philippines (Boysen & VanBergen, 2013). These researchers also point out that despite the existence of cases around the world, 82% of newly identified cases were from Western countries and 50% were from the United States and Canada alone. Similarly, Turkey accounted for 79% of cases in non-Western countries. These data would suggest that DID is not a universal response to traumatic events but may indeed be a culture-specific response (Boysen & VanBergen, 2013). This is not to say that people who believe that they have DID are "faking it." Rather, it would suggest that the behavior exists as the acting out of a culturally expected role (Lilienfeld et al., 1999). As we discuss in detail in the etiology section, DID may be the result of a cultural expectation regarding how someone should respond to such a traumatic event (Boyson & VanBergen, 2013).

DEVELOPMENTAL FACTORS. The average age of onset for depersonalization disorder (as defined in DSM-IV-TR) ranges from 15.9 to 22.8 years (Baker et al., 2003; Simeon et al., 2003) although children as young as age 8 have been diagnosed with DID (Hornstein & Putnam, 1992). However, the children who were given this diagnosis also had many other psychological disorders as well as unusual beliefs (i.e., delusions), unusual perceptual experiences (hallucinations, such as hearing voices when no one is present), and histories of suicidal ideation and attempts. This means that as with adults, DID, if it exists at all, rarely occurs alone, even in children (Putnam, 1993; Vincent & Pickering, 1988).

Etiology

LO 6.14 Describe how the controversy surrounding repressed/recovered memories has influenced the etiological theories of dissociative disorders.

Because dissociative disorders are very rare, there are few empirical data to help us understand how the disorders develop. Therefore, much of what has been written about the onset of dissociative disorders is based on clinical experience and impressions, not empirical data. In some instances, this theorizing has negatively affected individuals, often the parents of affected children, by falsely accusing them of committing child abuse. As you read the examples in this section, consider whether some of these behaviors remind you of the concept of *emotional contagion*, which we discussed in Chapter 1.

BIOLOGICAL FACTORS. Neurological disorders, such as temporal lobe epilepsy, head injury, tumor, cerebral vascular accident (stroke), migraine, and dementia, may produce symptoms such as blackouts, fugues, depersonalization, amnesia, anxiety and panic symptoms, and auditory, visual, and olfactory hallucinations (Lambert et al., 2002). Several empirical trials suggest that between 10 and 21% of patients with DID have abnormal brain activity (Sivec & Lynn, 1995). Therefore, although abnormal neurological function cannot account for the onset of all cases of dissociative disorders, some dissociative symptoms may result from neurological conditions.

Neuroanatomical and neurochemical studies of dissociative disorders are few (Şar et al., 2001; Simeon, Guralnik, Knutelska et al., 2001; Vermetten et al., 2006), and those that exist are limited by small sample sizes, lack of adequate control groups, or failure to exclude the presence of other disorders such as posttraumatic stress disorder. Actually, a comparison of people with DID and people with PTSD indicated few differences in brain anatomy and brain function (Loewenstein, 2005). The common denominator in both of these conditions may be chronic stress. As discussed in Chapter 4, the chronic stress associated with PTSD can produce changes in the hippocampus and amygdala, brain regions known to be involved in memory functions. Neurochemical changes may also occur. During periods of stress, the availability of neuropeptides and neurotransmitters (known collectively as *neuromodulators*) in these regions is altered, which affects establishing memory traces for specific events (Bremner et al., 1996). These neuromodulators may have both strengthening and diminishing effects on memory based on the level of stress and the type of neuromodulator.

PSYCHOSOCIAL FACTORS. According to its proponents, DID is a failure of the normal developmental process of "personality integration." The failure is hypothesized to result from traumatic experiences and disordered caregiver–child relationships during critical developmental periods. This leads to the development and elaboration of distinct personality states (International Society for the Study of Dissociation, 2005). The traumas are most commonly incidents of physical and/or sexual abuse that occur during childhood.

Consistent with the suggested association between abuse and somatic symptom and related disorders, data supporting the proposal that DID results from childhood trauma are correlational and based on samples of patients who are seeking treatment (Lynn et al., 2014). Some proponents of this relationship assert that many or virtually all patients with DID were severely abused as children, but no controlled investigations support these assertions. The available longitudinal studies of the adult effects of childhood sexual abuse do not include DID as one of the negative outcomes (e.g., Bulik et al., 2001; Piper & Merskey, 2004a). Of course, large epidemiological studies are sometimes conducted using telephone interviews, and researchers make decisions about how best to use the interview time. Sometimes rarely occurring disorders such as DID are not included in epidemiological surveys because they occur so infrequently. This means that the disorder may be present but undetected. However, even if some people who are sexually abused develop DID, this does not mean that all abuse victims develop DID or that DID is the only result of sexual abuse. In one large twin study, a history of childhood sexual abuse was related to increased risk for many different outcomes, such as depression, suicide attempts, conduct disorder, substance abuse, social anxiety, adult rape, and divorce (Nelson et al., 2002). Therefore, childhood sexual abuse appears to increase the risk for adult psychopathology in general, but it does not appear to predict the development of any one particular disorder (Bulik et al., 2001).

Despite the lack of strong empirical data, clinicians who specialize in DID still propose that dissociation is used to cope with traumatic experiences, blocking painful events from awareness and allowing the person to function as if nothing traumatic had happened (Sivec & Lynn, 1995). Although blocking painful events might help someone cope in the short term, its repeated use results in functional impairments. However, this is where some theorists jump from a behavioral explanation to an etiological theory without the corroborating evidence. They conclude that anyone who experiences dissociative symptoms *must have been abused.* Significant gaps in childhood memories are considered evidence of repeated trauma (Bass & Davis, 1988). Patients are often encouraged to "remember" the trauma as a way of overcoming their symptoms. There is a fallacy in this reasoning, however, because these theories ignore the evidence that memory gaps before the age of 6 are common in the general population (Holmes et al., 2005b). But what if people only "remember" abuse after a therapist explains that their symptoms are the result of unrecalled child abuse? Are these recovered memories or *false* memories?

The issue of *repressed memories* and *recovered memories* is an emotional and controversial one for psychology and mental health professionals. Consider the following example:

> In 1990, George Franklin Sr., age 51, was found guilty of the murder of 8-year-old Susan Kay Nason. What made the case unusual was that the murder occurred more than 20 years earlier, and the primary evidence was the recovered memory of Franklin's daughter, Eileen, who was also 8 years old at the time. Eileen's memory of the murder did not return at once but in bits and pieces. By the time it had all returned, Eileen described witnessing her father sexually assault Susan in the back of a van and then kill her by smashing her head with a rock. Many people believed Eileen's account even though many of the details could have been obtained from newspaper accounts. More disconcerting was the fact that many of the details she provided changed over time. For example, she initially stated that the event occurred in the morning. When later confronted with the fact that Susan had attended school that day, Eileen changed her testimony to state that the event occurred after school (from Loftus, 1993). Because of the inconsistency of Eileen's testimony, George Franklin's conviction was later overturned.

There is no way to determine whether Eileen's memories were fact or fiction, yet throughout the 1980s and 1990s, many people reported "recovered" memories, most often having to do with incidents of child abuse. Many therapists believed that these memories were absolute fact without considering that memory is fallible; in other words, memory can be inaccurate or, even in some cases, completely made up.

To understand the recovered memory controversy, understanding that memory is an active process is necessary. First, to remember something, you must have paid attention to it.

> Tom was walking down the street when he was physically assaulted. When describing the event to the police, he was unable to recall the face of his assailant.

Some theorists propose that such selective amnesia indicates that the person's mind has actively blocked this aspect of the traumatic event. However, experimental data suggest that under conditions of high arousal, people pay attention to the central feature of an event at the expense of less important details (McNally, 2005). Tom may not have remembered the face of his attacker because his attention was focused on the perpetrator's gun.

Second, most people do not understand that "memory does not operate like a videotape recorder" (McNally, 2005, p. 818). Remembering is an active process and always involves reconstruction. Even very strong memories may change over time. The morning after the space shuttle *Challenger* exploded, undergraduate students were asked to write down where they were and what they were doing when they heard the news (Neisser & Harsch, 1992). Nearly 3 years later, they were interviewed again. The students were highly confident about the truthfulness of their memory, but the researchers detected many inaccuracies in their recall of the events, including very basic facts such as where they were and what they were doing. In short, memory changes as time progresses.

Just by asking a misleading question, memory researchers have demonstrated that eyewitnesses can construct memories for events that did not occur. Ten months after a horrible plane crash that had national news coverage, people were asked, "Did you see the television film of the moment that the plane hit the apartment building?" Actually, no such film was available, but when asked this question, more than 60% of the people responded that they had seen the film and were able to describe details of television coverage *that did not exist* (Cronbag et al., 1996). Other studies also illustrate that memories of entirely fictionalized events can be constructed. As part of a study of "childhood memories," adult subjects were given three true stories about their childhood as well as a fourth, false story (i.e., that at age 5, they were lost in a mall; Loftus & Pickrell, 1995). During follow-up interviews, when adults described everything they could remember about the four situations, 25% of the participants provided elaborate details about the event that had never occurred.

Even if we leave aside the issue of repressed/recovered memories, controlled clinical trials still provide only limited evidence for the relationship between abuse and DID. There are two reasons for this controversial relationship. First, the descriptions of abuse often are not objectively documented. Second, the definition of abuse can be quite variable. In some studies, it is limited to acts of physical or sexual abuse. In other studies, abuse is defined broadly to include emotional abuse and emotional/physical neglect, situations that are much more difficult to objectively define and quantify. In still other studies, the samples consist solely of individuals already diagnosed with dissociative disorders with no adequate comparison groups, yet the results are described as "definitive" (Lewis et al., 1997).

With these limitations in mind, the data from controlled trials suggest that trauma exposure plays only a limited role. In one sample, trauma exposure accounted for only 4.4% of the dissociative symptoms (Briere et al., 2005). Emotional abuse plays an equally important role as, if not a larger role than, sexual abuse (Simeon, Guralnik, Schmeidler et al., 2001). More general environmental factors, such as a generally poor relationship between parent and child (even without specific acts of abuse), contribute more to the onset of these disorders than does emotional abuse (e.g., Nelson et al., 2002).

Therapists who adhere to a *posttraumatic model* of DID believe that a person "compartmentalizes" responses to trauma in the form of alternate personalities. They believe that different patient behaviors indicate the possible presence of alters even if the person is unaware of their existence (Piper & Mersky, 2004b). Some therapists report that alters emerge only after repeated requests from the therapist. Could these actions actually cause DID? When the therapist or the therapy itself contributes to the onset of a disorder, the cause is said to be *iatrogenic.* An **iatrogenic** disease is one that is inadvertently caused by a physician, by a medical or surgical treatment, or by a diagnostic procedure. The *sociocultural model* postulates that DID is an iatrogenic disorder that develops using cues from the media and therapists as well as from personal experiences and observations of others who have enacted multiple identities. These experiences and cues are legitimized and maintained by social reinforcement in therapeutic settings (Spanos, 1994; see "Examining the Evidence: Can Therapy Cause Dissociative Identity Disorder?").

Ethics and Responsibility

LO 6.15 Discuss how the research on recovered/false memories may affect our assumptions about child abuse and its aftermath.

What conclusions can we draw about the research on recovered/false memories? Even though a person provides a detailed memory and is confident that it is accurate, that does not always mean that the person remembered how an event really happened (Laney & Loftus, 2005). The issue of recovered/false memories is not simply an intellectual curiosity but also an important element in the controversy surrounding child abuse and, by extension, DID. It is important to remember that (1) some children do suffer abuse and (2) although some abused children may suffer from psychological disorders as adults, no clear link exists between abuse and DID because much of the available research does not include objective corroboration of child abuse and is based on cross-sectional, not longitudinal, studies (Lynn et al., 2014). Furthermore, despite the disagreement regarding recovered memories, all mental health professionals agree on one key point: memories of childhood abuse that were always present are almost always authentic as are those that are spontaneously remembered outside of a therapeutic setting (Holmes et al., 2005).

Examining the EVIDENCE

Can Therapy Cause Dissociative Identity Disorder?

- **The Facts** The number of cases of DID worldwide rose from 79 in 1970 to approximately 6,000 in 1986 (Elzinga et al., 1998), a period of time corresponding to the appearance of the book and movie *Sybil*. By 2000, the number of cases was estimated to be in the tens of thousands (Acocella, 1998). The *sociocultural model* proposes that therapists (and the media) can influence people to develop alternate identities. Might these influences explain the dramatically increased prevalence of DID?

- **The Evidence** Among DID patients, 80 to 100% have no knowledge of their alters before they began therapy (Dell & Eisenhower, 1990; Lewis et al., 1997; Putnam, 1989). As they continue in therapy, the number of alters reported by a person continues to increase (e.g., North et al., 1993). *Posttraumatic* model theorists address this phenomenon, explaining that patients with DID tend to hide their symptoms before treatment. Perhaps this is so, but are there alternative hypotheses?

- **Let's Examine the Evidence** Several lines of evidence suggest that therapists may shape people to produce alternative personalities (Lilienfeld et al., 1999).

  First, when people with no psychological disorders are given appropriate cues, they can successfully produce DID symptoms including reports of physical, sexual, and satanic abuse rituals (Stafford & Lynn, 2002).

  Second, both the increase in the number of patients with DID and the number of alters that appear during the course of treatment coincide with increased therapist awareness of the diagnostic features. In other words, the more the therapist believes in the diagnosis, the more likely the patients will be given the diagnosis.

  Third, one DID expert recommends to novice therapists that when an alter does not emerge spontaneously, "Asking to meet an alter directly is an increasingly accepted intervention" (Kluft, 1993, p. 29). Other advice includes giving the person the hypnotic suggestion that "everybody (meaning all the personalities) listen." Would such suggestions lead the patient to believe (i.e., shape the patient to believe) that other personalities must exist?

  Such shaping did occur in the case of children's testimony during the McMartin preschool molestation trial in California in the 1980s, a notorious case in which a number of day care workers were falsely accused and convicted of sexually molesting the children in their care. Later testimony refuted the original claims. Children who initially denied being molested by day care workers were repeatedly interviewed until, as one child later reported, "Anytime I would give them an answer they didn't like, they would ask me again and encourage me to give them the answer they were looking for" (Zirpolo, 2005). In effect, the children were encouraged to provide answers consistent with the therapist's preexisting beliefs.

- **Conclusion** The posttraumatic model asserts that most therapists do not diagnose DID because they neglect to sufficiently probe for its features (Ross, 1997). However, both basic laboratory and behavioral observation data suggest that college students and patients may be vulnerable to therapists' expectations and may produce alters because of suggestions (or probing) by a therapist. This evidence indicates that iatrogenesis and the sociocultural model explanation for the existence of DID cannot be discounted.

Treatment

LO 6.16 Summarize the state of the knowledge on how to treat dissociative disorders.

As noted, dissociative amnesia usually resolves without treatment. No controlled pharmacological trials for derealization disorder or DID have been conducted, but clinical reports suggest that antidepressant medications may be helpful. It is unclear, however, whether these medications work on core dissociative symptoms or treat the associated anxiety and depression. Little empirical data exist regarding treatment for DID (Brand et al., 2011). The same conclusion may apply to CBT approaches, which hypothesize that people with dissociative disorders misinterpret normal symptoms of fatigue, stress, or even substance intoxication as abnormal. CBT therapists challenge these misinterpretations by teaching the person to generate alternative explanations for their symptoms (a process known as cognitive restructuring). In some instances, people may avoid situations that elicit their symptoms, in which case exposure therapy (see Chapter 4) may help people enter these feared situations. Recall from Chapters 4 and 5 that exposure therapy requires putting the person in the situation that creates anxiety/distress and keeping him or her there until the anxiety/distress subsides. When the situation is a physical symptom, the person must be exposed to that symptom. In order to do this, the therapists in one of the first open trials (Weiner & McKay, 2012) used strobe light and 3D glasses to create unusual perceptual experiences, similar to what happens in a depersonalization episode. Once the symptom of depersonalization occurred, the person "sat" with the feeling until it dissipated. After four exposure sessions, the patients reported lower scores on a self-report of depersonalization and derealization experiences. Of course, we do not know if these changes would persist, and randomized controlled trials are necessary. But this study is a first attempt to apply these CBT strategies to treat dissociative disorders.

Learning Objective Summaries

LO 6.10 Discuss how dissociative amnesia is different from momentary forgetting or amnesia as a result of medical conditions.

Momentary forgetting is a common part of everyday life. Amnesia sometimes occurs after a medical condition or injury. Dissociative amnesia is the inability to recall important information, usually of a personal nature. Failure to recall events that occur during a certain period of time is known as localized amnesia, whereas generalized amnesia is a total inability to recall any aspect of one's life. Selective amnesia relates to the ability to not recall certain aspects of an event while recalling other parts of the event.

LO 6.11 Identify two ways in which the process of the diagnosis of DID differs from other psychological disorders.

Dissociative identity disorder (DID) is a very controversial diagnosis. Unlike most psychological disorders, the primary symptom (the existence of alternate identities) often emerges only after the individual has entered treatment. Most people seek psychotherapy because they have symptoms. Another difference is that the alternate personality or the "distinct personality state" is not clearly defined, making it difficult for some people to determine if it is clearly an alternate personality or perhaps just a very dramatic mood swing. Finally, few quantitative research studies exist, and most of the information is based on clinical description or clinical expertise.

LO 6.12 Describe the symptoms of depersonalization/derealization and when those feelings are most likely to occur.

Depersonalization is defined as experiencing feelings of unreality, detachment, or being an outside observer with respect to one's thoughts, feelings, sensations, body, or actions. Derealization is defined as experiencing feelings of unreality or detachment with respect to surroundings. These feelings often occur in the context of an extreme emotional state. To be considered a disorder, depersonalization or derealization must create distress or functional impairment.

LO 6.13 Understand one of the major challenges to establishing accurate estimates of the prevalence of dissociative disorders, including DID.

One of the major challenges to establishing accurate estimates of the prevalence of dissociative disorders is that structured diagnostic interviews do not assess for the presence of these disorders. Also, the diagnostic criteria are not the same in the two major diagnostic systems, the ICD and the DSM. Therefore, it is difficult to establish prevalence across countries.

LO 6.14 Describe how the controversy surrounding repressed/recovered memories has influenced the etiological theories of dissociative disorders.

Despite the reports that cases of DID exist around the world, 82% of newly identified cases were from Western countries and 50% were from the United States and Canada alone. Similarly, Turkey accounted for 79% of cases in non-Western countries. These data would suggest that DID is not a universal response to traumatic events but may indeed be a culture-specific response. An alternative hypothesis is that different diagnostic criteria, applied differently in different countries, affect the estimates of who suffers from these disorders.

LO 6.15 Discuss how the research on recovered/false memories may affect our assumptions about child abuse and its aftermath.

The theory that dissociative disorders, particularly DID, always follow the experience of child abuse (physical or sexual) has led some individuals to think that those who suffer dissociative disorders must have been abused. Because of this theory, some adults have been unjustly accused of abuse and end up facing criminal charges. Etiological theories, for what are real psychological symptoms, should not begin with preconceived notions.

LO 6.16 Summarize the state of the knowledge on how to treat dissociative disorders.

The treatment outcome literature for dissociative disorders is very small. Most of the information is based on clinical experience rather than randomized controlled trials. Clinical experience is often the starting point for the development of empirically supported treatments, but randomized, carefully controlled studies using objective outcome measures and large sample sizes are necessary to establish the efficacy of any intervention.

Critical Thinking Question

Most psychological disorders show a steady rise in prevalence from the mid-1980s through 2003. By contrast, the number of publications regarding dissociative amnesia and DID rose from low levels in the mid-1980s to a sharp peak in the 1990s followed by an equally sharp decline by 2003 (Pope et al., 2006). Worldwide, in 2003, the literature reported only 13 explicit cases of dissociative amnesia and DID. How would you explain this phenomenon?

Malingering

LO 6.17 Define malingering, and explain why it creates issues for clinicians in diagnosing disorders

You may have engaged in malingering behavior at some time if you ever feigned illness (played sick) in order to avoid going to school, taking a test, or engaging in some other activity. For most of us, these are isolated events. Some individuals, however, may feign psychological disorders in order to avoid criminal prosecution (see Chapter 15). It is extremely important for psychologists to be able to detect malingering. Yet, because diagnosing psychological disorders often depends upon a person's self-report ("yes, I feel sad" or "no, I do not hear voices"), how does a psychologist determine whether a person might be feigning a psychological disorder? As you

REAL People REAL Disorders

The Piano Man—Dissociative Disorder, Factitious Disorder, or Malingering?

For a time, he was the world's most enigmatic young man—a haunted, gaunt figure known only as the "Piano Man." On April 7, 2005, police found him in Kent, England, soaking wet in a suit with the labels cut out. He had no passport, no credit cards, and no money. He was mute. Police put him in the care of psychiatrists, who gave him a pen and paper in the hope he would write his name. Instead, he drew a detailed sketch of a grand piano. When they brought him a piano, it was reported that he played for hours at a time. His condition set off a media frenzy in Europe, both to discover his identity and to determine his condition.

Many mental health professionals thought that he might have autism spectrum disorder (see Chapter 13). His ability to play the piano was interpreted as an example of the highly specific talents often seen among people with this disorder. As discussed by a spokesperson for the National Autistic Society, the facts that he had ripped out the labels from his clothing and that he rarely made eye contact were further clues that he had autism spectrum disorder. A clinical psychologist commented that the behaviors could also suggest schizophrenia. Depression or posttraumatic stress disorder were also possibilities. Medical administrators denied that he was faking his symptoms. He was described as very nervous and anxious.

Five months later, a nurse went into his room and said, "Are you going to speak to us today?" He replied, "Yes, I think I will." He told the staff that he was German, had been working in Paris but had lost his job, and after a broken love affair, had traveled by train to Great Britain. He was trying to commit suicide when the police picked him up on the beach. He had worked previously with mentally ill patients and had copied some mannerisms that successfully fooled the staff, including two very senior doctors. He said he drew a piano because that was the first thing that came into his head. Contrary to previous reports, he didn't play the piano; he just kept tapping the same key. After his revelation, he was sent home to Germany.

SOURCE: http://www.mirror.co.uk/news/uk-news/piano-man-sh-am-554649

will see in the "Real People, Real Disorders" feature above, one possible explanation for the Piano Man's unusual behavior was that he was creating his psychological symptoms for personal gain (in this case, having a place to live and people to take care of him for a period of time).

After you finish reading this feature, decide for yourself. Did the Piano Man suffer from a dissociative disorder? Did he have factitious disorder? Did he have depression? Or was he malingering?

A growing concern on college campuses is students who do not have a history of attention deficit/hyperactivity disorder (ADHD) but who would like to get stimulant medication or increased testing time in order to enhance their academic performance. The challenge for psychologists is to identify students who are really suffering from ADHD (and may not have been diagnosed as a child) and who are in need of psychiatric medication. In some cases, cognitive measures, known as symptom validity tests (SVTs), which measure cognitive abilities and not reports of symptomatology, are useful parts of the diagnostic evaluation. For example, among college students seeking evaluation for ADHD, 31% failed a word memory test. In fact, even though these students were functioning at a cognitive level that allowed them to be admitted to college, they failed a test usually passed by people with severe traumatic brain injury (Suhr et al., 2008), indicating that they were faking memory problems. In another investigation, college students were asked to "fake ADHD" and were given information about the disorder from the Internet. When evaluated by diagnosticians blinded to whether the student really had ADHD or was faking, the two groups had equal scores on ADHD symptom profiles, indicating that they had adequately learned the symptoms of this disorder (Sollman et al., 2010). However, on tests of memory and concentration, the group pretending to have ADHD actually did *much worse* than students who had a legitimate diagnosis, indicating that these cognitive tests were much less susceptible to feigning a psychological disorder. The issue of malingering is an important and understudied area of psychology. Most people seeking psychological help do indeed have legitimate psychological symptoms. Detecting malingering behavior is important not only in forensic (criminal) evaluations or college campuses but in any diagnostic interview. The treatment of psychological disorders involves significant financial and professional resources, and it is important that these limited resources are not used inappropriately.

Learning Objective Summaries

LO 6.17 Define malingering, and explain why it creates issues for clinicians in diagnosing disorders.

Malingering is defined as the deliberate production of physical or psychological symptoms for the purpose of some type of personal gain. Detecting malingering behavior is important because the treatment of psychological disorders involves significant financial and professional resources, and it is important that these limited resources are not used inappropriately.

Critical Thinking Question

Do you think it is possible for excessive malingering to lead to somatic disorders? Why or why not?

Real SCIENCE Real LIFE

Nancy—A Case of Somatic Symptom Disorder

THE PATIENT

Nancy, 55 years old, comes to the psychiatric emergency room accompanied by her husband, George.

THE PROBLEM

Her complaint is as follows: "I have these fits and no one can find the cause." Nancy describes the sudden onset of seizures during which she falls down and shakes uncontrollably. She does not lose consciousness, and the seizures do not result in any injury. As a matter of fact, when she "falls," she usually falls slowly into a chair or onto the couch, suggesting some degree of control over her body movements. The last physician who she saw gave her husband some syringes with "antiseizure" medication, which he used to stop her seizures once they began.

After detailing the physical symptoms, the psychologist began to interview Nancy about her personal history. As a child, Nancy recalls her mother often taking her to the pediatrician. "My mother was very health conscious. She always worried about us when we were ill. If we had a fever or a headache, she would make us stay in bed, but she would stay in the room with us, playing games to keep us occupied. Once I was in the hospital to have my tonsils removed. This was before the time that parents were encouraged to stay in the hospital with their children. But my mother made such a fuss, the nurses let her stay. She showed me how much she loved me by refusing to leave me, even in the care of health professionals."

Nancy and George have been married for 35 years. She described her marriage as mediocre—she married George because she was pregnant. Her parents were both alcoholic, and as a child, she was subjected to a great deal of emotional abuse. Marriage was her way of getting out. George and Nancy have six children. Nancy never worked; her life revolved around her children. As a matter of fact, Nancy and George had nothing in common but their children. Recently, the youngest child moved out of the house. Now there was no one but Nancy and George, a marriage without communication or affection.

When asked how George was responding to her seizures, Nancy's face brightened. "It's the funniest thing," she said. "Ever since my seizures developed, George has become really attentive. He hasn't been this nice since I was pregnant. And I've been really lucky—George has been there every time that I've had a seizure to give me my medication. As soon as I get the injection, my tremors disappear." George had brought one of the syringes to the meeting. When he gave it to the psychologist, she could clearly see the words "saline injection" on the side. In fact, Nancy's antiseizure medication was salt water.

ASSESSING THE SITUATION

First, what would you say is the etiology of this disorder? How did it develop? Second, how would you treat it? Design a plan to help Nancy get over her symptoms.

THE TREATMENT

The therapist determined that Nancy was suffering from conversion disorder and that a number of environmental and social factors were maintaining her condition. However, because Nancy was convinced that her symptoms had a physical cause, the psychologist did not attempt to convince her otherwise. First, she had Nancy keep a log of what was happening every time that she had a "seizure." It became clear that her seizures occurred after conflict with her husband, children, and sister. In most instances, the conflict centered on Nancy's inability to assert herself. Therefore, treatment focused on assertiveness training and general social skills training to increase her ability to express her wants and desires to her family. In addition, the therapist instructed George that when a seizure occurred, he should give Nancy her medicine but should not focus on or discuss the seizure in any way. This decreased family attention on this behavior. The therapist also gave George and Nancy homework assignments to do one pleasant thing per week—having dinner out with friends, going to a movie, taking a French cooking class.

THE TREATMENT OUTCOME

After 6 months, Nancy's attacks had decreased from three times per week during the first month to only one in the past 8 weeks. She reported some increased marital satisfaction and was getting along better with her adult children. Her sister remained the only source of distress, but Nancy was vowing to continue to work on that relationship.

Key Terms

amnesia, p. 215
conversion disorder, p. 200
depersonalization/derealization disorder, p. 218
dissociative amnesia, p. 215
dissociative disorders, p. 214
dissociative fugue, p. 216
dissociative identity disorder, p. 216
factitious disorder, p. 203
factitious disorder imposed on another, p. 205
factitious disorder imposed on self, p. 204
iatrogenic, p. 223
illness anxiety disorder, p. 203
malingering, p. 203
pseudoseizures, p. 200
somatic symptom disorder, p. 199
somatic symptom and related disorders, p. 199

Chapter 7
Bipolar and Depressive Disorders

Chapter Learning Objectives

Bipolar and Related Disorders	**LO 7.1**	Recognize and differentiate bipolar and related disorders and their component symptoms.
	LO 7.2	Describe the prevalence of bipolar and related disorders in various segments of the population (sex, race, ethnicity, age).
	LO 7.3	Explain how the presentation of bipolar and related disorders differs across the life span.
	LO 7.4	Characterize patterns of comorbidity in bipolar and related disorders.
Depressive Disorders	**LO 7.5**	Recognize the symptoms of major depressive disorder.
	LO 7.6	Define persistent depressive disorder, and distinguish it from major depressive disorder.

	LO 7.7 Construct an argument for the inclusion of disruptive mood regulation disorder in DSM-5.
	LO 7.8 Recognize the symptoms of premenstrual dysphoric disorder and depressive disorder with peripartum onset.
	LO 7.9 Describe the prevalence of major depressive disorder in various segments of the population (sex, race, ethnicity, age).
	LO 7.10 Characterize the prevalence of major depressive disorder across the life span.
	LO 7.11 Characterize patterns of comorbidity in depressive disorders.
Suicide	**LO 7.12** Clarify the differences among suicidal ideation, suicide attempts, and death by suicide.
	LO 7.13 List factors associated with suicide, and detail the relationship between depression and suicidal ideation and behavior.
	LO 7.14 Explain the relation between mental illness and suicide attempts in children.
	LO 7.15 Identify risk factors associated with suicide attempts and death by suicide.
	LO 7.16 Discuss approaches to understanding factors associated with death by suicide.
	LO 7.17 Evaluate the current understanding of the preventability of suicide.
	LO 7.18 Discuss approaches to treatment after suicide attempts.
The Etiology of Bipolar and Depressive Disorders	**LO 7.19** Understand genetic, brain, and environmental factors that increase risk for bipolar and depressive disorders.
	LO 7.20 Contrast psychodynamic, behavioral, and cognitive theories of depressive disorders.
The Treatment of Bipolar and Depressive Disorders	**LO 7.21** Identify efficacious pharmacological and psychological treatments for bipolar disorder.
	LO 7.22 Identify efficacious pharmacological and psychological treatments for depressive disorders.
	LO 7.23 Evaluate appropriateness of treatment based on mood symptoms and patient characteristics.

Alexis was a senior in high school. She had good grades (As and Bs), was involved in extracurricular activities, and played varsity sports. Although she was a worrier by temperament, she had friends and a busy high school schedule.

In her senior year, she started losing interest in her activities. She quit the student newspaper and found it difficult to drag herself to practice. All she wanted to do was stay at home in her room—she stopped seeing her friends and avoided their phone calls.

Alexis went to bed at a decent hour but woke up first at 5 A.M. and then gradually earlier and earlier. Soon she was wide awake each morning at 3 A.M. and unable to fall back to sleep. She lost her appetite. Everything tasted like cardboard, and Alexis lost 7 pounds that she didn't have to lose. She felt restless. She was irritable with her younger brother and lashed out at her parents, which she had never done before. She stared at her homework for hours, reading the same paragraph again and again. Alexis's grades plummeted, and she became ineligible for athletics.

One of her teachers recommended that she see the school counselor, which she did grudgingly. Her thoughts became very dark, and she often felt there was no reason to live. Alexis considered killing herself and had begun to explore how she might do it.

Alexis had never felt this way before. She told the counselor that her maternal grandmother had been in a psychiatric hospital and that she had seen Prozac in her mother's medicine cabinet. The counselor contacted Alexis's mother and helped her set up an appointment with a psychiatrist immediately. As it turned out, Alexis's mother also had had several depressive episodes (often in the autumn months) and had been on medication for years. Alexis started antidepressant medication and saw a psychologist for cognitive-behavioral therapy to help her develop skills to combat the negative thought patterns that often accompany depression.

Alexis had loss of energy and appetite, trouble sleeping, and a very sad mood, and she could not identify a cause for her depressed mood. Alexis's symptoms are a clear example of a disorder characterized most prominently by a pervasive and unshakable low mood. Alexis's problems distressed her and bewildered those around her. Once a high-functioning and active girl both socially and athletically, she had become a social recluse. The cluster of signs and symptoms that Alexis experienced, including social withdrawal, lack of energy and interest, loss of appetite, insomnia, irritability, and restlessness, constitute a disorder known as *major depressive disorder*.

Major depressive disorder is just one type of disorder that affects mood. Actually, the bipolar and depressive disorders consist of several different conditions characterized by various degrees of depressed (low) or manic (high) moods. People with these syndromes have physical, emotional, and cognitive symptoms that may interfere with their ability to work, study, sleep, eat, interact with others, have sexual relations, and enjoy daily life. Although all of us have mood fluctuations from time to time, major depressive disorder is *not* the same as a transient "blue" mood or sad feelings, and mania is *not* the same as being elated. This chapter examines how and why the bipolar and depressive disorders involve more than just bad (or good) moods.

Bipolar and Related Disorders

Bipolar Disorder

LO 7.1 Recognize and differentiate bipolar and related disorders and their component symptoms.

Bipolar and depressive disorders are syndromes whose predominant feature is a disturbance in mood. The disturbance can take the form of mood that is abnormally low—**depression**—or abnormally high—**mania**. There are two categories: (1) bipolar and related disorders and (2) depressive disorders. The primary bipolar and related disorders include bipolar I, bipolar II, and cyclothymic disorder, each of which is characterized by both highs and lows in mood. The primary depressive disorders include disruptive mood dysregulation disorder, major depressive disorder, persistent depressive disorder (dysthymia), and premenstrual dysphoric disorder. These presentations are marked by low mood only. The critical features are the presence of depressed or elated mood (or both) and by the length of time or the specific times that the mood abnormalities persist.

Mood disturbance can include mood that is too low or too high, with the latter known as *mania*. Mania is different from elated mood in which excitement and good feelings naturally match a happy or an enjoyable experience. Rather, mania is high mood that is clearly excessive and is often accompanied by inappropriate and potentially dangerous behavior, irritability, pressured or rapid speech, and a false sense of well being (see "DSM-5: Bipolar I Disorder"). The side-by-side case studies illustrate the contrast between normal elation and mania. Because recurrent mania in the absence of any depressive episodes is extremely rare, the DSM does not recognize it as a separate disorder. Manic episodes almost always occur in tandem with episodes of depression, and a person who has only a single manic episode will very likely have depression as well. Generally, a person is said to suffer from **bipolar disorder** (formerly known as *manic-depressive disorder*) when both episodic depressed mood and episodic mania are present.

Bipolar disorder consists of dramatic shifts in mood, energy, and ability to function. It is a long-term episodic illness in which mood shifts between the two emotional "poles" of mania and depression. In a depressed period, a person may be all but immobile, feeling unable to get out of bed. In a manic period, the same person may be so full of energy as to try to start a new business, buy a house, and plan a trip around the world on the same day. At either extreme, the person cannot cope with the demands of everyday life. Periods of normal feelings and energy commonly occur between these mood changes.

Watch PROFILES OF BIPOLAR DISORDER

Bipolar disorder is commonly categorized as either **bipolar I** or **bipolar II** (see DSM-5: Bipolar I Disorder). The main difference is the degree of mania. In bipolar I, full-blown mania alternates with episodes of major depression; it also includes a single manic episode with or without periods of depression. In bipolar II disorder, *hypomania* alternates with

DSM-5

Criteria for Bipolar I Disorder

For a diagnosis of bipolar I disorder, it is necessary to meet the following criteria for a manic episode. The manic episode may have been preceded by and may be followed by hypomanic or major depressive episodes.

Manic Episode

A. A distinct period of abnormally and persistently elevated, expansive, or irritable mood and abnormally and persistently increased goal-directed activity or energy, lasting at least 1 week and present most of the day, nearly every day (or any duration if hospitalization is necessary).

B. During the period of mood disturbance and increased energy or activity, three (or more) of the following symptoms (four if the mood is only irritable) are present to a significant degree and represent a noticeable change from usual behavior:

1. Inflated self-esteem or grandiosity.
2. Decreased need for sleep (e.g., feels rested after only 3 hours of sleep).
3. More talkative than usual or pressure to keep talking.
4. Flight of ideas or subjective experience that thoughts are racing.
5. Distractibility (i.e., attention too easily drawn to unimportant or irrelevant external stimuli), as reported or observed.
6. Increase in goal-directed activity (either socially, at work or school, or sexually) or psychomotor agitation (i.e., purposeless non-goal-directed activity).
7. Excessive involvement in activities that have a high potential for painful consequences (e.g., engaging in unrestrained buying sprees, sexual indiscretions, or foolish business investments).

C. The mood disturbance is sufficiently severe to cause marked impairment in social or occupational functioning or to necessitate hospitalization to prevent harm to self or others, or there are psychotic features.

D. The episode is not attributable to the physiological effects of a substance (e.g., a drug of abuse, a medication, other treatment) or to another medical condition.

Note: A full manic episode that emerges during antidepressant treatment (e.g., medication, electroconvulsive therapy) but persists at a fully syndromal level beyond the physiological effect of that treatment is sufficient evidence for a manic episode and, therefore, a bipolar I diagnosis.

Hypomanic Episode

A. A distinct period of abnormally and persistently elevated, expansive, or irritable mood and abnormally and persistently increased activity or energy, lasting at least 4 consecutive days and present most of the day, nearly every day.

B. During the period of mood disturbance and increased energy and activity, three (or more) of the following symptoms (four if the mood is only irritable) have persisted, represent a noticeable change from usual behavior, and have been present to a significant degree:

1. Inflated self-esteem or grandiosity.
2. Decreased need for sleep (e.g., feels rested after only 3 hours of sleep).
3. More talkative than usual or pressure to keep talking.
4. Flight of ideas or subjective experience that thoughts are racing.
5. Distractibility (i.e., attention too easily drawn to unimportant or irrelevant external stimuli), as reported or observed.
6. Increase in goal-directed activity (either socially, at work or school, or sexually) or psychomotor agitation.
7. Excessive involvement in activities that have a high potential for painful consequences (e.g., engaging in unrestrained buying sprees, sexual indiscretions, or foolish business investments).

C. The episode is associated with an unequivocal change in functioning that is uncharacteristic of the individual when not symptomatic.

D. The disturbance in mood and the change in functioning are observable by others.

E. The episode is not severe enough to cause marked impairment in social or occupational functioning or to necessitate hospitalization. If there are psychotic features, the episode is, by definition, manic.

F. The episode is not attributable to the physiological effects of a substance (e.g., a drug of abuse, a medication, other treatment).

Note: A full hypomanic episode that emerges during antidepressant treatment (e.g., medication, electroconvulsive therapy) but persists at a fully syndromal level beyond the physiological effect of that treatment is sufficient evidence for a hypomanic episode diagnosis. However, caution is indicated so that one or two symptoms (particularly increased irritability, edginess, or agitation following antidepressant use) are not taken as sufficient for diagnosis of a hypomanic episode, nor necessarily indicative of a bipolar diathesis.

Note: Criteria A–F constitute a hypomanic episode. Hypomanic episodes are common in bipolar I disorder but are not required for the diagnosis of bipolar I disorder.

Major Depressive Episode

A. Five (or more) of the following symptoms have been present during the same 2-week period and represent a change from previous functioning; at least one of the symptoms is either (1) depressed mood or (2) loss of interest or pleasure.

Note: Do not include symptoms that are clearly attributable to another medical condition.

1. Depressed mood most of the day, nearly every day, as indicated by either subjective report (e.g., feels sad, empty, or hopeless) or observation made by others (e.g., appears tearful). (**Note:** In children and adolescents, can be irritable mood.)
2. Markedly diminished interest or pleasure in all, or almost all, activities most of the day, nearly every day (as indicated by either subjective account or observation).
3. Significant weight loss when not dieting or weight gain (e.g., a change of more than 5% of body weight in a month), or decrease or increase in appetite nearly every day. (**Note:** In children, consider failure to make expected weight gain.)
4. Insomnia or hypersomnia nearly every day.
5. Psychomotor agitation or retardation nearly every day (observable by others; not merely subjective feelings of restlessness or being slowed down).
6. Fatigue or loss of energy nearly every day.
7. Feelings of worthlessness or excessive or inappropriate guilt (which may be delusional) nearly every day (not merely self-reproach or guilt about being sick).
8. Diminished ability to think or concentrate, or indecisiveness, nearly every day (either by subjective account or as observed by others).
9. Recurrent thoughts of death (not just fear of dying), recurrent suicidal ideation without a specific plan, or a suicide attempt or a specific plan for committing suicide.

(continued)

B. The symptoms cause clinically significant distress or impairment in social, occupational, or other important areas of functioning.

C. The episode is not attributable to the physiological effects of a substance or another medical condition.

Note: Criteria A–C constitute a major depressive episode. Major depressive episodes are common in bipolar I disorder but are not required for the diagnosis of bipolar I disorder.

Note: Responses to a significant loss (e.g., bereavement, financial ruin, losses from a natural disaster, a serious medical illness or disability) may include the feelings of intense sadness, rumination about the loss, insomnia, poor appetite, and weight loss noted in Criterion A, which may resemble a depressive episode. Although such symptoms may be understandable or considered appropriate to the loss, the presence of a major depressive episode in addition to the normal response to a significant loss should also be carefully considered. This decision inevitably requires the exercise of clinical judgment based on the individual's history and the cultural norms for the expression of distress in the context of loss.

Bipolar I Disorder

A. Criteria have been met for at least one manic episode (Criteria A–D under "Manic Episode" above).

B. The occurrence of the manic and major depressive episode(s) is not better explained by schizoaffective disorder, schizophrenia, schizophreniform disorder, delusional disorder, or other specified or unspecified schizophrenia spectrum and other psychotic disorder.

episodes of major depression. **Hypomania** is a mood elevation that is clearly abnormal but not as extremely elevated as frank mania. Behaviorally, a person in a hypomanic state may be overly talkative, excitable, or irritable, but there are no impulsive acts or gross lapses of judgment that are common during mania (e.g., telephoning Washington to tell the president how to run the country). Hypomania is "mild mania" and lasts at least 4 days (American Psychiatric Association, 2013). More common than bipolar I, bipolar II disorder is defined by having at least one episode of major depression and at least one hypomanic event. Bipolar II can be especially difficult to diagnose because a person experiencing hypomania may associate these episodes with periods of high productivity or creativity and is less likely to report his or her symptoms as distressing or problematic.

> Jack felt on top of the world. He had never had his ideas flow so fast and furious. All week he needed only 2 hours of sleep per night, and he woke up totally refreshed and ready to go. He felt like a people magnet. He was funny, engaging, and full of energy. He was texting people at all hours of the night and couldn't figure out why other people were signing off when he was in such good form. He wished this feeling could last forever.

Actress Catherine Zeta-Jones revealed that she has struggled with bipolar II disorder, characterized by hypomanic episodes that alternate with periods of depression.

The frequency of mood elevations varies considerably across individuals and even within the same individual across time. Some people have episodes yearly or even less frequently. Mood shifts come out of the blue and are not necessarily in response to environmental events. In contrast, people with *rapid cycling bipolar disorder* have four or more severe mood disturbances within a single year (American Psychiatric Association, 2013). Even less common is an extremely rapid cycling pattern in which multiple shifts between manic and depressed mood occur within a single day. Finally, people who have symptoms of mania and depression at the same time suffer from a **mixed state**; symptoms can include agitation, insomnia, changes in appetite, psychosis, and suicidal thoughts. A person in a mixed state can feel very sad and very energized at the same time. See Figure 7.1 for an illustration of the episodic nature of bipolar I disorder, bipolar II disorder, and rapid cycling bipolar disorder.

Bipolar disorder requires lifelong maintenance treatment and clinical management (Mahli et al., 2010). Although some people with bipolar disorder are symptom free between episodes, many have some continuing symptoms. Even when controlled by medication, many

Figure 7.1 The Different Types of Bipolar Disorders.

Each type of bipolar disorder (bipolar I disorder, bipolar II disorder, and rapid cycling bipolar disorder) has a different course of illness.

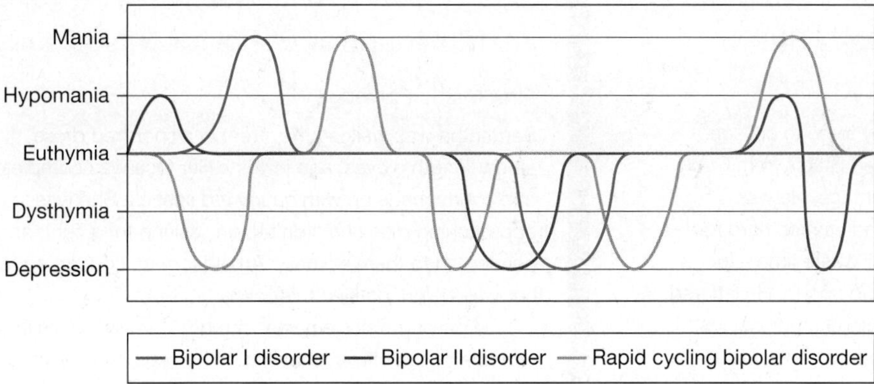

patients report mild to moderate residual symptoms between episodes—typically symptoms of depression rather than mania (Judd et al., 2002; Keller et al., 1993; Post et al., 2003). Most experience multiple recurrences, and some, despite treatment, have chronic unremitting symptoms (Pallaskorpi et al., 2015). Bipolar disorder is frequently depicted in literature as the mental illness that rests between the boundaries of creativity and madness, although this is not accurate (see "Examining the Evidence: Is There a Link Between Art and Madness?").

Another disorder, **cyclothymic disorder**, is characterized by fluctuations that alternate between hypomanic and depressive symptoms (Van Meter et al., 2012). In cyclothymia, the episodes are not as severe as with mania or major depression, but they persist for at least 2 years and, as a result of the cyclical and often unpredictable mood changes, cause impairment (Akiskal, 2001).

Epidemiology, Sex, Race, and Ethnicity

LO 7.2 Describe the prevalence of bipolar and related disorders in various segments of the population (sex, race, ethnicity, age).

Much less common than major depression, the lifetime prevalence of bipolar I and II is approximately 0.6% and 0.4%, respectively, according to the WHO World Mental Health Survey (Merikangas, Jin, et al., 2011). In North America, lifetime prevalence is slightly higher: 0.9 to 1.0% for bipolar I and 0.6 to 1.1% for bipolar II (Mcdonald et al., 2015; Merikangas et al., 2007). The average age of onset of the first manic or depressive episode is 18.4 years for bipolar I and 20.0 years for bipolar II (Merikangas, Jin, He et al., 2011). Bipolar disorder is unrelated to sex, race/ethnicity, and family income and is commonly comorbid with substance use disorders, anxiety disorders, and impulse control disorders (Fassassi et al., 2014; Merikangas, Jin et al., 2011).

In a manic state, people with bipolar disorder may act impulsively, such as spending excessive amounts of money.

The majority of studies suggest that the risk of developing bipolar I disorder is fairly equal across the sexes (for example, Mcdonald et al., 2015), although there is some suggestion that bipolar I may be more common in men and bipolar II in women (Diflorio & Jones, 2010; Merikangas, Jin et al., 2011). In the United States, lifetime prevalence is about 0.8% of males and 1.1% of females for bipolar I and 0.9% of males and 1.3% of females for bipolar II (Merikangas et al., 2007).

Although surveys suggest that bipolar disorder is found at equal rates across racial and ethnic groups (Breslau et al., 2006; Merikangas et al., 2007), a number of investigations spanning decades have reported that

SIDE by SIDE Case Studies

Dimensions of Behavior: From Adaptive to Maladaptive

Adaptive Behavior Case Study

Elation due to Academic Success

George was the first person in his family to go to college. His parents had immigrated to the United States from Cuba and had given him every possible advantage. He was valedictorian of his high school class and worked hard for the honor. He was never one to party or waste time—for him, school was all about academics and sports. He lettered in baseball and led his school to the state championships.

He got a full baseball scholarship to an Ivy League school. He was grateful for his athletic skills and was an All-American starting pitcher for the team, but political science was his first love.

George's teachers recognized that he had a keen sense of international relations, and they felt he had the potential to go far. Given his academic record and athletic success, they encouraged him to apply for a Rhodes Scholarship. George thought that the son of immigrants would never have a chance at getting a Rhodes. He was so convinced of this that after he sent in his application, he put it out of his mind, forgetting about the decision date.

When the letter arrived in the mail, his heart jumped into his throat. George talked himself down, reminding himself of the competition and his background. Then he opened the letter and found he had been selected. He started jumping up and down, knocking on everyone's dorm room, yelling, "You're not going to believe this!" He jumped into the shower with his clothes on, shouting, "Omigod, omigod!" When he called his parents, George was talking so fast in a combination of Spanish and English that they could not understand him. He was positively over the moon! But after the news sank in, he came down to earth, thrilled and honored by the possibilities his future held.

Maladaptive Behavior Case Study

First Manic Episode

Samantha was walking the street in a short red dress, elbow-length gloves, and jewelry. Her face was completely and overly made up with gaudy red lipstick. She was approaching men she didn't know, asking for a light, and coming on to them sexually. An older man, concerned for her well-being, notified the police.

In the psychiatric emergency room, Samantha was fawning over the police officer, showing off her legs. She kept walking across the room to strike up conversations with other patients—the topics were inappropriate and flirtatious. Her energy had an edge. She kept asking when she was going to be seen and "What's wrong with this joint that you can't get served?"

Given her disruptive behavior, the attending psychiatrist and the resident evaluated her immediately. During the interview, she told the resident he was a hottie and asked him what he was doing later that night. Her speech was rapid and pressured, the doctors couldn't get a question in edgewise, and whatever answers she gave were not to the questions they asked. The attending physician gave her a medication to calm her down until her parents could arrive. As it turned out, Samantha had just maxed out her credit cards buying all of the clothes, makeup, and jewelry she was wearing. Her parents had called in a missing persons report the previous evening and provided more information.

Her drug screen was negative, and there were no other medical reasons for her bizarre behavior. Her family history was positive for bipolar disorder, and this was her first manic episode. Samantha was admitted to the hospital and started on a course of lithium medication. She also received psychoeducation about bipolar disorder and lithium and started psychotherapy to help her adjust to living with her diagnosis.

whites are more likely to receive a diagnosis of bipolar disorder than African American individuals (Crishon et al., 2012; Kessler et al., 1994; Strakowski et al., 1996); although this may be true in terms of the actual number, closer scrutiny suggests that additional factors for this disparity might be at play. Whereas whites tend to be diagnosed with bipolar disorder, African Americans are more likely to receive a diagnosis in the schizophrenia spectrum (see Chapter 11 for a more extensive discussion of this issue). Whether this diagnostic difference is accurate or reflects racial variations affecting clinical presentation and expression of symptoms, access to care, help-seeking behaviors, and clinician judgment remains unknown (Haeri et al., 2011).

Developmental Factors in Bipolar Disorder

LO 7.3 Explain how the presentation of bipolar and related disorders differs across the life span.

Children do suffer from bipolar disorder, and the rate of bipolar diagnoses in children has increased over time (Blader & Carlson, 2007; Moreno et al., 2007). However, the symptoms may be very different from those seen in adults. In children, mania may be chronic rather than episodic, may cycle rapidly, or may appear as a mixed state (Geller et al., 2004). During a manic episode, children are more likely to display irritability and temper tantrums rather than a euphoric "high." These different symptoms make it difficult for mental health professionals to distinguish this disorder from other conditions such as attention deficit hyperactivity disorder, conduct disorder, oppositional defiant disorder, or even schizophrenia (Grimmer et al., 2014; National Institute of Mental Health, 2001; Weller et al., 1995) (see Chapter 11). Accurate diagnosis is critical because the onset of bipolar disorder in childhood or early adolescence may represent a different and possibly more severe condition than the condition that develops in adulthood (Perlis et al., 2004; Post et al., 2010).

On the other end of the age spectrum, lifetime prevalence of bipolar disorder in older adults (age 60 and older) is approximately 0.5 to 1.0% (Kessler, Berglund et al., 2005; Sajatovic & Chen, 2011) (see Chapter 14). After that age, manic and depressive symptoms often develop in association with medical illness, especially stroke (Van Gerpen et al., 1999). Older patients who may have had some elements of mania in younger years can experience manic symptoms later in life (Keck et al., 2001), and most older adults with bipolar disorder had first symptom onset earlier in life (Sajatovic et al., 2005). Recurrences among older adults are

Examining the EVIDENCE

Is There a Link Between Art and Madness?

- **The Facts** Throughout history, many remarkably talented artists have struggled through the tumultuous peaks and pitfalls associated with mood disturbances. In many cases, their personal experiences became the substance of their artistic expression. As Byron observed, "We of the craft are all crazy. Some are affected by gaiety, others by melancholy, but all are more or less touched." But is there really a relationship between art and madness?
- **The Evidence** In *Touched with Fire*, Johns Hopkins Professor Kay Redfield Jamison examined the lives, works, and familial pedigrees of writers, poets, artists, and musicians and described a common thread among them: volatile cycles of compelling imagination, exuberance, and intelligence countered by periods of grim isolation and melancholy. Emily Dickinson, T. S. Eliot, Ernest Hemingway, Victor Hugo, Michelangelo, Charles Mingus, Georgia O'Keeffe, Sylvia Plath, Peter Tchaikovsky, Vincent van Gogh, and Virginia Woolf are just a few on Jamison's list with probable cyclothymia (cycling between dysthymia and hypomania), major depression, or bipolar disorder. But without sound psychological and biological data to corroborate the diagnosis, these historical observations are not hard evidence that these individuals actually suffered from psychiatric illness. The question remains: what empirical evidence supports this link?
- **Let's Examine the Evidence** In his research, University of Kentucky Professor Arnold Ludwig found that writers had much higher rates of depression and mania than matched controls. In his work *The Price of Greatness*, he writes that members of the artistic professions or creative arts are more likely than others to suffer from a lifetime mental illness. Similarly, in *The Hypomanic Edge*, Johns Hopkins psychologist John Gartner notes that hypomania may be a common (and potentially positive) trait among those who thrive in Western, bigger-better-faster culture. A recent systematic review (Thys et al., 2014) "cautiously" supports an association between bipolar disorder and creativity, and polygenic risk scores for bipolar disorder (and schizophrenia) (i.e., how many risk alleles for the disorder an individual carries) also predict creativity (measured as artistic society membership or a creative profession) (Power et al., 2015), suggesting some shared genetic component between psychosis and creativity. Yet not all individuals who have mood disorders are creative, and not all artists have mood disorders. So is there another variable that may influence the relationship between mood disorders and creativity?
- **What Are Alternative Explanations for This Relationship?** Jamison suggests that mood disorders may foster imaginative thought, and she notes that diagnostic criteria for mania include "sharpened and unusually creative thinking." Combined with the breadth of deep emotions present in some mood disorders, such intellectual inspiration might lend itself to artistic creativity. "Ludwig speculates that those with mood disorders might be naturally drawn to artistic professions, given the potential normalization of the artistic temperament in such fields" (Jamison, 1993).
- **Conclusion** The link between creativity and mood disorders is still not well understood but potentially has many implications for artists, medicine, and society. When creativity is a necessary aspect of an individual's work, what are the potential implications of dampening this temperament with pharmacology? What if the person refuses to take medication because of the potential loss of creative ability? What are the implications of untreated depression? How would you feel if you were an artist and your best work occurred during what clinicians referred to as hypomanic episodes, which were often followed by depression? Would you give up your creativity (and perhaps your livelihood) for an opportunity to be free of severe mood swings?

more common, and intervals between mania and depression are shorter and the episodes longer than in younger patients (Keck et al., 2001; Oostervink et al., 2015).

Comorbidity

LO 7.4 Characterize patterns of comorbidity in bipolar and related disorders.

Bipolar disorder carries considerable medical and psychological comorbidity risk, and the effects are often bidirectional: the comorbid conditions may increase risk for developing bipolar disorder, and bipolar disorder (or its pharmacologic treatments) might increase the risk of some of the comorbid conditions. People with bipolar disorder are at increased risk for asthma, thyroid disease, migraine headaches, epilepsy, elevated lipids, heart disease, type 2 diabetes, kidney disease, and obesity (Krishnan, 2005; Kupfer, 2005; Forty et al., 2014). Other common comorbid psychological conditions are anxiety disorders (especially panic attacks), behavior disorders (including intermittent explosive disorder, attention deficit hyperactivity disorder, oppositional defiant disorder, and conduct disorder), and substance use disorders, with the majority of individuals with bipolar disorder endorsing three or more additional psychiatric disorders (Merikangas et al., 2007; Merikangas, Jin, He et al., 2011). Individuals with bipolar disorder might try to self-medicate with drugs or alcohol, drugs or alcohol might trigger or exacerbate manic or depressive episodes, or a third underlying trait (e.g., impulsivity) may contribute to both conditions.

Learning Objective Summaries

LO 7.1 Recognize and differentiate bipolar and related disorders and their component symptoms.

Bipolar disorder consists of dramatic shifts in mood, energy, and ability to function. It is a long-term episodic illness in which mood shifts between the two emotional "poles" of mania and depression. Bipolar disorder is commonly categorized as either bipolar I or bipolar II. The main difference between bipolar I and biolar II is the degree of mania. In bipolar I, full-blown mania alternates with episodes of major depression; it also includes a single manic episode with or without periods of depression. In bipolar II disorder, hypomania alternates with episodes of major depression. Cyclothymic disorder is characterized by fluctuations that alternate between hypomanic and depressive symptoms.

LO 7.2 Describe the prevalence of bipolar and related disorders in various segments of the population (sex, race, ethnicity, age).

The lifetime prevalence of bipolar I and II is approximately 0.6 to 1.0% and 0.4 to 1.1%, respectively. The average age of onset is late adolescence and young adulthood. Bipolar disorder is unrelated to sex, race/ethnicity, and socioeconomic status. Although research suggests that bipolar disorder is found at equal rates across racial and ethnic groups, whites are more likely to receive a diagnosis of bipolar disorder than African American individuals.

LO 7.3 Explain how the presentation of bipolar and related disorders differs across the life span.

In children, mania may be chronic rather than episodic, may cycle rapidly, or may appear as a mixed state. During a manic episode, children are more likely to display irritability and have temper tantrums rather experience elation. Recurrences among older adults are common, and intervals between mania and depression are shorter and the episodes longer than in younger patients.

LO 7.4 Characterize patterns of comorbidity in bipolar and related disorders.

People with bipolar disorder are at increased risk for medical comorbidities including asthma, thyroid disease, migraine headaches, epilepsy, elevated lipids, heart disease, type 2 diabetes, kidney disease, and obesity. They are also commonly at risk for comorbid psychological conditions including anxiety disorders, behavior disorders (including intermittent explosive disorder, attention deficit hyperactivity disorder, oppositional defiant disorder, and conduct disorder), and substance use disorders.

Critical Thinking Question

Sometimes individuals with bipolar disorder will express concern that medication "flattens" them out. Although they are typically fine with medication that helps minimize depressive episodes, they may miss the energy, decreased need for sleep, and excitement associated with manic episodes. Discuss ways to encourage long-term adherence to medication to prevent both future depressive and manic episodes.

Depressive Disorders

Major Depressive Disorder

LO 7.5 Recognize the symptoms of major depressive disorder.

The core symptom of **major depressive disorder** is a persistent sad or low mood that is severe enough to impair a person's interest in or ability to engage in normally enjoyable activities. In adults, depressed mood is central to major depressive disorder, but in children, the persistent mood disturbance may take the form of irritability or hostility. Major depressive disorder can be extremely debilitating, in part, because of other psychological, emotional, social, and physical problems that often accompany the persistent depressed mood. People with this disorder may feel completely worthless or extremely guilty, and they may be at risk for harming themselves. Major depressive disorder can affect a person physically by disrupting sleep, appetite, and sexual drive (see "DSM-5: Major Depressive Disorder"). Often, this means problems falling or staying asleep, feeling tired all the time, and having decreased appetite. However, about 40% of people diagnosed with major depressive disorder actually sleep and eat *more* than usual (referred to as "**atypical depression**"). Either way, the changes in sleep and appetite can lead to significant problems with attention and concentration and can increase an already overwhelming sense of inadequacy and inclination to withdraw from the world.

Watch MARTHA: MAJOR DEPRESSIVE DISORDER

Inability to fall asleep or stay asleep is one of the symptoms of depression.

Major depressive disorder is an episodic illness. During their lifetime, some individuals have only one episode (*single episode*), but others suffer from multiple episodes separated by periods of normal mood (*recurrent*). Major depressive disorder is a prevalent psychological disorder: approximately 16.2% of U.S. adults suffer from at least one episode of major depressive disorder in their lifetime and 6.6% over the last 12 months (Kessler et al., 2003). A single episode, according to DSM-5, lasts at least 2 weeks, but episodes can and often do persist for several months. Refer to Figure 7.2 for an illustration of the course of the different forms of depression.

In addition to symptoms that last for 2 weeks, another factor that distinguishes major depressive

Figure 7.2 The Different Forms of Depressive Disorders.

Contrast each of these patterns to normal mood fluctuations.

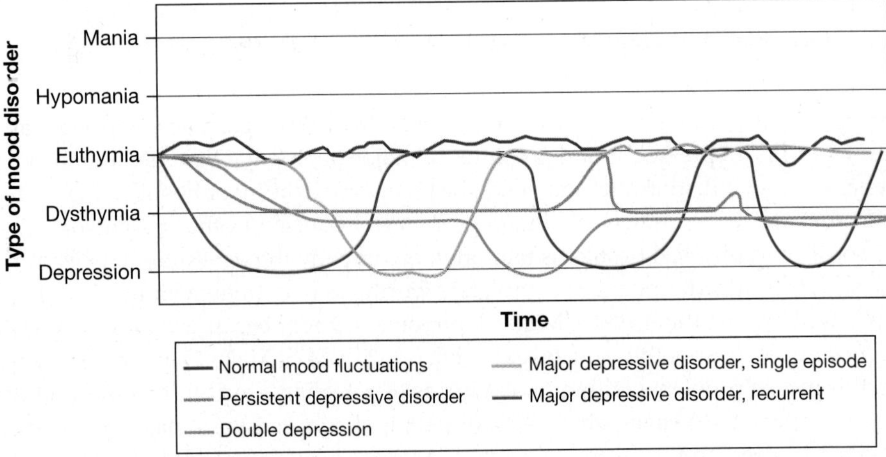

disorder from sad mood is that the symptoms must affect the person's ability to function in social or work settings. Symptoms of major depressive disorder may sometimes result from physical disorders such as Cushing's syndrome (hypercortisolism, or too much of the hormone cortisol) and hypothyroidism (lack of sufficient thyroid hormone); however, depression is not diagnosed if the symptoms are caused by medical conditions such as these. Special considerations apply when the depressed feelings result from a life event such as the death of a loved one (American Psychiatric Association, 2013). Finally, depression can occur even after events that are not typically associated with sadness, such as after having a baby.

DSM-5

Criteria for Major Depressive Disorder

A. Five (or more) of the following symptoms have been present during the same 2-week period and represent a change from previous functioning; at least one of the symptoms is either (1) depressed mood or (2) loss of interest or pleasure.

Note: Do not include symptoms that are clearly attributable to another medical condition.

1. Depressed mood most of the day, nearly every day, as indicated by either subjective report (e.g., feels sad, empty, hopeless) or observation made by others (e.g., appears tearful). (Note: In children and adolescents, can be irritable mood.)
2. Markedly diminished interest or pleasure in all, or almost all, activities most of the day, nearly every day (as indicated by either subjective account or observation).
3. Significant weight loss when not dieting or weight gain (e.g., a change of more than 5% of body weight in a month), or decrease or increase in appetite nearly every day. (Note: In children, consider failure to make expected weight gain.)
4. Insomnia or hypersomnia nearly every day.
5. Psychomotor agitation or retardation nearly every day (observable by others; not merely subjective feelings of restlessness or being slowed down).
6. Fatigue or loss of energy nearly every day.
7. Feelings of worthlessness or excessive or inappropriate guilt (which may be delusional) nearly every day (not merely self-reproach or guilt about being sick).
8. Diminished ability to think or concentrate, or indecisiveness, nearly every day (either by subjective account or as observed by others).
9. Recurrent thoughts of death (not just fear of dying), recurrent suicidal ideation without a specific plan, or a suicide attempt or a specific plan for committing suicide.

B. The symptoms cause clinically significant distress or impairment in social, occupational, or other important areas of functioning.

C. The episode is not attributable to the physiological effects of a substance or another medical condition.

Note: Criteria A–C represent a major depressive episode.

Note: Responses to a significant loss (e.g., bereavement, financial ruin, losses from a natural disaster, a serious medical illness or disability) may include the feelings of intense sadness, rumination about the loss, insomnia, poor appetite, and weight loss noted in Criterion A, which may resemble a depressive episode. Although such symptoms may be understandable or considered appropriate to the loss, the presence of a major depressive episode in addition to the normal response to a significant loss should also be carefully considered. This decision inevitably requires the exercise of clinical judgment based on the individual's history and the cultural norms for the expression of distress in the context of loss.

D. The occurrence of the major depressive episode is not better explained by schizoaffective disorder, schizophrenia, schizophreniform disorder, delusional disorder, or other specified and unspecified schizophrenia spectrum and other psychotic disorders.

E. There has never been a manic episode or a hypomanic episode.

Note: This exclusion does not apply if all of the manic-like or hypomanic-like episodes are substance-induced or are attributable to the physiological effects of another medical condition.

Persistent Depressive Disorder (Dysthymia)

LO 7.6 Define persistent depressive disorder, and distinguish it from major depressive disorder.

Persistent depressive disorder, or **dysthymia**, can best be conceptualized as a chronic state of depression (see "DSM-5: Persistent Depressive Disorder"). The symptoms are the same as those of major depression, but they are less severe. Whereas major depressive disorder is an episodic disorder with patients often achieving euthymia, or normal mood, between episodes, dysthymia is the consistent persistence of depressed mood. By definition, persistent depressive disorder lasts 2 or more years, and the individual is never without symptoms for more than 2 months (American Psychiatric Association, 2013). Although, on a day-to-day basis, the symptoms are typically milder than those of major depressive disorder, because they are so persistent, they may lead to severe outcomes (e.g., social isolation, high suicide risk) that affect not only the sufferer but also extended family and friends. Less severe symptoms may also result in people suffering from persistent depressive disorder for years before seeking treatment. Meanwhile, family and friends may turn away, often mislabeling the person as too moody and difficult.

Louise was under a constant gray cloud. She felt as if she had lived through the marriage of her daughter and the birth of her first two grandchildren like a zombie. She felt no joy, no wonder, and would rather stay home and cry than visit and play with her grandchildren. When all of the other women at church beamed about the accomplishments of their families, she could only feel guilty for not being part of her own children's lives.

DSM-5

Criteria for Persistent Depressive Disorder (Dysthymia)

This disorder represents a consolidation of DSM-IV-defined chronic major depressive disorder and dysthymic disorder.

A. Depressed mood for most of the day, for more days than not, as indicated by either subjective account or observation by others, for at least 2 years.

Note: In children and adolescents, mood can be irritable and duration must be at least 1 year.

B. Presence, while depressed, of two (or more) of the following:

1. Poor appetite or overeating.
2. Insomnia or hypersomnia.
3. Low energy or fatigue.
4. Low self-esteem.
5. Poor concentration or difficulty making decisions.
6. Feelings of hopelessness.

C. During the 2-year period (1 year for children or adolescents) of the disturbance, the individual has never been without the symptoms in Criteria A and B for more than 2 months at a time.

D. Criteria for a major depressive disorder may be continuously present for 2 years.

E. There has never been a manic episode or a hypomanic episode, and criteria have never been met for cyclothymic disorder.

F. The disturbance is not better explained by a persistent schizoaffective disorder, schizophrenia, delusional disorder, or other specified or unspecified schizophrenia spectrum and other psychotic disorder.

G. The symptoms are not attributable to the physiological effects of a substance (e.g., a drug of abuse, a medication) or another medical condition (e.g., hypothyroidism).

H. The symptoms cause clinically significant distress or impairment in social, occupational, or other important areas of functioning.

Note: Because the criteria for a major depressive episode include four symptoms that are absent from the symptom list for persistent depressive disorder (dysthymia), a very limited number of individuals will have depressive symptoms that have persisted longer than 2 years but will not meet criteria for persistent depressive disorder. If full criteria for a major depressive episode have been met at some point during the current episode of illness, they should be given a diagnosis of major depressive disorder. Otherwise, a diagnosis of other specified depressive disorder or unspecified depressive disorder is warranted.

People with persistent depressive disorder may also have major depressive episodes (this is known as **double depression**). The combination of episodic major depressive episodes superimposed on chronic low mood is often associated with poorer long-term outcome and higher relapse risk than either disorder alone (Keller et al., 1997; Rhebergen et al., 2009, 2010). In many instances, persistent depressive disorder is undiagnosed until the person has a major depressive episode. When the person seeks help for the more severe depressive symptoms, the longer history of dysthymia is identified. See Figure 7.2 for the time course of persistent depressive disorder and double depression.

Disruptive Mood Dysregulation Disorder

LO 7.7 Construct an argument for the inclusion of disruptive mood regulation disorder in DSM-5.

Disruptive mood dysregulation disorder (DMDD) is a new disorder making its first appearance in the DSM-5, and it is a controversial diagnosis. This category is reserved for children ages 6 to 18 years who have "severe recurrent temper outbursts that are grossly out of proportion in intensity or duration to the situation" (see "DSM-5: Disruptive Mood Dysregulation Disorder"). Arguments for inclusion of the disorder are to slow the rate of diagnoses of childhood bipolar disorder, which was being overdiagnosed in children with disruptive tendencies.

DSM-5

Criteria for Disruptive Mood Dysregulation Disorder

A. Severe recurrent temper outbursts manifested verbally (e.g., verbal rages) and/or behaviorally (e.g., physical aggression toward people or property) that are grossly out of proportion in intensity or duration to the situation or provocation.

B. The temper outbursts are inconsistent with developmental level.

C. The temper outbursts occur, on average, three or more times per week.

D. The mood between temper outbursts is persistently irritable or angry most of the day, nearly every day, and is observable by others (e.g., parents, teachers, peers).

E. Criteria A–D have been present for 12 or more months. Throughout that time, the individual has not had a period lasting 3 or more consecutive months without all of the symptoms in Criteria A–D.

F. Criteria A and D are present in at least two of three settings (i.e., at home, at school, with peers) and are severe in at least one of these.

G. The diagnosis should not be made for the first time before age 6 years or after age 18 years.

H. By history or observation, the age at onset of Criteria A–E is before 10 years.

I. There has never been a distinct period lasting more than 1 day during which the full symptom criteria, except duration, for a manic or hypomanic episode have been met.

Note: Developmentally appropriate mood elevation, such as occurs in the context of a highly positive event or its anticipation, should not be considered as a symptom of mania or hypomania.

J. The behaviors do not occur exclusively during an episode of major depressive disorder and are not better explained by another mental disorder (e.g., autism spectrum disorder, posttraumatic stress disorder, separation anxiety disorder, persistent depressive disorder [dysthymia]).

Note: This diagnosis cannot coexist with oppositional defiant disorder, intermittent explosive disorder, or bipolar disorder, though it can coexist with others, including major depressive disorder, attention-deficit/hyperactivity disorder, conduct disorder, and substance use disorders. Individuals whose symptoms meet criteria for both disruptive mood dysregulation disorder and oppositional defiant disorder should only be given the diagnosis of disruptive mood dysregulation disorder. If an individual has ever experienced a manic or hypomanic episode, the diagnosis of disruptive mood dysregulation disorder should not be assigned.

K. The symptoms are not attributable to the physiological effects of a substance or to another medical or neurological condition.

Arguments against the disorder are that (1) most children who receive this diagnosis already fit diagnostic criteria for other childhood disorders (e.g., oppositional defiant disorder and conduct disorder) and (2) there is poor reliability in the diagnosis across clinicians (Dobbs, 2012; Mayes et al., 2015). The harshest critics fear that this category is simply turning temper tantrums into a mental illness (Frances, 2012). Only time and experience will tell how well this diagnostic category differentiates a true mood syndrome from other non-mood-disorder syndromes of childhood and whether its existence reduces overdiagnosis of bipolar disorder in children (Margulies et al., 2012).

Depressive Disorders Related to Reproductive Events

LO 7.8 Recognize the symptoms of premenstrual dysphoric disorder and depressive disorder with peripartum onset.

PREMENSTRUAL DYSPHORIC DISORDER Many women will verify that there can be mood changes in the days preceding menstruation. However, **premenstrual dysphoric disorder** (PMDD) is a more severe form of these premenstrual changes that afflicts on average 1.3 to 4.6% of women of reproductive age (Epperson et al., 2012; Gehlert et al., 2009). PMDD follows a cyclic pattern and typically begins in the late luteal phase of the menstrual cycle (see "DSM-5: Premenstrual Dysphoric Disorder"). Mood symptoms can vary and include deep sadness or despair, anxiety and tension, anger or irritability, and panic. Changes in sleep, appetite, and libido can also emerge. PMDD not only affects the sufferers but can have significant effects on interpersonal relationships, which can be vulnerable to the extremes of emotionality often associated with the disorder.

The "baby blues" are common among new mothers, but major depressive disorder with peripartum onset is a serious psychological disorder. Celebrity Hayden Panettiere suffered from depression after the birth of her first child.

MAJOR DEPRESSIVE DISORDER WITH PERIPARTUM ONSET

All of the books painted such a rosy picture—the happy mothers breastfeeding, talking with other moms, developing that special bond with their new babies. What is wrong with me? Why do I just want this child to stop crying and go away? I can't bear to have my husband touch me. What kind of a mother am I? All the baby does is scream. Help me! Where's the joy? Why can't I feel what they're feeling?

—*Susan, new mother*

DSM-5

Criteria for Premenstrual Dysphoric Disorder

A. In the majority of menstrual cycles, at least five symptoms must be present in the final week before the onset of menses, start to *improve* within a few days after the onset of menses, and become *minimal* or absent in the week post menses.

B. One (or more) of the following symptoms must be present:

1. Marked affective lability (e.g., mood swings; feeling suddenly sad or tearful, or increased sensitivity to rejection).
2. Marked irritability or anger or increased interpersonal conflicts.
3. Marked depressed mood, feelings of hopelessness, or self-deprecating thoughts.
4. Marked anxiety, tension, and/or feelings of being keyed up or on edge.

C. One (or more) of the following symptoms must additionally be present, to reach a total of *five* symptoms when combined with symptoms from Criterion B above.

1. Decreased interest in usual activities (e.g., work, school, friends, hobbies).
2. Subjective difficulty in concentration.
3. Lethargy, easy fatigability, or marked lack of energy.
4. Marked change in appetite; overeating; or specific food cravings.
5. Hypersomnia or insomnia.
6. A sense of being overwhelmed or out of control.
7. Physical symptoms such as breast tenderness or swelling, joint or muscle pain, a sensation of "bloating," or weight gain.

Note: The symptoms in Criteria A–C must have been met for most menstrual cycles that occurred in the preceding year.

D. The symptoms are associated with clinically significant distress or interference with work, school, usual social activities, or relationships with others (e.g., avoidance of social activities; decreased productivity and efficiency at work, school, or home).

E. The disturbance is not merely an exacerbation of the symptoms of another disorder, such as major depressive disorder, panic disorder, persistent depressive disorder (dysthymia), or a personality disorder (although it may co-occur with any of these disorders).

F. Criterion A should be confirmed by prospective daily ratings during at least two symptomatic cycles. (**Note:** The diagnosis may be made provisionally prior to this confirmation.)

G. The symptoms are not attributable to the physiological effects of a substance (e.g., a drug of abuse, a medication, other treatment) or another medical condition (e.g., hyperthyroidism).

As many as 80% of new mothers develop the "baby blues" within 3 to 5 days of childbirth. These mild mood symptoms (tearfulness, sadness, mood swings, irritability, fatigue) generally subside 2 weeks postpartum—that is, after childbirth (Henshaw, 2003; O'Hara & McCabe, 2013). Although for many women the blues are transient, they are a risk factor for the development of postpartum depression (Reck et al., 2009). Many of the symptoms of peripartum depression are the same as major depressive disorder; however, mothers can feel overwhelmed, empty, disconnected from their child, and guilty because they feel they should be feeling the joy of motherhood.

The prevalence of depression with onset in the first 6 months postpartum ranges from 6.5 to 12.9% across studies, peaking at 2 and 6 months after delivery (Gavin et al., 2005; O'Hara & McCabe, 2013). Risk for this disorder is increased in women who experience vaginal bleeding, kidney or bladder infection, preterm labor, bed rest, hypertension, and blood transfusion during pregnancy (Sundaram et al., 2014).

This disorder not only negatively affects mothers' functioning but is also associated with temperamental, social, emotional, cognitive, physical health, and behavioral difficulties in the children (O'Hara & McCabe, 2013; Pearlstein et al., 2009). In very rare cases, women may suffer a condition known as postpartum mood episodes with psychotic features (see Chapter 11).

Epidemiology, Sex, Race, and Ethnicity

LO 7.9 **Describe the prevalence of major depressive disorder in various segments of the population (sex, race, ethnicity, age).**

Major depressive disorder is the most common psychiatric disorder in the United States (Kessler, Berglund, Demler et al., 2003, 2005; Kessler et al., 2010). According to the National

Comorbidity Survey Replication (NCS-R), approximately 16.2 to 19.2% of people over the age of 18 report major depressive disorder at some point in their lifetime, which according to current census statistics equates to 39.3 to 46.6 million U.S. adults (Kessler et al., 2005a). The mean age of onset of major depressive disorder for U.S. adults is 26.2 years, with younger age cohorts reporting earlier age of onset than older cohorts (Kessler et al., 2005a, 2010). Dysthymia is less common, affecting approximately 6.4% of the general population (Kessler et al., 1994). Depression ranks fourth in terms of the global burden of disease (WHO, 2011). Disease burden uses an indicator called *disability adjusted life years (DALY)*, which measures the total amount of healthy life lost to all causes whether from premature death or disability. People with depression reported a fivefold increase in the time away from work than people without depression (Kessler & Frank, 1997), an average of 27.2 lost workdays per year (Kessler, Akiskal, et al., 2006). Depression also exacts a considerable economic burden in the United States, reaching $210.5 billion in 2010 (up from $173.2 billion in 2005) (Greenberg et al., 2015). Clearly, major depression is a burden to both the individual and society.

Despite their commonality, depressive disorders do not occur with equal frequency across all sex, racial, and ethnic groups. Although the precise reasons are unknown, some differences—especially the disproportionate number of women affected by depression—have consistently been observed and remain a topic of considerable scientific debate.

DEPRESSION IN WOMEN Across cultures, almost twice as many women as men suffer from major depressive disorder (Ferrari et al., 2013; Kessler et al., 2003; Weissman et al., 1993, 1996); in the United States, lifetime prevalence among adult women is approximately 21.3% vs. 12.7% for adult men (Kessler et al., 1993). Depressive symptoms are more common among women who have few financial resources, are less educated, and are unemployed (McGrath et al., 1990). Even among women, rates of depression vary by age. There are no sex differences in prevalence of depression in young children, but rates diverge around age 10 years and remain higher in women through midlife (Noble, 2005). Reproductive events such as puberty, the premenstrual period, pregnancy, the postpartum period, and menopause all are risks for mood disturbances (Angold & Costello, 2006; Bennett et al., 2004; Driscoll, 2006; Harsh et al., 2009), suggesting that the ebb and flow of female hormones may have some role. Yet the precise manner in which hormonal fluctuations influence risk for major depressive disorders is unclear.

DEPRESSION IN RACIAL AND ETHNIC MINORITIES AND ACROSS CULTURES In the United States, non-Hispanic whites experience significantly higher rates of major depressive disorder than non-Hispanic black and Hispanic populations. The National Comorbidity Study-Replication reported a higher prevalence of major depression in non-Hispanic whites (17.9%) than non-Hispanic blacks (10.8%) or Hispanics (13.5%) (Breslau et al., 2005; Breslau et al., 2006). Non-Hispanic black and Hispanic individuals have lower lifetime risk for major depressive disorder than non-Hispanic whites, beginning in childhood, and this risk is especially lower in groups with the lowest education levels (Breslau et al., 2006).

Understanding racial, ethnic, and cultural differences requires an appreciation of culture and context. (Breslau et al., 2005) underscore the importance of exploring racial and ethnic factors that may be protective against the emergence of depression. Two factors, ethnic identity and religious participation, have been posited to be protective against depression (Breslau, 2006); however, they underscore that reasons for different rates of mental illness across racial and ethnic groups are complex and change over time.

A more fundamental question is whether the concept of depression is based primarily on a European (Western) understanding of mental illness. Many languages and cultures do not have words for depression, so simple translations of Western interview questions can complicate the diagnostic process, yielding inaccurate diagnosis and incorrect prevalence data. Overall, individuals from various cultures tend to report both psychological and physical symptoms of depression (Simon et al., 1999). Nonetheless, culturally appropriate terminology would ensure recognition of depression across cultures, races, and ethnic groups in addition to the enhanced treatment delivery and adherence (Patel, 2001).

Developmental Factors

LO 7.10 Characterize the prevalence of major depressive disorder across the life span.

The mean age of onset of major depressive disorder is about 26 years (Kessler, Berglund et al., 2005a; Kessler, Birnbaum et al., 2010). However, depression exists across all ages, and emerging data suggest that the risk of depression in children, adolescents, people with chronic illnesses, and older people (especially people with health problems) is increasing (National Institute of Mental Health, 2013).

A meta-analysis of 26 studies suggests that an estimated 2.8% of children under age 13 years and 5.6% of adolescents ages 13 to 18 years suffer from depression (Costello et al., 2006). An estimated 2.8 million adolescents ages 12 to 17 in the United States had at least one major depressive episode in the past year, representing 11.4% of the U.S. population ages 12 to 17 (SAMHSA, 2014). Although the diagnostic criteria are the same, the observable signs of depression may differ, and young people may lack the necessary vocabulary and insight to describe depressed mood. Warning signs can include nonspecific physical complaints, such as headaches, muscle aches, stomachaches, or tiredness; school absence or poor performance; unexplained irritability; crying spells; boredom; social withdrawal; alcohol or substance abuse; anger or hostility; relationship difficulties; and recklessness (National Institute of Mental Health, 2013). Especially if untreated, depression in adolescence can lead to school failure, alcohol or other drug use, and suicide (National Institute of Mental Health, 2013).

Developmental factors also influence the sex ratio of depression. Throughout childhood, girls and boys are equally likely to have depression. However, around ages 10 to 13 years, rates begin to climb for girls but remain constant or even decrease for boys (Cyranowski et al., 2000; Noble, 2005; Nolen-Hoeksema, 2001; Parker & Brotchie, 2004). By late adolescence, the 2:1 ratio (girls to boys) is established and thereafter remains fairly constant through midlife (Avenevoli et al., 2015). As yet there is no clear explanation for this developmental sex difference, but biological, psychological, and environmental factors may be involved. These factors may include hormones, self-consciousness about bodily changes during puberty, poor sense of competence, socioeconomic disadvantage, victimization, chronic life stressors, low self-esteem, and higher reactivity to stress. Any or all of these factors may converge to both increase risk and perpetuate mood disturbances in women (Angold & Costello, 2006; Noble, 2005; Nolen-Hoeksema, 2001; Parker & Brotchie, 2004).

Children as well as adolescents and adults may suffer from depression, but the signs and symptoms of the disorder may be different in children.

In addition to female sex, high *neuroticism* (i.e., the tendency to be sad, anxious, and emotionally reactive) is also associated with depression (Hakulinen et al., 2015). Children high on the neuroticism trait may be more vulnerable to major depressive disorder (and anxiety disorders) (Parker & Brotchie, 2004). Using the biopsychosocial model (see Chapter 1), hormonal influences on the female brain (the biological factor) may be particularly powerful in those with higher neuroticism (the psychological factor), thereby increasing their vulnerability to social stress (the social factor) and the likelihood of experiencing depression during and after puberty. Depression often goes unrecognized and untreated in children and adolescents (Wang et al., 2005). This is unfortunate because early-onset depression often persists, recurs, and continues into adulthood (van Loo et al., 2014; Weissman et al., 1999).

On the other end of the developmental spectrum, about 20.7% of those ages 50 to 64 years and 9.8% of those age 65 and older suffer from depression at some point in their lifetime (see Chapter 14) (Kessler, Birnbaum et al., 2010), and approximately 1.3% suffer from persistent depressive disorder/dysthymia (Kessler, Berglund et al., 2005). Older adults are also more likely to suffer from medical illnesses. Both the illnesses and the medications used to treat them can complicate the detection and diagnosis of depression (Árean & Reynolds, 2005). We are already seeing the emergence of depression earlier in life than previously; as the average age of the American population increases, researchers will be monitoring increases in the incidence of depression in late life (see Chapter 14).

Comorbidity

LO 7.11 Characterize patterns of comorbidity in depressive disorders.

Depression may co-occur with many medical conditions, including cardiovascular and respiratory diseases, central nervous system diseases, diabetes, thyroid disease, arthritis, cancer, and migraines (Fleischhacker et al., 2008; Gili et al., 2011). Coronary heart disease often coexists with depression, and depression can influence outcome from coronary illness (Charlson et al., 2013; Goldston & Baillie, 2008; van Melle et al., 2004). Major depressive disorder also commonly coexists with other psychiatric conditions. Nearly three-fourths (72.1%) of adults with lifetime major depressive disorder had at least one additional disorder including anxiety disorders (59.2%), substance use disorder (24%), and impulse control disorders (30%) (Kessler, Berglund et al., 2003; Kessler, Berglund et al., 2005). Adolescents with major depressive disorder are also at higher odds of having comorbid psychiatric disorders, including anxiety disorders, ADHD, behavior disorders, and substance use disorders (Avenevoli et al., 2015). Depression is also the most common comorbid disorder in eating disorders (Fernandez-Aranda et al., 2007) and often persists even after recovery from the eating disorder (Sullivan et al., 1998). In most cases, depression occurred before the other conditions.

Much research has been directed at understanding the relation between anxiety and depression. Twin studies examine how the same genetic and environmental factors can contribute to two different disorders. In fact, the genetic correlation between major depressive disorder and generalized anxiety disorder is 1.0 (Kendler, 1996; Kendler et al., 1992, 2007), suggesting that the same genetic factors influence the risk for both disorders. The twin-based genetic correlations between major depressive disorders and other anxiety disorders, including panic disorder, agoraphobia, and social phobia, are also quite high and range from 0.70 to 0.79 (Mosing et al., 2009). Genetically vulnerable individuals may develop major depressive disorder, generalized anxiety disorder, or both depending on their environmental experiences. In other words, genes provide the vulnerability to a negative mood state, and the environment shapes *which* negative mood state emerges. This conclusion—that depression and anxiety represent the same gene(s) but different environments—is one compelling explanation for why these two disorders co-occur so commonly. As yet, we have not unraveled the second part of the equation—namely, which environmental experiences result in depression, anxiety, or both?

Learning Objective Summaries

LO 7.5 Recognize the symptoms of major depressive disorder.

The core symptom of major depressive disorder is a persistent sad or low mood. Anhedonia or diminished or absent interest in typical pleasurable activities and changes in weight, sleep, appetite, activity level, energy, sex drive, and concentration can occur. People with this disorder experience feelings of worthlessness and guilt, and they are at risk for harming themselves.

LO 7.6 Define persistent depressive disorder, and distinguish it from major depressive disorder.

Persistent depressive disorder (dysthymia) is a chronic state of depression. The symptoms are the same as those of major depression, but they are less severe. Whereas major depressive disorder is episodic and marked by normal mood between episodes, persistent depressive disorder is the consistent persistence of depressed mood that lasts 2 or more years, and the individual is never without symptoms for more than 2 months.

LO 7.7 Construct an argument for the inclusion of disruptive mood regulation disorder in DSM-5.

Disruptive mood regulation disorder is reserved for children ages 6 to 18 years who display "severe recurrent temper outbursts that are grossly out of proportion in intensity or duration to the situation." The use of this diagnostic category is thought to slow the rate of diagnoses of childhood bipolar disorder, which was being overdiagnosed in children with disruptive tendencies.

LO 7.8 Recognize the symptoms of premenstrual dysphoric disorder and depressive disorder with peripartum onset.

PMDD is a cyclic disorder that typically begins in the late luteal phase of the menstrual cycle. Mood symptoms can vary and include deep sadness or despair, anxiety and tension, anger or irritability, or panic. Changes in sleep, appetite, and libido can also emerge. Postpartum depression occurs within the first 6 months of birth peaking at 2 and 6 months after delivery. Many of the symptoms of peripartum depression are the same as major depressive disorder; however, mothers can feel overwhelmed, empty, disconnected from their child, and guilty because they feel they should be feeling the joy of motherhood.

LO 7.9 Describe the prevalence of major depressive disorder in various segments of the population (sex, race, ethnicity, age).

Major depressive disorder is the most common psychiatric disorder in the United States. Almost twice as many women as men suffer from major depressive disorder. Non-Hispanic whites experience significantly higher rates of major depressive disorder than non-Hispanic black and Hispanic populations.

LO 7.10 Characterize the prevalence of major depressive disorder across the life span.

The mean age of onset of major depressive disorder is about 26 years. There are no sex differences in prevalence of depression in young children, but rates diverge around age 10 years and remain higher in women through midlife. An estimated 2.8% of children under age 13 years and 5.6% of adolescents ages 13 to 18 years suffer from depression. On the other end of the developmental spectrum, about 20.7% of those ages 50 to 64 years and 9.8% of those age 65 and older suffer from depression at some point in their lifetime.

LO 7.11 Characterize patterns of comorbidity in depressive disorders.

Depression may co-occur with many medical conditions, including cardiovascular and respiratory diseases, central nervous system diseases, diabetes, thyroid disease, arthritis, cancer, and migraines. Major depressive disorder also commonly coexists with other psychiatric conditions including anxiety disorders, substance use disorder, and impulse control disorders.

Critical Thinking Question

Depression is more common in women. It is associated with both reproductive events (e.g., puberty, the menstrual cycle, pregnancy and the postpartum period) and with socioeconomic disadvantage. How would you go about determining the relative contribution of biology and environment to depression in women?

Suicide

Although not all suicides are associated with depression, thoughts of suicide or of death are a frightening component of depression both for the sufferer and his or her family and friends. Suicide is one of the most perplexing of human behaviors and the most devastating outcome of depression. Its effects reach far beyond the person who dies and can have a deep and long-lasting impact on family, friends, the community, the nation, and sometimes even the world. Family members and friends may never understand what drove a person to suicide.

Suicide currently ranks as the 10th leading cause of death in the United States (CDC, 2015) and the 15th leading cause of death worldwide, accounting for 1.4% of global deaths and 56% of all violent deaths in 2012 (WHO, 2014). The World Health Organization (WHO, 2014) estimates that, every year, about 800,000 people die from suicide, yielding a "global" mortality rate of 11.4 per 100,000 (15.0 for males, 8.0 for females; based on data from 2012). For each adult who dies from suicide, there are likely an additional 20 or more suicide attempts (WHO, 2014). Globally, suicide rates have increased by 60% in the past 45 years but fell 9% between 2000 and 2012. Suicide is among the three leading causes of death among those ages 15 to 44 years in some countries, and the second leading cause of death among those 15 to 29 years of age (WHO, 2014). It is commonly believed that suicide rates are underreported because of suicide's sensitivity, because it is illegal in some countries, and due to the misclassification of cause of death in situations such as single-vehicle car accidents.

Figure 7.3 Global Suicide Rates.
Rates of suicide vary widely around the world.

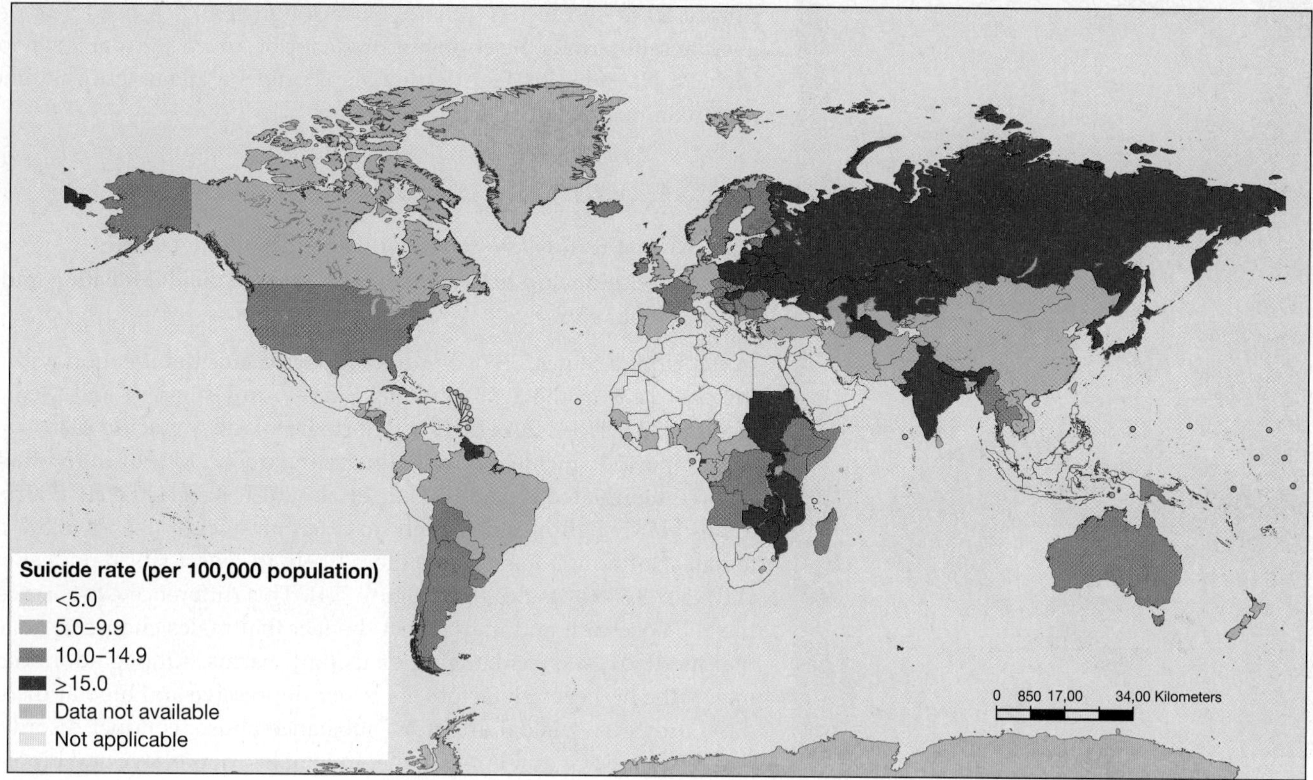

Suicide rates differ across the world (see Figure 7.3), with 75% of suicides occurring in low- and middle-income countries. According to the latest official figures released by WHO, the highest rates of male suicide are found in Guyana and Lithuania, with rates greater than 50 per 100,000. In contrast, rates of male suicide in the United States are 19.4 per 100,000 and in females 5.2 per 100,000 (WHO, 2014).

Suicidal Ideation, Suicide Attempts, and Death by Suicide

LO 7.12 Clarify the differences among suicidal ideation, suicide attempts, and death by suicide.

Suicidal ideation and behavior range from mere thoughts about suicide or death to plans about how to commit suicide to death by suicide. Although varying in intensity, at each level, these thoughts and behaviors should be taken seriously and should raise concern about the person's psychological well being.

Thoughts of death, also known as **suicidal ideation**, may take different forms. *Passive suicidal ideation* is a wish to be dead but does not include active planning about how to commit suicide. *Active suicidal ideation* includes thoughts about how to commit the act, including details such as where, when, and how. Although some suicidal acts are impulsive, detailed suicidal plans are of considerable clinical concern because they indicate premeditation and determination to complete the act.

Suicidal acts are evaluated based on lethality and intent. Some acts, occasionally called *parasuicides*, are behaviors such as superficial cutting of the wrists or overdoses of nonlethal amounts of medications. These acts are unlikely to result in death. However, intent cannot necessarily be inferred from lethality. For example, a woman who takes some pills to end her life may be unaware that the dose was not lethal; she may have fully intended to die.

Firearms in the home increase the risk of suicide.

In contrast, violent attempts such as hanging, self-inflicted gunshot wounds, and jumping from a building are almost always associated with serious intent. Previous attempts at suicide increase the risk of suicide 30 to 40 times (Harris & Barraclough, 1997). A history of deliberate self-harm is the strongest predictor of future suicidal behavior (Zahl & Hawton, 2004). All attempts should be taken seriously and require immediate treatment.

Who Commits Suicide?

LO 7.13 List factors associated with suicide, and detail the relationship between depression and suicidal ideation and behavior.

In the United States, 3.9% of adults reported suicidal ideation within the past year in the 2013 National Survey on Drug Use and Mental Health (SAMHSA, 2014), 1.1% reported making a suicide plan, and 0.6% reported suicide attempts (including about 13% of individuals who contemplated suicide) (Han et al., 2015; Kessler et al., 2005b). Males were slightly more likely to attempt suicide (0.6 vs. 0.5% of females), although females are more likely to report suicidal ideation (4.0% vs. 3.8% of males) (see Figure 7.4). This difference exists across the age spectrum and may reflect the fact that males choose more lethal methods, such as hanging or using firearms. Among adolescent males, the highest risk factors are major depressive and bipolar disorders, previous suicidal attempts, substance abuse, conduct disorder, and presence of a gun in the home. In females, depressive and bipolar disorders, previous suicidal attempts, and presence of a handgun in the home increase risk (Brent et al., 1999; Shaffer et al., 1996). Youth from socially disadvantaged backgrounds (less education and lower socioeconomic status) are at a higher risk of serious suicide attempts (Beautrais et al., 1997, 1998). Other factors associated with child and adolescent suicide are parent–child discord, family history of depression or substance abuse or suicidal behavior, being suspended or having dropped out of school, child/adolescent major depression, substance abuse, previous suicide attempt, a phenomenon called *drifting* (being generally disconnected from school, work, and family), sociodemographic disadvantage, and adverse family circumstances, (Beautrais et al., 1997; Gould, 1990; Pelkonen, 2003). In terms of immediate events likely to precipitate a suicide attempt, relationship breakdowns, interpersonal problems, and financial difficulties are most commonly reported in youth. One-third of those attempting suicide do not identify

Figure 7.4 Suicide in Boys and Girls Ages 10 to 24.

Across all three age groups, boys are more likely to commit suicide than girls.

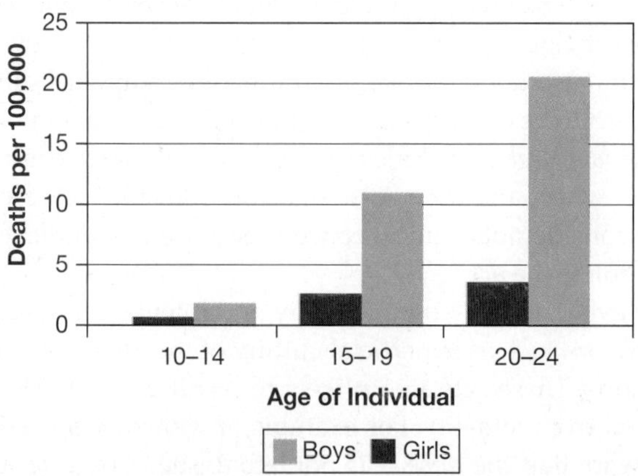

any specific precipitating factor (Beautrais et al., 1997). Among older people, chronic illness and decreasing social support may increase the risk of suicide (Conwell et al., 2002). (In Chapter 14, we discuss suicide in older adults.)

The likelihood of committing suicide also varies with race and ethnicity. In the United States, according to the 2013 National Survey on Drug Use and Health, the highest suicide rates were among American Indian/Alaskan Native (0.9%) and Hispanic (0.8%) individuals, followed by non-Hispanic blacks (0.6%), whites (0.5%), and Asians (0.2%).

Ethics and Responsibility

LO 7.14 Explain the relation between mental illness and suicide attempts in children.

Suicide in children and adolescents does occur and is a global public health concern (McLoughlin, 2015). In 2006, 56 American children under age 12 committed suicide, of whom 45 were boys and 11 girls (Price, 2010). From 2000 to 2009, global suicide rates for boys and girls ages 10 to 14 years were 1.52 and 0.94 per 100,000, respectively, which was a slight decrease for boys and increase for girls over the preceding decade (Kolves & De Leo, 2014). Most suicides in children involve hanging, with a smaller number involving firearms, asphyxiation, and poison (Vajani et al., 2007). Expert panelists at the 2010 American Psychological Association convention indicated that more than 90% of children who commit suicide have a psychological disorder, most often major depressive disorder. Suicidal ideation and attempts are also higher in children and adolescents with anxiety disorders, eating disorders, oppositional defiant disorder, and ADHD (Dickerson Mayes et al., 2015). History of sexual or physical abuse and a pattern of antisocial behavior—such as shoplifting, fighting, or starting fires—are also common. Some evidence suggests that young boys who think they might be gay are also at risk. The expert panel cautioned that parents and teachers often ignore warning signs, such as threats to kill themselves or frequent talk of suicide, because they just do not believe that young children would actually act out such behaviors.

Developmental issues can help in understanding suicide in children. First, because their brains are still developing, they might not realize the finality of suicide. Moreover, they are more impulsive than adults and may not be able to understand that the troubles they face are not necessarily permanent. As the panel emphasized, teachers and authorities must also work to prevent copycat suicide attempts. They need to avoid glamorizing suicide or presenting an overly positive image of the suicide victim as someone who children should try to model. Because suicides in children do occur, psychologists must assist parents and teachers in taking threats seriously and creating effective, developmentally tailored interventions for children at risk.

Explore ETHICS AND RESPONSIBILITY

Risk Factors for Suicide

LO 7.15 Identify risk factors associated with suicide attempts and death by suicide.

Many factors may affect the risk of acting on suicidal thoughts or impulses, but one of the strongest predictors is a history of prior attempts (Alberdi-Sudupe et al., 2011; Borges et al., 2006).

FAMILY HISTORY Suicidal behaviors run in families. This is demonstrated by both family studies and highly visible cases in which multiple family members across generations have committed suicide (see "Real People, Real Disorders: The Heritability of Suicide—The Hemingway and van Gogh Families"). However, family studies cannot disentangle the extent to which this familial factor is genetic or environmental. Twin studies of suicidal ideation and suicide attempts clearly implicate genetic influences, even when accounting for the effects of psychopathology (Althoff et al., 2012; Brent & Melhem, 2008; Pedersen & Fiske, 2010).

PSYCHIATRIC ILLNESS Although suicide does not always occur within the context of mental illness, approximately 90% of attempted suicides or deaths by suicide are committed by individuals who suffer from psychological disorders (Cavanagh et al., 2003; Kessler, Berglund, Borges, et al., 2005). Clinicians are seriously concerned about the relation between major depression and suicide. In the National Comorbidity Survey-Replication, 70% of individuals who attempted suicide had a mood disorder in the past 12 months (Kessler, Berglund, Borges, et al., 2005). Suicide attempts in bipolar disorder are approximately 60 times higher than the international population rate; they tend to occur during severe depressive or mixed states and are often deadly (Baldessarini et al., 2006). Approximately 50% of patients with bipolar disorder attempt suicide during their lifetime, and between 15 and 20% die by suicide (Harris & Barraclough, 1997; Jamison & Baldessarini, 1999). These trends are also evident in the National Comorbidity Survey-Replication: Adolescent Supplement, with 96.1% of adolescents with a lifetime history of suicide attempt meeting criteria for at least one psychiatric disorder, most notably major depression or dysthymia (75.7%) and oppositional defiant disorder (50.0%) (Nock et al., 2013).

Whereas depression strongly predicts suicide ideation, the presence of other disorders marked by anxiety and agitation (e.g., PTSD) and impulse dyscontrol (e.g., substance use disorders and conduct disorder) is more strongly associated with progressing to an actual plan or attempt (Nock et al., 2010). Moreover, a positive association exists between suicide attempts and number of comorbid disorders (i.e., the risk for suicide is greater among those with a lifetime history of more psychiatric disorders) (Nock et al., 2010). Patients with schizophrenia may act on auditory hallucinations ("hearing voices") commanding them to kill themselves.

BIOLOGICAL FACTORS Scientific advances have increased our understanding of the neurobiology of suicide. Intriguingly, true animal models of suicide have been challenging to create, as nonhuman suicidal behavior has not been observed; however, the use of animal models to distill components of suicidality (e.g., extreme social stress responses and impulsivity) have emerged, often focusing on the serotonergic system (Preti, 2011). In human studies, neuroimaging and brain autopsy studies reveal very low levels of serotonin in the brains of people who have committed suicide (Mann et al., 2001; Pandey, 2013). The biology and genetics of suicide appear to be at least partially independent of the biology of depression and other mental illnesses (Brent & Mann, 2005). In other words, depression alone does not lead to suicide, although it increases the risk. For example, behaviors such as impulsivity and pathological aggression, both of which are associated with low levels of serotonin, may also contribute to risk for suicidal behaviors. A recent GWAS of suicidal behavior, which included 577 cases (individuals who attempted suicide or died by suicide) and 1,233 controls, did not detect any SNPs that met genome-wide significance, although among the top SNPs were genes related to inflammatory response (*ADAMTS14, PSME2*), neuronal cell death (*STK3*), and brainstem motor neuron development (*TBX20*) (Galfalvy et al., 2015). Another genome-wide study examining copy number variations (CNVs) in

475 suicide attempters and completers vs. 1,133 controls did not yield any significant findings (Gross et al., 2015), and other GWAS studies of suicidal behavior have not yet produced robust, reproducible findings at the genome-wide significance level (Sokolowski et al., 2014). Undoubtedly this is due to the fact that these samples sizes are inadequate for the detection of small effects.

Understanding Death by Suicide

LO 7.16 Discuss approaches to understanding factors associated with death by suicide.

It is impossible to completely re-create the thoughts, circumstances, and triggers that lead to suicide. Although different approaches exist, they remain at best crude approximations of what actually occurs when the decision is made to end one's own life.

THE PSYCHOLOGICAL AUTOPSY Piecing together the events leading to suicide is complicated. Between one-fifth and one-third of those who commit suicide leave suicide notes, but these notes are not typically detailed accounts of what led to the act (Kuwabara et al., 2006). Putting together the information often involves a process known as a

REAL People REAL Disorders

The Heritability of Suicide—The Hemingway and van Gogh Families

In the mid-nineteenth century, the poet Alfred, Lord Tennyson described multiple melancholic relatives as "taint[s] of blood" (Jamison, 1993). Perhaps a more striking reality is that suicide may also be heritable as in the families of Ernest Hemingway and Vincent van Gogh.

Hemingway's family tree is tragically replete with suicide. Over two generations, four members committed suicide—the writer, his father, his brother, and his sister—and in 1996, the daughter of Ernest's oldest son, model Margaux Hemingway, died from a barbiturate overdose. Ernest was diagnosed with bipolar disorder, and a clear pattern of depression, rages, and mania exists in his family (Jamison, 1993; Lynn, 1987). Before the writer took his own life in 1961, he had been hospitalized and received electroconvulsive therapy for psychotic depression. The author's writing reflected the experience of his father's suicide: many of his characters come face to face with death and are admired for confronting death bravely and without emotional expression (Magill, 1983).

Suicide also runs strongly in the van Gogh family. Both Vincent van Gogh and his brother Cornelius took their own lives. Although Vincent van Gogh's condition has been debated for nearly a century, much evidence taken from letters and medical records suggests that the painter suffered from depression, possibly manic-depressive illness (Jamison, 1993). His brother Theo also had psychotic and manic-depressive symptoms, and his sister Wilhelmina suffered from chronic psychosis, spending most of her life in a mental institution. Before shooting himself in 1890, van Gogh wrote of his illness in a letter to his brother Theo as "a fatal inheritance, since in civilization the weakness increases from generation to generation."

Research corroborates the existence of these suicidal clusters. Researchers in Denmark compared 4,262 people who had committed suicide with healthy controls and evaluated their family histories of suicide and psychiatric illness (Qin et al., 2002). People with a family history of suicide were upward of three times more likely to commit suicide than those without a family history, and reviews of additional studies suggest increased odds of committing suicide of approximately three to five times in those with a family history (Baldessarini & Hennen, 2004; Brent & Mann, 2005, Petersen, 2013). Other studies have found that the familiality of suicide might be genetically transmitted.

The heritability of suicide complicates the already difficult matter of coping with a family member's suicide—a process that can leave survivors with complex emotions as well as a feeling of stigma surrounding the act of suicide. Organizations such as the American Foundation for Suicide Prevention (AFSP) provide support and treatment resources to survivors. Joining these efforts, Mariel Hemingway, the granddaughter of the writer, has become an outspoken advocate for suicide prevention.

psychological autopsy. Clinicians interview family, friends, coworkers, and health care providers to identify psychological causes in much the same way that a coroner searches for physical causes of death. A structured interview is sometimes used to reconstruct motives and circumstances. The interview addresses potential precipitants and stressors, motivation, lethality, and intentionality. For example, the interviewer may try to determine whether the person had distributed personal objects or written a will or other letters that would suggest deliberate suicidal intent.

Although this approach can help survivors understand factors that contributed to a suicide, it does little to diminish their anguish. Commonly, those left behind search for clues and blame themselves for not noticing them in time. For this reason, comments about suicide or passive death wishes should always be taken seriously. Dismissing such comments as passing moods or cries for attention can be a devastating error. If a person is troubled enough to mention suicide, then something is wrong, and getting professional help is critical.

Prevention of Suicide

LO 7.17 Evaluate the current understanding of the preventability of suicide.

Because suicide is a final act, interventions must focus on prevention. Indeed, suicide prevention has served as a model for prevention in other mental illness fields, and prevention research has examined variables spanning from the individual to the community level.

CRISIS INTERVENTION Suicide hotlines exist across the United States and are generally staffed by people with crisis intervention training. People with suicidal thoughts are urged to call these hotlines to receive support in the hope of preventing a suicide attempt. A counselor who determines that the caller is in immediate danger attempts to locate the person and send help immediately. Because hotlines are anonymous, it is virtually impossible to assess their specific effectiveness on a population level. However, even if the hotline provides only a referral for further psychiatric care, it represents a meaningful component of suicide prevention.

FOCUS ON HIGH-RISK GROUPS One approach to suicide prevention targets people with several known risk factors (Brent & Mann, 2005). The children of parents with mood disorders who have attempted suicide themselves are clearly an at-risk group. For those children, early detection and treatment of mood disturbances, substance abuse, and other comorbid symptoms could create an early connection with mental health professionals and provide parents and children with tools to deal with emerging symptoms before they become severe.

SOCIETAL LEVEL PREVENTION Using teacher and peer support, societal approaches try to "reconnect" youth who are drifting with social and emotional supports, thereby improving both their school and family functioning (Eggert et al., 1995; Thompson & Eggert, 1999; Thompson et al., 2000). A cluster-randomized controlled trial of three suicide prevention programs across 10 European countries found that a mental health program targeting adolescent students was effective at reducing suicidal ideation and suicide attempts over the subsequent 12 months, while there was no difference between the control group and groups assigned to gatekeeper training for teachers or screening by professionals (Wasserman et al., 2015). Effectiveness of primary prevention programs targeting university students has also been mixed (Harrod et al., 2014). Other interventions try to eliminate access to methods of committing suicide (Brent & Mann, 2005). Physically limiting access to suicide methods, including detoxification of domestic and motor gas, restricting access to firearms, banning highly lethal pesticides, limiting access to jump sites, and reducing quantities of pharmaceuticals available for a single purchase, may help to reduce suicide attempts and completions (Florentine & Crane, 2010). In Montreal, Canada, installation of bridge barriers reduced suicides by jumping from the bridge without increasing suicides at other bridges and jumping sites in the region (Perron et al., 2013). In Japan, the installation of blue LED lights (expected to have a calming effect) on train platforms decreased the number of suicides without simultaneously

Research HOT Topic

Suicide Barrier on the Golden Gate Bridge

In June 2014, the board of the Golden Gate Bridge, Highway, and Transportation District unanimously approved a $76 million funding plan for a suicide barrier on the bridge, which will consist of steel-cable nets 20 feet below both sides extending 20 feet outward. Caltrans ($22 million), state Mental Health Services Act funds ($7 million), the Golden Gate Bridge district ($20 million), and the Metropolitan Transportation Commission ($27 million) comprise the funding sources. According to the Bridge Rail Foundation, more than 1,600 individuals have committed suicide by jumping from the Golden Gate Bridge, including 38 in 2014 and 46 in 2013. The barrier is expected to be completed in 2019.

Researchers from the Human Cognitive Neurophysiology Research Laboratory in Martinez, California, conducted a cost-effectiveness analysis of the proposed suicide barrier, comparing the estimated costs over 20 years ($51.6 million at the time of the study) with estimated reductions in mortality (assuming that prevented suicides would attempt suicide via another, less lethal method). Based on suicide statistics from the San Francisco Bay Area over the period 1936–2006, they estimated that 286 lives would be saved over 20 years, with an average cost per life of $180,419. This is a small fraction of what the U.S. Department of Transportation estimates to be the minimal value of statistical life ($3.2 million), making the suicide barrier highly cost-effective in reducing suicide mortality (Atkins Whitmer & Woods, 2013).

SOURCES: http://www.sfgate.com/bayarea/article/Golden-Gate-Bridge-going-to-get-suicide-nets-5585482.phphttp://www.sfgate.com/bayarea/article/38-Golden-Gate-Bridge-suicides-last-year-after-6059465.php; http://www.mercurynews.com/crime-courts/ci_27177901/final-design-golden-gate-bridge-suicide-barrier-complete

increasing incidence of suicide at neighboring stations that did not receive the light intervention (Matsubayashi et al., 2014). Community-based prevention programs may also help to prevent suicide and suicide attempts, particularly in rural areas (Ono et al., 2013). Some evidence suggests that people who are determined to commit suicide will simply find alternative methods (Marzuk et al., 1992). It is not possible to eliminate every hazard (e.g., bridges and tall buildings), but limiting the availability of lethal weapons at least introduces a delay that creates an opening for intervention.

PREVENTING SUICIDAL CONTAGION The media's portrayal of suicides of famous people has been associated with copycat suicides (Gould, 1990). The careless inclusion of details about suicide attempts and the portrayal of those who commit suicide as tragic or flawed heroes or martyrs can lead to a pathological obsession with suicide as a solution to life's problems—especially in youth. In addition, suicide clusters, suicide pacts, and Internet sites that function as how-to or support groups that encourage suicide are frightening and dark portrayals of youth whose thinking is detached from reality.

When a youth commits suicide, schools often act immediately, intervening with *critical incident debriefing* (CID), a strategy that brings together people who witnessed a trauma to talk about the event and their reaction to it (Curtis, 1995). CID is a controversial intervention that when used incorrectly may do more harm than good (Bootzin & Bailey, 2005). However, when trained professionals join with school officials to administer CID appropriately, it may provide an outlet for those affected to express their fears and grief by talking about the event. They can also seek support and learn concrete ways to say "good-bye" to the suicide victim. CID can also help to identify fellow students at risk for suicide, allow students to process the death of a peer, and provide an accurate and balanced (rather than glorified) account of the pain and futility of suicide (Macy et al., 2004; Meilman & Hall, 2006).

Treatment After Suicide Attempts

LO 7.18 Discuss approaches to treatment after suicide attempts.

Serious suicide attempts require immediate medical care; however, prolonged psychological care beyond the effects of the attempt is sometimes necessary.

> Jackie was seriously depressed and felt that life was hopeless. She attempted suicide by jumping out of a fifth-story window. Although she shattered almost every bone in her body, she did not die. Now she faces a life with severe facial disfigurement, impaired ability to speak, and confinement to a wheelchair. All she thinks about is how to "finish the job." Jackie desperately needs help, now more than ever, to cope with and find some relief from her depressed mood and her physical ailments. But as long as she remains focused on ending her life, her mood is bound to stay depressed, making it very difficult for her to seek out and receive the help she deserves.

Deliberate self-harm is a major risk factor for suicide. Various psychological and psychosocial interventions reduce self-harm behavior and improve mood in people who previously attempted suicide. However, more studies are needed to determine the impact of these interventions in reducing subsequent suicide attempts or deaths by suicide (Hepp et al., 2004). All individuals should receive follow-up psychiatric care after an attempt, but data suggest that many people who attempt suicide do not receive proper psychotherapeutic attention afterward (Beautrais et al., 1997).

Learning Objective Summaries

LO 7.12 Clarify the differences among suicidal ideation, suicide attempts, and death by suicide.

Thoughts of death, also known as suicidal ideation, may take different forms. Passive suicidal ideation is a wish to be dead but does not include active planning about how to commit suicide. Active suicidal ideation includes thoughts about how to commit the act, including details such as where, when, and how. Suicidal acts are evaluated based on lethality and intent. Some acts, occasionally called parasuicides, are behaviors such as superficial cutting of the wrists or overdoses of nonlethal amounts of medications. These acts are unlikely to result in death. Suicide attempts could result in death by suicide.

LO 7.13 List factors associated with suicide, and detail the relationship between depression and suicidal ideation and behavior.

Males are more likely to attempt suicide and females are more likely to report suicidal ideation. Youth from socioeconomically disadvantaged backgrounds and those who are drifting (being generally disconnected from school, work, and family) are at increased risk. The presence of major depressive disorders and bipolar disorder increases risk of suicide.

LO 7.14 Explain the relation between mental illness and suicide attempts in children.

More than 90% of children who commit suicide have a psychological disorder, most often major depressive disorder. Suicidal ideation and attempts are also higher in children in adolescents with anxiety disorders, eating disorders, oppositional defiant disorder, and ADHD.

LO 7.15 Identify risk factors associated with suicide attempts and death by suicide.

The strongest predictor of suicide is a history of suicide attempts. Family history of suicide, the presence of psychiatric illnesses, behaviors such as impulsivity and pathological aggression, and genetic factors may also influence risk.

LO 7.16 Discuss approaches to understanding factors associated with death by suicide.

A psychological autopsy can attempt to re-create the thoughts, circumstances, and triggers that led to suicide. A structured interview that addresses potential precipitants and stressors, motivation, lethality, and intentionality can reconstruct motives and circumstances.

LO 7.17 Evaluate the current understanding of the preventability of suicide.

Suicide hotlines are common but anonymous, so evaluation of efficacy is not possible. Approaches to decrease risk of suicide by reconnecting youth may reduce ideation and attempts. Physically limiting access to suicide methods, such as detoxification of domestic and motor gas, restricting access to firearms, banning highly lethal pesticides, limiting access to jump sites, bridge guards, and reducing quantities of pharmaceuticals available for a single purchase, may help to reduce suicide attempts and completions

LO 7.18 Discuss approaches to treatment after suicide attempts.

Serious suicide attempts require immediate medical care; however, prolonged psychological care beyond the effects of the attempt is sometimes necessary. All individuals who attempt suicide should receive follow-up psychiatric care.

Critical Thinking Question

Suicide is a uniquely human behavior, although analogs have been reported in some animals. What features of humans as a species influence our desire to commit suicide?

The Etiology of Bipolar and Depressive Disorders

An occasional feeling of low mood is a universal human experience, and we usually can identify the reason. For example, if you missed going home for a holiday or if you did not do well on an important exam, it would be reasonable to feel down for a day or two. Other events—such as losing a job or ending an important relationship—are more stressful and could lead to the onset of a major depressive episode. However, sometimes depressive and bipolar disorders can seem mysterious, and symptoms can turn into full-blown episodes with no obvious cause. Research provides valuable clues into the causes of depressive and bipolar disorders, although no one perspective adequately explains their onset.

Biological Perspective

LO 7.19 Understand genetic, brain, and environmental factors that increase risk for bipolar and depressive disorders.

With the adoption of new technologies and methods, studies of genetics and biological determinants have provided exciting new insights about depression's underlying causes and risk factors. Twin and adoption studies provide evidence of heritability. Neuroimaging studies map out brain circuitry and function that are altered in the context of mood disorders. These studies, in turn, help shape our understanding of how environmental and sociocultural factors influence the course of depressive and bipolar disorders. All this information is being synthesized to develop new interventions and strategies for treating and managing bipolar and depressive disorders.

GENETICS AND FAMILY STUDIES Evidence converging from family, twin, and genetic studies indicates that genes influence the risk for major depressive disorder (Sullivan et al., 2000). This is not to say that genes alone cause depression. By definition, depression is a complex trait that is influenced by both genetic and environmental factors and their interaction. Family studies illustrate how mood disorders track across generations. Twin studies can tell us to what extent a mood disorder is influenced by genetic or environmental factors. Molecular genetic studies help us identify the actual genes that code for proteins that influence risk for mood disorders.

Bipolar disorder As illustrated by bipolar disorder's complex clinical picture, multiple factors are implicated in its etiology (American Psychiatric Association, 2005; Berk & Dodd, 2005; Keck et al., 2001; National Institute of Mental Health, 2001; Perlis et al., 2006). Family, twin, and adoption studies all support a strong familial and genetic component (Barnett & Smoller, 2009). Estimates of the heritability of bipolar disorder range from 59 to 87% (McGuffin et al., 2003).

Linkage studies have identified several areas of the genome that may harbor genes that influence susceptibility to bipolar disorder (Hayden & Nurnberger, 2006; Shinozaki & Potash, 2014). As part of the Psychiatric Genomics Consortium, a large-scale genome-wide association study (GWAS) was conducted of 7,481 individuals with bipolar disorder and 9,250 controls, together with a replication study of 4,496 cases and 42,422 controls. This major study confirmed genome-wide significant evidence of association with the *CACNA1C* gene, identified a new genetic target, *ODZ4*, and suggested that calcium channels may be involved in the etiology of both bipolar disorder and schizophrenia (Psychiatric GWAS Consortium Bipolar Disorder Working Group, 2011), although researchers are just beginning to explore how these channels may exert their influence (Uemura et al., 2015). Combining data from multiple GWAS studies has allowed researchers to identify several genes (*CACNA1C, DTNA, FOXP1, GNG2, ITPR2, LSAMP, NPAS3, NCOA2*, and *NTRK3*) and pathways associated with bipolar disorder: corticotropin-releasing hormone signaling, cardiac β-adrenergic signaling, phospholipase C signaling, glutamate receptor signaling, endothelin 1 signaling, and cardiac hypertrophy signaling (Nurnberger et al., 2014). A more recent GWAS study replicated earlier findings and also added two new significant loci: *ADCY2* and a region between *MIR2113* and *POU3F2* (Muhleisen et al., 2014). Further analysis of GWAS data also suggests that genetic variation in certain biological pathways may increase risk for not only bipolar disorder but also schizophrenia and major depression (Network and Pathway Analysis Subgroup of Psychiatric Genomics Consortium, 2015). Rare variants in genes related to neuronal excitability may also increase risk for bipolar disorder (Ament et al., 2015; Duan et al., 2014). Genetic variation may also help to predict response to treatment, such as lithium therapy (Chen et al., 2014). GWAS with even larger sample sizes are expected to open new doors to understanding the biology of mental illness.

Major depressive disorder Major depressive disorder runs in families. First-degree relatives of people with depression are two to three times more likely to suffer from depression than are first-degree relatives of people without depression (Sullivan et al., 2000). In particular, the genetic predisposition appears stronger in those individuals who suffer from recurrent depression and when there is an early age at onset (Sullivan et al., 2000). In addition to the family studies, twin studies estimate that the heritability of major depressive disorder is about 31 to 42% (Sullivan et al., 2000). That means that about one-third of the liability to major depressive disorder is due to genetic factors with the remaining risk due to environmental factors. Studies of monozygotic twins who are discordant for depressive disorders (i.e., one twin has depression and the other does not) suggest a role for epigenetic factors (i.e., DNA methylation) in risk for depression (Córdova-Palomera et al., 2015; Davies et al., 2014).

For depression, candidate gene association studies have focused on genes that regulate the *serotonergic system*, a network of neurons and neurotransmitters in the brain, one function of which is to regulate emotion (Levinson, 2005). Although several significant associations have been found, the available data do not yet solve the genetic puzzle. Genetic variation in *ACSM1*, which is involved in activation of fatty acids, is also associated with major depressive disorder (Li & Ji et al., 2015), as are gene expression clusters related to IL-6 signaling and NK cell pathways (Jansen et al., 2016).

As we noted in Chapter 2, GWAS do not focus on a single gene but scan the entire genome to identify genetic variants. A large GWAS mega-analysis that combined data from several studies compared single nucleotide polymorphisms (SNPs) from 9,240 individuals with major depressive disorder and 9,519 controls (Major Depressive Disorder Working Group of the Psychiatric-GWAS Consortium, 2013). The analysis did not reveal any SNPs that met the stringent genome-wide significance criterion. Although this sample size might seem like a very large number of research participants, the researchers estimated that much larger sample sizes will be needed to understand the role of genes in the onset of depression (Levinson et al., 2014). When low-coverage whole-genome sequencing was carried out on samples from Han Chinese women recruited through the CONVERGE Consortium (China, Oxford, and Virginia

Commonwealth University Experimental Research on Genetic Epidemiology) consortium (5,303 cases and 5,337 controls), genome-wide significant associations with major depression were found for two loci on chromosome 10, near the SIRT1 gene and on an intron of the *LHPP* gene (CONVERGE Consortium, 2015). The associations were replicated using a separate sample of Han Chinese individuals and in a subset of severe cases in the original sample. It is likely that the homogeneity of the sample (all female, Han Chinese with recurrent cases of major depression) contributed to the success of the study, as the results were not replicated in the aforementioned larger sample that included more heterogeneous cases from multiple European countries (Sullivan, 2015).

Ultimately, understanding depression involves understanding both genetic and environmental factors. Exploring this interaction may help determine why some people are more vulnerable to environmental stressors. New technologies and approaches will make it more likely that specific genes will be identified. Future research may identify genetic variants that influence response to medication (Biernacka et al., 2015; Fabbri et al., 2013) and perhaps to psychotherapy (Malhotra et al., 2004), allowing mental health professionals to target treatment to an individual, enhancing its likelihood of success.

NEUROIMAGING STUDIES Neuroimaging studies have begun to elucidate brain regions and pathways that may be implicated in bipolar and depressive disorders. In depression, functional neuroimaging studies have focused on four main brain regions: the amygdala, which is associated with memory and emotional responses to stimuli; the orbitofrontal cortex, which is responsible for cognitive processing and decision making; the dorsolateral prefrontal cortex, which is involved with affect regulation, planning, and decision making; and the anterior cingulate cortex, which is involved with error detection, motivation, and modulation of emotional responses (Koenigs & Grafman, 2009) (see Figure 7.5). Changes in the structure of the hippocampus and amygdala after treatment with electroconvulsive therapy (ECT) are associated with clinical response (Joshi et al., 2015).

In bipolar disorder, many of the brain regions implicated are involved with emotional reactivity and regulation and parallel findings for major depression. The amygdala, prefrontal cortex, anterior cingulate cortex, and hippocampus have shown differences in individuals with bipolar disorder compared with controls (Davidson et al., 2002; Mayberg et al., 2004).

Figure 7.5 Brain Views of Amygdala, Orbitofrontal Cortex, Dorsolateral Cortex, and Anterior Cingulate Cortex.

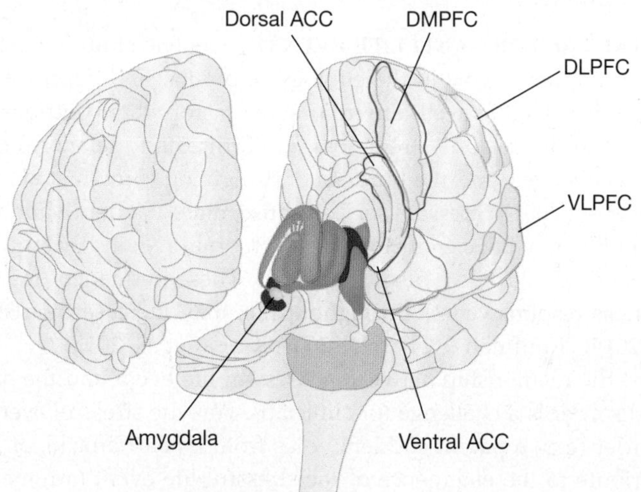

DLPFC: Dorsolateral prefrontal cortex
VLPFC: Ventrolateral prefrontal cortex
DMPFC: Dorsomedial prefrontal cortex
ACC: Anterior cingulate cortex

Experiences of loss and grief can contribute to the onset of depression.

These differences may partly reflect the effects of treatment, as individuals with bipolar disorder who were treated with lithium have smaller hippocampal and amygdala volumes than healthy controls, while the same is not true for those not treated with lithium (Hartberg et al., 2015). Overall, individuals with bipolar disorder have lower total brain volume than controls as well as thickness and white matter integrity differences (Maller et al., 2014).

fMRI studies of people with bipolar disorder engaging in emotional and cognitive tasks have identified abnormal brain activity in frontal, subcortical, and limbic regions (Yurgelun-Todd & Ross, 2006). An example of an emotional task would be looking at happy vs. angry faces. Compared with healthy controls, individuals with bipolar disorder performed more poorly on a test of facial emotion recognition, which was correlated with gray matter volume in the right middle cingulate gyrus (Maila de Castro et al., 2015). In a study of 527 adults (153 with and 374 without bipolar disorder) from 26 families with heavy genetic loading for bipolar disorder, neuroimaging and neurocognitive assessments revealed 32 significant brain–behavior associations (Fears et al., 2015). The sheer number of identified abnormalities makes it difficult to conclude that any single brain area is responsible for bipolar disorder. In fact, the symptoms of bipolar disorder may emerge from the dysfunction of interconnected brain networks (Adler et al., 2006).

Although intriguing, these studies were conducted with people who had the disorder, so we cannot use the data to draw conclusions regarding causality. An alternative hypothesis is that differences in brain function may be the *result* of the disorder (i.e., *biological scarring*) rather than its cause. To ultimately determine the role of neurobiology, we will need to conduct neuroimaging studies of individuals who are at risk for bipolar disorder but who do not yet show any symptoms (e.g., children of parents with bipolar disorder) and follow them over time. This research design could help determine whether any premorbid abnormalities exist and are associated with the development of bipolar and depressive disorders.

ENVIRONMENTAL FACTORS AND LIFE EVENTS Genetic studies suggest that biological factors play an important role in the etiology of bipolar and depressive disorders, but the environment is involved as well. Environmental factors that contribute to the onset of major depressive disorder include stress, loss, grief, threats to relationships, occupational problems, health challenges, and the burdens of caregiving (Brown et al., 1996; Kendler et al., 1998; Monroe et al., 2001). Stressors such as abuse, maternal deprivation, neglect, or loss that occur early in life may have enduring effects on brain regions that influence stress and emotion (Mandelli et al., 2015; see also Chapter 4). These permanent brain changes, such as heightened stress responsiveness throughout life, may increase the risk for depression (Cattaneo et al., 2015; ; Kaufman & Charney, 2001; Kumar et al., 2015).

Teasing apart the relationship between a stressful life event and the onset of a bipolar and depressive disorder is a challenge for clinicians. Was the stressful event truly independent of the disorder (e.g., a parent suddenly dies from a heart attack), or did the person's depression contribute to the emergence of the stressful life event (a romantic relationship ends)—a dependent life event?

> Right out of law school, John landed a prime job with a prominent law firm in his home city. The hours were grueling. At first, he was energized by the challenge, but after months of getting by on 4 hours of sleep per night, he started to have pervasive self-doubt about his abilities, forget

important facts about cases, and have altercations with his colleagues. He was late for work, and when he arrived, he looked disheveled and often disoriented. He was fired from his job and blamed his depression on this loss. In reality, the job stress precipitated the depression, and his job loss was a dependent life event.

Although stressful life events are commonly reported in first episodes of major depressive disorder, over time, recurrent episodes seem to be more independent of life events (Kendler et al., 2000).

An important question is why stressful life events seem to lead to depression in some people but not in others and whether genetic factors may play a role in determining sensitivity (Felger et al., 2015; Pishva et al., 2014). For example, women who are at high genetic risk for major depressive disorder not only report more stressful life events (Kendler & Karkowski-Shuman, 1997; Kendler & Prescott, 1999) but also are more sensitive to their effects (Kendler et al., 1995). This phenomenon is called *genetic control of sensitivity to the environment* (Kendler & Karkowski-Shuman, 1997). This basically means that two people can encounter the same stressful life event, but because of traits they possess that are under genetic control, one person experiences that event as more stressful than the other (Lopizzo et al., 2015; Riglin et al., 2015).

Watch RESILIENCE

Psychological Perspective

LO 7.20 Contrast psychodynamic, behavioral, and cognitive theories of depressive disorders.

Long before we understood the role of biology, clinicians and researchers sought psychological explanations for depressive disorders. Older psychological theories have evolved over time, and some factors, such as loss, have been consistently identified. Research has produced a complex picture that has questioned some early psychological theories and supported others. Nevertheless, these theories reflect our changing ideas of depression and provide a foundation for formulating new research questions and for designing new interventions.

PSYCHODYNAMIC THEORY Freud conceptualized depression as "anger turned inward" (Freud, 1917). The anger, he proposed, arises after the loss of an object—either real or imagined. In Freudian terms, an "object" is anything to which someone is emotionally attached (e.g., another person, an aspect of the self, an animal). The loss may be real, such as the death of a friend or of a romantic partner, or it may be a process that is completely

Research HOT Topic

Resiliency

How can people at high genetic risk or with high environmental exposure (or both) remain impervious to depression? Scientists have been studying how our underlying genetic makeup and neurobiology may dictate how we respond to stress, and researchers at the Cold Spring Harbor Laboratory in New York have honed in on one potential explanation (Wang et al., 2014). Because there is no true animal model of depression, they used a mouse model with a classic symptom (helplessness) that mirrors what is seen in humans with depression. In their learned helplessness paradigm, the mice first underwent two induction sessions with random electric foot shocks followed by a testing session where they were placed back in the same chamber for additional shocks but given the opportunity to escape to another safe chamber through an open door. Not surprisingly, most mice moved chambers to avoid the foot shocks, but about 20% did not—demonstrating learned helplessness. Because researchers were using genetically modified mice whose neurons glow green when activated, they were able to see if brain activity in any particular region differentiated the "resilient" mice from the "depressed" mice. The "depressed" group showed more nodes of connection (i.e., increased activity) in the medial prefrontal cortex (mPFC), which has been linked to emotion regulation as well as mood and anxiety disorders. Humans with depression show hyperactivity in this region. These findings were underscored by additional experiments whereby the researchers artificially enhanced activity in the mPFC in "resilient" mice, which caused them to no longer move chambers to avoid electric shocks. These results raise an interesting question: would the reverse work (i.e., if you inhibited activity in the mPFC, would mice become more resilient)? If so, this would support treatments such as deep brain stimulation (DBS) targeting the mPFC.

SOURCES: http://www.washingtonpost.com/national/health-science/why-are-some-depressed-others-resilient-scientists-home-in-on-part-of-the-brain/2014/06/05/db638498-e83f-11e3-a86b-362fd5443d19_story.html; http://time.com/119572/why-some-people-get-depressed-and-others-get-resilient/

contained in the unconscious below the person's level of awareness. An unconscious loss might be the loss of some aspect of youth about which the person was not actively aware. In "Mourning and Melancholia," Freud distinguished between these two terms. According to Freud, *melancholia* (a condition akin to major depression) is a "profoundly painful dejection, cessation of interest in the outside world, loss of the capacity to love, inhibition of all activity, and a lowering of the self-regarding feelings to a degree that finds utterance in self-reproaches and self-revilings, and culminates in a delusional expectation of punishment." To illustrate anger turned inward, Freud noted that melancholics were often highly self-accusatory—usually in ways that were not realistic or justified. These accusations were misdirected against the self; Freud believed that they were actually directed against someone whom the patient loved. Freud focused on internal representations of our relationships in the external world. He emphasized that the loss of a person in the real world leads to an internal loss, which is experienced as a psychic wound or a lesion in one's self-esteem.

Psychodynamic theorists consider depression and mania as intricately interlinked. They view hypomania and mania as defenses against the unwanted and intolerable experience of depression. Exaggerated self-esteem and grandiosity protect the person against confronting the underlying distressing thoughts associated with low self-esteem or self-loathing.

Both clinical experience and research support the hypothesis that loss (as well as other stressful life events) can precipitate depression. Advances in psychodynamic theory focus on the role of real-world relationships and loss in the emergence of depression rather than on unverifiable unconscious processes (Horner, 1974). Moreover, psychodynamic underpinnings contributed to the development of a successful intervention for depression called interpersonal psychotherapy (Klerman et al., 1984).

ATTACHMENT THEORY Guided by data from animal studies, John Bowlby examined how disruptions in mother–infant attachment could lead to depression and anxiety. According to Bowlby, attachment has evolutionary significance for survival and is related to maternal protection of offspring from predators. Bowlby proposed that a child's response to maternal separation consists of three stages: (1) protest; (2) despair, pain, and loss; and (3) detachment or denial of affection for the mother. Others have expanded

Bowlby's ideas to highlight how early attachment affects later life functioning and how disruptions in attachment lead to vulnerability to depression, anxiety, and problems with attachment in adulthood (Ainsworth, 1982). In a community sample of adolescents, perceived attachment security to one's parents, particularly the mother, was shown to predict trajectories of depressive symptoms from age 11 to 16 years, with greater perceived attachment security associated with lower odds of following a trajectory with greater depressive symptoms (Duchesne & Ratelle, 2014).

BEHAVIORAL THEORIES

> Charles is a widower. After his wife died, he decided to fill his time by volunteering at the hospital two blocks from his home. His volunteer work was fulfilling, and he won several hospital awards for his dedication to his work and the people whom he served. Financial pressures forced the hospital to close. Charles no longer felt comfortable driving, and there was no public transportation in his neighborhood. Now Charles had no way to occupy his time, no opportunity to feel needed, and no one to praise him for his work. Soon, Charles stopped getting dressed and told his children, who lived in another city, that there really was no reason to leave his house anymore.

Behavioral theory (e.g., Skinner, 1953) proposes that depression results from the withdrawal of reinforcement (aspects of the social environment) for healthy behaviors. Changes in reinforcement may result from decreases in the number and types of reinforcing stimuli and/or the inability to obtain reinforcement due to a lack of social skills (Lewinsohn, 1974), and decreased environmental reward has been shown to be associated with both self-reported and diagnosed depression (Carvalho et al., 2011). For example,

> Jana was always shy but had a close circle of friends whom she had to leave behind when she moved cross-country to a new city for what she thought would be a fabulous new job. Suddenly, there was no one with whom she felt close enough to go out to dinner or share her thoughts (i.e., there was a decrease in available social reinforcers). Her severe shyness prevented her from meeting new people (i.e., she was unable to obtain reinforcement because of a lack of social skills). Although she called her friends when she could, they could no longer drop by for a glass of wine or call her to go shopping. The longer she was in her new environment, the sadder she became. Her new colleagues saw a quiet person who did not smile, and they were not inclined to approach her.

LEARNING AND MODELING Many researchers have been interested in discovering how learning theory might play a role in the in etiology of depression (Dygdon & Dienes, 2013). Among them is Martin Seligman, who developed his theory of **learned helplessness** while exploring the effects of inescapable shock on avoidance learning (Landgraf et al., 2015; Seligman, 1975; Taylor et al., 2014). In his original experimental avoidance learning paradigm, dogs were restrained in a harness while several shocks (an unconditioned stimulus—UCS) were paired with a conditioned stimulus (CS)—in this case, a light. After the conditioning trials, the dogs were placed in a box where they could easily avoid a shock by jumping over a low barrier (see Figure 7.6). Surprisingly, most of the dogs failed to learn to avoid the shock. They remained sitting when the light came on, receiving shocks that they could easily have escaped. Seligman theorized that their earlier experience with inescapable shocks interfered with the dogs' ability to learn that escape was possible in a new situation. Seligman called this "learned helplessness." About a third of the dogs did learn to escape, suggesting that there are fundamental underlying differences in the likelihood of developing learned helplessness. Although we do not know the nature of these underlying differences, they may be either biologically or environmentally based.

Environmental factors, such as the loss of social support or social reinforcement, are significant in the onset and maintenance of depressive episodes.

Figure 7.6 Learned Helplessness.

After being in an inescapable situation, the dog is put in a situation from which escape from painful shock is possible. However, because of prior learning, most of the dogs did not try to escape the shock by jumping over the very small barrier.

SOURCE: Lilienfeld, S., et al. (2009). *Psychology: From inquiry to understanding*. Allyn & Bacon. Copyright © 2009. Reprinted by permission of Pearson Education.

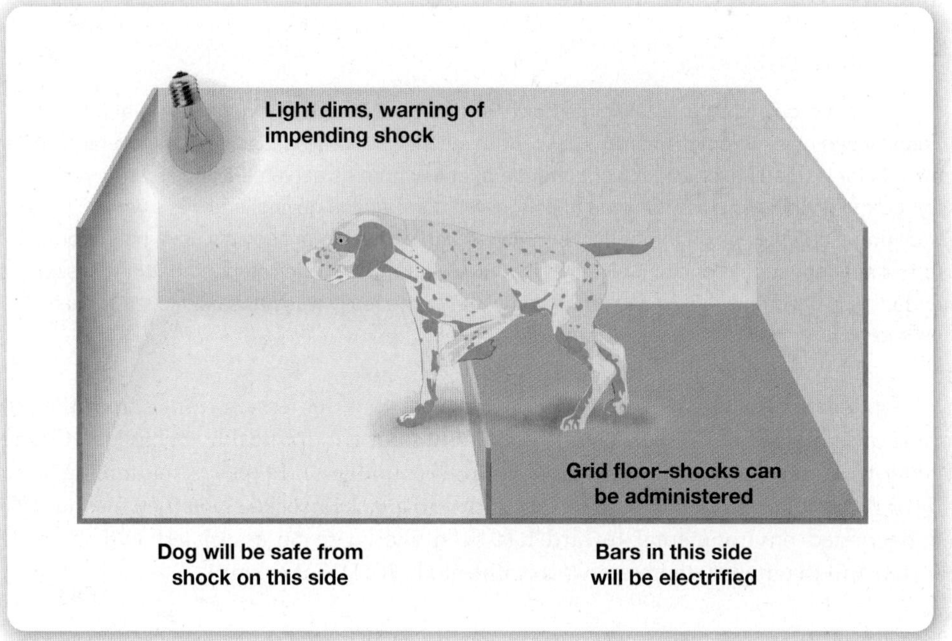

Learned helplessness proposes that externally uncontrollable environments (e.g., repeated abuse, failure at school or work, relationship failures) and presumably internally uncontrollable environments (e.g., pervasive low mood, thoughts of death) are inescapable stimuli that can lead to *dysphoria* (sadness or low mood) and major depressive disorder. Why some people develop learned helplessness and others do not may depend on whether the individual thinks the situation is inescapable (Abramson et al., 2002). If the situation is attributed to an internal cause that is personal, pervasive, and permanent (e.g., "I lost my job because I'm a loser and I'll always be a loser"), then helplessness, hopelessness, and depression may result. In contrast, if negative events are seen as external and impermanent (e.g., "I lost my job because my boss is a jerk. In my next job, I will work for someone better"), helplessness and depression are averted.

Three aspects of learning theory are relevant to understanding the development of depression. The first concerns individuals' appraisal of themselves, their lives, and others (Alloy et al., 2000; Beck, 1979). The second focuses on problem solving, whether an individual has a proactive (positive) or an avoidant approach to solving problems (D'Zurilla & Nezu, 1999). The third aspect focuses on the success of previous attempts to deal with stress (Folkman & Lazarus, 1985). Each of these factors appears to contribute to a person's vulnerability to depression and its chronicity.

COGNITIVE THEORY Aaron T. Beck, the father of cognitive therapy, proposed that thoughts cause feelings and behaviors and that *negative* thoughts can cause depressive feelings and behaviors. The theory proposes that *negative cognitive schemas* (patterns of negativistic thinking) can develop early in life and become part of an individual's self-concept (Beck, 1961, 1967; Sher, 2005). Negativistic thinking is characterized by persistently pessimistic and critical thoughts. Individuals with negativistic thinking are also more prone to low self-esteem (Verplanken et al., 2007). This thinking style contributes to the inability to find pleasure from previously pleasant experiences and to the social isolation commonly seen in depression (Cacioppo et al., 2010). Negative schemas can be identified by the presence of

Table 7.1 Common Thinking Errors

Dichotomous or "all or nothing" thinking: Thinking in "all-or-nothing" terms. *"If I can't do something perfectly, I may as well quit."*

Overgeneralizing: Condemning yourself as a total person on the basis of a single event. "I got a C on a psychology test—I will never be a psychologist."

Selective thinking: Concentrating on your weaknesses and forgetting your strengths. "It does not matter that I am a good singer. I cannot dance or act."

Catastrophizing: Only paying attention to the dark side of things, or overestimating the chances of disaster. "I didn't get into an Ivy League school. I'll never have a decent career."

Personalizing: Taking things personally that have little or nothing to do with you. "Jenny is so quiet. She must really be angry with me."

Personal Ineffectiveness: Assuming you can do nothing to change your situation. "Jack always criticizes me. I wish he would quit."

automatic thoughts, which are dysfunctional thoughts and represent beliefs about the self that become a habitual pattern of thinking: I'm a failure, I have no willpower, and I have no luck in love. Automatic thoughts tend to be extreme and counterproductive and produce negative feelings. They go untested, become fixed, and lead to *self-fulfilling prophecies* (e.g., you expect to fail and so you do). Beck proposed that individuals with depression experience a *negative cognitive triad*—negative thoughts about the self, the world, and the future. He described a variety of thinking errors that sustain the negative thoughts in the triad (see Table 7.1).

Learning Objective Summaries

LO 7.19 Understand genetic, brain, and environmental factors that increase risk for bipolar and depressive disorders.

Family, twin, and genetic studies indicate that genes influence the risk for bipolar and major depressive disorders. Several genes have been implicated in bipolar disorder and major depressive disorder through GWAS. Imaging studies have focused in on the amygdala, the orbitofrontal cortex, the dorsolateral cortex, and the anterior cingulate cortex in depression and bipolar disorder. Environmental factors that contribute to depression risk include stress, loss, grief, threats to relationships, occupational problems, health challenges, and the burdens of caregiving.

LO 7.20 Contrast psychodynamic, behavioral, and cognitive theories of depressive disorders.

Psychodynamic theories of depression range from seeing it as "anger turned inward" to more modern conceptualizations of real-world relationships and loss in the emergence of depression rather than on unverifiable unconscious processes. Behavioral theory proposes that depression results from the withdrawal of reinforcement for healthy behaviors. Learning theory also focuses on individuals' appraisal of themselves, their lives, and others; their problem-solving approach; and success of previous attempts to deal with stress. Cognitive theory proposes that thoughts cause feelings and behaviors and that *negative* thoughts can cause depressive feelings and behaviors.

Critical Thinking Question

Ming started feeling depressed at the end of her first year of college. Earlier that year, she had injured her knee, which kept her sidelined from the varsity women's soccer team. After she got a C on an important exam in biology, she began to question her ability to enter medical school, her longtime goal. In the spring, her father died suddenly of a heart attack. How do you think each of these events might have contributed to her depression?

The Treatment of Bipolar and Depressive Disorders

Several treatments are available for people who suffer from bipolar and depressive disorders, ranging from "talk" therapies to antidepressant medication and other biologically based treatments. Just as mood disorders may involve symptoms of the mind and body, treatment in some cases involves both psychotherapy and medication.

Bipolar Disorder

LO 7.21 Identify efficacious pharmacological and psychological treatments for bipolar disorder.

Medications are the primary treatment for bipolar disorder; psychotherapy alone is insufficient (American Psychiatric Association, 2005; Frye et al., 2014). However, psychotherapy may provide emotional support to both the patient and family members and help the patient develop behavioral strategies to cope with symptoms and stabilize his or her mood (Parikh et al., 2015). Psychotherapy reduces hospitalizations and improves daily functioning (Depression and Bipolar Support Alliance, 2006; National Institute of Mental Health, 2001). Different forms of psychotherapy are available to people with bipolar disorder, including cognitive-behavioral therapy, psychoeducation, family therapy, and interpersonal and social rhythm therapy (National Institute of Mental Health, 2001). Pilot testing has also established the potential efficacy of dialectical behavior therapy for adolescents with bipolar disorder (Goldstein et al., 2015). The field is moving toward translating results of genetic studies to develop genetically informed personalized interventions that will incorporate biomarkers of treatment response (Frye, 2014).

PSYCHOLOGICAL TREATMENTS Various types of psychotherapy benefit individuals with bipolar disorder when used adjunctively to effective pharmacotherapy (Miklowitz & Scott, 2009; Popovic et al., 2014).

Cognitive-behavioral therapy (CBT) Cognitive-behavioral therapy (CBT) for bipolar disorder develops skills to change inappropriate or negative thought patterns and behaviors. CBT appears to decrease depressive symptoms, improve outcome, and increase adherence to treatment recommendations (Lam et al., 2003; Miklowitz & Scott, 2009), but the results of randomized trials of CBT for bipolar disorder have not been consistent (Gomes et al., 2011; Scott et al., 2006). Psychoeducation teaches the patient about bipolar disorder, its treatment, and how to recognize warning signs or precursors of mood shifts. Early recognition can prompt patients to seek treatment, reduce the risk of relapse, and improve social and occupational functioning (Miklowitz & Scott, 2009). Education can also be informative for family and friends. Family-based treatment, sometimes initiated while an individual is still receiving inpatient care, focuses on developing strategies to reduce personal and familial stress and engage families in early recognition and treatment of impending mood shifts (Glick et al., 1993; Miklowitz & Scott, 2009).

Interpersonal and social rhythm therapy (IPSRT) Interpersonal and social rhythm therapy (IPSRT) (Frank et al., 1997) promotes adherence to regular daily routines (including regular sleep patterns). This treatment is based on interpersonal psychotherapy (Klerman et al., 1984) coupled with a social zeitgeber hypothesis (Grandin et al., 2006). (In German, social zeitgebers are "time givers." The word refers to persons, social demands, or tasks that set the biological clock.) The hypothesis states that the loss of social zeitgebers may result in unstable biological rhythms. In vulnerable individuals, this leads to manic or depressive episodes (Ehlers et al., 1988; Frank et al., 2005). Not getting enough sleep or getting too much sleep and not enough physical activity in one's day can both contribute to negative mood. Thus, patients treated under this therapeutic approach are coached to go to bed and get out of bed at the same time of day, every day. They are also advised to eat meals on a regular schedule during the day and to take breaks during long workdays whenever possible. They are encouraged to keep a reasonable and consistent schedule of social events. IPSRT increases the regularity of social rhythms in individuals with bipolar disorder, which in turn is associated with decreased likelihood of new affective episodes (Frank et al., 2005). IPSRT has been shown to reduce symptoms and improve social functioning in adolescents and young adults with bipolar disorder (Inder et al., 2015) and has been shown to be effective in a group treatment format (Hoberg et al., 2013). It may also be beneficial for adolescents at high risk of developing bipolar disorder (Goldstein et al., 2014).

A large multisite trial, the Systematic Treatment Enhancement Program for Bipolar Disorder (STEP-BD), compared the effects of three specialized psychosocial interventions for bipolar disorder—family-focused treatment, IPSRT, and CBT relative to a collaborative care condition (six sessions of relapse prevention) when delivered in conjunction with pharmacotherapy. Although the outcome did not differ significantly among the three specialist therapies, patients who received the specialty interventions fared better than those in the collaborative care condition, suggesting a role for psychotherapy in the management of bipolar disorder (Miklowitz et al., 2007).

BIOLOGICAL TREATMENTS Bipolar disorder requires care by a psychiatrist and treatment with medication. A patient in a manic or depressive episode may need hospitalization to be safe and to receive needed treatment. The most commonly used medication is lithium (American Psychiatric Association, 2005; Berk & Dodd, 2005; Keck et al., 2001), which moderates mood swings from manic to depressive episodes.

Lithium is a naturally occurring metallic element. Discovered by accident in the 1940s by John Cade, an Australian doctor, it was not widely used until the 1970s. For many years, lithium was used to treat bipolar disorder with no clear understanding of why it worked. Then, in 1998, researchers at the University of Wisconsin discovered that a neurotransmitter called *glutamate* was the key to its efficacy. Too much glutamate in the synapse causes mania, whereas too little causes depression. Lithium moderates glutamate levels in the brain, and therefore, it is an efficacious treatment for people with bipolar disorder. In a meta-analysis of seven treatment trials comparing lithium and placebo, lithium was more effective at preventing bipolar episodes (Severus et al., 2014).

Lithium is intended as a long-term therapy and must be taken consistently. Often when patients are *euthymic* (in a period of normal mood between depressive and manic episodes) or manic, they stop taking their medication either because they believe they are well or because they would like to keep experiencing some aspects of mania (e.g., increased energy, decreased need for sleep). Discontinuing the medication often leads to a clinical relapse. Patients must be monitored carefully because if the dose is not exactly right, toxic levels of lithium may build up in the bloodstream.

Anticonvulsant medications (normally used to treat epilepsy) are also used to manage bipolar disorder, sometimes in combination with lithium (American Psychiatric Association, 2005; Berk & Dodd, 2005; Keck et al., 2001), though a recent meta-analysis of seven treatment trials comparing lithium and anticonvulsants suggests that lithium is superior in preventing manic episodes (Severus et al., 2014). Other medications (such as atypical antipsychotics) may be added during depressive episodes (American Psychiatric Association, 2005; Berk & Dodd, 2005; Keck et al., 2001), but it is not clear whether they are effective for children, adolescents, or older adults (Keck et al., 2001). Even though episodes of mania and depression can be controlled, bipolar disorder is a long-term illness that currently has no cure. It is important for patients to stay on their medications, even when well, to keep the disease under control and reduce the chance of recurrent, worsening episodes.

Electroconvulsive therapy (ECT) can also be used in the treatment of bipolar disorder, particularly for severe depressive episodes, extreme or prolonged mania, or catatonia (NICE, 2003). It is used primarily when medications and psychotherapy are not effective, when a person is at high risk for suicide, or when use of medications is contraindicated, such as during pregnancy (National Institute of Mental Health, 2001) and has shown some efficacy in improving symptoms among those with treatment-resistant bipolar disorder (Medda et al., 2015; Schoeyen et al., 2015).

Depressive Disorders

LO 7.22 Identify efficacious pharmacological and psychological treatments for depressive disorders.

Because many medical illnesses can masquerade as depression, an important first step in treatment is a comprehensive physical exam (American Psychiatric Association, 2013). In addition to ruling out a medical cause (such as cancer, malnutrition, mild stroke, certain metabolic disorders), a complete review of current medications is important because certain drugs can have side effects (such as fatigue or hyperactivity that disrupts sleep) that mimic depression. Once these possibilities are ruled out, the next step is selecting an appropriate treatment strategy. Surprisingly, only about half of those with major depression obtain professional treatment, and of these, only about 22% receive clinically adequate care (Kessler et al., 2003).

In part, this inadequate treatment is due to the failure to recognize the symptoms, to the stigma associated with seeking care, or to the provider's lack of knowledge about evidence-based treatments. Campaigns such as Mental Health Month through the National Alliance on Mental Illness (https://www.nami.org/get-involved/raise-awareness) and "Real Stories of Depression" launched by the National Institute of Mental Health (http://www.nimh.nih.gov/health/topics/depression/men-and-depression/real-stories-of-depression/index.shtml) seek to improve mental health literacy by helping people recognize the signs of depression and providing a roadmap for seeking care.

Many efficacious treatments for major depression are available. Psychotherapy helps people express distressing emotions and learn more effective ways to deal with factors that may have contributed to or resulted from depression. Medications and other physical treatments (e.g., electroconvulsive therapy and deep brain stimulation) can help individuals who are too depressed to benefit from psychotherapy alone. Many choices exist, and often more than one approach is needed until an efficacious treatment is found (Ebmeier et al., 2006; Moore & McLaughlin, 2003).

PSYCHOLOGICAL TREATMENTS Psychological treatments focus on understanding how thoughts, perceptions, and behaviors influence depressed mood, and vice versa. Generally, these treatments are delivered by a trained clinician (in most cases a clinical psychologist or licensed clinical social worker) in individual or group settings and are an essential component of a comprehensive treatment plan for depression.

Cognitive-behavioral therapy (CBT) Cognitive-behavioral therapy (CBT) (Beck, 1979) is based on the premise that an individual can learn to think and behave differently, which can lead to improved mood. A key ingredient involves having patients record their thoughts, feelings, and behaviors (see Table 7.2). Through this monitoring, patients identify situations or triggers for low mood as well as situations associated with improved mood. Once triggers are identified, the patient learns to recognize and modify automatic or distorted thoughts and change behaviors to improve mood and functioning. CBT has shown widespread efficacy in treating depression in children and adolescents (Zhou et al., 2015) and has shown

Table 7.2 Thought Restructuring Record

After identifying a negative, automatic thought, a cognitive-behavioral therapist encourages the person with depression to replace that thought with a more positive idea. Reframing the situation in more positive terms often helps the person feel less negative about the self, the world, and the future.

Situation: Got a C on a test for which I studied really hard

Automatic Thought: I'm so stupid. I'll never get my degree

Emotion: Sad and discouraged

New Thought: This was the first test—next time, I'll be better prepared

Outcome: Concerned but motivated to continue in class

success in computer-, Internet-, and mobile-based versions (Ebert et al., 2015) in addition to traditional face-to-face therapy (individual or group-based) (Okumura & Ichikura, 2014).

> After keeping her mood and thought records, Bonita noticed that her moods were consistently worse as the weekends approached. Earlier in the week she was focused on work-related tasks, but then she noticed that around Wednesday, she started having thoughts like "Everyone else is making plans for the weekend, and I'm going to be all alone as usual." By Friday morning, she was consistently negative, and the thoughts would get worse: "I am a complete loser." "No one wants to be around me." Working with her therapist, Bonita challenged her negative thoughts with other thoughts that were more balanced, less "all or nothing." For example, she replaced "No one wants to be around me" with "I haven't given people the chance to see who I am; I have to take initiative." Once she recognized the weekly pattern, she used the negative thoughts as calls to action rather than as signs of an inevitable slide into a weekend of misery and loneliness.

Interpersonal psychotherapy (IPT) IPT is a focused, time-limited therapy developed by Klerman and Weissman (Klerman et al., 1984). It has its roots in the work of Harry Stack Sullivan, who emphasized the importance of current interpersonal relationships for mental health. Its core principle is that interpersonal problems can trigger depression and depression itself can influence interpersonal functioning.

> Sam had grown increasingly frustrated with his job since his new boss took over; they always disagreed about his effort, and his boss was constantly on his case. In addition, all of his coworkers avoided him in the break room, in large part because Sam always complained about the boss's heavy-handed tactics. He found himself having trouble getting up in the morning to go to work, and showing up late just led to more criticism. He withdrew from his coworkers and eventually from his wife, who was having trouble understanding Sam's sullen and angry mood. Losing his job was the last straw. Sam stopped coaching his son's baseball team because he was too ashamed to face the other dads, and he started staying out late at night to avoid the inevitably tough conversations with his wife about bills that were piling up.

IPT uses 12 to 16 sessions and focuses on an interpersonal problem area (e.g., grief, role transition, disputes, interpersonal deficits) that guides treatment. Therapeutic techniques include expression of mood, clarification of feelings, communication analysis, and behavior change. IPT is efficacious for mild to moderate depression (Cuijpers et al., 2011) and is also used to treat dysthymia, child/adolescent and late-life depression, postpartum depression, anxiety, and eating disorders (Fairburn, 1993; Frank et al., 1991; Lipsitz et al., 2006; Miniati et al., 2014; Mufson et al., 1994; Stuart, 1995; Zhou et al., 2014).

Behavioral activation Based on the theory that depression is maintained by a lack of positive reinforcement, early behavioral interventions focused on increasing access to pleasant, and therefore reinforcing, events through daily scheduling of pleasurable activities, social skills training, and time management strategies (e.g., Lewinsohn & Graf, 1973). *Behavioral activation treatment for depression* (BATD) (Dimidjian et al., 2011; Lejuez et al., 2001) modifies this approach, emphasizing increased contact with positive reinforcement for healthy behaviors, thereby increasing positive mood. For example, for someone who is stuck in a "dead-end" job, therapy may include scheduling weekly trips to the library to read about career development. With BATD, the therapist and patient develop a comprehensive list of goals in major life areas. Each week, they develop more specific goals and activities to be completed by the patient (Hopko et al., 2003). As the patient completes the goals, increased positive reinforcement helps reduce depressive symptoms (e.g., Lejuez et al., 2001). A modified behavioral activation treatment has been adapted for use with adolescents (McCauley et al., 2015).

BIOLOGICAL TREATMENTS Biological treatments are most often medications designed to alter mood-regulating chemicals in the brain (and body). These treatments are generally prescribed by a psychiatrist but may also be given by family practitioners (in part because of the stigma attached to seeking psychiatric care). These treatments are efficacious in reducing symptoms of moderate to severe depression, especially when combined with psychological treatment (NICE, 2004).

First-generation antidepressants—tricyclic antidepressants and monoamine oxidase inhibitors The first drugs marketed to treat depression were the monoamine oxidase inhibitors (MAOIs) and the tricyclic **antidepressants** (TCA), sometimes called *traditional* or *first-generation antidepressants*. MAOIs treat depression by inhibiting (preventing) the action of the enzyme monoamine oxidase. Normally, this enzyme breaks down the neurotransmitters norepinephrine, serotonin, and dopamine in the brain. By preventing the enzyme from doing its work, the availability of these neurotransmitters in the neural synapses is increased, which is believed to cause the antidepressant effect.

MAOIs are efficacious, especially in people who have depressive symptoms such as hypersomnia (sleeping too much) and weight gain (Thase & Kupfer, 1996). People who take MAOIs must not eat foods containing the substance tyramine because the interaction of the drug and these foods can cause extremely high blood pressure and possibly death. Foods containing tyramine include smoked, aged, or pickled meat or fish; sauerkraut; aged cheeses; yeast extracts; fava beans; beef or chicken liver; aged sausages; game meats; red and white wines; beer; hard liquor; avocados; meat extracts; caffeine-containing beverages; chocolate; soy sauce; cottage cheese; cream cheese; yogurt; and sour cream. Owing to their potentially dangerous side effects, MAOIs are usually prescribed only for people who have not responded to other medications.

Tricyclic antidepressants work by preventing the reuptake of various neurotransmitters in the brain—primarily norepinephrine and serotonin. By blocking the reuptake of the neurotransmitter back into the neuron, they remain in the synapse longer, thereby increasing their availability for activation of the next neuron. The name of these drugs comes from the fact that they share a three-ring molecular structure. Countless randomized clinical trials document their efficacy in adults compared with placebo controls (Arroll et al., 2005), but they are less efficacious in children and adolescents (Hazell & Mirzaie, 2013). Typically, patients take the medication for 6 to 8 weeks. If the response is positive, the medication may need to be continued for many months to prevent a relapse (Ebmeier et al., 2006). These medications must not be stopped abruptly. First-generation antidepressants are often accompanied by multiple side effects, including dry mouth, constipation, bladder problems, sexual problems, blurred vision, dizziness, daytime drowsiness, and increased heart rate. Thus, they are no longer the first choice for pharmacological treatment of depression (Gartlehner et al., 2005).

Second-generation antidepressants The second-generation antidepressants include **selective serotonin reuptake inhibitors** (SSRIs) and serotonin and norepinephrine reuptake inhibitors (SNRIs) (Hansen et al., 2005). Perhaps the best-known antidepressant is fluoxetine (Prozac), which was approved in 1987 by the U.S. Food and Drug Administration (FDA). We do not fully understand how most second-generation antidepressants work, but in general, they act by selectively inhibiting the reuptake of serotonin at the presynaptic neuronal membrane, restoring the normal chemical balance (see Figure 4.10). The SNRIs inhibit both serotonin and norepinephrine reuptake as well as that of dopamine (to a lesser extent).

The SSRIs and other second-generation antidepressants appear to be as efficacious as the TCAs and MAOIs (Gartlehner et al., 2005; Magni et al., 2013). They have fewer and milder side effects than the TCAs, and patients generally tolerate them well (Anderson, 2001; Hansen et al., 2005; Magni, 2013; Taylor et al., 2006). Side effects may include sexual problems, headache, nausea, nervousness, trouble falling asleep or waking often during the night, and jitteriness.

In the early 2000s, concerns grew about a potentially lethal adverse effect of SSRIs. Several highly publicized cases led the FDA to issue a "black box" warning label, stating that antidepressants increased the risk of suicidal thinking in children and adolescents with major depressive disorder. This is the most serious warning the FDA can issue for a prescription medication. Youth treated with SSRIs need to be monitored very closely, especially during the first 4 weeks, for intensification of depression, emergence of suicidal thoughts or behavior, or behavioral changes such as sleeplessness, agitation, or social withdrawal. These substances have not been prohibited despite their potentially dangerous side effects because they provide substantial benefits for adolescents with moderate and severe depression, including many with suicidal ideation (National Institute of Mental Health, 2005).

We do not fully understand the increases in suicidal thoughts and suicidal behavior that appear to be associated with SSRI medication. Some suspect that SSRIs improve physical symptoms before mood actually lifts. So, in the early stages of treatment, young people may feel more energy, and this increased energy and ongoing depressed mood increases the probability of acting on suicidal thoughts (Hall, 2006). A review of several studies ultimately concluded that the benefits of SSRI treatment far outweigh the risks, but caution and careful monitoring are necessary (Bridge et al., 2007; Richmond & Rosen, 2005).

Electroconvulsive therapy Drug therapies are not the only biological treatment for major depressive disorder. Electroconvulsive therapy (ECT) is one of the most efficacious treatments for major depression, especially for people who are severely depressed, have not responded to medication or psychotherapy, are unable to take antidepressants, are at serious risk of suicide, or present with psychotic symptoms (Micallef-Trigona, 2014; NICE, 2003; Ren et al., 2014; UK ECT Review Group, 2003). ECT has a remission rate of 60 to 75% in these treatment-resistant cases of depression and leads to rapid relief from depressive symptoms (Eranti et al., 2007; Husain et al., 2004). ECT can also be useful in the treatment of mania (Gitlin, 2006).

ECT dates to the 1930s and has a history that concerns many people decades after it was first used to treat psychotic disorders (Cerletti & Bini, 1938). When ECT was new, patients were not given muscle relaxants, and the resulting violent seizures often caused injuries. In addition, the electrodes were placed on both sides of the head, often resulting in substantial and permanent memory loss.

Today, a muscle relaxant is administered along with a brief period of general anesthesia before ECT is carried out. Electrodes, placed at precise locations on the scalp, deliver electrical impulses, which cause brief seizures in the brain. The seizures induced are not specific to one particular brain area and appear to influence the production of a number of neurotransmitters (Post et al., 2000). Exactly how ECT works remains a mystery, but it often leads to speedier improvement in severely depressed patients than either medication or psychotherapy (Husain et al., 2004).

Bitemporal ECT is the best characterized among the possible electrode placements, but one-side (unilateral) approaches are equally efficacious and may result in less memory loss. Bifrontal ECT was developed later in order to minimize exposure of the temporal lobes and reduce memory-related side effects. A systematic review and meta-analysis found that all three placements were equally efficacious in reducing depressive symptoms, with bifrontal ECT having a slight benefit in terms of cognitive outcomes (Dunne & McLoughlin, 2012). The most common side effects of the therapy as presently administered are confusion after the procedure and temporary amnesia (Ebmeier et al., 2006; UK ECT Review Group, 2003). ECT is usually administered several times a week for a number of weeks.

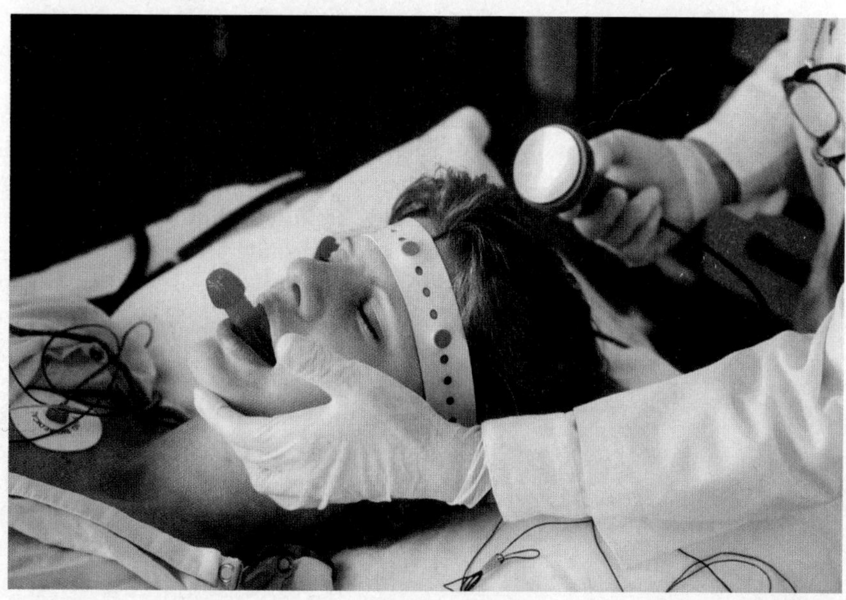

A clinician prepares a patient to undergo electroconvulsive therapy. Many precautions are taken to be sure that the patient is not injured and does not feel pain during the procedure.

Light therapy for major depressive disorder with a seasonal pattern The National Institute of Mental Health psychiatrist Norman Rosenthal first described **seasonal affective disorder** (SAD) in 1984. Now a specifier in DSM-5 states, "With a seasonal pattern this variant of major depressive disorder afflicts millions of people worldwide, and is characterized by depressive episodes that vary by season. Although some patients experience summer depression, most

Light therapy is sometimes used as a treatment for SAD.

are affected during December, January, and February. Symptoms of the winter pattern include increased appetite, increased sleep, weight gain, interpersonal difficulties, and a heavy, leaden feeling in one's limbs."

Patients with this variant are sometimes treated with *light therapy* (Terman & Terman, 2005). This involves exposure to an artificial source of bright light, usually a light box, a light visor, or a dawn simulator. These devices produce light that is approximately 10 times brighter than regular household lightbulbs. Light therapy sessions take place at the same time each day (usually in the morning) and generally last between 30 and 90 minutes. The patient sits by the light source, eyes open, so that light reaches the retina. Treatment usually begins with the onset of symptoms each winter and continues until spring.

Because full-spectrum light is not necessary to reap the benefits of light therapy, UV rays are filtered out to avoid damage to the eyes and skin. Nonetheless, there are occasional side effects, including photophobia (eye sensitivity to light), headache, fatigue, irritability, hypomania, and insomnia. In addition, light boxes are expensive and often are not covered by insurance. Despite these potential drawbacks, light therapy appears to be effective in a substantial proportion of cases of depression with a seasonal pattern (Lam & Levitt, 1999; Rohan et al., 2004).

Transcranial magnetic stimulation **Transcranial magnetic stimulation** (TMS), which received FDA approval in December 2008 for use in individuals with treatment-resistant depression, uses a magnetic coil placed over the patient's head to deliver a painless, localized electromagnetic pulse to a part of the brain (De Raedt et al., 2015). The magnetic field may be targeted to different cortical regions, but the most common form of TMS for depression treatment (repetitive TMS or rTMS) is typically carried out at high frequency over the left dorsolateral prefrontal cortex (DLPFC) (Wani et al., 2013). We do not know why the treatment works, but several clinical trials comparing it with a sham procedure have supported its use as a potentially effective alternative to ECT or medication (Ebmeier et al., 2006; Grunhaus et al., 2003; Janicak et al., 2002). TMS has fewer side effects than ECT (the most common being headache and pain at the stimulation site). Two recent systematic reviews and meta-analyses compared the efficacy of ECT vs. rTMS in the treatment of depression (Micallef-Trigona, 2014; Ren et al., 2014). Both found better efficacy in ECT vs. rTMS when examining treatment response, while Ren et al. (2014) also found that remission rates were higher for ECT treatment (52.9% vs. 33.6% for rTMS). (See Chapter 10 for a detailed description of TMS.)

Deep brain stimulation **Deep brain stimulation** (DBS) is a therapy targeting an area of the brain important for regulating negative mood changes, the subgenual cingulate region (Delaloye & Holtzheimer, 2014). DBS works by surgically implanting electrodes into specific, improperly functioning areas of the brain. These electrodes are attached by wire to a pulse generator (or "brain pacemaker") that is implanted into the chest wall. The electrodes continuously release tiny electrical impulses that deactivate (but do not kill) immediately surrounding brain cells. In this way, DBS inhibits abnormal activity in targeted parts of the brain and treats disorders characterized by overactivity. The FDA has approved DBS for use in treating Parkinson's disease and some types of bodily tremors. It has also been used to treat psychiatric disorders. DBS is FDA-approved for the treatment of obsessive-compulsive disorder (OCD), significantly improving anxiety, compulsions, and comorbid depression (Greenberg et al., 2006).

Several trials have been carried out on the use of DBS for treatment-resistant depression, targeting areas of the brain including the subcallosal cingulate cortex (SCC), the nucleus accumbens (NAcc), the anterior limb of the internal capsule (ALIC), the superolateral medial forebrain bundle (slMFB), the inferior thalamic peduncle (ITP), and the lateral habenular complex (LHb-c) (Gálvez et al., 2015). Across 7 trials, with 6 to 21 participants each and follow-up ranging from 3 to 67 months, DBS achieved response and remission rates of up to 92% and 67% respectively. The main adverse effects related to DBS are surgical complications from either the initial implant surgery or follow-up surgeries for battery replacement (Wani et al., 2013). Although more research is needed, especially in the form of sham-controlled trials, DBS may prove to be a promising intervention for people with refractory depression.

> June had suffered from recurrent depression for more than 20 years. She had been prescribed what seemed like every antidepressant on the planet and had two courses of electroconvulsive therapy. Occasionally she would find some relief, but she never seemed to be able to climb out of the pit of depression. When offered the opportunity for DBS, although frightened at first, she realized she had nothing to lose. Her experience was transformative. June reported experiencing an almost physical removal of weight from her shoulders. She said she could "see the light" for the first time in 20 years. Her description of a visceral and physical removal of weight underscored the extent to which depression had literally weighed her down both mentally and physically over the previous two decades.

Selecting a Treatment

LO 7.23 Evaluate appropriateness of treatment based on mood symptoms and patient characteristics.

With so many available options, clinicians and patients often feel challenged to determine the best treatment. The initial decision depends on several factors, including the nature and severity of symptoms, unipolar or bipolar features, psychotic features or suicidal intent, patient's age, preferences, tolerance of side effects, and treatments available in the patient's community.

Decades of placebo-controlled, randomized clinical trials indicate that major depressive disorder responds to both psychotherapy and pharmacotherapy. Interpersonal psychotherapy and CBT have the strongest empirical support (National Institute of Mental Health, 2001), and IPT may have specific beneficial effects on interpersonal functioning (Weissman, 1994). But psychodynamic approaches have not proved to be very useful (American Psychiatric Association, 2005). CBT may be less efficacious than medication in people who are severely depressed (Thase & Friedman, 1999). Combining medication and psychotherapy provides only moderate additional benefit over either treatment alone (Hollon et al., 1992). Although approximately 60% of patients respond to psychotherapeutic interventions, relapse may occur—especially if treatment is not maintained and if symptoms are not entirely remitted at the end of treatment (Prien & Kupfer, 1986). For both pharmacological and psychological interventions, continuation and maintenance treatment reduces relapse after the initial acute treatment phase ends. ECT is a viable option for individuals who are severely depressed or suicidal or cannot tolerate antidepressants.

For bipolar disorder, medication with lithium or anticonvulsants is the treatment of choice. Although drug treatment is effective, many patients continue to experience breakthrough episodes or lingering symptoms (Gitlin, 2006). Psychotherapy alone is not effective for bipolar disorder. Family therapy, interpersonal and social rhythm therapy, and cognitive-behavior therapy in combination with medication can help the patient adjust to having a chronic illness, adhere to a treatment plan, and avoid relapses (Craighead & Miklowitz, 2000; Frank et al., 1999).

Learning Objective Summaries

LO 7.21 Identify efficacious pharmacological and psychological treatments for bipolar disorder.

Medications are the primary treatment for bipolar disorder; psychotherapy alone is insufficient. Lithium and anticonvulsant medications are often used to manage bipolar disorder. Cognitive-behavioral therapy and interpersonal and social rhythm therapy can play an important role as it is a long-term disorder requiring continued care.

LO 7.22 Identify efficacious pharmacological and psychological treatments for depressive disorders.

Cognitive-behavioral therapy, interpersonal psychotherapy, and behavioral activation treatments are effective in the treatment of mild to moderate depression. A number of medications are used in the treatment of depression including the first-generation antidepressants (tricyclic antidepressants and monoamine oxidase inhibitors) as well as second-generation antidepressants including selective serotonin reuptake inhibitors (SSRIs) and serotonin and norepinephrine reuptake inhibitors (SNRIs).

LO 7.23 Evaluate appropriateness of treatment based on mood symptoms and patient characteristics.

Decisions regarding how to treat individuals with bipolar disorder and major depressive disorder should consider several factors, including the nature and severity of symptoms, unipolar or bipolar features, psychotic features or suicidal intent, patient's age, preferences, tolerance of side effects, and treatments available in the patient's community.

Critical Thinking Question

With only half of depressed individuals receiving health care and less than a quarter of them receiving adequate care, how could we improve health service delivery to individuals suffering from major depressive disorder?

Real SCIENCE Real LIFE

Latisha—Treatment of Major Depressive Disorder with Peripartum Onset

THE PATIENT

Latisha was a 22-year-old senior at a college in the Northeast. She appeared at Student Health complaining of sadness and tearfulness, a drop in her grades, and a sense of being lost about her future. She awakened too early in the morning, had lost her appetite, and had lost interest in the things that she normally enjoyed. She sometimes thought it would be better if she were dead. Because of her religion, Latisha stated that she would never commit suicide, but she wished that the Lord would take her life. She reported no symptoms of mania and no psychosis.

THE PROBLEM

Latisha had been in a stable relationship for 3 years. She and Ted had been inseparable, and everyone, including Latisha, thought they would graduate from college, get married, and live happily ever after. It felt like a slap in the face when Ted announced a month ago that he no longer wanted to be in a serious relationship. Soon Latisha saw him walking arm in arm with another woman. She was devastated. Even more important, she watched as her friends got jobs and chose their life paths after college, and after 3 changes of her major, she was lost and directionless.

Latisha came from a healthy and happy family. Her maternal grandmother, with whom she was quite close, had died a year ago. Latisha was not terribly independent, latching onto other people and following the crowd. Of note, her mother, two aunts, and her brother had all been treated with antidepressants. Latisha had never used drugs, drank alcohol occasionally, and had been drunk only a few times. She was physically healthy. Her only medications were vitamins and the birth control pill.

ASSESSING THE SITUATION

First, what would you say is the etiology of this disorder? What factors precipitated the illness? Second, which psychotherapy approach would you choose treat it? Why? Is there a role for medications? Design a plan to help Latisha get over her symptoms.

THE TREATMENT

The clinician diagnosed Latisha with major depressive disorder and recommended interpersonal psychotherapy (IPT). The therapist and Latisha together identified her main problem as role transitions; grief over Ted was secondary. Therapy focused on helping Latisha make the transition to independent life. She saw that she relied on others and that it was critical for her to make her own choices. With support from her therapist, she started to emerge from her depression after about 3 weeks and sought career counseling. After 8 weeks, her mood lifted. She started sleeping better, spent more time with her friends, and improved her grades.

Latisha completed graduate school and landed an excellent job as a media relations manager in a hospital associated with the university medical school. She married a supportive man, and all seemed well. Two months after the birth of her first child, at 27, Latisha was unable to shake a pervasive sense of feeling overwhelmed and was nearly incapacitated with depression.

She cried all day, could barely muster the energy to shower, and was unable to care for her baby. When the baby cried at night, she would just bury her head under the pillow and lament what a horrible mother she was.

After a thorough evaluation, a psychiatrist diagnosed Latisha with depression with peripartum onset. After 2 weeks on an SSRI, she was able to play with her daughter. Her sense of humor came back, and her husband felt comfortable leaving Latisha with the baby. After 5 weeks, she felt much better—although she still was not back to her normal self. She saw a psychologist who specialized in peripartum depression and began a course of CBT. After a few weeks, Latisha could recognize the cycle of automatic thoughts that perpetuated her low mood. Whenever she perceived herself as failing at a task of motherhood, she would think, "I'm a terrible mother." She worked to replace the thought with less self-deprecating thoughts. She eventually climbed back to her normal level of functioning and engaged in all aspects of mothering. After 12 weeks, she went back to work part-time. She felt some pangs of regret about leaving the baby in day care, but she was glad to be back at work and continued to enjoy time with her daughter.

THE TREATMENT OUTCOME

Latisha continued to take SSRIs for another year before the medication was gradually withdrawn. Her psychiatrist helped her to identify warning signs of depression because Latisha now had had two episodes in her lifetime. For her, changes in sleep and appetite signaled a need to seek treatment immediately. Therapy gave her new tools for life. She began using them in other aspects of her life as well when she recognized dysfunctional cognitions.

Key Terms

antidepressants, p. 270
atypical depression, p. 239
behavioral activation, p. 269
bipolar disorder, p. 231
bipolar I, p. 232
bipolar II, p. 232
bipolar and depressive disorders, p. 231
cyclothymic disorder, p. 235
deep brain stimulation, p. 272
depression, p. 231
disruptive mood regulation disorder, p. 242
double depression, p. 242
dysthymia, p. 241
electroconvulsive therapy, p. 267
hypomania, p. 234
learned helplessness, p. 263
lithium, p. 267
major depressive disorder, p. 239
mania, p. 231
mixed state, p. 234
persistent depressive disorder, p. 241
premenstrual dysphoric disorder, p. 242
psychological autopsy, p. 254
seasonal affective disorder, p. 271
selective serotonin reuptake inhibitors, p. 270
suicidal ideation, p. 249
transcranial magnetic stimulation, p. 272

Chapter 8

Feeding and Eating Disorders

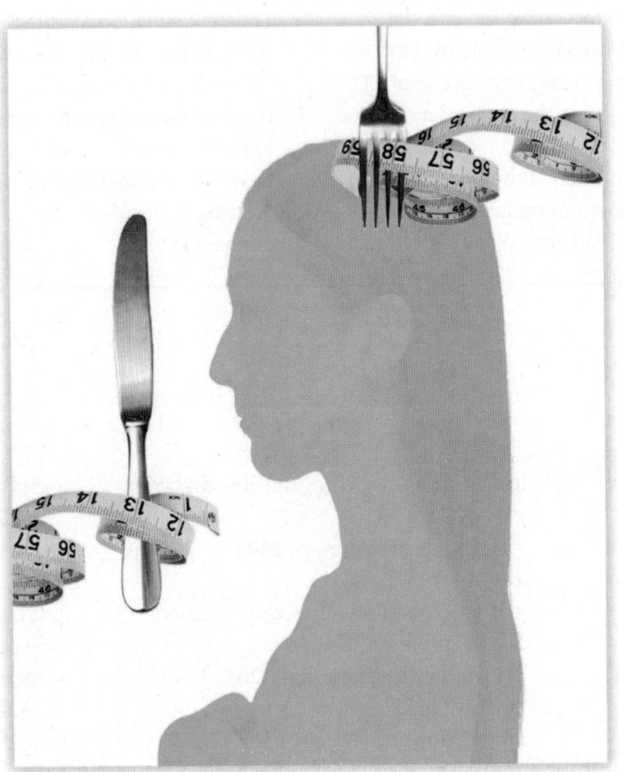

Chapter Learning Objectives

Anorexia Nervosa	**LO 8.1**	Describe the component features of anorexia nervosa.
	LO 8.2	Trace the occurrence of anorexia nervosa across various segments of the population and characterize its typical clinical course.
	LO 8.3	Characterize personality traits and patterns of comorbidity in anorexia nervosa.
Bulimia Nervosa	**LO 8.4**	Describe the component features of bulimia nervosa.
	LO 8.5	Trace the occurrence of bulimia nervosa across various segments of the population and characterize its typical clinical course.
	LO 8.6	Characterize personality traits and patterns of comorbidity in bulimia nervosa.
Binge-Eating Disorder	**LO 8.7**	Describe the component features of binge-eating disorder.
	LO 8.8	Trace the occurrence of binge-eating disorder across various segments of the population and characterize its typical clinical course.

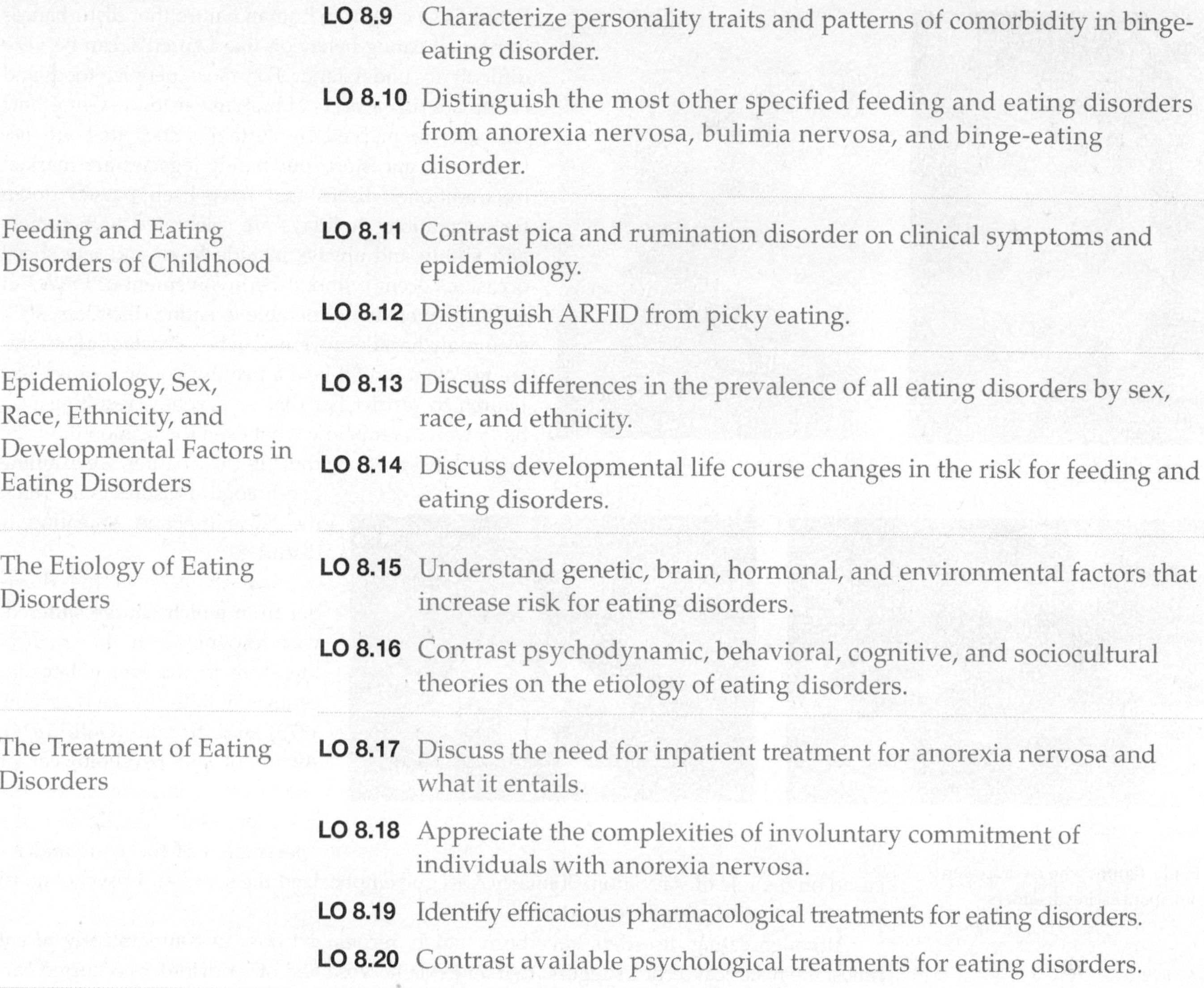

	LO 8.9	Characterize personality traits and patterns of comorbidity in binge-eating disorder.
	LO 8.10	Distinguish the most other specified feeding and eating disorders from anorexia nervosa, bulimia nervosa, and binge-eating disorder.
Feeding and Eating Disorders of Childhood	**LO 8.11**	Contrast pica and rumination disorder on clinical symptoms and epidemiology.
	LO 8.12	Distinguish ARFID from picky eating.
Epidemiology, Sex, Race, Ethnicity, and Developmental Factors in Eating Disorders	**LO 8.13**	Discuss differences in the prevalence of all eating disorders by sex, race, and ethnicity.
	LO 8.14	Discuss developmental life course changes in the risk for feeding and eating disorders.
The Etiology of Eating Disorders	**LO 8.15**	Understand genetic, brain, hormonal, and environmental factors that increase risk for eating disorders.
	LO 8.16	Contrast psychodynamic, behavioral, cognitive, and sociocultural theories on the etiology of eating disorders.
The Treatment of Eating Disorders	**LO 8.17**	Discuss the need for inpatient treatment for anorexia nervosa and what it entails.
	LO 8.18	Appreciate the complexities of involuntary commitment of individuals with anorexia nervosa.
	LO 8.19	Identify efficacious pharmacological treatments for eating disorders.
	LO 8.20	Contrast available psychological treatments for eating disorders.

Having excelled in middle school, Lauren was accepted into a prestigious boarding high school that focused on science and mathematics. At her pre-school physical, her pediatrician weighed her and said, "My, you are filling out nicely." Embarrassed, Lauren went home and scrutinized her body in the mirror. She saw her budding breasts and her expanding hips and did not like it one bit. She turned sideways and looked at the protrusion where her flat stomach used to be and was determined to make it go away. Marshaling her determination, she developed a strict regimen of running (2 miles in the morning, 5 miles in the evening) and a "healthy balanced diet" that followed the USDA MyPlate guidelines in terms of nutrients but contained only 400 calories per day. She rationalized that if she got something from all the major food groups, she'd be fine. But fats and oils made her nervous. She told her parents that she needed discipline to excel in this very competitive high school. She started wearing layers and layers of clothes, checking her weight on the scale four times per day, feeling her hipbones to make sure they were protruding, and skipping family meals.

At first her parents were impressed that she was taking her educational opportunity so seriously, but then they started to worry as her temper began to flare. If they ran out of one of her preferred foods, she would lash out at her mother for not having stocked up. She became more and more rigid and added 300 sit-ups to her exercise regimen before bed. One day, her mother accidentally walked into the bathroom as Lauren was getting into the shower, and she was shocked by the emaciated body she saw: ribs, vertebrae, a prominent clavicle. Her daughter looked like a concentration camp victim.

This discovery occurred 2 weeks before school was to start. Lauren's parents took her back to the pediatrician only to find that she had lost 30 pounds, dropping to 85 pounds at 5′5″. Their daughter was severely underweight. Rather than starting school in the fall, Lauren spent 2 months on an inpatient eating disorders unit where her weight gain was carefully monitored by a dietitian and physicians and where she received the support that she needed from a psychologist to regain a healthy weight and to deal with the underlying anxiety she felt about her ability to succeed in the high-pressure environment of the math and science school.

Dennis Quaid

Lady Gaga

Russell Brand

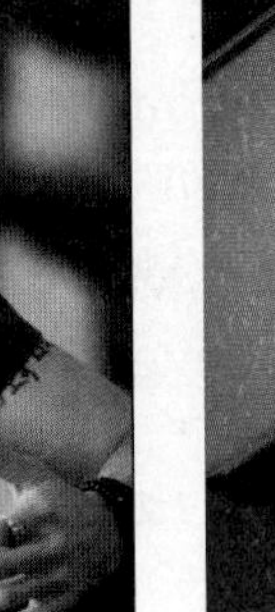

Katie Couric

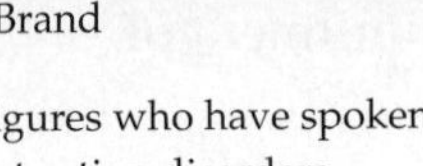

Public figures who have spoken out about eating disorders.

Eating is so central to human nature that disturbances in normal eating behavior, like Lauren's, can be very difficult to understand. For most people, food and eating are rich aspects of human existence. Our ethnic legacies are marked by certain dishes that are native to our ancestors; our family legacies are marked by traditional dishes that have been passed down for generations; holidays are celebrated with friends and family and always include food; and few social occasions occur without the involvement of food. But for those who are vulnerable to eating disorders, such seemingly harmless events can be devastatingly frightening. What would lead a healthy young woman like Lauren to restrict her diet so severely, resulting in a body weight far below what even the fashion industry might consider to be thin? In this chapter, we examine psychological disorders in which the basic function of eating is disturbed.

Anorexia nervosa, the disorder from which Lauren suffered, was recognized in the medical literature in the late nineteenth century in both France (Lasègue, 1873) and Britain (Gull, 1874). Aware of the psychological or "nervous" components of the disorder, Gull highlighted the "perversion of the will" and focused on the role of starvation. Similarly, Lasègue emphasized the social and psychological factors associated with the disorder.

Although eating disorders have been widely recognized only in comparatively recent times, the historical record suggests that anorexia nervosa and other disorders occurred earlier. Bell (1985) provides vivid accounts of saints who starved themselves pursuing purity or devotion to God. Intriguingly, this is a classic example of how social context may alter the clinical expression of a disorder. The self-starvation mirrored the symptoms that we see today in anorexia nervosa, yet the cultural context embedded the disorder in religion. Today, as in Lauren's case, we see the symptoms in a very different sociocultural context—one that is interpreted as a young woman's internalization of the ideal of extreme thinness.

Today almost everyone knows someone who has suffered from an eating disorder—from actors to politicians, acquaintances, and family members. (See photos above.) Anorexia nervosa (see "DSM-5: Anorexia Nervosa") has the highest mortality rate of any psychological disorder, yet after decades of research, we are only beginning to uncover the causes of this perplexing illness.

Anorexia Nervosa

Clinical Features of Anorexia Nervosa

LO 8.1 Describe the component features of anorexia nervosa.

Anorexia nervosa is a serious condition marked by a restriction of energy intake relative to needed energy requirements, resulting in significantly low body weight in the context of age, sex, developmental trajectory, and physical health. Younger patients fail to achieve the weight (and often height) increases expected as part of normal growth. Psychologists measure just how thin their patients are by calculating **body mass index (BMI)**.

Weight, in kilograms, is divided by height, in meters squared (kg/m^2). See Table 8.1 for the cutoffs for underweight, normal weight, overweight, and obese. Table 8.2 gives examples of just what these measures mean in terms of an average woman (5′6″) and an average man (5′11″). BMI is not a perfect measure in everyone. For example, a professional football player might be 6′3″ tall and weigh 240 pounds. According to the BMI charts, he would be considered to be obese (BMI = 30 kg/m^2). But in reality, the man has very little body fat and quite a bit of lean muscle. Moreover, he is in great physical shape. Another important consideration is when measuring BMI in children, both sex and age are considered, and the appropriate metric is BMI percentile.

Table 8.1 BMI Categories

BMI	Weight Status
Below 18.5	Underweight
18.5–24.9	Normal
25.0–29.9	Overweight
30.0 and above	Obese

Table 8.2 BMI to Weight Examples for Average Woman and Man

BMI	Woman 5′6″ Age 20 Weight (lbs.)	Man 5′11″ Age 20 Weight (lbs.)
13.0	80	93
18.5	114	132
21.0	130	150
25.0	155	179
30.0	186	215
40.0	248	287

SOURCE: http://www.cdc.gov/healthyweight/assessing/bmi/adult_BMI/english_bmi_calculator/bmi_calculator.html

Anorexia nervosa patients are noticeably thin—although they may conceal their *emaciation* (severe underweight) by wearing layers of clothes or otherwise hiding their bodies. According to the DSM-5, atypical anorexia nervosa can be diagnosed if an individual has lost a substantial amount of weight even if she or he remains within or above the normal weight range. Anorexia nervosa has two subtypes: restricting and binge eating/purging. In the classic restricting subtype, patients maintain their low weight only by reducing their caloric intake and increasing their physical activity. In the binge eating/purging subtype, individuals may engage in **binge eating** (eating an unusually large amount of food in a short period of time and feeling out of control), **purging** (self-inducing vomiting or using laxatives, diuretics [water pills], or enemas), or both behaviors. Binge eating occurs in about one-quarter and purging in about half of individuals with anorexia nervosa (Hoffman et al., 2012).

One clinical feature of anorexia nervosa that can be terribly perplexing to friends and families is an intense fear of gaining weight or becoming fat even though the person is seriously underweight. Individuals with anorexia nervosa, even in the most extreme phases of emaciation, fear weight gain. They are not merely afraid of becoming fat; they are terrified by even the smallest amount of weight gain. This is commonly expressed as "feeling fat," although the precise meaning of that phrase differs by individual, as "fat" is not truly a feeling.

DSM-5

Criteria for Anorexia Nervosa

A. Restriction of energy intake relative to requirements, leading to a significantly low body weight in the context of age, sex, developmental trajectory, and physical health. *Significantly low weight* is defined as a weight that is less than minimally normal or, for children and adolescents, less than that minimally expected.

B. Intense fear of gaining weight or of becoming fat, or persistent behavior that interferes with weight gain, even though at a significantly low weight.

C. Disturbance in the way in which one's body weight or shape is experienced, undue influence of body weight or shape on self-evaluation, or persistent lack of recognition of the seriousness of the current low body weight.

(F50.01) Restricting type: During the last 3 months, the individual has not engaged in recurrent episodes of binge eating or purging behavior (i.e., self-induced vomiting or the misuse of laxatives, diuretics, or enemas). This subtype describes presentations in which weight loss is accomplished primarily through dieting, fasting, and/or excessive exercise.

(F50.02) Binge-eating/purging type: During the last 3 months, the individual has engaged in recurrent episodes of binge eating or purging (i.e., self-induced vomiting or the misuse of laxatives, diuretics, or enemas).

Watch NATASHA: ANOREXIA

Other characteristics of anorexia nervosa exist, and patients may experience some or all of them. The first characteristic is experiential and possibly perceptual, in which patients *experience their weight or shape as large even when they are emaciated.* The mechanism of this perceptual distortion remains unknown, but it may work in the same way that some people who have been overweight and lose weight still perceive themselves as overweight. Betsy recalls,

> I remember during treatment when Anne, the dietitian, was working with me to include a muffin for breakfast. I put the muffin on my plate and just stared at it. It may as well have been a tarantula or a python. I took a bite and I could literally see my thighs getting fatter. The muffin was going straight to my thighs. After four bites, I just panicked and threw the muffin away. I had to go running to get rid of it.

The second characteristic is *placing undue importance on body weight and shape as a measure of self-evaluation.* People with anorexia nervosa are totally preoccupied by weight. In fact, their self-worth and self-esteem can be almost entirely determined by their weight or shape. Slight weight increases can lead to a downward spiral of mood and self-worth.

The third characteristic is *lack of recognition of the seriousness of the low body weight.* Even when facing severe medical complications, individuals with anorexia nervosa may insist that everything is fine. This creates considerable problems in reaching and accepting treatment and, on occasion, can result in patients being hospitalized involuntarily (see Chapter 15) because they are a clear danger to themselves. It remains unknown how they are able to survive in extreme negative energy balance (energy output > energy input) for so long.

Many individuals with anorexia nervosa see their bodies as larger than they actually are. The mechanism for this distortion remains unknown.

> Kaylee suffered from anorexia nervosa for 3 years, and her weight dropped precipitously from 120 to 70 pounds (BMI · 12 kg/m^2). Despite this dangerously low weight, she maintained her rigorous exercise schedule of running 5 miles per day, doing 400 sit-ups, and spending 1 hour on the exercise bike.

In previous versions of the diagnostic criteria for anorexia nervosa, **amenorrhea**, or the absence of menstruation for at least 3 consecutive months, was a requirement. Amenorrhea is a common response to starvation and weight loss as the body shuts down reproductive functioning in the face of famine. In recognition that there are no meaningful differences between individuals with anorexia nervosa who do and do not menstruate (Attia & Roberto, 2009; Gendall et al., 2006), this criterion was removed in DSM-5. Nonetheless, menstrual functioning should always be assessed in individuals with eating disorders as it can be an important indicator of severity.

Table 8.3 Features Associated with Anorexia Nervosa

Physical Features	Psychological/Behavioral Features
Dehydration	Cognitive impairment
Electrolyte imbalances (sodium, potassium levels)	Body checking (touching and pinching to measure fatness)
Osteoporosis (decreased bone density)	Depression
Lanugo hair (fine downy hair on body)	Anxiety
Dry brittle hair	Low self-esteem
Low body temperature	Ritualistic behaviors
Hypotension (low blood pressure)	Extreme perfectionism
Bradycardia (slow heart rate)	Self-consciousness
Growth retardation	
Bloating	
Constipation	
Fidgeting	
Loss of tooth enamel and dentin	

In addition to the diagnostic features, anorexia nervosa is associated with a long list of psychological and medical features. Psychologically, depression and anxiety are commonly present. Medically, patients often have slow heart rates, low blood pressure, reduced bone density, gastrointestinal disturbances, and lowered body temperature (which might explain their tendency to wear layers of clothes, even in warm temperatures) (Zipfel et al., 2015). Nearly every bodily system is adversely affected. Table 8.3 presents additional clinical features associated with anorexia nervosa.

Epidemiology and Course of Anorexia Nervosa

LO 8.2 Trace the occurrence of anorexia nervosa across various segments of the population and characterize its typical clinical course.

How common is anorexia nervosa? The lifetime prevalence of anorexia nervosa is 0.9% in women and 0.3% in men (Hudson et al., 2007). Many more girls and women (between 1 and 3%) suffer from less severe forms of anorexia nervosa (McKnight Investigators, 2003; Stice et al., 2013; Swanson, 2011; Wittchen et al., 1998), and individuals with these *subthreshold conditions* can experience significant social and occupational impairment. Many of our previous prevalence estimates are based on earlier versions of anorexia nervosa criteria, which included the amenorrhea criterion. Prevalence estimates may increase with the removal of that criterion in DSM-5 (Dellava et al., 2011; Mancuso et al., 2015; Ornstein et al., 2013). The lifetime prevalence of DSM-5 anorexia nervosa in adolescents has been estimated to be 1.7% in girls and 0.1% in boys (Smink et al., 2014).

Anorexia nervosa also occurs in boys and men, although less frequently. The disorder typically begins in adolescence, but more recently, young children and older adults have been reported to suffer from classic anorexia nervosa (Lask & Bryant-Waugh, 2000; Madden et al., 2009; Mangweth-Matzek et al., 2014; Pinhas et al., 2011). Puberty may be a high-risk period due to hormonal changes and dysregulations that interact with neurotransmitter functioning, brain maturity, and genetic factors.

Although the incidence rate (number of new cases) of anorexia nervosa remained stable over the past several decades, there has been an increase in the high-risk group of 15- to 19-year-old girls (Smink et al., 2012), which has the highest incidence of any age group (Micali et al., 2013). Accurate estimates are difficult to obtain because many individuals with anorexia nervosa are unable to recognize the seriousness of their low weight, and many people (especially those with subthreshold anorexia nervosa) never seek treatment.

We do know that anorexia nervosa tends to cluster in certain segments of the population. These segments include the entertainment industry and sports in which undue emphasis is placed on body shape and weight as part of performance. Actors, dancers, models, and athletes are at greater risk of developing the disorder than other groups. "Real People, Real Disorders: Karen Carpenter" presents the well-known story of the death of singer Karen Carpenter from anorexia nervosa.

Who develops anorexia nervosa, and what is life like during the illness and after recovery? Even after recovery, people who have suffered from anorexia nervosa tend to continue to have low BMIs (Dellava et al., 2011; Sullivan et al., 1998). In addition, they can suffer from **osteoporosis** (decreased bone density) (Franzoni et al., 2014; Misra, 2008), major depression (Mischoulon et al., 2011; Sullivan et al., 1998), neuropsychological impairment (Danner et al., 2012), and difficulties with fertility and childbirth (Hoffman et al., 2012). The course of anorexia nervosa can be protracted and often includes periods of relapse, remission, and crossover to bulimia nervosa. A substantial number of individuals who start with anorexia nervosa develop bulimic symptoms at some point during the course of their illness—usually during the first 5 years (Bulik et al., 1997; Castellini et al., 2011; Eckert et al., 1995; Eddy et al., 2008; Tozzi et al., 2005). Bardone-Cone et al. (2010) suggest that a stringent definition of recovery should be used—one that combines physical weight restoration with the absence of disordered eating behaviors as well as psychological recovery. When such a definition is operationalized, those in full recovery from an eating disorder are nearly indistinguishable from healthy individuals who have no eating disorder history.

Many people are surprised to discover that anorexia nervosa has the highest mortality rate of any psychiatric disorder, estimated to be 5% per decade of follow-up (Sullivan, 1995). People with anorexia nervosa are 5.2 to 10.5 times more likely to die than their age- and sex-matched peers (Birmingham et al., 2005; Chesney et al., 2014; Keshaviah et al., 2014), with reports of even higher standardized mortality ratios among adolescents and young adults ages 15 to 24 years (11.5 times) and adults ages 25 to 44 years (14.0 times) (Hoang et al., 2014). The principal causes of death include both direct effects of starvation and suicide (Birmingham et al., 2005; Rosling et al., 2011). For these reasons, friends and family members always need to take anorexia nervosa seriously. Thinking that it is just a phase or that someone will "snap out of it" is dismissing a potentially deadly disease.

Personality and Comorbidity in Anorexia Nervosa

LO 8.3 Characterize personality traits and patterns of comorbidity in anorexia nervosa.

When we look back at Lauren's case, we have to ask whether there were any hints in her personality that might hold the clue to why she developed this devastating illness. Some personality traits do seem to come before the eating disorder, get worse during the eating disorder, and often persist after recovery. The most important is *perfectionism*. People who develop anorexia nervosa are often described as model children and model students who set extremely high standards for themselves. They also apply that perfectionism to their pursuit of thinness and hold themselves to dieting standards above what others could possibly attain. Other common personality factors are *obsessionality* (going over and over things in their mind) and *neuroticism* (being a worrier and having difficulty shaking things off). Research in female twins also suggests that individuals with AN have a high need for order and are particularly sensitive to praise and reward (Atiye et al., 2015; Bardone-Cone et al., 2007; Bulik et al., 2007; Wade et al., 2008; Wonderlich et al., 2005). This cluster of personality traits may help explain why adolescence and young adulthood are typical periods of risk for the development of eating disorders. Many of the developmental tasks of this life period involve substantial change and encounters with unfamiliar stimuli (e.g., puberty, leaving home for college, dating). Such transitions can be challenging even for healthy youths. People who are worriers, tend toward unwavering perfectionism, and find change difficult

REAL People REAL Disorders

Karen Carpenter—The Dangers of Syrup of Ipecac

Karen Carpenter and her brother, Richard, were a famous 1970s musical duo. The siblings won three Grammy awards during their career and performed at the White House. Their worldwide popularity earned them a star on the Hollywood Walk of Fame. On February 4, 1983, Karen Carpenter died from complications associated with the binge eating/purging subtype of anorexia nervosa. Although her fans were aware of her diminishing size, her death came as a shock. It is believed that she died of heart failure caused by abuse of ipecac syrup, which she used to induce vomiting. Intended as a lifesaving remedy to induce vomiting in those who have ingested poison or overdosed on medication, syrup of ipecac is toxic and can be deadly. After Karen Carpenter's death, the dangers of ipecac were brought to public attention. One of its major dangers is that it is easily accessible. It is sometimes found in household first aid kits and can be bought in drugstores.

When used properly, the syrup is a valuable medical tool, but when used repeatedly or in increasingly high doses, it is highly toxic to the heart. Misuse of ipecac syrup can lead to irregular heartbeat, seizures, dehydration, lethargy, respiratory complications, hemorrhaging, shock, electrolyte abnormalities, high blood pressure, cardiac arrest, and death.

Karen Carpenter's tragic story exemplifies the dangers of syrup of ipecac abuse and has increased public awareness of the serious consequences of anorexia nervosa.

SOURCE: Read more about Karen Carpenter's life in *Little Girl Blue: The Life of Karen Carpenter (Schmidt, 2011).*

may experience this period of life as a trigger for an underlying predisposition to eating disorders. Addressing these fundamental underlying personality traits is often an important aspect of treatment.

People with anorexia often suffer from anxiety, depression, and other psychological disorders. Up to 80% will experience major depression at some time during their lives (Fernandez-Aranda et al., 2007), and up to 75% will suffer from anxiety disorders (Bulik et al., 1997; Godart et al., 2002; Kaye et al., 2004), especially obsessive-compulsive disorder (Kaye et al., 2004). It is particularly interesting that anxiety disorders, including social phobia, posttraumatic stress disorder, generalized anxiety disorder, and obsessive-compulsive disorder, are often present before an eating disorder develops (Kaye et al., 2004; Raney et al., 2008; Swinbourne et al., 2012). To some, this suggests that anxiety may increase a person's risk for developing anorexia nervosa. If this is the case, early detection and treatment of anxiety disorders might prevent the development of eating disorders, at least for some people. Even after recovery, depression and anxiety commonly persist (Sullivan et al., 1998). A subset of individuals with anorexia nervosa also have features of autism spectrum disorders, and their family members may be at greater risk (Baron-Cohen et al., 2013; Råstam & Wentz, 2003), although this pattern may not be specific to anorexia nervosa (Koch et al, 2015). Effective treatment for anorexia nervosa must address all comorbid disorders to completely restore healthy functioning.

Learning Objective Summaries

LO 8.1 Describe the component features of anorexia nervosa.

Anorexia nervosa is marked by a restriction of energy intake relative to needed energy requirements, resulting in significantly low body weight. Individuals have an intense fear of gaining weight or becoming fat, may perceive their body weight and shape inaccurately, put undue influence of shape and weight as related to their self-evaluation, or be unable to recognize the seriousness of the low body weight.

LO 8.2 Trace the occurrence of anorexia nervosa across various segments of the population and characterize its typical clinical course.

Anorexia nervosa is more common in females than males and typically begins around puberty, although it can onset at any age. The disorder does cluster in certain segments of the population in which emphasis is put on behaviors that restrict weight. The course of anorexia nervosa can be protracted and often includes periods of relapse, remission, and crossover to bulimia nervosa. Anorexia nervosa has the highest mortality rate of any psychiatric disorder.

LO 8.3 Characterize personality traits and patterns of comorbidity in anorexia nervosa.

Individuals with anorexia nervosa commonly display perfectionism, obesssionality, neuroticism, harm avoidance, and difficulties with change or when encountering unfamiliar stimuli. The majority of individuals with anorexia nervosa also suffer from major depressive disorder and anxiety disorders. The anxiety disorders typically begin before anorexia nervosa.

Critical Thinking Question

Jasmine lost 15 pounds and seemed to be exercising all the time. She was focused on only eating healthy foods and stopped having dinners with the family. When her mother raised concerns, her dad said that all three of his sisters had gone through phases like this. He recommended just waiting it out because, just like sucking her thumb and being afraid of the dark, this too will pass. Why should parents never dismiss weight preoccupation and excessive exercise as a harmless phase?

Bulimia Nervosa

Danielle was 21 years old when she first came to the eating disorders service. She reported 4 years of untreated binge eating and self-induced vomiting. Her high-risk binge times were in the evening when she would close the blinds in her kitchen and, in her words, "go hog wild." A typical binge included a gallon of ice cream, dry cereal straight from the box, and sometimes a whole package of cookies. Then she would switch from sweet to salty and start with chips and anything else she could find. In the past year, desperate to control her weight, she began taking laxatives. Her use started with some herbs from the health food store but soon progressed to stronger laxatives. First she took the recommended dose, but then she needed more to get the desired effect. In the months before she sought treatment, Danielle lost her job and was basically housebound in her parents' home. She was binge eating and purging more than 20 times per day and taking more than 70 laxatives each night. She had developed large ulcers and scrapes in her esophagus because she was pushing objects down her throat to induce vomiting. She had had two emergency room visits for dehydration. On one visit, a blood test showed her potassium level to be dangerously low. After she was stabilized medically, she was admitted to a partial hospitalization program for eating disorders. She had difficulty adhering to the hospital's nonsmoking rules, and she frequently disappeared from the treatment facility during the day. When faced with the ultimatum of adhering to the program rules or being discharged against medical advice, she opted to leave. Two days later, Danielle was again in the emergency room with dehydration, an irregular heartbeat, and a low potassium level. This time she was admitted to a medical floor for monitoring, later to be transferred to an inpatient eating disorders program.

Clinical Features of Bulimia Nervosa

LO 8.4 Describe the component features of bulimia nervosa.

Bulimia nervosa (see "DSM-5: Bulimia Nervosa") can occur at any body weight. It is characterized by recurrent episodes of binge eating in combination with recurrent inappropriate *compensatory behaviors* to prevent weight gain. Binge eating is the consumption of an amount of food in a discrete period of time that is definitely larger than most people would consume. Unlike simple overeating, the hallmark feature of a binge is a sense of lack of control over eating. The person cannot stop the urge to binge once it has begun or has difficulty ending the eating episode even when long past being full. Some patients talk about a trance

DSM-5

Criteria for Bulimia Nervosa

A. Recurrent episodes of binge eating. An episode of binge eating is characterized by both of the following:

1. Eating, in a discrete period of time (e.g., within any 2-hour period), an amount of food that is definitely larger than what most individuals would eat in a similar period of time under similar circumstances.
2. A sense of lack of control over eating during the episode (e.g., a feeling that one cannot stop eating or control what or how much one is eating).

B. Recurrent inappropriate compensatory behaviors in order to prevent weight gain, such as self-induced vomiting; misuse of laxatives, diuretics, or other medications; fasting; or excessive exercise.

C. The binge eating and inappropriate compensatory behaviors both occur, on average, at least once a week for 3 months.

D. Self-evaluation is unduly influenced by body shape and weight.

E. The disturbance does not occur exclusively during episodes of anorexia nervosa.

or a "binge mode" in which everything else melts away during this time. Running out of food, being interrupted by other people, feeling physically uncomfortable, guilt, or experiencing an extreme urge to purge usually stop the binge.

Placing an actual caloric level on what constitutes a binge is difficult. Most agree that about 1,000 calories is the minimum amount to be considered a binge—but in some cases, as many as 20,000 calories may be consumed, and there is considerable variability in the composition of binges (Fitzgibbon & Blackman, 2000). The way to judge is to ask whether the amount of food is more than a typical person would eat under similar circumstances. What is most important is whether overeating is coupled with a sense of loss of control (Latner et al., 2007). Indeed, some people (especially those with anorexia nervosa) might feel out of control even when they eat relatively small amounts of food. So someone with anorexia nervosa might say she binged after eating two cookies. The term *subjective binge* defines eating a typical or even small amount of food (e.g., a cookie) coupled with the feeling that the eating is out of control. This is in contrast to an *objective binge,* which is defined as eating a comparatively large amount of food plus feeling out of control.

The pattern of binge eating also varies. The frequency can range from occasionally to a few times per week to 20 or 30 times per day. Once per week for 3 months is the required frequency for a threshold diagnosis of bulimia nervosa. Some people become locked in an entrenched binge–purge cycle, which comes to dominate their lives. For Danielle, evenings were clearly her high-risk times for binge eating, and she became locked into a vicious cycle of binge eating and purging that could not be interrupted.

Inappropriate compensatory behaviors are any actions that a person uses to counteract a binge or to prevent weight gain. These behaviors include self-induced vomiting; misuse of laxatives, diuretics, enemas, or other agents; fasting; and excessive exercise. It is important to note that some people purge without binge eating (see "Other Specified Feeding and Eating Disorders"). People with bulimia nervosa tend to be either of normal weight or overweight. Many calories associated with the binge are absorbed (Kaye et al., 1993), and those calories lead to weight gain. Actually, laxatives, which work in the colon (after all of the nutrients have been absorbed in the stomach and the small intestine), are ineffective but dangerous purge agents. Minimal calories consumed are lost (Bo-Linn et al., 1983), but losing water and necessary electrolytes (such as potassium) makes abusing laxatives very dangerous.

In addition to the core symptoms of bulimia nervosa, many other physical and psychological features exist. Some are similar to those of individuals with anorexia nervosa, but others are quite distinct. Table 8.4 presents additional clinical features of bulimia nervosa.

Table 8.4 Features Associated with Bulimia Nervosa

Physical Features	Psychological/Behavioral Features
Dehydration	Depression
Electrolyte imbalances (sodium and potassium levels)	Low self-esteem
Acid reflux	Ritualistic behaviors
Ruptures of esophagus	Extreme perfectionism
Loss of tooth enamel and dentin	Self-consciousness
Swollen parotid glands	Anxiety
Gastrointestinal complications	Alcohol and drug abuse
Irregular menstruation	Irritability
Constipation	Impulsive spending
Bloating	Shoplifting

Epidemiology and Course of Bulimia Nervosa

LO 8.5 Trace the occurrence of bulimia nervosa across various segments of the population and characterize its typical clinical course.

Many people with bulimia nervosa keep their behavior secret because of the stigma and shame attached to it. Estimates based on previous DSM-IV-TR criteria suggest that the prevalence is about 1 to 3% for women and 0.1 to 0.5% for men across Westernized countries (Hoek & van Hoeken, 2003; Hudson et al., 2007; Keski-Rahkonen et al., 2009; Preti et al., 2009). When subthreshold forms of bulimia nervosa are included, the estimate is closer to 5 to 6%. This percentage range is probably more realistic because the frequency and duration criteria for bulimia in the DSM are really just arbitrary cutoffs. In other words, even if a person does not meet all the diagnostic criteria, engaging in any binge eating and purging is unhealthy and potentially dangerous. Prevalence estimates may increase somewhat with DSM-5 criteria, as the previous frequency and duration criteria were more stringent at twice per week for 3 months (Allen et al., 2013; Flament et al., 2015; Trace, 2012).

Is the incidence of bulimia nervosa rising? Few data exist to address this question, but individuals born after 1960 are at greater risk for the disorder (Kendler et al., 1991), suggesting that bulimia nervosa is a more "modern" phenomenon than anorexia nervosa. Eating disorder behaviors such as binge eating, purging, and restricting do appear to have risen in the decade between 1995 and 2005 (Hay et al., 2008), but research is inconclusive on whether the incidence of bulimia nervosa has been rising, falling, or remaining stable—studies have shown all three trends (Micali et al., 2013; Smink et al., 2012; Steinhausen & Jensen, 2015). Some contend that bulimia nervosa is more of a culture-bound syndrome than anorexia nervosa (Keel & Klump, 2003; Pike et al., 2014), reflecting the trend that began in the 1960s toward thinner cultural ideals of beauty. Bulimia nervosa tends to be more common in racial and ethnic minority groups (Marques et al., 2011) and in urban than in rural areas (Hoek et al., 1995; van Son et al., 2006). This suggests that environmental exposure, social learning, or information transfer may play a role in the development of this disorder. Many patients state that they first got the idea to purge from something they read or even from sports practices, such as techniques used to reach a lower weight class on wrestling teams. However, virtually all youth are exposed to this information at some time or another, so why do only a relatively small percentage develop the disorder? This question is considered in the section on genetics.

Who develops bulimia nervosa, and what is life like during the illness and after recovery? Like anorexia nervosa, bulimia nervosa is more common in females than males. The disorder typically starts somewhat later than anorexia nervosa—in middle to late adolescence or early adulthood—although even later onset is not uncommon (Keski-Rahkonen et al., 2009).

Bulimia nervosa is also associated with serious physical complications including fatigue, lethargy, cardiac arrhythmia, and gastrointestinal problems such as bloating, flatulence, constipation, decreased appetite, abdominal pain, borborygmi (stomach rumbling), and nausea (Chami et al., 1995; Sachs & Mehler, 2015). The disorder is hard on the body. Frequent vomiting leads to erosion of dental enamel, swelling of the parotid (salivary) glands, and calluses on the backs of the hands (Russell's signs) (Mitchell et al., 1991). Those who frequently misuse laxatives can have *edema* (bodily swelling), fluid loss and subsequent dehydration, electrolyte abnormalities, serious metabolic problems, and permanent loss of normal bowel function (Mitchell et al., 1991).

The mortality rate for bulimia nervosa is about 3.9% (Crow et al., 2009), and a meta-analysis of studies examining mortality rates in patients with eating disorders found a standardized mortality ratio of 1.9 for bulimia nervosa (Arcelus et al., 2011)—though one study in England found ratios of 4.1 (ages 15 to 24 years) and 7.7 (ages 25 to 44 years), suggesting much higher mortality (Hoang et al., 2014). In one 10-year outcome study, 11% of individuals continued to meet full diagnostic criteria for bulimia nervosa and 18.5% met criteria for the DSM-IV-TR residual diagnosis of **eating disorder not otherwise specified** (EDNOS); that is, their eating patterns were abnormal but did not actually fit the diagnostic criteria for any other eating disorder as defined in the DSM at the time. Approximately one-half to two-thirds of patients eventually achieve full or partial remission (Berkman et al., 2007; Smink et al., 2013).

Personality and Comorbidity in Bulimia Nervosa

LO 8.6 Characterize personality traits and patterns of comorbidity in bulimia nervosa.

People with bulimia nervosa share some personality features with those who have anorexia nervosa, primarily perfectionism and low self-esteem, but differences also exist. Unlike the classic restricting subtype of anorexia nervosa, people with bulimia tend to be more impulsive (acting before thinking) and have higher *novelty-seeking* (stimulus or sensation-seeking) behavior (Atiye et al., 2015; Bulik et al., 1995; Fassino et al., 2004; Steiger et al., 2004). They also score significantly higher on measures of *harm avoidance* than healthy controls (Atiye et al., 2015). These different personality factors are intriguing and reflect the symptom profiles of the disorders. Individuals with the restricting subtype of anorexia nervosa display more rigid and obsessional personalities—congruent with their rigid eating patterns. In contrast, people with bulimia nervosa exhibit more erratic and impulsive traits—consistent with the impulsive and fluctuating nature of alternating starving, binge eating, and compensatory behaviors.

REAL People REAL Disorders

Elton John: Bulimia Nervosa and Drug and Alcohol Abuse

Critics have proclaimed Elton John to be the biggest pop music sensation of the 1970s, and he is still composing and performing. This legendary performer has spent much of his life in the spotlight. Fans worldwide have read about his turbulent addiction to cocaine and alcohol as well as his love life, but fans may be less aware of his struggle with bulimia nervosa.

Born in 1947, Elton John was originally named Reginald Kenneth Dwight. By age 11, he had been awarded a scholarship to the Royal Academy of Music. At the height of his career, he admitted to being bisexual, being addicted to cocaine and alcohol, and suffering from bulimia nervosa. The world was shocked by his confession, particularly his struggle with bulimia, because it was unconventional at that time to hear of many men, much less a celebrity, suffering from this disorder.

Not atypically, Elton John's road to recovery was difficult. He faced obstacles once he decided to seek treatment because there were no Los Angeles clinics at the time that accepted patients needing rehabilitation for drug abuse and bulimia nervosa. In 1990, he checked into a Chicago hospital where he attended group therapy meetings, forged new friendships with other patients, and worked to overcome his problems. He declared himself recovered from bulimia nervosa later in 1990, ending his 14-year battle with the disorder.

REAL People REAL Disorders

Demi Lovato: Bulimia Nervosa and Self-Harm

Popular singer Demi Lovato has been a vocal advocate in the eating disorder community by discussing openly her nearly lifelong struggles with body image and weight. The former Disney star recalls experiencing body dissatisfaction as early as age 4 when she would look in the mirror and think she was fat. By age 12 she stopped eating and lost a lot of weight but still found no respite from her low self-esteem and body esteem. The life of a "tween" star was hectic and overwhelming, and she fell into a desperate pattern of starving, purging, and self-harm. Lovato revealed that her descent into cutting was largely driven by an overwhelming sense of anxiety, which she was desperate to escape. After a 3-month-long residential treatment in 2010 when she was also diagnosed with bipolar disorder, Lovato has been vocal about spreading the correct understanding of eating disorders by clarifying that they are an illness, not a choice. Tattoos on her wrists that say "Stay" and "Strong" with a heart both cover scars from cutting and are daily reminders of what she has overcome as well as the support she has had from family, friends, and fans in her recovery.

SOURCES: http://www.dailymail.co.uk/tvshowbiz/article-2111364/Demi-Lovato-reveals-battles-daily-eating-disorder-self-harm-issues.html

http://stealherstyle.net/tattoos/demi-lovatos-tattoo/

http://www.dailymail.co.uk/home/you/article-2100569/Actress-singer-Demi-Lovato--I-ll-fight-addiction-rest-life.html

Approximately 80% of patients with bulimia nervosa have another psychiatric disorder at some time in their lives (Fichter & Quadflieg, 1997); this is a very high rate. Some individuals have several disorders at the same time, and some continue to suffer from other disorders even after they recover from bulimia nervosa. The most common comorbid psychiatric conditions include anxiety disorders, major depression, substance use, and impulse control disorders (Braun et al., 1994; Brewerton et al., 1995; Bushnell et al., 1994; Fernandez-Aranda et al., 2006; Hudson et al., 2007). In a treatment-seeking sample of adolescents with bulimia nervosa, nearly half had comorbid depression, and high-risk behaviors such as alcohol use (65.8%), illegal drug use (30.3%), and cigarette use (42.1%) were common (Fischer & le Grange, 2007). The accompanying features ("Real People, Real Disorders") present the story of Elton John, who suffered from comorbid bulimia nervosa and drug and alcohol abuse, and Demi Lovato, who suffered from bulimia nervosa and self-harm.

Learning Objective Summaries

LO 8.4 Describe the component features of bulimia nervosa.

Bulimia nervosa is characterized by recurrent episodes of binge eating (eating an unusually large amount of food and feeling out of control) in combination with recurrent inappropriate compensatory behaviors to prevent weight gain such as self-induced vomiting; laxative, diuretic, or emetic use; fasting; or exercise. Self-evaluation is also unduly influenced by body shape and weight.

LO 8.5 Trace the occurrence of bulimia nervosa across various segments of the population and characterize its typical clinical course.

Bulimia typically begins in middle to late adolescence or early adulthood. It affects more women than men and can have a protracted course. One-half to two-thirds of patients eventually achieve full or partial remission. Mortality is elevated.

LO 8.6 Characterize personality traits and patterns of comorbidity in bulimia nervosa.

Individuals with bulimia nervosa share some personality features with those with anorexia nervosa such as perfectionism, harm avoidance, and low elf-esteem, but they also exhibit greater impulsivity and novelty seeking. Comorbid psychiatric disorders are common including anxiety disorders, major depression, substance use, and impulse control disorders.

Critical Thinking Question

About half of individuals with anorexia nervosa develop bulimia nervosa at some point during the course of their illness. Given that the disorders seem so different on the surface (anorexia nervosa characterized by restricting and bulimia nervosa with binge eating), how can you account for this high rate of diagnostic flux?

Binge-Eating Disorder

Janna was a 42-year-old emergency room nurse. She had been overweight since childhood. Her typical day started out late; she shunned both the scale and breakfast in the morning. She had to get the kids off to school and always prepared their breakfast, but she said her stomach didn't wake up until about 11 A.M. But then it woke up with a vengeance. On her 11 A.M. break, the vending machines "started calling her name." She started craving the prepackaged sandwiches she could get from the machines, loaded with packets of mayonnaise and relish. Once she got the salt cravings out of the way, she stopped by the candy machine. The best to satisfy the deep need inside of her was something with both chocolate and nuts—hit the sweet and salt cravings in one fell swoop. She had to get back to work in the afternoon, but she still had cravings. All she could think of was being alone in her kitchen after the kids were in bed and finally satisfying her needs. She would make it through the day with half of her mind on food the whole time. She fed the kids dinner, only eating a small salad herself. Once they were safely tucked in bed, she could have her "date with her pantry." Janna said that food was her best friend. It was always there when she needed it. It was the only one that listened to her sadness, her loneliness, and her pain. For those few hours, surrounded by chocolate cupcakes, chips, chocolates, and ice cream, she felt comfort. She would be infuriated if one of the kids woke up and interrupted her binge. Most nights, she would retire to her bedroom in tears. Her "friend" had an edge. She would lie in bed with thoughts of failure running through her head, thinking she would never get her eating and her life under control. The next morning she would wake up with what she called a "food hangover" and start the process all over again.

Clinical Features of Binge-Eating Disorder

LO 8.7 Describe the component features of binge-eating disorder.

Binge eating was first recognized in a subset of obese individuals by Stunkard in 1959. In 2013, with the publication of DSM-5, the American Psychiatric Association recognized

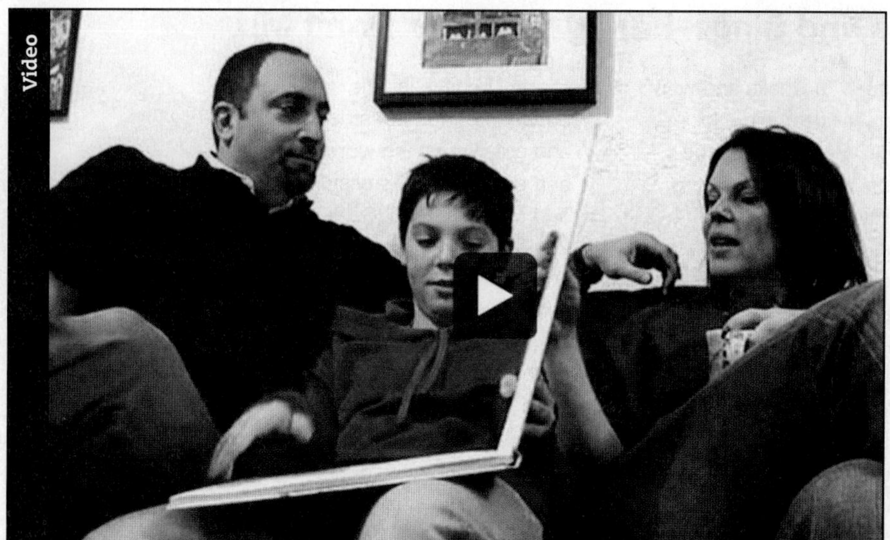

binge-eating disorder (BED) as an official diagnostic category (see "DSM-5: Binge-Eating Disorder"). BED is characterized by recurrent binge-eating behavior but without the recurrent inappropriate compensatory behaviors that are part of bulimia nervosa. "Real People, Real Disorders" presents the true story of tennis sensation Monica Seles's struggle with BED.

Epidemiology and Course of Binge-Eating Disorder

LO 8.8 Trace the occurrence of binge-eating disorder across various segments of the population and characterize its typical clinical course.

About 3.5% of women and 2% of men in the general population meet criteria for BED as defined in DSM-IV (Hudson et al., 2007), making BED the most common eating disorder. According to the World Health Organization (WHO) World Mental Health Surveys, the lifetime prevalence of BED is approximately 1.9% across a group of 14 mostly upper-middle- and high-income countries (Kessler et al., 2013). We expect that those estimates will increase somewhat as the frequency and duration criteria for BED changed from twice per week for 6 months in DSM-IV-TR to once per week for 3 months in DSM-5 (Mancuso et al., 2015; Trace et al., 2012). BED is found in approximately 5 to 8% of obese individuals (Bruce & Wilfley, 1996), and the lifetime prevalence of DSM-5 BED in adolescents is 2.3% for females and 0.7% for males (Smink et al., 2014).

In terms of outcome and mortality, data on long-term outcome of BED are rare, and it is unclear whether individuals with BED have increased mortality compared with age- and sex-matched peers (Smink et al., 2013). One study followed a clinical sample for 6 years after treatment to determine their long-term outcome; 57.4% of women had a good outcome, 35.7% an intermediate outcome, and 5.9% a poor outcome (Fichter et al., 1998). Only one patient had died. Six years later, 6% still had BED, 7.4% had developed bulimia nervosa, and 7.4% continued to have some form of EDNOS. BED can be a chronic condition—the average length of time a person is ill is 14.4 years—suggesting that BED is not just a passing phase (Pope et al., 2006). Individuals with BED also have lower health-related quality of life than the general population (Winkler et al., 2014). Individuals with BED are at increased risk for suicide attempts (Pisetsky et al., 2013; Welch, et al., 2016). "Side-by-Side Case Studies" highlights the critical differences between binge eating and overeating.

REAL People REAL Disorders

Monica Seles—Tennis and Binge-Eating Disorder Don't Mix

Monica Seles was ranked number 1 for 178 weeks and won nine Grand Slam singles titles, 53 career titles, and a bronze medal at the Sydney Olympics in 2000. Before 1993, she was unstoppable. During a quarterfinal match in Hamburg, Germany, in which Seles, then age 19, was leading 6–4, 4–3, Günter Parche, a fan who was obsessed with rival tennis star Steffi Graf, stabbed Seles between her shoulder blades with a 9-inch knife. Parche was sentenced to only 2 years' probation and psychological treatment. In her book *Getting a Grip*, Seles describes that incident as the point when her "reality was ripped away." She claims the emotional scars took much longer to heal than the physical ones, and food became her "comfort and her poison." For 9 years, although the press constantly commented on her size and the physical shape she was in, she vacillated between periods of strict dieting and gut-wrenching workouts and periods of depression and all-out binges (Seles, 2009). Her mood, self-esteem, and athletic self-confidence all became dependent on the number on the scale. She worked her way out of the trap by abandoning diets, restoring her love for food, and journaling. She describes the first step of her recovery as abandoning the search for answers outside of herself and instead "listening to the quiet voice inside.

Personality and Comorbidity in Binge-Eating Disorder

LO 8.9 Characterize personality traits and patterns of comorbidity in binge-eating disorder.

Less is known about the personality precursors to BED than about those to anorexia and bulimia nervosa. Although many investigations have explored the personality variables and the symptoms of binge eating, few have looked specifically at individuals with BED. What little we do know suggests that they score higher on measures of harm avoidance than healthy control individuals (Peterson et al., 2010), while there do not appear to be differences between individuals with BED and healthy controls on measures of novelty seeking, reward dependence, or persistence (Atiye et al., 2015). In addition, obese women with BED score lower on measures of self-directedness than obese women without BED, and both groups score lower than healthy controls (Fassino et al., 2002). Another study, which compared obese individuals with BED to both obese individuals without BED and normal weight controls on a number of personality variables, found no distinct differences between the obese individuals with and without binge eating. However, those two groups scored higher than normal weight controls on sensitivity to reward and to punishment, harm avoidance, impulsivity, and addictive personality traits (Davis et al., 2008).

Individuals with BED experience many of the same forms of comorbidity as those with anorexia and bulimia nervosa. In a treatment-seeking sample, nearly 74% reported at least one additional psychological disorder, with the most common being mood disorders, anxiety disorders, and substance use disorders (Grilo et al., 2009; Welch et al., in press). In the National Comorbidity Survey-Replication, 78.9% of individuals with BED endorsed psychiatric comorbidity, with nearly half (48.9%) endorsing three or more additional psychiatric disorders. The most common comorbid diagnoses were anxiety disorders (65.1%), mood disorders (46.4%), and impulse control disorders (43.3%) (Hudson et al., 2007). BED is also associated with risk for development of components of metabolic syndrome (which includes hypertension, dyslipidemia, and type 2 diabetes) as well as endocrine and gastrointestinal disorders (Hudson et al, 2010; Thornton, submitted). This increased risk for some of these conditions appears to be independent of the effects of obesity.

DSM-5

Criteria for Binge-Eating Disorder

A. Recurrent episodes of binge eating. An episode of binge eating is characterized by both of the following:

1. Eating, in a discrete period of time (e.g., within any 2-hour period), an amount of food that is definitely larger than what most people would eat in a similar period of time under similar circumstances.
2. A sense of lack of control over eating during the episode (e.g., a feeling that one cannot stop eating or control what or how much one is eating).

B. The binge-eating episodes are associated with three (or more) of the following:

1. Eating much more rapidly than normal.
2. Eating until feeling uncomfortably full.
3. Eating large amounts of food when not feeling physically hungry.
4. Eating alone because of feeling embarrassed by how much one is eating.
5. Feeling disgusted with oneself, depressed, or very guilty afterward.

C. Marked distress regarding binge eating is present.

D. The binge eating occurs, on average, at least once a week for 3 months.

E. The binge eating is not associated with the recurrent use of inappropriate compensatory behavior as in bulimia nervosa and does not occur exclusively during the course of bulimia nervosa or anorexia nervosa.

Other Specified Feeding and Eating Disorders

LO 8.10 Distinguish the most common other specified feeding and eating disorders from anorexia nervosa, bulimia nervosa, and binge-eating disorder.

As we have noted, the DSM criteria for anorexia nervosa, bulimia nervosa, and BED are very specific. In fact, many people who have eating disorders do *not* meet these criteria. Instead, they are given the diagnosis of other specified feeding and eating disorder (OSFED). DSM-5 lists five categories of OSFED. The first is *atypical anorexia nervosa,* in which a person has all the features of anorexia nervosa, except the person's weight is within or above the normal range despite significant weight loss. Next is *bulimia nervosa (of low frequency and/or limited duration),* in which a person meets all the criteria for bulimia nervosa, but the binge eating and compensatory behaviors happen less than once a week and/or for less than 3 months. Third is *binge-eating disorder (of low frequency and/or limited duration),* in which a person meets all the criteria of binge-eating disorder, but binge eating happens less than once a week and/or for less than 3 months. Fourth is *purging disorder,* in which a person uses purging behavior (e.g., self-induced vomiting or misuse of laxatives) to control their weight or shape, but they are not binge eating. Last is *night eating syndrome,* in which a person eats after waking

SIDE by SIDE Case Studies

Dimensions of Behavior: From Adaptive to Maladaptive

Adaptive Behavior Case Study

Overeating

Josh liked to eat. His mother loved having him come home from college because she could cook all of his favorite dishes. She knew that nothing would spoil in the refrigerator as it did when Josh was at college. Over spring break, he went home to freshly baked cookies, his favorite dinners, red velvet cupcakes, and gallons and gallons of milk! His mom went all out making sure the refrigerator and pantry were stocked with his favorite foods. At dinner, she offered seconds, and even though he was full, he did not want to hurt her feelings, so he ate second helpings. He felt really overstuffed but decided to take a run the next day and cut down a little. But he woke up to her famous apple coffee cake, and he just couldn't say no! That afternoon, he went to the gym because he was feeling bloated. In addition, he knew his mom had invited his grandparents over for a special meal that night. Josh ate a healthy portion size and took seconds, but he had no room for dessert. After dinner, he plopped down on the couch and watched football with his dad. He almost couldn't wait to get back to cafeteria food at school. Josh was overeating, but he was not out of control. He did not have an eating disorder.

Maladaptive Behavior Case Study

Binge-Eating Disorder

Brian had always had a healthy appetite. His grandmother always referred to him as "her best eater." Even when his schoolmates started teasing him about being overweight, his loving Italian grandmother still showered him with his favorite foods. Not one to turn down something tasty and not wanting to hurt his grandmother's feelings, he always obliged. He managed to keep his weight under control throughout high school by joining the swim team. But even with all of that training, he still always seemed to have an extra layer of fat compared with the other guys. Once he hit college, he stopped swimming, but he did not stop eating. His weight started creeping up, and with a full load and copyediting for a newspaper until the wee hours of the morning, he just didn't have time for exercise. He started to wonder what he was doing with his life, and his nights at the newspaper became more and more depressing. At first he ordered in a pizza and would eat and edit all night but stop at one pie. But then he found that a whole pizza simply was not satisfying some need he felt inside. He added garlic bread, then donuts to top it off with something sweet, and sometimes he would go home and eat even more in the dorm. He was disgusted with himself, but he couldn't stop. This was happening two or three times a week. One night, one of the section editors came back to the office late at night and found Brian surrounded by pizza boxes, donut boxes, chocolate wrappers, and gallons of soft drinks. The editor asked if they had been partying. Brian lied and said the other folks had just left and he offered to stay behind and clean up. His eating was out of control. Brian had binge-eating disorder.

Table 8.5 Brief Summary of Eating Disorders

Disorder	Symptoms
Anorexia nervosa	• Restriction of energy intake relative to requirements • Significantly low body weight • Intense fear of gaining weight or becoming fat • Persistent behavior that interferes with weight gain • Disturbance in the way one's body weight or shape is experienced • Undue influence of weight and shape on self-evaluation • Persistent lack of recognition of the seriousness of low body weight
Bulimia nervosa	• Recurrent binge eating • Recurrent compensatory behaviors • Undue influence of weight and shape on self-evaluation
Binge-eating disorder	• Recurrent binge eating • Eating much more rapidly than normal • Eating until feeling uncomfortably full • Eating large amounts of food when not feeling physically hungry • Eating alone because of feeling embarrassed by how much one is eating • Feeling disgusted with oneself, depressed, or very guilty afterward • Distress regarding binge eating is present • No recurrent inappropriate compensatory behaviors
Purging disorder	• Recurrent purging behaviors in the absence of binge eating
Night eating syndrome	• Eating after waking up in the night • Eating excessively after the evening meal

up during the night or eats excessively after the evening meal and they can recall the eating. These behaviors cause significant distress or impairment of normal functioning and are not the result of other factors, such as social norms or substance abuse. Individuals who do not meet criteria for OSFED or any of the primary eating disorders yet have symptoms of a feeding or eating disorder that cause significant distress or functional impairment are placed in the residual category of *unspecified feeding or eating disorder*.

Many changes were made to the previous diagnostic and classification system of eating disorders, in which the residual category used to be called eating disorder not otherwise specified (EDNOS) (American Psychiatric Association, 2004). Changes were made to that classification system because most people who sought treatment for an eating disorder received a diagnosis of EDNOS (Fairburn & Walsh, 2002; Turner & Bryant-Waugh, 2003). The DSM-IV classification system did not adequately capture eating-related pathology as it existed in the real world. Only time, clinical observation, and research will tell whether the revisions in DSM-5 more accurately capture the true landscape of eating disorders (Mancuso et al., 2015).

Learning Objective Summaries

LO 8.7 Describe the component features of binge-eating disorder.

BED is characterized by recurrent binge-eating behavior but without the recurrent inappropriate compensatory behaviors that are part of bulimia nervosa. Marked distress regarding the binge eating is present.

LO 8.8 Trace the occurrence of binge-eating disorder across various segments of the population and characterize its typical clinical course.

About 3.5% of women and 2% of men in the general population meet criteria for BED. BED can be a chronic condition, is associated with lower health-related quality of life, and is associated with increased risk for suicide attempts.

LO 8.9 Characterize personality traits and patterns of comorbidity in binge-eating disorder.

Individuals with BED report elevated harm avoidance and elevated sensitivity to reward and to punishment, impulsivity, and addictive personality traits.

LO 8.10 Distinguish the most common other specified feeding and eating disorders from anorexia nervosa, bulimia nervosa, and binge-eating disorder.

The OSFED category comprises atypical anorexia nervosa (all the features of anorexia nervosa except weight is within or above the normal range despite weight loss); bulimia nervosa (of low frequency and/or limited duration) (meets all the criteria for bulimia nervosa, but the binge eating and compensatory behaviors happen less than once a week and/or for less than 3 months); binge-eating disorder (of low frequency and/or limited duration) (meets all the criteria of binge-eating disorder, but binge eating happens less than once a week and/or for less than 3 months); purging disorder, in which a person uses purging behavior (e.g., self-induced vomiting or misuse of laxatives) to control their weight or shape but is not binge eating; and night eating syndrome, in which a person eats after waking up during the night or eats excessively after the evening meal and can recall the eating.

Critical Thinking Question

Skeptics have claimed that binge-eating disorder is simply the medicalization of gluttony. Discuss why this claim is patently untrue and dangerous.

Feeding and Eating Disorders Often Seen in Childhood

Before DSM-5, feeding-related conditions commonly seen in children were included in a category titled other disorders of childhood and adolescence. With the publication of DSM-5, these disorders were merged with the eating disorders category, thereby acknowledging some continuity of dysregulated eating patterns across developmental stages. This new arrangement could encourage additional research addressing how feeding disorders in childhood might be related to the eating disorders that typically emerge in adolescence and adulthood.

Many children, particularly infants and toddlers, are "picky eaters."

> Sarah was 5 years old. Although she had no medical problems, her height and weight were at the second percentile for her age. Sarah refused to eat any foods except peanut butter sandwiches and candy. When offered other foods, she would cry and hold her breath until her mother gave her a peanut butter sandwich.

Sarah had no need to eat other foods—when she held her breath, she got her way. Treatment consisted of offering Sarah other foods and teaching her mother to ignore her tantrums. In Sarah's case, abnormal eating was the result of environmental factors and was not really dangerous. But other disordered eating behaviors, *pica* and *rumination*, are conceptually more perplexing and difficult to treat.

Pica and Rumination Disorder

LO 8.11 Contrast pica and rumination disorder on clinical symptoms and epidemiology.

Pica is the persistent eating of nonnutritive, nonfood substances. The term comes from the Latin word for "magpie," a bird that voraciously consumes food and nonfood substances (Stiegler, 2005). Although more than 50% of children ages 18 to 36 months ingest nonfood items, this practice generally decreases with age (Mishori & McHale, 2014). According to one parent, "Over the last couple years we have pulled out of [our son's] throat: a set of keys, large bulldog clips, sticks, rocks, wads of paper, open safety pins, wire (from the screen, etc.). Plus all the stuff that he gets down before we can get it out: magnets from

DSM-5

Criteria for Pica

A. Persistent eating of nonnutritive, nonfood substances over a period of at least 1 month.

B. The eating of nonnutritive, nonfood substances is inappropriate to the developmental level of the individual.

C. The eating behavior is not part of a culturally supported or socially normative practice.

D. If the eating behavior occurs in the context of another mental disorder (e.g., intellectual disability [intellectual developmental disorder], autism spectrum disorder, schizophrenia) or medical condition (including pregnancy), it is sufficiently severe to warrant additional clinical attention.

the fridge, Barbie parts, paper, money, paper clips, etc." (Menard, cited in Stiegler, 2005). Although children with developmental disabilities constitute the largest group of people with pica, the disorder also occurs in people with intellectual disability, people with schizophrenia, and sometimes people with no psychological disorder. Among a group of adolescent and young adult females receiving residential treatment for eating disorders, 1.3% met DSM-5 criteria for pica (Delaney et al., 2015).

Pica occurs in various socioeconomic groups, both sexes, and all ages (Stiegler, 2005). Although its prevalence in the general population is uncertain (American Psychiatric Association, 2013), it may be more common among women (especially pregnant women), children, and people of lower socioeconomic status (Rose et al., 2000). Pica can result in serious health consequences, including anemia, heavy metal exposure/poisoning (lead, mercury, arsenic), parasitic infections, potassium abnormalities, abdominal pain, malnutrition, dental trauma, oral lacerations, gum disease, and erosion of tooth enamel (Mishori & McHale, 2014; Stiegler, 2005). Pica is associated with anemia and low hemoglobin (Hb), hematocrit (Hct), and plasma zinc (Zn) concentrations, but the direction of the causal relationship between pica and micronutrient deficiencies is unknown (Miao et al., 2015). Consuming safety pins, glass, or nails can obstruct or perforate the esophagus, stomach, or intestines. Finally, the ingestion of certain items may repulse caregivers or peers, leading to social isolation and/or rejection (Stiegler, 2005).

Cultural pica occurs in many countries. Some women in India consume soil and its by-products (mud, clay, ash, lime, charcoal, and brick) in response to pregnancy cravings (Nag, 1994). Some East African women consume soil for purposes of fertility (Abrahams & Parsons, 1996). Certain cultures in South America eat clay for its purported medicinal value (Rose et al., 2000). In the United States, eating kaolin (also known as white dirt, chalk, or white clay) occurs in the Piedmont region of Georgia (Grigsby et al., 1999) and parts of Mississippi (Ali, 2001).

Pica has many different causes. Iron and zinc deficiencies may result in the urge to ingest certain foods or substances, but many people without these conditions also engage in pica. Environmental factors (stress and impoverished living environments) or developmental disorders are important causal factors (Stiegler, 2001). Among people without psychological disorders, pica sometimes begins after stressful events such as surgery or the loss of a family member (Soykan et al., 1997). In a study of pregnant adolescents, 46% reported engaging in pica behavior, and several indicators of maternal iron status (serum ferritin, total body iron, and serum hepcidin) were significantly lower in the pica vs. non-pica group (Lumish et al., 2014).

In a rare eating disorder, **rumination disorder**, recently eaten food is effortlessly regurgitated into the mouth, followed by rechewing, reswallowing, or spitting it out. Rumination disorder occurs in both sexes and may begin in infancy, childhood, or adolescence (Chial et al., 2003; O'Brien et al., 1995). Episodes may occur several times per day and may last for more than an hour (Chial et al., 2003; Soykan et al., 1997). Because rumination resembles vomiting, some people are initially diagnosed with bulimia nervosa or gastroesophageal reflux disease (GERD). They sometimes undergo gastrointestinal surgical procedures and consult several physicians before getting a correct diagnosis (O'Brien et al., 1995).

DSM-5

Criteria for Rumination Disorder

A. Repeated regurgitation of food over a period of at least 1 month. Regurgitated food may be re-chewed, re-swallowed, or spit out.

B. The repeated regurgitation is not attributable to an associated gastrointestinal or other medical condition (e.g., gastroesophageal reflux, pyloric stenosis).

C. The eating disturbance does not occur exclusively during the course of anorexia nervosa, bulimia nervosa, binge-eating disorder, or avoidant/restrictive food intake disorder.

D. If the symptoms occur in the context of another mental disorder (e.g., intellectual disability [intellectual developmental disorder] or another neurodevelopmental disorder), they are sufficiently severe to warrant additional clinical attention.

As with pica, the overall prevalence of rumination disorder is unknown (American Psychiatric Association, 2013) but may be more common in children and adolescents as well as those with intellectual disabilities. In a study of Sri Lankan children ages 10 to 16 years, the prevalence of rumination syndrome was 5.1% (Rajindrajith et al., 2012). A meta-analysis of eating disorders in adults with intellectual disability suggests a prevalence of rumination of approximately 6% in this population (Gravestock, 2000). Rumination disorder cannot be diagnosed in the presence of another DSM-5 feeding or eating disorder, but rumination behavior has been reported in individuals with eating disorders, particularly bulimia nervosa (Delaney et al., 2015; Fairburn & Cooper, 1984; Larocca & Della-Fera, 1986). Medical complications of rumination disorder can include malnutrition, abdominal pain, bloating, weight loss, and electrolyte disturbances (Rajindrajith et al., 2012).

Avoidant/Restrictive Food Intake Disorder

LO 8.12 Distinguish ARFID from picky eating.

Avoidant/restrictive food intake disorder (ARFID) was introduced into the DSM-5 given the frequency with which children with certain types of presentations were given diagnoses of EDNOS (the DSM-IV residual category). ARFID captures the behavior of those children who exhibit restricted or otherwise inadequate eating. Although this is most common in children and adolescents, it can persist into adulthood. Because this is a new diagnostic category, its prevalence has not been well studied, but a recent survey of children and

Table 8.6 Brief Summary of Childhood Eating Disorders

Eating Disorder	Symptom
Pica	• Persistent ingestion of nonnutritive, nonfood substances • Eating of nonnutritive substances that is not culturally or socially normative
Rumination disorder	• Repeated regurgitation of food • Rechewing, reswallowing, or spitting out regurgitated food • Regurgitation not secondary to a gastrointestinal, medical, or other psychiatric disorder
ARFID	• Apparent lack of interest in eating or food • Avoidance based on the sensory characteristics of food • Concern about aversive consequences of eating • Failure to meet appropriate nutritional and/or energy needs • Significant weight loss or failure to gain weight • Significant nutritional deficiency • Dependence on enteral feeding or oral nutritional supplements • Marked interference with psychosocial functioning • Undereating not due to food unavailability or cultural practices

DSM-5

Criteria for Avoidant/Restrictive Food Intake Disorder

A. An eating or feeding disturbance (e.g., apparent lack of interest in eating or food; avoidance based on the sensory characteristics of food; concern about aversive consequences of eating) as manifested by persistent failure to meet appropriate nutritional and/or energy needs associated with one (or more) of the following:

1. Significant weight loss (or failure to achieve expected weight gain or faltering growth in children).
2. Significant nutritional deficiency.
3. Dependence on enteral feeding or oral nutritional supplements.
4. Marked interference with psychosocial functioning.

B. The disturbance is not better explained by lack of available food or by an associated culturally sanctioned practice.

C. The eating disturbance does not occur exclusively during the course of anorexia nervosa or bulimia nervosa, and there is no evidence of a disturbance in the way in which one's body weight or shape is experienced.

D. The eating disturbance is not attributable to a concurrent medical condition or not better explained by another mental disorder. When the eating disturbance occurs in the context of another condition or disorder, the severity of the eating disturbance exceeds that routinely associated with the condition or disorder and warrants additional clinical attention.

adolescents ages 8 to 13 years in Swiss primary schools found that 3.2% met criteria for ARFID (Kurz et al., 2014). In a retrospective chart review and case-control study of children and adolescents receiving treatment for eating disorders, 22.5% and 13.8% met DSM-5 criteria for ARFID, respectively (Fisher et al., 2014; Nicely et al., 2014). These patients were younger, more likely to be male, and had longer duration of illness than those with other eating disorder diagnoses. Those with ARFID also had greater prevalence of comorbid medical conditions, anxiety, pervasive developmental disorder, and learning disorders and less comorbid depression and other mood disorders.

Examples of ARFID include individuals who have little interest in feeding, eat only a very narrow range of foods (often due to sensory features of food), and/or restrict their food intake to regulate emotions, an emotional crisis, or an unpleasant experience. Although often misunderstood as "picky eating," these presentations can be associated with clinically significant levels of impairment in development or functioning and potentially severe medical complications.

Learning Objective Summaries

LO 8.11 Contrast pica and rumination disorder on clinical symptoms and epidemiology.

Pica is the persistent eating of nonnutritive, nonfood substances and is commonly seen in individuals with developmental disabilities, intellectual disability, and schizophrenia and sometimes people with no psychological disorder. In contrast, in rumination disorder, recently consumed food is regurgitated into the mouth and then rechewed, reswallowed, or spat out. Rumination disorder occurs in both sexes and may begin in infancy, childhood, or adolescence.

LO 8.12 Distinguish ARFID from picky eating.

ARFID captures the behavior of those children who exhibit restricted or otherwise inadequate eating. Examples include children who have little interest in feeding, eat only a very narrow range of foods (often due to sensory features of food), and/or restrict their food intake to regulate emotions, an emotional crisis, or an unpleasant experience. Unlike "picky eating," ARFID can be associated with clinically significant levels of impairment in development or functioning and potentially severe medical complications.

Critical Thinking Question

How could a parent distinguish between picky eating and ARFID in his or her child?

Epidemiology, Sex, Race, Ethnicity, and Developmental Factors in Eating Disorders

Unlike some psychological disorders, eating disorders do not affect everyone equally, nor do they occur with equal frequency across the life span. Understanding eating disorders requires a careful understanding of who develops them and when.

Sex, Race, and Ethnicity in Eating Disorders

LO 8.13 Discuss differences in the prevalence of all eating disorders by sex, race, and ethnicity.

Anorexia nervosa is more common in women and girls than in men and boys. According to the DSM-IV criteria, anorexia occurs in about 0.9% of women (Hudson et al., 2007; Preti et al., 2009) and 0.3% of men (Hudson et al., 2007). The lifetime prevalence of DSM-5 anorexia nervosa in adolescents has been estimated to be 1.7% in girls and 0.1% in boys (Smink et al., 2014). Although the precise reason for this imbalance remains unknown, many theories have been suggested, including internalization of pressures on females and males to attain a thin or lean ideal, objectification of the female body, and the influences of female hormones on appetite and weight regulation (Klump et al., 2006; Striegel-Moore & Bulik, 2007).

Like anorexia nervosa, there is a gender imbalance in bulimia nervosa with 0.88% of women and 0.12% of men reporting bulimia nervosa using DSM-IV criteria (Preti et al., 2009) The lifetime prevalence of DSM-5 bulimia nervosa in adolescents has been estimated to be 0.8% in girls and 0.1% in boys (Smink et al., 2014). Although the sex ratio for bulimia nervosa is imbalanced, the diagnostic criteria are somewhat sex biased. This is so because men tend to rely on nonpurging forms of compensatory behavior after binge eating, such as excessive exercise (Anderson & Bulik, 2003; Lewinsohn et al., 2002). Changing our definition of bulimia nervosa to include forms of compensatory behaviors more common in men could alter the sex ratio in this disorder (Anderson & Bulik, 2003; Woodside et al., 2001). Male athletes are among those who feel strong pressure to remain slim and who may focus excessive attention on their weight and body shape. Intriguingly, the relation among the component behaviors of eating disorders such as binge eating, exercising, purging, and desire for weight loss may also differ across the sexes (De Young et al., 2010).

Unlike anorexia and bulimia nervosa, the sex distribution of BED is more equal (Hay, 1998; Hudson et al., 2007). Using DSM-IV criteria, the prevalence of BED was estimated at 3.5% for women and 2% for men (Hudson et al., 2007). The lifetime prevalence of DSM-5 BED in adolescents has been estimated to be 2.3% in girls and 0.7% in boys (Smink et al., 2014).

Research HOT Topic

Gender Diversity in Eating Disorders Research

Biological and psychological research, including that on eating disorders, has historically focused on cisgender individuals, or those whose anatomy and gender identity align to allow them to fall neatly into the male/female sex binary (Boehmer, 2002; Diemer et al., 2015). Recently, however, research into the prevalence of eating disorders in gender-diverse individuals has blossomed proportionately with growing awareness of transgender and transsexual issues. Some of this research indicates that the prevalence of eating disorders and compensatory behaviors in non-cisgender populations are in fact higher than they are in cisgender individuals. Diemer et al. (2015), for example, found in a survey of more than 280,000 American college students that transgender individuals were far more likely than any other group to have been diagnosed with an eating disorder in the past year (15.82%; only 0.55% of the lowest-risk group, cisgender heterosexual men, had been diagnosed with an eating disorder in the past year). The body of research investigating eating disorders in transgender and other gender-diverse individuals is still growing, but it remains an important field of inquiry.

Unfortunately, we do not have adequate epidemiologic data to give us a clear picture of the racial and ethnic distribution of eating disorders and behaviors in the United States. One study (Striegel-Moore et al., 2003) assessing eating disorders in 2,054 young adult African American and white women (average age 21 years) found higher rates of anorexia and bulimia nervosa among white than black women. Of particular interest, no African American women were diagnosed with anorexia nervosa, compared with 1.5% of white women (Striegel-Moore et al., 2003). However, because the groups also differed on social class, it is not clear whether the difference in prevalence was due to racial or socioeconomic differences or both. A subsequent study using nationally representative data from the U.S. population found no racial/ethnic differences in lifetime prevalence of anorexia nervosa (Marques et al., 2011).

One group of researchers (Striegel-Moore et al., 2005) found different patterns of eating disorder symptoms across racial/ethnic groups. Binge eating in the absence of purging was more common in African American women, whereas purging in the absence of binge eating was more common in white women. Other researchers (Marques et al., 2011) found that the lifetime prevalence of "any binge eating" (defined as binge eating at least twice a week for 3 months with loss of control but without additional markers of distress) was significantly higher in Hispanics, African Americans, and Asians compared with non-Hispanic whites. In addition, there was a significantly higher lifetime prevalence of bulimia nervosa among Hispanics and African Americans than in non-Hispanic whites (Marques et al., 2011). Several studies, however, did not find racial or ethnic differences in the prevalence of recurrent binge eating (Reagan & Hersch, 2005; Smith et al., 1998; Striegel-Moore et al., 2001). The prevalence of binge eating also appears to be similar between Native American women and men and in whites (Striegel-Moore et al., 2011). The lack of data about these disorders in the diverse U.S. population is a significant gap in our knowledge.

For BED, fewer differences in prevalence exist across racial or ethnic groups (Smink et al., 2012), with no significant difference in lifetime prevalence across racial/ethnic groups (Marques et al., 2011). Preliminary data suggest that there may be increased risk for BED in lower socioeconomic classes (Langer et al., 1992; Warheit et al., 1993).

Developmental Factors in Eating Disorders

LO 8.14 Discuss developmental life course changes in the risk for feeding and eating disorders.

Despite the typical age of onset and the highly imbalanced sex ratio, principles of developmental psychology have not yet been adequately applied to examine the causes of eating disorders. Few studies have examined the relation between the feeding disorders of childhood, childhood weight problems, and the emergence of eating disorders in adolescence. Given the new placement of the childhood feeding disorders with the eating disorders, this section focuses on what we know about developmental factors in anorexia nervosa, bulimia nervosa, and BED.

Anorexia nervosa in childhood is uncommon, although the incidence may be increasing (Lask & Bryant-Waugh, 2000). Bulimia nervosa before puberty is rarely reported (Stein et al., 1998). Clinical reports suggest that disordered eating behaviors and attitudes are clearly present in some preadolescent girls (Killen et al., 1994; Leon et al., 1993). In one study, childhood predictors of disordered eating behaviors included the mother's own body dissatisfaction, internalization of the thin body ideal (or how much the person accepted society's pressure to be thin), bulimic symptoms, and maternal and paternal BMI, which predicted the emergence of childhood eating disturbance (Stice et al., 1999). The extent to which this familial relationship reflects environmental or genetic factors is unknown.

When anorexia nervosa begins in early adolescence, social and emotional development are clearly interrupted by its medical and psychological consequences (Bulik, 2002). The disorder itself and associated symptoms such as depression, anxiety, social withdrawal, difficulty eating in social situations, self-consciousness, fatigue, and medical complications can lead to isolation from peers and family. Often recovery requires facing challenges that normally would have been faced years before, such as establishing independence from family, developing trust in friendships, and dating and establishing romantic relationships. Although the physical toll of eating disorders is often emphasized, the social and psychological effects are equally disruptive. In addition, anorexia nervosa has dramatic effects on the family both emotionally and financially. Family meals often become battlegrounds marked by refusal to eat, power struggles about food, and frustration and tears. Parents struggle to understand as their child becomes increasingly unreachable and unable to think rationally about a function, eating, that to them seems a simple fact of life. The needs of siblings and other family members commonly become secondary to the demands of the eating disorder. This, coupled with the enormous expense of treatment, can wreak havoc on the most functional of families.

Addressing the issue of who develops bulimia nervosa, population-based studies of older children indicate that early menarche (onset of menstruation) may increase the risk for bulimia nervosa (Fairburn et al., 1997). Girls whose body fat percentage increases more rapidly and who develop mature figures earlier than their peers may develop greater body dissatisfaction. This may lead to early experimentation with behaviors designed to control eating and weight (Attie & Brooks-Gunn, 1989), which, in turn, increases the risk of developing eating disorders. For example, among middle school girls, higher body fat (an indication of maturational status) was associated with the development of eating problems 2 years later (Attie & Brooks-Gunn, 1989). Similarly, among 971 middle school girls (Killen et al., 1992), those who were more developmentally mature for their age were more likely to meet diagnostic criteria for bulimia nervosa. There may be important differences in family background as well. Compared with people with anorexia nervosa, the family background of individuals with bulimia nervosa also includes the same high achievement orientation. However, these families also have more problems with drug and alcohol dependence and higher frequency of sexual abuse than in anorexia nervosa. It is important to note, however, that sexual abuse is no more common in families of individuals with eating disorders than in families of individuals with other psychological illnesses.

We know even less about developmental factors associated with BED. Retrospective reports from obese women with BED indicate that binge eating before age 18 was associated with an earlier onset of obesity, dieting, and psychopathology (Marcus et al., 1995). Most studies indicate that BED generally begins in late adolescence or early adulthood (Hudson et al., 2006). Some people report that they began binge eating earlier in life (11 to 13 years old)—often before they even went on their first diet (Grilo & Masheb, 2000). Among children ages 6 to 12, those who reported binge eating gained an additional 15% of fat mass compared with children who said they did not binge (Tanofsky-Kraff et al., 2006).

Researchers also focus on children who report a loss of control over their eating without consuming an unambiguously large amount of food (i.e., loss of control [LOC] eating). LOC eating is often discussed in relation to children rather than binge eating because parents or other caregivers may limit the amount of food that is available or consumed on a given occasion, and because of their developmental stage, children are less capable of accurately quantifying the amount of food they consume. Studies of overweight youth report that LOC eating is associated with elevated eating-related distress, anxiety, depressive symptomatology, and lower self-esteem as well as post-meal confusion and fatigue (Tanofsky-Kraff et al., 2007; Tanofsky-Kraff, McDuffie, et al., 2009a). LOC eating may also be related to the rise in childhood obesity, as children at high risk for adult obesity (due to parent or child overweight) who report LOC eating have an increased rate of BMI growth over time and gain an additional 5 pounds per year compared with those without LOC eating (Tanofsky-Kraff, Yanovski, et al., 2009). The prevalence of LOC eating differs by sex and race/ethnicity, with higher prevalence reported by gay, lesbian, and bisexual adolescents (compared with heterosexual counterparts) (Austin et al., 2009). Binge eating is also more common in obese Caucasian youth than African American youth, with Hispanic youth falling in between (Elliott et al., 2013), which contrasts somewhat to a report of similar prevalence of LOC eating among Caucasian and African American youth in a study that included both healthy weight and overweight participants (Cassidy et al, 2012).

With the introduction of ARFID in DSM-5, selective eating in young children, as well as associated developmental factors, is gaining increased attention from researchers. In a cohort study of young children (n = 917; mean age 4 years), caregivers reported that 20.3%

engaged in selective eating—17.7% at a moderate level (restricted diet only) and 3.0% at a severe level (restricted diet that limited ability to eat with others) (Zucker et al., 2015). Compared with nonselective eaters, children with moderate or severe selective eating showed elevated symptoms of depression, social anxiety, and general anxiety as well as heightened aversion to food, reduced growth, and enhanced sensitivity to food texture, smell, visual cues, and motion (Zucker et al., 2015). Although some children may outgrow their selective eating patterns, the impairment associated with restrictive eating at a young age is concerning and may be a marker of increased risk for future disordered eating.

Learning Objective Summaries

LO 8.13 Discuss differences in the prevalence of all eating disorders by sex, race, and ethnicity.

Anorexia nervosa occurs in about 0.9% of women and 0.3% of men and bulimia nervosa in 0.88% of women and 0.12% of men; binge-eating disorder has a more equal sex ratio, occurring in 3.5% of women and 2% of men. Eating disorders including binge-eating symptomatology are as common, if not more common, in racial and ethnic minorities. Anorexia nervosa is somewhat less prevalent among African American individuals than whites.

LO 8.14 Discuss developmental life course changes in the risk for feeding and eating disorders.

Anorexia nervosa typically develops around puberty, bulimia nervosa in mid- to late adolescence or early adulthood, and binge-eating disorder in late adolescence or early adulthood, although many patients say they began binge eating in early childhood. Importantly, although these are the typical ages of onset, it can occur at any point across the life cycle. The childhood disorders of pica, rumination disorder, and ARFID typically onset in younger children.

Critical Thinking Question

How could early puberty influence body image and body dissatisfaction in young girls and thereby contribute to the development of eating disorders?

The Etiology of Eating Disorders

Although researchers have been studying eating disorders for decades, our understanding of their causes remains incomplete. Many theories have been proposed, ranging from purely sociocultural to purely biological. A complete understanding of the causes of eating disorders will no doubt require a reasonable synthesis of the different contributions of biology and environment.

Biological Perspectives

LO 8.15 Understand genetic, brain, hormonal, and environmental factors that increase risk for eating disorders.

Biological research has revolutionized our understanding of several psychological conditions. Classic examples are autism spectrum disorder (once thought to be caused by cold and distant mothers) and schizophrenia (once thought to be caused by a "schizophrenogenic" mother). We now know that autism spectrum disorder and schizophrenia are neurodevelopmental disorders. A neurobiological approach is now being used to help understand the biological basis of eating disorders. The use of animal models has considerably enhanced our understanding of eating disorders. Observing animals in the lab is one way to understand the underlying biology of the core symptoms of eating disorders. This research focuses on those aspects of the illness for which animal analogues exist. Although we cannot develop animal models of some of the psychological components of eating disorders, such as body dissatisfaction or body image distortion, we can develop models of

Figure 8.1 The hypothalamus has a central role in appetite and weight regulation.

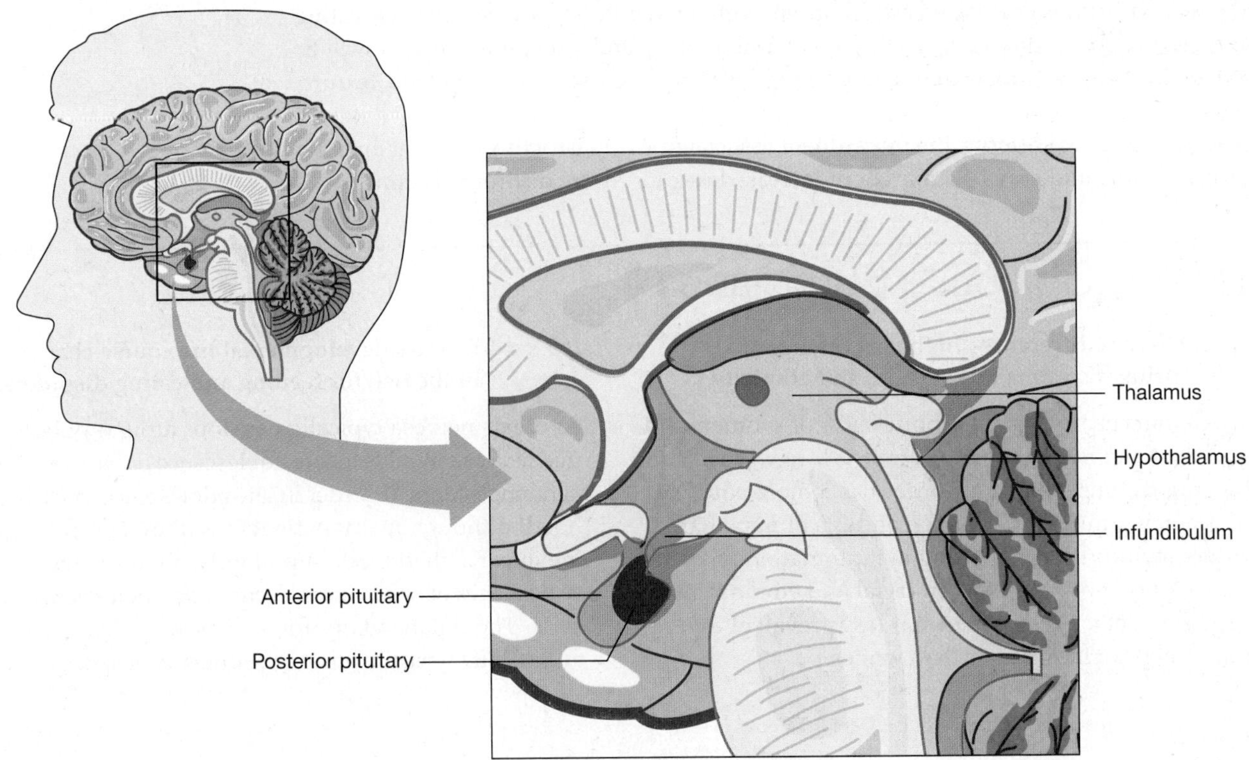

more behavioral components, such as food restriction and binge eating (see "New Research a Game Changer for Binge Eating").

ROLE OF THE HYPOTHALAMUS We know from animal studies that the hypothalamus (a region of the brain that regulates certain metabolic processes and other autonomic activities) is influential in appetite and weight control (see Figure 8.1). When researchers make surgical lesions in the *ventromedial hypothalamus* in mice, the mice overeat and become obese. In contrast, when lesions are made in the lateral hypothalamus, the mice reduce their food intake and lose weight. Therefore, the hypothalamus appears central to appetite and weight regulation in mice, but its function constitutes only one aspect of eating disorders (King, 2006). Furthermore, no evidence of consistent hypothalamic abnormalities has been observed in *humans* with eating disorders.

The hypothalamus is central to weight and appetite regulation, and when a rat's ventromedial hypothalamus is lesioned, great weight gain results. When a rat's lateral hypothalamus is lesioned, it becomes extremely thin.

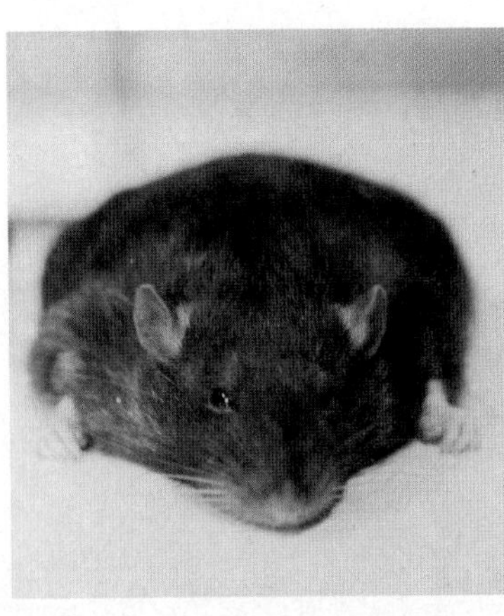

ACTIVITY-BASED ANOREXIA Another animal model for eating disorders focuses on the excessive hyperactivity seen in patients with anorexia nervosa, which persists even in the underweight state. In this rodent model, unlimited access to a running wheel, together with scheduled feeding, leads to increased running wheel activity and decreased feeding. Under these conditions, rodents can lose more than 20% of their body weight and can die from emaciation (Carrera et al., 2014; Gutierrez, 2013; Hillebrand et al., 2005; Routtenberg & Kuznesof, 1967). This model is intriguing because it captures one perplexing symptom of anorexia nervosa (hyperactivity) and uses that symptom to further understand its biological underpinnings and as a basis to understand pharmacological action (Adan et al., 2011). Breaking down complex psychological disorders into component parts and developing animal models for these component behaviors constitute a valuable scientific approach to understanding etiology.

ADDICTION MODEL OF BINGE EATING Are eating disorders characterized by binge eating similar to addictive disorders? To what extent are the same brain systems that are involved with alcohol and drug abuse also involved with binge eating? The Yale Food Addiction Scale (Gearhardt et al., 2009) was developed by modifying the DSM-IV diagnostic criteria for substance dependence to reflect addiction to food. The majority of

Research HOT Topic

New Research a Game Changer for Binge Eating

Sixty years ago scientists could electrically stimulate a region of a mouse's brain to cause the mouse to eat, whether hungry or not. Now researchers from University of North Carolina School of Medicine have pinpointed some of the precise cellular connections responsible for trigging that behavior. The finding, published in 2013 in the journal *Science*, lends insight into a cause for obesity and could lead to treatments for eating disorders such as anorexia and bulimia nervosa.

Optogenetic stimulation of BNST in mice.
Source: Josh Jennings

"The study underscores that obesity and other eating disorders have a neurological basis," said senior study author Garret Stuber, PhD, assistant professor in the department of psychiatry and department of cell biology and physiology at the University of North Carolina at Chapel Hill. "With further study, we could figure out how to regulate the activity of cells in a specific region of the brain and develop treatments."

Back in the 1950s, when scientists electrically stimulated a region of the brain called the lateral hypothalamus, they knew that they were stimulating many different types of brain cells. Stuber wanted to focus on one cell type—gaba neurons in the bed nucleus of the stria terminalis, or BNST. The BNST is an outcropping of the amygdala, the part of the brain associated with emotion. The BNST also forms a bridge between the amygdala and the lateral hypothalamus, the brain region that drives primal functions such as eating, sexual behavior, and aggression.

The BNST gabaneurons have a cell body and a long strand with branched synapses that transmit electrical signals into the lateral hypothalamus. Stuber and his team wanted to stimulate those synapses by using an optogenetic technique, an involved process that would let him stimulate BNST cells simply by shining light on their synapses.

Typically, brain cells don't respond to light. So Stuber's team used genetically engineered proteins—from algae—that are sensitive to light and used genetically engineered viruses to deliver them into the brains of mice. Those proteins then get expressed only in the BNST cells, including in the synapses that connect to the hypothalamus.

His team then implanted fiber optic cables in the brains of these specially bred mice, and this allowed the researchers to shine light through the cables and onto BNST synapses. As soon as the light hit BNST synapses the mice began to eat voraciously even though they had already been well fed. Moreover, the mice showed a strong preference for high-fat foods.

"They would essentially eat up to half their daily caloric intake in about 20 minutes," Stuber said. "This suggests that this BNST pathway could play a role in food consumption and pathological conditions such as binge eating."

Stimulating the BNST also led the mice to exhibit behaviors associated with reward, suggesting that shining

Watch OGENETIC STIMULATION

light on BNST cells enhanced the pleasure of eating. On the flip side, shutting down the BNST pathway caused mice to show little interest in eating, even if they had been deprived of food.

"We were able to really home in on the precise neural circuit connection that was causing this phenomenon that's been observed for more than 50 years," Stuber said.

The study suggests that faulty wiring in BNST cells could interfere with hunger or satiety cues and contribute to human eating disorders, leading people to eat even when they are full or to avoid food when they are hungry. Further research is needed to determine whether it would be possible to develop drugs that correct a malfunctioning BNST circuit.

"We want to actually observe the normal function of these cell types and how they fire electrical signals when the animals are feeding or hungry," Stuber said. "We want to understand their genetic characteristics—what genes are expressed. For example, if we find cells that become really activated after binge eating, can we look at the gene expression profile to find out what makes those cells unique from other neurons."

And that, Stuber said, could lead to potential targets for drugs to treat certain populations of patients with eating disorders.

SOURCE: UNC scientists identify brain circuitry that triggers overeating http://news.unchealthcare.org/news/2013/september/BNST

individuals who meet criteria for food addiction also meet criteria for BED, so additional fine-grained research is required to tease out subtle differences between the two (Schreiber et al., 2013).

Some neuropsychological systems that are associated with addiction-related processes, including systems related to impulsivity and the executive (decision-making) system, may play a role in the development of BED (Tanofsky-Kraff et al., 2013). These systems may involve the reinforcing value of food for individuals and whether they experience loss of control over eating. Using PET scans, it was observed that the caudate and putamen areas of the brains of obese individuals with BED release more dopamine after exposure to a food stimulus than do the brains of obese individuals without BED (Wang et al., 2011). This is an important finding because dopamine regulates our motivation to eat, suggesting that obese individuals with BED are getting stronger signals to eat when they are exposed to food stimuli. Likewise, obese individuals with moderate-to-severe binge eating showed a reduction in pallidum/putamen response to images of high-calorie food in an fMRI study after treatment with a mu-opioid receptor antagonist vs. placebo (Cambridge et al., 2013). In addition, based on functional MRI data, overweight individuals with BED show more activity in the orbitofrontal cortex when viewing pictures of food than either overweight or normal weight individuals without BED (Schienle et al., 2009). The orbitofrontal cortex is involved in decision making but also houses structures related to taste reward and olfaction.

Much like work on drugs and alcohol, stress reactivity also increases the reinforcing value of food for individuals with BED. Individuals without BED tend to find food less reinforcing under conditions of stress (Goldfield et al., 2008). However, further research is needed to better understand how the full range of impulsive and executive system processes relate to BED as well as how these brain circuit abnormalities compare with other addictive disorders.

NEUROENDOCRINE AND NEUROHORMONAL FACTORS Other approaches to understanding biological causes focus on how the neuroendocrine and neurohormonal systems (see Chapter 2) affect feeding behavior and impulse control. Several neurotransmitter systems reviewed in Chapter 2 have been implicated in regulating feeding behavior. We focus here on the role of serotonin and dopamine, although several other neurotransmitters may also have an influence on *feeding initiation* (starting eating), *satiety* (fullness), craving, and appetite (Badman & Flier, 2005; Gerald et al., 1996; O'Connor & Roth, 2005; Scammell & Saper, 2005). Serotonin and dopamine have been linked to changes in the psychological and behavioral features of eating disorders, such as impulsivity and obsessionality (Roth & Shapiro, 2001; Simansky, 2005; Swerdlow, 2001). Indeed, serotonin has been directly related to the development of eating disorders (Brewerton & Jimerson, 1996; Jimerson et al., 1997; Kaye, 1997). In patients who have been free from anorexia or bulimia nervosa for more than a year, cerebrospinal levels of serotonin metabolites remain high (Kaye et al., 1991, 1998). However, it is not clear whether this increased brain serotonin activity is the *result* of the disorder or if it was present earlier and could predispose someone to develop an eating disorder. Women recovered from anorexia and bulimia nervosa also show alterations in serotonin receptor activity in some cortical and limbic brain regions, and these changes are associated with increased drive for thinness and harm avoidance (Culbert et al., 2015). Moreover, the profile of individuals with anorexia suggests that they are able to maintain a state of denial and, with the exception of weight loss, find little pleasure in life. This led some researchers to suggest that dopamine, the primary neurotransmitter for pleasure, might be involved. Interacting abnormalities in the serotonin and dopamine systems have been hypothesized to contribute to some of the personality features of eating disorders, such as perfectionism, rigidity, and obsessionality in anorexia nervosa (Kaye et al., 2013). Data from PET studies indicate that individuals with anorexia might have a dopamine-related disturbance of reward mechanisms that contributed to their behavioral style of self-denial (Frank, 2015). Across the female menstrual cycle, changes in ovarian hormones are associated with changes in emotional eating and binge eating, and these associations are particularly strong among women who engage in binge eating (Klump et al., 2014). Among women with clinically diagnosed binge episodes, emotional eating and binge frequencies were higher when levels of both progesterone and estradiol were low.

BRAIN STRUCTURE AND FUNCTIONING STUDIES Structural brain abnormalities exist in patients with anorexia nervosa. Compared with healthy controls, women with anorexia may have reduced gray matter volume in the insula, frontal operculum, occipital, medial temporal, or cingulate cortex as well as reduced gray matter volume across the cerebellum, temporal, frontal, and occipital lobes, though some studies have also shown increased gray matter volume in certain brain regions. Individuals with anorexia nervosa may also have less gray matter volume in the cerebellum, temporal, frontal, and occipital cortex when compared with those with bulimia nervosa (Frank, 2015) People with bulimia nervosa have increased gray matter volumes in frontal and ventral striatal areas (Van den Eynde et al., 2012). Studies of recovered individuals suggest that many of these brain tissue abnormalities may recover with clinical improvement (Van den Eynde et al., 2012; Wagner et al., 2006).

In terms of functional brain differences (see Chapter 2 on functional MRI), Geisler and colleagues (Geisler, 2015) used resting state fMRI to model the brain as a network and found broad disturbance in information flows across brain networks in individuals with acute anorexia nervosa. They reported reduced local network efficiency in the thalamus and posterior insula and hypothesized that this could be related to abnormal representations of body size and hunger in these patients.

In a series of investigations comparing visual processing in anorexia nervosa and body dysmorphic disorder, Feusner and colleagues identified abnormalities in the functioning of the early visual system functioning, which may contribute to perceptual distortions associated with body distortion in anorexia and perceptions of bodily defects in body dysmorphic disorder (Li & Lai et al., 2015; Madsen et al., 2013).

One intriguing area of investigation is the response of individuals with eating disorders and obesity in comparison with healthy controls when processing visual food cues during fMRI. A review of 50 studies suggested that differences do emerge in two brain circuits: the limbic and paralimbic areas that are associated with the activation of salience and reward processes and prefrontal areas supporting cognitive control processes (Garcia-Garcia et al., 2013).

No studies of individuals with anorexia and bulimia nervosa examine brain structure before patients develop eating disorders, so it is not known whether these changes existed before the disorder developed or are the result of it. From a scientist–practitioner perspective, demonstrating that these changes persist after weight recovery does not provide evidence that these changes are causal. Indeed, starvation (or alternating starvation and binge eating) could cause lasting biological "scars," indicating that these changes were a result of the disorders, not the reason that they developed.

FAMILY AND GENETIC STUDIES In Chapter 2, we discussed how understanding the role of genetics involves first asking whether a disorder runs in families and, if so, designing twin and adoption studies to determine the extent to which the familial pattern is due to genetic or environmental factors. Several family and twin studies have been conducted on eating disorders.

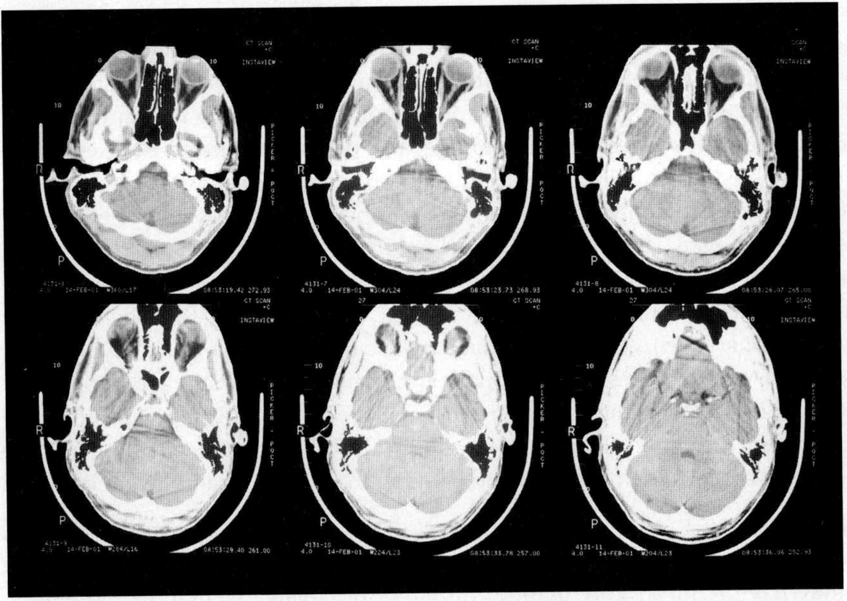

Acute anorexia nervosa in adolescents is associated with global thinning of cortical gray matter, which appears to be reversible with successful weight rehabilitation.

Family studies show that anorexia nervosa, bulimia nervosa, and BED clearly run in families (see "Examining the Evidence: Genes or Environment in Anorexia Nervosa?"). Relatives of individuals with anorexia and bulimia nervosa have approximately 10 times the lifetime risk of having an eating disorder as do relatives of people without eating disorders (Hudson et al., 1987; Lilenfeld et al., 1998; Strober et al., 2000). However, family members do not necessarily share the same eating disorder; rather, families often include members with anorexia nervosa, bulimia nervosa, and various types of EDNOS (the DSM-IV-TR residual category) (Lilenfeld et al., 1998; Strober et al., 2000). BED also runs in families independently of obesity (Hudson et al., 2006). Moreover, relatives of individuals with BED were 2.5 times more likely to be severely obese than were relatives of individuals without BED.

To what extent is this familial pattern due to genes and to what extent can it be attributed to the environment or modeling of unhealthy behaviors? Twin studies consistently show that eating disorders and related traits are moderately genetic (Bulik et al., 2000; Wade et al., 1999). The heritability of anorexia nervosa is estimated to be about 60% (Bulik et al., 2007; Wade et al., 2000) and the heritability of bulimia nervosa between 28 and 83% (reviewed in Bulik et al., 2000). The remaining variance (in both disorders) is attributable to individual specific environmental factors (see Chapter 2). For BED, the best current estimate of heritability is approximately 41% (Reichborn-Kjennerud et al., 2004). As a result of the consistent replication across samples and across countries, it appears that eating disorders are indeed influenced by genetic factors.

Armed with the results of the twin studies, genetic studies of eating disorders have gone one step further and begun to examine closely the areas of the genome that may influence the risk for anorexia and bulimia nervosa. To date, much less is known about the molecular genetics of BED, although studies are currently under way. For anorexia nervosa, one area of interest is on chromosome 1 (Devlin et al., 2002; Grice et al., 2002). Two genes have been isolated in that area—one related to serotonergic function and one to opioidergic function. Both are under study for their potential role in the development of anorexia nervosa (Bergen et al., 2003). Many other studies using the association approach (see Chapter 2) have explored genes that are known to influence appetite, weight regulation, and mood, again focusing on genes that influence the function of serotonin and dopamine and several other genes involved in functions central to the etiology of eating disorders.

For bulimia nervosa, a specific area of chromosome 10 has been identified as a "hot spot" (Bulik et al., 2003). Intriguingly, this area was also identified as a hot spot in a genetic study of obesity (Froguel, 1998). Genetic studies using the association approach have focused on many of the same genes targeted in the study of anorexic nervosa. Of particular interest, one genetic variation associated with the serotonin system (Steiger et al., 2005)

Examining the EVIDENCE

Genes or Environment in Anorexia Nervosa?

Is this just an example of the "fat phobic" environment terrorizing two young girls into anorexia nervosa, or could it be the manifestation of an underlying genetic predisposition?

Let's Examine the Evidence

- **The Role of Environment** The environment is a major contributor to eating disorders. Issues such as weight intolerance, teasing, fat phobia, and the societal pressure to be thin all contribute to young girls developing eating disorders. The teasing that the Kendall twins experienced was another powerful environmental influence: they made a pact never to be teased again. Twins also often have a special bond. In this case, their pact to diet was so strong that they both eventually died. A rational approach to preventing eating disorders would include a focus on decreasing bullying and teasing in school as well as putting pressure on the media and the modeling industry to stop flaunting unrealistic ideals of thinness.
- **The Facts** Twin sisters Michaela and Samantha Kendall considered themselves to be overweight at age 14 and started dieting to lose weight. The notion that they were overweight was not their own idea. The girls were taunted and ridiculed by classmates (their mother estimated that they weighed nearly 200 pounds before they started dieting). Although the dieting began innocently, it ended up being devastating. The girls had no idea how controlling eating disorders could be. Samantha abused laxatives and eventually became unable to control her bowels. She soiled her bedsheets almost nightly. Both twins became pregnant at age 22 but had abortions for fear of getting fat. The twins attracted international media attention in the 1990s when they appeared on the Maury Povich show and shared their heartbreaking struggles with eating disorders. Both sisters eventually died from complications of anorexia nervosa. Michaela died first, lying next to her twin sister in bed. After Michaela died in 1994, Samantha tried desperately to turn her life around and recover. Unfortunately, the damage to her body had already been done, and although Samantha managed a short recovery period, she died in October 1997.
- **The Role of Genetics** The fact that the Kendall twins already weighed nearly 200 pounds by age 14 suggests that they were indeed biologically predisposed to eating and weight dysregulation. Although they were teased in school, countless overweight kids get teased in school but never develop an eating disorder. The twins decided to go on their first diet together, and they never came off of it. Even though that first diet was a choice, once they were in negative energy balance (expended more calories than they took in), the anorexia took on a life of its own—because they were genetically predisposed. They were different because of their bodies' response to starvation. Indeed, most teens who are overweight and go on a diet have a hard time losing weight and often become obese adults. In the Kendall twins' situation, their weight dropped like a stone, and they were able to maintain that frightening low weight until their deaths. In this case, their biology trapped them in the prison of anorexia nervosa. A rational approach to preventing eating disorders would be to identify the genes that predispose to anorexia nervosa and develop medications to counteract the biological factors that inhibit eating and enable maintenance of low body weight.
- **Conclusion** Not nature *or* nurture but nature *and* nurture—it is highly unlikely that either nature or nurture alone caused the Kendall twins' anorexia nervosa. Whereas countless adolescents are teased about their weight, only a small fraction ever goes on to develop anorexia nervosa. What made them more vulnerable? What made their bodies respond to dieting differently than the majority of their peers? It is very likely that their genetic predisposition rendered them more sensitive to negative energy balance than others. Their ability to maintain such low intake and low weight is testimony to the fact that they were biologically different from their peers. A rational approach to preventing eating disorders would be to identify high-risk individuals based on their genotype. These individuals could then be provided strategies and tools to develop environments that would allow them to avoid situations of negative energy balance that could trigger an eating disorder.

SOURCE: Bateman, M. (1997, November 16). These are not just desserts. *The London Independent*.

found a relationship with symptoms such as impulsivity, affective instability, and insecure attachment in women with eating disorders that included binge eating and purging.

Three studies have used genome-wide association approaches to compare people with anorexia nervosa to people with no psychological disorder; however, none of these studies was sufficiently large to expect the identification of loci that meet the stringent criteria for genome-wide significance (Boraska et al., 2014; Nakabayshi et al., 2009; Wang et al., 2011). Results suggest that signal does exist in the data and that increased sample sizes will yield results. Based on results from genetic studies for other psychiatric disorders, as sample size increases, sometimes into the tens and hundreds of thousands, significant results emerge. Given that we expect hundreds of genes to be implicated, each of small effect, it is logical that large samples are necessary before their effects can be detected.

Advances in the understanding of the genetics of eating disorders have been meteoric over the past decade; however, genes cannot paint the entire picture. The most likely causal explanations will involve an interaction between genes and the environment. Just having risk genes does not mean that someone will develop an eating disorder. In fact, someone with several risk genes may never develop a disorder if she or he is not exposed to environmental factors that trigger the genetic predisposition. Although our genes establish our baseline risk, our environment can be protective (buffering) and/or triggering (risk enhancing). As with so many psychological disorders, the complex interplay between genes and the environment will be the key to understanding the emergence of these syndromes.

Psychological Perspectives

LO 8.16 Contrast psychodynamic, behavioral, cognitive, and sociocultural theories on the etiology of eating disorders.

Several psychological theories attempt to explain eating disorders. Some of these theories still contribute to our understanding of aspects of the disorders, but they are best considered together with what we know about biological risk factors.

PSYCHODYNAMIC PERSPECTIVES As we recall from Chapter 1, psychodynamic thinking focuses on the influence of early experience. Early psychoanalytic theory viewed anorexia nervosa as an attempt to defend against anxiety associated with emerging adult sexuality (Waller et al., 1940). Anorexia nervosa was considered an unconscious attempt to reverse or reject adult female sexuality via starvation to a prepubertal state (Dare et al., 1994). As psychoanalytic theory moved away from a narrow focus on sexuality, the explanation shifted to interpersonal relationships and the interpersonal context in which these disorders arose (Kaufman & Heiman, 1964). One of the key clinicians and writers in the field, Hilde Bruch (1973, 1978), introduced rich clinical descriptions of patients with anorexia nervosa in her book *The Golden Cage*. Through her careful insights and keen ability to understand what motivated her patients to maintain such rigid control on food intake, she identified features such as body image distortion and a pervasive sense of ineffectiveness as core aspects of anorexic pathology.

The fashion industry's emphasis on thinness has often been identified as a sociocultural factor contributing to the rising prevalence of eating disorders.

FAMILY MODELS OF EATING DISORDERS Early family models of eating disorders, especially anorexia nervosa, focused on patterns of family dysfunction among patients who sought treatment. Perhaps best known is the work of Argentinean psychiatrist Salvador Minuchin (Minuchin et al., 1978), who identified four dysfunctional patterns. He noted enmeshment, rigidity, overprotectiveness, and poor conflict resolution as characteristic of what he referred to as *psychosomatic families*. The word **enmeshment** described the overinvolvement of all family members in the affairs of any one member. *Rigidity* described the difficulty families faced in adapting to the changing developmental needs of their children, for example, children's increasing need for autonomy. Rigid families have great difficulty maturing along with their children. *Overprotectiveness* meant that parents shielded children from age-appropriate experiences. Finally, *poor conflict resolution* reflected the difficulties these families had in dealing with problematic, negative situations.

According to Minuchin's theory, family pathology was expressed as a psychosomatic illness in one child (in this case anorexia nervosa). He used the family mealtime to assess family functioning and as a therapeutic tool. His vivid examples of family meals provided insights into how families functioned at a high-risk time (namely, around food). Although his work brought the study of anorexia nervosa into the realm of scientific inquiry, his sample was biased toward families who could afford treatment at an academic center. Later studies suggested that his descriptions were oversimplified and that families of patients with anorexia nervosa were not so homogeneous (Kog et al., 1987). Many of the patterns he observed were results of the family living with anorexia nervosa rather than causal. Contemporary theories focus more on how to engage families in treatment rather than viewing them as causal agents (Lock & le Grange, 2012).

Family-based interventions for eating disorders often focus on family meals.

COGNITIVE-BEHAVIORAL THEORIES The cognitive-behavioral model focuses on distorted cognitions about body shape, weight, eating, and personal control that lead to and maintain unhealthy eating and weight-related behaviors. Consider the following classic example of a cognitive distortion. After eating one doughnut, someone with bulimia nervosa might think, "I've already blown it. I may as well go ahead and eat the whole dozen!" Proponents of a cognitive-behavioral model emphasize the power of thoughts to influence feelings and behaviors. In bulimia nervosa, distorted thoughts about food, shape, and weight lead to particular feelings and behaviors that then perpetuate the binge–purge cycle. Several cognitive-behavioral models of bulimia nervosa have been developed (Fairburn, 1981; Mitchell, 1990; Schnitzler et al., 2012).

SOCIOCULTURAL THEORIES Sociocultural models emphasize the Western cultural preoccupation with thinness as beauty. The sociocultural model follows the path from being exposed to the ideal of thinness, to internalizing this ideal, and then to observing a discrepancy between actual and ideal body to dissatisfaction with one's body (e.g., via body surveillance), to dietary restraint, and finally to restriction (Fitzsimmons-Craft et al., 2012; Stice & Shaw, 2002; Striegel-Moore et al., 1986). Because girls and women are often valued primarily for their appearance (Moradi et al., 2005), they are more likely to internalize the thin ideal. Subtle and overt messages to achieve the thin ideal can significantly affect a woman's self-esteem and body esteem. In general, exposure to media images of the thin ideal is associated with adverse consequences among college-age women (Stice & Shaw, 2002; Tiggemann & Pickering, 1996). Even brief exposure to a cosmetic surgery reality show can lead to decreased self-esteem—especially in individuals who have significantly internalized the thin ideal (Mazzeo et al., 2007). Internationalization of the thin ideal can also predict future social appearance comparison and body dissatisfaction (Rodgers et al., 2015).

Although the thin ideal primarily targets girls and women, sociocultural forces also operate on boys and men. Increasing emphasis on leanness and muscularity can contribute to males turning to unhealthy weight control behaviors, including using anabolic steroids to achieve the prized "six-pack" or "ripped" physical ideal (Kanayama et al., 2006). Just as for women, even brief exposure to media images of the thin body ideal can negatively affect men's views of their own bodies (Leit et al., 2002). Support for the role of sociocultural factors in eating disorders comes from a landmark study conducted by Becker and her colleagues in Fiji. In 1995, before television was available on the island, Becker and her team surveyed 63 Fijian secondary school girls who were on average 17 years old. Three years later, after television had saturated the island, the researchers surveyed 65 girls from the same schools, who were matched in age, weight, and other characteristics with the girls in the earlier group. Remarkably, whereas only 3% of the original girls had reported self-induced vomiting for weight control in the initial study, a full 15% reported such vomiting 3 years later (Becker et al., 2002). Additionally, new data indicate that the amount of television watching by someone's friends can influence a girl's body image even if the girl does not own or watch television herself (Becker et al., 2011). Thus, one's social network can strongly affect a person's risk for developing an eating disorder.

Four lines of evidence provide partial support for the sociocultural model (Striegel-Moore & Bulik, 2007). This evidence includes the imbalanced sex ratio in anorexia and bulimia nervosa, the increasing incidence of some eating disorders in parallel with the decreasing body size ideal for women, cross-cultural differences in the incidence or prevalence of eating disorders (with higher rates in cultures that value extreme female thinness), and the significant prospective relationship between internalization of the thin ideal and disordered eating.

Sociocultural theory cannot account for the development of all eating disorders. Virtually all young girls are exposed to the thin ideal, and many internalize it, yet only a few go on to develop full eating disorder syndromes (Striegel-Moore et al., 1986). The most plausible explanation is that environment affects individuals to different degrees and in different ways. The reason for this could rest in genetic factors and suggest gene × environment interactions as we discussed in Chapter 2 (Bulik, 2005; Culbert et al., 2015). A genetic predisposition may make an individual more vulnerable to behaviors such as dieting, which are triggered by exposure to sociocultural pressures toward thinness. Although the first diet may be nothing more than an unpleasant hunger-inducing experience for someone with low genetic vulnerability, for someone with high genetic vulnerability, the first diet may trigger the descent into full-blown anorexia nervosa. Another factor requiring further research is the role of increased average weight (which is increasing in children and young adults) and more frequent dieting (which starts earlier and affects many more people).

Learning Objective Summaries

LO 8.15 Understand genetic, brain, hormonal, and environmental factors that increase risk for eating disorders.

Anorexia nervosa, bulimia nervosa, and binge-eating disorder are all heritable, meaning that genetic factors play a significant causal role. Genes do not act alone as environmental factors such as societal thin ideal internalization, teasing and bullying, and childhood abuse can also increase risk for developing eating disorders. Both human and animal research studies are beginning to isolate areas and pathways in the brain that influence abnormal eating and appetite including brain regions involved in reward. Serotonin, dopamine, and several other neurotransmitters appear to influence feeding initiation (starting eating), satiety (fullness), craving, and appetite.

LO 8.16 Contrast psychodynamic, behavioral, cognitive, and sociocultural theories on the etiology of eating disorders.

Psychodynamic theories focus on early experience and the desire to reverse emerging sexuality. The cognitive-behavioral model focuses on distorted cognitions about body shape, weight, eating, and personal control that lead to and maintain unhealthy eating and weight-related behaviors. Sociocultural models emphasize the Western cultural preoccupation with thinness as beauty and the internalization of this ideal, which leads to observing a discrepancy between actual and ideal body to dissatisfaction with one's body (e.g., via body surveillance), to dietary restraint, and finally to restriction.

Critical Thinking Question

Zach was an exchange student in Japan. The food was all quite unfamiliar, and he was much larger (and hairier) than all of the Japanese boys in his class. He felt like an ogre in comparison to his new classmates. He also missed the familiarity of the food from home. He started skipping lunch and found that he felt much less self-conscious in the afternoon. His restricting got out of hand as he lost a lot of weight fast. His host family notified the school, and he was sent back home for medical care. Discuss the likely genetic and environmental factors that contributed to Zach developing anorexia nervosa.

The Treatment of Eating Disorders

Treatment goals for patients with anorexia nervosa, bulimia nervosa, and BED differ somewhat, although they have commonalities. The normalization and stabilization of eating behavior and weight are the central treatment goal for all eating disorders; however, the precise nature of the desired change differs. In anorexia nervosa, the initial goals are to increase caloric intake and weight gain so that later stages of treatment can deal more effectively with the psychological aspects of the disorder. For bulimia nervosa, when weight is usually within the healthy range, the focus of treatment is to normalize eating, eliminate binge eating and purging episodes, and improve the psychological aspects of the disorder. In BED, controversy exists over whether weight loss should be a therapeutic outcome for patients who are overweight or obese, as many people argue that repeated attempts to lose weight are often causal of BED. The best way to achieve the therapeutic goals is different for each disorder.

Inpatient Treatment for Anorexia Nervosa

LO 8.17 Discuss the need for inpatient treatment for anorexia nervosa and what it entails.

Treatment for anorexia nervosa can be difficult and is best accomplished by a multidisciplinary team. The first and most critical step is restoring weight. Psychotherapy is difficult to conduct when the patients are acutely ill because starvation impairs their ability to think. Psychotherapeutic approaches include individual psychotherapy (cognitive-behavioral, interpersonal, behavioral, supportive, and psychodynamic), family therapy (especially for younger patients), and group therapy. Individuals who are below 75% of their expected body weight should be hospitalized (APA Work Group on Eating Disorders, 2000).

Besides weight, other factors that influence the decision to hospitalize individuals suffering from anorexia nervosa include medical complications; suicide attempts or plans; failure to improve with outpatient treatment; comorbid psychiatric disorders; interference with school, work, or family; poor social support; pregnancy; and the unavailability of other treatment options (APA Work Group on Eating Disorders, 2000). Inpatient treatment involves highly specialized multidisciplinary teams, including psychologists, psychiatrists, internists or pediatricians, dietitians, social workers, and nurse specialists. At severely low weights, patients may be prescribed bed rest or have their activity limited for safety reasons and as a way to give their bodies a chance to start gaining weight. Typically, as patients eat and gain weight, they are given increasing privileges on the treatment unit. Often, a dietitian initially chooses menus for the patients. As patients get better and are able to make healthy choices, they take on responsibility for food selections in order to continue the weight gain. Inpatient treatment for anorexia nervosa can be very difficult for both the patients and their families. Treatment presents an unusual situation: patients are deeply afraid of giving up the symptoms (starvation and low weight), and the medicine the doctor offers is something the patients avoid (food). Developing a collaborative relationship is critical to decreasing patients' anxiety about weight gain and to making the hospitalization a success.

Ethics and Responsibility

LO 8.18 Appreciate the complexities of involuntary commitment of individuals with anorexia nervosa.

Involuntary treatment for anorexia nervosa by means of legal commitment occurs for a minority of patients with eating disorders, and this is sometimes a controversial action. Legal commitment is less controversial when the patient is suicidal, clearly intending to harm herself or himself. Yet part of the diagnostic criteria for anorexia nervosa is an inability to recognize the seriousness of the low weight, and patients with this disorder will not express an intent to harm themselves, although their behaviors may result in severe harm or death. Legally, self-starvation is generally considered a behavior that endangers life and constitutes a grave disability, thereby allowing civil commitment of patients with severe anorexia who refuse treatment (Applebaum & Rumpf, 1998).

Patients with anorexia nervosa show equivalent rates of weight gain during hospitalization whether they enter the hospital voluntarily or involuntarily as a result of a legal commitment process. Moreover, when asked later, patients who were committed involuntarily commonly report that their involuntary treatment was justified and view their treatment teams with good will (Watson et al., 2000). In principle, involuntary commitment should be viewed as an approach of last resort only after patients decline voluntary hospitalization, when their physical safety is at risk, and when there is likely to be therapeutic gain from hospitalization (Applebaum & Rumpf, 1998).

Discussions and clinical trials are emerging that explore how best to treat individuals with severe and enduring eating disorders (SE-ED) for whom multiple interventions fail to effect cure. A recent RCT of outpatient psychotherapy supported a shift of focus from weight regain and recovery to a therapeutic goal of improved quality of life (Touyz et al., 2013).

Explore ETHICS AND RESPONSIBILITY

Biological Treatments for Eating Disorders

LO 8.19 Identify efficacious pharmacological treatments for eating disorders.

PHARMACOLOGICAL TREATMENTS Although medications are commonly prescribed for the treatment of anorexia nervosa, none has yet been identified as effective (Watson & Bulik, 2013). A 2007 report highlighted the critical need for developing medications that target the core symptoms of anorexia nervosa (Bulik et al., 2007). For bulimia nervosa, the antidepressant fluoxetine (Prozac) appears to reduce the core symptoms of binge eating and purging and associated psychological features such as depression and anxiety, at least in the short term (Shapiro et al., 2007). In 1994, the Food and Drug Administration (FDA) approved fluoxetine for the treatment of bulimia. Although fluoxetine reduces the core symptoms, it is still unclear whether its effects are long lasting or associated with permanent remission. The optimal duration of treatment and the best strategy for maintaining treatment gains also remain unknown. For BED, several medications target the core symptoms of binge eating or weight loss. Evidence exists for the efficacy of second-generation antidepressants (as a class), topiramate (an anticonvulsant), and lisdesxmfetamine (an amphetamine that has received FDA approval) in the treatment of BED (Brownley et al., in press).

NUTRITIONAL COUNSELING For all eating disorders, nutritional rehabilitation is a necessary but not sufficient intervention. Although patients with anorexia nervosa often spend inordinate amounts of time pondering nutrition labels and counting calories, they are unable to apply this information to their own eating. Dietitians trained in the treatment of eating disorders are valuable members of the multidisciplinary team and can assess nutritional deficiencies in patients with anorexia nervosa, set appropriate goal weights, provide support, develop strategies for renormalization of eating, and calculate caloric requirements for weight gain (Mittnacht & Bulik, 2015). For bulimia nervosa and BED, dietitians can help the patient relearn appropriate portion sizes, eat meals in a normal way, and develop strategies for decreasing urges to binge. In addition, in BED, the dietitian can help determine appropriate caloric intake for either body weight maintenance or weight loss. Although an important adjunct, nutritional therapy is ineffective as a sole intervention and is unacceptable to patients, as reflected in high dropout rates when delivered as the only intervention (Hsu et al., 2001).

Psychological Treatments

LO 8.20 Contrast available psychological treatments for eating disorders.

COGNITIVE-BEHAVIORAL THERAPY As discussed in earlier chapters, cognitive-behavioral therapy (CBT) helps patients change patterns in thinking that contribute to their problems. The application of CBT to the treatment of eating disorders focuses on faulty cognitions about body shape, weight, eating, and personal control that lead to and perpetuate the dysfunction in eating and weight. The therapist addresses both relatively easily accessible thoughts, called *automatic thoughts*, which are often evaluative in nature, and deeper *core beliefs*, which are the guiding principles or self-truths of the individual. CBT involves identifying and challenging distorted cognitions about food, eating, and body shape and weight and replacing them with health-promoting alternatives. Studies that have dismantled the cognitive and behavioral components of CBT have shown that the cognitive component appears to be most critical in effecting behavior change.

For anorexia nervosa, preliminary evidence suggests that CBT may reduce relapse in adults after weight has been restored (Pike et al., 1996). CBT may be less effective when patients are extremely underweight. This therapy requires active cognitive effort, so patients whose cognitive processing is impaired by starvation may not be able to benefit from CBT during the acute stage of their illness (McIntosh et al., 2005). What we know about the efficacy of CBT for anorexia nervosa is limited to adults, for no studies have adequately evaluated developmentally tailored cognitive-behavioral treatments for adolescents.

Recovery rates from bulimia with CBT vary from 35 to 75% at 5 or more years of follow-up (Fairburn et al., 2000; Herzog et al., 1999). The rates differ in part because of varying definitions of recovery. However, approximately 33% of individuals with bulimia nervosa relapse, and the risk is highest during the year following treatment (Shapiro et al., 2007).

The cornerstone of CBT for bulimia nervosa is self-monitoring. Patients keep track of what they ate, whether it was a binge or purge episode, the situation they were in, who else was present, and their thoughts and feelings (see Figure 8.2). By analyzing the data, the patient and therapist can identify patterns of unhealthy behavior, including high-risk times and situations for binge eating and purging, which serves as a first step in establishing healthier behavior patterns. More recently, modern information technology has been adapted for self-monitoring including the use of smartphone apps and cell phone–based text messaging.

The next steps involve mastering the language and concepts of CBT, including recognizing thoughts, feelings, and behaviors that are associated with unhealthy eating behavior; learning to recognize cues for and consequences of disordered eating; learning to control automatic thoughts; and learning to restructure distorted cognitions that perpetuate unhealthy eating behaviors. The final goal of CBT is preventing relapse, and clinicians provide tools to patients for maintaining healthy behaviors (see Figure 8.3).

CBT is also effective in the treatment of BED (Brownley et al., in press). In the United Kingdom, self-help, often incorporating CBT principles, is recommended as a first step in treating this disorder (National Institute of Clinical and Health Excellence, 2004). Patients with BED might first be offered a self-help book or an online cognitive-behavioral program to use at their own pace. For some, this approach might be enough to put them on the path

Figure 8.2 Self-Monitoring via Text Message.

Patients type in their status and receive a return message from their therapist.

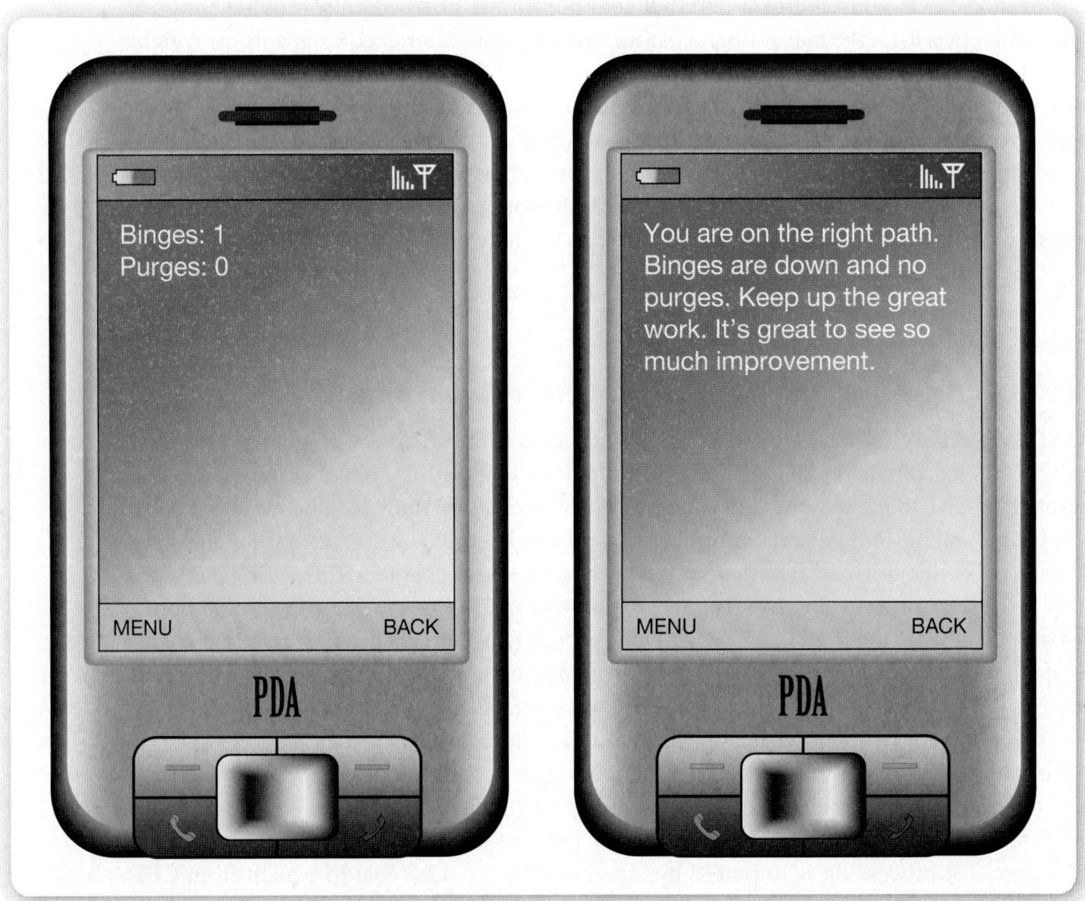

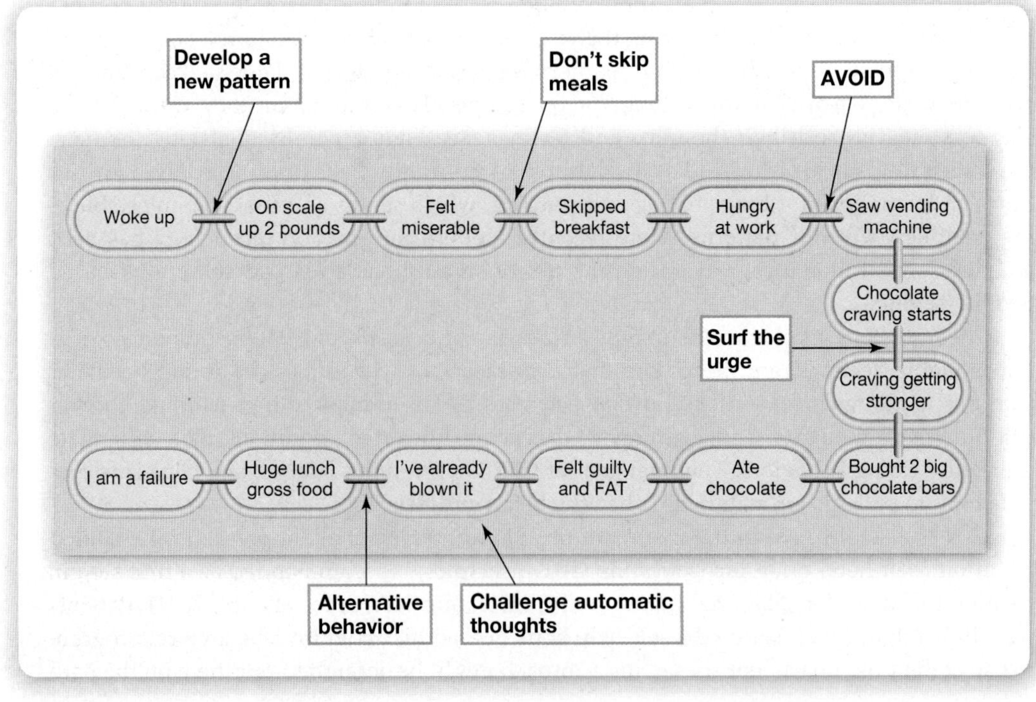

Figure 8.3 A Behavioral Chain.

Chaining allows the patient to map out how thoughts, feelings, and behaviors cascade to unhealthy consequences. The object of the technique is to help the patient learn strategies to break the chain at every link.

to recovery. At the next check-in, if doing well, they might be encouraged to continue. If they have made no progress or if their condition has deteriorated, they are referred for specialist treatment as a second step in care.

By extension, dialectical behavioral therapy (DBT) focuses on emotional dysregulation as the core problem in eating disorders and views symptoms as attempts to manage unpleasant emotional states. A small study of DBT for bulimia showed that patients receiving it had significantly greater decreases in binge eating and purging than did those on a waiting list and that abstinence was greater after DBT treatment than in the waiting-list group (Safer et al., 2001). DBT is also being explored as an intervention for anorexia nervosa (McCabe & Marcus, 2002) and BED (Chen et al., 2008; Masson et al., 2013). An open-label trial has also pilot-tested the integration of DBT and family-based therapy (FBT) for adolescents with bulimia nervosa (Murray et al., 2015). Additional studies are necessary before the efficacy of DBT for AN, BN, and BED can be determined (Bankoff et al., 2012; Brownley et al., in press).

INTERPERSONAL PSYCHOTHERAPY Initially developed for the treatment of depression, interpersonal psychotherapy (IPT) is a brief, time-limited psychotherapy (Klerman et al., 1984). IPT is based on the theory that, regardless of their cause, the current depressive symptoms are "inextricably intertwined" with the patient's interpersonal relationships. The goals of IPT for depression are to decrease depressive symptoms and to improve interpersonal functioning by enhancing communication skills in significant relationships. The adaptation of IPT for the treatment of bulimia nervosa (Fairburn et al., 1993), anorexia nervosa (McIntosh et al., 2000), and BED (Wilfley et al., 1993) applies the same principles of focusing on reducing symptoms related to eating disorders. IPT for eating disorders intervenes at the symptom and social functioning levels by addressing one of four problem areas: interpersonal disputes, role transitions, abnormal grief, or interpersonal deficits.

For anorexia nervosa, IPT has been found to be less effective at end treatment than a therapy based on supportive psychotherapy and sound clinical management or CBT, although across-group differences were no longer apparent at 5-year follow-up (McIntosh et al., 2005). For bulimia nervosa, IPT has been found to be as effective as CBT, but CBT shows more rapid decreases in bulimic symptoms (Fairburn et al., 1991, 1993). IPT, delivered both individually and in group therapy, has also shown preliminary efficacy in BED (Wilfley et al., 1993). It is interesting that a treatment that does not directly address the core symptoms of the eating disorder (especially bulimia and BED) but focuses solely on current interpersonal relationships produces results equivalent to CBT, which focuses specifically on the disordered eating and body image issues. How IPT helps to decrease the symptoms of bulimia nervosa and BED is unknown. Clearly, eating disorders often have profound effects on interpersonal relationships, and IPT highlights the many ways in which the eating disorder disrupts social functioning.

SPECIALIZED SUPPORTIVE CLINICAL MANAGEMENT Specialist supportive clinical management (SSCM) for anorexia nervosa is an outpatient treatment originally developed as a comparison treatment to CBT and IPT in a psychotherapy trial for AN (McIntosh et al., 2005, 2006). SSCM combines features of clinical management (Fawcett et al., 1987) and supportive psychotherapy (Dewald, 1994). Clinical management addresses core symptoms of AN, focusing on facilitating normal eating and the restoration of weight. Clinical management is good-quality clinical care from an experienced clinician, ensuring safety, providing care and education, and doing no harm as well as maintaining a therapeutic relationship that promotes adherence to recommended treatment (Fawcett, 1987; Joyce, 1995). The supportive therapy component addresses other life issues identified by the patient. Supportive psychotherapy aims to assist patients by providing a supportive therapeutic context with a warm, encouraging clinician in which the patient is encouraged to explore issues and make changes to relieve the intensity of distress and impairment associated with the presenting problems (Dewald, 1994). Supportive psychotherapy strategies include demonstrating support, acceptance, and affection toward the patient; working together to make changes; communicating optimism that goals are achievable; focusing on strengths; respecting defenses; and encouraging independent coping (Dewald, 1994). Subsequent to the original trial, three studies have found SSCM to be not significantly different to more complex therapies. SSCM is potentially more easily disseminated to a range of health professionals (Jordan et al., 2015).

FAMILY-BASED AND COUPLE-BASED THERAPY Based on early family theories of anorexia nervosa, Minuchin and Palazzoli have advocated therapy aimed at changing the dysfunctional family system (Minuchin et al., 1978; Palazzoli, 1978), modifying dysfunctional transactional family patterns, and reorganizing the family around healthier and more open communication (Minuchin et al., 1978). Family involvement is unquestionably critical in the treatment of anorexia nervosa especially in young patients who are not chronically ill (Russell et al., 1987). However, the early observations by Minuchin and others of the "typical" anorexia nervosa family have not been substantiated. Indeed, there is no one prototypic anorexic family. Modern approaches to family therapy for anorexia nervosa include conjoint family therapy in which all family members are treated together; separated family therapy in which parents are treated separately from their ill child; parent training that provides parents psychoeducation and tools to manage their child's eating disorder (Zucker et al., 2005); and a popular approach, family-based therapy (FBT), referred to as some as the Maudsley method, which focuses on parental control of the initial stages of renutrition (Lock et al., 2002, 2010). FBT hinges on seven principles:

1. Work with experts who know how to help you.
2. Work together as a family.
3. Don't blame your child or yourself for the problems you are having. Blame the illness.
4. Focus on the problem before you.
5. Don't debate with your child about eating—or weight-related concerns.
6. Know when to begin backing off.
7. Take care of yourself. You are the child's best hope.

The Maudsley approach empowers parents to take an active role in achieving successful treatment. This approach also includes therapist-assisted family meals.

Although family therapy is effective with adolescents, as currently conceptualized, it is less developmentally appropriate for adults with anorexia nervosa (Bulik et al., 2007), although couple-based interventions that join partners in recovery from anorexia nervosa and BED are being evaluated (Bulik et al., 2011, Kirby et al., 2015). A novel treatment called MANTRA (Maudsley Model of Anorexia Nervosa Therapy for Adults) is also exploring including family members in the treatment of adults with anorexia nervosa (Schmidt et al., 2015).

One clinical trial has shown initial promise for family-based treatment of bulimia nervosa (le Grange et al., 2007). There have been no clinical trials of family therapy for BED. See Table 8.7 for a summary of treatments.

TREATMENT OF EATING DISORDERS IN CHILDREN

Nina was 14 years old and had moderate intellectual disability. When not closely monitored, she would eat any foreign object that she found on the floor. The psychologist developed an overcorrection program that consisted of Nina's spitting out the object and throwing it away. Then she would be led to the bathroom to brush her teeth for 10 minutes using an antiseptic toothpaste. After 1 week of consistent overcorrection, Nina's pica was reduced by 60%.

Behavioral interventions, such as overcorrection, are also effective for pica (Call et al., 2015). If such procedures are done repeatedly and consistently, pica can be eliminated or greatly reduced (Foxx & Martin, 1975; Hagopian et al., 2011). Medications are not efficacious for the treatment of feeding disorders. Behavioral interventions such as habit reversal, relaxation training, and cognitive-behavioral therapy are efficacious for rumination disorder (Chial et al., 2003; Soykan et al., 1997). *Habit reversal* is a behavioral treatment in which a problem behavior is eliminated by consistently using a competing (i.e., alternative) behavior. In the case of rumination, the patient is taught *diaphragmatic* (deep) breathing, a competing response that eliminates rumination in most patients (Chial et al., 2003). As ARFID first appeared in DSM-5, evidence-based treatment guidelines have yet to emerge.

Table 8.7 Types of Therapy

Type of Therapy	Description
Cognitive-behavioral therapy	• Focuses on here and now • Addresses faulty cognitions about body shape, weight, eating, and personal control • Addresses automatic thoughts • Works on core beliefs
Dialectical behavioral therapy	• Focuses on emotional dysregulation • Views symptoms as attempts to manage unpleasant emotional states
Interpersonal psychotherapy	• Originally developed for treatment of depression • Sees eating disorder symptoms as "inextricably intertwined" with the patient's interpersonal relationships • Focuses on one of four problem areas: interpersonal disputes, role transitions, abnormal grief, or interpersonal deficits
Specialized supportive clinical management	• Combines elements of clinical management and supportive psychotherapy • Ensures safety, provides care and education, does no harm, maintains a therapeutic relationship that promotes adherence to recommended treatment • Addresses other life issues identified by the patient
Family-based treatment	• Parents in control of renutrition • Work together as a family • Empowers parents to take an active role in treatment
Couple-based treatment	• Includes partners in treatment context • Work together toward recovery

Learning Objective Summaries

LO 8.17 Discuss the need for inpatient treatment for anorexia nervosa and what it entails.

Inpatient treatment involves highly specialized multidisciplinary teams, including psychologists, psychiatrists, internists or pediatricians, dietitians, social workers, and nurse specialists. At severely low weights, patients may be prescribed bed rest or have their activity limited for safety reasons and to facilitate weight gain. Typically, as patients eat and gain weight, they are given increasing privileges on the treatment unit. Often, a dietitian initially chooses menus for the patients. As patients get better and are able to make healthy choices, they take on responsibility for food selection in order to continue the weight gain.

LO 8.18 Appreciate the complexities of involuntary commitment of individuals with anorexia nervosa.

Because individuals with anorexia nervosa often cannot recognize the seriousness of their low weight, their behaviors may result in severe harm or death. Legally, self-starvation is considered a behavior that endangers life and constitutes a grave disability, thereby allowing civil commitment of patients with severe anorexia who refuse treatment. In principle, involuntary commitment should be viewed as an approach of last resort only after patients decline voluntary hospitalization, when their physical safety is at risk, and when there is likely to be therapeutic gain from hospitalization.

LO 8.19 Identify efficacious pharmacological treatments for eating disorders.

No medications are effective in treating anorexia nervosa. Fluoxetine has been approved by the FDA for the treatment of bulimia nervosa, and lisdesxmfetamine has been approved for the treatment of BED; there is also evidence for efficacy of second-generation antidepressants (as a class) and topiramate (an anticonvulsant).

LO 8.20 Contrast available psychological treatments for eating disorders.

Cognitive-behavioral therapy is the evidence-based treatment of choice for bulimia nervosa and BED and may be helpful in anorexia nervosa after initial weight restoration. Interpersonal psychotherapy has also demonstrated efficacy in anorexia nervosa, bulimia nervosa, and binge-eating disorder although the trajectory of recovery may be slower than CBT. Family-based therapy (FBT) is a promising treatment for youth with anorexia and bulimia nervosa, and including family members and partners in treatment of adults with eating disorders may also be beneficial.

Critical Thinking Question

Marian recalls experiencing loss of control eating since she was a little girl. She was teased a lot for her frizzy hair and because her parents were obese. She would often go home after school and drown her hurt by eating sweets, hiding wrappers under her mattress until she could throw them away without being caught. At age 55, this pattern has persisted. Often in response to conflicts with others or situations at work in which she feels inadequate, she finds herself binge eating at home after work. Her doctor has told her to lose weight for her health, but that just makes her binge more, feeling like a complete failure. Discuss Marian's treatment options. What might you recommend and why? If your first choice doesn't work, what would you try next?

Real SCIENCE Real LIFE

Hannah—Detection and Treatment of Anorexia Nervosa in a Student Athlete

THE PATIENT

Hannah loved to run. In elementary school, she outran the boys. In middle school, she joined the cross-country team, was team captain, and won the conference championships. Running was her life, and she was good at it. She ran cross-country and the 3,000 throughout high school, racking up state championships in both. But that was just like Hannah—she was always driven to do her best, whether it was in academics or athletics. Even in first grade, she often cried and would tell her mother that she was worried that she did not do her best—and she had to be the best. So she was thrilled when she was awarded full athletic scholarships to two excellent universities. She chose a university two states away that excelled in women's track and field.

THE PROBLEM

The cross-country season started off well her freshman year, but Hannah had tendonitis problems during indoor track season. The trainers had her sit out the season so that she would be ready for the outdoor season. Not competing caused her great distress. She watched her teammates at home meets, listened to their tales of victory at away meets, and longed to be out there with them. She found it difficult to concentrate on her schoolwork. Previously an A student, she started to get Cs in chemistry and calculus. Not only that, but she also started to gain weight. Even though she was swimming and cross-training to try to stay in shape, it wasn't the same as being on the team. Carrying around an extra 10 pounds made her feel like she didn't belong on the team. She felt fat and disgusting. With only 1 month to go before the outdoor season, she felt desperate to get back into shape. She was limiting herself to 300 calories per day and was exercising about 6 hours a day—swimming, using an elliptical machine, running, doing hundreds of crunches on her dorm room floor—she never sat still. Her tendonitis improved a little, and she was able to start training with the team again—but she didn't stop her extra exercising. She was quickly back to her training weight, but the coach noticed that her running wasn't quite back to her previous outstanding level. He assumed that it was just from the time off and worked with her to increase her miles and try to improve her overall conditioning. The attention paid off, her running improved, she took second at the relays, and she was contributing to the team's success. But she started looking really thin. Her teammates noticed her in the locker room and were shocked that they could count every rib and vertebra. They went to the coach with their concerns. The coach listened but had a dilemma. NCAA finals were coming up, and they were well positioned to win—but not without Hannah. Could he wait until after the finals to talk to Student Health? He decided to sit on it for a couple of days and then decide.

ASSESSING THE SITUATION

First, what factors contributed to the development of Hannah's problem? What were the precipitating events? Second, how would you treat her problem? Design a plan to treat Hannah's eating disorder. What might the high risk factors be for relapse?

THE TREATMENT

Two days later, the coach got a call from EMS. One of his athletes had collapsed during a 15-mile training run and was being transported to the emergency room. He rushed to the ER and found Hannah hooked up to an IV, exhausted and dehydrated. She was tearful and determined to go to the finals, saying she was letting everyone down.

The coach told Hannah about the conversation he had had with her teammates. Avoiding talking about the finals, he told her that he would do whatever he could to work with her to get healthy and that was the only goal right now. The coach agonized over not having approached her immediately. Waiting 2 days could have meant her life.

At first, Hannah's treatment focused on support while she was being renourished. Her weight had dropped to 78 pounds, and she was 5′5″ (BMI · 13 kg/m^2). Her therapist noted that her thinking was very negative. It was unclear whether she was also suffering from depression or if her low mood and negative thoughts were simply secondary to starvation. Hannah continued to believe that she had let down the team, the school, her family, and herself. She also believed that she could run well only if she were the thinnest girl on the team. Initially, Hannah was afraid that the therapist's only goals were to make her fat and to keep her from running. However, she began to see that the therapist would indeed work with her to get her back to her sport but only after she was fully recovered. As her thinking cleared, her therapist had her begin self-monitoring—not only of her food intake but also of her urges to exercise and her thoughts. They worked together to ensure that she was eating properly and not engaging in unhealthy exercise that would make weight gain nearly impossible. She began to recognize patterns in her urges to exercise as well as some of the automatic thoughts that had maintained the eating-disordered behaviors. She realized that every time she saw a female athlete in revealing clothing, she started to feel as if she needed to get back to her waiflike weight. She would develop an overwhelming urge to go running or punish herself in the gym. Her therapist helped her to unpack the distorted thinking that fueled that urge ("I will be a successful runner only if I am back to my previous low weight") and helped her integrate the realization that her low weight actually interfered with her running rather than helping it. Gradually, Hannah became more and more confident in her ability to resist the urge to exercise, although she still felt waves of envy as she saw the thinner girls. As she gained weight, her mood improved, so her physician saw no immediate need for medication but did continue to monitor Hannah's mood over time to see whether the depression would return and medication might be required.

THE TREATMENT OUTCOME

The following year before cross-country season, and with Hannah's permission, a meeting was set up with Hannah, her parents, her coach, her athletic trainer, and her therapist. Together they developed a plan for Hannah's competitive season including reasonable training schedules and procedures for action if warning signs emerged. Hannah also talked openly about her struggle with her teammates, who were supportive of her efforts toward recovery.

In many ways, Hannah was a highly successful young woman—academically and athletically. The transition from high school to college, though exciting, posed significant challenges for her. Two states away from home, she was on her own in a highly competitive Division I school. Precisely those traits (competitiveness and determination) that made her a great success were her undoing after her injury. Hannah didn't have the personal tools to deal with this setback in a healthy way; instead, she went overboard with exercise as a means of feeling a sense of control over her situation. Once she was able to engage in a supportive relationship with her therapist, she was able to change her behavior, although many cues in the environment clearly led to urges to exercise. With the support of her family, therapist, trainer, coach, and teammates, Hannah was able to finish her competitive college career successfully.

Key Terms

amenorrhea, p. 280
anorexia nervosa, p. 278
avoidant/restrictive food intake disorder, p. 296
binge eating, p. 279
binge-eating disorder, p. 290
body mass index (BMI), p. 278
bulimia nervosa, p. 284
eating disorder not otherwise specified, p. 287
enmeshment, p. 308
inappropriate compensatory behavior, p. 285
osteoporosis, p. 282
pica, p. 294
purging, p. 279
rumination disorder, p. 295

Chapter 9

Gender Dysphoria, Sexual Dysfunctions, and Paraphilic Disorders

Chapter Learning Objectives

Human Sexuality	**LO 9.1**	Discuss the typical sexual response cycle in men and women.
	LO 9.2	Describe sex differences in biological and psychological components of sexual behaviors.
	LO 9.3	Describe the challenges of defining "normal sexual behavior" and how biological and cultural factors affect that definition.

Gender Dysphoria	**LO 9.4**	Discuss the concepts of gender identity, gender dysphoria, and transgender behavior.
	LO 9.5	Describe how gender dysphoria affects the individual and the family.
	LO 9.6	Identify how sex, race, and ethnicity affect the clinical presentation of gender dysphoria.
	LO 9.7	Identify the biological and psychological theories that may contribute to the onset of gender dysphoria.
	LO 9.8	Discuss the ethics of trying to "fix" a child's sexual orientation in utero.
	LO 9.9	Describe the interventions available to treat gender dysphoria, including any ethical considerations.
Sexual Dysfunctions	**LO 9.10**	Discuss the role of gender in the definition and development of sexual dysfunction.
	LO 9.11	Describe how understanding "normal" sexual behavior provides an important context when determining the presence of orgasmic disorders.
	LO 9.12	Identify the features of genito-pelvic pain/penetration disorder.
	LO 9.13	Identify the challenges to determining functional impairment for sexual dysfunctions.
	LO 9.14	Discuss how age, sex, race, and ethnicity affect the prevalence of sexual dysfunctions.
	LO 9.15	Understand the biological and psychological complexities involved in the etiology and treatment of sexual dysfunction.
	LO 9.16	After identifying the factors that may preclude people from seeking treatment, discuss the available biological and psychological treatments.
Paraphilic Disorders	**LO 9.17**	Describe the difference between pedophilic disorder and child molestation.
	LO 9.18	Describe the different paraphilic dysfunctions based on anomalous activity preferences.
	LO 9.19	Identify the limits of functional impairment in people with paraphilias.
	LO 9.20	Discuss how age, sex, race, and ethnicity affect the prevalence and clinical presentation of paraphilic disorders.
	LO 9.21	Identify the limitations of the current knowledge base regarding the etiology of paraphilic disorders.
	LO 9.22	Identify the most promising biological and psychosocial treatments for the paraphilic disorders and the ethical issues that affect the conduct of clinical research.

At 30 years old, Nicole was referred to the clinic by her gynecologist. All of her friends were married, and she thought that she should be too. But unlike her friends, she had no desire to engage in sexual acts and never had sexual desires, fantasies, or urges regarding men or women. This lack of desire included all forms of sexual intimacy. Nicole felt very uncomfortable with any physical contact, including hugging her family and her best friend. Although she dated in high school and college, the relationships always ended when the boy tried to kiss her or touch her breasts. Nicole was never sexually abused or the victim of sexual assault, but in middle school she had a serious problem with her spine and she walked with a limp. The other children called her "gimpy." After several surgeries and a year in a body cast, she returned to school. She had matured physically and the boys thought that she was attractive, but she remained very self-conscious of her body. Someone started a rumor that she had a sexual relationship with a recently fired science teacher. The rumor was not true, and the science teacher was fired for having child pornography on his computer, but no one knew the truth and the rumor spread. She had a few girlfriends in the high school band and some positive interactions with her church group.

A friend arranged a blind date with Amery, a man who was even shyer than Nicole. He was respectful and a real gentleman, and Nicole enjoyed his company. They went to movies, concerts, and dinners with friends, and Amery never asked for anything other than a quick goodnight kiss on her cheek, which Nicole endured. After 3 months, Amery desired more intimacy. Nicole had been hoping that her feelings about sex would change because he was such a great guy. But now they seemed to fight a lot. She described feelings of panic and disgust when Amery tried to hug her. In fact, she was so anxious that she rejected all of his romantic advances, even including holding hands. She volunteered to seek help, but Amery was angry and frustrated and broke off the relationship. Nicole was crushed—she was sure she would never find another guy as great as Amery.

Nicole suffered from a sexual dysfunction, and her situation highlights many of the issues that we address in this chapter. First, even people who long for a committed, loving relationship can have difficulty with sexual intimacy. Second, difficulties in sexual performance never occur in isolation. Biological, psychological, interpersonal, and environmental factors often contribute to the development and persistence of sexual dysfunction. Nicole was different in one respect. Unlike many other people, she decided to seek treatment for her intimacy issues. *Sexual dysfunctions* are one of the three types of disorders discussed in this chapter. They are defined as a clinically significant disturbance in the person's ability to respond sexually or experience sexual pleasure (American Psychiatric Association, 2013). Another category, *gender dysphoria*, describes individuals who feel a marked incongruence between their assigned gender and their experienced/expressed gender (American Psychiatric Association, 2013). It is not dissatisfaction with a sexual behavior or attitude but dissatisfaction with and distress over one's entire identity as male or female. **Paraphilic disorders** are yet a different category and consist of intense and persistent sexual interest that is not directed toward phenotypically normal, physically mature, consenting human partners (American Psychiatric Association, 2013). As these disorders illustrate, sexual behavior is complex and multifaceted. It is also the subject of frequent misunderstandings and misconceptions. To understand these behaviors and their impact, we first review our historic understanding of sexual function and dysfunction.

Human Sexuality

Perhaps because the subject is highly personal and often considered taboo, people find it difficult to discuss sexual attitudes and behaviors. This leads to many misconceptions about normal sexual functioning. One of the first formal attempts to understand sexual behavior occurred in 1938 when Alfred Kinsey, a professor of biology at Indiana University, interviewed Americans about their sexual practices. Kinsey published his findings in *Sexual Behavior in the Human Male* in 1948 and *Sexual Behavior in the Human Female* in 1953. The books created public and scientific controversies. The most serious scientific criticism was that Kinsey's samples were not representative of the general population in the United States. Nevertheless, over the course of his career, Kinsey and his staff interviewed approximately 18,000 Americans about their sexual practices, and his groundbreaking work was a significant force in the scientific study of sexuality.

Shortly after Kinsey's publications, William Masters, a gynecologist, and his wife, Virginia Johnson, a psychologist, began their own research program in human sexuality. In addition to interviews, Masters and Johnson actually recorded the physical responses of more than 700 adults as they engaged in sexual activity. They published their research in their books, *Human*

Sexual Response (1966) and *Human Sexual Inadequacy* (1970). In these books, they described the physical and psychological bases of sexual response, measured the body's sexual responses, examined deviations from normal sexual functioning, and developed treatments to address dysfunction. Much of what we know about the physical responses leading to orgasm stems from the work of Masters and Johnson.

Alfred Kinsey was one of the first scientists to investigate the sexual behaviors of men and women in the United States.

Sexual Functioning

LO 9.1 Discuss the typical sexual response cycle in men and women.

The basis of sexual functioning is the human sexual response cycle. Originally, Masters and Johnson described four stages of sexual functioning: arousal, plateau, orgasm, and resolution (Masters & Johnson, 1966). Helen Singer Kaplan, a psychotherapist who specialized in sex therapy, described sexual response as consisting of desire, excitement, and orgasm (Kaplan, 1979). Most contemporary explanations incorporate some combination of these terms, conceptualizing four phases of sexual response (see Figure 9.1). First is the *desire phase*, which begins in response to external or internal cues. This is followed by the *arousal phase*, characterized by physical and psychological signs of sexual arousal. In men, the most overt response is *penile tumescence*, which occurs as blood flow to the penis increases. In women, arousal is marked by *vasocongestion* (swelling of the blood vessels) in the genital area and vaginal lubrication. Psychologically, there is a positive emotional response. Next is the *orgasm phase*. Men have a feeling of the inevitability of ejaculation followed by actual ejaculation of seminal fluid. Women experience contractions in the outer third of the vagina. Both men and women also experience a strong subjective feeling of pleasure that is based in the brain rather than the genitalia. The *resolution phase* is more common in men than women. Physical arousal decreases followed by a refractory (resting) period during which penile erection cannot occur. Women may experience two or more orgasms before experiencing a resolution phase. Health and mental health professionals use this model of sexual response to understand sexual dysfunctions. However, this model may not be the best "fit" for understanding sexual behavior in men and women.

Sex Differences in Sexual Behaviors

LO 9.2 Describe sex differences in biological and psychological components of sexual behaviors.

All surveys of sexual practices indicate that men engage in more frequent sexual activity than do women. Does this mean that males have a stronger biological **sex drive**, defined as craving for sexual activity and pleasure? Most people assume that the answer is "yes," but that is not necessarily true. Men do think about sex more often than women do, are more

Figure 9.1 The Human Sexual Response Cycle.

The sexual response cycle typically consists of four phases. In contrast to men, women may have more than one orgasm prior to the resolution phase.

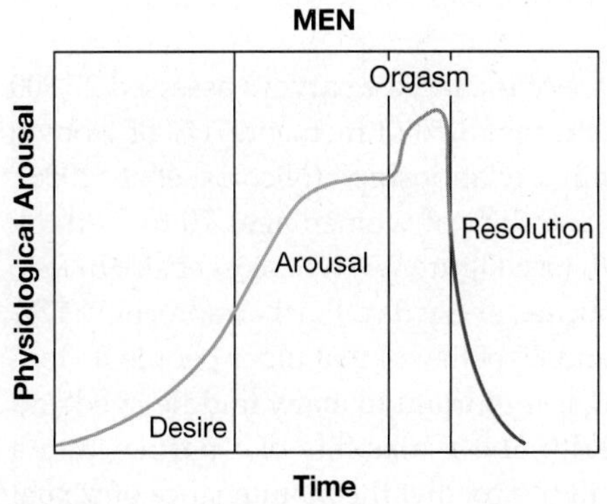

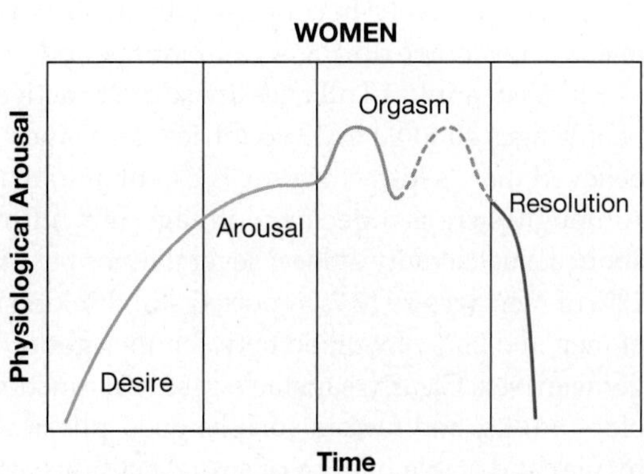

William Masters and Virginia Johnson observed sexual interactions of men and women, recording their physiological responses during different phases of sexual activity.

frequently sexually aroused, have more frequent and different fantasies, desire sex more often, desire more partners, masturbate more often, are less able or willing to go without sex, more often initiate sex, less often refuse sex, use more resources to get sex, make more sacrifices for sex, have a more favorable attitude toward and enjoy a wider variety of sexual practices, and rate themselves as having stronger sex drives than women. However, women have a higher capacity for sex, are biologically capable of engaging in sexual behavior for a longer period of time, are capable of more orgasms than men, and do not have a refractory period (Baumeister et al., 2001).

The way each sex defines sexual drive also differs. For many men, sexual desire is defined primarily by physical pleasure and sexual intercourse. Women appear to define sexual desire more broadly and include in their definition the need for emotional intimacy (Basson et al., 2002; Peplau, 2003). Female sexual responses may be more complicated than a biological-affective drive marked by sexual thoughts, fantasies, and a conscious urge to engage in sexual activity (Tiefer, 2001). Thus sexual desire may exist equally in both sexes when different definitions are applied. Understanding these differences is important because the current diagnostic system has evolved from a model of male sexual functioning and may not appropriately identify sexual dysfunction in women.

Biological sex also interacts with age to affect sexual behavior. In men, the effects of age are most apparent in genital response (inability to achieve an erection), whereas in women, the effects of age are most apparent in declining sexual interest (Bancroft et al., 2003). A psychological difference exists too. Unlike men, many women do not consider normal age-related changes in their sexuality or sexual practices to be problematic.

Understanding Sexual Behavior

LO 9.3 Describe the challenges of defining normal sexual behavior and how biological and cultural factors affect that definition.

Since the time of Kinsey and Masters and Johnson, research aimed at understanding sexual behavior has increased. Over the past 25 years, several large well-controlled surveys have been conducted: One targeted men ages 20 to 39 (Billy et al., 1993), a second targeted college-age women (DeBuono et al., 1990), and a third targeted adults ages 40 to 80 (Nicolosi et al., 2006). Surveys of typical sexual practices provide a context for understanding the deviations that are the topics of this chapter.

Over a 12-month period (see Figure 9.2), 95% of males between the ages of 18 and 30 and 87% of females between the ages of 18 and 22 years had vaginal intercourse (Billy et al., 1993; DeBuono et al., 1990). In addition, 74% of men and 86% of women orally stimulated the genitalia of their partner, and 79% and 65% were the recipients of oral stimulation by a partner, respectively. In contrast, only a minority (20% of males and 9% of females) engaged in anal intercourse during a 12-month period.

Indeed, adults of all ages are sexually active. One of the largest surveys assessed 27,900 people ages 40 to 80 in 29 countries. This study found that 82% of men and 76% of women believed that "satisfactory sex is essential to maintain a relationship" (Nicolosi et al., 2006). Although there is a decline with age, 48% of men and 25% of women ages 70 to 79 think about sexual activity at least several times per month (see Figure 9.3) (Nicolosi et al.). In fact, 22% of men ages 70 to 79 reported still thinking about sex every day. Furthermore, only 17% of men and 23% of women between the ages of 40 and 80 believed that older people no longer want sex. Clearly, satisfactory sexual functioning is important to many middle-aged and older adults, and factors such as good physical health, the availability of a partner, and a regular and stable pattern of sexual activity earlier in life predict the maintenance of sexual

Figure 9.2 Sexual Activity of Males Between Ages 18 and 30 and Females Between 18 and 22.

As this graph shows, both young men and women engage in a variety of different sexual behaviors, although the percentages differ by sex and by type of behavior.

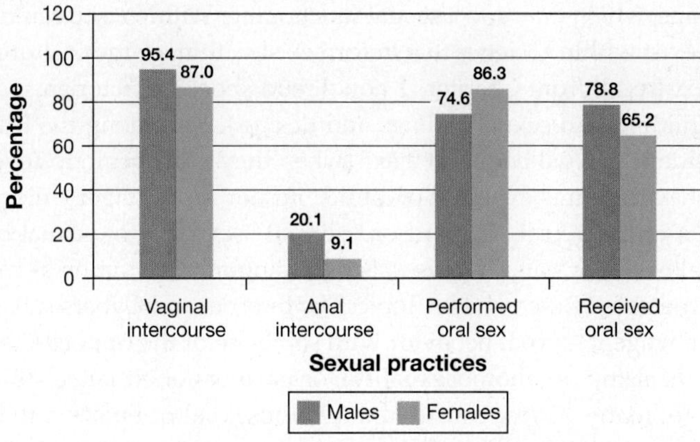

activity in old age (Corona et al., 2013). Consistent with their belief in its importance, 93% of men ages 40 to 49 are sexually active as are 53% of men ages 70 to 80 years (Nicolosi et al., 2004). For women ages 40 to 49, 88% were sexually active, as were 21% of women ages 70 to 80. As with younger adults, middle-aged and older men were more likely to think about and engage in sexual activity than were women.

Studies of sexuality and sexual behaviors in the United States have often neglected cultural considerations, particularly among Hispanic and Asian populations (Meston & Ahrold, 2007). Whereas sexual experiences among Hispanic undergraduate students in the United States appear similar to those of non-Hispanic whites (Cain et al., 2003), Asian students report less participation in intercourse, masturbation, oral sex, and petting (Meston et al., 1996), and Asian women reported lower frequencies of these behaviors than non-Asian women and Asian men. Similarly, Hispanic men had higher levels of sexual permissiveness than Hispanic women (Cain et al., 2003). Furthermore, African American women were more likely than white women to endorse the statement that engaging in sexual activity was

Figure 9.3 Frequency with Which Men and Women of Various Ages Think About Sexual Activity.

Across English-speaking populations, there is a decline in the frequency with which men and women think about sexual activity on a daily basis, but even at advanced ages, interest in sex does not disappear.

SOURCE: Nicolosi, A., Laumann, E. O., Glasser, D. B., Brock, G., King, R., & Gingell, C. (2006). Sexual activity, sexual disorders, and associated help-seeking behavior among mature adults in five Anglophone countries from the Global Survey of Sexual Attitudes and Behaviors (GSSAB). *Journal of Sex & Marital Therapy, 32,* 331–342. Copyright © 2006, Taylor & Francis Group (http://www.informaworld.com). Reprinted by permission of the publisher.

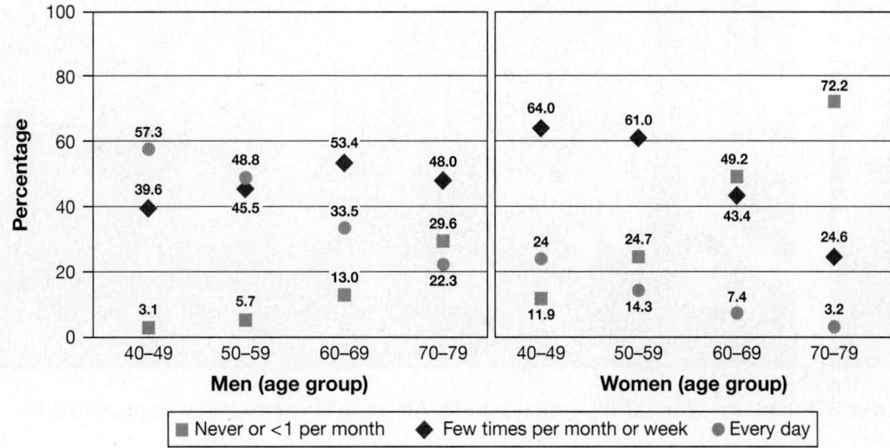

important, whereas Japanese and Chinese women were less likely than white women to agree with the idea that sex was important (Cain et al., 2003).

What constitutes sexuality and sexual behavior varies a great deal across cultures (Nieto, 2004). Some researchers have suggested that sexual attraction is not simply biological or sociocultural—it is an integrated response (Tolman & Diamond, 2001). We have already noted one biological factor, age, which may affect sexual functioning. Within a sociocultural context, sexual relationships exist within societies that in turn exist within a larger culture and also within a historical context (recall from Chapter 1 how Freud shocked Victorian society by suggesting that young children had sexual feelings and desires). Yet among the Khumbo of Nepal, children are considered sexual beings at age 5, when they must begin to cover their genitalia with clothing, behavior that is expected of adults but not the younger children (Nieto, 2004). Therefore, there is no universal standard of "normal" sexuality or sexual behavior. In fact, one type of sexual behavior, called *cybersex*, is becoming more common as more people have access to the Internet (see "Research Hot Topic: The Internet and Cybersex").

People may engage in sexual behavior with someone of the opposite sex (heterosexuality), someone of the same sex (homosexuality), or partners of either sex (bisexuality). Until about 25 years ago, many people considered a homosexual orientation to be a mental disorder, but for a long time it was not clear how many people engaged in sexual behaviors with someone of the same sex. One reason was that, given how difficult it is to get people to discuss sexuality, questions about same-sex practices were rarely included in surveys of adult sexual behaviors. In one of the first surveys (Billy et al., 1993), 2.3% of young men ages 20 to 39 reported that they had engaged in same-sex activity. This rate was consistent with a survey of men and women in the United States ages 18 to 70; 2% reported exclusive same-sex activity or sexual activity with both sexes (Leigh et al., 1993). These rates are also consistent with those in other Western countries. Population surveys of adults in Britain and France revealed that 3.6% of British men had engaged in sexual activity with another man on at least one occasion as had 4.1% of French men (Bajos et al., 1995).

Overall, it appears that 2 to 5% of men and 1 to 2% of women are exclusively same-sex attracted (Diamond, 1993; Laumann et al., 1994; Wellings et al., 1994). These rates appear to be consistent worldwide, although cultural customs and sanctions often dictate the frequency of same-sex *behavior* as opposed to a gay/lesbian or bisexual *identity*. In other words, people may feel sexual attraction toward someone of the same sex but may not act on that emotion because of religious or cultural practices. As with heterosexual attraction, there are sex differences in the strength of same-sex attraction; men are more likely to be exclusively

Appropriate dress for girls and women is dictated by culture. (Left) Typical dress for American teenagers. (Right) Typical dress for women in Esfahan, Iran.

attracted to the same sex, and women are more likely to describe themselves as attracted to both sexes (Bailey et al., 2000).

This sex difference may reflect more erotic plasticity among women (Rahman & Wilson, 2003); their sex drive is more likely to be influenced by cultural and social factors. Developmentally, same-sex attraction or bisexual attraction is often seen as experimentation in adolescents and young adults. The results of a 10-year longitudinal study of women from ages 19 to 29 years indicated that 67% of the women changed their sexual orientation self-label over that period of time and 33% changed their self-label two times or more. However, in contrast to an experimental or transitional hypothesis, over this critical period of time, more women adopted a bisexual label than gave it up (Diamond, 2008). Thus there does appear to be fluidity in sexual orientation among women, but it is not clear whether these changes in labeling or behavior continue to change as women continue to mature.

Scientists are now beginning to understand that sexual desire and romantic love emerge from different social behavioral systems that have different goals (Diamond, 2003). Sexual desire is controlled by the sexual mating system that has the goal of reproduction of the species (Fisher et al., 2002). Romantic attraction is controlled by the attachment or pair-bonding system that has the goal of an enduring relationship with another individual. Even though these systems often work together, it is possible that an individual, regardless of his or her sexual orientation, can be romantically attracted to people of either sex (Diamond, 2003).

Research HOT Topic

The Internet and Cybersex

According to the characters in the Broadway musical *Avenue Q*, "The Internet is for porn!" A more scientific examination of online sexual activities indicated that 13% of terms entered into Internet search engines were sex related and 4% (42,337 of the 1,000,000) of the most trafficked Internet websites were sex related (Ogas & Gaddam, 2011). Online sexual behavior covers a wide range of activities and in some cases may seem quite harmless. But cybersex, one type of online behavior, can result in personal distress and negatively affect areas of functioning. Researchers are beginning to study this increasingly common behavior.

- **How do we define cybersex?** Currently, there is no accepted definition. Some researchers include all Internet sex activity as cybersex. Others distinguish between *online sexual activity*, which may include viewing pornography, searching for information about sexual dysfunctions or sex therapy, and *cybersex*, defined as online communications about sexual activities, fantasies, and desires that occur with a partner in real time (Shaughnessy & Byers, 2014).

- **How many people engage in cybersex?** A Swedish study indicated that 30% of men and 34% of women had engaged in at least one cybersex experience (Daneback et al., 2005); 38% were between the ages of 18 and 24, and 13% were over age 50. Cybersex may occur with a person's primary partner, a known non-partner, or strangers (Shaughnessy & Byers, 2014).

- **What are the negative implications?** Cybersex use can result in changes in personality or sleep patterns, disregard for responsibility, loss of sexual interest in real-life partner sex, real-life infidelity, sexual exploitation, and divorce (Goldberg et al., 2008; Schneider, 2003; Southern, 2008). If sites charge a fee, users may incur huge debts. Employee productivity is at risk; 70% of Internet sexual activity occurs on weekdays between 9 A.M. and 5 P.M. (Southern, 2008). Downloading sexual material from certain sites may lead to charges of trafficking in child pornography (Cooper et al., 2004). Persons who are married or have a steady partner and who secretly engage in cybersex with a third party may be seen by a partner as engaging in cyberinfidelity (Döring, 2009), and online sexual harassment/solicitation may also occur.

- **Who is at risk for overuse of cybersex?** When questioned about their ability to control their online sexual activity, perhaps as many as 11.8 million people have problems controlling online sexual behavior (Goldberg et al., 2008) and 4.9% of women and 12.9% of men believe that they may have Internet sexual problems including inability to control their behavior, feeling depressed, feeling addicted, and feeling the need for treatment (Ross et al., 2012).

In summary, cybersex is clearly an emerging problem, but as yet our knowledge is based on clinical reports and survey research. However, its increasing prevalence and potentially harmful effects are motivating mental health professionals to initiate research in order to better understand and therefore be able to treat this behavior if it rises to the level of an addiction.

The development of sexual orientation appears to be based primarily on one's biology. In fact, more than half a century of research has not provided any support for etiology based on psychological theories (Rahman & Wilson, 2003). Based on twin studies, homosexual or same-sex orientation appears to be in part genetically determined (Långström et al., 2010). Among the 3,826 studied monozygotic and dizygotic same-sex twin pairs, genetic effects explained 0.34 to 0.39 of the variance in men, whereas the shared environment explained 0.00, and the individual-specific environment explained 0.61 to 0.66 of the variance. Among women, 0.18 to 0.19 of the variance was explained by genetic factors, 0.16 to 0.17 by shared environment, and 0.64 to 0.66 for unique environment. However, the largest molecular genetics study to date was not able to identify any specific genetic loci that reached genome-wide significance. (http://blog.23andme.com/wp-content/uploads/2012/11/Drabant-Poster-v7.pdf). Therefore, although there appears to be some genetic determination, the specific place where this heritability lies remains undetermined.

Other attempts to understand the biology of sexual orientation have focused on the role of sex hormones called *androgens*. Atypical levels or timing of androgens during fetal development (high or low, early or late) do not always create differences in secondary sexual characteristics, genital anatomy, or gonadal function, but they may affect sexual orientation. Some researchers have examined the relationship between homosexuality and (1) non-righthandedness, (2) differences in the ratio of the second (index) finger to the fourth (ring) finger, and (3) symmetry in patterns of fingerprint ridges. In the latter case, gay men show fingerprint patterns more like heterosexual women than they do heterosexual men. Although these three differences may be related to abnormal levels of androgens during prenatal development (Hiraishi et al., 2012); Rahman & Wilson, 2003), the data so far are not conclusive because the sample sizes in these studies are small. Also, the methods of determining a relationship are indirect. Specifically, this research uses physical features of adults to hypothesize about the presence of *prenatal hormones* that were present when the fetus was in the uterus (i.e., in utero). More direct, and perhaps more conclusive, evidence would come from directly measuring these hormones in utero.

More conclusive data have been reported for fraternal birth order in males. Across numerous and diverse samples (Gooren, 2006), gay men had a greater number of older brothers than did heterosexual men. One explanation for this phenomenon is that there is an incompatibility between the mother's immune system and the androgens that are in the male fetus. The mother's body responds to the presence of male androgens with an immune response in the form of antibodies (to fight off the androgens). These antibodies cross the placental barrier and affect fetal hormonal level. As the number of male-offspring pregnancies increases, this immunological response becomes stronger and may affect fetal brain masculinization, although it is unclear whether the entire brain is affected or only certain specific areas (Bogaert & Skorska, 2011). Estimates of risk indicate that each older brother increases a younger brother's risk by 33 to 48%, but overall, this accounts for only a small increase in overall prevalence. Furthermore, not all gay men have older brothers, and, of course, the theory cannot account for homosexuality or bisexuality among women (Gooren, 2006). Therefore, although this androgen theory may explain the origin of sexual orientation for some gay men, it will most likely remain only one of many potential etiologies.

Learning Objective Summaries

LO 9.1 Discuss the typical sexual response cycle in men and women.

For both men and women, the human sexual response consists of four phases: desire, arousal, orgasm, and resolution. Unlike men, some women are capable of more than one orgasm during a single response cycle.

LO 9.2 Describe sex differences in biological and psychological components of sexual behaviors.

Men think about sex more often than women do, are more frequently sexually aroused, have more frequent and different fantasies, desire sex more often, desire more partners, masturbate more often, are less able or willing to go without sex, more often initiate sex, less often refuse sex, use more resources to get sex, make more sacrifices for sex, have a more favorable attitude toward and enjoy a wider variety of sexual practices, and rate themselves as having stronger sex drives than women. However, women have a higher capacity for sex, are biologically capable of engaging in sexual behavior for a longer period of time, are capable of more orgasms than men, and do not have a refractory period.

LO 9.3 Describe the challenges of defining normal sexual behavior and how biological and cultural factors affect that definition.

The term *normal sexual behavior* is hard to define. Vaginal intercourse is the most frequently practiced sexual activity. Yet biological (age, sex) and cultural factors play a role in how frequently sexual activity occurs and what type of sexual behaviors are practiced. Although the frequency of sexual activity declines with age, satisfactory sexual functioning is considered important by people at any age.

Critical Thinking Question

Cybersex is defined as online communications about sexual activities, fantasies, and desires that occur with a partner in real time. Online sexual activity is a broader category that may include viewing pornography, searching for information about sexual dysfunctions, or searching for information about sex therapy. Discuss the advantages and disadvantages of having this material available to anyone. When might this accessibility be helpful? Who might be harmed as a result of this accessibility?

Gender Dysphoria

Tyler is 23 years old. He came to the psychology clinic after hearing one of the psychologists talking about depression on TV. He thought that the psychologist seemed very understanding, leading him to seek treatment. Tyler felt sad, but his real reason for coming to the clinic was that he "no longer wanted to be a man." Ever since he was a young child, Tyler felt like a girl. His happiest time was sneaking into his sister's room and putting on her pink dancing costume. In fact, he coveted any of his sister's clothing. His father was horrified and forced Tyler to play with guns, a football, anything that would help him "be a man." Tyler tried, but he always felt as if he were pretending. He felt that he was a woman trapped in a man's body.

How does a child know if he or she is a boy or a girl? The answer seems obvious, but it is not. Traditionally, *sex* was considered to be determined by genes, hormones, and physical genitalia, whereas *gender* could be defined as categories of male or female defined by cultural role expectations. Some researchers consider these definitions to be very simplistic (Lyons & Lyons, 2006), and the complex issue of defining these terms is outside the scope of abnormal psychology. But what if you have male genitalia yet you feel like a girl?

Gender Identity and Gender Dysphoria

LO 9. 4 Discuss the concepts of gender identity, gender dysphoria, and transgender behavior.

To understand Tyler's behavior and feelings, we need to explore the concept of *gender identity*, the personal understanding of oneself as male or female. Gender identity typically develops by age 3 or 4 (Bradley & Zucker, 1997). Usually, biological sex and gender identity match—boys who are genetically male describe themselves as boys, and girls who are genetically female describe themselves as girls. However, in cases of **gender dysphoria**, biological sex and gender identity do not match, as with Tyler, leading to distress and impairment.

Gender dysphoria (see "DSM-5: Gender Dysphoria") is not simply a momentary wish to be the opposite sex because of cultural or social advantages (e.g., "men have all the power"). It is a marked incongruence between the gender to which a person was assigned (usually

Cross-dressing may provide sexual gratification for some men; male entertainers sometimes dress as females to entertain the public.

at birth) and their experienced/expressed gender (American Psychiatric Association, 2013). Among children, gender dysphoria is apparent in repeated statements that the child *wants* to be the opposite sex or *is* the opposite sex; cross-dressing in clothing stereotypical of the other sex (as with Tyler); persistent fantasies of being the opposite sex or persistent preference for cross-gender roles in pretend play; a strong desire to participate in games and activities usually associated with the opposite sex; and strong preference for playmates of the opposite sex.

Several high-profile cases (e.g., Caitlyn Jenner discussed in this chapter) have brought this condition to the attention of the public, leading to increased understanding and appreciation of the pervasive discomfort and despair that individuals with gender dysphoria experience. Such high-profile cases have made it easier for individuals with profound gender dysphoria to seek options for undergoing sex reassignment surgery, for finding acceptable options for use of public facilities that are typically segregated by sex, and for encouraging the evolution of language that does not rely on traditional gender-binary terms.

In addition to identifying with the opposite sex, people with gender dysphoria have persistent discomfort with their own sex. Boys express disgust about their penis or testes, state that the penis will disappear, or state that it would be better not to have one. They avoid rough-and-tumble play or stereotypically male activities. Girls express persistent discomfort by refusing to sit on the toilet to urinate, stating that they have a penis or will grow one and that they do not want to grow breasts or begin menstruation. They also dislike female clothing, refusing to wear dresses. Among adolescents and adults, this is called **transgender behavior**.

It is important to differentiate between the terms **transsexualism** and *transvestic disorder*. The latter is the desire and perhaps even the need among heterosexual men to dress in women's clothes (American Psychiatric Association, 2013), but not the desire to *be* the opposite sex (Lawrence & Zucker, 2012; Sharma, 2007). (We discuss transvestic disorder later in this chapter in the section on paraphilic disorders.)

Because it is so rare, gender dysphoria is not a disorder that is included in epidemiological investigations, making its prevalence difficult to determine. The most commonly reported prevalence estimates are 1 in 7,400 to 12,800 for men and 1 in 30,000 to 52,100 for women (Lawrence & Zucker, 2012). As in Tyler's case, feeling trapped in one's body can lead to feelings of depression. In fact, people with gender dysphoria may have other psychiatric disorders, most commonly anxiety, depression, and personality disorders (Blosnich et al., 2013; Heylens et al., 2014; Taher, 2007; Zucker, 2004). However, these disorders do not occur more frequently among people with gender dysphoria than people with other psychiatric disorders (Heylens et al., 2014). They are also not the cause of gender dysphoria. Rather, these anxiety and depressive symptoms are a response to the condition and to the ridicule that people with gender dysphoria often face as a result of their behavior. Cross-gender identification sometimes becomes so strong that people have **sex reassignment surgery** (also known as gender affirmation surgery). This surgery consists of a series of procedures that matches their physical anatomy and their gender identity (see "Real People, Real Disorders: 'Call Me Caitlyn'").

Functional Impairment

LO 9.5 Describe how gender dysphoria affects the individual and the family.

Among young children, cross-gender behaviors are common, and their presence alone does not seem to create significant distress. However, these behaviors may result in peer

DSM-5

Criteria for Gender Dysphoria

Gender Dysphoria in Children

A. A marked incongruence between one's experienced/expressed gender and assigned gender, of at least 6 months' duration, as manifested by at least six of the following (one of which must be Criterion A1):

1. A strong desire to be of the other gender or an insistence that one is the other gender (or some alternative gender different from one's assigned gender).
2. In boys (assigned gender), a strong preference for cross-dressing or simulating female attire; or in girls (assigned gender), a strong preference for wearing only typical masculine clothing and a strong resistance to the wearing of typical feminine clothing.
3. A strong preference for cross-gender roles in make-believe play or fantasy play.
4. A strong preference for the toys, games, or activities stereotypically used or engaged in by the other gender.
5. A strong preference for playmates of the other gender.
6. In boys (assigned gender), a strong rejection of typically masculine toys, games, and activities and a strong avoidance of rough-and-tumble play; or in girls (assigned gender), a strong rejection of typically feminine toys, games, and activities.
7. A strong dislike of one's sexual anatomy.
8. A strong desire for the primary and/or secondary sex characteristics that match one's experienced gender.

B. The condition is associated with clinically significant distress or impairment in social, school, or other important areas of functioning.

Gender Dysphoria in Adolescents and Adults

A. A marked incongruence between one's experienced/expressed gender and assigned gender, of at least 6 months' duration, as manifested by at least two of the following:

1. A marked incongruence between one's experienced/expressed gender and primary and/or secondary sex characteristics (or in young adolescents, the anticipated secondary sex characteristics).
2. A strong desire to be rid of one's primary and/or secondary sex characteristics because of a marked incongruence with one's experienced/expressed gender (or in young adolescents, a desire to prevent the development of the anticipated secondary sex characteristics).
3. A strong desire for the primary and/or secondary sex characteristics of the other gender.
4. A strong desire to be of the other gender (or some alternative gender different from one's assigned gender).
5. A strong desire to be treated as the other gender (or some alternative gender different from one's assigned gender).
6. A strong conviction that one has the typical feelings and reactions of the other gender (or some alternative gender different from one's assigned gender).

B. The condition is associated with clinically significant distress or impairment in social, occupational, or other important areas of functioning.

rejection or social isolation, which can in turn lead to negative mood states (Bartlett et al., 2000). Sometimes the distress associated with gender dysphoria is not found in the child but in his or her parents. As one mother reported,

> He was very excited about [putting on a blouse of mine] and leaped and danced around the room. I didn't like it and I just told him to take it off and I put it away. He kept asking for it. He wanted to wear that blouse again. (Green, 1987, p. 2)

Among children with gender dysphoria, distress does not result from cross-gender behaviors but from being *prevented* from engaging in the desired behaviors. Among adults with gender dysphoria, lifetime prevalence of comorbid disorders ranges from 14% for current disorders to 71% for lifetime disorders (Hepp et al., 2005; Hoshiai et al., 2010). However, even when the existence of a second disorder was low, lifetime prevalence of suicidal ideation (74%) and self-mutilation (33%) were significant (Hoshiai et al., 2010), indicating the severity of distress that can accompany this disorder.

REAL People REAL Disorders

Caitlyn Jenner: "Call Me Caitlyn"

Bruce Jenner struggled with dyslexia in the classroom but excelled at sports. A knee injury ended his college football career, and after turning to track and field, he placed 10th in the decathlon at the 1972 Munich Olympic Games. Four years later, at the 1976 Montreal Olympic Games, Jenner not only won the gold medal but set an Olympic world record. After earning the title of World's Greatest Athlete, Jenner remained a public figure—appearing on the Wheaties cereal box and television shows and in a few movies and speaking engagements.

But in 2015, Jenner's physical appearance began to change, and on June 1, 2015, Jenner announced that she was a woman and that her name was Caitlyn. She appeared that same month on the cover of *Vanity Fair* and made her first public appearance at the Espy Awards, where she received the Arthur Ashe Award for Courage, given to individuals who "transcend sports." Her acceptance speech that night touched on the difficulty of her transition—harder than anything she could imagine and certainly harder than training for the Olympics. Caitlyn recalls gender dysphoria from her adolescence and has undergone hormone replacement therapy and cosmetic surgery.

Caitlyn used her spotlight that night to speak out for transgendered people who are physically assaulted or murdered or who commit suicide because of who they are. "If you want to call me names, make jokes, doubt my intentions, go ahead, because the reality is, I can take it. But for the thousands of kids out there coming to terms with being true to who they are, they should not have to take it."

SOURCES: http://www.nytimes.com/2015/06/02/business/media/jenner-reveals-new-name-in-vanity-fair-article.html
http://www.biography.com/people/bruce-jenner-307180

Sex, Race, and Ethnicity

LO 9.6 Identify how sex, race, and ethnicity affect the clinical presentation of gender dysphoria.

Occasional cross-gender behavior is common among elementary schoolchildren (Sandberg et al., 1993) and does not automatically indicate the presence of gender dysphoria. When present, gender dysphoria is usually first detected between ages 2 and 4. The earliest signs include persistent cross-gender dressing and play. Verbal wishes to be a member of the other sex do not usually occur before age 6 or 7 (Bartlett et al., 2000). Before puberty, there are five to seven preadolescent boys for every one preadolescent girl evaluated and treated for gender dysphoria (Bradley & Zucker, 1997; Zucker, 2004). By contrast, in adolescence, the ratio of boys to girls with gender dysphoria is virtually equal (Bradley & Zucker, 1997; Zucker, 2004). Among adults, and based mostly on studies from European countries, gender dysphoria is more common in males than females (Lawrence & Zucker, 2012).

Gender dysphoria exists even when contradicted by religious, moral, and social values (Taher, 2007). Sometimes, transsexual individuals do not self-identify unless they know that sympathetic health professionals and treatment are available. For example, once sex reassignment surgery was available in Singapore, transsexuals of Chinese, Malaysian, and Indian ethnicity began to seek treatment (Tsoi & Kok, 1995). The appearance of these patients contradicted previously held beliefs that transsexualism was rare among the Chinese (Tseng, 2003).

Although Western cultures recognize two gender categories, other cultures have a greater number of classifications. For example, in India, a third gender is known as the *hijra* (Nanda, 1985). Although most are biologically male, hijra are not considered to be male or female but to possess elements of both sexes. They usually dress as women and refer to themselves as female.

Similarly, in independent Samoa, males who are sexually attracted to men are referred to as *fa'afafine*, literally meaning "in the manner of a woman" (Vasey & Bartlett, 2007). Fa'afafine adults recalled engaging as children in significantly more female-typical behavior and significantly fewer male-typical behaviors (Bartlett & Vasey, 2006). Although some individuals reported that parents attempted to force them to behave in culturally prescribed ways, others reported that individuals were very tolerant of atypical gender choices.

Hijra are found in different cultures and are considered a third gender, neither masculine nor feminine.

Etiology

LO 9.7 Identify the biological and psychological theories that may contribute to the onset of gender dysphoria.

A number of theories explain the etiology of gender dysphoria, but virtually no empirical data support many of them. On the biological side, some hormonal data provide intriguing but non-specific evidence for a biological contribution to the development of this disorder. Psychosocial theories have examined the role of family, particularly parent–child relationships.

BIOLOGICAL THEORIES To date, little evidence suggests a genetic contribution to gender dysphoria. Neuroanatomical research has identified differences in the brains of men and women (Michel et al., 2001). One study found that the brains of male transsexuals were similar in size and shape to those of heterosexual women and unlike the brains of heterosexual men (Zhou et al., 1995). A more recent investigation reported that regional gray matter variation in male-to-female (MTF) transsexuals more closely resembled the pattern found in heterosexual men but that MTF transsexuals showed a significantly larger volume of regional gray matter in the right putamen compared with heterosexual men (Luders et al., 2009). These findings may suggest some differences in brain anatomy, but these findings have not been replicated and data from neuroanatomical and neurobiological studies remain contradictory and inconclusive.

A hormonal condition that may contribute to the development of gender dysphoria is *congenital adrenal hyperplasia* (CAH). Boys and girls with CAH are missing an enzyme necessary to make the hormones cortisol and aldosterone. As a result, the body produces too much of the male hormone androgen, causing early and inappropriate male sexual development in both sexes. At birth, girls with CAH have ambiguous genitalia, often appearing more male than female. As they grow, these girls develop male secondary sexual features such as a deep voice and facial hair. Boys with CAH begin puberty as early as 2 to 3 years of age.

In addition to physical differences, girls with CAH display more cross-gender identification (Pasterski et al., 2015) and cross-gender role behaviors (Cohen-Bendahan et al., 2005; Zucker, 2004) than girls without this condition. They do become more feminine with age, but some adult women with CAH (particularly those with the most severe form) have less heterosexual interest and are less feminine than those with no hormonal disorder (Hines et al., 2004; Long et al., 2004). We still do not know whether CAH, or any other hormonal imbalance, leads to the development of gender dysphoria. We do know that this condition affects prenatal hormonal levels, the development of physical sex characteristics, and gender behaviors. Understanding CAH may help us understand the development of gender dysphoria for some children.

Ethics and Responsibility

LO 9.8 Discuss the ethics of trying to "fix" a child's sexual orientation in utero.

For the past 20 years, efforts have been made to treat CAH before birth in an attempt to prevent the development of ambiguous sexual genitalia in females (Nimkarm & New, 2010). Because this disorder is a genetic condition, pregnant women whose fetus is at risk for CAH may be offered treatment with dexamethasone. When given prior to the ninth week of pregnancy and continued for a number of weeks, this steroid decreases the amount of androgen to which the fetus is exposed and may prevent genital ambiguity in affected females. Short-term follow-up data suggest that children exposed to dexamethasone before birth have normal growth and development (Hughes, 2006), but the data are few, long-term follow-up is not available, and the Food and Drug Administration does not approve the use of dexamethasone for CAH. However, the amount of prenatal exposure to androgen also appears to have some effect on sexual orientation: higher levels are associated with more masculine behaviors (Meyer-Bahlburg et al., 2008). The practice of prenatal dexamethasone administration has led some *bioethicists* (researchers who study the ethical and moral implications of new medical discoveries) to question whether this drug might be used by parents or promoted by physicians to prevent homosexual or bisexual orientations in girls (Dreger et al., 2010). The implication of this controversy is that something is inherently wrong with people who do not have a heterosexual orientation (Dreger et al., 2010). These ethical issues will likely occupy researchers for many years to come, but at this time, almost all involved agree that, for now, administration of dexamethasone for CAH should occur only in closely monitored clinical trials with substantial long-term follow-up.

Explore ETHICS AND RESPONSIBILITY

Interactive

PSYCHOSOCIAL THEORIES Psychoanalysts postulate that parental rejection may play a role in the onset of gender dysphoria. For example, if parents really wanted a girl but had a boy instead (Sharma, 2007), they may reject their son. That rejection may cause the boy to try to please the parent by behaving like a girl. Although parents who reinforce masculine or feminine behaviors increase the frequency of those behaviors, simple reinforcement alone does not appear to affect gender identity. One well-known case (Green & Money, 1969) suggests that biology is stronger than environmental forces.

> John and his brother were identical twins. During their circumcision, the physician's hand slipped and ablated (cut off) John's penis. After much discussion, the physicians and John's parents agreed that he should be raised as a girl, and he was renamed Joan. His parents dressed and

treated Joan as a girl, and at adolescence, Joan was given female hormone replacement therapy to encourage the development of secondary female sexual characteristics (breast development). Despite all the efforts, Joan never felt like a girl and often rebelled against adult efforts to make her behave like one. Finally, at age 14, her parents told her the truth. Interestingly, John recalled that he had suspected that he was a boy beginning in the second grade. In adulthood, John had sex reassignment surgery, lived as a man, married, and adopted three children (Diamond & Sigmundson, 1977). However, this story does not have a happy ending. John suffered from depression, and in 2004, at age 39, he committed suicide.

The reasons for John's suicide are unknown but probably include his unusual childhood and a strong family history of depression—John's mother and twin brother also suffered from depression (Colapinto, 2004). His twin brother died from an overdose of antidepressants, and John had twice attempted suicide when he was in his twenties. Although John's story has a sad ending, it provides an important insight: Environmental efforts alone cannot overcome biology and establish or change gender identity.

Watch TRAVIS: GENDER DYSPHORIA PART 1

Treatment

LO 9.9 Describe the interventions available to treat gender dysphoria, including any ethical considerations.

Few longitudinal studies of children with gender dysphoria have been conducted, but those data that are available suggest that only a minority of children who originally receive this diagnosis continue to be distressed about their gender into adulthood (Drescher & Pula, 2014; Zucker, 2008). In two follow-up studies conducted 10 to 15 years after the original diagnosis, between 12 and 27% of individuals were still classified as gender dysphoric (Drummond et al., 2008; Wallien & Cohen-Kettenis, 2008). In those studies, children who had the most severe symptoms of gender dysphoria were the ones still likely to have the disorder and most likely to have a homosexual or bisexual orientation. Among the adults who no longer had gender dysphoria, half of the boys and all of the girls had a heterosexual orientation (Wallien & Cohen-Kettenis, 2008).

Perhaps because the disorder is quite rare, no controlled trials for treatments of gender dysphoria have been conducted. Clinically, several different treatment approaches exist, some of which are available only in specialized clinics. The most common procedure for adults is surgical reassignment.

SEX REASSIGNMENT SURGERY Historically, treatment for adults with gender dysphoria attempted to change the person's social and sexual behaviors to match his or her biological sex. Currently, treatment focuses on helping adults live as their chosen gender identity, maximizing their psychological and social adjustment. The change to live as their chosen gender identity involves three phases: living as the desired gender, using hormone therapy, and undergoing sex reassignment surgery (Meyer et al., 2001b). Not every person who begins treatment completes the sex reassignment surgery (gender reassignment surgery) phase.

In the first stage, the person lives in the new gender role for at least 2 years (Meyer et al., 2001b). The person dresses and socializes in a manner consistent with the desired gender role, allowing the person to examine how this change affects every aspect of life. This step is considered absolutely necessary for the treatment program. The second step is hormone therapy. Testosterone is given to biological females and estrogen to biological males, reducing unwanted secondary sex characteristics and leading to the secondary sexual characteristics of the preferred sex. Initiation of hormone therapy has been associated with decreases in anxiety, depression, and emotional distress reported by people with gender dysphoria (Heylens et al., 2014). Not every individual proceeds to the third and final phase of gender reassignment surgery. For males transitioning to females, this includes surgical removal of the penis and the creation of a clitoris, labia, and artificial vagina. For females transitioning to males, it includes removal of the breasts, vagina, and uterus, the formation of a scrotum and testicular prostheses, and the creation of a neophallus (an artificial penis). The goal is to try to preserve sexual functioning in order to achieve optimal quality of life (Lawrence, 2003).

Compared with treatments for other psychological disorders, sex reassignment surgery is an extensive and radical procedure (Smith et al., 2005). Although early studies suggested that a percentage of those who had surgery were not satisfied with the results, more recent and long-term follow-up data indicate that the outcome has become more positive (Ruppin & Pfäfflin, 2015). Sex reassignment surgery eliminates gender dysphoria (Lawrence, 2003; Smith et al., 2005), improves body satisfaction and interpersonal relationships, and reduces anxiety and depression (Ruppin & Pfäfflin, 2015; Smith et al., 2001, 2005; Weyers et al., 2008). In one long-term follow-up study (Weyers et al., 2008), the participants described some difficulties with sexual arousal, lubrication, and pain. Across different studies, more than 95% of patients reported satisfaction with sex reassignment surgery (Lawrence, 2003; Smith et al., 2005). A few patients were dissatisfied; most commonly, those individuals lacked family support and/or had additional psychological disorders affecting overall functioning (Eldh et al., 1997; Landén et al., 1998).

Some adolescents with gender dysphoria seek sex reassignment surgery, and it is reasonable to question whether adolescents can make such an irreversible decision. Early sex reassignment surgery may prevent gender dysphoria during adolescence (Delemarre-van de Waal & Cohen-Kettenis, 2006), and the physical outcome is more satisfactory when secondary sex characteristics have not yet developed. However, such surgery requires absolute certainty because the intervention is nonreversible. Only a small number of adolescents receive sex reassignment therapy, and many questions remain about the procedure including at what age the surgery should occur and whether those adolescents who have surgery continue to feel positively about the procedure as adults. Official guidelines published by The Endocrine Society recommend against sex role change in prepubertal children (Shumer & Spack, 2013).

PSYCHOLOGICAL TREATMENT No randomized controlled trials of psychosocial interventions have been conducted. In the past, behavioral, psychoanalytic, and eclectic approaches attempted to alter the child's perception of her or his gender with her or his biological sex by focusing attention and reinforcement on same-sex activities and friendships, spending time with the same-sex parent, and having play dates with same-sex peers (Bradley & Zucker, 1997). Same-gender behaviors were rewarded (prizes given), and cross-gender behaviors were punished (prizes removed) (Rekers & Lovaas, 1974; Rekers & Mead, 1979; Rekers et al., 1974). The interventions were reported to be efficacious for some children, but these approaches have been criticized for forcing specific gender stereotypes (i.e., stereotypical masculine behaviors) (Bryant, 2006) onto young children, and they have fallen out of use.

Learning Objective Summaries

LO 9.4 Discuss the concepts of gender identity, gender dysphoria, and transgender behavior.

Gender identity is the personal understanding of oneself as male or female. Gender dysphoria, also known as transsexualism in adults, is a strong and persistent cross-gender identification and persistent discomfort with one's own sex. Transgender behavior is acting in ways that are more consistent with the gender roles assigned to someone of the other sex. Transsexualism differs from transvestic disorder, which consists of sexual arousal that occurs when dressing in female clothing.

LO 9.5 Describe how gender dysphoria affects the individual and the family.

Particularly in children, parents of children with gender dysphoria are more emotionally affected by the child's behavior than are the children. Parents will sometimes try to "force" the child to adhere to gender roles consistent with their biological sex, causing family conflict and emotional distress. Transgendered adults often report feeling sad and anxious, trapped in a physical body that is inconsistent with their feelings about "who they are."

LO 9.6 Identify how sex, race, and ethnicity affect the clinical presentation of gender dysphoria.

The disorder appears to be more common in males than females among adults and can have a pervasive effect on all aspects of functioning. Gender dysphoria is usually first detected between ages 2 and 4, with signs including persistent cross-gender dressing and play. Before puberty, there are five to seven preadolescent boys for every one preadolescent girl evaluated and treated for gender dysphoria, but the ratio during adolescence is virtually equal. Among adults, gender dysphoria is more common in males than females. Gender dysphoria is probably universal in scope, although in many instances transsexual individuals do not self-identify unless they know that sympathetic health professionals and treatments are available.

LO 9.7 Identify the biological and psychological theories that may contribute to the onset of gender dysphoria.

The cause of gender dysphoria is unknown but in some cases, may be related to a hormonal imbalance known as congenital adrenal hyperplasia (CAH). At birth, girls with CAH have ambiguous genitalia, often appearing more male than female. As they grow, these girls develop male secondary sexual features such as a deep voice and facial hair. Boys with CAH begin puberty as early as 2 to 3 years of age. It is not certain whether CAH, or any other hormonal imbalance, leads to the development of gender dysphoria, although this condition does affect prenatal hormonal levels, the development of physical sex characteristics, and gender behaviors.

LO 9.8 Discuss the ethics of trying to "fix" a child's sexual orientation in utero.

Efforts have been made to treat CAH before birth and prevent the development of ambiguous sexual genitalia in females by offering treatment with dexamethasone to pregnant women whose fetus is at risk for CAH. Bioethicists have questioned whether this drug might be used by parents or promoted by physicians to prevent homosexual or bisexual orientations in girls. The implication of this controversy is that something is inherently wrong with people who do not have a heterosexual orientation.

LO 9.9 Describe the interventions available to treat gender dysphoria, including any ethical considerations.

It is not ethical to try to change someone's gender identity to match physical sexual characteristics. Gender affirmation surgery (also called sex reassignment surgery) matches the person's physical anatomy with his or her gender identity and typically includes three phases: living in the desired gender role for a period of at least 2 years, hormonal therapy, and then sex reassignment surgery. Some individuals choose not to undergo the actual surgery. Gender affirmation therapy is not considered an option for prepubescent children.

Critical Thinking Question

Children with the most severe symptoms of gender dysphoria may continue to have gender dysphoria as an adult, but this outcome occurs in a minority of people with this disorder. Furthermore, the distress associated with gender dysphoria is often that of the parent, not the child. Applying what you know about diagnosis and treatment, would you recommend treatment of a child who has gender dysphoria symptoms to a parent?

Sexual Dysfunctions

As we discussed in the opening section of this chapter, many factors contribute to sexual performance including age, sex, and culture. Therefore, the diagnostic criteria for all **sexual dysfunctions** consist of an absence or an impairment of some aspect of sexual response *that causes significant distress and/or functional impairment and includes consideration of age, sex, and culture*. In some instances, the prevalence of a disorder changes when these factors are considered. In addition, a person's life circumstances, such as physical illness or physical separation from the sexual partner, must be considered when determining the presence or absence of a sexual dysfunction. With these issues in mind, we turn our attention to disorders of sexual functioning, which are classified as disorders of sexual desire, sexual arousal, orgasm, and pain.

Sexual Interest/Desire Disorders

LO 9.10 Discuss the role of gender in the definition and development of sexual dysfunction.

Sexual desire is an interest in sexual activity or objects or wishes to engage in sexual activity. Disorders of sexual desire/arousal are indicated by a diminished or absent interest in sexual activity and may include *male hypoactive sexual desire disorder, female sexual interest/arousal disorder*, and *erectile disorder*.

Male hypoactive sexual desire disorder is defined as persistently or recurrently deficient or absent sexual/erotic thoughts or fantasies and desire for sexual activity (American Psychiatric Association, 2013) (see "DSM-5: Sexual Interest/Desire Disorders"). Factors often associated with decreased sexual desire include low sexual satisfaction, the presence of another sexual dysfunction (such as pain), negative thoughts about sexuality, and other forms of psychological distress such as depression, anxiety, and couple distress (Trudel et al., 2001).

DSM-5

Criteria for Sexual Interest/Desire Disorders

Male Hypoactive Sexual Desire Disorder

A. Persistently or recurrently deficient (or absent) sexual/erotic thoughts or fantasies and desire for sexual activity. The judgment of deficiency is made by the clinician, taking into account factors that affect sexual functioning, such as age and general and sociocultural contexts of the individual's life.

B. The symptoms in Criterion A have persisted for a minimum duration of approximately 6 months.

C. The symptoms in Criterion A cause clinically significant distress in the individual.

D. The sexual dysfunction is not better explained by a nonsexual mental disorder or as a consequence of severe relationship distress or other significant stressors and is not attributable to these effects of a substance/medication or another medical condition.

Female Sexual Interest/Arousal Disorder

A. Lack of, or significantly reduced, sexual interest/arousal, as manifested by at least three of the following:

1. Absent/reduced interest in sexual activity.
2. Absent/reduced sexual/erotic thoughts or fantasies.
3. No/reduced initiation of sexual activity, and typically unreceptive to a partner's attempts to initiate.
4. Absent/reduced sexual excitement/pleasure during sexual activity in almost all or all (approximately 75%–100%) sexual encounters (in identified situational contexts or, if generalized, in all contexts).
5. Absent/reduced sexual interest/arousal in response to any internal or external sexual/erotic cues (e.g., written, verbal, visual).
6. Absent/reduced genital or nongenital sensations during sexual activity in almost all or all (approximately 75%–100%) sexual encounters (in identified situational contexts or, if generalized, in all contexts).

B. The symptoms in Criterion A have persisted for a minimum duration of approximately 6 months.

C. The symptoms in Criterion A cause clinically significant distress in the individual.

D. The sexual dysfunction is not better explained by a nonsexual mental disorder or as a consequence of severe relationship distress (e.g., partner violence) or other significant stressors and is not attributable to the effects of a substance/medication or another medical condition.

Erectile Disorder

A. At least one of the three following symptoms must be experienced on almost all or all (approximately 75%–100%) occasions of sexual activity (in identified situational contexts or, if generalized, in all contexts):

1. Marked difficulty in obtaining an erection during sexual activity.
2. Marked difficulty in maintaining an erection until the completion of sexual activity.
3. Marked decrease in erectile rigidity.

B. The symptoms in Criterion A have persisted for a minimum duration of approximately 6 months.

C. The symptoms in Criterion A cause clinically significant distress in the individual.

D. The sexual dysfunction is not better explained by a nonsexual mental disorder or as a consequence of severe relationship distress or other significant stressors and is not attributable to the effects of a substance/medication or another medical condition.

Alice was just not interested in sex anymore. She loved her husband; they had been married for 25 years and had three children ages 20, 18, and 15. Alice denied feeling depressed and had no history of sexual abuse. She was still menstruating regularly, so hormonal changes were not likely. Alice loved her husband Steve, but she no longer wanted an intimate relationship with him. Steven was frustrated and, at times, angry.

Female sexual interest/arousal disorder is defined as significantly reduced or absent sexual interest/arousal as indicated by reduced interest in sexual activity or lack of sexual excitement/pleasure/response during sexual activity. Symptoms can be primarily psychological or primarily physiological (Basson et al., 2003). When primarily psychological, the condition is sometimes called *subjective sexual arousal disorder*. In these cases, a physical response to sexual stimulation (e.g., vaginal lubrication) but no subjective feeling of sexual excitement or sexual pleasure may occur. In contrast, when primarily physiological (also called *genital sexual arousal disorder*), subjective feelings of sexual desire but no physiological response may occur. The third subgroup, *combined sexual arousal disorder*, includes lack of both subjective and physiological response. Female sexual interest/arousal disorder is a controversial diagnosis, and as defined in DSM-5, the prevalence is unknown. Some data suggest that low sexual interest is commonly reported in gynecological settings—up to 75% of women seeking routine care in one sample (Nusbaum et al., 2000).

Approximately 15% of men and 30% of women ages 19 to 59 in the United States experience dissatisfaction with their sexual desire (Laumann et al., 1999). Similar rates are found for men and women from the Middle East (21% and 43%, respectively) and from Southeast Asia (28% and 43%, respectively) (Laumann et al., 2005). Across cultures, this disorder is more frequent in women than men. However, because men and women may have different sexual goals and define sexual desire differently, we must be careful not to overinterpret these data. Patterns of male sexuality, for example, are not necessarily the best standard by which to compare the behaviors of females. Also, the media often report that inappropriate behavior on the part of well-known celebrities is the result of sexual addiction or hypersexuality (see "Research Hot Topic: Sexual Addiction and Hypersexual Disorder").

Erectile disorder is a common male sexual dysfunction known in the media as *erectile dysfunction* (formerly *impotence*). It is the repeated failure to obtain or maintain erections during partnered sexual activities (American Psychiatric Association, 2013). An important element of this definition is the word *repeated*. Most men experience an occasional episode of erectile dysfunction, usually caused by fatigue, stress, or anxiety. The diagnosis is not given unless there

Research HOT Topic

Sexual Addiction and Hypersexual Disorder

Jesse James and David Duohovny are only two among a number of recent celebrities who have announced that they were entering treatment for sexual addiction, now widely used to explain sexual behavior associated with progressive risk taking, loss of control, and significant psychosocial consequences such as discovery of infidelity by one's spouse. Although widely criticized in the media, some empirical support for sex as an addictive or dependency syndrome exists (Kafka, 2010). Self-identified sexual addicts describe withdrawal symptoms, unsuccessful attempts to control or reduce their behavior, and engaging in the behavior longer than they intended (Wines, 1997). However, the topic remains confusing because it is unclear whether this behavior (1) meets criteria for an addiction, (2) is a symptom of an underlying problem, or (3) merely represents bad decisions that often lead to significant distress for the marital partner (Levine, 2010; Steffens & Rennie, 2006).

Hypersexual disorder is a proposed sexual dysfunction characterized by increasing frequency and intensity of sexually motivated fantasies, arousal, urges, and behaviors along with an impulsivity component (Kafka, 2010). Behaviors that are consistently associated with hypersexual disorder include masturbation, pornography, sexual behavior with consenting adults, and cybersex, all of which can have significant adverse effects. Negative outcomes can include unplanned pregnancies, relationship breakups, marital separation and divorce, and the risk of sexually transmitted diseases including HIV. Attempting to empirically define hypersexual behavior remains a challenge for researchers, and much more research is needed to understand its clinical presentation, etiology, and course and prognosis. As researchers address these questions, the scientific validity of this proposed disorder will be confirmed or disproved, leading to improved understanding of another aspect of sexual behavior.

is consistent inability to achieve or maintain an erection or there is marked decrease in erectile rigidity. Significant distress and/or interpersonal difficulty must also occur.

Orgasmic Disorders

LO 9.11 Describe how understanding normal sexual behavior provides an important context when determining the presence of orgasmic disorders.

Another group of sexual dysfunctions include the orgasmic disorders: female orgasmic disorder, delayed ejaculation, and premature ejaculation (see "DSM-5: Orgasmic Disorders"). **Delayed ejaculation**, sometimes called *retarded ejaculation*, is a marked delay in or inability to achieve ejaculation despite adequate sexual stimulation. This disorder is not as common as premature ejaculation. Some men might consider delayed ejaculation to be an advantage as it could increase the sexual pleasure of a partner. In these cases, a diagnosis may not be warranted because there would not be any distress or functional impairment. However, some men who suffer from delayed ejaculation report frustration, distress, and sometimes pain (Brotto & Klein, 2007).

Female orgasmic disorder is defined as difficulty experiencing orgasm and/or markedly reduced intensity of orgasmic sensations. Sometimes called *anorgasmia*, the symptoms must occur on all or almost all sexual activity experiences. Before making a diagnosis, it is necessary to consider age, adequacy of sexual stimulation, and sexual experience. Interestingly, unlike most other sexual disorders, female orgasmic disorder is most common among younger women (Laumann et al., 1999).

> Alice's husband, Steven, was a senior stockbroker in a major brokerage house, and he was working 16 hours a day. He was stressed and anxious much of the time. Steven loved Alice but was frustrated that their sex life had not been good for some time. About 6 months ago, Steven had a heart attack and afterward had difficulty with sexual performance. Although he still had sufficient sexual desire, once he initiated sexual activity, he worried that he was straining his heart. Added to this, Alice was not responsive when they did have intercourse, so he felt pressure to "get it over with." Now he had developed a pattern of premature ejaculation.

Sometimes known as *rapid ejaculation* (see "Real Science, Real Life: Michael—Treatment of Sexual Dysfunction"), **premature (early) ejaculation** is a common male dysfunction and,

DSM-5

Criteria for Orgasmic Disorders

Delayed Ejaculation

A. Either of the following symptoms must be experienced on almost all or all occasions (approximately 75%–100%) of partnered sexual activity (in identified situational contexts or, if generalized, in all contexts), and without the individual desiring delay:

1. Marked delay in ejaculation
2. Marked infrequency or absence of ejaculation.

B. The symptoms in Criterion A have persisted for a minimum duration of approximately 6 months.

C. The symptoms in Criterion A cause clinically significant distress in the individual.

D. The sexual dysfunction is not better explained by a nonsexual mental disorder or as a consequence of severe relationship distress or other significant stressors and is not attributable to the effects of a substrance/medication or another medical condition.

Female Orgasmic Disorder

A. Presence of either of the following symptoms and experienced on almost all or all (approximately 75%–100%) occasions of sexual activity (in identified situational contexts or, if generalized, in all contexts):

1. Marked delay in, marked infrequency of, or absence of orgasm.
2. Markedly reduced intensity of orgasmic sensations.

B. The symptoms in Criterion A have persisted for a minimum duration of approximately 6 months.

C. The symptoms in Criterion A cause clinically significant distress in the individual.

D. The sexual dysfunction is not better explained by a nonsexual mental disorder or as a consequence of severe relationship distress (e.g., partner violence) or other significant stressors and is not attributable to the effects of a substance/medication or another medical condition.

depending on the definition, may affect approximately 30% of men (Laumann et al., 1999). The process of ejaculation consists of four phases. *Erection*, or penile tumescence, is the first phase and is controlled by the parasympathetic nervous system. The second phase is *emission*, in which semen is collected and transported in preparation for the third stage, *ejaculation*, which is the release of seminal fluids from the penis. This occurs when signals from nerves in the urethra reach the spinal cord and cause a reflex response. The sympathetic and somatic branches of the nervous system (see Chapter 2) are responsible for stages 2 and 3. The final stage, *orgasm*, is the subjective feeling of pleasure associated with ejaculation and is believed to be a cortical (brain) experience (Metz et al., 1997).

Premature ejaculation is defined as ejaculation during sexual activity with a partner that occurs within about 1 minute after vaginal penetration and before the individual wishes it (American Psychiatric Association, 2013). Among self-identified premature ejaculators, 90% ejaculated within 1 minute of vaginal insertion and 80% ejaculated within 30 seconds (Waldinger, 2002). In contrast, other samples of men who described themselves as premature ejaculators reported ejaculation that occurred before vaginal insertion or as long as 10 minutes after insertion, although most (79%) reported ejaculation ranging from before insertion to 2 minutes after penetration (Symonds et al., 2003).

A different definition involves an inability to inhibit ejaculation long enough for a partner to reach orgasm 50% of the time (Masters & Johnson, 1970). The advantage of this definition is that it is not tied to a specific number of minutes, but the disadvantage is that it depends on the partner's sexual response (Metz et al., 1997). This definition acknowledges that often sexual dysfunction may be a dysfunction of the couple, not of a single person, such as we saw earlier in the case of Steven and Alice.

Still other researchers (e.g., Kaplan, 1974) define premature ejaculation as simply a lack of control over ejaculation. To come to some consensus, the International Society for Sexual Medicine held a meeting of experts in the field. They agreed on the following definition of

SIDE by SIDE Case Studies

Dimensions of Behavior: From Adaptive to Maladaptive

Adaptive Behavior Case Study

Stress- and Alcohol-Induced Diminished Performance

Barry had had a really stressful week at school. He was in graduate school, and it was time for his dissertation proposal—a very important oral examination. He found that preparing the oral proposal took longer than he had expected. He stayed up all night preparing just to be sure he would be ready, and after the presentation, he was pretty confident that things had gone well. He wanted only to sleep, but it was Friday night and his wife's birthday. He had promised her dinner at a romantic restaurant, and he did not want to disappoint. Sarah looked beautiful, and he felt so lucky to be in love with such a beautiful woman. They drank a bottle of champagne to celebrate, and after dinner, they walked home. Sarah was giving him all the signals that she wanted a night of romance, and cognitively, so did Barry. But his body wasn't responding. No matter how hard he concentrated, he just could not achieve an erection. Sarah knew he was stressed and that he had had quite a bit of alcohol. When she realized what was happening, she pulled him close and told him they should just get some sleep. Although Barry was worried that something was wrong with him, the next time they had the chance to be together, he was rested and sober and did not have any problem achieving an erection.

Maladaptive Behavior Case Study

Erectile Dysfunction

Jack was always anxious around girls. He dated a little in high school but was always nervous, stumbling over his words, acting clumsy, and seeming to always make the wrong move. He had hoped that as he grew older, the anxiety would go away, but it did not. Instead, it seemed to get worse. The stakes got higher. In high school, the pressure to have sex was not so great, but in college it seemed to be everywhere. The girls dressed differently, the guys were always talking about their latest conquest, and Jack felt totally alone. He could barely talk to a woman, let alone think about engaging in sex. His first attempt at sexual intercourse was a failure—he was so nervous, he was unable to achieve a full erection. The girl pretended it did not matter, but she no longer answered his telephone calls. Then he decided to try a prostitute. He thought if he did not know the woman, he might not be so nervous. But he was wrong—he was nervous and the prostitute was impatient. She kept telling him to "hurry up" and "you only paid for an hour, honey, don't you want to use it?" His anxiety was so overwhelming, he just walked out. He tried with a different prostitute, and the same thing happened—despite his cognitive desire, he was unable to achieve an erection. Then he got drunk—alcohol always seemed to make him less nervous in social situations, so maybe it would help with sex. But that did not help either; the alcohol made things worse. Now, every time he finds a woman who is sexually attractive, he avoids any interaction with her. He feels that depression and loneliness are better than the humiliation of not being able to perform sexually.

DSM-5

Criteria for Premature (Early) Ejaculation

A. A persistent or recurrent pattern of ejaculation occurring during partnered sexual activity within approximately 1 minute following vaginal penetration and before the individual wishes it.

Note: Although the diagnosis of premature (early) ejaculation may be applied to individuals engaged in nonvaginal sexual activities, specific duration criteria have not been established for these activities.

B. The symptom in Criterion A must have been present for at least 6 months and must be experienced on almost all or all (approximately 75%–100%) occasions of sexual activity (in identified situational contexts or, if generalized, in all contexts).

C. The symptom in Criterion A causes clinically significant distress in the individual.

D. The sexual dysfunction is not better explained by a nonsexual mental disorder or as a consequence of severe relationship distress or other significant stressors and is not attributable to the effects of a substance/medication or another medical condition.

premature ejaculation for heterosexual males: "always or nearly always occurring before or within one minute of vaginal penetration, and the inability to delay ejaculation on all or nearly all vaginal penetrations, and negative personal consequences such as distress, bother, frustration and/or the avoidance of sexual intimacy" (McMahon et al., 2008, p. 347). As can be seen, the majority of research in this area has been conducted with heterosexual couples. More work is required to determine the extent to which patterns of dysfunction are similar in homosexual or bisexual individuals.

Premature ejaculation is considered *primary* when a man has suffered from this condition since his first sexual encounter. The preceding definition was limited to primary (or lifelong) premature ejaculation. *Secondary* premature ejaculation is the term used when a man initially had no difficulty controlling ejaculation but now ejaculates prematurely (such as Steven). Among men with secondary premature ejaculation, 75% have a physical disease that might account for it, while the other 25% do not have a physical disorder but do report relationship problems (Metz et al., 1997).

Genito-Pelvic Pain/Penetration Disorder

LO 9.12 Identify the features of genito-pelvic pain/penetration disorder

This disorder consists of persistent or recurrent difficulties with (1) vaginal penetration during intercourse, (2) vulvovaginal or pelvic pain during intercourse, (3) fear or anxiety about pain during vaginal penetration, and/or (4) tension/tightening of the pelvic floor muscles (see "DSM-5: Genito-Pelvic Pain/Penetration Disorder").

Among women seeking routine gynecological care, 72% report pain from sexual activity (Nusbaum et al., 2000). Even minimal attempts at sexual intercourse can result in dyspareunia, leading to severe distress and avoidance of sexual behavior. Although the diagnostic criteria for **genito-pelvic pain/penetration disorder** refer to pain in the vaginal or pelvic region, some men also report pain during sexual intercourse. Among men in Western countries, 3 to 5% report the presence of dyspareunia, which is pain during intercourse. (Laumann et al., 2005). Among gay men, 14% suffer frequent and severe pain during receptive anal sex, a condition sometimes known as *anodyspareunia* (Damon & Simon Rosser, 2005).

> Marianne is in love with Mateo. After several months of dating, they want to become sexually intimate. They have tried on several occasions, but every time, Marianne feels her vaginal muscles contract and she cries out in pain. It is not just being physically intimate with Mateo that causes pain. She has never been able to insert a tampon into her vagina. The physician wanted to perform an internal exam to rule out the presence of infection, which could cause pain. Although he tried to insert a speculum, Marianne cried out and asked to discontinue the examination.

DSM-5

Criteria for Genito-Pelvic Pain/Penetration Disorder

A. Persistent or recurrent difficulties with one (or more) of the following:

1. Vaginal penetration during intercourse.
2. Marked vulvovaginal or pelvic pain during vaginal intercourse or penetration attempts0
3. Marked fear or anxiety about vulvovaginal or pelvic pain in anticipation of, during, or as a result of vaginal penetration.
4. Marked tensing or tightening of the pelvic floor muscles during attempted vaginal penetration.

B. The symptoms in Criterion A have persisted for a minimum duration of approximately 6 months.

C. The symptoms in Criterion A cause clinically significant distress in the individual.

D. The sexual dysfunction is not better explained by a nonsexual mental disorder or as a consequence of a severe relationship distress (e.g., partner violence) or other significant stressors and is not attributable to the effects of a substance/medication or another medical condition.

Marianne's pain is sometimes called *vaginismus*, unwanted involuntary spasms of the vaginal muscles that interfere with intercourse or vaginal insertion. As with other categories of sexual pain disorder, few empirical studies have addressed the validity of this diagnosis. Subjective experience of a vaginal spasm does not always correlate with actual spasms measured during gynecological examination (Reissing et al., 2004), indicating the importance of psychological factors in this diagnosis. Furthermore, most women who report vaginismus also report the presence of dyspareunia (de Kruiff et al., 2000).

Any of the sexual dysfunctions may be classified according to the following dimensions: lifelong (always existed) vs. acquired (develops only after a period of normal functioning), generalized (sexual difficulties that are not limited to certain types of stimulation, situations, or partners) vs. situational (limited to certain situations, partners, or types of stimulation), and due to psychological factors vs. due to combined factors (psychological plus medical).

Functional Impairment

LO 9.13 Identify the challenges to determining functional impairment for sexual dysfunctions.

Any sexual dysfunction can lead to dissatisfaction. Depending on the particular complaint, between 65 and 87% of people with a sexual dysfunction report dissatisfaction (Fugl-Meyer & Sjögren Fugl-Meyer, 1999). Furthermore, sexual difficulties between partners are common. Among men with erectile disorder, lower sexual desire affected 60% and lack of sexual arousal affected 44% of their partners (Sjögren Fugl-Meyer & Fugl-Meyer, 2002). In addition, the existence of a sexual dysfunction, whether in one's partner or oneself, affects both individuals' sexual well-being. Compared with a control group, men with one or more sexual dysfunction reported decreased relationship happiness as well as decreased sexual satisfaction (Rosen et al., 2016). Their female partners also reported decreased sexual satisfaction and decreased relationship happiness when compared with a control group, although to a lesser degree than their male partners. In other instances, sexual disorders may sometimes affect sexual functioning without affecting overall functioning. Men who report premature ejaculation indicate that fulfilling a partner's need is an important part of their own sexual satisfaction (Rowland et al., 2004). While their disorder may affect their own self-esteem and ongoing sexual relationship, it does not always affect their overall relationship (Byers & Grenier, 2003). In one study, only 6% of men with premature ejaculation reported that they declined an opportunity for sexual intercourse because of their problem, and even this occurred only rarely (Grenier & Byers, 2001).

Reflecting society's reluctance to talk about sex is the fact that less than 19% of adults with sexual dysfunctions have ever sought professional help (Moreira et al., 2005). Even when the problem was frequent, 36% did not seek any advice. Among those who did, 55% sought support from family or friends, 19% went to media sources, and 32% sought medical advice (Nicolosi et al., 2006). When asked why they did not consult a professional, 72.1% said that they did not consider the behavior to be a problem, 53.9% did not think it was a medical problem, 22.7% were embarrassed to talk about it, and 12.2% did not have access to medical care. These data, once again, illustrate two important points. First, what one person considers a problem is not necessarily a problem for someone else. Second, even people who are frequently bothered by sexual dysfunctions may not realize that the problem can be treated or are reluctant to discuss it with a professional.

Epidemiology

LO 9.14 Discuss how age, sex, race, and ethnicity affect the prevalence of sexual dysfunctions.

Among one sample of 573 Australian men, 42.2% reported the presence of a sexual dysfunction (McCabe & Connaughton, 2014). The most frequent dysfunction was erectile dysfunction, followed by premature ejaculation, hypoactive sexual desire disorder, and delayed ejaculation, respectively. In a sample of 701 women seeking services in a primary care or

Table 9.1 Prevalence (%) of Sexual Difficulties in Men Ages 18 to 59

	Age			
Sexual Difficulty	**18–29**	**30–39**	**40–49**	**50–59**
Lacks interest in sex	14	13	15	17
Is unable to achieve orgasm	7	7	9	9
Climaxes too early	30	32	28	31
Finds sex not pleasurable	10	8	9	6
Is anxious about performance	19	17	19	14
Has trouble maintaining or achieving an erection	7	9	11	18

SOURCES: Brotto, L. A., & Klein, C. (2007). Sexual and gender identity disorders. In M. Hersen, S. M. Turner, & D. C. Beidel (Eds.). *Adult psychopathology and diagnosis* (6th ed.) (pp. 504–570). New York: John Wiley and Sons; Laumann, E. O., Paik, A., & Rosen, R. C. (1999). Sexual dysfunction in the United States. *The Journal of the American Medical Association, 281*, 537–544.

obstetrics/gynecology clinic, 7.4% reported acquired hypoactive sexual desire disorder (HSDD) (Rosen et al., 2012). The prevalence was lower in minority and postmenopausal women. Rates of HSSD were highest among perimenopausal women (ages 40 to 49) and immediate postmenopausal women (ages 50 to 59).

One of the most comprehensive studies of sexual dysfunction in the United States is the National Health and Social Life Survey, which used a sample of 3,159 Americans ages 18 to 59 years (Laumann et al., 1999). This study included face-to-face interviews and questionnaire data and found that sexual dysfunction existed among 43% of women and 31% of men. Tables 9.1 and 9.2 illustrate the prevalence of common sexual difficulties in men and women.

According to data in Tables 9.1 and 9.2, the presence of some sexual dysfunctions increases with age. Problems with erectile dysfunction in men and difficulty with vaginal lubrication in women appear to become more prevalent with increasing age (Fugl-Meyer & Sjögren Fugl-Meyer, 1999; Laumann et al., 1999).

Sexual dysfunctions occur across race and ethnicity. Comparisons of African American and white women indicate that, in general, African American women reported lower levels of sexual desire and pleasure than did white women, whereas white women were more likely to have pain. Both white and African American women reported more sexual difficulties than did Hispanic women (Laumann et al., 1999). In men, the results of the Boston Area Community Health (BACH) Survey indicate that 24.9% of African American and 25.3% of Hispanic men reported erectile dysfunction compared with 18.1% of white men (Kupelian et al., 2008) (see Figure 9.4). Although this would appear to suggest a higher prevalence of erectile dysfunction in the first two groups, these racial/ethnic differences appeared to be the result of socioeconomic differences. This suggests that rather than looking at factors within

Table 9.2 Prevalence (%) of Sexual Difficulties in Women Ages 18 to 59

	Age			
Sexual Difficulty	**18–29**	**30–39**	**40–49**	**50–59**
Lacks interest in sex	32	32	30	27
Is unable to achieve orgasm	26	28	22	23
Experiences pain during sex	21	15	13	8
Finds sex not pleasurable	27	24	17	17
Is anxious about performance	16	11	11	6
Has trouble lubricating	19	18	21	27

SOURCES: Brotto, L. A., & Klein, C. (2007). Sexual and gender identity disorders. In M. Hersen, S. M. Turner, & D. C. Beidel (Eds.). *Adult psychopathology and diagnosis* (6th ed.) (pp. 504–570). New York: John Wiley and Sons; Laumann, E. O., Paik, A., & Rosen, R. C. (1999). Sexual dysfunction in the United States. *The Journal of the American Medical Association, 281*, 537–544.

Figure 9.4 Prevalence of Erectile Dysfunction by Race and Socioeconomic Status.

Although simply examining the data by race/ethnicity would suggest group differences in the prevalence of erectile dysfunction, these differences disappeared when the researchers controlled for socioeconomic status.

SOURCES: Kupelian, V., Link, C. L., Rosen, R. C., & McKinlay, J. B. (2008). Socioeconomic status, not race/ethnicity, contributes to variation in the prevalence of erectile dysfunction: Results from the Boston Area Community Health (BACH) Survey. *Journal of Sexual Medicine, 5*, 1325–1333.

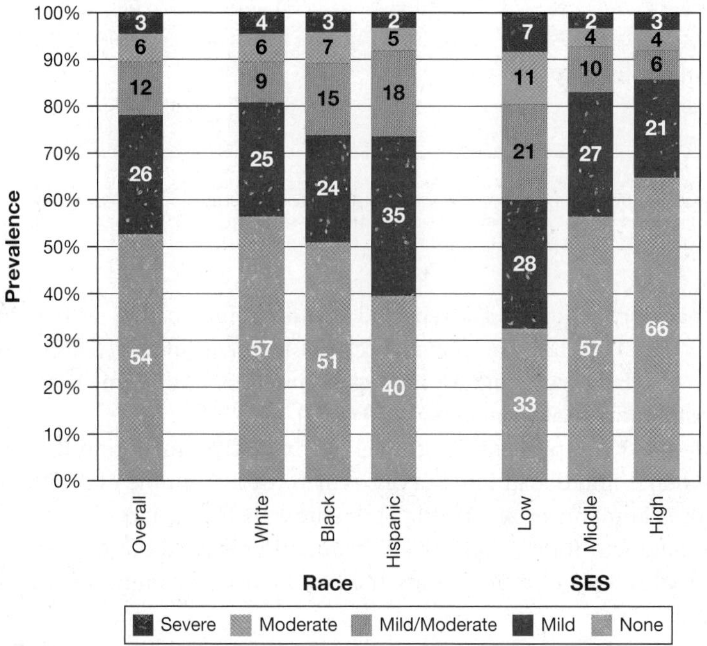

each group that might account for these differences, researchers need to pay attention to social and environmental factors, such as employment status, income, and living accommodations, that might predispose one to poor health.

In the Global Study of Sexual Attitudes and Behaviors, which assessed 27,500 adults between the ages of 40 and 80 in 29 countries, 28% of the men and 39% of the women reported ever having a sexual dysfunction (Nicolosi et al., 2004). Among men, 28% had at least one sexual dysfunction; premature ejaculation was most common (14%) followed by erectile difficulties (10%) (Nicolosi et al., 2004). Among women, 39% had at least one sexual problem; lack of sexual interest was most common (21%) with 16% reporting inability to achieve orgasm and 16% reporting vaginal lubrication difficulties. Across cultures, prevalence of erectile dysfunction is higher in Eastern Asia and Southeastern Asia (27.1% and 28.1%, respectively) than in Western countries. Men in Southeastern Asia also had higher prevalence of retarded ejaculation (Laumann et al., 2005). Similarly, women from Southeast Asia had the highest prevalence of female orgasmic disorder (41.2%) (Laumann et al., 2005).

Among one sample of 573 Australian men, 42.2% reported the presence of a sexual dysfunction (McCabe & Connaughton, 2014). The most frequent dysfunction was erectile dysfunction, followed by premature ejaculation, hypoactive sexual desire disorder, and delayed ejaculation, respectively.

Etiology

LO 9.15 Understand the biological and psychological complexities involved in the etiology and treatment of sexual dysfunction.

Some sexual dysfunctions are related to medical conditions, and a physical examination is necessary to rule out physical causes. In addition, medications for physical disorders such as hypertension and for psychological disorders such as depression may lead to sexual dysfunction as can the use of illicit drugs.

BIOLOGICAL FACTORS Biological conditions may affect sexual desire. Hormonal imbalances, such as hypothyroidism and hypogonadism (Maurice, 2005), can occur at any age and may decrease sexual interest directly by lowering the amount of sex hormones in the body. These conditions may also function indirectly by causing negative mood states, which in turn decrease sexual desire. Other hormonal imbalances are age related. Menopausal changes in women reduce estrogen, which affects vaginal lubrication and vaginal tissue elasticity, which in turn results in discomfort and possibly dyspareunia. In men, testosterone levels decrease with age (beginning in the thirties and forties). How this decline decreases sexual desire and performance is unclear (Isidori et al., 2005), but decreases in testosterone can lower sexual desire and produce erectile dysfunction.

Physical disorders, such as cardiovascular disease, hypertension, diabetes, kidney failure, and cancer, can decrease sexual desire or performance. Among men treated for diabetes, 28% had erectile dysfunction (Feldman et al., 1994). Men who have had surgery for prostate cancer may subsequently suffer from erectile dysfunction (Stanford et al., 2000). Alternatively, physical illness may impair sexual arousal indirectly by causing psychological distress, which may in turn decrease desire.

Androgens contribute to feelings of sexual desire in women as well as in men, although their specific effect on female sexual functioning is not yet known (Brotto & Klein, 2007). Women who have had their ovaries removed have lower levels of androgens, and this can decrease sexual desire. In addition, pelvic surgery, chemotherapy, and radiation treatment have been associated with dyspareunia, vaginal dryness, and hypoactive sexual desire (Amsterdam et al., 2006).

Alcohol and drugs can create temporary sexual dysfunction including premature ejaculation and delayed ejaculation in men and orgasmic disorders in men and women. Drugs that block dopamine receptors or serotonin reuptake in the brain can also delay ejaculation (Metz et al., 1997; Waldinger, 2002). Antidepressant medications, such as the selective serotonin reuptake inhibitors (SSRIs), improve mood but produce significant sexual side effects (Ferguson, 2001). They decrease physical response, inhibit the ability to achieve orgasm, and retard ejaculation in males, although they may improve psychological desire or arousal (see "Biological Treatments" later).

PSYCHOSOCIAL FACTORS Negative emotional states such as depression may be associated with sexual dysfunction. College women who were depressed were more likely than nondepressed women to report difficulties with sexual arousal, inability to achieve orgasm, and painful intercourse (e.g., Cyranowski et al., 2004; Frohlich & Meston, 2002). In addition, they reported less satisfaction with their sexual relationship and less pleasure during sexual activity. Among normally aging men (ages 40 to 70), depression and erectile dysfunction were strongly correlated, and this effect was independent of aging, health status, medication use, and hormones (Araujo et al., 1998). It is unclear whether low sexual desire is a cause or a result of depression—and the relationship may be different for different people.

Behavior theorists and sex therapists (Masters & Johnson, 1970) propose that anxiety and stress play a role in sexual dysfunction because both anxiety and premature ejaculation are associated with the sympathetic nervous system. Performance anxiety appears to be a major cause of erectile dysfunction and can cause other sexual dysfunctions as well. If a man experiences temporary dysfunction as a result of alcohol, stress, or anxiety, the temporary problem may become a concern, and erectile dysfunction may become a self-fulfilling prophecy. Sex theorists also suggest that premature ejaculation results from conditioning experiences involving the need to ejaculate quickly, such as hurried sexual contacts in parked cars (see "Real Science, Real Life: Michael—Treatment of Sexual Dysfunction"), sex with prostitutes, and engagement with sexual partners with whom there is a lack of intimacy (Metz et al., 1997). Although such patterns are sometimes present in the history of men with premature ejaculation, few empirical data address this issue (Grenier & Byers, 2001).

Factors such as couple distress or negative life events may result in temporary changes in sexual functioning in both sexes (Bancroft et al., 2003). Environmental events such as sexual assault may result in cases of genito-pelvic pain/penetration disorder (Weijmar Schultz & Van de Wiel, 2005). Such dysfunctions do not indicate permanent changes in biological functioning in contrast to those caused by aging.

Treatment

LO 9.16 After identifying the factors that may preclude people from seeking treatment, discuss the available biological and psychological treatments.

It is unfortunate that some people who are distressed by their sexual functioning never seek treatment because of ignorance or embarrassment. Many treatments are available with documented efficacy for improving sexual functioning.

BIOLOGICAL TREATMENTS Because low levels of certain hormones, particularly testosterone, may affect sexual functioning, physicians may prescribe testosterone replacement therapy. Available as an injection, patch, or gel, replacement therapy is efficacious for men with low testosterone and sexual desire (Isidori et al., 2005). Testosterone patches may also improve sexual desire and satisfaction among women who have undergone *hysterectomy* (removal of the uterus) or *oophorectomy* (removal of the ovaries) (Braunstein et al., 2005; Buster et al., 2005; Kingsberg, 2007; Shifren et al., 2000).

The relationship between depression and sexual functioning is complicated. Depression can decrease sexual desire. As noted earlier, some antidepressants that improve depressed mood (e.g., SSRIs) increase sexual *desire* but impair sexual *performance* by delaying ejaculation and inhibiting orgasm. The side effect of delayed ejaculation means that some men may be reluctant to take the medication to treat their depression. However, this side effect means that SSRIs may be a useful treatment for premature ejaculation by delaying ejaculation for several minutes (Althof et al., 2014). This illustrates how a medication's negative effect in one context may be a positive therapeutic effect when used differently. However, many individuals who use SSRIs or other medications for PE discontinue the medications because of the adverse side effects (Jern et al., 2014). In addition to the SSRIs, the drug Tramadol is in the class of drugs known as narcotics (**analgesic** drugs that act through the central nervous system). Various randomized controlled trials suggest that this medication may effectively treat premature ejaculation but has significant adverse effects such as erectile dysfunction (ED), nausea, and vomiting, among others (Martyn-St. James et al., 2015).

We noted at the beginning of this section that people with sexual dysfunctions often fail to seek treatment because they do not know that help is available. However, this cannot be said about pharmacological treatments for ED. In fact, it is difficult to watch television or read a newspaper without seeing an advertisement for Viagra, Levitra, or Cialis. The blockbuster drug Viagra (generic name sildenafil) was approved in early 1998 for the treatment of ED. Tadalafil (Cialis) and vardenafil (Levitra) soon followed. These drugs are known as *phosphodiesterase type-5* (PDE5) inhibitors. PDE5 is a molecule found in the *corpus cavernosum*, the spongy erectile tissue in the penis and the clitoris. PDE5 is involved in *detumescence* (loss of erection), so PDE5 inhibitors allow penile erection to occur. Since the introduction of these drugs, thousands of studies have examined the efficacy of PDE5 inhibitors for erectile dysfunction. All three drugs are more efficacious than placebo with 43 to 80% efficacy depending on the reason for the dysfunction (Lewis et al., 2005; Osterloh & Riley, 2002; Porst et al., 2001). The success of the PDE5 inhibitors for male erectile dysfunction has encouraged clinical trials of Viagra as a treatment for female sexual arousal disorder (see "Examining the Evidence: Viagra for Female Sexual Arousal Disorder").

Before the introduction of PDE5 inhibitors, erectile dysfunction was treated with a substance known as *prostaglandin E1*, which was either injected into the penis or inserted into the urethra. Positive effects ranged from 70 to 87% (Linet & Ogrinc, 1996; Padma-Nathan et al., 1997). However, the discomfort associated with the drug's administration makes many men unwilling to use it. A cream version of prostaglandin E1 applied externally to treat female sexual arousal disorder does not appear to be better than placebo (Padma-Nathan et al., 2003).

Finally, physical treatments can address erectile dysfunction. Penile implants are prosthetic devices that consist of a pump placed in the penis or scrotum that forces fluid into an inflatable cylinder, producing an erection. Similarly, vacuum devices consist of a plastic cylinder and a constriction ring that is placed around the penis. A vacuum is created using a pump, which produces an erection. The cylinder is then removed. Physical treatments are common when there is a physical reason for erectile dysfunction, such as diabetes or prostate surgery. Though efficacious and without side effects, they are awkward to use and do not always produce satisfactory results.

PSYCHOSOCIAL TREATMENTS First developed in the 1970s and 1980s, psychosocial treatments for sexual dysfunctions are efficacious (Hawton, 1995; Heiman, 2002), but many were studied in randomized controlled trials more than 20 years ago (Brotto & Klein, 2007). Although further and more sophisticated research is necessary, we now review the available and empirically supported treatments.

Sex therapy (Masters & Johnson, 1970) consists of teaching couples about sexual functioning, enhancing communication skills, and eliminating performance anxiety through specific couple's exercises. Using *sensate focus and nondemand pleasuring,* treatment focuses on decreasing performance anxiety and increasing communication. Sensate focus has three steps. Both partners must become comfortable at each level of intimacy before proceeding to the next step. The first step focuses simply on pleasurable, nonsexual touching. Partners take turns touching the other's body, but they are prohibited from touching the genitals and breasts. During the second step, partners touch any part of the other's body including the genitals and breasts. The focus

Examining the EVIDENCE

Viagra for Female Sexual Arousal Disorder

The success of Viagra in treating erectile dysfunction invariably led to questions about whether this medication might help other sexual dysfunctions. For example, given the high prevalence of sexual dysfunctions among women, would Viagra be a useful treatment for female hypoactive sexual desire disorder or female sexual arousal disorder?

- **The Evidence** PDE5 inhibitors block a molecule in the corpus cavernosum (spongy tissue) that creates detumescence in the penis. Corpus cavernosum tissue is also present in the clitoris of females. Six placebo-controlled trials have studied the efficacy of PDE5 inhibitors for women with female sexual arousal disorder. Two studies (Berman et al., 2003; Caruso et al., 2001) reported positive effects (enhanced orgasm, improved sexual satisfaction). However, four other studies (Basson & Brotto, 2003; Basson et al., 2002; Berman et al., 2003; Kaplan et al., 1999), including a very large multicenter trial that had a sample of 788 women (Basson et al., 2002), did not find any positive effects.

- **Let's Examine the Evidence** The studies that found positive outcomes for PDE5 inhibitors versus those that found no effects had methodological differences.

  First, positive effects occurred when the sample consisted of women with female sexual arousal disorder. No effects were found for samples of women with more heterogeneous sexual dysfunctions (such as hypoactive sexual desire disorder or both hypoactive sexual desire disorder and female sexual arousal disorder).

  Second, in one of the two positive trials (Caruso et al., 2001), women received both the active drug and the placebo (though at separate times), and each condition was compared with the baseline condition (no pill). When someone takes an active drug and later a placebo (or vice versa), the side effects of the medication may "unblind" the patients. Side effects, more likely to accompany active medication, allow participants to correctly guess which substance they are taking. When the dependent variable is a subjective report, such as "feel more aroused," knowing when you are taking the active medication could influence your judgment of how well the pill worked.

  Third, the outcome depends upon the specific question that is asked. PDE5 inhibitors appeared to be less effective for sexual *desire* when compared to sexual *arousal or sexual orgasm* or sexual *satisfaction* (Gao et al., 2016). Given the complex nature of female sexual arousal disorder, physicians are cautioned that prescribing PDE5 inhibitors for female sexual arousal disorder should be the *last* treatment option (Monte et al., 2014).

- **Conclusion** In contrast to the thousands of studies examining the efficacy of Viagra for erectile dysfunction, the few studies examining its effect on women present a mixed picture. Although the same biological tissue exists in both sexes, it appears that Viagra works for only a few women. What hypothesis might you suggest to account for these differences?

Vaginal dilators, of increasing sizes, are used to treat genito-pelvic pain/penetration disorder.

remains on the sensation of touching. Intercourse is not allowed. The third step involves mutual touching, eventually leading to sexual intercourse. Sex therapy is most effective for genito-pelvic pain/penetration disorder and erectile dysfunction that are psychological in origin (Hawton, 1995) and for female disorders of sexual interest or sexual arousal (what used to be known as female hypoactive sexual desire disorder) (Trudel et al., 2001). The long-term outcome is variable. In some instances, initial treatment effects were not maintained when patients were followed up several years later (Brotto & Klein, 2007).

Used by Masters and Johnson (1970) and Kaplan (1979), the *stop-squeeze technique* (Semans, 1956) is highly efficacious for premature (early) ejaculation. In this treatment, the sexual partner stimulates the penis until an ejaculatory urge occurs. At that point, sexual stimulation stops and the partner squeezes the glans of the penis (the tip) until the urge disappears. This sequence is repeated until the interval between initial sexual stimulation and ejaculatory urge lengthens. Then the couple practices briefly inserting the penis into the vagina without thrusting, and the practice continues until the man is able to control the timing of ejaculation and the couple reports sexual enjoyment. This treatment can be adapted for a man to use alone (see "Real Science, Real Life: Michael—Treatment of Sexual Dysfunction"). The stop-squeeze technique has a success rate of about 60% (Althof, 2006; Metz et al., 1997), although positive long-term outcome is achieved in only a minority of cases (Metz et al., 1997). With respect to delayed ejaculation/orgasm in males, no empirical data indicate that any one treatment is more efficacious than another one and that at the current time the selection of a treatment must be based on a clear understanding of etiological and maintenance factors (Althof, 2012).

For female orgasmic disorder, therapists commonly prescribe *directed masturbation* (Heiman & LoPiccolo, 1987; Masters & Johnson, 1970). Women focus on sexually erotic cues and use graduated stimulation to the genital area, particularly the clitoris. Allowing the woman to focus on sexual stimulation that is effective for her without worrying about a partner's behavior enables her to more effectively communicate her wishes to a partner. Approximately 90% of women treated with directed masturbation become orgasmic after this treatment (Heiman & LoPiccolo, 1987).

Treatment for genito-pelvic pain/penetration disorder is based on standard systematic desensitization (see Chapter 4) and uses different sizes of vaginal dilators. Using a hierarchical approach, the dilators are inserted into the vagina, by either the woman or her partner, while she practices relaxation. Over time, a woman becomes comfortable engaging in sexual activity. This procedure, sometimes coupled with cognitive-behavior therapy to challenge irrational beliefs such as "intercourse will always be painful," is a highly successful treatment (Kabakçi & Batur, 2003; Leiblum, 2000; ter Kuile et al., 2007).

Learning Objective Summaries

LO 9.10 Discuss the role of gender in the definition and development of sexual dysfunction.

Sexual dysfunction occurs in both men and women, but the nature of the dysfunction differs by sex. Whereas deficits in sexual performance are most common in men, lack of sexual desire is often the most common complaint among females. There are also differences between the sexes in the degree to which males and females perceive their sexual behavior to be problematic.

LO 9.11 Describe how understanding "normal" sexual behavior provides an important context when determining the presence of orgasmic disorders.

There are many factors that must be considered when determining the presence of orgasmic disorders. For example, age, physical state, or the depth of a woman's emotional connection with her partner may affect sexual functioning but may not necessarily indicate the presence of a sexual dysfunction. Some men might consider delayed ejaculation to be an advantage as it could increase the sexual pleasure of a partner. In these cases, a diagnosis may not be warranted because there would not be any distress or functional impairment.

LO 9.12 Identify the features of genito-pelvic pain/penetration disorder.

Persistent or recurrent difficulties with (1) vaginal penetration during intercourse, (2) vulvovaginal or pelvic pain during intercourse, (3) fear or anxiety about pain during vaginal penetration, and/or (4) tension/tightening of the pelvic floor muscles are the diagnostic features of this disorder. Although the diagnostic criteria for genito-pelvic pain/penetration disorder refer to pain in the vaginal or pelvic region, some men also report pain during sexual intercourse.

LO 9.13 Identify the challenges to determining functional impairment for sexual dysfunctions.

People are reluctant to talk about sexual functioning, and less than 20% seek professional help. When people have questions about sex, only 32% seek medical advice. Others go to family or friends, or media sources. Some people do not believe that the behavior is problematic, whereas others do not think that it is a medical problem. Additionally, a number of individuals are too embarrassed to talk about sexual functioning and some people do not have access to medical care. There are two important points to take away: what one person considers a problem is not necessarily a problem for someone else, and even people who are frequently bothered by sexual dysfunctions may not realize that the problem can be treated.

LO 9.14 Discuss how age, sex, race, and ethnicity affect the prevalence of sexual dysfunctions.

Age affects the frequency of sexual functioning and the type of sexual problems that are problematic. Sexual dysfunction exists in both sexes, but the types of problems differ in scope and frequency. Sexual dysfunctions exist across all races and ethnicities with some differences in the frequency of the disorder by race/ethnicity or country of origin.

LO 9.15 Understand the biological and psychological complexities involved in the etiology and treatment of sexual dysfunction.

Sexual dysfunctions may be related to medical conditions, surgical complications, or medications that are used to treat physical disorders. Hormonal imbalances may decrease sexual interest. Alcohol or other substance use may create temporary sexual dysfunctions. Negative emotional states such as depression, anxiety, and stress play a role in sexual dysfunction for both males and females. Psychological factors may also lead to sexual dysfunction, and in turn, sexual dysfunction can lead to psychological distress.

LO 9.16 After identifying the factors that may preclude people from seeking treatment, discuss the available biological and psychological treatments.

Embarrassment and the lack of realization that sexual problems can be treated may preclude people from seeking treatment. However, people who seek treatment may benefit from either biological or psychological interventions. On the biological side, medications and physical devices may restore sexual functioning. Behavioral interventions designed to address emotional distress, anxiety, and depression as well as teaching specific procedures to delay ejaculation or decrease sexual pain have been demonstrated to be efficacious for men and women. However, treatments that work with one sex are not always efficacious for the other sex.

Critical Thinking Question

Efficacious pharmacological and psychosocial treatments for men with sexual dysfunctions and efficacious psychosocial treatments for women are available. Because talking about sex has become more common among young adults in Western cultures, how might this affect our understanding of the prevalence and treatment of sexual dysfunctions? Do you think that this new "openness" would affect males and females in the same way?

Paraphilic Disorders

The term *paraphilia* is defined as "intense and persistent sexual interests other than sexual interest in genital stimulation or preparatory fondling with phenotypically normal, physically mature, consenting human partners" (American Psychiatric Association, 2013, p. 685). Paraphilic disorders are paraphilias that cause distress or impairment to the person or when the satisfaction of a paraphilia has caused harm or risk of harm to another person. Paraphilias sometimes concern the person's erotic activities whereas others concern the person's erotic targets. The public sometimes associates paraphilic disorders with criminal activity, but the relationship is not so simple. Some paraphilic disorders, such as *transvestic disorder*, are unusual but do not involve criminal activity. Other paraphilic disorders, however, such as *exhibitionistic disorder* or *pedophilic disorder*, may result in criminal charges. In addition, some sexual offenders, such as rapists, do not commit that act because of a paraphilia (McElroy et al., 1999). Therefore, not every paraphilic activity is criminal, but some may lead a person to engage in criminal acts.

Paraphilic disorders are sometimes classified into two groups: disorders based on anomalous (deviating from expected) target preferences or disorders based on anomalous activity preferences. Defining the limits of a paraphilia is difficult because some behaviors (such as physical restraint during sexual activity) do not necessarily cause distress or functional impairment for some adults (Krueger & Kaplan, 2001). Therefore, before any behavior is labeled a paraphilia, its impact in terms of distress and functional impairment must be considered.

Paraphilic Disorders Based on Anomalous Target Preferences

LO 9.17 Describe the difference between pedophilic disorder and child molestation.

In some instances, sexual urges, fantasies, or behaviors are associated with targets that deviate from what is considered normal or expected (see "DSM-5: Paraphilic Disorders Based on Anomalous Target Preferences"). Many different objects may be associated with sexual arousal, although certain categories, such as women's lingerie, occur more frequently. However, it is important to remember that not everything that a person identifies as "sexy" indicates the presence of deviant sexual arousal. A young man may find that seeing his girlfriend wearing lacy underwear enhances his sexual desire for her, but a person with a paraphilia would find the underwear alone arousing.

FETISHISTIC DISORDER

Michael was referred to the clinic after his second arrest for shoplifting. A high school senior who was a loner for most of his school career, Michael was overweight and clumsy and had bad acne. He had mediocre grades and was the classic "last kid to get picked for the team." He never had a girlfriend. Michael loved to cook. He spent hours in the kitchen baking because his goal was to become a pastry chef. In the first shoplifting offense, he was caught stealing a pair of red underpants from the

DSM-5

Criteria for Paraphilic Disorders Based on Anomalous Target Preferences

Fetishistic Disorder

A. Over a period of at least 6 months, recurrent and intense sexual arousal from either the use of nonliving objects or a highly specific focus on nongenital body part(s), as manifested by fantasies, urges, or behaviors.

B. The fantasies, sexual urges, or behaviors cause clinically significant distress or impairment in social, occupational, or other important areas of functioning.

C. The fetish objects are not limited to articles of clothing used in cross-dressing (as in transvestic disorder) or devices specifically designed for the purpose of tactile genital stimulation (e.g., vibrator).

Transvestic Disorder

A. Over a period of at least 6 months, recurrent and intense sexual arousal from cross-dressing, as manifested by fantasies, urges, or behaviors.

B. The fantasies, sexual urges, or behaviors cause clinically significant distress or impairment in social, occupational, or other important areas of functioning.

Pedophilic Disorder

A. Over a period of at least 6 months, recurrent, intense sexually arousing fantasies, sexual urges, or behaviors involving sexual activity with a prepubescent child or children (generally age 13 years or younger).

B. The individual has acted on these sexual urges, or the sexual urges or fantasies cause marked distress or interpersonal difficulty.

C. The individual is at least age 16 years and at least 5 years older than the child or children in Criterion A.

Note: Do not include an individual in late adolescence involved in an ongoing sexual relationship with a 12- or 13-year-old.

women's lingerie department. He avoided charges by telling the security guard that he wanted to buy his girlfriend a birthday present but didn't have enough money. The guard felt sorry for him and let him go. The second time, he wasn't so lucky. He had taken a bag of women's panties and was caught on the security camera masturbating with them in one of the men's changing rooms. When the store security guard called his mother, she was horrified. She searched his room and found stashes of women's underwear in the back of his drawers and under his bed. At the court-ordered assessment, Michael was reluctant to discuss his sexuality at all. He seemed indifferent to his fetishism and only hoped that this arrest would not interfere with his ability to get into a culinary academy.

Recurrent and intense sexual arousal (fantasies, urges, or behaviors) that involves nonliving objects or a highly specific focus on nongenital body parts is known as **fetishistic disorder**. It would be impossible to provide a complete list of fetish objects, but the most common are female underwear, stockings, footwear, or other apparel (American Psychiatric Association, 2013). It is important to add that the sexual arousal or behavior must be accompanied by clinically significant distress or impairment in order to be considered a disorder. Sexual arousal may occur after looking at or fondling, rubbing, licking, or smelling the object; seeing someone else wearing the object; or manipulating the object by cutting or burning it (Chalkley & Powell, 1983). We have virtually no empirical data on this disorder, although those who engage in fetishism are primarily men, and once established, the disorder is chronic (Brotto & Klein, 2007).

TRANSVESTIC DISORDER

Berk is a successful physician with a big secret. It started when he was a teenager. His sister had hung her bra over the shower rod. He was curious—how did girls wear them? What did it feel like? He found himself getting excited at the thought of the lacy bra against his skin. One day he took the bra and matching panties out of the fresh laundry. His sister never noticed. Whenever he wore them, he felt sexually aroused. Berk was shy and awkward around girls. He rationalized that he did not have time for girls—he had to study if he wanted to become a doctor. All through high school, college, medical school, and residency, he satisfied his sexual urges by wearing women's underwear underneath his shirt and pants. Now he was a physician, and he was interested in marrying and settling down. He was seeking treatment because he was quite distressed; he wanted to date an attractive nurse who seemed interested in him. But he did not feel the same sexual excitement thinking about her that he did when he thought about wearing the lacy underwear.

Also known as *cross-dressing*, **transvestic disorder** is recurrent and intense sexual arousal that results from cross-dressing and is accompanied by significant distress or impairment. Not every man who cross-dresses suffers from functional transvestic fetishism. Female impersonators, for example, wear women's clothing to impersonate female singers or actresses on stage; these performers are not necessarily sexually aroused when wearing the clothing or performing. Transvestic disorder occurs almost exclusively in men. Among one sample of cross-dressers, 60% were married and 83% of the wives were aware of their husband's activities (Docter & Prince, 1997). Among the wives, 28% completely accepted their husband's behavior, whereas 19% were described as completely antagonistic. The rest were reported to have less clear feelings.

PEDOPHILIC DISORDER **Pedophilic disorder** is defined as recurrent and intense sexual urges, sexually arousing fantasies, or behaviors involving sexual activity directed toward a prepubescent child or children (see "DSM-5: Paraphilic Disorders Based on Anomalous Target Preferences"). The sexual arousal may be toward girls, boys, or girls and boys. The diagnosis for this disorder is appropriate if the person has acted on the urges or fantasies but denies distress or functional impairment (American Psychiatric Association, 2013). Although the terms *pedophile* and *child molester* are sometimes used interchangeably, they are not synonymous. Someone with pedophilia could have urges or fantasies involving sexual activity with a child but never act on them. That person would not be a child molester. Yet much of what we know about pedophilia comes from samples of convicted child molesters and does not describe all of those who suffer from the disorder.

Table 9.3 Men's Pedophilic Acts with Boys and Girls

Male Perpetrator/Female Victim	Male Perpetrator/Male Victim
Has few victims	Has many victims (up to hundreds)
Offends repeatedly with same victim	Offends only once with a victim
Offends in victim's home	Offends away from victim's home
Offends with victim of mean age of 8 years	Offends with victim of mean age of 10 years
Is also attracted to older women	Is not attracted to adults of either sex
Is commonly married	Is single
Has had behavior since adulthood	Has had behavior since adolescence
Has characteristics of low income, unemployed, alcoholic, lower IQ, psychopathic	Is stable/employed, average IQ, "immature," prefers company of children to adults

SOURCE: McConaghy, N. (1993). *Sexual behavior: Problems and management*. New York: Plenum.

The most common pedophilic acts are fondling and genital exposure. Intercourse (oral, vaginal, or anal) is less common, and rape and abduction are the least common (Fagan et al., 2002). Perpetrators can be familial or nonfamilial. Among one offending group, 29% of offenders were natural parents, 29% other parents, and 40% other caretakers (Sedlak & Broadhurst, 1996). When the offender and the child are related, pedophilia is called *incest*. Although incest perpetrators share many similarities to perpetrators who abuse biologically unrelated children, incest victims are usually at the age of puberty. Younger children are most often the victims of nonbiologically related males with pedophilic disorder (Rice & Harris, 2002).

Girls are more often the victims of pedophilic disorder than are boys, although a perpetrator who prefers boys will often have a much higher number of victims (Abel & Osborn, 1992). Table 9.3 illustrates the difference between those who have heterosexual pedophilic disorder and homosexual pedophilic disorder. These differences include the number of victims involved, where the offenses occur, the sex and age of the victims, and whether the perpetrator is also sexually attracted to adults. Initially considered to be a disorder of men, evidence now indicates that some women suffer from pedophilia (Brotto & Klein, 2007; Fagan et al., 2002).

Pedophilic disorder involving fantasies or impulses about engaging in sexual behavior with children is not considered criminal unless the person acts on the sexual urges. In that case, the behaviors do constitute a crime and may bring the individual to the attention of the criminal justice system. Criminal behaviors are not simply limited to sexual acts with a minor child. Possessing sexual images of children (child pornography, even when obtained over the Internet) is a criminal offense. Because epidemiological studies do not include questions about pedophilic fantasies and behaviors, the prevalence of pedophilia in the general population is not known (Fagan et al., 2002). Furthermore, the percentage of child abusers who suffer from pedophilic disorder is also unknown.

Paraphilic Dysfunctions Based on Anomalous Activity Preferences

LO 9.18 Describe the different paraphilic dysfunctions based on anomalous activity preferences.

The common factor that groups these paraphilias together is that they are based on sexual activities that are considered anomalous (deviating from what is considered normal or expected) (see "DSM-5: Paraphilic Dysfunctions Based on Anomalous Activity Preferences"). These urges or fantasies must cause clinically significant distress or functional impairment in order to consider that the person has a disorder. Some behaviors in this category, such as exhibitionism, may elicit temporary startle reactions or annoyance from the victims. In addition, some of the behaviors in this category are not only deviant sexual behaviors but also criminal offenses, although the extent of the legal implications varies with the particular activity.

DSM-5

Criteria for Paraphilic Dysfunctions Based on Anomalous Activity Preferences

Exhibitionistic Disorder

A. Over a period of at least 6 months, recurrent and intense sexual arousal from the exposure of one's genitals to an unsuspecting person, as manifested by fantasies, urges, or behaviors.

B. The individual has acted on these sexual urges with a nonconsenting person, or the sexual urges or fantasies cause clinically significant distress or impairment in social, occupational, or other important areas of functioning.

Frotteuristic Disorder

A. Over a period of at least 6 months, recurrent and intense sexual arousal from touching or rubbing against a nonconsenting person, as manifested by fantasies, urges, or behaviors.

B. The individual has acted on these sexual urges with a nonconsenting person, or the sexual urges or fantasies cause clinically significant distress or impairment in social, occupational, or other important areas of functioning.

Voyeuristic Disorder

A. Over a period of at least 6 months, recurrent and intense sexual arousal from observing an unsuspecting person who is naked, in the process of disrobing, or engaging in sexual activity, as manifested by fantasies, urges, or behaviors.

B. The individual has acted on these sexual urges with a nonconsenting person, or the sexual urges or fantasies cause clinically significant distress or impairment in social, occupational, or other important areas of functioning.

C. The individual experiencing the arousal and/or acting on the urges is at least 18 years of age.

Sexual Masochism Disorder

A. Over a period of at least 6 months, recurrent and intense sexual arousal from the act of being humiliated, beaten, bound, or otherwise made to suffer, as manifested by fantasies, urges, or behaviors.

B. The fantasies, sexual urges, or behaviors cause clinically significant distress or impairment in social, occupational, or other important areas of functioning.

Sexual Sadism Disorder

A. Over a period of at least 6 months, recurrent and intense sexual arousal from the physical or psychological suffering of another person, as manifested by fantasies, urges, or behaviors.

B. The individual has acted on these sexual urges with a nonconsenting person, or the sexual urges or fantasies cause clinically significant distress or impairment in social, occupational, or other important areas of functioning.

EXHIBITIONISTIC DISORDER

> Max was not sure why he did it, but boy, it sure felt good. He experienced a tremendous urge that could not otherwise be satisfied—nothing else felt the same. When he felt the urge, he would dress in only a dark raincoat and ski mask. Right before dusk, he would drive to a part of town where he was not known. He would hide in the bushes until a woman walked by—he would jump out and open his raincoat, exposing his genitals. Usually the woman would scream. For Max, the possibility of being caught naked and the surprise of the victim were important elements of his sexual satisfaction.

Defined as recurrent and intense sexual arousal involving exposing one's genitals to an unsuspecting person, **exhibitionistic disorder** may also include the act of masturbation in front of a stranger. The shock of the victim is sometimes the sexually arousing component. Most often the perpetrator is male (Federoff et al., 1999), and most victims are female. Exhibitionistic disorder is a "high victim" crime. Among 142 people with a history of exhibitionistic disorder, there were a total of 72,074 victims (Tempelman & Stinnett, 1991). People who engage in this behavior are not different from the general population in terms of academic achievement, intelligence, socioeconomic status, or emotional adjustment (Brotto & Klein, 2007). They are more likely than people with other types of paraphilic disorders to be in committed relationships. They also are less likely than others to see their behavior as harmful to the victim (Cox & Maletzky, 1980).

FROTTEURISTIC DISORDER

> Kwan is a 20-year-old college student. Socially introverted since middle school, he has a few male friends and has had a few dates with girls. Around age 13, he realized that he became sexually aroused by fantasies about women he saw in the mall, at sports games, or at the movie theater. He had no interest in meeting them, but he was sexually aroused by the idea of rubbing his body against them. When Kwan was 17, he began to act on this urge. On a crowded morning subway ride, Kwan would brush his body up against women. He'd say "excuse me" as if he intended to pass them, but he'd linger for a few seconds to press his penis up against the woman's derriere or hip. Soon he was not satisfied just doing it once; by age 18, he was spending hours on the subway each day. He began to have fantasies of exclusive, caring relationships with his female victims. Once at college in a rural area, he worried that he would not be able to fulfill his sexual urge. He tried to stop and began dating a woman. However, his sexual compulsion was so powerful that actual romantic interactions with a partner left him unfulfilled. Kwan was very distressed. Then, in an abnormal psychology class, he heard the word *frotteurism*. He was astonished, ashamed, but also somewhat relieved—he was not the only one with this secret behavior.

Recurrent and intense sexual arousal in the form of urges, fantasies, or behaviors that involve touching or rubbing against a nonconsenting person is known as **frotteuristic disorder**. The word comes from the French word *frotter*, meaning "to rub." As in Kwan's case, the behavior occurs in public places such as crowded buses or subways. Areas of contact are primarily thighs, buttocks, genitals, or breasts. Usually the person fantasizes about a positive emotional relationship with the victim (American Psychiatric Association, 2013). What few data exist suggest that the disorder occurs almost exclusively in adolescent or young adult men who have many victims, are rarely arrested, and, when arrested, serve minimal sentences (Krueger & Kaplan, 1997).

VOYEURISTIC DISORDER **Voyeuristic disorder** involves sexually arousing urges, fantasies, and behaviors that are associated with seeing an unsuspecting person naked, undressing, or engaging in sexual activity (American Psychiatric Association, 2013). To be considered a disorder, the person must experience significant distress or perform actual voyeuristic acts. Although we have few empirical data, people with voyeurism are thought to have limited social skills, limited sexual knowledge, and problems with sexual dysfunction and intimacy (Marshall & Eccles, 1991).

SEXUAL MASOCHISM DISORDER AND SEXUAL SADISM DISORDER The terms *masochist* and *sadist* are commonly used in our society and do not always refer to sexual behaviors. However, sexual masochism and sexual sadism are diagnostic categories that involve pain and humiliation during sexual activity (see "DSM-5: Paraphilic Dysfunctions Based on Anomalous Activity Preferences"). It is important to understand that what defines these disorders is not a specific behavior but the resultant pain, humiliation, or suffering that creates sexual arousal.

> Jack had a secret. He experienced intense sexual arousal and orgasm when his supply of oxygen was cut off during sexual activity. When he could not find a partner willing to choke him while they engaged in intercourse, Jack would "do it himself"—using a chair and a rope to briefly hang himself while he masturbated. He was always extremely careful to have an escape route. One day he did not show up at a meeting. It was not like Jack to miss meetings, and his concerned colleagues went to his home. They found Jack, naked and dead, hanging from a ceiling beam, an overturned step ladder nearby.

Sexual masochism disorder is recurrent and intense sexual arousal that occurs as a result of being humiliated, beaten, bound, or otherwise made to suffer. The events actually occur and are not simulated. Pain may result from being slapped, spanked, or whipped. Humiliation may result from acts such as wearing diapers, licking shoes, or displaying one's naked body. Other acts might include being urinated or defecated on, self-mutilation, or, as in Jack's case, being deprived of oxygen (Brotto & Klein, 2007). Males and females who engage in sexual masochism may do so by mutual agreement and use a safety signal when they want to stop. Yet in some cases these activities lead to injury or death, as happened to Jack.

Sexual sadism disorder also involves the infliction of pain or humiliation, but in this case, the physical or psychological suffering is inflicted on another person. The disorder is found primarily among males. In some instances, the sadistic acts may be nonconsensual, resulting in the crime of sexual assault.

Watch JOCELYN: EXPLORING SADISM AND MASOCHISM

Many people who engage in sexual sadism had formerly engaged in sexual masochism (Baumeister, 1989). In some individuals, sexual fantasies and behaviors alternate between sadism and masochism (Abel et al., 1988; Arndt et al., 1985).

Functional Impairment

LO 9.19 Identify the limits of functional impairment in people with paraphilias.

People who have paraphilic disorders often have more than one. Among one group of sex offenders with a paraphilic disorder, 29% had two paraphilic disorders and 14% had three paraphilic disorders. Specifically, 81% met criteria for pedophilic disorder, 43% for frotteuristic disorder, 19% for sexual sadism disorder, 14% for voyeuristic disorder, and 14% for paraphilic disorder not otherwise specified (McElroy et al., 1999).

Despite their unusual sexual practices, people with paraphilic disorders are often indistinguishable from other people in nonsexual areas of functioning. They do not seek out pain or humiliation in other types of activities. They are described as well adjusted, successful, and above the norm on assessments of mental health (Brotto & Klein, 2007). Men with transvestic disorder are happy with their biological sex and gender identity. Their behaviors, occupations, and hobbies are typical of those found in other heterosexual males (Buhrich & McConaghy, 1985; Chung & Harmon, 1994). However, accidental deaths, such as Jack's, sometimes occur from oxygen deprivation. In the United States, England, Australia, and Canada, one or two deaths from this cause occur per 1 million people each year (American Psychiatric Association, 2000a).

Frotteuristic disorder and exhibitionistic disorder do have victims. Among one college sample, 44% report having been the victim of one of these behaviors in their lifetime

(Clark et al., 2014). As a result of these encounters, more than one-third report behavior changes (monitoring how close they stood to others) and feeling violated and disgusted. Although only rarely were these acts reported to the police, they are not "victimless" activities.

Epidemiology

LO 9.20 Discuss how age, sex, race, and ethnicity affect the prevalence and clinical presentation of paraphilic disorders.

As noted, most epidemiological surveys of psychological disorders do not ask questions about paraphilic disorders. Most people find these behaviors difficult to discuss, and it is highly unlikely that they would admit them to a stranger. Furthermore, in some instances, these behaviors could lead to criminal charges, making it even more unlikely that people would admit to them. Therefore, most of what we know about paraphilic disorders comes from people who seek or are referred for treatment or who have been apprehended as a result of their sexual behavior. This results in confusing and conflicting prevalence estimates. At this time, the most accurate statement is that paraphilic disorders are probably rare, but their actual prevalence remains unknown.

Almost all people with paraphilic disorders are men, but females with paraphilic disorder have been reported (Krueger & Kaplan, 2001). Sexual masochism disorder is also found among women, although the ratio is still approximately 20 males to 1 female (American Psychiatric Association, 2000a). Another sex difference is that women prefer less pain than men during sexually masochistic activities (Baumeister, 1989).

Cultural factors are particularly important to consider in the case of paraphilic disorders. For example, exhibitionistic disorder is considered a paraphilic disorder when cultural norms require wearing clothing that covers the genitalia. When exposure of the genitals is the norm, as in some tropical areas where clothing is not traditionally worn, the diagnosis of exhibitionistic disorder may not be appropriate (Tseng, 2003).

The most common age of onset for all paraphilic disorders is adolescence to young adulthood (Abel et al., 1985; American Psychiatric Association, 2013), although the disorders may begin at any age. Particularly in the case of pedophilic disorder, we usually think about children as the victims. However, young boys (some as young as age 4) have been known to sexually molest even younger children. In one sample, boys who abused younger children were an average of 8 years old at the time that they committed their first offense, and the victims averaged 6 years of age (Cavanagh-Johnson, 1988). The perpetrators used coercion to commit the offenses and knew the children that they victimized.

Across one sample of sex offenders, the average age of onset for a paraphilic disorder was 16 years but ranged from 7 to 38 years (McElroy et al., 1999). Compared with sexual offenders without paraphilic disorders, sexual offenders with a paraphilia were significantly younger when they committed their first sexual offense, had offended for a longer period of time before being arrested, had more victims, and were significantly more likely to suffer from anxiety, depression, substance abuse, and impulse control disorders (Krueger & Kaplan, 2001).

Etiology

LO 9.21 Identify the limitations of the current knowledge base regarding the etiology of paraphilic disorders.

The etiology of paraphilic disorders is unknown (Krueger & Kaplan, 2001), although various theories have been proposed. With respect to biology, several studies have examined the role of endocrine abnormalities in paraphilic disorders, but data have failed to document differences in those with paraphilic disorders (Krueger & Kaplan, 2001). Neuroanatomical and neurochemical studies have not detected specific brain abnormalities (Hucker et al., 1988; O'Carroll, 1989; Tarter et al., 1983), and few data support a role for genetics in the onset of paraphilic disorders (Krueger & Kaplan, 2001).

With respect to psychosocial theories, a commonly held belief is that people who abuse children were abused themselves. However, the available data do not support this contention. If estimates of abuse are correct, as many as 1 in 10 children may be sexually abused before the age of 18, but the vast majority of these children do not develop pedophilia (Murphy & Peters, 1992). Research tells us that a history of child abuse is not necessary or sufficient for the development of pedophilic disorder. In one sample, 28% of sex offenders reported a history of sexual abuse as children compared with 10% among a nonoffending community sample (Hanson & Slater, 1988). Although the rate among offenders is higher, it still means that almost three of four offenders did not have a history of childhood sexual abuse.

Behavioral conditioning theories have been proposed to explain the development of paraphilic disorders, but we have few empirical data. For example, if a person engages in a paraphilic disorder and achieves sexual release, engaging in that behavior is reinforced and likely to be repeated. In a similar vein, negative family environments and disrupted family structures have been hypothesized to play an etiological role, but these hypotheses are based primarily on isolated case reports with few supporting data (Brotto & Klein, 2007).

Treatment

LO 9.22 Identify the most promising biological and psychosocial treatments for the paraphilic disorders and the ethical issues that affect the conduct of clinical research.

Again, it is important to note that a diagnosis requires significant distress or functional impairment. People with paraphilic disorders often are not motivated to change because the sexual behavior is very reinforcing. It creates a pleasurable state and therefore is likely to be repeated. Individuals who seek treatment usually do so because the legal system mandates it, and individuals often discontinue treatment once legal oversight is terminated. Some investigators consider pedophilic disorder to be a chronic disorder with treatment directed toward stopping abuse and helping the perpetrator learn to control the deviant behavior (Fagan et al., 2002). Sometimes treatments are combined to achieve optimum results. Positive outcomes have been reported for these treatments, but the available data are few, and the sample sizes are small and far from conclusive.

Determining the efficacy of interventions requires accurate assessment of the problem before and after treatment. This is particularly difficult in the case of paraphilic disorders because most people are reluctant to discuss these behaviors. Furthermore, admitting to certain sexual behaviors may have legal consequences. Therefore, many researchers and some clinicians depend on objective measures of sexual arousal known as **plethysmography**: penile plethysmography for males and vaginal photoplethysmography for females. Most research has been directed at the *penile plethysmograph*, considered a reliable and valid form of assessing sexual arousal including deviant sexual arousal. The penile plethysmograph measures changes in penile tumescence when the man is shown sexually arousing or nonarousing stimuli. The stimuli usually consist of photographs of males and females, of all ages, against a plain background. The man is instructed to look at the slide, and his erectile response is recorded.

By identifying patterns of sexual arousal, penile plethysmography can distinguish between sexual and nonsexual offenders (although it is more accurate in detecting those who did not commit a sexual offense than those who did commit one) and between rapists or child molesters and nonoffenders (Barbaree & Marshall, 1989; Barsetti et al., 1998). Penile plethysmography also predicts violent recidivism among sexual offenders and informs clinicians and researchers about the efficacy of treatment (Lalumière & Quinsey, 1994; Seto, 2001). In the psychosocial treatment section, we also show how penile plethysmography can assess treatment outcome.

Despite the advances in understanding sexual deviations made possible by plethysmography, a number of ethical, social, and medical concerns surround its use (Abel et al., 1998).

Because the assessment uses nude photographs, one concern is the potential exploitation of children. Even when the photos are used solely for purposes of assessment and treatment, transporting them across state lines can result in arrest for trafficking in child pornography. Second, researchers must be concerned about the transmission of HIV/AIDS when the plethysmograph is used. Third, the device is very intrusive because it must be placed on the penis, and sometimes a technician's assistance is required. This raises questions about its use with adolescents, who later could accuse the technician of abuse. Finally, although it is difficult, some men can "beat the machine" and control their physiological response to appear less aroused than they actually are.

In response to these concerns, a new assessment strategy, the *visual reaction time task*, has been developed. This procedure measures the length of time that people look at slides of males and females (of all ages) who are wearing bathing suits. The theory is that people will look longer at the pictures that they find sexually arousing (e.g., heterosexual women should look longer at slides of adult males rather than children of either sex or adult females). The visual reaction time task appears to be as reliable and valid as penile plethysmography (Abel et al., 1988, 2004) and is more acceptable for use with adolescents (Abel et al., 2004).

BIOLOGICAL TREATMENT Surgical castration, though efficacious for some people, is no longer used to treat paraphilic disorders due to obvious legal and ethical constraints (Rösler & Witztum, 2000). Pharmacological interventions include SSRIs and antiandrogens. Because some forms of paraphilic disorder are considered to be compulsive in nature, the SSRIs were initially considered to have some promise due to their efficacy in treating obsessive-compulsive disorder (see Chapter 5), but to date, their efficacy for paraphilic disorders is not established (Gijs & Gooren, 1996; Rösler & Witztum, 2000).

The primary goal of *antiandrogen medications* is to reduce the sexual drive. Medroxyprogetertone acetate (Depo-Provera) and leuprolide acetate (Depo-Lupron) are testosterone-lowering medications currently used in the United States. Cyproterone acetate is available in Canada and Europe. These drugs inhibit *luteinizing hormone secretion*, which in turn is responsible for decreasing testosterone levels (Rösler & Witztum, 2000). Depending on the dosage used, there often is still enough testosterone for erectile function to allow sexual intercourse with an appropriate partner (Fagan et al., 2002). The drug controls behaviors such as pedophilic disorder, exhibitionistic disorder, and voyeuristic disorder as long as the patient continues to take the medication, but there are significant side effects and a high recidivism rate (an average of 27%) that limit its usefulness (Rösler & Witztum, 2000).

PSYCHOSOCIAL TREATMENT Among psychological interventions, behavioral and cognitive-behavioral treatments for paraphilic disorders are the most common psychosocial intervention and at this time are considered the most efficacious (Krueger & Kaplan, 2002; Marshall et al., 2006). The current empirical database has two limitations. First, the majority of research is based on sexual offenders who have been incarcerated. Second, randomized controlled trials are usually not possible because having no treatment control conditions for sexual offenders is unethical. Despite these limitations, behavioral and cognitive-behavioral treatments result in reduced recidivism rates compared with programs that use other approaches or compared with offenders who do not receive treatment due to lack of financial and therapeutic resources. Treatments based on learning theory have been applied to the treatment of paraphilic disorders since the 1970s and usually involve two parts: decreasing sexual arousal to inappropriate sexual stimuli and enhancing appropriate sexual behavior.

Eliminating or decreasing inappropriate sexual arousal Treatments based on classical and operant conditioning (see Chapter 1) have been successfully developed for various paraphilic disorders. **Satiation** involves exposing the person to the arousing stimuli and continuing that exposure for an extended period until the stimuli no longer produce positive, erotic feelings. For example, a man who fantasizes about exposing his genitals to adolescent females would be asked to imagine that fantasy and masturbate for an extended period of time (perhaps for 2 hours) until he reports an absence of sexual arousal or perhaps even aversion to the idea. A number of sessions must be conducted until even any initial sexual arousal is eliminated. **Covert sensitization** is a similar procedure in which the individual is asked to imagine doing the deviant act but also visualize the negative consequences that result from it. The scene is presented to the patient for a period of time and over repeated sessions until the patient reports that urges to engage in the deviant behavior have been eliminated.

For example, a patient who is troubled by urges to expose himself might be presented the following:

> You hear the teenage babysitter next door playing outside with the children. You feel the urge to stand in front of a window that faces that house and expose yourself. If you stand on a chair, you can expose your genitals and no one will see your face. You know it is wrong, but the urge keeps getting stronger. You climb into the window and pull down your pants. You hear the babysitter gasp—her voice trembles as she tells the children to get into the house. You feel so good. But before you can pull up your pants, the door opens and your mother screams. "Ben, what are you doing? How could you do this?" She is crying and you struggle to pull up your pants. Soon there is a pounding at your door—and when your mother opens it, still crying and screaming "What's wrong with you," the babysitter is at the door with a police officer. You stand there embarrassed and humiliated as the girl watches you, standing in your underwear, being arrested for exposing your genitals. As you are taken away, the entire neighborhood sees you, wearing just your underwear, being handcuffed and put into a police car. You are humiliated, your mother is humiliated, and tomorrow everyone will know what a pervert you are.

Olfactory aversion is the pairing of noxious but harmless odors (such as ammonia) with either sexual fantasies or sexual behaviors. It is an application of classical conditioning theory. Typically, the person is presented deviant sexual stimuli and then inhales the ammonia fumes, which cause burning and watering eyes, runny nose, and coughing. With repeated pairings, the deviant sexual behavior is suppressed, usually within a few weeks (Laws, 2001).

Cognitive-behavioral group therapy is the treatment of choice for those who suffer from pedophilic disorder. The intervention includes psychoeducational groups, anger management, assertiveness training, human sexuality, communication training, control of deviant sexual arousal, and relapse prevention in which participants are educated about identifying high-risk relapse situations (Studer & Aylwin, 2006). Cognitive-behavioral treatments include *cognitive restructuring* in which distorted or faulty cognitions ("I'll never be normal") are identified and more adaptive positive thoughts are substituted ("I can change"). A second cognitive-behavioral treatment is *empathy training* that teaches offenders to recognize the harmful aspects of their behavior and put themselves in the place of the victim to build empathy toward him or her. As noted, behavioral and cognitive-behavioral treatments are efficacious, but it is not clear that they produce permanent behavioral change for paraphilic disorders (Laws, 2001). Booster sessions are probably needed. In addition, these interventions are only one aspect of an overall treatment plan (Krueger & Kaplan, 2002).

Enhancing appropriate sexual interest and arousal Sex is a biological drive, and eliminating deviant sexual urges, fantasies, or behavior will be ineffective unless the person finds a more appropriate sexual outlet. To address this dimension of functioning, clinicians utilize interventions such as *social skills training* that teaches the person basic social conversation skills including initiating and maintaining conversations, using assertive behavior, and developing dating skills to establish relationships with appropriate adults. When a person with paraphilic disorder is in an established adult relationship, the aberrant sexual behavior may severely strain the relationship, particularly if there are legal complications. Therefore, *couples therapy* may be necessary. Finally, people with paraphilic disorders often lack a basic understanding of sexual behavior, particularly appropriate adult sexual behaviors, and treatment may therefore need to include *sex education* (Krueger & Kaplan, 2001).

Learning Obective Summaries

LO 9.17 Describe the difference between pedophilic disorder and child molestation.

Pedophilic disorder is a paraphilic disorder. *Sexual offender* and *child molester* are terms applied to people whose behaviors involve criminal sexual activities.

LO 9.18 Describe the different paraphilic dysfunctions based on anomalous activity preferences.

The common factor that groups these paraphilias together is that they are based on sexual activities that deviate from what is considered normal or expected. Individuals with these disorders get sexual satisfaction by exposing their genitals to others, rubbing their genitals against others, looking into the homes of unsuspecting persons who are in various stages of dress, or needing to receive/give pain during sexual activities. These urges or fantasies must cause clinically significant distress or functional impairment.

LO 9.19 Identify the limits of functional impairment in people with paraphilias.

To be considered a disorder, paraphilias must cause significant distress or functional impairment. In many instances, these functional impairments may be limited to the area of sexual functioning. People with paraphilic disorders are often indistinguishable from other people in nonsexual areas of functioning.

LO 9.20 Discuss how age, sex, race, and ethnicity affect the prevalence and clinical presentation of paraphilic disorders.

Most of what we know about paraphilic disorders is based on a treatment seeking sample. The most accurate statement is that paraphilic disorders are probably rare, but their actual prevalence remains unknown. Almost all people with paraphilic disorders are men, and most are adult age. There are no data on race and ethnicity.

LO 9.21 Identify the limitations of the current knowledge base regarding the etiology of paraphilic disorders.

The etiology of paraphilic disorders is unknown. Neuroanatomical and neurochemical studies have not detected specific brain abnormalities (Hucker et al., 1988; O'Carroll, 1989; Tarter et al., 1983), and few data support a role for endocrine or genetics in the etiology of these disorders. The commonly held belief that people who abuse children were abused themselves is not supported by data. Similarly, behavioral conditioning theories have been proposed to explain the development of paraphilic disorders, but there are few empirical data to support this contention.

LO 9.22 Identify the most promising biological and psychosocial treatments for the paraphilic disorders and the ethical issues that affect the conduct of clinical research.

Psychological interventions are the most efficacious treatment for paraphilic disorders, but many who suffer from these disorders either are reluctant to seek treatment or do not see the need for it. Often they participate in treatment only when required by court order and quit when they are no longer compelled to do so. Furthermore, because paraphilic disorders are unusual and often misunderstood, people who suffer from these disorders rarely seek treatment. This makes it difficult to conduct the clinical trials necessary to fully determine the efficacy of these treatments.

Critical Thinking Question

Do you think that culture might influence the expression or labeling of a certain behavior as a paraphilic disorder?

Real SCIENCE Real LIFE

Michael—Treatment of Sexual Dysfunction

THE PATIENT

Michael is 21 years old. His first real girlfriend just broke up with him, and he is sure it is because of his inadequate sexual performance. Michael is very shy around girls, and he admits that he does not even know how to talk to them. Furthermore, he has had few sexual experiences. He lost his virginity in the backseat of a car, and he said, "It was over before I knew it."

THE PROBLEM

Until now, Michael's sexual experience consisted of visits to local prostitutes during which he always felt rushed both by the woman and by the thought that he might get caught in a police raid. With his first real girlfriend, he often ejaculated before intromission. His girlfriend kept saying that it did not matter, but he knew that it did. His friends told him to think about baseball when having sex in an effort to delay ejaculation, but that did not work. Michael was desperate to get help.

ASSESSING THE SITUATION

What factors do you think might have contributed to Michael's problem, and what would you recommend for his treatment?

THE TREATMENT

The psychologist knew that premature ejaculation could be treated by the stop-squeeze technique, but Michael did not have a partner when he started treatment. The therapist began by explaining the rationale to Michael and educated him about the normal male sexual response cycle and the four-step process of ejaculation. This was important because Michael needed to learn to recognize the plateau phase in order to implement the procedure correctly. Once Michael understood these biological processes, the therapist taught him to use the procedure himself through masturbation. In session, the therapist discussed the procedure and used drawings to show Michael where and when to squeeze. The therapist developed a self-monitoring sheet so that Michael could track his progress. Michael was instructed to practice the procedure each day, trying to lengthen the time between his initial erection and ejaculation.

At each treatment session, Michael reported on his progress. In session, the therapist focused on social skills training, particularly heterosocial interactions and dating skills. As Michael's confidence grew, he was able to invite a girl to a movie. He did not attempt to engage in a sexual relationship at once but waited until he felt very comfortable. He continued to practice the stop-squeeze technique and did not visit any prostitutes in order not to impede his progress.

THE TREATMENT OUTCOME

After 3 months of dating, Michael and his girlfriend became sexually intimate. Michael reported that the first time was "not very long"—only about 3 minutes after intromission. His girlfriend attributed it to the fact that they had had a lot of wine that evening and told him not to worry. Because he did not feel rejected, Michael was able to try again. At the end of treatment, Michael was engaging in vaginal intercourse for about 5 minutes before ejaculation. He also had increased confidence in his ability to interact socially, not just sexually, with women.

Key Terms

analgesic, p. 348
covert sensitization, p. 361
delayed ejaculation, p. 340
erectile disorder, p. 339
exhibitionistic disorder, p. 355
female orgasmic disorder, p. 340
female sexual interest/arousal disorder, p. 339
fetishistic disorder, p. 353
frotteuristic disorder, p. 356
gender dysphoria, p. 329
genito-pelvic pain/penetration disorder, p. 343
male hypoactive sexual desire disorder, p. 338
olfactory aversion, p. 361
paraphilic disorder, p. 322
pedophilic disorder, p. 353
plethysmography, p. 359
premature (early) ejaculation, p. 340
satiation, p. 360
sex drive, p. 323
sex reassignment surgery, p. 330
sexual dysfunctions, p. 338
sexual masochism disorder, p. 356
sexual sadism disorder, p. 357
transgender behavior, p. 330
transsexualism, p. 330
transvestic disorder, p. 353
voyeuristic disorder, p. 356

Chapter 10

Substance-Related and Addictive Disorders

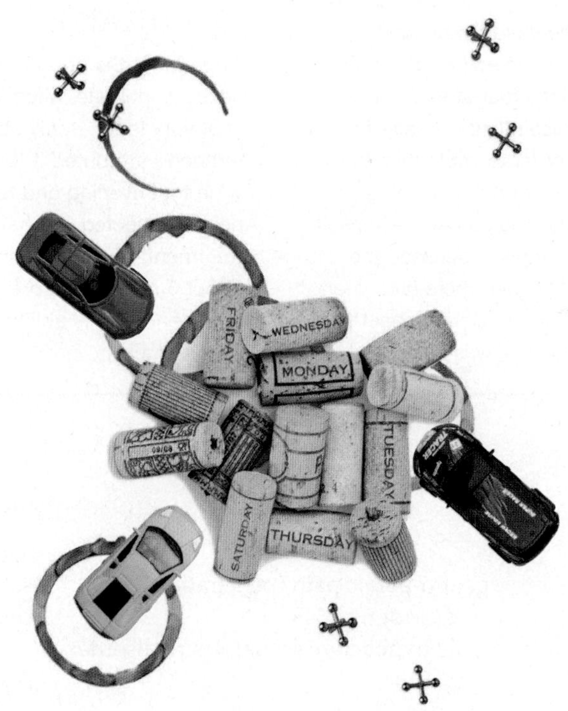

Chapter Learning Objectives

Substance-Related Disorders	**LO 10.1**	Enumerate the features that distinguish substance use disorders from substance use.
Commonly Used "Licit" Drugs	**LO 10.2**	Characterize the physical and psychological effects of caffeine consumption.
	LO 10.3	Describe the physical and psychological effects of nicotine and risks associated with its use.
	LO 10.4	Enumerate the adverse health effects of alcohol use disorder.
Illicit Drugs and Non-Substance-Related Disorders	**LO 10.5**	Describe the short- and long-term therapeutic and negative psychological and health consequences of marijuana use.
	LO 10.6	Characterize patterns of use and effects of CNS stimulants.
	LO 10.7	Summarize the mechanism of action of cocaine on the brain.

	LO 10.8 Compare and contrast patterns of use and effects of barbiturates and benzodiazepines.
	LO 10.9 Summarize the ways in which opioids can be taken and their effects on body and mind.
	LO 10.10 Describe typical effects of LSD and hallucinogens.
	LO 10.11 Explain how inhalants can permanently damage the brain.
	LO 10.12 Explain the concept of behavioral addictions and the debate about their inclusion in the DSM.
	LO 10.13 Characterize the demographic patterns of illicit drug use.
Etiology of Substance-Related Disorders	**LO 10.14** Illustrate the role that the brain's reward pathways play in addiction.
	LO 10.15 Explain how the principles of reinforcement apply to substance use disorders.
	LO 10.16 Elucidate the role of cultural and economic factors in substance use disorders.
	LO 10.17 Trace the developmental trajectory of risk for substance use disorders.
Treatment of Substance Use Disorders	**LO 10.18** Compare approaches and philosophies of cognitive, behavioral, and 12-step approaches to treatment of substance use disorders.
	LO 10.19 Evaluate the ethical complexities of confronting an impaired colleague.
	LO 10.20 Outline the core principles of biological interventions for substance use disorders.
	LO 10.21 Identify sex and racial/ethnic differences in treatment seeking for substance use disorders.

Karen wasn't sure this was the life she wanted. Before the kids, she and her husband had a fairly equal relationship—Scott helped with the cooking, and she helped with the cars—but now they had reverted to a traditional sex-role relationship. She felt trapped. She agreed to stay home with Baxter, age 2, and Otis, age 6, until they started school, while Scott climbed the ladder to partner in his law firm. Karen was a good mom, but when her third child, Jackson, was born, she felt like she was losing control. Making matters worse, Baxter was becoming jealous of the attention his new brother was getting and was becoming a terror on wheels.

Karen tried to talk with her husband, but he did not understand. Baxter never acted up when his dad was around and would sit and read quietly with him after work. Scott worked later and later every night.

Karen tried to talk with her mom and the other moms at the playground, but they rattled off advice that felt very judgmental to her. One particularly tough day, she put the kids down for their nap and decided to have a glass of wine to relax. What started out as an "innocent" drink in the afternoon soon snowballed into a full bottle by the time Scott came home. At first she carefully hid the bottles, but she soon realized that he wasn't paying any attention anyway. In fact, she stopped caring what he thought. Wine became her support system.

She rationalized her drinking and took steps to be safe. She did her errands in the morning and only started drinking around noon. However, she injured her back connecting a car seat, and things got worse. Her doctor prescribed some Vicodin (a narcotic painkiller) and recommended physical therapy. She passed on the therapy, but Vicodin made her feel as if nothing mattered—and it helped her back pain! So, still drinking her bottle of wine, she would now also pop a pill or two as needed. Sometimes she would pass out in bed.

One afternoon while she was dozing on the couch, Baxter threw something at Jackson that cut his forehead. Blood poured out of his little head. Panic stricken, Karen strapped the kids in their car seats and drove to the emergency room. It was raining, and she lost control of the car. When she woke up, everyone was safe, but she was in the hospital with her arm in a sling. She was okay, but because of her blood alcohol content of 0.12, she was charged with driving under the influence. Scott demanded that she stop drinking immediately. He was surprised to hear her say she didn't think she could stop. He realized then that Karen needed professional help.

In Karen's case, what started out as one "innocent" drink soon progressed to a serious problem that jeopardized her children's safety. Karen found that she needed to drink more and more—one glass of wine no longer allowed her to relax. Known as *tolerance*, this is one property of substances that can propel a person from simple use to a substance use disorder. How does this process occur? Why can some people stop at just one drink while others lack the internal "brakes" that keep them from spiraling into addiction? In this chapter, we discuss how biology, psychology, and culture interact to influence the development of substance use disorders.

Substance-Related Disorders

Basic Principles of Substance-Related Disorders

LO 10.1 Enumerate the features that distinguish substance use disorders from substance use.

Whether the drug is caffeine, nicotine, alcohol, or heroin, most people use substances at some point during their lifetime. Many people "use" substances occasionally without them producing any problems with social, educational, or occupational functioning. Examples are drinking caffeinated sodas daily, drinking a beer or two at weekend parties, having wine with dinner, or smoking marijuana occasionally—although some substances are legal and some are illegal depending on where you are.

The effect of substance use varies from mild (perking up after morning coffee) to extreme, which is known as **substance intoxication**. This is categorized in the current DSM as substance-induced disorder (American Psychiatric Association, 2013). The definition of *intoxication* includes several concepts. First, intoxication is reversible (one comes down from the intoxicated state) and substance specific (the features of intoxication vary with the substance ingested). In addition, intoxication results in maladaptive behavioral or psychological changes associated with the central nervous system. Finally, the effects of intoxication emerge during or shortly after drug use. Consider the sports fan who has had too much to drink at a game or someone who is unable to walk a straight line in a sobriety test. These individuals are experiencing intoxication. Intoxication can be an isolated event, or it can be a recurring state in the context of a **substance use** disorder.

Drawing the boundaries between alcohol use and an alcohol use disorder requires the knowledge of the frequency, duration, and severity of the behavior.

Distinguishing between substance use and problematic use can be complicated. Indeed, cultural norms vary—what is viewed as use in one culture may be regarded as abuse in another. Even legal ramifications differ across cultures. See, for example, Table 10.1 for the legal blood alcohol limit across a number of countries showing varying tolerances of alcohol behind the wheel.

In the DSM-5, substance use disorders refer to a cluster of cognitive, behavioral, and physiological symptoms indicating that the person continues to use a substance despite significant substance-related problems (see "DSM-5: Alcohol

Table 10.1 Legal Blood Alcohol Content (BAC) Limits Around the World

Country	BAC Limit (%)
Pakistan, Saudi Arabia, Armenia, Azerbaijan, the Czech Republic, Hungary, Jordan, Kyrgyzstan, Romania	0.00
China, Estonia, Poland	0.02
Serbia, Japan, Uruguay	0.03
Argentina, Australia, Austria, Belgium, Finland, France, Germany, Greece, Hong Kong, Israel, Italy, South Africa, Spain, Switzerland, Thailand, Taiwan, Turkey	0.05
United States, Malaysia, Mexico, New Zealand, Norway, Puerto Rico, Singapore, the United Kingdom	0.08

Data from http://www.bactrack.com/blogs/expert-center/35043525-typical-bac-limits-around-the-world

Use Disorder" for an example of the diagnostic criteria for a substance use disorder). In the DSM-5, two or more symptoms must be present to meet the criteria for a substance use disorder, with severity characterized based on the number of symptoms present: mild = 2–3 symptoms, moderate = 4–5 symptoms, and severe = 6 or more symptoms.

The substance-related disorders are divided into *substance use disorders* and *substance-induced disorders*. Substance-induced disorders include intoxication, withdrawal, and other substance/medication-induced mental disorders (e.g., psychotic disorders, depressive disorders, etc.). The DSM-5 defines **tolerance** as requiring an increased dose of a substance to achieve the desired effect or experiencing a markedly reduced effect when consuming the usual dose. It defines **withdrawal** as a syndrome that occurs when concentrations of a substance decline in an individual who had maintained prolonged and heavy use of a substance. The physical symptoms of withdrawal vary by the class of substance, but physiological withdrawal symptoms are most apparent with alcohol, opioids, and nicotine and, to a lesser extent, sedatives, hypnotics, anxiolytics, and caffeine.

DSM-5

Criteria for Alcohol Use Disorder

A. A problematic pattern of alcohol use leading to clinically significant impairment or distress, as manifested by at least two of the following, occurring within a 12-month period:

1. Alcohol is often taken in larger amounts or over a longer period than was intended.
2. There is a persistent desire or unsuccessful efforts to cut down or control alcohol use.
3. A great deal of time is spent in activities necessary to obtain alcohol, use alcohol, or recover from its effects.
4. Craving, or a strong desire or urge to use alcohol.
5. Recurrent alcohol use resulting in a failure to fulfill major role obligations at work, school, or home.
6. Continued alcohol use despite having persistent or recurrent social or interpersonal problems caused or exacerbated by the effects of alcohol.
7. Important social, occupational, or recreational activities are given up or reduced because of alcohol use.
8. Recurrent alcohol use in situations in which it is physically hazardous.
9. Alcohol use is continued despite knowledge of having a persistent or recurrent physical or psychological problem that is likely to have been caused or exacerbated by alcohol.
10. Tolerance, as defined by either of the following:
    - **a.** A need for markedly increased amounts of alcohol to achieve intoxication or desired effect.
    - **b.** A markedly diminished effect with continued use of the same amount of alcohol.
11. Withdrawal, as manifested by either of the following:
    - **a.** The characteristic withdrawal syndrome for alcohol (refer to Criteria A and B of the criteria set for alcohol withdrawal).
    - **b.** Alcohol (or a closely related substance, such as a benzodiazepine) is taken to relieve or avoid withdrawal symptoms.

In addition to tolerance and withdrawal, the behavioral features of substance use disorders include using more than the intended amount; desiring or attempting to cut down; spending time trying to acquire the substance; giving up social, occupational, or recreational activities because of substance use; and continuing use despite known physical or psychological problems caused by or exacerbated by the substance use.

Whether a person develops a substance use disorder depends in part on the drug's addictive potential and on the characteristics of the person using the drug. Some drugs such as heroin and alcohol produce more withdrawal symptoms. Some users are more prone to substance problems because of their genetic makeup, ongoing life stress, or immersion in a subculture that involves drug use (Daughters et al., 2007). Therefore, a combination of genetic and environmental factors determines liability to developing a substance use disorder.

Learning Objective Summaries

LO 10.1 Enumerate the features that distinguish substance use disorders from substance use.

Many people around the world use substances, often with few adverse effects; however, substance use disorders refer to a cluster of cognitive, behavioral, and physiological symptoms indicating that the person continues to use a substance despite significant substance-related problems. In addition to tolerance and withdrawal, the behavioral features of substance use disorders include using more than the intended amount; desiring or attempting to cut down; spending time trying to acquire the substance; giving up social, occupational, or recreational activities because of substance use; and continuing use despite known physical or psychological problems caused by or exacerbated by the substance use.

Critical Thinking Question

Many students are exposed to underage drinking in college. What factors do you think contribute to whether students engage in that behavior? What are some of the genetic and environmental factors that influence whether underage college drinking becomes a regular event or remains a rare behavior?

Commonly Used "Licit" Drugs

We focus first on three legal psychoactive drugs that are widely used in our society: caffeine, nicotine, and alcohol. Although the sale of caffeine has no formal restrictions, it is widely considered to be a poor source of energy for young children. Nonetheless, children are introduced to caffeine very early in life through carbonated beverages. In contrast, the purchase and use of nicotine and alcohol have age restrictions with penalties applicable to both the buyer and the seller. We look first at the drug with which millions of people start their day: caffeine.

Caffeine

LO 10.2 Characterize the physical and psychological effects of caffeine consumption.

"One doppio espresso...one triple grande latte...one espresso macchiato." Customers place orders like this every morning at countless coffee bars. **Caffeine** is a central nervous system (CNS) stimulant with a kick that boosts energy, mood, awareness, concentration, memory consolidation, and wakefulness. Caffeine may be consumed quite safely in moderation to produce these positive effects. Its less desirable side effects include headache, fatigue, depressed mood, inactivity, nausea, restlessness, trouble concentrating, irritability, and feeling "foggy" (Gonzalez de Mejia & Ramirez-Mares, 2014; Juliano & Griffiths, 2004). Coffee, a robust source of caffeine, has become an important part of our culture and often serves as a backdrop for socializing.

Figure 10.1 Coffee consumption worldwide

Caffeine is the most widely used drug in the world. The manner in which it is consumed is often influenced by cultural conditions.

SOURCE: Based on Coffee consumption, World Resources Institute, viewed 8th February, 2011, <http://www.wri.org>

World Coffee Consumption

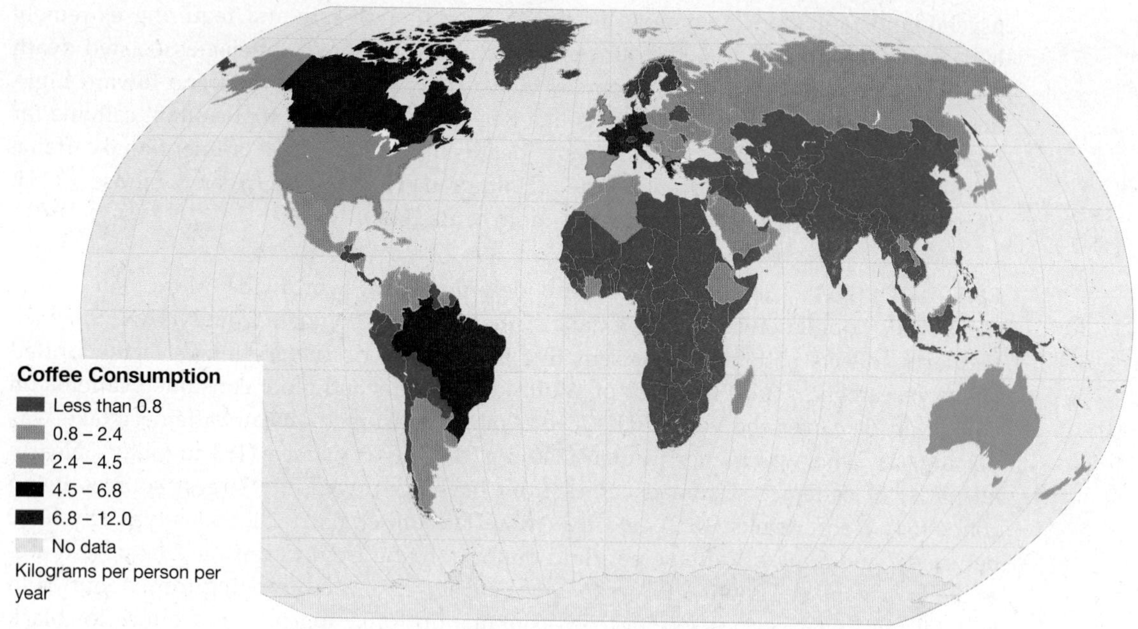

Although less harmful than most other substances, caffeine, like other stimulants, affects multiple organs within the body, and withdrawal after regular use produces short-term effects such as a "crash." It also has long-term effects, including tolerance, dependence, and withdrawal. However, there is no diagnosis for caffeine use disorder in the DSM-5, although there are DSM-5 diagnoses for caffeine intoxication and caffeine withdrawal (see "Functional Impairment" below). One diet soda a day can escalate to 10 during exam time to get the same level of alertness. If you then celebrate the end of exams with a back-to-nature camping trip where getting your coffee fix is not possible, you might find yourself with a blistering caffeine-withdrawal headache. Although caffeine's precise mechanism of action remains unknown, the neurotransmitters adenosine, dopamine, and serotonin may be involved in its effect on the brain (Carrillo & Benitez, 2000; Sturgess et al., 2010). Caffeine has a long half-life (i.e., it stays in the bloodstream for a long time), and some people can experience its effects 6 hours or more after their last dose (Statland & Demas, 1980).

FUNCTIONAL IMPAIRMENT Because just about everyone consumes caffeine in one form or another—in coffee and/or sodas—it is considered normal, and its potential health effects are often overlooked. On the one hand, habitual coffee consumption has been associated with lower risk for Parkinson's and Alzheimer's disease, certain cancers, type 2 diabetes, and all-cause mortality, and moderate intake (≤400 mg/day) is not associated with adverse effects in healthy adults (Gonzalez de Mejia & Ramirez-Mares, 2014). However, over time, caffeine may contribute to cardiovascular disorders (including hypertension and increased cholesterol), reproductive problems (including spontaneous abortion and effects on fetal growth), bone loss and osteoporosis, cancer, and psychiatric disturbances (Barone & Grice, 1994; Carrillo & Benitez, 2000; Garattini, 1993; Gonzalez de Mejia & Ramirez-Mares, 2014; Massey, 1998). For some people, the equivalent of five to eight cups of coffee per day may lead to anxiety and to respiratory, urinary, gastric, and cardiovascular distress (Carrillo & Benitez, 2000). While caffeine, at a minimum, elicits some physiological effects on healthy individuals, research indicates that caffeine provokes a significantly higher anxiety score in individuals carrying genes associated with anxiety disorders (e.g., panic disorder) as well as increased anxiety and induction of panic attacks in individuals with panic disorder and social anxiety disorder (Alsene et al., 2003; Nardi et al., 2009; Vilarim et al., 2011). Consuming large amounts of caffeine can produce acute caffeine intoxication, which includes physical symptoms such as headache, nausea, hyperventilation, restlessness, nervousness, excitement, insomnia, fever, flushed face, diuresis (increased urination), gastrointestinal disturbance, vomiting, muscle twitching, rambling flow of thought and speech, fast or irregular heartbeat, periods of inexhaustibility, and psychomotor agitation (Yamamoto et al., 2015). Although rare and requiring extremely high doses (roughly 50 to 100 8-ounce cups of coffee per day), caffeine-associated death can occur. Unfortunately, this outcome is increasingly likely with the trend toward high-dose beverages, such as energy drinks like Red Bull or Monster, that contain caffeine far in excess of a regular cup of coffee. Several deaths due to accidental or intentional caffeine supplement overdose have been reported (Holmgren et al., 2004; Kerrigan & Lindsey, 2005; Mrvos et al., 1989; Silva et al., 2014; Yamamoto et al., 2015).

EPIDEMIOLOGY Caffeine is the most widely used drug worldwide. More than 80% of the world's population consumes it daily (James, 1997). Using data from NHANES, which regularly collects nationally representative information on dietary intake in the United States, researchers found that 89% of adults age 19 years and older consumed caffeine on any given day over the years 2001–2010. Among consumers, mean caffeine intake was 211 mg/day and was higher in men (240 mg/day) than women (183 mg/day). Nearly all (98%) of caffeine consumed comes from beverages, with the largest sources being coffee (64%), soft drinks (18%), and tea (16%) (Fulgoni et al., 2015). Sodas typically have between 2 and 5 mg of caffeine per fluid ounce, ranging from Coca-Cola Classic (2.8 mg) at the lower end to Mountain Dew (4.6 mg) at the higher end (ranging from about 25 to 60 total mg in a 12-ounce serving). Tea contains up to 5.2 mg per fluid ounce for black tea (about 60 total mg in a 12-ounce serving), with slightly less in green tea (3.1 mg, or about 37 total mg in a 12-ounce serving). Coffee ranges from about 7 to 10 mg per ounce in instant coffee and lattes to more than 20 mg per ounce in brewed coffee (ranging from about 80 mg to well over 200 mg in a 12-ounce cup), and espresso has about 50 mg per ounce (about 150 total mg in a double 1.5-ounce serving; http://www.caffeineinformer.com/the-caffeine-database).

An emerging trend, especially among adolescent boys and young men, is the use of highly caffeinated energy drinks. These drinks typically start at about 10 mg per ounce and can exceed 200 mg per ounce in popular *energy shots*, which are recommended for dilution but often are taken in their packaged form (http://www.caffeineinformer.com/the-caffeine-database). Although energy drinks provide less than 1% of the daily caffeine for U.S. adults, their consumption has increased substantially in recent years (Fulgoni et al., 2015). According to the Eating and Activity in Teens (EAT) study, about 15% of U.S. adolescents in grades 6 to 12 consume energy drinks on a weekly basis (Larson et al., 2014), but other self-report surveys suggest that up to 50% of adolescents and young adults consume energy drinks (Seifert et al., 2011). About 6% of caffeine consumed in 2009–2010 by U.S. children and adolescents came from energy drinks (Branum et al., 2014). These drinks have now joined coffee as a legal drug that many use at moderate levels to boost energy but that also have the potential to produce negative side effects. They may provide a false sense of wakefulness that might replace adequate sleep. In developing adolescents, these effects can lead to especially problematic health consequences, and energy drink–related adverse events have been reported that include liver damage, kidney failure, agitation, seizures, tachycardia, hypertension, heart failure, and even death (Seifert et al., 2011).

Even more troubling is the consumption of caffeine pills or powdered caffeine, which received an FDA warning in 2014 after the deaths of two young men from caffeine overdose (FDA Consumer Advice on Powered Caffeine: http://www.fda.gov/food/recallsoutbreaksemergencies/safetyalertsadvisories/ucm405787.htm). A single teaspoon of pure caffeine is equivalent to consuming about 25 cups of coffee, making it easy to consume a lethal amount. At such a high concentration, adverse health effects can set in within minutes, including agitation and confusion, rapid and dangerously irregular heartbeat, nausea and vomiting, and the potential for seizures or death (AP/Huffington Post, 2014:

Table 10.2 Caffeine Content in Popular Drinks

Ingestible Substance (Amount)	Caffeine (mg)	mg/fl oz.
Brewed coffee, caffeinated (8 oz.)	95–200	23
Brewed coffee, decaffeinated (8 oz.)	2–12	0.7
Black tea (8 oz.)	42	5.2
Black tea (decaffeinated) (8 oz.)	5	0.6
Energy shots (variable)	80–500	5–714
Red Bull (8.2 oz.)	80	9.5
Mountain Dew (Diet or Regular) (12 oz.)	54	4.5
Coca-Cola Classic and Diet Coke (12 oz.)	34	2.8
Dr Pepper (12 oz.)	41	3.4
Caffeinated gum	40–100	n/a
Generic caffeine pill (1 pill)	100	n/a
Vivarin or NoDoz (1 caplet)	200	n/a
Caffeine powder 1/16 tsp.	200	n/a

SOURCES: http://www.caffeineinformer.com/the-caffeine-database
http://www.mayoclinic.org/healthy-lifestyle/nutrition-and-healthy-eating/in-depth/caffeine/art-20049372
http://www.cspinet.org/new/cafchart.htm.

http://www.huffingtonpost.com/2014/07/19/logan-stiner-caffeine-pow_n_5601775.html). Table 10.2 presents the caffeine content of a range of ingestible substances for comparison.

Nicotine

LO 10.3 Describe the physical and psychological effects of nicotine and risks associated with its use.

John looked around the group as the therapist said, "Congratulations. If you are going to quit, you'll need to plan for events that trigger your urge to smoke. So I'd like everyone to think about an upcoming situation when you will really need a cigarette." John almost laughed. Quitting smoking would be easy. He wouldn't even be here if his wife, Sandra, who was quitting with him, hadn't insisted John come with her. Sheila described how she liked to blow off steam at happy hour, drinking and smoking the stress away. Oscar described trying to drink his morning coffee without a cigarette. Mikey talked about how his work "smoke break" was the only way he managed to calm down and not strangle his boss. Cheryl, a high-powered lawyer, described how, after a big win, she would sit outside on "her bench" and smoke in celebration. When it was Sandra's turn, John was in a cold sweat and could barely concentrate. All this talk about smoking made him think he needed one right now. When the group leader called his name, he blurted out, "Right now, my trigger is right now!"

Especially for people who are genetically susceptible, **nicotine** is a highly addictive drug (Benowitz, 1988; U.S. Surgeon General's Report, 1988). Its most common source is the plant *Nicotiana tabacum*, which has been chewed and smoked for centuries. Cigarettes are the most common method of delivery, but other methods such as cigars, pipes, smokeless tobacco, and, most recently, e-cigarettes are widely available.

Nicotine can enter the bloodstream via the lungs (smoking), mucus membranes of the mouth or nose (chewing tobacco, using snuff), and even the skin (using a transdermal nicotine patch). Nicotine is both a stimulant and a sedative; its rapid action (8 to 10 seconds) and rapid effect are part of what makes the drug so rewarding or reinforcing. Many smokers report that nicotine produces temporary tension relief and helps with alertness and concentration. Furthermore, nicotine has strong social determinants. Indeed, subcultures centered on cigars and smokeless tobacco are common, and cigarette smoking provides an instant social affiliation, from smokers asking each other for a light at a bar to a few strangers standing outside a restaurant or office building chatting while they smoke.

E-cigarettes have become a popular method of nicotine delivery. Their use is called "vaping."

Nicotine also has pervasive physical effects. It stimulates the adrenal glands, causing a discharge of epinephrine (adrenaline), leading to a feeling of a "rush" or a "kick." This stimulation also leads to glucose release and increases blood pressure, respiration, and heart rate. Nicotine affects the pancreas by suppressing insulin secretion, leading to mild hyperglycemia (elevated blood sugar) in smokers. Central to its highly addictive potential, nicotine releases dopamine, directly affecting the brain's pleasure and motivation centers. The release of dopamine is believed to underlie the pleasurable sensations described by many smokers (National Institute on Drug Abuse, 2012).

FUNCTIONAL IMPAIRMENT Frequent use of nicotine leads not only to addiction but also to acute drug tolerance. Highly dependent smokers identify the first cigarette of the day as the hardest one to give up. Overnight, withdrawal has begun, and by morning the "craving" is quite strong. Moreover, giving up smoking leads to withdrawal symptoms that can last up to a month or more, making quitting very difficult. These symptoms may include depressed mood, insomnia, irritability, frustration or anger, anxiety, difficulty concentrating, restlessness, decreased heart rate, increased appetite, and weight gain.

The plant *Nicotiana tabacum* is dried and processed into cigarettes, cigars, pipe tobacco, and smokeless tobacco for consumption.

Tobacco use is the largest preventable cause of death in the world and is responsible for nearly 6 million deaths per year (WHO, 2011), including 480,000 per year in the United States (U.S. Department of Health and Human Services, 2014). In 1964, the U.S. Surgeon General's Advisory Committee on Smoking and Health first identified smoking as a leading contributor to preventable illness and premature death. Subsequent Surgeon General's reports underscore the severe impact of cigarette smoking, including increased risk for many types of cancer, cardiovascular disease, stroke, diabetes, tuberculosis, certain eye diseases, rheumatoid arthritis, and respiratory illnesses, including emphysema and chronic bronchitis (U.S. Department of Health and Human Services, 2014) (see Figure 10.2). Smoking during

Figure 10.2 The negative health consequences of smoking affect almost all bodily systems.

NOTE: The conditions in red are new diseases that have been causally linked to smoking.

SOURCE: USDHHS 2004, 2006, 2012.
http://www.surgeongeneral.gov/library/reports/50-years-of-progress/exec-summary.pdf.

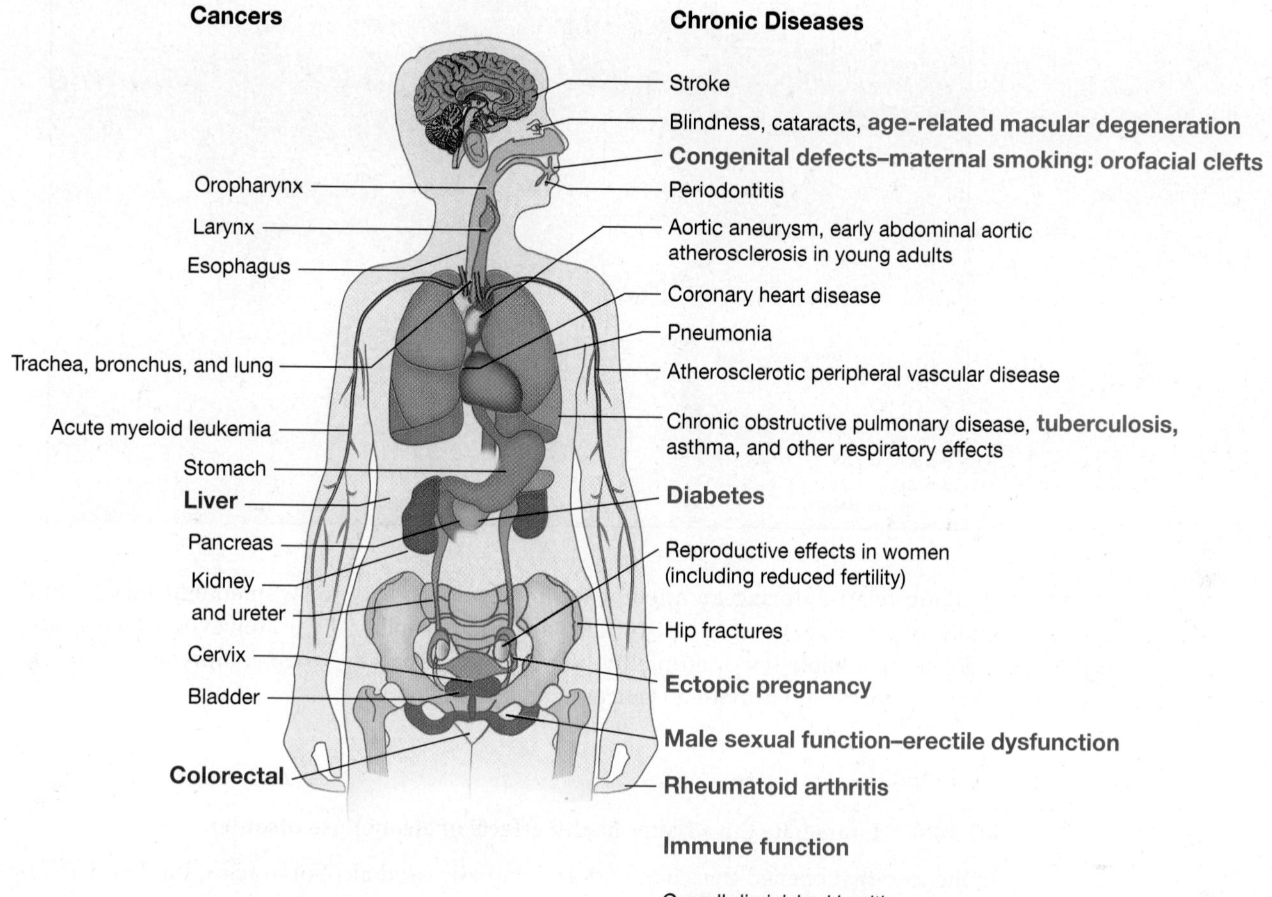

pregnancy is related to pregnancy complications, premature birth, low-birth-weight infants, stillbirth, and sudden infant death syndrome (SIDS) (Office of the U.S. Surgeon General, 2004). Concerted efforts to promote quitting have been partially successful: smoking rates have declined dramatically in the United States in the past 40 years (Centers for Disease Control and Prevention [CDC], 1994, 2004; Jamal et al., 2014). Most smokers are aware of the deleterious health effects, and it is estimated that 70% of smokers actually want to quit (U.S. Department of Health and Human Services, 2014). Approximately 43% of adult smokers have attempted to quit within the past year (U.S. Department of Health and Human Services, 2014).

EPIDEMIOLOGY In the past few decades, the number of people who smoke has declined dramatically, although statistics vary by demographic group. In 2013, 17.8% of adults (20.5% of men and 15.3% of women) in the United States smoked cigarettes, and rates varied by racial/ethnic group, from a low of 9.6% in Asians to a high of 26.8% in American Indians/Alaska Natives (CDC, 2014). Similarly, the number of high school students who reported smoking in the past month declined from 36% in 1997 to 24.6% in 2014. Despite these promising trends, 42.1 million adults and 4.6 million adolescents still smoke (Arrazola et al., 2015; CDC, 2015). Among high school students in 2014, e-cigarettes were the most common tobacco product used (13.4%), followed by hookahs (9.4%) and cigarettes (9.2%). These are substantial changes from only 3 years earlier in 2011, when cigarette use (15.2%) dwarfed that of e-cigarettes (1.5%) and hookah (4.1%) (CDC, 2015). Smoking cuts across all ethnic and racial groups and across all socioeconomic strata, although research indicates that African American adolescents start smoking at a later age than other groups (Kelder et al., 2003). Some evidence suggests that

Figure 10.3 Rates of tobacco use vary dramatically around the world.

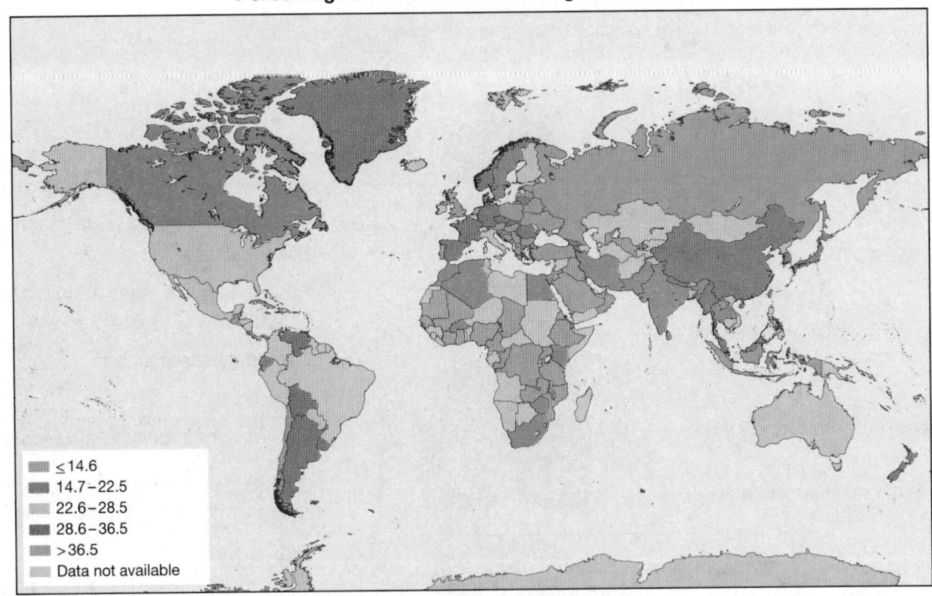

smoking relapse during an attempt to quit is more likely for women and racial/ethnic minorities (Caraballo et al., 2014; Doolan & Froelicher, 2006). However, other studies indicate no reliable sex or ethnicity differences in relapsing when comprehensive behavioral treatments are provided (Velicer et al., 2007).

Alcohol

LO 10.4 Enumerate the adverse health effects of alcohol use disorder.

In the case that opened this chapter, Karen initially used alcohol to relax, but her drinking eventually endangered her own and her children's health. Although many people find a

Examining the EVIDENCE

When It Comes to Decreasing Smoking, Australia Is Ahead of the Pack

As a result of sustained, concerted, and comprehensive public policy efforts from all levels of government and action from public health organizations, Australia has witnessed a dramatic decline in smoking rates across the country, dropping from more than 24% of the population in 1990 to about 13% of the population in 2013 (Nagelhout, 2015). Efforts have included bans on all cigarette advertisements on radio and television (1976), bans on smoking in restaurants (1994–2003), more than 25% increases in tax on cigarettes (2010), and, intriguingly, the introduction of "tobacco plain packaging" in 2012 that continues to evolve.

The goals of plain packaging are to reduce the attractiveness and appeal of tobacco products to consumers, particularly young people, to increase the noticeability and effectiveness of mandated health warnings, and to reduce the ability of the retail packaging of tobacco products to mislead consumers about the harms of smoking. All cigarettes are marketed in the same drab olive packages with graphic pictures of the effects of smoking on the front. The extent to which these graphic packages alone are contributing to decreases in smoking or whether the dramatic decrease reflects a relentless and comprehensive coordinated approach remains to be seen. Regardless, Australia is clearly ahead of the pack when it comes to safeguarding its population against the detrimental effects of both direct and passive exposure to smoking.

Australian cigarette plain pack.

drink stimulating, alcohol is actually a depressant. The active ingredient in any alcoholic drink, *ethyl alcohol*, is quickly absorbed via the stomach and intestines into the bloodstream. Then it is distributed throughout the body and quickly acts to depress the central nervous system. Although alcohol affects many neurotransmitter systems, its effect on receptors in the brain's *gamma aminobutyric acid* (GABA) system are particularly noteworthy. GABA is the brain's primary inhibitory neurotransmitter. So, by increasing GABA firing, alcohol inhibits other brain activity. This explains why alcohol is called a "depressant." Continued drinking leads to a slowing (depression) of the central nervous system, impairing motor coordination, decreasing reaction times, and leading to sad mood, impaired memory, poor judgment, and visual and auditory disturbances. Impairment ranges from mild feelings of being "tipsy" to more extreme levels of intoxication, or being drunk.

FUNCTIONAL IMPAIRMENT Although many people drink socially with little or no impairment, others who drink more regularly may experience tolerance. At first, one drink produced relaxation for Karen, but soon, she needed much more, and she eventually added another depressant (pain medicine) to achieve the same effect. Withdrawal symptoms from chronic heavy drinking can range from mild to severe. Signs and symptoms of alcohol withdrawal include tremors, anxiety, irritability, and agitation. Other effects include a craving for alcohol, insomnia, anxiety, increased pulse and respiration rates, increased body temperature and blood pressure, vivid dreams, hypervigilance, vomiting, headache, and sweating (Longo & Schuckit, 2014). In its most severe form, alcohol withdrawal includes experiencing hallucinations (false sensory perceptions) and seizures. Alcohol hallucinations begin within 1 to 2 days of stopping or cutting down and can be auditory, visual, or tactile. They may include a phenomenon known as *formication*, the sensation of having ants or bugs crawling all over the body. Seizures may also occur within 1 to 2 days of stopping drinking. Another withdrawal symptom, **delirium tremens** (DTs) characterized by disorientation, severe agitation, high blood pressure, and fever, usually begins about 3 days after general withdrawal symptoms begin and can last 1 to 8 days or more. This is a severe condition; 1 to 4% of individuals hospitalized with withdrawal delirium die from these metabolic complications, most often from hyperthermia, cardiac arrhythmia, complications from withdrawal seizures, or concomitant medical disorders (Longo & Schuckit, 2014).

Watch CHRIS: ALCOHOLISM

Depending on its severity, withdrawal can be treated with either careful monitoring (if mild) or the administration of benzodiazepines (see Chapter 4). Benzodiazepines can help decrease neuronal hyperactivity and reduce withdrawal symptoms as well as the risk of seizures and DTs. Alcohol and benzodiazepines have similar mechanisms of action, so individuals become *cross tolerant*—that is, their tolerance to one drug translates to tolerance of the other.

DSM-5

Criteria for Withdrawal Delirium (Delirium Tremens)

Criteria for alcohol withdrawal

1. Cessation of or reduction in heavy and prolonged use of alcohol
2. At least two of eight possible symptoms after reduced use of alcohol:
   Autonomic hyperactivity
   Hand tremor
   Insomnia
   Nausea or vomiting
   Transient hallucinations or illusions
   Psychomotor agitation
   Anxiety
   Generalized tonic–clonic seizures

Criteria for delirium

1. Decreased attention and awareness
2. Disturbance in attention, awareness, memory, orientation, language, visuospatial ability, perception, or all of these abilities that is a change from the normal level and fluctuates in severity during the day
3. Disturbances in memory, orientation, language, visuospatial ability, or perception
4. No evidence of coma or other evolving neurocognitive disorders

A patient who meets the criteria for both alcohol withdrawal and delirium is considered to have withdrawal delirium.

Although alcohol withdrawal can be associated with medical complications, excessive consumption of alcohol can also cause serious long-term health effects. **Alcohol cirrhosis** is a liver disease that occurs in about 10 to 15% of people with alcoholism. Cirrhosis is the slow deterioration and malfunction of the liver due to chronic injury. In the case of alcoholism, the injury is from alcohol exposure. Chronic alcohol consumption can impair the liver's ability to detoxify the blood, leading to the development of scar tissue. In turn, scar tissue obstructs blood flow and impairs the liver's function. Symptoms of alcohol cirrhosis include malnutrition, parotid enlargement, vascular spiders, palmar erythema, hepatosplenomegaly, portal hypertension, fluid and electrolyte redistribution, feminization, neuropathy, and encephalopathy (Huang et al., 2011).

Long-term alcohol abuse also harms the brain. Deficiencies in thiamine (vitamin B1) secondary to alcohol dependence, which accounts for up to 90% of thiamine deficiency, can cause **Wernicke-Korsakoff syndrome**, which has a prevalence of up to 12.5% in patients with alcoholism (Isenberg-Grzeda et al., 2012). The syndrome is characterized by a cluster of symptoms including (1) mental status changes (confusion, drowsiness, apathy, *amnesia* [see

The photo on the left shows a healthy liver; the photo on the right shows a diseased liver.

Chapter 14], and anxiety); (2) paralysis of the eye muscles and other eye signs; and (3) ataxia (lack of muscle coordination) or unsteadiness of gait (Isenberg-Grzeda et al., 2012). Because people with Wernicke-Korsakoff syndrome lose the ability to learn from experience, they almost always require custodial care, and 80% of individuals with this condition do not regain full cognitive function.

Characteristic features of fetal alcohol syndrome include a short palpebral fissure length (the distance from the inner to outer corner of the eye), a smooth philtrum (area between the nose and upper lip), and a thin upper lip.

Fetal alcohol syndrome (FAS) (first described by Jones & Smith, 1973), another severe consequence of alcohol use, occurs when a pregnant woman drinks alcohol and it passes through the placenta and harms the developing fetus. Though warnings against consuming alcohol while pregnant are commonplace, approximately 12% of pregnant women do so (Pruett et al., 2013). In addition to maternal alcohol consumption, three other criteria must be met for a diagnosis of FAS: (1) at least two of three classic identifiable facial anomalies, including short palpebral fissure lengths (distance from the inner to outer corner of the eye), a smooth philtrum (area between the nose and upper lip), and a thin upper lip; (2) prenatal or postnatal growth retardation (height or weight in the 10th percentile or less); and (3) central nervous system neurodevelopmental abnormalities. These could include small head size, structural brain abnormalities, and neurological problems such as impaired fine motor skills, hearing loss, poor eye–hand coordination, and abnormal gait. As the child develops, learning difficulties, poor school performance, and impulse control problems may occur, and individuals with a history of prenatal alcohol exposure are at higher risk for substance use and other psychiatric disorders (Pruett et al., 2013). A primary determinant of the severity of FAS is how much and how frequently the mother drinks (Abel & Hannigan, 1995), though research suggests that specific genes play a role in the variability of effects from prenatal alcohol exposure (Pruett et al., 2013). FAS can be avoided if women abstain from alcohol when pregnant. It is also wise to abstain if you are trying to get pregnant or think you might be pregnant.

EPIDEMIOLOGY, SEX, RACE, AND ETHNICITY After caffeine, alcohol is the most commonly used psychoactive substance (American Psychiatric Association, 2013). According to the National Epidemiologic Survey on Alcohol and Related Conditions III (NESARC-III), a nationally representative study of 36,309 U.S. adults conducted in 2012–2013, 12-month prevalence of DSM-5 alcohol use disorder (AUD) was 13.9%, while lifetime prevalence was 29.1% (Grant et al., 2015). Mean age of onset was 26.2 years, and AUD is associated with other psychiatric disorders, including other substance use disorders and some mood, anxiety, and personality disorders (Grant et al., 2015). Using DSM-IV criteria, the 12-month (12.7%) and lifetime (43.6%) prevalence of AUD have increased substantially since the 2001–2002 NESARC, when the rates were 8.5% and 30.3%, respectively (Grant et al., 2015). One intriguing question is whether these diagnoses remain stable over time. One longitudinal survey (Hasin et al., 1990) found that 4 years after initial diagnosis, 15% of individuals continued to meet the criteria for alcohol abuse, and 39% no longer met the diagnostic criteria for any alcohol-related disorder, although it is unclear whether these people were able to continue with more sustained abstinence. Cranford et al. (2014) examined trajectories of alcohol use over 2.5 to 3 years in adults (n = 364) with AUD, three-fourths of whom were entering alcohol treatment, and found that participants could be grouped into five trajectories: (1) moderate baseline → slow decline; (2) heavy baseline → stable abstinent; (3) heavy baseline → slow decline; (4) heaviest baseline → steep decline; and (5) heaviest baseline → stable heavy. The persistence of alcohol problems seems to be best predicted by the frequency of intoxication and the frequency of heavy drinking (more than five drinks a day) (Dawson, 2000).

Considerable differences exist in patterns of alcohol use disorders across sex and racial/ethnic groups. Lifetime prevalence of AUD is higher among males (36.0%) than females (22.7%) (Grant et al., 2015). Although men are at higher risk for AUD, women may be more vulnerable to the negative health consequences of heavy drinking (Dawson & Grant, 1993). In terms of race and ethnicity, the lifetime prevalence of AUD is highest among Native Americans (43.4%), followed by whites (32.6%), Hispanics (22.9%), African Americans (22.0%), and Asian or Pacific Islanders (15.0%) (Grant et al., 2015).

Learning Objective Summaries

LO 10.2 Characterize the physical and psychological effects of caffeine consumption.

Caffeine is a central nervous system (CNS) stimulant with a kick that boosts energy, mood, awareness, concentration, memory consolidation, and wakefulness. Its less desirable side effects include headache, fatigue, depressed mood, inactivity, nausea, restlessness, trouble concentrating, irritability, and feeling "foggy."

LO 10.3 Describe the physical and psychological effects of nicotine and risks associated with its use.

Nicotine stimulates the adrenal glands, causing a discharge of epinephrine (adrenaline), leading to a feeling of a "rush" or a "kick." This stimulation also leads to glucose release and increases blood pressure, respiration, and heart rate. Nicotine affects the pancreas by suppressing insulin secretion, leading to mild hyperglycemia (elevated blood sugar) in smokers. Nicotine releases dopamine, directly affecting the brain's pleasure and motivation centers. Frequent use of nicotine leads not only to addiction but also to acute drug tolerance. Tobacco use is the largest preventable cause of death in the world, resulting in increased risk for many types of cancer, cardiovascular disease, stroke, diabetes, tuberculosis, certain eye diseases, rheumatoid arthritis, and respiratory illnesses, including emphysema and chronic bronchitis.

LO 10.4 Enumerate the adverse health effects of alcohol use disorder.

Alcohol affects many neurotransmitter systems, particularly the gamma aminobutyric acid (GABA) system. Increased GABA firing inhibits other brain activity including sad mood, impaired memory, poor judgment, and visual and auditory disturbances. Withdrawal symptoms from chronic heavy drinking include tremors, anxiety, irritability, and agitation. Other effects include a craving for alcohol, insomnia, anxiety, increased pulse and respiration rates, increased body temperature and blood pressure, vivid dreams, hypervigilance, vomiting, headache, and sweating. Delirium tremens (DTs) characterized by disorientation, severe agitation, high blood pressure, and fever usually begins about 3 days after general withdrawal symptoms begin and can last 1 to 8 days or more. Cirrhosis of the liver is the slow deterioration and malfunction of the liver due to chronic exposure to alcohol. Wernicke-Korsakoff syndrome due to thiamine deficiency can lead to permanent dysfunction and includes (1) mental status changes (confusion, drowsiness, apathy, amnesia, and anxiety); (2) paralysis of eye muscles and other eye signs; and (3) ataxia or unsteadiness of gait.

Critical Thinking Question

In Western cultures, the use of caffeine, nicotine, and alcohol is common. What do these drugs contribute to our culture, and how would the Western world differ in the absence of these drugs?

Illicit Drugs and Non-Substance-Related Disorders

Each year, new and often dangerous drugs make their way into the population. Entry points vary from the drug underworld to the doctor's prescription pad—yet the desire for new mind-altering substances continues. Illicit drug use comes with steep emotional, social, legal, and financial costs, but for many individuals, the strong pull of the physiological high and/or the escape from the real world makes long-term abstinence difficult. We begin this section by focusing on marijuana. Although illegal in parts of the United States, it is legal in some other countries, such as the Netherlands, and is continuously under scrutiny for decriminalization, especially for medical use. We then examine other classes of drugs that have primary effects on the central nervous system—stimulants, depressants, and hallucinogens. Finally, we review inhalants and prescription medicines.

Marijuana

LO 10.5 Describe the short- and long-term therapeutic and negative psychological and health consequences of marijuana use.

Marijuana comes from the *Cannabis sativa* plant, which also produces the fiber known as *hemp*. Its leaves can be dried and used in food and drink, or—most frequently—smoked. According to the 2013 National Survey on Drug Use and Health (NSDUH), about 7.5% of individuals ages 12 and older were current (i.e., past month) users of marijuana, making it the most commonly used illicit drug in the United States (Substance Abuse and Mental Health Services Administration, 2014), although many states have laws legalizing marijuana use in some form. The active ingredient is **tetrahydrocannabinol** (THC). When marijuana is smoked, THC immediately enters the brain and lasts for 1 to 3 hours (National Institute on Drug Abuse, 2016). The user generally experiences a pleasant state of relaxation, intensified color and sound, and slowed perception of time. Mild effects include dry mouth, increased hunger ("the munchies") and thirst, trembling, fatigue, depression, and occasional anxiety or panic. The effects of marijuana depend on the dose and the user's characteristics or sensitivity. Also, THC content varies across preparations and methods of delivery. While low doses are commonly associated with relaxation, higher doses are associated with visual and auditory activity and fascination, increased heart rate and blood pressure, bloodshot eyes, and occasionally anxiety, panic, and paranoia.

How does marijuana produce these effects? Its active ingredient, THC, is received by special brain receptors called *cannabinoid receptors*, which influence pleasure, learning and memory, higher cognitive functions, sensory perceptions, and motor coordination (National Institute on Drug Abuse, 2016). Like most drugs of abuse, THC activates the brain's reward system by stimulating the release of dopamine, leading to the feelings of euphoria associated with being "high."

FUNCTIONAL IMPAIRMENT Adverse health effects related to acute use of marijuana include hyperemesis syndrome, impaired coordination and performance, anxiety, suicidal ideation, and

Figure 10.4 Marijuana Legalization in the United States as of June 2016.

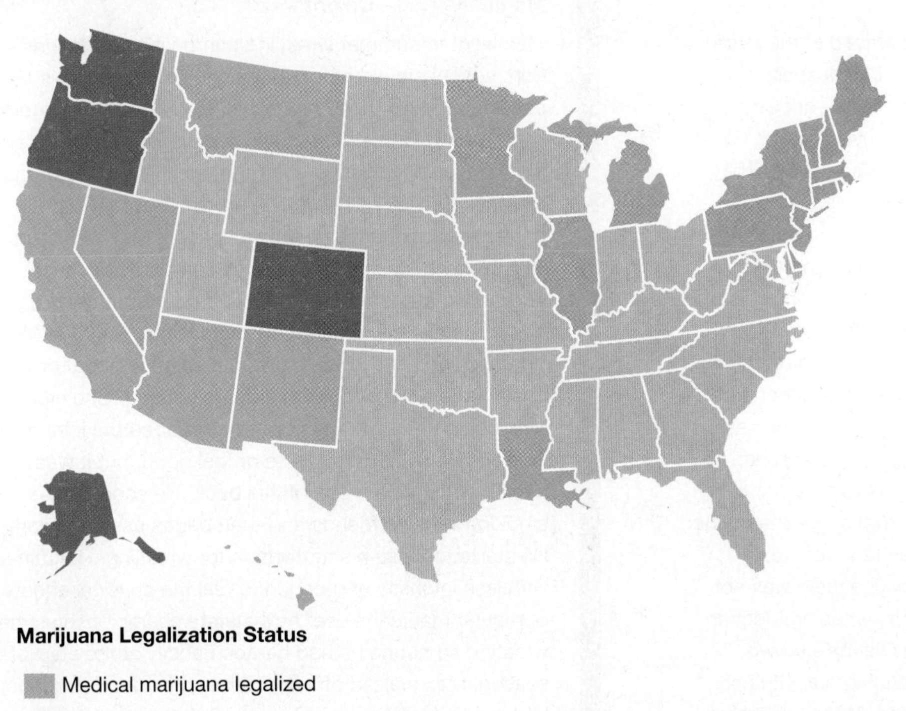

psychotic symptoms (Karila et al., 2014). Heavy marijuana use results in persistent memory loss; neurocognitive impairment of attention, learning skills, and motor movement; addiction; chronic respiratory and cardiovascular problems; and an increased risk of mood disorders as well as head, neck, and lung cancer (Karila et al., 2014). However, THC has medicinal effects as well. Two cannabinoids (dronabional and nabilone) are FDA-approved for treatment of nausea and vomiting associated with cancer chemotherapy and appetite stimulation in people with wasting illnesses such as AIDS or cancer (Hill, 2015). In addition, there is strong evidence to support the use of marijuana to treat chronic pain, neuropathic pain, and spasticity associated with multiple sclerosis (Hill, 2015) (see "Research Hot Topic: Medical Uses of Marijuana").

Evidence regarding tolerance to cannabis is unclear. Some studies report tolerance; others do not report a need for increased doses to achieve the same high. Craving for marijuana and withdrawal symptoms can make it difficult to quit (Budney et al., 2003). Withdrawal symptoms include anger, aggression, irritability, decreased appetite, sleep difficulties, anxiety/nervousness, and restlessness (Agrawal et al., 2008). In the 2001–2002 National Epidemiologic Survey on Alcohol and Related Disorders (NESARC), more than 43% of individuals who had used cannabis in the previous 12 months reported experiencing at least one withdrawal symptom, and 29% reported experiencing two or more. There were no overall differences in prevalence between men and women in experiencing withdrawal, though some individual symptoms were more commonly experienced by men or women (Agrawal et al., 2008).

EPIDEMIOLOGY Marijuana use is common in the United States, with 19.3 million individuals (7.5% of the population ages 12 and older) reporting having used marijuana in the past month in the 2013 National Survey on Drug Use and Health. This is an increase over the

SIDE by SIDE Case Studies

Dimensions of Behavior: From Adaptive to Maladaptive

Adaptive Behavior Case Study

Marijuana Use—No Disorder

Meghan was from a small town and arrived at the state university for her freshman year. She was desperate to fit in. Her roommate Glenna was from New York City and was very worldly. They got along well, even though Glenna disliked sports and anything that made her sweat. They went to their first college party together. Meghan was amazed to find everyone drinking alcohol and smoking marijuana. Glenna passed her a joint. Meghan held it for a minute while everyone stared at her. Glenna said, "Meghan's from a small town—we might have to show her how to inhale." So Meghan inhaled instead of making a scene. She partied hard that night and felt like one of the crowd. This was what she thought college life was supposed to be. Then Meghan started track, and her teammates invited her to a party. Some people were drinking alcohol, but many had soft drinks. No one pushed her to do drugs. Meghan invited Glenna to the track parties, but she found them dull because there was not enough "partying." For the rest of the semester, Meghan split her time between partying with Glenna's crowd, where she smoked to "fit in," and hanging out with her track buddies, where she drank sodas. At the end of the semester, she moved in with her track buddies, leaving the drugs and Glenna's friends behind.

Maladaptive Behavior Case Study

Marijuana Use—Disorder

Max went to summer wrestling camp while his friends from school stayed home and worked. He found his passion, and his friends found marijuana. At his welcome back party, Ronnie offered him a joint. Max's coach said that he would kick anyone off the team who used drugs, so Max refused. The guys teased him, but they didn't push too hard. During wrestling season, Max was around less, partly because he was busy and partly because he was afraid the coach would find out about the drugs. Over time, his friends became increasingly angry at Max's success and his "holier-than-thou" attitude about drugs. They made a big deal each time he refused. One night Max couldn't take it anymore—he grabbed the joint and inhaled deeply. It didn't taste or feel good, but it was a relief getting everyone off his back. He soon started smoking with his friends and then began using regularly. He started to lose his motivation for wrestling. He trained with less intensity and began to feel the physical effects of regular marijuana use. At the state championships, he wrestled someone he had beaten handily at the start of the season. Max started off well, but as the match continued, he found himself short of breath. Before he knew it, he was pinned and defeated.

Research HOT Topic

Medical Uses of Marijuana

The legalization of marijuana for medical use is a hot political topic across the nation. Each state is responsible for deciding whether medical marijuana use is legal and under what circumstances. As of June 2016, 25 states plus the District of Columbia have enacted laws to legalize medical marijuana: These include Alaska, Arizona, California, Colorado, Connecticut, Delaware, Hawaii, Illinois, Louisiana, Maine, Maryland, Massachusetts, Michigan, Minnesota, Montana, Nevada, New Hampshire, New Jersey, New Mexico, New York, Oregon, Pennsylvania, Rhode Island, Vermont, and Washington.

Researchers believe that marijuana has many therapeutic applications, including relief from nausea and appetite loss, reduction of pressure within the eye, reduction of muscle spasms, and relief from some forms of chronic pain. In 1997, the National Institute of Health formed a group of eight clinical trials experts. The group concluded that much of the existing evidence for medical marijuana use was anecdotal and that controlled clinical trials were necessary. There are now two FDA-approved cannabinoids in the United States, dronabinol and nabilone, which are approved for nausea and vomiting associated with cancer chemotherapy and appetite stimulation in wasting illnesses such as AIDS or cancer (Hill, 2015). As of March 2015, more than 40 clinical trials had been published examining other uses of medicinal marijuana, with strong evidence supporting treatment of chronic pain, neuropathic pain, and spasticity associated with multiple sclerosis. Studies examining treatment of Parkinson's disease, Crohn's disease, and amyotrophic lateral sclerosis have been less promising (Hill, 2015).

The value and safety of medical marijuana use are severely compromised when it is used in an unregulated manner and administered through smoking. Smoking marijuana is not particularly safe and can be ineffective for medicinal purposes for several reasons. First, medications work best when they are taken in an appropriate dose. Smoking does not provide a precise and controlled dose, and when the drug is obtained through nonregulated sources, purity cannot be guaranteed. A more problematic risk is smoking as a means of drug administration. It is a misconception that only cigarettes impair health; many of the same risks, as well as a few others, are evident when smoking marijuana. Ongoing research must address both the benefits and risks associated with marijuana for medicinal purposes. The scientific process should be allowed to evaluate the potential therapeutic effects of marijuana for certain disorders separately from the societal debate over the potential harmful effects of non-medical marijuana use.

period 2002–2008, when rates varied from 5.8 to 6.2% before rising to 6.7% in 2009 and then continuing to increase year by year. More than 80% of all illicit drug users in 2013 reported using marijuana, and about 65% of illicit drug users reported only using marijuana in the past month. About 35% of illicit drug users reported using drugs other than marijuana (including cocaine, heroin, hallucinogens, inhalants, and non-medical use of prescription drugs), and nearly 16% reported currently using both marijuana and other drugs (Substance Abuse and Mental Health Services Administration, 2014). In 2013, about 2.4 million individuals used marijuana for the first time, the majority of which (1.4 million, or 57%) were under the age of 18 at initiation. More males (9.7%) than females (5.6%) use marijuana (Substance Abuse and Mental Health Services Administration, 2014). In 2013, 4.2 million individuals (1.6% of the U.S. population ages 12 and older) were classified as having marijuana dependence or abuse, making up more than 60% of those meeting criteria for illicit drug dependence or abuse (Substance Abuse and Mental Health Services Administration, 2014).

CNS Stimulants

LO 10.6 Characterize patterns of use and effects of CNS stimulants.

Amber was an adult from an early age. Her mother was an alcoholic who brought home different men. When Amber was 13, one of the men molested her while her mother lay passed out on the sofa. These experiences took a toll on Amber. She had trouble making friends, and she was incapable of romantic intimacy. At 17, she worked at a clothing store. There she met Nicole, who was fun and easygoing, all the things Amber wasn't. One night after work, Nicole offered her a ride home and talked her into stopping at a rave. Nicole bought some pills and gave one to Amber. After about 30 minutes, Amber felt a wave come over her. The experience was unbelievable. She felt free and wanted to be intimate and close with those around her. The next day she slept through her shift at work. She had already missed several shifts because of her mother, and she was fired. She thought about going back to work to beg for her job, but instead she called Nicole to see if she had any more pills.

Figure 10.5 Use of Illicit Drugs.

The 2014 Monitoring the Future survey of drug use and attitudes reveals a wide range of drug use in the 8th and 12th grades.

SOURCE: University of Michigan, 2014 Monitoring the Future study. http://www.drugabuse.gov/publications/drugfacts/high-school-youth-trends.

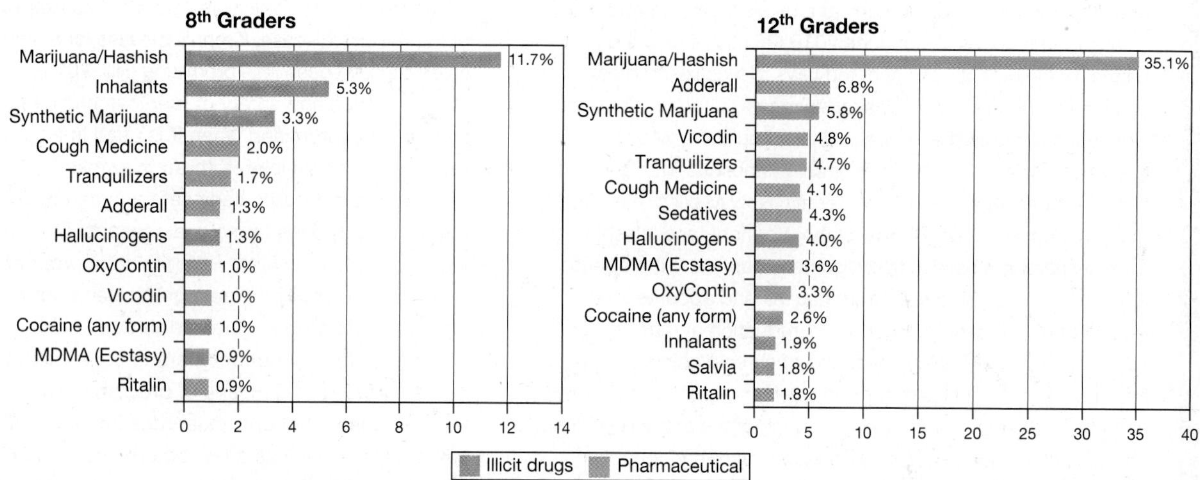

*Only 12th graders surveyed about sedatives use

Having already discussed the effects of two widely used legal stimulants (nicotine and caffeine), we now turn to the illegal stimulants: cocaine and amphetamines. The effects of both drugs include euphoria, increased energy, mental alertness, and rapid speech. Some people also feel a sense of power and courage, the ability to tackle otherwise daunting tasks, and increased feelings of intimacy and sexual arousal. However, the use of cocaine and amphetamines has serious short- and long-term adverse effects, including dangerous elevations in blood pressure and heart rate and cardiovascular abnormalities, potentially leading to heart attack, respiratory arrest, and seizures. These stimulants disrupt the normal communication among brain circuits by increasing dopamine, which leads to elevated mood and increased alertness. In high doses, increased dopamine and norepinephrine can lead to hallucinations, delusions, and paranoia (see Chapter 11).

Amphetamines come in many forms. Legitimate uses include the treatment of asthma, nasal congestion, attention deficit hyperactivity disorder (see Chapter 13), and narcolepsy (a sleep disorder). Because these drugs prolong wakefulness, sometimes people who need to stay awake for long periods of time—such as airline pilots, truckers, and students studying for exams—use them. They can also suppress appetite, making them attractive to some dieters. Amphetamines, also known as *uppers, bennies*, and *speed*, are manufactured in laboratories through reduction of ephedrine or pseudoephedrine. On the street, they are often cut (mixed) with cocaine, heroin, or dangerous toxic substances such as cyanide or strychnine (Greene et al., 2008). Three different preparations of amphetamines include *amphetamine* (Benzedrine), *dextroamphetamine* (Dexedrine), and *methamphetamine* (Methedrine). These drugs, swallowed in pill form or injected for a quicker kick, increase the release of dopamine, norepinephrine, and serotonin in the brain.

Other manufactured amphetamines, sometimes referred to as *designer drugs*, often spread rapidly throughout the community across sex, race, and socioeconomic status. One example, *methylenedioxymethamphetamine* (MDMA), interferes with the reuptake of serotonin. Initially used as an appetite suppressant, the pill form of MDMA (**Ecstasy**) has become a common "club" drug and a frequent trigger for emergency room visits. Similarly, **crystal methamphetamine** (ice, crank) is a form of methamphetamine that produces longer-lasting and more intense physiological reactions than the powdered form. It is smoked in glass pipes or injected—the high is rapid and intense and can last for 12 hours or more.

FUNCTIONAL IMPAIRMENT Use of amphetamines puts the adrenergic system into overdrive, causing tachycardia, tachypnea, diaphoresis, hypertension, hyperthermia, mydriasis, hyperreflexia, tremors, and a range of potential effects on the CNS, including hyperarousal, agitation, paranoia, hallucinations, disinhibition, and seizures. Hepatotoxicity and electrolyte abnormalities are also possible (Greene et al., 2008). Over time, users can become violent and aggressive and suffer from emaciation and malnutrition due to appetite suppression. Tolerance develops rapidly, often leading to rapid dose escalation. Additional effects of amphetamine toxicity are evident in many body systems, including cardiovascular (aortic dissection, arrhythmia, vasospasm, acute cardiomyopathy), CNS (euphoria, bruxism, intracerebral hemorrhage, anorexia), pulmonary (pulmonary edema), gastrointestinal (nausea, vomiting, diarrhea, gastrointestinal ischemia), metabolic (hyponatremia, acidosis), and muscular (muscle rigidity, rhabdomyolysis) (Greene et al., 2008). Withdrawal from extended highs produces "crashes" marked by depression, irritability, and prolonged periods of sleep.

EPIDEMIOLOGY According to the 2013 National Survey on Drug Use and Health, an estimated 595,000 Americans ages 12 years and older (0.2% of the population) were current users of methamphetamines (Substance Abuse and Mental Health Services Administration, 2013). Approximately 144,000 individuals were new users of methamphetamines within the prior 12 months, and the average age of initiating methamphetamine use was 18.9 years. For stimulants, prevalence is approximately equal by sex (0.5% in both males and females in a 1-month period) (Substance Abuse and Mental Health Services Administration, 2013). Among amphetamines users in the 2001–2002 National Epidemiologic Survey of Alcohol and Related Disorders, 56.2% were male and approximately one-third met DSM-IV criteria for abuse or dependence (Moss et al., 2012). Among persons admitted for treatment of substance abuse in 2001, approximately 6% (98,000 cases) were considered primary amphetamine users. Most people (71.0%) who are treated for amphetamine abuse do not use another substance. When they do report polydrug use, it is usually marijuana (47%), alcohol (36%), or cocaine (10%). Although data are limited, evidence suggests significantly higher use among whites than other groups (Hopfer et al., 2006), though some racial/ethnic minority groups may be at higher risk for certain health complications of methamphetamine use (Herbeck et al., 2013).

Cocaine

LO 10.7 Summarize the mechanism of action of cocaine on the brain.

> Namia was an up-and-coming model. At age 16 she traveled all the time. When she wasn't shooting or preparing for a shoot, she was exercising or working with her tutor trying to keep up with her schoolwork. What worried her most, however, was the pressure to stay impossibly thin. Namia was constantly hungry. Before fashion week, an older model saw her struggling, smoking cigarette after cigarette to curb her appetite. She introduced Namia to cocaine, snorting lines in the dressing room and saying, "This is the only way to get through the week . . . and you won't feel hungry at all!" She was right. For the next 2 days, Namia had a lot more energy. She seemed on top of everything else including her schoolwork. And then she crashed. Things spiraled out of control. One night right before a big show, she could barely move from exhaustion.

Cocaine, which comes from the leaves of the coca plant, is indigenous to South America. People have chewed coca leaves for centuries to provide relief from fatigue and hunger. Cocaine's introduction to the United States in the late 1800s was as a legal additive to cigars and cigarettes and, believe it or not, to Coca-Cola. Cocaine was also used as a painkiller because of its anesthetic effects. Once its addictive properties became known, its use declined.

The powdered form of cocaine can be snorted or dissolved in water and injected. Crack cocaine is a smoked form of rock crystal cocaine that is highly addictive, delivers large amounts of drug quickly via the lungs, and produces an immediate euphoric effect. The term *crack* refers to the crackling sound it makes when heated (National Institute on Drug Abuse, 2004b). Additives, such as local anesthetics, sugars, stimulants, toxins, or other substances (flour, cornstarch, etc.) may be used to increase potency, volume, or toxicity of the cocaine (Karila et al., 2012).

Characteristic lines of cocaine cut with a razor in preparation for inhalation, known as "snorting."

FUNCTIONAL IMPAIRMENT Cocaine is highly addictive. It increases synaptic levels of dopamine, serotonin, and norepinephrine, but its powerful stimulant effects are thought to be caused by inhibiting nerve cells' reabsorption of dopamine (Karila et al., 2012). When more dopamine is available in the synapses, the stimulation of the brain reward pathways increases and provides more positive feelings. Cocaine use increases euphoria, self-confidence, self-control, energy, motor activity, mental efficiency, alertness, and cognitive capacity and decreases appetite, anxiety, dysphoria, paranoia, and restlessness. When tolerance develops, use increases in order to get the initial euphoric effects. When users take larger doses, their exposure to the drug is increased, and they are more sensitive to its dangerous effects, such as anesthetic and convulsant effects. Hallucinations, aggressiveness, disorientation, tremors, convulsions, and increased body temperature can result from high doses (Karila et al., 2012). This phenomenon may account for reported deaths after relatively low doses (www.nida.nih.gov/researchreports/cocaine/cocaine.html). Cocaine addiction has negative health consequences for the cardiovascular, respiratory, central nervous, otolaryngological, gastrointestinal, and renal systems, and psychiatric comorbidity can include major depression, cocaine-induced paranoia or compulsive foraging, and panic attacks (Karila et al., 2012).

EPIDEMIOLOGY Cocaine is the second most trafficked and second most commonly used illicit drug worldwide after marijuana (Karila et al., 2012). North America is the largest market for cocaine, but worldwide, the number of cocaine users is estimated at 0.3 to 0.5% of the population ages 15 to 64 years (Pomara et al., 2012). In 2013, 1.5 million individuals 12 years and older (0.6% of the population) were estimated to be current cocaine users (use in the past month), and 855,000 individuals met criteria for cocaine dependence or abuse as defined in DSM-IV (Substance Abuse and Mental Health Services Administration, 2014). This is a decrease from the period 2002–2007, when the number of current users exceeded 2.0 million. More than 600,000 individuals (average age 20.3 years) initiated cocaine use in 2013, and 58,000 initiated use of crack cocaine. More than 90% of cocaine users reported using marijuana before they tried cocaine. More males (0.8%) than females (0.4%) reported cocaine use (Substance Abuse and Mental Health Services Administration, 2014). The highest rate of cocaine use was observed in American Indians/Alaska Natives (2.0%) followed by 1.6% of African Americans, 0.8% of non-Hispanic whites and Hispanics, 0.6% of Native Hawaiian or other Pacific Islanders, and 0.2% of Asians (Substance Abuse and Mental Health Services Administration, 2003).

Sedative Drugs

LO 10.8 Compare and contrast patterns of use and effects of barbiturates and benzodiazepines.

Leila, a nurse, was energetic and loved her work. Another nurse suggested having a poker night. Leila had never gambled, but that first night she cleaned up. After doing it again, she found herself enjoying gambling. As a nurse, she kept unusual hours and came home late at night stressed and looking for a way to relax. Unlike games with her friends, the Internet casino was always available. At first she was so excited about her wins and worried about getting back her losses that she hardly missed the sleep. Soon, however, she was cutting everything and everyone else out of her life. As her losses grew, she opened up new credit cards to get more money to win back her losses. She was convinced that she just needed one good streak to get everything back. When she could no longer open any more credit cards, she followed the advice of another nurse on an Internet gambling site and stole painkillers and Xanax from work to get some quick cash. At first, Leila took just a few pills. After an especially big loss, she felt suicidal. To calm down, she took one Xanax. This helped her walk away from the computer for a while and relax. Over time she needed more and more pills to sell and to take for herself until the hospital found out what she was doing and fired her.

Sedative drugs include two general classes: **barbiturates** and **benzodiazepines**, both of which are central nervous system *depressants*. This means that their mechanism of action is the opposite of the CNS *stimulants* discussed earlier. Initially used to treat anxiety and insomnia, barbiturates are now less commonly prescribed than benzodiazepines due to the high risk of abuse, dependence, and overdose.

Barbiturates, or "downers," act on the GABA-ergic system in a manner similar to alcohol. Common barbiturates include amobarbital (Amatol), pentobarbital (Nembutal), and secobarbital (Seconal). They can be swallowed or injected and are often used to counteract the effect of "uppers" or amphetamines. Initial benefits at low doses include disinhibition and euphoria in an attempt to alleviate feelings of anxiety. In the short term, barbiturate use leads to slurred speech, decreased respiration, fatigue, disorientation, lack of coordination, and dilated pupils. At higher doses, users can experience impaired memory and coordination, irritability, and paranoid and suicidal thoughts.

Benzodiazepines were originally prescribed (widely) for the treatment of anxiety, and they can be used responsibly and effectively for short-term treatment of anxiety and insomnia. However, their prolonged use or use without a prescription can be problematic. At high doses, the drugs produce light-headedness, vertigo, and muscle control problems. Valium, commonly known as "mother's little helper," would have been a drug that Karen might have been prescribed in the 1960s to deal with the stress of caring for young children. Other benzodiazepines include Xanax and Halcion. Although generally considered to be safer than barbiturates and to have lower potential for abuse and dependence when used as prescribed, they are not completely benign. One powerful benzodiazepine, Rohypnol ("roofies" or "date rape drug"), is available by prescription in many countries but not the United States. This drug is 7 to 10 times more potent than Valium and causes partial amnesia—which means that people given the drug often cannot remember certain events when they were intoxicated. It is this feature and its powerful effects that earned it the reputation of being associated with date rape.

FUNCTIONAL IMPAIRMENT If overused, both barbiturates and benzodiazepines can result in oversedation and problems in thinking and interacting with others. Although the drugs are legal if prescribed, their use by those without a prescription or their misuse by people for whom they are medically inappropriate often leads to theft and other dangerous strategies for obtaining the drugs. Tolerance for barbiturates develops rapidly, producing a high risk for overdose. Death results from depression of the brain's respiratory center. Withdrawal from barbiturates produces tremors, increased blood pressure and heart rate, sweating, and seizures. Tolerance and withdrawal also occur with benzodiazepines. The symptoms mirror alcohol withdrawal and include anxiety, insomnia, tremors, and delirium. Although benzodiazepines can be overused with problematic consequences, they have largely replaced barbiturates due to less potential for dependence and fewer side effects.

EPIDEMIOLOGY Benzodiazepine use is rather common in the United States, with 5% of adults filling a prescription in 2008—prevalence is higher among women and increases with age (Olfson, King, et al., 2015). In 2013, 251,000 individuals 12 years and older (0.1% of the population) were current non-medical users of sedatives, such as barbiturates and benzodiazepines (Substance Abuse and Mental Health Services Administration, 2014). Lifetime prevalence of non-medical use of benzodiazepines was 7.5% among a nationally representative sample of high school seniors (McCabe & West, 2014). Approximately 0.2% of new users of illicit drugs in 2013 initiated non-medical use of sedatives, and the average age at first use was 25.0 years. More than half of these new users obtained the drugs from a friend or relative, the majority of whom received the prescription from a doctor (Substance Abuse and Mental Health Services Administration, 2014). The drugs tend to be abused secondarily to other drugs (usually alcohol), most commonly by whites and by individuals who have high levels of education. In 2011, there were approximately 426,000 emergency room visits in the United States related to non-medical use of benzodiazepines, 24.2% of which also involved alcohol (Olfson et al., 2015). National epidemiological data suggest that approximately 4.2% of males and 7.9% of females reported nonmedical use of anti-anxiety drugs including benzodiazepines (Simoni-Wastila, 2000; Simoni-Wastila et al., 2004). These drugs are more frequently prescribed to women than to men, which may explain their higher rates of abuse by women (Simoni-Wastila et al., 2004).

Barbiturate use in the United States has varied over the past several decades. In 1975, its use peaked at 10.7%, but by 1992, only 2.8% of high school seniors reported using a barbiturate in the past year. Unfortunately, the "popularity" of barbiturates among youth has experienced a resurgence; the estimated prevalence of use for 12th graders in 2005 was about 7.0%.

Opioids

LO 10.9 Summarize the ways in which opioids can be taken and their effects on body and mind.

Patrick had no idea what a panic attack was, but he knew that sometimes his heart would race and he'd think he was losing his mind. Patrick mentioned this to his cousin one day at a family BBQ. Patrick's cousin, who playfully referred to himself as a street pharmacist, suggested that he might have something that would help take the edge off. Patrick wasn't crazy about sticking a needle in his arm, but he trusted his cousin. The drug gave him a calm feeling, making him numb to his usual feeling of hyperarousal.

Opium, used primarily to relieve physical pain, has been used and appreciated in various forms and cultures throughout history. Drugs such as heroin, morphine, and codeine are derived from the opium poppy and are classified as **opioids**. Methadone is an example of synthetic opioid. Thus, this class of drug spans the spectrum from legal and medically prescribed (though carefully controlled) drugs, such as codeine and morphine, to highly illegal and dangerous drugs, such as heroin. Opioids produce pain relief, euphoria, sedation, reduced anxiety, and tranquility. To produce their characteristic high, they mimic the effect of the body's natural opioids, such as endorphins or enkephalins, which the body releases in response to pain. Depending on the drug, dose, and method of delivery, opioids produce a broad range of effects. Besides pain relief and sedation, they cause narrowing of the pupils, constipation, flushed skin, itching, lowered blood pressure, slowed heart rate, low body temperature, nausea, vomiting, and slowed respiration (Benich, 2011). Opioids can be smoked, snorted, injected beneath the skin ("popped"), or mainlined (injected into the bloodstream).

FUNCTIONAL IMPAIRMENT Tolerance to opioids develops very rapidly, often after only 2 or 3 days. Users often increase their dosage, and when taking preparations of unknown strength (as in the case of street drugs), they can unwittingly self-administer lethal doses. Individuals at particularly high risk for developing opioid dependence include those who purchase street drugs, people employed in health care professions (due to easy access), and people on chronic pain medication for chronic pain syndromes (Benich, 2011). Similarly, administering a previously tolerated dose after a period of abstinence can lead to death from overdose (see "Real People, Real Disorders: Amy Winehouse—A Tragic End to a Life of Substance Abuse"). Heroin is dangerous because of its pharmacological effects and its underworld association with drug trafficking. The latter can include tainted preparations (to increase volume and profits), medical risks associated with sharing needles, and violence. All contribute to high mortality. Early withdrawal symptoms, which may appear as soon as 4 to 6 hours after stopping the drug, include rapid breathing, yawning, crying, sweating, and a runny nose. Withdrawal symptoms worsen with chronic use and may include hyperactivity, irritability, intensified awareness, agitation, insomnia, increased heart rate, hypertension, fever, dilated pupils, tremors, hot and cold flashes, aching muscles, loss of appetite, abdominal cramps, nausea, vomiting, and diarrhea (Merck & Co., 1995–2006). Withdrawal symptoms reach maximum intensity 36 to 72 hours after opioid cessation and can last up to 8 days, with milder symptoms continuing even longer, complicating the addict's task of quitting (Benich, 2011).

When opiates are popped or mainlined with shared or unsterilized needles, medical complications may include viral hepatitis and liver damage, infections at the injection site, and transmission of the human immunodeficiency virus (HIV), which causes AIDS. Lung and immune system problems can develop, as can neurological problems due to insufficient blood flow to the brain, potentially resulting in coma. Opioid use during pregnancy is particularly dangerous and can result in significant morbidity and mortality for mother and baby (Kaltenbach et al., 1998; Meyer, 2014).

EPIDEMIOLOGY Patterns of opiate use vary by age, socioeconomic status, education, and type of drug used. Many national surveys that target heroin use may underestimate prevalence because of the difficulty of surveying current users due to living situation, failure to disclose, or health status and hospitalizations secondary to the dangers of sharing needles (i.e., HIV, AIDS, and hepatitis). Among individuals ages 12 years and older, approximately 289,000 (or 0.1%) were current (within the past month) heroin users in 2013, with 681,000 individuals reporting past-year heroin use. Criteria for heroin abuse or dependence were met by 517,000 individuals. In 2013, 169,000 individuals ages 12 years and older used heroin for the first time, and the average age at first use was 24.5 years (Substance Abuse and Mental Health Services Administration, 2014).

Opiates other than heroin, such as codeine and morphine, are commonly prescribed for pain relief, particularly for people who are recovering from surgery. However, when not taken as directed, these prescribed drugs can also be abused. In North America, approximately 5% of the adult population (and even higher rates among adolescents) reported

REAL People REAL Disorders

Amy Winehouse—A Tragic End to a Life of Substance Abuse

Amy Winehouse (1983–2011) was one of the most successful new artists of the 2000s. Her music, a blend of R&B, pop, and jazz, was incredibly popular in her home country of England, across Europe, and in the United States. Her album, *Back to Black*, earned her five Grammy awards in 2008 including Best New Artist and Record of the Year. Sadly, Amy became as well known for her struggles with substance use as for her incredible musical talent.

Amy found her first big success in the United Kingdom with her debut album, *Frank*, which was released in 2003. It was during this time that her substance use started to spiral out of control. Amy would regularly show up to performances and interviews under the influence of alcohol and illegal drugs and be unable to perform. Her management team tried to persuade her to get help by entering rehab. Amy refused and instead wrote the hit song "Rehab" in which she repeatedly says that she won't go to rehab. Released as a single off *Back to Black*, "Rehab" would earn Amy a Grammy for Song of the Year.

Adding to Amy's issues with substance use was her relationship with Blake Fielder-Civil. Amy and Blake began dating in 2005, and Blake admits that he was the one to introduce Amy to hard drugs, including heroin. Their sometimes-violent, on-and-off relationship was fueled by addiction. Still, they eloped in 2007. Also in 2007, Amy slipped into a coma after overdosing on what she would later explain was a mix of heroin, cocaine, Ecstasy, ketamine, whisky, and vodka. Amy entered rehab briefly in 2008, but her substance issues continued.

Throughout 2007 and 2008, Amy was forced to cancel performances and entire tours due to her substance abuse. Amy and Blake separated in late 2008 and eventually divorced in 2009. It seemed as though Amy was gaining more control of her life throughout 2010 and early 2011, but her substance use issues clearly continued, and she died of accidental alcohol poisoning on July 23, 2011. Amy was 27 years old.

SOURCE: Amy Winehouse. (2013). *The Biography Channel website*. Retrieved March 21, 2013, from http://www.biography.com/people/amy-winehouse-244469.

non-medical prescription opioid use (Fischer et al., 2014). There is substantial overlap between opioid and nicotine dependence, with about 9 out of 10 individuals with opioid dependence also meeting criteria for nicotine dependence (Benich, 2011).

The Centers for Disease Control and Prevention (CDC) reported that fatal drug overdoses reached a new high in 2014, killing nearly 50,000 Americans (http://www.cdc.gov/media/releases/2015/p1218-drug-overdose.html). Since 2000, the rate of deaths from drug overdoses has increased 137%, including a 200% increase in the rate of overdose deaths involving opioids (opioid pain relievers and heroin). More than 60% of the overdose deaths were due to some form of opioid including heroin. Unlike previous decades, men and women of all races and ethnic groups and ages were affected by drug overdoses. More deaths were recorded from drug overdoses in the United States in 2014 than during any previous year on record.

LSD and Natural Hallucinogens

LO 10.10 Describe typical effects of LSD and hallucinogens.

Hallucinogens produce altered states of bodily perception and sensation, intense emotions, detachment from oneself and from the environment, and, for some users, feelings of insight with mystical or religious significance. The effects are caused by a disruption of the nerve cells that influence the transmission of the neurotransmitter serotonin (National Institute on Drug Abuse, 2005b), resulting in an experience of the world that is very different from reality.

As with marijuana, the perceptual changes are often intensified experiences in which people become fascinated by minute details. Objects can become distorted and appear to shift and change shape. All five senses can be affected. Depending on the situation and the person, such "trips" can be experienced as pleasant and fascinating or deeply disturbing and frightening.

Many naturally occurring and synthetic hallucinogens exist. Naturally occurring hallucinogens include *psilocybin* (magic mushrooms) and *mescaline* (a product of the peyote cactus). The most widely known synthetic hallucinogen, **lysergic acid diethylamide (LSD)**, gained notoriety in the 1960s counterculture movement when the drugs were believed to "expand the consciousness." LSD was first synthesized in the laboratory by Swiss chemist Albert Hoffman in 1938. His self-testing of the compound led him to report the following observations to the head of the pharmaceutical department in a report:

> Last Friday, April 16, 1943, I was forced to stop my work in the laboratory in the middle of the afternoon and to go home, as I was seized by a peculiar restlessness associated with a sensation of mild dizziness. On arriving home, I lay down and sank into a kind of drunkenness which was not unpleasant and which was characterized by extreme activity of imagination. As I lay in a dazed condition with my eyes closed (I experienced day-light as disagreeably bright) there surged upon me an uninterrupted stream of fantastic images of extraordinary plasticity and vividness and accompanied by an intense, kaleidoscope-like play of colors. This condition gradually passed off after about 2 hours. (http://www.psychedelic-library.org/hofmann.htm)

The web on the left was made by a regular spider, while the one on the right was made by a spider given marijuana.

FUNCTIONAL IMPAIRMENT Psychological symptoms such as emotional swings, panic, and paranoia can lead to bizarre or dangerous behavior. Tolerance builds up rapidly but fades after a few days. Hallucinogens do not produce classic withdrawal symptoms and are not physically addictive, but some users may experience perceptual distortions (hallucinations) long after all traces of the drug have left the system. This condition, *hallucinogen persisting perception disorder*, may result from stress or fatigue. The hallucinations and distortions can be persistent or come in periodic short bursts, or "flashbacks."

EPIDEMIOLOGY According to the 2013 National Survey on Drug Use and Health, approximately 1.3 million individuals ages 12 and older (0.5% of the population) were current (past month) users of hallucinogens (Substance Abuse and Mental Health Services Administration, 2014). The rate of current hallucinogen use is higher in males (0.7%) than females (0.3%) and more than three times higher (1.8%) among young adults ages 18 to 25 years. In 2013, an estimated 1.1 million individuals ages 12 and older used hallucinogens for the first time (average age 19.9 years), including 482,000 who initiated use of LSD (average age 19.7 years) (Substance Abuse and Mental Health Services Administration, 2014).

Inhalants

LO 10.11 Explain how inhalants can permanently damage the brain.

The drugs most commonly used by teenagers, **inhalants**, include substances such as nitrous oxide, amyl nitrite, cleaning fluid, gasoline, spray paint, other aerosol sprays, and glue that are used as a source of inhalable fumes (Substance Abuse and Mental Health Services Administration, 2014). Methods include direct inhalation (sniffing or snorting), using a plastic or paper bag (bagging), holding a soaked rag or cloth over the mouth or nose (huffing), and directly spraying aerosol cleaners into the mouth or nose (dusting) (Baydala, 2010). Inhalants are attractive because they are cheap, legal, and accessible and their effect is immediate

Figure 10.6 Myelin damage from inhalant exposure.

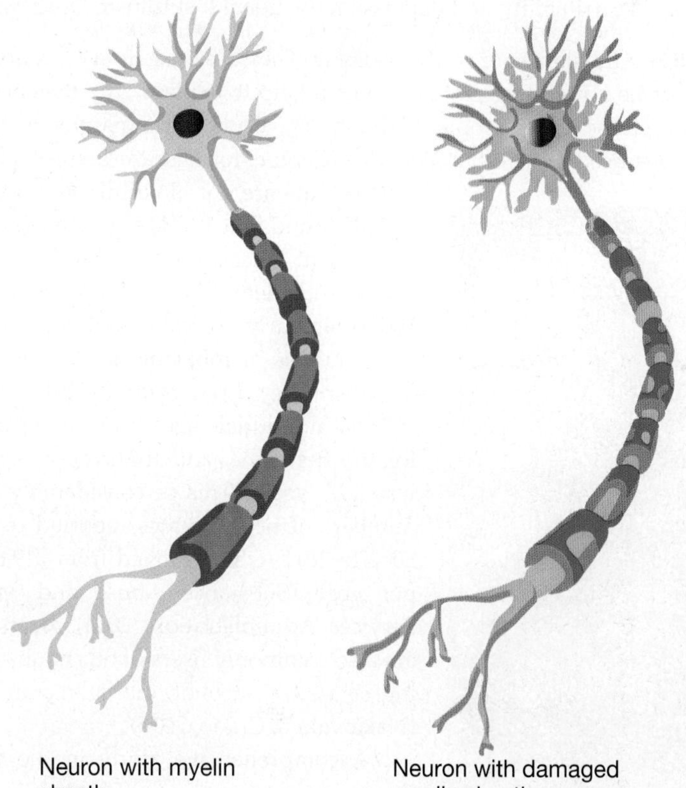

(Duncan & Lawrence, 2013). The reinforcing effects of inhalants, which start within minutes, include rapid onset of sedation, euphoria, and disinhibition as well as the sensation of heat and excitement believed to enhance sexual pleasure. Their immediate adverse effects include dizziness, drowsiness, confusion, slurred speech, and impaired motor skills. Other immediate, and potentially fatal, effects include irregular heartbeat and respiratory failure. Continued exposure or increasing concentration can lead to unconsciousness (Duncan & Lawrence, 2013; Maxwell, 2001). Inhalants act by quickly entering the bloodstream, dispersing throughout the body, and affecting the central nervous system and peripheral nervous system. Many different chemicals can be inhaled, so it is difficult to generalize about their effect. However, the vaporous fumes can change brain chemistry and may permanently damage the brain and central nervous system. Some of the chemicals that are inhaled include toluene (paint thinner, rubber cement), butane and propane gas (lighter fluid, fuel), fluorocarbons (asthma sprays), chlorinated hydrocarbons (dry-cleaning agents, spot removers), acetone (nail polish remover, permanent markers), benzene (varnishes, lacquers, resins), and nitrous oxide (aerosol cans, balloon tanks) (Baydala, 2010).

FUNCTIONAL IMPAIRMENT Chronic exposure to fumes, regardless of the type, can cause severe damage to all vital organs including the brain and bone marrow, leading to compromised red blood cell production and anemia. Inhalants can also have a profound effect on nerves because they can damage the myelin—the protective fatty tissue that surrounds and protects nerve fibers. Myelin assists with the rapid communication necessary for nerve fibers. Damage can lead to muscle spasms and tremors, causing permanent interference with basic functions such as walking, bending, and talking. Magnetic resonance imaging (MRI) studies of inhalant abusers have found changes in brain structure including shrinkage of the cerebral cortex, cerebellum, and brain stem. These changes lead to permanently impaired motor and cognitive abilities (Sherman, 2005), which may be indicated by irritability, tremor, ataxia, nystagmus, slurred speech, decreased visual acuity, and deafness. Other health effects of inhalant abuse can include cardiomyopathy, pulmonary debilitation, hepatitis, immune impairment, and certain types of cancer (Baydala, 2010). Chronic abuse of inhalants has been associated with impaired cognitive function, decreased IQ, anxiety, depression, increased impulsivity, and transition to illicit drug use (Duncan & Lawrence, 2013). When people stop using inhalants, withdrawal symptoms include weight loss, muscle weakness, disorientation, inattentiveness, irritability, and depression (National Institute on Drug Abuse, 2004a).

EPIDEMIOLOGY Inhalants are easily available: They are present in most homes, are inexpensive, and can be bought legally, all of which help to explain why they are often one of the first drugs used by young people. With tobacco, alcohol, and marijuana, they round out the top four drugs used by youth in America (Centers for Disease Control and Prevention, 2004b). Data are not plentiful, but a national survey in 2003 found that 10.7% of youth ages 12 to 17 used an inhalant at least once in their lifetime (Substance Abuse and Mental Health Services Administration, 2003). Similarly, an estimated 46.8 percent of past year initiates of inhalants in 2013 were under age 18 when they first used. In 2013, approximately 563,000 individuals age 12 and older used inhalants for the first time, and the average age of first use was 19.2 years. This is considerably less than the numbers of new initiates reported over the period 2002 to 2011, which ranged from 719,000 to 877,000 per year (Substance Abuse and Mental Health Services Administration, 2014). Users of inhalants are also commonly users of other substances, including cigarettes, alcohol, marijuana, and other drugs (Nakawaki & Crano, 2015).

Inhalants are often the drug of choice for youth of low socioeconomic status around the world.

A comprehensive study in the U.S. Midwest documented clear sex differences in inhalant use with males more likely to try them (21.7%) and more likely to use them on a monthly basis (9.4%); comparable figures for females were 13.5% and 5.8%, respectively (Ding et al., 2007). These data are consistent with national surveys (Substance Abuse and Mental Health Services Administration, 2006). Consistent patterns have also emerged for ethnicity and inhalant use, with whites and Hispanic youth being more likely to use inhalants and African Americans having the lowest rates (CDC, 2004b; Ding et al., 2007).

Non-Substance-Related Disorders

LO 10.12 Explain the concept of behavioral addictions and the debate about their inclusion in the DSM.

All of the substances that we have reviewed thus far are ingested into the body via one method or another. More recently, other behaviors have been proposed as possible *behavioral addictions* because they produce short-term positive effects that increase the behavior's frequency even though they also produce negative consequences (Grant et al., 2010). This concept is gaining favor based on similarities in observable behaviors, self-report, and neurobiological research. Considerable controversy remains about whether behaviors such as pathological gambling, kleptomania, compulsive buying, and excessive sexual activity (nonparaphilic hypersexuality; see Chapter 9) should be viewed as addictions. Other behaviors in this category, when repeated excessively, include tanning, Internet use, and computer/video game playing (Holden, 2010). In DSM-5, gambling disorder is included as a type of substance-related and addictive disorder under a subcategory of non-substance-related disorders due to research demonstrating the clinical, phenomenological, genetic, and neurobiological similarities between gambling and substance use disorders (Potenza, 2014). There was much discussion about whether Internet addiction should be included in DSM-5. However, the workgroup decided that additional research and studies were necessary before a determination on its inclusion is made. Other addictions related to sex, exercise, and shopping were also under consideration but were not ultimately included in DSM-5. Debate about whether one can classify "food addiction" as a diagnostic category is also ongoing (Moreno & Tandon, 2011; Potenza, 2014).

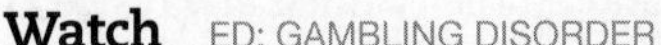

Watch ED: GAMBLING DISORDER

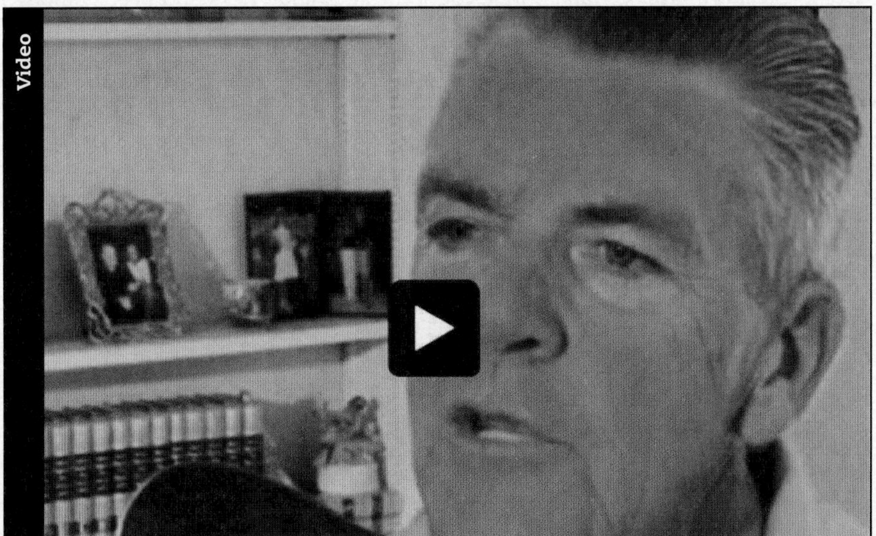

Arguments in favor of the concept of behavioral addictions are based on their many similarities to substance addictions. First, individuals with these behaviors commonly report strong urges or cravings to engage in the behavior (Grant et al., 2010). Second, these behaviors are commonly comorbid with substance use disorders (Cunningham-Williams et al., 1998). Third, many of the same neurotransmitter systems and brain regions appear to be operative in these behaviors as in substance use disorders (Potenza, 2008). Finally, similar treatment approaches appear to be efficacious in treating both behavioral addictions and substance use disorders (Grant et al., 2010). Although the controversy is far from settled, ongoing neurobiological research may help determine whether these pathological, repetitive, and all-consuming behaviors are actual addictions.

Sex, Ethnicity, Education, and Illicit Drug Use

LO 10.13 Characterize the demographic patterns of illicit drug use.

In the 2013 National Survey on Drug Use and Health, among individuals ages 12 years and older, the rate of current (past month) illicit drug use was higher for males (11.5%) than females (7.3%). A smaller gap between male and female illicit drug use (9.6% vs. 8.0%) is seen when considering adolescents ages 12 to 17 years only. Males were more likely than females to be current users of the following drugs: marijuana (9.7% vs. 5.6%), cocaine (0.8% vs. 0.4%), and hallucinogens (0.7% vs. 0.3%) (Substance Abuse and Mental Health Services Administration, 2014).

The pathway to drug addiction for women differs from that for men. Although women are less likely to abuse substances and tend to begin abusing substances at later ages, they often become dependent more quickly and experience more severe consequences of drug use over shorter periods of time (e.g., Hser et al., 2004). Substance use in women is also often associated with relationship issues; women with substance use disorders are more likely to have a partner who also uses illicit drugs (Westermeyer & Boedicker, 2000). Women are more likely than men to turn to alcohol use, binge drinking, and marijuana use when dealing with the breakup of a relationship (Larson & Sweeten, 2012). Women who use substances also have more psychiatric comorbidity compared with males who abuse substances with rates approximating 20% higher (Kessler et al., 1997). The disorders include anxiety, depression, borderline personality disorder (see Chapter 12), and posttraumatic stress disorder (Brooner et al., 1997; Cottler et al., 2001; Trull et al., 2000).

When attempting to understand the role of ethnicity, two problems arise. First, relatively little research has been conducted explicitly on the topic of ethnicity and drug use. Second, in most of the research, the role of ethnicity is confounded with low socioeconomic status. Thus, the relative impact of low socioeconomic status, poverty, and ethnicity must always be kept in mind when considering these data. Studies do indicate unique risks and needs among many minority individuals who misuse drugs. People from minority groups who live in inner-city areas are particularly vulnerable to drug use as a result of high levels of poverty, violence, and availability of street drugs (Avants et al., 2003). Data suggest, too, that illicit drug use differs across racial and ethnic boundaries. Specifically, in 2013, among persons ages 12 or older, the prevalence was lowest among Asians (3.1%). Prevalence estimates were 12.3% for American Indians and Alaska Natives, 10.5% for blacks, 17.4% for persons reporting two or more races, 9.5% for whites, 14.0% for Native Hawaiians or other Pacific Islanders, and 8.8% for Hispanics. There were no significant changes in rates of illicit substance abuse from 2012 to 2013 for any racial/ethnic group (Substance Abuse and Mental Health Services Administration, 2014).

Education level is also associated with illicit drug use among adults ages 18 years and older: it is lower among college graduates (6.7%) than among those who did not graduate from high school (11.8%), high school graduates (9.9%), and those with some college but no degree (10.8%) (Substance Abuse and Mental Health Services Administration, 2014).

Learning Objective Summaries

LO 10.5 Describe the short- and long-term therapeutic and negative psychological and health consequences of marijuana use.

Adverse health effects related to acute use of marijuana include hyperemesis syndrome, impaired coordination and performance, anxiety, suicidal ideation, and psychotic symptoms. Heavy marijuana use results in persistent memory loss; neurocognitive impairment of attention, learning skills, and motor movement; addiction; chronic respiratory and cardiovascular problems; and an increased risk of mood disorders as well as head, neck, and lung cancer. At the same time, the FDA has approved forms of marijuana for treatment of nausea and vomiting associated with cancer chemotherapy and appetite stimulation in people with wasting illnesses such as AIDS or cancer. In addition, there is strong evidence to support the use of marijuana to treat chronic pain, neuropathic pain, and spasticity associated with multiple sclerosis.

LO 10.6 Characterize patterns of use and effects of CNS stimulants.

Effects include euphoria, increased energy, mental alertness, and rapid speech. Some people also feel a sense of power and courage, the ability to tackle otherwise daunting tasks, and increased feelings of intimacy and sexual arousal. Adverse effects include dangerous elevations in blood pressure and heart rate and cardiovascular abnormalities, potentially leading to heart attack, respiratory arrest, and seizures.

LO 10.7 Summarize the mechanism of action of cocaine on the brain.

Cocaine increases synaptic levels of dopamine, serotonin, and norepinephrine, but its powerful stimulant effects are thought to be caused by inhibiting nerve cells' reabsorption of dopamine. When more dopamine is available in the synapses, the stimulation of the brain reward pathways increases and provides more positive feelings. Increased dopamine availability in synapses increases stimulation of the brain reward pathways, leading to positive feelings such as euphoria, self-confidence, self-control, energy, motor activity, mental efficiency, alertness, and cognitive capacity. Negative effects include decreases in appetite, anxiety, dysphoria, paranoia, and restlessness and in higher doses hallucinations, aggressiveness, disorientation, tremors, convulsions, and increased body temperature.

LO 10.8 Compare and contrast patterns of use and effects of barbiturates and benzodiazepines.

Both are sedative drugs that are central nervous system *depressants*. Initially used to treat anxiety and insomnia, barbiturates are now less commonly prescribed than benzodiazepines due to the high risk of abuse, dependence, and overdose. Barbiturate use leads to slurred speech, decreased respiration, fatigue, disorientation, lack of coordination, and dilated pupils. At higher doses, users can experience impaired memory and coordination, irritability, and paranoid and suicidal thoughts. Withdrawal from barbiturates produces tremors, increased blood pressure and heart rate, sweating, and seizures. Benzodiazepines were originally prescribed for the treatment of anxiety and can be used responsibly and effectively for short-term treatment of anxiety and insomnia. Withdrawal from benzodiazepines includes anxiety, insomnia, tremors, and delirium.

LO 10.9 Summarize the ways in which opioids can be taken and their effects on body and mind.

Opioids can be taken as pills, smoked, snorted, injected beneath the skin ("popped"), or mainlined (injected into the bloodstream). Opioids produce pain relief, euphoria, sedation, reduced anxiety, and tranquility. To produce their characteristic high, they mimic the effect of the opioids, such as endorphins or enkephalins, which the body releases in response to pain. Besides pain relief and sedation, they cause narrowing of the pupils, constipation, flushed skin, itching, lowered blood pressure, slowed heart rate, low body temperature, nausea, vomiting, and slowed respiration.

LO 10.10 Describe typical effects of LSD and hallucinogens.

Hallucinogens produce altered states of bodily perception and sensation, intense emotions, detachment from oneself and from the environment, and, for some users, feelings of insight with mystical or religious significance.

LO 10.11 Explain how inhalants can permanently damage the brain.

Chronic inhalant use can have a profound effect on nerves because they can damage the myelin—the protective fatty tissue that surrounds and protects nerve fibers. Damage can lead to muscle spasms and tremors, causing permanent interference with basic functions such as walking, bending, and talking. Imaging studies of inhalant abusers have found changes in brain structure including shrinkage of the cerebral cortex, cerebellum, and brain stem. These changes lead to permanently impaired motor and cognitive abilities, which may be indicated by irritability, tremor, ataxia, nystagmus, slurred speech, decreased visual acuity, and deafness.

LO 10.12 Explain the concept of behavioral addictions and the debate about their inclusion in the DSM.

Several behaviors, such as gambling, sex, video gaming, shopping, and "food," have been termed "behavioral addictions" because they produce short-term positive effects that increase the behavior's frequency even though they also produce negative consequences. Although they share many phenomenological similarities to substance use disorders, they differ in that no exogenous substances (except food) are involved. The discussion and research continues regarding whether these behaviors should be classified with other substance use disorders.

LO 10.13 Characterize the demographic patterns of illicit drug use.

Among individuals ages 12 years and older, the rate of current illicit drug use was higher for males than females. Between the ages of 12 and 17, the gap between the sexes gets smaller. Use does differ by sex, with males being more likely to use marijuana, cocaine, and hallucinogens. Illicit drug use tends to be lower in individuals with a college education; however, patterns of use across age groups, socioeconomic groups, and races and ethnicities are fluid and change with availability and trends.

> **Critical Thinking Question**
>
> Because various substances often lead to quite different "highs," what factors might influence drug choice across individuals?

Etiology of Substance-Related Disorders

Friends and family often cannot understand why someone continues to use drugs when so much is at stake. A husband whose marriage is in jeopardy apparently "chooses" to return to drinking knowing divorce will be the consequence. A man who has had one warning at work for a positive urine screen smokes marijuana on a weeknight knowing that another positive test means he will lose his job. A pregnant woman continues to smoke even while reading the warning label on the cigarette pack. What drives people to make these self-destructive choices? Once we blamed personal characteristics such as moral weakness or depravity, but as we have learned more about drug abuse, we have come to acknowledge the contribution of biological, behavioral, and sociocultural factors.

Biological Factors

LO 10.14 Illustrate the role that the brain's reward pathways play in addiction.

To understand the biology of substance use, we must appreciate the effects not only of each substance on biology but also of an individual's biology regarding potential to abuse alcohol or drugs.

FAMILY AND GENETIC STUDIES A substantial body of family, twin, adoption, and molecular genetic research has determined that both genes and environment affect the likelihood of substance abuse. After analyzing more than 17,500 MZ and DZ twin pairs from 14 different studies, researchers concluded that both genetic and environmental factors influence whether a person ever starts smoking, continues smoking, and becomes dependent on nicotine (Sullivan & Kendler, 1999). Environmental factors seem to be particularly important in determining whether a person (especially an adolescent) starts smoking, and genetic factors are more prominent in influencing whether the smoker progresses to nicotine dependence.

In addition, studies are under way to identify areas of the genome and specific susceptibility genes that may be important in nicotine dependence. The most studied of these genes are on chromosome 15, with single nucleotide polymorphisms (SNPs) of several genes coding for nicotine receptors (*CHRNA5-A3-B4*) having shown replicated associations with nicotine dependence in numerous studies (Hancock et al., 2015; Olfson et al., 2015). Common, low frequency variants as well as rare variants of these genes are associated with risk of nicotine dependence (Olfson et al., 2015). Several SNPs on chromosome 15 genes (*IREB2, HYKK, PSMA4, CHRNA5-A3-B4*) are also associated with *CHRNA5* methylation in the prefrontal cortex, frontal cortex, temporal cortex, and pons (Hancock et al., 2015). Though Tyndale et al. (2015) found the expected associations between *CHRNA5-A3-B4* genes and baseline tobacco consumption in a sample of Caucasian adults (n = 654) who were participating in a clinical trial of smoking cessation (nicotine patch vs. varenicline vs. placebo), they did not find any genome-wide significant associations between these genes and smoking cessation outcomes (Tyndale et al., 2015). Other researchers have found genome-wide significant associations with nicotine dependence on chromosomes 7, 8, and 14 but did not replicate associations with genes on chromosome 15 (*CHRNA5-A3-B4*) that code for nicotine receptors (Gelernter et al., 2015).

Genetic factors account for about 50 to 60% of the variance in liability for alcohol dependence in both men and women (Prescott, 2001). The search for candidate genes has focused on alcohol metabolism and genes involved in the dopamine, serotonin, GABA, opioid, cannabinoid, and choline pathways. Thus far, genes related to alcohol metabolism have produced the most robust findings, including those related to alcohol dehydrogenase and aldehyde dehydrogenase 2 as well as glutamatergic, dopaminergic, and serotonergic neurotransmitter signaling pathways (Hart & Kranzler, 2015; Samochowiec et al., 2014). Studies are under way to further explain how genes influence alcohol dependence. It is perhaps no coincidence that some overlap has been observed in the genes that influence both nicotine and alcohol dependence. Indeed, both disorders often co-occur, and at least some of the same genes may influence the risk of developing each type of dependence (Grucza & Beirut, 2007). In a candidate gene study of individuals with alcohol abuse (n = 101) and abstinence from alcohol dependence (n = 100) vs. healthy controls (n = 97), Plemenitas et al. (2015) did not find any significant associations between *TPH2* genotypes and alcohol dependence, though results suggested a potential role for genetic variability of *TPH2* in comorbid symptomatology. Zuo et al. (2015) conducted a GWAS meta-analysis of four independent cohorts (total n = 12,481) and found SNPs associated with alcohol dependence that were specific to individuals with European ancestry (*SERINC2, STK40, KIAA0040,* and *IPO11*) or African ancestry (*SLC6A11* and *CBLN2*) or common across both populations (*PTP4A1-PHF3*), all of which were located in various transcription factor binding sites. Polygenic risk analyses using GWAS data suggest that genetic risk for alcohol dependence is influenced by many loci with small effects, and much larger sample sizes, likely with tens of thousands of participants, may be needed to detect additional loci with significant associations to alcohol dependence (Hart & Kranzler, 2015).

Family, twin, and adoption studies are more difficult to conduct with illicit drug users because people who abuse substances are reluctant to report their use and to participate in research. However, we do know that genetic factors play a substantial role and that there may be additive effects of SNPs on genetic risk for nicotine, alcohol, marijuana, and cocaine dependence (Palmer et al., 2015). In a large Norwegian twin study, Kendler et al. (2006) reported heritability estimates for a range of illicit drug use (e.g., cannabis, stimulants, opiates, cocaine, and psychedelics) from 58 to 81%. The remaining variance was attributed to individual-specific environmental effects. Johnson et al. (2015) examined genetic associations with drug abuse in samples of European Americans (n = 6,845) and African Americans (n = 3,742) from the Urban Health Study, all of whom injected drugs and abused opioids, cocaine, marijuana, stimulants, or other drugs at least 10 times in the prior 30 days and found that a SNP in the *KAT2B* gene (part of the AMP and dopamine signaling pathways) was significantly associated with drug abuse in African Americans only. This result was replicated in a second African American cohort (Johnson et al., 2015).

We still do not know precisely what is inherited. We have not yet identified specific genes that explain why some people become addicted to substances while others do not. Although the complete picture remains unclear, neurobiology, cognition, personality, and behavior may all contribute to addiction liability.

NEUROBIOLOGY From a neurobiological perspective, alcohol and drugs act on several areas of the brain but especially the part of the brain that is involved with processing pleasurable feelings (the reward system) (Volkow & Baler, 2014). The reward circuitry includes the ventral tegmental area and the basal forebrain (see Figure 10.7). By using neuroimaging technology, we can observe how this pathway is activated in response to drug administration. Importantly, although dopamine is commonly considered the "pleasure" neurotransmitter, other neurotransmitters are also involved in the development and maintenance of addictive behaviors, including glutamate, gamma-aminobutyric acid (GABA), serotonin, norepinephrine, acetylcholine, corticotrophin-releasing factor, opioids, cannabinoids,

Figure 10.7 The Brain's Reward System.

The dopaminergic system is the primary reward system in the brain. Major structures in the system including the ventral tegmental area (VTA), the nucleus accumbens, and the prefrontal cortex are highlighted. Information travels from the VTA to the nucleus accumbens and then up to the prefrontal cortex.

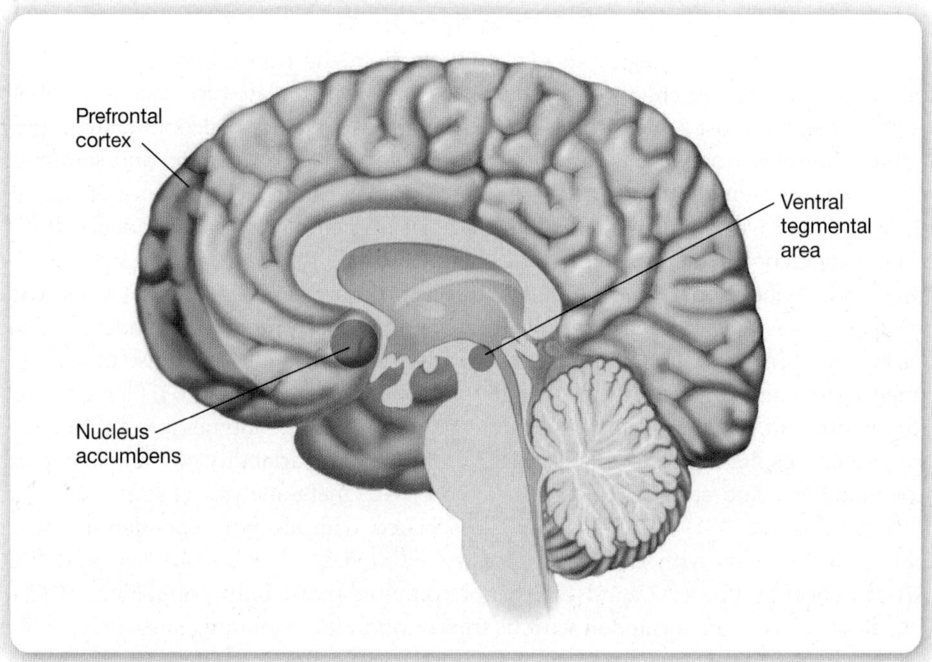

oxytocin, vasopressin, and neuropeptide Y (Hammond et al., 2014). Differences in brain circuitry related to emotional conflict, decision making, and the reward system (anterior cingulate cortex, prefrontal cortex, ventral tegmental area) are also evident in adolescents with parental history of substance use disorders (Qiao et al., 2015). In addition to the areas of the brain associated with reward processing, activity in other areas has been associated with negative affect and withdrawal states (central and peripheral noradrenergic systems) as well as craving states (prefrontal cortex, orbitofrontal, medial prefrontal, anterior cingulate, basolateral amygdala, insula, and hippocampus) (Hammond et al., 2014).

The endogenous opioid system is clearly involved in the reinforcing effect of opiates as well as that of alcohol and nicotine. This system is directly involved in how pleasurable we perceive the drug to be. As the treatment section of this chapter illustrates, administering an *opiate receptor antagonist*, which blocks the positive effect of the drug, is effective in decreasing alcohol use in humans (Garbutt et al., 1999). Serotonin appears to be associated with alcohol use (LeMarquand et al., 1994) and may also be associated with the reinforcing properties (positive effects) of cocaine (White & Wolf, 1991). In addition, low cerebrospinal fluid levels of 5-hydroxyindoleacetic acid (5-HIAA), which are associated with impulsivity and sensation seeking, have been found in individuals with substance use disorders (Grant et al., 2006). Sedative drugs may act primarily through the GABA system.

Thus several neurotransmitters are involved with the experience of reinforcement and reward associated with drug and alcohol use. In addition, genetic and environmental factors may combine to determine who is most vulnerable to the lure of such rewards. One hypothesis is that people at risk for drug and alcohol dependence have deficits in their brain reward pathway. For example, a person whose brain harbors low dopamine or exhibits hypodopaminergic traits may need a higher dose of a dopamine "fix" to feel good (Blum et al., 2000). This deficit could lead the person to seek a drug that would provide that good feeling. Likewise, repeated exposure to drugs or alcohol in individuals at high risk for substance dependence or abuse may influence neurocircuitry in such a way that the reward system is more reactive to that particular substance (Hammond et al., 2014). Maladaptive behaviors that could develop in an attempt to boost dopamine include addictive, impulsive, and compulsive behaviors. Although we need further research to verify this model, recognizing that substance use is the result of a chronically under-rewarded brain system can be a useful way for family and friends to understand the challenges that a person faces when trying to abstain from alcohol and drugs. This information also may help in developing approaches to treatment for substance dependence that focus on finding alternative rewarding experiences to replace those provided by drugs.

Watch NEUROTRANSMITTERS

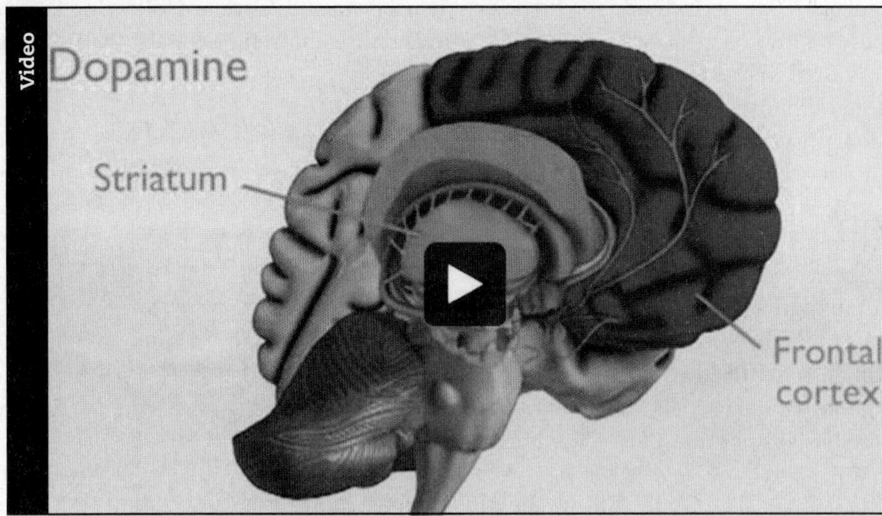

Psychological Factors

LO 10.15 Explain how the principles of reinforcement apply to substance use disorders.

Although biology plays a central role, psychological factors also influence critical aspects of drug use, such as the decision to try a drug (initiation), the decision to continue using the drug, the frequency with which a drug is used, and the decision to stop drug use.

BEHAVIORAL FACTORS—DRUGS AS REINFORCERS Drugs are reinforcing in several ways, and operant conditioning helps explain the role of drugs as reinforcers. First, drug-induced euphoria produces positive physical feelings and increases the likelihood that the drug will be used again. This is positive reinforcement. Negative reinforcement also maintains drug use when repeated use removes an unpleasant state. A person feeling tired and lethargic who grabs a cup of coffee removes that lethargic state and experiences negative reinforcement. Positive reinforcement processes are more directly implicated in the initial stages of addiction, with negative reinforcement mechanisms playing an increasingly important role as addiction progresses.

Drugs are reinforcers. They produce positive physical feelings, increasing the likelihood that they will be used again.

Conditioning through positive or negative reinforcement involves more than the simple act of using the drug. Environmental aspects, such as settings in which the drugs are taken, the people with whom drugs are used, or the paraphernalia used to administer the drugs, themselves become cues (signals) to begin drug use (Caprioli et al., 2007). This is why, for example, some people who are trying to quit smoking say, "I do OK till I go into a bar—once I start to drink, I really need a cigarette." This fits well with classical conditioning models of substance use (Domjan, 2005). In these models, external stimuli that have been paired with drug use produce some of the same bodily sensations that previously have been caused by the drug itself (i.e., the conditioned and unconditioned responses are similar). In this way, stimuli that previously had signaled the arrival of a drug (the sight of a person or passing a particular street corner) seem to set off a whole host of feelings and reactions that trigger drug use. In the case of drug-compensatory conditioned responses, regulatory bodily changes occur in the presence of conditioned stimuli (e.g., drug paraphernalia, fellow drug users) to counteract the anticipated effects of drugs or alcohol (Siegel et al., 2000). An individual who does not engage in substance use following these compensatory bodily changes feels considerable pain and discomfort (i.e., withdrawal). As a result, the individual may engage in substance use as a way to escape from or avoid withdrawal symptoms (Domjan, 2005).

Laboratory paradigms can test the reinforcing effects of various drugs from both operant and classical conditioning perspectives. For example, laboratory animals can be given either free access to alcohol or drugs, or they can be trained to work (press a lever) in order to receive a drug. Changing the reinforcement schedule (free versus work) helps the researcher determine how reinforcing the drug is to the animal, allowing comparisons of the relative reinforcing value of two drugs—for example, alcohol versus nicotine. Another approach—*conditioned place preference*—initially exposes the animal to two distinct but neutral environments (Cage A or Cage B). Then a drug is repeatedly paired with one of the environments (Cage A, for example). After the conditioning trials, the amount of time the animal spends in the "drug" environment helps establish its positive effects (Tzschentke, 2007).

COGNITIVE FACTORS Cognitive theories are based on the premise that how a person interprets a situation influences the decision to use a drug (Beck et al., 1993). A social setting may activate thoughts (e.g., "I am much more relaxed after I have a beer" or "a line of cocaine will make me more sociable") and make the person more likely to use the substance. Cognitions can also affect a person's reaction to physiological symptoms associated with anxiety and craving (Beck et al., 1993). A thought (e.g., "I cannot stand not having a cigarette") will increase awareness of cravings and enhance the reaction when craving occurs.

Based in social learning theory (Bandura, 1977a, 1977b), Bandura's social cognitive approach (1999) explores biased belief systems that maintain substance abuse. Briefly, several factors initiate and maintain substance use disorders: (1) positive drug outcome expectancies (e.g., "this drug will make me feel good"); (2) minimal negative expectancies (e.g., "I have never gotten caught"); and (3) poor self-efficacy beliefs regarding one's ability to cope without drugs (e.g., "I don't think I can survive another day of school without marijuana"). Although empirical studies have demonstrated a relation between positive outcome expectancies and substance use, such approaches rely on self-report of cognition, which is subject to bias.

Behavioral and cognitive theories focus on how expectations of outcome are associated with actual outcomes (i.e., relaxation, pleasure). The associations arise directly from the drug's effects as well as from environmental factors that are paired with those positive feelings. Repeated exposure to the drug and the associated cues bias the information that a person recalls about drug use (i.e., remembering the buzz but not the hangover) (McCusker, 2001). Lapses and relapses occur when the cues for use outweigh the positive features of abstinence (e.g., keeping a relationship).

Sociocultural, Family, and Environmental Factors

LO 10.16 Elucidate the role of cultural and economic factors in substance use disorders.

Among the factors associated with substance abuse, sociocultural dimensions are critical. Social, family, and environmental variables all combine with genetic predisposition to contribute to substance-related disorders. Many researchers have studied the contribution of family, peer, and socioeconomic factors to the development of substance-related disorders. In studies of both adolescents and adults, family and peer influence (Bailey et al., 2014; Van Ryzin et al., 2012; Wang et al., 2007), trauma (Edalati & Krank, 2015; Wills et al., 2001), and economic factors (Black & Krishnakumar, 1998; Boles & Miotto, 2003) have all been associated with increased substance use and abuse. Although these relationships highlight the importance of environmental variables, exactly how they interact with genetic predisposition remains unknown.

Cultural, family, and social factors also may buffer or protect against substance abuse. The use of alcohol and nicotine has been found to be strongly and inversely related to dimensions of religiosity (Kendler, Gardner, Thornton et al., 1997). For example, the more strongly people identify themselves as being religious, the less likely they are to smoke or abuse alcohol. Although these relationships—both risk and protective—highlight the role of environmental variables, our understanding demands an integrated perspective on the roles of genes and environment. However, considering that substance use may play an important role in some cultures is also important.

Developmental Factors

LO 10.17 Trace the developmental trajectory of risk for substance use disorders.

Many adolescents experiment with drugs, but most do not progress to abuse or dependence (Newcomb & Richardson, 1995). Introduction to substance use at a young age and heavy use during adolescence are two risk factors (Kandel & Davies, 1992). Further, drug-related problems (i.e., experiencing some symptoms without meeting full diagnostic criteria) in adolescence predict future substance use disorders, elevated levels of depression, and antisocial and borderline personality disorder symptoms (see Chapter 12) by age 24 (Rohde et al., 2001).

Drug involvement is typically progressive, beginning with substances that are legal for adults (e.g., alcohol, nicotine) followed by marijuana and then other illicit drugs (Anthony & Petronis, 1995). For this reason, some argue that adolescent marijuana use is a gateway to other drug use, but this statement often is misinterpreted. Marijuana is the initial illicit drug used before other more harmful drugs (Daughters et al., 2007; Haug et al., 2014). However, "gateway" is usually interpreted to mean that marijuana use somehow precipitates the use of other drugs. Precipitating factors might include environmental factors, such as increased access to other drugs, or pharmacological factors, in which case marijuana use might make one vulnerable to developing dependence on other drugs. It is also important to note that many people never "graduate" past marijuana at all and others may briefly experiment with other drugs but not progress to regular use (Tarter et al., 2006).

Regardless of whether marijuana is a gateway drug, more direct developmental consequences are associated with its use. If it is used chronically, any drug can have damaging effects with biological consequences such as compromised brain development. Chronic use also has social consequences such as "arrested development" in which normal developmental experiences and growth opportunities may be missed due to excessive marijuana use. Many individuals who use substances throughout their adolescence simply stop using on their own as they enter adulthood. For individuals who reach the point of developing a substance use disorder, however, recovery is more difficult even with treatment. For this reason, prevention efforts are especially relevant for adolescents. The most effective approaches focus on skills-based programs as opposed to providing information or using scare tactics (Nation et al., 2003).

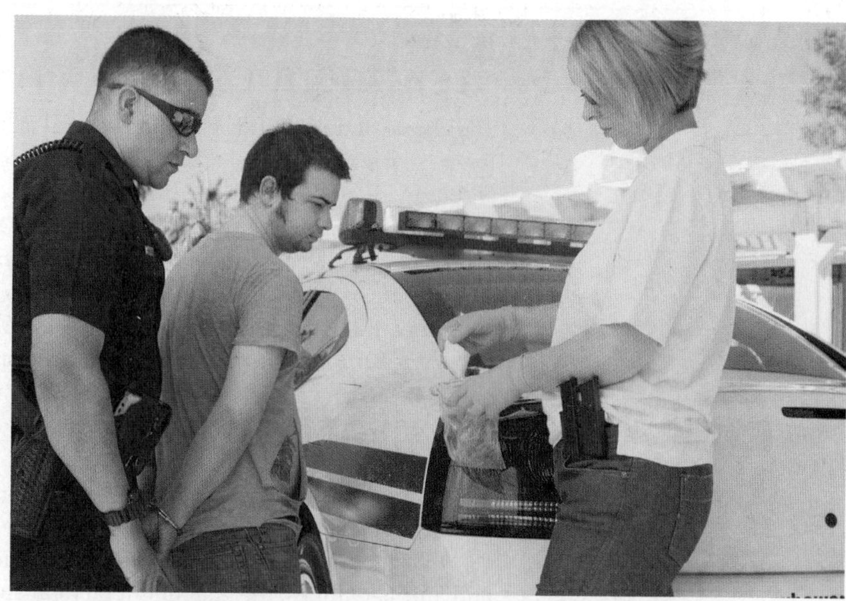

Low socioeconomic conditions and the absence of alternative reinforcers can increase the risk of engaging in substance abuse.

Learning Objective Summaries

LO 10.14 Illustrate the role that the brain's reward pathways play in addiction.

From a neurobiological perspective, alcohol and drugs act on several areas of the brain but especially the part of the brain that is involved with processing pleasurable feelings (the reward system). The reward circuitry includes the ventral tegmental area and the basal forebrain. One hypothesis is that people at risk for drug and alcohol dependence have deficits in their brain reward pathway. For example, a person whose brain shows "low dopamine or hypodopaminergic" traits may need a dopamine boost in order to feel good. Likewise, repeated exposure to drugs or alcohol in individuals at high risk for substance dependence or abuse may influence neurocircuitry in such a way that the reward system is more reactive to that particular substance.

LO 10.15 Explain how the principles of reinforcement apply to substance use disorders.

Drug-induced euphoria produces positive physical feelings and increases the likelihood that the drug will be used again. This is positive reinforcement. Negative reinforcement also maintains drug use when repeated use removes an unpleasant state. A person feeling tired and lethargic who grabs a cup of coffee removes that lethargic state and experiences negative reinforcement. Positive reinforcement processes are more directly implicated in the initial stages of addiction, with negative reinforcement mechanisms playing an increasingly important role as addiction progresses.

LO 10.16 Elucidate the role of cultural and economic factors in substance use disorders.

Social, family, and environmental variables all combine with genetic predisposition to contribute to substance-related disorders. Family and peer influence, trauma, and economic factors have all been associated with increased substance use and abuse. Cultural, family, and social factors also may buffer or protect against substance abuse. The use of alcohol and nicotine has been found to be strongly and inversely related to dimensions of religiosity.

LO 10.17 Trace the developmental trajectory of risk for substance use disorders.

Many adolescents experiment with drugs, but most do not progress to abuse or dependence. Introduction to substance use at a young age and heavy use during adolescence are two risk factors. Further, drug-related problems (i.e., experiencing some symptoms without meeting full diagnostic criteria) in adolescence predict future substance use disorders, elevated levels of depression, and antisocial and borderline personality disorder symptoms by young adulthood.

Critical Thinking Question

Although we discuss how genes and environment interact to influence the risk for drug abuse, can you describe a situation in which someone who is at low genetic risk might develop drug abuse solely due to environmental exposures? Similarly, can you describe a scenario in which someone with very high genetic liability would never develop a drug abuse problem?

Treatment of Substance Use Disorders

The choice of treatment is based on several factors, including which drug is being abused and the person's particular characteristics and resources. Treatment should be both multifaceted and individually tailored. Medical treatment both for detoxification and reduction of cravings for a substance may be useful, but the best evidence is for behavioral treatment approaches. For these disorders, treatment should be as intense and long lasting as possible. For severe substance use problems, residential treatment may help people recover away from potential substance use triggers (Reif, George et al., 2014a). Less intensive options, such as recovery housing (short-term housing after inpatient or residential care) or intensive outpatient treatment, are also a valuable component of continuum of care (McCarty et al., 2014; Reif, George et al., 2014). Although treatment is available across all ages and social strata, evidence indicates that minority individuals from low-income settings sometimes have difficulty finding adequate specialized treatments. We cover the treatment of substance abuse here broadly, highlighting evidence-based approaches when they exist.

Judging the effectiveness of an intervention is complex. For some drugs, such as heroin and amphetamines, the goal might be total abstinence and no relapse. For other drugs, such

Figure 10.8 Principles of Effective Treatment for Substance Use Disorders.

Because people abuse so many different substances and people who abuse substances have so many different characteristics, treatment for substance use disorders must be multifaceted.

SOURCE: Adapted from the National Institute on Drug Abuse (2014).

Adapted from the National Institute on Drug Abuse (2014).

1. No single treatment is appropriate for all individuals.
2. Treatment needs to be readily available.
3. Effective treatment attends to multiple needs of the individual, not just his or her drug use.
4. An individual's treatment and services plan must be assessed continually and modified as necessary to ensure that the plan meets the person's changing needs.
5. Remaining in treatment for an adequate period of time is critical for treatment effectiveness.
6. Counseling (individual and/or group) and other behavioral therapies are critical components of effective treatment for addiction.
7. Medications are an important element of treatment for many patients, especially when combined with counseling and other behavioral therapies.
8. Addicted or drug-abusing individuals with coexisting mental disorders should have both disorders treated in an integrated way.
9. Medical detoxification is only the first stage of addiction treatment and by itself does little to change long-term drug use.
10. Treatment does not need to be voluntary to be effective.
11. Possible drug use during treatment must be monitored continuously.
12. Treatment programs should provide assessment for HIV/AIDS, hepatitis B and C, tuberculosis and other infectious diseases, and counseling to help patients modify or change behaviors that place themselves or others at risk of infection.
13. Recovery from drug addiction can be a long-term process and frequently requires multiple episodes of treatment.

References

http://www.nida.nih.gov/PODAT/PODATindex.html, Retrieved June 7, 2013.

as alcohol, some researchers have argued that drinking moderately and in a controlled way may be an acceptable goal (see "Examining the Evidence: Controlled Drinking?"). Thus evaluating treatment efficacy can be daunting—especially when comorbid psychopathology, legal, or financial complications may interfere with treatment success.

Thirteen principles of effective treatment must be considered before deciding on a specific treatment approach. See Figure 10.8 for these guiding principles and a framework for approaching intervention as well as a glimpse into the complexity of treating these often intractable disorders. With these critical factors in mind, we now explore the various types of interventions.

Therapies Based on Cognitive and Behavioral Principles

LO 10.18 Compare approaches and philosophies of cognitive, behavioral, and 12-step approaches to treatment of substance use disorders.

Interventions based on cognitive and behavioral principles are efficacious in treating substance use disorders (Dutra et al., 2008). Each strategy targets the function of substance use and uses interventions that focus on the cognitive, behavioral, and/or environmental factors maintaining substance use.

AVOIDANCE OF THE STIMULUS In some treatments for substance use disorders, people may be instructed to avoid stimuli that are related to past drug use (e.g., fellow drug users, drug paraphernalia) (Read et al., 2001). Evidence for the usefulness of this strategy comes from studies of returning Vietnam veterans who were addicted to heroin while in Vietnam and treated before returning home (Robins & Slobodyan, 2003). The rate of relapse for these soldiers was significantly less than for comparable groups of civilians whose experience with heroin was on their home territory. One reason for the reduced relapse in veterans may have been their removal from the environment in which heroin use occurred. Although avoidance of drug-related stimuli can prevent the occurrence of cravings and relapse, many remain skeptical about the value of this approach. Long-term avoidance of all drug cues is virtually impossible for most people, and complete avoidance of drug-related stimuli fails to teach individuals more adaptive behaviors that are incompatible with taking drugs (Rohsenow et al., 1990).

RELAPSE PREVENTION A widely used cognitive-behavioral intervention is **relapse prevention** (RP; Marlatt & Gordon, 1985). RP uses *functional analysis* (see Chapter 3) to identify the antecedents and consequences of drug use and then to develop alternative cognitive and behavioral skills to reduce the risk of future drug use. Working together, the therapist and patient identify high-risk situations and the (1) trigger for that situation, (2) thoughts during that situation, (3) feelings experienced in response to the trigger and thoughts, (4) drug use behavior, and (5) positive and negative consequences of drug use. After analyzing this behavior chain, the therapist and patient develop strategies for altering thoughts, feelings, and behaviors to help avoid or manage situations that threaten the patient's commitment to abstinence (Wheeler et al., 2006).

In the relapse prevention model, a *lapse* is a single instance of substance use and a *relapse* is a complete return to pretreatment behaviors. A core feature of RP, **abstinence violation effect**, focuses on a person's cognitive and affective responses to engaging in a prohibited behavior. How a person responds to or interprets the lapse, and not the lapse itself, determines whether the lapse becomes a relapse (Collins & Lapp, 1991; Curry et al., 1987; Larimer et al., 1999; Shiffman et al., 1997). For example, if after having one drink, a recovered alcoholic says, "I'm a failure, I'm an incurable addict, I may as well give up," he or she has a higher chance of progressing to a relapse than someone whose response is "I had one drink, but that doesn't mean I have to have two. I can stop now, pour the rest of this away, and still be successful in my commitment to quit." The abstinence violation effect acknowledges that a person can have positive affective responses to a lapse independent of the cognitions (e.g., "That scotch felt good going down") (Hudson et al., 1992; Ward & Hudson, 1996). Attention to these cognitions is essential to successful relapse prevention. In other words, we cannot ignore the fact that drug use simply might be pleasurable. Acknowledging these positives can be explored in functional analysis or problem-solving therapy by focusing on finding both other pleasurable activities and other strategies aside from seeking pleasure to cope with negative events.

STAGES OF CHANGE AND MOTIVATIONAL ENHANCEMENT THERAPY (MET) Despite the severe impairment in social and occupational functioning that substance abuse causes, a drug's reinforcing effect can be so strong that the desire to use it overshadows any negative consequence. Two critical issues related to this situation are how to motivate people to enter treatment and how to tailor treatment to the motivational level of the individual. The **transtheoretical model** (TTM) proposes a five-stage sequential model of behavioral change (Prochaska & DiClemente, 1983). Limited awareness of the problem, few emotional reactions to substance abuse, and resistance to change characterize *precontemplation*. Individuals in the *contemplation* stage are more aware of the problem and weigh the positive and negative aspects of their substance abuse. The *preparation* stage is marked by a decision to take corrective action (within the next month), and the *action* stage is characterized by actual attempts to change environment, behavior, or experiences. Once entering the

Figure 10.9 Transtheoretical model of change.

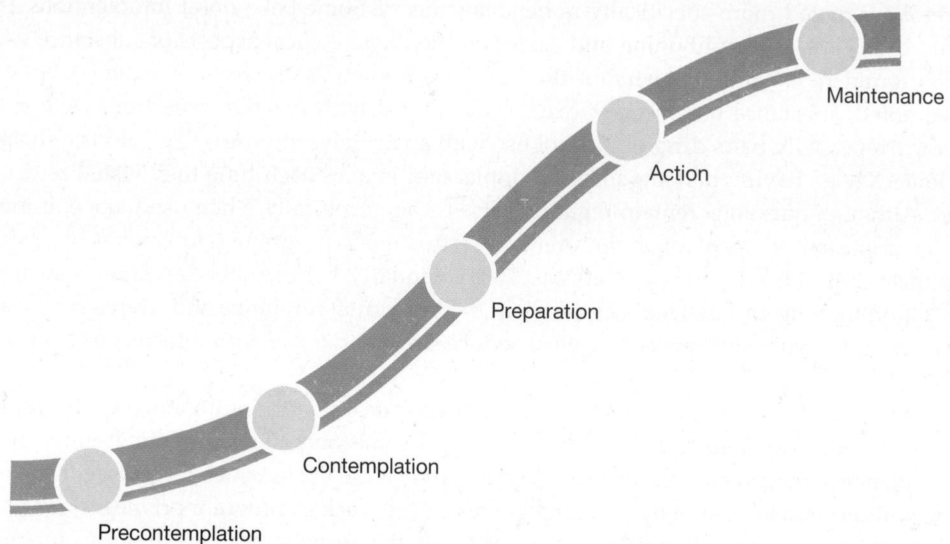

maintenance stage, individuals are acquiring and engaging in behaviors that are designed to prevent relapse (see Figure 10.9). Evidence strongly supports this model and its relevance for treating substance use disorders (Migneault et al., 2005).

Motivational interviewing begins by identifying each person's place on the TTM model as the entry to motivate people to change (VanBuskirk & Wetherell, 2014). This approach differs greatly from more traditional approaches that are more confrontational and require a patient to be ready to quit for therapy to proceed. Motivational interviewing (Miller, 1983; Miller & Rollnick, 1991) uses principles of motivational psychology to produce rapid, internally motivated change and to mobilize the patient's own resources for change. This may include focusing on patient strengths as opposed to weaknesses and getting the patient to collaborate in the selection of goals and how to achieve them. MET's goal is to help the individual move through the stages of change swiftly and effectively in order to achieve sustained treatment response. MET can be used alone or as preparation for other interventions. It is effective for adults across a wide range of substances (Tait & Hulse, 2003) but may be especially relevant for adolescents whose ambivalence about abstinence may be more common (Grenard et al., 2006; Tevyaw & Monti, 2004).

SKILLS TRAINING Skills training is an important part of cognitive-behavioral therapy. Skills training approaches are based on the idea that individuals with substance use disorders may lack some of the basic skills that are necessary for everyday coping. For this reason, these approaches are sometimes called *coping skills interventions*. Approaches targeting coping and social skills training are among the most widely used (O'Leary & Monti, 2002). According to this approach, interpersonal, environmental, and individual skill deficits pose a challenge to sobriety, and the goal is to teach the basic skills that enable substance users to manage problematic aspects of their life. The Community Reinforcement Approach (Hunt & Azrin, 1973; Meyers et al., 2003) is based on the same principles and includes a broad range of skills training including vocational counseling but especially targets identifying and building the substance user's social network and other support systems. Data support this approach both as a stand-alone treatment and as an adjunct to medication and other treatment approaches (Read et al., 2001).

Although complete abstinence is a goal of most approaches, treatments for alcohol use disorder such as behavioral self-control training focus on strategies to help the individual control alcohol use. Strategies include goal setting, self-monitoring, efforts to limit use, rewards for achieving goals, functional analysis of drinking situations, learning alternate coping skills, and relapse prevention. Considerable evidence supports the use of this approach (Walters, 2000).

BEHAVIORAL THERAPIES BASED ON CLASSICAL AND OPERANT CONDITIONING Although many interventions include both behavioral and cognitive components, several are rooted more specifically in behavior theory. Some behavioral interventions are focused on classical conditioning and center on the physiological aspects of substance use. One prominent example is **aversion therapy** (also known as *aversive conditioning*). As we have noted, substance use in most cases is associated with positive sensations. Aversion therapy repeatedly pairs drug or alcohol use with an aversive stimulus (e.g., electric shock) or images (e.g., having patients imagine unpleasant images each time they visualize drug use). Although questions remain regarding its efficacy, especially when used alone, it may be an important element of a comprehensive treatment program (Howard et al., 1991; Rimmele et al., 1995; Upadhyaya & Deas, 2008). Similarly, behavioral interventions such as relaxation training and biofeedback can help the individual minimize and overcome physiological urges to use substances as well as reduce stress and tension for which substance use may be a coping strategy.

Some behavioral interventions focus more directly on operant conditioning. For example, inpatient and residential treatment programs (and some outpatient programs) implement **contingency management approaches** (Prendergast et al., 2006) in which rewards (either concrete reinforcers such as money or intangible reinforcers such as program privileges) are provided for treatment compliance, such as having negative urine screens for drugs. Compared with 12 weeks of usual treatment alone, adding contingency management for methamphetamine users resulted in less drug use and longer periods of abstinence (Roll et al., 2006). This finding suggests that contingency management holds promise as a component of treatment for methamphetamine use.

Research on behavioral interventions is expanding to incorporate technology and to optimize delivery in the community (Dallery et al., 2015; Kiluk & Carroll, 2013). *Virtual reality therapies* that expose patients to alcohol and drugs, to social interactions that are associated with drug-seeking behaviors, and to peer pressure are excellent examples of the new wave of behavioral interventions that are being evaluated for efficacy (Hone-Blanchet et al., 2014).

TWELVE-STEP APPROACHES If you have ever seen a discreet advertisement for a meeting of "Friends of Bill W.," you saw a notice for an Alcoholics Anonymous (AA) meeting. Established in 1935 by "Bill W." Wilson and Robert Hilbrook Smith, AA's 12-step approach (see Figure 10.10) is based on the need for abstinence. It begins with the realization that the individual is powerless over the addiction, and it provides a structured approach to remaining sober. Members attend regular meetings and are assigned a sponsor whom they can call if they feel unable to maintain sobriety or need support (Donovan et al., 2013; Tusa & Burgholzer, 2013). Each year of sobriety is acknowledged, and social support is crucial. Based on the popularity of AA, additional 12-step approaches have been developed including Narcotics Anonymous (NA) and Overeaters Anonymous (OA).

While behavioral and cognitive-behavioral approaches focus on developing skills to control addiction, the 12-step approach emphasizes an unmanageable life, an inability to control addiction, and participants' belief that only a Higher Power can cure them of their addiction. Although the evidence base is not extensive, some studies suggest that AA is effective. Personal testimonies also attest to its power (Ouimette et al., 1997) as well as other aspects common to more empirically based treatment reviewed above such as structure, social support, and identification of nonsubstance rewards (Moos, 2008).

Group meetings help people struggling with substance use disorders find support and accountability.

Opinions remain divided on 12-step approaches. For people who have found the focus on God inconsistent with their own beliefs, a set of steps that is less focused on religion has been developed (e.g., Rational Recovery). Even without an extensive evidence base, if the 12-step programs are efficacious for only a percentage of addicted individuals, they deserve a place among available treatments.

Figure 10.10 Twelve Steps of Alcoholics Anonymous.

1. We admitted we were powerless over alcohol—that our lives had become unmanageable.
2. Came to believe that a Power greater than ourselves could restore us to sanity.
3. Made a decision to turn our will and our lives over to the care of God as we understood Him.
4. Made a searching and fearless moral inventory of ourselves.
5. Admitted to God, to ourselves and to another human being the exact nature of our wrongs.
6. Were entirely ready to have God remove all these defects of character.
7. Humbly asked Him to remove our shortcomings.
8. Made a list of all persons we had harmed, and became willing to make amends to them all.
9. Made direct amends to such people wherever possible, except when to do so would injure them or others.
10. Continued to take personal inventory and when we were wrong promptly admitted it.
11. Sought through prayer and meditation to improve our conscious contact with God as we understood Him, praying only for knowledge of His will for us and the power to carry that out.
12. Having had a spiritual awakening as the result of these steps, we tried to carry this message to alcoholics, and to practice these principles in all our affairs.

Ethics and Responsibility

LO 10.19 Evaluate the ethical complexities of confronting an impaired colleague.

Although psychologists treat substance use disorders, they too can suffer from these disorders, interfering with their ability to practice their profession. The American Psychological Association's "Ethical Principles of Psychologists and Code of Conduct" (see Chapter 15) states clearly that "[w]hen psychologists become aware of personal problems that may interfere with their performing work-related duties adequately, they take appropriate measures, such as obtaining professional consultation or assistance, and determine whether they should limit, suspend, or terminate their work-related duties" (American Psychological Association, 2002).

Explore ETHICS AND RESPONSIBILITY

When a psychologist is not yet aware or ready to admit that a problem with substance use exists, colleagues are ethically obligated to intervene. Yet despite their training, psychologists are often hesitant to confront impaired colleagues directly. They fear alienating them, being wrong in their suspicions, being labeled a whistle-blower, or feeling as if they crossed an inappropriate boundary (Pincus, 2003). Professional associations offer services, but the number of professionals who seek assistance voluntarily is smaller than the number of professionals estimated to be impaired (Floyd et al., 1998). Because psychology is a licensed profession, state licensing boards have guidelines about substance use in professionals and, depending on the problem and whether harm has occurred to a patient, disciplinary options can include monitoring the psychologist's work for a period of time, mandatory treatment, and even revoking the psychologist's license to practice. Colleague assistance programs play an important role in educating psychologists on reducing stress through self-care and in providing services for professionals who self-refer for help or are referred by others (American Psychological Association, 2006; Pincus, 2003; Pincus & Delfin, 2003). These programs also provide training, consultation, and support to psychologists who are concerned about a colleague. Ultimately through rehabilitation, professional monitoring, or other disciplinary action, the combined aims of the ethical principles of conduct and the oversight of licensure boards are designed to reduce the chances that an impaired psychologist could do harm by practicing psychology when competence is compromised (American Psychological Association, 2006).

Biological Treatments

LO 10.20 Outline the core principles of biological interventions for substance use disorders

Biological interventions play an important role in the treatment of substance use disorders. They can be used as the sole intervention or as an adjunct to psychological or community interventions. This is a burgeoning area of research as more is learned about the impact of drugs on the brain and the response of the brain to drugs (Verrico et al., 2013).

Withdrawal symptoms can be severe and occasionally lethal. **Detoxification**, medically supervised drug withdrawal, is necessary to treat substance use disorders—but it is only the first step. Medications can reduce withdrawal symptoms and decrease the likelihood of adverse effects (Agabio et al., 2013). For example, benzodiazepines can be administered to reduce the likelihood of an alcoholic developing DTs.

Agonist substitution is a type of therapy that substitutes a chemically similar safe medication for the drug of abuse (Stoops & Rush, 2013). *Chemically safe* means several things. First, the substitute drug binds with the same receptors as the target drug, thereby preventing any pharmacological effect ("high") of the target drug. Although the substitute shares many similarities with the target drug, it also differs in several key ways. The substitute works more slowly and has fewer acute pharmacological effects with no resulting high and subsequent crash. Although some potential for developing problems with the substitute drug may exist, these problems are typically far less severe than with the target drug. People taking an agonist substitution drug are still taking a drug regularly, but with few of the social, occupational, and physical impairments associated with the target drug. The most widely known agonist substitute is **methadone**, used as a replacement for heroin. Distributed under controlled conditions in "methadone clinics," methadone removes the substantial risk associated with obtaining and injecting heroin. Some individuals continue on methadone therapy indefinitely, but considerable evidence both in the United States (Gruber et al., 2008) and abroad (Hser et al., 2011) suggests that coupling methadone with counseling, individual psychotherapy, or contingency management improves treatment outcome.

The nicotine patch allows for controlled release of nicotine into the body and helps with smoking cessation.

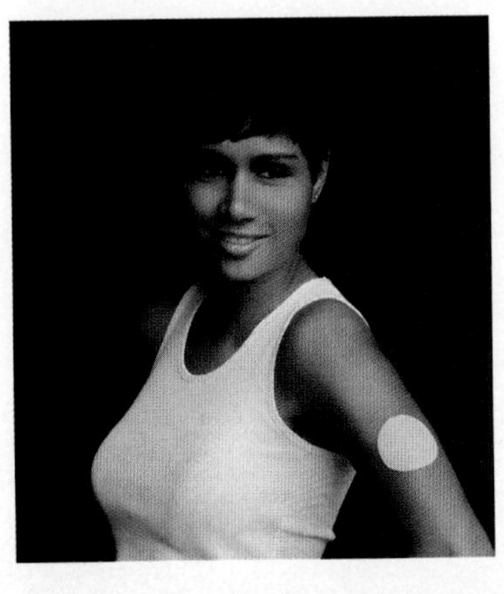

NICOTINE REPLACEMENT THERAPY Whereas methadone replacement substitutes one drug for another, some replacement therapies vary the *method* of drug delivery rather than the drug itself. **Nicotine replacement therapy (NRT)** is safe and effective when used as part of a comprehensive smoking cessation program. NRT is available over the counter as gum or a patch and by prescription as a puffer or inhaler or sublingual (under the tongue) lozenges. NRT replaces nicotine from cigarettes, reduces withdrawal symptoms, and helps the patient resist the urge to smoke. NRT approaches increase the odds of quitting approximately 1.5- to 2-fold both with and without additional counseling (Silagy et al., 2004).

ANTAGONIST TREATMENTS Because the positively reinforcing effects of drugs appear to be a major factor in their use, could drug use be discontinued if these sensations were blocked by a drug that *antagonized* (acted against) the action of the drug being abused? Several studies have examined the efficacy of the opioid antagonists *naltrexone* and *nalmefene* to treat alcohol use disorders (Woody, 2014). Naltrexone reduces the risk of relapse to drink heavily and the frequency of drinking when compared with placebo, but it does not substantially enhance abstinence (Garbutt et al., 1999). More recently, long-acting injectable preparations of naltrexone were found to reduce heavy drinking among alcohol-dependent patients during 6 months of therapy (Garbutt et al., 2005). Although antagonist drugs do not miraculously reverse drug use, they are a valuable pharmacological tool worth investigating further.

AVERSIVE TREATMENTS Similar to aversion therapy, aversive pharmacological interventions pair ingestion of the substance with a noxious physical reaction. The best known substance is *disulfiram*, or **Antabuse**. Disulfiram prevents the breakdown of *acetaldehyde* (a substance found in alcohol), and the buildup of this substance in the body produces the noxious feelings. While taking Antabuse, people who consume alcohol experience nausea, vomiting, and increased heart rate and respiration. Controlled studies of disulfiram reveal mixed results. Its use reduces drinking frequency, but minimal evidence has been found to support improved continuous abstinence rates (Garbutt et al., 1999). Discontinuing the drug is all that is required to return to drinking without the noxious symptoms.

VACCINES A truly novel approach to treatment is *immunopharmacotherapy*—or vaccination against drug use. A vaccine produces antibodies that bind to the targeted drug before it reaches the brain and therefore block its positive, reinforcing effects. Attaching drugs to proteins from the blood can trigger an immune response, and the body generates antibodies against the drugs. As early as 1974, researchers discovered that when rhesus monkeys already addicted to heroin were vaccinated, the monkeys significantly reduced the number

Table 10.3 Street Names for Drugs

Type of Drug	Street Names
Marijuana	pot, weed, reefer, dope, ganja, grass, herb, bud, green, trees, skunk, smoke, sinsemilla
Heroin	brown sugar, smack, horse, dope, H or Big H, junk, skag, skunk, white horse, China white
Cocaine	candy, snow, rock, flake, blow and toot, C, coke, bump, Charlie, white
Crack cocaine	apple jacks, basa, baseball, BJs, Baby T, badrock, beemers, candy, crumbs, dice, hotcakes, jelly beans, rocks, fat bags, nuggets, ice cubes, cookies, dip, crib, egg, fries, garbage rock, golf ball, goofball, hard rock, hubba, love, kangaroo, piles
Amphetamines	Bennie or Bennies, amped or ampes, benz or benzies, cartwheels, Blue Mollies or Black Mollies, speed, jelly beans or super jellies, hearts, uppers, pick me ups or wake me ups, wake ups, get ups, boot ups, sparkles, dexies or dexy, footballs, eye poppers or eye openers, lid poppers or lid openers, oranges, fast lightning or lightning
Methamphetamine	meth, ice, crank, speed, jibb, tina, glass, fire, chalk and crystal, crystal meth
Inhalants	laughing gas, poppers, snappers, whippets
LSD	A, acid, black star, blotter, boomers, cubes, Elvis, golden dragon, L, microdot, paper acid, pink robots, superman, twenty-five, yellow sunshine, ying yang
Barbiturates	barbs, reds, red birds, phennies, tooies, yellows, yellow jackets
Benzodiazepines	candy, downers, sleeping pills, tranks, totem poles, chill pills, french fries, tranqs, blues, z-bar, bricks, benzos
Prescription drugs	hillbilly heroin, oxy, oc, oxycotton, oxycet, percs, happy pills, vikes, Watson-387, tuss, big boys, cotton, percs, morph, kicker

SOURCE: Hser et al., 2011.

Examining the EVIDENCE
Controlled Drinking?

- **The Facts** Many conceptualizations (disease model) and treatment approaches (AA, therapeutic communities) for alcohol are based on the idea that complete abstinence is the only acceptable approach to overcoming alcohol dependence. Over the past 50 years, researchers have begun to question this all-or-nothing approach.
- **The Evidence** Mark and Linda Sobell conducted the best-known study of what is now called *controlled drinking* (Sobell & Sobell, 1973). Results indicated that people receiving behavioral treatment for alcoholism combined with learning skills to engage in nonproblematic drinking had significantly more "days functioning well" during a 2-year follow-up period than those receiving a treatment aimed at abstinence (Sobell & Sobell, 1973, 1978). Can individuals with alcohol use disorder be taught to control their drinking?
- **Let's Examine the Evidence** Although this research was well received, it also had detractors (Pendery et al., 1982) and inspired spirited criticism in sources such as the *New York Times* and the television news show *60 Minutes*, suggesting that the research was both flawed and potentially fraudulent. However, an independent investigation of the Sobells' research supported the integrity of this work on all counts. Alan Marlatt, a leading researcher in the area of alcohol, suggested that the media closely covered the critiques of the Sobells' work but paid little attention to the evidence supporting its integrity and validity (Marlatt et al., 1993). The controversy over controlled drinking still continues, but it has taken its toll on the scientific community, and research directly bearing on this question has been pursued less frequently than might be expected (Coldwell & Heather, 2006).
- **What Are Alternative Explanations for This Controversy?** Probably the clearest finding from this research is that controlled drinking approaches may be especially suited to individuals with less severe drinking problems (Sobell & Sobell, 1995), although other researchers question the apparent consensus that it is not a suitable approach for more severe drinkers (Heather, 1995). Today the spirit of controlled drinking lives on, but the name has not widely survived. "Harm reduction" is the most common name now used (Marlatt et al., 1993). Although harm reduction shares many of the same goals of controlled drinking, it has received less critical attack, and initial evidence is encouraging (Witkiewitz & Marlatt, 2006). Furthermore, treatment approaches such as motivational interviewing (Miller, 1983) place the client's preferences and goals at its center and allow patients to choose controlled drinking as a strategy for treatment. Yet it is notable that in many cases even motivational interviewing is conducted within settings favoring an abstinence-only approach (Coldwell & Heather, 2006).
- **Conclusion** Although no one would argue that abstinence is bad, researchers in the tradition of controlled drinking hope to provide alternatives for people who may be able to attain a normal and healthy life without completely avoiding alcohol.

of times they pressed a lever for heroin, indicating that the vaccine blocked the heroin high (Bonese et al., 1974). Since then, animal models have been developed for immunization against cocaine, nicotine, hallucinogens, and methamphetamine, suggesting the potential efficacy of these treatments in humans. Human clinical trials are under way for vaccines against cocaine and nicotine (Meijler et al., 2004). If effective, this intervention could have intriguing social ramifications. Will parents vaccinate their children against nicotine, alcohol, marijuana, and other drugs just as they do against polio, measles, and mumps? Will the tobacco companies resist the vaccines because they will infringe on the free market? Will prisoners who have committed drug-related crimes be vaccinated against their will? Many important ethical and social questions will arise as the efficacy of the immunopharmacotherapy approach becomes clear.

Sex and Racial/Ethnic Differences in Treatment

LO 10.21 Identify sex and racial/ethnic differences in treatment seeking for substance use disorders.

Women face unique barriers to obtaining treatment for substance use disorders, which may account for findings suggesting that women are less likely to enter treatment than men. For instance, limited access to child care and society's punitive attitude toward mothers who abuse drugs can keep them from admitting that they have a problem and seeking help (Allen, 1995). Women also differ from men in their response to treatment, although the data are inconsistent. Several studies have reported that women are more likely than men to drop out of substance abuse treatment, but this finding is far from conclusive (Bride, 2001; Joe et al., 1999; McCaul et al., 2001; Simpson et al., 1997).

Strikingly, 8.9 million individuals in the United States are estimated to have co-occurring mental health and substance use disorders (Priester et al., 2016). An integrative review suggests that the ability to access and engage in treatment is especially difficult for individuals with schizophrenia and intellectual disabilities. Women cited lack of trust in institutions, the absence of on-site child care, and fear of the criminal justice system (especially single mothers) as barriers to accessing treatment. Underrepresented minorities and individuals of low socioeconomic status view stigma associated with treatment to add to their already marginalized status (Eliason and Amodia, 2006). These researchers also suggest that societal oppression contributes to differential, inaccurate, and underdiagnosis of individuals who are racial/ethnic, gender, or sexual minorities.

Our ability to truly understand how best to prevent and treat substance use disorders will require a solid foundation of research that considers the specific needs and challenges associated with sex, ethnicity and race, and socioeconomic status. Considerable care must be taken not to assume that any particular conclusion applies to all groups.

Learning Objective Summaries

LO 10.18 Compare approaches and philosophies of cognitive, behavioral, and 12-step approaches to treatment of substance use disorders.

Relapse prevention, a cognitive-behavioral strategy, uses *functional analysis* to identify the antecedents and consequences of drug use and then to develop alternative cognitive and behavioral skills to reduce the risk of future drug use. Motivational interviewing identifies where people are on the transtheoretical model stages of change and then uses principles of motivational psychology to produce rapid, internally motivated change and to mobilize the patient's own resources for change. Behavior approaches may pair substance use with aversive stimuli (aversion therapy), provide rewards for treatment compliance (contingency management), or conduct exposure-based treatment (virtual reality therapy). Twelve-step programs begin with the realization that the individual is powerless over the addiction and provide a structured approach to remaining sober. Members attend regular meetings and are assigned a sponsor whom they can call if they feel unable to maintain sobriety or need support.

LO 10.19 Evaluate the ethical complexities of confronting an impaired colleague.

Colleagues are ethically obligated to intervene if they observe an impaired colleague. This can be a very difficult step to take for fear of alienating the individual, being wrong in their suspicions, being labeled a whistle-blower, or feeling as if they crossed an inappropriate boundary. As a licensed profession, state psychology licensing boards have guidelines about substance use in professionals and, depending on the problem and whether harm has occurred to a patient, disciplinary options can include monitoring the psychologist's work for a period of time, mandatory treatment, and even revoking the psychologist's license to practice.

LO 10.20 Outline the core principles of biological interventions for substance use disorders.

Detoxification refers to medically supervised drug withdrawal. Medications can reduce withdrawal symptoms and decrease the likelihood of adverse effects. Agonist substitution is a type of therapy that substitutes a chemically similar safe medication for the drug of abuse. Antagonist substitution blocks the reinforcing action of the drug being used. Aversive pharmacological interventions pair ingestion of the substance with a noxious physical reaction. Finally, immunopharmacotherapy—or vaccination against drug use—administers a vaccine that produces antibodies that bind to the targeted drug before it reaches the brain and therefore blocks its positive, reinforcing effects.

LO 10.21 Identify sex and racial/ethnic differences in treatment seeking for substance use disorders.

Women are less likely to enter treatment for substance use disorders and may be more likely to drop out. Reasons may include the absence of on-site childcare facilities and fear of social services. Treatment alternatives are also less available for individuals of low socioeconomic status and for racial and ethnic minorities. It is critical to note that "one size does not fit all" when it comes to the treatment of substance use disorders.

Critical Thinking

With some psychiatric illnesses, the patient and the therapist are "on the same side." They both want to take the symptoms away (e.g., "Doctor, please help me get rid of the phobia that interferes with my life"). With substance use disorders, this is often not the case. If you are the therapist, what are the therapeutic challenges of working with a patient whose goals may differ from yours?

Real SCIENCE Real LIFE

Jessica—Treating Poly-Substance Use

THE PATIENT

The court mandated Jessica, 36 years old, to 30 days of residential treatment at a community center.

THE PROBLEM

At the time of her arrest, Jessica was living with her boyfriend of 3 years, their 2-year-old son, and one child from a previous relationship. She had dropped out of high school but did get her GED. She had a series of low-paying jobs and most recently lost her job as a cashier at a diner after she stole money from the cash register. She depended financially on her boyfriend, whose source of income was unknown. When Jessica arrived at the facility, she denied substance use within the prior 24 hours and reported some physical and psychological discomfort due to withdrawal. She was agitated, her speech was pressured, and her thoughts and speech were disorganized. She denied any hallucinations or delusions.

At intake, Jessica met the criteria for current severe crack/cocaine and mild alcohol use disorder. In the past, she had used marijuana, amphetamines, and heroin. A previous HIV test was negative. Her family history was positive for heroin and cocaine use disorders (father), alcoholism (mother), and death by heroin overdose (brother). Her boyfriend was a crack user who was not interested in receiving treatment, and he had interfered with her earlier attempts to get sober. Jessica worried that her daughter was using drugs and engaging in unsafe sexual activity, which concerned her greatly because she hoped her daughter could escape the cycle of high-risk behaviors that characterized her family.

A complete behavioral analysis identified the triggers associated with her cocaine and alcohol use. Her boyfriend, a drug dealer, was a major trigger in her use. Continuing to depend on him financially would seriously increase her risk of relapse.

During her residential treatment, Jessica learned skills for resisting urges to use. She worked through lapse and relapse scenarios and planned strategies for remaining clean. She had several family meetings with her sister and brother-in-law to mobilize family support. The team also helped her mobilize her faith and organized several outings to her church to meet with people who knew her situation and would provide support after treatment. Jessica also attended AA meetings regularly while in treatment and planned to continue attendance after discharge. While in treatment, she was trained in parenting skills. Her daughter, who had indeed started using drugs herself, was referred for treatment. Her social worker helped Jessica to find job placement and low-cost housing.

ASSESSING THE SITUATION

First, discuss the genetic and environmental factors that led Jessica to develop substance use disorder. What are the complicating factors in Jessica's life that her treating clinician should pay attention to? Design a treatment plan for Jessica. What might the high-risk triggers be for relapse after Jessica achieves abstinence?

THE TREATMENT

Jessica's mandated treatment followed her arrest for stealing from the diner, which was her only arrest. She had had three previous contacts with the legal system when neighbors, fearing for her children, called the police in response to loud yelling and throwing objects against the wall. On each occasion, the police left, giving the couple a warning only. Jessica had denied any abuse or imminent danger to herself or her children.

The only hint that Jessica was interested in treatment for her addictions was her concern about her daughter and worry that her baby would be placed in foster care. Although she was clear that her boyfriend was not supporting her treatment, she did mention it to a sister as well as members of her church who she felt would support her.

In addition to her substance use problems, Jessica reported a period lasting for about the past 2 months when her mood had been consistently low. She reported decreased appetite and poor sleep.

Following the team's review of her initial assessment, they developed a preliminary treatment plan that identified four targets: treat her crack/cocaine use disorder, treat her alcohol use disorder, further evaluate her depression, and mobilize social support for continued abstinence. Her team felt that even though the treatment was court mandated, Jessica was sufficiently concerned about her children that they could enhance her desire to change her behaviors.

THE TREATMENT OUTCOME

At the end of the 30-day treatment, Jessica was afraid to be discharged. She felt as if she had only started to get clean, and she did not know what she would do without the daily support of the center staff. When she was admitted, she had feared that 30 days was a life sentence, but now she knew that it was really too short a time for true recovery. She was realistic about her chances of staying sober. She knew that the thought of financial security would tempt her to go back to her dealer boyfriend, but each time she considered that, she had to pair that desire with her concern for her children's welfare. She was stepped down to weekly sessions with her social worker to provide ongoing support and early identification of any lapses or relapses. Jessica continued to attend AA meetings at her church. Her sister helped out by providing child care while Jessica worked. In return, Jessica helped her sister with her housekeeping job.

At the 1-year anniversary of her discharge, Jessica was still sober. She managed to continue to attend AA, had become a regular member of her church community, and had become a better mother to her daughter, who had also remained drug free since her intervention. She continued to have mood fluctuations and noted honestly that at times she felt poorly equipped to put the required energy into remaining sober. However, her children remained her primary motivator, and her social and family supports helped carry her through the times of highest risk.

Key Terms

abstinence violation effect, p. 402
agonist substitution, p. 406
alcohol cirrhosis, p. 376
amphetamines, p. 382
Antabuse, p. 407
aversion therapy, p. 404
barbiturates, p. 385
benzodiazepines, p. 385
caffeine, p. 368
cocaine, p. 383
contingency management approaches, p. 404
crystal methamphetamine, p. 382
delirium tremens, p. 375
detoxification, p. 406
Ecstasy, p. 382
fetal alcohol syndrome, p. 377
hallucinogens, p. 388
inhalants, p. 389
lysergic acid diethylamide (LSD), p. 388
marijuana, p. 379
methadone, p. 406
nicotine, p. 371
nicotine replacement therapy (NRT), p. 406
opioids, p. 386
relapse prevention, p. 402
sedative drugs, p. 385
substance intoxication, p. 366
substance use, p. 366
tetrahydrocannabinol, p. 379
tolerance, p. 367
transtheoretical model, p. 402
Wernicke-Korsakoff syndrome, p. 376
withdrawal, p. 367

Chapter 11

Schizophrenia Spectrum and Other Psychotic Disorders

Chapter Learning Objectives

Psychotic Disorders

LO 11.1 Distinguish between a psychotic experience and the psychotic disorders.

LO 11.2 Understand that schizophrenia is not a condition involving "split personality," nor does it usually involve violent behavior toward others.

LO 11.3 Identify the positive, negative, and cognitive symptoms of schizophrenia.

LO 11.4 Describe how schizophrenia affects all aspects of personal functioning.

LO 11.5 Discuss how sex, race, and ethnicity affect the clinical presentation of schizophrenia.

	LO 11.6	Describe how developmental factors affect the clinical presentation of schizophrenia.
	LO 11.7	Identify the other psychotic disorders and how they differ from schizophrenia.
Etiology of Schizophrenia	**LO 11.8**	Discuss the neurodevelopmental model of schizophrenia.
	LO 11.9	Understand the interplay of genetic, biological, psychological, and environmental factors in the etiology of schizophrenia.
Treatment of Schizophrenia and Other Psychotic Disorders	**LO 11.10**	Identify efficacious pharmacological treatments for schizophrenia.
	LO 11.11	Identify efficacious psychological treatments for schizophrenia.

What I remember most is how disoriented and frightened I felt. With little warning, my world had simply shifted under my feet. Over a period of several months, I began to believe that messages were being left for me in graffiti across campus. I also began to believe that my phone was being tapped. My friends insisted I was mistaken. But no one knew enough to realize anything was wrong. And then one day everything changed.

One afternoon I realized the people on the radio were talking to me, much the way one has an intuition about a geometry proof, a sudden dawning of clarity or understanding. This clarity was more compelling than reality. It took me several weeks to put the pieces together. What I had known all my life was wrong. My friends were not real friends: at best they were neutral, at worst they were spies for the CIA. Graduate school was a luxury I was no longer allowed. There was a secret history of the world to which I now became attuned. It involved the NSA, the CIA, and the stealth bomber, which flew just out of sight in order to register details regarding my movements. An evil dictator was gathering power to himself and he meant to perpetuate a holocaust on the Nation. Only the American resistance, of which I was now a part, stood in his way.

As time passed I became proficient at reading code. Most of my days were spent reading and responding to the newspaper so that the resistance could gather its military and economic resources to retake territory that had been lost. I learned to communicate by deciphering bits of conversation, reading newspaper articles, and listening to songs on the radio. Everyone could read my mind, so unless I was engaged in conversation, I spoke mostly in my head. I could not read anyone else's mind so I remained dependent on the media for information.

Within 6 months, I became adept at coordinating different avenues of information. However, I was living a nightmare. When I shut my eyes, I saw neon-colored cartoon characters that zoomed in and out of my field of vision. They were so bright it hurt. At night I would keep my eyes open until I fell asleep from exhaustion. I also lived in terror of the evil dictator and his minions. I never knew where they might be or how to evade them. I begged my superiors to have me killed. When it became clear that this was not going to happen, I took matters into my own hands. Within the course of a week, I tried to commit suicide four times.

SOURCE: Weiner, S. K. (2003). First person account: Living with the delusions and effects of schizophrenia. *Schizophrenia Bulletin, 29*, 877–879.

Psychotic Disorders

Psychotic disorders are characterized by unusual thinking, distorted perceptions, and odd behaviors. People with a psychotic disorder are considered to be out of touch with reality and to be unable to think in a logical or coherent manner. They sometimes behave oddly, talking or mumbling to themselves or gesturing at someone that no one else can see. Some of the psychotic disorders are serious and chronic, while others are temporary states of confusion. Before we discuss the different disorders, it is necessary to understand the abnormal cognitive, perceptual, and behavioral symptoms that define these conditions.

What Is Psychosis?

LO 11.1 Distinguish between a psychotic experience and the psychotic disorders.

Psychosis is a severe mental condition characterized by a loss of contact with reality. This usually takes the form of a **delusion** (a false belief), a **hallucination** (a false sensory perception), or both. Both of these phenomena are illustrated in our opening case,

Delusions and hallucinations are characteristic of schizophrenia. The person who experiences them is in poor touch with reality and often behaves in ways that seem strange or bizarre.

which involves several false beliefs (being spied on, being part of a resistance movement) and false sensory perceptions (seeing cartoon characters that were not there). Such a dramatic loss of contact with reality can be quite frightening and can affect every aspect of functioning, even leading the affected person to behaviors as extreme as attempting suicide.

Although psychotic symptoms can be quite disturbing, hallucinations or delusions alone do not necessarily mean that a psychotic disorder, such as schizophrenia, is present. Psychotic symptoms may also occur among adults with other psychological disorders including bipolar disorder, major depressive disorder, posttraumatic stress disorder (PTSD), and substance-related disorders. Children with bipolar disorder, obsessive-compulsive disorder (OCD), autism spectrum disorder, and conduct disorder (see Chapter 13) also may have psychotic symptoms (Biederman et al., 2004).

> Nadia is 10 years old. She is sad and very irritable. She cries all the time and refuses to go to school. Her parents brought her to the clinic because of her school refusal behavior, but during the interview, she revealed to the clinician that for the past month, she has been hearing voices. One is the voice of Snow White, and the other voice sounds like an alien. They whispered "bad things" to her, but she will not say what the voices said to her. A month later, when Nadia's mood improved, she said the voices had gone away.

Psychotic experiences such as delusional thinking and hallucinations may also occur in people with physical illnesses such as brain tumors, major or mild neurocognitive disorder due to Alzheimer's disease and Parkinson's disease, and after physical damage to the brain such as brain injuries or exposure to toxic substances. When psychotic experiences occur suddenly, the presence of a serious brain-related medical condition must first be considered.

Finally, psychotic experiences sometimes occur even when no psychological disorder is present. Brief or limited psychotic experiences are common, occurring in 5 to 8% of adults (van Os et al., 2009), and may include thoughts of persecution, a feeling that someone is stealing or manipulating one's thoughts, or hearing voices or sounds no one else can hear. Additionally, individuals without psychotic disorders report that often, the voices are positive; they were not upset by the presence of the voices and felt in control of the experience (Honig et al., 1998). In contrast, people suffering from psychosis perceive the voices as negative and do not feel in control of the experience.

Psychotic symptoms may thus occur across many different physical conditions and psychological disorders and even at times among people with no apparent physical or psychological disorder. However, psychotic symptoms are most often considered as one of the defining characteristics of schizophrenia.

What Is Schizophrenia?

LO 11.2 Understand that schizophrenia is *not* a condition involving "split personality," nor does it usually involve violent behavior toward others.

Schizophrenia is a severe psychological disorder characterized by disorganization in thought, perception, and behavior. People with schizophrenia do not think logically, perceive the world accurately, or behave in a way that permits normal everyday life and work. They may worry that the government is spying on them or that voices on the radio are speaking directly to them—giving them instructions about how to behave or transmitting messages only they can understand. As a result of these delusions and/or hallucinations, they behave oddly, appearing to others to be talking to themselves or

SIDE by SIDE case studies

Dimensions of Behavior: From Adaptive to Maladaptive

Adaptive Behavior Case Study

Comforting Thoughts—Adaptive

Daphne had always had a close relationship with her mother. When her mother developed breast cancer, Daphne took care of her, taking a leave of absence from her job and moving in with her mother to make sure that she received the care that she needed. After her mother died, Daphne was devastated. She stayed on to settle her mother's affairs and sell her house. Daphne had mixed feelings when the house was sold. She had grown up there, and knowing that she would never come back was hard. After packing up the last of her belongings, she stood in the kitchen—the place where she and her mother had spent so many happy times. With tears in her eyes, she said, "Well Mom, I guess I have to go." Daphne tells everyone that clear as could be, her mother replied, "Yes, honey. Go live your life." Daphne often relives that moment, feeling comforted by her mother's last words.

Maladaptive Behavior Case Study

Scary Thoughts—Maladaptive

Amare had always had a pleasant relationship with his father-in-law, but last week they had some cross words. It was nothing really serious, and Amare planned to apologize when he saw his father-in-law again next week. However, before that could happen, his father-in-law had a heart attack and died. Amare became deeply depressed, regretting that he never had the chance to tell his father-in-law he was sorry. After the funeral, he started hearing voices accusing him of being a bad son-in-law and causing his father-in-law's death by his cross words and suggesting that perhaps he did not deserve to live. The voices would not let him sleep; they were loud and merciless, calling him "killer." About a week later, his wife found him in the bedroom, arguing with the voices and insisting that his wife had to be hearing them too. Frightened by his behavior, his wife called the police and had Amare hospitalized.

doing things such as barricading themselves inside their homes to prevent being kidnapped by an unseen enemy. Schizophrenia is a serious psychological disorder because the condition creates severe impairment and is often chronic even with the best available treatments. However, it is important to remember that among people with a diagnosis of schizophrenia, there is a great deal of variability in symptoms, treatment response, course, and outcome (Owen et al., 2016).

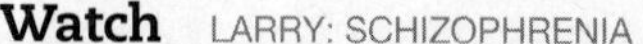

Watch LARRY: SCHIZOPHRENIA

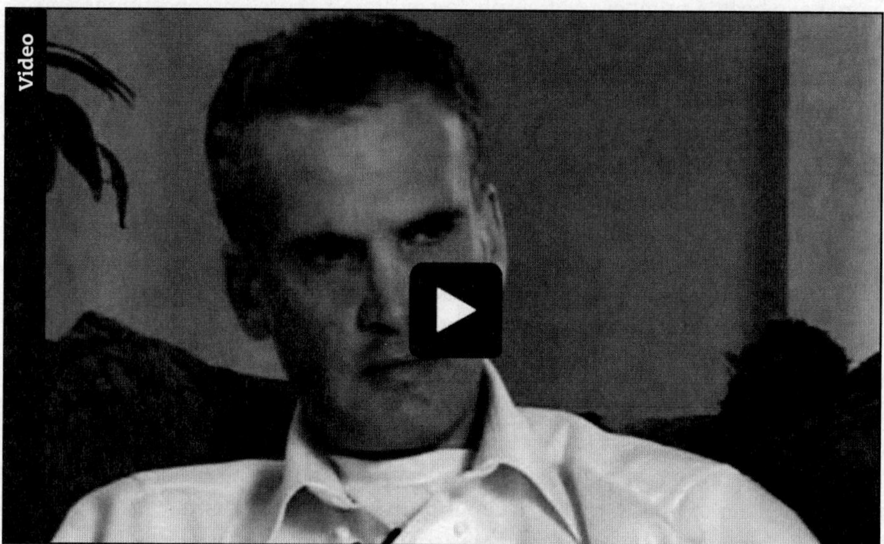

As discussed in Chapter 1, the German psychiatrist Emil Kraepelin and the Swiss psychiatrist Eugen Bleuler first defined schizophrenia more than 100 years ago. Kraepelin called this disorder **dementia praecox** to highlight its pervasive disturbances of perceptual and cognitive faculties (*dementia*) and its early life onset (*praecox*) and to distinguish it from the dementia associated with old age. Bleuler focused on four core symptoms of the disorder: ambivalence, disturbances of affect, disturbance of association, and preference for fantasy over reality (Tsuang et al., 2000). Bleuler renamed the condition *schizophrenia*, combining the Greek words for "split" (*schizo*) and "mind" (*phrene*), to highlight the splitting of thought, affect, and behavior that occurs among people with this disorder.

Because almost everyone has felt sad at some time, it is easy for most people to understand that depression is "extreme" sadness. However, it is difficult for people to understand the unusual symptoms of schizophrenia, a disorder that challenges mental health professionals as well. Yet during the past 100 years, our understanding of the clinical presentation, etiology, and treatment of schizophrenia has improved substantially. Before examining its symptoms, it is important to clarify several common misconceptions about schizophrenia.

Perhaps because it is so difficult to understand the experience of schizophrenia, many mistaken ideas about this disorder exist. This lack of understanding has led to many inaccurate media and literary portrayals of schizophrenia. Robert Louis Stevenson's *The Strange Case of Dr. Jekyll and Mr. Hyde* is a classic description of two contradictory personalities that exist within the same individual. Dr. Henry Jekyll is sensitive and kind; Mr. Edward Hyde is a violent murderer. Even today the term *Jekyll and Hyde* is used to describe behaviors that appear to be polar opposites yet exist within the same person. However, people with schizophrenia do *not* have "split personalities." The Greek word *schizo* describes the split between an individual's thoughts and feelings, not the splitting of the personality. Yet this misunderstanding is common. According to a Harris Poll conducted for the National Organization on Disability in the United States, about two-thirds of people surveyed believe that "split personality" is part of schizophrenia (http://www.abc.net.au/science/k2/moments/s1200266.htm).

A similar misconception is that schizophrenia involves multiple personalities. As discussed in Chapter 6, a condition called *dissociative identity disorder* (DID) does exist. People with DID are considered to have two or more distinct personalities, each with its own thoughts, feelings, and behaviors. As illustrated by novels such as *The Three Faces of Eve* and *Sybil*, one personality may be unaware of the other's behavior. However, each personality perceives, deals with, and interacts with the environment successfully. This ability to successfully negotiate with the environment is what differentiates people with schizophrenia from people with DID. Schizophrenia results in an inability to perceive the environment appropriately or deal with it adequately. In short, people with schizophrenia do *not* have split or multiple personalities.

There have been a number of attempts to counteract these misconceptions and to educate the general population about the origins of schizophrenia. Educational attempts have included online informational text (Wiesjahn et al., 2016) and a documentary film (Thonon et al., 2016). Both approaches were effective in changing public perceptions about the origins of schizophrenia and the negative stereotypes (people with schizophrenia are dangerous), although the long-term effects of these educational efforts are unknown.

Schizophrenia in Depth

LO 11.3 Identify the positive, negative, and cognitive symptoms of schizophrenia.

The symptoms of schizophrenia include delusions, hallucinations, disorganized speech, disorganized or catatonic behavior, and negative symptoms (see "DSM-5: Schizophrenia"). Delusions and hallucinations are sometimes called positive symptoms, but in this case, the term *positive* does not mean optimistic or upbeat; it denotes the *presence* of an abnormal behavior within the individual. **Positive symptoms**, the behaviors that people most often associate with schizophrenia, consist of unusual thoughts, feelings, and behaviors. They vary in intensity and in many cases are responsive to treatment (Tirupati et al., 2006).

One positive symptom of schizophrenia is the presence of delusions, which are fixed beliefs that are not changeable when presented with conflicting evidence (American Psychiatric Association, 2013; see Table 11.1 for a list of different types of delusions). **Persecutory delusions** are the most common. These consist of the belief that someone is harming or attempting to harm the person. Other delusions include the belief that the

Table 11.1 Types of Delusions and Hallucinations Found in People with Schizophrenia

Symptom	Example
Delusions	
Influence	Beliefs that behavior or thoughts are controlled by others including thought withdrawal, broadcasting, or insertion or mind reading by another person
Self-significance	Thoughts of grandeur, reference (random events, objects, and behaviors of others have a particular and unusual significance to oneself—such as the messages left in graffiti in the opening case), religion (believing that one is a supreme being), guilt, or sin
Persecution or paranoid	Thoughts that others are out to harm the person
Somatic	Belief that one's body is rotting away
Hallucinations	
Auditory	Noises or voices, perhaps speaking to or about the person
Visual	Visions of religious figures or dead people
Olfactory	Smells
Gustatory	Tastes
Somatic	Feelings of pain or deterioration of parts of one's body or feeling that things are crawling on or in the skin or the body

SOURCES: Kimhy, D., Goetz, R., Yale, S., Corcoran, C., & Malaspina, D. (2005). Delusions in individuals with schizophrenia: Factor structure, clinical correlates, and putative neurobiology. *Psychopathology, 38,* 338–344; Mueser, K. T., Bellack, A. S., & Brady, E. U. (1990). Hallucinations in schizophrenia. *Acta Psychiatrica Scandinavica, 82,* 26–29.

person is a special agent/individual (as in our opening case) (Appelbaum et al., 1999). Although most delusions are distressing in nature, sometimes the delusion is grandiose with negative events occurring when others do not act in accord with the delusional content.

> Kim was a college student of Korean descent and was hospitalized after he was found wandering around on the city streets, yelling at strangers because they did not bow when he walked by. Upon questioning, Kim revealed that he was the emperor of Korea and that people on the street were not giving him the deference appropriate to his royal status.

Other common delusions are **delusions of influence**, which include beliefs that others control one's behavior or thoughts. People with schizophrenia often believe that their thoughts are being manipulated by processes known as *thought withdrawal, thought broadcasting*, or *thought insertion*. People with delusions of influence believe that the government is inserting thoughts into their head or that evil forces, such as alien invaders, are "stealing" thoughts out of their head. In thought broadcasting, the person believes that his or her private thoughts are being revealed to others, usually by being transmitted over the radio or television.

A second positive symptom is hallucinations (which are perception-like experiences without an external stimulus, such as hearing voices when no one is there or seeing visions that no one else sees). Auditory hallucinations are most common (experienced by 71% of one sample; Mueser et al., 1990) and can range from simple noises to one or more voices of either sex. Voices are most commonly negative in quality and content but on occasion can be comforting or kind (Copolov et al., 2004). Auditory hallucinations that appear to be exclusive to people with schizophrenia are voices that keep a running commentary on the individual's behavior or several voices that have a conversation. Visual hallucinations are less common (14% in one sample) but do occur, often in people with the most severe form of the disorder (Mueser et al., 1990).

People with schizophrenia sometimes believe that their thoughts are being tampered with, for example, being removed from their heads or broadcast on TV. This is a *delusion*, a false belief.

DSM-5

Criteria for Schizophrenia

A. Two (or more) of the following, each present for a significant portion of time during a 1-month period (or less if successfully treated). At least one of these must be (1), (2), or (3):

1. Delusions.
2. Hallucinations.
3. Disorganized speech (e.g., frequent derailment or incoherence).
4. Grossly disorganized or catatonic behavior.
5. Negative symptoms (i.e., diminished emotional expression or avolition).

B. For a significant portion of the time since the onset of the disturbance, level of functioning in one or more major areas, such as work, interpersonal relations, or self-care, is markedly below the level achieved prior to the onset (or when the onset is in childhood or adolescence, there is failure to achieve expected level of interpersonal, academic, or occupational functioning).

C. Continuous signs of the disturbance persist for at least 6 months. This 6-month period must include at least 1 month of symptoms (or less if successfully treated) that meet Criterion A (i.e., active-phase symptoms) and may include periods of prodromal or residual symptoms. During these prodromal or residual periods, the signs of the disturbance may be manifested by only negative symptoms or by two or more symptoms listed in Criterion A present in an attenuated form (e.g., odd beliefs, unusual perceptual experiences).

D. Schizoaffective disorder and depressive or bipolar disorder with psychotic features have been ruled out because either 1) no major depressive or manic episodes have occurred concurrently with the active-phase symptoms, or 2) if mood episodes have occurred during active-phase symptoms, they have been present for a minority of the total duration of the active and residual periods of the illness.

E. The disturbance is not attributable to the physiological effects of a substance (e.g., a drug of abuse, a medication) or another medical condition.

F. If there is a history of autism spectrum disorder or a communication disorder of childhood onset, the additional diagnosis of schizophrenia is made only if prominent delusions or hallucinations, in addition to the other required symptoms of schizophrenia, are also present for at least 1 month (or less if successfully treated).

Common examples of visual hallucinations include seeing the devil or a dead relative or a friend. About 15% of hallucinations are *tactile* (touch). *Olfactory* (smell) and *gustatory* (taste) hallucinations are the least common types (11%).

> John was diagnosed with schizophrenia. Despite medication, he continued to have auditory hallucinations consisting of voices that talked to him or directed him to do certain things. John talked back to the voices or laughed aloud at something that they said. Each day, John came to the local mental health clinic for the free coffee provided to patients waiting for an appointment. He rarely had an appointment, but the staff was sympathetic toward him and would let him sit in the waiting room and drink coffee. He was never violent, but his behavior often disturbed the clinic patients unfamiliar with schizophrenia. On many occasions, John's behavior became too upsetting to the other patients, and the staff had to ask him to leave. Even though he was hallucinating, a staff member would approach him and say, "John, it is time to go now." Immediately, John would look up, greet the staff member by name, say, "Sure, see you tomorrow," and calmly leave the clinic.

John's behavior illustrates a very important point about people suffering with schizophrenia. Hallucinations may persist despite adequate medication dosages, but many patients are able to function at some level and maintain some contact with reality even while hallucinating.

Another positive symptom is disorganized thinking, which is usually assessed by abnormality of speech. When untreated, individuals with schizophrenia usually show strange speech patterns that indicate deterioration in their cognitive functioning. Some examples of this cognitive derailment or deterioration include **loose associations**, or thoughts that have little or no logical connection to the next thought (e.g., "I once worked at an Army base. It is important to soldier on. The Middle East—I like to travel, my favorite place is Arizona"). Another symptom is **thought blocking**, exemplified by unusually long pauses in the patient's speech that occur during a conversation. A third symptom is **clang associations** in which speech is governed by words that sound alike rather than words that have meaning (e.g., "I have bills, summer hills, bummer, drum solo"), rendering communication meaningless.

Another positive symptom is grossly disorganized or abnormal motor behavior. **Catatonia** is a condition in which a person is awake but is nonresponsive to external stimulation.

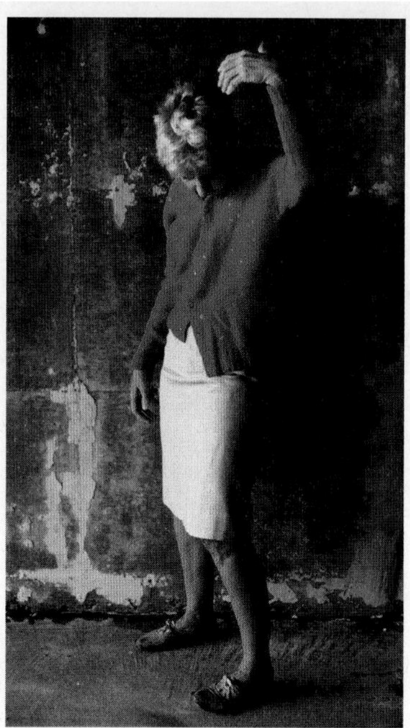

The catatonic feature of schizophrenia sometimes includes *waxy flexibility*, in which a person's limbs can be "posed" by someone else. The person remains in that position until he or she is moved again.

> The police brought Derek to the psychiatric emergency room. They found him standing naked in an alley downtown. He was mute, he did not make eye contact, and he seemed oblivious to the fact that the outside temperature was 35 degrees Fahrenheit. Because he would not speak or move on his own, Derek was hospitalized on the inpatient unit. The next morning, the nurses found him standing in the patient lounge, naked and motionless. They put him in pajamas and sat him in a chair—12 hours later, he was still sitting in the same position.

During a catatonic state, the patient may not move or make eye contact with others. He or she may be *mute* (without speech) or muscularly rigid (like a statue). When **waxy flexibility** is present, parts of the body (usually the arms) remain frozen in a particular posture when positioned that way by another person.

Positive symptoms may be quite dramatic, but they are not the only type of symptom. A second symptom category is the negative symptoms. In this case, the term *negative* does not refer to bad or horrific content but to the *absence* of behaviors that exist in the general population. In schizophrenia, **negative symptoms** are behaviors, emotions, or thought processes (cognitions) that exist in people without a psychiatric disorder but are absent (or are substantially diminished) in people with schizophrenia. Common negative symptoms include *diminished emotional expression, anhedonia, avolition* or apathy, *alogia*, and *psychomotor retardation*.

Diminished emotional expression describes reduced or immobile facial expressions and a flat, monotonic vocal tone that does not change even when the topic of conversation becomes emotionally laden. This inconsistency between a schizophrenic patient's facial expression and vocal tone and the content of his or her speech is one example of Bleuler's use of the word *split* to describe this disorder—for example, the patient may describe horrific thoughts with very little emotional expression in the face or voice. **Anhedonia** refers to a lack of capacity for pleasure: The person feels no joy or happiness. **Avolition**, or apathy, is an inability to initiate or follow through on plans. Often, relatives of people with schizophrenia interpret this apathy as simple laziness or a deliberate unwillingness to improve their life—an erroneous interpretation that can create distress and discord in the family environment (Mueser & McGurk, 2004). **Alogia** is a term used to describe decreased quality and/or quantity of speech. **Psychomotor retardation** describes slowed mental or physical activities. When psychomotor retardation affects cognition, for example, speech can be slowed to the point that it is difficult or impossible for others to follow the person's conversation. Unlike positive symptoms, which can be largely controlled by medication, negative symptoms are treatment-resistant; they tend to persist (Fenton & McGlashan, 1991) and restrict the person's ability to hold a job, go to school, or even take care of personal responsibilities such as bathing or dressing. See "DSM-5: Schizophrenia" for the symptoms that are necessary for a diagnosis of schizophrenia.

People with schizophrenia also have **cognitive impairments**. Deficits in cognitive abilities include impairments in visual and verbal learning and memory, inability to pay attention, decreased speed of information processing (how fast information is understood), and impaired abstract reasoning and executive functioning (ability to solve problems and make decisions; Green et al., 2004). To illustrate cognitive impairments, consider the following example of impaired abstract reasoning. People without schizophrenia interpret the phrase "People who live in glass houses should not throw stones" to mean that one should not criticize others when

Watch SYMPTOMS OF SCHIZOPHRENIA

they themselves also may have faults or flaws. However, many individuals with schizophrenia interpret that statement as follows: "It means that you should build a house with bricks because stones cannot break bricks." Cognitive deficits are one of the earliest signs of schizophrenia (Kurtz et al., 2005). Like negative symptoms, cognitive deficits are long-lasting and strongly correlated with functional impairment. However, for some people with schizophrenia, many aspects of cognitive functioning can remain in the normal or even the above-normal range (see "Real People, Real Disorders: Elyn Saks—*The Center Cannot Hold*").

In addition to general cognitive impairment, people with schizophrenia have a deficit in **social cognition**, which is the ability to perceive, interpret, and understand social information including other people's beliefs, attitudes, and emotions. People with schizophrenia are often deficient in the basic skills necessary for positive social interactions (Bellack et al., 1990; Penn et al., 2001) including the ability to perceive social nuances and engage in basic conversation. They show impairment in the ability to identify the emotional states of

REAL People REAL Disorders

Elyn Saks—*The Center Cannot Hold*

Professor Elyn Saks has schizophrenia. As a graduate student at Oxford University, she experienced auditory hallucinations and sought psychological treatment. Later during her time at Yale Law School, she required inpatient hospitalization and antipsychotic medication. She was told that her prognosis was "grave," that she was among the worst cases anyone had ever seen. "I would never live independently, hold a job, find a loving partner, get married. My home would be a board and care facility, my days spent watching TV in a day room with other people debilitated by mental illness. I would work at menial jobs."

Today Professor Saks is the Orrin B. Evans Professor of Law, Psychology, and Psychiatry and the Behavioral Sciences at the University of Southern California Gould Law School. She continues in therapy and takes medication but does not allow her symptoms to keep her from achieving her goals. She is an expert in mental health law and a recipient of the highly competitive "genius grant" from the McArthur Foundation. Saks's research suggests that many individuals with schizophrenia learn to manage their disorder not just through medication and therapy but by actively taking control. Some have identified triggers that precipitate symptoms, whereas others cognitively challenge the veracity of their hallucinations. One of the most frequent strategies to manage symptoms was work. As Professor Saks noted, "by engaging in work, the crazy stuff often recedes to the sidelines."

Elyn Saks

SOURCE: http://www.nytimes.com/2013/01/27/opinion/sunday/-schizophrenic-not-stupid.html?pagewanted=2&_r=0

other people and in the ability to comprehend sarcasm and lies (Sparks et al., 2010). People with schizophrenia also show reduced emotional responses to positive and negative events (Mathews & Barch, 2010). These skills, collectively known as social cognition, are necessary for effective academic, social, and occupational functioning (Green & Horan, 2010; Mathews & Barch, 2010) (see "Treatment of Schizophrenia and Other Psychotic Disorders").

A diagnosis of schizophrenia requires the presence of two of the five symptoms listed in criterion A (i.e., delusions, hallucinations, disorganized speech, grossly disorganized or catatonic behavior, or negative symptoms). So people with schizophrenia may have different symptoms. Common features of schizophrenia include paranoia, which includes delusions/hallucinations of a persecutory and frightening nature, and catatonia, which includes diminished motor activity—immobility (rigid posture, waxy flexibility)—and/or mutism unresponsive to commands or suggestions or excessive motor activity and/or **echolalia** (repeating verbatim what others say) that is purposeless in nature.

People with schizophrenia often have additional psychological disorders as well. Depression affects as many as 45% of people with schizophrenia (Leff et al., 1988), and approximately 5% commit suicide (Inskip et al., 1998; Palmer et al., 2005). Suicide rates are much higher during the initial onset of the disorder (Malla & Payne, 2005) and immediately before or after any inpatient hospitalization (Qin & Nordentoft, 2005). Acts of self-harm do not occur any more frequently for people with schizophrenia than for those with other psychological disorders. Factors that increase the likelihood of self-harm include previous depressed mood or previous suicide attempts, drug abuse, agitation or restlessness, fear of mental deterioration, or delusions or hallucinations that encourage such behavior (Symonds et al., 2006; Tarrier et al., 2006).

Approximately 47% of people with schizophrenia also have anxiety disorders (Kessler et al., 2005a). Because their disorder leaves schizophrenic patients vulnerable to victimization and violence as a result of poor living conditions or homelessness, PTSD is quite common, occurring in at least 43% of patient samples (Mueser et al., 2002). Substance-related disorder occurs among approximately 50% of individuals with schizophrenia (Regier et al., 1990). Among one group of patients with both schizophrenia and substance abuse, alcohol was the most commonly abused drug (89%), followed by marijuana (27%) and benzodiazepines (13%; Erkiran et al., 2006). Substance abuse results in more impairment in daily functioning than when schizophrenia occurs alone; people with both disorders are more likely to relapse and have to be rehospitalized, to be homeless, and to be noncompliant with their treatment (Drake & Brunette, 1998).

Could the use of alcohol or drugs by people with schizophrenia be a strategy to cope with or escape from negative symptoms such as the inability to feel pleasure (Drake & Mueser, 2002)? This is known as the *self-medication hypothesis* and has been the subject of much debate and controversy. A recent meta-analysis (i.e., a statistical procedure that analyzes the results of many different research studies) suggests that patients with both schizophrenia and substance use disorders have *fewer* negative symptoms than patients who do not abuse substances (Potvin et al., 2006). However, before concluding that substance abuse decreases symptoms (a cause-and-effect model), remember that all of these data are cross-sectional and correlational in nature (see Chapter 2). Actually, we can interpret the relationship between substance abuse and schizophrenia in two ways. First, substance abuse might relieve negative symptoms such as anhedonia or apathy, providing support for the self-medication hypothesis. Alternatively, those with fewer negative symptoms may simply be less likely to abuse these substances. Experimental and longitudinal designs rather than correlational studies are necessary to disentangle this issue.

Functional Impairment

LO 11.4 Describe how schizophrenia affects all aspects of personal functioning.

Dorrie was always shy and did not make friends easily. She was very bright and graduated summa cum laude from a local college in the South. She was admitted to a prestigious master's program in business administration in the Northeast. Soon after she arrived, she became very concerned about her safety and worried that others were out to harm her. She began to spend more and more time alone and bought a gun for her personal safety. One day, the school called her parents—Dorrie was walking around campus threatening to shoot the "undercover CIA agents." She was dismissed from the program, and her parents took her home. Her symptoms are now partially controlled by medication. She works part-time in the elementary school cafeteria but may never be able to live independently or fulfill her former academic potential.

Across their lifetime, more than 50% of people with schizophrenia have intermittent symptoms, and 20% have chronic symptoms and resultant disability (Barbato, 1998). There is a positive correlation between the severity of the symptoms of schizophrenia and the degree to which those symptoms impair the person's ability to function. Among 64 patients who were followed for 7 to 11 years after their hospitalization (first episode), 17.2% had stable remission, 57.8% had an unstable remission, and 25% never had a remission (Jaracz et al., 2015).

Any delay in receiving treatment increases the severity of the functional impairment. Although long-term outcome is significantly worse when the illness is untreated for a year (Harris et al., 2005), even smaller delays seriously affect the possibility of being able to live and function independently again. This means that treatment should begin as soon as possible to limit the chronic nature of the disorder.

Schizophrenia takes a significant human toll on the person and the family. Its social and economic burden makes it one of the 10 most debilitating (medical or psychological) conditions in the world in terms of disability-adjusted life years (Mueser & McGurk, 2004). Life expectancy for people with schizophrenia is reduced by 10 to 20 years (Chesney et al., 2014). Between 80 and 90% of people with schizophrenia are unemployed (Kooyman et al., 2007; Marwaha & Johnson, 2004). Among all of the psychological disorders, schizophrenia is one of the most serious conditions and was considered 100 years ago to have a progressively deteriorating course with little to no chance for recovery (Bleuler, 1911; Kraepelin, 1919). As a result of the discovery of effective treatments beginning in the 1960s, positive symptoms such as hallucinations and delusions may lessen and intensify again in severity over an individual's lifetime, resulting in periods of remission followed by relapse. Although the situation has improved somewhat since that time, the long-term outcome of schizophrenia is still quite poor (Jobe & Harrow, 2005), particularly for individuals who have what is known as the *treatment-resistant* type, which is defined as poor or no response to antipsychotic medication. Individuals with the treatment-resistant type have the most severe symptoms and worst community functioning (Iasevoli et al., 2016). In 2002, the estimated cost of this disorder was $62.7 billion (Wu et al., 2005).

Although the long-term outcome of this disorder is heterogeneous, there are people who had full remissions as well as those who had a chronic and debilitating course (Harrow et al., 2005; Lang et al. 2013). Over a 15-year follow-up period, 41% of patients with schizophrenia had a period of recovery defined as the presence of all of the following for 1 year: no psychotic symptoms, no negative symptoms, and demonstration of adequate psychosocial functioning (working at least half-time, moderate social activity, and no hospitalizations; Harrow et al., 2005). This definition of recovery is sometimes described as "recovery from" a serious mental disorder. Some researchers (e.g., Davidson & Roe, 2007) describe a second type of recovery similar to the conceptualization of recovery among people who were formerly substance dependent; that is, they are considered to be "in recovery." Using this definition, people in recovery from serious mental illnesses such as schizophrenia still may have symptoms of the disorder but are able to manage other aspects of their life such as work, education, friendships, and self-determination of life's various challenges. When this definition of recovery is used, perhaps as many as 50% of patients with schizophrenia are considered to be "in recovery."

Like substance-related disorder, coexisting depression increases the chance of a poor overall outcome. People who have both schizophrenia and depression are likely to be frequently hospitalized and to be unemployed (Sands & Harrow, 1999). Poorer general physical health and excessive medical morbidity (rates of illness) are also common among people with schizophrenia (Brown et al., 2000; Osby et al., 2000) including increased risk of infectious diseases (Rosenberg et al., 2001), physical injury as a result of violent victimization (Walsh et al., 2003), and smoking-related and other illnesses (De Leon et al., 1995). Adults with schizophrenia are 3.5 times more likely to die prematurely than the general population (Okfson et al., 2015). The most common cause of early death was cardiovascular disease.

Lung cancer also had a high mortality rate as did chronic obstructive pulmonary disease, influenza, and pneumonia. Accidental death was twice as common as suicide, and "non-suicidal" death from alcohol and other drugs was also a common cause of death. Clearly, clinicians who treat people with schizophrenia need to attend to physical illness/disease/health habits as well as their patients' mental status.

Cultural factors play a role in the course of schizophrenia; positive outcomes are more often found in developing countries than in developed nations. This may seem contradictory to what one would expect but may be the result of fewer social supports for people in more industrialized countries. In industrialized nations, people often leave home and family for better economic opportunities in a distant city and thus have limited family support when illness occurs. Cultural factors that are more prominent in developing countries and appear to be associated with better outcome for patients include differences in social structure, the more central role of the family in caring for psychiatrically ill patients, and differing beliefs about the etiology of the disorder (Tseng, 2003). For example, people in developing nations are more likely to accommodate deviance by a member of the community. They are more likely to keep a person with mental illness at home rather than seek hospitalization. Such cultures and lifestyles tend to be less complicated with fewer streets to navigate and more options for employment for those with less education, so it is easier for a patient with cognitive impairments to negotiate the environment. All of these factors have been associated with a more positive prognosis (Sartorius et al., 1978), and more recent studies continue to support the role of the family and community in affecting the outcome for people with schizophrenia (Tseng, 2003).

A common misconception about schizophrenia is that it is associated with violence. In fact, the rate of violence committed by people with schizophrenia (and other serious mental disorders) is higher than rates of violence for the general population (Hodgins et al., 1996). However, it is not higher (and in some cases it is lower) than among patients with other serious disorders such as depression and bipolar illness (Monahan et al., 2001a). Among patients with schizophrenia recently discharged from a psychiatric hospital, 8% committed a violent act during the first 20 weeks after hospitalization and 15% committed a violent act after the first year (Monahan et al., 2001). Definitions of violence include many different behaviors, some of which are considered minor acts (simple assault without injury or weapon use), whereas others represent more serious violence (assault using a lethal weapon, assault resulting in injury, threat with a lethal weapon, or sexual assault; Swanson et al., 2006). When examined by type of violence, the overall rate of violent acts committed by people with schizophrenia during a 6-month period was 19.1%, but only 3.6% were serious acts. An additional factor is that violent acts of any type are more often perpetrated by people with both schizophrenia and substance abuse than by people with schizophrenia alone (Erkiran et al., 2006).

People with schizophrenia are often the victims of violence. In some instances, their impaired cognitive and emotional status makes them easy targets. However, people with schizophrenia are also at risk for violence because their disorder limits their occupational choices and their income. Thus, their lower socioeconomic status means that they often live in neighborhoods where crime is common. Furthermore, some people with this disorder are homeless, and living on the streets also increases the likelihood of being a crime victim. Overall, the percentage of individuals with schizophrenia who are victimized (from crimes such as assault, rape, and robbery) ranges from 16% over a 1-year period (Walsh et al., 2003) to 34% when the time period is expanded to 3 years (Brekke et al., 2001). As with violence perpetration, most people with schizophrenia are the victims of nonviolent rather than violent crimes (Fitzgerald et al., 2005; Hiday et al., 2002).

People with schizophrenia are at risk for victimization by others. They often live in unsafe conditions, and their cognitive impairments make them easy targets.

People with schizophrenia are significantly impaired in many aspects of life functioning including self-care, independent living, interpersonal relationships, work, school, parenting, and leisure time (Mueser & McGurk, 2004). Not every person with this disorder is impaired in each of these areas, and in many instances, the presence of positive symptoms (which can be controlled with medication) is not associated with functional impairment. Rather, the disorder's cognitive deficits limit the ability to function effectively. Even a behavior as simple as getting dressed requires several different cognitive abilities (Bellack, 1992). *Executive functioning* (the ability to make decisions) is required to initiate the process of getting dressed, *memory* is required to recall where clothing articles are kept (drawers, closets), and *attention* is required in order to complete the process of getting dressed (not being distracted and, therefore, not finishing the process; Velligan et al., 2000).

Delusions and hallucinations distract people with schizophrenia, leaving them with only a limited ability to attend to their environmental surroundings. For example, people with schizophrenia are unable to observe or detect the social cues of other people, leading to awkward social interactions. Finally, deficits in memory and concentration may affect the ability to hold a job (Velligan et al., 2000). Work performance suffers when workers are unable to remember job assignments or follow instructions (e.g., "Mary, sweep the floor once an hour and every 30 minutes check to make sure the hair stylists have clean towels for their stations").

Epidemiology

LO 11.5 Discuss how sex, race, and ethnicity affect the clinical presentation of schizophrenia.

Schizophrenia is recognized around the world, and the prevalence is approximately the same in all cultures. The lifetime prevalence of schizophrenia averages 1%, ranging from 0.3 to 1.6% of the general U.S. population (Kessler, Berglund, Demler, Jin et al., 2005). This percentage is consistent across different populations, cultures, and level of industrialization (Combs et al., 2014). In any given year, between 16 and 40 of every 100,000 people develop schizophrenia (Jablensky, 2000). A higher incidence is associated with people who live in urban settings (perhaps a more complicated lifestyle), who move to a new area/country (perhaps resulting in social isolation and discrimination), and who are male. Schizophrenia is a very significant public health problem in terms of both its frequency and its disabling effects. Its onset can be either acute or gradual, and in many instances, *premorbid* (before the illness) features exist for many years before the actual psychotic symptoms emerge.

When the onset is gradual, the person often has some deterioration of functioning before the positive symptoms of the disorder emerge. In the *prodromal* phase, social withdrawal or deterioration in personal hygiene, such as not bathing or not changing clothes, may occur. The person may also have difficulty functioning properly at work or school. As the disorder progresses, the person enters the *acute* phase in which he or she exhibits the positive symptoms including hallucinations, delusions, and thought disorder. Negative symptoms are also present, but they are overshadowed by the psychotic behaviors. After the acute episode, some people with schizophrenia have a *residual phase*: The psychotic symptoms are no longer present, but the negative symptoms often remain. The continuing presence of negative symptoms sometimes prevents the person from being successfully employed or having satisfying social relationships.

The sexes differ significantly with regard to the age of onset for schizophrenia as well as its course and prognosis. Women tend to develop schizophrenia at a later age than men do. Perhaps because of this difference, women often have a milder form of the disorder and experience fewer hospital admissions and better social functioning (Mueser & McGurk, 2004). When the disorder develops later, individuals have more opportunity to achieve adolescent and young adult developmental milestones and develop better social functioning (e.g., graduating from high school or college or getting married). Of course, simply finding a difference between the sexes does not explain why that difference exists. The sex difference in age of onset may be related to hormonal and/or sociocultural factors. For example, the female hormone estrogen has a strong protective influence on brain development and is hypothesized to lessen the abnormal brain development commonly seen among those with schizophrenia (Goodman et al., 1996; see also "Etiology of Schizophrenia").

With respect to sociocultural factors, females are socialized from a very early age to be more socially competent than males, and they have more extensive social networks (Combs & Mueser, 2007). As is true for other areas, the answer to why sex differences exist may not be as simple as social competence or more extensive social networks. Both factors appear to be important influences in lessening the overall impact of schizophrenia among women.

Within the United States, symptoms of psychosis are consistent across various racial and ethnic groups including Korean Americans, African Americans, Latinos, and European Americans (Bae & Brekke, 2002). Although the *symptoms* of schizophrenia are common across racial and ethnic groups, rates at which a *diagnosis* of schizophrenia is given are not equally common, at least within the United States. African Americans are far more likely to receive a diagnosis of schizophrenia than are white people (e.g., Barnes, 2004; Bell & Mehta, 1980; Lawson et al., 1994) and Latino people (Minsky et al., 2003), particularly when the diagnosis is based on unstructured clinical interviews. Members of other ethnic groups, even when expressing very similar symptoms, are more frequently diagnosed with psychotic depression. Factors such as racial and ethnic biases, misinterpretation of patient reports due to a lack of understanding of cultural features, and racial differences in the presentation of psychiatric symptoms may bias clinicians' interpretation of patient symptoms (Barnes, 2004). For example, among some African Americans, the phrase "the witch is riding me" describes episodes of *isolated sleep paralysis*, a variant of panic disorder. However, the phrase is less familiar to white clinicians, who sometimes misinterpret this statement as a delusional belief. Such cultural insensitivity leads to misinterpretation of symptoms and inaccurate diagnosis (Minsky et al., 2003).

ETHICS AND RESPONSIBILITY Even if not deliberate, racial bias appears to be a very real factor in the diagnosis of schizophrenia. Most diagnoses are based on interviews in which the clinician and patient meet face to face, so the patient's race is known to the evaluator. Determining diagnoses based solely on a person's symptoms (without knowing race) could eliminate potential racial bias. When clinicians make a diagnosis based on a written transcript of a diagnostic interview rather than conducting an actual interview, African Americans are no more likely than European Americans to receive a diagnosis of schizophrenia (Arnold et al., 2004). These data suggest that a patient's characteristics (in this case, race), not just the symptoms, may play an important role in determining a diagnosis. This is a very important issue because the label of schizophrenia still carries a negative connotation and a poor prognosis. A mistake in diagnosis may result in unsuitable treatment with powerful medications being used inappropriately.

Explore ETHICS AND RESPONSIBILITY

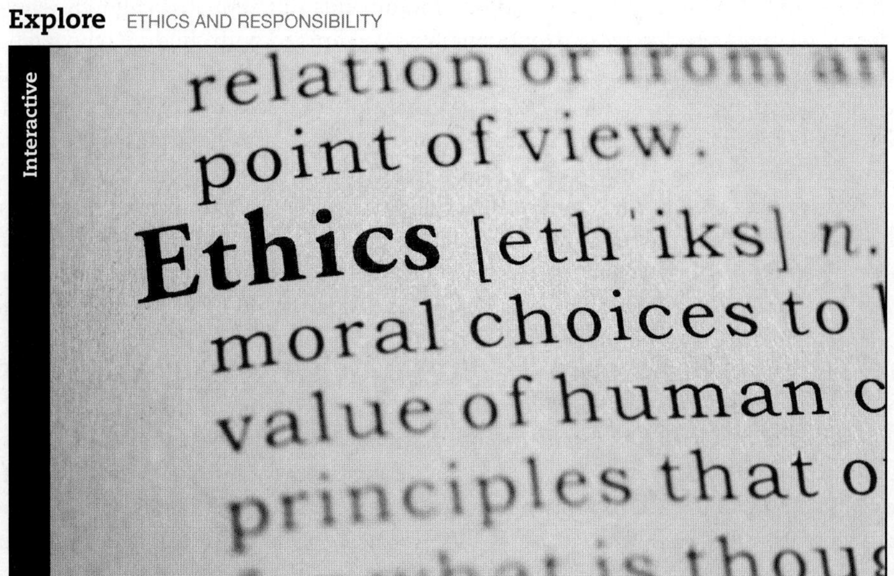

Inaccurate diagnosis may also result from inattention to cultural differences in behavior, lack of cultural competence among clinicians, language barriers and few bilingual therapists, and diagnostic errors as a result of inadequate clinical interviews conducted in busy outpatient clinics (Minsky et al., 2003). Eliminating racial and ethnic biases poses a significant challenge. Clinicians who are of the same race or ethnicity as the patient could reduce misunderstanding of cultural factors, but the United States has too few minority mental health professionals for that to be the single answer. Increasing cultural sensitivity and awareness of the issue is also important.

Developmental Factors

LO 11.6 Describe how developmental factors affect the clinical presentation of schizophrenia.

As children, adults who develop schizophrenia may have situational anxiety, nervous tension, depression, and "psychotic-like" experiences such as perceptual disturbances, magical thinking, and referential ideas (Owens et al., 2005). *Magical thinking* describes the belief that thinking about something can make it happen. For example, after you wish your parents were dead, they are involved in a serious car accident, and you conclude that your thoughts caused the accident. If you have *ideas of reference*, you interpret casual events as being directly related to you. For example, you walk by two people and they start to laugh—you wonder whether they are laughing at you. If you have *delusions of reference*, you would be sure that they were talking about you. These abnormalities in mood and perceptions have been reported consistently in childhood and suggest that some aspects of schizophrenia are present, though often undetected, long before the onset of the more dramatic positive symptoms.

Patients' childhood histories are usually collected retrospectively; that is, once the disorder is diagnosed, patients (or perhaps their parents) are asked to recall "how they were" before the symptoms began. These descriptions are compared with descriptions of people who do not suffer from the disorder. From a scientific perspective, this retrospective design is better than nothing at all, but it has a serious limitation. The cognitive deficits common among people with schizophrenia may limit the ability to recall premorbid functioning accurately. In addition, parents' recall of an adult child's early history may be affected by her or his more recent behaviors. Thus the current illness may bias any recollection of previous events. A prospective research design that would assess premorbid behaviors objectively before an illness developed is the preferable approach.

With respect to overt behaviors, impaired motor skills in children at high risk for the development of the disorder have been considered to be a biomarker for predicting who will develop schizophrenia in adulthood (Erlenmeyer-Kimling et al., 2000). Continued research in this area has found that poorer gross and fine motor skills differentiated children who have first-degree relatives affected by schizophrenia when compared with children who have first-degree relatives with other psychological disorders or children whose first-degree relatives do not have any psychological disorders. These conclusions were based on an analysis of a number of studies that had examined these groups. The strongest finding that was predictive of children who had a first-degree relative affected by schizophrenia was for impaired coordination. One limitation of this meta-analysis was that all of these studies were cross-sectional in nature. This means that although these children had poorer gross and fine motor skills, they were not "followed up" to determine if they developed schizophrenia in adulthood. As was discussed in Chapter 2, what would be needed is a prospective study to determine if children who have these skill deficits do indeed develop schizophrenia.

In one well-designed prospective study (Schiffman et al., 2004), all Danish youth ages 11 to 13 were videotaped under *standardized* (identical) conditions while they were eating lunch at school. Observers rated the children's behavior for sociability (smiles, laughs, initiates or responds to conversations), involuntary movements (right or left hand, facial movement, other abnormal movements), and general neuromotor signs (raised elbows, eye movements, other abnormal movements). Nineteen years later, when the participants were between the ages of 31 and 33, individuals unaware of their earlier behavioral ratings interviewed them. Twenty-six of the children had developed schizophrenia. Their behaviors at age 11 to 13 were compared with those of adults who had other disorders and to adults who had no disorder. Compared with both groups, adults with schizophrenia were significantly less sociable when they were children. Furthermore, compared with people who had a different psychiatric disorder (such as depression), people who developed schizophrenia had more subtle general neuromotor abnormalities as children. Because this study was prospective in design (not retrospective), it included the entire birth registry of all children born in Denmark during a specific time (therefore there was no selection bias that might have influenced the results), used objective measures (rather than subjective report), and included a psychological comparison group, these results provide strong evidence that poor sociability and abnormal motor functioning may be factors uniquely related to the onset of schizophrenia.

Studies have shown that adults with schizophrenia tended to be significantly less sociable when they were children.

Schizophrenia usually begins in late adolescence or early adulthood, but approximately 23% of patients develop the disorder after age 40 (Harris & Jeste, 1988; see also Chapter 14). About 1% of adults have schizophrenia (Mueser & McGurk, 2004), but only 0.01% of people under age 18 suffer from this disorder. Within this 0.01% group, more adolescents than children suffer from schizophrenia. When the disorder begins in childhood or adolescence (usually considered before age 18), it is called **early-onset schizophrenia** (EOS) and has severe biological and behavioral consequences.

Biologically, children with EOS lose more cortical gray matter than children without a psychological disorder (Kranzler et al., 2006) over a 5-year period (see Figure 11.1). This loss occurs on both sides of the brain and progresses from front to back (Vidal et al., 2006), indicating significant biological deterioration in brain functioning. Behaviorally, only between 8 and 20% of those with EOS ever achieve full symptom remission; most have persistent symptoms throughout their lifetimes (Eggers & Bunk, 1997; Röpcke & Eggers, 2005). Even when compared with patients with adult-onset schizophrenia or children with other forms of psychoses, patients with EOS are more impaired; they have additional psychotic episodes, need more continuing psychiatric care, and are more impaired in the area of social functioning and independent living (Hollis, 2000; Kranzler et al., 2006). Perhaps the only positive factor for children with EOS is that their IQ scores remain stable even 13 years after the disorder's onset (Gochman et al., 2005). Clearly, this is one disorder in which the earlier the onset, the more severe the outcome.

The long-term outcome is little better when the onset of schizophrenia occurs in adolescence. More than 10 years later, 83% of one sample had at least one additional episode that required inpatient treatment, and 74% were still receiving psychiatric treatment (Lay et al., 2000). Impairments in life functioning were common: 57% did not achieve their premorbid educational and occupational goals, 66% were socially disabled (were socially isolated, avoided social activities, were unable to do typical household chores, lived without a sexual relationship), and 75% depended financially on their parents or public assistance. People with EOS have also been found to be less likely to marry or remain married (Eaton, 1975; Munk-Jørgensen, 1987), especially if they were male, and less likely to go to college (Kessler et al., 1995).

Jermaine is 10 years old. When he was little, he played with the children in his preschool and was in the advanced reading class. Now he is behind in reading and gets into fights with his peers. He takes good-natured teasing very seriously and gets angry. He hides when other people come to his home. When he was younger, he was diagnosed with attention deficit hyperactivity disorder, depression, anxiety, and even autism spectrum disorder, but nothing seemed to fit. In all of his school pictures,

Figure 11.1 Gray Matter of Schizophrenics.

SOURCE: Thompson et al., http://users.loni.usc.edu/~thompson/MEDIA/PNAS/PNAS2001_article.pdf

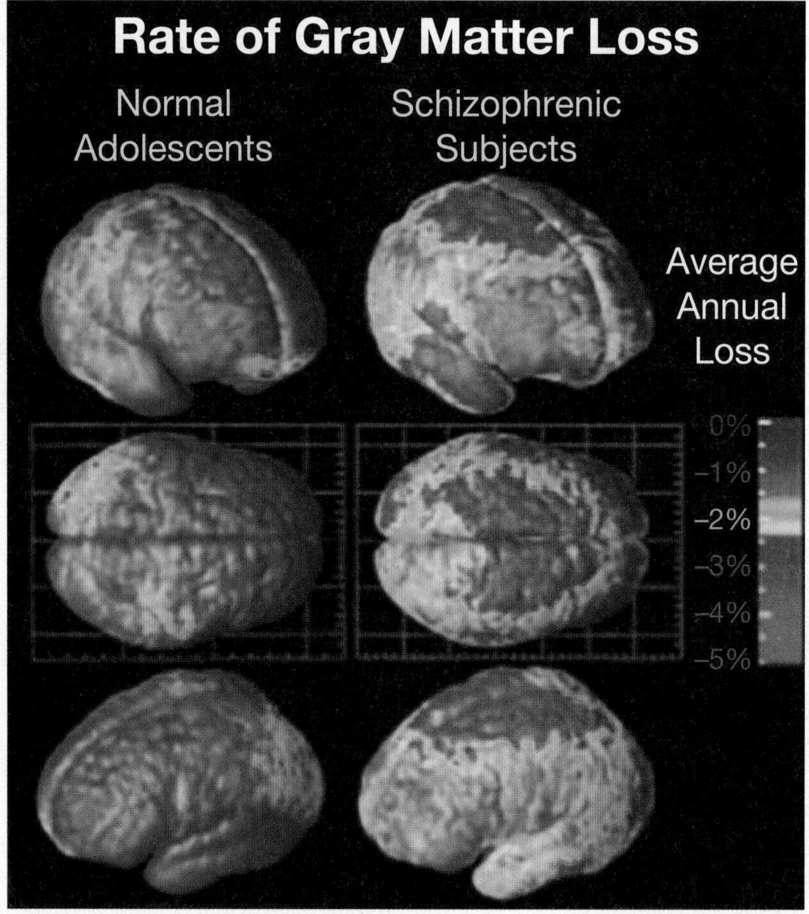

he has a blank look on his face. His frustrated parents brought him to a new psychologist for an evaluation. After listening to the lack of emotion in Jermaine's voice, the way he would suddenly seem distracted or smile inappropriately, the psychologist asked if he ever heard voices. Almost relieved, Jermaine started talking about the "good voices" and the "bad voices." The good ones, he explained, were trying to help him. The bad ones were trying to trick him into doing "bad things" so he would go to hell. All of the voices commented on his behavior, telling him he was "good" or "bad."

To summarize, even before delusions and hallucinations begin, children and adolescents with EOS are socially withdrawn, have difficulty interacting with peers, and have school adjustment problems (McClellan et al., 2003; Muratori et al., 2005). Because early onset does not allow much opportunity for normal social development, it is not surprising that the long-term outcome for those with EOS is worse than when schizophrenia begins in adulthood. Outcome is extremely poor when the disorder begins before age 14 (Remschmidt & Theisen, 2005).

Other Psychotic Disorders

LO 11.7 Identify the other psychotic disorders and how they differ from schizophrenia.

Schizophrenia is the most common type of psychotic disorder and the one that has been most thoroughly studied. However, psychotic experiences do not always mean that the person is suffering from schizophrenia. We discuss several other types of psychotic disorders next.

REAL People REAL Disorders

Andrea Yates and Postpartum Mood Disorder with Psychotic Features

Andrea Yates methodically drowned her five children (ages 6 months to 7 years) in the family bathtub on June 20, 2001. She was diagnosed with the DSM-IV-TR disorder known as postpartum psychosis. In DSM-5, her symptoms would meet criteria for recurrent postpartum mood disorders with psychotic features. After drowning her oldest son, she called the police, was arrested, and confessed to the crime. Her defense asserted that this disorder was the reason for the killings. Yates told her jail psychiatrist, "It was the seventh deadly sin. My children weren't righteous. They stumbled because I was evil. The way I was raising them, they could never be saved. They were doomed to perish in the fires of hell." Although all agreed that Mrs. Yates was psychotic, she was found guilty and sentenced to prison. However, her conviction was overturned, and in her second trial, the jury found her not guilty by reason of insanity. She was committed to a mental institution until she no longer needs treatment.

The birth of a baby is usually a happy and eagerly anticipated event, yet postpartum mood disorder with psychotic features occurs in 1 or 2 women out of every 1,000 who give birth (Robertson et al., 2005). Research suggests that both stressful life events and/or a preexisting psychological disorder (schizoaffective disorder, major depression, bipolar disorder) may be related to its onset (Kumar et al., 1993; Robertson et al., 2005). In some instances, hormonal changes that commonly occur a few days after childbirth also may contribute to the onset of this disorder, particularly in women who had a psychological disorder before they became pregnant (Kumar et al., 1993). As in other disorders, both biological and psychosocial factors appear to play a role.

Brief psychotic disorder is the sudden onset of any psychotic symptom, such as delusions, hallucinations, disorganized speech, or grossly disorganized or catatonic behavior. As its name indicates, this disorder may resolve after 1 day and does not last for more than 1 month. After the disorder remits (resolves itself), the person returns to a normal level of functioning. Often the disorder's onset is associated with significant psychosocial stressors, such as the death of a loved one or birth of a child (see "Real People, Real Disorders: Andrea Yates and Postpartum Mood Disorder with Psychotic Features").

The symptoms of **schizophreniform disorder** are identical to those of schizophrenia with two exceptions. First, the duration of the illness is shorter, ranging from at least 1 month to less than 6 months. In a few instances, the symptoms seem to disappear. In other instances, a person is treated successfully and never has another episode, although why treatment is successful in any particular case is not known.

The second difference between people with schizophrenia and those with schizophreniform disorder is that in the case of schizophreniform disorder, impaired social or occupational functioning is a possibility, but some people can still conduct their daily activities. For example,

> Jack was suspicious that his neighbors were listening in on his telephone conversations or were keeping a record of when he entered and left his apartment. However, he did not harbor those same suspicions about coworkers. Therefore, although he would not answer his telephone (because his neighbors might be listening) and was reluctant to leave his apartment (because the neighbors would mark down the time), he did leave once a day to go to work.

Individuals with **schizoaffective disorder** might be considered to have both schizophrenia and an affective disorder. That is, in addition to having the symptoms of a psychotic illness, the patient also suffers from a major depressive, manic, or mixed episode disorder at some point during the illness.

> Brian admitted himself to the hospital for depression. A talented painter, he had struggled for many years with mood swings, and his paintings reflected his mood. Lately, his friends were worried because his paintings were getting darker in color and in content. After a few days on the inpatient

unit, he came out of his room smiling and joking. He walked up to a nurse and said, "I am making you my director of overseas operations." He passed a research assistant and said, "You are my new head of human resources." He next told a psychiatrist he was being demoted to a shift work position. When the head nurse finally caught up to him and asked how he was feeling, he replied, "Wonderful, honey. I'm Mr. Mellon, the president of US Steel. If you are nice to me, I'll make you my personal assistant." He was so sure that he was the owner of a multinational corporation, and he became angry and belligerent when she tried to remind him that he was Brian the painter.

Schizoaffective disorder is a controversial diagnosis. It has been considered a type of schizophrenia, a type of mood disorder, or an intermediate condition between the two. When patients with schizophrenia, schizoaffective disorder, and mood disorders were compared, positive symptoms were more severe in people with schizophrenia than in people with schizoaffective disorder, but both groups had equally severe cognitive impairments (Evans et al., 1999). In some instances, diagnostic decisions are made on which group of symptoms (psychotic or mood) is considered to be more severe or more impairing.

Delusional disorder consists of the presence of a nonbizarre delusion (defined as an event that might actually happen; see Table 11.2).

Janice does not believe that she needs to see a mental health professional. She is confident that, despite all medical evidence to the contrary, she has cancer. Her belief is based on the fact that she can actually feel the cancer cells eating away at her body. She sits in the psychologist's office, calmly relating the fact that she has consulted at least 20 physicians, all of whom are wrong. Her family physician told her that he would not see her anymore unless she consulted a mental health professional.

People with delusional disorder do not have other psychotic symptoms except perhaps hallucinations that are directly related to the delusion (such as Janice's report of feeling the cancer cells eating away inside her). Also, in contrast to schizophrenia, few changes occur in the person's overall functioning other than the behaviors immediately surrounding the delusion (Janice's "doctor-shopping" to find someone who will treat her cancer). Because people with delusional disorder do not believe that they need treatment, it is not clear how many people suffer from this disorder.

When two or more individuals who have a close relationship share the same delusional belief, the disorder is known as **shared psychotic disorder** (folie à deux).

Dorien was a successful businessman. His cognitive faculties began to fade as he approached retirement. He had difficulty with daily activities, and his wife, Alicia, began to have cognitive problems as well (as a result of a mugging incident in which she sustained head injuries). Concerned about their safety, family members moved them to an assisted living environment where a medical staff monitored their activities. Dorien began complaining that he was being held against his will, that the staff was stealing his belongings, that his food was being poisoned, and that his family was trying to kill him. Initially, Alicia tried to convince him that none of this was real, but after a few weeks, she became convinced that her husband's beliefs were true. Alicia needed surgery and was transferred to a medical center and then to a rehabilitation center for physical therapy. As a result of her separation from Dorien, her delusional beliefs quickly disappeared.

Table 11.2 Common Delusional Themes Among Individuals with Delusional Disorder

Type	Content
Erotomanic	The person believes that someone of higher status is in love with him or her (sometimes found among "celebrity stalkers")
Grandiose	The person has feelings of inflated worth, power, knowledge, identity, or special relationships to a deity or a famous person
Jealous	The person's sexual partner is unfaithful
Persecutory	The person (or someone close to the person) is being badly mistreated
Somatic	The person has a medical condition or physical defect for which no medical cause can be found

Shared psychotic disorder begins when one person (sometimes termed the *inducer* or *the primary case*) develops a psychotic disorder with delusional content. The inducer is the dominant person in the relationship with a second individual (usually related by blood or marriage and living in close physical proximity) and, over time, imposes the delusional system on the second person, who then adopts the belief system and acts accordingly. If the relationship is interrupted (as happened for Dorien and Alicia), the delusional beliefs of the second person quickly disappear. Shared psychotic disorder is equally common among males and females and affects both younger and older patients. Among one sample, 90% of those suffering from this disorder were married couples, siblings, or parent–child dyads (many of whom were socially isolated from others). Dementia, depression, and mental retardation were common features among people with this disorder (Silveira & Seeman, 1995).

Learning Objective Summaries

LO 11.1 Distinguish between a psychotic experience and the psychotic disorders.

A psychotic experience is a single event that involves a loss of contact with reality and usually consists of a delusion or a hallucination. Psychotic experiences occur in people without any psychiatric disorder, people with medical illnesses, and people with many of the different psychological disorders discussed in this book. When psychotic experiences become frequent or continuous and create distress and/or functional impairment, they are called *psychotic disorders*.

LO 11.2 Understand that schizophrenia is not a condition involving "split personality," nor does it usually involve violent behavior toward others.

Terms such as *multiple personality* and *split personality* are not synonyms for schizophrenia. The term *schizophrenia* describes the "disconnect" among an individual's thoughts, feelings, and behavior, not the existence of one or more complete personalities within a single person. It is not synonymous with violent behavior.

LO 11.3 Identify the positive, negative, and cognitive symptoms of schizophrenia.

Schizophrenia is a serious psychological disorder characterized by disorganization in thought, perception, and behavior. People with schizophrenia do not think logically, perceive the world accurately, or behave in a way that permits normal everyday life and work. The positive symptoms of schizophrenia consist of hallucinations, delusions, and bizarre behaviors such as catatonia and waxy flexibility. Negative symptoms consist of diminished emotional expression, anhedonia, alogia, and avolition. Cognitive symptoms consist of deficits in visual and verbal learning and memory, ability to pay attention, speed of information processing, and abstract reasoning and executive functioning.

LO 11.4 Describe how schizophrenia affects all aspects of personal functioning.

Schizophrenia takes a significant human toll on the person and the family. It is one of the 10 most debilitating conditions (medical or psychological) in the world. Life expectancy for people with schizophrenia is reduced by 10 to 20 years, and between 80 and 90% of people with schizophrenia are unemployed.

LO 11.5 Discuss how sex, race, and ethnicity affect the clinical presentation of schizophrenia.

The lifetime prevalence of schizophrenia averages 1%, and this prevalence is consistent across different populations, cultures, and level of industrialization. When the onset is gradual, the person often has some deterioration of functioning before the positive symptoms emerge. In the *prodromal* phase, social withdrawal or deterioration in personal hygiene, such as not bathing or not changing clothes, may occur. The person may also have difficulty functioning properly at work or school. Race, culture, and ethnicity play a role in the diagnosis, etiology, and treatment of schizophrenia. Within the United States, the symptom pattern of people with schizophrenia is not different among various racial and ethnic groups. However, African American men appear to be diagnosed with schizophrenia at a higher rate than African American women or white people of either sex. Compared with people with schizophrenia who live in developed countries, people with schizophrenia who live in developing nations often have a more positive treatment outcome, possibly because their families are more supportive of and play a more supportive role in the patient's care.

LO 11.6 Describe how developmental factors affect the clinical presentation of schizophrenia.

The consequences of schizophrenia are more serious and long-lasting when the disorder begins in childhood, a condition known as early-onset schizophrenia (EOS). Children with EOS lose more cortical gray matter than children without a psychological disorder; this loss occurs on both sides of the brain and progresses from front to back, indicating significant biological deterioration in brain functioning. Behaviorally, few children with EOS ever achieve full symptom remission; most have persistent symptoms throughout their lifetimes. Compared with patients with adult-onset schizophrenia or children with other forms of psychoses, patients with EOS are more impaired; they have additional psychotic episodes, need more continuing psychiatric care, and are more impaired in the area of social functioning and independent living.

LO 11.7 Identify the other psychotic disorders and how they differ from schizophrenia.

In contrast to schizophrenia, which is considered to be a chronic disorder, other forms of psychosis may be time limited. Brief psychotic disorder, for example, may last for only 1 day. Schizophreniform disorder lasts no more than 6 months. Schizoaffective disorder is a condition in which psychotic symptoms and major depression are equal in severity and frequency. In this group of patients, the positive symptoms of psychosis are less severe than in those with schizophrenia alone.

Critical Thinking Question

Your friend is also in your abnormal psychology class. She was robbed at gunpoint the other day, and she confides to you that every time she walks down the street where the robbery occurred, she thinks that she sees the man who robbed her. Then the image disappears. She is afraid that she is developing schizophrenia. What would you tell her?

Etiology of Schizophrenia

Schizophrenia is a complex disorder. Its symptoms are quite dramatic and not easily understood by the general public. Many different theories about its development have been offered and, in some cases, discarded. Overall, a century of research has been more successful in ruling out than in establishing causes of schizophrenia. For example, it is now clear that this disorder is not caused by "poor" or "bad" parenting—a relief to families who have to cope with someone struggling with this disorder. It is now quite clear that schizophrenia probably involves many different elements. In this section, we examine the biological, psychological, and social/environmental factors that may play a role in the onset of schizophrenia.

Biological Factors

LO 11.8 Discuss the neurodevelopmental model of schizophrenia.

Based on research conducted over the past 50 years, the consensus that schizophrenia is a neurodevelopmental disorder is increasing. Research has established that this disorder has a genetic component and that abnormalities exist in both brain structure and brain function. This does not mean that we now thoroughly understand this complex disorder—we still have much to learn. However, we now know that no simplistic explanations and no single biological factor exist. The following describes what we know so far.

NEUROTRANSMITTERS The three different symptom categories that make up schizophrenia might suggest abnormalities in several different neurotransmitter systems. By far the most attention has been paid to neurotransmitters associated with the dramatic positive symptoms. For more than 50 years, schizophrenia has been considered to be a disorder associated with an excess of the neurotransmitter *dopamine*. The **dopamine hypothesis** emerged from clinical observations that chemical compounds such as amphetamines and *levadopa* (also called *L-dopa*, a drug used to treat Parkinson's disease) increase the amount of dopamine available in the neural synapse, which, in turn, can lead to the development or worsening of psychotic symptoms. In contrast, substances that decrease dopamine seem to be associated with the lessening of psychotic symptoms.

Watch NEUROTRANSMITTERS AND SCHIZOPHRENIA

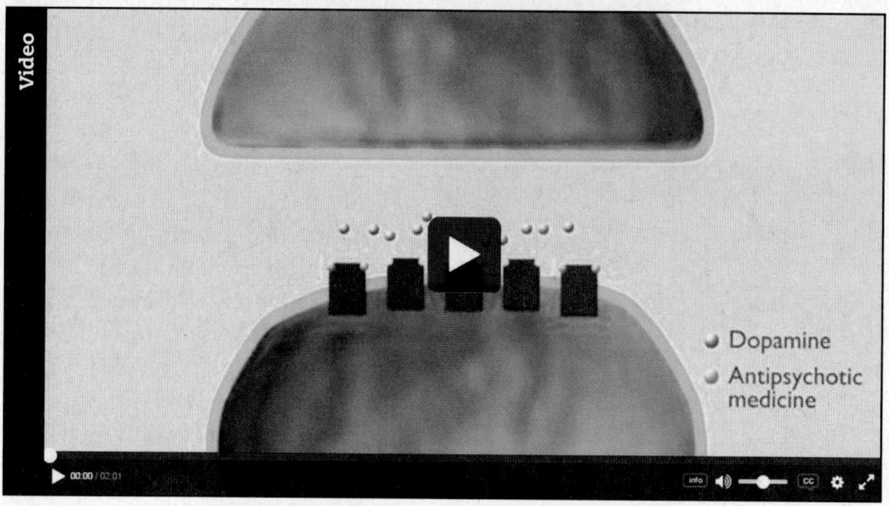

We just used the term *associated with* because a causal relationship between dopamine and schizophrenia has not been clearly established, and three possibilities must be considered. First, excessive dopamine could lead to the development of schizophrenia. Second, the chronic stress created by a disorder as serious as schizophrenia may create many different brain abnormalities including excess dopamine. Finally, both excess dopamine and schizophrenia could result from some third, currently unknown variable. Although the direction of this relationship remains uncertain, the existence of abnormal dopamine levels in the neural synapses of patients with schizophrenia has been established. The relationship is far from simple, however. It appears that *too much* dopamine in the limbic area of the brain may be responsible for positive symptoms (i.e., overactivity of behavior and perception), whereas *too little* dopamine in the cortical areas may be responsible for negative symptoms (i.e., impaired cognitive abilities and motivation; Howes & Murray, 2014). Therefore, dopamine abnormalities are not simply a matter of too much or too little in the brain. They may take the form of both excesses and deficits within the same individual. This finding may explain why medications that block dopamine levels reduce positive symptoms but do not change negative symptoms (see "Treatment of Schizophrenia and Other Psychotic Disorders").

As you will recall, the second category of symptoms found in people with schizophrenia are the negative symptoms, which are defined as an absence of behaviors that are found in people without the disorder. In many ways, the negative symptoms of schizophrenia (e.g., slowed speech, apathy) are similar to the psychomotor retardation symptoms found in depression. In Chapter 7, we discussed that these symptoms of depression may be related to the limited availability of *serotonin* (a different neurotransmitter) in certain neural synapses. It appears that serotonin deficits may also be present in the same brain areas in people with schizophrenia (Horacek et al., 2006). Finally, evidence exists in both animals and humans that a third set of neurotransmitters, *GABA and glutamate*, play an important role with respect to learning and remembering new material (Barch & Caeser, 2012; Moghaddam & Javitt, 2012). Therefore, deficits in these neurotransmitters may be associated with some of the negative and cognitive impairments (the third category of symptoms) found among people with schizophrenia (Addington et al., 2005; Owen et al., 2016), whereas dopamine dysfunction may result in the emergence of the positive symptoms (Owen et al., 2016).

GENETICS AND FAMILY STUDIES As with many other psychological disorders, schizophrenia "runs in families." Just because a parent has schizophrenia does not mean that the child will also develop the disorder. Genetically, the risk of developing schizophrenia is 15% if one parent has the disorder and 50% if both parents have it (McGuffin et al., 1995). Several twin studies around the world have revealed that genetic factors play a role in liability to the disorder. A large

Because they have the same genetic makeup, the risk that both monozygotic twins will develop schizophrenia is higher than for dizygotic twins or other non-twin siblings.

meta-analysis of 12 well-conducted twin studies yielded a heritability estimate of 81% (95% confidence interval, 73 to 90%) with additional evidence for the effects of common or shared environmental influences on liability to schizophrenia of about 11% (95% confidence interval, 3 to 19%) (Sullivan et al., 2003).

Our understanding of the genetics of schizophrenia is advancing rapidly. Scientific breakthroughs have been made secondary to researchers around the world coming together to create very large samples of DNA from people with schizophrenia. In 2014, the Schizophrenia Working Group of the Psychiatric Genomics Consortium reported a GWAS that included DNA from 36,989 cases and 113,075 controls. Achieving that large sample allowed them to examine 128 independent associations spanning 108 conservatively defined loci that met genome-wide significance. Eighty-three of the loci were novel—meaning they had not been discovered in previous studies, and many were enriched among genes that are expressed in the brain. Additional work has aimed to identify whether the implicated genes assort into identifiable molecular pathways and if these are shared across psychiatric disorders or unique to schizophrenia. Looking across schizophrenia, bipolar disorder, and major depressive disorder, the Network and Pathway Analysis Subgroup of Psychiatric Genomics Consortium (2015) identified an enrichment for genes in pathways related to histone methylation, immune and neuronal pathways, and pathways related to post-synaptic density—all pointing toward biological processes that may go awry to increase risk for developing schizophrenia and other major psychiatric disorders. Neuroscientists can now begin to prioritize the genes and drill down into their function to determine concretely how alterations or perturbations in those genes and pathways contribute to the development of schizophrenia. Expectations are that the action of hundreds of genes (polygenic influence) and epigenetic and environmental factors are likely to also play a role (see "Examining the Evidence: Genetics and Environment in the Development of Schizophrenia").

NEUROANATOMY The dramatic abnormalities in perception, thought, and behavior found among people with schizophrenia led naturally to consideration of brain abnormalities, which may be structural or functional. One consistent neuroanatomical abnormality found among people with schizophrenia is enlargement of the brain *ventricles* (Wright et al., 2000). The ventricles are cavities in the brain that contain cerebrospinal fluid (see Figure 11.2), which acts as a cushion to prevent brain damage if there is a blow to the head. In addition to enlarged ventricles, people with schizophrenia have a reduction in cortical (gray matter) and white matter areas of the brain (Haijma et al., 2013) compared with people with no disorder. Based on MRI data, some of these structural brain abnormalities, such as white matter reductions, clearly are present at the onset of the disorder (Haijma et al., 2013; Vita et al., 2006). Some of these same abnormalities exist in the non-ill parents of adults with schizophrenia (Ohara et al., 2006), the children of adults with schizophrenia (Diwadkar et al., 2006), and other non-ill relatives (McDonald et al., 2002). The consistency of these abnormalities coupled with their existence among people who do not show symptoms of the disorder (but who have a relative with the disorder) indicates that these abnormalities are not the result of the illness but are present before the positive symptoms emerge.

Figure 11.2 Ventricles of the Brain.

The brain's ventricles contain cerebrospinal fluid, which helps cushion the brain against injury. Compared with people with no disorder, people with schizophrenia have enlarged ventricles. Although the exact meaning of this difference is not clear, it is one piece of evidence suggesting a neurodevelopmental basis for the disorder.

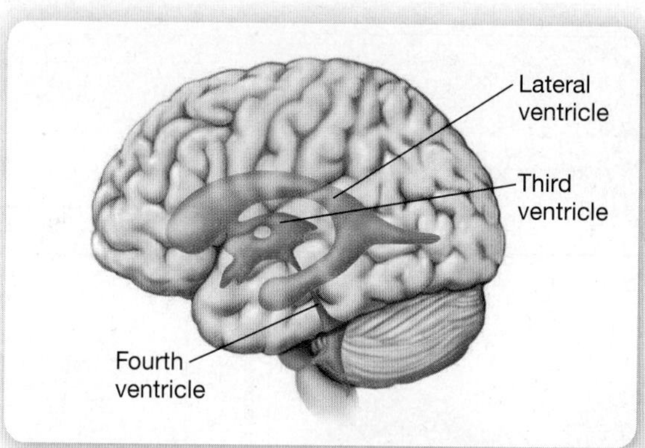

Both gray and white matter continues to decrease with the progression of the illness (Haijma et al. 2013; Sheffield et al., 2015), as does cortical thinning in several areas of the brain including the prefrontal cortex (Zhang et al., 2015), and gray matter reductions are larger in patients who take antipsychotic medications compared with those who did not. Additionally, functional connectivity is degraded (Sheffield et al., 2015). Functional connectivity describes different spatial areas of the brain that work together (they function as a unit for a specific purpose). When compared with people with no disorder, people with schizophrenia had significant decline in the cingulo-opercular network and the front-parietal network (both networks are involved with higher-order cognitive abilities). Additionally, people with schizophrenia had significantly lower node degree (the number of connections that a node has within a specific network) for the right anterior insula, left dorsolateral prefrontal cortex, and the dorsal anterior cingulate cortex (Sheffield et al., 2015) (see Figure 11.3).

Taken together, these data suggest that part of the reduction in brain volume in people with schizophrenia is most likely present before the onset of the disorder but that there is continued decline as the illness progresses (Haijma et al., 2013; Sheffied et al., 2015; Vita et al., 2012). Additionally, there is more gray matter, white matter, and functional connectivity loss in people with schizophrenia when compared with people with no disorder. People with schizophrenia who are treated with antipsychotic medications appear to have even greater losses when compared with people who have schizophrenia but who do not receive antipsychotic medications (Fusar-Poli et al., 2013; Haijma et al., 2013; Vita et al., 2012).

Abnormal brain structure exists not only at the macro level of enlarged ventricles and decreased cortical size. Differences are also evident at the basic cellular level of the brain. Brain abnormalities that appear specific to people with schizophrenia (compared with those with no psychiatric disorder or a different disorder) include mild structural disorganization at the level of the individual brain cells (evident at autopsy) and altered neuronal connections in multiple brain areas (Opler & Susser, 2005). This type of cellular disorganization cannot happen as a result of brain deterioration or aging; it can occur only early in the process of brain development (before birth). Studies of cerebral development indicate that this phase of cortex development occurs during the second trimester of pregnancy. Therefore, it is clear that these abnormalities develop long before the onset of the observable symptoms of schizophrenia.

VIRAL THEORIES AND OTHER PRENATAL STRESSORS There are now sufficient data, including the neuroanatomical data just discussed, to conclude that structural and functional brain abnormalities exist among people with schizophrenia. Genetics may contribute to this abnormal development but cannot alone account for the onset of schizophrenia. Another aspect that may affect fetal brain development is the prenatal environment. Prenatal factors identified as potentially associated with the later onset of schizophrenia include maternal

Figure 11.3 Node Degree and Age.

Parts of the brain form networks allowing for performance of complicated activities. In contrast to healthy controls, the efficiency of these networks declines with increasing age when people have schizophrenia.

SOURCE: Sheffield, J. M., Repovs, G., Harms, M. P., Carter, C. S., Gold, J. M., MacDonald, A. W.,…& Barch, D. M. (2015). Evidence for accelerated decline of functional brain network efficiency in schizophrenia. *Schizophrenia Bulletin,* doi:10.1093/schbul/sbv148.

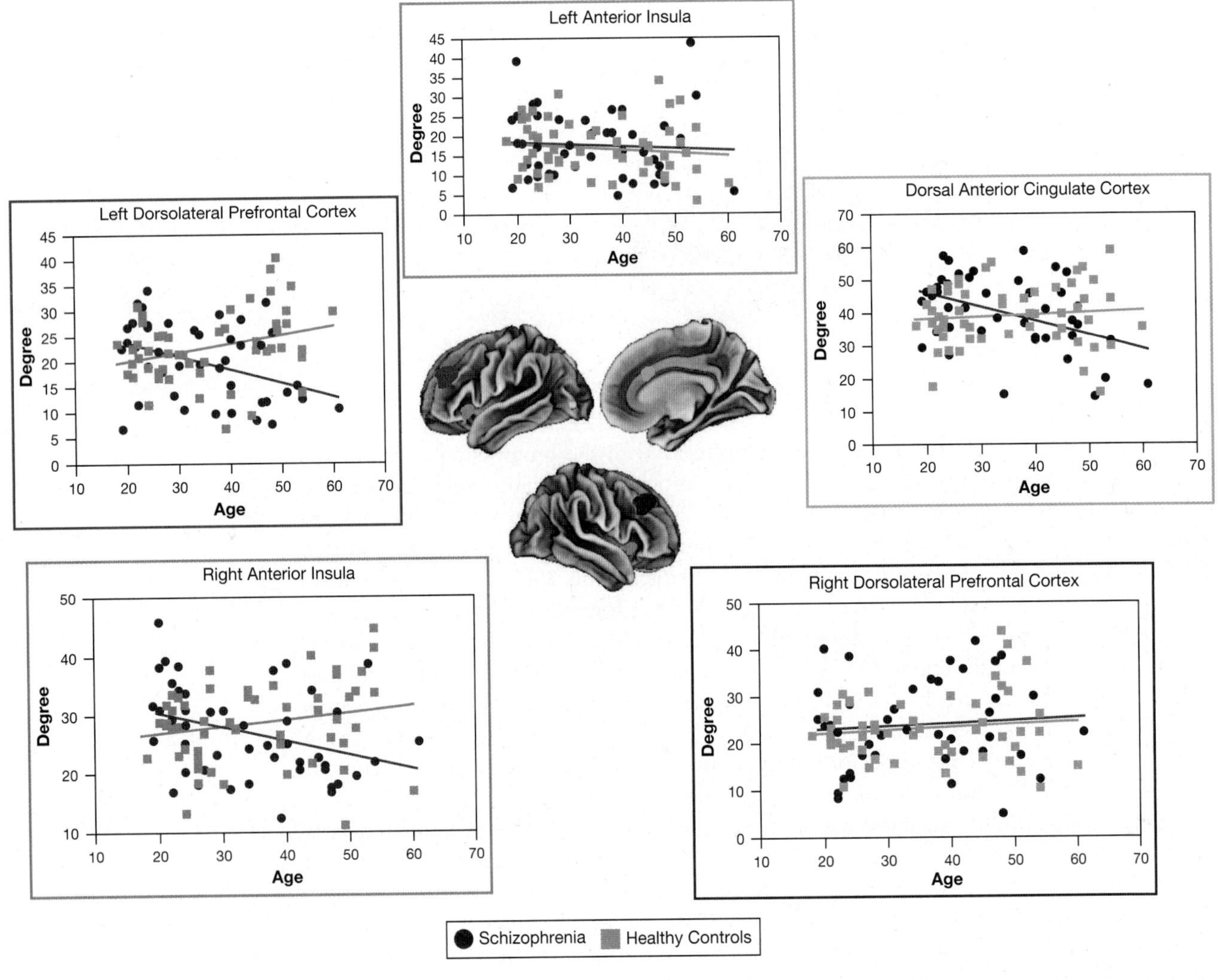

Examining the EVIDENCE

Genetics and Environment in the Development of Schizophrenia

Because genetically identical (MZ) twins are not 100% concordant for schizophrenia, a strict genetic etiology is unlikely. In fact, 80% of people with psychotic symptoms do not have a parent with the disorder, and in 60% of the cases, no family history can be identified (Gottesman, 2001). Therefore, other factors must contribute to this disorder. One such factor now receiving increased attention is the family environment.

- **The Evidence** In Finland, a national sample of children whose mothers had schizophrenia and were adopted away at birth was compared with children who were also adopted away but whose mothers did not have schizophrenia (Tienari et al., 2004). The family environment in the adoptive family was classified as disordered (high in criticism, conflict, constricted affect, and boundary problems) or healthy (low in criticism, conflict, constricted affect, and boundary problems). The children were interviewed at age 23 and again at age 44. As adults, 36.8% of the biological children of schizophrenic mothers who were raised in a disordered family environment developed a schizophrenic spectrum disorder, whereas only 5.8% of children of schizophrenic mothers who were reared in a healthy family environment developed one of these disorders. In contrast, the adoptive family environment was not a factor for those children whose mother did not have schizophrenia; 5.3% of children raised in disordered environments developed a schizophrenic spectrum disorder as did 4.8% of children raised in healthy family environments.

- **Examining the Evidence** These results suggest that a family environment high in conflict and criticism and low in expressions of emotion may be an important factor in the development of schizophrenia *but only when the child has a parent with schizophrenia.* Whereas overall, about 15% of offspring develop schizophrenia if one parent has the disorder, that percentage doubles when the children are raised in a disordered family environment even when they are not raised by a parent with the disorder.
- **What Do** These Data Illustrate About the Role of Genetics?
    1. Even when a person has a genetic predisposition to develop schizophrenia (mother has the disorder) and is raised in an environment that is not healthy, 63.2% do *not* develop a schizophrenic spectrum disorder.
    2. Although 36.8% developed a schizophrenic spectrum disorder, only 5.1% developed schizophrenia; many of the others had psychotic disorders or depression with psychosis. This means that what appears to be inherited is a general risk factor for psychosis, not necessarily for schizophrenia.
- **What Do** These Data Illustrate About the Role of the Environment?
    1. A conflictual or disorganized environment appears to increase the risk for a psychotic disorder but only among those who have relatives with schizophrenia.
    2. Even with no genetic risk and a healthy family environment, 4.8% of individuals still developed a schizophrenic spectrum disorder.
- **Conclusion** The answer to these questions is not simple because both biological and environmental factors appear to play a role. If you were a psychologist, how would you explain the outcome of this study to your female patient with schizophrenia who wants to have a child?

infections during pregnancy (Brown, 2012; Khandaker et al., 2013), influenza during the first or second trimester period (Brown et al., 2004), nutritional deprivation during early gestation (Brown, 2012), lead exposure during the second trimester (Opler & Susser, 2005), birth complications (Brown, 2011), and severe prenatal maternal stress (Khashan et al., 2008).

Among all of these prenatal risk factors, one of the most thoroughly investigated is maternal exposure to the influenza virus during pregnancy. In an initial report (Mednick et al., 1988), children of mothers who were exposed to an influenza virus during their second trimester (the second 3 months of pregnancy) were at greater risk of developing schizophrenia when they became adults. Since the publication of this study, the relationship of influenza and schizophrenia has been an area of continuous controversy. About 50% of the research literature confirms this initial relationship, but the other 50% is unable to detect any increased risk for schizophrenia following maternal influenza exposure. One reason for these inconsistent findings is that in many instances, determining whether the mother was exposed to influenza depended on the mother's recall rather than objective medical data. In one of the few studies for which objective evidence exists, exposure to influenza documented by presence of the virus in the mother's blood resulted in a sevenfold increase in the risk of the infant's developing schizophrenia when exposure occurred during the first, but not the second, trimester (Brown et al., 2004).

How could exposure to influenza be related to the development of schizophrenia? Because the influenza virus does not cross the placenta, the virus itself is not responsible for any abnormal brain development. However, when a pregnant woman (or anyone) contracts influenza, her immune system produces antibodies (in this case, IgG antibodies) to fight the infection. These antibodies cross the placental barrier and react with fetal brain *antigens* (a substance that stimulates production of antibodies), producing an immunological response that disrupts fetal brain development. In turn, abnormalities in *structural* brain development may then trigger *functional* abnormalities that in turn result in the onset of schizophrenia (Wright et al., 1999). Think about an automobile engine. If it is not built (structured) correctly, it will not run (function) correctly.

Although no direct studies in humans are available to support this hypothesis, the offspring of pregnant mice that are deliberately exposed to the influenza virus have a reduced number of cells in the cortex and hippocampal areas of the brain. This is a significant finding because these are the same neuroanatomical areas that have been identified as abnormal in patients with schizophrenia (Fatemi et al., 1999). Given the complex nature of schizophrenia, it is far too simplistic to conclude that it is caused simply by exposure to the influenza virus. Its etiology is probably much more complicated. Furthermore, it is important to note that many pregnant women are exposed to influenza each year and only 1% of adults develop schizophrenia. Therefore, other factors must play a role.

Many obstetric complications have positive but weak relationships to schizophrenia, but these do not appear to play a major role (Cannon et al., 2002). Overall, the definition of obstetric complications is very broad, and when applied across the general population, 25 to 30% of all pregnancies have some type of complication. So again, we cannot conclude that all children born to women with pregnancy complications will develop schizophrenia (Rapoport et al., 2005). These complications more likely signal the presence of other factors with a more direct role or indicate a general vulnerability to the development of various mental illnesses. In the case of schizophrenia, these factors when combined with a genetic predisposition may be the initial triggers leading to the development of the abnormal brain structures we have discussed.

A NEURODEVELOPMENTAL MODEL OF SCHIZOPHRENIA From a biological perspective, schizophrenia is best conceptualized as a neurodevelopmental disorder. Genetic and prenatal or perinatal (occurring at the time of birth) risk factors may set the stage for a disease process that encompasses biological, cognitive, and social changes that occur over time and result in schizophrenia (see Figure 11.4). Longitudinal studies using repeated fMRI neuroimaging (Rapoport et al., 2012) show that people with schizophrenia lose significant gray matter during adolescence through a normal biological process known as **synaptic pruning** that eliminates weaker synaptic contacts and enhances the already-strong ones (see Figure 11.5). For people with schizophrenia, synaptic pruning occurs at a rate faster than it does in people without schizophrenia, beginning in childhood and accelerating in adolescence. The timing of this acceleration coincides with the emergence of subtle behavioral, motor, and cognitive abnormalities (Jones et al., 1994; Walker et al., 1994). Impaired peer relationships, enhanced social isolation and social anxiety, disruptive behaviors in preadolescent boys, and withdrawal behaviors in preadolescent girls also occur during this time. All of these behaviors are associated with but not specific to the onset of schizophrenia in adulthood (Done et al., 1994).

However, schizophrenia is not simply a biological process. Although changes in different parts of the brain have been identified, no unique anatomical or functional abnormalities have been identified (Owen et al., 2016). What is meant by this statement is that some of the

Figure 11.4 Neurodevelopmental Model of Schizophrenia.

This general neurodevelopmental model indicates many different biological and environmental factors that probably contribute to the onset of schizophrenia.

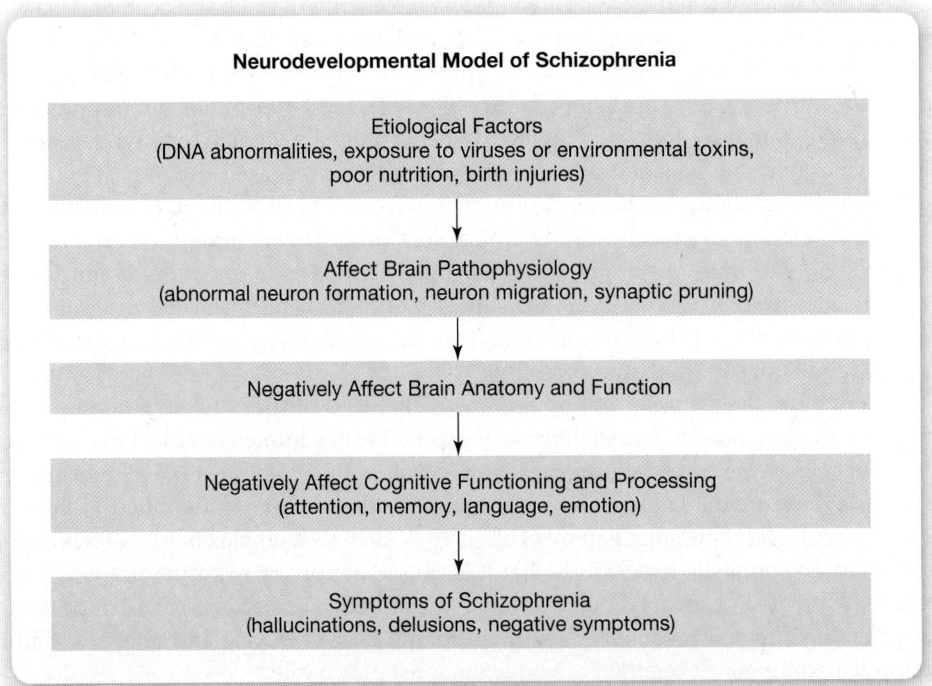

Figure 11.5 Synaptic Pruning.

Synaptic pruning (eliminating weak brain synapses) is accelerated in children with early onset schizophrenia, even in comparison to their healthy siblings.

SOURCE: Rapoport, J. L., Giedd, J. N., & Gogtay, N. (2012). Neurodevelopmental model of schizophrenia: Update 2012. *Molecular Psychiatry*, *17*, 1228–1238. & 2012 Macmillan Publishers Limited All rights reserved 1359-4184/12

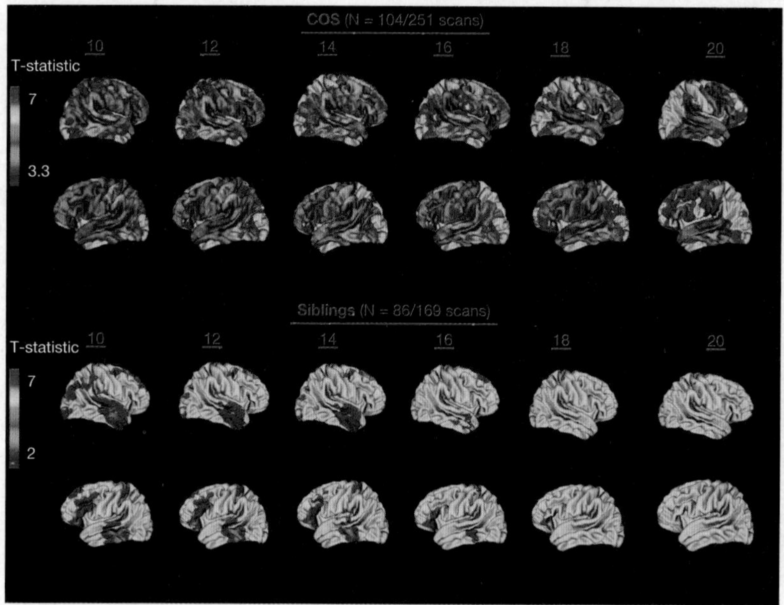

brain abnormalities seen in people with schizophrenia also occur in their relatives who never develop the disorder. This means that it is not just the neuroanatomical differences; other factors, such as psychological and environmental influences, probably contribute as well.

Family Influences

LO 11.9 Understand the interplay of genetic, biological, psychological, and environmental factors in the etiology of schizophrenia.

Historically, the "schizophrenogenic mother" was considered as an environmental factor representing either a cause and/or a response to the presence of schizophrenia in a child (Parker, 1982), even an adult child. This concept emerged from the clinical observations of mental health professionals who worked with families of patients with schizophrenia and who described patients' mothers as dominant, overprotective, and rejecting. However, controlled scientific investigations (including longitudinal designs) did not confirm the existence of such a behavior pattern (Hartwell, 1996). How do we reconcile the clinical observations with the empirical data? One explanation is that the concept of the "schizophrenogenic mother" was based in part on observations or descriptions of family interactions when the patient already had schizophrenia. However, the presence of a psychological disorder, particularly one that affects cognition and behavior as seriously as does schizophrenia, also affects family interactions. In many cases, parents must assume substantial responsibility for their children—even their adult children—and this could result in parents acting in a controlling and overprotective fashion perhaps out of necessity given their child's disorder. However, this does not mean that parents behaved in this way *before* the patient developed the disorder.

Ruling out poor parenting or a "bad" family environment highlights an important point: What science has determined is (or is not) the cause of a disorder is not necessarily the same as what people believe is responsible for their suffering. Earlier we noted that culture may affect the expression and interpretation of the symptoms of schizophrenia. Similarly, culture may also shape explanations of its etiology. Whereas white patients born in the United Kingdom gave a biological explanation for their illness (e.g., it is the result of physical illness or substance use) (McCabe & Priebe, 2004), second-generation United

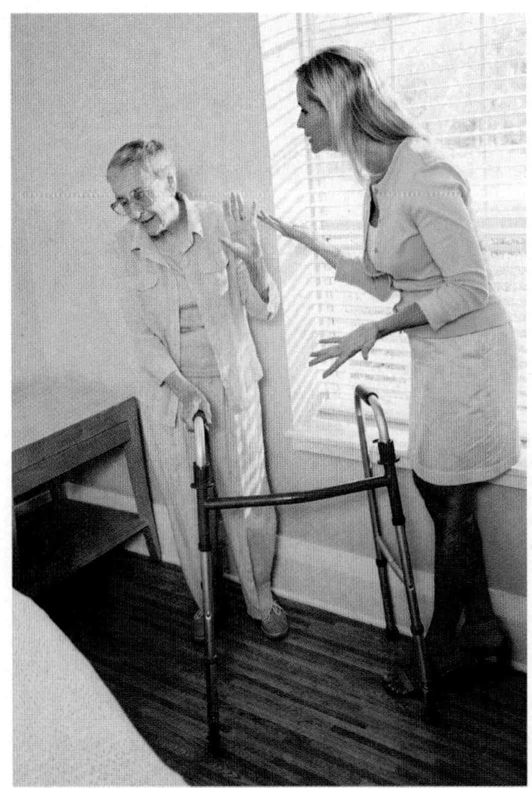

Negative and critical attitudes by family members are correlated with higher rates of relapse among schizophrenic patients.

Kingdom residents of African Caribbean, Bangladeshi, or West African descent were more likely to provide a social explanation (e.g., interpersonal problems/stress/negative childhood experiences) or a supernatural one (e.g., magic spells/evil forces).

Returning to our examination of familial factors, even though the notion of a "schizophrenogenic mother" is no longer accepted, environmental factors such as family interaction remain the subject of scientific scrutiny. The concept known as **expressed emotion** (EE) describes a family's emotional involvement and critical attitudes found among people with a psychological disorder, in this case, schizophrenia. Patients with schizophrenia who live in family environments that are high on EE variables (which include high levels of emotional overinvolvement and critical attitudes) are more likely to relapse and have higher rates of rehospitalization (e.g., Butzlaff & Hooley, 1998). High EE is an environmental stressor that may increase the likelihood of relapse among those with schizophrenia. However, a treatment designed to increase communication and problem-solving skills among families of a patient with schizophrenia was no more effective than the control condition of monthly family visits to a therapist (Schooler et al., 1997). This means that although high EE may predict relapse, it may not be possible to change these family patterns once they have been established.

Unlike the study presented in "Examining the Evidence: Genetics and Environment in the Development of Schizophrenia" (which was a prospective study), the relationship between high EE and relapse is based mainly on correlational data. Therefore, no conclusions about the role of EE as a *causal* factor are available. It is possible that high levels of emotional involvement and critical family attitudes emerge *after* the onset of the patient's disorder. Coping with someone with schizophrenia can be very stressful, and families worldwide feel its effects (Breitborde et al., 2009; Huang et al., 2009; Zahid & Ohaeri, 2010). Families experience financial and emotional burdens as well as negative health consequences (Dyck et al., 1999). In fact, the family interaction patterns identified as characteristic of EE have been identified with other disorders such as drug and alcohol abuse. High EE may reflect the emotional toll of living with a family member with any type of severely impairing mental disorder.

The relationship of EE to relapse and rehospitalization may be unique to white people. Whereas low levels of criticism and fewer intrusive behaviors by relatives were associated with better patient outcome for white patients, high levels of critical and intrusive behavior were associated with better outcomes for African American patients (Gurlak & De Mamani, 2015; Rosenfarb et al., 2006), again illustrating the need to consider culture, race, and ethnicity when studying abnormal behavior. Given these differences, the role of EE in the course of schizophrenia requires further study and should include attention to racial and ethnic group membership as well.

We noted that schizophrenia "runs in families." In some instances, the relatives of patients with schizophrenia also have schizophrenia; in other instances, they may have some behaviors associated with the disorder, such as exaggerated distrust of strangers, but not at a level that produces impairment. These relatives possess *traits* associated with schizophrenia, such as a deficit in social cognition. Although definitions of this construct differ, it is useful to think of social cognition as the "mental operations underlying social interactions, which include the human ability and capacity to perceive the intentions and dispositions of others" (Brothers, 1990, p. 28). Social cognition, sometimes called *social perception*, includes skills such as the ability to perceive when someone is interested in conversation or to interpret eye contact or a smile from a stranger.

Sigrid, age 20, was diagnosed with paranoid schizophrenia. She was hospitalized after she went to the local FBI office demanding the surveillance tapes that she believed it had collected regarding her daily activities. When Sigrid's mother, Linda, came to the unit for a consultation with the social worker, the social worker noticed that Linda did not make eye contact and asked the social worker at least 12 times who would have access to her daughter's hospital records.

Although Linda had never been treated for schizophrenia, her behavior indicated deficits in social cognition. A **gene–environment correlation** means that the same person who provides a patient's genetic makeup also provides the environment in which that person lives. Thus individuals who are at increased genetic risk for schizophrenia may also be exposed to environments that increase risk of developing symptoms of schizophrenia. Did Linda's mother contribute to her daughter's condition by virtue of shared genes or by fostering an environment limited in appropriate social cognition? In such a case, it is difficult to disentangle genetic and environmental influences on the development of a disorder—they are deeply intertwined.

Learning Objective Summaries

LO 11.8 Discuss the neurodevelopmental model of schizophrenia.

The neurodevelopmental model of schizophrenia is based on research indicating that the brain abnormalities commonly associated with schizophrenia occur early in the course of human development, sometimes prenatally. Genetic alterations, prenatal environmental factors, and obstetrical complications may begin an ongoing developmental process that encompasses biological, cognitive, and social changes occurring throughout a lifetime. An accelerated process of synaptic pruning in the brain may also be an important factor in the disorder's etiology.

LO 11.9 Understand the interplay of genetic, biological, psychological, and environmental factors in the etiology of schizophrenia.

Advances in neuroscience have allowed for a much better understanding of structural and functional brain abnormalities. Evidence indicates a genetic contribution to the development of schizophrenia. Twin and family studies illustrate the complex roles of genes and the environment in contributing to the development of schizophrenia. An important concept is synaptic pruning that eliminates weaker synaptic contacts and strengthens the already-strong ones. In people with schizophrenia, this process is accelerated and associated with behavioral, motor, and cognitive abnormalities. Biological factors may combine with environmental influences such as a disordered family environment to result in schizophrenia. Prenatal events associated with the disorder include biological factors such as exposure to influenza and environmental stressors such as maternal malnutrition. Environmental factors that are influential after birth include the family. For example, children of mothers with schizophrenia are more likely to develop the disorder if they are "adopted away" into a disordered family environment when compared to children who are adopted into a stable home environment. Psychological factors such as family support may help prevent relapse and rehospitalization.

Critical Thinking Question

A viral model for the development of schizophrenia is illustrated by studies examining exposure to the influenza virus in pregnant women. Given the number of people who catch the flu each year, how strong is the evidence for this theory?

Treatment of Schizophrenia and Other Psychotic Disorders

Much of the historical treatment of mental illnesses discussed in Chapter 1 actually describes treatment of psychotic disorders such as schizophrenia. Until the past 50 years, institutionalization and humane treatments such as those proposed by Pinel, Tuke, Rush, and Dix (see Chapter 1) were among the few courses of action available to treat these disorders or at least separate people suffering from psychological disorders from the rest of society. Surgical treatments in the form of primitive lobotomies were performed to decrease a patient's agitated, aggressive, or violent behavior. *Lobotomies* involved first administering anesthesia and then entering the person's brain either through a hole drilled in the skull or by inserting a device similar to an ice pick above the eyeball. The

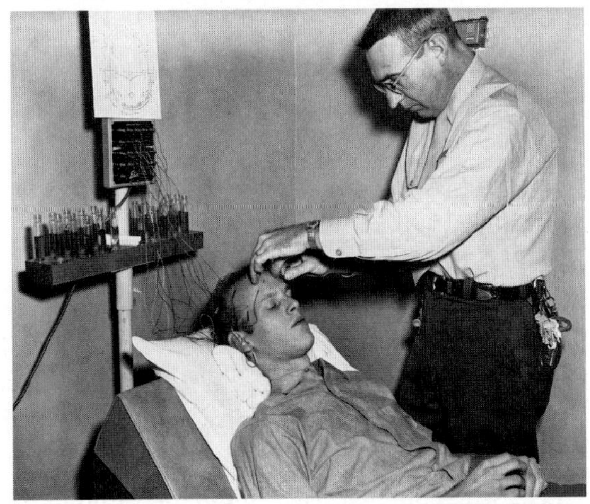

In the 1940s and 1950s, many people who were considered to have uncontrollable behavior were given a surgical treatment called a *lobotomy*. Although the treatment included different procedures, all were designed to sever some neuronal connections in the brain.

rationale for these procedures was that emotions were seated in the brain and that removing some of the brain matter would alleviate suffering (similar to *trephination* discussed in Chapter 1). The outcomes of lobotomies were generally negative and included cognitive and emotional deficits and in some cases death.

Until the middle of the twentieth century, no therapies actually reduced symptoms of the disorder. Hydrotherapy (water therapy) was used to calm agitated patients. Hospital staff would give patients prolonged baths (8 to 24 hours in length) or wrap them in wet sheets (either warm or cold) to reduce agitation (Harmon, 2009). During this time, sedative medication was another form of treatment to reduce agitation.

In the 1950s, the discovery of the medication chlorpromazine changed the treatment of schizophrenia. This medication treated the specific symptoms of the disorder, allowing patients to be discharged from the hospital (Drake et al., 2003). The ability of patients to leave the hospital led to the *community mental health movement*, which emphasized treatment, recovery, and reintegration into the community (Drake et al., 2009; see Chapter 15 for more information on this movement). Now in the twenty-first century, the situation has changed dramatically again; several effective treatments are available for people with schizophrenia. These treatments are far from universally or uniformly effective, but they constitute a great advance over what was available 100 years ago.

Pharmacological Treatment

LO 11.10 Identify efficacious pharmacological treatments for schizophrenia.

Pharmacotherapy (medication) is the treatment of choice for schizophrenia. The most common medication class is the **antipsychotics**, which block dopamine receptors at four different receptor sites labeled D1, D2, D3, and D4 (Horacek et al., 2006). However, blocking the receptor is not simply an all-or-nothing process. Depending on the particular drug, blocking may be temporary, permanent, partial, or complete, and the type of blocking affects how well the drug works. Antipsychotics have only limited effects, however. They do not improve the negative symptoms or the cognitive deficits found among people with schizophrenia (Owen et al., 2016). Antipsychotics are efficacious at decreasing positive symptoms and consist of two types: typical and atypical.

TYPICAL ANTIPSYCHOTICS Before the 1990s, the available antipsychotics (now called **conventional or typical antipsychotics**) effectively reduced the positive symptoms of schizophrenia but produced serious side effects. These included muscle stiffness, tremors, and **tardive dyskinesia**, a neurological condition characterized by abnormal and involuntary motor movements of the face, mouth, limbs, and trunk (Gray et al., 2005). The most common symptoms of tardive dyskinesia are movements of the tongue (lip licking, sucking, smacking, and fly-catching movements), jaw (chewing, grinding), face (grimacing, tics), and eyes (blinking, brow arching). Unfortunately, tardive dyskinesia appears to be a fairly common condition; after 15 years of treatment with typical antipsychotics, about 52% of patients will develop this side effect (Kane et al., personal communication, cited in Tarsy & Baldessarini, 2006). Tardive dyskinesia may begin months or years after the start of the medication (Margolese & Ferreri, 2007). Although it is not clear why this syndrome occurs, one possibility is that the typical antipsychotics create "supersensitivity" of the dopamine receptors, leading them to "overreact" and produce these abnormal movements (e.g., Dean, 2006). Unfortunately, discontinuation of the medication does not eliminate tardive dyskinesia, and it is likely that once the receptor sensitivity is altered, it cannot be easily reversed.

ATYPICAL ANTIPSYCHOTICS Since the 1990s, a group of medications called the **atypical antipsychotics** have been preferred for the treatment of schizophrenia in both adults and youth (Kranzler et al., 2005; Mueser & McGurk, 2004). These medications are considered as effective as traditional antipsychotics in treating positive symptoms, and they are much less likely to produce tardive dyskinesia. They also have some effects on negative symptoms and cognitive impairments (Mallinger et al., 2006). The medications do not help everyone, and one study found that over an 18-month period, more than 60% of patients who were prescribed one of these medications discontinued them due to side effects or lack of effectiveness (Lieberman et al., 2005). Still, the atypical antipsychotics may represent an improvement over their predecessors because they help reduce negative symptoms and produce fewer side effects (Fleischhacker & Widschwendter, 2006). Although they are less likely to produce tardive dyskinesia, they have their own side effects including producing diabetes and high triglycerides (a type of fat found in the blood). The most dangerous side effect is *agranulocytosis*, which is a lowering of the white blood cell count that could be fatal if not detected in time. Weight gain (sometimes severe) is another side effect that occurs in both children and adults (Kranzler et al., 2006). Therefore, although the atypical antipsychotics are now the most commonly prescribed medication for people with schizophrenia, whether they represent a *significant* improvement remains controversial (Lieberman et al., 2005). Newer biological treatments such as transcranial magnetic stimulation (TMS) attempt to change brain functioning through procedures other than medications (see "Research Hot Topic: Transcranial Magnetic Stimulation").

As illustrated in the sections on symptoms and etiology, cultural factors play a role in the treatment of schizophrenia. White patients more frequently preferred medication and

Research HOT Topic

Transcranial Magnetic Stimulation

Transcranial magnetic stimulation (TMS) is a noninvasive biological approach used to treat several psychological disorders including depression, obsessive-compulsive disorder, and schizophrenia. The goal of TMS is to provide stimulation to a targeted area of the cerebral cortex to change brain activity. Using a small coil placed over the scalp, a brief but powerful magnetic current passes through the scalp and skull. This induces an electrical current that produces *depolarization* (neuronal discharge) in the area beneath the coil and in functionally related areas (Hoffman et al., 2003). Based on the magnetic frequency used, the stimulation can produce an excitatory or inhibitory effect on the specific neurons (Saba et al., 2006). Although the actual treatment regimen has some variation, one treatment involves 8 minutes of stimulation on Day 1, 12 minutes on Day 2, and 16 minutes on the next 7 days (Hoffman et al., 2003). Side effects appear to be minimal and include brief headaches that are treated with standard over-the-counter medication and concentration and memory difficulties that last no more than 10 minutes after treatment (Hoffman et al., 2003).

The use of TMS in schizophrenia is based on neuroimaging studies that show specific areas of brain activity during auditory hallucinations. For example, areas important for speech perception become activated during periods of hallucinations (Hoffman et al., 2003). These findings have produced several hypotheses regarding the neuroanatomical basis of auditory hallucinations including (1) the hallucinated voice is the patient's inner speech that is misperceived as coming from outside the brain and (2) the hallucination is the result of a malfunction of the speech perception system—in effect, the system creates speech without any input from the outside (Lee et al., 2005). TMS changes the activity of these neurons, thereby decreasing (at least temporarily) the frequency of hallucinations.

Available data suggest that TMS is more effective than *sham TMS* (using the coil but not delivering the current) in reducing auditory hallucinations that are resistant to medication (Fitzgerald & Daskalakis, 2008; Hoffman et al., 2003) and reduced scores on self-report of positive symptoms (including hallucinations; Lee et al., 2005). There is mixed support for whether it is effective in reducing negative symptoms (Fitzgerald & Daskalakis, 2008; Quan et al., 2015; Wobrock et al., 2015) or cognitive functioning (Fitzgerald & Daskalakis, 2008; Wobrock et al., 2015). TMS does not appear to reduce delusions (Saba et al., 2006; Wobrock et al. 2015) or have an impact on overall illness severity (Quan et al., 2015). Very preliminary evidence suggests that TMS may reduce negative symptoms and enhance cognitive functioning. Also, its effects are time limited, there appears to be a placebo effect in some cases (Dollfus et al., 2016), and many studies were of poor quality and subject to biased reporting (Dougall et al., 2015). As discussed in Chapter 2, many differences in available experiments including sample sizes, strength of an intervention (in this case, strength of the magnetic field), and different outcome variables (in this case, hallucinations versus delusions) make it difficult to determine whether TMS is really effective for schizophrenia. More studies are needed. However, given the impairing nature of residual schizophrenic symptoms, this promising treatment is sure to be the object of much further study.

counseling treatments (McCabe & Priebe, 2004), whereas African Caribbeans were more likely to want counseling but not medication. In contrast, patients of Bangladeshi descent preferred a religious activity or no treatment at all, consistent with their beliefs that the cause of their illness was societal or spiritual in nature. Despite their different cultural backgrounds, all patients were equally likely to comply with their prescribed treatment. Therefore, different cultural preferences did not affect their willingness to accept offered treatments.

In addition to different treatment preferences, racial disparities exist in the frequency with which atypical antipsychotics are prescribed; white people are approximately six times more likely to receive these medications than African American individuals (Mallinger et al., 2006), who are more likely to receive the typical antipsychotics. The reasons for the different prescription rates are unclear because the symptoms of schizophrenia do not differ for these two groups. One factor to consider is the difference in the rate of side effects: African American patients may be at increased risk for medication-induced diabetes and agranulocytosis (Moeller et al., 1995), side effects more commonly found with the atypical antipsychotics. This might make some psychiatrists less likely to prescribe these medications to African Americans, but this alone would not seem to account for such a large disparity.

Any single study may not reveal the entire picture about the effectiveness of any particular drug. A meta-analysis (which uses advanced statistical procedures to combine the results of many different studies) examined the efficacy of different classes of medications for the treatment of schizophrenia using 168 randomized controlled trials of adult patients (Fusar-Poli et al., 2015). Second generation antipsychotics were found to reduce the negative symptoms of schizophrenia, as were antidepressants but to a lesser degree. First-generation antipsychotics had no effect on negative symptoms, and neither did brain stimulation. A different meta-analysis using 27 studies of children, adolescents, and young adults with schizophrenia was less encouraging; antipsychotics only had a small beneficial effect on psychotic symptoms where it had a medium negative effect on weight gain and discontinuation due to side effects, leading the authors to conclude that these medications are less efficacious for children, adolescents, and young adults than typical adult populations (Stafford et al., 2015).

One of the greatest challenges to effective pharmacological treatment for people with schizophrenia is medication compliance. Approximately 50% of patients never take their medication or do not take it as prescribed (Fenton et al., 1997). Medication noncompliance is associated with high relapse rates and poor treatment response (Ilott, 2005; Yamada et al., 2006). Noncompliance occurs among chronic patients and those recovering from their first episode (Kamali et al., 2006). The reasons for noncompliance are varied but include distress about side effects and embarrassment or stigma (Perkins et al., 2006; Yamada et al., 2006), more severe positive symptoms, lack of insight regarding symptoms, alcohol and drug abuse (Kamali et al., 2006), and lack of belief in the need for treatment or the benefit of medication (Perkins et al., 2006). Psychoeducation programs aimed at enhancing patients' understanding of medication compliance have produced only moderate results (Ilott, 2005). Interventions may need to tailor the education to each patient's specific concerns rather than only provide general information.

Psychosocial Treatment

LO 11.11 Identify efficacious psychological treatments for schizophrenia.

Antipsychotic medications are considered the treatment of choice for patients with schizophrenia. Although they have minimal to no efficacy on the primary symptoms of schizophrenia for children, adolescents, or adults (Fusar-Poli et al., 2015; Stafford et al., 2015), psychosocial strategies are used as *adjunctive* (supplemental) interventions that seek to further reduce primary symptoms and to decrease daily stress on the patient and/or family, increasing the patient's social skills and helping the patient find and maintain employment when possible. The United Kingdom's National Institute for Health and Care Excellence recommends that people with schizophrenia should be offered family psychoeducation and cognitive behavioral therapy as well as medication (Owen et al., 2016).

PSYCHOEDUCATION Schizophrenia is difficult on the patient and the family. Positive symptoms often require hospitalizing the patient, and negative symptoms strain family relationships and cause considerable conflict. For example, a patient who withdraws from family activities and neglects personal hygiene may face hostile criticism from family members. Because family environments characterized by high levels of emotional involvement and critical attitudes toward the patient (high EE) are associated with higher rates of relapse and higher rates of rehospitalization for some patients than others (e.g., Butzlaff & Hooley, 1998), an important treatment component is psychoeducation of the family and significant others. **Psychoeducation** is a process that educates patients and family members about the disorder; it provides the same type of information found in this chapter. The goal of the process is to reduce family members' distress and allow clinicians to increase the effectiveness of their work with the patient and caregiver. These programs reduce relapse rates and shorten length of hospitalization (Motlova et al., 2006; Pitschel-Walz et al., 2001). Although family psychoeducation does not affect the symptoms of the disorder directly, it helps family members understand and deal with the patient and the illness.

COGNITIVE-BEHAVIORAL TREATMENT Between 20 and 50% of people with schizophrenia continue to have hallucinations despite taking antipsychotic medication (Newton et al., 2005), creating continuing distress and negatively affecting social and occupational adjustment. Psychologists have used behavioral and cognitive-behavioral therapy (CBT) to reduce or eliminate psychotic symptoms, although their use is not common. The literature describing the efficacy of behavior therapy for schizophrenia dates back 35 years (Glaister, 1985; Nydegger, 1972), and CBT appears effective in reducing psychotic symptoms that remain even with the proper use of medication (Butler et al., 2006; Cather et al., 2005; Gaudiano, 2006). CBT consists of psychoeducation about psychosis and hallucinations, exploration of individual beliefs about hallucinations and delusions, education in using coping strategies to deal with the symptoms, and improving self-esteem (Wykes et al., 2005). Patients take medication while participating in CBT. In one investigation, group CBT significantly reduced the severity of hallucinations (compared with a control group) but only when the therapy was delivered by very experienced group therapists (Wykes et al., 2005). Group CBT for psychotic symptoms appears to be more effective when it is delivered early in the course of the illness (i.e., within the first 3 years of onset; Newton et al., 2005). Research is now examining why these two factors (very experienced therapists and treatment delivered within the first 3 years of symptom onset) may be so important.

There have been a number of attempts in the past decade to formally address the social cognitive deficits that are part of this disorder. Known as social cognition treatment, there are several different programs that are available. Although each is a little different, they attempt to teach skills such as changing attributional biases, emotional perception, social perception, theory of mind (the ability to attribute various mental states to oneself or others), and facial affect recognition using video instruction, role plays, and practice exercises. These programs appear most efficacious for training facial affect recognition and theory of mind but less efficacious for training attributional style. Only a few studies assessed social perception, but training appears to be efficacious for that skill as well. However, there are no long-term follow-up studies, so it is unclear if these treatment gains last, but if so, it would significantly improve the social functioning of people with this disorder.

Training in social perception skills often use faces portraying different emotions to teach people with schizophrenia to understand emotional expressions.

SOCIAL SKILLS TRAINING Impaired social functioning is a core symptom of schizophrenia, and behaviors such as social isolation and withdrawal often occur before psychotic symptoms appear. The inability to interact with others in a socially acceptable way interferes with social, occupational, and vocational functioning. Effective social skills are needed to interview for a job, maintain employment, establish social support networks, and go to college. Social skills training teaches the basics of social interaction including nonverbal skills such as eye contact, vocal tone, and voice volume and verbal skills such as initiating and maintaining conversations, expressing feelings, and acting assertively. Although not a comprehensive treatment for schizophrenia, social skills training has a long and successful history improving the social functioning of people with this disorder (Bellack, 2004), even those who are middle-aged or older (Granholm et al., 2005) and who have had the disorder for many years.

SUPPORTED EMPLOYMENT The ability to maintain full-time competitive employment is associated with higher rates of symptom improvement, enhanced leisure and financial satisfaction, and enhanced self-esteem (Bond, Resnick, Drake, Xi, et al., 2001). However, few patients with schizophrenia (between 10 and 20%; Mueser & McGurk, 2004) are able to work full-time. Schizophrenia begins for many people during the transition from adolescence to adulthood before they have experience with adult work activities. Supported employment is a psychosocial intervention that provides job skills to people with schizophrenia. The program includes a rapid job search approach; individual job placements that match patient preferences, strengths, and work experience (if any); follow-along support (continued contact with therapists and job counselors); and integration with the treatment team (Bond, Resnick, Drake, Rapp, et al., 2001). Such programs help people with schizophrenia find and maintain competitive employment, but there are not yet enough programs for all people who could benefit from them.

COMPREHENSIVE INTEGRATED CARE As we noted earlier in this chapter, schizophrenia is a complex disorder and requires a comprehensive approach to treatment. One comprehensive approach, called Navigate, consists of four components: personalized medication management, family psychoeducation, individualized resilience-focused illness self-management therapy, and supported education and employment (Rosenheck et al., 2016). This intervention addresses medication and psychological skill building as well as working with the family and providing support for education and employment. It is important to note that this was not just a group of interventions; they were provided in a coordinated fashion. When compared with treatment as usual, this comprehensive and integrated approach was more effective at improving quality of life for a sample of people with first-episode psychosis, and although it had higher outpatient and mental health costs than typical community care, the incremental cost-effectiveness comparisons demonstrated that in the long run, the comprehensive treatment was more cost-effective than community care.

Learning Objective Summaries

LO 11.10 Identify efficacious pharmacological treatments for schizophrenia.

Schizophrenia is a chronic disorder, and full symptom remission is rare. Pharmacological treatment is the primary intervention for schizophrenia, particularly the class of medication known as the atypical antipsychotics, which appear to help with both the positive and the negative symptoms. Use of the typical antipsychotics has declined because they are associated with an irreversible side effect known as tardive dyskinesia.

LO 11.11 Identify efficacious psychological treatments for schizophrenia.

Psychological interventions such as social skills training, cognitive-behavioral treatment, and supported employment are effective *adjunctive*, or additional, treatments that may reduce negative symptoms, reduce medication-resistant hallucinations and delusions, and enhance employment skills. Interventions that combine medication, psychosocial treatment, and family education/support may be needed for this very chronic and serious disorder.

Critical Thinking Question

Given that medications have side effects so severe that a subset of patients discontinues taking medication, why is cognitive-behavioral treatment not used first to treat the positive symptoms of schizophrenia?

Real SCIENCE Real LIFE

Kerry—Treating Schizophrenia

THE PATIENT

Kerry is 19 years old. He has always been a shy, quiet young man. Studious and respectful in high school, he had few friends and never dated. He was accepted at the state university 100 miles from home.

THE PROBLEM

During his first semester, he became concerned that people who were living in his dorm were "out to get him." His concerns extended to an instructor who wore a red shirt, which Kerry believed to be a sign of the devil. The archangel Michael began to speak to Kerry, commenting on his behavior and giving him instructions on how to behave. His roommate became alarmed not only because Kerry accused him of inserting thoughts into his head but also because Kerry stopped eating (he thought the food might have been poisoned) and bathing (in case the water was contaminated).

Kerry stopped going to classes and was reluctant to leave his room where he constantly examined light fixtures and electrical outlets for listening devices planted there by the FBI. He would call his parents at odd hours of the night, crying and pleading with them to make the voices go away. The next day he would call them and angrily accuse them of being in league with the devil, the FBI, or both. His bizarre behavior led to an inpatient hospitalization and a diagnosis of paranoid schizophrenia.

ASSESSING THE SITUATION

First, how would you explain the etiology of this disorder to his parents? How did it develop? Second, how would you treat it? Design a plan to help Kerry. What would you say is his prognosis?

THE TREATMENT

Kerry was treated with an atypical antipsychotic, which decreased his auditory hallucinations but did not eliminate them. Kerry was unable to tolerate the medication dosage considered necessary for optimal treatment outcome because of severe side effects, and he continued to express discomfort with auditory hallucinations. He was treated with cognitive-behavioral therapy (CBT) and felt that although he was better able to cope with the hallucinations on a daily basis, they still interfered with his ability to return to school or hold a job. Because he had achieved only a partial treatment response, Kerry had to take a leave of absence from school and returned home to live with his parents. The medical school near his parents' home was offering a research study using TMS, and Kerry enrolled as a participant. TMS decreased the frequency of his symptoms to the extent that he was then able to use the coping skills he acquired through CBT to deal with the remaining hallucinations. His negative symptoms were also somewhat improved. Although he was not able to return to college full-time, he was able to maintain half-time employment as a dishwasher in a restaurant.

THE TREATMENT OUTCOME

One year after treatment was completed, Kerry became depressed at his inability to return to his previous state of functioning. He stopped taking his medication and attempted to commit suicide by choking himself. He passed out before he suffocated and was hospitalized. After rehospitalization and reinstatement of his medication, Kerry was admitted to a partial hospitalization program in which he received group treatments such as social skills training and illness-management skills. Following his discharge, he was rehired at the restaurant and enrolled in one college course at a community college. Six months later, he moved out of his parents' house into a supported living facility, allowing him more independence. He continues to struggle with the hallucinations but has been able to use his coping skills to manage their severity.

Key Terms

alogia, p. 419
anhedonia, p. 419
antipsychotics, p. 442
atypical antipsychotics, p. 442
avolition, p. 419
brief psychotic disorder, p. 429
catatonia, p. 419
clang associations, p. 419
cognitive impairment, p. 419
conventional or typical antipsychotics, p. 442
delusion, p. 413
delusional disorder, p. 430
delusions of influence, p. 417
dementia praecox, p. 415
diminished emotional expression, p. 419
dopamine hypothesis, p. 432
early-onset schizophrenia, p. 427
echolalia, p. 421
expressed emotion, p. 440
gene–environment correlation, p. 441
hallucination, p. 413
loose associations, p. 418
negative symptoms, p. 419
persecutory delusions, p. 416
positive symptoms, p. 416
psychoeducation, p. 445
psychomotor retardation, p. 419
psychosis, p. 413
schizoaffective disorder, p. 429
schizophrenia, p. 414
schizophreniform disorder, p. 429
shared psychotic disorder, p. 430
social cognition, p. 420
synaptic pruning, p. 438
tardive dyskinesia, p. 442
thought blocking, p. 419
waxy flexibility, p. 419

Chapter 12

Personality Disorders

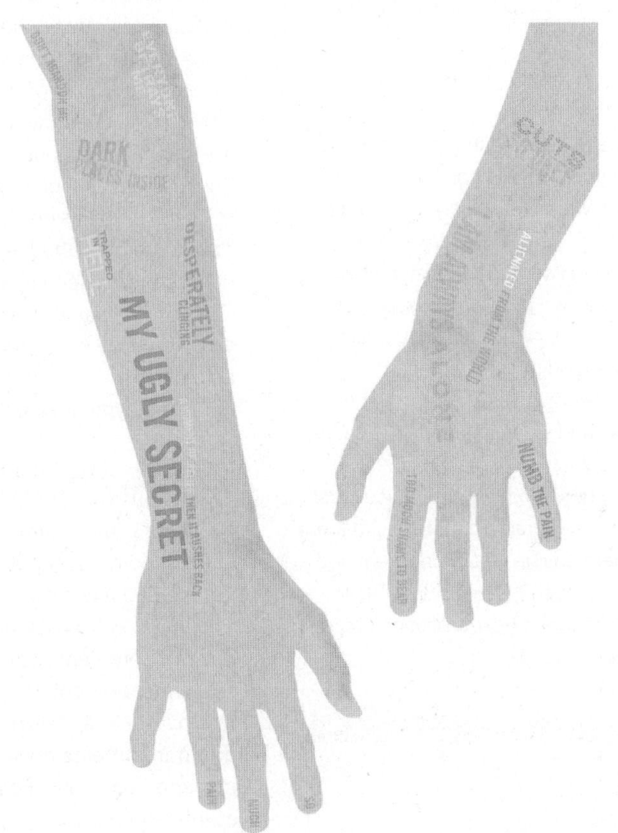

Chapter Learning Objectives

Defining Personality Disorders

LO 12.1 Distinguish between a personality trait and a personality disorder.

LO 12.2 Describe how the categorical approach to diagnosing a personality disorder differs from a dimensional approach.

Personality Disorder Clusters

LO 12.3 Describe the Cluster A personality disorders and their uniting characteristics.

LO 12.4 Describe the Cluster B personality disorders and their uniting characteristics.

LO 12.5 Describe the Cluster C personality disorders and their uniting characteristics.

LO 12.6 Evaluate various models of personality disorders.

LO 12.7 Debate the extent to which childhood personality predicts adult personality and personality disorders.

	LO 12.8	Clarify the manner in which personality disorders influence interpersonal functioning.
	LO 12.9	Trace the occurrence of personality disorders across various segments of the population.
Etiology of Personality Disorders	**LO 12.10**	Understand the role biology may play in the origin of personality pathology.
	LO 12.11	Compare psychological theories of personality disorders and discuss the role of culture on personality.
Treatment of Personality Disorders	**LO 12.12**	Discuss challenges in the treatment of personality disorders with psychotherapy.
	LO 12.13	Evaluate the effectiveness of medication in the treatment of various personality disorders.

Jacqui was a graduate student in mass communications. She was in danger of getting kicked out of her program. Her explanation was that the professors "just don't f**king get" her creativity. In her first year of grad school, Jacqui had become very close friends with a gay man in her class named Brad, and they partied a lot together. At first they got along well, but then she started pushing him to try more drugs and get "really wasted" with her.

After failing an assignment on a Friday, she went to his house to cry on his shoulder. He was very understanding, helped calm her down, and helped her work out a plan to talk with the professor. She told him he was the kindest friend in the world and she didn't know what she would do without his support. They went out drinking and dancing that night. She drank way too much and accused him of sexually assaulting her. She spread a rumor that he wasn't really gay and that was just a front so he could get closer to women and then rape them.

Her classmates seemed to turn on her after she started this rumor; they all came to his defense. She didn't go to class for a week and just stayed in her apartment and smoked weed. She was sick of everyone, but she felt so alone and empty. No one understood her.

The only thing that made her feel better was cutting. At first she made cuts on her thighs and abdomen where no one could see them. But then she decided she wanted to "wear" her scars. So she started cutting her arms and wearing short sleeves. She started flaunting her cuts. One night when she was alone in her apartment drinking, she cut too deep. Blood was pouring from her arm, and she was frightened.

She called Brad who, in an act of extreme kindness after her accusations, rushed her to the emergency room. The physician tended to her cut and talked with her about the cuts all over her body that were in various stages of healing. She called the on-call psychiatrist, who evaluated Jacqui on site and admitted her for a thorough psychiatric evaluation.

We commonly use adjectives to describe someone's typical behaviors, or personality *traits*: Jan is rigid and controlling, Kiara is outgoing and optimistic, Liza is flitty and distractible, Ty is condescending and arrogant, Rolfe is self-interested and untrustworthy. So when does behavior cross the line from trait to disorder? In some people, characteristic ways of seeing, interpreting, and behaving in the world develop over time in an inflexible and maladaptive way. If someone cannot adapt his or her characteristic approach to the world when necessary and that approach causes significant psychological distress either to the person or to others, then these *traits* may have crystallized into a personality *disorder*. In this chapter, we will discuss personality, personality traits, and personality disorders.

Defining Personality Disorders

What is the difference between a personality *trait* and a personality *disorder*? All people can be described in terms of specific patterns of personality, but not all have a disorder. Differentiating between traits and disorders is crucial for both diagnosis and treatment. This module will start us off by explaining how we define personality disorders.

Personality Trait vs. Personality Disorder

LO 12.1 Distinguish between a personality trait and a personality disorder.

To distinguish between a personality trait and a personality disorder, it is important to consider whether the trait has become rigid and maladaptive. We all have personality traits. Some of those traits might be quite appealing to others (e.g., graciousness, sense of humor), whereas others may be quite irritating to others (e.g., clinginess, vanity). In determining whether a trait or cluster of traits has crystallized into a personality disorder, it is important to determine whether they have become rigid and maladaptive.

A second relevant dimension to consider is that of clinical *state* versus a personality *trait*. A *state* refers to the expression of a personality characteristic that is related to a specific circumstance, clinical condition, or period of time. For example,

> Juan, who is usually even-tempered and easygoing, becomes emotionally unstable whenever he is under stress. He lashes out at people and vacillates between being nice and barking at people.

Juan's behavior is a function of his current life events and would be considered a state-dependent change—not his characteristic way of approaching the world. His behavior would be considered *ego-dystonic*, or distinctly different from the person's self-image.

Conversely, a *trait* refers to the specific and characteristic way someone approaches the world. It is unlikely to change across situations, time, and events. For example, if Juan's behavior tends to fluctuate unpredictably most of the time and others describe him as "dramatic" or "Jekyll and Hyde," this behavior would be considered a personality trait. It is *ego-syntonic*, or consistent with the individual's self-image.

If we observe Juan at any one time and note that his emotions vacillate more often than those of his peers, several explanations are possible. First, his emotional vacillation may not create any significant psychological distress for him or those around him but may simply reflect a colorful aspect of his unique personality. Alternately, our observation may not have detected important contextual information, namely that Juan is very upset lately because he has been having problems at work. After a comprehensive clinical evaluation, he may receive a diagnosis of major depressive disorder. A third possibility is that Juan's vacillation reflects an ingrained way that he interacts with the world that has caused him to lose relationships, jobs, and ties with his family. In this case, we would say that he has a *personality disorder*.

These three alternative explanations highlight several important aspects of a personality disorder diagnosis. First, it is critical to differentiate between a personality trait and a personality disorder. Second, personality disorders should never be diagnosed after a single brief behavioral observation because they represent enduring ways of dealing with the world. Third, clinicians should not diagnose personality disorders without knowing the surrounding context. So, before deciding whether someone has a personality disorder, a clinician must evaluate the person's problems within the larger diagnostic context: Is the person suffering from a personality disorder or from another disorder that is influencing his or her personality? For example, many people may seem to have a personality disorder (they are very emotional or abuse substances) when they are in the throes of an acute episode of another disorder (such as bulimia nervosa). It may be necessary to wait until the other disorder remits and then determine whether the troubling behaviors are still present.

Personality traits are observable from the early years. Many of our perceptions of others are based on our impressions of their personalities. From this picture, whom would you choose as each of these: "Most likely to succeed in business"? "Most likely to graduate from college"? "Most likely to lead a protest march"?

This example illustrates how difficult it is to diagnose a personality disorder: If Juan seeks treatment, the evaluating clinician must consider that his current state does not necessarily reflect his typical behavior. So, because we all have distinctive personality traits, how do we know when a personality state constitutes a maladaptive personality disorder? Because no strong evidence supports a clear boundary between personality traits and personality disorders as yet, the best way to think about them is as pathological amplifications of underlying traits.

Determining whether a behavior is a disorder must consider impairment and distress. This is a particular challenge for diagnosing personality disorders whose symptoms are difficult to quantify. Furthermore, personality disorders have few biological or observable signs. Personality disorders cannot be detected with a blood test, for example, and they must be distinguished from other psychological disorders. You might think of the other psychological disorders in the same manner as an acute medical illness that afflicts a person who functions relatively well in many aspects of life. In contrast, a personality disorder is not a dramatic or acute illness but a long-term, chronic, pervasive pattern of inflexible and maladaptive functioning. Personality disorders are not so much illnesses as a "way of being." They are typically apparent in late adolescence or early adulthood and may persist throughout life.

One particularly difficult distinction to make diagnostically is between personality disorders and other disorders that have a prolonged course, such as persistent depressive disorder (see Chapter 7). In terms of impairment, what separates the distress caused by disorders described in other chapters from the difficulty created by personality disorders? As we describe the various personality disorder clusters, we will illustrate the ways in which these disorders can impair social and occupational functioning. One interesting characteristic of these disorders is that they often cause more distress to other people than to the person with the disorder. Some people with personality disorders may feel very little distress or even none at all.

One way to understand what distinguishes personality disorders from the other disorders in this book is "the three P's." These disorders are patterns of behavior that are *persistent* (over time), *pervasive* (across people and situations), and *pathological* (clearly abnormal). A **personality disorder**, therefore, is "an enduring pattern of inner experience and behavior that deviates markedly from the expectations of the individual's culture, is pervasive and inflexible, has the onset in adolescence or early adulthood, is stable over time, and leads to distress and impairment" (American Psychiatric Association, 2013). Definitions of personality disorders have always highlighted symptom stability: These are not transient moods or temporary quirks of behavior but persistent behavioral features.

Dimensional Approach vs. Categorical Approach

LO 12.2 Describe how the categorical approach to diagnosing a personality disorder differs from a dimensional approach.

The DSM divides personality disorders into three clusters: **Cluster A**, "odd or eccentric"; **Cluster B**, "dramatic, emotional, or erratic"; and **Cluster C**, "anxious or fearful." These labels do not relate directly to the names of the individual disorders within the clusters but describe an overall style of behavior that cuts across the individual disorders. However, some researchers and clinicians question the validity of these clusters. Why? Because, as we have seen, personality traits are common to everyone—we all may have enduring tendencies to be somewhat eccentric, emotional, or fearful. Exactly at what point do these traits turn pathological?

According to the DSM, one either has or does not have a particular personality disorder. This is known as the *categorical* model of personality. Many researchers emphasize that a better model would use a *dimensional* approach that captures the full range of a trait.

A dimensional approach would consider personality to be on a continuum—for example, socially outgoing people on one end and extremely shy people on the other. (See Chapter 3 for more discussion of categorical versus dimensional classification.) Indeed, many prominent theories of personality focus more on dimensional than categorical models. The personality disorders work group that deliberated potential revisions for DSM-5 carefully considered a transition to a more dimensional model for personality disorders. In the end, no significant changes were made to the personality disorders section in DSM-5; however, future versions of the DSM may incorporate more dimensional measures.

SIDE by SIDE Case Studies

Dimensions of Behavior: From Adaptive to Maladaptive

Adaptive Case Study

Trait but No Disorder

Rasheed's wife calls him a "neatnik." He likes his closet in order; everything in his drawers is always neatly folded and tucked away, and he is brilliant at organizing their finances. His wife drives him crazy because she is more of a "piles" person—her clothes are in piles, her work papers are in piles—everything ends up in a pile. Even though it bugs him and he secretly wishes she were more like him, he learned after he tried to organize her things once early in their marriage never to touch her piles! Rasheed has a strong tendency to believe the old adage that "if you want something done right, you have to do it yourself," but he has come to learn that doing everything yourself does not really help other people learn how they can help you, and it just ends up causing more and more stress for you. So even though it irks him on some level when something is not done at work or at home as well as he knows he could do it, he can take a deep breath and let it go. His wife can sense his frustration sometimes and occasionally will just tease him about being wound so tight. At least he can laugh at himself ... and he can always hang out in his closet if he needs to be somewhere tidy!

Maladaptive Case Study

Personality Disorder

Jeff would be happiest if his life never varied. He is a 52-year-old married statistician with three children ages 18, 16, and 12. Every day for the past 15 years, he has risen at 5:30, exercised for 30 minutes while reading the paper, drunk two cups of coffee, eaten a bowl of cereal and a piece of fruit, and caught the same train to work. Each time that train was delayed, he anxiously looked at his watch and fretted about lost time in the office. The household was run to his specifications. If the kids were asked to fold laundry, they had to do it right. If they did it wrong, he gave them one chance to fix it, and if they still did it wrong, he did it himself. His motto was "if you want something done right, you have to do it yourself." He reviewed his children's homework fastidiously and grilled them if their grades slipped. Dinner was at 6:30. He played tennis on Tuesday and Thursday evenings. He had color-coded sticky notes with lists of things to do. But he was a prisoner of his lists. At times, he would sit at his desk, three different-colored lists in front of him, faced with scores of e-mails, and simply not know where to begin. As the lists became longer and the inbox fuller, he could become paralyzed by anxiety. One evening he developed chest pains on the tennis court, and his partner drove him to the ER. It was not a heart attack, but his blood pressure was sky high. His doctor had warned him countless times about his lifestyle, pressure, and anxiety, but he had never listened. The doctor called this his wake-up call. She gave him medications for the blood pressure and the name of a psychologist to help him deal with his driven and obsessive-compulsive personality style.

Learning Objective Summaries

LO 12.1 Distinguish between a personality trait and a personality disorder.

Personality traits represent a wide array of characteristics individuals can have. When a trait or cluster of traits becomes rigid or maladaptive and evolves into an ingrained way that an individual interacts with the world, then it is considered to be a disorder. To determine whether a personality disorder exists, one must consider impairment and distress. A personality disorder is an enduring pattern of inner experience and behavior that deviates markedly from the expectations of the individual's culture, is pervasive and inflexible, has the onset in adolescence or early adulthood, is stable over time, and leads to distress and impairment in social, occupational, or other important areas of functioning.

LO 12.2 Describe how the categorical approach to diagnosing a personality disorder differs from a dimensional approach.

The categorical approach as codified in the DSM-5 divides personality disorders into clusters and specific disorders within those clusters that share core traits. A dimensional model focuses more on a continuum of traits and recognizes that most people have varying degrees of certain traits, which when extreme can become maladaptive. The DSM-5 has not adopted a dimensional model of personality; however, it may emerge in future iterations of the manual.

Critical Thinking Question

What do you think of the dimensional versus categorical classification systems? If you could categorize personality disorders, which would you choose—or would you opt for a different system—and why?

Personality Disorder Clusters

Most mental health professionals follow the DSM categorical approach when characterizing, communicating about, and treating personality disorders. In the following sections, we present both a clinical description and a clinical example of each personality disorder. Keep in mind that impairment is the hallmark of these disorders and that, in many instances, impairment is judged from the perspective of others who are affected by the person's personality disorder. Also, remember the three P's (persistent, pervasive, pathological). To help clinicians understand the core features of all personality disorders, the DSM-5 presents a prototype set of criteria called "General Diagnostic Criteria for a Personality Disorder." A clinician would never give a person a diagnosis of general personality disorder, but in determining whether someone did have a diagnosable personality disorder, the clinician might check in with this prototype to determine whether the person actually did exhibit disturbances in all of the listed domains. It is a guideline that captures the essence of a personality disorder.

Cluster A: Odd or Eccentric Disorders

LO 12.3 Describe the Cluster A personality disorders and their uniting characteristics.

The common features of Cluster A personality disorders (see "DSM-5: Cluster A Disorders") are characteristic behaviors that others would consider odd, quirky, or eccentric (American Psychiatric Association, 2013). Disorders in Cluster A include features similar to those seen

DSM-5

General Diagnostic Criteria for a Personality Disorder

A. An enduring pattern of inner experience and behavior that deviates markedly from the expectations of the individual's culture. This pattern is manifested in two (or more) of the following areas:

1. Cognition (i.e., ways of perceiving and interpreting self, other people, and events).
2. Affectivity (i.e., the range, intensity, lability, and appropriateness of emotional response).
3. Interpersonal functioning.
4. Impulse control.

B. The enduring pattern is inflexible and pervasive across a broad range of personal and social situations.

C. The enduring pattern leads to clinically significant distress or impairment in social, occupational, or other important areas of functioning.

D. The pattern is stable and of long duration, and its onset can be traced back at least to adolescence or early adulthood.

E. The enduring pattern is not better explained as a manifestation or consequence of another mental disorder.

F. The enduring pattern is not attributable to the physiological effects of a substance (e.g., a drug of abuse, a medication) or another medical condition (e.g., head trauma).

Paranoia can include distrust and suspiciousness of family and friends (movie advertisement from the film *Black Swan*).

in psychosis and schizophrenia (see Chapter 11). Indeed, the dividing line between psychosis and Cluster A personality disorders is unclear. For example, family members of people with schizophrenia have higher rates of Cluster A personality disorders—suggesting possible continuity between psychotic disorders and Cluster A disorders (Erlenmeyer-Kimling et al., 1995; Kendler et al., 1993)

PARANOID PERSONALITY DISORDER **Paranoid personality disorder** is a pervasive distrust and suspiciousness of others such that their motives are interpreted as malevolent (American Psychiatric Association, 2013). While a little bit of paranoia can be adaptive in some situations (e.g., protecting oneself from dishonest individuals), paranoid personality disorder is characterized by unjustified and pervasive distrust. People with this disorder (1) believe without any evidence that others are out to exploit, harm, or deceive them; (2) bear grudges and are unforgiving of perceived insults; and (3) are hypervigilant for signs of disloyalty or untrustworthiness in friends, family, coworkers, and acquaintances (American Psychiatric Association, 2013). Typical beliefs of individuals with paranoid personality disorder may include "I cannot trust other people," "Other people have hidden motives," "If other people find out things about me, they will use them against me," "People often say one thing and mean something else," and "A person to whom I am close could be disloyal or unfaithful." Unfortunately, this distrust can extend to friends and family members and potentially damage relationships. In paranoid personality disorder, the suspiciousness does not extend to delusional thoughts. If delusions are present, a more serious condition probably exists, such as delusional disorder or paranoid schizophrenia.

DSM-5

Criteria for Cluster A Personality Disorders

Paranoid Personality Disorder

A. A pervasive distrust and suspiciousness of others such that their motives are interpreted as malevolent, beginning by early adulthood and present in a variety of contexts, as indicated by four (or more) of the following:

1. Suspects, without sufficient basis, that others are exploiting, harming, or deceiving him or her.
2. Is preoccupied with unjustified doubts about the loyalty or trustworthiness of friends or associates.
3. Is reluctant to confide in others because of unwarranted fear that the information will be used maliciously against him or her.
4. Reads hidden demeaning or threatening meanings into benign remarks or events.
5. Persistently bears grudges (i.e., is unforgiving of insults, injuries, or slights).
6. Perceives attacks on his or her character or reputation that are not apparent to others and is quick to react angrily or to counterattack.
7. Has recurrent suspicions, without justification, regarding fidelity of spouse or sexual partner.

B. Does not occur exclusively during the course of schizophrenia, a bipolar disorder or depressive disorder with psychotic features, or another psychotic disorder and is not attributable to the physiological effects of another medical condition.

Note: If criteria are met prior to the onset of schizophrenia, add "premorbid," i.e., "paranoid personality disorder (premorbid)."

Schizoid Personality Disorder

A. A pervasive pattern of detachment from social relationships and a restricted range of expression of emotions in interpersonal settings, beginning by early adulthood and present in a variety of contexts, as indicated by four (or more) of the following:

1. Neither desires nor enjoys close relationships, including being part of a family.
2. Almost always chooses solitary activities.

3. Has little, if any, interest in having sexual experiences with another person.
4. Takes pleasure in few, if any, activities.
5. Lacks close friends or confidants other than first-degree relatives.
6. Appears indifferent to the praise or criticism of others.
7. Shows emotional coldness, detachment, or flattened affectivity.

B. Does not occur exclusively during the course of schizophrenia, a bipolar disorder or depressive disorder with psychotic features, another psychotic disorder, or autism spectrum disorder and is not attributable to the physiological effects of another medical condition.

Note: If criteria are met prior to the onset of schizophrenia, add "premorbid," i.e., "schizoid personality disorder (premorbid)."

Schizotypal Personality Disorder

A. A pervasive pattern of social and interpersonal deficits marked by acute discomfort with, and reduced capacity for, close relationships as well as by cognitive or perceptual distortions and eccentricities of behavior, beginning by early adulthood and present in a variety of contexts, as indicated by five (or more) of the following:

1. Ideas of reference (excluding delusions of reference).
2. Odd beliefs or magical thinking that influences behavior and is inconsistent with subcultural norms (e.g., superstitiousness, belief in clairvoyance, telepathy, or "sixth sense"; in children and adolescents, bizarre fantasies or preoccupations).
3. Unusual perceptual experiences, including bodily illusions.
4. Odd thinking and speech (e.g., vague, circumstantial, metaphorical, overelaborate, or stereotyped).
5. Suspiciousness or paranoid ideation.
6. Inappropriate or constricted affect.
7. Behavior or appearance that is odd, eccentric, or peculiar.
8. Lack of close friends or confidants other than first-degree relatives.
9. Excessive social anxiety that does not diminish with familiarity and tends to be associated with paranoid fears rather than negative judgments about self.

B. Does not occur exclusively during the course of schizophrenia, a bipolar disorder or depressive disorder with psychotic features, another psychotic disorder, or autism spectrum disorder.

Note: If criteria are met prior to the onset of schizophrenia, add "premorbid," e.g., "schizotypal personality disorder (premorbid)."

Arun had done reasonably well as an undergraduate biology major and was now a graduate student in genetics. He was often concerned that fellow students were stealing his ideas or cheating from his papers, but he never filed any formal complaints. He had gone to a university close to home as an undergraduate and had lived with his parents. Grad school was the first time he was truly away from home. Arun's research focused on a specific gene associated with a rare form of deafness. He started suspecting that his supervisor had brought him to the university to take credit for his work and claim it as his own. One day, Arun gave his mentor a contract guaranteeing that the supervisor would not steal any of Arun's intellectual property. When the supervisor wouldn't sign, Arun became worried that he was out to get him. Arun wanted to go to the dean, but he knew that the dean and his supervisor were friends and were probably in cahoots anyhow. Arun started locking up his written work and bought extra security for his laptop. He even developed second datasets that were inaccurate so that if his supervisor stole the data and published them, the theft would be evident.

When his supervisor confronted him about how he was feeling, Arun interpreted it as yet another attempt to get access to his work. He began writing letters to the chancellor of the university, the governor of the state, and various state legislators, apprising them of the situation. When the chancellor contacted the dean, who then called Arun's supervisor, it became clear that Arun was disturbed. He was taken to Campus Health Services, where he was evaluated and diagnosed with paranoid personality disorder.

Arun's case illustrates several features of paranoid personality disorder. First, his pervasive suspiciousness led him to believe that conspiracies existed all around him. He questioned the loyalty and trustworthiness of fellow students and even departmental faculty. Arun had no evidence that others were trying to steal his data, but he nonetheless persisted in his beliefs. People around him would invariably have perceived him as abrasive, accusing, and suspicious. At first, his faculty adviser and the chancellor may have been willing to listen to and investigate his concerns, perhaps wondering if he had had a bad experience elsewhere that made him protective of his work. However, they soon realized that Arun was suspicious of them as well and that Arun's reality was different from their own.

A classic example of the interpersonal difficulties that accompany paranoid personality disorder is the suspicion of infidelity in a partner. At first, it looks like routine jealousy, but then it becomes clear that the suspicion goes far beyond any rational thought, and the partner can do nothing to dispel the fears. Another common feature of paranoid personality disorder is interpreting innocent events as being personally relevant or having personal meaning. For example, getting stuck in the longest line in the grocery store or being singled out for security screening in the airport could be viewed as a personal attack.

SCHIZOID PERSONALITY DISORDER **Schizoid personality disorder** is a pervasive pattern of detachment from social relationships and a restricted range of emotional expression in interpersonal settings (American Psychiatric Association, 2013). People with schizoid personality disorder may be introverted, solitary, emotionally unexpressive, and isolated. They derive little enjoyment from or show little interest in belonging to families or social groups. Often absorbed in their own thoughts and feelings, they can be afraid of relationships that require closeness and intimacy. People with this disorder also appear to be indifferent to others' opinions and frequently prefer tasks without human interaction (e.g., laboratory or computer tasks). They seem to experience few emotional extremes, such as anger or joy. Instead, they hover indifferently in the middle range of emotion. This disorder is also associated with the absence of enjoyment of sensory, bodily, or interpersonal experiences (American Psychiatric Association, 2013). Sometimes the detachment experienced by people with this disorder can lead to impairment in both social and occupational functioning. Often oblivious to normal social cues, these individuals cannot engage in the normal social discourse that maintains relationships and supports occupational success. The lack of social skills can be misinterpreted as aloofness. However, people with schizoid personality disorder usually do not have the hallucinations, delusions, or the complete disconnection from reality that occurs in untreated (or treatment-resistant) schizophrenia, although they may experience brief psychotic episodes, especially in times of stress.

> Jacob was a 24-year-old stable hand and was most comfortable when alone with the horses and mucking out stalls. He came in early in the morning, did his work, left late at night, and barely spoke to anyone. New people would try to engage him in conversation, but he just wasn't interested. People would sometimes interpret his lack of interest as arrogance and wonder what made him feel so special, but more often, they would wonder how anyone could go so long without talking to anyone. A new young rider brought her horse to the stables and took a liking to Jacob. Even though he seemed really distant, she thought he was attractive. She asked him out, but he seemed to have absolutely no interest in her—or anyone else. Jacob would visit his parents about once a month. His mother was a seamstress, and his father delivered mail. When he went home, he sometimes helped his mother rip out hems of pants she was altering, but the three basically sat in silence or worked while the TV was on.

In lay terms, Jacob would be called a loner or a hermit. He was not concerned by his lack of relationships and showed almost no emotional response when the young rider showed interest in him. His work reflected his preference for being alone. The horses placed no social demands on him. Yet it did not appear that his job gave him pleasure. In fact, it seemed routine and rote. If he was praised, he would accept tips, but he seemed to take no pride in his work and did not express appreciation for others' kind words. The image of Jacob and his parents sitting around watching TV and barely talking suggests that a schizoid style might run in the family and reflects the general lack of emotionality and engagement seen in these individuals.

SCHIZOTYPAL PERSONALITY DISORDER **Schizotypal personality disorder** is a pervasive pattern of social and interpersonal deficits marked by acute discomfort, reduced capacity for close relationships, cognitive or perceptual distortions, and behavioral eccentricities (American Psychiatric Association, 2013). Symptoms of schizotypal personality disorder are best described as a cluster of idiosyncrasies. People with this disorder may have offbeat, peculiar, or paranoid beliefs and thoughts. Moreover, they have difficulty forming relationships and have extreme social anxiety. During interpersonal interactions, people with this personality disorder may react inappropriately, show no emotion, or inappropriately talk to themselves. Another feature is "magical thinking," an erroneous belief that one can foretell the future or affect events by thinking certain thoughts. People with schizotypal personality disorder may harbor *ideas of reference*. These are incorrect interpretations that events around them have specific and unusual personal meaning. These interpretations are not as severe as *delusions of reference* (see Chapter 11), in which beliefs develop a delusional pattern. People with schizotypal personality disorder also report unusual perceptual experiences or have odd patterns of thinking and speech. Some people with this disorder display suspiciousness or paranoia, and their emotional expressions can be inappropriate and excessive or severely restricted.

The oddities found in people with schizotypal personality disorder are not restricted to thinking and behavior. Individuals may also have an odd, eccentric, or peculiar physical appearance reflected in their clothing and personal hygiene. These oddities, in addition to their excessive social anxiety and paranoia, may result in limited social relationships.

> Everyone on campus knew him as "the pigeon man." When students first saw him, they avoided him by crossing the street. Here was some guy talking to himself (without Bluetooth!). He slept at the local shelter, where the workers saw him as harmless. In fact, they told people that the pigeon man was more afraid of them than they should be of him. He rarely washed, had holes in his shoes, and held all of his possessions close to his body in a burlap bag when he slept at night. During the day, he dug scraps out of the trash, sat in the park on a bench surrounded by pigeons, fed them, and carried on extended conversations with the birds. Sometimes he laughed, and other times he looked positively angry at the birds. When he finished, he retreated back into his own little world, walking up and down the streets until it was time to go back to the shelter for a meal. His case manager confirmed that he did not have hallucinations or delusions and had never met diagnostic criteria for schizophrenia. Yet this odd pattern of behavior had been with him since middle school—his caption in the yearbook called him "bird boy."

The pigeon man's history of eccentric behavior around birds existed from childhood. Thus, his symptoms were persistent. Keeping his possessions in his burlap bag close to his body clearly reflected suspiciousness or paranoia about his belongings. Although he was not dangerous, he caused uneasiness in others, probably because of his personal appearance and erratic behaviors. Clearly, those around him did not share the pigeon man's experience with reality. He saw the world differently, although he never had a psychotic episode. Nonetheless, his sustained odd and eccentric behavior was sufficiently extreme to lead others to avoid him.

Cluster B: Dramatic, Emotional, or Erratic Disorders

LO 12.4 Describe the Cluster B personality disorders and their uniting characteristics.

The common features of Cluster B personality disorders are behaviors that are viewed as exaggerated, inflated, dramatic, emotional, or erratic (American Psychiatric Association, 2013) (see "DSM-5: Cluster B Disorders"). The four disorders in this cluster are marked by extreme and often colorful patterns of behavior. Other common features are the fluctuating nature of symptoms—often vacillating between extremes. These patterns can be particularly disrupting interpersonally, as the following cases illustrate.

ANTISOCIAL PERSONALITY DISORDER **Antisocial personality disorder** (ASPD) is a pervasive pattern of disregard for and violation of the rights of others (American Psychiatric Association, 2013). It is more common in males than in females. This personality disorder

Antisocial personality disorder often has its roots in childhood with antisocial behaviors such as theft and vandalism.

has been known throughout history, literature, and the legal system by many names, including *psychopathy, sociopathy*, and *dyssocial personality disorder*. This diagnosis is reserved for individuals who are at least 18 years old and who had symptoms of conduct disorder before age 15 (see Chapter 13), illustrating how the pattern of antisocial behavior begins in childhood and then crystallizes and intensifies over time. Common behaviors in youth include cruelty to animals and people, destruction of property, deceitfulness or theft, or serious violations of rules (American Psychiatric Association, 2013).

ASPD is somewhat easier to diagnose than other personality disorders because of its flagrant behaviors. Fundamentally, people with ASPD fail to conform to social norms, which often leads to legal difficulties, including arrests. They often lie, use aliases, con others for profit or enjoyment, destroy property, harass others, and engage in behaviors and actions that violate the basic rights, wishes, safety, and feelings of others (American Psychiatric Association, 2013) (see "Real People, Real Disorders: Jeffrey Dahmer: Antisocial Personality Disorder"). Associated features include being highly impulsive and engaging in problematic activities on the spur of the moment. This can result in physical fights, temper outbursts, physically abusive behavior, changes in residence, reckless driving, and other impulsive high-risk behaviors that threaten their own safety and well-being (e.g., sexual behavior, reckless driving or driving while intoxicated, causing motor vehicle accidents, drug use). Another common feature is irresponsibility, exhibited by unemployment, underemployment, or poor and erratic job performance and financial irresponsibility, including bad debts and failure to support their families or children. In addition, individuals with ASPD fail to take responsibility for their own actions and commonly blame the victims for inciting their behavior. Examples include saying that a rape victim deserved the assault because of her sexy clothes or blaming physical fights on the other guy (e.g., "he had it coming to him"). Individuals with this personality disorder are also often able to use their charm or persuasiveness to exploit others. Perhaps most disconcerting are the tendencies to minimize the consequences of their actions and to feel no remorse. Indeed, they may be completely indifferent to the consequences of their actions.

Brandon was raised in a family that included his father, mother, and younger sister, but he did not have a close relationship with anyone. Without parental supervision or involvement, Brandon was often in trouble at school for inappropriate conduct, even at an early age. Despite being very bright, his grades were poor because "he just doesn't care." At 13, he was sent to a youth detention center for breaking into a neighbor's house while high on marijuana, and soon after being released, he began carjacking.

At age 19, he was sent to state prison for 18 months for a felony. In prison, Brandon gained a reputation as a "gangsta" for his ability to intimidate other prisoners by physical force, and he had small teardrops tattooed onto his cheek. After he was released, he was arrested as an accomplice to murder in a drive-by shooting in a neighboring state. He was sent back to jail and then transferred to a federal prison.

In prison, Brandon often bragged about his ability to seduce women, always using fake names and, after gaining their trust, taking a good deal of their money. Brandon had no regrets about his behaviors. If anything, he viewed each incident as another notch in his belt. He could not communicate with others without ultimately resorting to violence. In the beginning, Brandon gained clout with other prisoners with his devil-may-care attitude, but other than a few individuals whom he seemed to have under his cunning influence, most of the other prisoners feared his ruthlessness.

The developmental nature of the disorder can be seen in the early misbehavior evident in childhood and adolescence. The severity of the misbehavior intensified as Brandon matured. He lacked empathy for his victims and had no remorse for his

DSM-5

Criteria for Cluster B Personality Disorders

Antisocial Personality Disorder

A. A pervasive pattern of disregard for and violation of the rights of others, occurring since age 15 years, as indicated by three (or more) of the following:

1. Failure to conform to social norms with respect to lawful behaviors, as indicated by repeatedly performing acts that are grounds for arrest.
2. Deceitfulness, as indicated by repeated lying, use of aliases, or conning others for personal profit or pleasure.
3. Impulsivity or failure to plan ahead.
4. Irritability and aggressiveness, as indicated by repeated physical fights or assaults.
5. Reckless disregard for safety of self or others.
6. Consistent irresponsibility, as indicated by repeated failure to sustain consistent work behavior or honor financial obligations.
7. Lack of remorse, as indicated by being indifferent to or rationalizing having hurt, mistreated, or stolen from another.

B. The individual is at least age 18 years.

C. There is evidence of conduct disorder with onset before age 15 years.

D. The occurrence of antisocial behavior is not exclusively during the course of schizophrenia or bipolar disorder.

Narcissistic Personality Disorder

A pervasive pattern of grandiosity (in fantasy or behavior), need for admiration, and lack of empathy, beginning by early adulthood and present in a variety of contexts, as indicated by five (or more) of the following:

1. Has a grandiose sense of self-importance (e.g., exaggerates achievements and talents, expects to be recognized as superior without commensurate achievements).
2. Is preoccupied with fantasies of unlimited success, power, brilliance, beauty, or ideal love.
3. Believes that he or she is "special" and unique and can only be understood by, or should associate with, other special or high-status people (or institutions).
4. Requires excessive admiration.
5. Has a sense of entitlement (i.e., unreasonable expectations of especially favorable treatment or automatic compliance with his or her expectations).
6. Is interpersonally exploitative (i.e., takes advantage of others to achieve his or her own ends).
7. Lacks empathy: is unwilling to recognize or identify with the feelings and needs of others.
8. Is often envious of others or believes that others are envious of him or her.
9. Shows arrogant, haughty behaviors or attitudes.

Borderline Personality Disorder

A pervasive pattern of instability of interpersonal relationships, self-image, and affects, and marked impulsivity, beginning by early adulthood and present in a variety of contexts, as indicated by five (or more) of the following:

1. Frantic efforts to avoid real or imagined abandonment. (**Note:** Do not include suicidal or self-mutilating behavior covered in Criterion 5.)
2. A pattern of unstable and intense interpersonal relationships characterized by alternating between extremes of idealization and devaluation.
3. Identity disturbance: markedly and persistently unstable self-image or sense of self.
4. Impulsivity in at least two areas that are potentially self-damaging (e.g., spending, sex, substance abuse, reckless driving, binge eating). (**Note:** Do not include suicidal or self-mutilating behavior covered in Criterion 5.)
5. Recurrent suicidal behavior, gestures, or threats, or self-mutilating behavior.
6. Affective instability due to a marked reactivity of mood (e.g., intense episodic dysphoria, irritability, or anxiety usually lasting a few hours and only rarely more than a few days).
7. Chronic feelings of emptiness.
8. Inappropriate, intense anger or difficulty controlling anger (e.g., frequent displays of temper, constant anger, recurrent physical fights).
9. Transient, stress-related paranoid ideation or severe dissociative symptoms.

(continued)

Histrionic Personality Disorder

A pervasive pattern of excessive emotionality and attention seeking, beginning by early adulthood and present in a variety of contexts, as indicated by five (or more) of the following:

1. Is uncomfortable in situations in which he or she is not the center of attention.
2. Interaction with others is often characterized by inappropriate sexually seductive or provocative behavior.
3. Displays rapidly shifting and shallow expression of emotions.
4. Consistently uses physical appearance to draw attention to self.
5. Has a style of speech that is excessively impressionistic and lacking in detail.
6. Shows self-dramatization, theatricality, and exaggerated expression of emotion.
7. Is suggestible (i.e., easily influenced by others or circumstances).
8. Considers relationships to be more intimate than they actually are.

behavior. Although not all individuals with antisocial personality disorder end up in prison, in Brandon's case, his early conduct problems were the first steps on a path to a lifetime of criminal behavior.

NARCISSISTIC PERSONALITY DISORDER **Narcissistic personality disorder** is a pervasive pattern of grandiosity (in fantasy or behavior), need for admiration, and lack of

REAL People REAL Disorders

Jeffrey Dahmer: Antisocial Personality Disorder

Jeffrey Lionel Dahmer (1960–1994), one of the most infamous serial killers in American history, murdered at least 17 men and boys between 1978 and 1991. Dahmer's killings were notably abhorrent, involving violent sodomy, necrophilia (sex with dead bodies), dismemberment, and cannibalism.

What causes someone to commit such heinous acts of violence against humanity? Insanity? Psychiatric illness? Evil? Any combination of these? In the case of Jeffrey Dahmer, several forensic experts addressed this question during his famous court case. While never formally diagnosed by expert witnesses, Dahmer appeared to have classic features of antisocial personality disorder. He showed no remorse for his crimes against others and acted in an impulsive, callous, manipulative, aggressive manner that reflected a failure to accept social norms. Moreover, many red flags appeared to be present in his childhood.

As a child, Dahmer reportedly dissected already-dead animals. At age 14, he began drinking alcohol, and at 18, soon after his parents' divorce, Dahmer committed his first murder. He invited the victim to his house and killed him because he "didn't want him to leave." By the summer of 1991, Dahmer was murdering approximately one person per week and, in a typical antisocial manipulation, used his charismatic nature to attract his victims, homosexual men and boys.

Commenting on this magnetism, Anne Schwartz, who covered the Dahmer story for the *Milwaukee Journal*, stated, "The day Jeffrey Dahmer was sentenced, I heard him read his statement to the court calmly and eloquently, and I wondered how easily I could have been conned." She continued, "He was an attractive man when he laughed.... I could see how so many were taken in by him."

With evidence overwhelmingly against him, Dahmer chose to plead not guilty by reason of insanity, arguing that his necrophiliac urges were so strong that he could not control them. The court found Dahmer guilty on 15 counts of murder and sentenced him to 15 life terms, totaling 937 years in prison. Dahmer served his time until late 1994, when he was beaten to death by a fellow inmate while on work detail in the prison gym.

Jeffrey Dahmer is an extreme example of how features of antisocial personality disorder can be associated with criminality. While all individuals who engage in antisocial behaviors are not criminals, 40% of convicted felons do meet the criteria for antisocial personality disorder. The line between mental illness and criminal behavior is not clear in this instance, and the distinction between illness and evil will no doubt be debated far into the future in hospitals, jails, and courtrooms.

SOURCES: http://www.criminalprofiling.com/Psychiatric-Testimony-of-Jeffrey-Dahmer_s115.html, http://www.crimelibrary.com/serial_killers/notorious/dahmer/19.html, http://www.tornadohills.com/dahmer/life.htm

empathy (American Psychiatric Association, 2013). People with this disorder have an exaggerated sense of self-importance and are often absorbed by fantasies of limitless success. Secondary to this preoccupation with their own superiority, they seek constant attention and may try to win admiration from others by flaunting or boasting about their perceived special abilities. This behavior often masks fragile self-esteem. Constant external praise or admiration allows them to continue to bolster their own grandiose sense of self.

People with narcissistic personality disorder often express a sense of entitlement, or a belief that they deserve only the best of everything and should associate only with others who are of similarly high caliber. For example, someone with narcissistic personality disorder might be unlikely to visit just any doctor for a minor complaint. She is always looking for the best or the most well-known, whether it is a doctor, a lawyer, or a hairstylist. The mundane will not do.

A corollary to this overestimated sense of accomplishment is the converse—namely, a devaluation of what others do or what others have accomplished. Those with narcissistic personality disorder can come off as haughty and arrogant as they constantly flaunt their imagined superiority. Their attitudes toward others can be patronizing and disdainful. People with narcissistic personality disorder are often so self-absorbed that they have a complete lack of empathy for others. They may be so preoccupied with their own need for praise and admiration that they are unable to understand other people's desires, needs, or feelings. People around them often come to feel ignored, devalued, or used.

Stephãn (originally Steven) had always been outwardly confident in his small-town high school. He felt that he transcended his Midwestern roots because he had traveled to Europe as a child. His edgy, electronic music and his interest in water polo were not as popular at his public high school as in the upper-crust private schools he had read about in the *New York Times* Sunday Edition. Stephãn felt that he was unique compared with other students. Generally looking down on what he thought were the "common" tastes of his school, he had few friends and generally kept his high self-opinion to himself.

However, during his first year at a prestigious East Coast liberal arts college, Stephãn's belief in his own uniqueness became intensified. He sought out friends based on whether he had seen them in the society columns of magazines or knew their parents were significant donors to the university. He was aloof and rude to professors and students in classes that he was "forced" to take due to university standards and complained of "wasting time in subjects that have nothing to do with being a CEO of a Fortune 500 company!" While quite charismatic, eloquent, and intelligent in his business courses, he often lied that his knowledge of economics came from his father, a prominent businessman who wrote for the *Wall Street Journal* (in reality his father was a convenience store owner).

Although quite successful in his academic pursuits, when faced with group projects, Stephãn was perceived by his peers as a nightmare to work with—always blaming them when he made small errors or pitting students against each other and then standing back to watch the arguments. He rarely wrote his own papers, saying, "Why waste my time when I can easily persuade one of the naïve, previous-valedictorian freshmen to do it for me?" While Stephãn desperately sought and often believed he had the admiration, attention, envy, or even fear of those around him, his classmates often saw him as arrogant and obnoxious.

As illustrated by this case, Stephãn created a persona that was legendary in his own mind. He considered himself vastly superior to others and grossly overestimated his abilities and prospects for the future. There was a deep disconnect between his beliefs (i.e., that everyone around him admired and respected him) and reality (i.e., that everyone around him found him to be quite insufferable and arrogant).

Although superficially confident, people with narcissistic personality disorder can experience extremes in mood and self-esteem. When their needs for admiration are not met, they may, at least temporarily, feel injured or defeated, resulting in low mood and social withdrawal.

BORDERLINE PERSONALITY DISORDER **Borderline personality disorder** is a pervasive pattern of unstable interpersonal relationships, self-image, affect, and impulsivity

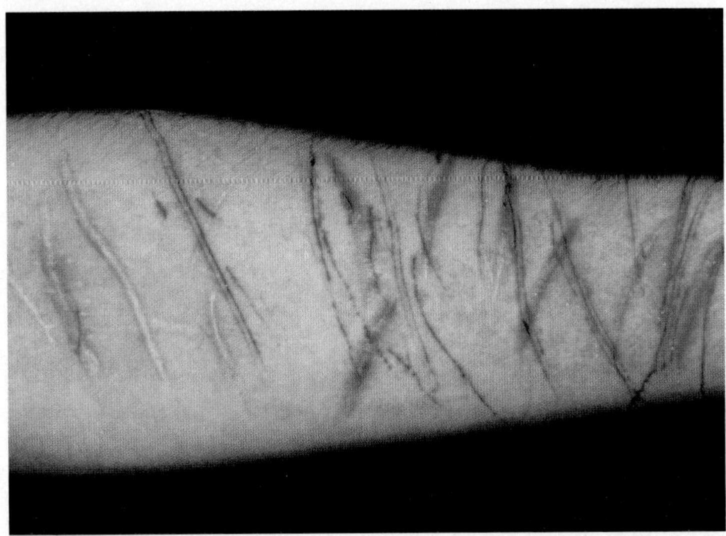

Borderline personality disorder is associated with multiple impulsive behaviors including self-harm.

(American Psychiatric Association, 2013). Its symptoms can be severe and rapidly fluctuating. Intense bouts of anger, depression, and anxiety may last for hours or as long as a day. As illustrated in Jacqui's case at the beginning of the chapter, other behaviors include impulsive hostility, self-injury, and drug or alcohol abuse. Cognitive distortions and an unstable and conflicted sense of self and self-worth can lead to frequent changes in long-term goals, career plans, jobs, friendships, gender identity, and values. Individuals may feel misunderstood, ill-treated, bored, or empty and have an unstable self-identity. At extreme times, the identity disturbance can be so severe that individuals with borderline personality disorder may feel as if they do not exist at all.

At the core of borderline personality disorder is a deep fear of abandonment. Minor separations or endings are misinterpreted as signs that they are being abandoned, left alone, or rejected and can lead to desperate attempts to remain connected and in contact with others. Examples include a therapist going on vacation or a partner having to go out of town for work. To prevent such separations, a person with borderline personality disorder may engage in impulsive and desperate behaviors such as self-mutilation or suicide attempts to keep the person near.

These destructive behaviors and personality style can lead to highly unstable social relationships. Idealization (intense positive feeling) is quickly replaced by devaluation (intense anger and dislike). A person with borderline personality disorder may immediately form an attachment to another person and idealize him or her. Then a minor conflict can lead to a rapid swing to the other extreme, and strong negative emotions toward the person develop. Impulsivity is another hallmark symptom and may include binge eating, shoplifting, gambling, irresponsible spending, unsafe sexual behaviors, substance abuse, or reckless driving.

Watch LIZ: BORDERLINE PERSONALITY DISORDER

Video

People with borderline personality disorder are also at high risk for suicide and self-harm (Krysinska et al., 2006; Paris, 2002) because of their tendency to perceive abandonment and to experience feelings of emptiness and nothingness. Self-mutilation can include cutting, burning, punching, and a variety of other behaviors that cause bodily injury. These can occur during *dissociative episodes* (in which there is a temporary detachment from reality). Some individuals report that self-harm releases underlying mounting tension. Others say that it helps them know that they can still experience feelings, and still others claim that it helps counteract a belief that they are somehow evil or tarnished.

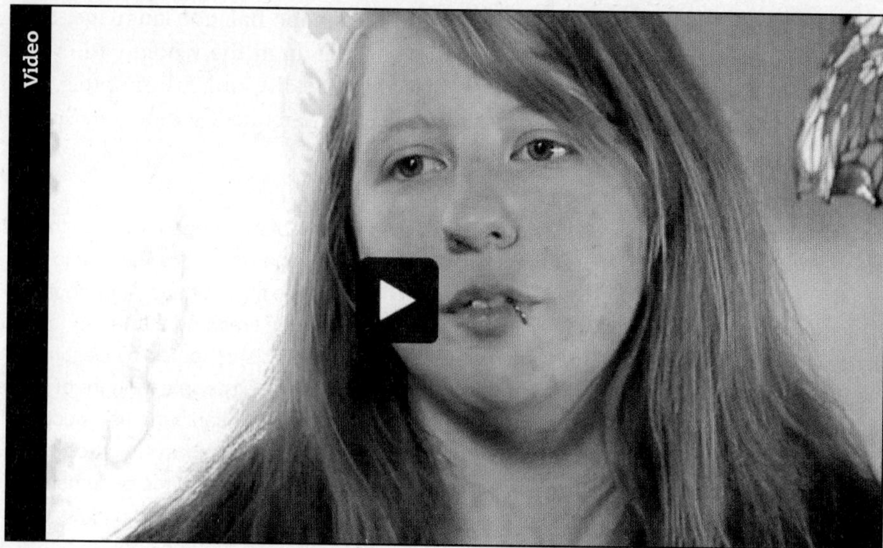

When people learn about borderline personality disorder, their first question is often "the borderline of what?" Historically, the term refers to the border between neurosis and psychosis, acknowledging that some, but not all, people with this disorder can experience transient psychotic episodes. Being around or in relationships with people with borderline personality disorder can be extremely challenging. Friends and partners feel like they are on an emotional roller coaster or that their value rises and falls like the stock market. Jacqui's mother would often say to her husband that she could never predict which Jacqui was going to come home from school or be on the phone, the loving and adoring one or the resentful, hateful one. Those around the person also experience the inconsistent sense of self that the sufferer does. The person is often considered exhausting and "high maintenance." Fostering a sense of stability both in terms of their internal experience and their network of social relationships is critical to leveling out the complex emotions of individuals with borderline personality disorder.

Given the extreme fluctuation in behavior seen in borderline personality disorder and the highs and lows seen in bipolar disorder (see Chapter 7), how does one best distinguish between these disorders? Recall that people with bipolar disorder have fluctuations in mood with periods of stability in between episodes. In borderline personality disorder, although mood does indeed fluctuate, so do other behaviors and emotions, such as feelings about others, feelings about the self, and moving between social approach versus withdrawal. Again, we return to the three P's: borderline personality disorder is *persistent, pervasive*, and *pathological* rather than episodic like bipolar disorder.

HISTRIONIC PERSONALITY DISORDER **Histrionic personality disorder** is a pattern of excessive emotion and attention-seeking behavior. *Histrionic* means "dramatic" or "theatrical," and people with this disorder incessantly "perform" and draw attention to themselves (American Psychiatric Association, 2013). At first, they are attractive and magnetic as they draw attention by their liveliness, colorful behavior, and flirtatiousness. Yet when no longer the center of attention, they engage in behaviors that draw the limelight back to them. Physical appearance and provocative and seductive behavior are often used to draw people into their circle, causing disruption in a variety of social and occupational settings.

The emotional expressions of people with histrionic personality disorder are pronounced but lack depth and shift rapidly. These changeable, shallow emotions create an impression of not being genuine and of faking their feelings. Histrionic speech also has a dramatic and shallow flair. Someone with this disorder might speak in lavish and colorful terms, express strong opinions, and behave in a dramatic manner, and her actions may seem overblown and insincere.

People with histrionic personality disorder consider relationships to be closer or more intimate than they actually are. Coupled with their dramatic flair for language, they may refer to a casual acquaintance as "one of my closest friends in the whole wide world" or describe degrees of closeness in relationships that are, in reality, quite distant (e.g., seeing a celebrity in a restaurant and subsequently stating that they frequently dine together at their favorite bistro).

> When she entered the party with Susan, her wife, Destiny was vibrant, gregarious, and the center of attention. She was in her element. At first, it was very charming. She easily told stories to complete strangers as if she had known them her whole life. But after four hours of Destiny's theatrical socializing and flirtatious behavior, Susan grew tired and started to feel like an accessory. This was the fourth party this week, and Susan felt disrespected by Destiny's flirting with others. One of Destiny's biggest concerns was what other people thought of her, and when she felt insecure, she lost her temper. It was often directed at Susan, who had become increasingly tired of bearing the brunt of this behavior. Because Destiny always needed to be in control and call the shots—fluctuating from enraged to contented based on the circumstances—Susan had thought of leaving her many times. Two weeks ago, Destiny grabbed a glass vase and threw it at the floor, screaming in a fit of rage when Susan suggested that they not go out to dinner because she had a stressful day at work. After the fight, Destiny withdrew from contact and didn't speak for days. When she became less angry, she was extremely sweet and solicitous toward Susan. Destiny's inexorable theatrics and need to be the center of attention eventually led to the end of the relationship.

Living with someone with histrionic personality disorder can be extremely challenging. Although initially alluring, Destiny, with her constant need to be the center of attention and her flirtatiousness with others, was unable to engage in a healthy and trusting emotional relationship with Susan. As evidenced by this case, behavior that is overly dramatic and demanding can be destructive to relationships.

ETHICS AND RESPONSIBILITY The label of borderline personality disorder has been associated with considerable stigmatization in the mental health field. Terms such as *difficult, treatment resistant, manipulative, demanding,* and *attention seeking* are commonly associated with borderline personality disorder (Aviram et al., 2006; Gallop & Wynn, 1987; Nehls, 1998). Such negative perceptions can lead to negative expectations, negative outcomes, and self-fulfilling prophecies. Indeed, negative expectations and perceptions by clinicians are consistent with the core fears of people with borderline personality disorder, who are sensitive to rejection and fearful of abandonment. These patients may react to clinicians' negative perceptions in a way that is harmful to themselves by withdrawing from treatment (Aviram et al., 2006). Clinicians' negative feelings and impressions may also manifest in behavioral responses, such as social distancing from patients, defensiveness, being less helpful, expressing less empathy, or expressing anger (Sansone & Sansone, 2013). Despite advances in the treatment of borderline personality disorder (see "Treatment of Personality Disorders"), stigmatization persists. Clinicians who use the term *borderline* loosely and inappropriately to label difficult patients can convey negative perceptions and negative expectations to other clinicians as well (Aviram et al., 2006). For all of these reasons, clinicians should give the diagnosis of borderline personality disorder only when the symptoms are consistent with the diagnostic criteria. They should seek supervision or specialized training if they are challenged by their own misperceptions or difficulties dealing with patients with this symptom profile.

Explore ETHICS AND RESPONSIBILITY

Cluster C: Anxious or Fearful Disorders

LO 12.5 Describe the Cluster C personality disorders and their uniting characteristics.

The common features of Cluster C are characteristic behaviors marked by considerable anxiety or withdrawal (American Psychiatric Association, 2013). The three disorders in this cluster share features that reflect some form of anxiety—social anxiety, obsessionality, or fear of independence. As you will see with each disorder, distinctions must be made between the personality disorder and other disorders that share some of the same clinical features. Again, recalling the distinction between "ways of being" versus illness can guide diagnostic decisions.

AVOIDANT PERSONALITY DISORDER **Avoidant personality disorder** (see "DSM-5: Cluster C Disorders") is a pervasive pattern of social inhibition, feelings of inadequacy, and hypersensitivity to negative evaluation (American Psychiatric Association, 2013). People with this disorder avoid social or occupational interactions for fear of rejection, criticism, or disapproval. Common patterns include being excessively shy and uncomfortable in social situations and worrying that what they say will be considered foolish by others. Other fears include blushing or crying in front of others and becoming very hurt by any real or perceived disapproval.

People with avoidant personality disorder may entirely avoid making new friends unless they have complete assurance that they will not be rejected. A common concern is that others will be critical or disapproving unless proved otherwise. This personality disorder can lead individuals to avoid intimate relationships entirely because of worries about being accepted. Avoidant individuals are hypervigilant to signs of rejection or criticism and may over- or misinterpret other people's comments about them.

Lou was a 35-year-old mechanic who rarely came out from under a car. Ever since he could remember, he had been basically terrified of talking to other people. Even though his grades were acceptable throughout high school, he was afraid that people would think he was "simple" because he never knew what to say. He avoided all school social events and group projects and would not attend graduation. He stayed in the garage all day working on cars. He quit work in one garage because he had to "cover" the front counter when the clerk went on breaks or lunch, and he could not deal with the phones and the customers. Lou would be under the cars worried that the phone would ring or he'd hear the bell on the counter. He did excellent work and was offered several promotions that would require him to supervise others, but he refused them because he did not know how to handle teams of people. To this day, Lou has never gone on a date. He eats alone in his house in front of the television every night and avoids all social contact. When Lou's mother found out he had refused promotions, she decided she had "had it" with his "ridiculous shyness" and brought him in for psychotherapy. Lou has been working for over a year with a therapist trying to develop skills to overcome his pervasive anxiety about the social world.

The core of avoidant personality is shyness and a sense of inadequacy that leads to significant impairment in life both socially and occupationally. People with this disorder may completely avoid talking about themselves or be very withdrawn or restrained due to their fear of potential criticism or disapproval. Others would describe them as quiet, shy, or "wallflowers." People perceive themselves as socially inadequate, inferior, and inept at social interaction. Social self-esteem and self-efficacy tend to be quite low (see "Examining the Evidence: Social Anxiety Disorder vs. Avoidant Personality Disorder").

DEPENDENT PERSONALITY DISORDER **Dependent personality disorder** is a pervasive and excessive need to be taken care of, which leads to submissive and clinging behavior and fears of separation (American Psychiatric Association, 2013). People with dependent personality disorder often have great difficulty making the simplest of everyday decisions, let alone larger life choices. This can result in a pattern of relying on others to make decisions and becoming paralyzed if advice and assistance are not available (e.g., not being able to leave the house without advice on which coat to wear). People with this disorder may become passive participants in the world and often allow others to take over responsibility for planning all aspects of their life. The degree of dependency is disproportionate to age-related norms and does not include situations in which depending on others is essential for survival (e.g., medically related dependence).

People with dependent personality disorder may also have trouble starting projects on their own. Having low confidence in their own ability and a chronic need to check with others for guidance and reassurance, they would rather follow than lead. Because of their exaggerated fears about their incompetence or inability to function or survive independently, a sense of helplessness can develop when they are left alone.

After the breakup of a significant relationship, people with dependent personality disorder quickly rebound into another one. They find it difficult to tolerate periods of independence and desperately embark on another dependent relationship to minimize intense anxiety and fears associated with being alone. These individuals may become so preoccupied with fears of being left alone that they go to extreme measures to arrange situations where they will have assurance of care.

Alicia was the younger of two sisters and her mother's favorite "because she was prettier." As a child, Alicia was indeed lovely, but she was very shy and clung to her mother's apron strings. She wet the bed until the age of 13 and had sleepovers only at her closest friend's house because she understood the problem and knew why she brought a plastic sheet. Alicia's mother was very opinionated and domineering. When she drank alcohol, she would get very loud. Alicia was always the one to quietly and gently ask her to be a little quieter. In high school, when Alicia's friends began dating, her mother always disapproved of the boys they dated. No one would ever be good enough for her Alicia. When it was time to decide about college, despite Alicia's good grades, her mother told her that college was a waste of time and suggested she get her realtor's license—that way she could live at home, save money, and make a good living. Alicia agreed and did as her mother suggested. Indeed, she was relieved because she was terrified of having to live alone or in a college dorm. She still went shopping for her mother and did errands for her parents regularly. At 37, she was still living at home. Her sister was married with children and constantly hassled her about "getting a life." Alicia loved playing with her little niece because Lily loved her unconditionally. Some of Alicia's brief relationships with men had bordered on the abusive. She never felt like she had the right to stand up for herself and thought she didn't really have opinions about anything. At least the men were there to care for her if she needed them. Whenever she brought one home to meet her parents, her mother never failed to find fault and interfere in the relationship. Alicia could not stand up to her mother or break away and become independent. She spent evenings in her room in tears worrying about her future and what would happen if her mother died and was no longer able to look after her.

Examining the EVIDENCE

Social Anxiety Disorder vs. Avoidant Personality Disorder

Since 1987, the diagnosis of both social anxiety disorder and avoidant personality disorder have been defined by fears of criticism and avoidance of activities that involve many different social interactions, not merely fears of public speaking (see Chapter 4). Both avoidant personality disorder and social anxiety disorder involve restraint in and avoidance of social situations. Because such overlap in the diagnostic criteria exists, are social anxiety disorder and avoidant personality disorder really two separate conditions?

- **The Facts** Only one criterion of avoidant personality disorder—"is reluctant to take personal risks or engage in new activities"—appears to differentiate its diagnostic criteria from social anxiety disorder. In 1992, based on several carefully controlled studies, researchers concluded that avoidant personality disorder and social anxiety disorder were overlapping constructs (Widiger, 1992). Yet the two categories continue to exist, suggesting that some view these conditions as qualitatively distinct. Why?
- **Let's Examine the Evidence** Early studies (Herbert et al., 1992; Holt et al., 1992; Turner et al., 1992) examined a host of variables, including the core characteristics of the disorders, the associated symptoms (such as depression), and etiology. Data from all these studies indicated that across all measures, individuals diagnosed with avoidant personality disorder had more severe problems, but the differences were quantitative, not qualitative. The difference appeared to be one of simple severity, not the qualitative distinction one would hope to find for these separate groups. More recent studies (Chambless et al., 2008; Huppert et al., 2008; Rettew, 2000) continue to search for qualitative distinctions, examining the same variables as the earlier studies but also including variables related to treatment outcome. Although statistical analysis appeared to be able to categorize people as either suffering from social anxiety disorder or avoidant personality disorder, the distinction disappeared when the severity of social anxiety disorder symptoms was statistically controlled. In other words, classification was still based solely on symptom severity. In each case, people with avoidant personality disorder had more severe symptoms and more functional impairment. In many studies, so many people qualified for a diagnosis of both disorders that classification appeared meaningless (Rettew, 2000).
- **Conclusion** Even though several controlled studies have tried to find qualitative differences between social anxiety disorder and avoidant personality disorder, few clear distinctions can be found. The primary difference remains the quantitative distinction of clinical severity, illustrating how early-onset anxiety disorders can become so pervasive that they can affect every aspect of daily functioning.

DSM-5

Criteria for Cluster C Personality Disorders

Avoidant Personality Disorder

A pervasive pattern of social inhibition, feelings of inadequacy, and hypersensitivity to negative evaluation, beginning by early adulthood and present in a variety of contexts, as indicated by four (or more) of the following:

1. Avoids occupational activities that involve significant interpersonal contact because of fears of criticism, disapproval, or rejection.
2. Is unwilling to get involved with people unless certain of being liked.
3. Shows restraint within intimate relationships because of the fear of being shamed or ridiculed.
4. Is preoccupied with being criticized or rejected in social situations.
5. Is inhibited in new interpersonal situations because of feelings of inadequacy.
6. Views self as socially inept, personally unappealing, or inferior to others.
7. Is unusually reluctant to take personal risks or to engage in any new activities because they may prove embarrassing.

Dependent Personality Disorder

A pervasive and excessive need to be taken care of that leads to submissive and clinging behavior and fears of separation, beginning by early adulthood and present in a variety of contexts, as indicated by five (or more) of the following:

1. Has difficulty making everyday decisions without an excessive amount of advice and reassurance from others.

(continued)

2. Needs others to assume responsibility for most major areas of his or her life.
3. Has difficulty expressing disagreement with others because of fear of loss of support or approval. (**Note:** Do not include realistic fears of retribution.)
4. Has difficulty initiating projects or doing things on his or her own (because of a lack of self-confidence in judgment or abilities rather than a lack of motivation or energy).
5. Goes to excessive lengths to obtain nurturance and support from others, to the point of volunteering to do things that are unpleasant.
6. Feels uncomfortable or helpless when alone because of exaggerated fears of being unable to care for himself or herself.
7. Urgently seeks another relationship as a source of care and support when a close relationship ends.
8. Is unrealistically preoccupied with fears of being left to take care of himself or herself.

Obsessive Compulsive Personality Disorder

A pervasive pattern of preoccupation with orderliness, perfectionism, and mental and interpersonal control, at the expense of flexibility, openness, and efficiency, beginning by early adulthood and present in a variety of contexts, as indicated by four (or more) of the following:

1. Is preoccupied with details, rules, lists, order, organization, or schedules to the extent that the major point of the activity is lost.
2. Shows perfectionism that interferes with task completion (e.g., is unable to complete a project because his or her own overly strict standards are not met).
3. Is excessively devoted to work and productivity to the exclusion of leisure activities and friendships (not accounted for by obvious economic necessity).
4. Is overconscientious, scrupulous, and inflexible about matters of morality, ethics, or values (not accounted for by cultural or religious identification).
5. Is unable to discard worn-out or worthless objects even when they have no sentimental value.
6. Is reluctant to delegate tasks or to work with others unless they submit to exactly his or her way of doing things.
7. Adopts a miserly spending style toward both self and others; money is viewed as something to be hoarded for future catastrophes.
8. Shows rigidity and stubbornness.

Despite the uncomfortable aspects of her life, Alicia remained with her mother at home where she felt someone would look after her and help her make critical decisions. She was preoccupied with worries about her future and fears about being unable to care for herself if her mother were no longer available. Alicia's degree of dependence had nothing to do with any physical condition or actual need for dependency on others and was clearly age inappropriate.

OBSESSIVE-COMPULSIVE PERSONALITY DISORDER **Obsessive-compulsive personality disorder** is a pervasive pattern of preoccupation with orderliness, perfectionism, and mental and interpersonal control at the expense of flexibility, openness, and efficiency (American Psychiatric Association, 2013). Even though the names are similar, it is important to distinguish between obsessive-compulsive disorder (Chapter 5) and obsessive-compulsive personality disorder. Whereas obsessive-compulsive disorder is marked by obsessions and compulsions (such as excessive hand washing, counting, ordering objects), obsessive-compulsive personality disorder is marked by traits such as orderliness, perfectionism, and rigidity. People with this personality disorder are classic examples of being unable to see the forest for the trees. Being hyperfocused on rules, trivial details, lists, or procedures can lead to losing sight of an overarching activity. A common behavior is checking and rechecking work to ensure complete accuracy. A strong feeling of self-doubt can lead to missing important work or school deadlines. The aspiration for perfection, which sometimes backfires, defines this disorder. For example, an individual may become so preoccupied with the details of perfecting part of a task that he or she never "pulls it all together" and does not complete the entire task. Students may recopy an assignment over and over in search of the "perfect" report but consequently not finish on time and miss the assignment deadline.

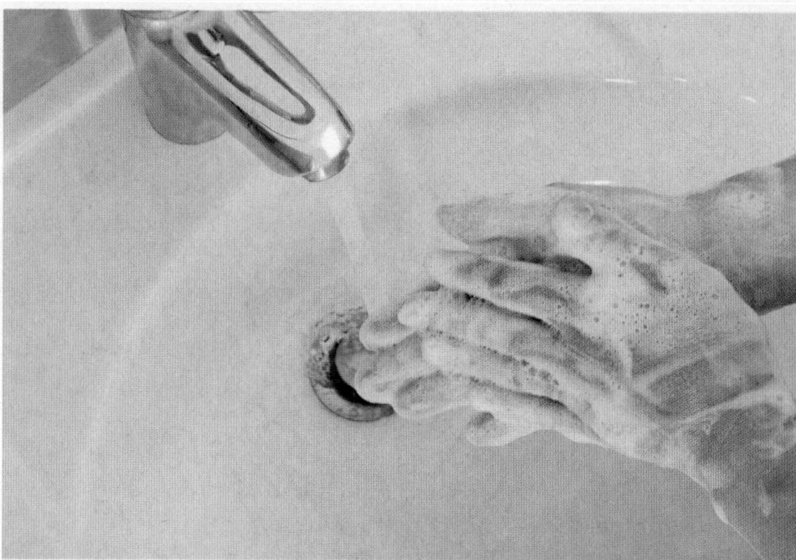

While obsessive-compulsive disorder is marked by obsessions and compulsions (such as excessive hand washing), obsessive-compulsive personality disorder is marked by traits such as orderliness, perfectionism, and rigidity.

This quest for perfection can often lead to a preoccupation with and devotion to work that leaves little or no time for leisure activities, pleasurable activities, or friendships and relationships. This is quite evident in the abnormal case study earlier in this chapter in which Jeff's entire life was focused on his work schedule (see Maladaptive Case Study). Anxiety increases if activities do not have a goal or a structure, and people with this disorder may even turn to structuring leisure time for themselves or their children. "Chilling" or "kicking back" is not in their vocabulary and, indeed, would be highly uncomfortable and even anxiety provoking. Others perceive them as rigid or stubborn.

Another common feature of obsessive-compulsive personality disorder is overconscientiousness and strict moral and ethical values that go beyond what is appropriate or normative for the person's cultural background or religious affiliation. This can result in holding oneself (and others) to extraordinarily high standards of moral and ethical conduct and merciless self-punishment if a rule is transgressed.

Another feature associated with obsessive-compulsive personality disorder includes being a "pack rat," unable to discard things that have no use or apparent sentimental value. Hoarded objects may seem completely useless (e.g., old cell phones, old junk mail). Delegation of work to others can also be a challenge, and the belief might be, like Jeff's, "If you want something done right, you have to do it yourself." This leads to feelings of being overwhelmed and unable to accomplish all tasks on the list. Rigidity and control may also extend to the financial area, in which people may feel compelled to pinch pennies or save for a rainy day, depriving themselves or their family of various things. The first purchases to be rejected are associated with pleasure or leisure and do not contribute in a direct or meaningful way to the accomplishment of tasks on the list. Like Jeff, the individual with obsessive-compulsive personality disorder is a prisoner of lists and "shoulds."

The Five-Factor Model: Toward a Dimensional Approach

LO 12.6 Evaluate various models of personality disorders.

Although the three clusters capture a broad range of personality disturbance, they are far from comprehensive. Sometimes people clearly have a personality disturbance (in that the traits are pervasive, persistent, and pathological and are more a "way of being" than an illness), yet they do not fit tightly into one of the disorder boxes. These individuals are given a diagnosis of personality disorder, not otherwise specified, which indicates that their symptoms may be a mixture of several disorders. Of all of the personality disorders, this is the most frequently used diagnosis in clinical practice (Verheul et al., 2007; Verheul & Widiger, 2004). Some people show features of or meet the criteria for more than one personality disorder (e.g., dependent and histrionic or obsessive-compulsive and paranoid), and reliability across clinicians in making personality disorder diagnoses is lower than for other psychiatric disorders (Bornstein, 2011).

Although it may be easy and diagnostically convenient to think of mental disorders (especially personality disorders) as clear-cut categories, they are not. Diagnostic nosology is a shifting construct, and the debate within the field about how personality disorders should be understood and described continues. Rather than a categorical model, some theorists propose and prefer a dimensional model of personality (see Chapter 3).

One well-known dimensional model is the five-factor model (FFM), which captures the "Big Five" personality dimensions: neuroticism, extraversion, openness to experience, agreeableness, and conscientiousness (Costa and McCrae, 1992). An individual would be rated as being maladaptively high or low on each dimension (see Figure 12.1). Integrating these dimensional factors of personality into current DSM-5 diagnoses may make these diagnostic categories more descriptive. For example, a person with schizoid personality disorder would score maladaptively low on extraversion while someone with borderline personality disorder would score maladaptively high on neuroticism (anxiousness). Proponents of a dimensional model (Widiger & Lowe, 2008) believe that it would provide a more comprehensive picture of personality and would eliminate the need to give several personality disorder diagnoses to describe behavior adequately. Because this approach highlights personality strengths, it could also reduce the stigma of labeling someone with a personality disorder.

Beyond the debate between categorical versus dimensional systems, the personality disorders described in DSM-5 may capture only a fraction of the personality-related problems of interest to patients and clinicians (McCrae et al., 2001). In one study (Westen & Arkowitz-Westen, 1998), 60% of patients treated for personality-related problems and distress did not meet criteria for a DSM-5 personality disorder. Yet personality problems, such as perfectionism and shyness, were among the reasons patients sought treatment.

Figure 12.1 The Five-Factor Model of Personality.

This model posits five primary dimensions of personality: extraversion, neuroticism, conscientiousness, agreeableness, and openness to experience.

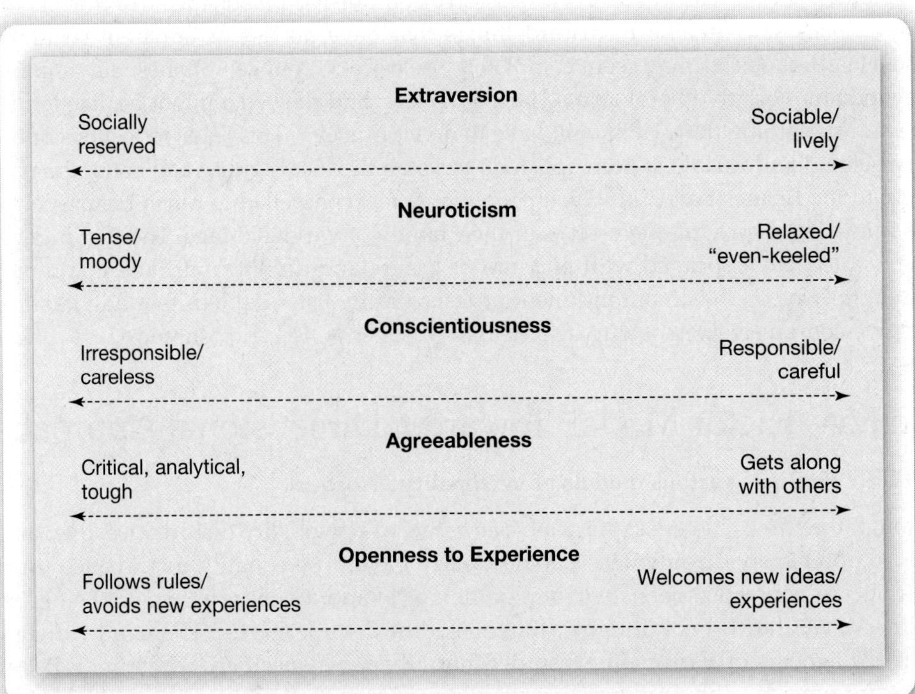

Rarely does someone seeking treatment fit perfectly into one of the personality disorder categories. Typically, people have a varied collection of symptoms that not only cut across disorders within a cluster but also sometimes across clusters. The psychologist's job is to evaluate and treat the complexity of the personality disturbance as it exists in the person rather than having the person's perspective limited by the published boundaries of any set of diagnostic criteria.

Developmental Factors and Personality Disorders

LO 12.7 Debate the extent to which childhood personality predicts adult personality and personality disorders.

The DSM helps clinicians make distinctions about the patient's current state in contrast to lifetime patterns of behavior, but the distinctions are not always entirely clear. For example, how long must a personality disturbance persist to qualify for a personality disorder diagnosis? When significant personality pathology exists in individuals under age 18, is a personality disorder diagnosis appropriate if personality is theoretically still under formation? While a diagnosis may be appropriate if the features are present for at least a year, diagnosing a personality disorder in someone under age 18 remains controversial, given the effects of brain maturation on the course of personality maturity (Ceballos et al., 2006; De Fruyt & De Clercq, 2014).

From a developmental perspective, many manifestations of personality disorders represent typical (although transient) childhood and adolescent behaviors. Dependency, anxiety, hypersensitivity, identity formation problems, conduct problems, histrionics, and testing the limits occur commonly during childhood and adolescence. In general, longitudinal follow-up studies show that such behaviors decrease over time, although high rates of personality disorder–type symptoms during childhood and adolescence are associated with increased risk for psychological disorders later in life. More flagrant symptoms (such as harming animals or risky sexual behavior) may be more serious red flags for later personality disturbance. As our understanding of personality formation emerges, evidence has accumulated that personality disorders originate very early in life and may at least in part be influenced by genetics. Elements of later personality may even be foreshadowed in the simple behaviors exhibited by babies and toddlers (De Clercq & De Fruyt, 2007). As we watch personality emerge in children, the difference between healthy development of individual personality features and the earliest symptoms of personality pathology remains unclear.

In community and clinical samples, adolescent personality disorders are associated with emotional distress and psychological impairment. In the Children in the Community study (Johnson et al., 2006)—a prospective longitudinal investigation of 593 families at four time points from childhood to adulthood (starting when children were ages 1 to 10 years)—low parental affection or nurturing was associated with elevated risk for antisocial, avoidant, borderline, paranoid, schizoid, and schizotypal personality disorders among adult offspring of these families. Aversive parental behavior (e.g., harsh punishment) was associated with an elevated risk for borderline, paranoid, and schizotypal personality disorders among adult offspring. Because this study controlled for offspring behavioral and emotional problems and parental psychiatric disorder, these findings suggest that parental rearing styles may be associated with the development of personality disorders in

Twin studies reveal that genes influence both personality traits and personality.

children. Conduct disorder and antisocial personality disorder represent the clearest case of progression from adolescence through adulthood (Johnson et al., 2006), and the former is, in fact, a requirement for diagnosis of the latter.

Distinguishing between signs and symptoms of adolescent borderline personality disorder and more typical fluctuations in adolescent personality may also enable early detection and treatment in an attempt to avoid a lifetime of turbulence and distress. Adolescent borderline personality disorder is marked by abandonment fears; unstable and intense interpersonal relationships; identity disturbance; impulsivity; suicidal behaviors; affective instability; chronic feelings of emptiness; inappropriate, intense anger and transient, stress-related paranoid ideation; and/or severe dissociative symptoms. Although many of these features may be observed in many adolescents, the personality disorder distinguishes itself in its severity, pervasiveness, and time course by persisting across developmental stages (Sharp & Fonagy, 2015).

Adolescent personality disorders are also associated with the presence of other psychological disorders. A young woman who shows persistent dependent traits throughout adolescence may find herself at increased risk for developing major depression during adulthood when she experiences loss. Applying dimensional approaches to understanding personality development in children may yield rich information. One longitudinal cohort study, the "Block Project," has followed 100 children since the age of 3 well into adulthood. The Block Project found that characteristic childhood personality and behavioral patterns predicted the later development of problems such as dysthymia. Boys who developed dysthymia by age 18 were observed to be aggressive, self-aggrandizing, and undercontrolled at age 7. Girls with later depressive tendencies were self-critical and overcontrolling as children (Block et al., 1991). Therefore, personality differences that exist in early childhood were associated with the later development of disorders such as depression, but different behaviors were important for boys and girls. However, we need to be careful that we do not immediately assume that every unusual childhood and adolescent behavior represents a risk factor for the emergence of a later psychological disorder. We do not yet fully appreciate the clinical significance of personality traits during childhood and adolescence.

In a longitudinal study of Norwegian twins, Reichborn-Kjennerud et al. (2015) demonstrated that features of borderline personality disorder and antisocial personality disorder were relatively stable across early and middle adulthood and that Cluster A disorders were highly stable over a 10-year observation period (Kendler et al., 2015). Moreover, in both of these studies, genetic factors were the primary contributor to the long-term stability of the disorders.

Comorbidity and Functional Impairment

LO 12.8 Clarify the manner in which personality disorders influence interpersonal functioning.

As each case in this chapter indicates, personality disorders produce substantial functional impairment, most obviously in interpersonal relationships. The person with borderline personality disorder alienates her friends and lovers with her rapidly fluctuating moods of adoration and hatred; the obsessive-compulsive father alienates his family with his rigid approach to the world; the son with schizoid personality disorder abandons his siblings and has few ties to the rest of the world. Perhaps not surprisingly, people with personality disorders create considerable distress for people around them and are often the topic of conversation because of the unusual and extreme aspects of who they are.

Personality disorders also often deeply affect occupational functioning. In a study of 2,770 young adults in Norway, the presence of any personality disorder was associated with significantly increased risk for disability pensioning (i.e., temporary or permanent leave from work due to disability) (Østby et al., 2014). From the person with avoidant personality disorder who declines promotions to avoid interpersonal contact, to the person with antisocial personality disorder who moves irresponsibly from job to job, to the person with histrionic personality disorder who flirts inappropriately to gain attention from coworkers, personality disorders can lead to occupational problems and failures. Needless to say, managers do not necessarily have the psychological background to understand that these patterns of behavior are secondary to a personality disorder. These behaviors result in poor or inappropriate performance and potentially loss of employment.

In addition to their problems with social and occupational functioning, people with personality disorders, in general, are at higher risk than other people for many other psychological disorders. In a sample of Dutch adults seeking outpatient psychiatric care, nearly all (93.9%) of those with a personality disorder met criteria for another comorbid psychological disorder (Wieland et al., 2015). Among Danish psychiatric patients, nearly half (46%) of individuals with personality disorders met criteria for a comorbid substance use disorder, most notably alcohol use disorder (38.6%) (Toftdahl et al., 2015). Cluster A personality disorders have been most strongly associated with dysthymia, major depression, social anxiety disorder, and mania (Grant, Hasin et al., 2004; Mattik & Newman, 1991). Borderline personality disorder is commonly comorbid with major depression (Sullivan et al., 1994), bulimia nervosa (Rosenvinge et al., 2000), and substance use disorders (Dulit et al., 1993; Skodol et al., 1999). Antisocial personality disorder often occurs within the context of substance abuse and other impulse control disorders (American Psychiatric Association, 2013; Dulit et al., 1993; Goldstein et al., 2007). Obsessive-compulsive personality disorder is often comorbid with anxiety disorders, mood disorders, and substance use disorders (Diedrich & Voderholzer, 2015). These high rates of comorbidity suggest that the clinical presentation and functional impairment of personality disorders can be compounded by the presence of other disorders. Furthermore, the combination results in significant personal distress and poses considerable treatment challenges. We will see that intervention must address not only the pervasive personality pathology but also the acute symptoms associated with comorbid disorders.

Epidemiology, Sex, Race, and Ethnicity

LO 12.9 Trace the occurrence of personality disorders across various segments of the population.

Few epidemiologic data on the prevalence of personality disorders are available. One reason is that personality disorders cannot be reliably diagnosed in a single setting. Most epidemiologic studies rely on a single diagnostic interview (at best) and a series of self-report questionnaires. Capturing the complexity of personality disorder diagnoses in cross-sectional epidemiological studies is a daunting and potentially unreliable task. We need to keep this in mind when considering the data that do exist.

In the general U.S. adult population, results from the National Epidemiologic Survey on Alcohol and Related Conditions revealed that as many as 21.5% of adult Americans meet criteria for at least one personality disorder (Trull et al., 2010) (see Figure 12.2). The specific prevalences reported in this study were paranoid (4.4%), schizoid (3.1%), schizotypal (3.9%), antisocial (3.8%), borderline (5.9%), histrionic (1.8%), narcissistic (6.2%), avoidant (2.4%), dependent (0.5%), and obsessive-compulsive (7.9%) (Trull et al., 2010). By applying more stringent criteria to the data from the National Epidemiologic Survey on Alcohol and Related Conditions (i.e., requiring distress or impairment for all personality disorder symptoms vs. distress or impairment for only one symptom), the lifetime prevalence of any personality disorder falls from 21.5% to 9.1%, which is in line with Lenzenweger et al.'s (2007) finding from the National Comorbidity Survey-Replication.

Our understanding of sex differences in personality disorders comes from epidemiological studies and studies of clinical populations. However, sex differences reported in clinical studies can be biased and may reflect the likelihood of the different sexes to seek treatment (or be brought in for treatment) rather than true sex differences. When we compare results across epidemiologic studies, two constant patterns emerge. First, antisocial personality disorder and schizotypal personality disorder are consistently more common in males (Alegria et al., 2013; Grant et al., 2004b; Pulay et al., 2009). Second, dependent and avoidant personality disorders tend to be more common in females (Grant et al., 2004b; Torgersen et al., 2001). Although in clinical settings, histrionic personality disorder tends to be diagnosed more

Figure 12.2 Prevalence of Personality Disorders, United States.

SOURCE: Based on data from National Epidemiologic Survey on Alcohol and Related Conditions/Trull et al., 2010

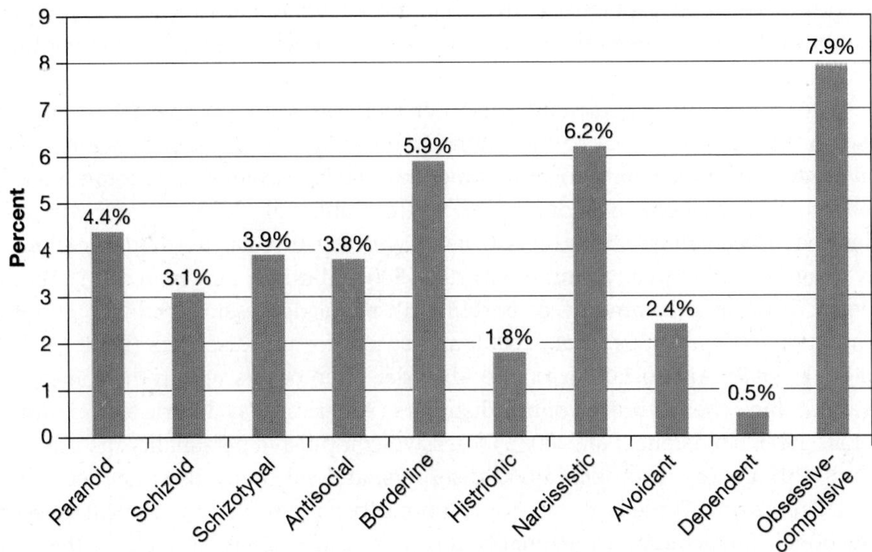

often in females and narcissistic personality disorder in males, this pattern is observed in some (Stinson et al., 2008; Torgersen et al., 2001) but not all (Grant et al., 2004b) epidemiologic studies. Beyond those differences, few consistent patterns emerge in terms of sex differences in personality disorders (Grant et al., 2008, 2012).

Few population-based data focus on racial and ethnic differences in personality disorders. According to epidemiologic research, borderline personality disorder is significantly more prevalent among Native American men and significantly less prevalent among Hispanic men and women and Asian women when compared with non-Hispanic whites (Grant et al., 2008). Data from the Epidemiological Catchment Area study (Robins et al., 1984) indicated similar estimates of histrionic personality disorder among African Americans and whites (Nestadt et al., 1990). Borderline personality disorder may be more common in nonwhite individuals belonging to lower socioeconomic groups (Swartz et al., 1990), and similar estimates of antisocial personality disorder were found among Mexican Americans, Puerto Ricans, and non-Hispanic whites (Canino et al., 1987; Karno et al., 1987). Compared to non-Hispanic whites, lifetime prevalence of narcissistic personality disorder is elevated in African American men and women and Hispanic women (Stinson et al., 2008), and schizotypal personality disorder is more prevalent in African American women and less prevalent in Asian men (Pulay et al., 2009).

The existing data on racial and ethnic factors in personality disorders must be viewed with considerable caution. We simply do not have adequate large-scale culturally sensitive studies that will provide data on racial and ethnic differences in either the prevalence or differences in clinical presentation of these disorders.

Learning Objective Summaries

LO 12.3 Describe the Cluster A personality disorders and their uniting characteristics.

The common features of Cluster A personality disorders are characteristic behaviors that others would consider odd, quirky, or eccentric and include paranoid personality disorder (pervasive distrust and suspiciousness of others such that their motives are interpreted as malevolent), schizoid personality disorder (pervasive pattern of detachment from social relationships and a restricted range of emotional expression in interpersonal settings), and schizotypal personality disorder (pervasive pattern of social and interpersonal deficits marked by acute discomfort, reduced capacity for close relationships, cognitive or perceptual distortions, and behavioral eccentricities).

LO 12.4 Describe the Cluster B personality disorders and their uniting characteristics.

The common features of Cluster B personality disorders are behaviors that are viewed as exaggerated, inflated, dramatic, emotional, or erratic and include antisocial personality disorder (pervasive pattern of disregard for and violation of the rights of others), borderline personality disorder (pervasive pattern of instability of interpersonal relationships, self-image, and affect, and marked impulsivity), histrionic personality disorder (pervasive pattern of excessive emotionality and attention seeking), and narcissistic personality disorder (pervasive pattern of grandiosity [in fantasy or behavior], need for admiration, and lack of empathy).

LO 12.5 Describe the Cluster C personality disorders and their uniting characteristics.

The common features of Cluster C are characteristic behaviors marked by considerable anxiety or withdrawal and include avoidant personality disorder (pervasive pattern of social inhibition, feelings of inadequacy, and hypersensitivity to negative evaluation), dependent personality disorder (pervasive and excessive need to be taken care of, which leads to submissive and clinging behavior and fears of separation), and obsessive-compulsive personality disorder (pervasive pattern of preoccupation with orderliness, perfectionism, and mental and interpersonal control at the expense of flexibility, openness, and efficiency).

LO 12.6 Evaluate various models of personality disorders.

In addition to the DSM classification model, other dimensional models exist that view personality on more of a continuum of traits. The popular five-factor model posits five primary dimensions of personality: extraversion, neuroticism, conscientiousness, agreeableness, and openness to experience.

LO 12.7 Debate the extent to which childhood personality predicts adult personality and personality disorders.

Personality traits originate very early in life and may at least in part be programmed at the genetic level. Elements of later personality may even be foreshadowed in the simple behaviors exhibited by babies and toddlers. Many manifestations of personality disorders represent typical and transient childhood and adolescent behaviors. Dependency, anxiety, hypersensitivity, identity formation problems, conduct problems, histrionics, and testing the limits occur commonly during childhood and adolescence. More flagrant symptoms (such as harming animals or risky sexual behavior) may be more serious red flags for later personality disturbance.

LO 12.8 Clarify the manner in which personality disorders influence interpersonal functioning.

Personality disorders produce substantial functional impairment in interpersonal relationships and often occupational functioning. People with personality disorders create considerable distress for people around them and are often the topic of conversation because of the unusual and extreme aspects of who they are.

LO 12.9 Trace the occurrence of personality disorders across various segments of the population.

In the general U.S. adult population, 21.5% of adult Americans meet criteria for at least one personality disorder. Antisocial personality disorder and schizotypal personality disorder are consistently more common in males. Dependent and avoidant personality disorders tend to be more common in females. Beyond those differences, few consistent patterns emerge in terms of sex differences in personality disorders. The existing data on racial and ethnic factors in personality disorders must be viewed with considerable caution. We simply do not have adequate large-scale culturally sensitive studies that will provide data on racial and ethnic differences in either the prevalence or differences in clinical presentation of these disorders.

Critical Thinking Question

Mental illnesses are often stigmatized. Do the descriptors for the three personality disorder clusters (A, "odd or eccentric"; B, "dramatic, emotional, or erratic"; and C, "anxious or fearful") seem derogatory to you? Do you think the names actually *are* derogatory, or do you think you may perhaps have been raised to have prejudice about such things? Discuss.

Etiology of Personality Disorders

What causes a persistent and maladaptive way of dealing with the world? Are there indicators early in life that predict the emergence of personality pathology? Can we use the same tools that we use with other psychological disorders to understand the causes of personality disorders? These are all critical and current questions that are being addressed with active research within the personality disorders field. As with other disorders, neither genetic underpinnings, chemical imbalances, psychological features, nor problematic social environments alone account for the development of personality pathology. Critical to understanding personality pathology is the convergence of both a biopsychosocial perspective and a full understanding of the developmental context. In the remaining sections of this chapter, we outline what is known about biological, psychological, and social factors and how they interact to result in disturbances in personality function.

Biological Perspectives

LO 12.10 Understand the role biology may play in the origin of personality pathology.

Ask any mother with more than one child and she will tell you that her babies had distinct and often quite different personalities from birth—and sometimes even from before birth (see "Research Hot Topic: Tracking Temperament from Childhood into Adulthood").

> In contrasting her children, Lashanda said, "Ronnie was a holy terror from the day he was born. He would scream and scream, and nothing could soothe him. In fact, it went back even further than that. Seems whenever I wanted to sleep when I was pregnant, he wanted to play. I didn't get a minute's rest for 9 months. It's amazing I had another one! Then came Jake. When I was pregnant, he slept when I slept. After he was born, I kept expecting him to be like Ronnie—throwing tantrums in the middle of the night, unable to be consoled. He might yell a little, I would come into his room, rub his back, he would pass a little gas, sigh, smile, roll over, and fall back to sleep. Those boys had different wiring!"

Temperament is influenced by genetics and may account for some of the variability in personality traits. Temperament refers to personality components that are biological or genetic in origin, observable from birth (perhaps before), and relatively stable across time and across various situations (Buss, 1999). For example, some children are born fussy and irritable, while others are mellow and calm. Even mothers of twins point out fundamental differences in the temperament of babies who developed at the same time in the womb. When these innate biological components interact with the outside world (i.e., experience), personality emerges (Cloninger et al., 1993). Thus, personality traits are a combination of temperament and experience. Personality disorders represent a dysfunctional outcome of this process, when certain traits become exaggerated and are applied in maladaptive ways.

Temperament, a part of personality that is believed to be biologically based, appears early in life.

Theories about the associations between personality dimensions and underlying biological or genetic markers await confirmatory data. In 1993, Cloninger proposed that associations between dimensions of temperament and specific neurotransmitter systems exist (Cloninger et al., 1993). As our understanding of temperament and neurobiology has progressed, it is clear that any simplistic theories that link one trait to one neurotransmitter will be replaced by more sophisticated models that account for complex biological underpinnings.

FAMILY AND GENETIC STUDIES Family and twin studies clearly indicate that both personality disorders (Barnow, 2013; Gjerde, 2012; Gunderson et al., 2011; Kendler, 2015; Kendler et al., 2007, 2008; Torgersen et al., 2012) and personality traits (Gjerde et al., 2015; Jang et al., 1996; Joyce et al., 2009; Reichborn-Kjennerud et al., 2015; Rettew et al., 2008) are familial and are influenced primarily by genetic factors. As with all complex traits, a single gene is not responsible for a single temperamental trait; the trait probably results from variations in several genes coupled with environmental influences.

Ongoing studies have explored genetic and environmental factors in personality disorders (Bae et al., 2013; Lubke et al., 2014). Large twin studies indicate that paranoid,

Figure 12.3 Heritability of Personality Disorders.

SOURCE: Kendler, K. S., Aggen, S. H., Czajkowski, N., Roysamb, E., Tambs, K., Torgersen, S., . . . Reichborn-Kjennerud, T. (2008). The structure of genetic and environmental risk factors for DSM-IV personality disorders: A multivariate twin study. *Archives of General Psychiatry, 65,* 1438–1446.

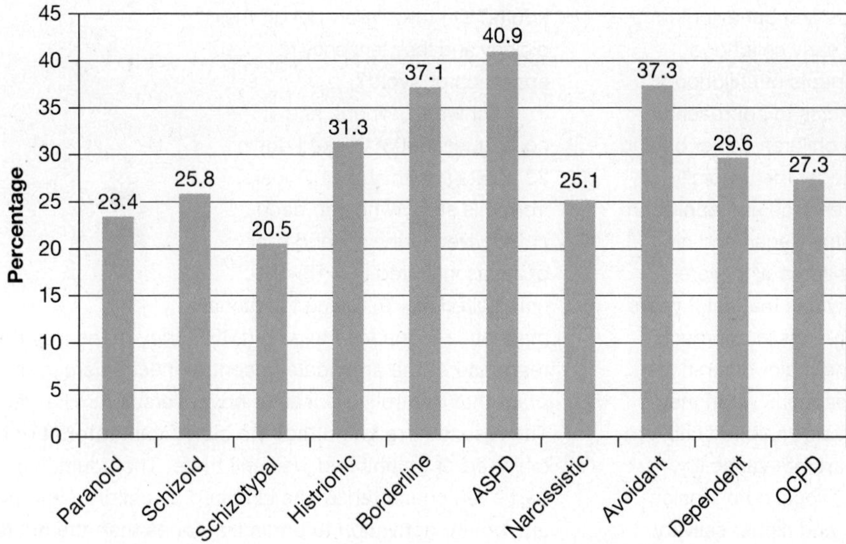

schizoid, and schizotypal personality disorders are all moderately heritable (Kendler et al., 2007, 2008). In a large multivariate twin study, heritability estimates across personality disorders ranged from the lower end (20.5% schizotypal and 23.4% paranoid) to the most heritable (borderline 37.1%, avoidant 37.3%, and antisocial 40.9%) (Kendler et al., 2008) (see Figure 12.3).

THE ROLE OF TRAUMATIC EVENTS Although one might consider traumatic events as transient environmental factors (and indeed they are), we now know that especially during critical developmental windows, they can have profound and long-term effects on brain biology (Goodman et al., 2004). People with some personality disorders report increased rates of childhood emotional abuse, physical abuse, and neglect (Battle et al., 2004; Bierer et al., 2003). In addition, childhood history of physical and/or sexual abuse has been associated with personality disorders (Herman et al., 1989; Ogata et al., 1990; Zanarini et al., 1989) although studies of discordant twins suggest that the effect may be quite small and the association between childhood trauma and personality disorders may better be accounted for by shared genetic factors (Berenz et al., 2013; Bornovalova et al., 2013). These associations provide an important clue to the biological mechanisms underlying the development of personality disorders. Early maltreatment is associated with problems in basic attachment. Attachment is one of the processes that provides the foundation for our ability later in life to relate to others interpersonally. Poor attachment is believed to interfere with brain structures that underlie development of the ability to think about the mental states of others, called *mentalization* (Fonagy et al., 1991). Early trauma and the subsequent disruption in attachment may lead to neurodevelopmental deficits in interpersonal functioning and create a pathway to the development of severe personality disturbance.

Poor attachment may play a role in the etiology of personality disorders, whereas good attachment may be a protective buffer.

A person's neurobiological responses to threat stimuli may be changed after traumatic events including childhood traumatic experiences. Alterations in arousal, fear conditioning, and emotional regulation have been observed in people who have a history of traumatic events (Arnsten, 1998; Bremner, 2007; Bremner et al., 1999; Mayes, 2000; Shin et al., 2005). These shifts in brain functioning are adaptive in the context of real danger, which requires a rapid automatic response to ensure survival.

Research HOT Topic

Tracking Temperament from Childhood into Adulthood

Temperament refers to the stable moods and behavior profiles that appear during infancy and early childhood. Two of the most extensively studied aspects of childhood temperament are the behavioral tendencies to approach or withdraw from unfamiliar stimuli. Some children cower behind their mother when confronted by a stranger (behaviorally inhibited children) while others eagerly engage and approach the stranger (uninhibited children). Jerome Kagan and his colleagues have followed a cohort of children who were categorized as inhibited or uninhibited within the first 2 years of life. In addition to the observed differences in approach/withdrawal, these researchers also found major differences in the children's underlying biological reactions when they were confronted with unfamiliar individuals. Inhibited children showed faster heart rates and more heart rate variability, pupillary dilation during cognitive tasks, vocal cord tension when speaking under moderate stress, and higher salivary cortisol levels than those who were uninhibited. Intriguingly, these differences remained throughout later childhood and adolescence. But what happens when the children become adults? Do they "grow out of" their biology and their tendency to approach or avoid?

Schwartz, Wright, and colleagues (2003) tracked down 22 adults (mean age 21.8 years) from this study who had been categorized in the second year of life as inhibited (n = 13) or uninhibited (n = 9). Using functional magnetic resonance imaging (fMRI), they measured the response of the amygdala (a central mechanism in our brain that controls arousal) to novel versus familiar faces. The researchers found that the biological footprint of being inhibited or uninhibited was still there. The adults who had been characterized as inhibited as children had more amygdalar activation to unfamiliar faces than the adults who had been classified as uninhibited. These findings show that some of the basic brain properties relating to temperament are preserved from infancy into early adulthood.

However, early trauma may permanently impair the biology of arousal regulation and fear conditioning, causing an inappropriate reaction even when danger is not imminent. Thus, trauma might lead to "overperceiving" and "overresponding" to threats. Early childhood trauma may have a permanent effect on brain development, which can set the stage for the emergence of maladaptive personality traits. Because many personality disorders represent maladaptive and, in many cases, exaggerated responses to seemingly innocuous interpersonal events, these fundamental neurobiological disturbances may well underlie the erratic and dysregulated responses to the world commonly seen in people with personality disorders.

BRAIN STRUCTURE AND FUNCTIONING STUDIES Modern assessment tools such as fMRI and PET scans enable us to examine the neurobiology of some personality disorders. Behaviorally, people with schizotypal personality disorder show the same psychotic-like cognitive and perceptual symptoms and cognitive disorganization as people with schizophrenia. Biologically, these two groups show both similarities and differences. Structurally, individuals with both schizophrenia and schizotypal personality disorder show abnormalities in *temporal lobe* volume (Siever et al., 2002), but the decrease in brain volume seen in the *frontal lobe* of people with schizophrenia is not found in people with schizotypal personality disorder (see Figure 12.4). Functionally, there are also subtle biological differences. Whereas both groups show decreased brain activity in the frontal cortex, only people with schizotypal personality disorder appear to be able to activate other regions of their brain as a way to compensate for this deficit (Siever et al., 2002).

With Cluster B disorders, studies examining people with borderline and antisocial personality disorders have focused on brain regions that control rage, fear, and impulsive automatic reactions (the prominent symptoms of the disorders). It appears that the hippocampus and amygdala may be as much as 16% smaller in people with borderline personality disorder than in people with no personality disorder. Traumatic experiences, which are common in people with borderline personality disorder, may create these neuroanatomical changes (Driessen et al., 2000). Neurobiological theories of antisocial personality disorder focus on individual differences in arousal or detection. One theory suggests that people at risk for antisocial personality disorder are in a chronic state of underarousal and that their

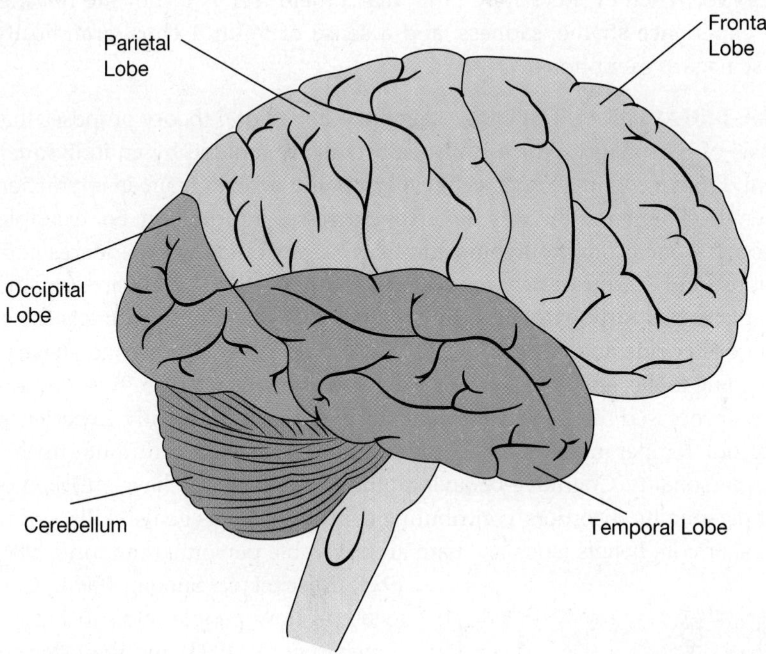

Figure 12.4 Individuals with schizophrenia and schizotypal personality disorder show abnormalities in the temporal lobe, but decreased frontal lobe volume is seen in individuals with schizophrenia.

behavior represents misguided attempts to seek stimulation (Quay, 1965). Another theory focuses on the apparent fearlessness of people with antisocial personality disorder and hypothesizes that they have a higher fear detection threshold than other people (Lykken, 1982). This difference in detection of fear allows them to enter calmly into situations that others would find overwhelmingly fear inducing.

Psychological and Sociocultural Perspectives

LO 12.11 Compare psychological theories of personality disorders and discuss the role of culture on personality.

An entire branch of psychology (personality psychology) deals with the psychological processes underlying healthy and maladaptive personality traits. For decades, various psychological theories dominated our understanding of their etiology. The two most prominent theories, which we review here, are the psychodynamic and the cognitive-behavioral perspectives.

PSYCHODYNAMIC INTERPRETATIONS Most psychodynamic theories focus on early parental interactions that shape behavioral traits that become personality disorders. Theories about the origins of borderline personality disorder, for example, associated a lack of parental acceptance to damaged self-esteem and fears of rejection (Gunderson, 1984). Indeed, this theory is generally consistent with the high rates of abuse and neglect reported by people with borderline personality disorders (Herman et al., 1989; Ogata et al., 1990). According to these theories, people tend to internalize negative parental attitudes, leaving them vulnerable to fears of abandonment and to self-hatred. In addition, they tend to treat themselves as they were treated by their parents. These attitudes prevent the development of mature, consistent, and positive perceptions of themselves and others. They also lead to a severe inability to regulate mood when faced with disappointment and difficulty in taking another's point of view.

The psychiatrist Otto Kernberg (1975) proposed a continuum of psychopathology from persistent, severe psychosis to severe personality disorders through neurotic to healthy functioning. Kernberg's work focused primarily on the development of borderline personality disorder but also encompassed other personality disorders. For example, people with narcissistic personality disorder construct a largely inflated view of themselves in order to maintain their self-esteem. On the outside, these individuals appear grandiose, but inside they are often very sensitive to even very minor attacks on the self. They create this enlarged perception of themselves in order to match the grandiose perception of their ideal in their own mind's eye. When events happen that make them feel as if they are not meeting this ideal, they experience shame, sadness, and a sense of failure. Thus, grandiosity protects against these negative emotions.

COGNITIVE-BEHAVIORAL THEORY Cognitive-behavioral theory proposes that learning is at the basis of personality, which is also substantially molded by an individual's unique environment. From a cognitive perspective, personality evolves from an interaction between a person's environment and the way he or she processes information. For example, imagine two adolescents—one is fairly outgoing and likes to seek out new experiences and the other is shy, anxious, and fearful of new experiences. Both are flying as unaccompanied minors when their plane hits turbulence and drops 10,000 feet. The first teen treats the experience like a roller coaster ride and basically says, "Wow, wild ride." The second shakes and cries, thinks he is going to die, and vows never to step into an airplane again. Two temperamentally different boys processed the same environmental event very differently. Experiences like this one—where our temperament and the environment intersect—contribute to the development of our personality. Cognitive-behavioral theory and therapy have enriched our understanding of personality disorders, contributing concepts such as goals, skills, self-regulation, and schemas, or core beliefs (such as "I am an unlovable person") (Bandura, 1986; Mischel, 1973; Mischel & Shoda, 1995). Considerable focus on how people learn to regulate moods (Linehan et al., 1993) and their development of core beliefs about themselves and their worlds (Beck et al., 2003) has transformed the theory into cognitive-behavioral treatments for personality disorders (see "Treatment of Personality Disorders").

Across cultures, different ideas of basic human concepts such as "self" may lead to very different conceptualizations and treatments of personality disorders. In Japan, the *self* is more of a collective concept than the individual *self* in the United States.

SOCIOCULTURAL THEORIES Sociocultural theories of personality go beyond the study of the individual to include a broader contextual view of personality development including culture as a critical element in shaping personality (Miller, 1997). Fundamental cultural differences can deeply influence the concept of personality. For example, consider the differences in the concept of "self" in Japanese and Western cultures. In Japanese culture, *self* includes both the personal self and that of the surrounding cultural community; in dominant Western culture, the *self* is considered independent and not contingent upon others (Markus & Kitayama, 1991). Clearly, this core conceptual difference could influence perceptions of what constitutes abnormal behavior.

Another factor that influences cross-cultural studies of personality is language. Classic Western personality measures may not capture cultural nuances of expression and language, such as the Japanese language term *amae*, meaning the need for dependency (Doi, 1973), or the Hindu language term *anasakti*, meaning nonattachment, a freedom from dependency that is associated with greater peace and mental health (Pande & Naidu, 1992). The similarities in personality disorders that we observe across cultures may simply reflect the imposition of Western language on non-Western cultures. Therefore, although the dimensional aspects of personality appear consistent across cultures, there are also cultural differences that will enrich our understanding of personality disorders (Poortinga & Van Hemert, 2001).

Learning Objective Summaries

LO 12.10 Understand the role biology may play in the origin of personality pathology.

Temperament is influenced by genetics and may account for some of the variability in personality traits. Temperament refers to personality components that are biological or genetic in origin, observable from birth (perhaps before), and relatively stable across time and across various situations. Personality traits and disorders are heritable, indicating that genetic factors play a role. Traumatic events, especially during critical developmental windows, can have long-term effects on brain biology and contribute to the emergence of personality disturbances.

LO 12.11 Compare psychological theories of personality disorders and discuss the role of culture on personality.

Psychodynamic theories focus on early parental interactions that shape the behavioral traits that become personality disorders. Cognitive approaches view personality as evolving from an interaction between a person's environment and the way he or she processes information. Cognitive-behavioral theories have explained personality disorders through concepts such as goals, skills, self-regulation, and schemas, or core beliefs. Sociocultural theories of personality go beyond the study of the individual to include a broader contextual view of personality development including culture and language as critical elements in shaping personality.

Critical Thinking Question

Sometimes defining the boundaries between personality disorder and criminal behavior found in someone like Jeffrey Dahmer can be a daunting task. If you were asked to think about when someone should be considered innocent due to a personality disorder versus guilty of criminal behavior, what types of issues would you consider? How would biology and history of trauma influence your thinking?

Treatment of Personality Disorders

Psychological Treatments

LO 12.12 Discuss challenges in the treatment of personality disorders with psychotherapy.

Treating enduring patterns of behavior is inherently different from treating acute disorders. No magic pill exists to change a person's personality style. Both patient and therapist must make subtle distinctions between healthy and maladaptive behavior patterns. The patient must understand the perspective of other people whom their disorder affects adversely. In addition, because these behavior patterns are long-standing, one cannot expect rapid improvement—particularly if the behavioral patterns reach back to early childhood and involve changes in brain functioning. Other significant challenges include just getting patients with personality disorders into treatment. Often the people around them are more interested in getting them treatment than the patients are themselves. Finally, the treatment can be especially complicated when people have more than one personality disorder and have an acute illness such as major depressive disorder, bipolar disorder, bulimia nervosa, or substance abuse. Such complications can pose treatment challenges for the most dedicated clinician. Patience, consistency, and persistence are valuable therapist characteristics that can facilitate treatment of personality disorders.

Only recently have we witnessed a surge of randomized controlled trials investigating the treatment of personality disorders. Although the overall amount of research remains small, studies have explored the efficacy of dynamic therapy and cognitive-behavioral therapy or their variants. The quality of the research varies because some studies focus on specific personality disorders, others on the personality disorder clusters, and still others on personality disorders in general. This makes the results of the studies difficult to interpret.

Most studies on specific personality disorders have focused on borderline or antisocial personality disorder. Although avoidant personality disorder and Cluster C disorders have received some research attention, there is a dearth of data on the treatment of Cluster A disorders. With this background in mind, we describe various treatments for personality disorders, their empirical basis, and the limitations of the available research. Given the broad and heterogeneous nature of this area, we present treatment approaches and data related to personality disorders generally and borderline personality disorder specifically.

Despite a limited number of treatment studies, recent data support the importance of psychotherapy in the treatment of personality disorders. While pharmacotherapy may help manage associated symptoms such as anxiety or depression, psychosocial treatments and excellent communication among all those delivering care are required for optimal management of personality disorders.

Early treatments for personality disorders were rooted in dynamic psychotherapy and adapted psychoanalytic techniques in long-term therapeutic approaches. Current treatment approaches differ somewhat according to disorder and often include components to address concurrent comorbid psychological disorders.

Treatment for Cluster A disorders can be challenging. When their core problem is distrust, it can be particularly difficult for people with paranoid personality disorder to trust the motives of a therapist. People with schizoid personality disorders have little desire for social interaction, so it is difficult to convince them that social interactions are often necessary and positively reinforcing (Beck et al., 2003). People with schizotypal personality disorder often benefit from cognitive-behavioral therapy that helps them develop appropriate thoughts and eliminate or modify odd or eccentric cognitions (Beck et al., 2003).

A form of cognitive-behavioral therapy focuses on the challenges inherent in treating people with the rapidly fluctuating symptoms of borderline personality disorder. This approach, *dialectical behavior therapy* (DBT), has considerable empirical support (Binks et al., 2006; Linehan et al., 2006). DBT is based on a model that focuses on the intersection of biological and environmental causes. DBT hypothesizes that the fundamental biological problem is in the emotion regulation system and may arise from genetics, intrauterine factors, traumatic early events, or some combination of these factors. The environmental component is any set of circumstances that punish, traumatize, or neglect this emotional vulnerability. Borderline personality disorder emerges from ongoing transactions between the individual and the environment with the individual becoming increasingly unable to regulate emotions and the environment becoming progressively more invalidating (Linehan et al., 2006). The emotional dysregulation in individuals with borderline personality disorder results from emotional vulnerability combined with deficits in the skills needed to regulate emotions. Intriguingly, at the age of 68, Dr. Linehan disclosed that as a youth she was hospitalized for suicidality, self-harm, and emotion dysregulation. At that time, she perplexed the mental health system and was inaccurately diagnosed with schizophrenia. In an interview with the *New York Times* she acknowledged that the treatment she developed, DBT, emerged from her own personal experience and provides the help she needed for so many years and never received.

DBT emphasizes discussion and negotiation between therapist and patient with a balance between the rational and the emotional and between acceptance and change. The patient and therapist establish a hierarchy of treatment goals, giving the highest priority to eliminating self-harm behaviors. DBT has many principles, but all patients receive skills training in several areas: mindfulness (to improve control of attention and the mind), interpersonal skills and conflict management, emotional regulation, distress tolerance, and self-management. These approaches help the patient to calm down what can feel like a chaotic internal

Table 12.1 The Four Key DBT Skills

Mindfulness (wise mind)
Distress tolerance
Emotion regulation
Interpersonal effectiveness

SOURCE: http://www.dbtselfhelp.com/html/dbt_skills_list.html

state, to pay attention to emotionally driven behavior, and to develop skills to manage feelings and impulses more effectively. Medications can also be used to assist with regulating the biological systems.

Compared with treatment as usual (what we call "talk therapy"), DBT and partial hospitalization (a day treatment program) produce superior treatment results (Brazier et al., 2006). Moreover, DBT may be more cost-effective than traditional therapy for borderline personality disorder. Other treatment strategies that are sometimes efficacious for borderline personality disorder include mentalization-based therapy (a psychoanalytically based intervention that aims to increase the reflective or mentalizing capacity of the individual, helping the person to understand and recognize the feelings he or she evokes in others and the feelings he or she experiences) (Bateman & Fonagy, 2004), inpatient therapy (Dolan et al., 1997), schema-focused therapy (helps people with BPD to identify their self-defeating core themes arising from unmet emotional needs in childhood and presenting as maladaptive coping styles in adulthood) (Young, 2003), and step-down programs characterized by short-term inpatient treatment followed by longer-term outpatient and community treatment (Chiesa et al., 2004, 2006). A review of these treatments suggests that psychotherapy definitely plays a role in the management of borderline personality disorder, with DBT being the most widely studied; however, the evidence base is not robust, and methodologically rigorous replication studies are required (Stoffers et al., 2012).

Dialectical behavior therapy blends Zen practice with cognitive-behavior therapy and teaches concepts such as "mindfulness," or being aware of one's experiences and emotional state. Here Dr. Marsha Linehan (the developer of DBT) and her students, Trevor Schraufnagel and Andrada Neacsiu, illustrate mindfulness practice of therapists at the start of DBT team meetings.

Disappointingly, there is very little evidence for the efficacy of psychotherapy on the treatment of antisocial personality disorder (Gibbon et al., 2010). The evidence base is poor in part because of the difficulty in engaging and retaining individuals with this personality disorder in treatment. However, to date, no psychotherapeutic intervention holds promise in addressing the core features of this condition.

Pharmacological Treatments

LO 12.13 Evaluate the effectiveness of medication in the treatment of various personality disorders.

Medications including antidepressants, mood stabilizers (drugs that even out the highs and lows seen in mood disorders), and antipsychotics are often prescribed for borderline personality disorder. These drugs target sudden mood swings, impulsivity, and aggression. A comprehensive review of all pharmacological interventions for borderline personality disorder reveals some beneficial effects with second-generation antipsychotics, mood stabilizers, and dietary supplementation by omega-3 fatty acids, although the effects are not robust (Stoffers et al., 2010). Moreover, antidepressants were not particularly effective unless comorbid conditions such as depression were present. Importantly, no medications were effective in ameliorating the symptoms of chronic feelings of emptiness, identity disturbance, and abandonment. The atypical antipsychotics (see Chapter 11) may be helpful for patients with borderline personality disorder who have psychotic-like, impulsive, or suicidal symptoms (Grootens & Verkes, 2005). It is critical to understand that remission from borderline personality disorder does occur. In a 6-year prospective outcome study (Zanarini et al., 2003), 34.5% of patients met criteria for remission at 2 years, 49.4% at 4 years, 68.6% at 6 years, and 73.5% over entire follow-up. Moreover, only 5.9% of patients whose symptoms remitted showed a recurrence of symptoms at a later time.

Less success has been achieved in the treatment of antisocial personality disorder. The state of research is so fragmented and insufficient that no conclusions can be drawn regarding the efficacy of treatment of the condition with medication. Single, unreplicated trials report some diminution of specific symptoms (often related to substance abuse or aggression), but no medication has proven useful in addressing the totality of antisocial personality disorder symptoms (Khalifa et al., 2010).

Learning Objective Summaries

LO 12.12 Discuss challenges in the treatment of personality disorders with psychotherapy.

Treating long-standing patterns of behavior is challenging in psychotherapy. Because these behavior patterns are long-standing, one cannot expect rapid improvement. Other significant challenges include just getting patients with personality disorders into treatment. One approach, *dialectical behavior therapy* (DBT), has considerable empirical support and is based on a model that focuses on the intersection of biological and environmental causes. DBT hypothesizes that the fundamental biological problem is in the emotion regulation system and may arise from genetics, intrauterine factors, traumatic early events, or some combination of these factors. DBT emphasizes discussion and negotiation between therapist and patient with a balance between the rational and the emotional and between acceptance and change.

LO 12.13 Evaluate the effectiveness of medication in the treatment of various personality disorders.

Medications including antidepressants, mood stabilizers (drugs that even out the highs and lows seen in mood disorders), and antipsychotics are often prescribed for borderline personality disorder. These drugs target sudden mood swings, impulsivity, and aggression. A comprehensive review of all pharmacological interventions for borderline personality disorder reveals some beneficial effects with second-generation antipsychotics, mood stabilizers, and dietary supplementation by omega-3 fatty acids, although the effects are not robust. Little empirical evidence exists to evaluate pharmacological interventions in other personality disorders.

Critical Thinking Question

Individuals with personality disorders experience the world through a different lens. Pick a personality disorder and discuss the differences in perspective through which someone with that disorder may view typical events of any given day. What might it feel like to perceive the world in that manner, and how might that influence individuals around you?

Real SCIENCE Real LIFE

Kayla—Life Transitions and Borderline Personality Disorder

THE PATIENT

Kayla was a senior in high school when she began to worry her parents and friends. Her family had moved to a new state in the summer before her senior year. In her previous school, she had been relatively popular, very involved with acting and student government, and, according to her mother, a well-behaved but sensitive and moody girl. She desperately did not want to move. She had a circle of friends and was worried that the new high school would be filled with cliques and she would have trouble making friends.

THE PROBLEM

Soon after they moved, there was a dramatic transformation in Kayla. She dyed her hair black, started wearing black eye makeup and black clothing, and rarely spoke at home. She would come home from school, throw her books down, and hide out in her room. She avoided meals with the family and always seemed to be brooding. Whenever anyone showed concern for her well-being, she returned their concern with anger and pushed them away. On the night of her referral, she came running into her mother's bedroom screaming that she was afraid she was going to die. Blood poured from her right arm. Her mother bandaged her up to stop the bleeding and took her directly to the emergency room. There she discovered that this wasn't the first time Kayla had cut herself. Under her long black sleeves and skirt, her arms and thighs were covered with cuts. That night she had gone too deep and was scared.

ASSESSING THE SITUATION

First, what factors would you say contributed to the development of this disorder? What were the precipitating events? Second, how would you treat it? Design a plan to help Kayla develop better strategies for emotion regulation.

THE TREATMENT

Kayla was admitted to the inpatient unit for evaluation. The psychiatrist diagnosed her with major depression and borderline personality traits and recommended medication and psychotherapy. She also cautioned Kayla about drinking and using drugs while taking the medication and warned her of the potential negative interactions. She referred Kayla to a therapist who specialized in dialectical behavioral therapy (DBT).

Kayla desperately did not want to go into therapy and on the first day adopted a stance that the therapist called "I dare you to care about me" and clearly intended to test all the limits. The therapist was no stranger to this personality style and recognized how chaotic and nonconstant the world must seem from Kayla's eyes. She knew the key was consistency and firm compassion.

As therapy progressed, there were numerous ups and downs. Two trips to the emergency room for cutting returned the focus to the self-destructive behaviors. Gradually, Kayla was able to apply the emotion regulation skills she had learned in group at the times when cutting seemed like the only option. She was able to begin to focus on thoughts or behaviors that got in the way of developing a reasonable quality of life, behavioral skills, and, finally, self-validation and self-respect.

All of the "rules" frustrated Kayla at first, but after she became accustomed to this type of therapy, she understood that the rules existed because if she were injured or dead or doing things to interfere with her therapy, there was little point in working on the rest. Moreover, she really wanted to work on other issues, which provided the motivation for her to work on "first things first." After many advances and steps backward over the course of a year and a half of therapy, Kayla began to accept herself for who she was while working on changing some of her unhealthy ways of dealing with problems by putting her DBT skills to use.

They established a therapeutic contract that centered on honesty. The DBT approach used a broad array of cognitive and behavioral strategies to help Kayla learn to accept herself just as she was within the context of trying to teach her how to change, starting with her self-harming cutting behavior. The therapist took a firm problem-solving stance, but as is typical with DBT, she recognized that it would be too much to try to get all the skills training accomplished in one individual session per week. She therefore contracted for additional weekly group therapy. The group focused on the development of skills in emotion regulation, distress tolerance, interpersonal effectiveness, self-management, and core mindfulness (a way of learning how best to observe, describe, and participate in the world around you). As she learned these skills in group, Kayla's individual therapy could focus on ways to best integrate these skills into daily life. Though reluctant at first to attend a group with "a bunch of 'emos,'" Kayla signed a contract with her therapist promising to attend. Kayla's therapist agreed to continue working with her in individual therapy only if Kayla would also attend weekly groups for the following year as well as follow some of the basic rules of therapy. After a roller coaster of emotions about what she was undertaking, Kayla signed the contract. The therapist told her that the therapy was very structured and specific in terms of what was considered most important to talk about. If Kayla was feeling suicidal or performing any life-threatening or self-damaging behaviors, such as cutting, her therapist wouldn't allow her to address anything else.

The next important issue was focusing on anything that got in the way of therapy. For example, about 6 months into therapy, Kayla brought in a gift for her therapist. It was a button that read, "Your caring about me is starting to piss me off." Sometimes it was really hard for Kayla to accept the compassionate side of her therapist's stance. Deep down, she feared she wasn't worth being cared about. With the message inherent in the gesture, the focus of the therapy shifted directly to targeting Kayla's feelings about the therapist and her ability to accept being cared for.

THE TREATMENT OUTCOME

Kayla graduated from high school and was accepted at the local college. No longer on her parents' insurance, she transferred her care to the Campus Health Services where she kept up with both individual and group therapy. The therapist occasionally wondered how she fared in the transition to college and after leaving the group. Several years later, an e-mail arrived in the therapist's inbox announcing her college graduation and her plans to become a high school counselor.

Key Terms

antisocial personality disorder, p. 457
avoidant personality disorder, p. 465
borderline personality disorder, p. 461
Cluster A, p. 451
Cluster B, p. 451
Cluster C, p. 451
dependent personality disorder, p. 466
histrionic personality disorder, p. 463
narcissistic personality disorder, p. 460
obsessive-compulsive personality disorder, p. 468
paranoid personality disorder, p. 454
personality disorder, p. 451
schizoid personality disorder, p. 456
schizotypal personality disorder, p. 456
temperament, p. 476

Chapter 13

Neurodevelopmental, Disruptive, Conduct, and Elimination Disorders

Chapter Learning Objectives

Intellectual Disability (Intellectual Developmental Disorder)

LO 13.1 Identify the three domains clinicians use to diagnose intellectual disability.

LO 13.2 Describe the social and occupational impairments that result from intellectual disability.

LO 13.3 Understand etiological factors that contribute to the development of intellectual disabilities.

LO 13.4 Identify efficacious strategies for treatment of intellectual disabilities.

Specific Learning Disorders	**LO 13.5**	Identify the elements that characterize specific learning disorders.
	LO 13.6	Discuss the etiology of specific learning disorder.
	LO 13.7	Identify efficacious treatments for specific learning disorder.
Autism Spectrum Disorder	**LO 13.8**	Identify the two core features of autism spectrum disorder.
	LO 13.9	Describe the functional impairments that result from autism spectrum disorder.
	LO 13.10	Discuss the etiology of autism spectrum disorder.
	LO 13.11	Identify efficacious treatments for autism spectrum disorder.
Attention Deficit Hyperactivity Disorder	**LO 13.12**	Define the core features of attention deficit hyperactivity disorder.
	LO 13.13	Describe the functional impairments that result from ADHD.
	LO 13.14	Identify the etiological factors that contribute to the development of ADHD.
	LO 13.15	Identify efficacious treatments for ADHD.
Conduct Disorder and Oppositional Defiant Disorder	**LO 13.16**	Describe the behaviors that comprise conduct disorder and oppositional defiant disorder.
	LO 13.17	Describe the functional impairments that result from conduct disorder and oppositional defiant disorder.
	LO 13.18	Discuss the etiology of conduct disorder and oppositional defiant disorder.
	LO 13.19	Describe the efficacious treatments for conduct disorder and oppositional defiant disorder.
Elimination Disorders	**LO 13.20**	Describe the four types of enuresis.
	LO 13.21	Describe the social consequences of encopresis.

Jeremy is 12 years old and in seventh grade. He is doing well academically but has significant difficulty with social relationships. He is unaware of social conventions and does not make eye contact with other people. He speaks loudly, often asks inappropriate questions, and makes inappropriate and often irrelevant statements or noises. When conversing, Jeremy engages in lengthy monologues on topics that interest him (dinosaurs, plumbing, and cars) and fails to pick up on others' lack of interest. He has no friends, and peers often ridicule and reject him. He sometimes behaves in ways that are self-injurious, pulling his hair, picking his skin, and hitting himself on the head.

Jeremy first displayed unusual behaviors at 18 months of age. He licked the pavement, chewed on rocks, and put strange things in his mouth. He did not like to be hugged and pushed his parents away if they attempted any physical contact. At age 2, he did not yet speak. He simply grunted or led his mother by the hand to communicate. He began speech therapy shortly thereafter and by age 3 was talking in complete sentences. As a young child, Jeremy lined up toy cars. He never played with the entire car but would spin the wheels over and over. He did not play with other children but stood alone watching them. Now, at 12, Jeremy becomes upset by any change in routine, insisting on dressing in a certain order (e.g., socks, then pants, then shirt). He is also hypersensitive to sound; he can hear a siren miles away and covers his ears in crowded noisy places such as shopping malls.

Throughout this book, we have used a developmental perspective to understand abnormal behavior, and this perspective informs our understanding of psychological disorders in two ways. First, it is important to understand that childhood and adolescence are stages of life characterized by critical physical, cognitive, and emotional development. With respect to physical development, infants first acquire the ability to raise their head, then roll over, sit up, crawl, and finally walk. Physical maturation also includes brain development. The human brain triples in weight during a child's first 2 years, reaching 90% of its adult weight by the time the child is 5. Along with brain size, *cognitive abilities* increase throughout infancy and childhood. Children learn to think and solve problems, and their memory improves. During adolescence, they develop the cognitive abilities to understand and use abstract concepts, such as justice and beauty. Adolescents can engage in hypothetical thinking, imagining, for example, the worst thing that could happen to them. Adolescents also begin to use *metacognition*: They can think about thinking, for example, exploring the best way to solve a problem.

Along with physical and cognitive maturity, children also develop *emotionally*. Early in elementary school, children understand basic emotions (happy, sad, mad, scared), but they often attribute facial expression to an external event (e.g., "she is smiling because she is holding a puppy") rather than to an internal emotional state (e.g., "she is smiling because she is happy"). With increasing maturity, adolescents recognize more subtle emotions, such as disgust, worry, and surprise, and associate facial expressions with internal emotional states.

How does understanding this path of human development help us understand psychological disorders in childhood? Quite simply, until children have achieved basic physical, cognitive, and emotional developmental milestones, psychological disorders may express themselves differently in childhood than they do in adulthood. (Recall our discussions of anxiety, depression, and schizophrenia among others.) For example, young children cannot *worry* about future events until they have the ability to *think* about future events. Because of these developmental differences, mental health professionals acknowledge that although many psychological disorders may have roots in childhood, they are not often fully manifested until late adolescence or even adulthood.

Using this same developmental perspective, we find that other psychological disorders are more common in children than adults. They are present at birth or emerge during childhood and present significant challenges for those who suffer from them. Some of these disorders, such as intellectual disability or autism, may continue to exist throughout adulthood. In other instances, physical, cognitive, and/or emotional maturation may function to change the symptoms, lessen their impact, or even make them disappear. This often happens with disorders of elimination, for example. Many different disorders emerge during childhood and adolescence. Some, such as learning disorders, affect specific aspects of functioning such as academic achievement. We begin this chapter by discussing intellectual disability, a common disorder that affects many different aspects of functioning.

Intellectual Disability (Intellectual Developmental Disorder)

People have different abilities—whether it is the ability to do math problems, to play an instrument, or to read a map. Each person has particular strengths and limitations, which can be affected by a variety of environmental factors. For example, the amount of sleep a child gets can affect success in school, and a child whose family can afford to pay for tutoring or private lessons may improve a particular skill. Even the extent to which that skill is valued by one's culture can influence how a child performs. Most people understand intellectual disability to mean below-average intellectual functioning (see "DSM-5: Intellectual Disability (Intellectual Developmental Disorder)"). How we measure what is average or below average, however, is quite controversial. When psychologists measure intelligence, they use a standardized, individualized test. Each person's score is calculated and converted to a standardized scale for which the mean score is 100 and the standard deviation is 15. In the past, a person's test score was called an intelligence quotient (IQ). Although the calculations that

DSM-5

Criteria for Intellectual Disability (Intellectual Developmental Disorder)

Intellectual disability (intellectual developmental disorder) is a disorder with onset during the developmental period that includes both intellectual and adaptive functioning deficits in conceptual, social, and practical domains. The following three criteria must be met:

A. Deficits in intellectual functions, such as reasoning, problem solving, planning, abstract thinking, judgment, academic learning, and learning from experience, confirmed by both clinical assessment and individualized, standardized intelligence testing.

B. Deficits in adaptive functioning that result in failure to meet developmental and sociocultural standards for personal independence and social responsibility. Without ongoing support, the adaptive deficits limit functioning in one or more activities of daily life, such as communication, social participation, and independent living, across multiple environments, such as home, school, work, and community.

C. Onset of intellectual and adaptive deficits during the developmental period.

Note: The diagnostic term *intellectual disability* is the equivalent term for the ICD-11 diagnosis *of intellectual developmental disorders.* Although the term *intellectual disability* is used throughout this manual, both terms are used in the title to clarify relationships with other classification systems. Moreover, a federal statute in the United States (Public Law 111-256, Rosa's Law) replaces the term *mental retardation with intellectual disability,* and research journals use the term *intellectual disability*. Thus, *intellectual disability* is the term in common use by medical, educational, and other professions and by the lay public and advocacy groups.

were used to determine IQ score are not used today, the term *IQ score* has remained, and we use it in this chapter. When psychologists talk about average intelligence, they are referring to the range of intelligence test scores that falls 1 standard deviation above or below the mean score of 100. Therefore, people with IQ scores between 85 and 115 are considered to have average intelligence (as measured by that particular test). In DSM-5, a person's IQ score is not part of the diagnostic criteria and thus alone cannot be used to determine that a person meets criteria for intellectual disability. Rather, the IQ score or a score from a standardized test of intellectual functioning is used as information to help in estimating the extent of impairment for this diagnosis. (See Chapter 3 for more on intelligence testing.)

Defining Intellectual Ability

LO 13.1 Identify the three domains clinicians use to diagnose intellectual disability.

The criteria for the diagnosis of **intellectual disability** reflects the approach that no single test of cognitive functioning should be used to determine the diagnosis. Instead, intellectual disability is described as a disorder that includes both intellectual deficits and adaptive functioning deficits in three distinct domains (American Psychiatric Association, 2013). Clinicians evaluate potential deficits in three distinct areas/domains, which reflect how well the individual copes with everyday tasks. These three domains are conceptual (language, reading, writing, math, reasoning, knowledge, and memory), social (empathy, social judgment, interpersonal communication, and friendship skills), and practical (personal care, job responsibilities, money management, recreation, and organization skills). The labels that are used to specify the extent of the deficits in intellect and adaptive functioning are mild, moderate, severe, and profound. The DSM-5 includes descriptions of these different levels of impairment to help the clinician make a decision regarding which of the labels is most appropriate. The onset of intellectual disability is always before the age of 18.

> Cathy was a pleasant young woman of 24 years with appropriate skills for everyday social interaction. Although she was able to shower independently, someone had to first check the water temperature because otherwise she would burn herself. Although she understood that hamburgers (her favorite food) had to be cooked before eating, her only attempt to cook independently had set the kitchen on fire. As a young woman, she was interested in men but did not understand basic concepts of sexual reproduction.

Clearly, Cathy had great difficulty functioning independently in the areas of self-care, home living, and health and safety, and she had been this way as a child.

In addition to the core diagnostic features, comorbid conditions (such as all of the other disorders discussed in this book) occur at a high rate among people with intellectual disability (Matson & Cervantes, 2013). Physical disorders and medical illness are also common among people with intellectual disability (Gentile et al., 2014; Matson & Cervantes, 2013); diabetes and sleep problems are common co-occurrences (Gentile et al., 2014).

Functional Impairment

LO 13.2 Describe the social and occupational impairments that result from intellectual disability.

As we have noted, adaptive impairment is necessary for a diagnosis of intellectual disability, but the extent and type of impairment are variable. In addition to deficits in intellectual functioning, impaired communication, social skills deficits, and motor impairments are common features of this disability (Matson & Cervantes, 2013). Adults with mild to moderate intellectual disability function in the community with minimal to moderate support. They might be in a group home in which a small number of adults live together under a counselor's supervision. Some adults are also able to hold traditional jobs in the community, such as working in a grocery store. In one national survey of community providers (Domin & Butterworth, 2013), about 15% of individuals with intellectual and developmental disabilities were working in individual jobs for pay, whereas an additional 10% participated in group-supported employment such as work crews. Sometimes an intervention known as *supported employment* provides training and a job coach to help people succeed in meaningful jobs (Banks et al., 2010; see Chapter 11). Adults with more significant cognitive impairments may work in a *sheltered workshop*, which is usually a free-standing workplace where workers perform tasks for businesses, such as sending out large mailings, packing items for shipment, or assembling certain products. People who work in sheltered workshops are paid wages and learn job skills such as coming to work on time, completing a task assignment, and taking direction from a supervisor.

In schools, *mainstreaming* could be considered supportive education for children with intellectual disability. *Mainstreaming* means that whenever possible, children with disabilities are included in regular classroom settings, allowing participation in typical childhood experiences. Whereas children with intellectual disability may need separate classroom instruction for mathematics, they may take the same physical education classes as the general student body. Inclusion in regular classroom settings promotes the acceptance of people with intellectual disability and enhances their self-esteem.

Mainstreaming children with Down syndrome into regular classroom settings helps develop acceptance and understanding of individual differences.

About 1 to 3% of the general population has an intellectual disability (American Psychiatric Association, 2013). The majority of people with a diagnosis of intellectual disability—about 85%—fall into the mild disability range. Controversy continues regarding the relationship between low IQ scores and racial or ethnic minority status in the United States. Many IQ tests do not account for cultural differences in verbal expressions of ideas, language, and behaviors. Furthermore, even within the United States, different racial and ethnic groups identify different behaviors as contributing to the definition of intelligence, and many of these behaviors (creativity, "street smarts," social skills) are not included in most standardized intelligence tests. Although differences in IQ scores among various racial and ethnic groups remain, the meaning of the difference is not clear. What is important to know is that no credible scientific support exists for a genetic explanation for group differences.

More boys than girls have a diagnosis of intellectual disability, but these sex differences are primarily among those with mild intellectual disability and may result from differences in children's verbal abilities. At younger ages, girls have superior verbal language skills (Joseph, 2000), and this may affect their test performance. No sex differences are found among children with the more severe forms of intellectual disability (Richardson et al., 1986).

Etiology

LO 13.3 Understand etiological factors that contribute to the development of intellectual disabilities.

Throughout this book, we have often introduced discussions of etiology with cautionary statements that the cause of a disorder is unknown. However, there are numerous known causes for intellectual disability. Many are biological, and others are environmental. For about 35% of people with intellectual disability, the cause is one of the disorders identified in Table 13.1. Many genetic disorders may produce intellectual disability (Walker & Johnson, 2006). When a genetic cause exists, the disorder is apparent at birth or shortly thereafter. In other cases, intellectual disability may result from environmental factors, a number of which are preventable. We next examine the best-known causes of intellectual disability beginning with the biological factors. Given the recency of DSM-5 criteria, this discussion of etiology is based on the DSM-IV-TR criteria.

GENETIC FACTORS Named for the British geneticist John Langdon Haydon Down (Czarnetzki et al., 2003), **Down syndrome** (trisomy 21) describes the unusual condition in which a chromosomal set has three chromosomes (i.e., trisomy) rather than the usual set of two. This error occurs during the cell division of a sperm or ovum—the chromosome pair does not divide as it should. Instead, the chromosomes "stick together." Later, when the sperm fertilizes the ovum, rather than each (sperm and ovum) contributing one chromosome to the 21st pair, three are present. People with Down syndrome have three #21 chromosomes in every cell in their body, giving them a total of 47 rather than the usual 46 chromosomes. Other trisomy conditions (trisomy 13, trisomy 18) exist and may also result in intellectual disability, but Down syndrome is by far the most common condition.

Children with Down syndrome have distinctive facial features including oblique eye fissures (slanted eyes), epicanthic eye folds (folds of skin in the corner of the eye), a flat nasal bridge, protruding tongues, short stocky stature, a very short neck, and small ears. Virtually every person with Down syndrome has intellectual disability, most commonly in the mild to moderate range, meaning that they are able to attend school, learn basic living skills, and function in a structured environment. Children with

Table 13.1 Frequency of Intellectual Disability by Type of Disorder

Types of Disorders	Frequency
Prenatal genetic disorders including Down syndrome, tuberous sclerosis, phenylketonuria, fragile X, "familial MR," Williams syndrome, Prader-Willi syndrome	32%
Malformation of unknown causes including neural tube defects and Cornelia deLange Syndrome	8%
External prenatal causes including human immunodeficiency virus (HIV) infection, fetal alcohol syndrome, prematurity	12%
Perinatal (birth) causes including encephalitis, neonatal asphyxia, hyperbilirubinemia	11%
Postnatal causes including encephalitis, lead poisoning, deprivation, trauma, tumor.	8%
Unknown causes	25%

SOURCE: Practice parameters for the assessment and treatment of children, adolescents, and adults with mental retardation and comorbid mental disorders. (1999, December). *Journal of the American Academy of Child and Adolescent Psychiatry, 38*(12)(Suppl.), 5S–31S. Copyright © 1999 by the American Academy of Child and Adolescent Psychiatry. Reprinted by permission.

Table 13.2 Relationship of Maternal Age to Incidence of Down Syndrome

Maternal Age	Incidence of Down Syndrome	Maternal Age	Incidence of Down Syndrome
20	1 in 2,000	35	1 in 350
21	1 in 1,700	36	1 in 300
22	1 in 1,500	37	1 in 250
23	1 in 1,400	38	1 in 200
24	1 in 1,300	39	1 in 150
25	1 in 1,200	40	1 in 100
26	1 in 1,100	41	1 in 80
27	1 in 1,050	42	1 in 70
28	1 in 1,000	43	1 in 50
29	1 in 950	44	1 in 40
30	1 in 900	45	1 in 30
31	1 in 800	46	1 in 25
32	1 in 720	47	1 in 20
33	1 in 600	48	1 in 15
34	1 in 450	49	1 in 10

SOURCE: http://www.ndss.org/Down-Syndrome/What-Is-Down-Syndrome/ Reprinted with permission from the National Down Syndrome Society.

Down syndrome may also have numerous medical problems including heart defects, intestinal abnormalities, visual and hearing impairments, and respiratory ailments (Roubertoux & Kerdelhúe, 2006). About 1 of every 1,000 children is born with Down syndrome, although the specific rate varies with maternal age; much higher rates occur among older mothers (see Table 13.2). Biological factors, such as fewer available ova or decreases in female hormones, are considered to be the reason why older mothers are more likely to have children with Down syndrome, but the specific mechanisms by which these factors might operate are not known (Waburton, 2005). Many environmental factors also have been proposed as causes, including maternal smoking, maternal alcohol use, radiation, and fertility drugs, but none of these factors has been confirmed (Sherman et al., 2007).

Down syndrome is a chromosomal abnormality that results in three chromosomes on the 21st pair—the third group from the left in the bottom row. The 23rd pair (bottom right) is an XY, so this profile is a boy.

In children with Down syndrome, almost all brain structures are smaller than normal (Roubertoux & Kerdelhúe, 2006; Teipel et al., 2004). Another characteristic is the presence of plaques and neurofibrillary tangles, usually found among adults with major or mild neurocognitive disorder due to Alzheimer's disease (see Chapter 14). In people with Down syndrome, this deterioration begins at about age 8 and progresses, accelerating rapidly between the ages of 35 and 45 (Lott & Head, 2005). The result is that almost all people with Down syndrome have some evidence of Alzheimer's disease by age 40.

Phenylketonuria (PKU) is a genetic disorder in which the body cannot break down the amino acid *phenylalanine* because an essential enzyme is absent. Without the enzyme, phenylalanine accumulates in the body, causing mental and physical abnormalities (dos Santos et al., 2006). PKU occurs in about 0.01% of the population with large variations by race and ethnicity. Whites and Native Americans have the highest rate, with much lower rates among African Americans, Hispanics, and Asians (Hellekson, 2001). In the United States, every infant is screened at birth for PKU, resulting in few untreated cases of the disorder. Treatment requires daily dietary supplements and a severely restricted low-protein diet. Milk and dairy products, meat, eggs, wheat, beans, corn, peanuts, lentils, and other grains are prohibited (dos Santos et al., 2006), and compliance with these restrictions can be quite poor. This diet must be continued until at least age 8 to prevent intellectual disability; discontinuation of the diet at the time of adolescence is controversial (Hellekson, 2001). Most physicians and researchers advise continuing the diet for life (Perez-Duenas et al., 2006).

Fragile X syndrome (FXS) is the most commonly inherited cause of intellectual disability (Sundaram et al., 2005; Valdovinos, 2007) and occurs when a DNA series makes too many copies of itself and "turns off" a gene on the X chromosome. When the gene is turned off, cells do not make a necessary protein, and without the protein, FXS occurs. In addition to intellectual disability, children with FXS have behavioral disorders such as hyperactivity, temper tantrums, irritability, poor eye contact, self-stimulation, and self-injurious behaviors (Crawford et al., 2002; Valdovinos, 2007). Perhaps because girls have two X chromosomes (i.e., they have a "spare" X chromosome), they are only half as likely as boys to have FXS (1 out of 4,000 males and 1 out of 8,000 females).

Other genetic disorders that can result in intellectual disability include *tuberous sclerosis complex* (*TSC*) and *Lesch-Nyhan syndrome*. Resulting from mutations on at least two different genes (Sundaram et al., 2005), TSC affects 1 in every 30,000 people in the United States. In children with TSC, benign tumors affect all body organs including the brain and result in developmental delays, seizures, and learning disabilities. About 50% of people with TSC have intellectual disability (Leung & Robson, 2007). Lesch-Nyhan syndrome is a rare genetic disorder that is transmitted on the X chromosome. Because it is a recessive trait, it occurs only in boys. Girls, who have two X chromosomes, are protected from the disorder. Like PKU, this disorder involves a missing enzyme. When the genetic defect is present, excess uric acid accumulates throughout the body. Lesch-Nyhan syndrome causes many different behavioral problems including cognitive dysfunction, intellectual disability, and aggressive and impulsive behaviors. Intellectual disability is usually moderate but can range from profound to mild (Olson & Houlihan, 2000). Nearly all children with this disorder develop persistent and severe self-injurious behavior, sometimes with permanent physical damage.

ENVIRONMENTAL FACTORS When genes are not the cause of intellectual disability, factors such as the prenatal or postnatal environment may be responsible. Prenatal influences associated with the presence of intellectual disability include uterine environmental toxins (maternal alcohol use, infections), premature birth, hypoxia (lack of oxygen to the brain, often during birth), and fetal malnutrition. Postnatal factors include malnutrition, bacterial and viral infections, lead exposure, and social factors such as poverty, low environmental stimulation, and poor maternal education (Walker & Johnson, 2006). However, it is important to understand that unlike genetic disorders such as Down syndrome, the presence of these environmental factors does not automatically lead to intellectual disability. For example, many children live in impoverished environments yet have average or above average IQs.

The leading known preventable environmental cause of intellectual disability is drinking alcohol during pregnancy, which can result in **fetal alcohol syndrome** (FAS; West & Blake, 2005; see Chapter 10). According to the Centers for Disease Control and Prevention, rates of fetal alcohol syndrome vary widely, ranging from 0.2 to 1.5 per 1,000 live births in different areas of the United States. Drinking alcohol during pregnancy can affect the physical development of the fetus including brain development. In addition to intellectual disability, fetal alcohol syndrome is associated with birth defects, abnormal facial features, growth problems, central nervous system abnormalities, memory problems, impaired academic achievement, vision or hearing impairment, and behavioral problems (see Figure 13.1). Children with FAS used medical resources at a yearly rate nine times as high as children without FAS ($16,859 vs. $1,859; Amendah et al., 2011).

Another preventable environmental cause of intellectual disability is exposure to lead, which can enter the bodies of young children in different ways. Many older homes contain lead-based paint, which can peel off and be eaten by young children, who have a tendency to put many things in their mouth. Also, when the paint becomes old and worn, the chips may be ground into tiny particles that mix with dust, which are then inhaled. Ingestion or inhalation leads to a buildup of lead in the body (Brown et al., 2006). Even low levels of exposure to lead in childhood are associated with low intelligence. High

Figure 13.1 Parts of the Brain That Can Be Affected by Maternal Alcohol Consumption.

When a woman drinks during pregnancy, many parts of the fetal brain can be damaged.

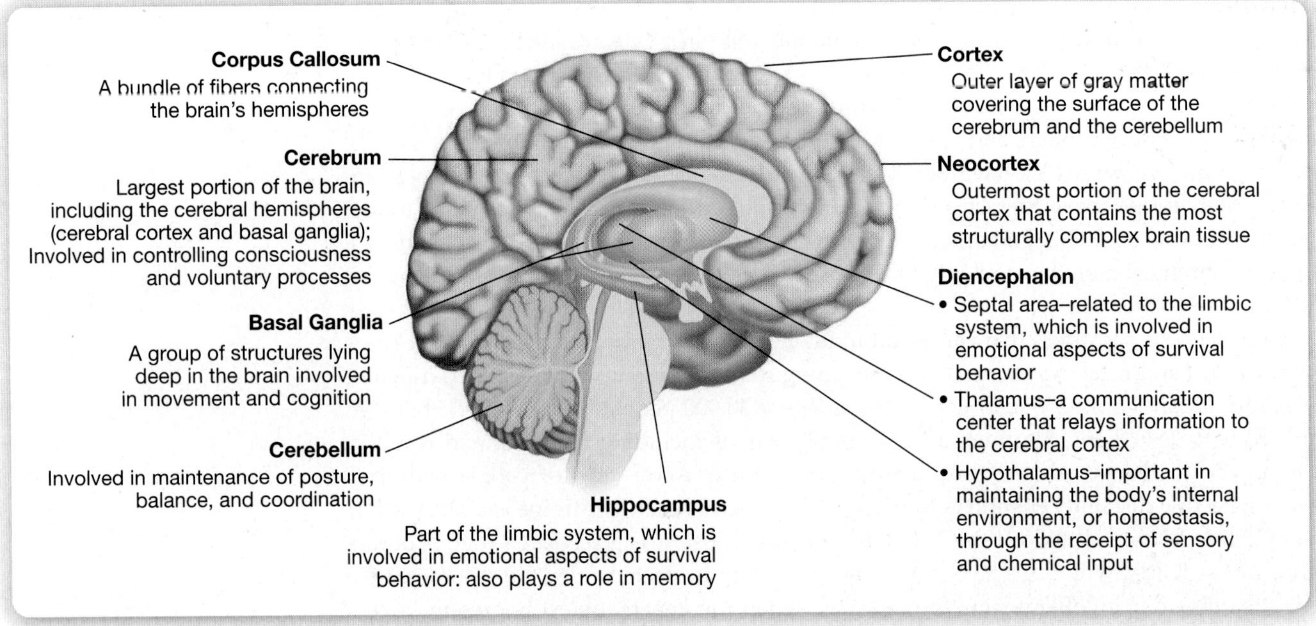

levels of exposure are associated with substantially lower IQ scores (Needleman & Gatsonis, 1990). Even years later, adults who were exposed to lead in childhood still had academic difficulties and behavior problems (Needleman & Gatsonis 1990). For more information on lead exposure in houses, see Chapter 15.

In many cases of mild intellectual disability, the specific cause is unknown. **Cultural-familial retardation** is defined as "retardation due to psychosocial disadvantage" (Weisz, 1990). Whereas severe intellectual disability exists across all socioeconomic levels, mild intellectual disability is more common among children in the lower socioeconomic classes (Stromme & Magnus, 2000), which include residents of poverty-stricken inner-city areas and poor rural areas as well as migrant workers.

Among the lowest socioeconomic classes, the prevalence of mild intellectual disability ranges from 10 to 30% of the American school-age population (Popper et al., 2004). However, sociocultural retardation is not limited to the United States: The same factors have been identified in European countries as well (Gillerot et al., 1989).

The reason for the association between lower socioeconomic status and mild intellectual disability is unclear, but both biological and environmental factors may contribute. In the early years of life, the brain is still developing. Environmental factors such as poor nutrition, lack of access to early educational enrichment (e.g., preschool, educational toys), or restricted access to medical care may negatively affect brain development, leading to lower IQ scores.

Treatment

LO 13.4 Identify efficacious strategies for treatment of intellectual disabilities.

Until recently, many people with intellectual disability were housed in institutions. Few community resources were available for them, and parents were encouraged to institutionalize their child where it was assumed that necessary extensive care would be available. There was even hope that proper environmental care might reduce deficits, although leaving the institution was not a long-term goal of placement (Brosco et al., 2006). In fact, most people who were institutionalized remained there for the rest of their lives. Today about 90% of people with intellectual disability live with families or in community placements, such as group homes. Intellectual disability is not reversible, but many children can learn

Figure 13.2 Prevalence of Specific Causes of Intellectual Disability over Time.

During the past 50 years, advances in medical science have decreased the prevalence of intellectual disability. Data from Brosco et al. (2006) *Archives of Pediatrics & Adolescent Medicine, 160*, 302–309.

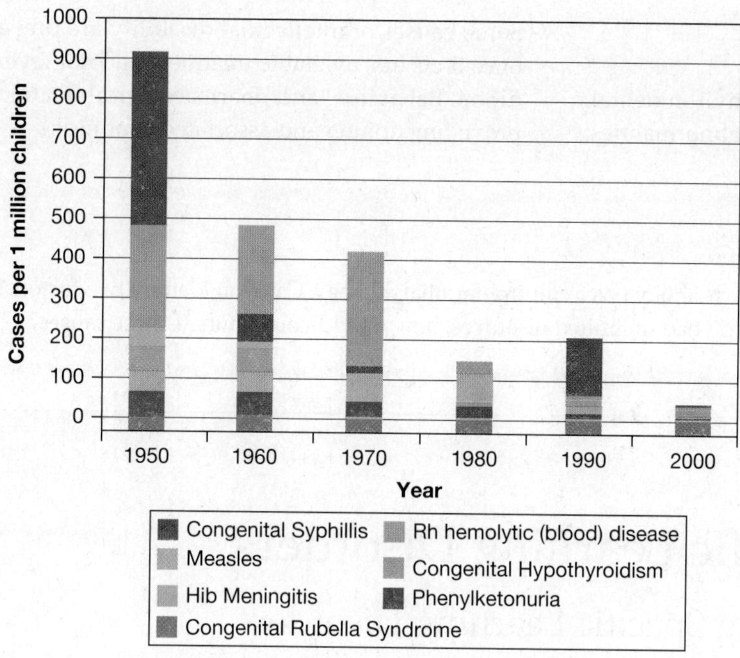

basic academic and adaptive functioning skills. Psychological treatments focus on teaching skills that facilitate community adjustment, such as self-care, independent living, and job maintenance. Behavioral procedures such as *shaping* (rewarding successive approximations of desired behavior) and *chaining* (teaching small, discrete behaviors and then putting them together) allow children with intellectual disability to learn simple tasks such as putting on a pair of pants or more complicated behaviors such as going to the bank and cashing a check.

Medical treatments to reduce diseases that cause intellectual disability have decreased its general prevalence. The number of children with intellectual disability as a result of measles and whooping cough has decreased since the introduction of successful vaccinations for these diseases (Brosco et al., 2006) (see Figure 13.2). Medication does not treat the core symptoms of intellectual disability but is sometimes used for coexisting psychological disorders such as attentional or aggressive behaviors. Overall, people with intellectual disability respond to medication in the same way as others, but rates of response are poorer and side effects more common (Handen & Gilchrist, 2006).

Learning Objective Summaries

LO 13.1 Identify the three domains clinicians use to diagnose intellectual disability.

Intellectual disability (intellectual developmental disorder) is characterized by intellectual and adaptive functioning deficits in three domains: conceptual (language, reading, writing, math, reasoning, knowledge, and memory), social (empathy, social judgment, interpersonal communication, and friendship skills), and practical (personal care, job responsibilities, money management, recreation, and organization skills).

LO 13.2 Describe the social and occupational impairments that result from intellectual disability.

Intellectual disability is characterized by both intellectual and adaptive functioning deficits in conceptual, social, and practical domains. Intellect and adaptive functioning exist along a continuum and can range from mild to severe or profound. Impaired communication, social skills deficits, and motor impairments are common among individuals with intellectual disabilities and can affect social and occupational functioning. Some individuals can work independently; others require a supportive group environment.

LO 13.3 Understand etiological factors that contribute to the development of intellectual disabilities.

Intellectual disability, both biological and environmental, has many different causes including genetic abnormalities, medical disorders, and parental behaviors such as alcohol abuse during pregnancy.

LO 13.4 Identify efficacious strategies for treatment of intellectual disabilities.

Some causes of intellectual disability are preventable, but once it occurs, available treatments do not reverse the condition. Behavioral and pharmacological treatment may improve functioning and associated conditions.

Critical Thinking Question

A significant proportion of mild intellectual disability has a cultural-familial etiology. Can you identify two factors leading to this type of intellectual disability, and if you had unlimited resources, how would you eliminate these causes?

Specific Learning Disorders

Defining Specific Learning Disorders

LO 13.5 Identify the elements that characterize specific learning disorders.

A universal task of education is to teach children basic skills such as reading, writing, and mathematics. Yet a number of public schoolchildren in the United States have at least average intelligence but have difficulty mastering these basic academic tasks (American Psychiatric Association, 2013). **Specific learning disorder** (see "DSM-5: Specific Learning Disorder") is defined by difficulties learning and using academic skills (reading, writing, arithmetic, or mathematical reasoning) (American Psychiatric Association, 2013). Academic skills are below what is expected for chronological age and cause interference in daily functioning, as confirmed by standardized achievement measures and clinical assessment. Affecting both sexes, these disorders can result in demoralization, low self-esteem, and school dropout rates that are higher than those in the general population.

When a clinician makes a diagnosis of specific learning disorder, she includes a specifier of one (or more) of the following: with impairment in reading, with impairment in written expression, or with impairment in mathematics. *Impairment in reading* is sometimes known as *dyslexia*. Impairments in reading can include problems with word recognition, reading rate or fluency, or reading comprehension. Children with reading impairments may display oral reading errors such as distortions, substitutions, or omissions of words. Silent reading disabilities include reading very slowly and making comprehension errors. These children often also have difficulty with spelling. Early theories emphasized vision and visual perceptual difficulties such as reversal of letters. However, advances in neurobiology and neuropsychology indicate that reading disorders most likely result from a diminished ability to recognize and produce sounds (*phonemes*) that when put together form words (Shaywitz et al., 2007). Instruction in reading is based on phonics, the process of "sounding out" a word by converting its visual representation into the appropriate sounds. Difficulty recognizing and articulating sounds leads to a cascade of negative events. "Sounding out" words is slow and requires effort; thus, reading is less fluent. Sounding out also requires more concentration to identify and pronounce difficult words, leaving fewer attentional resources for reading comprehension and leading to mental fatigue and behavioral avoidance (Kronenberger & Dunn, 2003). As researchers continue to study reading problems, it is becoming clearer that this is not a single disorder—there may be at least 17 different types of reading impairments (Zoccolotti & Friedmann, 2010).

DSM-5

Criteria for Specific Learning Disorder

A. Difficulties learning and using academic skills, as indicated by the presence of at least one of the following symptoms that have persisted for at least 6 months, despite the provision of interventions that target those difficulties:

1. Inaccurate or slow and effortful word reading (e.g., reads single words aloud incorrectly or slowly and hesitantly, frequently guesses words, has difficulty sounding out words).
2. Difficulty understanding the meaning of what is read (e.g., may read text accurately but not understand the sequence, relationships, inferences, or deeper meanings of what is read).
3. Difficulties with spelling (e.g., may add, omit, or substitute vowels or consonants).
4. Difficulties with written expression (e.g., makes multiple grammatical or punctuation errors within sentences; employs poor paragraph organization; written expression of ideas lacks clarity).
5. Difficulties mastering number sense, number facts, or calculation (e.g., has poor understanding of numbers, their magnitude, and relationships; counts on fingers to add single-digit numbers instead of recalling the math fact as peers do; gets lost in the midst of arithmetic computation and may switch procedures).
6. Difficulties with mathematical reasoning (e.g., has severe difficulty applying mathematical concepts, facts, or procedures to solve quantitative problems).

B. The affected academic skills are substantially and quantifiably below those expected for the individual's chronological age, and cause significant interference with academic or occupational performance, or with activities of daily living, as confirmed by individually administered standardized achievement measures and comprehensive clinical assessment. For individuals age 17 years and older, a documented history of impairing learning difficulties may be substituted for the standardized assessment.

C. The learning difficulties begin during school-age years but may not become fully manifest until the demands for those affected academic skills exceed the individual's limited capacities (e.g., as in timed tests, reading or writing lengthy complex reports for a tight deadline, excessively heavy academic loads).

D. The learning difficulties are not better accounted for by intellectual disabilities, uncorrected visual or auditory acuity, other mental or neurological disorders, psychosocial adversity, lack of proficiency in the language of academic instruction, or inadequate educational instruction.

Note: The four diagnostic criteria are to be met based on a clinical synthesis of the individual's history (developmental, medical, family, educational), school reports, and psychoeducational assessment.

Children may also have *impairments in mathematics*, sometimes called *dyscalculia. Mathematics impairments* involve the diminished ability to understand mathematical terms, operations, or concepts; recognize numerical symbols or arithmetic signs; or copy numbers or figures correctly. Difficulty performing mental calculations may lead affected children to rely on external devices, such as counting on their fingers. They also often have difficulty with the logic of word problems.

The third specific learning disorder specifier, *impairment in written expression*, also called *dysgraphia*, is more than sloppy handwriting. It includes having difficulty composing grammatically correct sentences; making frequent grammatical, punctuation, or spelling errors; and experiencing diminished ability to organize coherent written paragraphs. Effective writing requires different cognitive, visual, and motor skills including knowledge of vocabulary and grammar, eye–hand coordination and hand movement, and memory (Pratt & Patel, 2007). Deficits in any of these areas can lead to impairment. Children with impairments in writing have no trouble presenting material orally but struggle with putting those same ideas into written form. Their written sentences are short, difficult to understand, and riddled with spelling and grammatical errors.

Between 5 and 10% of school children, perhaps up to 4 million, may suffer from specific learning disorder, most commonly persistent problems in reading (Pratt & Patel, 2007; Shaywitz et al., 2007), which may affect between 2 and 8% of all children. Reading problems that meet diagnostic criteria for specific learning disorder are more common in boys, but the reason is not clear. One hypothesis is that it may not be more common but *more commonly identified* because associated behavioral disorders, such as attention deficit hyperactivity disorder (ADHD), lead to a referral to a mental health professional. Difficulty with phonics and reading may lead to the identification of specific learning disorder as early as the preschool years. By contrast, persistent problems of written expression are often not apparent until third or fourth grade when there are increased demands to present ideas in writing. Children with mild symptoms may be difficult to identify and may be described by parents or teachers as messy, unfocused, or disorganized (Pratt & Patel, 2007). As adults, children with mild symptoms compensate by developing a working vocabulary in their occupational area that allows them to function effectively. However, they still have difficulty with unfamiliar words. Their reading may be accurate but not fluent or automatic (Shaywitz et al., 2007).

Children with specific learning disorder are more likely to drop out of school, limiting their opportunities for employment (American Psychiatric Association, 2013). They also often feel demoralized by their disabilities and report low self-esteem. Children with specific learning disorder may also have other childhood emotional and behavioral problems such as ADHD, conduct disorder, depression, and anxiety disorders.

Etiology

LO 13.6 Discuss the etiology of specific learning disorder.

The etiology of specific learning disorder is unclear. As we begin to identify many different types of reading and writing difficulties, we must recognize that these impairments probably do not arise from a single neurological abnormality but from different neurocognitive impairments (Zoccolotti & Friedman, 2010) or the inability of several brain areas to work together.

Much more is known about the etiology of reading difficulties than about mathematics or writing difficulties. Structural and functional magnetic imaging studies and positron emission tomography (PET) studies have identified various areas of the brain that appear to be important for reading (Shaywitz et al., 2007) (see Figure 13.3). Again, why a child would have abnormal brain functioning is not entirely clear, but genetics appears to play a significant role. Concordance rates for reading impairment are 71% for monozygotic twins and 49%

Figure 13.3 Areas of the Brain Involved in Reading Disorder.

Reading is a complex process that involves several areas of the brain.

SOURCE: Shaywitz, S. (2003). *Overcoming dyslexia: A new and complete science-based program for reading problems at any level* (p. 34). New York: Alfred A. Knopf. Copyright © 2003 Sally Shaywitz. Reprinted by permission of the publisher.

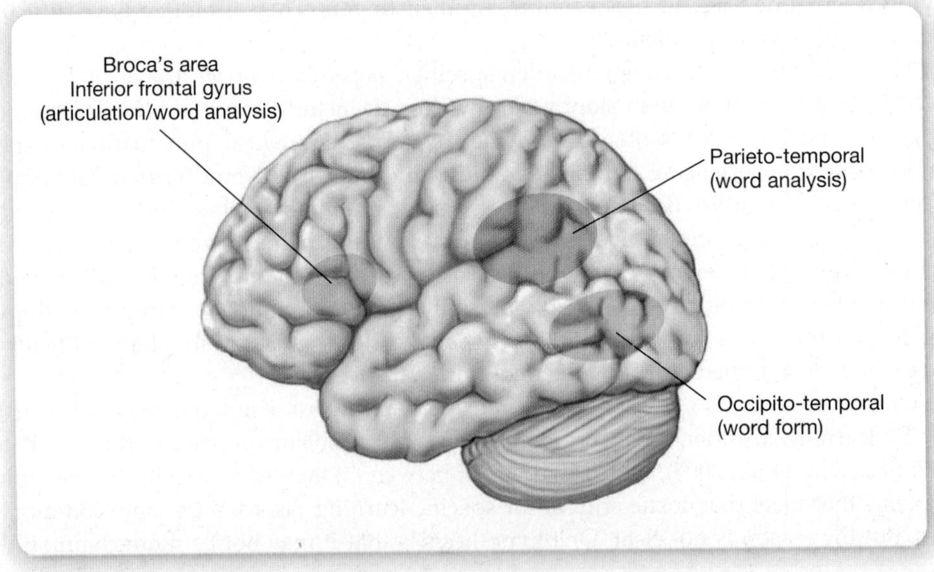

for dizygotic twins (Castles et al., 1999). We have much to learn about the biological basis of reading difficulties, but what is clear now is that the impairment does not result from the inheritance of one single gene. It is likely that a number of different genes are involved.

Treatment

LO 13.7 Identify efficacious treatments for specific learning disorder.

Treatment for specific learning disorder usually occurs in the educational setting. Intervention for reading begins early and focuses on developing the skills necessary for phonological processing and fluent reading with later emphasis on reading for comprehension (Kronenberger & Dunn, 2003). See Figure 13.4 for the trajectory of reading scores for good and poor readers. As the data show, poor readers can make significant progress in their reading skills, but they never achieve the skill level possessed by good readers at the same age. As children mature and gains are consolidated, intervention shifts to disability accommodation (Pratt & Patel, 2007), such as more time for reading and test taking and the use of computers, tape recorders, or recorded books to allow effective functioning in academics and occupational environments.

Treatment for mathematics includes arithmetic drills and memorization. Because writing is considered to result from difficulties in the written expression of ideas, children first engage in simple writing tasks such as keeping a diary. As their basic writing skills improve, they are given more challenging writing tasks.

ETHICS AND RESPONSIBILITY The lack of efficacious traditional treatments for specific learning disorder with impairment in reading has led some parents to turn to complementary or alternative medicine (Bull, 2009). Among one sample of 148 children with this disorder, 55.4% of their parents reported using nontraditional approaches including diets and nutritional supplements (42.6%), homeopathic medicines (19.6%), and chiropractic manipulations (19.6%). Other approaches used by these parents included

Figure 13.4 Reading Skills in Good Readers Compared with Those Who Have Reading Impairment.

Over time, differences in reading skills between good readers (children without reading difficulties) and poor readers (those with reading disorder, or dyslexia) remain constant. This shows that children with reading impairment are not just "slow" at acquiring skills but have a specific reading deficit.

SOURCE: Shaywitz, S. (2003). *Overcoming dyslexia: A new and complete science-based program for reading problems at any level* (p. 34). New York: Alfred A. Knopf. Copyright © 2003 Sally Shaywitz. Reprinted by permission of the publisher.

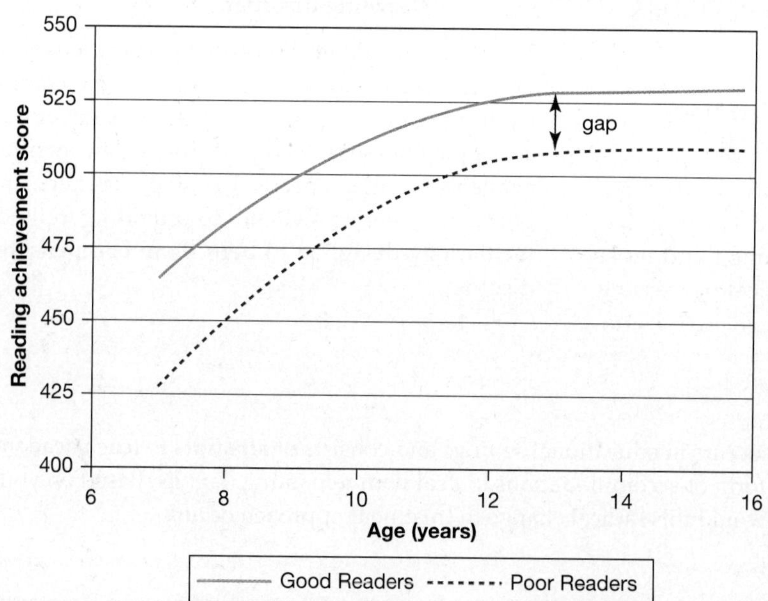

aromatherapy, acupuncture, massage, and reflexology. Although scientists must always be open to new ideas and approaches to a problem, to date none of these interventions has been scientifically verified as an efficacious treatment for this disorder. Mental health professionals who work with parents and children with these disorders are obligated to explain to parents that these procedures, while probably not harmful, have not yet been shown to be helpful.

Explore ETHICS AND RESPONSIBILITY

Learning Objective Summaries

LO 13.5 Identify the elements that characterize specific learning disorders.

Specific learning disorder is defined by difficulties learning and using academic skills (reading, writing, arithmetic, or mathematical reasoning). The academic skills are below what is expected for chronological age and interfere with daily functioning, as confirmed by standardized achievement measures and clinical assessment.

LO 13.6 Discuss the etiology of specific learning disorder.

Specific learning disorder may be in the area of reading, mathematics, and writing. Of the specific learning disorder specifiers, reading is the most common and most likely represents a difficulty in phonological processing resulting from abnormalities in different areas of the brain. Genetics appear to play a major role in the etiology of reading problems. The etiology of specific learning disorders in mathematics or writing is unknown.

LO 13.7 Identify efficacious treatments for specific learning disorder.

Teaching phonological processing – how letters and groups of letters represent sounds—can improve reading disability, but people with reading disorders never read as well as people without reading disorders. Few interventions are available for other specific learning disorders, and at some point, intervention switches to providing individuals with technology designed to help them compensate for their disorder.

Critical Thinking Question

Treatment for specific learning disorder occurs in educational settings and consists of attempts to teach academic skills. At later ages, treatment takes the form of accommodations to deal with remaining deficits. Based on your knowledge of brain development, why would this radical change in treatment approach occur?

Autism Spectrum Disorder

Defining Autism Spectrum Disorder

LO 13.8 Identify the two core features of autism spectrum disorder.

As in the case of Jeremy at the beginning of this chapter, some childhood behavioral abnormalities are evident very early in life. Most children spontaneously say "mama" or "dada" before age 1. But Jeremy did not speak until age 3 when he had speech therapy. Jeremy also had unusual social behaviors. He refused to make eye contact, spoke too loudly, asked inappropriate questions, and made inappropriate statements or noises. In addition to holding his toy car and spinning the wheels over and over, he showed other stereotyped behaviors. (These are repetitive behaviors that serve no observable social functions, such as hand flapping, spinning, and ritualistic pacing). Such behaviors are characteristic of **autism spectrum disorder** and consist of deficits in social communication and social interaction and the presence of restrictive and repetitive behavior patterns (American Psychiatric Association, 2013) (See "DSM-5: Autism Spectrum Disorder").

DSM-5

Criteria for Autism Spectrum Disorder

A. Persistent deficits in social communication and social interaction across multiple contexts, as manifested by the following, currently or by history (examples are illustrative, not exhaustive; see text):

1. Deficits in social-emotional reciprocity, ranging, for example, from abnormal social approach and failure of normal back-and-forth conversation; to reduced sharing of interests, emotions, or affect; to failure to initiate or respond to social interactions.
2. Deficits in nonverbal communicative behaviors used for social interaction, ranging, for example, from poorly integrated verbal and nonverbal communication; to abnormalities in eye contact and body language or deficits in understanding and use of gestures; to a total lack of facial expressions and nonverbal communication.
3. Deficits in developing, maintaining, and understanding relationships, ranging, for example, from difficulties adjusting behavior to suit various social contexts; to difficulties in sharing imaginative play or in making friends; to absence of interest in peers.

***Specify* current severity:**

Severity is based on social communication impairments and restricted, repetitive patterns of behavior (see Table 2).

B. Restricted, repetitive patterns of behavior, interests, or activities, as manifested by at least two of the following, currently or by history (examples are illustrative, not exhaustive; see text):

1. Stereotyped or repetitive motor movements, use of objects, or speech (e.g., simple motor stereotypies, lining up toys or flipping objects, echolalia, idiosyncratic phrases).
2. Insistence on sameness, inflexible adherence to routines, or ritualized patterns of verbal or nonverbal behavior (e.g., extreme distress at small changes, difficulties with transitions, rigid thinking patterns, greeting rituals, need to take same route or eat same food every day).
3. Highly restricted, fixated interests that are abnormal in intensity or focus (e.g., strong attachment to or preoccupation with unusual objects, excessively circumscribed or perseverative interests).
4. Hyper- or hyporeactivity to sensory input or unusual interest in sensory aspects of the environment (e.g., apparent indifference to pain/temperature, adverse response to specific sounds or textures, excessive smelling or touching of objects, visual fascination with lights or movement).

***Specify* current severity:**

Severity is based on social communication impairments and restricted, repetitive patterns of behavior (see Table 2).

C. Symptoms must be present in the early developmental period (but may not become fully manifest until social demands exceed limited capacities, or may be masked by learned strategies in later life).

(continued)

D. Symptoms cause clinically significant impairment in social, occupational, or other important areas of current functioning.

E. These disturbances are not better explained by intellectual disability (intellectual developmental disorder) or global developmental delay. Intellectual disability and autism spectrum disorder frequently co-occur; to make comorbid diagnoses of autism spectrum disorder and intellectual disability, social communication should be below that expected for general developmental level.

Note: Individuals with a well-established DSM-IV diagnosis of autistic disorder, Asperger's disorder, or pervasive developmental disorder not otherwise specified should be given the diagnosis of autism spectrum disorder. Individuals who have marked deficits in social communication, but whose symptoms do not otherwise meet criteria for autism spectrum disorder, should be evaluated for social (pragmatic) communication disorder.

In 1943, the psychiatrist Leo Kanner described children with *autistic disturbances of affective contact*, highlighting behaviors that are central to this disorder and are apparent before 30 months of age (Rutter, 1978). Key features of autism spectrum disorder include *deficits in social communication and social interaction* (Klin, 2006) across multiple contexts including delays in acquiring spoken language, the inability to make eye contact and to recognize facial expressions, and a lack of interest in social interaction. Other deficits include the inability to start or continue a conversation and stereotyped or unusual language, such as *echolalia*, the repetition of the last word, sound, or phrase that was heard.

The second characteristic of autism spectrum disorder is *restricted and repetitive patterns of behavior, interests, or activities*, which includes intense preoccupation with a particular interest.

> Adi has a fascination with pipes and turbines. When he encounters one, he stops and stares, refusing to leave. His parents often find him in the basement staring at the furnace. He knows everything about the mechanics of large machinery and talks incessantly about the advantages and disadvantages of various systems, types of piping, and so on.

Repetitive and stereotyped patterns also include intense adherence to routines (e.g., eating or bedtime rituals) and self-injurious behaviors (e.g., eye gouging, head banging, hand biting). Why children engage in these behaviors is unclear, but some clinicians hypothesize that these behaviors allow the child to stop an aversive environmental stimulus such as a hug (Matson et al., 1996). For children with limited communication abilities, self-injurious behaviors may be a way to express emotions such as anger or pain (Volkmar & Wiesner, 2009). The diagnostic criteria for autism spectrum disorder include the ability to specify the level of support service that an individual requires. These levels are "requiring support," "requiring substantial support," and "requiring very substantial support."

Watch DAVID: ASPERGER'S SYNDROME

Infants with autism spectrum disorder are often described as being "too good" and never crying. They lack social interest, do not play interactive or imitative games (such as peek-a-boo), are extremely sensitive to touch and sound, and have abnormal sleep patterns with nighttime awakenings that last for several hours. They also have rigid eating behaviors, refusing to eat certain foods because of the smell, texture, or taste.

Approximately 60 to 75% of children with autism spectrum disorder have IQs below 70 (Barbaresi et al., 2006; Bethea & Sikich, 2007). Behavioral problems such as hyperactivity, impulsivity, social anxiety, general anxiety, irritability, and aggression are common (Bethea & Sikich, 2007), as are depression and phobias (Matson & Nebel-Schwalm, 2007).

Functional Impairment

LO 13.9 Describe the functional impairments that result from autism spectrum disorder.

Autism spectrum disorder is a lifelong impairment that affects the entire family; only about one-third of all people with this disorder are ever able to live independently (Klin, 2006). However, deficits in the core areas do improve with age, and there are always exceptions to this generally bleak outlook (see "Real People, Real Disorders: Temple Grandin, Ph.D.").

Children often are socially isolated, desiring social interaction but seeking it inappropriately: interrupting others, engaging in one-sided conversations about a favorite topic, and speaking too loudly and too rapidly. Some children with autism spectrum disorder require special classroom placement, whereas other children are able to function academically in traditional classroom settings. However, because of their social difficulties, their classmates often bully, tease, or ignore them, resulting in social isolation at school.

The prevalence of autism spectrum disorder has increased dramatically in recent years (see "Examining the Evidence: Vaccines Do Not Produce Autism Spectrum Disorder"). Before 1994, the median prevalence of autism was 0.05% (Fombonne, 2005). The most recent estimate is that 1 in every 68 children (14.7% of the general population) may have autism spectrum disorder (Centers for Disease Control and Prevention [CDC], http://www.cdc.gov/ncbddd/autism/data.html) (see Table 13.3). However, the increased *prevalence* (proportion of people in the general population who have a disorder) of autism spectrum disorder cannot be attributed to an increase in *incidence* (number of new cases of a disorder during a given time interval). It is likely that changes in diagnostic criteria, diagnostic practices, special education policies, and the availability of diagnostic services are contributing factors (Fombonne, 2005; Klin, 2006).

Overall, autism spectrum disorder is more common among boys than among girls, with 3.5 to 4 boys for every 1 girl diagnosed (Bethea & Sikich, 2007; Nicholas et al., 2008). Currently, no data exist to indicate that the prevalence of autism spectrum disorder differs by race, ethnicity, or social class (Fombonne, 2005; Klin, 2006).

The onset of autism spectrum disorder is always before age 3, and the core features are often clearly present by age 2 or 3 (Lord et al., 2006; Maenner et al., 2013). Parents sometimes

Table 13.3 Identified Prevalence of Autism Spectrum Disorder

ADDM Network 2000–2010 Combining Data from All Sites

Surveillance Year	Birth Year	Number of ADDM Sites Reporting	Prevalence per 1,000 Children (Range)	This is About 1 in X Children...
2000	1992	6	6.7	1 in 150
2002	1994	14	6.6	1 in 150
2004	1996	8	8.0	1 in 125
2006	1998	11	9.0	1 in 110
2008	2000	14	11.3	1 in 88
2010	2002	11	14.7	1 in 68

REAL People REAL Disorders

Temple Grandin, Ph.D.

Temple Grandin, Ph.D., is a professor of animal science at Colorado State University. She obtained her B.A. at Franklin Pierce College, her M.S. in animal science at Arizona State University, and her Ph.D. in animal science from the University of Illinois. She has written more than 300 articles and several books. One book, *Animals in Translation*, was a *New York Times* best-seller. Her writings on animal grazing behaviors have helped reduce stress on animals during handling, and in North America, about half of the cattle in livestock yards are handled in a system that she designed.

Dr. Grandin has autism spectrum disorder. She didn't speak until she was 3½ years old, communicating by screaming, peeping, and humming. In 1950, she was labeled "autistic," and professionals recommended that she be institutionalized. The book she eventually wrote, *Emergence: Labeled Autistic*, stunned the world. Until then, most people had assumed that this disorder prevented achievement or productivity in life. She speaks about her disorder because, she says, "I have read enough to know that there are still many parents, and, yes, professionals, too, who believe that 'once autistic, always autistic.' This dictum has meant sad and sorry lives for many children diagnosed, as I was in early life, as autistic. To these people, it is incomprehensible that the characteristics of autism can be modified and controlled. However, I feel strongly that I am living proof that they can."

recognize that something is wrong at a much earlier age, perhaps as early as 12 to 18 months. However, symptoms may change dramatically between infancy and early childhood (Charman et al., 2005; Lord et al., 2006). Although it is possible that autism spectrum disorder can be reliably detected at 18 to 24 months (Lord et al., 2006), symptoms are more stable beginning at age 3, allowing for a more accurate diagnosis.

The long-term outcome of autism spectrum disorder is variable. In one controlled longitudinal study (Eaves & Ho, 2008), 46% of children who were diagnosed with this disorder had a poor outcome as young adults, 32% had a fair outcome, and 21% had a good to very good outcome. IQ remained stable from childhood to adulthood. Emotional problems were present among 62% of the sample, most commonly obsessive-compulsive disorder or another anxiety disorder. Only 27% had ever been employed for an average of 5 hours per week and most often in a sheltered workshop. More than half of the adults were living at home (56%) or in a group home or foster care (35%). Despite these figures, some adults with autism spectrum disorder, such as Dr. Temple Grandin, do achieve success.

Etiology

LO 13.10 Discuss the etiology of autism spectrum disorder.

Autism spectrum disorder is a neurodevelopmental disorder associated with the presence of different genetic syndromes and chromosomal abnormalities (Barbaresi et al., 2006). Although its specific genetic mechanism is not yet known, the estimated heritability is higher than 90% (Gupta & State, 2007). Evidence from neuroscience and genetic research indicates that more than 60 genetic and metabolic conditions are associated with autism. This means that it is more likely that autism spectrum disorder represents people with a range of severity and functional impairment (Eichler & Zimmerman, 2008). Contemporary genetic research suggests that large spontaneous deletions or duplications of areas in the genome are among the molecular causes of autism spectrum disorder (Weiss et al., 2008).

Interestingly, whereas advancing maternal age is associated with Down syndrome and intellectual disability, advancing paternal age may be associated with an increased prevalence of autism spectrum disorder (Gabis et al., 2010; Reichenberg et al., 2006). However, as with Down syndrome and maternal age, it is not clear how a father's advanced age might lead to development of the disorder.

One indication of the neurodevelopmental basis of autism spectrum disorder is unusually accelerated head and brain growth during the first few years of life. At birth, children

Examining the EVIDENCE

Vaccines Do Not Produce Autism Spectrum Disorder

- **Fact 1** Forty years ago, 4 of every 10,000 children were diagnosed with autism spectrum disorder. The rate now is 1 out of 68 children (http://www.cdc.gov/ncbddd/autism/data.html).
- **Fact 2** Childhood inoculations (measles-mumps-rubella, or MMR, vaccine) occur between 12 and 18 months of age.
- **Fact 3** Some children with autism spectrum disorder appear to develop normally until about age 2 when developmental regression appears.
- **Possible Conclusion?** Because the incidence of autism spectrum disorder appears to have increased when the MMR vaccine became common, the vaccine caused the rise in rates (Wakefield, 1999).
- **Let's Examine the Evidence** Wakefield (1999) described a *correlational relationship* between vaccination and autism spectrum disorder, but it was wrongly interpreted as causation. Other studies appeared to confirm this parallel upward trend. However, the studies did not manipulate the variable of interest (MMR vaccine), which would be necessary to conclude causation. When researchers examined variations in the diagnosis of autism spectrum disorder *before* and *after* the termination of a vaccine program (Honda et al., 2005), rates rose when the vaccine was administered. However, *rates continued to rise* after the vaccine was discontinued. If the MMR vaccine were responsible, the rate should have *decreased* once the program was discontinued (but it did not).
- **What are possible alternative explanations for the increased rate of autism spectrum disorder?**
  1. **Change in diagnostic practices**. Until recently, a child with intellectual disability was not given a second diagnosis of autism even if autism spectrum disorder was present. Now both diagnoses can be given, leading to a rise in the total number of autism spectrum disorder diagnoses.
  2. **Changes in diagnostic criteria**. Forty years ago, the term *autism* was restricted to children who would now represent the very extremely impaired end of the spectrum. Now, children with the same behaviors, although milder in severity, are included in the diagnosis of autism spectrum disorder (Rutter, 2005), leading to a rise in the total number of children diagnosed with one of the disorders.
- **Conclusion** Environmental or biological contributors to autism cannot be discounted, but there are no data that the MMR vaccination is a cause for autism spectrum disorder (DeStefano et al., 2013; Taylor et al., 2014). After examining all the evidence, the editors of the respected medical journal *BMJ* published an editorial concluding that Wakefield's article reporting a link between the MMR vaccine and autism spectrum disorder was fraudulent (Godlee et al., 2011). Vaccines do not produce autism spectrum disorder.

later diagnosed with autism spectrum disorder have a head circumference at the 25th percentile for all infants. Between 6 and 14 months of age, head circumference and brain size reaches the 84th percentile, far exceeding the growth rate for typically developing children (Bethea & Sikich, 2007; Courchesne & Pierce, 2005).

In addition to the abnormal growth rate, diagnostic imaging (MRI, fMRI, and PET scans) provides data that suggest subtle structural and organizational abnormalities in the brains of at least some children with autism spectrum disorder. Particularly affected is the anterior cingulate cortex, an area that integrates verbal information with emotional tone and observation of personally important faces. When shown pictures of familiar and significant faces, children without autism spectrum disorder show activation in the anterior cingulate cortex while children with autism spectrum disorder do not (Pierce et al., 2004). This would suggest that children with autism spectrum disorder do not have the same neurochemical reaction when they see familiar faces as do typically developing children.

Another area of the brain that appears to be underactivated in children with autism spectrum disorder is the fusiform gyrus (Pierce et al., 2001). This area is important in the recognition of facial expression, although it remains unclear if this area is underactivated when viewing faces of family members or only faces of strangers (Pierce & Redcay, 2008). Severe underactivation of this area appears to be related to severe social impairment (Schultz et al., 2001). Advanced

In response to viewing faces of familiar people and strangers, brain activity occurs in both people with autism spectrum disorder and people with no disorder. However, when the two groups are compared, there is stronger activation in people with no disorder and more areas of the brain are activated.

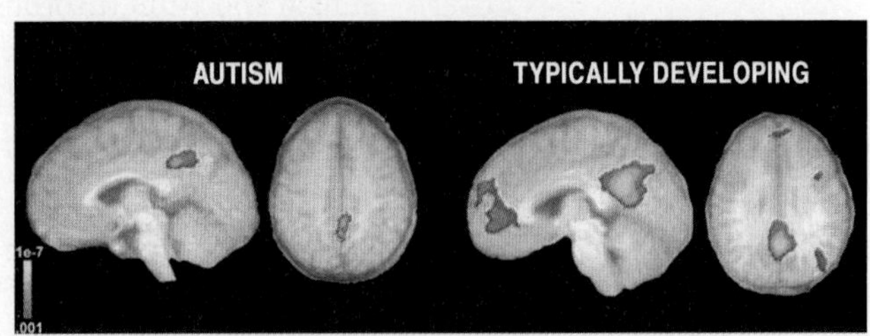

neuroimaging now allows us to examine not just brain *regions* but brain *networks*, and it now appears that recognition of facial expression might involve not just the fusiform gyrus and the amygdala but also networks found within the cortex and the subcortex of the brain (Nomi & Uddin, 2015). This would suggest that there could be a biological basis for this social impairment. If the part of the brain that recognizes faces is not functioning properly, children miss social cues that others "automatically" use to engage in pleasurable social interactions. It is not yet clear whether therapy can change this biological deficit.

There are many avenues of exciting new research about the neurological bases of autism spectrum disorder, but there are many medical misunderstandings about its causes. One theory is that autism spectrum disorder is caused by the measles-mumps-rubella (MMR) vaccine (see "Examining the Evidence: Vaccines Do Not Produce Autism Spectrum Disorder"). Another theory without empirical support is that autism spectrum disorder is caused by thimerosal (a mercury-containing preservative used in vaccines). Why would such theories develop if no evidence supports them? One reason is that in a desperate search for explanations, parents often misinterpret or overinterpret research data in their quest to find a cause for this disorder. Despite the current lack of evidence, some parents refuse to allow their children to be vaccinated for childhood medical disorders, thereby exposing their children to diseases that may result in physical handicaps such as blindness, intellectual disability, or even death.

ETHICS AND RESPONSIBILITY Throughout history, there have also been psychological misunderstandings about the etiology of autism spectrum disorder. In the 1950s and 1960s, psychosocial theories proposed that "refrigerator mothers" (parents who were emotionally unresponsive to their infants) were responsible for its development (Klin, 2006). This concept was discredited in the 1970s when it became clear that the roots of the disorder were neurobiological. Parents do play a critical role in the early detection and treatment for children with this disorder (see "Treatment"), but they do *not* cause autism spectrum disorder. Currently, scientists have many theories regarding the etiology of autism spectrum disorder and the reasons for the increase in its prevalence over the past 20 years. Researchers point to changing diagnostic criteria, diagnostic substitution, and the decreasing age at which the diagnosis can be assigned (Leonard et al., 2010). Unfortunately, many people in the general population do not accept the current scientific theories but instead adhere to theories of causality that have been discredited, such as vaccines and gluten in the diet (Mulloy et al., 2010, 2011). Other environmental factors considered by non–mental health professionals as valid potential theories to explain increases in autism spectrum disorder include (1) medical technologies such as ultrasound scans and cesarean sections; (2) drug use/exposure to toxins; (3) changing lifestyles such as working mothers, stress, and indoor air quality; and (4) technology effects such as carbon monoxide exposure, nuclear power stations, and cell phone towers (Russell et al., 2009). Researchers must be sure to be respectful of others' ideas—not discounting every theory outright but seeking to educate the public about the validity of these hypotheses based on solid science. Failure by scientists to address these theories or pseudotheories in a respectful scientific manner may result in children not getting needed medical services or being subjected to interventions that hold nothing but false promises.

Treatment

LO 13.11 Identify efficacious treatments for autism spectrum disorder.

Early and intensive behavioral treatment improves the long-term outcome for children with autism spectrum disorder (Barbaresi et al., 2006). Behavioral interventions typically target five groups of problem behaviors: aberrant behaviors, social skills, language, daily living skills, and academic skills (Matson & Smith, 2008; White et al., 2007). For all categories except aberrant behaviors, treatment consists of *positive reinforcement and shaping*, which teaches new and needed behaviors (such as saying a word, putting on clothes, completing homework). Clinicians teach parents to train their children in these skills. *Applied behavior analysis* (ABA) is a behavioral intervention that uses shaping and positive reinforcement to improve social, communication, and behavioral skills by intensively training (shaping) and rewarding (reinforcing) specific behaviors. Introduced by O. Ivar Lovaas (1987), applied behavior analysis (conducted for 40 hours per week for more than 2 years) improved the behaviors in 9 of 19 children with autism spectrum disorder (47%) to the extent that they were indistinguishable from children without the disorder. Although subsequent studies did not replicate this high success rate, empirical data show that ABA is effective, particularly when provided individually for at least 20 hours per week and started before age 4 (Barbaresi et al., 2006).

In the case of aberrant behaviors, self-injury is an unfortunate part of the clinical syndrome and must be treated quickly or serious and permanent injury or even death may result. Mildly *aversive procedures* (e.g., a short spray of warm water to the face) quickly and painlessly disrupt such behaviors. When such treatments are combined with positive approaches to behavior change, self-injurious behaviors can be reduced or eliminated (Matson et al., 1996). Aversive procedures are used (1) in very specific instances, (2) when the child's health or welfare is at risk, and (3) under the supervision of a qualified professional. Procedures such as a spray of warm water or placing lemon juice on the tongue are quite effective. Mild electric shocks were used in the past but are now used rarely, if at all, and only when less aversive procedures are not effective and there is danger of severe physical damage (such as brain injury as a result of repeated head banging). Decisions about aversive procedures should never be made by a single person but only after consultation with other professionals and perhaps an ethics committee.

Social skills training has been used to address the social deficits commonly found among individuals with autism spectrum disorder. Most commonly delivered in group format, these interventions target teaching discrete social skills (eye contact, vocal tone) and providing generalization experiences to transfer those skills from the clinic to naturalistic settings (White et al., 2014). Incorporating peers into the treatment program (to increase socialization in the child's own environment) may increase the effectiveness of these social skills training programs and therefore enhance abilities to interact effectively in many different social environments.

No medications are efficacious for the social or communication deficits found in children with autism spectrum disorder (Barbaresi et al., 2006). Atypical antipsychotic drugs (see Chapter 11) may manage behaviors such as tantrums, aggression, and self-injurious behavior (McCracken et al., 2002; White et al., 2014) and improve restricted, repetitive, and stereotyped patterns of behaviors, interests, and activities (McDougle et al., 2005). Stimulants reduce hyperactivity but are not as effective as they are in children with ADHD (Research Units on Pediatric Psychopharmacology [RUPP]Autism Network, 2005). Selective serotonin reuptake inhibitors (SSRIs) are safe, but it is not clear if they are really effective. They may decrease repetitive behaviors (Hollander et al., 2005) but increase behavioral agitation in a population already prone to this behavior (Kolevzon et al., 2006).

Learning Objective Summaries

LO 13.8 Identify the two core features of autism spectrum disorder.

The two core features of autism spectrum disorder are (1) persistent deficits in social communication and social interaction as manifested by deficits in social-emotional reciprocity or nonverbal communicative behaviors used for social interaction and (2) restricted, repetitive patterns of behavior, interests, or activities, as manifested by at least two of the following: stereotyped or repetitive motor movements, use of objects, or speech; insistence on sameness, inflexible adherence to routines, or ritualized patterns of verbal or nonverbal behavior; highly restricted, fixated interests that are abnormal in intensity or focus; and hyper- or hyporeactivity to sensory input or unusual interest in sensory aspects of the environment.

LO 13.9 Describe the functional impairments that result from autism spectrum disorder.

Autism spectrum disorder is a lifelong condition. Autism spectrum disorder is characterized by deficits in social communication and social interaction across multiple contexts as well as restricted and stereotypical behaviors, interests, and activities. Children often are socially isolated, desiring social interaction but seeking it inappropriately.

Some children with autism spectrum disorder require special classroom placement. The long-term outcome of autism spectrum disorder is variable, and fewer than 25% of children diagnosed with this disorder have a good to very good outcome as adults.

LO 13.10 Discuss the etiology of autism spectrum disorder.

It is now assumed that autism spectrum disorder is a neurobiologically based disorder. Different areas of the brain function differently in people with autism spectrum disorders. The reason for the differential functioning is not yet clear but probably includes genetic factors. Environmental "causes" of this disorder are unproven and in some cases have been disproven.

LO 13.11 Identify efficacious treatments for autism spectrum disorder.

Despite increased understanding, we cannot yet offer treatments that entirely reverse the effects of this disorder. Early and intense interventions can produce symptom improvement and enhance the long-term outcome. Social skills training may enhance the ability to interact effectively with others, and medications may be useful to treat the self-injurious behaviors that sometimes accompany this disorder.

Critical Thinking Question

Autism spectrum disorder is neurobiological in nature and appears to have a genetic basis. When children with autism spectrum disorder are looking at faces, certain areas of their brains, such as the fusiform gyrus, do not appear to have the same level of reactivity as the brains of children with no disorder. How does this neurobiological finding relate to the children's ability to interact in a socially appropriate manner with others?

Attention Deficit Hyperactivity Disorder

Being active is part of childhood, whether it is playing games at recess, being involved in organized sports, or just wrestling with a sibling. An important developmental process involves the ability to control physical activity and direct it toward the achievement of identified goals. Most children achieve this developmental milestone. However, for a subset of children, physical activity is not goal directed but just excessively overactive, resulting in negative outcomes such as household disruption, academic underachievement, and poor social relationships. These children suffer from *attention deficit hyperactivity disorder*, a common behavior disorder to which we now turn our attention.

Identifying Attention Deficit Disorder

LO 13.12 Define the core features of attention deficit disorder.

Ronnie (see "Side-by-Side Case Studies") had a situational problem that was resolved by proper school placement and a challenging curriculum. Jason has **attention deficit hyperactivity disorder (ADHD)** (see "DSM-5: Attention Deficit Hyperactivity Disorder"), a prevalent, early-onset childhood disorder that affects many aspects of functioning. The symptoms of ADHD fall into two categories. First are symptoms of *inattentiveness*, such as daydreaming, distractibility, and an inability to focus on or complete a task. The second component consists of *hyperactivity* (excessive energy, restlessness, excessive talking, and an inability to sit still) (Biederman, 2005) and *impulsivity* (blurting out answers, interrupting others' conversations, and inability to take turns). Children with ADHD cannot inhibit their responses and do not wait to generate a plan before they act. If they are inattentive, they cannot pay attention in order to store information. Finally, their inability to concentrate keeps them from focusing on one particular idea or activity in order to develop a plan of action or way to behave. Some children have predominantly inattentive presentation (showing only inattention symptoms), and others have a predominantly hyperactive/impulsive presentation (showing only hyperactive/impulsive symptoms). Still other children have a combined presentation, with symptoms from all three components.

Jason is an example of a child who has ADHD combined type. Other children, like Allie, have ADHD but are not hyperactive, displaying only attentional problems.

> Allie is 12 years old. She has been having problems paying attention since she was in the second grade, and currently she is having problems at home and at school. She always had difficulty following directions and avoiding careless mistakes, and that affects her schoolwork. Allie's assignments are incomplete, her grades are poor, and her teacher thinks that she just does not care. At home her mom gets frustrated with the length of time that Allie needs to finish her homework. She has difficulty following instructions and organizing tasks and loses things, but she never gets in trouble at home or school for not being able to stay in her seat. During the interview, Allie tapped her foot and played with a pencil.

ADHD is most commonly diagnosed in early elementary school. Establishing the diagnosis early (i.e., during the preschool years) is challenging because many symptoms (short attention span, difficulty sitting still, high activity level) are developmentally appropriate during toddlerhood (Blackman, 1999). When ADHD is diagnosed at the preschool age, the combined type is most common (Lahey et al., 1998; Wilens et al., 2002). When diagnosed at this early age, children continue to have ADHD symptoms during the elementary school years (Lahey et al., 2004).

Watch JIMMY: ADHD

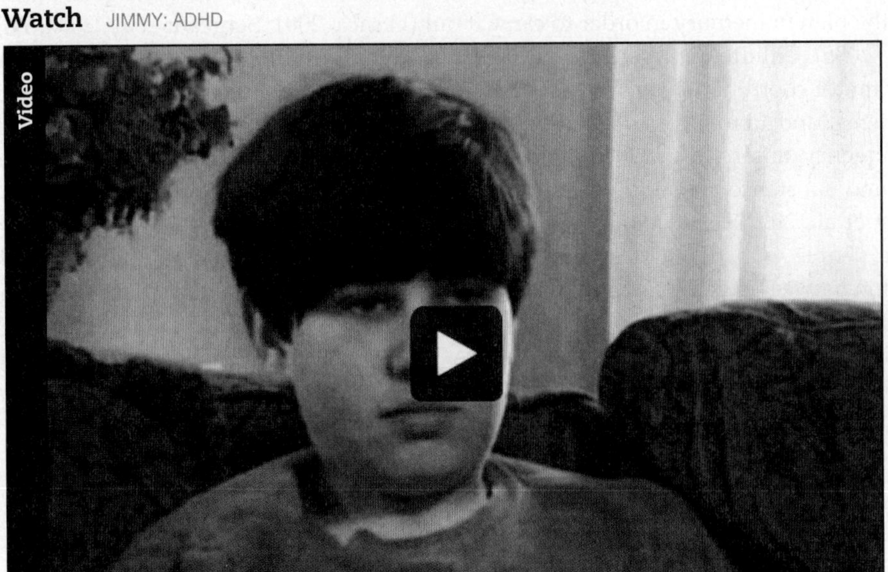

Across cultures, 3 to 5% of children have ADHD (Biederman, 2005; Canino et al., 2004; Costello et al., 2003; Graetz et al., 2001; Rohde et al., 2005; Wolraich et al., 1998). Boys are four to five times more likely than girls to have ADHD (Costello et al., 2003). Boys with ADHD may have more severe symptoms or may suffer more impairment than others, making it more likely that their parents will seek treatment. Compared with boys, girls with ADHD have different impairments. They are more likely to have the predominantly inattentive subtype, less likely to have a learning disability, less likely to have problems in school or in their spare time, and less likely to have comorbid depression, oppositional defiant disorder, or conduct disorder (Biederman et al., 2002; Spencer et al., 2007). Teachers rate boys with ADHD as more inattentive and hyperactive/impulsive than girls with this disorder (Greene et al., 2001; Hartung et al., 2002).

Until about 20 years ago, ADHD was thought to disappear at or shortly after puberty (Smith et al., 2000). It is now clear that adolescents and adults also suffer from ADHD (Biederman, 2005). In a large national survey of psychiatric disorders in adolescents, the lifetime prevalence of ADHD among adolescents was 8.1%, and the disorder is significantly more common among boys than girls (12.1% vs. 3.9%; Kessler et al, 2014). Some adults were diagnosed in childhood, but a substantial number are diagnosed for the first time in adulthood. The prevalence of ADHD among adults is unclear but seems to range from 2% to 5.5% (Mongia & Hechtman, 2012; Moriyama et al. 2013). Determining ADHD in adults is a challenge and is controversial. Some of the diagnostic criteria (inability to sit still in class, difficulty playing quietly) are obviously not valid for adults. Also, deciding whether an adult had such symptoms before age 12 is difficult because it is often based solely on retrospective self-report (McGough & Barkley, 2004). In DSM-5, the diagnostic criteria for ADHD are valid for adults as well as children, with the need for five symptoms (rather than six symptoms) for a reliable diagnosis (American Psychiatric Association, 2013).

Children, adolescents, and adults with ADHD often have other disorders including conduct problems (Kessler et al., 2014; Wilens et al., 2002), mood disorders, anxiety disorders, and learning disabilities (Biederman, 2005; Kessler et al, 2014; Mongia & Hechtman, 2012), and substance abuse disorders (Kessler et al., 2014; Mogia & Hechtman, 2012). Similarly, among adults with ADHD, anxiety disorders are most common followed by mood disorders, substance abuse, and antisocial personality disorder.

Functional Impairment

LO 13.13 Describe the functional impairments that result from ADHD.

ADHD is associated with a deficit in executive functioning, which includes the cognitive abilities needed to formulate a goal, plan a series of actions to achieve the goal, and maintain the plan in memory in order to carry it out (Lesaca, 2001; Sergeant et al., 2002; Willcutt et al., 2005). Children with ADHD have more accidents and injuries (perhaps as a result of poor motor coordination), poor peer relationships, and academic underachievement, sleep problems, and family stress (Biederman, 2005; Daley, 2006). Among adolescents, school delinquency, failure to graduate from high school, suicidal ideation and attempts, smoking, and substance abuse are common (Biederman & Faraone, 2005; Kessler et al., 2014; Smith et al., 2000). Even though the association between suicide and ADHD is strongest when people with ADHD also have comorbid depression, there is still a significant correlation between suicide and ADHD even when controlling for the presence or absence of a comorbid depressive disorder. Children with ADHD are at 80% risk of injuries requiring medical attention as are 50% of adults with ADHD (Nigg, 2012). Finally, perhaps because of inattentiveness and impulsivity, adolescents with ADHD have a higher risk of injury and

SIDE by SIDE Case Studies

Dimensions of Behavior: From Adaptive to Maladaptive

Adaptive Behavior Case Study

Boyish Exuberance

Ronnie is 6 years old. He has older brothers and loves "rough and tumble" play. He has broken a few family possessions but not more than his brothers. He does not like to sit quietly for a long period of time; reading has never been his favorite activity. However, 90% of the time he finishes activities that he starts. He was eager to start first grade. He gets good grades and has been sent to the principal only once, for talking out of turn. Sitting still in first grade is hard—he says school is boring. Psychological testing revealed a superior IQ score, and when he started the gifted and talented program, his out-of-seat behavior disappeared and he no longer found school boring.

Maladaptive Behavior Case Study

Attention Deficit Hyperactivity Disorder

Jason is 7 years old. He has trouble at school academically and complains that he hates school. He has no friends and is constantly picked on by the other children. He wants to socialize, but he always ends up fighting. He is genuinely puzzled about why other children do not like him. Jason is impulsive—he interrupts others, butts in line, and disrupts organized games. He cannot sit still, does not pay attention in class, and will not follow the rules at home. His mother reports that he has been a "wild child" since age 3. During the clinic interview, Jason does not sit in the chair. At times, he lies down on the floor and a few moments later, he is standing on the windowsill.

DSM-5

Criteria for Attention Deficit Hyperactivity Disorder

A. A persistent pattern of inattention and/or hyperactivity-impulsivity that interferes with functioning or development, as characterized by (1) and/or (2):

1. Inattention: Six (or more) of the following symptoms have persisted for at least 6 months to a degree that is inconsistent with developmental level and that negatively impacts directly on social and academic/occupational activities:

Note: The symptoms are not solely a manifestation of oppositional behavior, defiance, hostility, or failure to understand tasks or instructions. For older adolescents and adults (age 17 and older), at least five symptoms are required.

a. Often fails to give close attention to details or makes careless mistakes in schoolwork, at work, or during other activities (e.g., overlooks or misses details, work is inaccurate).
b. Often has difficulty sustaining attention in tasks or play activities (e.g., has difficulty remaining focused during lectures, conversations, or lengthy reading).
c. Often does not seem to listen when spoken to directly (e.g., mind seems elsewhere, even in the absence of any obvious distraction).
d. Often does not follow through on instructions and fails to finish schoolwork, chores, or duties in the workplace (e.g., starts tasks but quickly loses focus and is easily sidetracked).
e. Often has difficulty organizing tasks and activities (e.g., difficulty managing sequential tasks; difficulty keeping materials and belongings in order; messy, disorganized work; has poor time management; fails to meet deadlines).
f. Often avoids, dislikes, or is reluctant to engage in tasks that require sustained mental effort (e.g., schoolwork or homework; for older adolescents and adults, preparing reports, completing forms, reviewing lengthy papers).
g. Often loses things necessary for tasks or activities (e.g., school materials, pencils, books, tools, wallets, keys, paperwork, eyeglasses, mobile telephones).
h. Is often easily distracted by extraneous stimuli (for older adolescents and adults, may include unrelated thoughts).
i. Is often forgetful in daily activities (e.g., doing chores, running errands; for older adolescents and adults, returning calls, paying bills, keeping appointments).

2. Hyperactivity and impulsivity: Six (or more) of the following symptoms have persisted for at least 6 months to a degree that is inconsistent with developmental level and that negatively impacts directly on social and academic/occupational activities:

Note: The symptoms are not solely a manifestation of oppositional behavior, defiance, hostility, or a failure to understand tasks or instructions. For older adolescents and adults (age 17 and older), at least five symptoms are required.

a. Often fidgets with or taps hands or feet or squirms in seat.
b. Often leaves seat in situations when remaining seated is expected (e.g., leaves his or her place in the classroom, in the office or other workplace, or in other situations that require remaining in place).
c. Often runs about or climbs in situations where it is inappropriate. (**Note:** In adolescents or adults, may be limited to feeling restless.)
d. Often unable to play or engage in leisure activities quietly.
e. Is often "on the go," acting as if "driven by a motor" (e.g., is unable to be or uncomfortable being still for extended time, as in restaurants, meetings; may be experienced by others as being restless or difficult to keep up with).
f. Often talks excessively.
g. Often blurts out an answer before a question has been completed (e.g., completes people's sentences; cannot wait for turn in conversation).
h. Often has difficulty waiting his or her turn (e.g., while waiting in line).
i. Often interrupts or intrudes on others (e.g., butts into conversations, games, or activities; may start using other people's things without asking or receiving permission; for adolescents and adults, may intrude into or take over what others are doing).

B. Several inattentive or hyperactive-impulsive symptoms were present prior to age 12 years.

C. Several inattentive or hyperactive-impulsive symptoms are present in two or more settings (e.g., at home, school, or work; with friends or relatives; in other activities).

D. There is clear evidence that the symptoms interfere with, or reduce the quality of, social, academic, or occupational functioning.

E. The symptoms do not occur exclusively during the course of schizophrenia or another psychotic disorder and are not better explained by another mental disorder (e.g., mood disorder, anxiety disorder, dissociative disorder, personality disorder, substance intoxication or withdrawal).

Perhaps because of their inattentiveness, children with ADHD are more likely to have childhood accidents such as falling off of their bicycles.

are more likely to have automobile accidents and to be involved in criminal behavior than other adolescents (Smith et al., 2000).

Symptoms of ADHD appear to improve at different rates. Symptoms of inattention decline only minimally as children mature, while hyperactivity/impulsivity symptoms show a much higher rate of decline, particularly from elementary school through mid-adolescence (Spencer et al., 2007). About 50% of children diagnosed with ADHD will continue to have the disorder during adolescence (Biederman et al., 1998; Smith et al., 2000). The outlook is even better for adults. Most adults who had ADHD as children will no longer have the disorder by age 30 to 40, but about 50% will still have some functional impairment (Biederman & Faraone, 2005).

Etiology

LO 13.14 Identify the etiological factors that contribute to the development of ADHD.

ADHD is considered to be a neurodevelopmental disorder with genetic, biological, and environmental influences. Like many other disorders, ADHD "runs in families," with between 20 and 25% of family members of someone with ADHD also having symptoms. Twin studies also support its heritability. A mean heritability of 77% (Biederman, 2005) suggests a substantial genetic influence, including at least six genetic markers that identify it (Nigg, 2012), and it appears that different genes may be associated with the inattentive and hyperactivity dimensions (Nikolas & Burt, 2010). We do not know yet how these genetic abnormalities contribute to ADHD, and there is no evidence that ADHD is a *genetic condition* in the way that Down syndrome is a genetic condition. Instead, prenatal and early environmental experiences may alter the expression of the gene in susceptible individuals (Nigg, 2012). Many neuroimaging studies now document differences in the brains of children with ADHD and children with no disorder. However, it now appears that instead of permanent structural differences, ADHD may be characterized by delays

Watch BRAIN MATURATION OF CHILDREN WITH ADHD COMPARED TO CONTROL in brain maturation. This delayed development has been documented in studies of brain volumes (Castellanos et al., 2002), cortical thickness (Shaw et al. 2006), and neural connectivity (Sripada et al., 2014). For example, the age at which brains attain peak cortical thickness was delayed in children with ADHD by approximately 3 years, with the largest difference occurring in the frontal lobes where the delay could be as long as 5 years (Rubia, 2007). In short, the difference between the brains of children with ADHD and children with no disorder is one of timing as to when the brain matures. Consistent with the behaviors of children with ADHD, who often appear more immature than what is expected for their chronological age (more active, more impulsive, shorter attention span), these research data suggest that their brains are less mature as well. Brain maturation occurs but, as noted above, is delayed by several years when compared with their peers.

Treatment

LO 13.15 Identify efficacious treatments for ADHD.

When making the decision to treat ADHD, clinicians must consider the child's age (3-year-old children should not be expected to sit still for the same length of time as 10-year-olds) and level of functional impairment at home, school, and other activities. Treatment should aim at restoring behavior to age-appropriate standards (Chronis et al., 2006).

Both pharmacological and behavioral interventions have been used effectively to treat ADHD. Stimulant medications, such as Ritalin, have a 40-year record of efficacy for ADHD's core symptoms (Biederman & Faraone, 2005). The drugs work by enhancing the neurotransmission of dopamine and norepinephrine (Spencer et al., 2004). These two neurotransmitters play an important role in brain functions such as self-control, attention, and thinking. Stimulants are short-acting medications and may need to be taken several times a day, sometimes making compliance difficult. These drugs decrease ADHD's core symptoms, but whether they affect other areas of functioning, such as academic achievement, is less clear (Hechtman & Greenfield, 2003; Wells et al., 2000).

The use of stimulants to treat ADHD is controversial. First, up to 30% of children may not respond to stimulant medication (Chronis et al., 2006). Second, side effects include emotional problems, sleep disturbance, appetite decrease, and irritability. The symptoms are more frequent among preschool children (Daley et al., 2009). Stimulant medication may affect physical stature. Children who take stimulants grow more slowly than other children, and recent prescribing practices mean that children are now taking these medications at higher doses, during the summer as well as the school year, and for many more years than in the past. The increase in medication use raises concerns about how these drugs affect height (Lerner & Wigal, 2008). A slower-than-normal rate of growth is greatest in the first year of use; it continues in the second year and appears to end in the third year. When considering stimulants as part of treatment for ADHD, parents and mental health professionals must balance the advantages of reducing symptoms against the potential for shorter stature.

For preschool children, parenting programs are recommended as the first treatment for children with ADHD. Medication should be used only when parent training is not efficacious (Daley et al., 2009). The Preschool ADHD Treatment Study was a multicenter research study that evaluated the use of a common stimulant, methylphenidate, in preschoolers with ADHD. Parent management training was also part of the treatment program. Initial outcome data suggested that the stimulant medication was superior to placebo in reducing ADHD symptoms, but only 21% of those on the optimal dose of the medication and 13% on placebo achieved remission (Greenhill et al., 2006). Six years later, 70.9% of the children were still taking ADHD medications (Vitiello et al., 2015), indicating that not all children had the same response but many continued to need medications to control their symptoms.

In addition to medication and parenting programs, additional psychosocial treatments for school-age children with ADHD include behavioral parent training, classroom behavioral management (daily report cards), social skills training, and an intensive outpatient/summer treatment program (Chronis et al., 2006; Pelham & Fabiano, 2008). *Behavioral parent training* teaches parents how to reward positive behaviors and decrease negative behaviors. In addition to improving core ADHD symptoms and sometimes classroom behavior (Chronis et al., 2006; Pelham et al., 1998), behavioral parent training improves parenting behavior and may also decrease stress on parents (Chronis et al., 2004). The *Daily Report Card* is a classroom behavioral management program that targets school-relevant goals such as completing homework and staying in one's seat (Chronis et al., 2004; Smith et al., 2000). Teachers record classroom behavior on a report card and parents use a reward system to reinforce positive school behaviors. A third behavioral treatment, social skills training, teaches children with ADHD to interact appropriately with others (taking turns, allowing others to decide which game to play). Social skills training appears to be particularly efficacious when combined with behavioral parent training (e.g., Pfiffner & McBurnett, 1997).

Because of the range and severity of their behavioral problems, children with ADHD may require intensive and comprehensive treatment programs. The Summer Treatment Program (Pelham et al., 2000) is an 8-week, all-day program that includes a point system, daily report cards, social skills training, academic skills training, problem-solving training, and sports training in a day camp atmosphere. It includes weekly parent management training and has been found to be an efficacious intervention for children with ADHD, decreasing symptoms and increasing associated behavioral functioning (e.g., Pelham et al., 2000, 2004).

The Collaborative Multimodal Treatment (MTA) Study of Children with ADHD is the largest controlled clinical trial comparing behavioral treatment (using the components just described), medication (primarily stimulant medication), a combination of behavioral treatment and medication, and standard community care for preadolescent children with ADHD. At the end of the treatment program, all four treatments improved children's symptoms, but children in the medication only and children in the combined group showed significantly more improvement than children in behavioral treatment alone or community care (MTA Cooperative Group, 1999). Do the results of this study mean that behavioral intervention is not useful for ADHD or, at the least, that it does not add value over medication? When an alternative method of data analysis was used, children who received medication and behavior therapy had a superior outcome over medication alone, which contradicts the original outcome (Conners et al., 2001). Thus, even though this was the largest child treatment study ever funded by the National Institute of Mental Health, its results are unclear and subject to various interpretations.

Among adolescents and adults, medication and behavior therapy produce similar outcomes on the symptoms of ADHD (Mongia & Hechtman, 2012; Moriyama et al., 2013; Sibley et al. 2014), although behavior therapy may produce more overall benefits on measures of impairment (as opposed to symptoms; Sibley et al., 2014). Among adults, improvement in time management, organization and planning, problem solving, motivation, and emotion regulation are primary treatment goals (Mongia & Hechtman, 2012).

Learning Objective Summaries

LO 13.12 Define the core features of attention deficit hyperactivity disorder.

The core features of attention deficit hyperactivity disorder (ADHD) are inattention and hyperactivity/impulsivity. These behaviors are manifested in different ways and occur in different settings, such as school and home.

LO 13.13 Describe the functional impairments that result from ADHD.

ADHD, once considered a disorder that affected only children, is now understood in some cases to continue into adolescence and adulthood. ADHD has variable symptoms and a complicated and complex etiology. The disorder creates significant functional impairment in many aspects of life. ADHD affects educational, social, familial and occupational functioning.

LO 13.14 Identify the etiological factors that contribute to the development of ADHD.

ADHD may be characterized by delays in brain maturation as documented by differences in brain volumes, cortical thickness, and neural connectivity. The age at which brains attain peak cortical thickness appears to be delayed in children with ADHD by approximately 3 years, with the largest difference occurring in the frontal lobes where the delay could be as long as 5 years. In short, the difference between the brains of children with ADHD and children with no disorder is one of timing as to when the brain matures.

LO 13.15 Identify efficacious treatments for ADHD.

Both pharmacological and behavioral interventions are efficacious for the treatment of ADHD, but the use of stimulants in very young children is controversial due to potential side effects such as limiting physical growth. No interventions appear to be particularly efficacious in addressing the academic impairment that is so often part of this disorder.

Critical Thinking Question

A friend in your abnormal psychology class thinks that he has ADHD, but he was never evaluated or diagnosed as a child. How could he go about collecting empirical evidence to demonstrate he had the disorder as a child?

Conduct Disorder and Oppositional Defiant Disorder

All of the disorders discussed this far in this chapter are included in the broad diagnostic category of *neurodevelopmental disorders*. Two other disorders that appear commonly in children are *conduct disorder* and *oppositional defiant disorder*. These disorders are included in a different diagnostic category called *disruptive, impulse control, and conduct disorders*. There are a number of disorders included in this diagnostic category, but we include these two disorders in this chapter as they occur in childhood. Although considered separate disorders, conduct disorder and oppositional defiant disorder are characterized by deviant, and sometimes unlawful, behaviors. They are among the most difficult disorders to treat, are the most common reason that a child is brought to a mental health clinic (Loeber et al., 2000), and often lead to incarceration in the juvenile justice system.

Defining Conduct Disorder and Oppositional Defiant Disorder

LO 13.16 Describe the behaviors that comprise conduct disorder and oppositional defiant disorder.

Conduct disorder (CD) (see "DSM-5: Conduct Disorder"), by far the more serious disorder, is a repetitive and persistent pattern of in which the basic rights of others or major age-appropriate societal norms or rules are violated (American Psychiatric Association, 2013). Behaviors fall into four different categories: aggression to people or animals, destruction of property, deceitfulness or theft, and serious rule violations.

For a diagnosis of conduct disorder, the first category, *aggression to people and animals*, includes what is commonly known as *bullying behavior*—making threats or intimidation directed toward others, such as initiating physical fights, stealing, physical cruelty or forcing someone to engage in sexual activity. Such children are also physically cruel toward people and animals. The second category is *destruction of property*, such as vandalism or deliberate fire setting. We emphasize that this is a behavioral pattern—not simply an isolated incident of property destruction, as often happens when siblings fight. The third component is *deceitfulness or theft* and includes activities such as breaking into houses or cars, lying, and nonconfrontational theft—shoplifting or forgery. The fourth component includes *serious violations of rules*, such as breaking parental curfews, running away from home overnight, and school truancy.

DSM-5

Criteria for Conduct Disorder

A. A repetitive and persistent pattern of behavior in which the basic rights of others or major age-appropriate societal norms or rules are violated, as manifested by the presence of at least three of the following 15 criteria in the past 12 months from any of the categories below, with at least one criterion present in the past 6 months:

Aggression to People and Animals

1. Often bullies, threatens, or intimidates others.
2. Often initiates physical fights.
3. Has used a weapon that can cause serious physical harm to others (e.g., a bat, brick, broken bottle, knife, gun).
4. Has been physically cruel to people.
5. Has been physically cruel to animals.
6. Has stolen while confronting a victim (e.g., mugging, purse snatching, extortion, armed robbery).
7. Has forced someone into sexual activity.

Destruction of Property

8. Has deliberately engaged in fire setting with the intention of causing serious damage.
9. Has deliberately destroyed others' property (other than by fire setting).

Deceitfulness or Theft

10. Has broken into someone else's house, building, or car.
11. Often lies to obtain goods or favors or to avoid obligations (i.e., "cons" others).
12. Has stolen items of nontrivial value without confronting a victim (e.g., shoplifting, but without breaking and entering; forgery).

Serious Violations of Rules

13. Often stays out at night despite parental prohibitions, beginning before age 13 years.
14. Has run away from home overnight at least twice while living in the parental or parental surrogate home, or once without returning for a lengthy period.
15. Is often truant from school, beginning before age 13 years.

B. The disturbance in behavior causes clinically significant impairment in social, academic, or occupational functioning.

C. If the individual is age 18 years or older, criteria are not met for antisocial personality disorder.

DSM-5

Criteria for Oppositional Defiant Disorder

A. A pattern of angry/irritable mood, argumentative/defiant behavior, or vindictiveness lasting at least 6 months as evidenced by at least four symptoms from any of the following categories, and exhibited during interaction with at least one individual who is not a sibling.

Angry/Irritable Mood

1. Often loses temper.
2. Is often touchy or easily annoyed.
3. Is often angry and resentful.

Argumentative/Defiant Behavior

4. Often argues with authority figures or, for children and adolescents, with adults.
5. Often actively defies or refuses to comply with requests from authority figures or with rules.

6. Often deliberately annoys others.
7. Often blames others for his or her mistakes or misbehavior.

Vindictiveness

8. Has been spiteful or vindictive at least twice within the past 6 months.

Note: The persistence and frequency of these behaviors should be used to distinguish a behavior that is within normal limits from a behavior that is symptomatic. For children younger than 5 years, the behavior should occur on most days for a period of at least 6 months unless otherwise noted (Criterion A8). For individuals 5 years or older, the behavior should occur at least once per week for at least 6 months, unless otherwise noted (Criterion A8). While these frequency criteria provide guidance on a minimal level of frequency to define symptoms, other factors should also be considered, such as whether the frequency and intensity of the behaviors are outside a range that is normative for the individual's developmental level, gender, and culture.

B. The disturbance in behavior is associated with distress in the individual or others in his or her immediate social context (e.g., family, peer group, work colleagues), or it impacts negatively on social, educational, occupational, or other important areas of functioning.

C. The behaviors do not occur exclusively during the course of a psychotic, substance use, depressive, or bipolar disorder. Also, the criteria are not met for disruptive mood dysregulation disorder.

Cecily is 8 years old. Her mother describes her as a "behavior problem." Specifically, Cecily often loses her temper and throws tantrums, particularly when she does not get her own way. She is not physically aggressive but argues with her parents whenever they ask her to do something and is constantly disobedient. She refused to clean up her room unless her parents gave her $10. She deliberately teases her baby brother and then laughs when he cries. Her mother describes her as spiteful. Her older sister received an award for an art project. The day after her sister brought the trophy home, it was discovered broken in half and the art project destroyed. When her mother confronted Cecily about it, Cecily blamed it on her 1-year-old brother.

Cecily's behaviors are characteristic of **oppositional defiant disorder (ODD)**, another disruptive behavior disorder (see "DSM-5: Oppositional Defiant Disorder"). ODD is a pattern or angry/irritable mood, argumentative/defiant behavior, or vindictiveness (American Psychiatric Association, 2013). It is important to understand that this is a consistent pattern of behavior and that the behavior occurs with at least one person who is not a sibling. Whereas the behaviors that are part of conduct disorder (deliberate fire setting, armed robbery, deliberate cruelty to people or animals) are inappropriate at any age, some behaviors that are part of ODD must be considered within a developmental context. For example, temper tantrums are common among 2-year-olds. However, Cecily was not 2 years old, and her temper tantrums were not simply an expression of typical toddler frustration.

The first symptoms of ODD occur during the preschool years (American Psychiatric Association, 2013), and it almost always begins before early adolescence. Unlike ADHD and conduct disorder, characterized by disruptive behaviors in several settings, it is common for children with ODD to behave negatively only at home. At their core, both of these disorders have a pattern of negative behaviors directed against people and society. We examine them together throughout the remainder of this section.

Functional Impairment

LO 13.17 Describe the functional impairments that result from conduct disorder and oppositional defiant disorder.

These disorders, and particularly CD, are associated with academic failure, substance abuse, risky sexual behavior, and criminal activities. For each child diagnosed with ODD or CD, the societal cost of these extreme behaviors ranges from $1.7 million to $2.3 million

(Petitclerc & Tremblay, 2009), and CD is responsible for a loss of 5.75 million disability-adjusted life years (Erskine et al., 2014). Many children with ODD and conduct disorder have additional disorders, and the combination negatively affects outcome. Coexisting ADHD is common in boys (Nock et al., 2006, 2007). Commonly co-occurring disorders among girls include anxiety and mood disorders, and girls with both conduct disorder and depression are at increased risk for suicidal behaviors (Keenan et al., 1999). Substance abuse is a common problem among children with conduct disorder (Keenan et al., 1999; Nock et al., 2006). For girls, conduct disorder is also associated with early pregnancy (Keenan et al., 1999). As adults, some children with either ODD or conduct disorder will have antisocial personality disorder.

In community samples, the prevalence of conduct disorder ranges from about 2 to 16% for boys and 1 to 10% for girls (Loeber et al., 2009). For ODD, prevalence estimates range from about 3 to 16% in community samples (Loeber et al., 2000). Both disorders are more prevalent among children from lower socioeconomic classes and from the worst inner-city neighborhoods (see Loeber et al., 2000). Boys are more likely to have a diagnosis of ODD than girls (13.4% vs. 9.1%, respectively, by age 16; Costello et al., 2003). Initially, conduct disorder in girls was relatively understudied because so few girls engage in physical fights. However, it is now clear that girls engage in *relational aggression*, which includes peer alienation, ostracism, manipulating social networks, circulating slanderous rumors, and character defamation (Ehrensaft, 2005; Keenan et al., 1999). When physical aggression does occur, boys target strangers and girls target family members or intimate partners (Ehrensaft, 2005). Conduct disorder is stable across time, meaning that children who are diagnosed with this condition usually do not outgrow it. Some children with ODD will develop CD, but others who initially receive a diagnosis of ODD will develop depression or anxiety disorder (Loeber et al., 2000; Rowe et al., 2010).

From a developmental perspective, some mental health clinicians have questioned whether preschool children can be diagnosed with ODD or conduct disorder. For preschoolers, some symptoms of CD are developmentally impossible (forcible sexual activity, truancy), developmentally improbable (fire setting, stealing with confrontation), or developmentally imprecise (often loses temper; Wakschlag et al., 2010). If we think about the core features of CD, there appear to be four elements: temper loss, aggression, noncompliance, and low concern for others. Using a developmental perspective, temper loss in a toddler may be displayed by crying and throwing oneself on the ground; in an adolescent, it may involve the physical assault of another person. Preschoolers do not have access to knives or guns, but they might use sticks or stones for weapons (Keenan & Wakschlag, 2002). Similarly, older children may steal cars, whereas preschool children may steal candy. Behaviors that are part of ODD and CD may change again when adolescents reach adulthood, at which time the diagnosis is antisocial personality disorder (see Chapter 12). Using this developmental perspective, it is clear that disruptive behavior disorders exist at all ages even if expressed differently at various developmental stages.

Less likely than boys to engage in physical aggression, girls with conduct problems often engage in relational aggression—such as teasing and ostracizing other girls.

Etiology

LO 13.18 Discuss the etiology of conduct disorder and oppositional defiant disorder.

Little is known about the cause of ODD because virtually all of the research on genetics, neuroanatomy, and neurochemistry has been directed at CD. Some evidence for a familial relationship between CD and adult antisocial personality disorder exists, but to date, genetic studies have not provided specific clues. Potential environmental causes include prenatal factors such as maternal smoking or substance abuse, pregnancy and birth complications, and postnatal environmental toxins such as lead. Psychological disorders in parents, poor parenting behaviors, child abuse, and socioeconomic status may also play a causal role. Any of these factors may be associated with CD or ODD, but it is highly unlikely that any one factor will be identified as important for all children with disruptive disorders (Waldman et al., 2011).

Treatment

LO 13.19 Describe the efficacious treatments for conduct disorder and oppositional defiant disorder.

Most mental health clinicians agree that psychosocial interventions should be the first line of treatment. Medication, particularly when used alone, has been unsuccessful in treating the core symptoms of ODD and conduct disorder (Bassarath, 2003) (see "Research Hot Topic: Psychiatric Medication Use in Children"). There are very few controlled treatment trials for children with ODD or CD and even fewer with samples in which the children do not also have other disorders. However, given those limitations, atypical antipsychotic drugs such as risperidone reduce symptoms of aggression in children with ODD and CD (Bassarath, 2003; Pandina et al., 2006).

Conduct problems are particularly challenging, and there are a number of interventions that have demonstrated efficacy (Powell et al., 2014). At the younger ages, interventions consist primarily of parent training approaches, although anger control training and problem-solving training may also be used. With adolescents, group interventions sometimes occur in the schools.

An effective behavioral treatment for ODD and CD is parent management training (Patterson & Gullion, 1968) (see the discussion of behavioral parent training in the section on ADHD treatment). For ODD and CD, parent management training is more efficacious than treatment as usual or no treatment (Brestan & Eyberg, 1998; Farmer et al., 2002; van den Wiel et al., 2002; Webster-Stratton et al., 1988). Particularly efficacious for preadolescent children, it may reduce criminal arrests, decrease time spent in institutions, and decrease self-reported delinquency compared with usual care or no treatment (Woolfenden et al., 2002).

A community-based intervention for ODD and CD is multisystemic therapy (MST), an intensive case-management approach to treatment (Henggeler et al., 1998). MST includes interventions conducted in the clinic, at home, at school—wherever the need exists. The choice of treatment is flexible—individual therapy, family therapy, social work interventions to assist in family functioning, and therapists always "on call" to provide needed services. MST, provided primarily to adolescent populations, is an efficacious intervention that not only decreases symptoms of conduct disorder but also decreases incarceration in both hospitals and juvenile justice settings (Henggeler et al., 1999).

Research HOT Topic

Psychiatric Medication Use in Children

Psychiatric medications comprise one of the largest groups of drugs manufactured by pharmaceutical companies. Most medications undergo rigorous development, and data are collected by controlled trials, such as those described throughout this book. Some research examines whether people can tolerate the medication and determines its most effective dose. If successful, active medication is compared with placebo to determine efficacy. In many instances, medication trials use adult samples. If approved by the Food and Drug Administration (FDA), a drug may be given to children even if it was not tested on children.

Over the past three decades, an increasing number of children have been prescribed medication for behavioral or emotional disorders. Between 1987 and 1996, total psychotropic medication use for youth increased two- to threefold, and by 1996, these medications were prescribed for children as often as for adults (Zito et al., 2003). This dramatic increase occurred even though there were still relatively few clinical data from studies of children.

Perhaps even more troubling is that medication prescriptions for preschoolers also increased dramatically between 1991 and 1995 (Zito et al., 2000). Rarely, if at all, are preschool children included in clinical trials. Some children are taking two or more medications; empirical data about the drugs are based almost exclusively on case reports and small, nonblinded trials (Safer et al., 2003). Thus, these powerful medications are being prescribed to children with few if any empirical data to back their use.

The American Academy of Child and Adolescent Psychiatry issued specific guidelines and precautions for the use of medications in children under 5 years old (American Academy of Child and Adolescent Psychiatry, 2012). Specifically, (1) the evaluation for using medication should be conducted by a clinician with specialized expertise in very young children, (2) developmental considerations for using medication in young children (such as potentially limiting growth) must be considered, (3) antipsychotic medications should be used with extreme care due to their potential serious side effects, and (4) given the very limited evidence for the use of medications in young children, developmental interventions (such as speech therapy or occupational therapy) or psychosocial interventions (e.g., behavior therapy or parent-child therapies) should be used first. Although medications may be necessary for specific behaviors (aggression in children with autism spectrum disorder), medications must be used with extreme caution in this age range.

Learning Objective Summaries

LO 13.16 Describe the behaviors that comprise conduct disorder and oppositional defiant disorder.

Conduct disorder is a persistent pattern of behavior that includes aggression to people and animals, destruction of property, deceitfulness or theft, and serious violations of rules. Oppositional defiant disorder consists of behaviors such as an angry/irritable mood, argumentative/defiant behavior, or vindictiveness.

LO 13.17 Describe the functional impairments that result from conduct disorder and oppositional defiant disorder.

Conduct disorder and ODD might be considered to be disorders of "misbehavior" and include activities such as disobedience, lying for no apparent reason, truancy, and other delinquent activities. Some children with ODD may develop conduct disorder as adolescents. Conduct disorder exists in girls but is sometimes overlooked if clinicians do not look for evidence of relational, rather than physical, aggression.

LO 13.18 Discuss the etiology of conduct disorder and oppositional defiant disorder.

Some evidence for a familial relationship between CD and adult antisocial personality disorder exists, but to date, genetic studies have not provided specific clues. Potential environmental causes for CD and ODD include prenatal factors such as maternal smoking or substance abuse, pregnancy and birth complications, and postnatal environmental toxins such as lead. Psychological disorders in parents, poor parenting behaviors, child abuse, and socioeconomic status may also play a causal role.

LO 13.19 Describe the efficacious treatments for conduct disorder and oppositional defiant disorder.

CD and ODD are very difficult disorders to treat. Behavioral and cognitive-behavioral treatments such as parent management training and problem-solving training are efficacious treatments for CD and ODD. There are very limited data for the efficacy of medications in the treatment of this disorder.

Critical Thinking Question

Boys with conduct disorder engage in physical aggression whereas girls engage in emotional aggression. Knowing what you know about biological and social factors, why do you think that these different forms of aggression might exist? Do you think that one form of aggression is more damaging than another?

Elimination Disorders

An important aspect of physical development is controlling bladder and bowel functions, which usually happens in the preschool years. Lack of control after this time may indicate the presence of enuresis or encopresis, which comprise what are known as eliminations disorders (see "DSM-5: Elimination Disorders").

DSM-5

Criteria for Elimination Disorders

Enuresis

A. Repeated voiding of urine into bed or clothes, whether involuntary or intentional.

B. The behavior is clinically significant as manifested by either a frequency of at least twice a week for at least 3 consecutive months or the presence of clinically significant distress or impairment in social, academic (occupational), or other important areas of functioning.

C. Chronological age is at least 5 years (or equivalent developmental level).

D. The behavior is not attributable to the physiological effects of a substance (e.g., a diuretic, an antipsychotic medication) or another medical condition (e.g., diabetes, spina bifida, a seizure disorder).

Encopresis

A. Repeated passage of feces into inappropriate places (e.g., clothing, floor), whether involuntary or intentional.

B. At least one such event occurs each month for at least 3 months.

C. Chronological age is at least 4 years (or equivalent developmental level).

D. The behavior is not attributable to the physiological effects of a substance (e.g., laxatives) or another medical condition except through a mechanism involving constipation.

Enuresis

LO 13.20 Describe the four types of enuresis.

Enuresis is the repeated voiding of urine into one's clothing or bedding. It may occur during the day (diurnal enuresis), at night (nocturnal enuresis), or both times (diurnal and nocturnal). *Primary* enuresis describes a condition in which a child has never achieved urinary continence (voiding urine is fully out of the child's control); *secondary* enuresis occurs if a child who was once fully continent loses that control. Primary nocturnal enuresis, or bed-wetting, is the most common form of the disorder.

Each year, approximately 15% of children with enuresis recover without treatment (Jalkut et al., 2001). Although enuresis may distress children and parents, little actual research has examined which children recover without the need for treatment. Enuresis occurs worldwide with prevalence estimates ranging from 5 to 15% for 5-year-olds, 1.5% to 5% among 9- to 10-year-olds, and 1% among people 15 years and older (American Psychiatric Association, 2013, Brown et al., 2010). Among children, boys are more likely than girls to be diagnosed with enuresis (Brown et al., 2010).

Despite many years of study, it is not clear whether children with enuresis have weaker bladders than other children (Jalkut et al., 2001). Enuresis does run in families, and it appears that there is a clear genetic component (Fritz et al., 2004). Between 30 and 40% of children with enuresis have parents who had primary nocturnal enuresis (Jalkut et al., 2001), and monozygotic twins are twice as likely to be concordant for enuresis than dizygotic twins. Multigenerational family studies have implicated areas on four different chromosomes that may hold genes contributing to the cause of enuresis (see Mikkelsen, 2001). However, psychosocial and environmental factors cannot be overlooked (Brown et al., 2010). Environmental and psychological factors that may contribute to the development of secondary enuresis include behavioral disturbances, stressful life events, and delayed achievement of initial bladder control (Eidlitz-Markus et al., 2000; Jalkut et al., 2001), suggesting that both genetic and environmental factors may be the most appropriate model for understanding the development of enuresis.

For enuresis, the most empirically supported treatment is the *enuresis alarm* (Caldwell et al., 2013; Mikkelsen, 2001), initially known as the *bell-and-pad* method when it was introduced in 1902 (Pander cited in Jalkut et al., 2001). The system consists of a battery-operated alarm or vibrator that is connected to a thin wire attached to the child's underwear, sleeping pad, or bedding. When urination begins, the alarm awakens the child, who then goes to the toilet. Over time, the child becomes sensitized to the sensations of a full bladder and awakens before urination. The average success rate for enuresis alarms, defined as 14 consecutive dry nights, is 65% (Butler & Gasson, 2005), but the average relapse rate is 42%. Relapse rates are higher when the intervention is short (less than 7 weeks).

Currently, the most common medication for enuresis is desmopressin acetate (DDAVP), which reduces nighttime urinary output and the number of enuretic episodes. Tricyclics (amitriptyline and desipramine) are also used. Although they appear effective when compared with placebo, the reduction in enuretic episodes varies greatly, the medications are less efficacious than bed-wetting alarms, and only a small percentage continue to "stay dry" once the medication is withdrawn (Caldwell et al., 2016; Fritz et al., 2004).

Encopresis

LO 13.21 Describe the social consequences of encopresis.

Jake is 7 years old. He lives with his parents and a 3-year-old brother. He soils his underwear one or two times per day, always during the daytime. Jake refuses to sit on the toilet, and he shows other oppositional behaviors as well. He interacts well with his peers and is a good student. Jake has been soiling for more than 4 years. He was never adequately toilet trained and describes defecation as very painful. He does not change his soiled underwear unless he is told to do so. There are no behavioral consequences for soiling; as a matter of fact, his mother leaves a stack of his clean underwear in the bathroom. His father tries to pressure Jake to use the toilet.

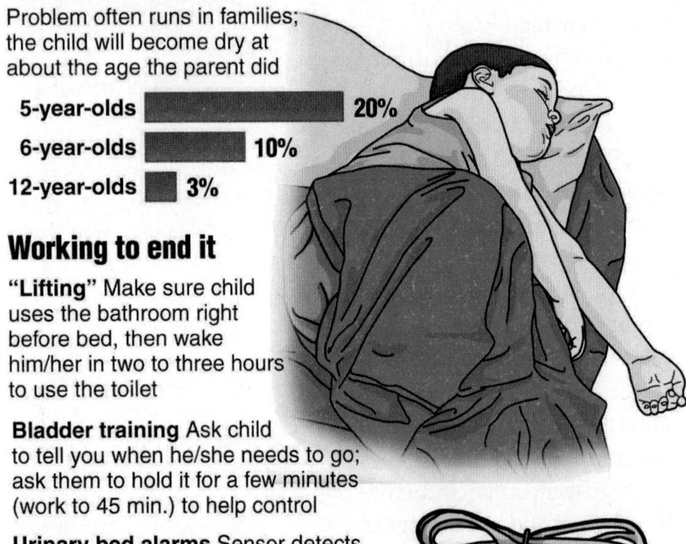

An alarm device is often used in the treatment of enuresis. A moisture sensor is attached to the child's underwear and detects moisture, triggering an alarm that awakens the child to get up and use the toilet.

Encopresis is the repeated passage of feces on or into inappropriate places, whether voluntary or intentional, by someone over age 4 (see "DSM-5 Elimination Disorders"). Encopresis can be intentional or accidental and, like enuresis, may be primary or secondary.

Children with encopresis often feel ashamed and avoid social interaction. They may be ostracized by peers and be the target of anger, punishment, and rejection by others including family (American Psychiatric Association, 2013). Compared with children with no disorder, children with encopresis had higher parent and teacher ratings of anxiety, depression, and behavioral problems, but only 20% had significant functional impairment or substantial distress (Cox et al., 2002). About 1% of 5-year-old children suffer from encopresis (American Psychiatric Association, 2013), but they account for 3% of all pediatric appointments and 25% of pediatric gastroenterology appointments (Brooks et al., 2000). Among children, boys are more likely than girls to be diagnosed with encopresis (American Psychiatric Association, 2013).

The etiology of encopresis is rarely studied. About 80% of children with encopresis have chronic constipation, and in 90% of all cases of chronic constipation, there is no obvious medical or functional cause (Issenman et al., 1999; van Dijk et al., 2007). Encopresis is often the result of withholding the stool, perhaps as a result of previous painful defecation experiences or extremely hard stools. This leads to chronic constipation and subsequent involuntary leakage of feces as a result of stool impaction (van Dijk et al., 2007).

Medical treatment for encopresis consists of enemas to clear the bowel and laxatives to deal with constipation. However, this intervention is usually considered to be only the first stage and is followed by behavioral interventions to "promote proper toileting behavior" (daily toilet sitting and use of positive reinforcement). The medical-behavioral intervention is superior to medical treatment alone (Brazzelli et al., 2011; Brooks et al., 2000), with improvement rates ranging from 65 to 78% (Borowitz et al., 2002; Cox et al., 1998).

Learning Objective Summaries

LO 13.20 Describe the four types of enuresis.

Enuresis is the repeated voiding of urine into one's clothing or bedding. It may occur during the day (diurnal enuresis), at night (nocturnal enuresis), or both times (diurnal and nocturnal). Children with primary enuresis have never achieved urinary control, whereas secondary enuresis describes children who were once fully continent but have lost that control.

LO 13.21 Describe the social consequences of encopresis.

Encopresis, the repeated passage of feces on or into inappropriate places by someone over age 4, can be intentional or accidental. Children with encopresis often feel ashamed and avoid social interaction, and they may be ostracized by peers. They may be the target of anger, punishment, and rejection by others including family.

Critical Thinking Question

Your friend's 5-year-old little brother has primary nocturnal enuresis. After reading this chapter, she approaches you and asks if she should talk to her parents about taking him to a psychologist. What would you advise knowing what you know about biological development? How would your advice change if the little brother was 10 years old? What if he was 15 years old?

Real SCIENCE Real LIFE

Danny—The Treatment of Social Anxiety Disorder and Autism Spectrum Disorder

THE PATIENT

Danny is 12 years old. He lives with his two older brothers and his parents. From birth, Danny's mother described him as "different." He would not cuddle with her. If someone tried to hold him, he would arch his back and twist away. He is very smart and does well in school, but he has no friends and is often sad. Although he claims that he wants to be left alone, he has tears in his eyes when he says it. At recess, he stands away from the other children but watches them intently.

THE PROBLEM

Danny has a complicated developmental history. He appears to be anxious, has some difficulty paying attention, and is socially awkward. At age 8, he was diagnosed with ADHD and severe depression for which he was treated with medication. The medication for depression seemed to help, but the medication for ADHD was ineffective. He has difficulty writing, and he sometimes shows a lack of awareness of dangerous situations. He appears incredibly anxious around people. His mother began to worry that Danny was different when he was in first grade. By the time he was in third grade, she was convinced that he was different. She brought him at age 12 to the clinic for a thorough evaluation and treatment recommendations.

Danny agreed with his mother's report of his behavior but added that he would really like to have friends but no one wanted to be friends with him. On a self-report measure of social anxiety, Danny scored in the "definite social anxiety disorder" range. He described feeling anxious when someone talked to him or he tried to talk to someone else. The interviewer noted that Danny made little eye contact during the interview and spoke in a very monotonic voice. At the time of the assessment, he was not depressed and he did not display any behaviors consistent with ADHD.

ASSESSING THE SITUATION

First, how would you explain the etiology of this disorder to Danny's parents? How did it develop? Second, how would you treat it? Design a plan to help Danny. What changes can you hope to make?

THE TREATMENT

The clinician administered a structured diagnostic interview that revealed the following: Danny's problems started when he was about 2 years old. He had achieved all of his developmental milestones (walking, talking, bladder and bowel control) at the typical ages. His difficulties appeared to be in the social realm. He is reluctant to make eye contact, rarely smiles at people, has little understanding of jokes or sarcasm, has no friends, and needs constant reminders to "use his manners." He also develops obsessions with certain activities—science and solar systems, steam pipes, and video games. He does not like to be touched even by his parents and is extremely sensitive to sound.

Danny was diagnosed with autism spectrum disorder and social anxiety disorder.

Danny participated in a social skills training group that consisted of four boys, all of whom were diagnosed with autism spectrum disorder. The group met once per week for 12 weeks, and the topics included initiating, maintaining, and ending a conversation; skills for joining groups; giving and receiving compliments; refusing unreasonable requests; asking others to change their behavior; and using the telephone. In addition to learning this verbal content, the group therapist worked with Danny on making eye contact and varying his vocal tone. After each group meeting, the boys met for an hour with four peer helpers (boys who were friendly and outgoing) who had agreed to participate in the activities and work with the boys. All of the boys went to an activity (miniature golf, bowling, pizza parlors), and Danny was encouraged to practice that day's social skill with the peers. He was also given a homework assignment each week that was geared to the content of the group activity. For example, if the group had practiced introducing oneself to another person, Danny's homework was to introduce himself to one new person every day. At the end of 12 weeks, Danny's social skills were reassessed. He had learned many of the skills necessary to make friends. His mom reported that he still had fewer friends than most boys but he had made two new friends since joining the group. His score on the self-report measure of social anxiety had decreased from the "definite social anxiety disorder" range to the "possible social anxiety disorder" range. Danny told the interviewer that he had learned some skills but was too nervous to try them out.

THE TREATMENT PROGRESS

Because he was still anxious and avoided social interactions, the therapist decided to conduct exposure therapy with Danny to address his social anxiety. The therapist, Danny, and his mother identified three anxiety-provoking situations: asking others questions, talking on the telephone, and having conversations with peers. In order for Danny to practice asking questions, he was given a survey task. Accompanied by the therapist, he was taken to a crowded environment and instructed to approach people, asking them to complete a short survey (topic depended upon the environment). With respect to the telephone, Danny first practiced calling stores and requesting information. Later he called family and classmates to ask questions and carry on a conversation (the last step on the hierarchy). Because exposure therapy is designed to eliminate anxiety, Danny remained in the situation, continuing the task, until he could do it without any distress. Furthermore, he did not move to the next task until he was able to perform the previous task without any initial distress.

THE TREATMENT OUTCOME

After 10 sessions, Danny's mother reported that she observed Danny playing at recess and initiating conversations at the bus stop. In addition, he now maintained conversations with his grandparents and visiting relatives. He had been invited to a friend's house for a sleepover for the first time in his life. She reported that he had hugged her and his friend's mother for the first time. Danny reported that he was not shy anymore, and this was supported by his score on the self-report inventory, which was now in the "no social anxiety disorder" range.

It is important to note that this treatment addressed Danny's social interactions by increasing his social skills and decreasing his anxiety. Danny still met criteria for autism spectrum disorder based on other behaviors—he could still become fixated on unusual activities and topics, had great difficulty writing, had difficulty understanding humor and sarcasm, and did not always enjoy physical contact with others.

Key Terms

Chapter 14
Aging and Neurocognitive Disorders

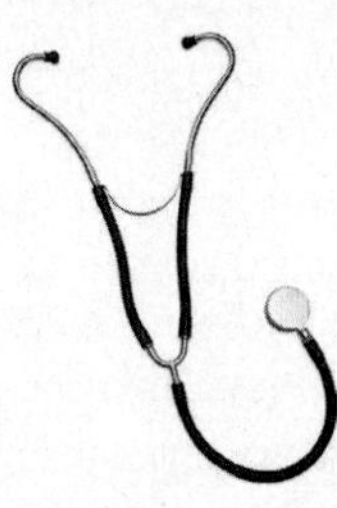

Chapter Learning Objectives

Symptoms and Disorders of Aging	**LO 14.1**	Recognize geropsychology as an important area of psychological research and practice.
	LO 14.2	Describe variables that predict successful aging.
	LO 14.3	Understand the ways in which aging may affect the expression and treatment of psychological symptoms and disorders in older adults.
Depression and Bipolar Disorder	**LO 14.4**	Explain the unique characteristics of depression and bipolar disorder in older adults.
	LO 14.5	Describe the prevalence rates and impact of depression and bipolar disorder in older adults with attention to differences related to age, race, and ethnicity.

	LO 14.6	Recognize the potential causes of depression in later life.
	LO 14.7	Describe different treatment approaches for older adults with depression and bipolar disorder.
Anxiety Disorders	**LO 14.8**	Understand symptoms of anxiety that are common for older adults and how these differ from anxiety in younger people.
	LO 14.9	Describe the prevalence and impact of anxiety disorders among older adults with attention to differences related to sex, race, and ethnicity.
	LO 14.10	Describe patterns of onset and potential causes of anxiety in later life.
	LO 14.11	Summarize pharmacological and psychosocial treatments that can be used to treat anxiety in older people.
Substance-Related Disorders and Psychosis	**LO 14.12**	Understand differences in the symptoms of substance use disorders in older and younger adults.
	LO 14.13	Describe the prevalence and impact of substance use disorders with particular attention to gender differences.
	LO 14.14	Summarize etiological factors and treatment models for substance use disorders in later life.
	LO 14.15	Understand differences in the symptoms of psychosis for older and younger adults.
	LO 14.16	Describe the prevalence of psychosis in older adults and differences due to sex, race, and ethnicity.
	LO 14.17	Summarize possible causes of and strategies for treating psychosis in older adults.
Neurocognitive Disorders	**LO 14.18**	Describe the symptoms and prevalence of delirium in older adults.
	LO 14.19	Understand the possible causes of and treatments for delirium.
	LO 14.20	Understand the symptoms of major and mild neurocognitive disorders (NCDs).
	LO 14.21	Summarize potential biological and nonbiological factors that may play a role in the onset of NCD.
	LO 14.22	Discuss pharmacological and psychological treatment strategies for major and minor NCDs.

Richard was born in 1933. His father died when he was 8, and things became very difficult for him and his mother. She had to work hard as a seamstress to make ends meet, and as a young teenager, Richard started to deliver newspapers to help with the finances. He felt sad and lonely much of the time but didn't want to let his mother know because she was working so hard and did not need another worry. Richard thought a lot about his father; he didn't understand why God had taken him away from their family. It just didn't make sense.

As he grew older, Richard never really lost his sense of loss or sadness, but he did notice that when he worked hard at school or a job, he didn't notice the sadness so much. So he worked even harder and earned a scholarship to college. His grades there were excellent, and he decided to go to medical school. While he was working as an intern, he met and married a lovely woman named Claire. Richard and Claire wanted to start a family, but it took a long time for Claire to conceive. When she finally did, Richard thought maybe he would again be able to feel happiness. However, the baby was stillborn, and Claire's next pregnancy ended in a miscarriage. They decided not to try again. It was just too painful. Richard threw himself into his work even more. He worked 12-hour days in his orthopedic practice, filling his time with patients, reading, and teaching. He and his wife did pleasant things during his off hours, and they had an agreeable relationship, but he just never felt happy. As Richard approached 65 years of age, he knew it was time to retire. He dreaded life without work, but it was time.

Soon after Richard stopped working, he began to feel lost. He didn't have any hobbies, and he had never taken time to make friends outside of work. Claire was busy with her volunteer and church activities, but Richard had never been able to join her at church because he just didn't believe there was a God. Too many bad things had happened to him, and there was so much suffering in the world. As the days passed, Richard tried to find things to occupy his time, but nothing was fun. He started having trouble sleeping, and his stomach hurt all the time. He had no appetite and began losing weight. He started spending most days in the house, watching TV and ruminating about his past and all the suffering in the world. Claire tried to get him to go out with her, but he was too despondent. He couldn't concentrate long enough to have a conversation, and he couldn't remember details of what he and others talked about. He had trouble remembering people's names, and he just didn't have the energy to meet new people.

Despite what many people believe, feeling sad is not a normal part of aging. Many adults do experience psychological symptoms and cognitive decline as they age, but older adults may experience and express psychological symptoms differently from younger adults in part because of the physical, cognitive, and social changes that accompany aging. Understanding the issues that are unique to aging helps clinicians identify and treat the psychological problems associated with old age.

The population of older adults in the United States is increasing rapidly (see Figure 14.1). As the baby boom generation (those born between 1945 and 1964) continues to age, this trend will accelerate. In 2000, there were 35 million adults age 65 and older in the United States, representing 16% of the population. By 2030, this figure is expected to reach 70 million (http://www.aoa.gov/Aging_Statistics/future_growth/future_growth.aspx#age), or 25% of the population (see Figure 14.1). With so many older adults in our society and the number increasing rapidly, we need to understand well the issues that confront older people. As we age, changes occur in our physical functioning (more medical problems, decreased sensory capacity), social functioning (retirement, reduced social networks as friends and family face health challenges), and cognitive abilities (changes in attention, learning, and memory). All of these are important factors that provide a unique sociocultural context in which to understand abnormal behavior in older adults.

Figure 14.1 Aging Population.

The size of the older adult population is increasing dramatically, and this trend is expected to continue over the next 30+ years.

SOURCE: http://www.aoa.gov/Aging_Statistics/future_growth/future_growth.aspx#age

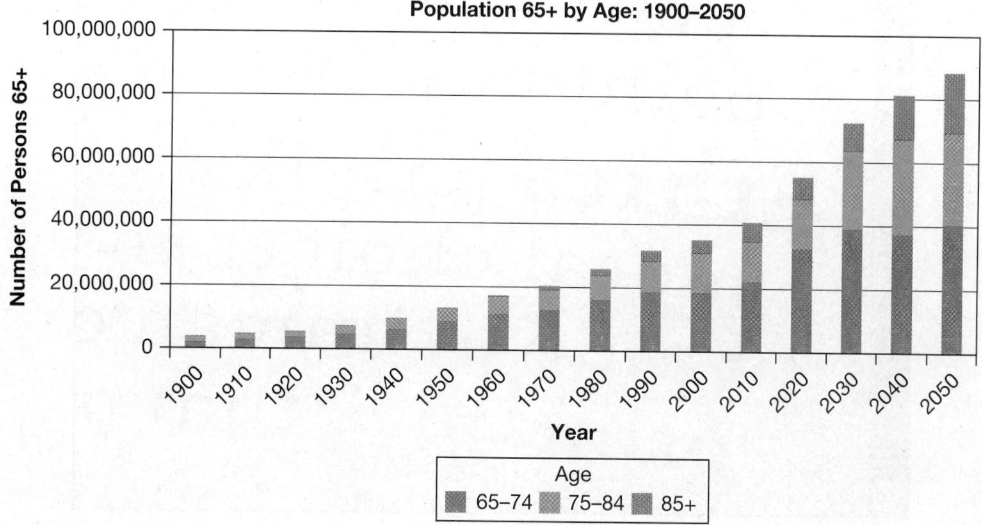

Although the older population is growing rapidly, the number of health professionals available who specialize in geriatric care lags far behind.

Symptoms and Disorders of Aging

Geropsychology as a Unique Field

LO 14.1 Recognize geropsychology as an important area of psychological research and practice.

Geropsychology is a subdiscipline of psychology that addresses issues of aging with particular attention to patterns of normal development, individual differences, and psychological problems that are unique to older persons (usually those age 65 and older). Childhood has long been recognized as a developmental stage with unique challenges, and children experience and express psychological symptoms in unique ways. Geropsychology expands this developmental approach to include the challenges and psychological symptoms older adults face, such as physical changes, lifestyle shifts, and role changes.

The field of geropsychology is expanding rapidly with increasing numbers of professional organizations and training programs that focus on providing services to meet the needs of older people (Qualls et al., 2005). Research efforts are also increasing as we strive to understand patterns of typical late-life development, unique problems that older adults experience, and strategies for improving their quality of life. Nevertheless, tremendous gaps still exist in our knowledge of psychological symptoms and disorders among older people and in our ability to identify and treat them. Furthermore, the number of researchers, educators, and health care professionals with specialized training and expertise in geriatrics is insufficient to meet the needs of this growing segment of our society. In keeping with the developmental focus of this book, we hope to identify some of the unique ways in which psychological problems affect people in the later decades of life.

ETHICS AND RESPONSIBILITY Most psychologists who provide clinical services see older people, but many training programs do not provide sufficient education and experience in geropsychology. The American Psychological Association has published a set of guidelines to help psychologists evaluate their competence to provide care for older adults (American Psychological Association, 2014). The guidelines suggest that psychologists

Explore ETHICS AND RESPONSIBILITY

Interactive

work within their areas of competence and seek consultation or additional training when needed. Psychologists working with older adults are encouraged to have knowledge of the aging process, the nature of cognitive and psychological problems among older people, and the assessment tools and treatment procedures specific to working with older adults. The importance of interfacing with other disciplines (e.g., medicine, social work) is also emphasized as a means of providing comprehensive care. Working with older patients requires adequate knowledge and training for ethical practice.

Successful Aging

LO 14.2 Describe variables that predict successful aging.

> Leonard is the picture of successful aging. He is 86 and lives alone in the house where he has lived for the past 50 years. Leonard retired many years ago, but he continues to spend time in his home office every day. He checks the Internet to keep up with current events, maintains e-mail contact with friends and college classmates, and writes a regular column for the alumni magazine. Leonard is also active in a number of civic organizations, takes a nap every day, and enjoys a cocktail before dinner. When his wife died 2 years ago, Leonard was sad, but he began to spend more time with friends and neighbors, inviting them to his home for afternoon visits. Over time, his home became a center for neighborhood socializing. The neighbors listen to his stories about life during the Korean War, enjoying his sense of humor and positive attitude. Leonard also continues to take a short walk each evening. Although he can't go very far now that his hip hurts, he always has a smile for any neighbor who is passing by. Leonard's optimism about life is infectious; his neighbors often remark that he is more energetic and positive than they are although many are 50 years younger. Leonard has some "rules" for aging well. A few of these include (1) use your brain every day, (2) stay active, (3) socialize with younger people, and (4) entertain younger ideas.

Although Leonard is not a psychologist, his philosophy and lifestyle reflect much of what is known about *successful aging*. Approximately one-third of older adults are judged to be aging successfully (Depp & Jeste, 2006), although rates are higher when people are asked to rate themselves (subjective successful aging) than when criteria are more objective (Jeste et al., 2010). Despite the use of 29 different definitions of successful aging in 28 studies (Depp & Jeste, 2006), common themes of successful aging include perceived good health and an active lifestyle, freedom from disability, continued independence in functioning, absence of cognitive impairment, and positive social relationships (Blazer, 2006; Phelan & Larson, 2002). One theory of positive aging is known as the *selective optimization and compensation* model (Grove et al., 2009). This model suggests that people age more successfully when they modify their goals and choices to make best use of their personal characteristics. These adjustments often require compensating for age-related limitations that reduce one's ability to reach previously valued goals.

> Max is an aging fisherman who used to be out on a boat every weekend. He can't fish any longer, but he can spend time reading magazines about fishing, watching television shows about fishing, and trading old fishing stories with his buddies at the local coffee shop.

Leonard also made choices that make the most of his ability to engage in rewarding activities and optimize his social, mental, and physical functioning.

Psychological Symptoms and Disorders Among Older People

LO 14.3 Understand the ways in which aging may affect the expression and treatment of psychological symptoms and disorders in older adults.

In the United States, 14 to 20% of older adults living in the community have a mental health or substance use condition (Institute of Medicine [IOM], 2012). Even more have significant problems that do not meet the diagnostic criteria for a psychological disorder but nonetheless create unnecessary distress, reduced functional ability, and poor quality of life. The prevalence of psychological symptoms and disorders is even higher in treatment settings such as hospitals, nursing homes, and home health care (Hybels & Blazer, 2015) and among patients with chronic medical illness (Kunik et al., 2005). The personal and societal costs associated with psychological symptoms in older people are high, and simply not enough appropriately trained professionals are available to help (Bartels & Smyer, 2002; IOM, 2012).

Many older adults with psychological problems never receive treatment. This issue is a particular problem among racial and ethnic minorities, many of whom live in underserved, low-income communities (Bao et al., 2011; Joo et al., 2010). Many older people with psychological symptoms do not seek treatment because they fear that others will think they are "crazy" (stigma), they lack sufficient resources (e.g., money, ability to find a therapist), or they experience logistical limitations (e.g., inability to drive to the clinician's office). Those who do seek help may approach a religious leader or make an appointment with their physician instead of pursuing specialized mental health care. Even in a medical setting, however, many psychological symptoms and disorders go unrecognized. Additionally, when problems are identified, treatment is often inadequate (Roundy et al., 2005). One reason for inadequate recognition and treatment in a medical clinic is the limited time that physicians now spend with patients during office visits, resulting in insufficient time for assessing and treating mental health problems. **Ageism**, however, is an equally serious issue. Many older adults and their doctors still consider psychological distress to be a normal part of aging and therefore not something that requires treatment. Reactions such as the following are common:

- Of course you feel down. You were recently diagnosed with a serious heart condition. It is normal for you to feel less energetic.
- I also would feel anxious if I had been forced to retire and didn't have enough money to support my wife and myself into older age. Who wouldn't be anxious in this situation?
- Oh, yes, I understand your concerns about your memory—I lose things all the time!

About one-third of older adults continue to experience good health and active lives in their later years. Successful aging is encouraged by positive social relationships and continuing mental activity.

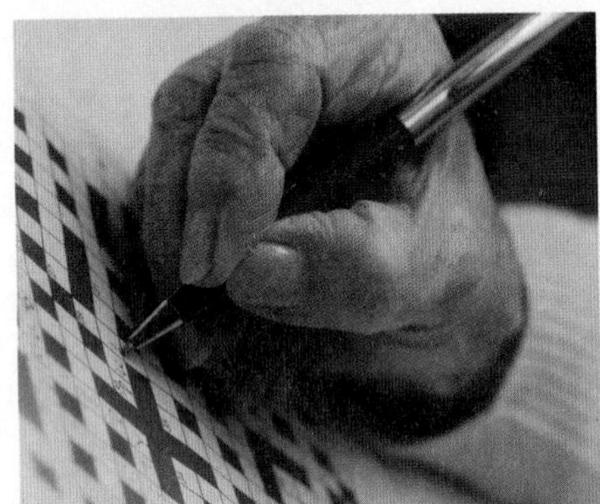

These comments ignore the fact that psychological symptoms and disorders are *not* a normal part of aging. Many emotional disorders experienced by older adults are treatable, and even when the progressive, neurobiological disorders associated with aging cannot be reversed (e.g., major neurocognitive disorder due to Alzheimer's disease or Parkinson's disease), quality of life can be improved.

Although it is commonly recognized that psychological symptoms are often different for adults and children, only recently have clinicians and researchers begun to understand how aging also may affect the kinds of psychological symptoms that adults experience and report. Older adults often report less negative mood and distress than younger adults (Goldberg et al., 2003), and prevalence rates for DSM-based disorders are lower in older than younger people (Reynolds et al., 2015). It is not entirely clear, however, whether these differences reflect distinctive experiences or simply different ways that people describe or express their moods. In Chapter 4, for example, we noted that boys and girls differ in how much fear they *express*, not how much fear they *experience*. Similarly, older adults often focus more on physical symptoms than on psychological symptoms of distress, and this may be another reason why they seek treatment from primary care physicians rather than mental health clinicians.

> Glenda denied feeling anxious but reported that her back and neck muscles were tight all the time, so much so that they hurt. She wasn't able to sit comfortably for long periods anymore, and her stomach "acted up" frequently when stressful events occurred. She was hoping for some help to decrease her muscle pain and reduce her indigestion and occasional diarrhea.

Focusing on physical symptoms complicates the identification of psychological disorders in older people, particularly for primary care physicians who are less experienced in this area. The increase in medical problems as people age further complicates the diagnostic challenge. Many medical diseases and treatments create symptoms that mimic psychological disorders. For example, symptoms of diabetes include weight loss and lethargy, which are common symptoms of depression, and chronic obstructive pulmonary disease causes breathing difficulties that are also associated with anxiety. Even a seemingly harmless medication like a decongestant can cause nervousness, sleeplessness, and increased blood pressure or heart rate, which also are symptoms of anxiety. When older adults have both medical and psychological difficulties, recognizing psychological problems is a huge challenge.

Although psychological difficulties in older age are often thought to be mainly cognitive (e.g., dementia, now known as major neurocognitive disorder), many of the disorders that older people face are the same ones that affect younger people, such as depression, anxiety, and substance abuse (Hybels et al., 2009). Within each category of difficulties experienced by older people, understanding normal age-related changes in physical, social, and cognitive functioning enables us to provide a developmental context for evaluating these disorders. As with other age groups, *comorbidity* (multiple disorders occurring together) also occurs.

Learning Objective Summaries

LO 14.1 Recognize geropsychology as an important area of psychological research and practice.

Geropsychology is a subdiscipline of psychology that addresses issues of aging. Given the rapidly growing population of older adults, more psychologists with experience in this area are needed. To practice or conduct research with older people, a psychologist needs to have specific training in geropsychology.

LO 14.2 Describe variables that predict successful aging.

Successful aging is associated with perceptions of good health, an active lifestyle, continued independence in functioning, lack of disability, absence of cognitive impairment, and positive social relationships. Older people age more successfully when they adapt their goals and choices to age-related changes and limitations.

LO 14.3 Understand the ways in which aging may affect the expression and treatment of psychological symptoms and disorders in older adults.

Older and younger adults experience and/or describe psychological symptoms in different ways. These symptoms also are often unrecognized and untreated among older people, particularly racial and ethnic minorities, because of perceived stigma, lack of resources, and logistic limitations. Comorbid medical problems also complicate the ability to recognize psychological symptoms among older people.

Critical Thinking Question

You are a geropsychologist who wants to improve the recognition of psychological symptoms among older patients in a primary care clinic. Given the differences in experience and expression of symptoms among older people, what strategies might you use to improve recognition?

Depression and Bipolar Disorder

Symptoms of Depression and Bipolar Disorder in Older Adults

LO 14.4 Explain the unique characteristics of depression and bipolar disorder in older adults.

Aging is associated with various types of losses (e.g., death of a loved one, changes in job or financial status, deterioration in physical abilities) and uncertainty about the future (e.g., ability to retain independence, future changes in health status, death). It should not be surprising, then, that depression is one of the most common psychological problems that older adults face. However, depression is not a natural consequence of aging.

Pat devoted her life to being a wife and mother. She raised five children and supported her husband through a very busy career. When Bob retired 3 years ago, Pat expected to spend the rest of her life traveling with him and visiting her children and grandchildren who lived across the country. However, Bob died suddenly of a heart attack just 6 months after he retired. Pat felt lost. She had no one with whom to share her thoughts. Her friends, whose husbands were still living, called less often. When she did go out with them, she felt like a "fifth wheel." She traveled alone to see her children and their families, and that wasn't enjoyable either. Pat found herself feeling apathetic about life in general, but she didn't know why. She cried more often, and she had trouble concentrating even when she was watching what used to be a favorite television show. She also had new medical symptoms—her heart pounded often, and she felt full and bloated even when she ate small amounts of food. Pat had lost some weight and was tired most of the time, but she had trouble staying asleep throughout the night. Her family thought she ought to get more involved in the church, but she just didn't have the energy. Her daughter thought she was depressed, but Pat knew she wasn't crazy. She was just getting older and adjusting to life as a widow.

Most depressive and bipolar disorders are diagnosed in older and younger adults using the same criteria. However, as Pat's case illustrates, older adults are often reluctant to acknowledge psychological symptoms, not wanting to be viewed as "crazy," and they focus on different symptoms than younger people. Older adults more often report increased physical symptoms (e.g., fatigue, appetite loss), sleep difficulties, and cognitive problems (e.g., memory and concentration) and fewer emotional symptoms (e.g., worthlessness, guilt) than younger adults (DiNapoli & Scogin, 2014). Overlapping symptoms of depression

Watch SAMHSA TREATMENT OF DEPRESSION IN OLDER ADULTS | EVIDENCE-BASED PRACTICES

and common medical illnesses in older adults also complicate the recognition and diagnosis of depression, as do associated cognitive difficulties that include problems with attention, speed of information processing, and **executive dysfunction** (difficulty planning, thinking abstractly, initiating and inhibiting actions, etc.). These cognitive symptoms of depression can occur even when a major or mild neurocognitive disorder (see "Neurocognitive Disorders") is not present (Kindermann et al., 2001; Lockwood et al., 2000). In fact, older adults with depression can sometimes appear to have a major neurocognitive disorder that actually resolves after appropriate treatment for depression.

Medical disorders can also produce depressive disorders that are unique to older adults. For example, *depressive disorder due to another medical condition* can be diagnosed in the context of cerebrovascular disease (disease of the arteries that supply blood to the brain). This type of depression, which has been referred to as **vascular depression** or **depression executive dysfunction syndrome of late life**, includes increased difficulties with language (e.g., speaking fluently, naming objects), increased apathy and slowed movements, and less agitation and guilt than other forms of depression (Alexopoulos, 2004). Depression that occurs among people with major neurocognitive disorder due to Alzheimer's disease also is associated with unique symptoms, including increased irritability and social isolation (Olin et al., 2002).

The possibility of suicide associated with major depressive disorder is a particular concern for older people (Conwell et al., 2011). Suicide rates increase dramatically with age (Figure 14.2), although patterns vary significantly as a result of gender and race. Both black and white women show decreasing rates of suicide from midlife to older adulthood (Conwell et al., 2011), although as is the case for younger adults, women have higher rates of suicide attempts than men (Alexopoulos, 2004). White men are at highest risk for completing suicide, although black men also show a peak in suicide during later life (Conwell et al., 2011). Most older adults who commit suicide have seen their physician within 1 month of their death (Luoma et al., 2002), suggesting that many suicides might be preventable.

Figure 14.2 Suicide Rate by Gender, Age, and Race.

Suicide rates vary significantly with gender, age, and race. White men are at highest risk for completing suicide, although black men also show a peak in suicide during later life.

SOURCE: Conwell, Y., Van Orden, K., & Caine, E.D. (2011). Suicide in older adults. *Psychiatric Clinics of North America, 34*(2), 451–468. Figure 1.

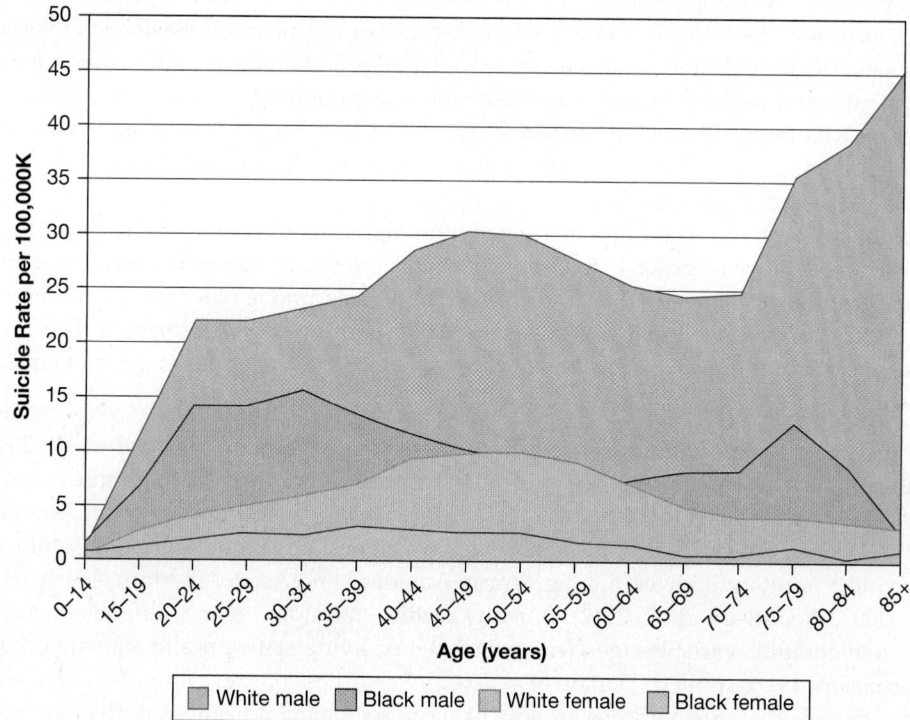

Risk factors for suicide in older people overlap with those in younger adults and include depression and another DSM disorder, financial problems, poor medical health, cognitive difficulties, and reduced social connectedness (Alexopoulos, 2004; Conwell et al., 2011).

Few adults develop mania or bipolar disorder after the age of 65. Many adults who do show initial signs of bipolar disorder in later life have a history of major depressive disorder. Similarly, older people who have manic symptoms later in life may have had elements of the disorder earlier in life (Keck et al., 2001). When bipolar disorder occurs in older adults, the intervals between manic and depressive shifts are shorter and the episode duration is longer relative to younger people (Keck et al., 2001). Late-onset bipolar disorder also is associated with increased risk for neurological abnormalities, mortality, and psychotic symptoms (Beyer, 2015; Ceglowski et al., 2014).

Prevalence and Impact

LO 14.5 Describe the prevalence rates and impact of depression and bipolar disorder in older adults with attention to differences related to sex, race, and ethnicity.

In the general population, major depressive disorder affects 3 to 4% of older adults, and persistent depressive disorder (dysthymia) occurs in 0.6 to 1.6% of older people (Byers et al., 2010; IOM, 2012). These percentages are lower than those found among younger adults, possibly due to different experience and expression of symptoms, although as many as 25% of older people have depressive symptoms that fail to meet diagnostic criteria but can still create significant distress and impairment (Hybels et al., 2009). Depressive disorders and symptoms are also more common in medical settings (Kunik et al., 2005) and among older adults who are homebound (Bruce et al., 2002) or have cognitive impairment (Alexopoulos, 2004). In these populations, the prevalence of major depressive disorder is as high as 14%, and about half of the people have clinically significant depressive symptoms.

The prevalence of bipolar disorder among older adults ranges from 0.08 to 0.9% (Beyer, 2015; Byers et al., 2010; IOM, 2012). As is the case for depressive disorders, these general figures are lower than among younger adults, but the disorder is more common among older adults in residential and hospital settings (Beyer, 2015).

Bipolar and depressive disorders and symptoms can affect daily functioning and even survival in older adults, much as they do in younger adults. Consider two older adults with the same medical condition, one of whom also has major depressive disorder and the other of whom does not. The patient with both a medical disorder and major depressive disorder has an increased risk of death and not simply because of the increased likelihood of suicide. Depression significantly affects the outcomes of medical conditions. People with major depressive disorder and medical illness recover less well, use more health care services, and create higher costs for the health care system (Prina et al., 2012). Late-life depression also is associated with decreased quality of life, poorer physical and social functioning, and increased cognitive difficulties (DiNapoli & Scogin, 2014).

Bipolar disorder in later life is associated with high rates of comorbid substance abuse, major neurocognitive disorder, PTSD, and anxiety disorder as well as increased rates of medical and neurological illnesses (Beyer, 2015). Mortality rates among older adults with bipolar disorder also are elevated and perhaps even higher than among older people with major depressive disorder (Beyer, 2015), although the reason for the higher rate is not yet known.

SEX, RACE, AND ETHNICITY As is the case for younger adults, depressive disorders among older people occur more often in women than in men (Woodward et al., 2012). But in contrast to younger adults, depressive symptoms and disorders are more common among Hispanic older adults, particularly those who are least acculturated in American society (González et al., 2001). Prevalence rates are highest among non-Hispanic white and Latino older adults and lowest among African American and Asian American elderly (Ford et al., 2007; Woodward et al., 2012). In many studies, racial and ethnic differences change when demographic variables (gender, marital status, living status, health status) and economic factors are controlled (Dunlop et al., 2003). Regardless of prevalence, however, older Hispanics and African Americans are less likely to seek mental health care than are older whites (Alvidrez et al., 2005; Blazer et al., 2000). As noted earlier, suicide rates in older populations are highest among white men (Conwell et al., 2011). African American and Hispanic adults have lower rates of suicide than whites. Rates of suicide among Asian adults (Japanese, Chinese, and Korean Americans) increase with age and are comparable to those of whites (Sakauye, 2004). Asian American and white older adults also report elevated levels of suicidal ideation relative to African American older people (Bartels et al., 2002).

With increasing age come increasing challenges for older adults. Friends pass away and children move to distant cities, potentially creating an environment that can lead to loneliness and depression.

Etiology of Depression in Later Life

LO 14.6 Recognize the potential causes of depression in later life.

Depressive disorders in late life appear to have causes much like those in younger people. In many cases, late-life depression simply reflects the persistence or recurrence of an earlier episode. However, it is important to identify the original age of onset for depressive disorders (early versus late) because this may have treatment implications (McMahon, 2004). Older adults with *early-onset depression* (typically defined as onset before age 35 or 45) more often have a family history of depression, probably reflecting the genetic contributions discussed in Chapter 6 (Alexopoulos, 2004). In contrast, people with *late-onset depression* are more likely to have coexistent cognitive impairment and more evidence of brain abnormalities, suggesting the presence of brain deterioration (Alexopoulos, 2004). Late-onset depression seems to occur more often in the context of vascular, neurological, or other physical diseases that are associated with genetic causes, such as Parkinson's disease, cerebrovascular disease, and Alzheimer's disease. For those with late-onset depression, symptoms of depressive disorders sometimes precede diagnosis of the medical condition by months or years (McMahon, 2004).

Researchers are examining the role of specific genetic factors in the emergence of late-life depression, although genetic factors appear to play a weaker role than for depression in earlier adulthood, and no clear candidate genes have been established (Blazer & Steffens, 2015). For example, some studies have shown a correlation between the *apo-lipoprotein (APOE) e4 allele* and late-life depression, but this finding has not always been replicated. We also need to remember that this kind of correlation (between the gene and depression) may merely reflect an underlying and stronger association between *APOE4* and major neurocognitive disorder (Plassman & Steffens, 2004). That is, the gene may be related to the onset of major neurocognitive disorder, and the depressive disorder may result from the cognitive impairment, not the effects of the gene. Other biological factors that may contribute to the etiology of depression in older adults include limitations in physical functioning and increased prevalence of chronic illness.

These biological factors likely interact with psychological and social variables to explain the etiology of late-life depression from a biopsychosocial perspective (see Figure 14.3; Blazer, 2010). Psychological factors may include decreased involvement in physical activity and pleasurable activities (e.g., Fred was no longer able to play tennis or run due to his severe arthritis) and maladaptive cognitions (e.g., Fred also thought he was too old to make new friends). Older adults also experience learned helplessness due to perceived loss of control over their environments. Psychological *protective factors* such as increased maturity and previous life experiences, however, may help reduce the impact of biological factors (Gatz, 2000). Unique social factors and stressful life events also may influence the onset of depression in later life. A number of challenges, for example, often accompany retirement and/or a loved one's death. These secondary effects include an increased sense of loss, a change in social status, and reduced income. Reduced social support that frequently occurs with aging also may be a contributing factor (DiNapoli & Scogin, 2014).

Look for biological, psychological, and social factors that may contribute to Walter's depression:

> Walter (age 87) and his wife Dorothy (age 85) recently moved to an assisted living facility. The responsibilities of keeping up their house and yard had become too much for them. Cleaning the house, mowing the lawn, and doing small repairs were no longer easy chores. Running errands had even become difficult given the limitations in Walter's vision that resulted from the initial

Figure 14.3 Biopsychosocial Approach to Depression in Later Life.

Depression with onset in later life is often considered to have a combination of causes that include biological, psychological, and social factors.

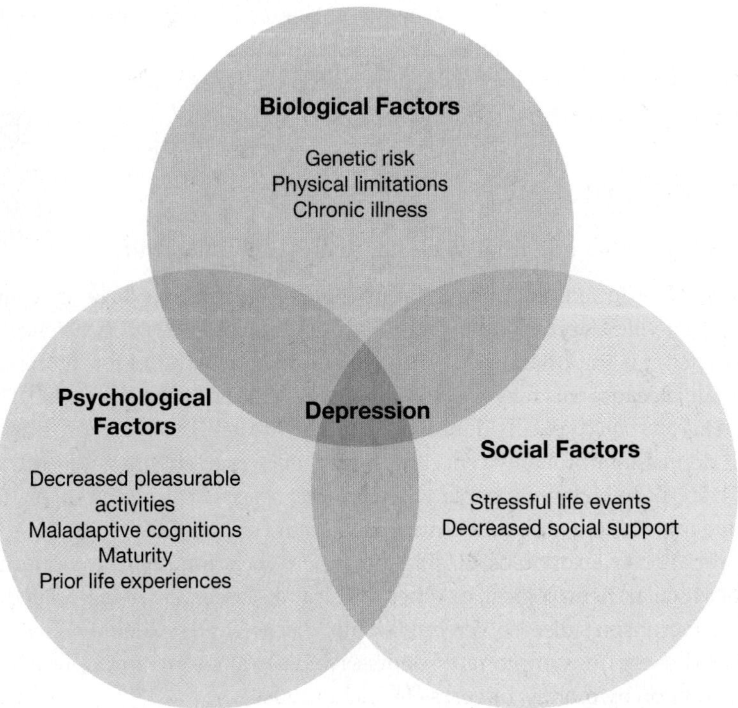

stages of macular degeneration (an eye disease). Although Walter and Dorothy hated to move from the house and neighborhood where they had lived for more than 50 years, their children convinced them that moving into a smaller place where they would have day-to-day help was better. After the move, though, Walter never seemed to regain his strength. He began to feel tired most of the time, and his energy and interest in socializing decreased. He played cards with other residents occasionally, and he went out to lunch when his daughter came to visit. But he missed his old neighborhood and church friends. He was able to attend church services only occasionally when someone came to get him, and he just didn't enjoy it the way he used to. He felt old and not very useful. His spirits perked up when his grandchildren came to see him, but they never stayed very long, and he had trouble hearing them because they talked too fast. Dorothy became concerned when he started to lose weight and just didn't seem hungry most of the time. Walter also never slept very well anymore except when he took sleeping pills. He often felt that he was just waiting to die.

Treatment of Depression and Bipolar Disorder in Older People

LO 14.7 Describe different treatment approaches for older adults with depression and bipolar disorder.

Because depressive disorders can accompany so many medical diseases, treatment must begin with a physical evaluation to rule out any medical causes, such as thyroid abnormalities, anemia, or diabetes. Once a diagnosis of major depressive disorder is established, treatment options include pharmacological and psychological interventions.

Medications used to treat major depressive disorder in younger adults (see Chapter 6) are also effective with older patients (Blazer & Steffens, 2015; Shanmugham et al., 2005). Selective serotonergic reuptake inhibitors (SSRIs) and serotonin-norepinephrine reuptake inhibitors (SNRIs) are most often used. Age-related changes in the body's metabolism increase older adults' sensitivity to medication in terms of both positive response and side effects. As a result, doses are typically increased more slowly and the dosage necessary for a positive response is lower than for younger adults (Blazer & Steffens, 2015). Electroconvulsive therapy (ECT) is used infrequently but is valuable for patients who have such severe symptoms that they cannot wait for the medication to have an effect or for those who fail to respond to alternative treatments.

Lithium is used as a treatment for bipolar disorder, but doses for elderly patients are lower than those used in younger patients and serious side effects can occur (Beyer, 2015). Because lithium can worsen cognitive impairment and create delirium (a syndrome described in more detail later), it must be used carefully (Young, 2005). Valproate, an anticonvulsant medication, also can be effective for late-life bipolar disorder, and ECT is sometimes used, although data to support this approach are limited to case studies (Beyer, 2015).

Psychological treatments also are efficacious for late-life depression (DiNapoli & Scogin, 2014), and older adults often prefer these approaches over medication (Gum et al., 2010). The greatest amount of empirical support exists for behavioral and cognitive-behavioral therapies (CBT). Behavioral activation and CBT are effective for late-life depression (see Chapter 6), as is a variation of CBT called **problem-solving therapy** (PST). CBT has been delivered effectively via *bibliotherapy,* and PST is useful for people who are experiencing executive dysfunction (Areán et al., 2010). Recent studies have demonstrated the benefits of these approaches in a variety of settings where older adults receive care (see "Research Hot Topic: Translating Research in Geropsychology to the Real World"). Other psychological treatments that appear beneficial for late-life depression are interpersonal therapy and brief psychodynamic therapy (see Chapter 6). **Reminiscence therapy**, used more uniquely with older adults, focuses on patients' recall of significant past events and how they managed distress (DiNapoli & Scogin, 2015). Case management, an intervention that helps older adults obtain access to financial, legal, housing, and health care resources, also is an effective treatment for depression among low-income older adults (Alexopoulos et al., 2016).

Learning Objective Summaries

LO 14.4 Explain the unique characteristics of depression and bipolar disorder in older adults.

Depression is one of the most common mental health problems among older adults. Compared with younger adults, older people with depression more often report physical symptoms, sleep problems, and cognitive difficulties. Overlapping medical and psychological problems make it difficult to diagnose depression in older adults. Suicide is a particular concern for older adults, particularly men. Few people develop bipolar disorder after age 65.

LO 14.5 Describe the prevalence rates and impact of depression and bipolar disorder in older adults with attention to differences related to age, race, and ethnicity.

Depression and bipolar disorders occur less frequently among older than younger adults, possibly due to differences in the experience or expression of psychological symptoms. Prevalence is higher among older people in residential and health care settings. These disorders affect mortality, quality of life, physical and social functioning, and cognitive difficulties among older adults. Depressive disorders occur more often among older women than older men. Prevalence is highest among non-Hispanic white and Latino older adults and lowest among African American and Asian American elderly. African American and Latino older adults are less likely to seek mental health care.

LO 14.6 Recognize the potential causes of depression in later life.

Biological, psychological, and social factors likely contribute to the onset of depression in later life. Biological factors include genetics, physical limitations, and chronic illness. Psychological factors include decreased positive activities and maladaptive thinking. Maturity and life experiences may be protective psychological factors. Social factors include stressful life events and reduced social support.

LO 14.7 Describe different treatment approaches for older adults with depression and bipolar disorder.

Medications that are useful for younger adults with depression and bipolar disorder are also effective for older adults, but doses are typically lower. Psychological treatments also are effective, particularly behavioral activation, cognitive-behavioral treatment, and problem-solving therapy. Case management is useful for treating depression among low-income older adults.

Critical Thinking Question

What are some of the major similarities and differences in the nature, etiology, and treatment of depression in older and younger adults?

Anxiety Disorders

Symptoms of Anxiety Disorders in Older Adults

LO 14.8 Understand symptoms of anxiety that are common for older adults and how these differ from anxiety in younger people.

As with depression, the diagnostic criteria for anxiety disorders are consistent across the life span (see Chapter 4), but important differences exist in the nature of anxiety and worry among older adults. These differences include developmental/life-cycle issues, age-related variations in the experience or expression of symptoms, and the presence of medical disorders that can complicate differential diagnosis.

With respect to life-span issues, worries reported by older people reflect the problems that arise in later stages of life. For example, older people tend to worry more about their own health and the welfare of loved ones but less about work and interpersonal relationships relative to younger and middle-aged adults (Miloyan et al., 2014). Fears of falling are common among older adults (Li et al., 2003), and they often worry about stressful life transitions (e.g., retirement, loss of a spouse or partner), added caregiving responsibilities (when spouses/partners or aging parents require significant assistance), and economic and legal issues associated with reduced income, increased health care costs, and end-of-life planning (American Psychological Association, 2014). Other potentially stressful events include changes in physical health, vision, hearing, sleep, continence, energy levels, memory, and increased disability (Brenes et al., 2005; Lenze et al., 2001; American Psychological Assocation, 2014; see Table 14.1). Anxiety can result from these physical changes or may contribute to worsening physical symptoms and lead to poorer physical health, sleep disruption, and memory problems.

As with depression, older adults also experience and express anxiety differently than younger adults. For example, older people use fewer psychological terms to describe anxiety (e.g., *concerns*, *fret*, or *think too much* rather than *worry* or *anxiety*; Lenze

Watch PATIENT AND PROVIDER DESCRIPTIONS OF ANXIETY

Table 14.1 Common Worries/Concerns Expressed by Older Adults

- Fear of falling
- Worries about health
- Life transitions—retirement, loss of a spouse or partner
- Caregiving responsibilities
- Reduced income and increased health care costs
- End-of-life issues, fear of death

et al., 2015), and they are less able than younger adults to identify accurately the symptoms of anxiety (Wetherell et al., 2009). Older adults also emphasize physical symptoms (Lenze et al., 2005), making recognition of anxiety disorders particularly difficult when medical illnesses are present. Many medical problems have physical symptoms that are common in anxiety (e.g., shortness of breath, chest pain, muscle pain or stiffness, gastrointestinal distress), and many medications produce anxiety-related side effects. For example, some blood pressure medications can create heart rate abnormalities, and bronchodilators that treat breathing disturbance can create nervousness, trembling, and increased heart rate.

Anxiety overlaps significantly with depression among people of all ages, but this overlap is even more common among older adults and leads to poorer treatment response (Lenze et al., 2015). Anxiety symptoms are more stable and consistent over time than depression, and research suggests that anxiety may be a significant risk factor for the emergence of late-life depression (Lenze et al., 2015; Schoevers et al., 2005). As such, treatment of anxiety may help to prevent depression, at least in some cases.

Prevalence and Impact

LO 14.9 Describe the prevalence and impact of anxiety disorders among older adults with attention to differences related to sex, race, and ethnicity.

Although anxiety disorders receive less attention than depression from clinicians and researchers, they are actually more common and considered one of the most significant mental health problems affecting older adults. Up to 11.6% of older adults in the United States suffer from some kind of anxiety disorder (Byers et al., 2010; Reynolds et al., 2015). Prevalence in other countries ranges from 5.4 to 14.2% (Miloyan et al., 2014). Although anxiety disorders occur less often among older than younger adults (Wolitzky-Taylor et al., 2010), anxiety disorders are more common than major depressive disorder in later life (Byers et al., 2010; Reynolds et al., 2015). As with depression, anxiety is more common among older patients in medical settings (Kunik et al., 2005; Tolin et al., 2005), and prevalence is high among older adults with cognitive impairment (Seignourel et al., 2008).

Among the anxiety disorders in late life, specific phobias, social anxiety disorder, and generalized anxiety disorder (GAD) are most common (Byers et al., 2010; IOM, 2012; Reynolds et al., 2015). The largest number of late-life anxiety studies have focused on GAD, which occurs in as much as 7% of the general population (Wolitzky-Taylor et al., 2010) and 11% of patients in medical clinics (Tolin et al., 2005). Clinically significant anxiety that does not meet diagnostic criteria is even more common (20 to 40%) (Brenes et al., 2005; Kunik et al., 2003; Wittchen et al., 2002). These figures actually may underestimate true prevalence because, as we discussed earlier, anxiety can be difficult to recognize, particularly in medical settings and for people with comorbid chronic illness. GAD may be the most difficult anxiety disorder to diagnose because its physical symptoms (sleep disturbance, fatigue, restlessness, difficulty concentrating; see Chapter 4) overlap the most with symptoms of normal aging, medical conditions, and medications used commonly in later life.

Anxiety in older adults is associated with less physical activity and poorer functioning, more negative perceptions of health, decreased life satisfaction, and more loneliness (Cully et al., 2006; Kim et al., 2000). Older adults with anxiety have more physical disabilities (Brenes et al., 2005; Lenze et al., 2001) and poorer quality of life (Porensky et al., 2009; Wetherell et al., 2004) than those who do not experience it. They also use more health care services (Porensky et al., 2009; Stanley et al., 2001) and are more dependent on others to function (Naik et al., 2004). Anxiety in later life increases the risk of death (Brenes et al., 2007; van Hout et al., 2004). As in other age groups, anxiety disorders are associated with significant distress and impaired functioning.

SEX, RACE, AND ETHNICITY As with younger adults, anxiety disorders in later life are more common among women (Wolitzky-Taylor et al., 2010; Woodward et al., 2012), although studies have not always considered the fact that women have longer life expectancies when determining prevalence. Furthermore, not all community data indicate that sex is a significant risk factor for anxiety in later life (Ford et al., 2007). Thus, it is unclear whether the differences in the prevalence of anxiety disorders are accurate or merely reflect the higher number of women in the older population.

The prevalence of late-life anxiety disorders differs based on race and ethnicity. Non-Hispanic white people and Latinos have the highest rates of anxiety disorders, particularly GAD and social anxiety disorder (Jimenez et al., 2010; Woodward et al., 2012). Among Latinos, rates of GAD are higher for those born in the United States than those who are immigrants (Jimenez et al., 2010). Anxiety disorders are less common among Asian American and African American older adults (Ford et al., 2007), although current diagnostic criteria may not reflect well the experience of these minority groups, thereby artificially reducing available prevalence rates. GAD occurs frequently among older Puerto Rican medical patients (11%; Tolin et al., 2005), and anxiety disorders in this population are associated with increased depression, high levels of suicidality, poor self-perceptions of health (e.g., a view of oneself as "sickly"), and increased use of health services (Diefenbach et al., 2004).

Culture-bound syndromes (see Chapter 4) also occur among older adults. They may be more common among older people due to lower education, less assimilation to the majority culture, and higher rates of foreign-born adults (Sakauye, 2004). In one study, 26% of older Puerto Rican primary care patients reported experiencing *ataque de nervios* (see Gloria, below). *Ataques* in this sample were associated with both anxiety and depressive disorders, particularly GAD and major depressive disorder, and they were characterized by anger, anxiety, dissociation, yelling or screaming, losing control, and seeking medical attention (Tolin et al., 2007).

> Gloria was a 58-year-old Puerto Rican woman who attended a Hispanic women's support group. During one meeting, she shared significant distress about her daughter, who was in a stormy dating relationship and moving away from family values in her behavior. Gloria was very upset with the way things were going. After the topic of group discussion changed, she fell on the floor and began shaking violently as if she were having a seizure. However, her face wasn't turning blue, she didn't lose bowel or bladder control, and she wasn't biting her tongue. The group leader was unable to console Gloria or decrease her symptoms. The ambulance was called to take her to the ER.

Etiology of Anxiety Disorders in Later Life

LO 14.10 Describe patterns of onset and potential causes of anxiety in later life.

Most anxiety disorders have their onset in childhood and young adulthood (Chapter 4), but anxiety can begin in later life. Some studies suggest a *bimodal distribution* of onset such that a significant proportion of older adults report long-term or lifetime symptoms of anxiety while another large subset indicates more recent onset (Lenze et al., 2015). In the latter cases, stressful life events (financial stress, increased physical disability, loss of social support, etc.) may play a causal role. Some studies suggest no differences in clinical symptoms related to age of onset (Lenze et al., 2015), but other data indicate more severe symptoms among patients with earlier onset and more serious functional limitations due to physical problems among those with later onset (Le Roux et al., 2005).

Certainly, the biological and psychological theories proposed to explain the onset of anxiety reviewed in Chapter 4 are relevant for older people, particularly those who have suffered from anxiety since their younger years. In addition, the biopsychosocial model of late-life depression described earlier in this chapter is also applicable to the development of anxiety among older adults. Biological factors contributing to anxiety onset can include genetics, physical limitations, and chronic illness. One large twin study, for example, suggested that approximately 25% of the variance in liability for GAD among older adults (ages 55 to 74) resulted from genetic factors (Mackintosh et al., 2006). In addition, physical limitations and chronic illness are risk factors for anxiety onset, as are maladaptive thoughts, behavioral avoidance and stressful life events. Consider chronic obstructive pulmonary disease (COPD), a common lung disease in later life with symptoms including shortness of breath and catastrophic thoughts about physical symptoms. These same symptoms are also characteristic of panic disorder, and COPD-related symptoms may precipitate anxiety syndromes in chronically ill people who worry excessively about medical symptoms and associated difficulties.

> Curtis had severe COPD that required oxygen therapy 24 hours a day. He was concerned about his medical condition whenever he went on an outing with his family. Even mild shortness of breath during an outing caused Curtis to feel panicky—thinking that he might not be able to breathe and that he might die. As he became more worried, his breathing worsened and he sometimes experienced dizziness, sweating, and shakiness. Doctors told Curtis and his family that not all of these symptoms would be expected based on his COPD and current treatments, but Curtis worried that the doctors might be missing something. He also began to feel concerned that he was slowing his family down when they were out, and he chose to stay home alone more often. As a result, Curtis felt even more anxious about going out.

Treatment of Anxiety Disorders in Later Life

LO 14.11 Summarize pharmacological and psychosocial treatments that can be used to treat anxiety in older people.

As with depression, ruling out physical illnesses that may be producing anxiety-like symptoms is necessary. Treatments for anxiety disorders in older adults are similar to those used for younger people, with most research examining pharmacological and psychosocial (primarily cognitive-behavioral) treatments.

Because older adults often seek help for mental health problems in a medical setting, most treatment for anxiety involves the use of medication. Among older adults, benzodiazepines are prescribed most frequently; they are given to as many as 43% of patients with persistent anxiety (Schuurmans et al., 2005). Older adults use benzodiazepine medications at a higher rate than younger adults (Olfson et al., 2015), and data indicate that these medications are superior to placebo in reducing symptoms of anxiety (Martin et al., 2007). However, benzodiazepines can create serious side effects for older adults including impaired cognitive functioning, slowed motor behavior and reaction times, and increased risks of falls and motor vehicle accidents. Long-term use also can create dependence. Thus, care must be taken in using these medications for older people, and alternative medications generally are preferred.

Antidepressants, such as selective serotonin reuptake inhibitors (SSRIs), are effective for older adults with anxiety disorders (Katz et al., 2002; Lenze et al., 2009; Schuurmans et al., 2006). These medications have fewer side effects than benzodiazepines and are recommended as the first-line pharmacological treatment. Even antidepressants have side effects, however, and older people often prefer psychosocial treatment over pharmacotherapy when they have a choice (Gum et al., 2010; Wetherell et al., 2004).

Most studies of psychological treatments have examined cognitive-behavioral therapy (CBT), which is well suited for older people because it is time-limited, directive, and collaborative. Modifying the treatment by slowing the pace, using different learning strategies to teach skills, and minimizing distractions may be helpful for some older people. CBT is efficacious for older adults with GAD (Gonçalves & Byrne, 2012) and panic disorder (Hendriks et al., 2014), although response is not always as robust for older adults as for younger adults (Wetherell et al., 2013b). Case studies have also demonstrated the potential value of acceptance and commitment therapy (see Chapters 4 and 5) for late-life anxiety (Wetherell et al., 2011). Nevertheless, additional modifications are needed to improve the outcomes of CBT for older adults and increase access to these interventions for older people who experience significant barriers to receiving care, including the lack of accessible and qualified providers, the cost of treatment, and transportation limitations (see Research Hot Topic: Translating Geropsychology Treatment Research into the Real World).

Research HOT Topic

Translating Geropsychology Treatment Research into the Real World

Much is now known about the treatment of anxiety and depression among older adults based on controlled clinical trials conducted in academic clinical settings (medical school psychiatry clinics, university psychology clinics, etc.). People who participate in those studies, however, are often not representative of older adults in the "real world." They are often healthier, better educated, and mostly white, calling into question how study outcomes relate to more diverse groups of older adults. Furthermore, many older people, particularly minorities, never seek care from specialized mental health settings. More often, they are treated by their primary care physicians, where anxiety and depression are often unrecognized. Still other older people are too fragile and unhealthy even to get to a medical clinic, and they either receive no care or obtain home health care through a community-based agency, where again psychological problems can be overlooked. Even when anxiety and depression are recognized in these settings, care is often inadequate or substandard relative to evidence-based standards. Recent research has begun to test modified treatment and delivery approaches designed to increase access to evidence-based mental health care for older adults with anxiety and depression.

Recent models of late-life depression treatment have utilized a **collaborative care** approach, which involves integrated pharmacological and psychosocial treatments facilitated by a *depression care manager* who might be a psychologist, nurse, or social worker. This kind of treatment is effective for reducing depression and suicidal ideation among Medicare home health patients (Lohman et al., 2015). Telephone-based delivery of CBT for anxiety also is effective for rural, older adults (Brenes et al., 2015), and nonexpert, bachelor-level providers working under the supervision of licensed mental health professionals can be trained to deliver effective treatment for late-life anxiety (Stanley et al., 2014). Community–academic partnerships also can facilitate improved delivery of care for older adults with anxiety or depression in community service settings (e.g., social service agencies, churches, community centers). In these partnerships, input from community leaders, consumers, and clinical scientists is used to create culturally relevant and person-centered approaches to meet the needs of underserved older adults (Areán et al., 2012; Jameson et al., 2012). In one recent community–academic partnership project, an innovative model of CBT-based treatment was developed to incorporate attention to religion and/or spirituality, which was expected to increase participation from African American older adults who endorse high levels of religious involvement. An initial pilot study of this intervention showed positive outcomes for worry and anxiety among older adults from low-income, underserved, mostly minority communities (Stanley et al., 2016).

Learning Objective Summaries

LO 14.8 Understand symptoms of anxiety that are common for older adults and how these differ from anxiety in younger people.

Older adults worry more about their own health, the welfare of others, falling, and stressful life transitions (retirement, death of a loved one) and less about work and interpersonal relationships relative to younger adults. They also use fewer psychological terms to describe anxiety and tend to emphasize physical symptoms. Comorbid medical problems common in older adults make diagnosis of anxiety more difficult than for younger people.

LO 14.9 Describe the prevalence and impact of anxiety disorders among older adults with attention to differences related to sex, race, and ethnicity.

Up to 11.6% of older adults in the United States suffer from an anxiety disorder. Anxiety disorders are less common among older than younger adults, but they are more common than depression in later life. Anxiety in older people is associated with less physical activity and poorer functioning, increased health care use, and higher risk of death. Anxiety disorders occur more often for older women than older men. Older non-Hispanic white and Latino adults have the highest rates of anxiety disorders. Prevalence in African American and Asian American adults is lower. Current diagnostic criteria may not represent well the experience and expression of anxiety in racial or ethnic minority adults, thus underestimating true prevalence.

LO 14.10 Describe patterns of onset and potential causes of anxiety in later life.

Anxiety disorders in older adults may have a bimodal distribution of onset. Causes of anxiety in later life are likely due to biological (genetics, physical limitations, comorbid medical disorders), psychological (maladaptive thoughts, behavioral avoidance), and social (stressful life events) factors.

LO 14.11 Summarize pharmacological and psychosocial treatments that can be used to treat anxiety in older people.

Benzodiazepines are frequently used to treat anxiety in older adults, but these medications put people at risk for impaired cognitive functioning, slowed motor behaviors, falls, and motor vehicle accidents. Antidepressants are preferable and effective, but older adults often favor psychosocial treatments. CBT is an effective treatment for anxiety in older adults, but new models of care that expand the traditional content and delivery of CBT are being developed to increase access to treatment.

Critical Thinking Question

Your grandmother has recently retired, and she seems more anxious. She denies feeling anxious, but she is agitated and complains about a lot of physical symptoms (e.g., reflux, headaches, sore muscles). She also was recently diagnosed with diabetes, so she now has to watch her diet more closely. How might the changes in her life be putting her at risk for development of an anxiety disorder?

Substance-Related Disorders and Psychosis

When most people think of older adults with psychological problems, they may not picture an older man who goes to bed drunk at night or a woman who has paranoid delusions. Yet older people suffer from substance abuse problems and psychotic disorders just as some younger people do. As with depression and anxiety, less is known about these disorders among older people than among younger adults. Nevertheless, substance misuse and psychotic symptoms can affect the quality of life and functioning of older people, and research is beginning to address the unique nature, causes, and treatment of these problems.

Substance-Related Disorders in Older Adults

LO 14.12 Understand differences in the symptoms of substance use disorders in older and younger adults.

> Harold was a 72-year-old divorced man who always enjoyed social events. He could have a few drinks, smoke a few cigarettes, enjoy his friends, and wake up feeling fine the next day. Even as he got older, he could "hold his own" at a party. One night when he was driving home from a gathering, he swerved to miss a car that he thought was too close to the line and ran off the road. His car suffered some damage, and he hurt his back and neck. The doctor gave him some pain medication, which made things much easier. He was already taking a mild tranquilizer for anxiety—but that was from a different doctor. He was sure there would be nothing wrong with adding one pill a day. When he started to have more trouble sleeping because of the pain, he decided to take one extra pill—and sometimes added a beer. That made it even easier to relax. Before long, Harold couldn't get to sleep without the tranquilizer, a double dose of pain medication, and a beer.

Alcohol and other substance-related disorders are underappreciated problems for older adults. The number of adults age 50 and over who have a substance-related disorder is expected to double from 2.8 million in 2002–2006 to 5.7 million in 2020 (Wu & Blazer, 2011). Overuse of alcohol, misuse of prescription medications (e.g., benzodiazepines, sedatives, narcotic painkillers), and tobacco abuse are the most common problems (Lin et al., 2011; Wu & Blazer, 2014). Although the diagnostic criteria are the same as for younger adults (see Chapter 10), the symptoms are not always consistent. Among older people, alcohol abuse is less often associated with antisocial behavior, legal problems, unemployment, and low socioeconomic status than among younger adults. Instead, problematic

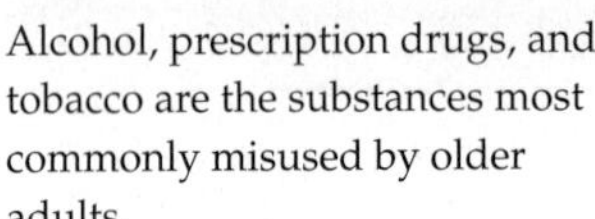
Alcohol, prescription drugs, and tobacco are the substances most commonly misused by older adults.

substance use in older adults may be recognized only as the individuals increasingly depend on others (who then have more opportunity to observe patterns of use) and/or as substance use affects medical illnesses and their treatment (Blazer & Nagy, 2004) or patient safety (car accidents, falls, etc.).

The National Institute on Alcohol Abuse and Alcoholism (NIAAA) recommends that adults age 65 and over have no more than one drink per day, or seven drinks per week, with no more than two drinks on any one occasion (Barry & Blow, 2014; Oslin & Mavandadi, 2009). In the United States, a standard drink is defined as 12 grams of alcohol. However, as with younger adults, alcohol use disorder in late life is defined not simply by the number of drinks but also by use that has adverse consequences (medical, social, or psychological) and negatively affects functioning. Determining adverse consequences may be challenging because older adults often have fewer obligations outside the home and fewer social contacts.

> Bill reported drinking five glasses of wine each evening, but he drank at home and did not drive. He also no longer had to get up early in the morning to get to work. Therefore, he denied any problems due to alcohol use. Does Bill have alcohol use disorder?

Similarly, overuse of prescription drugs (e.g., benzodiazepines, opioids) is a significant problem that may often be unrecognized among older adults (Kalapatapu & Sullivan, 2010). Patients may be prescribed medications by multiple physicians who are unaware of other medications the patients may be taking. Many older adults tend to take less medication than they are prescribed, but the average older adult takes multiple prescription medications each day, leading to increased risk of adverse effects. Over-the-counter medications can complicate drug interactions even further. In many cases, prescription abuse among older adults is noticed only when signs of toxicity or withdrawal occur.

Prevalence and Impact of Substance Use in Older Adults

LO 14.13 Describe the prevalence and impact of substance use disorders, with particular attention to gender differences.

Tobacco is the most commonly abused substance in older adults, although the prevalence of tobacco dependence is lower than among younger people (Blazer & Wu, 2012). Nevertheless, more than 17.1 million adults over the age of 50 reported smoking within the previous month (National Survey on Drug Use and Health, 2006). The serious negative health consequences of smoking are well known (cancer, heart disease, COPD, osteoporosis, etc.), and tobacco use disorders account for more disability and mortality among older adults than all other substance use disorders combined (Atkinson, 2004).

In the United States, prevalence estimates for alcohol-related disorders (DSM-IV alcohol abuse and dependence) among older adults range from 2.1 to 8.1% for men and 1.0 to 1.3% for women (Wu & Blazer, 2014). Rates are increasing as baby boomers age (Mavandadi & Oslin, 2015), but as with other psychological conditions, alcohol use often goes unrecognized among older adults (IOM, 2012). Many older people (50 to 70%) report that they do not drink alcohol (Oslin & Mavandadi, 2009). In some cases, abstinence has been lifelong; for other people, abstinence followed the onset of an illness. If older adults who decide to abstain from alcohol have a prior history of alcohol-related disorders, they may be at risk for future problematic drinking during periods of stress.

Risky or problem drinking (excessive alcohol use that may not meet diagnostic criteria for substance-related disorders) occurs more frequently than alcohol-related disorders, perhaps affecting as many as 16.7% of men and 10.9% of women (Wu & Blazer, 2014). *Binge drinking* (three or more drinks on the same occasion for women; four or more drinks on the same occasion for men; Barry & Blow, 2014) also is a problem for older adults, with prevalence of 19.6% among men and 6.3% among women (Wu & Blazer, 2014). Approximately one-third of older adults with alcohol-related disorders develop the disorder in later life, but many of these individuals may have been risky drinkers in their earlier years. When the disorder begins later in life, symptoms are typically milder and more circumscribed, and less family history is reported. Late onset occurs more often among women (Atkinson, 2004).

Admitted substance-related disorders are rare among older adults, with prevalence estimates near 0% (IOM, 2012; Oslin & Mavandadi, 2009), although drug use is also underrecognized among older adults and rates are rising as baby boomers age. For example, among adults age 65 and older, the percentage of admissions to substance abuse treatment facilities between 1995 and 2005 increased from 6.6 to 10.5% for opioid/heroin addiction (SAMHSA, 2007). Similar increases were found for cocaine (2.1 to 4.4%) and sedatives (0.5 to 1.3%). In the United States, one-third of all prescription medications are used by older adults (Kalapatapu & Sullivan, 2010), and they are particularly likely to be prescribed benzodiazepines. As many as 15% of older people at any one time have such a prescription (Atkinson, 2004). Although there is little misuse, physical and psychological dependence can result from long-term use (4 to 12 months). When these drugs are used for chronic insomnia, tolerance may be particularly problematic, although most surveys of substance-related disorders do not consider this type of misuse.

Despite low rates of actual disorders, alcohol and other substances can have significant detrimental effects. Of particular concern are age-related physical changes (decreased lean body mass and total body water related to total fat, increased central nervous system sensitivity, etc.) that decrease the body's ability to *metabolize* (break down) drugs. This age-related decline increases the potential for side effects and toxicity from alcohol and other substances. The same amount of alcohol, for example, produces higher blood alcohol levels and more impaired performance in older adults than it does in younger people (Atkinson, 2004; Oslin & Mavandadi, 2009). Therefore, continuing to drink the same amount of alcohol can lead to increased problems of abuse as a person ages. Excessive alcohol use can result in falls and motor vehicle accidents, decreased sexual interest and impotence, medical problems, and increased risk of delirium, major or mild neurocognitive disorder, dehydration, and gait problems (Mavandadi & Oslin, 2015; Oslin, 2004). In addition, abuse increases the risk of problematic drug interactions (Mavandadi & Oslin, 2015) and can interfere with the treatment of chronic medical problems, such as hypertension and diabetes.

SEX, RACE, AND ETHNICITY As already noted, older men have higher rates of alcohol abuse and dependence, risky drinking, and binge drinking than older women. These differences are consistent across various ethnic and racial groups (Atkinson, 2004). Women, however, are at higher risk for negative consequences because they do not metabolize alcohol as quickly as men do and need less alcohol to suffer the intoxicating effects (Epstein et al., 2007). Illicit drug use is more common in older men, but women are at higher risk for prescription drug abuse (Kalapatapu & Sullivan, 2010).

Overall prevalence of alcohol- and drug-related disorders appears to be comparable among older white, African American, and Hispanic subgroups (IOM, 2012). Drinking is uncommon among older Chinese Americans (Kirchner et al., 2007). African Americans (23%) smoke more cigarettes than non-Hispanic whites and Hispanics (National Survey on Drug Use and Health, 2006).

Etiology and Treatment of Substance-Related Disorders

LO 14.14 Summarize etiological factors and treatment models for substance use disorders in later life.

ETIOLOGY Theories regarding the development of alcohol- and substance-related disorders in younger adults also apply to older people (see Chapter 10), particularly when the disorder started early in life. Across the life span, some people have a steady use pattern whereas others use alcohol and substances more progressively or variably. When the onset of misuse occurs later in life, there is less evidence that genetic factors are operative, but there is often a personal history of habitual use and/or risky drinking (Atkinson, 2004). Vulnerability to misuse also increases with medical frailty and the need for multiple medications (Mavandadi & Oslin, 2015). Likewise, benzodiazepine overuse increases when patients have a history of alcohol-related disorders.

TREATMENT OF SUBSTANCE-RELATED DISORDERS Most of the research on treating substance-related disorders in older adults focuses on risky or problematic drinking (Barry & Blow, 2014; Oslin & Mavandadi, 2009). Treatment is aimed at both prevention and early intervention. Interventions are typically brief (one to four contacts) and include motivational exercises, family support, education including direct feedback about problematic drinking, and specific advice on reducing alcohol use. *Behavioral self-control procedures* (e.g., keeping a drinking diary, behavioral contracting) are also sometimes used. In primary care settings, these brief interventions have had positive results for at-risk drinking in older adults (Moore et al., 2011; Oslin, 2005), with decreases in average number of drinks per week at 13 to 34% (Barry & Blow, 2014).

For older adults with diagnosed alcohol- or substance-related disorders rather than risky drinking, treatment outcomes are comparable across age groups when older and younger adults are treated together (Atkinson & Misra, 2002). Older patients, however, tend to be more adherent to treatment recommendations (Oslin et al., 2002) and have better outcomes when treatment is age specific (Mavandadi & Oslin, 2015). Age-specific treatment may foster better peer relationships and longer retention in treatment, which may enhance treatment outcomes. Older women respond better to alcohol treatment than men (Mavandadi & Oslin, 2015).

Medications such as naltrexone (see Chapter 10) are safe and beneficial for the treatment of late-life alcohol-related disorder (Mavandadi & Oslin, 2015). Another drug, disulfiram (Antabuse), is commonly used to prevent drinking in younger adults. However, this drug can be dangerous for older patients if they drink while taking the medication. Antidepressant medication can be useful for reducing drinking if patients experience depression along with alcohol-related disorders.

Benzodiazepine dependence is usually treated by gradual discontinuation of the drug. However, the outcome is poor if the drug has been used for a long time. When treatment is successful, it improves cognitive functioning and reduces anxiety, depression, and insomnia. Some symptoms may remain, and older adults are at increased risk for return usage (Atkinson, 2004). Smoking cessation treatments that are efficacious for younger adults (e.g., brief interventions in primary care, transdermal nicotine patch therapy) are also efficacious for older patients (Atkinson, 2004).

Psychosis in Older Adults

LO 14.15 Understand differences in the symptoms of psychosis for older and younger adults.

Older adults, like younger ones, can experience some of the most severe psychological disorders that include symptoms of psychosis. In many cases, the diagnostic categories used to describe these disorders are the same for older and younger adults (see Chapter 11). We focus here on different characterizations of schizophrenia that are used to describe subgroups of older patients and on psychotic symptoms that arise in the context of depression and major neurocognitive disorders.

For most older adults with schizophrenia, onset occurs in younger adulthood and the disorder continues into older age (Maglione et al., 2015). In most cases, the disorder is relatively stable over the lifetime, but for a minority of older adults with schizophrenia (10 to 20%), there is either worsening or improvement of symptoms over time. Generally, the symptoms of schizophrenia are the same for older and younger adults, although older adults with the disorder also experience cognitive changes that are typical for increasing age.

When the disorder begins later in life (after age 40), a unique pattern of related symptoms develops. Although **late-onset schizophrenia** is associated with many of the same risk factors as earlier onset (family history, genetic risk, and childhood maladjustment) (Jeste et al., 2009; Pearman & Batra, 2012), this pattern of onset is associated with lower average severity of positive symptoms (delusions, hallucinations) and less impairment in learning, abstraction, and flexibility of thinking (Maglione et al., 2015). People with late-onset schizophrenia also report higher premorbid functioning (better functioning before the disorder started) and more successful occupational and marital histories (Pearman & Batra, 2012).

Schizophrenia in older adults is usually a continuation of a disease process that began at an earlier age. In some cases, however, schizophrenia can begin at older ages.

Very-late-onset schizophrenia-like psychosis is a heterogeneous category with onset after age 60. In the very-late-onset subgroup, psychotic symptoms typically result from a stroke, tumor, or other *neurodegenerative* change. Because these symptoms occur after a period of normal neurobiological development, very-late-onset schizophrenia differs from other forms of schizophrenia, which are considered *neurodevelopmental* (see Chapter 11). Very-late-onset schizophrenia-like psychosis is associated with less genetic susceptibility, less evidence of childhood maladjustment, a relative lack of thought disorder, and fewer negative symptoms (Jeste et al., 2009; Maglione et al., 2015).

Psychotic symptoms also occur frequently for people with major neurocognitive disorder due to Alzheimer's disease (AD) (Ropacki & Jeste, 2005), usually 3 to 4 years after the Alzheimer's diagnosis. The psychotic symptoms associated with AD are different from those in late-life schizophrenia (Maglione et al., 2015; see Table 14.2). Persecutory delusions and delusions of theft are common.

> Hazel repeatedly told her daughter that the man across the hall in her nursing home was stealing from her. She was certain that he came into her room when she was sleeping and took her things.

Misidentification of a caregiver also occurs frequently, as do visual hallucinations.

> Hazel regularly referred to her daughter, who visited her daily, as "that woman who comes here to clean my room." When she was awake in the middle of the night, Hazel also frequently looked out her window and saw fires burning and children dying, but no one would come to help.

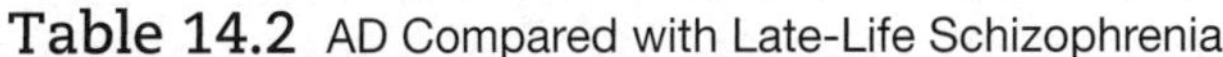

Table 14.2 AD Compared with Late-Life Schizophrenia

Symptoms of psychosis vary when they occur in the context of Alzheimer's Disease or late-life schizophrenia.

Psychosis of AD vs. Late-Life Schizophrenia	
Psychosis of AD	**Late-Life Schizophrenia**
• 30 to 50% prevalence	• <1% prevalence
• Bizarre delusions rare	• Bizarre delusions frequent
• Misidentifications common	• Misidentifications rare
• Mostly visual hallucinations	• Mostly auditory hallucinations
• Suicidality rare	• Suicidality frequent
• Past history rare	• Past history common
• Remission frequent	• Remission uncommon
• Antipsychotic doses low	• Antipsychotic doses moderate

A past history of psychosis is rare in people who develop psychotic symptoms during the course of AD, and these symptoms often remit during the later stages of cognitive decline. Psychotic symptoms also occur for older adults with depression. For these individuals, hallucinations are uncommon, but delusions of persecution or of having an incurable illness often occur. Deluisions in late-life depression are typically classified as *mood congruent* (with a depression theme) or *mood incongruent* (without a depressive theme).

Prevalence and Impact of Psychosis in Older Adults

LO 14.16 Describe the prevalence of psychosis in older adults and differences due to sex, race, and ethnicity.

Schizophrenia occurs in 0.1 to 0.5% of people age 65 and above (Ceglowski et al., 2014). Fewer than 10% have onset after age 40, and less than 1% report onset of symptoms after age 60 (Ceglowski et al., 2014). Psychotic symptoms are more common among people who are hospitalized or living in nursing homes. Schizophrenia in later life is tremendously debilitating, significantly affecting functioning, quality of life, health care use and costs, and mortality (Van Citters et al., 2005). Poor functioning is associated with worse cognitive performance, little education, and severe negative symptoms (Evans et al., 2003).

Approximately 40% of people with AD develop psychotic symptoms (Maglione et al., 2015), and these individuals have increased executive dysfunction, greater overall cognitive decline, and increased risk of death relative to people with AD and no psychosis (Ceglowski et al., 2014; Maglione et al., 2015). Caregiver distress also is higher when people with AD also have psychosis, and rates of nursing home placement are higher. Up to 30% of people with late-life depression experience psychotic symptoms. These people have increased rates of suicidal ideation and intent, poorer social support, and the presence of bipolar disorder (Blazer & Steffens, 2015).

SEX, RACE, AND ETHNICITY Late-onset schizophrenia is more common among women but begins at an earlier age for men (Jeste et al., 2009). Neuroendocrine changes, increased longevity of women, and differential psychosocial stressors may explain these sex-related differences. Estrogen, for example, may serve as an *endogenous antipsychotic* (a naturally occurring substance that functions in the same way as an antipsychotic medication). In this instance, until menopause, estrogen may prevent psychotic symptoms in women who are biologically at risk for schizophrenia (Maglione et al., 2015).

As noted in Chapter 11, the symptoms of psychosis and schizophrenia are similar across racial and ethnic groups, although, as is the case for younger adults, psychosis and inaccurate diagnoses of schizophrenia are more common among African American older adults (Faison & Armstrong, 2003). Contributing factors include clinician bias, lack of culturally appropriate assessment instruments, and misinterpretation of psychotic symptoms. Latinos with schizophrenia are more likely to live with family but are less likely to receive services.

Spirituality and witchcraft are often used to explain these unusual symptoms among African American, Hispanic, and Native American populations (Sakauye, 2004). Hallucinations with religious content actually may represent normal religious experience in some cultures (Faison & Armstrong, 2003), and thoughts that might be classified as paranoid for some patients actually may represent "healthy" or "normal" reactions to discrimination-related trauma or immigration experiences. Finally, herbal medications used in some cultures can cause psychotic symptoms when combined with some antidepressant or antipsychotic medications.

Etiology and Treatment of Psychosis in Older Adults

LO 14.17 Summarize possible causes of and strategies for treating psychosis in older adults.

ETIOLOGY Late-onset schizophrenia shares many possible etiological factors with schizophrenia that begins earlier in life. Brain abnormalities are similar to those in patients with earlier onset including enlarged ventricles, increased density of dopamine receptors, and reduced size of the superior temporal gyrus (see Chapter 11).

Some etiological factors, such as hypothesized differences in hormonal changes and psychosocial stressors, may produce later onset in women. In addition, some studies have suggested that late-onset schizophrenia is associated with deficits in hearing and vision. Other studies, however, suggest that older adults with early or late onset receive poor correction for sensory impairments (e.g., not getting the appropriate glasses), suggesting that generally poorer health care may explain this relation (Maglione et al., 2015).

As noted earlier, very-late-onset schizophrenia-like psychosis is generally associated with neurological damage, such as a stroke or tumor. In these cases, there is no evidence of a direct genetic role, although both genetic and environmental factors may contribute to medical conditions, such as stroke, that then produce psychotic symptoms. When psychosis occurs in people with AD, more severe cognitive impairment is present (see "Neurocognitive Disorders"). Patients with both disorders have increased degeneration in the brain, higher levels of norepinephrine, and decreased levels of serotonin (Maglione et al., 2015).

TREATMENT OF PSYCHOSIS As with younger adults, the primary treatments for schizophrenia for older adults include the typical and atypical antipsychotic medications. However, treatment response may differ across age groups. Physical and emotional differences in cognitive and social functioning, age-related changes in metabolism and neurotransmitter receptor sensitivity, medical illnesses, and use of other medications may affect response to antipsychotic medication. Little research has examined the efficacy of antipsychotic medications specifically in older adults, but available data suggest modest improvements in a range of symptoms (Van Critters et al., 2005). The atypical antipsychotics (e.g., Abilify, Zyprexa) produce better outcomes and fewer side effects than do the typical antipsychotics (e.g., Haldol, chlorpromazine). Because older adults show increased medication sensitivity and much higher rates of movement-related side effects (e.g., tardive dyskinesia; see Chapter 11), medication doses are typically 25 to 50% lower than for younger adults (Maglione et al., 2015).

When psychosis occurs in the context of major neurocognitive disorders, antipsychotic medications produce modest effects with atypical variants performing best (Schneider et al., 2006; Weintraub & Katz, 2005). As age increases, medication dosage decreases. Because psychotic symptoms frequently remit in the later stages of the neurocognitive disorder, long-term use of medications is often not necessary (Maglione et al., 2015). Patients with major neurocognitive disorders are particularly sensitive to medication side effects, and even the atypical antipsychotic medications can produce sedation, fluctuation in blood pressure, and increased risk of mortality (Schneider et al., 2005).

Only a small number of studies have tested the utility of psychological treatments for schizophrenia in older adults, but skills training and CBT in various combinations have positive effects (e.g., Ceglowski et al., 2014; Granholm et al., 2005; Jeste et al., 2009). These interventions help patients challenge their delusional beliefs and change behaviors related to medication noncompliance and health care management. Patients also learn social, communication, and life skills (e.g., organization and planning, financial management) aimed at improving overall functioning. Among patients with psychosis and neurocognitive disorder, family support and education are important along with training to the caregiver on coping skills and behavioral management of problematic behaviors, such as aggression toward caregivers.

Learning Objective Summaries

LO 14.12 Understand differences in the symptoms of substance use disorders in older and younger adults.

Overuse of alcohol, prescription medications, and tobacco are the most common substance use problems among older adults. Substance use problems are less often recognized among older than younger adults and are less often associated with antisocial behavior and legal problems. Recommended daily use of alcohol is less for older than younger adults, and problems with prescription drug use may be enhanced for older adults due to increased use of other prescription and over-the-counter medications.

LO 14.13 Describe the prevalence and impact of substance use disorders with particular attention to gender differences.

Prevalence of alcohol-related disorders, risky drinking, and binge drinking is higher for older men than older women, but women are at greater risk for prescription drug abuse. Other substance-related disorders are uncommon among older adults, although rates are increasing as baby boomers age. Alcohol and other substances have a greater impact for older people, particularly older women, based on age- and sex-related changes in the body's ability to metabolize substances.

LO 14.14 Summarize etiological factors and treatment models for substance use disorders in later life.

Theories regarding the development of alcohol and substance use disorders in younger adults apply to older people, particularly when the disorder started earlier in life. When the onset of misuse starts in later life, there is less evidence of genetic factors, but a history of habitual or risky use is often present. Treatment research for alcohol use focuses mostly on prevention, with attention to risky drinking, and brief non-medication interventions are effective.

LO 14.15 Understand differences in the symptoms of psychosis for older and younger adults.

For older adults, psychosis occurs in the context of disorders like schizophrenia. In most cases, onset of schizophrenia is in younger adulthood and persists into older age. Late-onset schizophrenia begins after age 40 and is associated with less severe positive symptoms and less cognitive impairment. Very-late-onset schizophrenia-like psychosis develops after age 60, usually as a result of stroke, tumor, or other neurodegenerative change. Psychosis that accompanies AD is characterized by persecutory delusions, misidentification, and visual hallucinations.

LO 14.16 Describe the prevalence of psychosis in older adults and differences due to sex, race, and ethnicity.

Schizophrenia occurs in 0.1 to 0.5% of adults age 65 and older. Late-onset schizophrenia is more common in women, possibly as a result of the natural antipsychotic effects of estrogen. Symptoms of psychosis and schizophrenia are similar across racial and ethnic groups, but schizophrenia is often inaccurately diagnosed among African Americans.

LO 14.17 Summarize theories of etiology and strategies for treating psychosis in older adults.

Similar etiological factors and brain abnormalities occur in early- and late-onset schizophrenia. Sensory deficits associated with late-onset schizophrenia may actually be the result of inadequate treatment. Very-late-onset schizophrenia-like psychosis is associated with neurological damage. Treatments for schizophrenia in late life include the same medications used with younger adults but at significantly lower dosages. Psychological treatments also can be effective.

Critical Thinking Question

Why are alcohol- and substance-related disorders such serious problems for older adults even though prevalence is lower among them than among younger people?

Neurocognitive Disorders

Neurocognitive disorders (NCDs; disorders of thinking) affect older adults more than the other syndromes discussed in this chapter. As older people live longer and the population of older people continues to increase, more and more people will suffer from these cognitive dysfunctions. Some level of cognitive decline (e.g., in memory, attention, speed of processing information) is associated with normal aging. However, *delirium* and *major and mild neurocognitive disorders* are disorders that represent deficits in cognitive abilities significantly affecting older people.

Delirium

LO 14.18 Describe the symptoms and prevalence of delirium in older adults.

The primary feature of **delirium** (see "DSM-5: Delirium") is an acute or sudden change in attention (e.g., the person cannot follow a conversation or focus on a task at hand) and awareness (e.g., the person is unable to orient to the environment). Delirium also can be associated with disorganized thinking and language (e.g., the person's speech is jumbled and doesn't reflect a logical sequence of ideas). These changes in awareness can involve decreased wakefulness and stupor (*hypoactive type*), severe insomnia and hyperarousal (*hyperactive type*), or a combination of the two (Saczynski & Inouye, 2015). The symptoms of delirium can wax and wane within or across days, but their acute onset (within hours to a few days) differentiates delirium from major neurocognitive disorder, which has a more gradual and progressive course.

Dorothy was an 82-year-old widow who had been given a diagnosis of AD 5 years previously. She lived in a nursing home, and her daughter Mary visited her almost every day. Dorothy often repeated herself and couldn't keep track of scheduled activities, but when the staff came to remind her, she was able to wheel herself to the game room to participate in activities such as watching movies, playing bingo, and attending ice cream socials. She had developed a friendship with her roommate, and she was always glad to see her daughter. Dorothy couldn't live on her own anymore, but she had adjusted reasonably well to life in the nursing home. One week, however, a major virus spread through the building, and everyone got sick—including Dorothy. Mary was worried about her, but the staff were doing their best to treat everyone and contain the spread of the virus. As Dorothy's symptoms worsened, she was coughing up phlegm and having increased difficulty breathing, with associated chest pain and a fever. The doctor diagnosed her with pneumonia and arranged for her to go to the hospital. When Mary met her at the hospital that evening, Dorothy was different. She was thrashing about in the bed, asking for Harry (her husband who had died many years before), and she grabbed Mary's arm and wouldn't let go even when Mary told her she was hurting her. Dorothy seemed frightened and didn't know where she was. The doctor came in and told Mary that these symptoms were common for people with dementia, but Mary knew her mother and told him that this was different. He decided that Dorothy might be experiencing delirium as a result of the changes in her physical health and nutrition, medications, and environment.

PREVALENCE AND IMPACT Prevalence of delirium is low in the community (1 to 2%), but the condition is a frequent complication of hospitalization among older adults. Among older hospitalized adults, the prevalence of delirium ranges from 29 to 64%, and the disorder is particularly problematic in intensive care units where incidence is as high as 82% (Saczynski & Inouye, 2015). Delirium also is common among older patients seen in the emergency room (30%) and those who have had surgery (15 to 53%; Fearing & Inouye, 2009). Over the past 10 years, prevalence estimates have been increasing, perhaps as a result of briefer hospital stays that do not allow sufficient time for full recovery from surgery (Liptzin, 2004). People with major NCD are at a significantly higher risk of experiencing delirium (Fearing & Inouye, 2009; McCusker et al., 2011). Among all older adults, delirium is associated with longer hospital stays (Ely et al., 2001; Thomason et al., 2005), more complications following surgery, poorer post-hospitalization functioning, increased risk of institutional placement (Liptzin, 2004), and higher rates of mortality (Saczynski & Inouye, 2015). Although most people recover from delirium, for older adults the recovery process may occur over several weeks.

SEX, RACE, AND ETHNICITY Men are at higher risk for delirium than women (Fearing & Inouye, 2009; Liptzin, 2004). However, incorrectly diagnosed women more often receive a diagnosis of major depressive disorder, and misdiagnosed men are more frequently given no diagnosis (Armstrong et al., 1997). African Americans and non-African Americans have similar rates of delirium (Campbell et al., 2014).

Etiology and Treatment of Delirium

LO 14.19 Understand possible causes of and treatments for delirium.

ETIOLOGY Delirium is associated with a range of biological and environmental factors (Liptzin, 2004; Raskind et al., 2004), but medication use is the cause in 40% of cases (Saczynski & Inouye, 2015). Medication toxicity occurs more easily among older

DSM-5

Criteria for Delirium

A. A disturbance in attention (i.e., reduced ability to direct, focus, sustain, and shift attention) and awareness (reduced orientation to the environment).

B. The disturbance develops over a short period of time (usually hours to a few days), represents a change from baseline attention and awareness, and tends to fluctuate in severity during the course of a day.

C. An additional disturbance in cognition (e.g., memory deficit, disorientation, language, visuospatial ability, or perception).

D. The disturbances in Criteria A and C are not better explained by another preexisting, established, or evolving neurocognitive disorder and do not occur in the context of a severely reduced level of arousal, such as coma.

E. There is evidence from the history, physical examination, or laboratory findings that the disturbance is a direct physiological consequence of another medical condition, substance intoxication or withdrawal (i.e., due to a drug of abuse or to a medication), or exposure to a toxin, or is due to multiple etiologies.

adults because they metabolize drugs differently and often take multiple medications that could interact to produce adverse drug effects. Other biological causes of delirium include infection, metabolic disorders (e.g., hypothyroidism or hypoglycemia), neurological disorders (e.g., head trauma, stroke, seizure, or meningitis), malnutrition or severe dehydration, and alcohol or drug intoxication or withdrawal. The risk of delirium increases with age and cognitive impairment. In some cases, episodes of delirium may be the first symptom of an underlying major neurocognitive disorder (Raskind et al., 2004).

Environmental factors also increase the risk for delirium during hospitalization, including the use of physical restraints, more than three medications, and/or a bladder catheter (Saczynski & Inouye, 2015; Weber et al., 2004). Risk factors that contribute to dehydration, poor nutrition, and sleep deprivation are also important. How these factors interact is not entirely clear, but delirium is associated with dysfunction in the prefrontal cortex, thalamus, and basal ganglia. Furthermore, a number of neurotransmitters may be involved (e.g., dopamine, serotonin, GABA, acetylcholine) (Liptzin, 2004; Saczynksi & Inouye, 2015; Trzepacz et al., 2002). Although the onset of delirium is complicated, determining its origin is necessary because for some older adults, appropriate intervention (rehydration, stopping medication) may reverse its symptoms.

TREATMENT In up to 70% of people delirium is often not recognized (Saczynski & Inouye, 2015). As a first step, screening for known risk factors (e.g., major NCD, substance use) is necessary. Precautions to minimize delirium include monitoring medications, ensuring proper nutrition and hydration, and managing the patient's sleep–wake cycle (Liptzin, 2004; Weber et al., 2004). When symptoms occur despite prevention strategies, early detection is important to reduce the episode's duration and impact.

Delirium is frightening to patients' families, so education and supportive care are important. Treatment of delirium also involves manipulating the environment (Fearing & Inouye, 2009). Beneficial environmental manipulations include reducing sensory stimulation (e.g., quiet room, low-level lighting), providing orientation through visual cues such as family pictures and clocks, encouraging the presence of family members, minimizing the use of physical restraints, and maintaining a regular day–night routine with open blinds, limited daytime sleeping, and minimal nighttime wakening for vital signs and other medical procedures (Fearing & Inouye, 2009; Liptzin, 2004). If medication is needed to manage severe agitation, low-dose antipsychotic medications can help keep the patient safe and reduce symptoms. When delirium is due to withdrawal of alcohol or other sedatives, short-acting benzodiazepines may be used (Liptzin, 2004).

Major and Mild Neurocognitive Disorders

LO 14.20 Understand the symptoms of major and mild neurocognitive disorders (NCDs).

Major neurocognitive disorder (major NCD) and **mild neurocognitive disorder** (mild NCD) are both characterized by a decline from a previous level of performance in various cognitive domains (e.g., attention, executive function, learning and memory, language; see "DSM-5: Major or Mild Neurocognitive Disorder Due to Alzheimer's Disease"). In major NCD, the decline is significant and interferes with the individual's ability to function independently (e.g., the person needs help with complex activities such as managing medications or paying bills; he or she may not recognize or be able to name objects or people). The term **dementia** was used in the DSM-IV to describe the symptoms of major NCD in older adults, and many clinicians and patients still use this term routinely. In mild NCD, the person can function independently, but tasks take longer and may require the use of *compensatory strategies* (e.g., the individual can still pay bills but needs to keep and recheck

SIDE by SIDE Case Studies

Dimensions of Behavior: From Adaptive to Maladaptive

Adaptive Case Study

Occasional Forgetfulness

Antonia is a 72-year-old Hispanic woman who worked as an administrative assistant in an elementary school for 35 years before she retired at age 65. She was much loved by her coworkers and the children at her school, but she was looking forward to spending more time with her grandchildren and helping out with various volunteer opportunities through her church. Indeed, Antonia found her retirement years very rewarding. She stayed in contact with coworkers who were also friends, and she enjoyed having more time to spend with her husband. Antonia did notice, however, as the years went by that she didn't think as quickly as she used to. She also began to have trouble recalling people's names, which was particularly embarrassing especially when she had known the person for many years. Antonia also misplaced things more often, but her friends said they were having similar experiences, and she always eventually found what she thought she'd lost. Her cognitive symptoms did not get in the way of her functioning, so she just chalked the changes up to normal "aging" and continued to enjoy her retirement life by volunteering at church, taking her grandchildren to the park, doing crossword puzzles, and walking her dog.

Maladaptive Case Study

Major Neurocognitive Disorder

Ernest is a 73-year-old African American male who was the pastor of a small, rural church for 30 years before he retired 10 years ago. He married for the first time when he was 25 and had three children. His wife left their family when the children were 7, 5, and 4 years old. Ernest raised the children on his own with help from his sister, who lived nearby. At age 60, when he was nearing retirement, he married a woman who was 10 years younger. He and his new wife developed an active retirement life filled with traveling, visiting relatives and friends, and playing bridge.

About 4 years ago, Ernest began to have memory problems. He regularly lost his keys and glasses, and he began to rely more on lists when he went about his daily chores and errands. Over time, he became more confused, and he had trouble keeping his lists organized. He began to have difficulty finding the right words to express his thoughts, and his wife noticed that he often repeated himself, telling her the same things several times a day. Ernest had always been very quick with numbers and calculations, but he began to have trouble keeping his mind focused on balancing his checkbook. He made calculation errors and couldn't remember where to record various pieces of financial information. He also got more and more confused during bridge games. As Ernest developed more serious cognitive limitations, he started to feel anxious and depressed. He had always been a cheerful man who was full of life, but as his cognitive difficulties grew, he started to withdraw from social engagements at church and in the community because he was worried that others would notice. He also felt less interested in activities that he used to enjoy. His wife was quite worried about him and how she would be able to continue to care for him if he got more confused.

a list to remember which bills have been paid; taking medications correctly requires careful sorting and labeling; reading a book requires rereading to remember characters and plot). In these NCDs, cognitive difficulties are not accompanied by changes in consciousness or alertness as in delirium.

The symptoms of major NCD are particularly devastating. They gradually rob people of their ability to function independently, and the disorder creates significant emotional problems for patients and their families, who suffer along with them through prolonged periods of increasing dysfunction. Treatments are available to slow progression of the disorders and improve quality of life, but these conditions remain one of the most common and debilitating disorders of older age.

Major and mild NCDs are typically diagnosed only after extensive interviews and history taking with the patient and close relatives or friends, cognitive testing (sometimes neuropsychological testing) and observation, a thorough medical evaluation, and sometimes a neuroimaging test (e.g., CT or MRI; Kimchi & Lyketsos, 2015; Lyketsos, 2009). To diagnose one of these disorders, clinicians compare cognitive difficulties with prior levels of functioning. Understanding the potential etiology is important because reversible causes, although infrequent, can include vitamin deficiency (particularly B-12), thyroid dysfunction, drug toxicity, and normal pressure hydrocephalus (an abnormal increase of cerebrospinal fluid in the brain's ventricles, or cavities) (Clarfield, 2003). In most cases, however, NCD reflects a progressive pattern of cognitive disability and functional impairment.

Watch ALVIN: DEMENTIA (ALZHEIMER'S TYPE)

DSM-5

Criteria for Major or Mild Neurocognitive Disorder Due to Alzheimer's Disease

Major Neurocognitive Disorder

A. Evidence of significant cognitive decline from a previous level of performance in one or more cognitive domains (complex attention, executive function, learning and memory, language, perceptual-motor, or social cognition) based on:

1. Concern of the individual, a knowledgeable informant, or the clinician that there has been a significant decline in cognitive function; and
2. A substantial impairment in cognitive performance, preferably documented by standardized neuropsychological testing or, in its absence, another quantified clinical assessment.

B. The cognitive deficits interfere with independence in everyday activities (i.e., at a minimum, requiring assistance with complex instrumental activities of daily living such as paying bills or managing medications).

C. The cognitive deficits do not occur exclusively in the context of a delirium.

D. The cognitive deficits are not better explained by another mental disorder (e.g., major depressive disorder, schizophrenia).

Mild Neurocognitive Disorder

A. Evidence of modest cognitive decline from a previous level of performance in one or more cognitive domains (complex attention, executive function, learning and memory, language, perceptual motor, or social cognition) based on:

1. Concern of the individual, a knowledgeable informant, or the clinician that there has been a mild decline in cognitive function; and
2. A modest impairment in cognitive performance, preferably documented by standardized neuropsychological testing or, in its absence, another quantified clinical assessment.

B. The cognitive deficits do not interfere with capacity for independence in everyday activities (i.e., complex instrumental activities of daily living such as paying bills or managing medications are preserved, but greater effort, compensatory strategies, or accommodation may be required).

C. The cognitive deficits do not occur exclusively in the context of a delirium.

D. The cognitive deficits are not better explained by another mental disorder (e.g., major depressive disorder, schizophrenia).

Major and mild NCDs are subtyped according to the presumed etiology of the symptoms. Major or mild neurocognitive disorder due to Alzheimer's disease (commonly known as **Alzheimer's disease** [AD]) has a gradual onset and continuing cognitive decline. **Major or mild vascular neurocognitive disorder** is diagnosed when cerebrovascular disease, such as stroke, is a potential cause of cognitive dysfunction. **Substance/medication-induced major or mild neurocognitive disorder** reflects cognitive impairment associated with substance use (abuse of a drug or a medication). Major or mild NCDs also may be the result of medical conditions such as HIV, head trauma, Parkinson's disease and Huntington's disease, or other medical illness (Kimchi & Lyketsos, 2015). In many cases, the disorder likely results from multiple etiologies (Lyketsos, 2009).

Major NCD due to AD is by far the most common subtype of NCD, accounting for up to 75% of all patients (Chapman et al., 2006; Kimchi & Lyketsos, 2015). It has a slow and progressive course of cognitive decline. Early noticeable signs can include forgetting recent conversations, events, or names; repeating statements or questions; getting lost while driving to familiar places; and experiencing difficulty with calculations (Alzheimer's Association, 2015; Chapman et al., 2006; Raskind et al., 2004). Sometimes early symptoms indicate a diagnosis of mild NCD, whereas in other cases the symptoms meet criteria for major NCD. It is not clear whether mild NCD is simply an early stage of major NCD or a separate disorder (see "Examining the Evidence: Is Mild Neurocognitive Disorder a Precursor of Major Neurocognitive Disorder or a Separate Syndrome?"). A diagnosis of major NCD due to AD in the early stages does not imply cognitive incompetence, and many people with AD are able to maintain a positive quality of life for a number of years after diagnosis. As the disorder progresses, however, AD results in more severe impairments in the ability to use language, make decisions, and engage in self-care (see "Real People, Real Disorders: Pat Summitt: Decreasing the Stigma of Alzheimer's Disease"). Behavioral problems also occur and include disrupted sleep, wandering, irritability, and aggression. The rate of progressive deterioration in cognitive capabilities and functioning increases as the severity of the disease worsens (Morris, 2005a).

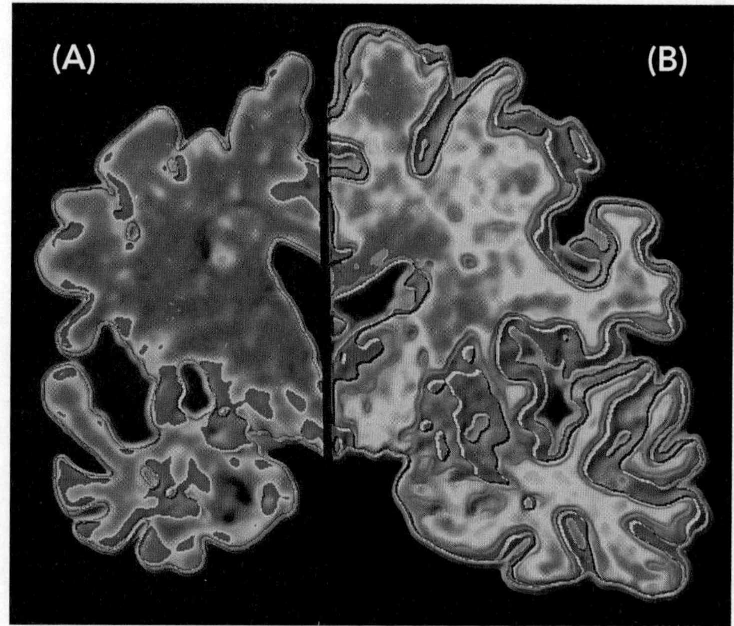

At left, a brain slice from a patient with major neurocognitive disorder due to Alzheimer's disease; at right, the brain of someone without this disorder. The brain on the left is shrunken due to the death of nerve cells.

> Virginia's difficulties were not so obvious at first. In fact, only her husband and best friend realized what was happening. She was able to hide her memory and language difficulties using jokes about her increasing age and self-imposed memory strategies (e.g., writing notes to herself, sticking to usual routines) along with support from her husband. However, as time went on, these strategies were less effective, and other people began to notice how much trouble she was having. Virginia's friends at her Bible study group realized that she was having significant trouble tracking conversations and understanding what she was reading.

A long period of gradual deterioration such as Virginia's is typical of this disease and can be devastating to family and friends of the person affected. Caregiver burden is a significant associated problem given the course and duration of the disease, and many people with AD or other major NCDs spend their final years in a nursing home (Alzheimer's Association, 2015).

We now know that AD involves the presence of **neurofibrillary tangles** (NFT), composed of an abnormal form of the tau protein within neurons, and **cerebral senile plaques** (SP), deposits of beta-amyloid protein that form between the cells in the hippocampus, cerebral cortex, and other regions of the brain (Chapman et al., 2006; Kimchi & Lyketsos, 2015; Morris, 2006).

Examining the EVIDENCE

Is Mild Neurocognitive Disorder a Precursor of Major Neurocognitive Disorder or a Separate Syndrome?

- **The Facts:** The symptoms of mild NCD differ from major NCD primarily with regard to severity. In mild NCD, cognitive impairment is greater than expected for the person's age and education but not severe enough to interfere with independent functioning. People with mild NCD can function independently through the use of accommodations or compensatory strategies, whereas people with major NCD require assistance from others to carry out daily activities. A number of different terms have been used to describe symptoms of mild NCD in older adults, including mild cognitive impairment (MCI) and cognitive impairment not dementia (CIND). Given that the primary differences between the mild and major forms of cognitive impairment relate to severity, is mild NCD simply a precursor of major NCD?

  MCI, a term previously used to describe mild NCD, occurs in 10 to 20% of people over age 65 (Langa & Levine, 2014). **Amnestic MCI** is a subtype of mild NCD in which cognitive complaints focus on memory difficulties (Petersen et al., 2001). Determining the nature and predictive value of MCI or mild NCD may be important in establishing prevention strategies or early treatment.

- **What Data Support Mild NCD (MCI) as a Precursor of Major NCD?**
  1. Approximately 46% of people with MCI progress to a diagnosis of major NCD within 3 years (Kimchi & Lyketsos, 2015), and the majority develop major NCD eventually (Lyketsos, 2009).
  2. People with mild MCI and the *APOE4* allele gene are at increased risk for developing major NCD (Kimchi & Lyketsos, 2015).
  3. Neuroimaging and neuropathology studies suggest that people with MCI share features with Alzheimer's disease including hippocampal atrophy and neurofibrillary tangles (Petersen et al., 2001).
  4. Amnestic MCI appears to be a precursor for AD (Morris, 2005; Peterson et al., 2009).

- **What Data Refute Mild NCD as a Precursor of Major NCD?**
  1. Approximately one-third of people with MCI improve such that their cognitive difficulties are no longer noticeable in the next few years (Kimchi & Lyketsos, 2015).
  2. *Conversion rates* (the rates at which people with MCI progress to a diagnosis of major NCD) vary widely across studies (Langa & Levine, 2014), perhaps due to difficulties in diagnosing MCI and other mild NCDs.
  3. Symptoms similar to those of MCI can result from many different causes including major depressive disorder, substance-related disorders, and side effects of medications (Morris, 2005b).
  4. Medication treatments for major NCD (cholinesterase inhibitors [CEIs]) are not effective for MCI.

- **Conclusions.** For the majority of people with mild NCD (MCI), conversion to major NCD occurs with the passage of time. This relation is particularly strong between amnestic MCI and the development of AD. However, a good proportion of people with mild NCD will recover cognitive abilities over time. As such, all people with mild NCD should be monitored regularly for any worsening of symptoms and may benefit from interventions to reduce other risk factors (Langa & Levine, 2014).

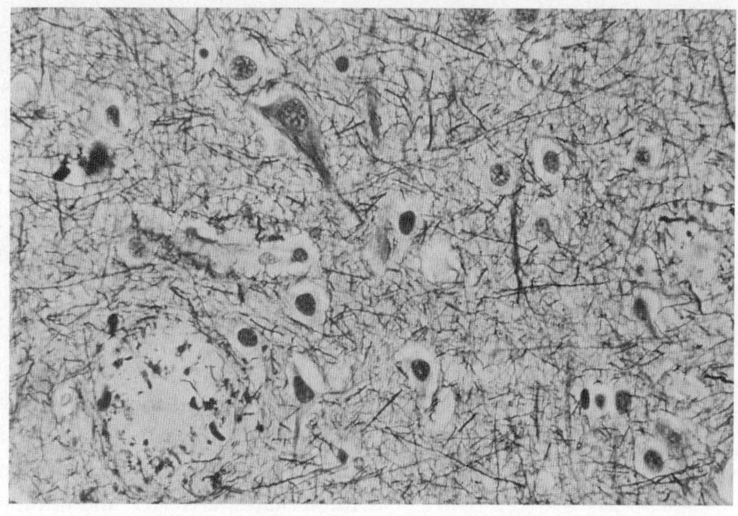

A microscopic examination of brain tissue taken from a patient with Alzheimer's disease reveals the neurofibrillary tangles (dark triangular shapes at left) and cerebral senile (amyloid) plaques (dark round shapes at right) associated with this disorder.

Increased frequency of NFTs and SPs accompanies normal aging, but people with AD have excessive amounts. Autopsies indicate that current clinical procedures for diagnosing AD are largely accurate (Kimchi & Lyketsos, 2015; Morris, 2005a). Brain changes associated with AD, however, likely begin years or even decades before symptoms are evident, suggesting the possibility of early identification and prevention once reliable biomarkers are developed (Alzheimer's Association, 2015; Kimchi & Lyketsos, 2015). Possible biomarkers may include levels of beta-amyloid and tau in the cerebrospinal fluid. Given heterogeneity in the association of brain changes and manifestation of AD symptoms, the experience of AD may have more to do with the location of the NFTs and SPs and the neurotransmitter systems that are affected (Kimchi & Lyketsos, 2015; Lyketsos, 2009).

Major or mild vascular NCD is diagnosed when a patient's history, laboratory tests, and/or brain imaging studies indicate cognitive impairment as a result of cardiovascular disease, such as stroke, transient ischemic attack (TIA, or mini-stroke), coronary artery disease, or untreated high blood pressure. In these conditions, blockages of blood vessels result in tissue death, or *infarction*, in the brain. Damage may be to a single, major vessel or to a number of smaller ones (Morris, 2005a). Vascular NCD can resemble AD with regard to clinical presentation, but it may also be associated with a more sudden onset, more focal or "patchy" cognitive deficits, and more stepwise progression of cognitive difficulties (Chapman et al., 2006). However, vascular NCD rarely occurs alone, and in most cases, people with major NCD have evidence of both AD and vascular NCD. "Pure" cases of AD and vascular NCD are rare.

REAL People REAL Disorders

Pat Summitt: Decreasing the Stigma of Alzheimer's Disease

"Earlier this year the doctors at the Mayo Clinic diagnosed me with an early-onset dementia—Alzheimer's type."

—*Pat Summitt, August 23, 2011, in a public statement made from her home in Blount County, TN*

Although Alzheimer's disease typically appears in people who are 65 years or older, it can have particularly devastating effects on adults who are much younger (called early-onset Alzheimer's disease). Pat Summitt, head women's basketball coach for the Lady Volunteers (or "Lady Vols") at the University of Tennessee, received this diagnosis in the summer of 2011 at the age of 59. Summitt initially contacted her doctors at the end of the 2011 basketball season, feeling like she had been having trouble thinking throughout the season. She originally thought her symptoms resulted from medication she was taking for arthritis, but an evaluation at the Mayo Clinic revealed early-onset dementia—Alzheimer's type. Her grandmother also suffered from this same disorder.

Pat Summitt is described as an "icon" of women's basketball, leading the Lady Vols to eight national championships and 1,071 career wins. This record trumps any other coach, man or woman, in the NCAA. Summitt's career also includes a silver medal as a player on the 1976 United States Olympics team and a gold medal as a coach for the 1984 team.

Following her public statement and conversations with her players, Summitt continued to work as a coach during the 2011–2012 season, but she relied more heavily on assistant coaches. The team finished the season with a 27–9 record.

A "We Back Pat" campaign arose among her fans and supporters almost overnight, and in November 2011 Summitt announced the formation of the Pat Summitt Foundation Fund to support research. Summitt's courage in being open about her disease was influential in increasing public awareness and reducing the stigma of AD. After her diagnosis, she continued to receive numerous awards and honors, including the Presidential Medal of Freedom on April 19, 2012. Sadly, on June 27, 2016, at the young age of 64, Summitt passed away peacefully surrounded by family. http://sportsillustrated.cnn.com/2011/basketball/ncaa/08/23/Pat.Summitt.dementia/index.html?hpt=hp_c2; http://espn.go.com/womens-college-basketball/story/_/id/6888321/tennessee-lady-vols-pat-summitt-early-onset-dementia; http://patsummitt.org/our_role/pats_story.aspx

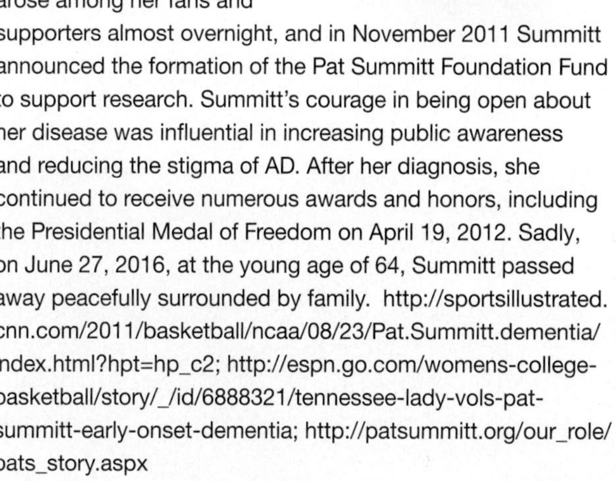

Substance use, in particular alcohol-related disorder, can lead to dementia that is difficult to differentiate from AD. In *substance/medication-induced major or mild NCD*, however, abstinence may stop or even reverse cognitive decline and cortical damage (Atkinson, 2004). Substance use may also increase vulnerability to other forms of dementia and the risk for other contributing factors, such as head trauma, infectious disease, and vitamin deficiency.

A number of medical conditions are also associated with NCDs. These syndromes result from damage that occurs primarily in the inner layers of the brain and frequently emerge during the later stages of HIV and in Parkinson's and Huntington's diseases.

PREVALENCE AND IMPACT In 2005, 29.3 million people worldwide were estimated to have major NCD, at a cost of $315.4 billion in health care (Brodaty et al., 2011). By 2030, the percentage of people with NCD is expected to reach 65 million (Kimchi & Lyketsos, 2015), with an associated increase in health care costs. The prevalence of major NCD increases dramatically with advancing age (Figure 14.4). As noted earlier, AD is the most common type, diagnosed in up to 75% of cases. Approximately 11% of people age 65 and over in the United States have AD, and another 200,000 have early-onset AD (Alzheimer's Association, 2015). Despite these high prevalence figures, many patients with NCD remain undiagnosed and untreated (Morris, 2005a).

The impact of NCD on patients, their families, and the health care system is enormous.

> Gene finally had to move in with his daughter, Sarah, and her family because he just couldn't function independently anymore. Although Sarah knew this was the right thing to do, it was hard on everyone. Someone had to be with him most of the time, and it was difficult for everyone to watch Gene, who had once been a vibrant man with many interests and skills, gradually deteriorate to a point where he couldn't remember their names.

As cognitive abilities and functional capacity deteriorate, negative emotional, social, and behavioral outcomes occur (Kunik et al., 2003; Lyketsos, 2009). In the early stages, social and emotional withdrawal is common. Remember how Ernest started to withdraw from activities at church and in the community for fear that people would notice his memory problems? Up to 50% of patients with AD also have depressive symptoms (Chi et al., 2014), and as many as 70% have anxiety symptoms (Seignourel et al., 2008). These figures are not surprising given the significant distress patients experience as a result of this deteriorating, debilitating condition. Anxiety and depression that are comorbid with AD result in more behavioral problems and increased limitations in daily activities (Seignourel et al., 2008; Starkstein et al., 2008). The

Figure 14.4 The Prevalence of Major NCD Increases with Age.

Although individual studies report different prevalence estimates, all research shows that the disorder becomes more prevalent as people get older.

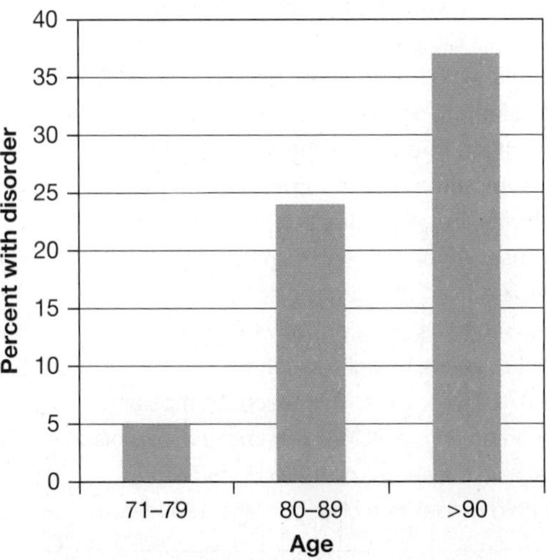

combination also increases social disability, decreases independence (Porter et al., 2003; Schultz et al., 2004), and increases the need for moving to a nursing home (Gibbons et al., 2002).

People with major NCD have more frequent coexisting medical conditions and reduced life expectancy. AD, in fact, is the sixth-leading cause of death in the United States (Theis et al., 2013). Major NCD also affects the treatment of medical conditions. Cognitively impaired people are often unaware of changes in symptoms and treatment needs, and they have limited capacity to participate in health care decision making, self-care, or other health care plans (Boise et al., 2004; Brauner et al., 2000).

As Gene's memory and ability to express himself decreased, Sarah had to accompany him to all doctor appointments and coordinate all of his medical care.

Major NCD also affects family caregivers. Wives, daughters, and daughters-in-law have the heaviest burden of care including assistance with nutrition and exercise, providing memory aids and activities for daily living, and making behavioral plans to manage associated mood and behavior problems (Chapman et al., 2006). Caregivers are at increased risk themselves for depression and anxiety (Alzheimer's Association, 2015; Cooper et al., 2007; Schoenmakers et al., 2010).

For Sarah, taking care of her father was a full-time job. It limited the amount of time she could give to her children, making her feel guilty and sad. It was also difficult to remain patient when she had to answer the same questions over and over.

Family caregiver stress is the most common reason for placing people with NCD in assisted living facilities (Alzheimer's Association, 2015). Use of health services and health care costs are also significantly higher than for people with similar chronic conditions but no NCD. In fact, the annual cost of health care for people with major NCD is three times as high as the cost for people without the disorder (Alzheimer's Association, 2015).

SEX, RACE, AND ETHNICITY AD is more frequent in women than men (Alzheimer's Association, 2015; Reisberg et al., 2003). Older African Americans and Hispanics also are more likely than older whites to have major NCD, although these differences may be accounted for to some degree by variations in socioeconomic variables, language and literacy, health-related factors (e.g., prevalence of chronic illnesses), and culturally based measures of cognitive functioning (Alzheimer's Association, 2015). Among Koreans, Japanese, and Chinese, cases of AD and vascular NCDs have increased over the past 25 years, and the most likely factors are the environmental or dietary changes associated with increased Westernization (Sakauye, 2004).

The increase in AD and vascular NCDs among Koreans, Japanese, and Chinese is likely due to dietary changes associated with Western influences.

Etiology

LO 14.21 Summarize potential biological and nonbiological factors that may play a role in the onset of NCD.

ETIOLOGY OF NCD As with all complex conditions, NCDs most likely result from multiple genetic and environmental factors. Family studies suggest increased rates of AD in people with a first-degree relative with the disorder, and twin studies support the potential role of genetic factors (Kimchi & Lyketsos, 2015). Early-onset AD (before age 65), which accounts for 1% of all Alzheimer's disease cases, is associated

Table 14.3 Risk and Protective Factors for NCD

Risk Factors	Protective Factors
Increasing age	Advanced education
Family history of NCD	Physical activity
Presence of e4 variant of *APOE* gene	Dietary factors (increased omega 3; decreased fat and cholesterol; vitamins C, D, and E)
Cardiovascular disease and associated factors (smoking, obesity, diabetes, hypertension)	Moderate alcohol use (especially red wine)
	Engagement in social and mental activities

with mutations in at least one of three different genes (Morris, 2005b). In most cases, signs and symptoms arise after age 65. Increasing age itself is one of the strongest predictors of NCD with the risk increasing by 0.5 to 1.0% per year after the age of 70 (Tsuang & Bird, 2004). Most cases with later onset are associated with multiple genes, but a specific mutation (e4) of the *APOE* gene greatly increases the risk of these disorders by at least 50%, probably through an impact on the age of onset (Lyketsos, 2009; Morris, 2005b; Tsuang & Bird, 2004). People with mild NCD who have this variant of the *APOE* gene are at increased risk for developing major NCD (see "Examining the Evidence: Is Mild Neurocognitive Disorder a Precursor of Major Neurocognitive Disorder or a Separate Syndrome?"). However, this mutation is neither necessary nor sufficient; only 40 to 65% of people with AD have this gene variant (Alzheimer's Association, 2015). Genome-wide assessment studies (GWASs) have identified up to 11 additional genes that may have a role in the etiology of AD, some of which may be linked to pathways that involve cholesterol metabolism and immune system functioning (Kimchi & Lyketsos, 2015).

Environmental and other nongenetic factors interact with genetic factors to influence the onset of NCD. For example, genetic factors appear to be less important after age 85 (Silverman et al., 2003). Cardiovascular disease and associated behaviors and illnesses (e.g., smoking, obesity, diabetes, hypertension) are linked to an increased risk of AD and other NCDs (Alzheimer's Association, 2015). In addition, certain *protective factors* may reduce the risk of cognitive decline (Table 14.3). Advanced education seems to reduce the risk of dementia (Gurland, 2004), possibly by creating cognitive reserves such as increased coping skills that minimize the impact of cognitive deterioration. Advanced education may also increase neuronal connections that counterbalance noticeable changes in memory as NFTs and SPs develop (Bourgeois et al., 2003). In addition, older adults with increased education may use more of their frontal lobes; that is, they may have neurobiological reserves that facilitate coping with cognitive deterioration (Springer et al., 2005). Other potential protective factors include physical activity, diet (e.g., increased intake of omega-3 polyunsaturated fatty acids; decreased fat and cholesterol intake; vitamins C, D, and E), moderate use of alcohol, and increased engagement in social and mental activities (e.g., doing puzzles, playing a musical instrument, using a computer) (Almeida et al., 2012; Alzheimer's Association, 2015; Lyketsos, 2009). Prevention strategies are important as they improve quality of life and decrease health care costs. Even a 1-year delay in the onset of NCD would result in 12 million fewer cases around the world by the year 2050, and this decrease would lower the health care burden (Brodaty et al., 2011).

Treatment

LO 14.22 Discuss pharmacological and psychological treatment strategies for major and minor NCDs.

No treatment yet has been developed that successfully reverses or modifies the progression of NCD (Kimchi & Lyketsos, 2015). For now, available treatments target delaying the expression of symptoms, prolonging independent functioning, improving quality of life, managing associated emotional and behavioral symptoms, and providing support and assistance to patients and caregivers. Treatments include pharmacological and psychological approaches. Medications known as *cholinesterase inhibitors* (CEIs; e.g., Aricept, Exelon) have positive effects on cognition and global functioning relative to placebo for people with AD (Deardorff et al., 2015). AD is associated with the destruction of neurons that release the neurotransmitter acetylcholine. Because it is not yet possible to regenerate these acetylcholine-producing neurons, CEIs block the enzyme that breaks down this neurotransmitter. This process increases the remaining level of acetylcholine in the brain. CEIs do not reverse the damage to the neurons but merely allow whatever neurotransmitter is left to function more effectively. Improvements with these drugs are greatest in the early stages of AD before extensive neurobiological damage has been done. The use of CEIs is not dramatic with regard to cognition or function, but they may slow down evidence of decline and delay movement to a nursing home (Kimchi & Lyketsos, 2015). These medications, however, do not improve symptoms for people with minor NCD nor reduce rates of conversion to major NCD (Kimchi & Lyketsos, 2015; Langa & Levine, 2014).

Other medical treatments target cardiovascular risk factors (e.g., cholesterol, diabetes, hypertension). A large meta-analysis, however, showed that using statins (drugs to reduce cholesterol) does not prevent cognitive decline or the incidence of major NCD (McGuinness et al., 2016). As the severity of AD and other major NCDs increases, another medication (memantine or Namenda) can be added to block overproduction of the neurotransmitter glutamate (Kimchi & Lyketsos, 2015), which plays a role in learning and memory. High doses of vitamin E also appear to slow the progress of symptoms, but very high doses of vitamin E may increase mortality (Dysken et al., 2014; Miller et al., 2005). Medications can also control the noncognitive symptoms including emotional disturbance, aggression, agitation, psychotic symptoms, and sleep disturbance. Antidepressant medications are useful to treat depression and other emotional symptoms (Chi et al., 2014). Antipsychotic medications can reduce delusions, hallucinations, agitation, and aggression. Because these drugs can have very serious side effects (increased risk of seizures, tardive dyskinesia, cardiovascular adverse events, and mortality), they should be used cautiously.

Psychological interventions do not affect disease progression directly but may significantly minimize its impact and improve quality of life. These strategies include changing the environment to ensure patient safety (e.g., walking aids to prevent falls, driving limitations or discontinuation), structuring daily routines, and facilitating appropriate nutrition, exercise, and social engagement (Kimchi & Lyketsos, 2015). Caregivers play a major role in helping patients make these changes, providing assistance with activities of daily living (household chores, transportation, health care appointments, and sometimes dressing, toileting, and eating), correct use of medications, managing behavioral and psychological symptoms (agitation, aggression, depression, anxiety), and hiring/supervising others who provide care (Alzheimer's Association, 2015). The burden of caregiving is tremendous.

Cognitive functioning can also be improved by cognitive training strategies that enhance comprehension, learning, and memory even among people with severe NCD (Bayles & Kim, 2003; Bourgeois et al., 2003; Sitzer et al., 2006). Behavioral interventions may reduce agitation and aggression (Gallagher & Herrmann, 2015), anxiety (Paukert et al., 2010), and depression (Teri et al., 2003). Caregivers also benefit from cognitive-behavioral interventions to manage stress, increase coping skills, and decrease depression (Cooper et al., 2007; Gallagher-Thompson & Coon, 2007). Using the Internet to deliver these interventions may be a cost-effective and less-burdensome method by which to reach caregivers (Blom et al., 2013). Although some studies have shown a positive effect of exercise programs for people with NCD, a recent meta-analysis failed to demonstrate positive effects of exercise on cognitive functioning or depression (Forbes et al., 2015). People with NCD and their caregivers frequently need help with identifying community resources to provide assistance and support (Kimchi & Lyketsos, 2015).

Learning Objective Summaries

LO 14.18 Describe the symptoms and prevalence of delirium in older adults.

The primary feature of delirium is an acute or sudden change in attention and awareness. Symptoms include disorganized thinking and language, decreased wakefulness and stupor, and/or severe insomnia and hyperarousal. Symptoms may wax and wane within or across days. Prevalence of delirium is low in the community, but the condition is a frequent complication of hospitalization among older adults. Men are at higher risk for delirium than women.

LO 14.19 Understand the possible causes of and treatments for delirium.

Possible causes of delirium include medication use, infection, disease, malnutrition or dehydration, and alcohol or drug intoxication or withdrawal. Treatment begins with manipulating the environment to reduce sensory stimulation, increase orientation, minimize the use of physical restraints, and maintain a regular day–night routine. If medication is needed, low-dose antipsychotic medications can be useful. Education and supportive care for the patient and family also are important.

LO 14.20 Understand the symptoms of major and mild neurocognitive disorders.

Major NCD and minor NCD are both characterized by a decline from a prior level of performance across cognitive domains (e.g., attention, executive function, learning and memory, language). In major NCD the decline interferes with the ability to function independently. In minor NCD the individual can still function independently with accommodations and compensatory strategies. Major and minor NCDs are subtyped according to the expected etiology of the symptoms.

LO 14.21 Summarize potential biological and nonbiological factors that may play a role in the onset of NCD.

NCDs likely result from genetic and environmental factors. Genetic risk factors have been identified for early and late onset AD. A specific mutation (e4) of the *APOE* gene increased the risk of these disorders by 50%, probably through an impact on the age of onset. Cardiovascular factors also affect the risk for major NCD. Protective factors include advanced education, physical activity, nutrition, alcohol use, engagement in social and mental activities, and use of nonsteroidal anti-inflammatory drugs.

LO 14.22 Discuss pharmacological and psychological treatment strategies for major and minor NCDs.

No treatment yet is available to reverse or modify the progression of NCD. Available treatments target delaying the expression of symptoms, prolonging independent functioning, improving quality of life, managing associated emotional and behavioral symptoms, and providing support and assistance to patients and caregivers. CEIs are medications with positive effects on cognition and global functioning for people with AD. These medications, however, do not improve symptoms for people with minor NCD. Psychological interventions include changing the environment to ensure patient safety, structuring daily routines, and facilitating appropriate nutrition, exercise, and social engagement. Caregivers also benefit from psychological interventions to manage stress.

Critical Thinking Question

Your grandmother is showing signs of memory loss. Think about what other signs and symptoms her doctor might look for to decide if she is developing minor or major NCD. If she is diagnosed with minor NCD, what treatments do you think the doctor will recommend?

Real SCIENCE Real LIFE

Charlotte—The Psychopathology and Treatment of Anxiety Disorder in an Older Adult

THE PATIENT

Charlotte is a 78-year-old widow who was always a worrier and a perfectionist. Her parents were loving but often critical when her school performance or other behavior wasn't perfect. Charlotte was very successful in her early years. She completed a college degree and worked as a bank teller and supervisor for 8 years before she married and had children. She stopped working when she had her first baby but remained busy with volunteer work during the years when she raised her three children. Throughout her life, despite outward success, Charlotte was always worried that things might not turn out well enough. She was concerned that her children were not doing well enough in school, that she was not a good enough mother, that her home wasn't clean and orderly enough, and that she and her husband might not have enough money to support themselves as they got older.

THE PROBLEM

Despite this persistent worry over the years, Charlotte functioned well in her roles as a wife, mother, and volunteer. When her husband died 5 years ago, however, she realized just how much she had relied on him for reassurance. Without him around to remind her that she was doing a good job and that their children were well adjusted, she had more trouble easing her mind of the worries. She began to spend many hours a day worrying about various things—whether people liked her, how well her grandchildren were doing in school, whether she was doing enough to help at church, and how she would be able to support herself if she developed serious medical problems.

Charlotte also began to experience significant sleep difficulties. She fell asleep easily but woke up frequently during the night, sometimes to go to the bathroom but always with many worries on her mind. Her arthritis also seemed to be getting worse, possibly because of increased muscle tension, and she developed serious problems such as back and neck pain. Charlotte found herself more irritable and snappy with her children, and she noticed difficulties with her memory and concentration. She misplaced things regularly and spent a lot of time looking for her keys, purse, and calendar. She also had difficulty concentrating when she sat down to read, and her children noticed that she was irritable and preoccupied most of the time.

DIAGNOSIS

Charlotte initially contacted the clinic for an evaluation of her memory. She was worried that she might have Alzheimer's disease. As part of Charlotte's initial evaluation, she also was assessed for the full range of possible psychiatric disorders. Cognitive evaluations showed no excessive deficits in her memory or thinking, but her symptoms met the criteria for generalized anxiety disorder. She also had symptoms of depression but not with sufficient severity for a diagnosis of major depressive disorder.

ASSESSING THE SITUATION

Based on what you've read of Charlotte's background, problem, and diagnosis, what type of treatment would you recommend, and what evidence would you use to justify this decision?

THE TREATMENT

Initial treatment strategies involved teaching Charlotte how to identify different symptoms of anxiety—for example, physical tension, worry-related thoughts, and behavioral avoidance. Simple self-monitoring forms were created that included spaces for recording various symptoms. As Charlotte became more familiar with her anxiety symptoms, she realized just how often she worried about things. She also learned how to identify physical symptoms of anxiety (e.g., muscle tension) that she had never noticed before.

Next, Charlotte began to learn skills to reduce her anxiety. The goal of this phase of the treatment was to give her a "toolbox" of skills to choose from to manage anxiety. The first skill that she learned was deep breathing. Charlotte used this skill to decrease her anxiety when she noticed her body tensing up. She also learned how to identify and challenge her worry-related thoughts (e.g., "I am a terrible grandmother; my grandchildren don't think I'm any fun.") and substitute them with more realistic thoughts (e.g., "My grandchildren love me. We usually have fun together. It is okay if sometimes they prefer to spend time with someone else."). She also learned how to solve problems instead of just worrying about them and how to push herself to face her worries (e.g., leading prayers at church even though she was afraid she'd say the "wrong" words).

THE TREATMENT OUTCOME

Over a period of 3 months, Charlotte learned many skills, and she began to worry less and felt that her life was more fulfilling.

Key Terms

ageism, p. 530
Alzheimer's disease, p. 555
Amnestic MCI, p. 556
cerebral senile plaques, p. 556
collaborative care, p. 542
delirium, p. 550
dementia, p. 553
depression executive dysfunction syndrome of late life, p. 533
executive dysfunction, p. 533
geropsychology, p. 553
late-onset schizophrenia, p. 547
major neurocognitive disorder, p. 553
major or mild vascular neurocognitive disorder, p. 555
mild neurocognitive disorder, p. 553
neurofibrillary tangles, p. 556
problem-solving therapy, p. 537
reminiscence therapy, p. 537
substance/medication-induced major or mild neurocognitive disorder, p. 555
vascular depression, p. 533
very-late-onset schizophrenia-like psychosis, p. 547

Chapter 15

Abnormal Psychology: Legal and Ethical Issues

Chapter Learning Objectives

Law, Ethics, and Issues of Treatment	LO 15.1	Identify the five aspirational goals related to the science and practice of psychology.
	LO 15.2	Discuss the positive and negative aspects of deinstitutionalization.
	LO 15.3	Understand the difference between criminal and civil commitment.
	LO 15.4	Identify the reasons for involuntary commitment for psychiatric services.
	LO 15.5	Identify differences between three legal terms used in criminal commitment proceedings.

Privacy, Confidentiality, and Privilege in Abnormal Psychology	**LO 15.6**	Define the distinct but related terms of *privacy, confidentiality*, and *privilege*.
	LO 15.7	Describe how HIPAA provides protection for health information and the unique protections provided to mental health treatment.
	LO 15.8	Discuss the duty to warn mandate and how it affects the concept of patient confidentiality.
Licensing, Malpractice Issues, and Prescription Privileges	**LO 15.9**	Understand the various ways that licensing protects the public.
	LO 15.10	Identify at least two behaviors that would be considered malpractice.
	LO 15.11	Identify the advantages and disadvantages of psychologists' having prescription privileges.
Research and Clinical Trials	**LO 15.12**	Describe documents crucial to the development of rights for research participants.
	LO 15.13	Discuss the special considerations that must occur when children participate in psychological research.
	LO 15.14	Understand the need for and proper use of control groups in psychological research.
	LO 15.15	Give reasons why some cultural groups may be reluctant to participate in research.

Colorado therapists Julie Ponder and Connell Watkins were convicted of reckless child abuse and sentenced to 16 years in prison after a young girl died during a "rebirthing" therapy session in April 2000. During the rebirthing session, 10-year-old Candace Newmaker was wrapped tightly in a blanket and pushed on with pillows in an effort to re-create the birth process. Watkins, who was neither licensed nor registered to conduct therapy, held the rebirthing session in her home. At the trial, jurors saw and heard Candace on video begging for her life from under her fabric "womb." The *Denver Rocky Mountain News* published excerpts of dialogue from the video providing a firsthand account of Candace's last hour of life. Throughout the 70-minute tape, Candace begs the therapists to get off of her and let her breathe. At one point, as she cries and pleads for her life, the four adults present pushed even harder on the girl, putting all their adult weight on top of the 70-pound fourth-grader. Here are excerpts from the tape:

CANDACE NEWMAKER: I can't do it. (Screams) I'm gonna die.
JULIE PONDER: Do you want to be reborn or do you want to stay in there and die?
CANDACE NEWMAKER: Quit pushing on me, please.... I'm gonna die now.
JULIE PONDER: Do you want to die?
CANDACE NEWMAKER: No, but I'm about to.... Please, please I can't breathe....
CANDACE NEWMAKER: Can you let me have some oxygen? You mean, like you want me to die for real?
JULIE PONDER: Uh huh.
CANDACE NEWMAKER: Die right now and go to heaven?
JULIE PONDER: Go ahead and die right now. For real. For real.
CANDACE NEWMAKER: Get off. I'm sick. Get off. Where am I supposed to come out? Where? How can I get there?
CONNELL WATKINS: Just go ahead and die. It's easier.... It takes a lot of courage to be born.
CANDACE NEWMAKER: You said you would give me oxygen.
CONNELL WATKINS: You gotta fight for it.... (Candace vomits and defecates.)
CONNELL WATKINS: Stay in there with the poop and vomit.
CANDACE NEWMAKER: Help! I can't breathe. I can't breathe. It's hot. I can't breathe....
CONNELL WATKINS: Getting pretty tight in there.
JULIE PONDER: Yep.... less and less air all the time.
JULIE PONDER: She gets to be stuck in her own puke and poop.
CONNELL WATKINS: Uh huh. It's her own life. She's a quitter.
CANDACE NEWMAKER: No.... (This is Candace's last word.)

The women's lawyers tried to convince the jury that Candace was a severely troubled young girl and was lying when she said she could not breathe. Watkins stated in a message to her supporters saying that "somehow the 10-year-old inexplicably stopped breathing." A day after the verdict, Colorado became the first state to make rebirthing therapy illegal. The court case did not address the issue that in Colorado a license is not required to practice psychotherapy.

The tragic case of Candace Newmaker illustrates what can happen when untrained (or undertrained) therapists use a treatment for which there is no scientific support. Certainly, this is a very dramatic example, but many therapists use untested or poorly tested treatments every day. Why would these therapists use such a dangerous procedure? There are many reasons including lack of clinical experience, inability to appropriately evaluate the supporting research, and mistakes about treatment efficacy because of conclusions based on correlational, not causal, data (Doust & Del Mar, 2004). Some therapists deny that empirical data alone should be used to determine whether a therapy works. They argue that *clinical expertise* is equally important (American Psychological Association Task Force on Evidence-Based Practice, 2005). However, from the scientist–practitioner perspective that we have used throughout this book, clinical experience alone is no substitute for data that emerge from well-controlled, internally and externally valid, empirical studies.

In this chapter, we examine legal, ethical, and professional issues relevant to understanding abnormal behavior and its treatment. Why do we include these issues in a book on abnormal psychology? Quite simply, by offering clinical services or conducting research, psychologists assume obligations to patients, to research participants, and to society. To the person seeking treatment, psychologists have the responsibility of practicing in their area of expertise, using treatments that are not harmful (and that preferably have a strong scientific basis), and never doing anything that would sacrifice their patients' health and safety. Furthermore, patients have the right to choose whether to participate in treatment, to choose the type of treatment (pharmacological, psychological), and to expect that their participation in therapy will remain confidential. In a research study, participants have the right to be fully informed of all study requirements and the right to refuse to participate. Their participation in a project must clearly involve more benefits than risks, and their rights and dignity must be respected.

As a society, we sometimes decide that protecting the public from potential risk is more important than the rights of an individual in treatment or the needs of a researcher. To protect the public, psychologists must inform appropriate third parties if a patient threatens bodily harm to another person. Sometimes courts decide that people with mental illness who have been arrested for a crime can be forced to take medications to treat their condition. In these instances, basic rights such as the right to confidentiality and the right to refuse treatment are compromised to protect society. In the next section, we examine society's laws and psychologists' ethical obligations when they provide clinical services.

Law, Ethics, and Issues of Treatment

Many laws regulate common activities such as driving a car, buying and consuming alcohol, voting, and getting married. Other laws strictly prohibit actions such as driving while intoxicated, breaking and entering, and assault. Still other laws regulate the practice of various professions, such as psychology, to protect vulnerable people from unqualified practitioners.

Defining Ethics

LO 15.1 Identify the five aspirational goals related to the science and practice of psychology.

In contrast to laws, **ethics** are accepted values that provide guidance in making sound moral judgments (Nagy, 2011). Groups including families, religions, colleges, and professional

Table 15.1 The Five Aspirational Goals Related to the Science and Practice of Psychology

Aspirational Goals	Definition
Beneficence and nonmaleficence	Psychologists always work to benefit their patients and are always careful not to do anything that causes harm.
Fidelity and responsibility	Psychologists seek to establish relationships of trust and are aware of their responsibilities to patients, colleagues, and society in general.
Integrity	Psychologists promote honesty and truthfulness in their science, teaching, and practice.
Justice	Psychologists promote fairness and equality for all persons. Everyone has equal access to psychology's contributions and services.
Respect for people's rights and dignity	Psychologists value the worth of everyone and uphold rights to privacy, confidentiality, and self-determination.

organizations develop them to guide their members' behavior. In psychology, the American Psychological Association's code of ethics guides the behavior of most psychologists. The code of ethics covers five core values: beneficence and nonmaleficence, fidelity and responsibility, integrity, justice, and respect for people's rights and dignity (American Psychological Association, 2010; see Table 15.1).

When psychologists join a professional organization such as the American Psychological Association or the Association for Psychological Science, they agree to behave in a manner consistent with the association's code of ethics. Failure to do so could result in expulsion from the association. Read the following paragraph and identify which ethical principles were violated.

> Dr. Smith is conducting research on psychotherapy. He recruits his students to participate in the research project, promising them extra credit in class. He promises that any information they provide will remain confidential. After looking at the research videotapes, he realizes that the responses from the participants illustrate "classic" responses, and he decides to use the tapes in a professional workshop he will do next month.

Dr. Smith violated the aspirational goals of *integrity* (he was not honest about how he would use the videotapes). He also violated the aspirational goal of *respect for people's rights and dignity* because showing the videos at a workshop without the permission of his students violates their right to confidentiality.

Other guidance on professional practice comes from state laws. Each state has a licensing board that sets the criteria for who can practice as a psychologist. When psychologists apply for a license, they must agree to adhere to the state's code of ethics (similar to that of many professional organizations) as well as its laws and statutes. If psychologists fail to do so, the state could revoke their license, resulting in an inability to practice. Both licensing laws and codes of ethics promote positive behavior, and the vast majority of psychologists adhere to both sets of standards.

Even when ethical standards are being carefully upheld, psychologists and society struggle to provide optimal treatment to people with psychological disorders. Throughout history, favored approaches to treatment have varied. One of the most dramatic changes has been the shift in views regarding the need for institutionalizing patients. Currently, we are in a phase of deinstitutionalization.

Deinstitutionalization

LO 15.2 Discuss the positive and negative aspects of deinstitutionalization.

Since the time of Hippocrates, physicians have advocated removing patients from society and housing them in environments where treatment can be provided in a humane setting (see Chapter 1). This idea sparked the nineteenth-century "humane movement," which advocated the *removal* of mentally ill persons from the community to hospital-like or

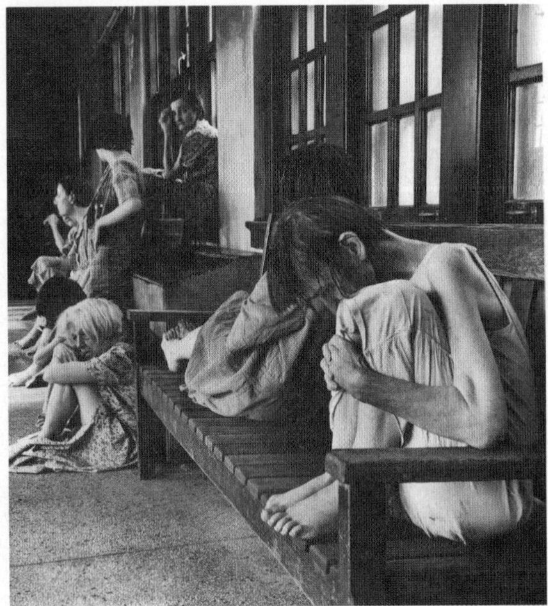

Until the late 1960s, people with psychological disorders were hospitalized in restrictive settings, and most were simply confined without treatment. Few efficacious psychotherapies or medications existed at that time.

residential settings where they could receive appropriate and adequate care. But many such hospitals and residences proved so inadequate—even harmful—that a twentieth-century movement arose to get patients out of institutions and back into the community. At the time, the idea was that needed care would be provided in smaller, more homelike environments where patients could live with fewer restrictions.

Confining patients in hospitals was common mainly because until the 1960s, few treatments controlled aggressive behaviors effectively, making institutionalization the simplest way to protect the public. Institutionalization was also common for people with schizophrenia and mood disorders because effective medications for serious psychological disorders had yet to be discovered. In the United States, state hospitals cared for increasing numbers of people with psychological disorders from their inception in the 1800s to their peak in 1955. At that time, psychiatric institutions had 559,000 beds, and institutionalization was the most common form of psychological treatment (Talbott, 1979/2004). By mid-century, however, it was the institutional setting that was considered inhumane. Hospitals were grossly understaffed, treatment was primarily limited to medications, and few, if any, patients were ever discharged. Few psychosocial treatments were available, and most patients spent their days in their beds or watching television. Discharging patients from these institutions so that they could obtain better care in the community was promoted as the humane alternative.

Beginning in the 1960s, effective medications became available, and treatment options expanded dramatically. Many mental health professionals and others outside the profession believed that when properly medicated, people with serious psychological disorders could function outside institutions if appropriate medical and community support were provided. So began the process of **deinstitutionalization**, the release of inpatients from hospitals to community treatment settings. Proponents of deinstitutionalization argued that community care would be better and cheaper than institutional care, particularly when medications constituted at least part of the treatment. Although medications could not cure serious mental illnesses, they could control seriously disordered *behavior*, allowing some people to leave the locked wards and contribute to society. If we look only at the reductions in numbers of hospitalized patients, the deinstitutionalization movement was very successful. In 2005, there were only 59,403 state mental hospital beds available in the United States, and in 2010, that number had decreased to 43,318 (http://www.tacreports.org/bedstudy; see Figure 15.1). The small number of beds available in 2010 was the same number of beds as there was in 1850, when the movement to provide humane care of the mentally ill began.

Figure 15.1 Patients in Public Psychiatric Hospitals per Total Population.

Over time, the number of people hospitalized in public psychiatric hospitals increased dramatically and then decreased. The rate is now the same as it was in 1850.

Based on data from http://tacreports.org/storage/documents/no_room_at_the_inn-2012.pdf

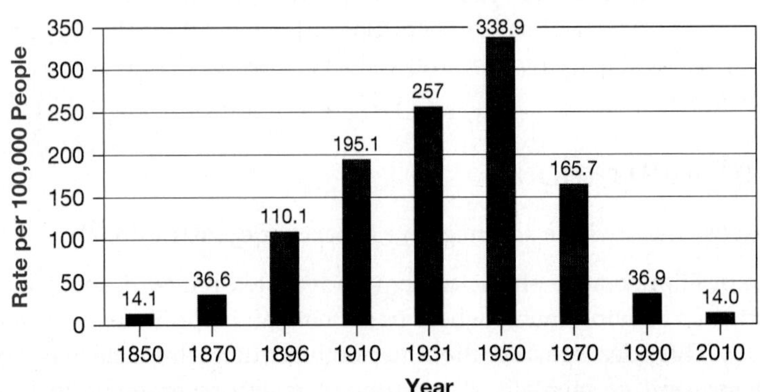

Looking back through a 50-year lens, deinstitutionalization clearly reduced the number of people involuntarily housed in state mental hospitals, but as early as 1979, signs emerged that the community care solution would fail (Talbott, 1979/2004). While the total number of people hospitalized for reasons of mental illness decreased during this time, the number of people with mental illness in state and federal prisons, local jails, and other locked settings *increased* dramatically (Lamb & Weinberger, 2005). These data suggest that the movement never achieved its original objective: to allow those with psychological disorders to reintegrate into the community.

Why did the deinstitutionalization movement fail? Perhaps the most important reason was that discharged patients did not receive the outpatient care and supervision they needed. Outpatient clinics, many of which were state funded, were understaffed and could not provide the treatment needed by patients with severe and chronic disorders. Furthermore, the available staff was often inadequately trained to deal with people suffering from severe psychological disorders. Patients with schizophrenia, for example, did not keep clinic appointments and stopped taking their medication, allowing their psychotic symptoms to reemerge. Without continued treatment, their mental status deteriorated and many patients became a danger to themselves and society, again necessitating forced removal from the community, sometimes to prisons.

The lack of appropriate follow-up care for deinstitutionalized patients illustrates the basic flaw in the deinstitutionalization process, which involves much more than unlocking the hospital doors and allowing patients to leave. Discharged patients must have appropriate places in the community where they can live, get psychological support, and have easy access to mental health services. Furthermore, most of the patients had been unemployed for many years, so they needed vocational counseling and vocational rehabilitation services to help them reenter the workforce. Many people with psychological disorders who were released from hospitals quickly became homeless. This additional negative effect of deinstitutionalization became a major social problem in many cities.

When people with psychological disorders are released from institutions but not given appropriate social supports, they may have difficulty coping with the demands of everyday life. A significant number become homeless.

Psychiatric Commitment

LO 15.3 Understand the difference between criminal and civil commitment.

One of the most negative effects of deinstitutionalization was that many people with psychological disorders ended up living on city streets. Their disheveled appearance and active psychotic symptoms created concern and sometimes fear among community residents (Talbott, 1979/2004), although people with mental disorders are far more often victims of violence than perpetrators (Brekke et al., 2001). According to statistics gathered in 2011, 30% of people who are homeless have mental health problems, and about 50% of that subset of people also have substance abuse disorders (http://homeless.samhsa.gov/ResourceFiles/hrc_factsheet.pdf); the rate of mental illness in the homeless population is higher than the rate in the overall population (15.7%; Cougnard et al., 2006).

At particularly high risk for homelessness are people with schizophrenia or bipolar disorder. Once they leave an institutionalized setting, patients with these disorders often stop taking their medication, and their symptoms return (see Chapters 7 and 11). Among people with serious mental illnesses who were being treated in a large public mental health system, 15% were homeless, including 20% of people with schizophrenia, 17% with bipolar disorder, and 9% with depression (Folsom et al., 2005). The risk of homelessness is higher among people who were young, male, Caucasian, or African American. People who were more likely to be homeless were also more likely to have substance use disorders.

Psychological disorders are also common among children who are homeless. The prevalence of mental health problems among homeless preschool children ranges from 10 to 26%, a percentage that is not higher than children living in stable housing (Bassuk et al., 2015). However, the risk of mental health problems in school-age children ranges from 24 to 40%, a rate that was two to four times higher than a comparison group of housed schoolchildren. It is not clear if these school-age children had mental health problems before they were homeless or if the problems developed after homelessness occurred. In either case, it is important to note that many of these children are in need of mental health services and are least likely to receive them.

Homelessness among patients with severe mental illness is an international problem. In rural China, 7.8% of people with schizophrenia were homeless at some point during a 10-year period (Ran et al., 2006). People most likely to be homeless had ramshackle or unstable housing, had a family history of schizophrenia, had no income, and were unmarried. Among French patients with schizophrenia, people who were homeless were more likely to be male and single, to abuse drugs, and to have had frequent hospitalizations (Cougnard et al., 2006). Across cultures, poor social support and substance use increase the likelihood of homelessness among the mentally ill.

If we consider deinstitutionalization as a process rather than a singular event, it appears that homelessness among people with psychological disorders is not a problem of deinstitutionalization per se but the implementation of the process. Successful deinstitutionalization requires continued outpatient care as well as the skills and resources for living independently (Lamb & Bachrach, 2001). When this does not occur, recently discharged patients may find themselves returning temporarily to locked or structured institutions (including jail) and/or requiring rehospitalization (Lamb & Weinberger, 2005). Even when an adequate community treatment plan exists, patients' adjustment is difficult, and in one sample, only 33% of recently discharged patients were living stable lives in the community and did not require rehospitalization (Lamb & Weinberger, 2005). Clearly, clinicians working with seriously mentally ill people need to be able to identify which patients need which resources to move successfully from a hospital to a community setting. When patients with psychological disorders cannot care for themselves in the community or if they become a danger to themselves or others, they may have to be institutionalized against their will, a process known as *civil commitment*.

Civil Commitment

LO 15.4 Identify the reasons for involuntary commitment for psychiatric services.

> Miguel was brought to the psychiatric emergency room by ambulance. His landlord had called the police because smoke was coming from under Miguel's apartment door. When the police finally broke down the door, they found him burning the furniture. He explained that about a month ago, he became suspicious about his coworkers. He feared that they were reading his mind, so he quit his job. Without any other source of income, he was unable to pay his bills and the electric company shut off his heat. To stay warm, he was burning his furniture in the fireplace, creating a significant fire hazard to everyone in the building.

Miguel's behavior (burning furniture in the fireplace) constituted a danger to himself and to others living in the building. **Civil commitment** is a state-initiated procedure that forces involuntary treatment on people who are judged to have a mental illness, present a danger to themselves (including the inability to care for themselves) or others (Appelbaum, 2006a), and refuse to participate in treatment voluntarily. During the early twentieth century, civil commitment usually meant inpatient hospitalization, and sometimes it still does.

However, with the deinstitutionalization movement, there has been a shift to **outpatient commitment**: "a court order directing a person suffering from severe mental illness to comply with a specified, individualized treatment plan that has been designed to prevent relapse and deterioration. Persons appropriate for this intervention are those who need ongoing psychiatric care owing to severe illness but who are unable or unwilling to engage in ongoing, voluntary, outpatient care" (Lamb & Weinberger, 2005, p. 530). Outpatient commitment is more coercive than voluntary treatment but is less coercive than inpatient hospitalization (Swartz & Monahan, 2001) because the person remains in the community with continued access to social supports.

In some instances, outpatient commitment is a condition for being discharged from a hospital. It is also an alternative to hospitalization for people who are currently in the community and whose condition is deteriorating. Outpatient commitment also may be used as a preventive measure for people considered to be at high risk for psychological deterioration and possible hospitalization (Monahan & Bonnie et al., 2001). There is continued controversy regarding the effectiveness of outpatient commitment for positive treatment outcomes (Steadman et al., 2001; Swartz et al., 2001; Zanni & Stavis, 2007), but patients have better success when therapy is sustained (commitment lasts for more than 6 months) and intensive (approximately seven contacts per month). With this type of planning, hospital admissions are reduced following initiation of outpatient commitment (Swartz et al., 1999; Zanni & Stavis, 2007).

Nevertheless, outpatient commitment is controversial (Geller, 2006; Swanson & Swartz, 2014). The American Psychiatric Association considers outpatient commitment a "useful tool in an overall program of intensive outpatient services aiming to improve compliance, reduce rehospitalization rates, and decrease violent behavior among a subset of the severely and chronically mentally ill" (Gerbasi et al., 2000). However, some members of the public, mental health law advocates, and clinicians oppose treatment coercion of any type, considering it an infringement of civil liberties, an extension of social control, and the alienation of the mentally ill from available treatments and treatment providers (Swartz & Monahan, 2001). In some instances, patients receive social services (welfare benefits and subsidized housing) only if they agree to participate in treatment. In other instances, patients must agree to outpatient commitment to avoid additional severe restrictions (jail, inpatient hospitalization). Most states have an outpatient commitment law, although the specifics of who can be committed to outpatient treatment vary by state (Geller, 2006). To date, there are few empirical data, in the form of randomized controlled trials, that support the effectiveness of court-ordering people to engage in treatment (Geller, 2006), although it is likely impossible to conduct randomized controlled trials in this case (Swanson & Swartz, 2014). Forcing someone to participate in treatment raises ethical concerns for many people (Monahan et al., 2001). In instances such as Miguel's, his right to refuse treatment ended when his actions (burning furniture in his fireplace) put the public (others in the building) at risk.

> Miguel was hospitalized for a week at which time he denied the presence of hallucinations or delusions. He was discharged to a group home where the staff could monitor his medication compliance.

To ensure that he continued to comply with all aspects of this treatment, Miguel was under an outpatient civil commitment order.

Criminal Commitment

LO 15.5 Identify differences between three legal terms used in criminal commitment proceedings.

Civil commitment is a response to behavior that poses a danger to the self or others. **Criminal commitment** occurs when a person with a psychological disorder commits a crime. Within the courtroom, those who are criminally committed may be judged not guilty by reason of insanity, guilty but mentally ill, or incompetent to stand trial. Such court cases are often widely publicized, such as the trials of James Eagan Holmes and Andrea Yates (see Chapters 1 and 11). Despite the media coverage, misconceptions surround what is commonly known as the *insanity defense*.

MENTAL ILLNESS VS. INSANITY

> On March 30, 1981, John W. Hinckley Jr. attempted to assassinate President Ronald Reagan. Hinckley was obsessed with the actress Jodie Foster and had been stalking her for some time. He made numerous attempts to gain her attention including trying to assassinate the

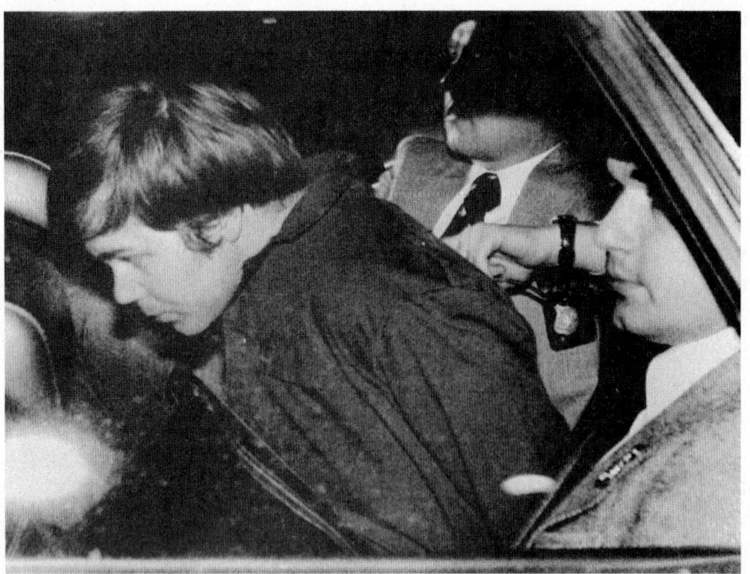

John Hinckley, who attempted to assassinate President Ronald Reagan, was found not guilty by reason of insanity.

president. Hinckley claimed that he had repeatedly watched the movie *Taxi Driver* in which a disturbed man plots to assassinate a presidential candidate. Hinckley shot and severely injured President Reagan, Reagan's press secretary James Brady, a police officer, and a Secret Service agent. A jury found Hinckley not guilty by reason of insanity, and for the past 30 years, he was confined to Saint Elizabeth's Hospital in Washington, DC, for treatment of depression and psychosis, although since 2009 he has been able to visit his parents for several days at a time. In 2015, both the hospital and Hinckley's family argued that it is time for his release, which occurred in August 2016.

For a person to be found guilty of a crime, the state must demonstrate that the accused committed the illegal act and behaved with criminal intent (Scott, 2010). **Not guilty by reason of insanity** (NGRI) is a legal decision that describes people who commit a crime but whose psychological disorder prevents them from understanding the seriousness and illegality of their actions. Therefore, they are considered not to have criminal intent. Andrea Yates, for example, was initially convicted of murdering her five children, but in a second trial, she was found NGRI. A jury found her incapable of understanding her actions because of her psychotic illness. Not every state allows for an NGRI defense, and medical professionals have long been divided on whether those with psychological disorders who commit crimes should be held accountable.

Charles Julius Guiteau shot President James Garfield in 1881. Garfield did not die until 80 days later as a result of infection rather than the gunshot itself. Guiteau appeared to be delusional, yet he was tried and executed for the assassination despite the protests of some medical professionals. His autopsy revealed chronic brain inflammation and other symptoms consistent with a diagnosis of neurosyphilis, a neuropsychological disorder (Paulson, 2006).

Understanding that insanity is a *legal* term, not a psychological disorder, is important. An insanity evaluation typically determines whether a person is so mentally ill that he or she is not responsible for the criminal acts that occurred (Scott, 2010). How such a determination is made differs by state, but in most cases, it is based on one of two insanity rules. The first is the **M'Naghten Rule**, established in England in 1843.

Daniel M'Naghten, possibly as a result of paranoid schizophrenia, believed that the English Tory party was persecuting him. He planned to kill the British prime minister but killed the prime minister's secretary instead.

M'Naghten was tried for the crime, but the court ruled that he was acquitted by reason of insanity. The public did not like the verdict, and the court developed specific guidelines. A person is presumed to be sane and the defense must prove one of the following: (1) at the time the act was committed, the person was suffering from a "defect or disease of the mind" and did not know the nature or quality of the action or (2) he or she did know the nature or quality of the action but did not know that the action was wrong.

There have been several changes to the standard originally established by the M'Naghten Rule. In 1929, the District of Columbia added an "irresistible impulse" test, allowing consideration of whether the defendant suffered from a "diseased mental condition" that did not allow the resistance of an irresistible impulse, acknowledging the idea of volition (freedom to choose or the ability to control behavior). The standard was changed again in 1954 when a judge in the U.S. Court of Appeals created the *Durham*

Rule, which held that an accused person is not criminally responsible if the unlawful act was the result of a mental disease (Scott, 2010). Because of this rule, the court decision hung on the testimony of an expert witness—if the witness said the person had a mental disease, the court had little choice but to find the defendant not criminally responsible. Therefore, the Durham Rule was discarded and replaced by the American Law Institute (ALI) model penal code definition (American Law Institute, 1962). This code states that a person is not responsible for criminal acts if the psychological disorder results in the inability to appreciate the wrongful conduct *or* if the person is unable to conform her or his conduct to the requirement of the law (i.e., the person cannot control her or his behavior).

Finally, the *Insanity Defense Reform Act* of 1984 states that as a result of mental illness, the defendant lacks the capacity to appreciate the nature and quality or wrongfulness of the act. Compared with the M'Naghten test, which is based solely on a cognitive standard (did the person understand his or her actions and know they were wrong?), the more recent criteria consider cognition *or* volition (Scott, 2010).

Committing an illegal act is not the same as committing a crime. To be convicted of committing a crime, a person must possess ***mens rea***, which is Latin for a guilty mind or criminal intent. To be considered guilty of committing a crime, the person must engage in illegal behavior and have *criminal intent*. In many instances, people with psychological disorders lack the intent to commit the crime with which they are charged.

> Eric Clark had been acting oddly for years, convinced that Flagstaff, Arizona, was populated by hostile space aliens. He slept surrounded by a burglar alarm made from fishing line and wind chimes. He decided that the police were aliens as well, and when he was stopped for driving erratically through a residential neighborhood, he shot and killed a Flagstaff police officer (Appelbaum, 2006b).

Clark's lawyers contended that he lacked *mens rea* because his delusions interfered with his ability to recognize that the victim was a police officer, not a hostile space alien. Unfortunately, Arizona law does not allow the introduction of mental illness when juries consider criminal intent. Thus, without being able to introduce his psychotic disorder, Clark was convicted and sentenced to 25 years in prison.

Eric Clark's inability to use the insanity defense is more common than most people believe. Among the many misconceptions about the plea of NGRI (Scott, 2010) is that it is overused. In fact, NGRI is used in less than 1% of all felony cases and is successful only 15 to 25% of the times that it is used. This means that very few people successfully use an insanity defense (see "Real People, Real Disorders: Kenneth Bianchi, Patty Hearst, and Dr. Martin Orne").

Another common misperception is that people who are acquitted as NGRI are simply set free. In fact, as has happened to John Hinckley, most people who are acquitted as NGRI are hospitalized for periods of time as long as, and sometimes longer than, they would have served if found guilty of the crime. Finally, the NGRI defense is not limited to murder cases, and despite public opinion, people who are acquitted are no more likely to be rearrested than those who are convicted felons (Pasewark & McGinley, 1986; Steadman & Braff, 1983).

Remember that NGRI is an affirmative defense: If it is successful, the individual is not subject to criminal incarceration but is subject to civil proceedings regarding confinement (Scott, 2010). This means that the person does not go to jail but may be required to go to an inpatient treatment facility and receive treatment. In contrast, a person who is found **guilty but mentally ill** (GBMI) or *guilty except insane* is considered criminally guilty and is subject to criminal penalties such as incarceration in a penal institution. The addition of "but mentally ill" acknowledges the presence of a psychological disorder when the offense was committed but does not change the person's criminal responsibility. Although proponents of GBMI hoped that it would address the public's concerns regarding NGRI, it has not done so. Specifically, GBMI has not reduced the number of NGRI acquittals (perhaps because that number is already so small). Of even

Table 15.2 Prison and Jail Inmates with Mental Health Problems.

Characteristic	Percent of Inmates in		
	State Prison	Federal Prison	Local Jail
All inmates	56.2	44.8	64.2
Sex			
Male	55.0	43.6	62.8
Female	73.1	61.2	75.4
Race			
White, not Hispanic	62.2	49.6	71.2
Black, not Hispanic	54.7	45.9	63.4
Hispanic	46.3	36.8	50.7
Other	61.9	50.3	69.5
Age			
24 or younger	62.6	57.8	70.3
25–34	57.9	48.2	64.8
35–44	55.9	40.1	62.0
45–54	51.3	41.6	52.5
55 or older	39.6	36.1	52.4

James, D. J., & Glaze, L. E. (2006). Mental health problems of prison and jail inmates. *Bureau of Justice Statistics Special Report.* Washington, DC: Office of Justice Programs, U.S. Department of Justice.

more concern to mental health professionals, GBMI does not ensure that the defendant receives treatment while in prison (Scott, 2010).

MENTAL HEALTH PROBLEMS IN JAILS AND PRISONS As we noted, one of the unfortunate outcomes of deinstitutionalization is that many people with psychological disorders often end up in jails or prisons. The reasons for their incarceration are many but may include diminished capacity and poor judgment, substance use disorders that lead to criminal activity to support their addiction, and charges such as vagrancy or trespassing. The number of people who are in jails and prisons is quite high with some variation based on age, sex, and race (see Table 15.2).

Despite the substantial number of inmates who are suffering from psychological disorders, prisoners may not always receive the treatment that they need. In other instances, people with psychological disorders may be so impaired that they are not even capable of assisting with their own legal defense. This is known as *being incompetent to stand trial*, the issue to which we now turn our attention.

INCOMPETENCE TO STAND TRIAL

Elizabeth Ann Smart, age 14, was kidnapped from her bedroom on June 5, 2002. She was found alive 9 months later not far from her home in the company of two homeless adults, Brian David Mitchell and Wanda Ileen Barzee. It was alleged that Mitchell and Barzee kidnapped Elizabeth to be Mitchell's second wife. After his arrest, a psychological competency evaluation revealed that Mitchell suffered from a delusional disorder. Although he understood the charges against him, he had an impaired capacity to (1) disclose to counsel pertinent facts, events, and states of mind and engage in reasoned choice of legal strategies and options; (2) manifest appropriate courtroom behavior; and (3) testify relevantly. During court appearances, Mitchell would begin to sing and had to be forcibly removed from the courtroom. His

Watch ELIZABETH SMART INTERVIEW

disorder substantially interfered with his relationship with counsel and his ability to participate in the proceedings against him. On July 26, 2005, he was found incompetent to stand trial and was committed to the custody of the executive director of the Utah Department of Human Services for treatment intended to restore him to competency.

In March 2010, a federal judge ruled that Mitchell was faking mental illness, and on November 1, 2010, his trial began. However, because Mitchell disrupted the court proceedings by singing hymns when he entered the courtroom, he watched his trial on video from his holding cell. In December 2010, Brian David Mitchell was found guilty of the kidnapping of Elizabeth Smart. As the verdict was announced, Mitchell loudly sang, "He died, the Great Redeemer died." He is serving a life sentence in the United States Penitentiary in Tuscon, Arizona.

An accused person who is considered to be so functionally impaired as to be unable to assist in his or her own defense is considered incompetent to stand trial. Under U.S. justice, to receive a fair trial, someone accused of illegal behavior must have a rational and factual understanding of court procedures and must be able to consult with his or her lawyer and assist in the defense. Determining whether a defendant is competent to stand trial is the job of a specially trained mental health professional who assesses the person's competency to assist in his or her defense. Although few empirical data exist, 77.5% of people in one sample who were referred for evaluation were found to be incompetent (Stafford & Wygant, 2005). They were more likely to have a psychotic diagnosis than people found to be competent. Psychiatric treatment restored competency in 47% of the individuals initially determined to be incompetent so that they could later stand trial. However, medicating patients just so that they can be tried for illegal behaviors they committed when they lacked criminal intent raises serious ethical issues.

THE RIGHT TO REFUSE MEDICATION/TREATMENT When faced with serious, disabling, or terminal illnesses, people often make choices about treatments. They might refuse treatments that produce serious side effects or do not improve their quality of life. U.S. law accepts the right to refuse treatment and respects the wishes of competent individuals. The use of an *advance directive* (a document that specifies in advance the types of treatments a patient wishes to receive or not receive) allows family members or others responsible to act in accord with the person's wishes. In some states, advance directives exist for the treatment of mental illness as well. But does that right extend to someone who committed a crime but was found to be incompetent to stand trial as a result of a psychological disorder?

Brian David Mitchell initially was judged by the court to be incompetent to stand trial for the crime of kidnapping and imprisoning Elizabeth Ann Smart. Later a judge ruled he was faking, and he was found guilty of the crimes.

Dr. Charles Sell was charged with Medicaid fraud, mail fraud, and submitting false insurance claims. He had a 20-year history of abnormal behavior, beginning with his belief that communists had contaminated the gold that he used for filling teeth. Over the years, he suffered from many different psychotic symptoms. He had occasionally been treated with antipsychotics but stopped taking the medication. He continued to have hallucinations and delusional beliefs including telling the police that "God told me every [FBI] person I kill, a soul will be saved" (Appelbaum, 2003). In 1999, Sell was examined and found mentally incompetent to stand trial. He was hospitalized to determine whether there was a probability that he would ever become competent. After 2 months, the staff recommended that he take antipsychotic medication. Dr. Sell refused, and the medical staff went to court seeking the right to administer antipsychotic medication against his will (Annas, 2004). In 2005, Sell pleaded no contest to charges of fraud and conspiracy to kill a federal agent. He spent 8 years without trial in federal prison. The U.S. District Judge sentenced him to time served, 6 months in a halfway house, and 3 years on parole.

While patients in mental hospitals are often medicated against their will if they are a danger to staff or to other patients, this was not the case for Dr. Sell. He was not a danger to hospital personnel, so forcible medication was solely to restore his competence for trial. The U.S. Supreme Court ruled in this case that someone could be involuntarily medicated solely for the purpose of restoring competency only if (1) important governmental interests were at stake (e.g., having a fair but speedy trial), (2) forced medication made it "substantially likely that the defendant will be competent" and "substantially unlikely that the drug will have effects that renders the trial unfair," (3) no less intrusive means were available, and (4) the medication is "medically appropriate" (Annas, 2004). What did this ruling mean for Dr. Sell? He could not be forced to take medication until these issues were resolved. Should a patient be forced to accept treatment if his behavior is not harmful to himself or others? When psychologists participate in legal proceedings, they must balance society's rights with the American Psychological Association's ethical principles of beneficence and nonmaleficence as well as respect for people's rights and dignity.

REAL People REAL Disorders

Kenneth Bianchi, Patty Hearst, and Dr. Martin Orne

In October 1977 and February 1978, 10 women were found tortured, strangled to death, and abandoned in the hills surrounding Los Angeles, thus giving the offender the name the Hillside Strangler. The police finally arrested cousins Kenneth Bianchi and Angelo Buono, both of whom had committed the crimes. After his capture, Bianchi claimed that he had a multiple personality disorder (MPD—now called DID or dissociative identity disorder; see Chapter 6) and that he was insane. Two experts in the disorder examined Bianchi and reported the existence of a second personality, Steve. Both experts agreed that Bianchi was insane, even though people with dissociative identity disorder usually have at least three separate personalities and Bianchi did not.

Martin Orne, M.D., Ph.D. (1927–2000), was a preeminent scientist who conducted research in many different areas of psychology including hypnosis, memory, and lie detection. Because of his expertise in basic studies of memory and lie detection, Dr. Orne had developed procedures to determine when people were faking a diagnosis or faking being hypnotized.

Called by the prosecution to conduct an additional examination of Mr. Bianchi, Dr. Orne first discussed MPD with him. Bianchi told Dr. Orne about Steve. Dr. Orne told Bianchi that it was rare for someone with MPD to have only two personalities—most people had at least three. Dr. Orne then hypnotized Bianchi, and suddenly a third personality named Bill appeared. In his court testimony, Dr. Orne pointed out that he was not better than the other clinicians, but he showed that Bianchi faked a third personality because of Dr. Orne's prehypnotic suggestion. Dr. Orne also identified another clue that Bianchi was faking MPD. During his initial examination of Mr. Bianchi, Dr. Orne asked him, under hypnosis, to imagine that his lawyer was sitting in the room; Bianchi actually stood up, walked across the room, shook hands with the imagined attorney, and insisted that Dr. Orne had to be seeing the attorney as well. Dr. Orne testified that people under deep hypnosis do not get out of their seats and attempt to shake somebody's hand unless told by the hypnotist to do so. Dr. Orne did not tell Bianchi to do that. Furthermore, deeply hypnotized subjects do not insist that others also see the image. Later, police discovered that Bianchi had numerous books on psychology, diagnostic testing, hypnosis, and criminal law in his home, suggesting that he could have studied how to present himself in an "insane" manner.

Bianchi

Orne

Dr. Orne was not always a witness for the prosecution. In 1976, Patricia Hearst, the heiress who had been abducted by an American radical group known as the Symbionese Liberation Army (SLA), was arrested and tried for participating in a bank robbery. Hearst's lawyers said that her abduction and torture were responsible for her actions, whereas the prosecution suggested that Hearst's appearance during the robbery (she was casually holding a gun) suggested that she was there of her own free will. Although initially concerned that she was faking, Dr. Orne conducted numerous tests, giving her many opportunities to exaggerate or fabricate her story. Unlike Bianchi, Ms. Hearst never picked up on any cues, and according to Dr. Orne, she "really, simply didn't lie" (Woo, 2000). In summary, Dr. Orne was a scientist–practitioner who developed scientific methods in a laboratory setting and then applied his research in clinical and legal settings. His work is the embodiment of the scientist–practitioner model of psychology.

Learning Objective Summaries

LO 15.1 Identify the five aspirational goals related to the science and practice of psychology.

The science and practice of clinical psychology are guided by aspirational principles: beneficence and nonmaleficence, fidelity and responsibility, integrity, justice, and respect for people's rights and dignity.

LO 15.2 Discuss the positive and negative aspects of deinstitutionalization.

The deinstitutionalization movement developed to stop the process of hospitalizing psychiatric patients for the rest of their lives. However, despite the promise of deinstitutionalization, one unfortunate outcome has been the lack of appropriate living arrangements for those with psychological disorders. The result is that many people with severe psychological disorders have not been successful in achieving community integration, resulting in homelessness or return to other state facilities such as jail.

LO 15.3 Understand the difference between criminal and civil commitment.

Civil commitment is a legal process that mandates treatment for people when there is concern that they may be a danger to themselves or others. Patients may be committed to inpatient treatment or outpatient treatment, which is far more common. Criminal commitment occurs when someone commits a crime and may result from jury decisions of not guilty by reason of insanity (NGRI) or guilty but mentally ill (GBMI). Criminal commitment involves removal from society; the person is committed to a psychiatric ward within a penal institution.

LO 15.4 Identify the reasons for involuntary commitment for psychiatric services.

Involuntary commitment for treatment is considered appropriate when a person is a danger to herself or himself or to another person. Therefore, a person who threatens to commit suicide or threatens to harm another person may be committed to a psychiatric care facility against her or his will. Similarly, a person may be committed if she or he is so disabled as to be unable to take care of basic needs (does not eat or drink or take care of other activities of daily living).

LO 15.5 Identify differences between three legal terms used in criminal commitment proceedings.

Insanity is a legal term, not a psychological disorder. For a person to be found guilty of a crime, the state must demonstrate that the accused committed the illegal act and behaved with criminal intent. Not guilty by reason of insanity (NGRI) is a legal decision that describes people who commit a crime but whose psychological disorder prevents them from understanding the seriousness and illegality of their actions. Therefore, they are considered not to have criminal intent. Rarely are patients with serious psychological disorders found to be NGRI. They are also unlikely to be found guilty but mentally ill (GBMI).

Critical Thinking Question

Patients and mental health professionals alike value the right to refuse treatment. The interesting paradox is that even when patients clearly lack the capacity to understand their actions, their negative behavior so concerns the public that there is pressure to restore their mental faculties so that they can be imprisoned for their actions. In such instances, society's need for patients to be accountable for their actions appears to override patients' right to refuse treatment. Is it ethical to treat people who are criminally insane to punish them for committing a horrific crime?

Privacy, Confidentiality, and Privilege in Abnormal Psychology

Fiona has obsessive-compulsive disorder. She has many intrusive thoughts, but the most frightening is that when using a sharp knife, she loses control and stabs her son, severely injuring or perhaps even killing him. Fiona loves her son and is a good mother. She is horrified about these thoughts and does not want to act on them. Yet she is so afraid that she will lose control that she has taken all the knives out of the house (including the butter knives). She has also removed all the scissors. She made an appointment to see a psychologist, but she is worried. What if the psychologist thinks she is crazy?

Psychologists must adhere to the concept known as *privilege*. Even if called to testify in court, they cannot be compelled to reveal what a client told them in a therapy session.

As we have noted throughout this book, psychological disorders are accompanied by significant emotional distress. Part of this distress relates to patients' concerns that they are "crazy" or that others will think that they are "crazy." To help patients feel comfortable, mental health professionals agree that what is discussed within the therapy session will not be revealed to others. The terms *privacy, confidentiality,* and *privilege* describe environments that provide protection against unwilling disclosure of patient information. There are, however, certain conditions in which the therapist must violate these protections, and we address these exceptions later in the chapter when we examine the issue of duty to warn.

Privacy, Confidentiality, and Privilege

LO 15.6 Define the distinct but related terms of *privacy, confidentiality,* and *privilege*.

The concept of **privacy** has a long history in the United States and is the basis for many laws. The right to privacy limits the access of other people to one's body or mind including one's thoughts, beliefs, and fantasies (Smith-Bell & Winslade, 1994).

> Fiona has not told anyone about her intrusive thoughts. At this time, her thoughts are private.

Privacy is a right of the individual who alone can give it away. When a person reveals thoughts, behavior, and feelings to another person, privacy is lost. In the context of therapy, the private information shared with a therapist is considered confidential. **Confidentiality** is an agreement between two parties (in this case, the therapist and patient) that private information revealed during therapy will not be discussed with others.

> Although it makes her quite uncomfortable, Fiona tells the psychologist, Dr. Jones, about her thoughts. Because she and her therapist have established a therapeutic relationship, the content of her intrusive thoughts is now considered confidential. Dr. Jones may not disclose it to others.

The psychologist agrees to keep confidential the information that the patient reveals. Even if the patient decides to discuss that information, the psychologist still is bound by confidentiality.

The third concept is **privilege**, a legal term that prevents a therapist from revealing confidential information during legal proceedings. You may have heard the term *privileged communication*, which is often used to describe conversations between a lawyer and client. Sometimes physicians and psychologists hold privilege, meaning that they are legally protected against being forced to reveal confidential information in a legal proceeding. If communication is privileged, the psychologist cannot be compelled to reveal it in court (or any other legal setting). Privileged communication is not an automatic right of the therapist or the patient. Whereas confidentiality is considered to be an ethical commitment, state law establishes privilege. For mental health clinicians, privilege extends to therapists who are licensed to practice therapy in a particular state.

> Dr. Jones is a licensed psychologist. Therefore, should she ever be subpoenaed in a court case, Dr. Jones would not have to testify about Fiona's mental status or the nature of the treatment because that is privileged information.

Although confidentiality is often assumed to be absolute, it does not apply in certain situations. Psychologists discuss these situations with the patient at the start of treatment. For example, a graduate student in clinical psychology in training to provide therapy requires supervision by a senior psychologist. In supervisory sessions, the trainee shares patient information with the supervisor to make sure that the treatment is conducted appropriately. In this case, the supervisor is bound by the same confidentiality standard as the therapist.

Other situations that require or call for exceptions to confidentiality include instances in which patients make their mental health an aspect of a lawsuit or a criminal defense strategy (such as insanity pleas or malpractice lawsuits). In these cases, neither confidentiality nor privilege applies because the case cannot be decided without knowledge of the situation. Confidentiality is also limited when health insurance companies require information about diagnosis and aspects of treatment (number of sessions, frequency of sessions) to provide payment for mental health treatment.

When treating a child, confidentiality issues become more complicated than with most adults. Some information must be shared with parents whereas other information remains confidential.

Disclosing confidential information is also necessary during civil commitment proceedings when involuntary treatment is necessary because the individual presents a danger to self (such as wanting to commit suicide) or others (a deliberate expression of intent to harm another person).

> Fiona denied any thoughts of hurting herself. She vehemently denied that she wanted to harm her son and, in fact, had taken steps to make sure that it would not happen (removing the knives and scissors from the house).

Therefore, she did not need involuntary commitment, and the psychologist did not have to violate confidentiality. Finally, confidentiality must also be breached when adults admit that they are physically or sexually abusing children or elders in which case the therapist must report the abuse to the appropriate state authorities.

When the patient is a minor child or an adolescent, other exceptions to confidentiality apply, and, again, therapists discuss these issues at the start of treatment so that the minor and the parent or guardian can make an informed decision about participating in therapy. With respect to children and adolescents, mental health clinicians, including psychologists, are required by state law to report physical, sexual, or emotional abuse to the proper state authorities, thereby violating confidentiality. State laws may cover other behaviors (such as substance abuse) because parents have a right to information about their child's treatment. Each state has its own guidelines. Exceptions to confidentiality also apply when a child or an adolescent is actively contemplating suicide or homicide as is the case for adults. Psychologists violate confidentiality to keep their patients and others physically safe. In certain instances, breaking confidentiality is a medical or legal necessity. In other cases, unfortunately, it can occur as a result of carelessness. To help safeguard patient confidentiality, the federal government enacted a law discussed next.

Health Insurance Portability and Accountability Act (HIPAA)

LO 15.7 Describe how HIPAA provides protection for health information and the unique protections provided to mental health treatment.

When you check in at your doctor's office, particularly if you are a new patient, you sign various consent forms including one with the abbreviation **HIPAA**, which stands for **Health Insurance Portability and Accountability Act**. Although HIPAA was originally designed to protect Americans who had been previously ill from losing their health insurance when they changed jobs, HIPAA also provided a uniform standard for transmission of health care claims forms, thereby streamlining the health care system. Legislators took the opportunity to include safeguards to protect patients' confidential health information. HIPAA is a complicated system of laws and regulations, but two of its components, security and privacy, have implications for psychological treatment as it relates to protected health information.

The HIPAA security rule attempts to ensure patient confidentiality by securing administrative, physical, and technical office procedures. Psychologists and physicians restrict information to only those people who have a right to know it. The security rule also requires keeping information received on fax machines, written on telephone message pads, and even written on sign-in sheets from being viewed by an unauthorized person, usually defined as someone who does not work in the office.

Protected health information (PHI) refers to facts about your health or health care maintained as a medical record or transmitted to another person. The HIPAA privacy rule requires that psychologists must obtain a patient's consent before using any PHI to carry out treatment, health care operations, or submitting information in order to be paid. In other words, when you sign the HIPAA consent form, you agree to allow your clinician to share your health information with (1) other health care professionals who may be involved in your treatment, (2) companies responsible for billing your insurance or paying your physician for services, and (3) companies responsible for arranging medical or legal reviews of services and auditing of medical care facilities. It also covers some other business-related functions, but they are less relevant to psychology. HIPAA consent does not include permission to share records with an employer or a school. Similarly, the psychologist's patient notes (called *psychotherapy notes* or *process notes*) are not considered part of the information included in the general HIPAA consent.

Therefore, although consent is almost always necessary before a psychologist can reveal content of the therapy session, exceptions exist. When a patient expresses a threat or desire to hurt others, the confidentiality of the therapeutic relationship becomes secondary to a *duty to warn* the third parties who may be at risk.

Duty to Warn

LO 15.8 Discuss the duty to warn mandate and how it affects the concept of patient confidentiality.

In 1969, University of California student Prosenjit Poddar sought therapy with a psychologist at the university's student health center because a young woman named Tatiana Tarasoff had spurned his affections. The psychologist believed that Poddar was dangerous because he had a pathological attachment to Tarasoff and he told the psychologist that he had decided to purchase a gun. The therapist notified the police both verbally and in writing. He did not warn Ms. Tarasoff because that would have violated patient–psychologist confidentiality. Poddar was questioned by the police, who found him to be rational. They made him promise to stay away from Tarasoff. Two months later, however, on October 27, 1969, Poddar killed Tarasoff. The Supreme Court of California found that the defendants (the Regents of the University of California) had a **duty to warn** Ms. Tarasoff or her family of the danger. In a second ruling, the court charged therapists with a duty to use reasonable care to protect third parties against dangers posed by patients. In short, the court found that a person has no right to confidentiality when the patient's actions might put the public at risk. The original Tarasoff decision applied only to the state of California, but since that time other states have adopted a duty to warn, although the specifics of the law vary by state.

More than 30 years later, the Tarasoff decision (as it is known) still has broad implications for the mental health profession. One is that society does not always hold confidentiality in the same high esteem as do therapists and patients. Society sometimes dictates that safeguarding the public welfare, particularly in the case of potential homicide, is more important than confidentiality. However, duty to warn is a slippery slope. What if the potential threat is not outright death, as was the case for Tatiana Tarasoff, but bodily infection?

> Michael is 33 years old. He has been married for 8 years and has two children. He had an affair with a neighbor several years ago. His wife never knew about the affair. He recently discovered that the neighbor died of AIDS. Michael had an HIV test, which was positive. He told his therapist that he had no intention of telling his wife about his test results (Chenneville, 2000).

If Michael were your patient, what would you counsel him to do? The laws are not clear in this type of situation. Depending on the particular state where Michael lived, the therapist may be *permitted* to make a disclosure to the health department or Michael's spouse, *required* to make a disclosure to the health department or Michael's spouse, or *required* to maintain confidentiality at all costs.

PREDICTION OF DANGEROUSNESS The psychologist's duty to warn is based on the belief that mental health clinicians have the ability to predict human behavior. Psychologists and psychiatrists are often asked to determine how likely it is that a person will become violent when the need for civil commitment is an issue (Skeem et al., 2006). In the past, mental health professionals were unable to predict patient dangerousness at a rate higher than chance alone (Steadman, 1983). In some instances, clinical intuition may help predict dangerousness. In an emergency room, male patients who worried clinicians (based on a diagnostic evaluation but no real empirical data) were more likely than other patients to subsequently commit violent acts and be involved in serious violence (Lidz et al., 1993).

Over the past decade, the ability of mental health clinicians to predict patient violence has significantly improved through the use of *actuarial* (quantitative) prediction measures, particularly when the prediction is based on specific psychological *symptoms* (such as anger or sadness), not psychological *disorders* (major depressive disorder, schizophrenia; Skeem et al., 2006). In particular, anger/hostility is predictive of violence over both short-term (1-week) and long-term (6-month) follow-up periods (Gardner et al., 1996; Skeem et al., 2006). Other symptoms such as anxiety, depression, or delusional beliefs did not predict acts of violence, at least not in the short term (Skeem et al., 2006).

Learning Objective Summaries

LO 15.6 Define the distinct but related terms of *privacy, confidentiality,* and *privilege.*

Privacy is a right of the individual who alone can give it away. When private information is shared with a therapist, the information can be considered confidential. Confidentiality is an agreement between two parties (in this case, the therapist and patient) with the understanding that private information revealed during therapy will not be discussed with others. Privilege is a legal term and it means that a licensed therapist cannot be compelled to reveal confidential information during legal proceedings.

LO 15.7 Describe how HIPAA provides protection for health information and the unique protections provided to mental health treatment.

The HIPAA privacy rule requires that psychologists must obtain a patient's consent before sharing your health information with (1) other health care professionals who may be involved in your treatment, (2) companies responsible for billing your insurance or paying your physician for services, and (3) companies responsible for arranging medical or legal reviews of services and auditing of medical care facilities. HIPAA consent does not include permission to share records with an employer or a school. Similarly, the psychologist's patient notes (called psychotherapy notes or process notes) are not considered part of the information included in the general HIPAA consent.

LO 15.8 Discuss the duty to warn mandate and how it affects the concept of patient confidentiality.

Sometimes confidentiality must be violated. Such cases include behaviors that are considered dangerous to the patient or others, abuse of children or elders, or substance abuse by children or adolescents. If a patient threatens to harm another person and that person can be identified, psychologists in some states have a duty to warn the threatened person as well as the police. Actuarial predictions allow psychologists to predict violence at levels better than chance alone. One factor that appears to play a role is patients' anger and hostility.

Critical Thinking Question

Remember Michael, who did not want to tell his wife that he had HIV. What if instead of being married, Michael were single, had gotten HIV as a result of a single encounter with someone he had met in a bar, and now was so angry that he told his therapist that he intended to go out and infect every woman that he could? Does a psychologist have a duty to warn in this instance?

Licensing, Malpractice Issues, and Prescription Privileges

Requiring mental health professionals to have a license serves several functions. It sets minimum standards of training and education, and it protects the public from unskilled or dangerous mental health services or providers. Insurance companies recognize the importance of licensing: They usually will not pay for psychological services unless the professional has a license.

Licensing

LO 15.9 Understand the various ways that licensing protects the public.

Psychologists who wish to provide professional services in certain settings must be licensed by the state in which they practice. Psychologists who do not provide professional services (such as cognitive psychologists, biological psychologists, or social psychologists) are not required to be licensed. State law specifies who can use the word *psychologist*, who can provide specific psychological services, and what type of training a person must have to practice psychology. Licensing laws vary by state, and there are many ways that nonqualified individuals can practice what some consider a form of therapy. In some states, people who are not psychologists but who wish to provide therapy can do so by avoiding the use of the words *psychology* and *psychologist* and instead using the term *psychotherapy*.

State laws protect the public by setting forth the minimal acceptable level of training and experience necessary for the practice of psychology. Most states have very similar requirements including a doctorate in psychology and 2 years of postdoctoral experience (or 1-year predoctoral internship and 1-year postdoctoral experience). The psychologist must also pass a national exam and a state exam. Once licensed, psychologists must adhere to the laws and the code of ethics. Failure to do so could result in loss of the license or claims of malpractice. Furthermore, to maintain their license, psychologists must engage in *continuing education* by continuing to attend workshops, read articles, and participate in other professional activities to refine and improve their knowledge and skills in psychology.

Malpractice

LO 15.10 Identify at least two behaviors that would be considered malpractice.

Psychologists, like all professionals, must meet certain standards when caring for their patients, legally defined as "that degree of care which a reasonably prudent person should exercise in same or similar circumstances" (Black, 1990, p. 1405). For example, although the law does not require all psychologists to use the same form of therapy, the care they do provide must meet commonly accepted professional standards (Baerger, 2001). If care is not consistent with standards, the psychologist may be guilty of **malpractice**: "professional misconduct or unreasonable lack of skill" (Black, 1990, p. 959). Although psychologists are less likely to be sued for malpractice than are physicians, the number of lawsuits filed against psychologists increases each year.

The most common reason that a psychologist is sued for malpractice is a result of a custody evaluation. It is common for the parent who does not get custody to identify the psychologist as the person responsible for the negative outcome.

Few studies of malpractice offenses committed by mental health clinicians (either psychiatrists or psychologists) exist, but in one anonymous survey, 3.5% of psychologists engaged in an inappropriate relationship. The majority of offenders were male psychologists who established a relationship with former female patients (Lamb et al., 2003). The American Psychological Association prohibits interpersonal relationships between psychologists and patients until at least 2 years after the therapy has ended and only when several other conditions can be met. Malpractice lawsuits are filed against psychologists when there is suspicion of a negligent or improper diagnosis. Malpractice accusations tend to involve child custody evaluation decisions intended to assess how best to meet the child's psychological needs. To arrive at their decisions, psychologists assess parenting abilities, the child's needs, and the resulting parent–child fit (American Psychological Association, 1994). Child custody evaluation is a high-risk task for a psychologist, who must remain neutral in a highly charged situation such as a divorce. Joint physical custody is the most common custody decision today (Bow & Quinnell, 2001). In the second most common decision, the mother is granted custody and the father has visitation rights. Parents who disagree with a custody decision may file a complaint with the state ethics board and/or file a malpractice suit. Among psychologists who conducted custody evaluations, ethics complaints were filed against 35%, and 10% were sued for malpractice (Bow & Quinnell, 2001).

In addition to child custody cases, malpractice claims include failure to obtain informed consent for treatment, negligent psychotherapy, and negligent release or dangerous acts. For example, grief-stricken family members sometimes blame a mental health professional for not preventing a patient's suicide (a claim of negligent release or dangerous acts), although predicting this type of behavior can be very difficult. Such charges were the sixth most common malpractice complaint in one survey of psychologists who had malpractice insurance (Bongar et al., cited in Baerger, 2001).

In summary, psychologists must adhere to both an ethical code of behavior and state laws and regulations. Licensure ensures that the professional has met minimum educational and training standards, but it does *not* guarantee that the therapist will always behave ethically. When unethical behaviors have occurred, a psychologist may be sued for malpractice.

Prescription Privileges

LO 15.11 Identify the advantages and disadvantages of psychologists' having prescription privileges.

What is the difference between a psychologist and a psychiatrist? The easy answer used to be "A psychiatrist is a physician who can prescribe medication, and a psychologist is a doctoral-level health care provider who cannot prescribe medication." That distinction is no longer quite so clear. During the past two decades, some psychologists have sought and received the legal right to prescribe medication for psychological disorders. Prescription privileges, the legal right to prescribe medication, are a controversial issue throughout the psychological community (Heiby, 2002).

Medications are an important part of the treatment of many psychological disorders, and in some cases, such as schizophrenia, the primary treatment. Although psychiatrists have always been free to use both psychotherapy and medication, psychologists have traditionally provided only psychological treatment. When their patients need medication, most psychologists arrange for treatment by a physician. Some psychologists believe that splitting treatment in this way is not in the best interest of the patient because different therapists may provide the patient different, and sometimes conflicting, viewpoints. With the ability to prescribe medications, these psychologists believe that they would be able to provide both medication and psychotherapy just as psychiatrists do.

Psychologists propose several reasons for prescription privileges. First, many psychologists have hospital admitting privileges, enabling them to treat the emotional components related to physical health problems such as stress caused by cancer, serious disabilities, or heart disease. These psychologists view the ability to write prescriptions as a natural extension of their practice (Norfleet, 2002; Welsh, 2003). Second, graduate programs in clinical psychology already offer courses in psychophysiology and psychopharmacology, which are necessary but not sufficient for prescribing medication. Therefore, psychologists already have some of the training necessary for prescribing medications. Third, because medications are the treatment of choice for some disorders, such as schizophrenia, prescription privileges would allow psychologists to treat patients who might not have access to treatment. Many people lack access to psychiatrists and obtain their medication from general practitioners who are much less knowledgeable about psychological disorders than psychologists. Allowing psychologists to prescribe medications would guarantee treatment by someone with specialized knowledge of abnormal behavior.

Other psychologists (Albee, 2002) suggest that prescribing medication undermines psychology's unique contributions to understanding behavior, such as the role of learning and the importance of the environment. From this perspective, seeking prescription privileges suggests that psychologists no longer value psychology's contributions and deemphasizes the efficacy of highly effective psychological treatments.

Psychologists would also need additional training to prescribe medications safely and would require an undergraduate education that would include some of the courses found in a premedicine curriculum (Sechrest & Coan, 2002). Providing appropriate biological training at the graduate level would extend the length of training (Wagner, 2002), which already averages about 6 years.

In the past few years, psychologists have gained the right to prescribe medication in New Mexico, Louisiana, and the island of Guam (Stambor, 2006), as have appropriately trained psychologists working in the Department of Defense, Indian Health Service, and the U.S. Public Health Service. If prescription privileges become part of the treatment arsenal for psychologists, medication providers will face controversial issues that relate to the marketing and funding of pharmacological treatment.

Psychiatric drugs are considered a booming business; they are the best-selling medications in the United States. During 2009, psychiatric drugs accounted for $14.6 billion of the overall prescription drug sales in the United States, which totaled $300 billion (http://www.ngpharma.com/article/psychiatric-drugs-a-booming-business). They are among the industry's most profitable drugs. Their use is increasing both among adults and children. See Figure 15.2 for the number of children prescribed medication over a six month period between 2011 and 2012.

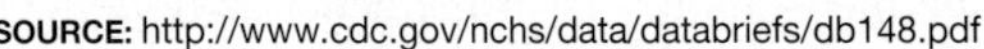

Figure 15.2 Percentage of Children Prescribed Medication During Past Six Months for Behavioral and Emotional Problems by Sex and Age Group, and Race and Hispanic Origin: United States, 2011–2012.

SOURCE: http://www.cdc.gov/nchs/data/databriefs/db148.pdf

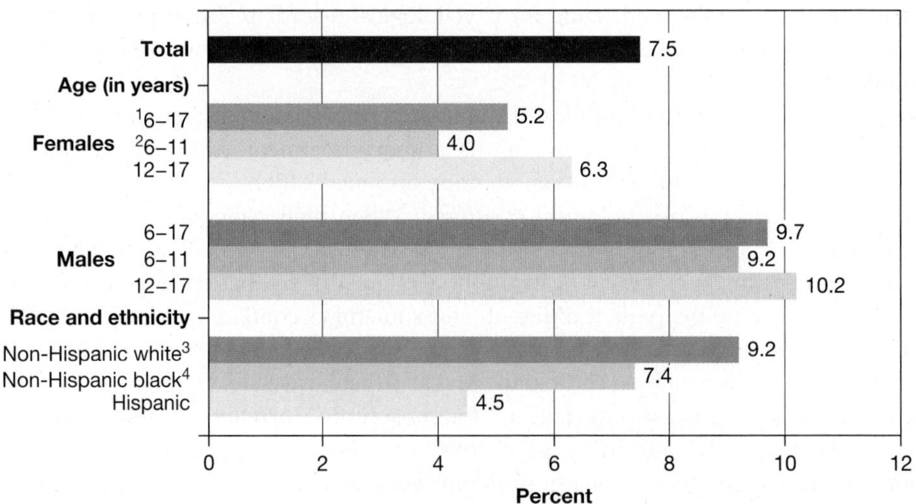

[1]Females aged 6–17 years significantly different from males aged 6–17 years. Females aged 6–11 years significantly different from males aged 6–11 years, and females aged 12–17 years significantly different from males aged 12–17 years.

[2]Females aged 6–11 years significantly different from females aged 12–17 years.

[3]Non-Hispanic white children significantly different from non-Hispanic black and Hispanic children.

[4]Non-Hispanic black children significantly different from Hispanic children.

The potential influence of the pharmaceutical industry extends far beyond public media advertisements. In one survey, 60% of published medication trials in psychiatry received funding from a pharmaceutical company (Perlis et al., 2005), although having pharmaceutical company support did not guarantee a positive outcome for the medication. Until recently, pharmaceutical companies provided promotional materials (pens, mouse pads, etc.) to potential medication prescribers. Although such gifts are now prohibited, health professionals must always be careful to guard against marketing influences when deciding on forms of therapy.

Learning Objective Summaries

LO 15.9 Understand the various ways that licensing protects the public.

States regulate the practice of psychology to safeguard the public against those who are not qualified to perform these services. The practice of psychology requires a doctoral degree, at least 2 years of supervised experience, and passing a national and state licensing examination.

LO 15.10 Identify at least two behaviors that would be considered malpractice.

Malpractice lawsuits against psychologists are uncommon, but when they occur, the reasons include inappropriate sexual behavior and dissatisfaction with child custody decisions.

LO 15.11 Identify the advantages and disadvantages of psychologists' having prescription privileges.

The advantages of holding prescription privileges include the ability to provide comprehensive care for their patients. As part of their current training psychologists already have some of the education necessary to prescribe medications, and privileges would allow psychologists to provide medications to people who might not have access to treatment. Disadvantages include the possibility that the psychological profession might no longer value psychology's contributions, it might deemphasize the efficacy of highly effective psychological treatments, and psychologists would need additional training in order to prescribe effectively and safely.

Critical Thinking Question

The ability to prescribe medication leads to potentially vulnerable exposure to pharmaceutical marketing campaigns, all of which seek to have their drug prescribed to patients. Given their extensive background in research training, do you think that psychologists would be able to resist this influence more than physicians can?

Research and Clinical Trials

We have approached the study of abnormal behavior from a scientist–practitioner perspective, highlighting how designing, conducting, and understanding research in abnormal behavior contribute to theories of etiology and approaches to treatment. When treatments are not based on science, they may result in harmful consequences. The use of unscientific theories and unsubstantiated treatments can result in the waste of time and money and public mistrust of therapy. But research itself comes with its own ethical issues. Here we focus on four important areas: the rights of research participants, special rights and issues for children and adolescents, the use of placebo controls, and the importance of conducting research that reflects the diversity of the U.S. population.

Rights of Participants in Research

LO 15.12 Describe documents crucial to the development of rights for research participants.

On December 9, 1946, the U.S. military initiated a tribunal against 23 German physicians and administrators for war crimes and other crimes against humanity. During World

War II, some German physicians conducted a euthanasia program, systematically killing people who they deemed unworthy to live. In a second program, physicians conducted pseudoscientific medical experiments on thousands of concentration camp prisoners (Jews, Poles, Russians, and Gypsies) without their consent (http://www.ushmm.org/research/doctors/). Most participants died or were permanently injured as a result of this inhumane experimentation. Sixteen doctors were found guilty; seven of them were executed.

The horrific and senseless nature of these "experiments" prompted the development of the **Nuremberg Code** (1947), which established directives for experimentation with human subjects. This code specifies that subjects must voluntarily consent to participate in clinical research. Furthermore, participants should know the nature, duration, and purpose of the research as well as its methods and means and all inconveniences and hazards that could be reasonably expected as a result of participation. The experiment must be conducted by qualified individuals, and the participants must be allowed to withdraw from the research study at any time (Trials of War Criminals before the Nuremberg Military Tribunals, 1949).

A second document developed as a result of Nazi atrocities is the **Declaration of Helsinki**, first adopted by the World Medical Assembly in 1964 and reaffirmed on subsequent occasions (http://history.nih.gov/research/downloads/helsinki.pdf). This document also sets forth basic guidelines for the conduct of research including the need for clearly formulated experimental procedures, a careful assessment of risks compared with benefits, and the provision of adequate information to the participants including the aims, methods, benefits and risks, and the freedom to withdraw. The Declaration of Helsinki does not specify how these principles are to be implemented; that is left to federal, state, and local governments and professional organizations.

A third document relevant to research conducted in the United States is the **Belmont Report**, which in 1979 created the National Commission for the Protection of Human Subjects of Biomedical and Behavioral Research. The Belmont Report identified three basic principles to guide behavioral and biomedical research with human subjects. The first is *respect for persons*, including the beliefs that (1) individuals should be treated as autonomous agents capable of independent thought and decision-making abilities and (2) persons who have limited or diminished autonomy (such as prisoners or those with limited cognitive ability) are entitled to special protections and should not be coerced or unduly influenced to participate in research activities.

The second principle is *beneficence*, meaning that researchers (1) do no harm (as in the Hippocratic Oath) and (2) maximize potential benefits and minimize possible harm. In short, the study's potential benefits must outweigh the perceived risks (Striefel, 2001), both to the individual and to society at large.

The third and final principle is *justice*: The benefits and burdens of research must be imposed equally. For example, all research on heart disease (much of it funded by the federal government) traditionally was conducted using male participants, so men were primarily benefiting from the results. Only later did researchers begin to study heart disease and its treatment in women. This example illustrates how the *benefits* of research were not being equally distributed; only one sex benefited from the efforts of scientists. The principle of justice was violated in the Tuskegee experiment and perhaps in the Baltimore lead paint study; we discuss both at greater length in the "Cultural Perceptions Regarding Research" section. In general, the recruitment of research participants must consider whether some classes of participants (welfare recipients, specific racial or ethnic minorities, or persons confined to institutions) are selected simply because they are easily accessible or easily manipulated. In short, no one group should be selected as research participants because of their availability, lack of power, or the possibility of easy manipulation (Striefel, 2001).

Also important to the research process is **informed consent**. Potential participants must understand the aims and methods of the research, what they will be asked to do, and what types of information they will be asked to provide. They must also understand the risks and benefits of research participation. Before starting a research study, the psychologist, or anyone else who wishes to conduct research with human participants, submits his or her research plan to an **institutional review board** (IRB). This board is charged by the researcher's institution with reviewing and approving the research using the guidelines just mentioned. An informed consent form, describing all aspects of the study in layperson's language, is included with the research plan. If you participated in research in your introductory psychology class, you probably signed a consent form.

Informed consent is based on the idea that providing enough information will allow cognitively competent people to understand the research process and make a voluntary and rational decision about participation. However, this assumption is not necessarily true. In one study examining the effects of a treatment, 62% of people who read the consent form and agreed to participate in the study failed to understand that treatment would be applied in a standard fashion and not individualized to their needs, or they overestimated the benefit of participating because they did not fully understand the study's methodology (e.g., use of a placebo control group that would provide little to no therapeutic benefit; Appelbaum et al., 2004).

When it came to understanding the disclosed risk, 25% failed to recall any risk listed in the informed consent document, whereas 45.8% understood the risks of the experimental *treatment* but not the risks of the experimental *design* (Lidz, 2006), such as the possibility of being assigned to the placebo control group. So, despite the profession's efforts to ensure that research participants are fully informed, many people take part in studies lacking full information about the risks and benefits they can expect.

Considerations with Children and Adolescents

LO 15.13 Discuss the special considerations that must occur when children participate in psychological research.

> Oscar, 14 years old, was extremely anxious in social situations. His parents brought him to the clinic to participate in a research study to treat social phobia and signed the consent form for Oscar's participation. When Oscar refused to sign the assent form, his father asked the investigator to leave the room, guaranteeing that his son would sign the form "in the next 10 minutes."

Although parental or guardian consent is necessary for children and adolescents to participate in research, ethical guidelines require that whenever they are able to do so, children and adolescents should be allowed to *assent* to their own participation. Although the ability to give assent varies with the individual child, by age 14, adolescents can understand and make decisions that are similar to the way adults do (Caskey & Rosenthal, 2005). In Oscar's case, the investigator could not enroll him in the study because it was clear that Oscar did not wish to participate, although his parents wanted him to do so.

To honor the principle of *beneficence*, investigators who study children and adolescents must protect the welfare of the participants. Researchers, like clinicians, must violate confidentiality when there is evidence of sexual or physical abuse. In certain instances, researchers must report alcohol or substance abuse to parents (Caskey & Rosenthal, 2005). Finally, *justice* in this case means that adolescents deserve the opportunity to participate in and benefit from research important to the adolescent population. Some adults believe that asking adolescents whether they have thought about committing suicide will instill such thoughts and urges in people who have never considered this behavior. Psychologists know that this is simply not true, yet many school districts will not allow research that includes questions about suicide. This denies treatment opportunities to adolescents who are seriously depressed and contemplating suicide. In this case, the principle of justice is not fulfilled because adolescents are denied an opportunity to participate in potentially important and helpful research.

Many of the same considerations surrounding the ability of children to consent to participate in research also apply to older adults who have cognitive difficulties and to prisoners who may feel coerced to participate because of their incarcerated status. When the research involves people from racial or ethnic minority groups, additional considerations include making sure that (1) assessments are culturally valid, (2) group differences are not attributed to race or ethnicity when they may be just as likely to result from other demographic variables such as socioeconomic status or level of education, (3) behaviors or developmental patterns of the white majority are not considered the "normal" standard for mental health, (4) research is not coercive, and (5) research teams include someone who is culturally competent (Fisher et al., 2002).

Using Control Groups in Psychological Research

LO 15.14 Understand the need for and proper use of control groups in psychological research.

The most rigorous types of scientific research have designs that involve the use of a control group (see Chapter 2). The different types of control groups include a wait list or no-treatment control group, a pill placebo or psychological placebo control group, or another active treatment group. Placebo control groups are used to understand the effects of time (some conditions, such as a cold, resolve with the passage of time) and/or the effects of clinical attention or education (e.g., people are relieved to know that their response to a traumatic event is typical and not a sign of pathology; see Chapter 4). However, questions often arise as to how and when the use of control groups is ethical (see "Research Hot Topic: The Use of Placebo in Clinical Research").

ETHICS AND RESPONSIBILITY Sometimes the use of a placebo control condition is not clinically acceptable. The possibility of denying treatment to a suicidal patient cannot be justified when treatments are available. Among children, the ethical use of a placebo is becoming increasingly complex. Scientifically, we know that placebo effects are more pronounced in children than in adults; specifically, more children than adults have a positive (therapeutic) response to placebo medication (Weimer et al., 2013). One reason for this difference may be that children may not understand the concept of a placebo (i.e., that it is an inactive treatment). Children, who are accustomed to getting medication from a physician for physical illness, may believe that the placebo pill will also make them well. When they take a pill to treat a bacterial infection, a blood test will reveal that the infection has been cured. However, the outcome of most psychological research is based on the patient's report of changed feelings; there is no "psychological blood test" to independently determine symptom improvement. Therefore, children's reports may be biased based on their belief that they took a pill and so should be feeling better. Adult reports also may be biased by taking a pill, but an adult's cognitive maturity increases the likelihood that the concept of a placebo is understood. To control the assumption (at any age) that taking a pill will make you better, it is clear that placebo controls are necessary, especially for children (Weimer et al., 2013). In summary, placebo controls are necessary for valid scientific research, but ethical issues continue to challenge scientist–practitioners interested in providing effective treatments to children.

Explore ETHICS AND RESPONSIBILITY

Cultural Perceptions Regarding Research

LO 15.15 Give reasons why some cultural groups may be reluctant to participate in research.

An interesting and little-known fact about the world's mental health database is that the vast majority of research has been conducted in the United States using white college students (Sue, 1999) who represent less than 5% of the world's population. The National Institutes of Health have recognized this inequity and now mandate that study samples recruited for federally funded research be representative of the U.S. population. However, when researchers, particularly white researchers, try to recruit a diverse sample, they often find that historical events have created a climate of cultural mistrust. People familiar with the now-infamous **Tuskegee experiment** may worry that they will be mistreated and their rights ignored. In that experiment, each of the three core values of research (respect for persons, beneficence, and justice) was violated.

In 1932, the Public Health Service, working with the Tuskegee Institute, began a study to determine the long-term effects of syphilis. Nearly 400 poor African American men with syphilis from Macon County, Alabama, were enrolled. They were never told that they had syphilis, nor were they ever treated for it. According to the Centers for Disease Control and Prevention, the men were told that they were being treated for "bad blood," a local term that described several illnesses including syphilis, anemia, and fatigue. For participating in the study, the men were given free medical exams, free meals, and free burial insurance. When the study began, no proven treatment for syphilis existed. But even after penicillin became a standard cure in 1947, the medicine was withheld from these men. The Tuskegee scientists wanted to continue to study how the disease spread through the body. Of course,

Research HOT Topic

The Use of Placebo in Clinical Research

Placebo-controlled trials are considered rigorous tests used to determine the effectiveness of a new treatment. Deep brain stimulation (DBS), for example, has shown preliminary effectiveness for depression that does not respond to medication. The procedure involves implanting an electrode within the part of the brain that is associated with mood. Electrical impulses are transmitted to and stimulate brain cells in the part of the brain that regulates mood. Although used to treat depression, the Food and Drug Administration has not yet approved DBS specifically for this purpose, and its effectiveness has not been demonstrated compared with placebo. Imagine that a researcher proposes to conduct a randomized, controlled trial in which one group receives DBS and the second group undergoes the surgical procedure in the brain but the wire is not connected to the stimulator. Is the use of a placebo ethical?

- **Argument in Favor of the Surgical Placebo** Article II.3 of the Declaration of Helsinki states: "In any medical study, every patient—including those of a control group, if any—should be assured of the best proven diagnostic and therapeutic method. This does not exclude the use of inert placebo in studies where no proven diagnostic or therapeutic method exists." The study that the researcher proposes might provide some additional support for the use of DBS, particularly in a group of patients who have not responded to standard medication treatments. However, the researchers must consider the potentially harmful consequences from surgery that has no benefit.
- **Argument Against the Use of the Surgical Placebo** Surgical placebo for DBS involves actual neurosurgery, an invasive procedure. In addition to potential complications of the procedure itself, consequences of the placebo implant include reaction to anesthesia and post-operative infection (La Vaque & Rossiter, 2001). Does the potential for symptom remission in a group with medication-resistant depression outweigh the potential for harm from surgical placebo?
- **Conclusion** When no known standard exists, using a placebo as a control condition to test a new treatment might be appropriate until the efficacy of a new intervention is known and available to the public. In the case of DBS or other invasive medical procedures, the risks associated with neurosurgery are the same whether or not the device is operative. In fact, those in the placebo condition have brain surgery for no therapeutic reason, a very substantial medical risk with no benefit. Of course, if participants in the placebo group are later allowed to have the implant activated, *then* the benefits may outweigh the risks for people whose depressive symptoms have not responded to any currently accepted conventional treatment.

In the Tuskegee experiment, medical treatment was knowingly withheld from patients who suffered from a deadly disease so that the disease could be studied. This unethical experiment on human beings was one factor that led to the development of review boards for institutional research.

in some cases, the disease killed the patient. The experiment lasted four decades until public health workers leaked the story to the media in 1972. By then, dozens of the men had died, and many wives and children had been infected. After the National Association for the Advancement of Colored People (NAACP) filed a class-action lawsuit in 1973, a $9 million settlement was divided among the study's participants. Free health care was given to the men who were still living and to infected wives, widows, and children.

Not until 1997 did the government formally apologize for the unethical study. President Clinton delivered the apology, saying that what the government had done was profoundly and morally wrong. "To the survivors, to the wives and family members, the children and the grandchildren, I say what you know: No power on Earth can give you back the lives lost, the pain suffered, the years of internal torment and anguish. What was done cannot be undone. But we can end the silence. We can stop turning our heads away. We can look at you in the eye and finally say on behalf of the American people, what the United States government did was shameful, and I am sorry."

The use of IRBs to review research proposals before an investigator can begin a research study guards against many potential abuses of research participants. For example, it is highly unlikely that Watson's experiment with Little Albert could be conducted today. Yet even with all of the current regulations of research activities, some studies still provoke controversy, particularly when the subjects are children. From 1993 to 1995, the Kennedy Krieger Institute (KKI) in Baltimore, Maryland, conducted a study to determine the short- and long-term effects of environmental lead in older homes. Lead is a natural element in the environment, but concentrations of lead in the blood are naturally quite low. In the United States, higher-than-acceptable lead levels usually result from two sources: lead in gasoline and the leaded paint chips and dust associated with deteriorating lead paint. The elimination of lead from gasoline and paint decreased blood level concentrations in children dramatically, although older homes with lead paint remain a source of concern. High lead levels lead to cognitive impairment (low IQ scores), inattention, hyperactivity, aggression, and delinquency (Committee on Environmental Health, American Academy of Pediatrics, 2005).

In Baltimore, attempts to remove lead paint through lead abatement procedures reduced lead dust levels by 80%, and KKI agreed to conduct a study to examine three different abatement procedures (some representing only partial abatement). In addition to these three experimental groups, there were two control groups, one in which no further abatement occurred and one in which the homes were newer and presumably lead free.

Some of the homes were occupied at the start of the study. In other instances, "inner city families who likely had no choice but to rent non-abated properties elsewhere in Baltimore" were recruited to live in the study houses (Lead Based Paint Study Fact Sheet, cited in Nelson, 2002). This resulted in two groups of children: those already living in a study home and those recruited to move into these homes. Inducements to move into the houses and participate in the study included T-shirts, food stamps, and $5 to $10 payments. For most of the children in the homes, the additional abatement procedures lowered levels of lead in the children. However, the study had some negative effects; lead levels increased in some children. In one instance, parental notification was delayed by 9 months. Mothers of two study participants later filed lawsuits, stating that they had not been fully informed about the goals of the study and were not promptly notified of the high levels of lead in their children's blood. If they had this information, they would not have agreed to participate in the study.

This study raises many ethical and moral issues (see "Examining the Evidence: Children and Nontherapeutic Research"). One is the issue of *justice* set forth in the Belmont Report. Was the research unethical if the family's only alternative was to live in other homes that had not undergone any abatement procedures? Should social deprivation be a reason for conducting a "natural experiment," or are researchers taking advantage of the

Examining the EVIDENCE

Children and Nontherapeutic Research

Before gaining approval, all proposed research must be reviewed to ensure that the study provides benefit and does not subject participants to undue risk or harm. In the case of the KKI lead-based paint study, concerns were raised that this study did not provide sufficient benefit and exposed children to undue risk. Do parents have the right to enroll their children in "nontherapeutic" research?

Let's Examine the Evidence

- **Was There a Direct Benefit for the Children Who Participated in the Study?** The research project offered monitoring of blood levels and notification to the parents if the blood level exceeded a certain standard. But testing is not treatment, and the study did not provide treatment if living in the house resulted in high blood levels of lead in the child (Nelson, 2002).

  Recall that there were two groups: children who were already living in the targeted houses and children who were recruited to live in them. Enticing someone to move into a house that contains lead can hardly be viewed as providing a benefit. For children already living in such homes, the research project offered the benefit of lead abatement. Therefore, the research offered a benefit only to those already living in a house known to contain lead (Spriggs, 2006).
- **Did the Procedure Present More Than Minimal Risk to the Subjects?** Monthly blood testing to determine the level of lead exposure presents only minimal risk. However, living in a home while lead removal occurs involves more than minimal risk because lead levels may increase when the lead is being removed. Parents were not informed that the three different methods might not have equal benefit. Is it only minimally risky to recruit families to live in houses that have had potentially ineffective methods of lead reduction? Do parents deserve the right to know that there was uncertainty about the benefits of these different procedures? Would your answer be different if the researchers told you that it was the best available option for these children?
- **Did the Consent Form Allow Parents to Make a Fully Informed Decision?** The consent document did not inform the parents about (1) the primary aim of the study (to examine the effectiveness of three different methods of lead removal), (2) the different methods used, (3) the importance of blood monitoring and the impact of high lead levels on the development of young children, and (4) the risks of inadequate lead removal (Nelson, 2002). Without this information, did parents have the opportunity to give fully informed consent?
- **Conclusion** The court noted that the institutional review board did not adequately consider the risks to the participants. Would you agree? Because removing lead from homes is an important societal goal, how could you change the study to address the issues raised above?

participants' social predicament (Spriggs, 2006)? In other words, is it acceptable to induce low-income children to live in partially lead-abated houses because the alternative might have been worse?

In both the Tuskegee experiment and the Baltimore lead paint study, groups with limited or diminished autonomy were put at risk. Poorly designed experiments such as these have led to grave mistrust among certain minority populations. This cultural mistrust, however, is not the only challenge facing those who wish to conduct sensitive, cross-cultural research. Some members of minority groups are unfamiliar with aspects of the research process, such as telephone interviews about psychological disorders (Okazaki & Sue, 1995). Uncomfortable telephone interviews about personal issues such as anxiety and depression may interfere with valid data collection. Another challenge occurs when survey instruments constructed in English are translated into other languages. For example, English cultural expressions such as "shake off the blues" have no literal Spanish translation, making the phrase meaningless to Hispanic populations. Without cultural sensitivity, any data collected will be meaningless (Rogler, 1999).

Issues of cultural diversity affect all aspects of the research process from the initial development of the project to recruitment of participants, to the study design and selection of assessment methods, and to how the data are collected and interpreted. All result in scientific data that can be biased and not appropriate to much of the world's population (Turner & Beidel, 2003). Many aspects of human behavior probably have no differences among racial and ethnic groups. However, until scientists begin to adequately address these issues, our understanding of abnormal behavior, indeed of all human behavior, will be limited.

Learning Objective Summaries

LO 15.12 Describe documents crucial to the development of rights for research participants.

Participation in research must be a choice; potential participants should never be coerced or misled. The Nuremberg Code, the Declaration of Helsinki, and the Belmont Report are important documents that set standards (rights of participants, beneficence, and justice) that any research project must meet. Informed consent implies that the researcher provides a complete explanation of the research project: the aims and methods of the study, what participants will be asked to do, and what type of information participants will be asked to provide.

LO 15.13 Discuss the special considerations that must occur when children participate in psychological research.

When children are research participants, parental consent is needed before the study begins. As age appropriate, child assent is needed, and that assent may be oral or written. As children mature, the assent form looks more like parental consent. Extra precautions are taken when children participate in research to make sure that the research has potential benefit to children.

LO 15.14 Understand the need for and proper use of control groups in psychological research.

Use of placebo controls is a controversial area of clinical research. They are necessary when no established treatments exist or when there is a suspicion that time or attention alone may change behavior. Once an effective treatment is established, comparing a new treatment to an established one rather than a placebo may be the most ethical approach.

LO 15.15 Give reasons why some cultural groups may be reluctant to participate in research.

Lack of attention to these standards is reflected in the maltreatment of research participants in cases such as the Tuskegee experiment and the Baltimore lead paint study. In turn, these experiments, as well as cultural insensitivity, have left many racial and ethnic minority groups mistrustful of research and research participation.

Critical Thinking Question

Mr. A. brings his daughter to participate in a study comparing treatments for childhood social phobia. The researcher is required to get one parent to sign the consent form and checks that Mom and Dad are married (they are). The researcher mentions that it is unusual for a father to bring a child for treatment—usually it is the mom. Dad replies that it is easier for him to do it because he is self-employed. Dad provides a cell phone number and the home number as a backup. The little girl never misses an appointment—Dad always brings her. When trying to schedule the 3-month follow-up appointment, Dad's cell phone does not seem to be working, so the research assistant calls the house. Mom answers, and when the research assistant says she is calling to schedule the 3-month follow-up appointment for the research study, Mom screams, "What research study?"

How would you handle this situation? Did the researcher commit any ethical violations? Was trust broken? If so, can it be repaired?

Real Science Real Life

Gregory Murphy—Psychiatry and the Law

On April 19, 2000, 8-year-old Kevin Shifflett was playing in the front yard of his great-grandmother's house in northern Virginia with some other children when he was stabbed 18 times by a stranger in an unprovoked attack. The suspect, Gregory D. Murphy, had been convicted for an unprovoked assault and had been paroled from prison only 12 days earlier. A note found in Murphy's hotel room said, "Kill them raceess whiate kidd's anyway." As the killer headed toward Kevin, he yelled something about hating white people. Kevin was white, and Murphy is African American.

First, it is important to consider whether Gregory Murphy's actions meet the definition for abnormal behavior. At one court hearing soon after his arrest, Murphy was verbally explosive in the courtroom, calling the judge a racist. At a later hearing, he attacked his lawyer, knocking him unconscious. It took at least five deputies to subdue Murphy. The new defense attorney asked for a competency hearing to determine whether Murphy was mentally competent to stand trial for the murder of Kevin Shifflett. If incompetent, Murphy could be forced to take medication to restore his sanity after which he would be tried for murder. Relying on a 1992 U.S. Supreme Court ruling, the state would have to show that it had considered less intrusive alternatives and that those drugs were medically appropriate for his safety and the safety of others or that treatment would be necessary to adjudicate Murphy's guilt or innocence.

The court had to determine whether Gregory Murphy was competent. By December 2000, the competency evaluation determined that Murphy suffered from psychosis, exhibiting both paranoia and delusions. His defense team suggested that the symptoms resulted from an organic brain disorder. An electroencephalogram (EEG) test, which measures brain waves, would be needed to confirm or rule out an organic cause for his unpredictable and aggressive behavior.

An important issue to consider was whether abnormal EEG activity would prove an organic cause. An EEG requires placing electrodes on a person's head to record his or her brain activity. The irony was that Murphy's delusions included beliefs that he had been attached to a machine since age 5, that the machine had influenced him for many years, and that he had arranged for "legal assistance" to turn off the machine. Murphy allowed the electrodes to be placed on his scalp but then refused to allow the machine to be turned on. He was transferred to a state psychiatric facility.

The parents of Kevin Shifflett filed a wrongful death suit against the state of Virginia and a parole officer based on documents indicating that state officials were warned that Murphy "has the ingredients of a high degree of future dangerousness." The lawsuit faulted the state for failing to civilly commit Murphy because "prison officials knew or should have known" that he suffered from a mental illness. The suit further charged that as a condition of Murphy's release, he had to stay with his parents and be monitored electronically. Installation of the electronic monitoring requirement was delayed. However, the monitoring system would not have notified anyone where Murphy was, only that he had left home. Kevin's parents finally withdrew their suit once government lawyers clarified that the electronic monitoring was not required.

Murphy's defense team learned that during his previous incarcerations, he had tested positive for syphilis, but no records existed regarding his treatment. It is important to consider whether issues of race and culture may have played a role in the defendant's lack of treatment. If Murphy had advanced neurosyphilis, this could explain his psychotic behavior. A spinal tap would be needed to confirm the diagnosis. However, the information that Murphy may have suffered delusions from age 5 would discount the idea that his abnormal behavior was the result of untreated syphilis. Furthermore, Murphy refused to submit to a spinal tap.

Prosecution attorneys petitioned the court to force Murphy to take medication—not only for his safety and the safety of others but also to treat his illness and restore him to competency. The defense team argued that because the defendant might suffer from neurosyphilis, antibiotic medication, not antipsychotic medication, was appropriate. However, the court ruled that antipsychotic medication was appropriate.

Several months later, a forensic psychiatrist testified that a spinal tap was not necessary to rule out neurosyphilis because Murphy's condition had not deteriorated over the past several months as would be expected if he had a progressive organic illness. The defense team argued that antipsychotic medications could have dangerous and permanent side effects and should not be used until the possible organic illness was ruled out. However, the judge would not vacate the order to medicate Murphy.

Finally, a spinal tap determined that Murphy did not have neurosyphilis. Murphy continued to receive antipsychotic medications, and his behavior became less aggressive. At one point, he asked the judge to appoint Johnnie Cochran as his attorney if he was tried on a capital murder charge. The request for representation by Johnnie Cochran, a famous trial lawyer, would confirm some level of contact with reality since he knew the name of the famous defense attorney. However, he continued to be found incompetent to stand trial.

Since the murder, Murphy has had competency evaluations at 6-month intervals but remains incompetent to stand trial. Although the psychologist found that his psychotic symptoms were largely in remission, the evaluations revealed that Murphy has a low intellect and puts facts together in simplistic ways. Murphy remains in custody and will never be released without going to trial.

ASSESSING THE SITUATION

What are your feelings about this case? Should a person with a serious, debilitating mental illness be medicated against his will in order to stand trial for his actions? Weigh the right of the patient to refuse treatment vs. the right of the family to have justice delivered and closure for themselves. What would change if Murphy had stood trial and been sentenced to life imprisonment (or death)?

Information on this case was drawn from articles in the *Washington Post* filed by reporters Patricia Davis, Josh White, Brooke A. Masters, and Tom Jackman.

Key Terms

Belmont report, p. 586
civil commitment, p. 570
confidentiality, p. 578
criminal commitment, p. 571
Declaration of Helsinki, p. 586
deinstitutionalization, p. 568
duty to warn, p. 580
ethics, p. 566
guilty but mentally ill, p. 573
Health Insurance Portability and Accountability Act (HIPAA), p. 579
informed consent, p. 586
institutional review board, p. 586
M'Naghten Rule, p. 572
malpractice, p. 582
mens rea, p. 573
not guilty by reason of insanity, p. 572
Nuremberg Code, p. 586
outpatient commitment, p. 570
privacy, p. 578
privilege, p. 578
Tuskegee experiment, p. 589

Glossary

A

ABAB. Also called *reversal*; a type of single case design where A represents a baseline phase and B represents a treatment phase; the two phases are alternated to examine their impact on behavior.

Abnormal behavior. Conduct that is inconsistent with the individual's developmental, cultural, and societal norms and that creates emotional distress or interferes with daily functioning.

Abstinence violation effect. The core feature of relapse prevention, which focuses on a person's cognitive and affective responses to re-engaging in a prohibited behavior.

Acceptance and commitment therapy (ACT). A therapy that teaches (1) becoming aware of experiences "in the moment", (2) accepting and dealing with distressing thoughts and feelings, (3) clarifying values, and (4) using those values to change behavior.

Addictive behavior. Repetitive or compulsive engagement in a behavior despite negative consequences to the physical, mental, social, or financial well-being that is associated with strong urges to perform the behavior and a sometimes hedonic pleasure during the behavior.

Ageism. The tendency to attribute a multitude of problems to advancing age; in abnormal psychology, this bias results in decreased recognition of psychological symptoms and disorders that warrant treatment.

Agonist substitution. A type of therapy that substitutes a chemically similar medication for the drug of abuse.

Agoraphobia. A fear of being in public places or situations where escape might be difficult or help unavailable if a panic attack occurs.

Alcohol cirrhosis. A liver disease that occurs in about 10 to 15% of people with alcoholism.

Alogia. The decreased quality and/or quantity of speech.

Alzheimer's disease. The most common form of dementia, characterized by a gradual onset and continuing cognitive decline, which includes memory loss, difficulties with language and decision making, and ultimately inability to care for self.

Amenorrhea. The absence of menstruation for at least 3 consecutive months.

Amnesia. The inability to recall important information, usually occurring after a medical condition or event.

Amnestic MCI. A mild cognitive impairment, a form of mild neurocognitive disorder, in which cognitive complaints focus on memory difficulties.

Amphetamines. A group of stimulant drugs that prolong wakefulness and suppress appetite.

Analgesic. Pain reducing.

Anhedonia. The lack of capacity for pleasure; a condition in which a person does not feel joy or happiness.

Animal magnetism. A force that Mesmer believed flowed within the body and, when impeded, resulted in disease.

Anorexia nervosa. A serious condition marked by a restriction of energy intake relative to energy requirements resulting in significantly low body weight.

Antabuse. An aversive medication that pairs the ingestion of a drug with a noxious physical reaction.

Antidepressants. A group of medications designed to alter mood-regulating chemicals in the brain and body that are effective in reducing symptoms of depression.

Antipsychotics. A class of medications that blocks dopamine receptors at neuron receptor sites.

Antisocial personality disorder. A pervasive pattern of disregard for and violation of the rights of others.

Anxiety. A common emotion characterized by physical symptoms, future-oriented thoughts, and escape or avoidance behaviors.

Anxiety disorder. A group of disorders characterized by heightened physical arousal, cognitive/subjective distress, and behavioral avoidance of feared objects/situations/events.

Anxiety proneness. See trait anxiety

Attention deficit hyperactivity disorder (ADHD). A common childhood disorder characterized by inattentiveness, hyperactivity, and impulsivity.

Atypical antipsychotic. A group of medications that effectively treats positive symptoms, is much less likely to produce tardive dyskinesia, and has some effect on negative symptoms and cognitive impairments.

Atypical depression. A variant of major depressive disorder marked by increased sleep and appetite.

Autism spectrum disorder. Consists of deficits in social communication and social interaction and the presence of restrictive and repetitive behavior patterns.

Aversion therapy. A treatment approach that repeatedly pairs drug or alcohol use with aversive stimuli or images.

Avoidant personality disorder. A pervasive pattern of social inhibition, feelings of inadequacy, and hypersensitivity to negative evaluation.

Avoidant/restrictive food intake disorder (ARFID). A disorder that captures the behavior of those children who exhibit restricted or otherwise inadequate eating.

Avolition. The inability to initiate or follow through on plans.

B

Barbiturates. Sedatives that act on the GABA system in a manner similar to alcohol.

Behavioral activation. A treatment for depression that focuses on increasing pleasant, and therefore reinforcing, events through daily scheduling of pleasurable activities, social skills training, and time management strategies.

Behavioral avoidance test. The behavioral assessment strategy used to assess avoidance behavior by asking a patient to approach a feared situation as closely as possible.

Behavioral genetics. The field of study that explores the role of genes and environment in the transmission of behavioral traits.

Behavioral inhibition. A temperamental feature characterized by withdrawal from (or failure to approach) novel people, objects, or situations.

Behavioral observation. The measurement of behavior as it occurs by someone other than the person whose behavior is being observed.

Behaviorism. The theory that the only appropriate objects of scientific study are behaviors that can be observed and measured directly.

Belmont Report. The document that sets forth three basic principles to guide behavioral and biomedical research with human subjects: respect for persons, beneficence, and justice.

Beneficence. The core ethical principle ensuring that researchers a) do no harm and b) maximize possible benefits and minimize possible harms.

Benzodiazepines. A group of sedatives that can be used responsibly and effectively for the short term but still have addictive properties.

Binge eating. Consuming a larger amount of food than most people would eat in a discrete period of time and having a sense that eating is out of control.

Binge-eating disorder. A condition characterized by regular binge eating behavior but without the inappropriate compensatory behaviors that are part of bulimia nervosa.

Bibliotherapy. Psychological treatment that occurs through the use of reading materials.

Biofeedback. A process in which patients learn to modify physical responses such as heart rate, respiration, and body temperature.

Biological challenge studies. Studies in which a biological agent is given to trigger symptoms.

Biological marker studies. Studies that compare biological variables across groups.

Biological scarring. The process by which years of living with a disorder causes changes in the brain.

Biopsychosocial model. A theoretical perspective that suggests that health is determined by complex interactions among biological, psychological, and social factors.

Biopsychosocial perspective. The idea that biological, psychological, and social factors probably contribute to the development of abnormal behavior and that different factors are important for different individuals.

Bipolar disorder. A state of both episodic depressed mood and episodic mania.

Bipolar I. Full-blown mania that alternates with episodes of major depression.

Bipolar II. Hypomania that alternates with episodes of major depression.

Bipolar and depressive disorders. Syndromes whose predominant feature is a disturbance in mood.

Body dysmorphic disorder. An overwhelming concern that some part of the body is ugly or misshapen.

Body-focused repetitive behavior. Repetitive behaviors that cause physical damage to oneself, including repetitive hair pulling, skin picking, and nail biting.

Body mass index (BMI). The formula for weight, in kilograms, divided by height, in meters squared (kg/m^2).

Borderline personality disorder. A pervasive pattern of instability in interpersonal relationships, self-image, and affect with marked impulsive features such as frantic efforts to avoid real or imagined abandonment.

Brain stem. A part of the brain located at its base that controls fundamental biological functions such as breathing.

Brief psychotic disorder. The sudden onset of any psychotic symptom that may resolve after 1 day and does not last for more than 1 month.

Bulimia nervosa. A disorder characterized by recurrent episodes of binge eating in combination with inappropriate compensatory behavior aimed at undoing the effects of the binge or preventing weight gain.

C

Caffeine. A central nervous system stimulant that boosts energy, mood, awareness, concentration, and wakefulness.

Candidate gene association study. A study that compares one or a few genes in a large group of individuals who have a specific trait or disorder with a well-matched group of individuals who do not have the trait or disorder.

Case study. A comprehensive description of an individual (or group of individuals) that focuses on the assessment or description of abnormal behavior or its treatment.

Catatonia. A condition in which a person is awake but is nonresponsive to external stimulation.

Central nervous system. One part of the human nervous system that includes the brain and the spinal cord.

Cerebral cortex. The largest part of the forebrain; contains structures that contribute to higher cognitive functioning including reasoning, abstract thought, perception of time, and creativity.

Cerebral senile plaque. Intercellular deposits of beta-amyloid protein that are found in the brains of patients with Alzheimer's disease.

Civil commitment. A state-initiated procedure that forces involuntary treatment on people who are judged to have a mental illness and who present a danger to themselves (including the inability to care for themselves) or others.

Clang associations. Conditions in which a person's speech is governed by words that sound alike rather than words that have meaning.

Classical conditioning. A form of learning in which a conditioned stimulus (CS) is paired with an unconditioned stimulus (UCS) to produce a conditioned response (CR).

Clinical assessment. The process of gathering information about a person and his or her environment to make decisions about the nature, status, and treatment of psychological problems.

Clinical interviews. Conversations between an interviewer and a patient, the purpose of which is to gather information and make judgments related to assessment goals.

Clinical significance. An observed change that is meaningful in terms of clinical functioning.

Cluster A. A group of personality disorders that includes characteristic ways of behaving that can be viewed as odd, quirky, or eccentric; includes paranoid, schizoid, and schizotypal personality disorders.

Cluster B. A group of personality disorders that includes characteristic ways of behaving that can be viewed as exaggerated, inflated, dramatic, emotional, or erratic; includes antisocial, borderline, narcissistic, and histrionic personality disorders.

Cluster C. A group of personality disorders that includes characteristic ways of behaving that are marked by considerable anxiety or withdrawal; includes avoidant, dependent, and obsessive-compulsive personality disorders.

Cocaine. A stimulant that comes from the leaves of the coca plant that is indigenous to South America.

Cognitive impairment. The diminishment in visual and verbal learning and memory, inability to pay attention, decreased speed of information processing, and inability to engage in abstract reasoning, any or all of which may be found in different psychotic disorders.

Cohort. A group of people who share a common characteristic and move forward in time as a unit.

Cohort studies. The study of a group of people who share a common characteristic and move forward in time as a unit.

Collaborative care. An approach to mental health care that involves integrated pharmacological and psychosocial treatments facilitated by a depression or anxiety care manager who might be a psychologist, nurse, or social worker.

Comorbidity. The presence of more than one disorder.

Compulsions. Repetitive behaviors or mental acts that are extensive, time-consuming, and distressful; compulsions are typically performed in response to obsessions or according to rigid rules.

Conduct disorder (CD). The continuous and repeated pattern of violating the basic rights of others or breaking societal rules including aggression toward people or animals, destruction of property, deceitfulness or theft, and serious rule violations.

Confidentiality. An agreement between two parties (in this case, the therapist and patient) that private information revealed during therapy will not be discussed with others.

Consent form. A form agreeing to the terms of a study and indicating that one understands their rights as a participant.

Contracting. The strategy that relies on setting up a reinforcement program to encourage healthy behavior.

Contingency management approach. A treatment approach in which rewards are provided for treatment compliance.

Control group. The comparison group for an experimental study in which the variable to be studied is absent.

Controlled group design. An experiment in which groups of participants are exposed to different conditions, at least one of which is experimental and one of which is a control.

Conventional or typical antipsychotics. Medications that effectively reduce the positive symptoms of schizophrenia but produce serious side effects.

Conversion disorder. A pseudoneurological complaint such as motor or sensory dysfunction that is not fully explained by the presence of a medical condition.

Correlation. The relationship between variables.

Correlation coefficient. A statistical figure that describes the direction and strength of a correlation.

Covert sensitization. A treatment that uses prolonged, imaginal exposure to engagement in a sexually deviant act but also imagining the negative consequences that result from it.

Criminal commitment. A court-ordered procedure that forces involuntary mental health treatment on a person with a psychological disorder who commits a crime.

Cross-sectional design. A research design in which participants are assessed once for the specific variable under investigation.

Crystal methamphetamine. A form of methamphetamine that produces longer-lasting and more intense physiological reactions than the powdered form.

Cultural-familial retardation. The mild intellectual disability that is more common among children in the lower socioeconomic classes and is considered retardation due to psychosocial disadvantage.

Culture. The shared behavioral patterns and lifestyles that differentiate one group of people from another.

Culture-bound syndrome. The abnormal behaviors that are specific to a particular location or group.

Cyclothymic disorder. A condition characterized by fluctuations that alternate between hypomanic symptoms and depressive symptoms.

D

Declaration of Helsinki. A document that sets forth basic guidelines for the conduct of research including the need for clearly formulated experimental procedures, a careful assessment of risks compared with benefits, and the provision of adequate information to the participants.

Deep brain stimulation. Surgically implanting electrodes in to targeted areas of the brain to treat depression and other psychological disorders.

Deinstitutionalization. The release of inpatients from hospitals to community treatment settings.

Delayed ejaculation. The delay of or inability to achieve orgasm despite adequate sexual stimulation; sometimes known as *retarded ejaculation*.

Delirium. A disturbance in consciousness that typically occurs in the context of a medical illness or after ingesting a substance.

Delirium tremens. A symptom characterized by disorientation, severe agitation, high blood pressure, and fever, which can last up to 3 to 4 days after stopping drinking.

Delusion. A false belief.

Delusional disorder. A condition in which a person has a nonbizarre delusion, no other psychotic symptoms, and few changes in overall functioning other than the behaviors immediately surrounding the delusion.

Delusions of influence. The belief that other people are controlling one's thoughts or behaviors.

Dementia. A term used in DSM-IV to describe major neurocognitive disorder.

Dementia praecox. The original name for schizophrenia coined by Kraepelin to highlight its pervasive disturbances of perceptual and cognitive faculties (*dementia*) and its early life onset (*praecox*) and to distinguish it from the dementia associated with old age.

Dependent personality disorder. A pervasive and excessive need to be taken care of by others that leads to dependency and fears of being left alone.

Dependent variable. The variable in a controlled experiment that is assessed to determine the effect of the independent variable.

Depersonalization/derealization disorder. Feelings of being detached from one's body or mind; a state of feeling as if one is an external observer of one's own behavior.

Depression. A mood that is abnormally low.

Depression executive dysfunction syndrome of late life. A type of depression among older adults, also known as vascular depression, that is associated with increased difficulties with language, increased apathy and slowed movements, and less agitation and guilt than other forms of depression.

Detoxification. A medically supervised drug withdrawal.

Developmental trajectory. The idea that common symptoms of a disorder may vary depending on a person's age.

Diagnosis. The identification of an illness.

Diagnostic and Statistical Manual of Mental Disorders (DSM). A classification of mental disorders originally developed in 1952; has been revised over subsequent years and is a standard of care in psychiatry and psychology.

Diathesis-stress model of abnormal behavior. The idea that psychological disorders may have a biological or psychological predisposition (diathesis) that lies dormant until environmental stress occurs and the combination produces abnormal.

Differential diagnosis. A process in which a clinician weighs how likely it is that a person has one diagnosis instead of another.

Dimensional approach. An approach to understanding behavior that considers it from a quantitative perspective (a little shy, moderately shy, a lot shy), not a qualitative perspective (shy or not shy).

Diminished emotional expression. Reduced or immobile facial expressions and a flat, monotonic vocal tone that does not change even when the topic of conversation becomes emotionally laden.

Disruptive mood regulation disorder. A disorder for children ages 6 to 18 years who have "severe recurrent temper outbursts that are grossly out of proportion in intensity or duration to the situation."

Dissociative amnesia. An inability to recall important information, usually of a personal nature, that follows a stressful or traumatic event.

Dissociative disorders. A set of disorders characterized by disruption in the usually integrated functions of consciousness, memory, identity, or perception of the environment.

Dissociative fugue. A disorder involving loss of personal identity and memory, often involving a flight from a person's usual place of residence.

Dissociative identity disorder. The presence within a person of two or more distinct personality states, each with its own pattern of perceiving, relating to, and thinking about the environment and self.

Dopamine hypothesis. The theory that a cause of schizophrenia is the presence of too much dopamine in the neural synapses.

Double depression. A combination of episodic major depressions superimposed on chronic low mood.

Down syndrome. The unusual condition in which chromosome 21 has three copies (i.e., trisomy) rather than the usual two.

Duty to warn. The duty of therapists to use reasonable care to protect third parties from dangers posed by patients.

Dysthmia. Also known as persistent depressive disorder, marked by chronic depression lasting two years or more.

E

Early-onset schizophrenia. A form of schizophrenia that develops in childhood or adolescence (usually before age 18).

Eating disorder not otherwise specified. A DSM-IV-TR residual diagnostic category for people who had eating disorders that did not match the classic profile of anorexia nervosa or bulimia nervosa.

Echolalia. The verbatim repetition of what others say.

Ecstasy. The pill form of *methylenedioxymethamphetamine* (MDMA), a common "club" drug and a frequent trigger for emergency room visits.

Effectiveness research. Research that maximizes external validity. Participants are more similar to the types of patients treated in routine care; emphasis is given to the cost–benefit ratio of treatment; and results are representative of treatment in the real world.

Efficacy research. Research designs that attempt to maximize internal validity.

Ego psychology. A form of psychodynamic theory that focuses on conscious motivations and healthy forms of human functioning.

Electroconvulsive therapy (ECT). The controlled delivery of electrical impulses, which cause brief seizures in the brain and reduce depressed mood.

Emotional contagion. The automatic mimicry and synchronization of expressions, vocalizations, postures, and movements of one person by another.

Encopresis. The repeated elimination of feces on or into inappropriate places such as the floor or clothing by someone over age 4.

Endocrine system. A system in the body that regulates bodily functions but uses hormones rather than nerve impulses to do so.

Enmeshment. The overinvolvement of all family members in the affairs of any one member.

Enuresis. The voiding of urine into one's clothing or bedding.

Epidemiology. A research approach that focuses on the prevalence and incidence of disorders and the factors that influence those patterns.

Epigenetics. Heritable changes in gene expression.

Erectile disorder. A condition with persistent and recurrent inability to maintain an adequate erection until completion of sexual activity.

Ethics. The accepted values that provide guidance to make sound moral judgments.

Excoriation (skin-picking) disorder. Recurrent skin picking resulting in skin lesions.

Executive dysfunction. The condition characterized by difficulty planning, thinking abstractly, initiating, and inhibiting actions.

Exhibitionistic disorder. The recurrent fantasies, urges, or behaviors involving exposing one's genitals to an unsuspecting stranger.

Experimental epidemiology. A research method in which the scientist manipulates exposure to either causal or preventive factors.

Experimental group. The group of individuals in a controlled group design who experience the independent variable.

Exposure. The crucial ingredient in behavior therapy in which a person learns to overcome fears by actual or imagined contact with the feared object or event.

Exposure and response prevention. A behavioral treatment for obsessive compulsive disorder that includes (1) exposure to feared stimuli and associated obsessions, and (2) response prevention, which involves preventing rituals, mental acts, and avoidance behaviors that serve to reduce anxiety associated with obsessions.

Expressed emotion. A concept used to describe the level of emotional involvement and critical attitudes that exist within the family of a patient with schizophrenia.

External validity. The ability to generalize study findings to situations and people outside the experimental setting. External validity often decreases with increased internal validity.

F

Factitious disorder. The condition in which physical or psychological signs or symptoms of illness are intentionally produced in what appears to be a desire to assume a sick role.

Factitious disorder imposed on another. A condition in which one person induces illness symptoms in someone else.

Factitious disorder imposed on self. A condition in which a person self engages in deceptive practices to produce signs of illness.

Family accommodation. A family's reaction to a member who has obsessive compulsive disorder that involves performing rituals for the person with OCD (e.g., providing repeated reassurance, checking for the person).

Familial aggregation. The process of examining whether family members of a person with a particular disorder are more likely to have that disorder than family members of people without the disorder.

Female orgasmic disorder. A condition with persistent and recurrent delay or absence of orgasm following the normal excitement phase; sometimes called *anorgasmia*.

Female sexual interest/arousal disorder. A condition with persistent or recurrent inability to maintain adequate vaginal lubrication and swelling response until the completion of sexual activity.

Fetal alcohol syndrome. A condition in babies that occurs when pregnant mothers drink alcohol and it passes through the placenta and harms the developing fetus; it is the leading known preventable environmental cause of intellectual disability.

Fetishistic disorder. The sexual arousal (fantasies, urges, or behaviors) that involves nonliving objects (not limited to female clothing used in cross-dressing).

Fight or flight. A general discharge of the sympathetic nervous system activated by stress or fear that includes accelerated heart rate, enhanced muscle activity, and increased respiration.

Forebrain. A part of the brain that includes the limbic system, basal ganglia, and cerebral cortex.

Fragile X syndrome (FXS). The most commonly inherited cause of intellectual disability; occurs when the presence of too many copies of a specific DNA series "turns off" a gene on the X chromosome. When the gene is turned off, cells do not make a necessary protein, and without it, FXS occurs.

Frontal lobe. One of the four lobes of the brain; seat of reasoning, impulse control, judgment, language, memory, motor function, problem solving, and sexual and social behavior that sends messages to the bodily organs via hormones.

Frotteuristic disorder. The consistent and intense sexually arousing fantasies, sexual urges, or behaviors involving touching and rubbing against a nonconsenting person.

Functional analysis. A strategy of behavioral assessment in which a clinician attempts to identify causal links between problem behaviors and environmental variables; also called *behavioral analysis* or *functional assessment*.

Functional neuroimaging. The use of technologies such as PET and fMRI that detect brain function.

G

Gender dysphoria. A strong and persistent cross-sex identification in which a person's biological sex and gender identity do not match.

Gene–environment correlation. The fact that biological parents pass on genotypes to their children, and also provide home environments that are correlated with their genotypes.

Generalized anxiety disorder. The excessive worry about future events, past transgressions, financial status, and the health of oneself and loved ones.

Genito-pelvic pain/penetration disorder. The consistent genital pain associated with sexual intercourse.

Genome-wide association study. An unbiased search of the human genome comparing cases and controls on genetic variants scattered across the genome for evidence of association.

Genome-wide linkage analysis. A technique that uses samples of families with many individuals who are ill with the same disorder or large samples of relatives who have the same disorder to identify genomic regions that may hold genes that influence a trait.

Geropsychology. A subdiscipline of psychology that addresses issues of aging including normal development, individual differences, and psychological problems unique to older persons.

Goodness of fit. The idea that behavior is problematic or not problematic depending on the environment in which it occurs.

Grooming behavior. A behavior observed across species that serves social and hygienic roles (e.g., picking and pulling to clean or maintain body appearance).

Guilty but mentally ill. A legal decision in which a person is considered criminally guilty and is subject to criminal penalties. The addition of the phrase *but mentally ill* acknowledges the presence of a psychological disorder when the offense was committed but does not change the person's criminal responsibility.

H

Habituation. Dissipation of anxiety that occurs during exposure treatment.

Hallucination. A false sensory perception.

Hallucinogens. Drugs that produce altered states of bodily perception and sensations, intense emotions, detachment from self and environment, and, for some users, feeling of insight with mystical or religious significance.

Health Insurance Portability and Accountability Act (HIPAA). A system of laws and regulations that protect the security and privacy of health information; provides protection for the privacy of certain individually identifiable health data, referred to as protected health information (PHI).

Health psychology. A subfield of psychology that uses its principles and methods to understand how attitudes and behaviors influence health and illness.

Heritability. The percentage of variance in liability to the disorder accounted for by genetic factors.

Hippocampus. The brain region that is part of the limbic system that also has a role in memory formation.

Histrionic personality disorder. A pervasive pattern of excessive emotionality and attention seeking.

Hoarding disorder. A disorder characterized by the persistent difficulty in discarding or parting with possessions, regardless of their actual value.

Hormones. Chemical messengers that are released into the bloodstream and act on target organs.

Hypomania. A mood elevation that is clearly abnormal yet not as extreme as frank mania.

I

Iatrogenic. The term describing a disease that may be inadvertently caused by a physician, by a medical or surgical treatment, or by a diagnostic procedure.

Illness anxiety disorder. The condition of experiencing fears or concerns about having an illness that persists despite medical reassurance.

Imaginal desensitization. A psychological treatment process that involves imagining a fear or urge, combined with a coping response such as relaxation or guided imagery, that facilitates reduction of the fear or urge.

Impulse control disorders. Disorders characterized by repetitive behaviors over which a person feels a lack of control; typically, these behaviors violate the rights of others or put the individual in conflict with societal norms or authority figures.

Inappropriate compensatory behavior. Any actions that a person uses to counteract a binge or to prevent weight gain.

Incidence. The number of new cases that emerge in a given population during a specified period of time.

Independent variable. The variable in a controlled experiment that the experimenter controls.

Informed consent. The concept that all people who participate in research must understand its aims and methods, what they will be asked to do, and what types of information they will be asked to provide. In addition, they must understand the risks and benefits of research participation and, based on that information, have the right to agree or refuse to participate in any research project.

Inhalants. The vapors from a variety of chemicals that yield an immediate effect of euphoria or sedation and can cause permanent damage to all organ systems including the brain.

Institutional review board. A committee charged by the researcher's institution with reviewing and approving scientific research.

Intellectual disability. Impairments of general mental abilities that impact functioning in conceptual, social, and practical domains.

Intelligence quotient. A score of cognitive functioning that compares a person's performance to his or her age-matched peers.

Intelligence test. A test that measures intelligence quotient (IQ).

Internal validity. The extent to which a study's design allows conclusions that an intervention (independent variable) caused changes in the outcome (dependent variable).

International Classification of Diseases and Related Health Problems (ICD). A classification system for mental disorders developed in Europe that is an international standard diagnostic system for epidemiology and many health management purposes.

Interrater agreement. The amount of agreement between two clinicians who are using the same measure to rate the same symptoms in a single patient.

K

Kleptomania. A disorder characterized by a failure to resist urges to steal items that are not needed for personal use or monetary value.

L

Late-onset schizophrenia. The schizophrenia that first appears after age 40.

Learned helplessness. A term meaning that externally uncontrollable environments and presumably internally uncontrollable environments are inescapable stimuli that can lead to depression.

Left hemisphere. The region of the brain primarily responsible for language and cognitive functions.

Life-span developmental diathesis-stress model. A model that considers the role of biological predispositions, stressful life events, and personal protective factors in the etiology of depression.

Limbic system. The brain region involved with the experience of emotion, the regulation of emotional expression, and the basic biological drives such as aggression, sex, and appetite.

Lithium. A naturally occurring metallic element used to treat bipolar disorder.

Longitudinal design. A research design in which participants are assessed at least two times and often more over a certain time interval.

Loose association. A thought that has little or no logical connection to the next one.

Lysergic acid diethylamide (LSD). A synthetic hallucinogen, first synthesized in 1938.

M

M'Naghten Rule. A legal principle stating that a person is not responsible for his actions if (1) he did not know what he was doing or (2) he did not know that his actions were wrong.

Major depressive disorder. A persistent sad or low mood that is severe enough to impair a person's interest in or ability to engage in normally enjoyable activities.

Major neurocognitive disorder. A disorder that represents deficits in cognitive abilities significantly affecting older people.

Major or mild vascular neurocognitive disorder. A disorder diagnosed when a patient's history, laboratory tests, and/or brain imaging studies indicate cognitive impairment as a result of cardiovascular disease, such as stroke, transient ischemic attack (TIA, or mini-stroke), coronary artery disease, or untreated high blood pressure.

Male hypoactive sexual desire disorder. A condition with reduced or absent sexual desires or behaviors, either with a partner or through masturbation.

Malingering. A condition in which physical symptoms are produced intentionally to avoid military service, criminal prosecution, or work or to obtain financial compensation or drugs.

Malpractice. Professional misconduct or unreasonable lack of skill.

Mania. A persistent mood that is abnormally high.

Marijuana. A drug derived from the *Cannabis sativa* plant that produces mild intoxication.

Mass hysteria. A situation in which a group of people share and sometimes even act upon a belief that is not based in fact (e.g., tarantism and lycanthropy).

***Mens rea*.** Latin term for guilty mind or criminal intent.

Meta-analysis. A method of data analysis that pools findings across multiple independent studies addressing a similar question.

Methadone. The most widely known agonist substitute; used as a replacement for heroin.

Midbrain. A portion of the brain stem that coordinates sensory information and movement; includes the reticular activating system, the thalamus, and the hypothalamus.

Mild neurocognitive disorder. A disorder of cognitive decline that afflicts older people in which the person can still function independently, but tasks take longer and may require the use of compensatory strategies.

Mindfulness. Being aware of one's experience "in the moment" and doing so in a non-judgmental fashion.

Mixed state. A state characterized by symptoms of mania and depression that occur at the same time.

Molecular genetics. The study of the structure and function of genes at a molecular level.

N

Narcissistic personality disorder. A pervasive pattern of grandiosity, need for admiration from others, and lack of empathy.

Negative symptoms. The behaviors, emotions, or thought processes (cognitions) that exist in people without a psychiatric disorder but are absent (or are substantially diminished) in people with schizophrenia.

Neuroanatomy. The brain structure.

Neurofibrillary tangles. The twisted protein fibers within neurons found in the brains of patients with Alzheimer's disease.

Neuroimaging. The technology that takes pictures of the brain.

Neuron. A nerve cell found throughout the body, including in the brain.

Neuroscience. The study of the structure and function of the nervous system and the interaction of that system and behavior.

Neurotransmitters. Chemical substances that are released into the synapse and transmit information from one neuron to another.

Nicotine. A highly addictive component of tobacco that is considered to be both a stimulant and a sedative.

Nicotine replacement therapy (NRT). A safe and effective therapy used as part of a comprehensive smoking cessation program.

Nonshared environmental factors. Environmental factors that are not shared between twins but which may influence the onset of psychological disorders.

Normative. A comparison group that is representative of the entire population against which a person's score on a psychological test is compared.

Normative comparison. A method of interpreting assessment data that involves comparing a person's score with the scores of a sample of people who are representative of the entire population (with regard to characteristics such as age, sex, ethnicity, education, and geographic region) or with the scores of a subgroup who are similar to the person being assessed.

Not guilty by reason of insanity. A legal decision that describes people who commit a crime but who are prevented by a psychological disorder from understanding the seriousness and illegality of their actions.

Nuremberg Code. The directives for experimentation with human subjects that specify that voluntary consent is absolutely essential for clinical research.

O

Obsessional neurosis. A term used to describe the symptoms of obsessive compulsive disorder at the time when psychoanalytic theories of etiology were developed.

Obsessions. Recurrent, persistent, and intrusive thoughts.

Obsessive-compulsive and related disorders. A group of disorders for which obsessive compulsive disorder is the "centerpiece," and all related disorders are thought to have significant overlap with this disorder in terms of clinical features, family/genetic risk factors, neuroanatomical abnormalities, behavioral mechanisms for symptom onset, and treatment response.

Obsessive-compulsive disorder. A condition involving obsessions (intrusive thoughts), often combined with compulsions (repetitive behaviors) that can be extensive, time consuming, and distressful.

Obsessive-compulsive personality disorder. A pervasive preoccupation with orderliness, perfectionism, and mental and interpersonal control to the point of distress.

Occipital lobe. One of four lobes of the brain; located at the back of the skull; center of visual processing.

Olfactory aversion. A treatment pairing an extremely noxious but harmless odor (such as ammonia) with either sexual fantasies or sexual behaviors.

Operant conditioning. A form of learning in which behavior is acquired or changed by the events that happen afterward.

Opioids. A drug group derived from the opium poppy, which includes heroin, morphine, and codeine.

Oppositional defiant disorder (ODD). The negative, hostile, or defiant behaviors that are less severe than those found in conduct disorder.

Osteoporosis. A condition of decreased bone density.

Outcome evaluation. One primary goal of psychological assessment that helps us know whether patients are getting better, when treatment is "finished," or when it is necessary to modify an approach that is not achieving its aims.

Outpatient commitment. A court order that directs a person to comply with a specified, individualized outpatient mental health treatment plan.

P

Panic attack. A discrete period of intense fear or discomfort (subjective distress) and a cascade of physical symptoms.

Panic disorder. A disorder in which the person has had at least one panic attack and worries about having more attacks.

Paranoid personality disorder. A pervasive distrust and suspiciousness of others such that their motives are interpreted as malevolent.

Paraphilic disorder. The intense, persistent, and frequently occurring sexual urges, fantasies, or behaviors that involve unusual situations, objects, or activities.

Parasympathetic nervous system. The part of the autonomic nervous system that counteracts the effects of system activation by slowing down heart rate and respiration, returning the body to a resting state.

Parietal lobe. One of four lobes of the brain; integrates sensory information from various sources and may be involved with visuospatial processing.

Pedophilic disorder. The consistent and intense sexually arousing fantasies, sexual urges, or behaviors involving sexual activity with a child or children not yet 14 years old; the person involved is at least 16 years old and at least 5 years older than the child or children.

Peripheral nervous system. One part of the human nervous system that includes the sensory–somatic nervous system (controls sensations and muscle movements) and the autonomic nervous system (controls involuntary movements).

Persecutory delusion. A patient's belief that someone is persecuting her or him or that the person is a special agent/individual.

Persistent depressive disorder. A chronic state of depression in which the symptoms are the same as those of major depression but are less severe.

Personality disorder. An enduring pattern of inner experience and behavior that deviates from the norm, is pervasive and inflexible, has an onset in adolescence or early adulthood, is stable across time, and leads to distress or impairment.

Personality test. A psychological test that measures personality characteristics.

Phenomenology. A school of thought that holds that one's subjective perception of the world is more important than the world in actuality.

Phenylketonuria. A genetic disorder in which the body cannot break down the amino acid *phenylalanine*; if untreated, it leads to the development of intellectual disability.

Pica. The recurrent, compulsive consumption of nonnutritive items.

Placebo control. The group in a clinical trial that receives treatment which is similar to the experimental treatment but without the active ingredients (e.g., a pill that looks exactly like the real medication but in fact has no active medication).

Placebo effect. Effect in which symptoms are diminished or eliminated not because of any specific treatment but because the patient believes that a treatment is effective.

Plethysmography. A method to measure sexual arousal in men or women.

Polypharmacy. The practice of prescribing more than one medication for a single disorder.

Positive symptoms. A group of schizophrenic symptoms including unusual thoughts, feelings, and behaviors that vary in intensity and in many cases are responsive to treatment.

Posttraumatic stress disorder. The emotional distress that occurs after an event involving actual or threatened death, serious injury, or a threat to physical integrity and that leads to avoidance of stimuli associated with the trauma, feelings of emotional numbness, and persistent symptoms of increased sympathetic nervous system arousal.

Premature (early) ejaculation. The consistent ejaculation with minimal sexual stimulation before, immediately upon, or shortly after penetration and before the person wishes it.

Prevalence. The number of cases of a disorder in a given population at a designated time.

Premenstrual dysphoric disorder (PMDD). A more severe form of premenstrual changes that afflict 3 to 8% of women of reproductive age.

Privacy. A right that limits the access of other people to one's body or mind including one's thoughts, beliefs, and fantasies.

Privilege. A legal term that prevents a therapist from revealing confidential information during legal proceedings.

Proband. The person with a particular disorder in a familial aggregation study.

Problem-solving therapy. A cognitive behavioral treatment that helps people learn the steps of solving problems to reduce depression and/or anxiety.

Projective test. A test derived from psychoanalytic theory in which people are asked to respond to ambiguous stimuli.

Pseudoseizure. A sudden change in behavior that mimics epileptic seizures but has no organic basis.

Psychoanalysis. A theory of abnormal behavior originated by Sigmund Freud that was based on the belief that many aspects of behavior were controlled by unconscious innate biological urges that existed from infancy.

Psychoeducation. The teaching of patient and families about the patient's disorder in order to reduce familial distress and equip them to work effectively with the patient.

Psychological autopsy. An attempt to identify psychological causes of suicide by interviewing family, friends, coworkers, and health care providers.

Psychological challenge studies. A study or assessment methodology that requires people to confront objects or situations while neuro-imaging procedures are used to scan suspected areas of the brain for enhanced activity.

Psychometric properties. A set of properties, including standardization, reliability, and validity, that helps us evaluate how well an assessment instrument works and affects how confident we can be in the testing results.

Psychomotor retardation. A condition in which a person has slowed mental or physical activities.

Psychoneuroimmunology. The study of the relations between social, psychological, and physical responses.

Psychophysiological assessment. The evaluation strategies that measure brain structure, brain function, and nervous system activity.

Psychosis. A severe mental condition characterized by a loss of contact with reality.

Punishment. The application of something painful or the removal of something positive.

Purging. Self-inducing vomiting or using laxatives, diuretics (water pills), or enemas to reverse the effects of a binge or to induce weight loss.

Pyromania. A disorder characterized primarily by the deliberate and intentional setting of fires for pleasure.

R

Random assignment. The most critical feature of a randomized controlled design in which each participant has an equal probability of being assigned to each experimental or control condition.

Reinforcement. A contingent event that strengthens the response that precedes it.

Relapse prevention. The treatment approach that uses functional analysis to identify the antecedents and consequences of drug use and then develops alternative cognitive and behavioral skills to reduce the risk of future drug use.

Reliability. The extent to which a psychological assessment instrument produces consistent results each time it is given.

Reminiscence therapy. A treatment for depression used with older adults that focuses on patients' recall of significant past events and how they managed distress.

Reversal. See ABAB.

Reversible dementia. The condition that occurs when the full syndrome of dementia appears to be present but resolves after appropriate treatment for another disorder; also known as *pseudodementia*.

Right hemisphere. The region of the brain associated with creativity, imagery, and intuition.

Rumination disorder. The regurgitation of recently eaten food into the mouth followed by either rechewing, reswallowing, or spitting it out.

S

Satiation. A treatment that uses prolonged, imaginal exposure to arousing sexual stimuli until it no longer produces positive, erotic feelings.

Schizoaffective disorder. A condition in which, in addition to all of the symptoms of schizophrenia, the patient suffers from a major depressive, manic, or mixed episode disorder at some point during the illness.

Schizoid personality disorder. A pervasive pattern of social detachment and a limited expression of emotion in interpersonal contexts.

Schizophrenia. A severe psychological disorder characterized by disorganization in thought, perception, and behavior.

Schizophreniform disorder. A condition with symptoms that are identical to those of schizophrenia except that its duration is shorter (less than 6 months) and it results in less impairment in social or occupational functioning.

Schizotypal personality disorder. A pervasive pattern of social and interpersonal deficits marked by acute discomfort, reduced capacity for close relationships, cognitive or perceptual distortions, and behavioral eccentricities.

Scientist–practitioner model. An approach to psychological disorders based on the concept that when providing treatment to people with psychological disorders, the psychologist relies on the findings of research and in turn, when conducting research, the psychologist investigates topics that help to guide and improve psychological care.

Screening. An assessment process that attempts to identify psychological problems or predict the risk of future problems among people who are not referred for clinical assessment.

Seasonal affective disorder. A subtype of major depression that is characterized by depressive episodes that vary by season.

Sedative drugs. A substance group including barbiturates and benzodiazepines, which are central nervous system depressants and cause sedation and decrease anxiety.

Selective serotonin reuptake inhibitor (SSRI). A group of medications that selectively inhibit the reuptake of serotonin at the presynaptic neuronal membrane, restoring the normal chemical balance; drugs thought to correct serotonin imbalances by increasing the time that the neurotransmitter remains in the synapse.

Self-monitoring. A procedure within behavioral assessment in which the patient observes and records his or her own behavior as it happens.

Self-referent comparisons. Comparison of responses on a psychological instrument with a person's own prior performance.

Separation anxiety disorder. The severe and unreasonable fear of separation from a parent or a caregiver.

Sex drive. The physical and/or psychological craving for sexual activity and pleasure.

Sex reassignment surgery. A series of behavioral and medical procedures that matches an individual's physical anatomy to gender identity.

Sexual dysfunction. The absence or impairment of some aspect of sexual response that causes distress or impairment considering age, sex, and culture.

Sexual masochism disorder. A person's consistent intense sexually arousing fantasies, sexual urges, or behaviors involving actual acts of being humiliated, beaten, bound, or otherwise made to suffer.

Sexual sadism disorder. The consistent sexual arousal that occurs when one inflicts acts of humiliation, beating, bondage, or acts of suffering on another person.

Shared environmental factors. Environmental variables that may influence the onset of psychological disorders that are shared among twins or family members.

Shared psychotic disorder. A condition in which two or more persons who have a close relationship share the same delusional belief; also known as *folie à deux*.

Single-case design. An experimental study conducted with a single individual.

Social anxiety disorder. A pervasive pattern of social timidity characterized by fear that the person will behave in a way that will be humiliating or embarrassing.

Social cognition. The ability to perceive, interpret, and understand social information including other people's beliefs, attitudes, and emotions.

Sociocultural model. The idea that abnormal behavior must be understood within the context of social and cultural forces.

Somatic symptom and related disorders. A condition defined as the presence of one or more somatic symptoms plus abnormal/excessive thoughts, feelings, and behaviors regarding the symptoms.

Specific learning disorder. A condition involving persisent difficulty in reading, writing, arithmetic or mathematics.

Specific phobias. Marked fear or anxiety about a specific object or situation that leads to significant disruption in daily functioning.

Standardization. Standard ways of evaluating scores on psychological assessments that can involve normative or self-referent comparisons (or both).

Structural neuroimaging. The use of technologies such as CAT and MRI that explore neuroanatomy.

Structured interview. A clinical interview in which the clinician asks a standard set of questions, usually with the goal of establishing a diagnosis.

Substance intoxication. The acute effects of substance use.

Substance use disorder. A cluster of cognitive, behavioral, and physiological symptoms indicating that an individual continues to use a substance despite significant substance-related problems.

Substance/medication-induced major or mild neurocognitive disorder. The cognitive impairment associated with substance use.

Suicidal ideation. A condition characterized by thoughts of death.

Sympathetic nervous system. The part of the autonomic nervous system that activates the body for the fight-or-flight response. When activated, the sympathetic nervous system increases heart rate and respiration, allowing the body to perform at peak efficiency.

Synapse. A space between neurons.

Synaptic pruning. A process in which weaker synaptic contacts in the brain are eliminated and stronger connections are enhanced.

T

Talking cure. A therapy in the form of discussion of psychological distress with a trained professional, leading to the elimination of distressing symptoms.

Tardive dyskinesia. A neurological condition characterized by abnormal and involuntary motor movements of the face, mouth, limbs, and trunk.

Temperament. Personality components that are biological or genetic in origin, observable from birth (or perhaps before), and relatively stable across time and situations.

Temporal lobe. One of four lobes of the brain; associated with understanding auditory and verbal information, labeling of objects, and verbal memory.

Test-retest reliability. The extent to which a test produces similar scores over time when given to the same individual(s).

Tetrahydrocannabinol. The active ingredient in marijuana.

Thought-action fusion. A type of obsessive thinking that involves equating a thought about a behavior with performing the behavior itself.

Thought blocking. An unusually long pause or pauses in a patient's speech that occur during a conversation.

Tolerance. The diminished response to a drug after repeated exposure to it.

Trait anxiety. A personality trait that exists along a dimension; those individuals high on this dimension are more "reactive" to stressful events and therefore more likely, given the right circumstances, to develop a disorder; also called *anxiety proneness*.

Transcranial magnetic stimulation. Treatment for depression that uses a magnetic coil placed over the patient's head to deliver a painless, localized electromagnetic pulse to a part of the brain.

Transgender behavior. The behavioral attempt to pass as the opposite sex through cross-dressing, disguising one's own sexual genitalia, or changing other sexual characteristics.

Translational research. A scientific approach that focuses on communication between basic science and applied clinical research.

Transsexualism. Another term for *gender dysphoria* commonly used to describe the condition when it occurs in adolescents and adults.

Transtheoretical model. A five-stage sequential model of behavioral change.

Transvestic disorder. The sexual arousal in men that results from wearing women's clothing and is accompanied by significant distress or impairment.

Treatment refractory. Resistance to positive effects of treatment.

Trephination. The process in which a circular instrument was used to cut away sections of the skull, possibly in an attempt to release demons from the brain.

Trichotillomania. Repetitive hair pulling that results in noticeable hair loss.

Tuskegee experiment. An infamous historical study in which core values of research (respect for persons, beneficence, and justice) were violated.

U

Unstructured interview. A clinical interview in which the clinician decides what questions to ask and how to ask them.

V

Validity. The degree to which a test measures what it is intended to assess.

Vascular depression. A mood disorder that occurs in the context of cerebrovascular disease.

Vasovagal syncope. A common physiological response consisting of slow heart rate, low blood pressure, and loss of consciousness that sometimes occurs in people with blood/illness/injury phobias.

Very-late-onset schizophrenia-like psychosis. A schizophrenic-like disorder but with symptoms that do not include deterioration in social and personal functioning.

Vicarious conditioning. A distinct type of learning in which the person need not actually do the behavior in order to acquire it.

Viral infection theory. The theory that during the prenatal period or shortly after birth, viral infections could cause some psychological disorders.

Voyeuristic disorder. The consistent intense sexually arousing fantasies, sexual urges, or behaviors centered on observing an unsuspecting person who is naked, disrobing, or engaging in sexual activity.

W

Waxy flexibility. A condition in which parts of the body (usually the arms) remain frozen in a particular posture when positioned that way by another person.

Wernicke-Korsakoff syndrome. A condition caused by deficiencies in thiamine secondary to alcohol dependence.

Withdrawal. A set of symptoms associated with physical dependence on a drug that occur when the drug is no longer taken.

Worry. The apprehensive (negative) expectations or outcomes about the future or the past that are considered to be unreasonable in light of the actual situation.

References

Abel, E. L., & Hannigan, J. H. (1995). Maternal risk factors in fetal alcohol syndrome: Provocative and permissive influences. *Neurotoxicology and Teratology, 17,* 445–462.

Abel, G. G., Mittelman, M. S., & Becker, J. V. (1985). Sexual offenders: Results of assessment and recommendations for treatment. In H. W. Ben-Gron (Ed.), *Clinical criminology* (pp. 191–205). Toronto: M. M. Graphics.

Abel, G. G., & Osborn, C. (1992). The paraphilias: The extent and nature of sexually deviant and criminal behavior. *Clinical Forensic Psychiatry, 15,* 675–687.

Abel, G. G., Becker, J. V., Cunningham-Rathner, J., Mittelman, M., & Rouleau, J. L. (1998). Multiple paraphilic diagnoses among sex offenders. *Bulletin of the American Academy of Psychiatry and the Law, 16,* 153–168.

Abel, G. G., Huffman, J., Warberg, B., & Holland, C. L. (1998). Visual reaction time and plethysmography as measures of sexual interest in child molesters. *Sexual Abuse: A Journal of Research and Treatment, 10,* 81–95.

Abel, G. G., Jordan, A., Rouleau, J. O. L., Emerick, R., Barboza-Whitehead, S., & Osborn, C. (2004). Use of visual reaction time to assess male adolescents who molest children. *Sexual Abuse: A Journal of Research and Treatment, 16,* 225–265.

Abrahams, P. W., & Parsons, J. A. (1996). Geophagy in the tropics: A literature review. *Geographical Journal, 162,* 63–72.

Abramowitz, J. S., & Jacoby, R. J. (2015). Obsessive-compulsive and related disorders: A critical review of the new diagnostic class. *Annual Review of Clinical Psychology, 11,* 165–186.

Abramowitz, J. S., Moore, E. L. (2007). An experimental analysis of hypochondriasis. *Behavior Research and Therapy, 45,* 413–424.

Abramson, L., Seligman, M., & Teasdale, J. (1978). Learned helplessness in humans: Critique and reformulation. *Journal of Abnormal Psychology, 87,* 49–74.

Abramson, L. Y., Alloy, L. B., Hankin, B. L., Haeffel, G. J., MacCoon, D. G., & Gibb, B. E. (2002). Cognitive vulnerability-stress models of depression in a self-regulatory and psychobiological context. In I. H. Gotlib and C. L. Hammen (Eds.) *Handbook of depression* (pp. 268–294). New York: Guilford Press.

Acarturk, C., Cuijpers, P., van Straten, A., & de Graaf, R. (2009). Psychological treatment of social anxiety disorder: A meta-analysis. *Psychological Medicine, 39,* 241–254.

Achiam-Montal, M., Tibi, L., & Lipsitz, J. D. (2013). Panic disorder in children and adolescents with noncardiac chest pain. *Child Psychiatry and Human Development, 44,* 742–750.

Acocella, J. (1998, April 6). The politics of hysteria, *The New Yorker,* 64–79.

Adan, R. A., Hillebrand, J. J., Danner, U. N., Cardona Cano, S., Kas, M. J., & Verhagen, L. A. (2011). Neurobiology driving hyperactivity in activity-based anorexia. *Current Topics in Behavioral Neurosciences, 6,* 229–250.

Addington, A. M., Gornick, M., Duckworth, J., Spron, A., Gogtay, N., Bobb, A., … Balkissoon, R. (2005). *GAD1* (2q31.1), which encoded glutamic acid decarboxylase (*GAD67*), is associated with childhood-onset schizophrenia and cortical gray matter volume loss. *Molecular Psychiatry, 10,* 581–588.

Adler, C. M., DelBello, M. P., & Strakowski, S. M. (2006). Brain network dysfunction in bipolar disorder. *CNS Spectrums, 11,* 312–320.

Agabio, R., Preti, A., & Gessa, G. L. (2013). Efficacy and tolerability of baclofen in substance use disorders: A systematic review. *European Addiction Research, 19,* 325–345.

Agarwal, S., & Lau, C. T. (2010). Remote health monitoring using mobile phones and Web services. *Telemedicine and e-Health, 16,* 603–607.

Agrawal, A., Pergadia, M. L., & Lynskey, M. T. (2008). Is there evidence for symptoms of cannabis withdrawal in the national epidemiologic survey of alcohol and related conditions? *The American Journal of Addictions, 17,* 199–208.

Aigner, M., Graf, A., Freidl, M., Prause, W., Weiss, M., Kaup-Eder. B., … Bach, M. (2003). Sleep disturbances in somatoform pain disorder. *Psychopathology, 36,* 324–328.

Ainsworth, M. (1982). Attachment: Retrospect and prospect. In C. Parkes and J. Stevenson-Hinde (Eds.), *The place of attachment in human behavior* (pp. 3–30). New York: Basic Books.

Akiskal, H. S. (2001). Dysthymia and cyclothymia in psychiatric practice a century after Kraepelin. *Journal of Affective Disorders, 62,* 17–31.

Albee, G. W. (2002). Just say no to psychotropic drugs! *Journal of Clinical Psychology, 58,* 635–648.

Alberdi-Sudupe, J., Pita-Fernandez, S., Gomez-Pardinas, S. M., Iglesias-Gil-de-Bernabe, F., Garcia-Fernandez, J., Martinez-Sande, G., … Pertega-Diaz, S. (2011). Suicide attempts and related factors in patients admitted to a general hospital: A ten-year cross-sectional study (1997–2007). *BMC Psychiatry, 11,* 51.

Alegria, A. A., Blanco, C., Petry, N. M., Skodol, A. E., Liu, S. M., Grant, B., & Hasin, D. (2013). Sex differences in antisocial personality disorder: Results from the National Epidemiological Survey on Alcohol and Related Conditions. *Personality Disorders: Theory, Research, and Treatment, 4,* 214–222.

Alexopoulos, G. (2004). Late-life mood disorders. *Comprehensive textbook of geriatric psychiatry, 3,* 609–653.

Alexopoulos, G. S., Raue, P. J., McCulloch, C., Kanellopoulos, D., Seirup, J. K., Sirey, J. A., … Areán, P. A. (2016). Clinical case management versus case management with problem-solving therapy in low-income, disabled elders with major depression: A randomized clinical trial. *The American Journal of Geriatric Psychiatry, 24,* 50–59.

Alfano, C. A., Beidel, D. C., & Turner, S. M. (2002). Cognition in childhood anxiety: Conceptual, methodological and developmental issues. *Clinical Psychology Review, 22,* 1029–1038.

Alfano, C. A., Beidel, D. C., & Turner, S. M. (2006). Cognitive correlates of social phobia among children and adolescents. *Journal of Abnormal Child Psychology, 34,* 189–201.

Ali, Z. (2001). Pica in people with intellectual disability: A literature review of aetiology, epidemiology and complications. *Journal of Intellectual & Developmental Disability, 26,* 205–215.

Allen, K. (1995). Barriers to treatment for addicted African-American women. *Journal of the National Medical Association, 87,* 751–756.

Allen, K. L., Byrne, S. M., Oddy, W. H., & Crosby, R. D. (2013). DSM-IV-TR and DSM-5 eating disorders in adolescents: Prevalence, stability, and psychosocial correlates in a population-based sample of male and female adolescents. *Journal of Abnormal Psychology, 122,* 720–732.

Alloy, L. B., Abramson, L. Y., Whitehouse, W. G., Hogan, M. E., Tashman, N. A., Steinberg, D. L., … Donovan, P. (2000). The Temple-Wisconsin Cognitive Vulnerability to Depression Project: Lifetime history of axis I psychopathology in individuals at high and low cognitive risk for depression. *Journal of Abnormal Psychology, 109,* 403–418.

Almeida, O. P., Yeap, B. B., Alfonso, H., Hankey, G. J., Flicker, L., & Norman, P. E. (2012). Older men who use computers have lower risk of dementia. *PLOS ONE, 7,* e44239.

Alper, K., Devinsky, O., Perrine, K., Vazquez, B., & Luciano, D. (1993). Nonepileptic seizures and childhood sexual and physical abuse. *Neurology, 43,* 1950–1953.

Alsene, K., Deckert, J., Sand, P., & de Wit, H. (2003) Association between A2a receptor gene polymorphisms and caffeine-induced anxiety. *Neuropsychopharmacology,* 28, 1694–702.

Althof, A. E. (2006). The psychology of premature ejaculation: Therapies and consequences. *Journal of Sexual Medicine, 3* (4 Suppl), 324–331.

Althof, A. E. (2012). Psychological interventions for delayed ejaculation/orgasm. *International Journal of Impotence Research, 24,* 131–136.

Althof, S. E., McMahon, C. G., Waldinger, M. D., Serefoglu, E. C., Shindel, A. W., Adaikan, G., … Torres, L. O. (2014). An update of the International Society of Sexual Medicine's guidelines for the diagnosis and treatment of premature ejaculation (PE). *Journal of Sexual Medicine,* 1, 1392–1422.

Althoff, R. R., Hudziak, J. J., Willemsen, G., Hudziak, V., Bartels, M., & Boomsma, D. I. (2012). Genetic and environmental contributions to self-reported thoughts of self-harm and suicide. *American Journal of Medical Neuropsychiatric Genetics Part B, 159B,* 120–127.

Alvidrez, J., Areán, P. A., & Stewart, A. L. (2005). Psychoeducation to increase psychotherapy entry for older African Americans. *The American Journal of Geriatric Psychiatry, 13,* 554–561.

Alzheimer's Association. (2015). *2015 Alzheimer's disease facts and figures.* Retrieved from https://www.alz.org/facts/downloads/facts_figures_2015.pdf.

Amendah, D. D., Grosse, S. D., & Bertrand, J. (2011). Medical expenditures of children in the United States with fetal alcohol syndrome. *Neurotoxicology and Teratology, 33,* 322–324.

Ament, S. A., Szelinger, S., Glusman, G., Ashworth, J., Hou, L., Akula, N., … Roach, J. C. (2015). Rare variants in neuronal excitability genes influence risk for bipolar disorder. *Proceedings of the National Academy of Sciences, 112,* 3576–3581.

American Academy of Child and Adolescent Psychiatry. (2012). *A guide for community child serving agencies on psychotropic medications for children and adolescents.* Retrieved from http://www.aacap.org/App_Themes/AACAP/docs/press/guide_for_community_child_serving_agencies_on_psychotropic_medications_for_children_and_adolescents_2012.pdf. Washington, DC.

American Law Institute. (1962). *Model penal code: Proposed official draft.* Philadelphia: American Law Institute.

American Psychiatric Association. (1952). *Diagnostic and statistical manual of mental disorders* (1st ed.). Washington, DC: American Psychiatric Press.

American Psychiatric Association. (1968). *Diagnostic and Statistical Manual of Mental Disorders* (2nd ed.). Washington, DC: American Psychiatric Press.

American Psychiatric Association. (1974). Position statement on homosexuality and civil rights. *American Journal of Psychiatry, 131,* 497.

American Psychiatric Association. (1980). *Diagnostic and Statistical Manual of Mental Disorders* (3rd ed.). Washington, DC: American Psychiatric Press.

American Psychiatric Association (1987). *Diagnostic and Statistical Manual of Mental Disorders: Edition III-R* (3rd ed.-revised). Washington, DC: American Psychiatric Press.

American Psychiatric Association. (2000). *Diagnostic and Statistical Manual of Mental Disorders* (4th ed., text revision). Washington, DC: American Psychiatric Press.

American Psychiatric Association. (2005). Practice guidelines for the treatment of patients with bipolar disorder. *American Journal of Psychiatry, 59*(4 Suppl), 1–50.

American Psychiatric Association (2006). *Gay, lesbian, and bisexual issues.* Retrieved from http://www.healthyminds.org/glbissues.cfm.

American Psychiatric Association (2013). *Diagnostic and Statistical Manual of Mental Disorders* (5th ed.). Washington, DC: American Psychiatric Association.

American Psychological Association. (1994). Guidelines for child custody evaluations in divorce proceedings. *American Psychologist, 49,* 677–680.

American Psychological Association. (2002). Ethical principles of psychologists and code of conduct. *American Psychologist, 57,* 1060–1073.

American Psychological Association. (2005). *Report of the 2005 Presidential Task Force on Evidence-Based Practice.* Washington, DC:American Psychological Association.

American Psychological Association. (2006). Advancing Colleague Assistance in Professional Psychology [CAP monograph]. Retrieved from http://www.apa.org/practice/resources/assistance/monograph.pdf

American Psychological Association. (2010). *Ethical principles of psychologists and code of conduct.* Washington, DC: American Psychological Association.

American Psychological Association. (2014). Guidelines for psychological practice with older adults. *The American Psychologist, 69,* 34.

Amsterdam, A., Carter, J., & Krychman, M. (2006). Prevalence of psychiatric illness in women in an oncology sexual health population: A retrospective pilot study. *Journal of Sexual Medicine, 3,* 292–295.

Anastasi, A., & Urbina, S. (1997). *Psychology testing* (7th ed.). Upper Sadle River, New Jersey: Prentice Hall.

Anderson, C., & Bulik, C. M. (2003). Gender differences in compensatory behaviors, weight and shape salience, and drive for thinness. *Eating Behaviors, 57*, 161–178.

Anderson, I. M. (2001). Meta-analytical studies on new antidepressants. *British Medical Bulletin, 57*, 161–178.

Anderson, L. M., Freeman, J. B., Franklin, M. E., & Sapyta, J. J. (2015). Family-based treatment of pediatric obsessive- compulsive disorder: Clinical considerations and application. *Child and Adolescent Psychiatric Clinics of North America, 24*, 535–555.

Anderson, P. L., Price, M., Edwards, S. M., Obasaju, M. A., Schmertz, S. K., Zimand, E., & Calamaras, M. R. (2013). Virtual reality exposure therapy for social anxiety disorder: A randomized controlled trial. *Journal of Consulting and Clinical Psychology, 81*, 751–760.

Andrews, G., Stewart, G., Allen, R., & Henderson, A. S. (1990). The genetics of six anxiety disorders: A twin study. *Journal of Affective Disorders, 19*, 23–29.

Andrews, G., & Hobbs, M. J. (2010). Andrews, G., & Hobbs, M. J. The effect of the draft DSM-5 criteria for GAD on prevalence and severity. *Australian New Zealand Journal of Psychiatry, 44*, 784–790.

Andrews, G., Hobbs, M. J., Borkovec, T. D., Beedo, K., Craske, M. G., Heimberg, R. G., … Stanley, M. A. (2010). Generalized worry disorder: A review of DSM-IV generalized anxiety disorder and options for DSM-V. *Depression & Anxiety, 27*, 134–147.

Andriasano, C., Chiesa, A., & Serretti, A. (2013). Newer antidepressants and panic disorder: A meta-analysis. *International Clinical Psychopharmacology, 28*, 33–45.

Angelakis, I., Gooding, P., Tarrier, N., & Panagioti, M. (2015). Suicidality in obsessive compulsive disorder (OCD): A systematic review and meta-analysis. *Clinical Psychology Review, 39*, 1–15.

Angold, A., & Costello, E. J. (2006). Puberty and depression. *Child and Adolescent Psychiatric Clinics of North America, 15*, 919–937, ix.

Annas, J. D. (2004). Forcible medication for courtroom competence—The case of Charles Sell. *New England Journal of Medicine, 350*, 2297–2301.

Anthony, J.C., & Petronis K.R. (1995) Early-onset drug use and risk of later drug problems. *Drug and Alcohol Dependence*, 40, 9–15.

Antony, M. M., & Barlow, D. H. (2002). Specific phobia. In D. H. Barlow. (Ed.), *Anxiety and its disorders: The nature and treatment of anxiety and panic* (2nd ed., pp. 380–417). New York: Guilford.

APA Working Group on Eating Disorders. (2000). Practice guideline for the treatment of patients with eating disorders (Rev. ed.). *American Journal of Psychiatry, 157*, 1–39.

Appelbaum, P. S. (2003). Treating incompetent defendants: The Supreme Court's decision is a tough sell. *Psychiatric Services, 54*, 1335–1341.

Appelbaum, P. S. (2006a). Commentary: Psychiatric advance directives at a crossroads—When can PADs be overridden? *Journal of the American Academy of Psychiatry and the Law, 34*, 395–397.

Appelbaum, P. S. (2006b). Insanity, guilty minds, and psychiatric testimony. *Psychiatric Services, 57*, 1370–1372.

Appelbaum, P. S., Lidz, C., & Grisso, T. (2004). Therapeutic misconception in clinical research: Frequency and risk factors. *IRB: A Review of Human Subjects Research, 26*, 1–8.

Appelbaum, P. S., Robbins, P. C., & Roth, L. H. (1999). Dimensional approach to delusions: Comparison across types and diagnoses. *American Journal of Psychiatry, 156*, 1938–1943.

Applebaum, P. S., & Rumpf, T. (1998). Civil commitment of the anorexia patient. *General Hospital Psychiatry, 156*, 1938–1943.

Araujo, A., Durante, R., Feldman, H. A., Goldstein, I., & McKinlay, J. B. (1998). The relationship between depressive symptoms and male erectile dysfunction: Cross-sectional results from the Massachusetts Male Aging Study. *Psychosomatic Medicine, 60*, 458–465.

Arcelus, J., Mitchell, A. J., Wales, J., & Nielsen, S. (2011). Mortality rates in patients with anorexia nervosa and other eating disorders. A meta-analysis of 36 studies. *Archives of General Psychiatry, 68*, 724–731.

Areán, P. A., & Reynolds, C. F., 3rd. (2005). The impact of psychosocial factors on late-life depression. *Biological Psychiatry, 58*, 277–282.

Areán, P. A., Raue, P., Mackin, R. S., Kanellopoulos, D., McCulloch, C., & Alexopoulos, G. S. (2010). Problem-solving therapy and supportive therapy in older adults with major depression and executive dysfunction. *American Journal of Psychiatry, 167*, 1391–1398.

Areán, P. A., Raue, P. J., Sirey, J. A., & Snowden, M. (2012). Implementing evidence-based psychotherapies in settings serving older adults: Challenges and solutions. *Psychiatric Services, 63*, 605–607.

Armstrong, S. C., Cozza, K. L., & Watanabe, K. S. (1997). The misdiagnosis of delirium. *Psychosomatics, 38*, 433–439.

Arndt, W., Foehl, J., & Good, F. (1985). Specific sexual fantasy themes: A multidimensional study. *Journal of Personality and Social Psychology, 48*, 472–480.

Arnold, I. A., de Waal, M. W., Eekhof, J. A., & van Hemert, A. M. (2006). Somatoform disorder in primary care: Course and the need for cognitive-behavioral treatment. *Psychosomatics, 47*, 498–503.

Arnold, L. M., Keck, P. E., Jr., Collins, J., Wilson, R., Fleck, D. E., Corey, K. B., … Strakowski, S.M. (2004). Ethnicity and first-rank symptoms in patients with psychosis. *Schizophrenia Research, 67*, 207–213.

Arnstern, A. F. (1998). The biology of being frazzled. *Science, 280*, 1711–1712.

Arrazola, R. A., Singh, T., Corey, C. G., Husten, C. G., Neff, L. J., Apelberg, B. J., … Centers for Disease Control and Prevention. (2015). Tobacco use among middle and high school students—United States, 2011–2014. *Morbidity and Mortality Weekly Report (MMWR), 64*, 381–385.

Arroll, B., Macgillivray, S., Ogston, S., Reid, I., Sullivan, F., Williams, B., & Crombie, I. (2005). Efficacy and tolerability of tricyclic antidepressants and SSRIs compared with placebo for treatment of depression in primary care: A meta-analysis. *The Annals of Family Medicine, 3*, 449–456.

Ashley-Koch, A. E., Garrett, M. E., Gibson, J., Liu, Y., Dennis, M. F., Kimbrel, N. A., Veterans Affairs Mid-Atlantic Mental Illness Research, Education, and Clinical Center Workgroup, … Hauser, M. A. (2015). Genome-wide association study of posttraumatic stress disorder in a cohort of Iraq-Afghanistan era veterans. *Journal of Affective Disorders, 184*, 225–234.

Ask, H., Torgersen, S., Seglem, K. B., & Waaktaar, T. (2014). Genetic and environmental causes of variation in adolescent anxiety symptoms: A multiple-rater twin study. *Journal of Anxiety Disorders, 28*, 363–371.

Atiye, M., Miettunen, J., & Raevuori-Helkamaa, A. (2015). A meta-analysis of temperament in eating disorders. *European Eating Disorders Review, 23*, 89–99.

Atkins Whitmer, D., & Woods, D. L. (2013). Analysis of the cost effectiveness of a suicide barrier on the Golden Gate Bridge. *Crisis, 34*, 98–106.

Atkinson, R. M. (2004). Substance abuse. In J. Sadavoy, L. F. Jarvik, G. T. Grossberg, & B. S. Meyers (Eds.), *Comprehensive textbook of geriatric psychiatry* (3rd ed., pp. 723–761). New York: W.W. Norton & Co.

Atkinson, R. M., & Misra, S. (2002). Further strategies in the treatment of aging alcoholics. In A.M. Gurnack, R.M. Atkinson, & N.J. Osgood (Eds.), *Treating alcohol and drug abuse in the elderly* (pp. 50–71). New York: Springer Verlag.

Attia, E., & Roberto, C. A. (2009). Should amenorrhea be a diagnostic criterion for anorexia nervosa? *International Journal of Eating Disorders, 42*, 581–589.

Attie, I., & Brooks-Gunn, J. (1989). Development of eating problems in adolescent girls: A longitudinal study. *Developmental Psychology, 25*, 70–75.

Austin, S. B., Ziyadeh, N. J., Corliss, H. L., Rosario, M., Wypij, D., Haines, J., … Field, A. E. (2009). Sexual orientation disparities in purging and binge eating from early to late adolescence. *Journal of Adolescent Health, 45*, 238–245.

Avants, S., Marcotte, D., Arnold, R., & Margolin, A. (2003). Spiritual beliefs, world assumptions, and HIV risk behavior among heroin and cocaine users. *Psychology of Addictive Behaviors, 17*, 159–162.

Avenevoli, S., Swendsen, J., He, J. P., Burstein, M., & Merikangas, K. R. (2015). Major depression in the national comorbidity survey-adolescent supplement: Prevalence, correlates, and treatment. *Journal of the American Academy of Child & Adolescent Psychiatry, 54*, 37–44 e32.

Aviram, R. B., Brodsky, B. S., & Stanley, B. (2006). Borderline personality disorder, stigma, and treatment implications. *Harvard Review of Psychiatry, 14*, 249–256.

Ayers, C., Ly, P., Howard, I., Mayes, T., Porter, B., & Iqbal, Y. (2013). Hoarding severity predicts functional disability in late-life hoarding disorder patients. *International Journal of Geriatric Psychiatry, 29*, 741–746.

Ayers, C. R., Saxena, S., Espejo, E., Twamley, E. W., Granholm, E., & Wetherell, J. L. (2014). Novel treatment for geriatric hoarding disorder: An open trial of cognitive rehabilitation paired with behavior therapy. *The American Journal of Geriatric Psychiatry, 22*, 248–252.

Ayers, C. R., Wetherell, J. L., Golshan, S., & Saxena, S. (2011). Cognitive-behavioral therapy for geriatric compulsive hoarding. *Behaviour Research and Therapy, 49*, 689–694.

Ayoub, C. C., Schreier, H. A., & Keller, C. (2002). Munchausen syndrome by proxy: Presentations in special education. *Child Maltreatment, 7*, 149–159.

Ayoub, C. C., O'Connor, E., Rappolt-Schlichtmann, G., Fischer, K. W., Rogosch, F. A., Toth, S. L., & Cicchetti, D. (2006). Cognitive and emotional differences in young maltreated children: A translational application of dynamic skill theory. *Developmental Psychopathology, 18*, 679–706.

Azrin, N., & Nunn, R. (1977). *Habit control: Stuttering, nailbiting, hairpulling, and tics*. New York: Simon & Schuster.

Badman, M., & Flier, J. (2005). The gut and energy balance: Visceral allies in the obesity wars. *Science, 307*, 1909–1914.

Bae, H. T., Sebastiani, P., Sun, J. X., Andersen, S. L., Daw, E. W., Terracciano, A., … Perls, T. T. (2013). Genome-wide association study of personality traits in the long life family study. *Frontiers in Genetics, 4*, 65.

Bae, S. W., & Brekke, J. S. (2002). Characteristics of Korean-Americans with schizophrenia: A cross-ethnic comparison with African-Americans, Latinos, and Euro-Americans. *Schizophrenia Bulletin, 28*, 703–717.

Baerger, D. R. (2001). Risk management with the suicidal patient: Lessons from case law. *Professional Psychology: Research and Practice, 32*, 359–366.

Bailey, J. A., Samek, D. R., Keyes, M. A., Hill, K. G., Hicks, B. M., McGue, M., … Hawkins, J. D. (2014). General and substance-specific predictors of young adult nicotine dependence, alcohol use disorder, and problem behavior: Replication in two samples. *Drug and Alcohol Dependence, 138*, 161–168.

Bailey, J. M., Kirk, K. M., Zhu, G., Dunne, M. P., & Martin, N. G. (2000). Do individual differences in sociosexuality represent genetic or environmentally contingent strategies? *Journal of Personality and Social Psychology, 78*, 537–545.

Bajos, N., Wadsworth, J., Ducot, B., Johnson, A. M., Le Pont, F., Wellings, K., … Field, J. (1995). Sexual behaviour and HIV epidemiology: Comparative analysis in France and Britain: The ACSF Group. *AIDS, 9*, 735–743.

Baker, D., Hunter, E., Lawrence, E., Medford, N., Patel, M., Senior, C., … David, A. S. (2003). Depersonalization disorder: Clinical features of 204 cases. *British Journal of Psychiatry, 182*, 428–433.

Baker, J. R., & Hudson, J. L. (2015). Children with social phobia have lower quality friendships than children with other anxiety disorders. *Anxiety, Stress, & Coping: An International Journal, 28*, 500–513.

Baldessarini, R. J., Tondo, L., Davis, P., Pompili, M., Goodwin, F. K., & Hennen, J. (2006). Decreased risk of suicides and attempts during long-term lithium treatment: A meta-analytic review. *Bipolar Disorders, 8* (5 Pt 2), 625–639.

Baldessarini, R. J., & Hennen, J. (2004). Genetics of suicide: An overview. *Harvard Review of Psychiatry, 12*, 1–13.

Bancroft, J., Loftus, J., & Long, J. S. (2003). Distress about sex: A national survey of women in heterosexual relationships. *Archives of Sexual Behavior, 32*, 193–208.

Bandelow, R., Boerner, R. J., Kapser, S., Linden. M., Wittchen, H. U., & Möller, H. J. (2013). The diagnosis and treatment of generalized anxiety disorder. *Deutsches Aerzteblatt International, 110*, 300–310.

Bandura, A. (1977a). Self-efficacy theory: Toward a unifying theory of behavioural change. *Psychological Review, 84*, 191–215.

Bandura, A. (1977b). *Social learning theory*. Englewood Cliffs, NJ: Prentice Hall.

Bandura, A. (1986). *Social foundations of thought and action*. Englewood Cliffs, NJ: Prentice Hall.

Bankoff, S. M., Karpel, M. G., Forbes, H. E., & Pantalone, D. W. (2012). A systematic review of dialectical behavior therapy for the treatment of eating disorders. *Eating Disorders, 20*, 196–215.

Banks, P., Jahoda, A., Dagnan, D., Kemp, J., & Williams, V. (2010). Supported employment for people with intellectual disability: The effect of job breakdown on psychological well-being. *Journal of Applied Research in Intellectual Disabilities, 24*, 344–354.

Bao, Y., Alexopoulos, G. S., Casalino, L. P., Ten Have, T. R., Donohue, J. M., Post, E. P., … Bruce, M. L. (2011). Collaborative depression care management and disparities in depression treatment and outcomes. *Archives of General Psychiatry, 68*, 627–636.

Barahona-Corrêa, J. B., Camacho, M., Castro-Rodrigues, P., Costa, R., & Oliveira-Maia, A. J. (2015). From thought to action: How the interplay between neuroscience and phenomenology changed our understanding of obsessive-compulsive disorder. *Frontiers in Psychology, 6*, 1798.

Barbaree, H. E., & Marshall, W. L. (1989). Erectile responses among heterosexual child molesters, father-daughter incest offenders, and matched non-offenders: Five distinct age preference profiles. *Canadian Journal of Behavioural Science, 21*, 70–82.

Barbaresi, W. J., Katusic, S. K., & Voigt, R. G. (2006). Autism: A review of the state of the science for pediatric primary health care clinicians. *Archives of Pediatrics & Adolescent Medicine, 160*, 1167–1175.

Barbato, A. (1998). Psychiatry in transition: Outcomes of mental health policy shift in Italy. *Australian and New Zealand Journal of Psychiatry, 32*, 673–679.

Barbor, T. F., Higgins-Biddle, J. C., Saunders, J. B., & Monteiro, M. G. (2001). *AUDIT: The Alcohol Use Disorders Identification Test guidelines for use in primary care: World Health Organization* (2nd ed). Geneva: World Health Organization Department of Mental Health and Substance Dependence.

Barch, D. M., & Caeser, A. (2012). Cognition in schizophrenia: Core psychological and neural mechanisms. *Trends in Cognitive Science, 16*, 27–34.

Bardone-Cone, A. M., Harney, M. B., Maldonado, C. R., Lawson, M. A., Robinson, D. P., Smith, R., & Tosh, A. (2010). Defining recovery from an eating disorder: Conceptualization, validation, and examination of psychosocial functioning and psychiatric comorbidity. *Behavior Research and Therapy, 48*, 194–202.

Barlow, D. H. (2002). *Anxiety and its disorders: The nature and treatment of anxiety and panic* (2nd ed.). New York: Guilford Press.

Barnes, A. (2004). Race, schizophrenia, and admission to state psychiatric hospitals. *Administration and Policy in Mental Health, 31*, 241–252.

Barnett, J. H., & Smoller, J. W. (2009). The genetics of bipolar disorder. *Neuroscience, 164*, 331–343.

Barnow, S., Aldinger, M., Arens, E. A., Ulrich, I., Spitzer, C., Grabe, H. J., & Stopsack, M. (2013). Maternal transmission of borderline personality disorder symptoms in the community-based Greifswald Family Study. *Journal of Personality Disorders, 27*, 806–819.

Baron-Cohen, S., Jaffa, T., Davies, S., Auyeung, B., Allison, C., & Wheelwright, S. (2013). Do girls with anorexia nervosa have elevated autistic traits? *Molecular Autism, 4*, 24.

Barone, J., & Grice, H. (1994). Seventh International Caffeine Workshop, Santorini, Greece, June 13–17, 1993. *Food Chemistry and Toxicology, 32*, 65–77.

Barry, K. L., & Blow, F. C. (2014). Substance use, misuse, and abuse. In N. A. Pachana & K. Laidlaw (Eds.), *The Oxford handbook of clinical geropsychology* (pp. 549–570). New York: Oxford University Press.

Barsade, S. G. (2002). The ripple effect: Emotional contagion and its influence on group behaviour. *Administrative Science Quarterly, 47*, 644–675.

Barsetti, I., Earls, C. M., Lalumière, M. L., & Bélanger, N. (1998). The differentiation of intrafamilial and extrafamilial heterosexual child molesters. *Journal of Interpersonal Violence, 13*, 275–286.

Barsky, A. J., & Klerman, G. L. (1983). Overview: Hypochondriasis, bodily complaints, and somatic styles. *The American Journal of Psychiatry, 140*, 273–283.

Barsky, A. J., Wyshak, G., & Klerman, G. L. (1990). The somatosensory amplification scale and its relationship to hypochondriasis. *Journal of Psychiatric Research, 24*, 323–334.

Barsky, A. J., Orav, H. J., & Bates, D. W. (2005). Somatization increases medical utilization and costs independent of psychiatric and medical comorbidity. *Archives of General Psychiatry, 62*, 903–910.

Bartels, S. J., & Smyer, M. A. (2002). Mental disorders of aging: An emerging public health crisis? *Generations, 26*, 14–20.

Bartlett, N. H., Vasey, P. L., & Bukowski, W. M. (2000). Is gender identity disorder in children a mental disorder? *Sex Roles, 43*, 753–785.

Bartlett, N. H., & Vasey, P. L. (2006). A retrospective study of childhood gender-atypical behavior in Samoan Fa'afafine. *Archives of Sexual Behavior, 35*, 659–666.

Bass, E., & Davis, L. (1998). *The courage to heal*. New York: Harper & Row.

Bassarath, L. (2003). Medication strategies in childhood aggression: A review. *Canadian Journal of Psychiatry, 48*, 367–373.

Bassiony, M. M. (2005). Social anxiety disorder and depression in Saudi Arabia. *Depression and Anxiety, 21*, 90–94.

Basson, R., McInnes, R., Smith, M. D., Hodgson, G., & Koppiker, N. (2002). Efficacy and safety of sildenafil citrate in women with sexual dysfunction associated with female sexual arousal disorder. *Journal of Women's Health & Gender-Based Medicine, 11*, 367–377.

Basson, R., & Brotto, L. A. (2003). Sexual psychophysiology and effects of sildenafil citrate in oestrogenised women with acquired genital arousal disorder and impaired orgasm: A randomised controlled trial. *International Journal of Obstetrics and Gynaecology, 110*, 1014–1024.

Bassuk, E. L., Richard, M. K., & Tsertsvadze, A. (2015). The prevalence of mental illness in homeless children: A systematic review and meta-analysis. *Journal of the American Academy of Child and Adolescent Psychiatry, 54*, 86–96.

Bateelan, N. M., de Graaf, R., Penninx, B. W., van Balkom, A. J., Vollebergh, W. A., & Beekman, A. T. (2010). The 2-year prognosis of panic episodes in the general population. *Psychological Medicine, 40*, 147–157.

Batelaan, N. M., de Graaf. R., Spijker, J., Smit, J. H., vam Balkom, A. J., Vollebergh, W. A., & Beekman, A. T. (2010). The course of panic attacks in individuals with panic disorder and subthreshold panic disorder: A population-based study. *Journal of Affective Disorders, 12*, 30–38.

Bateman, M. (1997, November 16). These are not just desserts. *The London Independent*.

Bateman, M., & Fonagy, P. (2004). *Psychotherapy for borderline personality disorder: Mentalisation based treatment*. Oxford, England: Oxford University Press.

Battle, C. L., Shea, M. T., Johnson, D. M., Yen, S., Zlotnick, C., Zanarini, M. C., ... Morey, L. C. (2004). Childhood maltreatment associated with adult personality disorders: Findings from the Collaborative Longitudinal Personality Disorders Study. *Journal of Personality Disorders, 18*, 193–211.

Baumeister, R. F. (1989). *Masochism and the self*. Hillsdale, NJ: Erlbaum.

Baumeister, R.F., Catanese, D,R., & Vohs, K.D. (2001). Is there a gender difference in strength of sex drive? *Personality and Social Psychology Review, 5*, 242–273.

Baxter, L. R. (1992). Neuroimaging studies of obsessive-compulsive disorder. *Psychiatric Clinics of North America, 15*, 871–884.

Baydala, L. (2010). Inhalant abuse. *Paediatrics & Child Health, 15*, 443–454.

Bayles, K. A., & Kim, E. S. (2003). Improving the functioning of individuals with Alzheimer's disease: Emergence of behavioral interventions. *Journal of Communication Disorders, 36*, 327–343.

Beard, C., Weisberg, R. B., & Keller, M. B. (2010). Health-related quality of life across the anxiety disorders: Findings from a sample of primary care patients. *Journal of Anxiety Disorders, 24*, 559–564.

Beautrais, A. L., Joyce, P. R., & Mulder, R. T. (1997). Precipitating factors and life events in serious suicide attempts among youths aged 13 through 24 years. *Journal of the American Academy of Child & Adolescent Psychiatry, 36*, 1543–1551.

Beautrais, A. L., Joyce, P. R., & Mulder, R. T. (1998). Psychiatric illness in a New Zealand sample of young people making serious suicide attempts. *New Zealand Medical Journal, 111*(1060), 44–48.

Beck, A., Wright, F., Neewman, C., & Liese, B. (1993). *Cognitive therapy of substance abuse*. New York: Guilford Press.

Beck, A., & Steer, R. (1993). *Beck anxiety inventory manual*. San Antonio, TX: The Psychological Corporation: Harcourt Brace & Company.

Beck, A., Steer, R., & Brown, G. (1996). Manual for the beck depression inventory. San Antonio, TX: The Psychological Corporation.

Beck, A. T. (1961). A systematic investigation of depression. *Comprehensive Psychiatry*, 2(3), 163-170.

Beck, A. T. (1962). A systematic investigation of depression. *Comprehensive Psychiatry, 2*, 163–170.

Beck, A. T. (1967). *Depression: Clinical, experimental and theoretical aspects*. New York: Hoeber.

Beck, A. T. (1979). *Cognitive therapy for depression*. New York: Guilford Press.

Beck, A. T., Davis, D. D., & Freeman, A. M. (2003). *Cognitive therapy of personality disorders*. New York: Guildford Press.

Beck, A. T., Emery, G. & Greenberg, R. L. (1985). *Anxiety disorders and phobias: A cognitive perspective*. New York: Basic Books.

Beck, H. P., Levinson, S., & Irons, G. (2009). Finding Little Albert: A journey to John B. Watson's infant laboratory. *American Psychologist, 64*, 605–614.

Becker, A. E., Burwell, R. A., Gilman, S. E., Herzog, D. B., & Hamburg, P. (2002). Eating behaviours and attitudes following prolonged exposure to television among ethnic Fijian adolescent girls. *British Journal of Psychiatry, 180*, 509–514.

Becker, A. E., Fay, K. E., Agnew-Blais, J., Khan, A. N., Striegel-Moore, R. H., & Gilman, S.E. (2011). Social network media exposure and adolescent eating pathology in Fiji. *British Journal of Psychiatry, 198*, 43–50.

Beesdo-Baum, K., Knappe, S., Fehm, L., Höfler, M., Lieb, R., Hofmann, S. G., & Wittchen, H. U. (2012). The natural course of social anxiety disorder among adolescents and young adults. *Acta Psychiatrica Scandinavica, 126*, 411–425.

Beesdo-Baum, K., Jenjahn, E., Höfler, M., Lueken, U., Becker, E. S., & Hoyer, J. (2012). Avoidance, safety behaviour, and reassurance seeking in generalized anxiety disorder. *Depression and Anxiety, 29*, 948–957.

Beidel, D. C., & Turner, S. M. (1997). At risk for anxiety: I. Psychopathology in the offspring of anxious parents. *Journal of the American Academy of Child and Adolescent Psychiatry, 36*, 918–924.

Beidel, D. C., & Turner, S. M. (1998). *Shy children, phobic adults: The nature and treatment of social phobia*. Washington, DC: American Psychological Association Books.

Beidel, D. C., & Turner, S. M. (2005). *Childhood anxiety disorders: A guide to research and treatment*. New York: Routledge.

Beidel, D. C., Turner, S. M., Sallee, F. R., Ammerman, R. T., Crosby, L. A., &, Pathak, S. (2007). SET-C vs. fluoxetine in the treatment of childhood social phobia. *Journal of the American Academy of Child and Adolescent Psychiatry, 46*, 1622–1632.

Beidel, D. C., Rao, P. A., Scharfstein, L., Wong, N., & Alfano, C. A. (2010). Social skills and social phobia: An investigation of DSM-IV subtypes. *Behaviour Research Therapy, 48*, 992–1001.

Beidel, D. C., Alfano, C. A., Kofler, M. J., Rao, P. A., Scharfstein, L., & Wong Sarver, N. (2014). The impact of social skills training for social anxiety disorder: A randomized controlled trial. *Journal of Anxiety Disorders, 28*, 908–918.

Beidel, D. C., Turner, S. M., & Morris, T. L. (1995). A new inventory to assess childhood social anxiety and phobia: The Social Phobia and Anxiety Inventory for Children. *Psychological Assessment, 7*, 73–79.

Belar, C.D., & Pewrry, N.W. (1992). Natonal Conference on Scientist-Practitioner Education and Training in the Professional Practice of Psychology. *American Psychologist, 47, 71–75*.

Bell, C. C., & Mehta, H. (1980). The misdiagnosis of black patients with manic depressive illness. *Journal of the National Medical Association, 72*, 141–145.

Bell, R. M. (1985). *Holy anorexia*. Chicago: University of Chicago Press.

Bellack, A. S., Morrison, R. L., Wixted, J. T., & Mueser, K. T. (1990). An analysis of social competence in schizophrenia. *British Journal of Psychiatry, 156*, 809–818.

Bellack, A. S. (1992). Cognitive rehabilitation for schizophrenia: Is it possible? Is it necessary? *Schizophrenia Bulletin, 18*, 51–57.

Bellack, A. S. (2004). Skills training for people with severe mental illness. *Psychiatric Rehabilitation, 27*, 375–391.

Bellino, S., Zizza, M., Paradiso, E., Rivarossa, A., Fulcheri, M., & Bogetto, F. (2006). Dysmorphic concern symptoms and personality disorders: A clinical investigation in patients seeking cosmetic surgery. *Psychiatry Research, 144*, 73–78.

Bellis, M. D. (2004). Neurotoxic effects of childhood trauma: Magnetic resonance imaging studies of pediatric maltreatment-related posttraumatic stress disorder versus nontraumatized children with generalized anxiety disorder. In J. M. Gorman. (Ed.), *Fear and anxiety: The benefits of translational research* (pp. 151–170). Washington, DC: American Psychiatric Publishing, Inc.

Benich, J. J., 3rd. (2011). Opioid dependence. *Primary Care, 38*, 59–70.

Benko, C. R., Farias, A. C., Farias, L. G., Pereira, E. F., Louzada, F. M., & Cordeiro, M. L. (2011). Potential link between caffeine consumption and pediatric depression: A case-control study. *BMC Pediatrics, 11*, 73.

Bennett, H. A., Einarson, A., Taddio, A., Koren, G., & Einarson, T. R. (2004). Prevalence of depression during pregnancy: Systematic review. *Obstetrics and Gynecology, 103*, 698–709.

Benowitz, N. (1988). Pharmacological aspects of cigarette smoking and nicotine addiction. *New England Journal of Medicine, 319*, 1318–1330.

Berenz, E. C., Amstadter, A. B., Aggen, S. H., Knudsen, G. P., Reichborn-Kjennerud, T., Gardner, C. O., & Kendler, K. S. (2013). Childhood trauma and personality disorder criterion counts: A co-twin control analysis. *Journal of Abnormal Psychology, 122*, 1070–1076.

Bergen, A. W., van den Bree, M. B., Yeager, M., Welch, R., Ganjei, J. K., Haque, K., … Kaye, W. H. (2003). Candidate genes for anorexia nervosa in the 1p33–36 linkage region: Serotonin 1D and delta opioid receptor loci exhibit significant association to anorexia nervosa. *Molecular Psychiatry, 8*, 397–406.

Berk, M., & Dodd, S. (2005). Bipolar II disorder: A review. *Bipolar Disorders, 7*, 11–21.

Berkman, N. D., Lohr, K. N., & Bulik, C. M. (2007). Outcomes of eating disorders: A systematic review of the literature. *International Journal of Eating Disorders, 40*, 293–309.

Berman, J. R., Berman, L. A., Toler, S. M., Gill, J., & Haughie, S., & Sildenafil Study Group. (2003). Safety and efficacy of sildenafil citrate for the treatment of female sexual arousal disorder: A double-blind, placebo controlled study. *Journal of Urology, 170*, 2333–2338.

Bethea, T. C., & Sikich, L. (2007). Early pharmacological treatment of autism: A rationale for developmental treatment. *Biological Psychiatry, 61*, 521–537.

Beyer, J. L. (2015). Bipolar and related disorders. In D. C. Steffens, D. G. Blazer, & M. E. Thakur (Eds.), *Textbook of geriatric psychiatry* (5th ed., pp. 283–308). Washington, DC: American Psychiatric Publishing.

Biederman, J. (2005). Attention-deficit/hyperactivity disorder: a selective overview. *Biological Psychiatry, 57*, 1215–1220.

Biederman, J., Mick, E., Faraone, S. V., Braaten, E., Doyle, A., Spencer, T., … Johnson, M.A. (2002). Influence of gender on attention deficit hyperactivity disorder in children referred to a psychiatric clinic. *American Journal of Psychiatry, 159*, 36–42.

Biederman, J., Petty, C., Faraone, S. V., & Seidman, L. (2004). Phenomenology of childhood psychosis: Findings from a large sample of psychiatrically referred youth. *Journal of Nervous and Mental Disease, 192*, 607–614.

Biederman, J., & Faraone, S. V. (2005). Attention-deficit hyperactivity disorder. *Lancet, 366*, 237–248.

Biederman, J., Petty, C. R., Hirshfeld-Becker, D. R., Henin, A., Faraone, S. V., Fraire, M., … Rosenbaum, J. F. (2007). Developmental trajectories of anxiety disorders in offspring at high risk for panic disorder and major depression. *Psychiatry Research, 153*, 245–252.

Bierer, L. M., Yehuda, R., Schmeidler, J., Mitropoulou, V., New, A. S., Silverman, J. M., & Siever, L. J. (2003). Abuse and neglect in childhood: Relationship to personality disorder diagnoses. *CNS Spectrums, 8*, 737–754.

Biernacka, J. M., Sangkuhl, K., Jenkins, G., Whaley, R. M., Barman, P., Batzler, A., … Weinshilboum, R. (2015). The International SSRI Pharmacogenomics Consortium (ISPC): A genome-wide association study of antidepressant treatment response. *Translational Psychiatry, 5*, e553.

Billy, J. O., Tanfer, K., Grady, W. R., & Klepinger, D. H. (1993). The sexual behavior of men in the United States. *Family Planning Perspectives, 25*, 52–60.

Binks, C. A., Fenton, M., McCarthy, L., Lee, T., Adams, C. E., & Duggan, C. (2006). Psychological therapies for people with borderline personality disorder. *Cochrane Database of Systematic Reviews, 1*, CD005652.

Binzer, M., & Kullgren, G. (1998). Motor conversion disorder: A prospective 2 to 5 years follow-up study. *Psychosomatics, 39*, 519–527.

Birmingham, C., Su, J., Hlynsky, J., Goldner, E., & Gao, M. (2005). The mortality rate from anorexia nervosa. *International Journal of Eating Disorders, 38*, 143–46.

Bisson, J. I., Jenkins, P. L., Alexander, J., & Bannister, C. (1997). Randomised controlled trial of psychological debriefing for victims of acute burn trauma. *The British Journal of Psychiatry, 171*, 78–81.

Bjornsson, A. S., Sibrava, N. J., Beard, C., Moitra, E., Weisberg, R. B., Benítez, C. I., & Keller, M. B. (2014). Two-year course of generalized anxiety disorder, social anxiety disorder, and panic disorder with agoraphobia in a sample of Latino adults. *Journal of Consulting and Clinical Psychology, 82*, 1186–1192.

Black, H. (1990). *Black's law dictionary*. St. Paul, MN: West.

Black, M. M., & Krishnakumar, A. (1998). Children in low-income, urban settings: interventions to promote mental health and well-being. *American Psychologist, 53*, 635.

Blackman, J. A. (1999). Attention-deficit/hyperactivity disorder in preschoolers. Does it exist and should we treat it? *Pediatric Clinics of North America, 46*, 1011–1025.

Blader, J. C., & Carlson, G. A. (2007). Increased rates of bipolar disorder diagnoses among U.S. child, adolescent, and adult inpatients, 1996–2004. *Biological Psychiatry, 62*, 107–114.

Blashfield, R., & Livesley, W. J. (1999). Classification. In T. Millon, P. H. Blaney, & R. D. Davis (Eds.), *Oxford textbook of psychopathology* (pp. 3–28). New York: Oxford University Press.

Blazer, D. G. (2006). Successful aging. *The American Journal of Geriatric Psychiatry, 14*, 2–5.

Blazer, D. G. (2010). The origins of late-life depression. *Psychiatric Annals, 40*, 13–18.

Blazer, D. G., Hybels, C. F., Simonsick, E. M., & Hanlon, J. T. (2000). Marked differences in antidepressant use by race in an elderly community sample: 1986–1996. *American Journal of Psychiatry, 157*, 1089–1094.

Blazer, D. G., & Steffens, D. C. (2015). Depressive disorders. In D. C. Steffens, D. G. Blazer, & M. E. Thakur (Eds.), *Textbook of geriatric psychiatry* (5th ed., pp. 243–282). Washington, DC: American Psychiatric Publishing.

Blazer, D. G., & Wu, L.T. (2012). Patterns of tobacco use and tobacco-related psychiatric morbidity and substance use among middle-aged and older adults in the United States. *Aging & Mental Health, 16*, 296–304.

Bleiberg, K. L., & Markowitz, J. C. (2005). A pilot study of interpersonal psychotherapy for posttraumatic stress disorder. *American Journal of Psychiatry, 162*, 181–183.

Bleuler, E. (1911/1950). *Dementia praecox or the group of schizophrenias*. New York: International Universities Press.

Bloch, M. H., & Storch, E. A. (2015). Assessment and management of treatment-refractory obsessive-compulsive disorder in children. *Journal of the American Academy of Child & Adolescent Psychiatry, 54*, 251–262.

Block, J. H., Gjerde, P. F., & Block, J. H. (1991). Personality antecedents of depressive tendencies in 18-year-olds: A prospective study. *Journal of Personality and Social Psychology, 60*, 726–738.

Blom, M. M., Bosmans, J. E., Cuijpers, P., Zarit, S. H., & Pot, A. M. (2013). Effectiveness and cost-effectiveness of an internet intervention for family caregivers of people with dementia: Design of a randomized controlled trial. *BMC Psychiatry, 13*, 17.

Blosnich, J. R., Brown, G. R., Shiperd, J., Kauth, M., Piegari, R. I., & Bossarte, R. M. (2013). Prevlaence of gender identity disorder and suicide risk among transgender veterans utilizing veterans health administration care. *American Journal of Public Health, 103*, e27.

Blum, K., Braverman, E. R., Holder, J. M., Lubar, J. F., Monastra, V. J., Miller, D., … Comings, D. E. (2000). Reward deficiency syndrome: A biogenetic model for the diagnosis and treatment of impulsive, addictive, and compulsive behaviors. *Journal of Psychoactive Drugs, 32*(Suppl: I–IV), 1–112.

Bo-Linn, G. W., Santa Ana, C. A., Morawski, S. G., & Fordtran, J. S. (1983). Purging and calorie absorption in bulimic patients and normal women. *Annals of Internal Medicine, 99*, 14–17.

Boehmer, U. (2002). Twenty years of public health research: Inclusion of lesbian, gay, bisexual, and transgender populations. *American Journal of Public Health, 92*, 1125–1130.

Bogaert, A. F., & Skorska, M. (2011). Sexual orientation, fraternal birth order and the maternal immune hypothesis: A review. *Frontiers in Neuroendocrinology, 32*, 247–254.

Bohne, A., Keuthen, N. J., Wilhelm, S., Deckersbach, T., & Jenike, M. A. (2002). Prevalence of symptoms of body dysmorphic disorder and its correlates: A cross-cultural comparison. *Psychosomatics, 43*, 486–490.

Bohne, A., Wilhelm, S., Keuthen, N. J., Florin, I., Baer, L., & Jenike, M. A. (2002). Prevalence of body dysmorphic disorder in a German college student sample. *Psychiatry Research, 109*, 101–104.

Boise, L., Neal, M. B., & Kaye, J. (2004). Dementia assessment in primary care: Results from a study in three managed care systems. *The Journals of Gerontology Series A: Biological Sciences and Medical Sciences, 59*, M621–M626.

Boles, S. M., & Miotto, K. (2003). Substance abuse and violence: A review of the literature. *Aggression and Violent Behavior, 8*, 155–174.

Bonanno, G. A. (2004). Loss, trauma, and human resilience. *American Psychologist, 59*, 20–28.

Bond, G. R., Becker, D. R., Drake, R. E., Rapp, C. A., Meisler, N., Lehman, A. F., … Blyler, C. R. (2001a). Implementing supported employment as an evidence-based practice. *Psychiatric Services, 52*, 313–322.

Bond, G. R., Resnick, S. G., Drake, R. E., Xie, H., McHugo, G. J., & Bebout, R. R. (2001b). Does competitive employment improve nonvocational outcomes for people with severe mental illness? *Journal of Consulting and Clinical Psychology, 69*, 489–501.

Bonese, K., Wainer, B., Fitch, F., Rothberg, R., & Schuster, C. (1974). Changes in heroin self-administration by a rhesus monkey after morphine immunisation. *Nature, 252*, 708–710.

Bootzin, R. R., & Bailey, E. T. (2005). Understanding placebo, nocebo, and iatrogenic treatment effects. *Journal of Clinical Psychiatry, 61*, 871–880.

Boraska, V., Franklin, C. S., Floyd, J. A., Thornton, L. M., Huckins, L. M., Southam, L., … Bulik, C. M. (2014). A genome-wide association study of anorexia nervosa. *Molecular Psychiatry, 19*, 1085–1094.

Borges, G., Angst, J., Nock, M. K., Ruscio, A. M., & Kessler, R. C. (2007). Risk factors for the incidence and persistence of suicide-related outcomes: A 10-year follow-up study using the National Comorbidity Surveys. Journal of Affective Disorders, 105, 25–33.

Bornovalova, M. A., Huibregtse, B. M., Hicks, B. M., Keyes, M., McGue, M., & Iacono, W. (2013). Tests of a direct effect of childhood abuse on adult borderline personality disorder traits: A longitudinal discordant twin design. *Journal of Abnormal Psychology, 122*, 180–194.

Bornstein, R. F. (2011). Toward a multidimensional model of personality disorder diagnosis: Implications for DSM-5. *Journal of Personality Assessment, 93*, 362–369.

Bouchard, T. J., Lykken, D. T., McGue, M., Segal, N. L., & Tellegen, A. (1990). Sources of human psychological differences: The Minnesota study of twins reared apart. *Science, 250*, 223–228.

Bourgeois, J. A., Seaman, J. S., & Servis, M. E. (2003). Delirium, dementia, and amnestic disorders. *Clinical Psychiatry*, 259–308.

Bourgeois, M. S., Camp, C., Rose, M., White, B., Malone, M., Carr, J., & Rovine, M. (2003). A comparison of training strategies to enhance use of external aids by persons with dementia. *Journal of Communication Disorders, 36*, 361–378.

Bow, J. N., & Quinnell, F. A. (2001). Psychologists' current practices and procedures in child custody evaluations: Five years after American Psychological Association Guidelines. *Professional Psychology: Research and Practice, 32*, 261–268.

Bowe, A., & Rosenheck, R. (2015). PTSD and substance use disorder among veterans: Characteristics, service utilization and pharmacotherapy. *Journal of Dual Diagnoses, 11*, 22–32.

Bowman, E. S., & Markand, O. N. (1996). Psychodynamics and psychiatric diagnoses of pseudoseizure subjects. *American Journal of Psychiatry, 153*, 57–63.

Boyle, M. (2000). Emil Kraepelin. In A. E. Kazdin. (Ed.), *Encyclopedia of Psychology* (Vol. 4, pp. 458–460). Washington, DC: American Psychological Association.

Boysen, G. A., & VanBergen, A. (2013). A review of published research on adult dissociative identity disorder: 2000–2010. *The Journal of Nervous and Mental Disease, 201*, 5–11.

Bradley, S. J., & Zucker, K. J. (1997). Gender identity disorder: A review of the past 10 years. *Journal of the American Academy of Child and Adolescent Psychiatry, 36*, 872–880.

Brand, B. L., Myrick, A. C., Loewenstein, R. J., Classen, C. C., Lanius, R., McNary, S. W., … Putnam, F. W. (2011). A survey of practices and recommended treatment interventions among expert therapists treating patients with Dissociative Identity Disorder and Dissociative Disorder Not Otherwise Specified. *Psychological Trauma: Theory, Research, Practice, and Policy, 4*, 490–500.

Branum, A. M., Rossen, L. M., & Schoendorf, K. C. (2014). Trends in caffeine intake among U.S. children and adolescents. *Pediatrics, 133*, 386–393.

Braun, D. L., Sunday, S. R., & Halmi, K. A. (1994). Psychiatric comorbidity in patients with eating disorders. *Psychological Medicine, 24*, 859–867.

Brauner, D. J., Muir, J. C., & Sachs, G. A. (2000). Treating nondementia illnesses in patients with dementia, *Journal of the American Medical Association, 283*, 3230–3235.

Braunstein, G. D., Sundwall, D. A., Katz, M., Shifren, J. L., Buster, J. E., Simon, J. A., … Watts, N. B. (2005). Safety and efficacy of a testosterone patch for the treatment of hypoactive sexual desire disorder in surgically menopausal women. *Archives of Internal Medicine, 165*, 1582–1589.

Brazier, J., Tumur, I., Holmes, M., Ferriter, M., Parry, G., Dent-Brown, K., & Paisley, S. (2006). Psychological therapies including dialectical behaviour therapy for borderline personality disorder: A systematic review and preliminary economic evaluation. *Health Technology Assessment, iii, ix–xii*(1–117).

Brazzelli, M., Griffiths, P. V., Cody, J. D., & Tappin, D. (2011). Behavioural and cognitive interventions with or without other treatments for the management of faecal incontinence in children. *Cochrane Database of Systematic Reviews, 12*, CD002240.

Breitborde, N. J. K., Lopez, S. R., Chang, C., Kopelowicz, A., & Zarate, R. (2009). Emotional over-involvement can be deleterious for caregivers' health. *Social Psychiatry and Psychiatric Epidemiology, 44*, 716–723.

Brekke, J. S., Prindle, C., Bae, S. W., & Long, J. D. (2001). Risks for individuals with schizophrenia who are living in the community. *Psychiatric Services, 52*, 1358–1366.

Bremner, J. D. (2006). Traumatic stress: Effects on the brain. *Dialogues in Clinical Neuroscience, 8*, 445–461.

Bremner, J. D. (2007). Neuroimaging in posttraumatic stress disorder and other stress-related disorders. *Neuroimaging Clinics of North America, 17*(ix), 523–538.

Bremner, J. D., Randall, P., Scott, T. M., Bronen, R. A., Seibyl, J. P, Southwick, S. M, … Innis, R. B. (1995). MRI-based measurement of hippocampal volume in patients with combat-related posttraumatic stress disorder [see comments]. *American Journal of Psychiatry, 152*, 973–981.

Bremner, J. D., Krystal, J. H., Charney, D. S., & Southwick, S. M. (1996). Neural mechanisms in dissociative amnesia for childhood abuse: Relevance to the current controversy surrounding the "false memory syndrome." *American Journal of Psychiatry, 153*, 71–82.

Bremner, J. D., Randall, P., Vermetten, E., Staib, L., Bronen, R. A., Mazure, C., … Charney, D. S. (1997). Magnetic resonance imaging-based measurement of hippocampal volume in posttraumatic stress disorder related to childhood physical and sexual abuse—A preliminary report. *Biological Psychiatry, 41*, 23–32.

Bremner, J. D., Narayan, M., Staib, L. H., Southwick, S. M., McGlashan, T., & Charney, D. S. (1999). Neural correlates of memories of childhood sexual abuse in women with and without posttraumatic stress disorder. *American Journal of Psychiatry, 156*, 1787–1795.

Brenes, G. A., Danhauer, S. C., Lyles, M. F., Hogan, P. E., & Miller, M. E. (2015). Telephone-delivered cognitive behavioral therapy and telephone-delivered nondirective supportive therapy for rural older adults with generalized anxiety disorder: A randomized clinical trial. *JAMA Psychiatry, 72*, 1012–1020.

Brenes, G. A., Guralnik, J. M., Williamson, J. D., Fried, L. P., Simpson, C., Simonsick, E. M., & Penninx, B. W. (2005). The influence of anxiety on the progression of disability. *Journal of the American Geriatrics Society, 53*, 34–39.

Brenes, G. A., Kritchevsky, S. B., Mehta, K. M., Yaffe, K., Simonsick, E. M., Ayonayon, H. N., … Penninx, B. W. (2007). Scared to death: Results from the Health, Aging, and Body Composition study. *The American Journal of Geriatric Psychiatry, 15*, 262–265.

Brent, D. A., Baugher, M., Bridge, J., Chen, T., & Chiappetta, L. (1999). Age- and sex-related risk factors for adolescent suicide. *Journal of the American Academy of Child & Adolescent Psychiatry, 38*, 1497–1505.

Brent, D. A., & Mann, J. J. (2005). Family genetic studies, suicide, and suicidal behavior. *American Journal of Medical Genetics C Seminars in Medical Genetics, 133*, 13–24.

Brent, D. A., & Melhem, N. (2008). Familial transmission of suicidal behavior. *Psychiatric Clinics of North America, 31*, 157–177.

Brent, D. A., & Mann, J. J. (2005). Family genetic studies, suicide, and suicidal behavior. *American Journal of Medical Genetics Part C: Seminars in Medical Genetics, 133C*, 13–24.

Breslau, J., Kendler, K. S., Su, M., Aguilar-Gaxiola, S., & Kessler, R. C. (2005). Lifetime risk and persistence of psychiatric disorders across ethnic groups in the United States. *Psychological Medicine, 35*, 317–327.

Breslau, J., Aguilar-Gaxiola, S., Kendler, K. S., Su, M., Williams, D., & Kessler, R. C. (2006). Specifying race-ethnic differences in risk for psychiatric disorder in a USA national sample. *Psychological Medicine, 36*, 57–68.

Breslau, N., & Kessler, R.C. (2001). The stressor criterion in DSM-IV posttraumatic stress disorder: An empirical investigation. *Biological Psychiatry, 50*, 699–704.

Brestan, E. V., & Eyberg, S. M. (1998). Effective psychosocial treatments of conduct-disordered children and adolescents: 29 years, 82 studies, and 5,272 kids. *Journal of Clinical Child Psychology, 27*, 180–189.

Breton, J. J., Bergeron, L., Valla, J. P., Bertiaume, C., Gauder, N., Lambert, J., … Lepine, S. (1999). Quebec child mental health survey: Prevalence of DSM-III-R mental health disorders. *Journal of Child Psychology and Psychiatry, 40*, 375–384.

Brewerton, T., Lydiard, R., Herzog, D., Brotman, A., O'Neil, P., & Ballenger, J. (1995). Comorbidity of Axis I psychiatric disorders in bulimia nervosa. *Journal of Clinical Psychiatry, 56*, 77–80.

Brewerton, T., & Jimerson, D. (1996). Studies of serotonin function in anorexia nervosa. *Psychiatry Research, 62*, 31–42.

Bride, B. (2001). Single-gender treatment of substance abuse: Effect on treatment retention and completion. *Social Work Research, 25*, 223–232.

Bridge, J. A., Iyengar, S., Salary, C. B., Barbe, R. P., Birmaher, B., Pincus, H. A., … Brent, D. A. (2007). Clinical response and risk for reported suicidal ideation and suicide attempts in pediatric antidepressant treatment: A meta-analysis of randomized controlled trials. *Journal of the American Medical Association, 297*, 1683–1696.

Briere, J., Weathers, F. W., & Runtz, M. (2005). Is dissociation a multidimensional construct? Data from the Multiscale Dissociation Inventory. *Journal of Traumatic Stress, 18*, 221–231.

Brodaty, H., Breteler, M., DeKosky, S. T., Dorenlot, P., Fratiglioni, L., Hock, C., … De Strooper, B. (2011). The world of dementia beyond 2020. *Journal of the American Geriatrics Society, 59*, 923–927.

Brooks, R. C., Copen, R. M., Cox, D. J., Morris, J., Borowitz, S., & Sutphen, J. (2000). Review of the treatment literature for encopresis, functional constipation, and stool-toileting refusal. *Annals of Behavioral Medicine, 22*, 260–267.

Brooner, R. K., King, V. L., Kidorf, M., Schmidt, C. W., Jr., & Bigelow, G. E. (1997). Psychiatric and substance use comorbidity among treatment-seeking opioid abuser. *Archives of General Psychiatry, 54*, 71–80.

Brosco, J. P., Mattingly, M., & Sanders, L. M. (2006). Impact of specific medical interventions on reducing the prevalence of mental retardation. *Archives of Pediatrics & Adolescent Medicine, 160*, 302–309.

Brothers, L. (1990). The social brain: A project for integrating primate behavior and neurophysiology in a new domain. *Concepts in Neuroscience, 1*, 27–61.

Brotto, L. A., & Klein, C. (2007). Sexual and gender identity disorders. In S. M. Turner, M. Hersen, & D. C. Beidel (Eds.), *Adult psychopathology and diagnosis* (5th ed., pp. 504–570). New York: John Wiley and Sons.

Brown, A. S., Begg, M. D., Gravenstein, S., Schaefer, C. A., Wyatt, R. J., Brenahan, M., … Susser, E. S. (2004). Serological evidence of prenatal influenza in the etiology of schizophrenia. *Archives of General Psychiatry, 61*, 774–780.

Brown, A. S. (2011). The environment and susceptibility to schizophrenia. *Progress in Neurobiolgy, 93*, 23–58.

Brown, A. S. (2012). Epidemiologic studies of exposure to prenatal infection and risk of schizophrenia and autism. *Developmental Neurobiology, 72*, 1272–1276.

Brown, G. W., Harris, T. O., & Eales, M. J. (1996). Social factors and comorbidity of depressive and anxiety disorders. *British Journal of Psychiatry Supplement, 30*, 50–57.

Brown, L. T., Mikell, C. B., Youngerman, B. E., Zhang, Y., McKhann, G. M., & Sheth, S. A. (2016). Dorsal anterior cingulotomy and anterior capsulotomy for severe, refractory obsessive-compulsive disorder: A systematic review of observational studies. *Journal of Neurosurgery, 124*, 77–89.

Brown, M. J., McLaine, P., Dixon S., & Simon, P. (2006). A randomized, community-based trial of home visiting to reduce blood lead levels in children. *Pediatrics, 117*, 147–153.

Brown, M. L., Pope, A. W., & Brown, E. J. (2010). Treatment of primary nocturnal enuresis in children: A review. *Child: Care, Health and Development, 37*, 153–160.

Brown, R. J., Schrag, A., & Trimble, M. R. (2005). Dissociation, childhood interpersonal trauma, and family functioning in patients with somatization disorder. *American Journal of Psychiatry, 162*, 899–905.

Brown, S., Inskip, H., & Barraclough, B. (2000). Causes of the excess mortality of schizophrenia. *British Journal of Psychiatry, 177*, 212–217.

Brown, T. A., Campbell, L. A., Lehman, C. L., Grisham, J. R., & Mancill, R. B. (2001). Current and lifetime comorbidity of the DSM-IV anxiety and mood disorders in a large clinical sample. *Journal of Abnormal Psychology, 110*, 585–599.

Browne, H. A., Gair, S. L., Scharf, J. M., & Grice, D. E. (2015). Genetics of obsessive-compulsive disorder and related disorders. *Psychiatric Clinics of North America, 37*, 319–335.

Brownley, K. A., Berkman, N. D., Peat, C. M., Lohr, K. N, Cullen, K. E., & Bulik, C. M. (2016). An evidence-based review and meta-analysis of treatment effectiveness and course of illness in adults with binge-eating disorder. *Annals of Internal Medicine.*

Bruce, B., & Wilfley, D. (1996). Binge eating among the overweight population: A serious and prevalent problem. *Journal of the American Dietetic Association, 159*, 1367–1374.

Bruce, M. L., McAvay, G. J., Raue, P. J., Brown, E. L., Meyers, B. S., Keohane, D. J., … Weber, C. (2002). Major depression in elderly home health care patients. *American Journal of Psychiatry, 159*, 1367–1374.

Bruce, S. E., Machan, J. T., Dyck, I., & Keller, M. B. (2001). Infrequency of "pure" GAD: Impact of psychiatric comorbidity on clinical course. *Depression and Anxiety, 14*, 219–225.

Bruch, H. (1973). *Eating disorders*. New York: Basic Books.

Bruch, H. (1978). *The golden cage*. Cambridge, MA: Harvard University Press.

Brühl, A. B., Designore, A., Komossa, K., & Weidt, S. (2014). Neuroimaging in a social anxiety disorder: A meta-analytic review resulting in a new neurofunctional model. *Neuroscience and Biobehavioral Reviews, 47*, 260–280.

Brunello, N., Davidson, J. R., Deahl, M., Kessler, R. C., Mendlewicz, J., Racagni, G., … Zohar, J. (2001). Posttraumatic stress disorder: Diagnosis and epidemiology, comorbidity and social consequences, biology and treatment. *Neuropsychobiology, 43*, 150–162.

Bryant, K. (2006). Making gender identity disorder of childhood: Historical lessons for contemporary debates. *Sexuality Research & Social Policy, 3*, 23–38.

Budney, A., Moore, B., Vandrey, R., & Hughes, J. (2003). The time course and significance of cannabis withdrawal. *Journal of Abnormal Psychology, 112*, 393–402.

Buhrich, N., & McConaghy, N. (1985). Preadult feminine behaviors of male transvestites. *Archives of Sexual Behavior, 14*, 413–419.

Bulik, C. M. (2002). Eating disorders in adolescents and young adults. *Child and Adolescent Psychiatric Clinics of North America, 11*, 201–218.

Bulik, C. M. (2005). Exploring the gene-environment nexus in eating disorders. *Journal of Psychiatry & Neuroscience, 30*, 335–339.

Bulik, C. M., Sullivan, P., Carter, F., & Joyce, P. (1995). Temperament, character, and personality disorder in bulimia nervosa. *Journal of Nervous and Mental Disease, 183*, 593–598.

Bulik, C. M., Sullivan, P., Fear, J., & Joyce, P. (1997). Eating disorders and antecedent anxiety disorders: A controlled study. *Acta Psychiatric Scandinavica, 96*, 101–107.

Bulik, C. M., Sullivan, P., Wade, T., & Kendler, K. (2000). Twin studies of eating disorders: A review. *International Journal of Eating Disorders, 27*, 1–20.

Bulik, C. M., Prescott, C. A., & Kendler, K. S. (2001). Features of childhood sexual abuse and the development of psychiatric and substance use disorders. *British Journal of Psychiatry, 179*, 444–449.

Bulik, C. M., Berkman, N. D., Brownley, K. A., Sedway, J. A., & Lohr, K. N. (2007). Anorexia nervosa treatment: A systematic review of randomized controlled trials. *International Journal of Eating Disorders, 40*, 310–320.

Bulik, C. M., Baucom, D. H., Kirby, J. S., & Pisetsky, E. (2011). Uniting couples (in the treatment of) anorexia nervosa. *International Journal of Eating Disorders, 44*, 19–28.

Bulik, C. M., Devlin, B., Bacanu, S. A., Thornton, L., Klump, K. L., Fichter, M. M., … Kaye, W. H. (2003). Significant linkage on chromosome 10p in families with bulimia nervosa. *American Journal of Human Genetics, 72*, 200–207.

Bulik-Sullivan, B., Finucane, H. K., Anttila, V., Gusey, A., & Day, F. R. (2015). An atlas of genetic correlations across human diseases and traits. *Nature Genetics, 47*,1236–1241..

Bull, L. (2009). Survey of complementary and alternative therapies used by children with specific learning difficulties (dyslexia). *International Journal of Language & Communication Disorders, 44*, 224–235.

Bunnell, B. E., & Beidel, D. C. (2013). Incorporating technology into the treatment of a 17 year old girl with selective mutism. *Clinical Case Studies, 12*, 291–306.

Burns, D. D. (1989). *The feeling good handbook*. New York: William Morrow and Company.

Burstein, M., Beesdo-Baum, J. P., & Merikangas, K. R. (2014). Threshold and subthreshold generalized anxiety disorder among US adolescents: Prevalence, sociodemographic, and clinical characteristics. *Psychological Medicine, 44*, 2351–2362.

Burton, P. R., McNiel, D. E., & Binder, R. L. (2012). Firesetting, arson, pyromania, and the forensic mental health expert. *Journal of the American Academy of Psychiatry and the Law Online, 40*, 355–365.

Bushnell, J. A., Wells, E., McKenzie, J. M., Hornblow, A. R., Oakley-Browne, M. A., & Joyce, P. R. (1994). Bulimia comorbidity in the general population and in the clinic. *Psychological Medicine, 24*, 605–611.

Buss, D. M. (1999). *Social adaptation and five major factors of personality*. New York: Guilford Press.

Buster, J. E., Kingsberg, S. A., Aguirre, O., Brown, C., Breaux, J. G., Buch, A., … Casson, P. (2005). Testosterone patch for low sexual desire in surgically menopausal women: A randomized trial. *Obstetrics and Gynecology, 105*, 944–952.

Butcher, J. N., Dahlstorm, W. G., Tellegen, A. M., & Kaemmer, B. (1989). *Minnesota Multiphasic Personality Inventory-2: Manual for administration and scoring*. Minneapolis: University of Minnesota Press.

Butler, A. C., Chapman, J. E., Forman, E. M., & Beck, A. T. (2006). The empirical status of cognitive–behavioral therapy: A review of meta-analyses. *Clinical Psychology Review, 26*, 17–33.

Butler, R. J., & Gasson, S. L. (2005). Enuresis alarm treatment. *Scandinavian Journal of Urology and Nephrology, 39*, 349–357.

Butterfield, M. I., Forneris, C. A., Feldman, M. E., & Beckham, J. C. (2000). Hostility and functional health status in women veterans with and without posttraumatic stress disorders: A preliminary study. *Journal of Traumatic Stress, 13*, 735–741.

Butzlaff, R. L., & Hooley, J. M. (1998). Expressed emotion and psychiatric relapse: A meta-analysis. *Archives of General Psychiatry, 55*, 547–552.

Byers, A. L., Yaffe, K., Covinsky, K. E., Friedman, M. B., & Bruce, M. L. (2010). High occurrence of mood and anxiety disorders among older adults: The National Comorbidity Survey Replication. *Archives of General Psychiatry, 67*, 489–496.

Byers, E. S., & Grenier, G. (2003). Premature or rapid ejaculation: Heterosexual couples' perceptions of men's ejaculatory behavior. *Archives of Sexual Behavior, 32*, 261–270.

Cacioppo, J. T., Hawkley, L. C., & Thisted, R. A. (2010). Perceived social isolation makes me sad: 5-year cross-lagged analyses of loneliness and depressive symptomatology in the Chicago Health, Aging, and Social Relations Study. *Psychology & Aging, 25*, 453–463.

Cain, V. S., Johannes, C. B., Avis, N. E., Molte, B., Shocken, M., Skurnick, J., & Ory, M. (2003). Sexual functioning and practices in a multi-ethnic study of midlife women: Baseline results from SWAN. *Journal of Sex Research, 40*, 266–277.

Caldwell, P. H. Y., Nankivell, G., & Sureshkumar, P. (2013). Simple behavioural interventions for nocturnal enuresis in children. *Cochrane Database of Systematic Reviews, 7*, CD003637.

Caldwell, P. H., Sureshkumar, P., & Wong, W. C. (2016). Tricyclic and related drugs for nocturnal enuresis in children. *Cochrane Database of Systematic Reviews, 1*, CD002117.

Call, N. A., Simmons, C. A., Mevers, J. E., & Alvarez, J. P. (2015). Clinical outcomes of behavioral treatments for pica in children with developmental disabilities. *Journal of Autism and Developmental Disorders, 45*, 2105–2114.

Cambridge, V. C., Ziauddeen, H., Nathan, P. J., Subramaniam, N., Dodds, C., Chamberlain, S. R., … Fletcher, P. C. (2013). Neural and behavioral effects of a novel mu opioid receptor antagonist in binge-eating obese people. *Biological Psychiatry, 73*, 887–894.

Campbell, N. L., Cantor, B. B., Hui, S. L., Perkins, A., Khan, B. A., Farber, M. O., … Boustani, M. A. (2014). Race and documentation of cognitive impairment in hospitalized older adults. *Journal of the American Geriatrics Society, 62*, 506–511.

Canino, G., Shrout, P. E., Rubio-Stipec, M., Bird, H. R., Bravo, M., Ramirez, R., … Martínez-Taboas, A. (2004). The DSM-IV rates of child and adolescent disorders in Puerto Rico. *Archives of General Psychiatry, 61*, 85–93.

Canino, G. J., Bird, H. R., Shrout, P. E., Rubio-Stipec, M., Bravo, M., Martinez, R., … Guevara, L. M. (1987). The prevalence of specific psychiatric disorders in Puerto Rico. *Archives in General Psychiatry, 44*, 727–725.

Cannon, M., Jones, P. B., & Murray, R. M. (2002). Obstetric complications and schizophrenia: Historical and meta-analytic review. *American Journal of Psychiatry, 159*, 1080–1092.

Cannon, W. B. (1929). *Bodily changes in pain, hunger, fear and rage*. New York: Appleton.

Caprioli, D., Celentano, M., Paolone, G., & Badiani, A. (2007). Modeling the role of environment in addiction. *Progress in Neuro-Psychopharmacology & Biological Psychiatry, 31*, 1639–1653.

Caraballo, R. S., Kruger, J., Asman, K., Pederson, L., Widome, R., Kiefe, C. I., … Jacobs, D. R., Jr. (2014). Relapse among cigarette smokers: The CARDIA longitudinal study—1985–2011. *Addictive Behaviors, 39*, 101–106.

Carmin, C. N., & Wiegartz, P. S. (2000). Successful and unsuccessful treatment of obsessive-compulsive disorder in older adults. *Journal of Contemporary Psychotherapy, 30*, 181–193.

Carrera, O., Fraga, A., Pellon, R., & Gutierrez, E. (2014). Rodent model of activity-based anorexia. *Current Protocols in Neuroscience, 67*, 9.47.1-9.47.11.

Carrigan, M. H., & Randall, C. L. (2003). Self-medication in social phobia: A review of the alcohol literature. *Addictive Behavior, 28*, 269–284.

Carrillo, J., & Benitez, J. (2000). Clinically significant pharmacokinetic interactions between dietary caffeine and medications. *Clinical Pharmacokinetics, 39*, 127–153.

Carter, C. S. (1998). Neuroendocrine perspectives on social attachment and love. *Psychoneuroendocrinology, 23*, 779–818.

Caruso, S., Intelisano, G., Lupo, L., & Agnello, C. (2001). Premenopausal women affected by sexual arousal disorder treated with sildenafil: A double-blind, cross-over, placebo-controlled study. *British Journal of Obstetrics and Gynaecology, 108*, 623–628.

Carvalho, J., Trent, L. R., & Hopko, D. R. (2011). The impact of decreased environmental reward in predicting depression severity: Support for behavioral theories of depression. *Psychopathology, 44*, 242–252.

Caskey, J. D., & Rosenthal, S. L. (2005). Conducting research on sensitive topics with adolescents: Ethical and developmental considerations. *Developmental and Behavioral Pediatrics, 26*, 61–67.

Caspi, A., Sugden, K., Moffitt, T., Taylor, A., Craig, I., Harrington, H., … Poulton, R. (2003). Influence of life stress on depression: Moderation by a polymorphism in the *5-HTT* gene. *Science, 301*(5631), 386–389.

Cassidy, O. L., Matheson, B., Osborn, R., Vannucci, A., Kozlosky, M., Shomaker, L. B., … Tanofsky-Kraff, M. (2012). Loss of control eating in African-American and Caucasian youth. *Eating Behaviors, 13*, 174–178.

Castellanos, F. X., Lee, P. P., Sharp, W., Jeffries, N. O., Greenstein, D. K., Clasen, L. S., … Rapoport, J. L. (2002). Developmental trajectories of brain volume abnormalities in children and adolescents with attention-deficit/hyperactivity disorder. *Journal of the American Medical Association, 288*, 1740–1748.

Castellini, G., Lo Sauro, C., Mannucci, E., Ravaldi, C., Rotella, C. M., Faravelli, C., & Ricca, V. (2011). Diagnostic crossover and outcome predictors in eating disorders according to DSM-IV and DSM-V proposed criteria: A 6-year follow-up study. *Psychosomatic Medicine, 73*, 270–279.

Castles, A., Datta, H., Gayan, J., & Olson, R. K. (1999). Varieties of developmental reading disorder: Genetic and environmental influences. *Journal of Experimental Child Psychology, 72*, 73–94.

Cather, C., Penn, D., Otto, M. W., Yovel, I., Mueser, K. T., & Goff, D. C. (2005). A pilot study of functional cognitive behavioral therapy (fCBT) for schizophrenia. *Schizophrenia Research, 74*, 201–209.

Cattaneo, A., Macchi, F., Plazzotta, G., Veronica, B., Bocchio-Chiavetto, L., Riva, M. A., & Pariante, C. M. (2015). Inflammation and neuronal plasticity: A link between childhood trauma and depression pathogenesis. *Frontiers in Cellular Neuroscience, 9*, 40.

Cavanagh, J. T., Carson, A. J., Sharpe, M., & Lawrie, S. M. (2003). Psychological autopsy studies of suicide: A systematic review. *Psychological Medicine, 33*, 395–405.

Ceballos, N. A., Houston, R. J., Hesselbrock, V. M., & Bauer, L. O. (2006). Brain maturation in conduct disorder versus borderline personality disorder. *Neuropsychobiology, 54*, 94–100.

Cederlöf, R., Rantasalo, I., Floderus-Myrhed, B., Hammar, N., Kaprio, J., Koskenvuo, M., … Sarna, S. (1982). A cross-national epidemiological resource: The Swedish and Finnish cohort studies of like-sexed twins. *International Journal of Epidemiology, 11*, 387–390.

Ceglowski, J., DeDios, L. V., & Depp, C. (2014). Psychosis in older adults. In N. A. Pachana & K. Laidlaw (Eds.), *The Oxford handbook of clinical geropsychology* (pp. 490–526). New York: Cambridge University Press.

Center for Behavioral Health Statistics and Quality (SAMHSA). (2014). *Behavioral health trends in the United States: Results from the 2014 National Survey on Drug Use and Health (HHS Publication No. SMA 15-4927, NSDUH Series H-50)*. Retrieved from http://www.samhsa.gov/data/sites/default/files/NSDUH-FRR1-2014/NSDUH-FRR1-2014.pdf

Centers for Disease Control and Prevention. (1994). Cigarette smoking among adults—United States, 1993. *Morbidity and Mortality Weekly Reports, 43*, 925–930.

Centers for Disease Control and Prevention. (2004). Prevalence of cigarette use among 14 racial/ethnic populations—United States, 1999–2001. *Morbidity and Mortality Weekly Reports, 53*, 49–52.

Centers for Disease Control and Prevention. (2004b). Youth risk behavior surveillance United States, 2003. *Morbidity and Mortality Report Weekly, 53*, 1–96.

Centers for Disease Control and Prevention (2006). *Youth Risk Behavior Surveillance—United States, 2005. MMWR (Morbidity and Mortality Weekly Report) Surveillance Summary, 55* (SS-5), 1–108.

Centers for Disease Control and Prevention (2013). *Deaths: Final data for 2013*. Retrieved from http://www.cdc.gov/nchs/data/nvsr/nvsr64/nvsr64_02.pdf

Centers for Disease Control and Prevention. (2015). *Leading causes of death*. Retrieved from http://www.cdc.gov/nchs/fastats/leading-causes-of-death.htm

Centers for Disease Control and Prevention. (2015). Drug overdose deaths hit record numbers in 2014. *CDC Newsroom Releases*. Retrieved from http://www.cdc.gov/media/releases/2015/p1218-drug-overdose.html

Cerletti, U., & Bini, L. (1938). Un nuovo metodo di shock-terapia: "L'elettroshock." *Bollettino ed Atti della Reale Accademia Medica di Roma, 64*, 136–38.

Chalkley, A. J., & Powell, G. E. (1983). The clinical description of forty-eight cases of sexual fetishism. *British Journal of Psychiatry, 142*, 292–295.

Chambless, D. L., Fydrich, T., & Rodebaugh, T. L. (2008). Generalized social phobia and avoidant personality disorder: Meaningful distinction or useless duplication? *Depression & Anxiety, 25*, 8–19.

Chambless, D. L., & Williams, K. E. (1995). A preliminary study of African Americans with agoraphobia: Symptom severity and outcome of treatment with in vivo exposure. *Behavior Therapy, 26*, 501–515.

Chami, T. N., Andersen, A. E., Crowell, M. D., Schuster, M. M., & Whitehead, W. E. (1995). Gastrointestinal symptoms in bulimia nervosa: Effects of treatment. *The American Journal of Gastroenterology, 90*, 88–92.

Chapman, D. P., Williams, S. M., Strine, T. W., Anda, R. F., & Moore, M. J. (2006). Dementia and its implications for public health. *Prevention of Chronic Disease, 3*, 1–13.

Chapman, T. F., Manuzza, S., & Fyer, A. J. (1995). Epidemiology and family studies of social phobia. In M. R. Liebowitz, R. G. Heimberg, D. A. Hope & F. R. Schneier (Eds.) *Social phobia: Diagnosis, assessment, and treatment* (pp. 21–40). New York: The Guilford Press.

Charlson, F. J., Moran, A. E., Freedman, G., Norman, R. E., Stapelberg, N. J., Baxter, A. J., … Whiteford, H. A. (2013). The contribution of major depression to the global burden of ischemic heart disease: A comparative risk assessment. *BMC Medicine, 11*, 250.

Charman, T., Taylor, E., Drew, A., Cockerill, H., Brown, J. A., & Baird, G. (2005). Outcome at 7 years of children diagnosed with autism at age 2: Predictive validity of assessments conducted at 2 and 3 years of age and pattern of symptom change over time. *Journal of Child Psychology and Psychiatry, 46*, 500–513.

Chen, C. H., Lee, C. S., Lee, M. T., Ouyang, W. C., Chen, C. C., Chong, M. Y., … for the Taiwan Bipolar Consortium. (2014). Variant *GADL1* and response to lithium therapy in bipolar I disorder. *The New England Journal of Medicine, 370*, 119–128.

Chen, E. Y., Matthews, L., Allen, C., Kuo, J. R., & Linehan, M. M. (2008). Dialectical behavior therapy for clients with binge-eating disorder or bulimia nervosa and borderline personality disorder. *International Journal of Eating Disorders, 41*, 505–512.

Chenneville, T. (2000). HIV, confidentiality, and duty to protect: A decision-making model. *Professional Psychology: Research and Practice, 31*, 661–670.

Chesney, E., Goodwin, G. M., & Fazel, S. (2014). Risks of all-cause and suicide mortality in mental disorders: A meta-review. *World Psychiatry, 13*, 153–160.

Chess, S., & Thomas, A. (1991). Perspectives on individual differences. In J. Strelaou and A. Angleitner (Eds.), *Explorations in temperament: International perspectives on theory and measurement* (pp. 15–28). New York: Plenum Press.

Chi, S., Yu, J. T., Tan, M. S., & Tan, L. (2014). Depression in Alzheimer's disease: Epidemiology, mechanisms, and management. *Journal of Alzheimer's Disease, 42*, 739–755.

Chial, H. J., Camilleri, M., Williams, D. E., Litzinger, K., & Perrault, J. (2003). Rumination syndrome in children and adolescents: Diagnosis, treatment, and prognosis. *Pediatrics, 111*, 158–162.

Chiesa, M., Fonagy, P., Holmes, J., & Drahorad, C. (2004). Residential versus community treatment of personality disorders: A comparative study of three treatment programs. *American Journal of Psychiatry, 161*, 1463–1470.

Chiesa, M., Fonagy, P., & Holmes, J. (2006). Six-year follow-up of three treatment programs to personality disorder. *Journal of Pesonality Disorders, 20*, 493–509.

Chou, K. L. (2009). Panic disorder in older adults: Evidence from the National Epidemiologic Survey on Alcohol and Related Conditions. *International Journal of Geriatric Psychiatry, 25*, 822–832.

Chrishon, K., Anderson, D., Arora, G., & Bailey, T. K. (2012). Race and psychiatric diagnostic patterns: Understanding the influence of hospital characteristics in the National Hospital Discharge Survey. *Journal of the National Medical Association, 104*, 505–509.

Chronis, A., Jones, H. A., & Raggi, V. L. (2006). Evidence-based psychosocial treatments for children and adolescents with attention-deficit/hyperactivity disorder. *Clinical Psychology Review, 26*, 486–502.

Chronis, A. M., Chacko, A., Fabiano, G. A., Wymbs, B. T., & Pelham, W. E., Jr. (2004). Enhancements to the behavioral parent training paradigm for families of children with ADHD: Review and future directions. *Clinical Child and Family Psychology Review, 7*, 1–27.

Chung, Y. B., & Harmon, L. W. (1994). The career interests and aspirations of gay men: How sex-role orientation is related. *Journal of Vocational Behavior, 45*, 223–239.

Clarfield, A. M. (2003). The decreasing prevalence of reversible dementias: An updated meta-analysis. *Archives of Internal Medicine, 163*, 2219–2229.

Clark, C. W. (1997). The witch craze in 17th-century Europe. In W. G. Bringman, H.E. Luck, R. Miller, & C. Early (Eds.), *A pictorial history of psychology* (pp. 23–29). Carol Stream, IL: Quintessence Publishing Co, Inc.

Clark, S. K., Jeglic, E. L., Calkins, C., & Tatar, J. R. (2014). More than a nuisance: The prevalence and consequences of frotteurism and exhibitionism. *Sexual Abuse: A Journal of Research and Treatment, 1*, 1–17.

Clauss, J. A., & Blackford, J.U. (2012). Behavioral inhibition and risk for developing social anxiety disorder: A meta-analytic study. *Journal of the American Academy of Child and Adolescent Psychiatry, 51*, 1066–1075.

Clinical Research News (2004). Studies of capsulotomy, cingulotomy. *Clinical Research News, 39*, 28.

Cloninger, C. R., Svrakic, D. M., & Przybeck, T. R. (1993). A psychobiological model of temperament and character. *Archives of General Psychiatry, 50*, 975–990.

Cohen-Bendahan, C. C., van de Beek, C., & Berenbaum, S. A. (2005). Prenatal sex hormone effects on child and adult sex-typed behavior: Methods and findings. *Neuroscience and Biobehavioral Reviews, 29*, 353–384.

Colapinto, J. Gender gap. What were the real resons behind David Reimer's suicide? *Slate Magazine*. Retrieved from http://www.slate.com/authors.john_colapinto.html

Coldwell, H., & Heather, N. (2006). Introduction to the special issue. *Addiction Research and Theory, 14*, 1–5.

Collins, R. L., & Lapp, W. M. (1991). Restraint and attributions: Evidence of the abstinence violation effect in alcohol consumption. *Cognitive Therapy and Research, 15*, 69–84.

Combs, D. R., & Mueser, K. T. (2007). Schizophrenia. In M. Hersen, S. Turner, and D. Beidel (Eds.), *Adult psychopathology and diagnosis (6th ed.*, pp. 261–315). New York: John Wiley and Sons.

Combs, D. R., Mueser, K. T., & Drake, E. (2014). Schizophrenia. In D. C. Beidel B.C. Frueh, & M. Hersen (Eds.), *Adult psychopathology and diagnosis* (*7th ed.*, pp. 165–216). New York: Wiley.

Committee on Environmental Health, American Academy of Pediatrics. (2005). Lead exposure in children: Prevention, detection, and management. *Pediatrics, 116*, 1036–1046.

Compas, B. E., & Gotlib, I. H. (2002). *Introduction to clinical psychology: Science and practice*. New York, NY: McGraw-Hill Humanities, Social Sciences & World Languages.

Compton, S. N., March, J. S., Brent, D., Albano, A. M., Weersing, R., & Curry, J. (2004). Cognitive-behavioral psychotherapy for anxiety and depressive disorders in children and adolescents: An evidence-based medicine review. *Journal of the American Academy of Child & Adolescent Psychiatry, 43*, 930–959.

Conners, C. K., Epstein, J. N., March, J. S., Angold, A., Wells, K. C., Klaric, J., … Newcorn, J. H. (2001). Multimodal treatment of ADHD in the MTA: An alternative outcome analysis. *Journal of the American Academy of Child and Adolescent Psychiatry, 40*, 159–167.

CONVERGE Consortium. (2015). Sparse whole-genome sequencing identifies two loci for major depressive disorder. *Nature, 523*(7562), 588–591.

Conwell, Y., Duberstein, P. R., & Caine, E. D. (2002). Risk factors for suicide in later life. *Biological Psychiatry, 52*, 193–204.

Conwell, Y., Duberstein, P. R., Hirsch, J. K., Conner, K. R., Eberly, S., & Caine, E. D. (2010). Health status and suicide in the second half of life. *International Journal of Geriatric Psychiatry, 25*, 371–379.

Conwell, Y., Van Orden, K., & Caine, E. D. (2011). Suicide in older adults. *Psychiatric Clinics of North America, 34*, 451–468.

Cooper, A., Delmonico, D. J., Griffin-Shelley, E., & Mathy, R. M. (2004). Online sexual activity: An examination of potentially problematic behaviors. *Sexual Addiction & Compulsivity, 11*, 120–143.

Cooper, C., Balamurali, T., & Livingston, G. (2007). A systematic review of the prevalence and covariates of anxiety in caregivers of people with dementia. *International Psychogeriatrics, 19*, 175–195.

Copolov, D. L., Mackinnon, A., & Trauer, T. (2004). Correlates of the affective impact of auditory hallucinations in psychotic disorders. *Schizophrenia Bulletin, 30*, 163–171.

Córdova-Palomera, A., Fatjo-Vilas, M., Gasto, C., Navarro, V., Krebs, M. O., & Fananas, L. (2015). Genome-wide methylation study on depression: Differential methylation and variable methylation in monozygotic twins. *Translational Psychiatry, 5*, e557.

Corkin, S. (1968). Acquisition of motor skill after bilateral medial temporal-lobe excision. *Neuropsychologia, 6*, 255–265.

Corona, G., Rastrelli, G., Maseroli, E., Forti, G., & Maggi, M. (2013). Sexual function of the ageing male. *Best Practice and Research Clinical Endocrinology and Metabolism, 27*, 581–601.

Coryell, W., & Norten, S. G. (1981). Briquet's syndrome (somatization disorder) and primary depression: Comparison of background and outcome. *Comprehensive Psychiatry, 22*, 249–256.

Costa, P. T. J., & McCrae, R. R. (1992). *Revised NEO Personality Inventory (NEO-PI-R) and NEO Five-Factor Inventory (NEO-FFI) manual*. Odessa, FL: Psychological Assessment Resources:

Costelllo, J. E., Erkanli, A., & Angold, A. (2006). Is there an epidemic of child or adolescent depression? *Journal of Child Psychology & Psychiatry, 47*, 1263–1271.

Costello, E. J., Mustillo, S., Erkanli, A., Keeler, G., & Angold, A. (2003). Prevalence and development of psychiatric disorders in childhood and adolescence. *Archives of General Psychiatry, 60*, 837–844.

Costello, E. J., Egger, H. L., & Angold, A. (2005a). The developmental epidemiology of anxiety disorders: Phenomenology, Prevalence, and Comorbidity. *Child & Adolescent Psychiatric Clinics of North America, 14*, 631–648.

Costello, E. J., Egger, H., & Angold, A. (2005). 10-year research update review: The epidemiology of child and adolescent psychiatric disorders; I. Methods and public health burden. *Journal of the American Academy of Child & Adolescent Psychiatry, 44*, 972–986.

Cottler, L. B., Nishith, P., & Compton, W. M., III. (2001). Gender differences in risk factors for trauma exposure and post-traumatic stress disorder among inner-city drug abusers in and out of treatment. *Comprehensive Psychiatry, 42*, 111–117.

Cougnard, A., Grolleau, S., Lamarque, F., Beitz, C., Brugère, S., & Verdoux, H. (2006). Psychotic disorders among homeless subjects attending a psychiatric emergency service. *Social Psychiatry and Psychiatric Epidemiology, 41*, 904–910.

Courchesne, E., & Pierce, K. (2005). Brain overgrowth in autism during a critical time in development: Implications for frontal pyramidal neuron and interneuron development and connectivity. *International Journal of Developmental Neuroscience, 23*, 153–170.

Cox, D. J., & Maletzky, B. M. (1980). Victims of exhibitionism. In D. J. Cox and R. J. Daitzman (Eds.), *Exhibitionism: Description, assessment, and treatment* (pp. 289–293). New York: Garland.

Cox, D.J., Sutphen, J., Borowitz, S., Kovatchev, B., & Ling, W. (1988). Contribution of behavior therapy an biofeedback to laxative theapy in the treatment of pediatric encopresis. *Annals of Behavioral Medicine, 20*, 70–76.

Cox, D. J., Morris, J. B., Jr., Borowitz, S. M., & Sutphen, J. L. (2002). Psychological differences between children with and without chronic encopresis. *Journal of Pediatric Psychology, 27*, 585–591.

Crabtree, F. A. (2000). Mesmer, Franz Anton. In A.E. Kazdin (Ed.), *Encyclopedia of psychology* (Vol. 4, pp. 200–201). Washington, DC: American Psychological Association.

Craig, T. K., Bialas, I., Hodson, S., & Cox, A. D. (2004). Intergenerational transmission of somatization behaviour: 2. Observations of joint attention and bids for attention. *Psychological Medicine, 34*, 199–209.

Craighead, W. E., & Miklowitz, D. J. (2000). Psychosocial interventions for bipolar disorder. *Journal of Clinical Psychiatry, 61*, 58–64.

Cranford, J. A., Krentzman, A. R., Mowbray, O., & Robinson, E. A. (2014). Trajectories of alcohol use over time among adults with alcohol dependence. *Addictive Behaviors, 39*, 1006–1011.

Craske, M. G., Kircanski, K., Epstein, A., Wittchen, H. U., Pine, D. S., Lewis-Fernandez, R., … DSM V Anxiety, Obsessive-Compulsive Spectrum, Posttraumatic and Dissociative Disorder Work Group. (2010). Panic disorder: A review of DSM-IV panic disorder and proposals for DSM-V. *Depression & Anxiety, 27*, 93–112.

Craske, M. G., Niles, A. N., Burklund, L. J., Wolitzky-Taylor, K. B., Vilardaga, J. C., Arch, J. J., … Lieberman, M. D. (2014). Randomized controlled trial of cognitive behavioral therapy and acceptance and commitment therapy for social phobia: Outcomes and moderators. *Journal of Consulting and Clinical Psychology, 82*, 1034–1048.

Crawford, D. C., Meadows, K. L., Newman, J. L., Taft, L. F., Scott, E., Leslie, M., … Sherman, S.L. (2002). Prevalence of the fragile X syndrome in African-Americans. *American Journal of Medical Genetics and Neuropsychiatric Genetics, 110*, 226–233.

Creed, F., & Barsky, A. (2004). A systematic review of the epidemiology of somatisation disorder and hypochondriasis. *Journal of Psychosomatic Research, 56*, 291–408.

Crider, A., Glaros, A. G., & Gevirtz, R. N. (2005). Efficacy of biofeedback-based treatments for temporomandibular disorders. *Applied Psychophysiology and Biofeedback, 30*, 333–345.

Crime, H. (2014, June). Death of teen Logan Stiner puts focus on caffeine powder dangers. *Huffington Post*. Retrieved from http://www.huffingtonpost.com/2014/07/19/logan-stiner-caffeine-pow_n_5601775.html

Crimlisk, H. L., Bhatia, K., Cope, H., David, A., Marsden, D. C., & Ron, M. A. (1998). Slater revisited: 6 year follow up study of patients with medically unexplained motor symptoms. *British Medical Journal, 316*(7131), 582–586.

Chrishon, K., Anderson, D., Arora, G., & Bailey, T. K. (2012). Race and psychiatric diagnostic patterns: understanding the influence of hospital characteristics in the National Hospital Discharge Survey. *Journal of the National Medical Association, 104*, 505–509.

Cronbag, H. F. M., Wagenaar, W. A., & van Koppen, P. J. (1996). Crashing memories and the problem of "source monitoring." *Applied Cognitive Psychology, 10*, 95–104.

Cuffe, S. P., McKeown, R. E., Addy, C. L., & Garrison, C. Z. (2005). Family and psychosocial risk factors in a longitudinal epidemiological study of adolescents. *Journal of the American Academy of Child and Adolescent Psychiatry, 44*, 121–129.

Cuijpers, P., Sijbrandij, M., Koole, S., Huibers, M., Berking, M., & Andersson, G. (2014). Psychological treatment of generalized anxiety disorder: A meta-analysis. *Clinical Psychology Review, 34*, 130–140.

Cuijpers, P., Geraedts, A. S., van Oppen, P., Andersson, G., Markowitz, J. C., & van Straten, A. (2011). Interpersonal psychotherapy for depression: A meta-analysis. *American Journal of Psychiatry, 168*, 581–592.

Culbert, K. M., Racine, S. E., & Klump, K. L. (2015). Research review: What we have learned about the causes of eating disorders—A synthesis of sociocultural, psychological, and biological research. *Journal of Child Psychology & Psychiatry, 56*, 1141–1164.

Cully, J. A., Graham, D. P., Stanley, M. A., Ferguson, C. J., Sharafkhaneh, A., Souchek, J., & Kunik, M. E. (2006). Quality of life in patients with chronic obstructive pulmonary disease and comorbid anxiety or depression. *Psychosomatics, 47,* 312–319.

Cunningham-Williams, R. M., Cottler, L. B., Compton, W. M., III, & Spitznagel, E. L. (1998). Taking chances: Problem gamblers and mental health disorders—Results from the St. Louis Epidemiologic Catchment Area Study. *American Journal of Public Health, 88,* 1093–1096.

Curry, S., Marlatt, G., & Gordon, J. (1987). Abstinence violation effect: Validation of an attributional construct with smoking cessation. *Journal of Consulting and Clinical Psychology, 55,* 145–149.

Curtis, J. M. (1995). Elements of critical incident debriefing. *Psychological Reports, 77,* 91–96.

Cyranowski, J., Frank, E., Young, E., & Shear, M. (2000). Adolescent onset of the gender difference in lifetime rates of major depression. *Archives of General Psychiatry, 57,* 21–27.

Cyranowski, J. M., Bromberger, J., Youk, A., Matthews, K., Kravitz, H. M., & Powell, L. H. (2004). Lifetime depression history and sexual function in women at midlife. *Archives of Sexual Behavior, 33,* 539–548.

Czajkowski, N., Røysamb, E., Reichborn-Kjennerud, T., & Tambs, K. (2010). A population based family study of symptoms of anxiety and depression: The HUNT study. *Journal of Affective Disorders, 125,* 335–360.

Czarnetzki, A., Blin, N., & Pusch, C.M. (2003). Down's syndrome in ancient Europe. *The Lancet, 362,* 1000.

D'Zurilla, T. J., & Nezu, A. M. (1999). *Problem-solving therapy: A Social Competence Approach to Clinical Intervention.* New York: Springer.

Dagöö, J., Asplund, R. P., Bsenko, H. A., Hjerling, S., Holmberg, A., Westh, S., … Andersson, G. (2014). Cognitive behaviour therapy versus interpersonal psychotherapy for social anxiey disorder delivered via smartphone and computer: A randomized controlled trial. *Journal of Anxiety Disorders, 28,* 410–417.

Daley, D. (2006). Attention deficit hyperactivity disorder: A review of the essential facts. *Child: Care, Health & Development, 32,* 193–204.

Daley, D. D., Jones, K. K., Hutchings, J. J., & Thompson, M. M. (2009). Attention deficit hyperactivity disorder in pre-school children: Current findings, recommended interventions and future directions. *Child: Care, Health & Development, 35,* 754–766.

Dallery, J., Jarvis, B., Marsch, L., & Xie, H. (2015). Mechanisms of change associated with technology-based interventions for substance use. *Drug and Alcohol Dependence, 150,* 14–23.

Damon, W., & Simon Rosser, B. R. (2005). Anodyspareunia in men who have sex with men: Prevalence, predictors, consequences and the development of DSM diagnostic criteria. *Journal of Sex & Marital Therapy, 31,* 129–141.

Daneback, K., Cooper, A., & Månsson, S. A. (2005). An internet study of cybersex participants. *Archives of Sexual Behavior, 14,* 321–328.

Danner, U. N., Sanders, N., Smeets, P. A., van Meer, F., Adan, R. A., Hoek, H. W., & van Elburg, A. A. (2012). Neuropsychological weaknesses in anorexia nervosa: Set-shifting, central coherence, and decision making in currently ill and recovered women. *International Journal of Eating Disorders, 45,* 685–694.

Dare, C., le Grange, D., Eisler, I., & Rutherford, J. (1994). Redefining the psychosomatic family: Family process of 26 eating disorder families. *International Journal of Eating Disorders, 16,* 211–226.

Daughters, S., Bornovalova, M., Correia, C., & Lejuez, C. (2007). Psychoactive substance use disorders: Drugs. In M. Hersen, S. M. Turner, & D. C. Beidel (Eds.), *Adult psychopathology and diagnosis* (5th ed., pp. 201–233). Hoboken, NJ: John Wiley & Sons.

Davidson, J. R. T. (2004). Use of benzodiazepines in social anxiety disorder, generalized anxiety disorder, and posttraumatic stress disorder. *Journal of Clinical Psychiatry, 65,* 29–33.

Davidson, J. R. T. (1993, March). Childhood histories of adult social phobics. *Paper presented at the Anxiety Disorders Association of America Annual Convention. Charleston, SC.*

Davidson, R. J., Pizzagalli, D., & Nitschke, J. B. (2002). The representation and regulation of emotion in depression: Perspectives from affective neuroscience. In I. Gotlib and C. Hammen (Eds.), *Handbook of depression* (pp. 219–244). New York: Guilford Press.

Davidson, L., & Roe, D. (2007). Recovery from versus recovery in serious mental illness: One strategy for lessening confusion plaguing recovery. *Journal of Mental Health, 16,* 459–470.

Davies, M. N., Krause, L., Bell, J. T., Gao, F., Ward, K. J., Wu, H., … Wang, J. (2014). Hypermethylation in the ZBTB20 gene is associated with major depressive disorder. *Genome Biology, 15,* R56.

Davis, C., Levitan, R. D., Carter, J., Kaplan, A. S., Reid, C., Curtis, C., … Kennedy, J. L. (2008). Personality and eating behaviors: A case-control study of binge eating disorder. *International Journal of Eating Disorders, 41,* 243–250.

Davis, M. L., Smits, J. A., & Hofmann, S. G. (2014). Update on the efficacy of pharmacotherapy for social anxiety disorder: A meta-analysis. *Expert Opinion in Pharmacotherapy, 15,* 2281–2291.

Dawson, D., & Grant, B. (1993). Gender effects in diagnosing alcohol abuse and dependence. *Journal of Clinical Psychology, 49,* 298–307.

Dawson, D. (2000). Drinking patterns among individuals with and without DSM-IV alcohol use disorders. *Journal of Studies on Alcohol, 61,* 111–120.

Day, D. O., & Moseley R. L. (2010). Munchausen by proxy syndrome. *Journal of Forensic Psychology Practice, 10,* 13–36.

De Clercq, B., & De Fruyt, F. (2007). Childhood antecedents of personality disorder. *Current Opinions in Psychiatry, 20,* 57–61.

De Fruyt, F., & De Clercq, B. (2014). Antecedents of personality disorder in childhood and adolescence: Toward an integrative developmental model. *Annual Review of Clinical Psychology, 10,* 449–476.

de Kruiff, M. E., ter Kuile, M. M., Weijenborg, P. T., & van Lankveld, J. J. (2000). Vaginismus and dyspareunia: Is there a difference in clinical presentation? *Journal of Psychosomatic Obstetrics and Gynaecology, 21,* 149–155.

De Raedt, R., Vanderhasselt, M. A., & Baeken, C. (2015). Neurostimulation as an intervention for treatment resistant depression: From research on mechanisms towards targeted neurocognitive strategies. *Clinical Psychology Review, 41,* 61–69.

De Young, K. P., Lavender, J. M., & Anderson, D. A. (2010). Binge eating is not associated with elevated eating, weight, or shape concerns in the absence of the desire to lose weight in men. *International Journal of Eating Disorders, 43,* 732–736.

Dean, C. E. (2006). Antipsychotic-associated neuronal changes in the brain: Toxic, therapeutic, or irrelevant to the long-term outcome of schizophrenia? *Progress in Neuro-Psychopharmacology and Biological Psychiatry, 30,* 174–189.

Deardorff, W. J., Feen, E., & Grossberg, G. T. (2015). The use of cholinesterase inhibitors across all stages of Alzheimer's disease. *Drugs & Aging, 32,* 537–547.

DeBuono, B.A., Zinner, S.H., Daamen, M., & McCormack, W. (1990). Sexual behavior of college women in 1975, 1986, and 1989. *New England Journal of Medicine, 322,* 821–825.

Decker, H. S. (2004). The psychiatric works of Emil Kraeplein: A many faceted story of modern medicine. *Journal of the History of the Neurosciences, 13,* 248–276.

Delaloye, S., & Holtzheimer, P. E. (2014). Deep brain stimulation in the treatment of depression. *Dialogues in Clinical NeuroSciences, 16,* 83–91.

Delaney, C. B., Eddy, K. T., Hartmann, A. S., Becker, A. E., Murray, H. B., & Thomas, J. J. (2015). Pica and rumination behavior among individuals seeking treatment for eating disorders or obesity. *International Journal of Eating Disorders, 48,* 238–248.

Delemarre-van de Waal, H. A., & Cohen-Kettenis, P. T. (2006). Clinical management of gender identity disorder in adolescents: A protocol on psychological and paediatric endocrinology aspects. *European Journal of Endocrinology, 155,* S131–S137.

Dell, P. F., & Eisenhower, J. W. (1990). Adolescent multiple personality disorder: A preliminary study of eleven cases. *Journal of the American Academy of Child & Adolescent Psychiatry, 29,* 359–366.

Dell'Osso, B., Altamura, A. C., Allen, A., Marazziti, D., & Hollander, E. (2006). Epidemiologic and clinical updates on impulse control disorders: A critical review. *European Archives of Psychiatry and Clinical Neuroscience, 256,* 464–475.

Dellava, J. E., Hamer, R. M., Kanodia, A., Reyes-Rodríguez, M. L., & Bulik, C. M. (2011). Diet and physical activity in women recovered from anorexia nervosa: A pilot study. *International Journal of Eating Disorders, 44,* 376–382.

Department of Health and Human Services. (1999). Women living long, living well. *Federal Register,* 6903–6904.

Depp, C. A., & Jeste, D. V. (2006). Definitions and predictors of successful aging: A comprehensive review of larger quantitative studies. *The American Journal of Geriatric Psychiatry, 14,* 6–20.

Depression and Bipolar Support Alliance. (2006). Signs and symptoms of mood disorders. Retrieved from http://www.DBSAlliance.org

Derewicz, M. (2013). UNC scientists identify brain circuitry that triggers overeating. Retrieved from http://news.unchealthcare.org/news/2013/september/BNST

Derogatis, L. R., & Lynn, L. L. (1999). Psychological tests in screening for psychiatric disorder. In M. E. Maruish (Ed.), *The use of psychological testing for treatment planning and outcomes assessment* (2nd ed., pp. 41–79). Mahwah, NJ: Lawrence Erlbaum Associates.

DeStefano, F., Price, C. S., & Weintraub, E. S. (2013). Increasing exposure to antibody-stimulating proteins and polysaccharides in vaccines is not associated with risk of autism. *Journal of Pediatrics, 163,* 561–567.

Devlin, B., Bacanu, S. A., Klump, K. L., Bulik, C. M., Fichter, M. M., Halmi, K. A., … Kaye, W. H. (2002). Linkage analysis of anorexia nervosa incorporating behavioral covariates. *Human Molecular Genetics, 11,* 689–696.

Dewald, P. A. (1994). Principles of supportive psychotherapy. *American Journal of Psychotherapy, 48,* 505–518.

Diamond, L. (1993). Homosexuality and bisexuality in different populations. *Archives of Sexual Behaviour, 22,* 291–310.

Diamond, L. M. (2003). What does sexual orientation orient? A biobehavioral model distinguishing romantic love and sexual desire. *Psychological Review, 110,* 173–192.

Diamond, L. M. (2008). Female bisexuality from adolescence to adulthood: Results from a 10-year longitudinal study. *Developmental Psychology, 44,* 5–14.

Diamond, M., & Sigmundson, K. (1977). Sex reassignment at birth: Long-term review and clinical implications. *Archives of Pediatric and Adolescent Medicine, 151,* 298–304.

Dickerson Mayes, S., Calhoun, S. L., Baweja, R., & Mahr, F. (2015). Suicide ideation and attempts in children with psychiatric disorders and typical development. *Crisis, 36,* 55–60.

Didie, E. R., Tortolani, C., Walters, M., Menard, W., Fay, C., & Phillips, K. A. (2006). Social functioning in body dysmorphic disorder: Assessment considerations. *Psychiatric Quarterly, 77,* 223–229.

Diedrich, A., & Voderholzer, U. (2015). Obsessive-compulsive personality disorder: A current review. *Current Psychiatry Reports, 17,* 2.

Diefenbach, G. J., Robison, J. T., Tolin, D. F., & Blank, K. (2004). Late-life anxiety disorders among Puerto Rican primary care patients: Impact on well-being, functioning, and service utilization. *Journal of Anxiety Disorders, 18,* 841–858.

Diemer, E. W., Grant, J. D., Munn-Chernoff, M. A., Patterson, D. A., & Duncan, A. E. (2015). Gender identity, sexual orientation, and eating-related pathology in a national sample of college students. *Journal of Adolescent Health, 57,* 144–149.

Diflorio, A., & Jones, I. (2010). Is sex important? Gender differences in bipolar disorder. *International Review of Psychiatry, 22,* 437–452.

Dimidjian, S., Barrera, M., Jr., Martell, C., Munoz, R. F., & Lewinsohn, P. M. (2011). The origins and current status of behavioral activation treatments for depression. *Annual Review of Clinical Psychology, 7,* 1–38.

Dimsdale, J. E., Creed, F., Escobar, J., Sharpe, M., Wulsin, L., Barsky, A., … Levenson, J. (2013). Somatic symptom disorder: An important change in DSM. *Journal of Psychosomatic Research, 75,* 223–228.

Dimsdale, J. E., & Levenson, J. (2013). What's next for somatic symptom disorder? *American Journal of Psychiatry, 170,* 1393–1395.

DiNapoli, E., & Scogin, F. R. (2014). Late-life depression. In N. A. Pachana & K. Laidlaw (Eds.), *The Oxford handbook of clinical geropsychology* (pp. 412–435). New York: Oxford University Press.

Ding, K., Torabi, M. R., Perera, B., Jun, M. K., & Jones-McKyer, E. L. (2007). Inhalant use among Indiana school children, 1991–2004. *American Journal of Health Behavior, 31,* 24–34.

Diwadkar, V. A., Montrose, D. M., Dworakowski, D., Sweeney, J. A., & Keshavan, M. S. (2006). Genetically predisposed offspring with schizotypal features: An ultra high-risk group for schizophrenia. *Progress in Neuro–Psychopharmacology & Biological Psychiatry, 30,* 230–238.

Dobbs, D. (2012). *The new temper tantrum disorder.* Retrieved from http://www.slate.com/articles/double_x/doublex/2012/12/disruptive_mood_dysregulation_disorder_in_dsm_5_criticism_of_a_new_diagnosis.html

Docter, R. F., & Prince, V. (1997). Transvestism: A survey of 1032 cross-dressers. *Archives of Sexual Behavior, 26,* 589–605.

Doi, T. (1973). *The anatomy of dependence.* Tokyo: Kodansha International.

Dolan, B. M., Warren, F., & Norton, K. (1997). Change in borderline symptoms one year after therapeutic community treatment for severe personality disorders. *British Journal of Psychiatry, 171,* 274–279.

Dollfus, S., Lecardeur, L., Morello, R., & Etard, O. (2016). Placebo response in repetitive transcranial magnetic stimulation trials of treatment of auditory hallucinations in schizophrenia: A meta-analysis. *Schizophrenia Bulletin, 42,* 301–308.

Domes, G., Heinrichs, M., Michel, A., Berger, C., & Herpertz, S. C. (2007). Oxytocin improves "mind-reading" in humans. *Biological Psychiatry, 61,* 731–733.

Domin, D., & Butterworth, J. (2013). The role of community rehabilitation providers in employment for persons with intellectual and developmental disabilities: Results of the 2010–2011 national survey. *Intellectual and Developmental Disabilities,* 51, 215–225.

Domjam, M. (2005). Pavlovian conditioning: A functional perspective. *Annual Review of Psychology, 56,* 179–206.

Done, D.J., Crow, T.J., Johnstone, E.C., & Sacker, A. (1994). Childhood antecedents of schizophrenia and affective illness: Social adjustment at ages 7 and 11. *British Medical Journal, 309,* 699–703.

Donohue, B., Thevenin, D. M., & Runyon, M. K. (1997). Behavioral treatment of conversion disorder in adolescence. A case example of Globus Hystericus. *Behavior Modification, 21,* 231–251.

Donovan, D. M., Ingalsbe, M. H., Benbow, J., & Daley, D. C. (2013). 12-step interventions and mutual support programs for substance use disorders: An overview. *Social Work in Public Health, 28*(3–4), 313–332.

Doolan, D., & Froelicher, E. (2006). Efficacy of smoking cessation intervention among special populations: Review of the literature from 2000 to 2005. *Nursing Research, 55(Suppl),* S29–S37.

Dorahy, M. J., Brand, B. L., Sar, V., Kruger, C., Stavropoulos, P., Martinez-Taboas, A., … Middleton, W. (2014). Dissociative identity disorder: An empirical overview. *Australian & New Zealand Journal of Psychiatry, 48,* 402–417.

dos Santos, L. L., de Castro Magalhãs, M., Januário, J. N., Burle de Agular, M. J., & Santos Carvalho, M. R. (2006). The time has come: A new scene for PKU treatment. *Genetics and Molecular Research, 5,* 33–44.

Dougall, N., Maayan, N., Soares-Weiser, K.., McDermott, L.M., & McIntosh, A. (2015). Transcranial magnetic stimulation for schizophrenia. *Schizophrenia Bulletin, 41,* 1220–1222.

Dougherty, D. D., Baer, L., Cosgrove, G. R., Cassem, E. H., Price, B. H., Nierenberg, A. A., … Rauch, S. L. (2002). Prospective long-term follow-up of 44 patients who received cingulotomy for treatment-refractory obsessive-compulsive disorder. *American Journal of Psychiatry, 159,* 269–275.

Doust, J., & Del Mar, C. (2004). Why do doctors use treatments that do not work? *British Medical Journal (Clinical Research Ed.), 328,* 474–475.

Drake, R. E., & Brunette, M. F. (1998). Complications of severe mental illness related to alcohol and drug use disorders. In M. Galanter (Ed.), *Recent developments in alcoholism: Vol. 14: The consequences of alcoholism* (pp. 285–299). New York: Plenum Press.

Drake, R. E., & Mueser, K. T. (2002). Co-occurring alcohol use disorder and schizophrenia. *Alcohol Research and Health, 26,* 99–102.

Drake, R. E., Green, A. I., Mueser, K. T., & Goldman, H. H. (2003). The history of community mental health treatment and rehabilitation for persons with severe mental illness. *Community Mental Health Journal, 39,* 427–440.

Drake, R. E., Essock, S. M., & Bond, G. R. (2009). Implementing evidence-based practices for people with schizophrenia. *Schizophrenia Bulletin, 35,* 704–713.

Dreger, A., Feder, E. K., & Tamar-Mattis, A. (2010, June 29). Preventing homosexuality (and uppity women) in the womb? *The Bioethics Forum.* Retrieved from http://thehastingscenter.org/Bioethicsforum/Post.aspx?id=4754&blogis=140

Drescher, J., & Pula, J. (2014). Ethical issues reside by the treatment of gender-variant prepubescent children. *Hasting Center Report, 44,* S17–S22.

Driessen, M., Herrmann, J., Stahl, K., Zwaan, M., Meier, S., Hill, A., … Petersen, D. (2000). Magnetic resonance imaging volumes of the hippocampus and the amygdala in women with borderline personality disorder and early traumatization. *Archives in General Psychiatry, 57,* 1115–1122.

Driscoll, J. W. (2006). Postpartum depression: The state of the science. *Journal of Perinatal and Neonatal Nursing, 20,* 40–42.

Drummond, K. D., Bradley, S. J., Peterson-Badall, M., & Zucker, K. J. (2008). A follow-up study of girls with gender identity disorder. *Developmental Psychology, 44,* 34–45.

Duan, J., Shi, J., Fiorentino, A., Leites, C., Chen, X., Moy, W., … Gejman, P. V. (2014). A rare functional noncoding variant at the GWAS-implicated MIR137/MIR2682 locus might confer risk to schizophrenia and bipolar disorder. *The American Journal of Human Genetics, 95,* 744–753.

Duchesne, S., & Ratelle, C. F. (2014). Attachment security to mothers and fathers and the developmental trajectories of depressive symptoms in adolescence: Which parent for which trajectory? *Journal of Youth and Adolescence, 43,* 641–654.

Dulit, R. A., Fye, R. M. R., Miller, F. T., Sacks, M. H., & Frances, A. J. (1993). Gender differences in sexual preference and substance abuse of inpatients with borderline personality disorder. *Journal of Personality Disorders, 7,* 182–185.

Duncan, J. R., & Lawrence, A. J. (2013). Conventional concepts and new perspectives for understanding the addictive properties of inhalants. *Journal of Pharmaceutical Sciences, 122,* 237–243.

Dunlop, D. D., Song, J., Lyons, J. S., Manheim, L. M., & Chang, R. W. (2003). Racial/ethnic differences in rates of depression among preretirement adults. *American Journal of Public Health, 93,* 1945–1952.

Dunn, G. E., Paolo, A. M., Ryan, J. J., & Van Fleet, J. N. (1994). Belief in the existence of multiple personality disorder among psychologists and psychiatrists. *Journal of Clinical Psychology, 50,* 454–457.

Dunne, R. A., & McLoughlin, D. M. (2012). Systematic review and meta-analysis of bifrontal electroconvulsive therapy versus bilateral and unilateral electroconvulsive therapy in depression. *The World Journal of Biological Psychiatry, 13,* 248–258.

Dutra, L., Stathopoulou, G., Basden, S., Leyro, T., Powers, M., & Otto, M. (2008). A meta-analytic review of psychosocial interventions for substance use disorders. *American Journal of Psychiatry, 165,* 179–187.

Dyck, D. G., Short, R., & Vitaliano, P. P. (1999). Predictors of burden and infectious illness in schizophrenia caregivers. *Psychosomatic Medicine, 61,* 411–419.

Dygdon, J. A., & Dienes, K. A. (2013). Behavioral excesses in depression: A learning theory hypothesis. *Depression & Anxiety, 30,* 598–605.

Dysken, M. W., Sano, M., Asthana, S., Vertrees, J. E., Pallaki, M., Llorente, M., … Malphurs, J. (2014). Effect of vitamin E and memantine on functional decline in Alzheimer disease: The TEAM-AD VA cooperative randomized trial, *Journal of the American Medical Association, 311,* 33–44.

Eaton, W. W. (1975). Marital status and schizophrenia. *Acta Psychiatrica Scandinavica, 52,* 320–329.

Eaves, L. C., & Ho, H. H. (2008). Young adult outcome of autism spectrum disorders. *Journal of Autism and Developmental Disabilities, 38,* 739–747.

Ebbeling, C. B., & Ludwig, D. S. (2010). Pediatric obesity prevention initiatives: More questions than answers. *Archives of Pediatrics & Adolescent Medicine, 164,* 1067–1069.

Ebersole, J. S. (2002). *Current practice of clinical electroencephalography.* Philadelphia: Lippincott Williams & Wilkins.

Ebert, D. D., Zarski, A. C., Christensen, H., Stikkelbroek, Y., Cuijpers, P., Berking, M., & Riper, H. (2015). Internet and computer-based cognitive behavioral therapy for anxiety and depression in youth: A meta-analysis of randomized controlled outcome trials. *PLOS ONE, 10,* e0119895.

Ebmeier, K. P., Donaghey, C., & Steele, J. D. (2006). Recent developments and current controversies in depression. *Lancet, 367*(9505), 153–167.

Eckert, E. D., Halmi, K. A., Marchi, P., Grove, W., & Crosby, R. (1995). Ten-year follow-up of anorexia nervosa: Clinical course and outcome. *Psychological Medicine, 25,* 143–156.

Edalati, H., & Krank, M. D. (2015). Childhood maltreatment and development of substance use disorders: A review and a model of cognitive pathways. *Trauma Violence, & Abuse, pii: 1524838015584370.*

Eddy, K. T., Dorer, D. J., Franko, D. L., Tahilani, K., Thompson-Brenner, H., & Herzog, D. B. (2008). Diagnostic crossover in anorexia nervosa and bulimia nervosa: Implications for DSM-V. *American Journal of Psychiatry, 165,* 245–250.

Edginton, B. (1997). Moral architecture: the influence of the York Retreat on asylum design. *Health & Place, 3,* 91–99.

Eggers, C., & Bunk, D. (1997). The long-term course of childhood-onset schizophrenia: A 42-year follow-up. *Schizophrenia Bulletin, 23,* 105–117.

Eggert, L. L., Thompson, E. A., Herting, J. R., & Nicholas, L. J. (1995). Reducing suicide potential among high-risk youth: Tests of a school-based prevention program. *Suicide and Life Threatening Behavior, 25,* 276–296.

Ehlers, C. L., Frank, E., & Kupfer, D. J. (1988). Social zeitgebers and biological rhythms: A unified approach to understanding the etiology of depression. *Archives of General Psychiatry, 45,* 948–952.

Ehrensaft, M. K. (2005). Interpersonal relationships and sex differences in the development of conduct problems. *Clinical Child and Family Psychology Review, 8,* 39–63.

Eichler, E. E., & Zimmerman, A. W. (2008). A hot spot of genetic instability in autism. *New England Journal of Medicine, 358,* 737–739.

Eidlitz-Markus, T., Shuper, A, & Amir, J. (2000). Secondary enuresis: post-traumatic stress disorder in children after car accidents. *Israeli Medical Association Journal, 2,* 135–137.

Einat, H., Yuan, P., & Manji, H.K. (2005). Increased anxiety-like behaviors and mitochondrial dysfunction in mice with targeted mutation of the Bel-2 gene: Further support for the involvement of mitochondrial function in anxiety disorders. *Behavior and Brain Research, 165,* 172–180.

Eisen, A. (1999). *Recommendations for the practice of clinical neurophysiology.* Amsterdam: Elsevier.

Eisendrath, S. J., & Young, J. Q. (2005). Factitious physical disorders: A review. In M. Maj, H.S. Akiskal, J. E. Mezzich, & A. Okasha (Eds.), *Somatoform disorders* (pp. 325–351). Hoboken, NJ: John Wiley & Sons.

El Alaoui, S., Hedman, E., Kaldo, V., Hesser, H., Kraepelien, M., Andersson, E., … Lindefors, N. (2015). Effectiveness of Internet-based cognitive-behavior therapy for social anxiety disorder in clinical psychiatry. *Journal of Consulting and Clinical Psychology, 83,* 902–914.

Eldh, J., Berg, A., & Gustafsson, M. (1997). Long-term follow up after sex reassignment surgery. *Scandinavian Journal of Plastic and Reconstructive Surgery and Hand Surgery, 31,* 39–45.

Eliason, M. J., & Amodia, D. S. (2006). A descriptive analysis of treatment outcomes for clients with co-occurring disorders: The role of minority identifications. *Journal of Dual Diagnosis, 2,* 89–109.

Elliott, C. A., Tanofsky-Kraff, M., & Mirza, N. M. (2013). Parent report of binge eating in Hispanic, African American and Caucasian youth. *Eating Behaviors, 14,* 1–6.

Ely, E., Gautam, S., Margolin, R., Francis, J., May, L., Speroff, T., … Inouye, S. (2001). The impact of delirium in the intensive care unit on hospital length of stay. *Intensive Care Medicine, 27,* 1892–1900.

Elzinga, B. M., van Dyck, R., & Spinhoven, P. (1998). Three controversies about dissociative identity disorder. *Clinical Psychology and Psychotherapy, 3,* 13–23.

Epperson, C. N., Steiner, M., Hartlage, S. A., Eriksson, E., Schmidt, P. J., Jones, I., & Yonkers, K. A. (2012). Premenstrual dysphoric disorder: Evidence for a new category for DSM-5. *American Journal of Psychiatry, 169,* 465–475.

Epstein, E. E., Fischer-Elber, K., & Al-Otaiba, Z. (2007). Women, aging, and alcohol use disorders. *Journal of Women & Aging, 19,* 31–48.

Eranti, S., Mogg, A., Pluck, G., Landau, S., Purvis, R., Brown, R. G., … McLoughlin, D. M. (2007). A randomized, controlled trial with 6-month follow-up of repetitive transcranial magnetic stimulation and electroconvulsive therapy for severe depression. *American Journal of Psychiatry, 164,* 73–81.

Erkiran, M., Özünalan, H., Evren, C., Aytaçlar, S., Kirisci, L., & Tarter, R. (2006). Substance abuse amplifies the risk for violence in schizophrenia spectrum disorder. *Addictive Behaviors, 31,* 1797–1805.

Erlenmeyer-Kimling, L., Squires-Wheeler, E., Adamo, U. H., Bassett, A. S., Cornblatt, B. A., Kestenbaum, C. J., …

Gottesman, II. (1995). The New York High-Risk Project. Psychoses and cluster A personality disorders in offspring of schizophrenic parents at 23 years of follow-up. *Archives in General Psychiatry, 52*, 857–865.

Erlenmeyer-Kimling, L., Rock, D., Roberts, S. A., Janal, M., Kestenbaum, C., Cornblatt, B., … Gottsman, I. I. (2000). Attention, memory, and motor skills as childhood predictors of schizophrenia-related psychoses: The New York High-Risk Project. *American Journal of Psychiatry, 157*, 1416–1422.

Erskine, H. E., Ferrari, A. J., Polanczyk, G. V., Moffitt, T. E., Murrary, C. J. L., Vos, T., … Scott, J. G. (2014). The global burden of conduct disorder and attention-deficit/hyperactivity disorder in 2010. *Journal of Child Psychology and Psychiatry, 55*, 328–336.

ESEMed/MHEDEA 2000 Investigators. (2004). Prevalence of mental disorders in Europe: Results from the European Study of the Epidemiology of Mental Disorders (ESEMeD). *Acta Psychiatrica Scandivavia, 109*(420 Suppl), 21–27.

Evans, J. D., Heaton, R. K., Paulsen, J. S., McAdams, L. A., Heaton, S. C., & Jeste, D. V. (1999). Schizoaffective disorder: A form of schizophrenia or affective disorder. *Journal of Clinical Psychiatry, 60*, 874–882.

Evans, J. D., Heaton, R. K., Paulsen, J. S., Palmer, B. W., Patterson, T., & Jeste, D. V. (2003). The relationship of neuropsychological abilities to specific domains of functional capacity in older schizophrenia patients. *Biological Psychiatry, 53*, 422–430.

Exner, J. E., Jr., & Erdberg, P. (2005). *The Rorschach, advanced interpretation*. New York, NY: John Wiley & Sons.

Fabbri, C., Di Girolamo, G., & Serretti, A. (2013). Pharmacogenetics of antidepressant drugs: An update after almost 20 years of research. *American Journal of Medical Genetics, Part B Neuropsychiatric Genetics, 162B*, 487–520.

Fagan, P. J., Wise, T. N., Schmidt, C. W., Jr., & Berlin, F. S. (2002). Pedophilia. *Journal of the American Medical Association, 288*, 2458–2465.

Fairburn, C. G. (1981). A cognitive-behavioural approach to the treatment of bulimia. *Psychological Medicine, 11*, 707–711.

Fairburn, C. G., & Cooper, P. J. (1984). Rumination in bulimia nervosa. *British Medical Journal (Clinical Research Edition), 288*, 826–827.

Fairburn, C., Jones, R., Peveler, R., Hope, R., & O'Connor, M. (1993). Psychotherapy and bulimia nervosa: Longer-term effects of interpersonal psychotherapy, behavior therapy, and cognitive-behavioral therapy. *Archives of General Psychiatry, 50*, 419–428.

Fairburn, C. G. (1993). Interpersonal psychotherapy for bulimia nervosa. In C.G. Fairburn and K. D. Brownell (Eds.), *Eating disorders and obesity: A comprehensive handbook* (2nd ed., pp. 171–177). New York: Guilford Press.

Fairburn, C. G., Welch, S. L., Doll, H. A., Davies, B. A., & O'Connor, M. E. (1997). Risk factors for bulimia nervosa: A community-based case-control study. *Archives of General Psychiatry, 54*, 509–517.

Fairburn, C. G., Cooper, Z., Doll, H. A., Norman, P., & O'Connor, M. (2000). The natural course of bulimia nervosa and binge eating disorder in young women. *Archives of General Psychiatry, 57*, 659–665.

Fairburn, C. G., & Walsh, B. (2002). Atypical eating disorders (eating disorders not otherwise specified). In C.G. Fairburn and K.D. Brownell (Eds.), *Eating disorders and obesity: A comprehensive handbook* (2nd ed., pp. 171–177). New York: Guilford Press.

Fairburn, C. G., Jones, R., Peveler, R. C., Carr, S. J., Solomon, R. A., O'Connor, M. E., … Hope, R. A. (1991). Three psychological treatments for bulimia nervosa. A comparative trial. *Archives of General Psychiatry, 48*, 463–469.

Faison, W. E., & Armstrong, D. (2003). Cultural aspects of psychosis in the elderly. *Journal of Geriatric Psychiatry and Neurology, 16*, 225–231.

Fang, A., Matheny, N. L., & Wilhelm, S. (2014). Body dysmorphic disorder. *Psychiatric Clinics of North America, 37*, 287–300.

Faravelli, C., Salvatori, S., Galassi, F., Aiazzi, L., Drei, C., & Cabras, P. (1997). Epidemiology of somatoform disorders: A community survey in Florence. *Social Psychiatry and Psychiatric Epidemilogy, 32*, 24–29.

Farmer, E. M., Compton, S. N., Burns, B. J., & Robertson, E. (2002). Review of the evidence base for treatment of childhood psychopathology: Externalizing disorders. *Journal of Consulting and Clinical Psychology, 70*, 1267–1302.

Farr, C. B. (1994). Benjamin Rush and American psychiatry. *American Journal of Psychiatry, 151*, 65–73.

Fassassi, S., Vandeleur, C., Aubry, J. M., Castelao, E., & Preisig, M. (2014). Prevalence and correlates of DSM-5 bipolar and related disorders and hyperthymic personality in the community. *Journal of Affective Disorders, 167*, 198–205.

Fassino, S., Leombruni, P., Pierò, A., Daga, G. A., Amianto, F., Rovera, G., & Rovera, G. G. (2002). Temperament and character in obese women with and without binge eating disorder. *Comprehensive Psychiatry, 43*, 431–437.

Fassino, S., Amianto, F., Gramaglia, C., Facchini, F., & Abbate Daga, G. (2004). Temperament and character in eating disorders: Ten years of studies. *Eating and Weight Disorders, 9*, 81–90.

Fatemi, S. H., Emamian, E. S., Kist, D., Sidwell, R. W., Nakajima, K., Akhter, P., … Bailey, K. (1999). Defective corticogenesis and reduction in immunoreactivity in cortex and hippocampus of prenatally infected neonatal mice. *Molecular Psychiatry, 4*, 145–154.

Fava, G. A., Grandi, S., Rafanelli, C., Ruini, C., Conti, S., & Belluardo, P. (2001). Long-term outcome of social phobia treated by exposure. *Psychological Medicine, 31*, 899–905.

Fawcett, J., Epstein, P., Fiester, S. J., Elkin, E., & Autry, J. H. (1987). Clinical management—Imipramine/placebo administration manual. *Psychopharmacology Bulletin, 23*, 309–321.

Food and Drug Administration. (2014). *FDA consumer advice on pure powdered caffeine*. Retrieved from http://www.fda.gov/food/recallsoutbreaksemergencies/safetyalertsadvisories/ucm405787.htm

Fearing, M. A., & Inouye, S. K. (2009). Delirium. *Focus, 7*, 53–63.

Fears, S. C., Schur, R., Sjouwerman, R., Service, S. K., Araya, C., Araya, X., … Bearden, C. E. (2015). Brain structure-function associations in multi-generational families genetically enriched for bipolar disorder. *Brain, 138*(Pt 7), 2087–2102.

Federoff, J. P., Fishell, A., & Federoff, B. (1999). A case series of women evaluated for paraphilic sexual disorder. *Canadian Journal of Human Sexuality, 8*, 127–140.

Fein, G., & Calloway, E. (1993). Electroencephalograms and event-related potentials in clinical psychiatry. In D. L. Dunner (Ed.), *Current psychiatric therapy* (pp. 18–26). Philadelphia: W.B. Saunders.

Feldman, H. A., Goldstein, I., Hatzichristou, D. G., Krane, R. J., & McKinlay, J. B. (1994). Impotence and its medical and psychosocial correlates: Results of the Massachusetts Male Aging Study. *Journal of Urology, 151*, 54–61.

Felger, J. C., Haroon, E., & Miller, A. H. (2015). Risk and resilience: Animal models shed light on the pivotal role of inflammation in individual differences in stress-induced depression. *Biological Psychiatry, 78*, 7–9.

Fenton, W. S., & McGlashan, T. H. (1991). Natural history of schizophrenia subtypes: II. Positive and negative symptoms and long term course. *Archives of General Psychiatry, 48*, 978–986.

Fenton, W. S., Blyler, C. R., & Heinssen, R. K. (1997). Determinants of medication compliance in schizophrenia: Empirical and clinical findings. *Schizophrenia Bulletin, 48*, 978–986.

Ferguson, J. M. (2001). The effects of antidepressants on sexual functioning in depressed patients: A review. *Journal of Clinical Psychiatry, 62*(3 Suppl), 22–34.

Fernández-Aranda, F., Jiménez-Murcia, S., Alvarez-Moya, E. M., Granero, R., Vallejo, J., & Bulik C. M. (2006). Impulse control disorders in eating disorders: Clinical and therapeutic implications. *Comprehensive Psychiatry, 47*, 482–488.

Fernandez-Aranda, F., Pinheiro, A. P., Tozzi, F., Thornton, L. M., Fichter, M. M., Halmi, K. A., … Bulik, C. M. (2007). Symptom profile of major depressive disorder in women with eating disorders. *Australian and New Zealand Journal of Psychiatry, 41*, 24–31.

Ferrari, A. J., Charlson, F. J., Norman, R. E., Patten, S. B., Freedman, G., Murray, C. J., … Whiteford, H. A. (2013). Burden of depressive disorders by country, sex, age, and year: Findings from the global burden of disease study 2010. *PLOS Med, 10*, e1001547.

Fichter, M., & Quadflieg, N. (1997). Six-year course of bulimia nervosa. *International Journal of Eating Disorders, 22*, 361–384.

Fichter, M. M., Quadflieg, N., & Gnutzmann, A. (1998). Binge eating disorder: Treatment outcome over a 6-year course. *Journal of Psychosomatic Research, 44*(3–4), 385–405.

Finkenbine, R., & Miele, V. J. (2004). Globus hystericus: A brief review. *General Hospital Psychiatry, 26*, 76–82.

Finn, S. E., & Martin, H. (2010). Therapeutic assessment: Using psychological testing as brief therapy. In K. F. Geisinger (Ed). *APA handbook of testing and assessment in psychology, Vol. 2, Testing and assessment in clinical and counseling psychology* (pp. 453–465). Washington, DC: American Psychological Association.

Fischer, B., Keates, A., Buhringer, G., Reimer, J., & Rehm, J. (2014). Non-medical use of prescription opioids and prescription opioid-related harms: Why so markedly higher in North America compared to the rest of the world? *Addiction, 109*, 177–181.

Fischer, S., & le Grange, D. (2007). Comorbidity and high-risk behaviors in treatment-seeking adolescents with bulimia nervosa. *International Journal of Eating Disorders, 40*, 751–753.

Fisher, C. B., Hoagwood, K., Boyce, C., Duster, T., Frank, D. A., Grisso, T., … Trimble, J. E. (2002). Research ethics for mental health science involving ethnic minority children and youths. *American Psychologist, 57*, 1034–1040.

Fisher, M. M., Rosen, D. S., Ornstein, R. M., Mammel, K. A., Katzman, D. K., Rome, E. S., … Walsh, B. T. (2014). Characteristics of avoidant/restrictive food intake disorder in children and adolescents: A "new disorder" in DSM-5. *Journal of Adolescent Health, 55*, 49–52.

Fisher, R. A. (1936). Has Mendel's work been rediscovered? *Annals of Science, 1*, 115–137.

Fitzgerald, P. B., deCastella, A. R., Filia, K. M., Filia, S. L., Benitez, J., & Kulkarni, J. (2005). Victimization of patients with schizophrenia and related disorders. *Australian and New Zealand Journal of Psychiatry, 39*, 169–174.

Fitzgerald, P. B., & Daskalakis, Z. J. (2008). A review of repetitive transcranial magnetic stimulation use in the treatment of schizophrenia. *The Canadian Journal of Psychiatry, 53*, 567–576.

Fitzgibbon, M. L., & Blackman, L. R. (2000). Binge eating disorder and bulimia nervosa: Differences in the quality and quantity of binge eating episodes. *International Journal of Eating Disorders, 27*, 238–243.

Fitzsimmons-Craft, E. E., Harney, M. B., Koehler, L. G., Danzi, L. E., Riddell, M. K., & Bardone-Cone, A. M. (2012). Explaining the relation between thin ideal internalization and body dissatisfaction among college women: The roles of social comparison and body surveillance. *Body Image, 9*, 43–49.

Flament, M. F., Buchholz, A., Henderson, K., Obeid, N., Maras, D., Schubert, N., … Goldfield, G. (2015). Comparative distribution and validity of DSM-IV and DSM-5 diagnoses of eating disorders in adolescents from the community. *European Eating Disorders Review, 23*, 100–110.

Flavell, J. H., Flavell, E. R., & Green, F. L. (2001). Development of children's understanding of connections between thinking and feeling. *Psychological Science, 12*, 430–432.

Fleischhacker, W. W., Cetkovich-Bakmas, M., De Hert, M., Hennekens, C. H., Lambert, M., Leucht, S., … Lieberman, J. A. (2008). Comorbid somatic illnesses in patients with severe mental disorders: Clinical, policy, and research challenges. *Journal of Clinical Psychiatry, 18*, e1–e6.

Fleischhacker, W.W., & Widschwendter, C.G. (2006). Treatment of schizophrenia patients: Comparing new-generation antipsycotics to each other. *Current Opinions in Psychiatry, 19*, 128–134.

Flessner, C. A., Busch, A. M., Heideman, P. W., & Woods, D. W. (2008). Acceptance-enhanced behavior therapy (AEBT) for trichotillomania and chronic skin picking: Exploring the effects of component sequencing. *Behavior Modification, 32*, 579–594.

Flessner, C. A., Mouton-Odum, S., Stocker, A. J., & Keuthen, N. J. (2009). StopPicking.com: Internet-based treatment for self-injurious skin picking. *Dermatology Online Journal, 13*, 3.

Flessner, C. A., Knopik, V. S., & McGeary, J. (2012). Hair pulling disorder (trichotillomania): Genes, neurobiology, and a model for understanding impulsivity and compulsivity. *Psychiatry Research, 199*, 151–158.

Flint, J. (2002). Genetic effects on an animal model of anxiety. *FEBS Letters, 529*, 131–134.

Flint, A. J. (2004). Anxiety disorders. In J. Sadavoy, G. T. Grossberg, & B. S. Meyers (Eds.), *Comprehensive textbook of geriatric psychiatry* (3rd ed., pp. 687–699). New York: W.W. Norton & Co.

Florentine, J. B., & Crane, C. (2010). Suicide prevention by limiting access to methods: A review of theory and practice. *Social Science & Medicine, 70*, 1626–1632.

Floyd, M., Myszka, M., & Orr, P. (1998). Licensed psychologists' knowledge and utilization of a state association colleague assistance committee. *Professional Psychology: Research and Practice, 29*, 594–598.

Foley, D. L., Pickles, A., Maes, H. M., Silberg, J. L., & Eaves, L. J. (2004). Course and short-term outcomes of separation anxiety disorder in a community sample of twins. *Journal of the American Academy of Child and Adolescent Psychiatry, 43*, 1107–1114.

Folkman, S., & Lazarus, R. S. (1985). If it changes it must be a process: Study of emotion and coping during three stages of a college examination. *Journal of Personality and Social Psychology, 48*, 150–170.

Folkman, S., & Lazarus, R. S. (1986). Stress-processes and depressive symptomatology. *Journal of Abnormal Psychology, 95*, 107–113.

Folsom, D. P., Hawthorne, W., Lindamer, L., Filmer, T., Bailey, A., Golshan, S., … Jeste, D. V. (2005). Prevalence and risk factors for homelessness and utilization of mental health services among 10,340 patients with serious mental illness in a large public mental health system. *American Journal of Psychiatry, 162*, 370–376.

Folstein, S. E., & Rosen-Sheidley, B. (2001). Genetics of austim: Complex aetiology for a heterogeneous disorder. *Nature Reviews Genetics, 2*, 943–955.

Fombonne, E. (2005). The changing epidemiology of autism. *Journal of Applied Research in Intellectual Disabilities, 18*, 281–294.

Fonagy, P., Steele, M., & Moran, G. (1991). The capacity for understanding mental states: The reflective self in parent and child and its significance for security of attachment. *Infant Mental Health Journal, 12*, 200–217.

Fontana, A., Rosenheck, R., & Desai, R. (2010). Female veterans of Iraq and Afghanistan seeking care from VA specialized PTSD programs: Comparison with male veterans and female war zone veterans of previous eras. *Journal of Women's Health, 19*, 751–757.

Foote, B., Smolin, Y., Kaplan, M., Legatt, M. E., & Lipschitz, D. (2006). Prevalence of dissociative disorders in psychiatric outpatients. *American Journal of Psychiatry, 163*, 623–629.

Forbes, D., Forbes, S. C., Blake, C. M., Thiessen, E. J., & Forbes, S. (2015). Exercise programs for people with dementia. *Cochrane Database of Systematic Reviews, 4*, CD006489.

Ford, B. C., Bullard, K. M., Taylor, R. J., Toler, A. K., Neighbors, H. W., & Jackson, J. S. (2007). Lifetime and 12-month prevalence of Diagnostic and Statistical Manual of Mental Disorders, disorders among older African Americans: Findings from the National Survey of American Life. *The American Journal of Geriatric Psychiatry, 15*, 652–659.

Ford, C. V. (2005). Deception syndrome: Factitious disorders and malingering. In J. L. Levenson (Ed.), *The American psychiatric publishing textbook of psychosomatic medicine* (pp. 297–309). Washington, DC: American Psychiatric Press.

Forty, L., Ulanova, A., Jones, L., Jones, I., Gordon-Smith, K., Fraser, C., … Craddock, N. (2014). Comorbid medical illness in bipolar disorder. *The British Journal of Psychiatry, 205*, 465–472.

Foxx, R. M., & Martin, E. D. (1975). Treatment of scavenging behavior (coprophagy and pica) by overcorrection. *Behaviour Research and Theapy, 13*, 153–162.

Frances, A. (2012). DSM-5 is a guide not a bible: Simply ignore its 10 worst changes. Retrieved from http://www.huffingtonpost.com/allen-frances/dsm-5_b_2227626.html

Frances, A. (2013). DSM-5 somatic symptom disorder. *The Journal of Nervous and Mental Disease, 201*, 530–531.

Frank, E., Kupfer, D. J., Wagner, E. F., McEachran, A. B., & Corner, C. (1991). Efficacy of interpersonal psychotherapy as a maintenance treatment of re-current depression: Contributing factors. *Archives of General Psychiatry, 48*, 1053–1059.

Frank, E., Swartz, H. A., Mallinger, A. G., Thase, M. E., Weaver, E. V., & Kupfer, D. J. (1999). Adjunctive psychotherapy for bipolar disorder: Effects of changing treatment modality. *Journal of Abnormal Psychology, 108*, 579–587.

Frank, E., Hlastala, S., Ritenour, A., Houck, P., Tu, X. M., Monk, T. H., … Kupfer, D. J. (1997). Inducing lifestyle regularity in recovering bipolar disorder patients: Results from the maintenance therapies in bipolar disorder protocol. *Biological Psychiatry, 41*, 1165–1173.

Frank, E., Kupfer, D. J., Thase, M. E., Mallinger, A. G., Swartz, H. A., Fagiolini, A. M., … Monk, T. (2005). Two-year outcomes for interpersonal and social rhythm therapy in individuals with bipolar I disorder. *Archives of General Psychiatry, 62*, 996–1004.

Frank, G. K. (2015). Recent advances in neuroimaging to model eating disorder neurobiology. *Current Psychiatry Reports, 17*, 559.

Frank, G. K., Bailer, U. F., Henry, S. E., Drevets, W., Meltzer, C. C., Price, J. C., … Kaye, W. H. (2005). Increased dopamine D2/D3 receptor binding after recovery from anorexia nervosa measured by positron emission tomography and [11c]raclopride. *Biological Psychiatry, 58*, 908–912.

Frank, L., Basch, E., & Selby, J. V. (2014). The PCORI perspective on patient-centered outcomes research. *Journal of the American Medical Association, 312*(15), 1513–1514.

Franklin, M., Kratz, H., Freeman, J., Ivarsson, T., Heyman, I., Sookman, D., … March, J. (2015). Cognitive-behavioral therapy for pediatric obsessive-compulsive disorder: Empirical review and clinical recommendations. *Psychiatry Research, 227*, 78–92.

Franzoni, E., Ciccarese, F., Di Pietro, E., Facchini, G., Moscano, F., Iero, L., … Bazzocchi, A. (2014). Follow-up of bone mineral density and body composition in adolescents with restrictive anorexia nervosa: Role of dual-energy X-ray absorptiometry. *European Journal of Clinical Nutrition, 68*, 247–252.

Freeman, J., Sapyta, J., Garcia, A., Compton, S., Khanna, M., Flessner, C., … Benito, K. (2014). Family-based treatment of early childhood obsessive-compulsive disorder: The Pediatric Obsessive-Compulsive Disorder Treatment Study for Young Children (POTS Jr)—A randomized clinical trial. *JAMA Psychiatry, 71*, 689–698.

Freire, R. C., Sergio Machado, S., Arias-Carrion, O., & Nardi, A. E. (2014). Current pharmacological interventions in panic disorder. *CNS & Neurological Disorders—Drug Targets, 13*, 1057–1065.

Fremont, W. P. (2004). Childhood reactions to terrorism-induced trauma: A review of the past 10 years. *Journal of the American Academy of Child and Adolescent Psychiatry, 43*, 381–392.

Freud, S. (1917). Mourning and melancholia. In J. Strachey (Ed.), *The standard edition of the complete psychological works of Sigmund Freud, 1953–1974* (Vol. 14, p. 248). London: Hogarth Press.

Freud, S. (1963). The sense of symptoms. In J. Strachey, *The standard edition of the complete psychological works of Sigmund Freud* (Vol. 16, pp. 264–269). London: Hogarth Press.

Frías, Á., Palma, C., Farriols, N., & González, L. (2015). Comorbidity between obsessive-compulsive disorder and body dysmorphic disorder: Prevalence, explanatory theories, and clinical characterization. *Neuropsychiatric Disease and Treatment, 11*, 2233–2244.

Fridlund, A. J., Beck, H. P., Goldie, W. D., & Irons, G. (2012). Little Albert: A neurologically impaired child. *History of Psychology, 15*, 302–327.

Friedl, M. C., & Draijer N. . (2000). Dissociative disorders in Dutch psychiatric inpatients. *The American Journal of Psychiatry, 157*, 1012–1013.

Fritz, G., Rockney, R., & the Work Group on Quality Issues. (2004). Practice parameter for the assessment and treatment of children and adolescents with enuresis. *Journal of the American Academy of Child and Adolescent Psychiatry, 43*, 1540–1550.

Froguel, P. (1998). The genetics of complex traits: From diabetes mellitus to obesity. *Pathologie Biologie (Paris), 46*, 713–714.

Frohlich, P. F., & Meston, C. M. (2002). Sexual functioning and self-reported depressive symptoms among college women. *Journal of Sex Research, 39*, 321–325.

Frost, R. O., Tolin, D. F., Steketee, G., Fitch, K. E., & Selbo-Bruns, A. (2009). Excessive acquisition in hoarding. *Journal of Anxiety Disorders, 23*, 632–639.

Frye, M. A., Prieto, M. L., Bobo, W. V., Kung, S., Veldic, M., Alarcon, R. D., … Tye, S. J. (2014). Current landscape, unmet needs, and future directions for treatment of bipolar depression. *Journal of Affective Disorders, 169 Suppl 1*, S17–23.

Fugl-Meyer, A. R., & Sjögren Fugl-Meyer, K. (1999). Sexual disabilities, problems and satisfaction in 18–74 year old Swedes. *Scandinavian Journal of Sexology, 2*, 79–105.

Fulgoni, V. L., 3rd, Keast, D. R., & Lieberman, H. R. (2015). Trends in intake and sources of caffeine in the diets of US adults: 2001–2010. *The American Journal of Clinical Nutrition, 101*, 1081–1087.

Fuller-Thomson, E., Lateef, R., & Sulman, J. (2015). Robust association between inflammatory bowel disease and generalized anxiety disorder: Findings from a nationally representative Canadian study. *Inflammatory Bowel Disease, 21*, 2341–2348.

Fusar-Poli, P., Smieskova. R., Kempton, M. J., Ho, B. C., Andreasen, N. C., & Borgwardt, S. (2013). Progressive brain changes in schizophrenia related to antipsychotic treatment? A meta-analysis of longitudinal MRI studies. *Neuroscience and Biobehavioral Reviews, 37*, 1680–1691.

Fusar-Poli, P., Papanastasiou, E., Stahl, D., Rocchetti, M., Carpenter, W., Shergill, S., & McGuire, P. (2015). Treatments of negative symptoms in schizophrenia: Meta-analysis of 168 randomized placebo-controlled trials. *Schizophrenia Bulletin, 41*, 892–899.

Gabis, L., Raz, R., & Kesner-Baruch, Y. (2010). Paternal age in autism spectrum disorders and ADHD. *Pediatric Neurology, 43*, 300–303.

Galfalvy, H., Haghighi, F., Hodgkinson, C., Goldman, D., Oquendo, M. A., Burke, A., … Mann, J. J. (2015). A genome-wide association study of suicidal behavior. *American Journal of Medical Neuropsychiatric Genetics Part B, 168*, 557–563.

Gallagher, D., & Hermann, N. (2015). Agitation and aggression in Alzheimer's disease: an update on pharmacological and psychosocial approaches to care. *Neurodegenerative Disease Management, 5*, 75–83.

Gallagher-Thompson, D., & Coon, D. W. (2007). Evidence-based psychological treatments for distress in family caregivers of older adults. *Psychology and Aging, 22*, 37–51.

Gallop, R., & Wynn, F. (1987). The difficult inpatient: Identification and response by staff. *Canadian Journal of Psychiatry, 32*, 211–215.

Gálvez, J. F., Keser, Z., Mwangi, B., Ghouse, A. A., Fenoy, A. J., Schulz, P. E., … Soares, J. C. (2015). The medial forebrain bundle as a deep brain stimulation target for treatment resistant depression: A review of published data. *Progress in Neuro-Psychopharmacology & Biological Psychiatry, 58*, 59–70.

Ganiats, T. G. (2015). Redefining the chronic fatigue syndrome. *Annals of Internal Medicine, 162*, 653–654.

Gao, L., Yang, L., Qian, S., Li, T., Han, P., & Yuan, J. (2016). Systematic review and meta-analysis of phosphodiesterase type 5 inhibitors for the treatment of female sexual dysfunction. *International Journal of Obstetrics and Gynaecology, 133*, 139–45.

Garattini, S. (1993). *Caffeine, coffee, and health*. New York: Raven Press.

Garb, H. N., Wood, J. M., Lilienfeld, S. O., & Nezworski, M. T. (2005). Roots of the Rorschach controversy. *Clinical Psychology Review, 25*, 97–118.

Garbutt, J., West, S., Carey, T., Lohr, K., & Crews, F. (1999). Pharmacological treatment of alcohol dependence: A review of the evidence. *Journal of the American Medical Association, 281*, 1318–1325.

Garbutt, J., Kranzler, H., O'Malley, S., Gastfriend, D., Pettinati, H., Silverman, B., … the Vivitrex Study Group. (2005). Efficacy and tolerability of long-acting injectable naltrexone for alcohol dependence: A randomized controlled trial. *Journal of the American Medical Association, 293*, 1617–1625.

Garcia-Garcia, I., Narberhaus, A., Marques-Iturria, I., Garolera, M., Radoi, A., Segura, B., … Jurado, M. A. (2013). Neural responses to visual food cues: Insights from functional magnetic resonance imaging. *European Eating Disorders Review, 21*, 89–98.

Gardner, H. (2011). *Frames of mind: The theory of multiple intelligences*. New York, NY: BasicBooks.

Gardner, W., Lidz, C. W., Mulvey, E. P., & Shaw, E. C. (1996). Clinical versus actuarial predictions of violence in patients with mental illness. *Journal of Consulting and Clinical Psychology, 64*, 602–609.

Gartlehner, G., Hansen, R. A., Carey, T. S., Lohr, K. N., Gaynes, B. N., & Randolph, L. C. (2005). Discontinuation rates for selective serotonin reuptake inhibitors and other second-generation antidepressants in outpatients with major depressive disorder: A systematic review and meta-analysis. *International Clinical Psychopharmacology, 20*, 59–69.

Gatz, M. (2000). Variations on depression in later life. In S. H. Qualls & N. Abeles (Eds.), *Psychology and the aging revolution: How we adapt to longer life* (pp. 173–196). Washington, DC: American Psychological Association.

Gaudiano, B. A. (2006). Is symptomatic improvement in clinical trials of cognitive-behavioral therapy for psychosis clinically significant? *Journal of Psychiatric Practice, 12*, 11–23.

Gavin, N. I., Gaynes, B. N., Lohr, K. N., Meltzer-Brody, S., Gartlehner, G., & Swinson, T. (2005). Perinatal depression: A systematic review of prevalence and incidence. *Obstetrics and Gynecology, 106*, 1071–1083.

Gearhardt, A. N., Corbin, W. R., & Brownell, K. D. (2009). Preliminary validation of the Yale Food Addiction Scale. *Appetite, 52*, 430–436.

Gehlert, S., Song, I. H., Chang, C. H., & Hartlage, S. A. (2009). The prevalence of premenstrual dysphoric disorder in a randomly selected group of urban and rural women. *Psychological Medicine, 39*, 129–136.

Geisler, D., Borchardt, V., Lord, A. R., Boehm, I., Ritschel, F., Zwipp, J., ... Ehrlich, S. (2016). Abnormal functional global and local brain connectivity in female patients with anorexia nervosa. *Journal of Psychiatry & Neuroscience, 41*, 6–15.

Gelernter, J., Kranzler, H. R., Sherva, R., Almasy, L., Herman, A. I., Koesterer, R., ... Farrer, L. A. (2015). Genome-wide association study of nicotine dependence in American populations: Identification of novel risk loci in both African-Americans and European-Americans. *Biological Psychiatry, 77*, 493–503.

Gelinas, B. L., & Gagnon, M. M. (2013). Pharmacological and psychological treatments of pathological skin-picking: A preliminary meta-analysis. *Journal of Obsessive-Compulsive and Related Disorders, 2*, 167–175.

Geller, B., Tillman, R., Craney, J. L., & Bolhofner, K. (2004). Four-year prospective outcome and natural history of mania in children with a prepubertal and early adolescent bipolar disorder phenotype. *Archives of General Psychiatry, 61*, 459–467.

Geller, J. L., & Morrissey, J. P. (2004). Asylum within and without asylums. *Psychiatry Services, 55*, 1128–1130.

Geller, J. L. (2006). The evolution of outpatient commitment in the USA: From conundrum to quagmire. *International Journal of Law and Psychiatry, 29*, 234–248.

Gendall, K., Joyce, P., Carter, F., McIntosh, V. V., Jordan, J., & Bulik, C. (2006). The psychobiology and diagnostic significance of amenorrhea in patients with anorexia nervosa. *Fertility and Sterility, 85*, 1531–1535.

Gentile, J. P., Gillig, P. M., Stinson, K., & Jensen, J. (2014). Toward impacting medical and psychiatric comorbidities in persons with intellectual/developmental disabilities: An initial prospective analysis. *Innovations in Clinical Neuroscience, 11*, 22–26.

Gerald, C., Walker, M., Criscione, L., Gustafson, E., Batzl-Hartmann, C., Smith, K., ... Schaffhauser, A. O. (1996). A receptor subtype involved in neuropeptide-Y-induced food intake. *Nature, 382*, 168–171.

Gerbasi, J. D., Bonnie, R. B., & Binder, R. L. (2000). Resource document on mandatory outpatient treatment. *Journal of the American Academy of Psychiatry and Law, 28*, 127–144.

Gibbon, S., Duggan, C., Stoffers, J., Huband, N., Vollm, B. A., Ferriter, M., & Lieb, K. (2010). Psychological interventions for antisocial personality disorder. *Cochrane Database of Systematic Reviews*, 6, CD007668.

Gibbons, L. E., Teri, L., Logsdon, R., McCurry, S. M., Kukull, W., Bowen, J., ... Larson, E. (2002). Anxiety symptoms as predictors of nursing home placement in patients with Alzheimer's disease. *Journal of Clinical Geropsychology, 8*, 335–342.

Gijs, L., & Gooren, L. (1996). Hormonal and psychopharmacological interventions in the treatment of paraphilias: An update. *Journal of Sex Research, 33*, 273–290.

Gilbertson, M. W., Shenton, M. E., Ciszewski, A., Kasai, K., & Lasko, N. B., Orr, S. P., & Pitman, R. K. (2002). Smaller hippocampal volume predicts pathologic vulnerability to psychological trauma. *Nature Neuroscience, 5*, 1242–1247.

Gili, M., Garcia-Toro, M., Vives, M., Armengol, S., Garcia-Campayo, J., Soriano, J. B., & Roca, M. (2011). Medical comorbidity in recurrent versus first-episode depressive patients. *Acta Psychiatric Scandinavica, 123*, 220–227.

Gilleland, J., Suveg, C., Jacob, M. L., & Thomassin, K. (2009). Understanding the medically unexplained: Emotional and familial influences on children's somatic functioning. *Child: Care, Health and Development, 35*, 383–390.

Gillerot, Y., Koulischer, L., Yasse, B., & Wetzburger, C. (1989). The geneticist and the so-called "sociocultural" familial mental retardation. *Journal de Génétique Humaine, 37*, 103–112.

Gitlin, M. (2006). Treatment-resistant bipolar disorder. *Molecular Psychiatry, 11*, 227–240.

Gjerde, L. C., Czajkowski, N., Roysamb, E., Ystrom, E., Tambs, K., Aggen, S. H., ... Knudsen, G. P. (2015). A longitudinal, population-based twin study of avoidant and obsessive-compulsive personality disorder traits from early to middle adulthood. *Psychological Medicine, 45*, 3539–3548.

Gladstone, G. L., Parker, G. B., Mitchell, P. B., Wilhelm, K. A., & Malhi, G. S. (2005). Relationship between self-reported childhood behavioral inhibition and lifetime anxiety disorders in a clinical sample. *Depression and Anxiety, 22*, 103–113.

Glaister, B. (1985). A case of auditory hallucination treated by satiation. *Behaviour Research and Therapy, 23*, 213–215.

Glazener, C. M., & Evans, J. H. (2002). Simple behavioural and physical interventions for nocturnal enuresis in children. *Cochrane Database of Systematic Reviews*, CD003637.

Gleaves, D. H., May, M. C., & Cardeña, E. (2001). An examination of the diagnostic validity of dissociative identity disorder. *Clinical Psychology Review, 21*, 577–608.

Glick, I. D., Clarkin, J. F., Haas, G. L., & Spencer, J. H., Jr. (1993). Clinical significance of inpatient family intervention: Conclusions from a clinical trial. *Hospital and Community Psychiatry, 44*, 869–873.

Gochman, P. A., Greenstein, D., Sporn, A., Gogtay, N., Keller, B., Shaw, P., & Rapoport, L. (2005). IQ stabilization in childhood-onset schizophrenia. *Schizophrenia Research, 77*, 271–277.

Godart, N., Flament, M., Perdereau, F., & Jeammet, P. (2002). Comorbidity between eating disorders and anxiety disorders: A review. *International Journal of Eating Disorders, 32*, 253–270.

Godlee, F., Smith, J., & Marcovitch, J. (2011). Wakefield's article linking MMR vaccine and autism was fraudulent. *British Medical Journal, 342*, c7452.

Gökalp, P. G., Tükel, R., Solmaz, D., Demir, T., Kiziltan, E., Demir, D., & Babaoðlu, A. N. (2001). Clinical features and co-morbidity of social phobics in Turkey. *European Psychiatry, 16*, 115–121.

Gold, L. (2005). American Psychiatric Association honors Dorothea Dix with first posthumous fellowship. *Psychiatric Services, 56*, 502.

Goldberg, D. P., & Hillier, V. F. (1979). A scaled version of the General Health Questionnaire. *Psychological Medicine, 9*, 139–145.

Goldberg, J. H., Breckenridge, J. N., & Sheikh, J. I. (2003). Age differences in symptoms of depression and anxiety: Examining behavioral medicine outpatients. *Journal of Behavioral Medicine, 26*, 119–132.

Goldberg, P. D., Peterson, B. D., Rosen, K. H., & Sara, M. L. (2008). Cybersex: The impact of a contemporary problem on the practices of marriage and family therapists. *Journal of Marital and Family Therapy, 34*, 469–480.

Golden, C. J., Purisch, A. D., & Hammeke, T. A. (1980). *The Luria-Nebraska Neuropsychological Battery: Manual* (Rev. ed.). Los Angeles: Western Psychological Services.

Goldfield, G. S., Adamo, K. B., Rutherford, J., & Legg, C. (2008). Stress and the relative reinforcing value of food in female binge eaters. *Physiology & Behavior, 93*, 579–587.

Goldstein, A. J., & Chambless, D. L. (1978). A reanalysis of agoraphobia. *Behavior Therapy, 9*, 47–59.

Goldstein, R. B., Dawson, D. A., Saha, T. D., Ruan, W. J., Compton, W. M., & Grant, B. F. (2007). Antisocial behavioral syndromes and DSM-IV alcohol use disorders: Results from the National Epidemiologic Survey on Alcohol and Related Conditions. *Alcoholism: Clinical and Experimental Research, 31*, 814–828.

Goldstein, T. R., Fersch-Podrat, R., Axelson, D. A., Gilbert, A., Hlastala, S. A., Birmaher, B., & Frank, E. (2014). Early intervention for adolescents at high risk for the development of bipolar disorder: Pilot study of interpersonal and social rhythm therapy (IPSRT). *Psychotherapy, 51*, 180–189.

Goldstein, T. R., Fersch-Podrat, R. K., Rivera, M., Axelson, D. A., Merranko, J., Yu, H., ... Birmaher, B. (2015). Dialectical behavior therapy for adolescents with bipolar disorder: Results from a pilot randomized trial. *Journal of Child and Adolescent Psychopharmacology, 25*, 140–149.

Goldston, D. B., Molock, S. D., Whitbeck, L. B., Murakami, J. L., Zayas, L. H., & Nagayama Hall, G. C. (2008). Cultural considerations in adolescent suicide prevention and psychosocial treatment. *American Psychologist, 63*, 14–31.

Goldston, K., & Baillie, A. J. (2008). Depression and coronary heart disease: A review of the epidemiological evidence, explanatory mechanisms and management approaches. *Clinical Psychology Review, 28*, 288–306.

Gomes, B. C., Abreu, L. N., Brietzke, E., Caetano, S. C., Kleinman, A., Nery, F. G., & Lafer, B. (2011). A randomized controlled trial of cognitive behavioral group therapy for bipolar disorder. *Psychotherapy and Psychosomatics, 80*, 144–150.

Gonçalves, D. C., & Byrne, G. J. (2012). Interventions for generalized anxiety disorder in older adults: Systematic review and meta-analysis. *Journal of Anxiety Disorders, 26*, 1–11.

Gonçalves, R., Pderozo, A. L., Coutinho, E. S. F., Figueira, I., & Ventura, P. (2012). Efficacy of virtual reality exposure therapy in the treatment of PTSD: A systematic review. *PLOS ONE, 7*, e48469.

Gonzalez de Mejia, E., & Ramirez-Mares, M. V. (2014). Impact of caffeine and coffee on our health. *Trends in Endocrinology & Metabolism, 25*, 489–492.

González, H. M., Haan, M. N., & Hinton, L. (2001). Acculturation and the prevalence of depression in older Mexican Americans: Baseline results of the Sacramento Area Latino Study on Aging. *Journal of the American Geriatrics Society, 49*, 948–953.

Goodman, M., New, A. S., & Siever, L. J. (2004). Trauma, genes, and the neurobiology of personality disorders. *Annals of the New York Academy of Sciences, 1032*, 104–116.

Goodman, W. K., Grice, D. E., Lapidus, K. A., & Coffey, B. J. (2014). Obsessive-compulsive disorder. *Psychiatric Clinics of North America, 37*, 257–267.

Goodman, Y., Bruce, A. J., Cheng, B., & Mattson, M. P. (1996). Estrogens attenuate and corticosterone exacerbates excitotoxicity, oxidative injury and amyloid beat-peptide toxicity in hippocampal neurons. *Journal of Neurochemistry, 5*, 1836–1844.

Gooren, L. (2006). The biology of human psychosexual differentiation. *Hormonal Behavior, 50*, 589–601.

Gottesman, I. I. (2001). Psychopathology through a life span-genetic prism. *American Psychologist, 56*, 867–878.

Gould, M. S. (1990). Teenage suicide clusters. *Journal of the American Medical Association, 263*, 2051–2052.

Gould, R. L., Coulson, M. C., & Howard, R. J. (2012). Efficacy of cognitive behavioral therapy for anxiety disorders in older people: A meta-analysis and meta-regression of randomized controlled trials. *Journal of the American Geriatrics Society, 60*, 218–229.

Grabe, H. J., Meyer, C., Hapke, U., Rumpf, H. J., Freyberger, H. J., Dilling, H., & John, U. (2003). Somatoform pain disorder in the general population. *Psychotherapy and Psychosomatics, 72*, 88–94.

Graetz, B.W., Sawyer, M.G., Hazell, PlL., Arney, F., & Baghurst, P.L. (2001). Validity of DSM-IV ADHD subtypes in a natonally representative sample of Australian children and adolescents. *Journal of the American Academy of Child and Adolescent Psychiatry, 40*, 1410–1417.

Graham, J. R. (2000). *MMPI-2: Assessing Personality and Psychopathology* (3rd ed.). New York: Oxford University Press.

Grandin, L. D., Alloy, L. B., & Abramson, L. Y. (2006). The social zeitgeber theory, circadian rhythms, and mood disorders: Review and evaluation. *Clinical Psychology Review, 26*, 679–694.

Granholm, E., McQuaid, J. R., McClure, F. S., Auslander, L. A., Perivoliotis, D., Pedrelli, P., ... Jeste, D. V. (2005). A randomized, controlled trial of cognitive behavioral social skills training for middle-aged and older outpatients with chronic schizophrenia. *American Journal of Psychiatry, 162*, 520–529.

Grant, B. F., Hasin, D. S., Stinson, F. S., Dawson, D. A., Chou, S. P., Ruan, W. J., & Pickering, R. P. (2004). Prevalence, correlates, and disability of personality disorders in the United States: Results from the national epidemiologic survey on alcohol and related conditions. *Journal of Clinical Psychiatry, 65*, 948–958.

Grant, B. F., Chou, S. P., Goldstein, R. B., Huang, B., Stinson, F. S., Saha, T. D., ... Ruan, W. J. (2008). Prevalence, correlates, disability, and comorbidity of DSM-IV borderline personality disorder: Results from the Wave 2 National Epidemiologic Survey on Alcohol and Related Conditions. *Journal of Clinical Psychiatry, 69*, 533–545.

Grant, B. F., Goldstein, R. B., Saha, T. D., Chou, S. P., Jung, J., Zhang, H., ... Hasin, D. S. (2015). Epidemiology of DSM-5 alcohol use disorder: Results from the National Epidemiologic Survey on Alcohol and Related Conditions III. *JAMA Psychiatry, 72*, 757–766.

Grant, J. E., Brewer, J. A., & Potenza, M. N. (2006). The neurobiology of substance and behavioral addictions. *CNS Spectrums, 11*, 924–930.

Grant, J. E. (2006). Understanding and treating kleptomania: New models and new treatments. *The Israel Journal of Psychiatry and Related Sciences, 43*, 81–87.

Grant, J. E., Potenza, M. N., Weinstein, A., & Gorelick, D. A. (2010). Introduction to behavioral addictions. *American Journal of Drug and Alcohol Abuse, 36*, 233–241.

Grant, J. E., & Kim, S. W. (2007). Clinical characteristics and psychiatric comorbidity of pyromania. *The Journal of Clinical Psychiatry, 68*, 1478–1722.

Grant, J. E., Kim, S. W., & Odlaug, B. L. (2009). A double-blind, placebo-controlled study of the opiate antagonist, naltrexone, in the treatment of kleptomania. *Biological Psychiatry, 65*, 600–606.

Grant, J. E., Mooney, M. E., & Kushner, M. G. (2012). Prevalence, correlates, and comorbidity of DSM-IV obsessive-compulsive personality disorder: Results from the National Epidemiologic Survey on Alcohol and Related Conditions. *Journal of Psychiatric Practice, 46*, 469–475.

Grant, J. E., & Potenza, M. N. (2008). Gender-related differences in individuals seeking treatment for kleptomania. *CNS Spectrums, 13*, 235–245.

Grant, J. E., Schreiber, L. R., & Odlaug, B. L. (2013). Phenomenology and treatment of behavioural addictions. *Canadian Journal of Psychiatry, 58*, 252–259.

Grant, J. E., & Stein, D. J. (2014). Body-focused repetitive behavior disorders in ICD-11. *Revista Brasileira de Psiquiatria, 36*, 59–64.

Gravestock, S. (2000). Eating disorders in adults with intellectual disability. *Journal of Intellectual Disability Research, 44* (Pt. 6), 625–637.

Gray, R., Parr, A. M., & Robson, D. (2005). Has tardive dyskinesia disappeared? *Mental Health Practice, 8*, 20–22.

Green, M., & Horan, W. P. (2010). Social cognition in schizophrenia. *Current Directions in Psychological Science, 19*, 243–248.

Green, M. F., Nuechterlein, K. H., Gold, J. M., Barch, D. M., Coehen, J., Essock, S., … Keefe, R. S. (2004). Approaching a consensus battery for clinical trials in schizophrenia: The NIMH-MATRICS conference to select cognitive domains and test criteria. *Biological Psychiatry, 56*, 301–307.

Green, R., & Money, J. (1969). *Transsexualism and sex reassignment.* Baltimore, MD: Johns Hopkins University Press.

Green, R. (1987). *The "Sissy Boy Syndrome" and the development of homosexuality.* New Haven, CT: Yale University Press.

Greenberg, B. D., Malone, D. A., Friehs, G. M., Rezai, A. R., Kubu, C. S., Malloy, P. F., … Rasmussen, S. A. (2006). Three-year outcomes in deep brain stimulation for highly resistant obsessive-compulsive disorder. *Neuropsychopharmacology, 31*.

Greenberg, P. E., Sisitsky, T., Kessler, R. C., Finkelstein, S. N., Berndt, E. R., Davidson, J. R., … Fyer, A. J. (1999). The economic burden of anxiety disorders in the 1990s. *The Journal of Clinical Psychiatry, 60*, 427–435.

Greenberg, P. E., Fournier, A. A., Sisitsky, T., Pike, C. T., & Kessler, R. C. (2015). The economic burden of adults with major depressive disorder in the United States (2005 and 2010). *Journal of Clinical Psychiatry, 76*, 155–162.

Greene, R. W., Biederman, J., Faraone, S. V., Monuteaux, M. C., Mick, E., Fine, C. S., … Goring, J. C. (2001). Social impairment in girls with ADHD: Patterns, gender comparisons, and correlates. *Journal of the American Academy of Child and Adolescent Psychiatry, 40*, 704–710.

Greene, S. L., Kerr, F., & Braitberg, G. (2008). Review article: Amphetamines and related drugs of abuse. *Emergency Medicine Australasia, 20*, 391–402.

Greenhill, L., Kollins, S., Abikoff, H., McCracken, J., Riddle, M., Swanson, J., … Cooper, T. (2006). Efficacy and safety of immediate-release methylphenidate treatment for pre-schoolers with ADHD. *Journal of the American Academy of Child and Adolescent Psychiatry, 45*, 1284–1293.

Gren-Landell, M., Bjorklind, A., Tillfors, M., Furkarm, T., Svedin, C. G., & Andersson, G. (2009). Evaluation of the psychometric properties of a modified version of the Social Phobia Screening Questionnaire for use in adolescents. *Child and Adolescent Psychiatry and Mental Health, 3*, 36.

Grenard, J., Ames, S., Pentz, M., & Sussman, S. (2006). Motivational interviewing with adolescents and young adults for drug-related problems. *International Journal of Adolescent Medical Health, 18*, 53–67.

Grenier, G., & Byers, E. S. (2001). Operationalizing premature or rapid ejaculation. *Journal of Sex Research, 38*, 369–378.

Grenier, S., Préville, M., Boyer, R., & O'Connor, K. (2009). Prevalence and correlates of obsessive-compulsive disorder among older adults living in the community. *Journal of Anxiety Disorders, 23*, 858–865.

Grice, D. E., Halmi, K. A., Fichter, M. M., Strober, M., Woodside, D. B., Treasure, J. T., … Berrettini, W. H. (2002). Evidence for a susceptibility gene for anorexia nervosa on chromosome 1. *American Journal of Human Genetics, 70*, 787–792.

Grigsby, R. K., Thyer, B. A., Waller, R. J., & Johnston, G. A., Jr. (1999). Chalk eating in middle Georgia: A culture-bound syndrome of pica? *Southern Medical Journal, 92*, 190–192.

Grilo, C. M., & Masheb, R. M. (2000). Onset of dieting vs binge eating in outpatients with binge eating disorder. *International Journal of Obesity and Related Metabolic Disorders, 24*, 404–409.

Grilo, C. M., White, M. A., & Masheb, R. M. (2009). DSM-IV psychiatric disorder comorbidity and its correlates in binge eating disorder. *International Journal of Eating Disorders, 42*, 228–234.

Grimmer, Y., Hohmann, S., & Poustka, L. (2014). Is bipolar always bipolar? Understanding the controversy on bipolar disorder in children. *F1000Prime Rep, 6*, 111.

Grob, G. N. (1994). *The mad among us: A history of the care of America's mentally ill.* Cambridge, MA: Harvard University Press.

Grootens, K. P., & Verkes, R. J. (2005). Emerging evidence for the use of atypical antipsychotics in borderline personality disorder. *Pharmapsychiatry, 38*, 20–23.

Gross, J. A., Bureau, A., Croteau, J., Galfalvy, H., Oquendo, M. A., Haghighi, F., … Turecki, G. (2015). A genome-wide copy number variant study of suicidal behavior. *PLOS ONE, 10*, e0128369.

Grove, L. J., Loeb, S. J., & Penrod, J. (2009). Selective optimization with compensation: A model for elder health programming. *Clinical Nurse Specialist, 23*, 25–32.

Grove, W. M. (2005). Clinical versus statistical prediction: The contribution of Paul E. Meehl. *Journal of Clinical Psychology, 61*, 1233–1243.

Grove, W. M., Zald, D. H., Lebow, B. S., Snitz, B. E., & Nelson, C. (2000). Clinical versus mechanical prediction: A meta-analysis. *Psychological Assessment, 12*, 19–30.

Grover, S., & Ghosh, A. (2014). Somatic symptom and related disorders in Asians and Asian Americans. *Asian Journal of Psychiatry, 7*, 77–79.

Gruber, V. A., Delucchi, K. L., Kielstein, A., & Batki, S. L. (2008). A randomized trial of 6-month methadone maintenance with standard or minimal counseling versus 21-day methadone detoxification. *Drug and Alcohol Dependence, 94*, 199–206.

Grucza, R., & Beirut, L. (2007). Co-occurring risk factors for alcohol dependence and habitual smoking: Update on findings from the Collaborative Study on the Genetics of Alcoholism. *Alcohol Research & Health, 29*, 172–177.

Grunhaus, L., Schreiber, S., Dolberg, O. T., Polak, D., & Dannon, P. N. (2003). A randomized controlled comparison of electroconvulsive therapy and repetitive transcranial magnetic stimulation in severe and resistant nonpsychotic major depression. *Biological Psychiatry, 53*, 324–331.

Guarnaccia, P. J., Lewis-Fernandez, R., Pincay, I. M., Shrout, P., Guo, J., Torres, M., … Alegria, M. (2010). Ataque de nervios as a marker of social and psychiatric vulnerability: Results from the NLAAS. *International Journal of Social Psychiatry, 56*, 298–309.

Guglielmi, V., Vulink, N. C., Denys, D., Wang, Y., Samuels, J. F., & Nestadt, G. (2014). Obsessive-compulsive disorder and female reproductive cycle events: Results from the OCD and Reproduction Collaborative Study. *Depression and Anxiety, 31*, 979–987.

Gull, W. W. (1874). Anorexia nervosa (apepsia hysterica, anorexia hysterica). *Transactions of the Clinical Society of London, 7*, 22–28.

Gum, A. M., Iser, L., & Petkus, A. (2010). Behavioral health service utilization and preferences of older adults receiving home-based aging services. *The American Journal of Geriatric Psychiatry, 18*, 491–501.

Gunderson, J. (1984). *The borderline patient.* Washington, DC: American Psychiatric Press.

Gunderson, J. G., Zanarini, M. C., Choi-Kain, L. W., Mitchell, K. S., Jang, K. L., & Hudson, J. I. (2011). Family study of borderline personality disorder and its sectors of psychopathology. *Archives of General Psychiatry, 68*, 753–762.

Gupta, A. R., & State, M. W. (2007). Recent advances in the genetics of autism. *Biological Psychiatry, 61*, 429–437.

Gurak, K., & Weisman de Mamani, A. (2015). Caregiver expressed emotion and psychiatric symptoms in African-Americans with schizophrenia: An attempt to understand the paradoxical relationship. *Family Process*, Oct 23. doi: 10.1111/famp.12188. [Epub ahead of print].

Gureje, O., Simon, G. E., Ustun, T. B., & Goldberg, D. P. (1997). Somatization in cross-cultural perspective: A World Health Organization study in primary care. *American Journal of Psychiatry, 154*, 989–995.

Gurland, B. J. (2004). Epidemiology of psychiatric disorders. In J. Sadavoy, L. F. Jarvik, G. T. Grossberg, & B. S. Meyers (Eds.), *Comprehensive textbook of geriatric psychology* (3rd ed., pp. 3–37). New York: W.W. Norton & Co.

Gurvits, T. V., Shenton, M. E., Hokama, H., Ohta, H., Lasko, N. B., Gilbertson, M. W., … Pitman, R. K. (1996). Magnetic resonance imaging study of hippocampal volume in chronic, combat-related posttraumatic stress disorder. *Biological Psychiatry, 40*, 1091–1099.

Gurwitch, R. J., Kees, M., & Becker, S.M. (2002). In the face of tragedy: Placing children's reactions to trauma in a new context. *Cognitive and Behavioral Practice, 9*, 286–295.

Gutierrez, E. (2013). A rat in the labyrinth of anorexia nervosa: Contributions of the activity-based anorexia rodent model to the understanding of anorexia nervosa. *International Journal of Eating Disorders, 46*, 289–301.

Haagen, J. F., Smid, G. E., Knipscheer, J. W., & Kleber, R. J. (2015). The efficacy of recommended treatments for veterans with PTSD: A metaregression analysis. *Clinical Psychology Review, 40*, 184–194.

Haas, L. F. (1993). Benjamin Rush (1745–1813). *Journal of Neurology, Neurosurgery, and Psychiatry, 56*, 741.

Haas, L. F. (2001). Jean Martin Charcot (1825–1893) and Jean Baptise Charcot (1867–1936). *Journal of Neurology, Neurosurgery, and Psychiatry, 71*, 524.

Haeri, S., Williams, J., Kopeykina, I., Johnson, J., Newmark, A., Cohen, L., & Galynker, I. (2011). Disparities in diagnosis of bipolar disorder in individuals of African and European descent: A review. *Journal of Psychiatric Practice, 17*, 394–403.

Hagopian, L. P., Rooker, G. W., & Rolider, N. U. (2011). Identifying empirically supported treatments for pica in individuals with intellectual disabilities. *Research in Developmental Disabilities, 32*, 2114–2120.

Haijma, S. V., Van Haren, N., Cahn. W., Koolschijn, C. M. P., Hulshoff Pol, H. E., & Kahn, R. S. (2013). Brain volumes in schizophrenia: A meta-analysis in over 18,000 subjects. *Schizophrenia Bulletin, 39*, 1129–1138.

Hakulinen, C., Elovainio, M., Pulkki-Raback, L., Virtanen, M., Kivimaki, M., & Jokela, M. (2015). Personality and depressive symptoms: Individual participant meta-analysis of 10 cohort studies. *Depression & Anxiety, 32*, 461–470.

Hall, W. D. (2006). How have the SSRI antidepressants affected suicide risk? *Lancet*, 1959–1962.

Hammond, C. J., Mayers, L. C., & Potenza, M. N. (2014). Neurobiology of adolescent substance use and addictive behaviors: Treatment implications. *Adolescent Medicine: State of The Art Reviews, 25*, 15–32.

Han, B., Compton, W. M., Gfroerer, J., & McKeon, R. (2015). Prevalence and correlates of past 12-month suicide attempt among adults with past-year suicidal ideation in the United States. *Journal of Clinical Psychiatry, 76*, 295–302.

Hancock, D. B., Wang, J. C., Gaddis, N. C., Levy, J. L., Saccone, N. L., Stitzel, J. A., … Johnson, E. O. (2015). A multiancestry study identifies novel genetic associations with CHRNA5 methylation in human brain and risk of nicotine dependence. *Human Molecular Genetics, 24*, 5940–5954.

Handen, B. L., & Gilchrist, R. (2006). Practitioner review: Psychopharmacology in children and adolescents with mental retardation. *Journal of Child Psychology and Psychiatry, 47*, 871–882.

Hanna, G. H. (2000). Clinical and family-genetic studies of childhood obsessive-compulsive disorder. In W. K. Goodman, & J. D. Maser (Eds.), *Obsessive-compulsive disorder: Contemporary issues in treatment* (pp. 87–103). Mahwah, NJ: Lawrence Erlbaum Associates, Publishers.

Hansen, R. A., Gartlehner, G., Lohr, K. N., Gaynes, B. N., & Carey, T. S. (2005). Efficacy and safety of second-generation antidepressants in the treatment of major depressive disorder. *Annals of Internal Medicine, 143*, 415–426.

Hanson, R. K., & Slater, S. (1988). Sexual victimization in the history of sexual abuses: A review. *Annals of Sex Research, 1*, 485–499.

Harmon, R. B. (2009). Hydrotherapy in state mental hospitals in the mid-twentieth century. *Issues in Mental Health Nursing, 30*, 491–494.

Harris, E. C., & Barraclough, B. (1997). Suicide as an outcome for mental disorders. A meta-analysis. *British Journal of Psychiatry, 170*, 205–228.

Harris, M. G., Henry, L. P., Harrigan, S. M., Purcell, R., Schwartz, O. S., Farrelly, S. E., … McGorry, P. D. (2005). The relationship between duration of untreated psychosis and outcome: An eight-year prospective study. *Schizophrenia Research, 70*, 85–93.

Harris, M. J., & Jeste, D. V. (1988). Late-onset schizophrenia: An overview. *Schizophrenia Bulletin, 14*, 39–45.

Harrod, C. S., Goss, C. W., Stallones, L., & DiGuiseppi, C. (2014). Interventions for primary prevention of suicide in university and other post-secondary educational settings. *Cochrane Database of Systematic Reviews, 10*, CD009439.

Harrow, M., Grossman, L. S., Jobe, T. H., & Herbener, E. S. (2005). Do patients with schizophrenia ever show periods of recovery? *Schizophrenia Bulletin, 31*, 723–734.

Harsh, V., Meltzer-Brody, S., Rubinow, D. R., & Schmidt, P. J. (2009). Reproductive aging, sex steroids, and mood disorders. *Harvard Review of Psychiatry, 17*, 87–102.

Hart, A. B., & Kranzler, H. R. (2015). Alcohol dependence genetics: Lessons learned from genome-wide association studies (GWAS) and post-GWAS analyses. *Alcoholism: Clinical and Experimental Research, 39*, 1312–1327.

Hartberg, C. B., Jorgensen, K. N., Haukvik, U. K., Westlye, L. T., Melle, I., Andreassen, O. A., & Agartz, I. (2015). Lithium treatment and hippocampal subfields and amygdala volumes in bipolar disorder. *Bipolar Disorders, 17*, 496–506.

Hartung, C. M., Willcutt, E. G., Lahey, B. B., Pelham, W. E., Loney, J., Stein, M. A., & Keenan, K. (2002). Sex differences in young children who meet criteria for attention deficit hyperactivity disorder. *Journal of Clinical Child and Adolescent Psychology, 31*, 453–464.

Hartwell, C. E. (1996). The schizophrenogenic mother concept in American psychiatry. *Psychiatry, 59*, 274–297.

Hasin, D., Grant, B., & Endicott, J. (1990). The natural history of alcohol abuse: Implications for definitions of alcohol use disorders. *American Journal of Psychiatry, 147*, 1537–1541.

Haug, S., Nunez, C. L., Becker, J., Hamel, G., & Schaub, M. P. (2014). Predictors of onset of cannabis and other drug use in male young adults: Results from a longitudinal study. *BMC Public Health, 14*, 1202.

Hawton, K. (1995). Treatment of sexual dysfunctions by sex therapy and other approaches. *The British Journal of Psychiatry, 167*, 307–314.

Hay, P. (1998). The epidemiology of eating disorder behaviors: An Australian community-based survey. *International Journal of Eating Disorders, 23*, 371–382.

Hay, P. J., Mond, J., Buttner, P., & Darby, A. (2008). Eating disorder behaviors are increasing: Findings from two sequential community surveys in South Australia. *PLOS ONE, 3*, e1541.

Hayden, E. P., & Nurnberger, J. I., Jr. (2006). Molecular genetics of bipolar disorder. *Genes, Brain, and Behavior, 5*, 85–95.

Hayes, S. C., Wilson, K. G., Gifford, E. V., Follette, V. M. & Strosahl, K. (1996). Experimental avoidance and behavioral disorders: A functional dimensional approach to diagnosis and treatment. *Journal of Consulting and Clinical Psychology, 64*, 1152–1168.

Hayes, S. L., Storch, E. A., & Berlanga, L. (2009). Skin picking behaviors: An examination of the prevalence and severity in a community sample. *Journal of Anxiety Disorders, 23*, 314–319.

Haynes, S. N., & O'Brien, W. H. (2003). *Principles and practice of behavioral assessment*. New York: Kluwer Academic/ Plenum Publishers.

Hayward, C., Killen, J. D., Kraemer, H. C., & Taylor, C. B. (1998). Linking self-reported childhood behavioral inhibition to adolescent social phobia. *Journal of the American Academy of Child & Adolescent Psychiatry, 37*, 1308–1316.

Hayward, C., Killen, J. D., Kraemer, H. C., & Taylor, C. B. (2000). Predictors of panic attacks in adolescents. *Journal of the American Academy of Child and Adolescent Psychiatry, 39*, 207–214.

Hazell, P., & Mirzaie, M. (2013). Tricyclic drugs for depression in children and adolescents. *Cochrane Database of Systematic Reviews, 18*, CD002317.

Heather, N. (1995). The great controlled drinking consensus: Is it premature? *Addiction, 90*, 1160–1163.

Hechtman, L., & Greenfield, B. (2003). Long-term use of stimulants in children with attention deficit hyperactivity disorder. *Pediatric Drugs, 5*, 787–794.

Hedman, E., Ljótsson, E., Rück, C., Bergström, J., Andersson, G., Kaldo, V., ... Lindefors, N. (2013). Effectiveness of internet-based cognitive behaviour therapy for panic disorder in routine psychiatric care. *Acta Psychiatrica Scandinavica, 128*, 457–467.

Heffner, C. L. (1999–2003). Chapter 3: Section 6: Freud's ego defense mechanisms. In C.L. Heffner. Editor (Ed.), *Psychology 101*. AllPsych and Heffner Media Group, Inc., www.allpsych.com.

Heiby, E. M. (2002). Concluding remarks on the debate about prescription privileges for psychologists. *Journal of Clinical Psychology, 58*, 709–722.

Heim, C., Newport, D. J., Miller, A. H., & Nemeroff, C. B. (2000). Long-term neuroendocrine effects of childhood maltreatment. *Journal of the American Medical Association, 284*, 2321.

Heim, C., & Nemeroff, C. (1999). The impact of early adverse experiences on brain systems involved in the pathophysiology of anxiety and affective disorders. *Biological Psychiatry, 46*, 1509–1522.

Heiman, J., & LoPiccolo, J. (1987). *Become orgasmic: A sexual and personal growth program for women*. New York: Simon & Schuster.

Heiman, J. R. (2002). Sexual dysfunction: Overview of prevalence, etiological factors, and treatments. *Journal of Sexual Research, 39*, 73–78.

Hellekson, K. L. (2001). NIH consensus statement on phenylketonuria. *American Family Physician, 63*, 1430–1432.

Hellström, K., Fellenius, J., & Ost, L. G. (1996). One versus five sessions of applied tension in the treatment of blood phobia. *Behaviour Research and Therapy, 34*, 101–112.

Hendriks, G. J., Kampman, M., Keijsers, G. P., Hoogduin, C. A., & Voshaar, R. C. O. (2014). Cognitive-behavioral therapy for panic disorder with agoraphobia in older people: A comparison with younger patients. *Depression and Anxiety, 31*, 669–677.

Henggeler, S. W., Schoenwald, S. K., Borduin, C. M., Rowland, M. D., & Cunningham, P. B. (1998). *Multisystemic treatment of antisocial behavior in children and adolescents*. New York: Guilford Press.

Henggeler, S. W., Rowland, M. D., Randall, J., Ward, D. M., Pickrel, S. G., Cunningham, P. B., ... Santos, A. B. (1999). Home-based multisystemic therapy as an alternative to the hospitalization of youths in psychiatric crisis: Clinical outcomes. *Journal of Clinical Child Psychology, 38*, 1381–1389.

Henshaw, C. (2003). Mood disturbance in the early puerperium: A review. *Archives of Women's Mental Health, 6*, S33–S42.

Hepp, U., Wittmann, L., Schnyder, U., & Michel, K. (2004). Psychological and psychosocial interventions after attempted suicide: An overview of treatment studies. *Crisis, 25, 108–117.*

Hepp, U., Kraemer, B., Schnyder, U., Miller, N., & Delsignore, A. (2005). Psychiatric comorbidity in gender identity disorder. *Journal of Psychosomatic Research, 58*, 259–261.

Herbeck, D. M., Brecht, M. L., & Pham, A. Z. (2013). Racial/ ethnic differences in health status and morbidity among adults who use methamphetamine. *Psychology, Health & Medicine, 18*, 262–274.

Herbert, J. D., Hope, D. A., & Bellack, A. S. (1992). Validity of the distinction between generalized social phobia and avoidant personality disorder. *Journal of Abnormal Psychology, 101*, 332–339.

Herbert, J. D., Gaudiano, B. A., Rheingold, A. A., Moitra, E., Myers, V. H., Dalrymple, K. L. & Brandsma, L. L. (2009). Cognitive behavior therapy for generalized social anxiety disorder in adolescents: A randomized controlled trial. *Journal of Anxiety Disorders, 23*, 167–177.

Herman, J. L., Perry, J. C., & van der Kolk, B. A. (1989). Childhood trauma in borderline personality disorder. *American Journal of Psychiatry, 146*, 490–495.

Herpertz-Dahlmann, B., Seitz, J., & Konrad, K. (2011). Aetiology of anorexia nervosa: From a "psychosomatic family model" to a neuropsychiatric disorder? *European Archives in Psychiatry and Clinical Neuroscience, 261* (Suppl 2), S177–S181.

Herzog, D. B., Dorer, D. J., Keel, P. K., Selwyn, S. E., Ekeblad, E. R., Flores, A. T., ... Keller, M. B. (1999). Recovery and relapse in anorexia and bulimia nervosa: A 7.5-year follow-up study. *Journal of the American Academy of Child and Adolescent Psychiatry, 38*, 829–837.

Hettema, J., Prescott, C., & Kendler, K. (2001). A population-based twin study of generalized anxiety disorder in men and women. *The Journal of Nervous and Mental Disease, 189*, 413–420.

Hettema, J. M., Prescott, C. A., Myers, J. M., Neale, M. C., & Kendler, K. S. (2005). The structure of genetic and environmental risk factors for anxiety disorders in men and women. *Archives in General Psychiatry, 62*, 182–189.

Heylens, G., Verroken, C., De Cock, S., T'Sjoen, G., & De Cypere, G. (2014). Effects of different steps in gender reassignment therapy on psychopathology: A prospective study of persons with a gender identity disorder. *Journal of Sexual Medicine, 11*, 119–126.

Heylens, G., Elaut, E., Kreukels, B. P. C., Paap, M. C. S., Cerwenka, S., Richter-Appelt, H., ... De Cuypere, G. (2014). Psychiatric characteristics in transsexual individuals: Multicentre study in four European countries. *The British Journal of Psychiatry, 204*, 151–156.

Hezel, D. M., & McNally, R. J. (2015). A theoretical review of cognitive biases and deficits in obsessive-compulsive disorder. *Biological Psychology*, pii: S0301-0511(15)30073-9.

Hibbard, S. (2003). A critique of Lilienfeld et al.'s (2000) The scientific status of projective techniques. *Journal of Personality Assessment, 80*, 260–271.

Hill, K. P. (2015). Medical marijuana for treatment of chronic pain and other medical and psychiatric problems: A clinical review. *Journal of the American Medical Association, 313*, 2474–2483.

Hillebrand, J. J., Koeners, M. P., de Rijke, C. E., Kas, M. J., & Adan, R. A. (2005). Leptin treatment in activity-based anorexia. *Biological Psychiatry, 58*, 165–171.

Hines, M., Brook, C., & Conway, G. S. (2004). Androgen and psychosexual development: Core gender identity, sexual orientation and recalled childhood gender role behavior in women and men with congenital adrenal hyperplasia (CAH). *Journal of Sex Research, 41*, 75–81.

Hiraishi, K., Sasaki, S., Shikishima, C., & Ando, J. (2012). The second to fourth digit ration (2D:4D) in a Japanese twin sample. *Archives of Sexual Behavior, 41*, 711–724.

Hoang, U., Goldacre, M., & James, A. (2014). Mortality following hospital discharge with a diagnosis of eating disorder: National record linkage study, England, 2001–2009. *International Journal of Eating Disorders, 47*, 507–515.

Hoberg, A. A., Ponto, J., Nelson, P. J., & Frye, M. A. (2013). Group interpersonal and social rhythm therapy for bipolar depression. *Perspectives in Psychiatric Care, 49*, 226–234.

Hodgins, S., Mednick, S. A., Brennan, P. A., Schulsinger, F., & Engberg, M. (1996). Mental disorder and crime: Evidence from a Danish birth cohort. *Archives of General Psychiatry, 53*, 489–496.

Hoek, H., & van Hoeken, D. (2003). Review of the prevalence and incidence of eating disorders. *International Journal of Eating Disorders, 34*, 383–396.

Hoek, H. W., Bartelds, A. I., Bosveld, J. J., van der Graaf, Y., Limpens, V. E., Maiwald, M., & Spaaij, C. J. (1995). Impact of urbanization on detection rates of eating disorders. *American Journal of Psychiatry, 152*, 1272–1278.

Hoffman, E. R., Gagne, D. A., Thornton, L. M., Klump, K. L., Brandt, H., Crawford, S., ... Bulik, C. M. (2012). Understanding the association of impulsivity, obsessions, and compulsions with binge eating and purging behaviours in anorexia nervosa. *European Eating Disorders Review, 20*, e129–e136.

Hoffman, R. E., Hawkins, K. A., Gueorguieva, R., Boutros, N. N., Rachid, F., Carroll, K., & Krystal, J.H. (2003). Transcranial magnetic stimulation of left temporoparietal cortex and medication-resistant auditory hallucinations. *Archives of General Psychiatry, 60*, 49–56.

Hofmann, S. G., Anu Asnaani, M. A., & Hinton, D. E. (2010). Cultural aspects in social anxiety and social anxiety disorder. *Depression & Anxiety, 27*, 1117–1127.

Hoge, C. W., Terhakopian, A., Castro, C. A., Messer, S. C., & Engel, C. C. (2007). Association of posttraumatic stress disorder with somatic symptoms, health care visits, and absenteeism among Iraq war veterans. *American Journal of Psychiatry, 164*, 150–153.

Hoge, E. A., Bui, E., Marques, L., Metcalf, C. A., Morris, L. K., Robinaugh, D.J., ... Simon, N. M. (2013). Randomized controlled trial of mindfulness meditation for generalized anxiety disorder: Effects on anxiety and stress reactivity. *Journal of Clinical Psychiatry, 74*, 786–792.

Holden, C. (2010). Behavioral addictions debut in proposed DSM-V. *Science, 327*, 935.

Holgate, S. T., Komaroff, A. L., Mangan, D., & Wessley, S. (2011). Chronic fatigue syndrome: Understanding a complex illness. *Nature Views for Neuroscience, 12*, 539–544.

Hollander, E., Phillips, A., Chaplin, W., Zagursky, K., Novotny, S., Wasserman, S., & Iyengar, R. (2005). A placebo controlled crossover trial of liquid fluoxetine on repetitive behaviors in childhood and adolescent autism. *Neuropsychopharmacology, 30*, 582–589.

Hollis, C. (2000). Adult outcomes of child- and adolescent-onset schizophrenia: Diagnostic stability and predictive validity. *American Journal of Psychiatry, 157*, 1652–1659.

Hollon, S. D., DeRubeis, R. J., Evans, M. D., Wiemer, M. J., Garvey, M. J., Grove, W. M., & Tuason, V. B. (1992). Cognitive therapy and pharmacotherapy for depression: Singly and in combination. *Archives of General Psychiatry, 49*, 774–781.

Holmes, E. A., Brown, R. J., Mansell, W., Fearon, P., Hunter, E. C. M., Frasquilho, F., & Oakley, D. A. (2005). Are there two qualitatively distinct forms of dissociation? A review and some clinical implications. *Clinical Psychology Review, 25*, 1–23.

Holmgren, P., Norden-Pettersson, L., & Ahlner, J. (2004). Caffeine fatalities—Four case reports. *Forensic Science International, 139*, 71–73.

Holt, C. S., Heimberg, R. G., & Hope, D. A. (1992). Avoidant personality disorder and the generalized subtype of social phobia. *Journal of Abnormal Psychology, 101*, 318–325.

Honda, H., Shimizu, Y., & Rutter, M. (2005). No effect of MMR withdrawal on the incidence of autism: A total population study. *Journal of Child Psychiatry and Psychology, 46*, 572–579.

Hone-Blanchet, A., Wensing, T., & Fecteau, S. (2014). The use of virtual reality in craving assessment and cue-exposure therapy in substance use disorders. *Frontiers in Human Neuroscience, 8*, 844.

Honig, A., Romme, M., Ensink, B., Escher, S. D., Pennings, M. H. A., & Devries, M. W. (1998). Auditory hallucinations: A comparison between patients and nonpatients. *Journal of Nervous and Mental Disease, 186*, 646–651.

Honigman, R. J., Phillips, K. A., & Castle, D. J. (2004). A review of psychosocial outcomes for patients seeking cosmetic surgery. *Plastic and Reconstructive Surgery, 113*, 1229–1237.

Hopfer, C., Mendelson, B., & Van Leeuwen, J. (2006). Club drug use among youths in treatment for substance abuse. *The American Journal of Addictions, 15*, 94–99.

Hopko, D. R., Lejuez, C. W., Ruggiero, K. J., & Eifert, G. H. (2003). Contemporary behavioral activation treatments for depression: Procedures, principles, and progress. *Clinical Psychology Review, 23*, 699–717.

Horacek, J., Bubenikova-Valesova, V., Kopecek, M., Palenicek, T., Dockery, C., Mohr, P., & Höschl, C. (2006). Mechanism of action of atypical antipsychotic drugs and the neurobiology of schizophrenia. *CNS Drugs, 20*, 389–409.

Horner, A. (1974). Early object relations and the concept of depression. *International Journal of Psychoanalysis, 1*, 337–340.

Hornstein, N. L., & Putnam, F. W. (1992). Clinical phenomenology of child and adolescent dissociative disorders. *Journal of the American Academy of Child & Adolescent Psychiatry, 31*, 1077–1085.

Horowitz, K., Gorfinkle, K., Lewis, O., & Phillips, K. A. (2002). Body dysmorphic disorder in an adolescent girl. *Journal of the American Academy of Child and Adolescent Psychiatry, 41*, 1503–1509.

Hoshiai, M., Matsumoto, Y., Sato, T., Ohnishi, M., Okabe, N., Kishimoto, Y., & Kuroda, S. (2010). Psychiatric comorbidity among patients with gender identity disorder. *Psychiatry and Clinical Neuroscience, 64*, 514–519.

Houy, E., Debono, B., Dechelotte, P., & Thibaut, F. (2007). Anorexia nervosa associated with right frontal brain lesion. *International Journal of Eating Disorders, 40*, 758–761.

Howard, M., Elkins, R., & Rimmele, C. (1991). Chemical aversion treatment of alcohol dependence. *Drug and Alcohol Dependence, 29*, 107–143.

Howes, O. D., & Murray, R. M. (2014). Schizophrenia: An integrated sociodevelopmental-cognitive model. *Lancet, 383*(9929), 1677–1687.

Hser, Y., Huang, Y., Teruga, C., & Anglin, M. (2004). Gender differences in treatment outcomes over a three-year period: A path model analysis. *Journal of Drug Issues, 34*, 419–440.

Hsu, L. K., Rand, W., Sullivan, S., Liu, D. W., Mulliken, B., McDonagh, B., & Kaye, W. H. (2001). Cognitive therapy, nutritional therapy, and their combination in the treatment of bulimia nervosa. *Psychological Medicine, 31*, 871–879.

Huang, X. Y., Jung, B. J., Sun, F. K., Lin, J. D., & Chen, C. C. (2009). The experiences of carers in Taiwanese culture who have long-term schizophrenia in their families. *Journal of Psychiatric and Mental Health Nursing, 16*, 874–883.

Huang, Y. W., Yang, S. S., & Kao, J. H. (2011). Pathogenesis and management of alcoholic liver cirrhosis: A review. *Journal of Hepatic Medicine: Evidence and Research, 3*, 1–11.

Hucker, S.J., Langevin, R., Wortzman, G., Dickey, R., Bain, J., Handy, L., … Wright, P. (1988). Cerebral damage and dysfunction in sexually aggressive men. *Annals of Sex Research, 1*, 33–47.

Hudson, J., Lalonde, J., Pindyck, L., Bulik, C. M., Crow, S., McElroy, S. L., … Pope, H. G., Jr. (2006). Binge-eating disorder as a distinct familial phenotype in obese individuals. *Archives of General Psychiatry, 63*, 313–319.

Hudson, J. I., Hiripi, E., Pope, H. G., & Kessler, R. C. (2007). The prevalence and correlates of eating disorders in the National Comorbidity Survey Replication. *Biological Psychiatry, 61*, 348–358.

Hudson, J. I., Lalonde, J. K., Coit, C. E., Tsuang, M. T., McElroy, S. L., Crow, S. J., … Pope, H. G., Jr. (2010). Longitudinal study of the diagnosis of components of the metabolic syndrome in individuals with binge-eating disorder. *The American Journal of Clinical Nutrition, 91*, 1568–1573.

Hudson, J. I., Pope, H. G., Jr., Jonas, J. M., Yurgelun-Todd, D., & Frankenburg, F. R. (1987). A controlled family history study of bulimia. *Psychological Medicine, 17*, 883–890.

Hudson, S., Ward, T., & Marshall, W. (1992). The abstinence violation effect in sexual offenders: A reformulation. *Behavior Research and Therapy, 30*, 435–441.

Hughes, I. (2006). Prenatal treatment of congenital adrenal hyperplasia: Do we have enough evidence? *Treatments in Endocrinology, 5*, 1–6.

Hunt, G., & Azrin, N. (1973). A community-reinforcement approach to alcoholism. *Behaviour Research and Therapy, 11*, 91–104.

Hunter, E. C., Baker, D., Phillips, M. L., Sierra, M., & David, A. S. (2005). Cognitive-behaviour therapy for depersonalisation disorder: An open study. *Behavior Research and Therapy, 43*, 1121–1130.

Hunter, E. C., Salkovskis, P. M., & David, A. S. (2014). Attributions, appraisals, and attention for symptoms in depersonalisation disorder. *Behavior Research and Therapy, 53*, 20–29.

Huppert, J. D., Strunk, D. R., Ledley, D. R., Davidson, J. R., & Foa, E. B. (2008). Generalized social anxiety disorder and avoidant personality disorder: Structural analysis and treatment outcome. *Depression & Anxiety, 25*, 441–448.

Hurwitz, T. A., & Prichard, J. W. (2006). Conversion disorder and fMRI. *Neurology, 67*, 1914–1915.

Husain, M. M., Rush, A. J., Fink, M., Knapp, R., Petrides, G., Rummans, T., … Kellner, C. H. (2004). Speed of response and remission in major depressive disorder with acute electroconvulsive therapy (ECT): A Consortium for Research in ECT (CORE) report. *Journal of Clinical Psychiatry, 65*, 485–491.

Hybels, C. F., & Blazer, D. G. (2015). Demography and epidemiology of psychiatric disorders in late life. In D. C. Steffens, D. G. Blazer, & M. E. Thakur (Eds.), *Textbook of geriatric psychiatry, DSM-5 edition* (pp. 3–32). Washington, DC: American Psychiatric Association.

Hybels, C. F., Blazer, D. G., & Hays, J. C. (2009). Demography and epidemiology of psychiatric disorders in late life. In D. G. Blazer & D.C. Steffens (Eds.). *The American psychiatric publishing of the textbook of geriatric psychiatry*, 4th ed., 19–43.

Iasevoli, F., Giordano, S., Ballette, R., Latter, G., Formato, M.V., Prinzivalli, E., … de Bartolomeis, A. (2016). Treatment resistant schizophrenia is associated with the worst community functioning among severely-ill highly disabling psychiatric conditions and is the most relevant predictor of poorer achievements in functional milestones. *Progress in NeuroPsychopharmacology and Biological Psychiatry, 65*, 34–48.

Iervolino, A. C., Perroud, N., Fullana, M. A., Guipponi, M., Cherkas, L., Collier, D. A., & Mataix-Cols, D. (2009). Prevalence and heritability of compulsive hoarding: A twin study. *American Journal of Psychiatry, 166*, 1156–1161.

Ilott, R. (2005). Does compliance therapy improve use of antipsychotic medication? *British Journal of Community Nursing, 10*, 514–519.

Inder, M. L., Crowe, M. T., Luty, S. E., Carter, J. D., Moor, S., Frampton, C. M., & Joyce, P. R. (2015). Randomized, controlled trial of interpersonal and social rhythm therapy for young people with bipolar disorder. *Bipolar Disorders, 17*, 128–138.

Inskip, H. M., Harris, E. C., & Barraclough, B. (1998). Lifetime risk of suicide for affective disorder, alcoholism, and schizophrenia. *British Journal of Psychiatry, 172*, 35–37.

Institute of Medicine. (2012). *Mental health and substance use workforce for older adults: In whose hands?* Washington, DC: Institute of Medicine.

International Society for the Study of Dissociation. (2005). Guidelines for treating dissociative identity disorder in adults. *Journal of Trauma & Dissociation, 6*, 69–149.

Ipser, J. C., & Stein, D. J. (2012). Evidence-based pharmacotherapy of post-traumatic stress disorder (PTSD). *International Journal of Neuropsychopharmacology, 15*, 825–840.

Ipser, J. C., Sander, C., & Stein, D. J. (2009). Pharmacotherapy and psychotherapy for body dysmorphic disorder. *Cochrane Database of Systematic Reviews, 1*.

Isenberg-Grzeda, E., Kutner, H. E., & Nicolson, S. E. (2012). Wernicke-Korsakoff-syndrome: Under-recognized and under-treated. *Psychosomatics, 53*, 507–516.

Isidori, A. M., Giannetta, E., Gianfrilli, D., Greco, E. A., Bonifacio, V., Aversa, A.,… Lenzi, A. (2005). Effects of testosterone on sexual function in men: Results of a meta-analysis. *Clinical Endocrinology, 63*, 381–394.

Isomura, K., Boman, M., Ruck, C., Serlachius, E., Larsson, H., Lichtenstein, P., & Mataix-Cols, D. (2015). Population-based, multi-generational family clustering study of social anxiety disorder and avoidant personality disorder. *Psychological Medicine, 45*, 1581–1589.

Jablensky, A. (2000). Epidemiology of schizophrenia: The global burden of disease and disability. *European Archives of Psychiatry & Clinical Neuroscience, 250*, 274–285.

Jacobson, N. S., & Truax, P. (1991). Clinical significance: A statistical approach to defining meaningful change in psychotherapy research. *Journal of Consulting and Clinical Psychology, 59*, 12–19.

Jalkut, M. W., Lerman, S. E., & Churchill, B. M. (2001). Enuresis. *Pediatric Urology, 48*, 1461–1488.

Jamal, A., Agaku, I. T., O'Connor, E., King, B. A., Kenemer, J. B., & Neff, L. (2014). Current cigarette smoking among adults—United States, 2005–2013. *Morbidity and Mortality Weekly Report (MMWR), 63*, 1108–1112.

James, D. J., & Glaze, L. E. (2006). *Mental health problems of prison and jail inmates*. Retrieved from http://www.bjs.gov/content/pub/pdf/mhppji.pdf

James, K. (1997). *Understanding caffeine: A biobehavioral analysis*. Thousand Oaks, CA: Sage Publications.

Jameson, J. P., Shrestha, S., Escamilla, M., Clark, S., Wilson, N., Kunik, M., … Varner, I. L. (2012). Establishing community partnerships to support late-life anxiety research: Lessons learned from the calmer life project. *Aging & Mental Health, 16*, 874–883.

Jamison, K. (1993). *Touched with fire: Manic-depressive illness and the artistic temperament*. New York: Free Press/Macmillan.

Jamison, K. R., & Baldessarini, R. J. (1999). Effects of medical interventions on suicidal behavior. *Journal of Clinical Psychiatry, 60*(Suppl. 2), 4–6.

Jang, K. L., Livesley, W. J., & Vernon, P. A. (1996). Heritability of the big five personality dimensions and their facets: A twin study. *Journal of Personality, 64*, 577–591.

Janicak, P. G., Dowd, S. M., Martis, B., Alam, D., Beedle, D., Krasuski, J., … Viana, M. (2002). Repetitive transcranial magnetic stimulation versus electroconvulsive therapy for major depression: Preliminary results of a randomized trial. *Biological Psychiatry, 51*, 659–667.

Jansen, R., Penninx, B. W., Madar, V., Xia, K., Milaneschi, Y., Hottenga, J. J., … Sullivan, P. F. (2016). Gene expression in major depressive disorder. *Molecular Psychiatry, 21*, 444.

Jaracz, K., Górna, K., Kiejda, J., Grabowska-Fudala, B., Jaracz, J., & Suwalska, A. (2015). Psychosocial functioning in relation to symptomatic remission: A longitudinal study of first episode schizophrenia. *European Psychiatry, 30*, 907–913.

Jenkins, E. J., & Bell, C.C. (1994). Violence among inner city high school students and posttraumatic stress disorder. In S. Friedman (Ed.), *Anxiety disorders in African Americans*. New York: Springer.

Jennings, J. H., Rizzi, G., Stamatakis, A. M., Ung, R. L., & Stuber, G. D. (2013). The inhibitory circuit architecture of the lateral hypothalamus orchestrates feeding. *Science, 341*(6153), 1517–1521.

Jensen, K. P., Stein, M. B., Kranzler, H. R., Yang, B. Z., Farrer, L. A., & Gelernter, J. (2014). The alpha-endomannosidase gene (MANEA) is associated with panic disorder and social anxiety disorder. *Translational Psychiatry, 4*, e353.

Jern, P., Johansson, A., Piha, J., Westberg, L., & Santtila, P. (2014). Antidepressant treatment of premature ejaculation. *International Journal of Impotence Research, 27*, 75–80.

Jeste, D. V., Depp, C. A., & Vahia, I. V. (2010). Successful cognitive and emotional aging. *World Psychiatry, 9*, 78–84.

Jeste, D. V., Lanouette, N. M., & Vahia, I. V. (2009). Schizophrenia and paranoid disorders. In D. C. Blazer & D. C. Steffens (Eds.), *Textbook of geriatric psychiatry* (pp. 317–332). Washington, DC: American Psychiatric Publishing, inc.

Jhung, K., Ku, J., Kim, S. J., Lee, H., Kim, K. R., An, S. K., … Lee, E. (2014). Distinct functional connectivity of limbic network in the washing type obsessive–compulsive disorder. *Progress in Neuro-Psychopharmacology and Biological Psychiatry, 53*, 149–155.

Jimenez, D. E., Alegría, M., Chen, C. N., Chan, D., & Laderman, M. (2010). Prevalence of psychiatric illnesses in older ethnic minority adults. *Journal of the American Geriatrics Society, 58*, 256–264.

Jimerson, D. C., Wolfe, B. E., Metzger, E. D., Finkelstein, D. M., Cooper, T. B., & Levine, J. M. (1997). Decreased serotonin function in bulimia nervosa. *Archives of General Psychiatry, 54*, 529–534.

Jobe, T. H., & Harrow, M. (2005). Long-term outcome of patients with schizophrenia: A review. *Canadian Journal of Psychiatry, 50*, 892–900.

Joe, G., Simpson, D., & Broome, K. (1999). Retention and patient engagement models for different treatment modalities in DATOS. *Drug and Alcohol Dependence, 57* (113–125).

Johnson, E. O., Hancock, D. B., Levy, J. L., Gaddis, N. C., Page, G. P., Glasheen, C., … Kral, A. H. (2015). *KAT2B* polymorphism identified for drug abuse in African Americans with regulatory links to drug abuse pathways in human prefrontal cortex. *Addiction Biology*.

Johnson, J. G., Cohen, P., Kasen, S., & Brook, J. S. (2006). Dissociative disorders among adults in the community, impaired functioning, and axis I and II comorbidity. *Journal of Psychiatric Research, 40*, 131–140.

Johnson, J. G., Cohen, P., Chen, H., Kasen, S., & Brook, J. S. (2006). Parenting behaviors associated with risk for offspring personality disorder during adulthood. *Archives of General Psychiatry, 63*, 579–587.

Jones, K. L., & Smith, D. W. (1973). Recognition of the fetal alcohol syndrome in early infancy. *Lancet, 302*, 999–1001.

Jones, P., Rodgers, B., Murray, R., & Mormot, M. (1994). Child development risk factors for adult schizophrenia in the British 1946 birth cohort. *Lancet, 344*, 1398–1402.

Joo, J. H., Morales, K. H., de Vries, H. F., & Gallo, J. J. (2010). Disparity in use of psychotherapy offered in primary care between older African-American and White adults: Results from a practice-based depression intervention trial. *Journal of the American Geriatrics Society, 58*, 154–160.

Jordan, J., McIntosh, V. V. W., Joyce, P. R., & Bulik, C. M. (2015). *Encyclopedia for eating disorders*. Singapore: Springer Science.

Joseph, R. (2000). The evolution of sex differences in language, sexuality, and visual-spatial skills. *Archives of Sexual Behavior, 20*, 35–66.

Joshi, S. H., Espinoza, R. T., Pirnia, T., Shi, J., Wang, Y., Ayers, B., … Narr, K. L. (2015). Structural plasticity of the hippocampus and amygdala induced by electroconvulsive therapy in major depression. *Biological Psychiatry, pii: S0006-3223*(15), 00154–00157.

Joyce, P. R. (1995). The clinical management of depression. In P. R. Joyce, S. E. Romans, P. M. Ellis, & T. S. Silverstone (Eds.), *Affective disorders* (pp. 35–46). Christchurch: Christchurch School of Medicine.

Joyce, P. R., McHugh, P. C., Light, K. J., Rowe, S., Miller, A. L., & Kennedy, M. A. (2009). Relationships between angry-impulsive personality traits and genetic polymorphisms of the dopamine transporter. *Biological Psychiatry, 66*, 717–721.

Judd, L. L., Akiskal, H. S., Schettler, P. J., Endicott, J., Maser, J., Solomon, D. A., … Keller, M. B. (2002). The long-term natural history of the weekly symptomatic status of bipolar I disorder. *Archives of General Psychiatry, 59*, 530–537.

Juliano, L. M., & Griffiths, R. R. (2004). A critical review of caffeine withdrawal: empirical validation of symptoms and signs, incidence, severity, and associated features. *Psychopharmacology, 176*, 1–29.

Kabakçi, E., & Batur, S. (2003). Who benefits from cognitive behavioral therapy for vaginismus? *Journal of Sex & Marital Therapy, 29*, 277–288.

Kafka, M. (2010). Hypersexual disorder: A proposed diagnosis for DSM-V. *Archives of Sexual Behavior, 39*, 377–400.

Kagan, J. (1982). *Psychological research on the human infant: An evaluative summary*. WT Grant Foundation.

Kalapatapu, R. K., & Sullivan, M. A. (2010). Prescription use disorders in older adults. *The American Journal on Addictions, 19*, 515–522.

Kaltenbach, K., Berghell, V., & Finnegan, L. (1998). Opioid dependence during pregnancy. *Obstetrics and Gynecology Clinics of North America, 25*, 151.

Kamali, M., Kelly, B. D., Clarke, M., Browne, S., Gervin, M., Kinsella, A., … O'Callaghan, E. (2006). A prospective evaluation of adherence to medication in first episode schizophrenia. *European Psychiatry, 21*, 29–33.

Kampov-Polevoy, A., Garbutt, J., & Khalitov, E. (2003). Family history of alcoholism and response to sweets. *Alcoholism, Clinical, and Experimental Research, 11*, 1743–1749.

Kanayama, G., Barry, S., Hudson, J. I., & Pope, H. G. (2006). Body image and attitudes toward male roles in anabolic-androgenic steroid users. *American Journal of Psychiatry, 163*, 697–703.

Kandel, D., & Davies, M. (1992). Progression to regular marijuana involvement: Phenomenology and risk factors for near-daily use. In M.D. Glantz & R. Pickens (Eds.), *Vulnerability to drug abuse* (pp. 211–253). Washington, DC: American Psychological Association.

Kanton, W. J., & Walker, E. A. (1998). Medically unexplained symptoms in primary care. *Journal of Clinical Psychiatry, 59*, 15–21.

Kaplan, H. S. (1974). *The new sex therapy*. New York: Brunner Mazel.

Kaplan, H. S. (1979). *Disorders of sexual desire*. New York: Brunner Mazel.

Kaplan, S. A., Reis, R. B., Kohn, I. J., Ikeguchi, E. F., Laor, E., Te, A. E., & Martins, A.C. (1999). Safety and efficacy of sildenafil in postmenopausal women with sexual dysfunction. *Urology, 53*, 481–486.

Karavidas, M. K., Tsai, P.-S., Yucha, C., McGrady, A., & Lehrer, P. M. (2006). Thermal biofeedback for primary Raynaud's phenomenon: A review of the literature. *Applied Psychophysiology and Biofeedback, 31*, 203–216.

Karila, L., Petit, A., Lowenstein, W., & Reynaud, M. (2012). Diagnosis and consequences of cocaine addiction. *Current Medicinal Chemistry, 19*, 5612–5618.

Karila, L., Roux, P., Rolland, B., Benyamina, A., Reynaud, M., Aubin, H. J., & Lançon, C. (2014). Acute and long-term effects of cannabis use: A review. *Current Pharmaceutical Design, 30*, 4112–4118.

Karno, M., Hough, R. L., Burnam, M. A., Escobar, J. I., Timbers, D. M., Santana, F., & Boyd, J. H. (1987). Lifetime prevalence of specific psychiatric disorders among Mexican Americans and non-Hispanic whites in Los Angeles. *Archives in General Psychiatry, 44*, 695–701.

Katon, W. J., & Walker, E. A. (1998). Medically unexplained symptoms in primary care. *Journal of Clinical Psychiatry*, 59 Suppl 20, 15–21.

Katz, I. R., Reynolds, C. F., Alexopoulos, G. S., & Hackett, D. (2002). Venlafaxine ER as a treatment for generalized anxiety disorder in older adults: Pooled analysis of five randomized placebo-controlled clinical trials. *Journal of the American Geriatrics Society, 50*, 18–25.

Kaufman, J., & Charney, D. (2001). Effects of early stress on brain structure and function: Implications for understanding the relationship between child maltreatment and depression. *Development and Psychopathology, 13*, 451–471.

Kaufman, M. R., & Heiman, M. (1964). *Evolution of psychosomatic concepts: Anorexia nervosa: A paradigm*. New York: International Universities Press.

Kawakami, N., Takeshima, T., Ono, Y., Uda, H., Hata, Y., Nakane, Y., … Kikkawa, T. (2005). Twelve-month prevalence, severity, and treatment of common mental disorders in communities in Japan: Preliminary finding from the World Mental Health Japan Survey 2002–2003. *Psychiatry and Clinical Neuroscience, 59*, 441–452.

Kaye, W. (1997). Anorexia nervosa, obsessional behavior, and serotonin. *Psychopharmacology Bulletin, 33*, 335–344.

Kaye, W. H., Gwirtsman, H. E., George, D. T., & Ebert, M. H. (1991). Altered serotonin activity in anorexia nervosa after long-term weight restoration. Does elevated cerebrospinal fluid 5-hydroxyindoleacetic acid level correlate with rigid and obsessive behavior? *Archives of General Psychiatry, 48*, 556–562.

Kaye, W. H., Bulik, C. M., Thornton, L., Barbarich, N., & Masters, K. (2004). Comorbidity of anxiety disorders with anorexia and bulimia nervosa. *American Journal of Psychiatry, 161*, 2215–2221.

Kaye, W. H., Greeno, C. G., Moss, H., Fernstrom, J., Fernstrom, M., Lilenfeld, L. R., … Mann, J. J. (1998). Alterations in serotonin activity and psychiatric symptoms after recovery from bulimia nervosa. *Archives of General Psychiatry, 55*, 927–935.

Kaye, W. H., Weltzin, T. E., Hsu, L. K., McConaha, C. W., & Bolton, B. (1993). Amount of calories retained after binge eating and vomiting. *American Journal of Psychiatry, 150*, 969–971.

Kaye, W. H., Wierenga, C. E., Bailer, U. F., Simmons, A. N., & Bischoff-Grethe, A. (2013). Nothing tastes as good as skinny feels: The neurobiology of anorexia nervosa. *Trends in Neuroscience, 36*, 110–120.

Kayiran, S., Dursun, E., Dursun, N., Ermutlu, N., & Karamürsel, S. (2010). Neurofeedback intervention in fibromyalgia syndrome; a randomized, controlled, rater blind clinical trial. *Applied Psychophysiology and Biofeedback, 35*, 293–302.

Kazdin, A. E. (2003). *Research design in clinical psychology* (4th ed.). Boston: A Pearson Education Company.

Keck, P. E., Jr., McElroy, S. L., & Arnold, L. M. (2001). Bipolar disorder. *Medical Clinics of North America, 85*, 645–661.

Keefe, J. R., McCarthy, K. S., Dinger, U., Zilcha-Mano, S., & Barber, J. P. (2014). A meta-analytic review of psychodynamic therapies for anxiety disorders. *Clinical Psychology Review, 34*, 309–323.

Keel, P. K., & Klump, K. (2003). Are eating disorders culture-bound syndromes? Implications for conceptualizing their etiology. *Psychological Bulletin, 129*, 747–769.

Keenan, K., Loeber, R., & Green, S. (1999). Conduct disorder in girls: A review of the literature. *Clinical Child and Family Psychology Review, 2*, 3–19.

Keenan, K., & Wakschlag, L. S. (2002). Can a valid diagnosis of disruptive behavior disorder be made in preschool children? *American Journal of Psychiatry, 159*, 351–358.

Kelder, S., Prokhorov, A., Barroso, C., Murray, N., Orpinas, P., & McCormick, L. (2003). Smoking differences among African American, Hispanic, and White middle school students in an urban setting. *Addictive Behaviors, 28*, 513–522.

Keller, M. B., Lavori, P. W., Coryell, W., Endicott, J., & Mueller, T. I. (1993). Bipolar I: A five-year prospective follow-up. *Journal of Nervous and Mental Disease, 181*, 238–245.

Keller, M. B., Hirschfeld, R. M., & Hanks, D. (1997). Double depression: A distinctive subtype of unipolar depression. *Journal of Affective Disorders, 45*, 65–73.

Keller, M. B. (2003). The lifelong course of social anxiety disorder: A clinical perspective. *Acta Psychiatrica Scandinavica, 108*, 85–94.

Kendler, K.S., Myers, J., Precott, C.A. & Neale, M.C. (2001). The genetic epidemiology of irrational fears and phobias in men. *Archives of General Psychiatry, 58*, 257–265.

Kendler, K., Kessler, R. C., Walters, E. E., MacLean, C., Neale, M. C., Heath, A. C., & Eaves, L.J. (1995). Stressful life events, genetic liability, and onset of an episode of major depression in women. *American Journal of Psychiatry, 152*, 833–842.

Kendler, K. (1996). Major depression and generalized anxiety disorder: Same genes, (partly) different environments: Revisited. *British Journal of Psychiatry, 168*, 68–75.

Kendler, K., & Karkowski-Shuman, L. (1997). Stressful life events and genetic liability to major depression: Genetic control of exposure to the environment? *Psychological Medicine, 27*, 539–547.

Kendler, K., Gardner, C., & Prescott, C. (1997). Religion, psychopathology, and substance use and abuse: A multimeasure, genetic-epidemiologic study. *American Journal of Psychiatry, 154*, 322–329.

Kendler, K., & Prescott, C. (1999). A population-based twin study of lifetime major depression in men and women. *Archives of General Psychiatry, 56*, 39–44.

Kendler, K., Gardner, C., Gatz, M., & Pedersen, N. (2007). The sources of co-morbidity between major depression and generalized anxiety disorder in a Swedish national twin sample. *Psychological Medicine, 37*, 453–462.

Kendler, K. S., MacLean, C., Neale, M. C., Kessler, R. C., Heath, A. C., & Eaves, L. J. (1991). The genetic epidemiology of bulimia nervosa. *American Journal of Psychiatry, 148*, 1627–1637.

Kendler, K. S., Neale, M. C., Kessler, R. C., Heath, A. C., & Eaves, L. J. (1992). Major depression and generalized anxiety disorder: Same genes, (partly) different environments? *Archives of General Psychiatry, 49*, 716–722.

Kendler, K. S., McGuire, M., Gruenberg, A. M., O'Hare, A., Spellman, M., & Walsh, D. (1993). The Roscommon family study III: Schizophrenia-related personality disorders in relatives. *Archives of General Psychiatry, 50*, 781–788.

Kendler, K. S., Karkowski, L. M., & Prescott, C. A. (1998). Stressful life events and major depression: Risk period, long-term contextual threat, and diagnostic specificity. *Journal of Nervous and Mental Disease, 186*, 661–669.

Kendler, K. S., Thornton, L. M., & Gardner, C. O. (2000). Stressful life events and previous episodes in the etiology of major depression in women: An evaluation of the "kindling" hypothesis. *American Journal of Psychiatry, 157*, 1243–1251.

Kendler, K. S. (2001). Twin studies of psychiatric illness: An update. *Archives of General Psychiatry, 58*, 1005–1014.

Kendler, K. S., Hettema, J. M., Butera, F., Gardner, C. O., & Prescott, C. A. (2003). Life event dimensions of loss, humiliation, entrapment, and danger in the prediction of onsets of major depression and generalized anxiety. *Archives of General Psychiatry, 60*, 789–796.

Kendler, K. S. (2005). Toward a philosophical structure for psychiatry. *American Journal of Psychiatry, 162*, 433–440.

Kendler, K. S. (2013). What psychiatric genetics has taught us about the nature of psychiatric illness and what is left to learn. *Molecular Psychiatry, 18*, 1058–1066.

Kendler, K. S., Aggen, S. H., Czajkowski, N., Roysamb, E., Tambs, K., Torgersen, S., … Reichborn-Kjennerud, T. (2008). The structure of genetic and environmental risk factors for DSM-IV personality disorders: A multivariate twin study. *Archives in General Psychiatry, 65*, 1438–1446.

Kendler, K. S., Aggen, S. H., Neale, M. C., Knudsen, G. P., Krueger, R. F., Tambs, K., … Reichborn-Kjennerud, T. (2015). A longitudinal twin study of cluster A personality disorders. *Psychological Medicine, 45*, 1531–1538.

Kent, D. A., Tomasson, K., & Coryell, W. (1995). Course and outcome of conversion and somatization disorders: A four-year follow-up. *Psychosomatics, 36*, 136–144.

Keppel-Benson, Ollendick, T. H, & Benson, M. J. (2002). Post-traumatic stress in children following motor vehicle accidents. *Journal of Child Psychology & Psychiatry, 43*, 203–212.

Kernberg, O. (1975). *Borderline conditions and pathological narcissism*. New York: Jason Aronson.

Kerrigan, S., & Lindsey, T. (2005). Fatal caffeine overdose: Two case reports. *Forensic Science International, 153*, 67–69.

Keshaviah, A., Edkins, K., Hastings, E. R., Krishna, M., Franko, D. L., Herzog, D. B., … Eddy, K. T. (2014). Re-examining premature mortality in anorexia nervosa: A meta-analysis redux. *Comprehensive Psychiatry, 55*, 1773–1784.

Keski-Rahkonen, A., Hoek, H. W., Linna, M. S., Raevuori, A., Sihvola, E., Bulik, C. M., … Kaprio, J. (2009). Incidence and outcomes of bulimia nervosa: A nationwide population-based study. *Psychological Medicine, 39*, 823–831.

Kessler, R. C. (2003). The impairments caused by social phobia in the general population: Implications for intervention. *Acta Psychiatrica Scandinavca, 108*, 19–27.

Kessler, R. C., Adler, L. A., Berglund, P., Green, J. G., McLaughlin, K. A., Fayyad, J., … Zaslavsky, A. M. (2014). The effects of temporally secondary co-morbid mental disorders on the associations of DSM-IV ADHD with adverse outcomes in the US National Comorbidity Survey Replication Adolescent Supplement (NCS-A). *Psychological Medicine, 44*, 1779–1792.

Kessler, R. C., Aguilar-Gaxiola, S., Alonso, J., Chatterji, S., Lee, S., Ormel, J., … Wang, P. S. (2009). The global burden of mental disorders: An update from the WHO World Mental Health (WMH) Surveys. *Journal for Epidemiology and Psychiatric Sciences, 18*, 23–33.

Kessler, R. C., Akiskal, H. S., Ames, M., Birnbaum, H., Greenberg, P., Hirschfeld, R. M., … Wang, P. S. (2006). Prevalence and effects of mood disorders on work performance in a nationally representative sample of U.S. workers. *American Journal of Psychiatry, 163*, 1561–1568.

Kessler, R. C., Berglund, P., Borges, G., Nock, M., & Wang, P. S. (2005). Trends in suicide ideation, plans, gestures, and attempts in the United States, 1990–1992 to 2001–2003. *Journal of the American Medical Association, 293*, 2487–2495.

Kessler, R. C., Berglund, P., Demler, O., Jin, R., Koretz, D., Merikangas, K. R., … National Comorbidity Survey Replication (2003). The epidemiology of major depressive disorder: Results from the National Comorbidity Survey Replication (NCS-R). *Journal of the American Medical Association, 289*, 3095–3105.

Kessler, R. C., Berglund, P. A., Chiu, W. T., Deitz, A. C., Hudson, J. I., Shahly, V., … Xavier, M. (2013). The prevalence and correlates of binge eating disorder in the World Health Organization World Mental Health Surveys. *Biological Psychiatry, 73*, 904–914.

Kessler, R. C., Berglund, P., Chiu, W. T., Demler, O., Heeringa, S., Hiripi, E., & Zheng, H. (2004). The US National Comorbidity Survey Replication (NCS-R): Design and field procedures. *International Journal of Methods in Psychiatric Research, 13*, 69–92.

Kessler, R. C., Berglund, P., Demler, O., Jin, R., Merikangas, K. R., & Walters, E. E. (2005). Lifetime prevalence and age-of-onset distributions of DSM-IV disorders in the National Comorbidity Survey Replication. *Archives of General Psychiatry, 62*, 593–602.

Kessler, R. C., Birnbaum, H., Bromet, E., Hwang, I., Sampson, N., & Shahly, V. (2010). Age differences in major depression: Results from the National Comorbidity Survey Replication (NCS-R). *Psychological Medicine, 40*, 225–237.

Kessler, R. C., Birnbaum, H., Demler, O., Falloon, I. R., Gagnon, E., Guyer, M., … Walters, E. (2005). The prevalence and correlates of nonaffective psychosis in the National Comorbidity Survey Replication (NCS-R). *Biological Psychiatry, 58*, 668–676.

Kessler, R. C., Brandenburg, N., & Lane, M. (2005). Rethinking the duration requirement for generalized anxiety disorder: Evidence from the National Comorbidity Survey Replication. *Psychological Medicine, 35*, 1073–1082.

Kessler, R. C., Chiu, W. T., Jin, R., Ruscio, A. M., Shear, K., & Walters, E. E. (2006). The epidemiology of panic attacks, panic disorder, and agoraphobia in the National Comorbidity Survey Replication. *Archives of General Psychiatry, 63*, 415–424.

Kessler, R. C., Crum, R. M., Warner, L. A., Nelson, C. B., Schulenberg, J., & Anthony, J. C. (1997). Lifetime co-occurrence of DSM-III-R alcohol abuse and dependence with other psychiatric disorders in the National Comorbidity Survey. *Archives of General Psychiatry, 54*, 313–321.

Kessler, R. C., Foster, C. L., Saunders, W. B., & Stang, P. E. (1995). Social consequences of psychiatric disorders, I: Education attainment. *The American Journal of Psychiatry, 152*, 1026–1032.

Kessler, R. C., & Frank, R. G. (1997). The impact of psychiatric disorders on work loss days. *Psychological Medicine, 27*, 861–873.

Kessler, R. C., McGonagle, K. A., Swartz, M., Blazer, D. G., & Nelson, C. B. (1993). Sex and depression in the National Comorbidity Survey. 1: Lifetime prevalence, chronicity and recurrence. *Journal of Affective Disorders, 29*(2–3), 85–96.

Kessler, R. C., McGonagle, K. A., Zhao, S., Nelson, C. B., Hughes, M., Eshleman, S., … Kendler, K. S. (1994). Lifetime and 12-month prevalence of DSM-III-R psychiatric disorders in the United States. Results from the National Comorbidity Survey. *Archives of General Psychiatry, 51*, 8–19.

Kessler, R. C., Petukhova, M., Sampson, N. A., Zaslavsky, A. M., & Wittchen, H. U. (2012). Twelve-month and lifetime prevalence and lifetime morbid risk of anxiety and mood disorders in the United States. *International Journal of Methods in Psychiatric Research, 21*, 169–184.

Kessler, R. C., & Wang, P.S. (2008). The descriptive epidemiology of commonly occurring mental disorders in the United States. *Annual Review of Public Health, 29*, 115–129.

Keuthen, N. J., Altenburger, E. M., & Pauls, D. (2014). A family study of trichotillomania and chronic hair pulling. *American Journal of Medical Genetics Part B: Neuropsychiatric Genetics, 165*, 167–174.

Khabdaker, G. M., Zimbron, J., Lewis, G., & Jones, P. B. (2013). Prenatal maternal infection, neurodevelopment and adult schizophrenia: A systematic review of population-based studies. *Psychological Medicine, 43*, 239–257.

Khalifa, N., Duggan, C., Stoffers, J., Huband, N., Vollm, B. A., Ferriter, M., & Lieb, K. (2010). Pharmacological interventions for antisocial personality disorder. *Cochrane Database of Systematic Reviews, 8*, CD007667.

Khan, A., Leventhal, R. M., Khan, S. & Brown, W. A. (2002). Suicide risk in patients with anxiety disorders: A meta-analysis of the FDA database. *Journal of Affective Disorders, 68*(2–3), 183–190.

Khabdaker, G. M., Zimbron, J., Lewis, G., & Jones, P. B. (2013). Prenatal maternal infection, neurodevelopment, and adult schizophrenia: A systematic review of population-based studies. *Psychological Medicine, 43*, 239–257.

Khashan, A. S., Abel. K.M., McNamee, R., Pedersen, M. G., Webb, R. T., Baker, P. N., … Mortensen, P. B. (2008), Higher risk of offspring schizophrenia following antenatal maternal exposure to severe adverse life events. *Archives of General Psychiatry, 65*, 146–152.

Khran, L. E., Li, H., & O'Connor, M. K. (2003). Patients who strive to be ill: Factitious disorder with physical symptoms. *American Journal of Psychiatry, 160*, 1163–1168.

Kihlstrom, J. F. (2001). Dissociative disorders. In P. B. Sutker & H. E. Adams (Eds.), *Comprehensive handbook of psychopathology* (3rd ed., pp. 259–276). New York: Plenum.

Killen, J., Hayward, C., Hammer, L., Wilson, D., Miner, B., Taylor, C. B., … Shisslak, C. (1992). Is puberty a risk factor for eating disorders? *American Journal of Diseases of Children, 146*, 323–325.

Killen, J., Taylor, C., Hayward, C., Wilson, D., Haydel, K., Hammer, L., … Kraemer, H. (1994). Pursuit of thinness and onset of eating disorder symptoms in a community sample of adolescent girls: A three-year prospective analysis. *International Journal of Eating Disorders, 16*, 227–238.

Kiluk, B. D., & Carroll, K. M. (2013). New developments in behavioral treatments for substance use disorders. *Current Psychiatry Reports, 15*, 420.

Kim, H. F. S., Kunik, M. E., Molinari, V. A., Hillman, S. L., Lalani, S., Orengo, C. A., … Goodnight-White, S. (2000). Functional impairment in COPD patients: The impact of anxiety and depression. *Psychosomatics, 41*, 465–471.

Kim, J. E., Dager, S. R., & Lyoo, I. K. (2012). The role of the amygdala in the pathophysiology of panic disorder: Evidence from neuroimaging studies. *Biology of Mood & Anxiety Disorders, 2*, 20.

Kim, S. J., Lee, H. S., & Kim, C. H. (2005). Obsessive-compulsive disorder, factor-analyzed symptom dimensions, and serotonin transporter polymorphism. *Neuropsychobiology, 52*, 176–782.

Kimchi, E. Z., & Lyketsos, C. G. (2015). Dementia and mild neurocognitive disorders. In D. C. Steffens, D. G. Blazer, & M. E. Thakur (Eds.), *Textbook of geriatric psychiatry, DSM-5 edition* (pp. 177–242). Washington, DC: American Pychiatric Association.

Kimhy, D., Goetz, R., Yale, S., Corcoran, C., & Malaspina, D. (2005). Delusions in individuals with schizophrenia: Factor structure, clinical correlates, and putative neurobiology. *Psychopathology, 38*, 338–344.

Kindermann, S. S., Kalayam, B., Brown, G. G., Burdick, K. E., & Alexopoulos, G. S. (2001). Executive functions and P300 latency in elderly depressed patients and control subjects. *The American Journal of Geriatric Psychiatry, 8*, 57–65.

King, B. M. (2006). The rise, fall, and resurrection of the ventromedial hypothalamus in the regulation of feeding behavior and body weight. *Physiology & Behavior, 87*, 221–244.

Kingsberg, S. (2007). Testosterone treatment for hypoactive sexual desire disorder in postmenopausal women. *Journal of Sexual Medicine, 4*(3 Suppl), 227–234.

Kirby, J. S., Runfola, C. D., Fischer, M. S., Baucom, D. H., & Bulik, C. M. (2015). Couple-based interventions for adults with eating disorders. *Eating Disorders: The Journal of Treatment and Prevention, 23*, 356–365.

Kirchner, J. E., Zubritsky, C., Cody, M., Coakley, E., Chen, H., Ware, J. H., … Miles, K. M. (2007). Alcohol consumption among older adults in primary care. *Journal of General Internal Medicine, 22*, 92–97.

Kirmayer, L. J. (2001). Cultural variations in the clinical presentation of depression and anxiety: Implications for diagnosis and treatment. *Journal of Clinical Psychiatry, 62*, 22–28; discussion 29–30.

Kirmayer, L. J., Groleau, D., Looper, K. J., & Dao, M. D. (2004). Explaining medically unexplained symptoms. *Canadian Journal of Psychiatry, 49*, 663–672.

Kirmayer, L. J., & Looper, K. J. (2007). Somatoform disorders. In M. Hersen, S.M. Turner, & D. C. Beidel (Eds.), *Adult Psychopathology and Diagnosis* (5th ed.). New York: John Wiley & Sons.

Kirmayer, L. J. & Robbins, J. M. (1996). Patients who somatize in primary care: A longitudinal study of cognitive and social characteristics. *Psychological Medicine, 265*, 937–951.

Klassen, B. J., Porcerelli, J. H., & Markova, T. (2013). The effects of PTSD symptoms on health care resource utilization in a low-income, urban primary care setting. *Journal of Traumatic Stress, 26*, 636–639.

Klein, R. G. (1995). Is panic disorder associated with childhood separation anxiety disorder? *Clinical Neuropharmacology, 18*, S7–S14.

Klerman, G. L., Weissman, M. M., Rounsaville, B. K., & Chevron, E. (1984). *Interpersonal psychotherapy of depression*. New York: Basic Books.

Klesges, R. C., Obarzanek, E., Kumanyika, S., Murray, D. M., Klesges, L. M., Relyea, G. E., … McClanahan, B. S. (2010). The Memphis Girls' health Enrichment Multi-site Studies (GEMS): An evaluation of the efficacy of a 2-year obesity prevention program in African American girls. *Archives of Pediatrics & Adolescent Medicine, 164*, 1007–1014.

Klin, A. (2006). Autism and Asperger syndrome: An overview. *Revista Brasileira de Psiquiatria, 28* (1 Suppl), S3–S11.

Kluft, R. P. (1993). Multiple personality disorder. In D. Spiegel (Ed.), *Dissociative disorders: A clinical review* (pp. 17–44). Lutherville, MD: Sidran Press.

Klump, K. L., Gobrogge, K. L., Perkins, P. S., Thorne, D., Sisk, C. L., & Breedlove, S. M. (2006). Preliminary evidence that gonadal hormones organize and activate disordered eating. *Psychological Medicine, 36*, 539–546.

Klump, K. L., Racine, S. E., Hildebrandt, B., Burt, S. A., Neale, M., Sisk, C. L., … Keel, P. K. (2014). Ovarian hormone influences on dysregulated eating: A comparison of associations in women with versus without binge episodes. *Clinical Psychological Science, 2*, 545–559.

Koch, S. V., Larsen, J. T., Mouridsen, S. E., Bentz, M., Petersen, L., Bulik, C., … Plessen, K. J. (2015). Autism spectrum disorder in individuals with anorexia nervosa and in their first- and second-degree relatives: Danish nationwide register-based cohort-study. *British Journal of Psychiatry, 206*, 401–407.

Kocovski, N. L., Fleming, J. E., Hawley, L. L., Huta, V., & Antony, M. M. (2013). Mindfulness and acceptance-based group therapy versus traditional cognitive behavioral group therapy for social anxiety disorder: A randomized controlled trial. *Behaviour Research and Therapy, 51*, 889–898.

Koenigs, M., & Grafman, J. (2009). The functional neuroanatomy of depression: Distinct roles for ventromedial and dorsolateral prefrontal cortex. *Behavioural Brain Research, 201*, 239–243.

Koessler, L., Maillard, L., Benhadid, A., Vignal, J.-P., Braun, M., & Vespignani, H. (2007). Spatial localization of EEG electrodes. *Neurophysiologie Clinique/Clinical Neurophysiology, 37*, 97–102.

Kog, E., Vertommen, H., & Vandereycken, W. (1987). Minuchin's psychosomatic family model revised: A concept-validation study using a multitrait-multimethod approach. *Family Process, 26*, 235–253.

Kohn, R., Westlake, R. J., Rasmussen, S. A., Marsland, R. T., & Norman, W. H. (1997). Clinical features of obsessive-compulsive disorder in elderly patients. *The American Journal of Geriatric Psychiatry, 5*, 211–215.

Kolb, B., & Whishaw, I. Q. (1996). *Fundamentals of human neuropsychology* (4th ed.). New York.

Kolevzon, A., Mathewson, K. A., & Hollander, E. (2006). Selective serotonin reuptake inhibitors in autism: A review of efficacy and tolerability. *Journal of Clinical Psychiatry, 67*, 407–414.

Kõlves, K., & De Leo, D. (2014). Suicide rates in children aged 10–14 years worldwide: Changes in the past two decades. *British Journal of Psychiatry, 205*, 283–285.

Kooyman, I., Dean, K., Harvey S., & Walsh, E. (2007). Outcomes of public concern in schizophrenia. *British Journal of Psychiatry, 50*, s29–s36.

Koran, L. M., Aboujaoude, E. N., & Gamel, N. N. (2007). Escitalopram treatment of kleptomania: An open-label trial followed by double-blind discontinuation. *The Journal of Clinical Psychiatry, 68*, 422–427.

Kosfeld, M., Heinrichs, M., Zak, P. J., Fischbacher, U., & Fehr, E. (2005). Oxytocin increases trust in humans. *Nature, 435*, 673–676.

Kossowsky, J., Pfaltz, M. C., Schneider, S., Taeymans, J., Locher, C., & Gaab, J. (2013). The separation anxiety hypothesis of panic disorder revisited: A meta-analysis. *American Journal of Psychiatry, 170*, 768–781.

Kossowsky, J., Wilhelm, F. H., Rogh, W. T., & Schneider, S. (2012). Separation anxiety disorder in children: Disorder-specific responses to experimental separation from the mother. *Journal of Child Psychology and Psychiatry, 53*, 178–187.

Kovacs, M. (1992). *The Children's Depression Inventory (CDI) manual*. Toronto, ON: Multi-Health Systems.

Kozlowska, K., Nunn, K. P., Rose, D., Morris, A., Ouvrier, R. A., & Varghese, J. (2007). Conversion disorder in Australian pediatric practice. *Journal of the American Academy of Child & Adolescent Psychiatry, 46*, 68–75.

Kraepelin, E. (1919/1971). *Dementia praecox and paraphrenia*. New York: Robert E. Krieger Publishing Co.

Krahn, L. E., Li, H., & O'Connor, M. K. (2003). Patients who strive to be ill: Factitious disorder with physical symptoms. *American Journal of Psychiatry, 160*, 1163–1168.

Kranzler, H. N., Roofeh, D., Gerbino-Rosen, G., Dombrowski, C., McMeniman, M., DeThomas, C., & Kumra, S. (2005). Clozapine: Its impact on aggressive behavior among children and adolescents with schizophrenia. *Journal of the American Academy of Child and Adolescent Psychiatry, 44*, 53–63.

Kranzler, H. N., Kester, H. M., Gerbino-Rosen, G., Henderson, I. N., Youngerman, J., Beauzile, G., … Kumra, S. (2006). Treatment-refractory schizophrenia in children and adolescents: An update on clozapine and other pharmacological interventions. *Child and Adolescent Psychiatric Clinics of North America, 15*, 135–159.

Krebs, G., & Heyman, I. (2015). Obsessive-compulsive disorder in children and adolescents. *Archives of Disease in Childhood, 100*, 495–499.

Krem, M. M. (2004). Motor conversion disorders reviewed from a neuropsychiatric perspective. *Journal of Clinical Psychiatry, 65*, 783–790.

Krishnan, K. R. (2005). Psychiatric and medical comorbidities of bipolar disorder. *Psychosomatic Medicine, 67*, 1–8.

Kroenke, K., & Mangelsdorff, A. D. (1989). Common symptoms in ambulatory care: Incidence, evaluation, therapy, and outcome. *American Journal of Medicine, 86*, 262–266.

Kroenke, K. & Spitzer, R. L. (1998). Gender differences in the reporting of physical and somatoform symptoms. *Psychosomatic Medicine, 60*, 150–155.

Kronenberger, W. G., & Dunn, D. W. (2003). Learning disorders. *Neurological Clinics of North America, 21*, 941–952.

Krueger, R. B., & Kaplan, M. (1997). Frotteurism: Assessment and treatment. In D. R. Laws and W. O'Donohue (Eds.), *Sexual Deviance. Theory, assessment, and treatment* (pp. 131–151). New York: Guilford Press.

Krueger, R. B., & Kaplan, M. S. (2001). The paraphilic and hypersexual disorders: An overview. *Journal of Psychiatric Practice, 7*, 391–403.

Krueger, R. B., & Kaplan, M. S. (2002). Behavioral and psychopharmacological treatment of the paraphilic and hypersexual disorders. *Journal of Psychiatric Practice, 8*, 21–32.

Krueger, R. F., Watson, D., & Barlow, D. H. (2005). Introduction to the special section: Toward a dimensionally based taxonomy of psychopathology. *Journal of Abnormal Psychology, 114*, 491–493.

Krysinska, K., Heller, T. S., & De Leo, D. (2006). Suicide and deliberate self-harm in personality disorders. *Current Opinions in Psychiatry, 19*, 95–101.

Kuhn, E., Greene, C., Hoffman, J., Nguyen, T., Wald, L., Schmidt, J., … Ruzek, J. (2014). Preliminary evaluation of PTSD Coach, a smartphone app for post- traumatic stress symptoms. *Military Medicine, 179*, 12–18.

Kuhn, T. S. (1962). *The structure of scientific revolutions*. Chicago: University of Chicago Press.

Kumar, P., Slavich, G. M., Berghorst, L. H., Treadway, M. T., Brooks, N. H., Dutra, S. J., … Pizzagalli, D. A. (2015). Perceived life stress exposure modulates reward-related medial prefrontal cortex responses to acute stress in depression. *Journal of Affective Disorders, 180*, 104–111.

Kumar, R., Marks, M., Wieck, A., Hirst, D., Campbell, I., & Checkley, S. (1993). Neuroendocrine and psychosocial mechanisms in post-partum psychosis. *Progress in NeuroPsychopharmacology and Biological Psychiatry, 17*, 571–579.

Kunik, M., Veazey, C., Cully, J., Souchek, J., Graham, D., Hopko, D., … Wray, N. (2008). COPD education and cognitive behavioral therapy group treatment for clinically significant symptoms of depression and anxiety in COPD patients: A randomized controlled trial. *Psychological Medicine, 38*, 385–396.

Kunik, M. E., Roundy, K., Veazey, C., Souchek, J., Richardson, P., Wray, N. P., & Stanley, M. A. (2005). Surprisingly high prevalence of anxiety and depression in chronic breathing disorders. *Chest Journal, 127*, 1205–1211.

Kunik, M. E., Snow, A. L., Molinari, V. A., Menke, T. J., Souchek, J., Sullivan, G., & Ashton, C. M. (2003). Health care utilization in dementia patients with psychiatric comorbidity. *The Gerontologist, 43*, 86–91.

Kupelian, V., Link, C. L., Rosen, R. C., & McKinlay, J. B. (2008). Socioeconomic status, not race/ethnicity, contributes to variation in the prevalence of erectile dysfunction: Results from the Boston Area Community Health (BACH) Survey. *Journal of Sexual Medicine, 5*, 1325–1333.

Kupfer, D. J. (2005). The increasing medical burden in bipolar disorder. *The Journal of the American Medical Association, 293*, 2528–2530.

Kurtz, M. M., Seltzer, J. C., Ferrand, J. L., & Wexler, B. E. (2005). Neurocognitive function in schizophrenia at a 10-year follow-up: A preliminary investigation. *CNS Spectrums, 10*, 277–280.

Kurz, S., van Dyck, Z., Dremmel, D., Munsch, S., & Hilbert, A. (2015). Early-onset restrictive eating disturbances in primary school boys and girls. *European Child & Adolescent Psychiatry, 24*, 779–785.

Kushner, M. G., Sher, K. J., & Beitman, B. D. (1990). The relationship between alcohol problems and the anxiety disorders. *American Journal of Psychiatry, 147*, 685–695.

Kuwabara, H., Shioiri, T., Nishimura, A., Abe, R., Hideyuki, N., Ueno, Y., … Someya, T. (2006). Differences in characteristics between suicide victims who left notes or not. *Journal of Affective Disorders, 94*, 145–149.

Lackner, J.M., Gudleski, G.D., & Blanchard, E.B. (2004) Beyond abuse: The association among parenting style, abdominal pain, and somatization in IBS patients. (2004). *Behavior Research and Therapy, 42*, 41–56.

La Greca, A., Silverman, W. K., Vernberg, E. M., & Prinstein, M. J. (1996). Symptoms of posttraumatic stress in children after Hurricane Andrew: A prospective study. *Journal of Consulting and Clinical Psychology, 64*, 712–723.

La Vaque, T. J., & Rossiter, T. (2001). The ethical use of placebo controls in clinical research: The Declaration of Helsinki. *Applied Psychophysiology and Biofeedback, 26*, 23–37.

Ladouceur, R., Gosselin, P., & Dugas, M. J. (2000). Experimental manipulation of uncertainty. *Behaviour Research and Therapy, 38*, 933–941.

LaGreca, A., Silverman, W. K., Vernberg, E. M., & Prinstein, M. J. (1996). Symptoms of posttraumatic stress in children after Hurricane Andrew: A prospective study. *Journal of Consulting and Clinical Psychology, 64*, 712–723.

Lahey, B.B., Pelham, W.E., Stein, M.A., Loney, J., Trapani, C., Nugent, K., … Baumann, B. (1998). Validity of DSM-IV attention deficit hyperactivity disorder for younger children. *Journal of the American Academy of Child and Adolescent Psychiatry, 37*, 695–702.

Lahey, B.B., Pelham, W.E., Loney, J., Kipp, H., Ehrhardt, A., Lee, S.S., … Masetti, G. (2004). Three year predictive validity of DSM-IV attention deficit hyperactivity disorder in children diagnosed at 4–6 years of age. *American Journal of Psychiatry, 162*, 2014–2020.

Lake, J. (2007). Emerging paradigms in medicine: Implications for the future of psychiatry. *Explore: The Journal of Science and Healing, 3*, 467–477.

Lalonde, J. K., Hudson, J. I., Gigante, R. A., & Pope, H. G., Jr. (2001). Canadian and American psychiatrists' attitudes toward dissociative disorders diagnoses. *Canadian Journal of Psychiatry, 46*, 407–412.

Lalumière, M. L., & Quinsey, V. L. (1994). The discriminability of rapists from non-sex offenders using phallometric measures: A meta-analysis. *Criminal Justice and Behavior, 21*, 150–157.

Lam, D. H., Watkins, E. R., Hayward, P., Bright, J., Wright, K., Kerr, N., … Sham, P. (2003). A randomized controlled study of cognitive therapy for relapse prevention for bipolar affective disorder: Outcome of the first year. *Archives in General Psychiatry, 60*, 145–152.

Lam, R., & Levitt, A. (1999). *Canadian consensus guidelines for the treatment of seasonal affective disorder*. Vancouver, Canada: Clinical & Academic Publishing.

Lamb, D. H., Catanzaro, S. J., & Moorman, A. S. (2003). Psychologists reflect on their sexual relationships with clients, supervisees, and students: Occurrence, impact, rationales and collegial intervention. *Professional Psychology: Research and Practice, 34*, 102–107.

Lamb, H. R., & Bachrach, L. I. (2001). Some perspectives on deinstitutionalization. *Psychiatric Services, 52*, 1039–1045.

Lamb, H. R., & Weinberger, L. E. (2005). The shift of psychiatric inpatient care from hospitals to jails and prisons. *Journal of the American Academy of Psychiatry and the Law, 33*, 529–534.

Lambert, M. J., & Lambert, J. M. (1999). Use of psychological tests for assessing treatment outcome. In M. E. Maruish (Ed.), *The use of psychological testing for treatment planning and outcomes assessment* (2nd ed., pp. 115–151). Mahwah, NJ: Lawrence Erlbaum Associates.

Lambert, M. V., Sierra, M., Phillips, M. L., & David, A .S. (2002). The spectrum of organic depersonalization: A review plus four new cases. *Journal of Neuropsychiatry and Clinical Neurosciences, 14*, 141–154.

Lambie, I., & Randell, I. (2011). Creating a firestorm: A review of children who deliberately light fires. *Clinical Psychology Review, 31*, 307–327.

Landén, M., Wålinder, J., Hambert, G., & Lundsström, B. (1998). Factors predictive of regret in sex reassignment. *Acta Psychiatrica Scandinavica, 97*, 284–289.

Landgraf, D., Long, J., Der-Avakian, A., Streets, M., & Welsh, D. K. (2015). Dissociation of learned helplessness and fear conditioning in mice: A mouse model of depression. *PLOS ONE, 10*, e0125892.

Laney, C., & Loftus, E. F. (2005). Traumatic memories are not necessarily accurate memories. *Canadian Journal of Psychiatry, 50*, 823–828.

Lang, F. U., Kösters, M., Lang, S., Becker, T., & Jäger, M. (2013). Psychopathological long-term outcome of schizophrenia— A review. *Acta Psychiatrica Scandinavica, 127*, 173–182.

Langa, K. M., & Levine, D. A. (2014). The diagnosis and management of mild cognitive impairment: A clinical review. *Journal of the American Medical Association, 312*, 2551–2561.

Langer, L., Warheit, G., & Zimmerman, R. (1992). Epidemiological study of problem eating behaviors and related attitudes in the general population. *Addictive Behaviors, 16*, 167–173.

Långström, N., Rahman, Q., Carlström, E., & Lichtenstein, P. (2010). Genetic and environmental effects on same-sex sexual behavior: A population study of twins in Sweden. *Archives of Sexual Behavior, 39*, 75–80.

Larimer, M., Palmer, R., & Marlatt, G. (1999). Relapse prevention: An overview of Marlatt's cognitive-behavioral model. *Alcohol Research & Health, 23*, 151–160.

Larocca, F. E., & Della-Fera, M. A. (1986). Rumination: Its significance in adults with bulimia nervosa. *Psychosomatics, 27*, 209–212.

Larson, N., Dewolfe, J., Story, M., & Neumark-Sztainer, D. (2014). Adolescent consumption of sports and energy drinks: Linkages to higher physical activity, unhealthy beverage patterns, cigarette smoking, and screen media use. *Journal of Nutrition Education and Behavior, 46*, 181–187.

Larson, M., & Sweeten, G. (2012). Breaking up Is Hard to Do: Romantic Dissolution, Offending, and Substance Use During the Transition to Adulthood. *Criminology, 50*, 605–636.

Lasègue, E.-C. (1873). On hysterical anorexia. *Medical Times and Gazette, 265–266*, 367–369.

Lask, B., & Bryant-Waugh, R. (2000). *Anorexia nervosa and related eating disorders in children and adolescence*. Hove, East Sussex, United Kingdom: Psychology Press.

Latner, J. D., Hildebrandt, T., Rosewall, J. K., Chisholm, A. M., & Hayashi, K. (2007). Loss of control over eating reflects eating disturbances and general psychopathology. *Behavior Research and Therapy, 45*, 2203–2211.

Laub, G. (2012). What happened to the girls in Le Roy? Retrieved from http://www.nytimes.com/2012/03/11/magazine/teenage-girls-twitching-le-roy.html

Laumann, E. O., Gagnon, J. H., Michael, R. T., & Michaels, S. (1994). *The social organization of sexuality: Sexual practices in the United States*. Chicago: University of Chicago Press.

Laumann, E. O., Paik, A., & Rosen, R. C. (1999). Sexual dysfunction in the United States. *Journal of the American Medical Association, 281*, 537–544.

Laumann, E. O., Nicolosi, A., Glasser, D. B., Paik, A., Gingell, C., Moreira, E., & Wang, T. (2005). Sexual problems among women and men aged 40–80 y: prevalence and correlates identified in the Global Study of Sexual Attitudes and Behaviors. *International Journal of Impotence Research, 17*, 39–57.

Lawrence, A. A. (2003). Factors associated with satisfaction or regret following male-to-female sex reassignment surgery. *Archives of Sexual Behavior, 32*, 299–315.

Lawrence, A. A., & Zucker, K. J. (2012). Gender identity disorders. In M. Hersen and D.C. Beidel (Eds.), *Adult psychopathology and diagnosis* (6th ed.). New York: Wiley.

Laws, D. R. (2001). Olfactory aversion: Notes on procedure, with speculations on its mechanism of effect. *Sexual Abuse: A Journal of Research and Treatment*, 275–287.

Lawson, W. B., Hepler, N., Holiday, J., & Cuffel, B. (1994). Race as a factor in inpatient and outpatient admissions and diagnosis. *Hospital and Community Psychiatry, 45*, 72–74.

Lay, B., Blanz, B., Hartmann, M., & Schmidt, M. H. (2000). The psychosocial outcome of adolescent-onset schizophrenia: A 12-year follow-up. *Schizophrenia Bulletin, 26*, 801–816.

le Grange, D., Crosby, R. D., Rathouz, P. J., & Leventhal, B. L. (2007). A randomized controlled comparison of family-based treatment and supportive psychotherapy for adolescent bulimia nervosa. *Archives of General Psychiatry, 64*, 1049–1056.

Le Roux, H., Gatz, M., & Wetherell, J. L. (2005). Age at onset of generalized anxiety disorder in older adults. *The American Journal of Geriatric Psychiatry, 13*, 23–30.

LeBeau, R. T., Glenn, D., Liao, B., Wittchen,H. U., Beedo-Baum, K., Ollendick, T., & Craske, M. G. (2010). Specific phobia: A review of DSM-IV specific phobia and preliminary recommendations for DSM-V. *Depression & Anxiety, 27*, 148–167.

Lecrubier, Y., Wittchen, H. U., Faravelli, C., Bobes, J., Patel, A., & Knapp, M. (2000). A European perspective on social anxiety disorder. *European Psychiatry, 15*, 5–16.

Lee, B., & Newberg, A. (2005). Religion and health: A review and critical analysis. *Journal of Religion and Science, 40*, 443–468.

Leff, J., Tress, K., & Edwards, B. (1988). The clinical course of depressive symptoms in schizophrenia. *Schizophrenia Research, 1*, 25–30.

Leiblum, S. R. (2000). Vaginimus: A most perplexing problem. In S. R. Leiblum & R. C. Rosen (Eds.), *Principles and practice of sex therapy* (pp. 181–202). New York: Guilford Press.

Leigh, B. C., Temple, M. T., & Trocki, K. F. (1993). The sexual behavior of US adults: Results from a national survey. *American Journal of Public Health, 83*, 1400–1408.

Leit, R. A., Gray, J. J., & Pope, H. G. (2002). The media's representation of the ideal male body: A cause for muscle dysmorphia? *International Journal of Eating Disorders, 31*, 334–338.

Lejuez, C. W., Hopko, D. R., & Hopko, S. D. (2001). A brief behavioral activation treatment for depression: Treatment manual. *Behavior Modification, 25*, 255–286.

LeMarquand, D., Pihl, R., & Benkelfat, C. (1994). Serotonin and alcohol intake, abuse, and dependence: Clinical evidence. *Biological Psychiatry, 36*, 326–337.

Lenze, E. J., Karp, J. F., Mulsant, B. H., Blank, S., Shear, M. K., Houck, P. R., & Reynolds, C. F. (2005). Somatic symptoms in late-life anxiety: Treatment issues. *Journal of Geriatric Psychiatry and Neurology, 18*, 89–96.

Lenze, E. J., Mohlman, J., & Wetherell, J. L. (2015). Anxiety, obsessive-compulsive, and trauma-related disorders. In D. C. Steffens, D. G. Blazer, & M. E. Thakur (Eds.), *Textbook of geriatric psychiatry, DSM-5 edition* (pp. 333–371). Washington, DC: American Psychiatric Association.

Lenze, E. J., Rogers, J. C., Martire, L. M., Mulsant, B. H., Rollman, B. L., Dew, M. A., … Reynolds, C. F. (2001). The association of late-life depression and anxiety with physical disability: A review of the literature and prospectus for future research. *American Journal of Geriatric Psychiatry, 9*, 113–135.

Lenze, E. J., Rollman, B. L., Shear, M. K., Dew, M. A., Pollock, B. G., Ciliberti, C., … Spitznagel, E. (2009). Escitalopram for older adults with generalized anxiety disorder: A randomized controlled trial. *Journal of the American Medical Association, 301*, 295–303.

Lenzenweger, M. F., Lane, M. C., Loranger, A. W., & Kessler, R. C. (2007). DSM-IV personality disorders in the National Comorbidity Survey Replication. *Biological Psychiatry, 62*, 553–564.

Leon, G., Fulkerson, J., Perry, C., & Cudeck, R. (1993). Personality and behavioral vulnerabilities associated with risk status for eating disorders in adolescent girls. *Journal of Abnormal Psychology, 102*, 438–444.

Leonard, D., Brann, S., & Tiller, J. (2005). Dissociative disorders: Pathways to diagnosis, clinician attitudes, and their impact. *Australian & New Zealand Journal of Psychiatry, 39*, 940–946.

Leonard, H., Gixon. G., Whitehouse, A. J. O., Bourke, J., Aiberti, K., Nassar, N.,… Glasson, E.J. (2010). Unpacking the complex nature of the autism epidemic. *Research in Autism Spectrum Disorders, 4*, 548–554.

Lerner, M., & Wigal, T. (2008). Long-term safety of stimulant medications used to treat children with ADHD. *Journal of Psychosocial Nursing and Mental Health Services, 46*, 39–48.

Lesaca, T. (2001). Executive functions in parents with ADHD. *Psychiatric Times, XVIII*, Issue 11.

Leung, A. K. C., & Robson, W. L. M. (2007). Tuberous sclerosis complex: A review. *Journal of Pediatric Health Care, 21*, 108–114.

Levine, S. B. (2010). What is sexual addiction? *Journal of Sex and Marital Therapy, 36*, 261–275.

Levinson, D. F. (2005). Meta-analysis in psychiatric genetics. *Current Psychiatry Reports, 7*, 143–151.

Levinson, D. F., Mostafavi, S., Milaneschi, Y., Rivera, M., Ripke, S., Wray, N. R., & Sullivan, P. F. (2014). Genetic studies of major depressive disorder: Why are there no genome-wide association study findings and what can we do about it? *Biological Psychiatry, 76*, 510–512.

Lewinsohn, P., Seeley, J., Moerk, K., & Striegel-Moore, R. H. (2002). Gender differences in eating disorder symptoms in young adults. *International Journal of Eating Disorders, 32*, 426–440.

Lewinsohn, P. M., & Graf, M. (1973). Pleasant activities and depression. *Journal of Consulting and Clinical Psychology, 41*, 261–268.

Lewinsohn, P. M. (1974). A behavioral approach to depression. In R. J. Friedman & M. M. Katz. (Ed.), *Psychology of depression: Contemporary theory and research* (pp.157–185). Oxford: Wiley.

Lewis, D. O., Yeager, C. A., Swica, Y., Pincus, J. H., & Lewis, M. (1997). Objective documentation of child abuse and dissociation in 12 murderers with dissociative identity disorder. *American Journal of Psychiatry, 143*, 1703–1710.

Lewis, R. W., Sadovsky, R., Eardley, I., O'Leary, M., Seftel, A., Wang, W. C.,… Ahuja, S. (2005). The efficacy of tadalafil in clinical populations. *Journal of Sexual Medicine, 2*, 517–531.

Lewis-Fernandez, R. (1998). A cultural critique of the DSM-IV dissociative disorders section. *Transcultural Psychiatry, 35*, 387–400.

Li, F., Fisher, K. J., Harmer, P., McAuley, E., & Wilson, N. L. (2003). Fear of falling in elderly persons: Association with falls, functional ability, and quality of life. *The Journals of Gerontology Series B: Psychological Sciences and Social Sciences, 58*, P283–P290.

Li, W., Ji, W., Li, Z., He, K., Wang, Q., Chen, J., … Shi, Y. (2015). Genetic association of *ACSM1* variation with schizophrenia and major depressive disorder in the Han Chinese population. *American Journal of Medical Genetics, Part B, Neuropsychiatric Genetics, 168B*, 144–149.

Li, W., Lai, T. M., Bohon, C., Loo, S. K., McCurdy, D., Strober, M., … Feusner, J. (2015). Anorexia nervosa and body dysmorphic disorder are associated with abnormalities in processing visual information. *Psychological Medicine, 45*, 2111–2122.

Libbey, J. E., Sweeten T. L., McMahon, W. M., & Fujinami, R. S. (2005). Autistic disorder and viral infections. *Journal of NeuroVirology, 11*, 1–10.

Libow, J. A. (2000). Child and adolescent illness falsification. *Pediatrics, 105*, 336–342.

Lidz, C. W., Mulvey, E. P., & Gardner, W. (1993). The accuracy of predictions of violence to others. *Journal of the American Medical Association, 269*, 1007–1011.

Lidz, C. W. (2006). The therapeutic misconception and our models of competency and informed consent. *Behavioral Sciences and the Law, 24*, 535–540.

Lieb, R., Wittchen, H., Höfler, M., Fuetsch, M., Stein, M., & Merikangas, K. (2000). Parental psychopathology, parenting styles, and the risk of social phobia in offspring: A prospective-longitudinal community study. *Archives of General Psychiatry, 57*, 859–866.

Lieberman, J. A., Stroup, T. S., McEvoy, J. P., Swartz, M. S., Rosenheck, R. A., Perkins, D. O., … Severe, J. (2005). Effectiveness of antipsychotic drugs in patients with chronic schizophrenia. *New England Journal of Medicine, 353*, 1209–1223.

Lilenfeld, L., Kaye, W. H., Greeno, C., Merikangas, K., Plotnikov, K., Pollice, C., … Nagy, L. (1998). A controlled family study of restricting anorexia and bulimia nervosa: Comorbidity in probands and disorders in first-degree relatives. *Archives of General Psychiatry, 55*, 603–610.

Lilienfeld, A. M., & Lilienfeld, D. E. (1980). *Foundations of epidemiology* (2nd ed.). New York: Oxford University Press.

Lilienfeld, S. C. (2007). Psychological treatments that cause harm. *Perspectives on Psychological Science, 2*, 53–70.

Lilienfeld, S. O., Lynn, S. J., Kirsch, I., Chaves, J. F., Sarbin, T. R., & Ganaway, G. K. (1999). Dissociative identity disorder and the sociocognitive model: Recalling the lessons of the past. *Psychological Bulletin, 125*, 507–523.

Lilienfeld, S. O., Wood, J. M., & Garb, H. N. (2000). The scientific status of projective techniques. *Psychological Science in the Public Interest, 1*, 27–66.

Lin, J. C., Karno, M. P., Grella, C. E., Warda, U., Liao, D. H., Hu, P., & Moore, A. A. (2011). Alcohol, tobacco, and nonmedical drug use disorders in US adults aged 65 years and older: Data from the 2001–2002 National Epidemiologic Survey of Alcohol and Related Conditions. *The American Journal of Geriatric Psychiatry, 19*, 292–299.

Linaker, O. M. (2000). Dangerous female psychiatric patients: Prevalence and characteristics. *Acta Psychiatrica Scandinavica, 101*, 67–72.

Linehan, M. M., Heard, H., & Armstrong, H. (1993). Naturalistic follow-up of a behavioral treatment for chronically parasuicidal borderline patients. *Archives of General Psychiatry, 50*, 971–974.

Linehan, M. M., Comtois, K. A., Murray, A. M., Brown, M. Z., Gallop, R. J., Heard, H. L., … Lindenboim, N. (2006). Two-year randomized controlled trial and follow-up of dialectical behavior therapy vs therapy by experts for suicidal behaviors and borderline personality disorder. *Archives of General Psychiatry, 63*, 757–766.

Linet, O. I., & Ogrinc, F. G. (1996). Efficacy and safety of intracavernosal alprostadil in men with erectile dysfunction. The Alprostadil Study Group. *New England Journal of Medicine, 334*, 873–877.

Linton, S. J. (2002). A prospective study of the effects of sexual or physical abuse on back pain. *Pain, 96*, 347–351.

Lipsitz, J. D., Markowitz, J. C., Cherry, S., & Fyer, A. J. (1999). Open trial of interpersonal psychotherapy for the treatment of social phobia. *American Journal of Psychiatry, 156*, 1814–1816.

Lipsitz, J. D., Gur, M., Miller, N. L., Forand, N., Vermes, D., & Fyer, A. J. (2006). An open pilot study of interpersonal psychotherapy for panic disorder (IPT-PD). *Journal of Nervous and Mental Disease, 194*, 440–445.

Liptzin, B. (2004). Delirium. In J. Sadavoy, L. F. Jarvik, G. T. Grossberg, & B. S. Meyers (Eds.), *Comprehensive textbook of geriatric psychiatry* (3rd ed., pp. 525–544). New York: W.W. Norton & Co.

Litz, B. T., Gray, M. J., Bryant, R. A., & Adler, A. B. (2002). Early intervention for trauma: Current status and future directions. *Clinical Psychology: Science and Practice, 9*, 112–134.

Ljótsson, B., Hesser, H., Andersson, E., Lindfors, P., Hursti, T., Rück, C., … Hedman, E. (2013). Mechanisms of change in an exposure-based treatment for irritable bowel syndrome. *Journal of Consulting and Clinical Psychology, 81*, 1113–1126.

Lochner, C., du Toit, P. L., Zungu-Dirwayi, N., Marais, A., van Kradenburg, J., Seedat, S., … Stein, D. J. (2002). Childhood trauma in obsessive-compulsive disorder, trichotillomania, and controls. *Depression and Anxiety, 15*, 66–68.

Lock, J., le Grange, D., Agras, W. S., & Dare, C. (2002). *Treatment manual for anorexia nervosa: A family-based approach*. New York: Guilford Press.

Lock, J., Le Grange, D., Agras, W. S., Moye, A., Bryson, S. W., & Jo, B. (2010). Randomized clinical trial comparing family-based treatment with adolescent-focused individual therapy for adolescents with anorexia nervosa. *Archives of General Psychiatry, 67*, 1025–1032.

Lock, J. & le Grange, D. (2012). *Treatment manual for anorexia nervosa, second edition: A family-based approach*. New York: Guilford Press.

Lockwood, K. A., Alexopoulos, G. S., Kakuma, T., & Van Gorp, W. G. (2000). Subtypes of cognitive impairment in depressed older adults. *The American Journal of Geriatric Psychiatry, 8*, 201–208.

Loeber, R., Burke, J. D., Lahey, B. B., Winters, A., & Zera, M. (2000). Oppositional defiant and conduct disorder: A review of the past 10 years, Part I. *Journal of the American Academy of Child and Adolescent Psychiatry, 39*, 1468–1484.

Loeber, R., Burke, J., & Pardini, D. A. (2009). Perspectives on oppositional defiant disorder, conduct disorder, and psychopathic features. *Journal of Child Psychology and Psychiatry, 50*, 133–142.

Loewenstein, R. J. (2005). Psychopharmacologic treatments for dissociative identity disorder. *Psychiatric Annals, 35*, 666–673.

Loftus, E. F. (1993). The reality of repressed memories. *American Psychologist, 48*, 518.

Loftus, E. F., & Pickrell, J. E. (1995). The formation of false memories. *Psychiatric Annals, 25*, 720–725.

Logue, M. W., Amstadter, A. B., Baker, D. G., Duncan, L., Koenen, K. C., Liberzon, I., … Uddin, M. (2015). The Psychiatric Genomics Consortium Post-traumatic Stress Disorder Workgroup: Post-traumatic stress disorder enters the age of large-scale genomic collaboration. *Neuropsychopharmacology, 40*, 2287–2297.

Lohman, M. C., Raue, P. J., Greenberg, R. L., & Bruce, M. L. (2016). Reducing suicidal ideation in home health care: Results from the CAREPATH depression care management trial. *International Journal of Geriatric Psychiatry, 7*, 708–716.

Long, D. N., Wisniewski, A. B., & Migeon, C. J. (2004). Gender role across development in adult women with congenital adrenal hyperplasia due to 21-hydroxylase deficiency. *Journal of Pediatric Endocrinology & Metabolism, 17*, 1367–1373.

López, S. R., & Guarnaccia, P. J. (2000). Cultural psychopathology: Uncovering the social world of mental illness. *Annual Review of Psychology, 51*, 571–598.

López, S. R., & Guarnaccia, P. J. (2007). Cultural dimensions of psychopathology: The social world's impact on mental illness. In J. E. Maddux &. B. A. Winstead. (Eds.), *Psychopathology: Foundations for a contemporary understanding* (pp. 19–38). New York: Routledge.

Lopizzo, N., Bocchio Chiavetto, L., Cattane, N., Plazzotta, G., Tarazi, F. I., Pariante, C. M., … Cattaneo, A. (2015). Gene-environment interaction in major depression: Focus on experience-dependent biological systems. *Frontiers in Psychiatry, 6*, 68.

Lord, C., Risi, S., DiLavore, P. S., Shulman, C., Thurn, A., & Pickles, A. (2006). Autism from 2 to 9 years of age. *Archives of General Psychiatry, 63*, 694–701.

Lott, I. T., & Head, E. (2005). Alzheimer disease and Down syndrome: Factors in pathogenesis. *Neurobiology of Aging, 26*, 383–389.

Low, N. C., Cui, L., & Merikangas, K. R. (2008). Community versus clinic sampling: Effect on the familial aggregation of anxiety disorders. *Biological Psychiatry, 63*, 884–890.

Lubke, G. H., Laurin, C., Amin, N., Hottenga, J. J., Willemsen, G., van Grootheest, G., … Boomsma, D. I. (2014). Genome-wide analyses of borderline personality features. *Molecular Psychiatry, 19*, 923–929.

Luchins, A. S. (2001). Moral treatment in asylums and general hospitals in 19th-century America. *The Journal of Psychiatry, 123*, 312–330.

Luders, E., Sanchez, F. J., Gaser, C., Toga, A. W., Narr, K. L., Hamilton, L. S., & Vilain, E. (2009). Regional gray matter variation in male-to-female transsexualism. *Neuroimage, 46*, 904–907.

Lugo Steidel, A., & Contreras, J. (2003). A new Familism Scale for use with Latino populations. *Hispanic Journal of Behavioral Sciences, 25*, 312–330.

Lukaschek, K., Kruse, J., Emeny, R. T., Lacruz, M. E., Rothe, A. V., & Ladwig, K. H. (2013). Lifetime traumatic experiences and their impact on PTSD: A general population study. *Social Psychiatry and Psychiatric Epidemilogy, 48*, 525–532.

Lumish, R. A., Young, S. L., Lee, S., Cooper, E., Pressman, E., Guillet, R., & O'Brien, K. O. (2014). Gestational iron deficiency is associated with pica behaviors in adolescents. *Journal of Nutrition, 144*, 1533–1539.

Luoma, J. B., Martin, C. E., & Pearson, J. L. (2002). Contact with mental health and primary care providers before suicide: A review of the evidence. *American Journal of Psychiatry, 159*, 909–916.

Lyketsos, C. G. (2009). Dementia and milder cognitive syndromes. In D. C. Blazer & D. C. Steffens (Eds.), *Textbook of geriatric psychiatry* (pp. 243–260). Washington,DC: American Psychiatric Publishing, Inc.

Lykken, D. (1982). Fearlessness: Its carefree charms and deadly risks. *Psychology Today, 16*, 20–28.

Lynn, K. S. (1987). *Hemingway*. New York: Simon & Schuster.

Lynn, S. J., Berg, J. M., Lilienfeld, S. O., Merckelbach, H., Giesbrecht, T., Accardi, M., & Cleere, C. (2014). Dissociative disorders. In D. C. Beidel, B.C. Frueh, & M, Hersen (Eds.), *Adult psychopathology and diagnosis* (7th ed.)(pp. 407–540). New York: John Wiley and Sons.

Lyons, A. P., & Lyons, H. D. (2006). The new anthropology of sexuality. *Anthropologica, 48*, 153–157.

Mackintosh, M. A., Gatz, M., Wetherell, J. L., & Pedersen, N. L. (2006). A twin study of lifetime generalized anxiety disorder (GAD) in older adults: Genetic and environmental influences shared by neuroticism and GAD. *Twin Research and Human Genetics, 9*(01), 30–37.

Macy, R. D., Behar, L., Paulson, R., Delman, J., Schmid, L., & Smith, S. F. (2004). Community-based, acute posttraumatic stress management: A description and evaluation of a psychosocial-intervention continuum. *Harvard Review of Psychiatry, 12*, 217–228.

Madden, S., Morris, A., Zurynski, Y. A., Kohn, M., & Elliot, E. J. (2009). Burden of eating disorders in 5–13-year-old children in Australia. *Medical Journal of Australia, 190*, 410–414.

Madsen, S. K., Bohon, C., & Feusner, J. D. (2013). Visual processing in anorexia nervosa and body dysmorphic disorder: Similarities, differences, and future research directions. *Journal of Psychiatric Research, 47*, 1483–1491.

Maenner, M.J., Schieve, L.A., Rice, C.E., Cunniff, C., Giarell, E., Kirby, R.S.,… Durkin, M.S. (2013). Frequency and pattern of documented diagnostic features and the age of autism identification. *Journal of the American Academy of Child and Adolescnt Psychiatry, 52*, 805–820.

Magee, W. J., Eaton, W. W., Wittchen, H. U., McGonagle, K. A., & Kessler, R. C. (1996). Agoraphobia, simple phobia, and social phobia in the National Comorbidity Survey. *Archives of General Psychiatry, 53*, 159–168.

Magill, F. (1983) Ernest Hemingway. In F.N. Magill & C. Rollyson (Eds.), *The critical survey of long fiction*. New York: Salem Press.

Maglione, J. E., Vahia, I. V., & Jeste, D. V. (2015). In D. C. Steffens, D. G. Blazer, & M. E. Thakur (Eds.) *Textbook of geriatric psychiatry, DSM-5 edition* (pp. 309–332). Washington, DC: American Psychiatric Association.

Magni, L. R., Purgato, M., Gastaldon, C., Papola, D., Furukawa, T. A., Cipriani, A., & Barbui, C. (2013). Fluoxetine versus other types of pharmacotherapy for depression. *Cochrane Database of Systematic Reviews, 17*, CD004185.

Magno Zito, J., Safer, D. J., dosReis, S., Gardner, J. F., Boles, M., & Lynch, F. (2000). Trends in the prescribing of psychotropic medications to preschoolers. *Journal of the American Medical Association, 283*, 1025–1030.

Magno Zito, J., Safer, D. J., dosReis, S., Gardner, J. F., Magder, L., Soeken, K., Boles, M.,… Riddle, M. A. (2003). Psychotropic practice patterns for youth. *Archives of Pediatrics & Adolescent Medicine, 157*, 17–25.

Magruder, K., Frueh, B.C., Knapp, R., Davis, L., Hamner, M. B., Martin, R. H., Gold, P. B., & Arana, G. W. (2005). Prevalence of posttramatic stress disorder in Veterans Affairs primary care clinics. *General Hospital Psychiatry, 27*, 169–179.

Maher, W. B., & Maher, B. A. (1985). Psychopathology: I. From ancient times to the eighteenth century. In G. A. Kimble & K. Schlesinger (Eds.), *Topics in the history of psychology* (Vol. 2). Hillsdale, NJ: Erlbaum.

Maila de Castro, L. N., Albuquerque, M. R., Malloy-Diniz, L., Nicolato, R., Neves, F. S., de Souza-Duran, F. L.,… Corrêa, H. (2015). A voxel-based morphometry study of gray matter correlates of facial emotion recognition in bipolar disorder. *Psychiatry Research: Neuroimaging, 233*(2), 158–164.

Maj, M. (2005). "Psychiatric comorbidity": An artefact of current diagnostic systems? *The British Journal of Psychiatry, 186*, 182–184.

Major Depressive Disorder Working Group of the Psychiatric Genomics Consortium, Ripke, S., Wray, N. R., Lewis, C. M., Hamilton, S. P., Weissman, M. M., … Sullivan, P. F. (2013). A mega-analysis of genome-wide association studies for major depressive disorder. *Molecular Psychiatry, 18*, 497–511.

Mak, L., Streiner, D. L., & Steiner, M. (2015). Is serotonin transporter polymorphism (5-HTTLPR) allele status a predictor for obsessive-compulsive disorder? A meta-analysis. *Archives of Women's Mental Health, 18*, 435–445.

Malhi, G. S., Adams, D., & Berk, M. (2010). The pharmacological treatment of bipolar disorder in primary care. *Medical Journal of Australia, 193*(4 Suppl), S24–30.

Malhotra, A., Murphy, G., & Kennedy, J. (2004). Pharmacogenetics of psychotropic drug response. *American Journal of Psychiatry, 161*, 780–796.

Malla, A. K., & Payne, J. (2002). Computed tomography of the brain morphology of patients with first-episode schizophrenic psychosis. *Journal of Psychiatry & Neuroscience, 27*, 650–671.

Malla, A. K., & Payne, J. (2005). First-episode psychosis: Psychopathology, quality of life, and functional outcome. *Schizophrenia Bulletin, 31*, 650–671.

Maller, J. J., Thaveenthiran, P., Thomson, R. H., McQueen, S., & Fitzgerald, P. B. (2014). Volumetric, cortical thickness, and white matter integrity alterations in bipolar disorder type I and II. *Journal of Affective Disorders, 169*, 118–127.

Mallinger, J. B., Fisher, S. G., Brown, T., & Lamberti, J. S. (2006). Racial disparities in the use of second-generation antipsychotics for the treatment of schizophrenia. *Psychiatric Services, 57*, 133–136.

Mancuso, S. G., Newton, J. R., Bosanac, P., Rossell, S. L., Nesci, J. B., & Castle D, J. (2015). Classification of eating disorders: Comparison of relative prevalence rates using DSM-IV and DSM-5 criteria. *British Journal of Psychiatry, 206, 519–520.*

Mandelli, L., Petrelli, C., & Serretti, A. (2015). The role of specific early trauma in adult depression: A meta-analysis of published literature. Childhood trauma and adult depression. *European Psychiatry, 30*, 665–680.

Mangweth-Matzek, B., Hoek, H. W., Rupp, C. I., Lackner-Seifert, K., Frey, N., Whitworth, A. B., … Kinzl, J. (2014). Prevalence of eating disorders in middle-aged women. *International Journal of Eating Disorders, 47*, 320–324.

Mann, J. J., Brent, D. A., & Arango, V. (2001). The neurobiology and genetics of suicide and attempted suicide: A focus on the serotonergic system. *Neuropsychopharmacology, 24*, 467–477.

Mansueto, C. (2013). Trichotillomania (hair pulling disorder): Conceptualization and treatment. *Independent Practitioner, 33*, 120–127.

March, J. S., Parker, J. D., Sullivan, K., Stallings, P., & Conners, K. (1997). The Multidimensional Anxiety Scale for children (MASC): Factor structure, reliability, and validity. *Journal of the American Academy of Child and Adolescent Psychiatry, 36*, 554–565.

March, J. S., Franklin, M. E., Leonard, H. L., & Foa, E. B. (2004). Obsessive-compulsive disorder. In T.L. Morris & J.S. March (Eds). *Anxiety disorders in children and adolescents* (pp. 212–240). New York: Guilford.

Marcus, M. D., Moulton, M. M., & Greeno, C. G. (1995). Binge eating onset in obese patients with binge eating disorder. *Addictive Behaviors, 20*, 747–755.

Margolese, H.W., & Ferreri, F. (2007). Management of conventional antipsychotic-induced tardive dyskinesia. *Journal of Psychiatry and Neuroscience, 32*, 72,

Margulies, D. M., Weintraub, S., Basile, J., Grover, P. J., & Carlson, G. A. (2012). Will disruptive mood dysregulation disorder reduce false diagnosis of bipolar disorder in children? *Bipolar Disorders, 14*, 488–496.

Markowitz, J. C., Petkova, E., Neria, Y., Van Meter, P. E., Zhao, Y., Hembree, E., … Marshall, R. D. (2015). Is exposure necessary? A randomized clinical trial of interpersonal psychotherapy for PTSD. *American Journal of Psychiatry, 172*, 430–440.

Markus, H. R., & Kitayama, S. (1991). Culture and the self: Implications for cognition, emotion and motivation. *Psychological Review, 98*, 244–253.

Marlatt, G. A., & Gordon, J. R. (1985). *Relapse prevention: Maintenance strategies in the treatment of addictive behaviors*. New York: Guilford Press.

Marlatt, G., Larimer, M., Baer, J., & Quigley, L. (1993). Harm reduction for alcohol problems: Moving beyond the controlled drinking controversy. *Behavior Therapy, 24*, 461–504.

Marques, L., Alegria, M., Becker, A. E., Chen, C. N., Fang, A., Chosak, A., & Diniz, J. B. (2011). Comparative prevalence, correlates of impairment, and service utilization for eating disorders across US ethnic groups: Implications for reducing ethnic disparities in health care access for eating disorders. *International Journal of Eating Disorders, 44*, 412–420.

Marshall, W. L., & Eccles, A. (1991). Issues in clinical practice with sex offenders. *Journal of Interpersonal Violence, 6*, 68–93.

Marshall, W. L., Marshall, L. E., & Serran, G. A. (2006). Strategies in the treatment of paraphilias: A critical review. *Annual Review of Sex Research, 17*, 167–182.

Martin, J. L. R., Sainz-Pardo, M., Furukawa, T. A., Martin-Sanchez, E., Seoane, T., & Galan, C. (2007). Review: Benzodiazepines in generalized anxiety disorder: Heterogeneity of outcomes based on a systematic review and meta-analysis of clinical trials. *Journal of Psychopharmacology, 21*, 774–782.

Martin, N., Boomsma, D., & Machin, G. (1997). A twin-pronged attack on complex traits. *Nature Genetics, 17*, 387–392.

Martinez-Barrondo, S., Saiz, P. A., Morales, B., Garcia-Portilla, M. P., Coto, E., Alvarez, V., & Bobes, J. (2005). Serotonin gene polymorphisms in patients with panic disorder. *Actas Espania Psiquiatrica, 33*, 210–215.

Martyn-St. James, M., Cooper, K., Kaltenthaler, E., Dickinson, K., Cantrell, K. Wylie, K., … Hood, C. (2015). Tramadol for premature ejaculation: A systematic review and meta-analysis. *BMC Urology, 15*, 6.

Maruish, M. E. (1999). Introduction *The use of psychological testing for treatment planning and outcomes assessment* (2nd ed., pp. 1–39). Mahwah, NJ.: Lawrence Erlbaum Associates.

Marwaha, S., & Johnson, S. (2004). Schizophrenia and employment—A review. *Social Psychiatry and Psychiatric Epidemiology, 39*, 337–349.

Marzuk, P., Leon, A., Tardiff, K., Morgan, E., Stajic, M., & Mann, J. (1992). The effect of access to lethal methods of injury on suicide rates. *Archives of General Psychiatry, 49*, 451–458.

Mashour, G. A., Walker, E. E., & Martuza, R. L. (2005). Psychosurgery: Past, present, and future. *Brain Research Reviews, 48*, 409–419.

Masi, G., Millepiedi, S., Mucci, M., Poli, P., Bertini, N., & Milantoni, L. (2004). Generalized anxiety disorder in referred children and adolescents. *Journal of the American Academy of Child and Adolescent Psychiatry, 43*, 752–760.

Massey, L. (1998). Caffeine and the elderly. *Drugs and Aging, 13*, 43–50.

Masson, P. C., von Ranson, K. M., Wallace, L. M., & Safer, D. L. (2013). A randomized wait-list controlled pilot study of dialectical behaviour therapy guided self-help for binge eating disorder. *Behaviour Research and Theapy, 51*, 723–728.

Masters, W. H., & Johnson, V. E. (1966). *Human sexual response*. Boston: Little, Brown.

Masters, W. H., & Johnson, V. E. (1970). *Human sexual inadequacy*. Boston: Little Brown.

Mataix-Cols, D. (2014). Hoarding disorder. *The New England Journal of Medicine, 70*, 2023–2030.

Mathews, C. A., Delucchi, K., Cath, D., Willemsen, G., & Boomsma, D. (2014). Partitioning the etiology of hoarding and obsessive-compulsive symptoms. *Psychological Medicine, 44*, 2867–2876.

Mathews, J. R., & Barch, D. M. (2010). Emotion responsivity, social cognition, and functional outcome in schizophrenia. *Journal of Abnormal Psychology, 119*, 50–59.

Matson, J. L., Benavidez, D. A., Compton, L. S., Paclawskyj, T., & Baglio, C. (1996). Behavioral treatment of autistic persons: A review of research from 1980 to the present. *Research in Developmental Disabilities, 17*, 433–465.

Matson, J. L., & Nebel-Schwalm, M. S. (2007). Comorbid psychopathology with autism spectrum disorder in children: An overview. *Research in Developmental Disabilities, 28*, 341–352.

Matson, J. L., & Smith, K. R. M. (2008). Current status of intensive behavioral interventions for young children with autism and PDD-NOS. *Research in Autism Spectrum Disorders, 2*, 60–74.

Matson, J. L., & Cervantes, P. E. (2013). Comorbidity among persons with intellectual disabilities. *Research in Autism Spectrum Disorders, 7*, 1318–1322.

Matsubayashi, T., Sawada, Y., & Ueda, M. (2014). Does the installation of blue lights on train platforms shift suicide to another station?: Evidence from Japan. *Journal of Affective Disorders, 169*, 57–60.

Mattheisen, M., Samuels, J. F., Wang, Y., Greenberg, B. D., Fyer, A. J., McCracken, J. T., … Grados, M. A. (2015). Genome-wide association study in obsessive-compulsive disorder: Results from the OCGAS. *Molecular Psychiatry, 20*, 337–344.

Mattik, R., & Newman, C. (1991). Social phobia and avoidant personality disorder. *International Review of Psychiatry, 3*, 163–173.

Mattis, S. (2001). *Dementia rating scale-2: Professional manual*. Lutz, FL: Psychological Assessment Resources.

Maurice, W. L. (2005). Male hypoactive sexual desire disorder. In R. Balon & R. T. Segraves (Eds.), *Handbook of sexual dysfunction* (pp. 76–109). Boca Raton, FL: Taylor & Francis.

Mavandadi, S., & Oslin, D. W. (2015). Substance-related and addictive disorders. In D.C. Steffens, D.C. Blazer, & M. E. Thakur (Eds). *The American Psychiatric Publishing Textbook of Geriatric Psychiatry*, 5th ed., Washington, DC: American Psychiatric Publishing.

Maxwell, J. (2001). Deaths related to the inhalation of volatile substances in Texas: 1988–1998. *American Journal of Drug and Alcohol Abuse, 27*, 689–697.

Mayberg, H. S., Keightley, M., Mahurin, R. K., & Brannan, S. K. (2004). Neuropsychiatric aspects of mood and affective disorders. In S.C. Yudofsky & R.E. Hales (Eds.), *Essentials of neuropsychiatry and clinical neurosciences* (pp. 489–517). Washington, DC: American Psychiatric Publishing.

Mayes, L. C. (2000). A developmental perspective on the regulation of arousal states. *Seminars in Perinatology, 24*, 267–279.

Mayes, R., & Horwitz, A. V. (2005). DSM-III and the revolution in the classification of mental illness. *Journal of the History of the Behavioral Sciences, 41*, 249–267.

Mayes, S. D., Mathiowetz, C., Kokotovich, C., Waxmonsky, J., Baweja, R., Calhoun, S. L., & Bixler, E. O. (2015). Stability of disruptive mood dysregulation disorder symptoms (irritable-angry mood and temper outbursts) throughout childhood and adolescence in a general population sample. *Journal of Abnormal Child Psychology, 43*, 1543–1549.

Mayou, R. A., Ehlers, A., & Hobbs, M. (2000). Psychological debriefing for road traffic accident victims. Three-year follow-up of a randomised controlled trial. *The British Journal of Psychiatry, 176*, 589–593.

Mazzeo, S. E., Trace, S. E., Mitchell, K. S., & Gow, R. W. (2007). Effects of a reality TV cosmetic surgery makeover program on eating disordered attitudes and behaviors. *Eating Behaviors, 8*, 390–397.

McCabe, J. E., & Marcus, M. D. (2002). Is dialectical behavior therapy useful in the management of anorexia nervosa? *Eating Disorders, 10*, 335–337.

McCabe, M. P., & Connaughton, C. (2014). How the prevalence rates of male sexual dysfunction vary using different criteria. *International Journal of Sexual Health, 26*, 229–237.

McCabe, R., & Priebe, S. (2004). Explanatory models of illness in schizophrenia: Comparison of four ethnic groups. *British Journal of Psychiatry, 185*, 25–30.

McCabe, S. E., & West, B. T. (2014). Medical and nonmedical use of prescription benzodiazepine anxiolytics among U.S. high school seniors. *Addictive Behaviors, 39*, 959–964.

McCarty, D., Braude, L., Lyman, D. R., Dougherty, R. H., Daniels, A. S., Ghose, S. S., & Delphin-Rittmon, M. E. (2014). Substance abuse intensive outpatient programs: Assessing the evidence. *Psychiatric Services, 65*, 718–726.

McCaul, M., Svikis, D., & Moore, R. (2001). Predictors of outpatient treatment retention: Patient versus substance use characteristics. *Drug and Alcohol Dependence, 62*, 9–17.

McCauley, E., Gudmundsen, G., Schloredt, K., Martell, C., Rhew, I., Hubley, S., & Dimidjian, S. (2015). The adolescent behavioral activation program: Adapting behavioral activation as a treatment for depression in adolescence. *Journal of Clinical Child and Adolescent Psychology, 20*, 1–14.

McClellan, J., Breiger, D., McCurry, C., & Hlastala, S. A. (2003). Premorbid functioning in early-onset psychotic disorders. *Journal of the American Academy of Child and Adolescent Psychiatry, 42*, 666–673.

McConaghy, N. (1993). *Sexual behavior: Problems and management*. New York: Plenum.

McCracken, J. T., McGough, J., Shah, B., Cronin, P., Hong, D., Aman, M. G., … for Research Units on Pediatric Psychopharmacology Autism Network (2002). Risperidone in children with autism and serious behavioral problems. *New England Journal of Medicine, 347*, 314–321.

McCrae R. R., Yang., J., Costa, P. T. Jr., Dai, X., Yao, S., Cai, T., & Gao, B. (2001). Personality profiles and the prediction of categorical personality disorders. *Journal of Personality, 69*, 155–174.

McCusker, C. (2001). Cognitive biases and addiction: An evolution in theory and method. *Addiction, 96*, 47–56.

McCusker, J., Cole, M. G., Voyer, P., Monette, J., Champoux, N., Ciampi, A., … Belzile, E. (2011). Prevalence and incidence of delirium in long-term care. *International Journal of Geriatric Psychiatry, 26*, 1152–1161.

McDonald, C., Grech, A., Toulopoulou, T., Schulze, K., Chapple, B., Sham, P.,… Murray, R. M. (2002). Brain volumes in familial and non-familial schizophrenic probands and their unaffected relatives. *American Journal of Medical Genetics and Neuropsychiatric Genetics, 114*, 616–625.

McDonald, K. C., Bulloch, A. G., Duffy, A., Bresee, L., Williams, J. V., Lavorato, D. H., & Patten, S. B. (2015). Prevalence of bipolar I and II disorder in Canada. *Canadian Journal of Psychiatry, 60*, 151–156.

McDougle, C. J., Scahill, L., Aman, M. G., McCracken, J. T., Tierney, E., Davies, M., … Shah, B. (2005). Risperidone for the core symptom domains of autism: Results from the study by the Autism Network of the Research Units on Pediatric Psychopharmacology. *American Journal of Psychiatry, 162*, 1142–1148.

McElroy, S. L., Soutullo, C. A., Taylor, P., Jr., Nelson, E. B., Beckman, D. A., Brusman, L. A.,… Keck, P. E. (1999). Psychiatric features of 36 men convicted of sexual offenses. *Journal of Clinical Psychiatry, 60*, 414–420.

McGough, J. J., & Barkley, R. A. (2004). Diagnostic controversies in adult attention deficit hyperactivity disorder. *American Journal of Psychiatry, 161*, 1948–1956.

McGrath, E., Keita, G. P., Stickland, B. R., & Russo, N. F. (1990). *Women and depression: Risk factors and treatment issues*. Washington, DC: American Psychological Association.

McGuffin, P., Owen, M. J., & Farmer, A. E. (1995). Genetic basis of schizophrenia. *Lancet, 346*, 678–682.

McGuffin, P., Rijsdijk, F., Andrew, M., Sham, P., Katz, R., & Cardno, A. (2003). The heritability of bipolar affective disorder and the genetic relationship to unipolar depression. *Archives of General Psychiatry, 60*, 497–502.

McGuinness, B., Craig, D., Bullock, R., & Passmore, P. (2016). Statins for the prevention of dementia. *The Cochrane database of systematic reviews, 1*, 2–47.

McGuire, J. F., Ung, D., Selles, R. R., Rahman, O., Lewin, A. B., Murphy, T. K., & Storch, E. A. (2014). Treating trichotillomania: A meta-analysis of treatment effects and moderators for behavior therapy and serotonin reuptake inhibitors. *Journal of Psychiatric Research, 58*, 76–83.

McIntosh, V. V., Bulik, C. M., McKenzie, J. M., Luty, S. E., & Jordan, J. (2000). Interpersonal psychotherapy for anorexia nervosa. *International Journal of Eating Disorders, 27*, 125–139.

McIntosh, V. V., Jordan, J., Carter, F. A., Luty, S. E., McKenzie, J. M., Bulik, C. M., … Joyce, P. R. (2005). Three psychotherapies for anorexia nervosa: A randomized, controlled trial. *The American Journal of Psychiatry, 162*, 741–747.

McIntosh, V. V., Jordan, J., Luty, S. E., Carter, F. A., McKenzie, J. M., Bulik, C. M., & Joyce, P. R. (2006). Specialist supportive clinical management for anorexia nervosa. *International Journal of Eating Disorders, 39*, 625–632.

McKnight Investigators. (2003). Risk factors for the onset of eating disorders in adolescent girls: Results of the McKnight longitudinal risk factor study. *American Journal of Psychiatry, 160*, 248–254.

McLoughlin, A. B., Gould, M. S., & Malone, K. M. (2015). Global trends in teenage suicide: 2003–2014. *International Journal of Medicine, 108*, 765–780.

McMahon, C. G., Althof, S., Waldinger, M. D., Porst, H., Dean, J., Sharlip, I., … International Society for Sexual Medicine Ad Hoc Committee for Definition of Premature Ejaculation (2008). An evidence-based definition of lifelong premature ejaculation. *BJU International, 102*, 338–350.

McMahon, F. J. (2004). Genetics of mood disorders and associated psychopathology. In J. Sadavoy, L. F. Jarvik, G. T. Grossberg, & B. S. Meyers (Eds.), *Comprehensive textbook of geriatric psychiatry* (3rd ed., pp. 85–104). New York: W.W. Norton & Co.

McNally, R. J. (1995). Automaticity and the anxiety disorders. *Behaviour Research and Therapy, 33*, 747–754.

McNally, R. J. (1999). EMDR and mesmerism: A comparative historical analysis. *Journal of Anxiety Disorders, 13* (1–2), 225–236.

McNally, R. J. (2001). Vulnerability to anxiety disorders in adulthood. In R. E. Ingram & J. M. Price (Eds.), *Vulnerability to psychopathology: Risk across the lifespan* (pp. 304–321). New York: Guilford Press.

McNally, R. J. (2005). Debunking myths about trauma and memory. *Canadian Journal of Psychiatry, 50*, 817–822.

McNally, R. J. (2009). Can we fix PTSD in DSM-V? *Depression and Anxiety, 26*, 597–600.

Medda, P., Toni, C., Mariani, M. G., De Simone, L., Mauri, M., & Perugi, G. (2015). Electroconvulsive therapy in 197 patients with a severe, drug-resistant bipolar mixed state: Treatment outcome and predictors of response. *Journal of Clinical Psychiatry, 76*, 1168–1173.

Medina-Moira, M. E., Borges, G., Lara, C., Benjet, C., Blanco, J., Fleiz, C., … Zambrano, J. (2005). Prevalence, service use, and demographic correlates of 12-month DSM-IV psychiatric disorders in Mexico: Results from the Mexican National Comorbidity Survey. *Psychological Medicine, 35*, 1773–1783.

Mednick, S. A., Machon, R. A., Huttunen, M. O., & Bonett, D. (1988). Adult schizophrenia following prenatal exposure to an influenza epidemic. *Archives of General Psychiatry, 45*, 189–192.

Meijler, M., Matsushita, M., Wirsching, P., & Janda, K. (2004). Development of immunopharmacotherapy against drugs of abuse. *Current Drug Discovery Technology, 1*, 77–89.

Meilman, P. W., & Hall, T. M. (2006). Aftermath of tragic events: The development and use of community support meetings on a university campus. *Journal of American College Health, 54*, 382–384.

Mendlowicz, M. V., & Stein, M. B. (2000). Quality of life in individuals with anxiety disorders. *The American Journal of Psychiatry, 157*, 669–682.

Merck Manual Professional (1995–2006).*Drug use and dependence*. Retrieved from http://www.merck.com/mmpe/sec15/ch198/ch198a.html?qt=drug%20use%20and%20dependence&alt=sh

Merikangas, K. R., Akiskal, H. S., Angst, J., Greenberg, P. E., Hirschfeld, R. M., Petukhova, M., & Kessler, R. C. (2007). Lifetime and 12-month prevalence of bipolar spectrum disorder in the National Comorbidity Survey replication. *Archives of General Psychiatry, 64*, 543–552.

Merikangas, K. R., He, J. P., Brody, D., Fisher, P. W., Bourdon, K., & Koretz, D. S. (2010). Prevalence and treatment of mental disorders among US children in the 2001–2004 NHANES. *Pediatrics, 125*, 75–81.

Merikangas, K. R., Jin, R., He, J. P., Kessler, R. C., Lee, S., Sampson, N. A.,… Zarkov, Z. (2011). Prevalence and correlates of bipolar spectrum disorder in the world mental health survey initiative. *Archives of General Psychiatry, 68*, 241–251.

Merikangas, K. R., He, J. P., Burstein, M., Swendsen, J., Avenevoli, S., Case, B., … Olfson, M. (2011). Service utilization for lifetime mental disorders in U.S. adolescents: Results of the National Comorbidity Survey-Adolescent Supplement (NCS-A). *Journal of the American Academy of Child and Adolescent Psychiatry, 50*, 32–45.

Meston, C. M., Trapnell, P. D., & Gorzalka, B. B. (1996). Ethnic and gender differences in sexuality: Variations in sexual behavior between Asian and non-Asian university students. *Archives of Sexual Behavior, 25*, 33–72.

Meston, C. M., & Ahrold, T. (2007). Ethnic, gender, and acculturation influences on sexual behaviors. *Archives of Sexual Behavior, 33*, 223–234.

Metz, M. E., Pryor, J. L., Nesvacil, L. J., Abuzzahab, F. Sr., & Koznar, J. (1997). Premature ejaculation: A psychophysiological review. *Journal of Sex & Marital Therapy, 23*, 3–23.

Mewton, L., Wong, N., & Andrews, G. (2012). The effectiveness of internet cognitive behavioural therapy for generalized anxiety disorder in clinical practice. *Depression and Anxiety, 29*, 843–849.

Meyer, G. J., Erdberg, P., & Shaffer, T. W. (2007). Toward international normative reference data for the comprehensive system. *Journal of Personality Assessment, 89*(S1), S201–S216.

Meyer, G. J., Finn, S. E., Eyde, L. D., Kay, G. G., Moreland, K. L., Dies, R. R., … Reed, G. M. (2001). Psychological testing and psychological assessment: A review of evidence and issues. *American Psychologist, 56*, 128–165.

Meyer, M. (2014). The perils of opioid prescribing during pregnancy. *Obstetrics and Gynecology Clinics of North America, 41*, 297–306.

Meyer, W. I., Bockting, W. O., Cohen-Kettenis, P., Coleman, E., DiCeglie, D., Devor, H., … Laub, D. (2001). The Harry Benjamin International Gender Dysphoria Association's standards of care for gender identity disorders (6th ed.). *Journal of Psychology & Human Sexuality, 13*, 1–30.

Meyer-Bahlburg, H. F. L., Dolezal, C., Baker, S., & New, M. I. (2008). Sexual orientation in women with classical or non-classical congenital adrenal hyperplasia as a function of degree of prenatal androgen excess. *Archives of Sexual Behavior, 37*, 85–99.

Meyers, L. (2008). The lingering storm. *American Psychological Associaton Monitor 39*, 50. Retrieved from http://www.apa.org/monitor/2008/04/katrina.aspx

Meyers, R., Smith, J., & Lash, D. (2003). The community reinforcement approach. In M. Gelerntner (Ed.), *Recent developments in alcoholism: Vol. 16: Research on alcoholism treatment* (pp. 183–195). New York: Kluwer Academic/Plenum Publishers.

Miao, D., Young, S. L., & Golden, C. D. (2015). A meta-analysis of pica and micronutrient status. *American Journal of Human Biology, 27*, 84–93.

Micali, N., Hagberg, K. W., Petersen, I., & Treasure, J. L. (2013). The incidence of eating disorders in the UK in 2000–2009: Findings from the General Practice Research Database. *British Medical Journal Open, 3*.

Micallef-Trigona, B. (2014). Comparing the effects of repetitive transcranial magnetic stimulation and electroconvulsive therapy in the treatment of depression: A systematic review and meta-analysis. *Depression Research and Treatment, 2014*, 135049.

Michel, A., Mormont, C., & Legros, J. J. (2001). A psychoendocrinological overview of transsexualism. *European Journal of Endocrinology, 145*, 365–376.

Migneault, J., Adams, T., & Read, J. (2005). Application of the transtheoretical model to substance abuse: Historical development and future directions. *Drug and Alcohol Review, 24*, 437–438.

Mihura, J. L., Meyer, G. J., Bombel, G., & Dumitrascu, N. (2015). Standards, accuracy, and questions of bias in Rorschach meta-analyses: Reply to Wood, Garb, Nezworski, Lilienfeld, and Duke (2015). *Psychological Bulletin, 141*, 250–260.

Mihura, J. L., Meyer, G. J., Dumitrascu, N., & Bombel, G. (2013). The validity of individual Rorschach variables: Systematic reviews and meta-analyses of the comprehensive system. *Psychological Bulletin, 139*, 548–605.

Mikkelsen, E. J. (2001). Enuresis and encopresis: Ten years of progress. *Journal of the American Academy of Child and Adolescent Psychiatry, 40*, 1146–1158.

Miklowitz, D. J., & Scott, J. (2009). Psychosocial treatments for bipolar disorder: Cost-effectiveness, mediating mechanisms, and future directions. *Bipolar Disorders, 11*, 110–122.

Miklowitz, D. J., Otto, M. W., Frank, E., Reilly-Harrington, N. A., Wisniewski, S. R., Kogan, J. N., … Sachs, G. S. (2007). Psychosocial treatments for bipolar depression: A 1-year randomized trial from the Systematic Treatment Enhancement Program. *Archives of General Psychiatry, 64*, 419–426.

Milak, M. S., Parsey, R. V., Keilp, J., Oquendo, M. A., Malone, K. M., & Mann, J. J. (2005). Neuroanatomic correlates of psychopathologic components of major depressive disorder. *Archives of General Psychiatry, 62*, 397–408.

Miller, E. R., Pastor-Barriuso, R., Dalal, D., Riemersma, R. A., Appel, L. J., & Guallar, E. (2005). Meta-analysis: High-dosage vitamin E supplementation may increase all-cause mortality. *Annals of Internal Medicine, 142*, 37–46.

Miller, J. G. (1997). Theoretical issues in cultural psychology. In J. W. Berry, Y. H. Poortinga, & J. Pandey (Eds.), *Handbook of cross-cultural psychology* (2nd ed., pp. 85–128). Boston: Allyn and Bacon.

Miller, W. (1983). Motivational interviewing with problem drinkers. *Behavioural Psychotherapy, 11*, 147–172.

Miller, W., & Rollnick, S. (1991). *Motivational interviewing: Preparing people to change addictive behavior*. New York: Guilford Press.

Millstein, D. J., Orsillo, S. M., Hayes-Skelton, S. A., & Roemer, L. (2015). Interpersonal problems, mindfulness, and therapy outcome in an acceptance-based behavior therapy for generalized anxiety disorder. *Cognitive Behavioral Therapy, 44*, 1–11.

Miloyan, B., Byrne, G. J., & Pachana, N. A. (2014). Late-life anxiety. In NA Pachana & K Laidlaw (Eds.) *Oxford Handbook of Clinical Geropsychology: International Perspectives* (pp. 470–489). USA: Oxford University Press.

Mineka, S., & Cook, M. (1986). Immunization against the observational conditioning of snake fear in rhesus monkeys. *Journal of Abnormal Psychology, 95*, 307–318.

Mineka, S., & Zinbarg, R. (2006). A contemporary learning theory perspective on the etiology of anxiety disorders: It's not what you thought it was. *American Psychologist, 61*, 10–26.

Miniati, M., Callari, A., Calugi, S., Rucci, P., Savino, M., Mauri, M., & Dell'Osso, L. (2014). Interpersonal psychotherapy for postpartum depression: A systematic review. *Archives of Women's Mental Health, 17*, 257–268.

Minsky, S., Vega, W., Miskimen, T., Gara, M., & Escobar, J. (2003). Diagnostic patterns in Latino, African American, and European American psychiatric patients. *Archives of General Psychiatry, 60*, 637–644.

Minuchin, S., Rosman, B. L., & Baker, L. (1978). *Psychosomatic families: Anorexia nervosa in context*. Cambridge, MA: Harvard University Press.

Miranda, A. O., & Fraser, L. D. (2002). Culture-bound syndromes: Initial perspectives from individual psychology. *The Journal of Individual Psychology, 58*, 422–433.

Mischel, W. (1973). Toward a cognitive social learning reconceptualization of personality. *Psychology Review, 39*, 351–364.

Mischel, W., & Shoda, Y. (1995). A cognitive-affective system of personality: Reconceptualizing situations, dispositions, dynamics and invariance in personality structure. *Psychology Review, 102*, 246–268.

Mischoulon, D., Eddy, K. T., Keshaviah, A., Dinescu, D., Ross, S. L., Kass, A. E., … Herzog, D. B. (2011). Depression and eating disorders: Treatment and course. *Journal of Affective Disorders, 130*, 470–477.

Mishori, R., & McHale, C. (2014). Pica: An age-old eating disorder that's often missed. *Journal of Family Practice, 63*, E1–E4.

Misra, M. (2008). Long-term skeletal effects of eating disorders with onset in adolescence. *Annals of the New York Academy of Sciences, 1135*, 212–218.

Mitchell, J., Specker, S., & De Zwaan, M. (1991). Comorbidity and medical complications of bulimia nervosa. *Journal of Clinical Psychiatry, 52*, 13–20.

Mitchell, J. E. (1990). *Bulimia nervosa*. Minneapolis: University of Minnesota Press.

Mittnacht, A. M., & Bulik, C. M. (2015). Best nutrition counseling practices for the treatment of anorexia nervosa: A Delphi study. *International Journal of Eating Disorders, 48*, 111–122.

Mobascher, A., Bohus, M., Dahmen, N., Dietl, L., Giegling, I., Jungkunz, M., … Lieb, K. (2014). Association between dopa decarboxylase gene variants and borderline personality disorder. *Psychiatry Research, 219*, 693–695.

Mochcovitch, M. D., da Rocha Freire, R. C., Garcia, R. F., & Nardi, A. E. (2014). A systematic review of fMRI studies in generalized anxiety disorder: Evaluating its neural and cognitive basis. *Journal of Affective Disorders, 167*, 336–342.

Moeller, F. G., Chen, Y. W., Steinberg, J. L., Petty, F., Ripper, G. W., Shah, N., & Garver, D. L. (1995). Risk factors for clozapine discontinuation among 805 patients in the VA hospital system. *Annals of Clinical Psychiatry, 7*, 167–173.

Moghaddam, B., & Javitt, D. C. (2012). From revolution to evolution: The glutamate hypothesis of schizophrenia and its implication for treatment. *Neuropsychopharmacology, 37*, 4–15.

Mohammadi, M. R., Ghanizadeh, A., Rahgozar, M., Noorbala, A. A., Davidian, H., Afzali, H. M., … Mesgarpour, B. (2004). Prevalence of obsessive-compulsive disorder in Iran. *BMC Psychiatry, 4*, 1.

Mojtabai, R., Stuart, E. A., Hwang, I., Susukida, R., Eaton, W. W., Sampson, N., & Kessler, R. C. (2015). Long-term effects of mental disorders on employment in the National Comorbidity Survey ten-year follow-up. *Social Psychiatry and Psychiatric Epidemiology, 50*, 1657–1668.

Monahan, J. (2001). Major mental disorders and violence: Epidemiology and risk assessment. In G.F. Pinard, L. Pagani (Eds.), *Clinical assessment of dangerousness: Empirical contributions* (pp. 89–102). New York: Cambridge University Press.

Monahan, J., Bonnie, R. J., Appelbaum, P. S., Hyde, P. S., Steadman, H. J., & Swartz, M. S. (2001). Mandated community treatment: Beyond outpatient commitment. *Psychiatric Services, 52*, 1198–1205.

Mongia, M., & Hechtman, L. (2012). Cognitive behavior therapy for adults with attention-deficit/hyperactivity disorder: A review of recent randomized controlled trials. *Current Psychiatry Reports, 14*, 561–567.

Monroe, S. M., Harkness, K., Simons, A. D., & Thase, M. E. (2001). Life stress and the symptoms of major depression. *Journal of Nervous and Mental Disease, 189*, 168–175.

Monte, G. L., Graziano, A., Piva, I., & Marci, R. (2014). Women taking the "blue pill" (sildenafil citrate): Such a big deal? *Drug Design, Development, and Therapy, 8*, 2251–2254.

Moore, A. A., Blow, F. C., Hoffing, M., Welgreen, S., Davis, J. W., Lin, J. C., … Gould, R. (2011). Primary care-based intervention to reduce at-risk drinking in older adults: A randomized controlled trial. *Addiction, 106*, 111–120.

Moore, K., & McLaughlin, D. (2003). Depression: The challenge for all healthcare professionals. *Nursing Standard, 17*, 45–52.

Moos, R. (2008). Active ingredients of substance use-focused self-help groups. *Addiction, 103*, 387–396.

Moradi, B., Dirks, D., & Matteson, A. V. (2005). Roles of sexual objectification experiences and internalization of standards of beauty in eating disorder symptomatology: A test and extension of objectification theory. *Journal of Counseling Psychology, 51*, 420–428.

Moreira, E. D., Brock, G., Glasser, D. B., Nicolosi, A., Laumann, E. O., Paik, A.,… Gingell, C. (2005). Help-seeking behaviour for sexual problems: The global study of sexual attitudes and behaviors. *International Journal of Clinical Practice, 59*, 6–16.

Moreno, C., & Tandon, R. (2011). Should overeating and obesity be classified as an addictive disorder in DSM-5? *Current Pharmaceutical Design, 17*, 1128–1131.

Moreno, C., Laje, G., Blanco, C., Jiang, H., Schmidt, A. B., & Olfson, M. (2007). National trends in the outpatient diagnosis and treatment of bipolar disorder in youth. *Archives of General Psychiatry, 64*, 1032–1039.

Morgan, D. L., & Morgan, R. K. (2001). Single-participant research design: Bringing science to managed care. *American Psychologist, 56*, 119–127.

Moriyama, T. S., Bolanczyk, G. V., Terzi, F. S., Faria, K. M., & Rohde, L. A. (2013). Psychopharamcology and psychotherapy for the treatment of adults with ADHD—A systematic review of available meta-analyses. *CNS Spectrums, 18*, 296–306.

Morris, J. (2005a). Early-stage and preclinical Alzheimer disease. *Alzheimer Disease and Associated Disorders, 19*, 163–165.

Morris, J. C. (2005b). Dementia update 2005. *Alzheimer Disease & Associated Disorders, 19*, 100–117.

Morris, J. C. (2006). Mild cognitive impairment is early-stage Alzheimer disease: Time to revise diagnostic criteria. *Archives of Neurology, 63*, 15.

Morris, S., Jaffee, S., Goodwin, G., & Franklin, M. (2015). Hoarding in children and adolescents: A review. *Child Psychiatry and Human Development*.

Mosing, M. A., Gordon, S. D., Medland, S. E., Statham, D. J., Nelson, E. C., Heath, A. C., … Wray, N. R. (2009). Genetic and environmental influences on the co-morbidity between depression, panic disorder, agoraphobia, and social phobia: A twin study. *Depression & Anxiety, 26*, 1004–1011.

Moss, H. B., Chen, C. M., & Yi, H. Y. (2012). Measures of substance consumption among substance users, DSM-IV abusers, and those with DSM-IV dependence disorders in a nationally representative sample. *Journal of Studies on Alcohol and Drugs, 73*, 820–828.

Motlova, L., Dragomirecka, E., Spaniel, F., Goppoldova, E., Zalesky, R., Selepova, P., & Höschl, C. (2006). Relapse prevention in schizophrenia: Does group family psychoeducation matter? One year prospective follow-up field study. *International Journal of Psychiatry in Clinical Practice, 10*, 38–44.

Mouton-Odum, S., Keuthen, N. J., Wagener, P. D., & Stanley, M. A. (2006). StopPulling.com: An interactive, self-help program for trichotillomania. *Cognitive and Behavioral Practice, 13*, 215–226.

Mowrer, O. (1960). Basic research methods, statistics and decision theory. *The American Journal of Occupational Therapy: Official Publication of the American Occupational Therapy Association, 14*, 199–205.

Mrvos, R., Reilly, P., Dean, B., & Krenzelok, E. (1989). Massive caffeine ingestion resulting in death. *Veterinary and Human Toxicology, 31*, 571–572.

MTA Cooperative Group. (1999). A 14-month randomized clinical trial of treatment strategies for attention-deficit/hyperactivity disorder. *Archives of General Psychiatry, 56*, 1073–1086.

Mueser, K. T., Bellack, A. S., & Brady, E. U. (1990). Hallucinations in schizophrenia. *Acta Psychiatrica Scandinavica, 82*, 26–29.

Mueser, K. T., Rosenberg, S. D., Goodman, L. A., & Trumbetta, S. L. (2002). Trauma, PTSD, and the course of schizophrenia: An interactive model. *Schizophrenia Research, 53*, 123–143.

Mueser, K. T., & McGurk, S. R. (2004). Schizophrenia. *Lancet, 363*, 2063–2072.

Mufson, L., Moreau, D., Weissman, M., Wickramaratne, P., Martin, J., & Samoilov, A. (1994). Modification of interpersonal psychotherapy with depressed adolescents (IPTA-A): Phase I and II studies. *Journal of the American Academy of Child & Adolescent Psychiatry, 33*, 695–705.

Muhleisen, T. W., Leber, M., Schulze, T. G., Strohmaier, J., Degenhardt, F., Treutlein, J., … Cichon, S. (2014). Genome-wide association study reveals two new risk loci for bipolar disorder. *Nature Communications, 5*, 3339.

Mulloy, A., Lang, R., O'Reilly, M., Sigafoos, J., Lancioni, G., & Rispoli, M. (2010). Gluten-free and casein-free diets in treatment of autism spectrum disorders: A systematic review. *Research in Autism Spectrum Disorders, 4*, 328–339.

Mulloy, A., Lang, R., O'Reilly, M., Sigafoos, J., Lancioni, G., & Rispoli, M. (2011). Addendum to "Gluten-free and casein-free diets in treatment of autism spectrum disorders: A systematic review." *Research in Autism Spectrum Disorders, 5*, 86–88.

Munk-Jørgensen, P. (1987). First-admission rates and marital status of schizophrenics. *Acta Psychiatrica Scandinavica, 76*, 210–216.

Muratori, F., Salvadori, F., D'Arcangelo, G., Viglione, V., & Picchi, L. (2005). Childhood psychopathological antecedents in early onset schizophrenia. *European Psychiatry, 20*, 309–314.

Muris, P., Schmidt, H., & Merckelbach, H. (1999). The structure of specific phobia symptoms among children and adolescents. *Behaviour Research and Therapy, 37*, 863–868.

Muris, P., & Ollendick, T.H. (2015). Children who are anxious in silence: A review on selective mutism, the new anxiety disorder in DSM-5. *Clinical Child and Family Psychology Review, 18*, 151–169.

Muris, P., Hendriks, E., & Bot, S. (2016). Children of few words: relations among selective mutism, behavioral inhibition, and (social) anxiety symptoms in 3-to 6-year-olds. *Child Psychiatry & Human Development, 47*, 94–101.

Murphy, D., & Peters, J. M. (1992). Profiling child sexual abusers. Psychological considerations. *Criminal Justice and Behavior, 19*, 24–37.

Murray, S. B., Anderson, L. K., Cusack, A., Nakamura, T., Rockwell, R., Griffiths, S., & Kaye, W. H. (2015). Integrating family-based treatment and dialectical behavior therapy for adolescent bulimia nervosa: Preliminary outcomes of an open pilot trial. *Eating Disorders, 23*, 336–344.

Muse, L. A., Harris, S. G., & Feild, H. S. (2003). Has the inverted-U theory of stress and job performance had a fair test? *Human Performance, 16*, 349–364.

Naaijen, J., Lythgoe, D. J., Amiri, H., Buitelaar, J. K., & Glennon, J. C. (2015). Fronto-striatal glutamatergic compounds in compulsive and impulsive syndromes: A review of magnetic resonance spectroscopy studies. *Neuroscience & Biobehavioral Reviews, 52*, 74–88.

Nagelhout, G. E., Osman, A., Yong, H. H., Huang, L. L., Borland, R., & Thrasher, J. F. (2015). Was the media campaign that supported Australia's new pictorial cigarette warning labels and plain packaging policy associated with more attention to and talking about warning labels? *Addictive Behaviors, 49*, 64–67.

Nagy, T. F. (2011). *Essential ethics for psychologists: A primer for understanding and mastering core issues*. Washington, DC: American Psychological Association.

Naik, A. D., Concato, J., & Gill, T. M. (2004). Bathing disability in community-living older persons: Common, consequential, and complex. *Journal of the American Geriatrics Society, 52*, 1805–1810.

Nakabayashi, K., Komaki, G., Tajima, A., Ando, T., Ishikawa, M., Nomoto, J., … Shirasawa, S. (2009). Identification of novel candidate loci for anorexia nervosa at 1q41 and 11q22 in Japanese by a genome-wide association analysis with microsatellite markers. *Journal of Human Genetics, 54*, 531–537.

Nakawaki, B., & Crano, W. (2015). Patterns of substance use, delinquency, and risk factors among adolescent inhalant users. *Substance Use & Misuse, 50*, 114–122.

Namanzi, M. R. (2001). Avicenna, 980–1037. *American Journal of Psychiatry, 158*, 1796.

Nanda, S. (1985). The hijras of India: Cultural and individual dimensions of an institutionalized third gender role. *Journal of Homosexuality, 11*, 35–54.

Nardi, A. E., Lopes, F. L., Freire, R. C., Veras, A. B., Nascimento, I., Valenca, A. M., … Zin, W. A. (2009). Panic disorder and social anxiety disorder subtypes in a caffeine challenge test. *Psychiatry Research, 169*, 149–153.

Nathan, P. E., & Langenbucher, J. W. (1999). Psychopathology: Description and classification. *Annual Review of Psychology, 50*, 79–107.

Nation, M., Crusto, C., Wandersman, A., Kumpfer, K. L., Seybolt, D., Morrissey-Kane, E., & Davino, K. (2003). What works in prevention. Principles of effective prevention programs. *American Psychologist, 58*, 449–456.

National Institute of Clinical and Health Excellence. (2004). *National Institute of Clinical and Health Excellence*. Retrieved from http://www.nice.org.uk/page.aspx?o=101239

National Institute for Health and Care Excellence (NICE) (2004). *Core interventions in the treatment and management of anorexia nervosa, bulimia nervosa, and related eating disorders*. Retrieved from http://www.nice.org.uk/page.aspx? o=101239

National Institute for Health and Care Excellence (NICE) (2003). *Technology appraisal guidance 59: Electroconvulsive treatment, technology appraisal guidances*. Retrieved from: https://www.nice.org.uk/guidance/ta59

National Institute for Health and Care Excellence (NICE) (2004). *Depression: Management of depression in primary and secondary care*. Retrieved from London: https://www.nice.org.uk/guidance/cg23

National Institute of Mental Health. (2001). *Bipolar disorder*. Retrieved from http://www.nimh.nih.gov/publicat/bipolar.cfm

National Institute of Mental Health. (2003). Older adults: Depression and suicide facts. *Depression*. Retrieved from http://www.nimh.nih.gov/publicat/elderlydepsuicide.cfm

National Institute of Mental Health. (2005). *Antidepressant medications for children and adolescents: Information for parents and caregivers*. Retrieved from http://www.nimh.nih.gov/healthinformation/antidepressant_child.cfm

National Institute of Mental Health. (2013). *Depression*. (NIH Publication No. TR 13-3561). Retrieved from http://www.nimh.nih.gov/health/publications/depression-easy-to-read/depression-trifold-new_150043.pdf

National Institute on Drug Abuse. (2012) *Is nicotine addictive?* Retreived from Bethesda Maryland: https://www.drugabuse.gov/publications/research-reports/tobacco/nicotine-addictive.

National Institute on Drug Abuse. (2012a). *Inhalant abuse*. Retrieved from Bethesda, MD: https://www.drugabuse.gov/drugs-abuse/inhalants.

National Institute on Drug Abuse (2014) Principles of drug abuse treatment for criminal justice populations - A research-based guide https://www.drugabuse.gov/publications/principles-drug-abuse-treatment-criminal-justice- populations/principles.

National Institute on Drug Abuse. (2016) *DrugFacts: Marijuana*. Retreived from Bethesda, MD: https://www.drugabuse.gov/publications/drugfacts/marijuana.

National Institute on Drug Abuse. (2005a). *Marijuana*. Bethesda, MD: National Institutes of Health.

National Institute on Drug Abuse. (2005b). *Hallucinogens and Dissociative Drugs*. Bethesda, MD: National Institutes of Health.

National Public Radio. (2012). The curious case of teen tics in Le Roy, NY. Retrieved from http://www.npr.org/2012/03/10/148372536/the-curious-case-of-teen- tics-in-le-roy-n-y

National Survey on Drug Use and Health. (2006). *Substance use among older adults: 2002 & 2003 update.* Retrieved from http://www.oas.samhsa.gov

Nag, M. (1994, September). Beliefs and practices about food during pregnancy. *Economic and Political Weekly,* 2427–2438.

Neal-Barnett, A., Flessner, C., Franklin, M. E., Woods, D. W., Keuthen, N. J., & Stein, D. J. (2010). Ethnic differences in trichotillomania: Phenomenology, interference, impairment, and treatment efficacy. *Journal of Anxiety Disorders, 24,* 553–558.

Needleman, H. L., & Gatsonis, C. A. (1990). Low-level lead exposure and the IQ of children. A meta-analysis of modern studies. *Journal of the American Medical Association, 263,* 673–678.

Nehls, N. (1998). Borderline personality disorder: Gender stereotypes, stigma, and limited system of care. *Issues in Mental Health Nursing, 19,* 97–112.

Neisser, U., & Harsch, N. (1992). Phantom flashbulbs: False recollections of hearing the news about Challenger. In E. Winograd & U. Neisser (Eds.), *Affect and accuracy in recall: Studies of flashbulb memories* (Vol. 4, pp. 9–31). Cambridge, MA: Cambridge University Press.

Nelson, E. C., Grant, J. D., Bucholz, K. K., Glowinski, A., Madden, P. A. F., Reich, W., & Heath, A. C. (2000). Social phobia in a population-based female adolescent twin sample: Comorbidity and associated suicide-related symptoms. *Psychological Medicine, 30,* 797–804.

Nelson, E. C., Heath, A. C., Madden, P. A., Cooper, M. L., Dinwiddie, S. H., Bucholz, K. K., … Martin, N. G. (2002). Association between self-reported childhood sexual abuse and adverse psychosocial outcomes. *Archives of General Psychiatry, 59,* 139–145.

Nelson, R. M. (2002). Appropriate risk exposure in environmental health research. The Kennedy-Krieger lead abatement study. *Neurotoxicology and Teratology, 24,* 445–449.

Nestadt, G., Romanoski, A. J., Chahal, R., Merchant, A., Folstein, M. F., Gruenberg, E. M., & McHugh, P. R. (1990). An epidemiological study of histrionic personality disorder. *Psychological Medicine, 20,* 413–422.

Nestoriuc, Y., & Martin, A. (2007). Efficacy of biofeedback for migraine: A meta-analysis. *Pain, 128,* 111–127.

Network and Pathway Analysis Subgroup of Psychiatric Genomics Consortium. (2015). Psychiatric genome-wide association study analyses implicate neuronal, immune and histone pathways. *Nature Neuroscience, 18,* 199–209.

Neubauer, K., von Auer, M., Murray, E., Petermann, F., Helbig-Lang, S., & Gerlach, A. L. (2013). Internet-delivered attention modification training as a treatment for social phobia: A randomized controlled trial. *Behaviour Research and Therapy, 51,* 87–97.

Newcomb, M., & Richardson, M. A. (1995). Substance use disorders. In C. Webster-Stratton & R.W. Dahl. (Eds.), *Advanced abnormal child psychology* (pp. 411–431). Hillsdale, NJ: Lawrence Erlbaum Associates.

Newman, M. G., Llera, S. J., Erickson, T. M., Przeworski, A., & Castonguay, L. G. (2013). Worry and generalized anxiety disorder: A review and theoretical synthesis of evidence on nature, etiology, mechanisms, and treatment. *Annual Review of Clinical Psychology, 9,* 275–297.

Newton, E., Landau, S., Smith, P., Monks, P. N., Sherrill, S., & Wykes, T. (2005). Early psychological intervention for auditory hallucinations. *Journal of Nervous and Mental Disease, 193,* 58–61.

Ni, X., Chan, K., Bulgin, N., Sicard, T., Bismil, R., McCain, S., & Kennedy, J. L. (2006). Association between serotonin transporter gene and borderline personality disorder. *Journal of Psychatric Research, 40,* 448–453.

Ni, X., Bismil, R., Chan, K., Sicard, T., Bulgin, N., McCain, S., & Kennedy, J. L. (2006). Serotonin 2A receptor gene is associated with personality traits, but not to disorder, in patients with borderline personality disorder. *Neuroscience Letters, 408,* 214–219.

Nicely, T. A., Lane-Loney, S., Masciulli, E., Hollenbeak, C. S., & Ornstein, R. M. (2014). Prevalence and characteristics of avoidant/restrictive food intake disorder in a cohort of young patients in day treatment for eating disorders. *Journal of Eating Disorders, 2,* 21.

Nicholas, J. S., Charles, J. M., Carpenter, J. A., King, L. B., Jenner, W., & Spratt, E. G. (2008). Prevalence and characteristics of children with autism spectrum disorders. *Annals of Epidemiology, 18,* 130–136.

Nicolosi, A., Laumann, E. O., Glasser, D. B., Moreira, E. D., Jr., Paik, A., & Gingell, C. for the Global Study of Sexual Attitudes and Behaviors Investigators' Group. (2004). Sexual behavior and sexual dysfunctions after age 40: The global study of sexual attitudes and behaviors. *Urology, 64,* 991–997.

Nicolosi, A., Laumann, E. O., Glasser, D. B., Brock, G., King, R., & Gingell, C. (2006). Sexual activity, sexual disorders and associated help-seeking behavior among mature adults in five Anglophone countries from the Global Survey of Sexual Attitudes and Behaviors (GSSAB). *Journal of Sex & Marital Therapy, 32,* 331–342.

Niedermeyer, E. (1999). Historical aspects. In E. Neidermeyer & F. L. Da Silva (Eds.), *Electroencephalography: Basic principles, clinical applications and related fields* (pp. 1–13). Lippincott Williams & Wilkins.

Nieto, J. A. (2004). Children and adolescents as sexual beings: Cross-cultural perspectives. *Child and Adolescent Psychiatric Clinics of North America, 13,* 461–477.

Nigg, J. T. (2012). Future directions in ADHD etiology research. *Journal of Clinical Child & Adolescent Psychology, 41,* 524–533.

Nikolas, M. A., & Burt, S. (2010). Genetic and environmental influences on ADHD symptom dimensions of inattention and hyperactivity: A meta-analysis. *Journal of Abnormal Psychology, 119,* 1–17.

Nimkarm, S., & New, M.I. (2010). Congenital adrenal hyperplasia due to 21-hydroxylase deficiency: A paradigm for prenatal diagnosis and treatment. *Annals of the New York Academy of Sciences, Mar,* 1192:5-11.

Nivard, M. G., Nbarek, H., Hottenga, J. J., Smit, J. H., Jansen, R., Penninx, B. W., … Boomsma, D. I. (2014). Further confirmation of the association between anxiety and CTNND2: Replication in humans. *Genes, Brain, and Behavior, 13,* 195–201.

Noble, R. E. (2005). Depression in women. *Metabolism, 54* (5 Suppl 1), 49–52.

Nock, M. K., Kazdin, A. E., Hiripi, E., & Kessler, R. C. (2006). Prevalence, subtypes and correlates of DSM-IV conduct disorder in the National Comorbidity Survey Replication. *Psychological Medicine, 36,* 699-697-610.

Nock, M. K., Kazdin, A. E., Hiripi, E., & Kessler, R. C. (2007). Lifetime prevalence, correlates, and persistence of oppositional defiant disorder: Results from the National Comorbidity Survey Replication. *Journal of Child Psychology and Psychiatry, 48,* 703–713.

Nock, M. K., Green, J. G., Hwang, I., McLaughlin, K. A., Sampson, N. A., Zaslavsky, A. M., & Kessler, R. C. (2013). Prevalence, correlates, and treatment of lifetime suicidal behavior among adolescents: Results from the National Comorbidity Survey Replication Adolescent Supplement. *JAMA Psychiatry, 70,* 300–310.

Nock, M. K., Hwang, I., Sampson, N. A., & Kessler, R. C. (2010). Mental disorders, comorbidity and suicidal behavior: Results from the National Comorbidity Survey Replication. *Molecular Psychiatry, 15,* 868–876.

Nolen-Hoeksema, S. (2001). Gender differences in depression. *Current Directions in Psychological Science, 10,* 173–176.

Nomi, J. S., & Uddin, L. Q. (2015). Face processing in autism spectrum disorders: From brain regions to brain networks. *Neuropsychologia, 71,* 201–216.

Nordsletten, A., Reichenberg, A., Hatch, S. L, Fernández de la Cruz, L., Pertusa, A., Hotopf, M., & Mataix-Cols, D. (2013). Epidemiology of hoarding disorder. *The British Journal of Psychiatry: The Journal of Mental Science, 203,* 445–452.

Norfleet, M. A. (2002). Responding to society's needs: Prescription privileges for psychologists. *Journal of Clinical Psychology, 58,* 599–610.

North, C. S., Ryall, J. E. M., Ricci, D. A., & Wetzel, R. D. (1993). *Multiple personalities, multiple disorders.* New York: Oxford University Press.

Novy, D. M., Stanley, M. A., Averill, P., & Daza, P. (2001). Psychometric comparability of English-and Spanish-language measures of anxiety and related affective symptoms. *Psychological Assessment, 13,* 347–355.

Nurnberger, J. I., Jr., Koller, D. L., Jung, J., Edenberg, H. J., Foroud, T., Guella, I. … Psychiatric Genomics Consortium Bipolar Group. (2014). Identification of pathways for bipolar disorder: A meta-analysis. *JAMA Psychiatry, 71,* 657–664.

Nusbaum, M. R., Gamble, G., Skinner, B., & Heiman, J. (2000). The high prevalence of sexual concerns among women seeking routine gynecological care. *Journal of Family Practice, 49,* 229–232.

Nydegger, R. V. (1972). The elimination of hallucinatory and delusional behavior by verbal conditioning and assertive training: A case study. *Journal of Behavior Therapy and Experimental Psychiatry, 3,* 225.

Obsessive Compulsive Cognitions Working Group. (1997). Cognitive assessment of obsessive-compulsive disorder. *Behaviour Research and Therapy, 35,* 667–681.

O'Carroll, R. (1989). A neuropsychological study of sexual deviation. *Sexual and Marital Therapy, 4,* 59–63.

O'Brien, M. D., Bruce, B. K., & Camilleri, M. (1995). The rumination syndrome: Clinical features rather than manometric diagnosis. *Gastroenterology, 108,* 1024–1029.

O'Connor, K., & Roth, B. (2005). Finding new tricks for old drugs: An efficient route for public-sector drug discovery. *Nature Reviews Drug Discovery, 4,* 1005–1014.

O'Donovan, M. C. (2015). What have we learned from the Psychiatric Genomics Consortium. *World Psychiatry, 14,* 291–293.

O'Hara, M. W., & McCabe, J. E. (2013). Postpartum depression: Current status and future directions. *Annual Review of Clinical Psychology, 9,* 379–407.

O'Leary, T., & Monti, P. (2002). Cognitive-behavioral therapy for alcohol addiction. In S. G. Hoffmann (Ed.), *Treating chronic and severe mental disorders: A handbook of empirically supported interventions* (pp. 234–257). New York: Guilford Press.

Office of the U.S. Surgeon General. (2004). *The health consequences of smoking: A report of the Surgeon General.* Retrieved from http://www.surgeongeneral.gov/library/smokingconsequences/

Ogas, O., & Gaddam, S. (2011). *A billion wicked thoughts.* New York: NY Penguin.

Ogata, S. N., Silk, K. R., Goodrich, S., Lohr, N. E., Westen, D., & Hill, E. M. (1990). Childhood sexual and physical abuse in adult patients with borderline personality disorder. *American Journal of Psychiatry, 147,* 1008–1013.

Ohara K., Sato, Y., Tanabu, S., Yoshida, K., & Shibuya, H. (2006). Magnetic resonance imaging study of the ventricle-brain ratio in parents of schizophrenia subjects. *Progress in Neuro-Psychopharmacology & Biological Psychiatry, 30,* 89–92.

Okazaki, S., & Sue, S. (1995). Methodological issues in assessment research with ethnic minorities. *Psychological Assessment, 7,* 367–375.

Olfson. M., Gerhard, T., Huang, C., Crystal, S., & Stroup, T. S. (2015). Premature mortality among adults with schizophrenia in the United States. *JAMA Psychiatry, 72,* 1172–1181.

Okumura, Y., & Ichikura, K. (2014). Efficacy and acceptability of group cognitive behavioral therapy for depression: A systematic review and meta-analysis. *Journal of Affective Disorders, 164,* 155–164.

Olatunji, B. O., Deacon, B. J., & Abramowitz, J. S. (2009). The cruelest cure? Ethical issues in the implementation of exposure-based treatments. *Cognitive and Behavioral Practice, 16,* 172–180.

Olatunji, B. O., Kauffman, B. Y., Meltzer, S., Davis, M. L., Smits, J. A., & Powers, M. B. (2014). Cognitive-behavioral therapy for hypochondriasis/health anxiety: A meta-analysis of treatment outcome and moderators. *Behaviour Research and Therapy, 58,* 65–74.

Olde Hartman, T. C., Borghuis, M. S., Lucassen, P. L., van de Laar, F. A., Speckens, A. E., & van Weel, C. (2009). Medically unexplained symptoms, somatisation disorder, and hypochondriasis: Course and prognosis. A systematic review. *Journal of Psychosomatic Research, 66,* 363–377.

Oleseon, O. F., Bennike, B., Hansen, E. S., Koefoed, P., Woldbye, D. P., Bolwig, T. G., & Mellerup, E. (2005). The short/long polymorphism in the serotonin transporter gene promoter is not associated with panic disorder in a Scandinavian sample. *Psychiatric Genetics, 15,* 159.

Olfson, E., Saccone, N. L., Johnson, E. O., Chen, L. S., Culverhouse, R., Doheny, K., … Bierut, L. J. (2016). Rare, low frequency and common coding variants in CHRNA5 and their contribution to nicotine dependence in European and African Americans. *Molecular Psychiatry, 21,* 601–607.

Olfson, M., King, M., & Schoenbaum, M. (2015). Benzodiazepine use in the United States. *JAMA Psychiatry, 72,* 136–142.

Olfson. M., G., T., Huang, C., Crystal, S., & Stroup, T. S. (2015). Premature mortality among adults with schizophrenia in the United States. *JAMA Psychiatry, 72,* 1172–1181.

Olin, J. T., Schneider, L. S., Katz, I. R., Meyers, B. S., Alexopoulos, G. S., Breitner, J. C., … Devanand, D. P. (2002). Provisional diagnostic criteria for depression of Alzheimer disease. *The American Journal of Geriatric Psychiatry, 10,* 125–128.

Ollendick, T., & King, N. J. (1991). Origins of childhood fears: An evaluation of Rachman's theory of fear acquisition. *Behaviour Research and Therapy, 29*, 117–123.

Ollendick, T. G., Öst, L. G., Reuterskiöld, L., & Costa, N. (2010). Comorbidity in youth with specific phobias: Impact of comorbidity on treatment outcome and the impact of treatment on comorbid disorders. *Behavior Research and Therapy, 48*, 827–831.

Ollendick, T. H., King, N. J., & Muris, P. (2004). Phobias in children and adolescents. In M. Maj, H. S. Akiskal, J. J. Lopez-Ibor, & A. Okasha (Eds.), *Phobias* (pp. 245–279). Wiley: London.

Ollendick, T. H., Grills, A. E., & Alexander, K. L. (2014). Fears, worries, and anxiety in children and adolescents. In F. Petermann & C. A. Essau (Eds.), *Anxiety disorders in children and adolescents* (pp. 1–35). New York: Psychology Press.

Olson, L., & Houlihan, D. (2000). A review of behavioral treatments used for Lesch-Nyhan syndrome. *Behavior Modification, 24*, 202–222.

Ono, Y., Sakai, A., Otsuka, K., Uda, H., Oyama, H., Ishizuka, N., … Yonemoto, N. (2013). Effectiveness of a multimodal community intervention program to prevent suicide and suicide attempts: A quasi-experimental study. *PLOS ONE, 8*, e74902.

Oostervink, F., Nolen, W. A., Kok, R. M., & Board, E. A. (2015). Two years' outcome of acute mania in bipolar disorder: Different effects of age and age of onset. *International Journal of Geriatric Psychiatry, 30*, 201–209.

Opler, M. G. A., & Susser, E. S. (2005). Fetal environment and schizophrenia. *Environmental Health Perspectives, 113*, 1239–1242.

Ori, R., Amos, T., Bergman, H., Soares-Weiser, K., Ipser, J. C., & Stein, D. J. (2015). Augmentation of cognitive and behavioural therapies (CBT) with d-cycloserine for anxiety and related disorders. *Cochrane Database of Systematic Reviews, 5*, CD007803.

Ornstein, R. M., Rosen, D. S., Mammel, K. A., Callahan, S. T., Forman, S., Jay, M. S., … Walsh, B. T. (2013). Distribution of eating disorders in children and adolescents using the proposed DSM-5 criteria for feeding and eating disorders. *Journal of Adolescent Health, 53*, 303–305.

Osby, U., Correia, N., Brandt, L., Ekbom, A., & Sparen, P. (2000). Mortality and causes of death in schizophrenia in Stockholm County, Sweden. *Schizophrenia Research, 45*, 21–28.

Oslin, D. (2005). Brief interventions in the treatment of at-risk drinking in older adults. *Psychiatric Clinics of North America, 28*, 897–991.

Oslin, D. W. (2004). Late-life alcoholism: Issues relevant to the geriatric psychiatrist. *The American Journal of Geriatric Psychiatry, 12*, 571–583.

Oslin, D. W., & Mavandadi, S. (2009). Alcohol and drug problems. In D. C. Blazer & D. C. Steffens (Eds.), *Textbook of geriatric psychiatry* (pp. 409–428). Washington, DC: American Psychiatric Publishing, Inc.

Oslin, D. W., Pettinati, H., & Volpicelli, J. R. (2002). Alcoholism treatment adherence: Older age predicts better adherence and drinking outcomes. *The American Journal of Geriatric Psychiatry, 10*, 740–747.

Öst, L.-G., Havnen, A., Hansen, B., & Kvale, G. (2015). Cognitive behavioral treatments of obsessive–compulsive disorder. A systematic review and meta-analysis of studies published 1993–2014. *Clinical Psychology Review, 40*, 156–169.

Ost, L. G. (1996). Long-term effects of behavior therapy for specific phobia. In M. Mavissakalian and R. R. Prien (Eds.), *Long-term treatments of anxiety disorders* (pp. 121–170). New York: Plenum.

Ost, L. G. (1992). Blood and injection phobia: Background and cognitive, physiological, and behavioral variables. *Journal of Abnormal Psychology, 101*, 68–74.

Østby, K. A., Czajkowski, N., Knudsen, G. P., Ystrom, E., Gjerde, L. C., Kendler, K. S., … Reichborn-Kjennerud, T. (2014). Personality disorders are important risk factors for disability pensioning. *Social Psychiatry and Psychiatric Epidemilogy, 49*, 2003–2011.

Osterloh, I. H., & Riley, A. (2002). Clinical update on sildenafil citrate. *British Journal of Clinical Pharmacology, 53*, 219–223.

Otowa, T., Maher, B. S., Aggen, S. G., McClay, J. L., van den Oord, E. J., & Hettema, J. M. (2014). Genome-wide and gene-based association studies of anxiety disorders in European and African American samples. *PLOS ONE, 9*, e112559.

Otto, M. W., Pollack, M. H., Maki, K. M., Gould, R. A., Worthington, J. J., Smoller, J. W., & Rosenbaum, J. F. (2001). Childhood history of anxiety disorders among adults with social phobia: Rates, correlates, and comparisons with patients with panic disorder. *Depression and Anxiety, 14*, 209–213.

Ouimette, P. C., Finney, J. W., & Moos, R. H. (1997). Twelve-step and cognitive-behavioral treatment for substance abuse: A comparison of treatment effectiveness. *Journal of Consulting and Clinical Psychology, 65*, 230–240.

Overall, J., & Gorham, D. (1988). The Brief Psychiatric Rating Scale (BPRS): Recent developments in in ascertainment and scaling. *Psychopharmacology Bulletin, 24*, 97–99.

Owen, M. J., Sawa, A., & Martensen, P. B. (2016). Schizophrenia. *Lancet*, S014.

Owens, D. G., Miler, P., Lawrie, S. M., & Johnstone, E. C. (2005). Pathogenesis of schizophrenia: A psychopathological perspective. *British Journal of Psychiatry, 186*, 386–393.

Ozer, E. J., Best, S. R., Lipsey, T. L,. & Weiss, D. S. (2003). Predictors of posttraumatic stress disorder and symptoms of adults: A meta-analysis. *Psychological Bulletin, 129*, 52–75.

Padma-Nathan, H., Brown, C., Fendl, J., Salem, S., Yeager, J., & Harning, R. (2003). Efficacy and safety of topical alprostadil cream for the treatment of female sexual arousal disorder (FSAD): A double-blind, multicenter, randomized, and placebo-controlled clinical trial. *Journal of Sex & Marital Therapy, 29*, 329–344.

Padma-Nathan, H., Hellstrom, W. J., Kaiser, F. E., Labasky, R. F., Lue, T. F., Nolten, W. E., … Place, V. A. (1997). Treatment of men with erectile dysfunction with transurethral alprostadil. Medicated Urethral System for Erection (MUSE) Study Group. *New England Journal of Medicine, 336*, 1–7.

Palazzoli, M. (1978). *Self-starvation: From individual to family in the treatment of anorexia nervosa*. New York: Jason Aronson.

Pallaskorpi, S., Suominen, K., Ketokivi, M., Mantere, O., Arvilommi, P., Valtonen, H., … Isometsa, E. (2015). Five-year outcome of bipolar I and II disorders: Findings of the Jorvi Bipolar Study. *Bipolar Disorders, 17*, 363–374.

Palmer, B. W., Pankrantz, V. S., & Bostwick, J. M. (2005). The lifetime risk of suicide in schizophrenia: A reexamination. *Archives of General Psychiatry, 62*, 247–253.

Palmer, R. H., Brick, L., Nugent, N. R., Bidwell, L. C., McGeary, J. E., Knopik, V. S., & Keller, M. C. (2015). Examining the role of common genetic variants on alcohol, tobacco, cannabis, and illicit drug dependence: Genetics of vulnerability to drug dependence. *Addiction, 110*, 530–537.

Pande, N., & Naidu, R. K. (1992). Anasaki and health: A study of non-attachment. *Psychology & Developing Societies, 4*, 91–104.

Pandey, G. N. (2013). Biological basis of suicide and suicidal behavior. *Bipolar Disorders, 15*, 524–541.

Pandina, G. J., Aman, M. G., & Findling, R. L. (2006). Risperidone in the management of disruptive behavior disorders. *Journal of Child and Adolescent Psychopharmacology, 16*, 379–392.

Parikh, S. V., Hawke, L. D., Velyvis, V., Zaretsky, A., Beaulieu, S., Patelis-Siotis, I., … Cervantes, P. (2015). Combined treatment: Impact of optimal psychotherapy and medication in bipolar disorder. *Bipolar Disorders, 17*, 86–96.

Paris, J. (2002). Chronic suicidality among patients with borderline personality disorder. *Psychiatric Services, 53*, 738–742.

Paris, J. (2012). The rise and fall of dissociative identity disorder. *The Journal of Nervous and Mental Disease, 200*, 1076–1079.

Park, J. M., Rahman, O., Murphy, T. K., & Storch, E. A. (2012). Early childhood trichotillomania: Initial considerations on phenomenology, treatment, and future directions. *Infant Mental Health Journal, 33*, 163–172.

Parker, G. (1982). Researching the schizophrenogenic mother. *Journal of Nervous and Mental Disease, 170*, 452–462.

Parker, G. B., & Brotchie, H. L. (2004). From diathesis to dimorphism: The biology of gender differences in depression. *Journal of Nervous and Mental Disease, 192*, 210–216.

Pasewark, R., & McGinley, H. (1986). Insanity plea: National survey of frequency and success. *Journal of Psychiatry and Law, 13*, 101–108.

Pasterski, V., Zucker, K. J., Hindmarsh, P. C., Hughes, I. A., Acerini, C., Spencer, D…. Hines, M. (2015). Increased cross-gender identification independent of gender role behaviour in girls with congenital adrenal hyperplasia: Results from a standardized assessment of 4- to 11-year-old children. *Archives of Sexual Behavior, 44*, 1363–1375.

Patel, V. (2001). Cultural factors and international epidemiology. *British Medical Bulletin, 57*, 33–45.

Patterson, G. R., & Gullion, M. E. (1968). *Living with children: New methods for parents and teachers*. Champaign, IL: Research Press.

Paukert, A. L., Calleo, J., Kraus-Schuman, C., Snow, L., Wilson, N., Petersen, N. J., … Stanley, M. A. (2010). Peaceful Mind: An open trial of cognitive-behavioral therapy for anxiety in persons with dementia. *International Psychogeriatrics, 22*, 1012–1021.

Pauls, D. L., Alsobrook, J. P., Goodman, W, Rasmussen, S., & Leckman, J. F. (1995). A family study of obsessive-compulsive disorder. *American Journal of Psychiatry, 152*, 76–84.

Pauls, D. L., Abramovitch, A., Rauch, S. L., & Geller, D. A. (2014). Obsessive-compulsive disorder: An integrative genetic and neurobiological perspective. *Nature Reviews Neuroscience, 15*, 410–424.

Paulson, G. (2006). Death of a president and his assassin—Errors in their diagnosis and autopsies. *Journal of the History of the Neurosciences, 15*, 77–91.

Pearlstein, T., Howard, M., Salisbury, A., & Zlotnick, C. (2009). Postpartum depression. *American Journal of Obstetrics and Gynecology, 200*, 357–364.

Pearman, A., & Batra, A. (2012). Late-onset schizophrenia: A review for clinicians. *Clinical Gerontologist, 35*, 126–147.

Pedersen, N. L., & Fiske, A. (2010). Genetic influences on suicide and nonfatal suicidal behavior: Twin study findings. *European Psychiatry, 25*, 264–267.

Pedersen, N. L., McClearn, G., Plomin, R., & Friberg, L. (1985). Separated fraternal twins: Resemblance for cognitive abilities. *Behavior Genetics, 15*, 407–419.

Pelham, W. E., Fabiano, G. A., Gnagy, E. M., Greiner, A. R., & Hoza, B. (2004). Intensive treatment: Summer treatment program for children with ADHD. In E. D. Hibbs, & P. S. Jensen (Eds.), *Psychosocial treatment for child and adolescent disorders: Empirically based strategies for clinical practice* (2nd ed.). Washington, DC: American Psychological Association Press.

Pelham, W. E., & Fabiano, G. A. (2008). Evidence-based psychosocial treatments for attention-deficit/hyperactivity disorder. *Journal of Clinical Child and Adolescent Psychology, 37*, 184–214.

Pelham, W. E. J., Wheeler, T., & Chronis, A. (1998). Empirically supported psychosocial treatments for attention deficit hyperactivity disorder. *Journal of Clinical Child Psychology, 27*, 190–205.

Pelham, W. E. J., Gnagy, E. M., Greiner, A. R., Hoza, B., Hinshaw, S. P., Swanson, J. M., … McBurnett, K. (2000). Behavioral versus behavioral and pharmacological treatment in ADHD children attending a summer treatment program. *Journal of Abnormal Child Psychology, 28*, 507–525.

Pelkonen, M., & Marttunen, M. (2003). Child and adolescent suicide: Epidemiology, risk factors, and approaches to prevention. *Pediatric Drugs, 5*, 243–265.

Pendery, M., Maltzman, I., & West, L. (1982). Controlled drinking by alcoholics? New findings and a reevaluation of a major affirmative study. *Science, 217*, 169–175.

Penn, D. L., Combs, D. R., & Mohamed, S. (2001). Social cognition and social functioning in schizophrenia. In P. W. Corrigan, & D. L. Penn (Eds.), *Social cognition and schizophrenia* (pp. 97–122). Washington, DC: APA Press.

Peplau, L. A. (2003). Human sexuality: How do men and women differ? *Current Directions in Psychological Science, 12*, 37–40.

Perez-Duenas, B., Pujol, J., Soriano-Mas, C., Ortiz, H., Artuch, R., Vilaseca, M.S., & Campistol, J. (2006). Global and regional volume changes in the brains of patients with phenylketonuria. *Neurology, 66*, 1074–1078.

Peris, T. S., & Piacentini, J. (2013). Optimizing treatment for complex cases of childhood obsessive compulsive disorder: A preliminary trial. *Journal of Clinical Child & Adolescent Psychology, 42*, 1–8.

Perkins, D. O., Johnson, J. L., Hamer, R. M., Zipursky, R. B., Keefe, R. S., Centorrhino, F., … Tohen, M. (2006). Predictors of antipsychotic medication adherence in patients recovering from a first psychotic episode. *Schizophrenia Research, 83*, 53–63.

Perkonigg, A., Kessler, R. C., Storz, S., & Wittchen, H. U. (2000). Traumatic events and post-traumatic stress disorder in the community: Prevalence, risk factors, and comorbidity. *Acta Psychiatric Scandinavica, 101*, 46–59.

Perlis, R. H., Perlis, C. S., Wu, Y., Hwang, C., Joseph, M., & Nierenberg, A. A. (2005). Industry sponsorship and financial conflict of interest in the reporting of clinical trials in psychiatry. *American Journal of Psychiatry, 163*, 225–231.

Perlis, R. H., Brown, E., Baker, R. W., & Nierenberg, A. A. (2006). Clinical features of bipolar depression versus major depressive disorder in large multicenter trials. *American Journal of Psychiatry, 163*, 225–231.

Perlis, R. H., Miyahara, S., Marangell, L. B., Wisniewski, S. R., Ostacher, M., DelBello, M. P., … STEP-BD Investigators. (2004). Long-term implications of early onset in bipolar disorder: Data from the first 1000 participants in the systematic treatment enhancement program for bipolar disorder (STEP-BD). *Biological Psychiatry, 55*, 875–881.

Perron, S., Burrows, S., Fournier, M., Perron, P. A., & Ouellet, F. (2013). Installation of a bridge barrier as a suicide prevention strategy in Montréal, Québec, Canada. *American Journal of Public Health, 103*, 1235–1239.

Pertusa, A., Frost, R. O., Fullana, M. A., Samuels, J., Steketee, G., Tolin, D., … Mataix-Cols, D. (2010). Refining the diagnostic boundaries of compulsive hoarding: A critical review. *Clinical Psychology Review, 30*, 371–386.

Petersen, L., Sorensen, T. I., Andersen, P. K., Mortensen, P. B., & Hawton, K. (2013). Genetic and familial environmental effects on suicide—An adoption study of siblings. *PLOS ONE, 8*, e77973.

Petersen, R. C., Doody, R., Kurz, A., Mohs, R. C., Morris, J. C., Rabins, P. V., … Winblad, B. (2001). Current concepts in mild cognitive impairment. *Archives of Neurology, 58*, 1985–1992.

Petersen, R. C., Roberts, R. O., Knopman, D. S., Boeve, B. F., Geda, Y. E., Ivnik, R. J., … Jack, C. R. (2009). Mild cognitive impairment: Ten years later. *Archives of Neurology, 66*, 1447–1455.

Peterson, C. B., Thuras, P., Ackard, D. M., Mitchell, J. E., Berg, K., Sandager, N., … Crow, S. J. (2010). Personality dimensions in bulimia nervosa, binge eating disorder, and obesity. *Comprehensive Psychiatry, 51*, 31–36.

Petitclerc, A., & Tremblay, R. E. (2009). Childhood disruptive behavior disorders: Review of their origin, development, and prevention. *The Canadian Journal of Psychiatry, 54*, 222–231.

Petkus, A. J., Gatz, M., Reynolds, C. A., Kremen, W. S., & Wetherell, J. L. (2015). Stability of genetic and environmental contributions to anxiety symptoms in older adulthood. *Behavior Genetics*, 1–14.

Petronis, A. (2010). Epigenetics as a unifying principle in the aetiology of complex traits and diseases. *Nature, 465*, 721–727.

Pfiffner, L. J., & McBurnett, K. (1997). Social skills training with parent generalization: Treatment effects for children with attention deficit disorder. *Journal of Consulting and Clinical Psychology, 65*, 749–757.

Phelan, E. A., & Larson, E. B. (2002). "Successful aging"—Where next? *Journal of the American Geriatric Society, 50*, 1306–1308.

Phillips, K. A., Coles, M. E., Menard, W., Yen, S., Fay, C., & Weisberg, R. B. (2005). Suicidal ideation and suicide attempts in body dysmorphic disorder. *Journal of Clinical Psychiatry, 66*, 717–725.

Phillips, K. A., Didie, E. R., Menard, W., Pagano, M. E., Fay, C., & Weisberg, R. B. (2006). Clinical features of body dysmorphic disorder in adolescents and adults. *Psychiatry Research, 141*, 305–314.

Phillips, K. A., & Dufresne, R. G. (2002). Body dysmorphic disorder: A guide for primary care physicians. *Primary Care: Clinics in Office Practice, 29*, 99–111.

Phillips, K. A., & Menard, W. (2006). Suicidality in body dysmorphic disorder: A prospective study. *American Journal of Psychiatry, 163*, 1280–1282.

Phillips, K. A., Wilhelm, S., Koran, L. M., Didie, E. R., Fallon, B. A., Feusner, J., & Stein, D. J. (2010). Body dysmorphic disorder: Some key issues for DSM-V. *Depression and Anxiety, 27*, 573–591.

Pierce, K., Muller, R. A., Ambrose, J., Allen, G., & Courchesne, E. (2001). Face processing occurs outside the fusiform "face area" in autism: Evidence for functional MRI. *Brain, 124*, 2059–2073.

Pierce, K., Haist, R., Sedaghat, F., & Courchesne, E. (2004). The brain response to personally familiar faces in autism: Findings of fusiform activity and beyond. *Brain, 127*, 2703–2716.

Pierce, K., & Redcay, E. (2008). Fusiform function in children with an autism spectrum disorder is a matter of "who." *Biological Psychiatry, 64*, 552–560.

Pike, K., Loeb, K., & Vitousek, K. (1996). Cognitive-behavioral therapy for anroexia nervosa and bulimia nervosa. In J.K. Thompson (Ed.), *Eating disorders, obesity, and body image: A practical guide to assessment and treatment.* Washington, DC: APA Books.

Pike, K. M., Hoek, H. W., & Dunne, P. E. (2014). Cultural trends and eating disorders. *Current Opinions in Psychiatry, 27*, 436–442.

Pincus, J. (2003, August). *Intervening with distressed and impaired colleagues.* Paper presented at the meeting of the American Psychological Association, Toronto, Ontario, Canada.

Pincus, J., & Delfin, P. E. (2003, October). *Intervening with distressed and impaired colleagues.* Workshop presented at the fall ethics conference of the Pennsylvania Psychological Association, Exton, PA.

Pinhas, L., Morris, A., Crosby, R. D., & Katzman, D. K. (2011). Incidence and age-specific presentation of restrictive eating disorders in children: A Canadian Paediatric Surveillance Program study. *Archives of Pediatrics & Adolescent Medicine, 165*, 895–899.

Piotrowski, C. (1995). A review of the clinical and research use of the Bender-Gestalt Test *Perceptual and Motor Skills, 81*, 1272–1274

Piper, A. & Mersky, H. (2004a). The persistence of folly: A critical examination of dissociative identity disorder. Part 1: The excesses of an improbable concept. *Canadian Journal of Psychiatry, 49*, 592–600.

Piper, A. & Merskey, H. (2004b). The persistence of folly: Critical examination of dissociative identity disorder. Part II. The defence and decline of multiple personality or dissociative identity disorder. *Canadian Journal of Psychiatry, 49*, 678–683.

Pisetsky, E. M., Thornton, L. M., Lichtenstein, P., Pedersen, N. L., & Bulik, C. M. (2013). Suicide attempts in women with eating disorders. *Journal of Abnormal Psychology, 122*, 1042–1056.

Pishva, E., Drukker, M., Viechtbauer, W., Decoster, J., Collip, D., van Winkel, R., … Kenis, G. (2014). Epigenetic genes and emotional reactivity to daily life events: A multistep gene-environment interaction study. *PLOS ONE, 9*, e100935.

Pitschel-Walz, G., Leucht, S., Bauml, J., Kissling, W., & Engel, R. R. (2001). The effect of family interventions on relapse and rehospitalization in schizophrenia—A meta-analysis. *Schizophrenia Bulletin, 27*, 73–92.

Pittenger, C., & Bloch, M. H. (2014). Pharmacological treatment of obsessive-compulsive disorder. *Psychiatric Clinics of North America, 37*, 375–391.

Plassman, B. L., & Steffens, D. C. (2004). Genetics. In D. G. Blazer, D. C. Steffens, & E. W. Busse (Eds.), *Textbook of geriatric psychiatry* (3rd ed., pp. 109–120). Washington, DC: American Psychiatric Publishing, Inc.

Plemenitas, A., Kores Plesnicar, B., Kastelic, M., Porcelli, S., Serretti, A., & Dolzan, V. (2015). Genetic variability in tryptophan hydroxylase 2 gene in alcohol dependence and alcohol-related psychopathological symptoms. *Neuroscience Letters, 604*, 86–90.

Plomin, R., DeFries, J. C., Knopik, V. S., & Neiderheiser, J. (2013). *Behavioral genetics* (6th ed.). New York: W. H. Freeman & Co.

Plomin, R., DeFries, J. C., McLearn, G. E., & Rutter, M. (1994). *Behavioral genetics* (3rd ed.). New York: W. H. Freeman & Co.

Polderman, T. J., Benyamin, B., De Leeuw, C. A., Sullivan, P. F., Van Bochoven, A., Visscher, P. M., & Posthuma, D. (2015). Meta-analysis of the heritability of human traits based on fifty years of twin studies. *Nature Genetics, 47*, 702–709.

Politi, P., Minoretti, P., Falcone, C., Martinelli, V., & Emanuele, E. (2006). Association analysis of the functional *Ala111Glu* polymorphism of the glyoxalase I gene in panic disorder. *Neuroscience Letters, 396*, 163–166.

Pomara, C., Cassano, T., D'Errico, S., Bello, S., Romano, A. D., Riezzo, I., & Serviddio, G. (2012). Data available on the extent of cocaine use and dependence: Biochemistry, pharmacologic effects, and global burden of disease of cocaine abusers. *Current Medicinal Chemistry, 19*, 5647–5657.

Poortinga, Y. H., & Van Hemert, D. A. (2001). Personality and culture: Demarcating between the common and the unique. *Journal of Personality Disorders, 69*, 1033–1060.

Pope, H. G., Oliva, P. S., & Gruber, A. J. (1999). Attitudes toward DSM-IV dissociative disorders diagnoses among board-certified American psychiatrists. *American Journal of Psychiatry, 156*, 321.

Pope, H. G., Jr., Lalonde, J. K., Pindyck, L. J., Walsh, T., Bulik, C. M., Crow, S. J., … Hudson, J. I. (2006). Binge eating disorder: A stable syndrome. *American Journal of Psychiatry, 163*, 2181–2183.

Pope, H. G. J., Barry, S., Bodkin, A., & Hudson, J. I. (2006). Tracking scientific interest in the dissociative disorders: A study of scientific publication output 1984–2003. *Psychotherapy and Psychosomatics, 75*, 19–24.

Popovic, D., Yildiz, A., Murphy, P., & Colom, F. (2014). Unexplored areas of psychotherapy in bipolar disorder. *Harvard Review of Psychiatry, 22*, 373–378.

Popper, C. W., Gammon, G. D., West, S. A., & Bailey, C. E. (2004). Disorders usually first diagnosed in infancy, childhood, or adolescence. In R. E. Hales & S. G. Yudofsky (Eds.), *Essentials of clinical psychiatry* (2nd ed., pp. 591–735). Washington, DC: American Psychiatric Publishing.

Porensky, E. K., Dew, M. A., Karp, J. F., Skidmore, E., Rollman, B. L., Shear, M. K., & Lenze, E. J. (2009). The burden of late-life generalized anxiety disorder: Effects on disability, health-related quality of life, and healthcare utilization. *The American Journal of Geriatric Psychiatry, 17*, 473–482.

Porst, H., Rosen, R., Padma-Nathan, H., Goldstein, I., Giuliano, F., Ulbrich, E., & Bandel, T. (2001). The efficacy and tolerability of vardenafil, a new, oral, selective phosphodiesterase type 5 inhibitor, in patients with erectile dysfunction: The first at-home clinical trial. *International Journal of Impotence Research, 13*, 192–199.

Porter, V. R., Buxton, W. G., Fairbanks, L. A., Strickland, T., O'Connor, S. M., Rosenberg-Thompson, S., & Cummings, J. L. (2003). Frequency and characteristics of anxiety among patients with Alzheimer's disease and related dementias. *The Journal of Neuropsychiatry and Clinical Neurosciences, 15*, 180–186.

Post, R. M., Speer, A. M., Weiss, S. R., & Li, H. (2000). Seizure models: Anticonvulsant effects of ECT and rTMS. *Progress in Neuro-Psychopharmacology & Biological Psychiatry, 24*, 1251–1273.

Post, R. M., Denicoff, K. D., Leverich, G. S., Altshuler, L. L., Frye, M. A., Suppes, T. M., … Nolen, W. A. (2003). Morbidity in 258 bipolar outpatients followed for 1 year with daily prospective ratings on the NIMH life chart method. *Journal of Clinical Psychiatry, 64*, 680–690.

Post, R. M., Leverich, G. S., Kupka, R. W., Keck, P. E., Jr., McElroy, S. L., Altshuler, L. L., … Nolen, W. A. (2010). Early-onset bipolar disorder and treatment delay are risk factors for poor outcome in adulthood. *Journal of Clinical Psychiatry, 71*, 864–872.

Potenza, M. N. (2008). The neurobiology of pathological gambling and drug addiction: An overview and new findings. *Philosophical Transactions of the Royal Society of London. Series B, Biological Sciences, 363*(3181–3189).

Potenza, M. N. (2014). Non-substance addictive behaviors in the context of DSM-5. *Addictive Behaviors, 39*, 1–2.

Potvin, S., Sepehry, A. A., & Stip, E. (2006). A meta-analysis of negative symptoms in dual diagnosis schizophrenia. *Psychological Medicine, 36*, 431–440.

Power, R. A., Steinberg, S., Bjornsdottir, G., Rietveld, C. A., Abdellaoui, A., Nivard, M. M., … Stefansson, K. (2015). Polygenic risk scores for schizophrenia and bipolar disorder predict creativity. *Nature Neuroscience, 18*, 953–955.

Pratt, H. D., & Patel, D. R. (2007). Learning disorders in children and adolescents. *Primary Care: Clinics in Office Practice, 34*, 361–374.

Prendergast, M., Podus, D., & Finney, J. (2006). Contingency management for treatment of substance use disorders: A meta-analysis. *Addiction, 101*, 1546–1560.

Prescott, C. (2001). The genetic epidemiology of alcoholism: Sex differences and future directions. In T.J. Peters, J.H. Foster, D.P. Agarwal & H.K. Seitz (Eds.), *Alcohol in health and disease* (pp. 125–149). New York: Marcel Dekker.

Preti, A. (2011). Animal model and neurobiology of suicide. *Progress in Neuro-Psychopharmacology & Biological Psychiatry, 35*, 818–830.

Preti, A., Girolamo, G., Vilagut, G., Alonso, J., Graaf, R., Bruffaerts, R.,… ESEMeD-WMH Investigators. (2009). The epidemiology of eating disorders in six European countries: Results of the ESEMeD-WMH project. *Journal of Psychiatric Research, 43*, 1125–1132.

Price, M. (2010). Suicide among pre-adolescents. *APA Monitor, 41*, 52.

Prien, R. F., & Kupfer, D. J. (1986). Continuation drug therapy for major depressive episodes: How long should it be maintained? *American Journal of Psychiatry, 143*, 18–23.

Priester, M. A., Browne, T., Iachini, A., Clone, S., DeHart, D., & Seay, K. D. (2016). Treatment access barriers and disparities among individuals with co-occurring mental health and substance use disorders: An integrative literature review. *Journal of Substance Abuse Treatment, 61*, 47–59.

Prina, A. M., Deeg, D., Brayne, C., Beekman, A., & Huisman, M. (2012). The association between depressive symptoms and non-psychiatric hospitalisation in older adults. *PLOS One, 7*(4), e34821.

Prochaska, J., & DiClemente, C. (1983). Stages and processes of self-change of smoking: Toward an integrative model of change. *Journal of Consulting and Clinical Psychology, 51*, 390–395.

Pruett, D., Waterman, E. H., & Caughey, A. B. (2013). Fetal alcohol exposure: Consequences, diagnosis, and treatment. *Obstetrical & Gynecological Survey, 68*, 62–69.

Psychiatric GWAS Consortium Bipolar Disorder Working Group. (2011). Large-scale genome-wide association analysis of bipolar disorder identifies a new susceptibility locus near *ODZ4*. *Nature Genetics, 43*, 977–983.

Psychological Assessment Resources. (2003). Computerized Wisconsin Card Sort Task version 4 (WCST).

Pulay, A. J., Stinson, F. S., Dawson, D. A., Goldstein, R. B., Chou, S. P., Huang, B., … Grant, B. F. (2009). Prevalence, correlates, disability, and comorbidity of DSM-IV schizotypal personality disorder: Results from the wave 2 national epidemiologic survey on alcohol and related conditions. *The Primary Care Companion: Journal of Clinical Psychiatry, 11*, 53–67.

Pulular, A., Levy, R., & Stewart, R. (2013). Obsessive and compulsive symptoms in a national sample of older people: Prevalence, comorbidity, and associations with cognitive function. *The American Journal of Geriatric Psychiatry, 21*, 263–271.

Putnam, F. W., Guroff, J. J., Silberman, E. K., Barban, L. & Post, R. M. (1986). The clinical phenomenology of multiple personality disorder: Review of 100 recent cases. *Journal of Clinical Psychiatry, 47*, 285–293.

Putnam, F. W. (1989). *Diagnosis and treatment of multiple personality disorder*. New York: Guilford Press.

Putnam, F. W. (1993). Dissociative disorders in children: Behavioral profiles and problems. *Child Abuse & Neglect, 17*, 39–45.

Qiao, J., Wang, Z., Geronazzo-Alman, L., Amsel, L., Duarte, C., Lee, S., … Hoven, C. W. (2015). Brain activity classifies adolescents with and without a familial history of substance use disorders. *Frontiers in Human Neuroscience, 9*, 219.

Qin, P., Agerbo, E., & Mortensen, P. B. (2002). Suicide risk in relation to family history of completed suicide and psychiatric disorders: A nested case-control study based on longitudinal registers. *Lancet, 360*, 1126–1130.

Qin, P., & Nordentoft, M. (2005). Suicide risk in relation to psychiatric hospitalization: Evidence based on longitudinal registers. *Archives of General Psychiatry, 62*, 427–432.

Qualls, S. H., Segal, D. L., Benight, C. C., & Kenny, M. P. (2005). Geropsychology training in a specialist geropsychology doctoral program. *Gerontology & Geriatrics Education, 25*, 21–40.

Quan, W. X., Zhu, X. L., Qiao, H., Zhang, W. F., Tan, S. P., Zhou, D. F., & Wang, X. Q. (2015). The effects of high-frequency repetitive transcranial magnetic stimulation (rTMS) on negative symptoms of schizophrenia and the follow-up study. *Neuroscience Letters, 584*, 197–201.

Quay, H. C. (1965). Psychopathic personality as pathological stimulation-seeking. *American Journal of Psychiatry, 122*, 180–183.

Rachman, S. (1977). The conditioning theory of fear-acquisition: A critical examination. *Behaviour Research and Therapy, 15*, 375–387.

Rachman, S. J., & Hodgson, R. J. (1980). *Obsessions and compulsions*. Englewood Cliffs, NJ: Prentice-Hall.

Radloff, L. S. (1977). The CES-D scale a self-report depression scale for research in the general population. *Applied Psychological Measurement, 1*, 385–401.

Rahman Q., & Wilson, G. D. (2003). Born gay? The psychobiology of human sexual orientation. *Personality and Individual Differences, 34*, 1337–1382.

Raimundo Oda, A. M. G., Banzato, C. E. M., & Dalgalarrondo, P. (2005). Some origins of cross-cultural psychiatry. *History of Psychiatry, 16*, 155–169.

Rajindrajith, S., Devanarayana, N. M., & Crispus Perera, B. J. (2012). Rumination syndrome in children and adolescents: A school survey assessing prevalence and symptomatology. *BMC Gastroenterology, 12*, 163.

Ran, M.S., Chan, C.L.W., Chen, E.Y.H., Xiang, M.Z., Caine, E.D., & Conwell, Y. (2006). Homelessness among patients with schizophrenia in rural China: a 10 year cohort study. *Acta Psychiatrica Scandinavica, 114*, 118–123.

Raney, T. J., Thornton, L. M., Berrettini, W., Brandt, H., Crawford, S., Fichter, M. M., … Mitchell, J. (2008). Influence of overanxious disorder of childhood on the expression of anorexia nervosa. *International Journal of Eating Disorders, 41*, 326–332.

Ranta, K., Kaltiala-Heino, R., Rantanen, P., & Marttunen, M. (2009). Social phobia in Finnish general adolescent population: Prevalence, comorbidity, individual and family correlates, and service use. *Depression and Anxiety, 26*, 528–536.

Raphael, K. G., Widom, C. S., & Lange, G. (2001). Childhood victimization and pain in adulthood: A prospective investigation. *Pain, 92*, 283–293.

Rapoport, J. L., Addington, A. M., Frangou, S., & Psych, M. R. (2005). The neurodevelopmental model of schizophrenia: Update 2005. *Molecular Psychiatry, 10*, 434–449.

Raskind, M., Bonner, L. T., & Reskind, E. R. (2004). Cognitive disorders. In D.G. Blazer, D. C. Steffens, & E. W. Busse (Eds.), *Textbook of geriatric psychiatry* (3rd ed., pp. 207–229). Washington, DC: American Psychiatric Publishing, Inc.

Råstam, M, G. C., & Wentz, E. (2003). Outcome of teenage-onset anorexia nervosa in a Swedish community-based sample. *European Child & Adolescent Psychiatry, 12*(Suppl 1), I78–190.

Read, J., Kahler, C., & Stevenson, J. (2001). Bridging the gap between alcoholism treatment research and practice: Identifying what works and why. *Professional Psychology: Research and Practice, 32*, 227–238.

Reagan, P., & Hersch, J. (2005). Influence of race, gender, and socioeconomic status on binge eating frequency in a population-based sample. *International Journal of Eating Disorders, 38*, 252–256.

Reck, C., Stehle, E., Reinig, & Mundt, K. C. (2009). Maternity blues as a predictor of DSM-IV depression and anxiety disorders in the first three months postpartum. *Journal of Affective Disorders, 113*, 77–87.

Regier, D. A., Farmer, M. E., Rae, D. S., Locke, B. A., Keith, S. J., Judd, L. L., & Centers for Disease Control and Prevention. (1990). Comorbidity of mental disorders with alcohol and other drug abuse. *Journal of the American Medical Association, 264*, 2511–2518.

Reichborn-Kjennerud, T., Bulik, C. M., Sullivan, P., Tambs, K., & Harris, J. (2004). Psychiatric and medical symptoms in binge eating in the absence of compensatory behaviors. *Obesity Research, 12*, 1445–1454.

Reichborn-Kjennerud, T., Czajkowski, N., Ystrom, E., Orstavik, R., Aggen, S. H., Tambs, K., … Kendler, K. S. (2015). A longitudinal twin study of borderline and antisocial personality disorder traits in early to middle adulthood. *Psychological Medicine, 45*, 3121–3131.

Reichenberg, A., Gross, R., Weiser, M., Bresnahan, M., Silverman, J., Harlap, S., & Centers for Disease Control and Prevention. (2006). Advanced paternal age and autism. *Archives of General Psychiatry, 63*, 1026–1032.

Reif, S., George, P., Braude, L., Dougherty, R. H., Daniels, A. S., Ghose, S. S., & Delphin-Rittmon, M. E. (2014). Recovery housing: Assessing the evidence. *Psychiatric Services, 65*, 295–300.

Reif, S., George, P., Braude, L., Dougherty, R. H., Daniels, A. S., Ghose, S. S., & Delphin-Rittmon, M. E. (2014a). Residential treatment for individuals with substance use disorders: Assessing the evidence. *Psychiatric Services, 65*, 301–312.

Reinholt, N., & Krogh, J. (2014). Efficacy of transdiagnostic cognitive behaviour therapy for anxiety disorders: A systematic review and meta-analysis of published outcome studies. *Cognitive Behaviour Therapy, 43*, 171–184.

Reisberg, B., Doody, R., Stöffler, A., Schmitt, F., Ferris, S., & Möbius, H. J. (2003). Memantine in moderate-to-severe Alzheimer's disease. *New England Journal of Medicine, 348*, 1333–1341.

Reissing, E. D., Binik, Y. M., Khalifé, S., Cohen, D., & Amsel, R. (2004). Vaginal spasm, pain, and behavior: An empirical investigation of the diagnosis of vaginismus. *Archives of Sexual Behavior, 33*, 5–17.

Reitan, R. L., & Davidson. (1974). *Halstead-Reitan Neuropsychological Battery*. Reitan Neuropsychology Laboratories. University of Arizona.

Rekers, G. A., & Lovaas, O. I. (1974). Behavioral treatment of deviant sex-role behaviors in a male child. *Journal of Applied Behavior Analysis, 7*, 173–190.

Rekers, G. A., Lovaas, O. I., & Low, B. (1974). The behavioral treatment of a "transsexual" preadolescent boy. *Journal of Abnormal Child Psychology, 2*, 99–116.

Rekers, G. A., & Mead, S. (1979). Early intervention for female sexual identity disturbance: Self-monitoring of play behavior. *Journal of Abnormal Child Psychology, 7*, 405–423.

Remschmidt, H., & Theisen, F. M. (2005). Schizophrenia and related disorders in children and adolescents. *Journal of Neural Transmission, 69*(Suppl), 121–141.

Ren, J., Li, H., Palaniyappan, L., Liu, H., Wang, J., Li, C., & Rossini, P. M. (2014). Repetitive transcranial magnetic stimulation versus electroconvulsive therapy for major depression: A systematic review and meta-analysis. *Progress in Neuro-Psychopharmacology & Biological Psychiatry, 51*, 181–189.

Repetti, R. L., Taylor, S. E., & Seeman, T. E. (2002). Risky families: Family social environments and the mental and physical health of offspring. *Psychological Bulletin, 128*, 330–366.

Research Units on Pediatric Psychopharmacology (RUPP) Autism Network. (2005). Randomized, controlled, cross-over trial of methylphenidate in pervasive developmental disorders with hyperactivity. *Archives of General Psychiatry, 62*, 1266–1274.

Rettew, D. C. (2000). Avoidant personality disorder, generalized social phobia, and shyness: Putting the personality back into personality disorders. *Harvard Review of Psychiatry, 8*, 283–297.

Rettew, D. C., Rebollo-Mesa, I., Hudziak, J. J., Willemsen, G., & Boomsma, D. I. (2008). Non-additive and additive genetic effects on extraversion in 3314 Dutch adolescent twins and their parents. *Behavior Genetics, 38*, 223–233.

Reynolds, K., Pietrzak, R. H., El-Gabalawy, R., Mackenzie, C. S., & Sareen, J. (2015). Prevalence of psychiatric disorders in US older adults: Findings from a nationally representative survey. *World Psychiatry, 14*, 74–81.

Reynolds, K. J., Vernon, S. D., Bouchery, E., & Reeves, W. C. (2004). The economic impact of chronic fatigue syndrome. *Cost Effectiveness and Resource Allocation, 2*, 4.

Rhebergen, D., Beekman, A. T., de Graaf, R., Nolen, W. A., Spijker, J., Hoogendijk, W. J., & Penninx, B. W. (2010). Trajectories of recovery of social and physical functioning in major depression, dysthymic disorder and double depression: A 3-year follow-up. *Journal of Affective Disorders, 124*, 148–156.

Rhebergen, D., Beekman, A. T., Graaf, R., Nolen, W. A., Spijker, J., Hoogendijk, W. J., & Penninx, B. W. (2009). The three-year naturalistic course of major depressive disorder, dysthymic disorder and double depression. *Journal of Affective Disorders, 115*, 450–459.

Rice, M. E., & Harris, G. T. (2002). Men who molest their sexually immature daughters: Is a special explanation required? *Journal of Abnormal Psychology, 111*, 329–339.

Richardson, S. A., Katz, M., & Koller, H. (1986). Sex differences in number of children administratively classified as mildly mentally retarded: An epidemiological review. *American Journal of Mental Deficiency, 91*, 250–256.

Richmond, T. K., & Rosen, D. S. (2005). The treatment of adolescent depression in the era of the black box warning. *Current Opinion in Pediatrics, 17*, 466–472.

Riglin, L., Collishaw, S., Shelton, K. H., McManus, I. C., Ng-Knight, T., Sellers, R., … Rice, F. (2015). Higher cognitive ability buffers stress-related depressive symptoms in adolescent girls. *Development and Psychopathology*, 1–13.

Rigotti, N., Neer, R., Skates, S., Herzog, D., & Nussbaum, S. (1991). The clinical course of osteoporosis in anorexia nervosa: A longitudinal study of cortical bone mass. *Journal of the American Medical Association, 265*, 1133–1137.

Rimmele, C., Howard, M., & Hilfrink, M. (1995). Aversion therapies. In K. Reid, M. Hester, & R. William (Eds.), *Handbook of alcoholism treatment approaches: Effective alternatives* (2nd ed., pp. 134–147). Needham Heights, MA: Allyn & Bacon.

Ritchie, K., Norton, J., Mann, A., Carrière, I., & Ancelin, M.-L. (2013). Late-onset agoraphobia: General population incidence and evidence for a clinical subtype. *American Journal of Psychiatry, 170*, 790–798.

Robbins, J. M., & Kirmayer, L. J. (1996). Transient and persistent hypochondriacal worry in primary care. *Psychological Medicine, 26*, 575–589.

Roberson-Nay, R., Eaves, L. J., Hettema, J. M., Kendler, K. S., & Silberg, J. L. (2012). Childhood separation anxiety disorder and adult onset panic attacks share a common genetic diathesis. *Depression and Anxiety, 29*, 320–327.

Robertson, E., Jones, I., Haque, S., Holer, R., & Craddock, N. (2005). Risk of puerperal and non-puerperal recurrence of illness following bipolar affective puerperal (post-partum) psychosis. *British Journal of Psychiatry, 186*, 258–259.

Robins, L., & Slobodyan, S. (2003). Post-Vietnam heroin use and injection by returning US veterans: Clues to preventing injection today. *Addiction, 98*, 1053–1060.

Robins, L. N., Helzer, J. E., Weissman, M. M., Orvaschel, H., Gruenberg, E., Burke, J. D., & Regier, D. A. (1984). Lifetime prevalence of specific psychiatric disorders in three sites. *Archives in General Psychiatry, 41*, 949–958.

Robinson, P. H., Kukucska, R., Guidetti, G., & Leavey, G. (2015). Severe and enduring anorexia nervosa (SEED-AN): A qualitative study of patients with 20+ years of anorexia nervosa. *European Eating Disorders Review, 23*, 318–326.

Robinson, T. N., Matheson, D. M., Kraemer, H. C., Wilson, D. M., Obarzanek, E., Thompson, N. S., … Fujimoto, M. (2010). A randomized controlled trial of culturally tailored dance and reducing screen time to prevent weight gain in low-income African American girls: Stanford GEMS. *Archives of Pediatrics & Adolescent Medicine, 164*, 995–1004.

Roccatagliata, G. (1997). Classical psychopathology. In W. G. Bringman, H. E. Luck, R. Miller, & C. Early, (Eds.), *A pictorial history of psychology*. Carol Stream, IL: Quintessence Publishing Co, Inc.

Rode, S., Salkovskis, P. M., & Jack, T. (2001). An experimental study of attention, labeling, and memory in people suffering from chronic pain. *Pain, 94*, 193–203.

Rodgers, R. F., McLean, S. A., & Paxton, S. J. (2015). Longitudinal relationships among internalization of the media ideal, peer social comparison, and body dissatisfaction: Implications for the tripartite influence model. *Developmental Psychology, 51*, 706–713.

Rogler, L. H. (1999). Methodological sources of cultural insensitivity in mental health research. *American Psychologist, 54*, 424–433.

Rohan, K. J., Lindsey, K. T., Roecklein, K. A., & Lacy, T. J. (2004). Cognitive-behavioral therapy, light therapy, and their combination in treating seasonal affective disorder. *Journal of Affective Disorders, 80*, 273–283.

Rohde, L. A., Szobot, C., Polanczyk, G., Schmitz, M., Martins, S., & Tramontina, S. (2005). Attention-deficit/hyperactivity disorder in a diverse culture: Do research and clinical findings support the notion of a cultural construct for the disorder? *Biological Psychiatry, 57*, 1436–1441.

Rohde, P., Lewinsohn, P., Kahler, C., Seeley, J., & Brown, R. (2001). Natural course of alcohol use disorders from adolescence to young adulthood. *Journal of the American Academy of Child and Adolescent Psychiatry, 40*, 83–90.

Rohsenow, D., Niaura, R., Childress, A., Abrams, D., & Monti, P. (1990). Cue reactivity in addictive behaviors: Theoretical and treatment implications. *International Journal of the Addictions, 25*, 957–993.

Roid, G. H., & Miller, L. J. (1997). *Examiner's manual: Leiter International Performance Scale—Revised*. Wood Dale: Stoelting.

Roll, J. M., Petry, N. M., Stitzer, M. L., Brecht, M. L., Peirce, J. M., McCann, M. J., … Kellogg, S. (2006). Contingency management for the treatment of methamphetamine use disorders. *American Journal of Psychiatry, 163*, 1993–1999.

Romanelli, R. J., Wu, F. M., Gamba, R., Mojtabai, R., & Segal, J. B. (2014). Behavioral therapy and serotonin reuptake inhibitor pharmacotherapy in the treatment of obsessive-compulsive disorder: A systematic review and meta-analysis of head-to-head randomized controlled trials. *Depression and Anxiety, 31*, 641–652.

Ropacki, S. A., & Jeste, D. V. (2005). Epidemiology of and risk factors for psychosis of Alzheimer's disease: A review of 55 studies published from 1990 to 2003. *American Journal of Psychiatry, 162*, 2022–2030.

Röpcke, B., & Eggers, C. (2005). Early-onset schizophrenia. *European Child & Adolescent Psychiatry, 14*, 341–350.

Rosario-Campos, M. C., Leckman, J. F., Mercadante, M. T., Shavitt, R. G., da Silva Prado, H., Sada, P., … Miguel, E. C. (2001). Adults with early-onset obsessive-compulsive disorder. *American Journal of Psychiatry, 158*, 1899–1903.

Rose, E. A., Porcecelli, J. H., & Neale, A. V. (2000). Pica: Common but commonly missed. *Journal of the American Board of Family Practice, 13*, 353–358.

Rosen, R. C., Connor, M. K., Miyasato, G., Shifren, J. L., Fisher, W. A., … Schobelock, M. J. (2012). Sexual desire problems in women seeking healthcare: A novel study design for ascertaining prevalence of hypoactive sexual desire disorder in clinic-based samples of U.S. women. *Journal of Women's Health, 21*, 505–515.

Rosen, R. C., Heiman, J. R., Long, J. S., Fisher, W. A., & Sand, M. S. (2016). Men with sexual problems and their partners: Findings from the International Survey of Relationships. *Archives of Sexual Behavior, 45*, 159–173.

Rosenberg, S. D., Goodman, L. A., Osher, F. G., Swartz, M. S., Essock, S. M., Butterfield, M. I., … Salyers, M. P. (2001). Prevalence of HIV, hepatitis B, and hepatitis C in people with severe mental illness. *American Journal of Public Health, 91*, 31–37.

Rosenfarb, I. S., Bellack, A. S., & Aziz, N. (2006). Family interactions in the course of schizophrenia in African-American and white patients. *Journal of Abnormal Psychology, 115*, 112–120.

Rosenheck, R., Leslie, D., Sint, K., Lin, H., Robinson, D. G., Schooler, N. R., … Kane, J. M. (2016). Cost-effectiveness of comprehensive, integrated care for first episode psychosis in the NIMH RAISE early treatment program. *Schizophrenia Bulletin*, sbv224.

Rosenvinge, J. H., Martinussen, M., & Ostensen, E. (2000). The comorbidity of eating disorders and personality disorders: A meta-analytic review of studies published between 1983 and 1998. *Eating and Weight Disorders, 5*, 52–61.

Rösler, A., & Witztum, E. (2000). Pharmacotherapy of paraphilias in the next millennium. *Behavioral Sciences and the Law, 18*, 43–56.

Rosling, A. M., Sparen, P., Norring, C., & von Knorring, A. L. (2011). Mortality of eating disorders: A follow-up study of treatment in a specialist unit 1974–2000. *International Journal of Eating Disorders, 44*, 304–310.

Ross, C. A. (1997). *Dissociative identity disorder: Diagnosis, clinical features and treatment of multiple personality*. New York: John Wiley & Sons.

Ross, M. W., Mansson, S. A., & Daneback, K. (2012). Prevalence, severity, and correlates of problematic sexual Internet use in Swedish men and women. *Archives of Sexual Behavior, 41*, 459–466.

Roth, B., & Shapiro, D. (2001). Insights into the structure and function of 5-HT2 family serotonin receptors reveal novel strategies for therapeutic target development. *Expert Opinion on Therapeutic Targets, 5*, 685–695.

Rothbart, R., & Stein, D. J. (2014). Pharmacotherapy of trichotillomania (hair pulling disorder): An updated systematic review. *Expert Opinion on Pharmacotherapy, 15*, 2709–2719.

Rothbaum, B. O., Hodges, L., Anderson, P. L., Price, L., & Smith, S. (2002). Twelve-month follow-up of virtual reality and standard exposure therapies for the fear of flying. *Journal of Consulting and Clinical Psychology, 70*, 428–432.

Rothbaum, B. O., Price, M., Jovanovic, T., Norrholm, S. D., Gerardi, M., Dunlop, B., … Ressler, K. J. (2014). A randomized, double-blind evaluation of d-cycloserine or alprazolam combined with virtual reality exposure therapy for posttraumatic stress disorder in Iraq and Afghanistan War veterans. *American Journal of Psychiatry, 171*, 640–648.

Roubertoux, P. L., & Kerdelhúe, B. (2006). Trisomy 21: From chromosomes to mental retardation. *Behavior Genetics, 36*, 346–354.

Roundy, K., Cully, J. A., Stanley, M. A., Veazey, C., Souchek, J., Wray, N. P., & Kunik, M. E. (2005). Are anxiety and depression addressed in primary care patients with chronic obstructive pulmonary disease? A chart review. *Primary Care Companion to the Journal of Clinical Psychiatry, 7*, 213–218.

Routtenberg, A., & Kuznesof, A. (1967). Self-starvation of rats living in activity wheels on a restricted feeding schedule. *Journal of Comparative Physiology and Psychology, 64*, 414–421.

Rowe, R., Costello, E. J., Angold, A., Copeland, W. E., & Maughan, B. (2010). Developmental pathways in oppositional defiant disorder and conduct disorder. *Journal of Abnormal Psychology, 119*, 726–738.

Rowland, D., Perelman, M., Althof, S., Barada, J., McCullough, A., Bull, S., … Ho, K. F. (2004). Self-reported premature ejaculation and aspects of sexual functioning and satisfaction. *Journal of Sexual Medicine, 1*, 225–232.

Roy-Byrne, P. P., Craske, M. G., Stein, M. B., Sullivan, G., Bystritsky, A., Katon, W., … Sherbourne, C. D. (2005). A randomized effectiveness trial of cognitive-behavioral therapy and medication for primary care panic disorder. *Archives of General Psychiatry, 62*, 290–298.

Roy-Byrne, P. P., Sherbourne, C. D., Craske, M. G., Stein, M. B., Katon, W., Sullivan, G., … Bystritsky, A. (2003). Moving treatment research from clinical trials to the real world. *Psychiatric Services, 54*, 327–332.

Rubia, K. (2007). Neuro-anatomic evidence for the maturational delay hypothesis of ADHD. *Proceedings of the National Academy of Sciences, 104*, 19663–19664.

Ruitenberg, A., van Swieten, J. C., Witteman, J. C., Mehta, K. M., van Duijn, C. M., Hofman, A., & Breteler, M. M. (2002). Alcohol consumption and risk of dementia: The Rotterdam Study. *Lancet, 359*, 281–286.

Ruppin, U., & Pfäfflin, F. (2015). Long-term follow-up of adults with gender identity disorder. *Archives of Sexual Behavior, 44*, 1321–1329.

Russell, G., Kelly, S., & Golding, J. (2009). A qualitative analysis of lay beliefs about the aetiology and prevalence of autistic spectrum disorders. *Child: Care, Health, and Development, 36*, 431–436.

Russell, G. F. M., Szmukler, G. I., Dare, C., & Eisler, I. (1987). An evaluation of family therapy in anorexia and bulimia nervosa. *Archives of General Psychiatry, 44*, 1047–1056.

Rutter, M. (1978). Diagnosis and definitions of childhood autism. *Journal of Autism and Developmental Disorders, 8*, 139–161.

Rutter, M. (2005). Incidence of autism spectrum disorders: Changes over time and their meaning. *Acta Pediatrica, 94*, 2–15.

Saba, G., Verdon, C. M., Kalalou, K., Rocamora, J. F., Dumortier, G., Benadhira, R., … Januel, D. (2006). Transcranial magnetic stimulation in the treatment of schizophrenic symptoms: A double blind sham controlled study. *Journal of Psychiatric Research, 4*, 147–152.

Sachs, K., & Mehler, P. S. (2015). Medical complications of bulimia nervosa and their treatments. *Eating and Weight Disorders-Studies on Anorexia, Bulimia and Obesity*, 1–6.

Saczynski, J. S., & Inouye, S. K. (2015). In D. C. Steffens, D. G. Blazer, & M. E. Thakur (Eds.), *Textbook of geriatric psychiatry, DSM-5 edition* (pp. 155–175). Washington, DC: American Psychiatric Association.

Safer, D. J., Magno Zito, J., & dosReis, S. (2003). Concomitant psychotropic medication for youths. *American Journal of Psychiatry, 160*, 438–449.

Safer, D. L., Telch, C. F., & Agras, W. S. (2001). Dialectical behavior therapy for bulimia nervosa. *American Journal of Psychiatry, 158*, 632–634.

Sagan, C. (1996). *The demon-haunted world: Science as a candle in the dark*. New York: Ballentine Books.

Sajatovic, M., Blow, F. C., Ignacio, R. V., & Kales, H. C. (2005). New-onset bipolar disorder in later life. *The American Journal of Geriatric Psychiatry, 13*, 282–289.

Sajatovic, M., & Chen, P. (2011). Geriatric bipolar disorder. *Psychiatric Clinics of North America, 34*, 319–333, vii.

Sakauye, K. (2004). Ethnocultural aspects of aging in mental health. In J. Sadavoy, L. F. Jarvik, G. T. Grossberg, & B. S. Meyers (Eds.), *Comprehensive text book of geriatric psychiatry* (pp. 225–250). New York: WW Norton & Co.

Salkovskis, P. M. (1989). Somatic problems. In K. Hawton, P. M. Salkovskis, J. W. Kirk, & D. M. Clark (Eds.), *Cognitive-behavioural approaches to adult psychiatric disorder: A practical guide* (pp. 235–276). Oxford: Oxford University Press.

Sallet, P. C., Elkis, H., Alves, T. M., Oliveria, J. R., Sassi, E., de Castro, C. C., Busatto, G. F., & Gattaz, W. F. (2003). Reduced cortical folding in schizophrenia: An MRI morphometric study. *American Journal of Psychiatry, 160*, 1606–1613.

Samochowiec, J., Samochowiec, A., Puls, I., Bienkowski, P., & Schott, B. H. (2014). Genetics of alcohol dependence: A review of clinical studies. *Neuropsychobiology, 70*, 77–94.

Samuels, J. F., Bienvenu, O. J., Grados, M. A., Cullen, B., Riddle, M. A., Liang, K.-Y., … Nestadt, G. (2008). Prevalence and correlates of hoarding behavior in a community-based sample. *Behaviour Research and Therapy, 46*, 836–844.

Sanchez, M. M., Ladd, C. O., & Plotsky, P. M. (2001). Early adverse experience as a developmental risk factor for later psychopathology: Evidence from rodent and primate models. *Developmental Psychopathology, 13*, 419–449.

Sandberg, D. E., Meyer-Bahlburg, H. F., Ehrhardt, A. A., & Yager, T. J. (1993). The prevalence of gender-atypical behavior in elementary school children. *Journal of the American Academy of Child and Adolescent Psychiatry, 32*, 306–314.

Sands, J. R., & Harrow, M. (1999). Depression during the longitudinal course of schizophrenia. *Schizophrenia Bulletin, 25*, 157–171.

Sansone, R. A., & Sansone, L. A. (2013). Responses of mental health clinicians to patients with borderline personality disorder. *Innovations in Clinical Neuroscience, 10*, 39–43.

Sapolsky, R. M., Uno, H., Rebert, C. S., & Finch, C. E. (1990). Hippocampal damage associated with prolonged glucocorticoid exposure in primates. *The Journal of Neuroscience, 10*, 2897–2902.

Sar, V., Akyüz, G., & Dogan, O. (2007). Prevalence of dissociative disorders among women in the general population. *Psychiatry Research, 149*, 169–176.

Şar, V., Unal, S. N., Kiziltan, E., Kundakci, T., & Ozturk, E. (2001). HMPAO SPECT study of regional cerebral blood flow in dissociative identity disorder. *Journal of Trauma & Association, 2*, 5–25.

Şar, V., & Ross, C.A. (2006). Dissociative disorders as a confounding factor in psychiatric research. *Psychiatric Clinics of North America, 29*, 129–144.

Sartorius, N., Jablensky, A., & Shapiro, R. (1978). Cross-cultural differences in the short-term prognosis of schizophrenic psychosis. *Schizophrenia Bulletin, 4*, 102–113.

Savitz, J. B., Rauch, S. L., & Devets, W.C. (2013). Clinical application of brain imaging for the diagnosis of mood disorders: The current state of play. *Molecular Psychiatry, 18*, 528–539.

Scaini, S., Belotti, R., & Ogliari, A. (2014). Genetic and environmental contributions to social anxiety across different ages: A meta-analytic approach to twin data. *Journal of Anxiety Disorders, 7*, 650–656.

Scammell, T. E., & Saper, C. B. (2005). Orexin, drugs and motivated behaviors. *Nature Neuroscience, 8*, 1286–1288.

Scharfstein, L. A., & Beidel, D. C. (2015). Social skills and social acceptance in children with social anxiety disorder. *Journal of Clinical Child and Adolescent Psychology, 44*, 826–838.

Schienle, A., Schafer, A., Hermann, A., & Vaitl, D. (2009). Binge-eating disorder: Reward sensitivity and brain activation to images of food. *Biological Psychiatry, 65*, 654–661.

Schiffman, J., Walker, E., Ekstrom, M., Schulsinger, F., Sorensen, H., & Mednick, S. (2004). Childhood videotaped social and neuromotor precursors of schizophrenia: A prospective investigation. *American Journal of Psychiatry, 161*, 2021–2027.

Schizophrenia Working Group of the Psychiatric Genomics Consortium. (2014). Biological insights from 108 schizophrenia-associated genetic loci. *Nature, 511*, 421–427.

Schmidt, R. (2011). *Little girl blue: The life of Karen Carpenter*. Chicago, IL: Chicago Review Press.

Schmidt, U., Magill, N., Renwick, B., Keyes, A., Kenyon, M., Dejong, H., … Landau, S. (2015). The Maudsley Outpatient Study of Treatments for Anorexia Nervosa and Related Conditions (MOSAIC): Comparison of the Maudsley Model of Anorexia Nervosa Treatment for Adults (MANTRA) with specialist supportive clinical management (SSCM) in outpatients with broadly defined anorexia nervosa: A randomized controlled trial. *Journal of Consulting and Clinical Psychology, 83*, 796–807.

Schneider, J. P. (2003). The impact of compulsive cybersex behaviours on the family. *Sexual and Relationship Therapy, 18*, 329–354.

Schneider, L. S., Dagerman, K., & Insel, P. S. (2006). Efficacy and adverse effects of atypical antipsychotics for dementia: Meta-analysis of randomized, placebo-controlled trials. *The American Journal of Geriatric Psychiatry, 14*, 191–210.

Schneider, L. S., Dagerman, K. S., & Insel, P. (2005). Risk of death with atypical antipsychotic drug treatment for dementia: Meta-analysis of randomized placebo-controlled trials. *Journal of the American Medical Association, 294*, 1934–1943.

Schnitzler, C. E., von Ranson, K. M., & Wallace, L. M. (2012). Adding thin-ideal internalization and impulsiveness to the cognitive-behavioral model of bulimic symptoms. *Eating Behaviors, 13*, 219–225.

Schoenmakers, B., Buntinx, F., & Delepeleire, J. (2010). Factors determining the impact of caregiving on caregivers of elderly patients with dementia. A systematic literature review. *Maturitas, 66*, 191–200.

Schoevers, R. A., Deeg, D., Van Tilburg, W., & Beekman, A. (2005). Depression and generalized anxiety disorder: Co-occurrence and longitudinal patterns in elderly patients. *The American Journal of Geriatric Psychiatry, 13*, 31–39.

Schoeyen, H. K., Kessler, U., Andreassen, O. A., Auestad, B. H., Bergsholm, P., Malt, U. F., … Vaaler, A. (2015). Treatment-resistant bipolar depression: A randomized controlled trial of electroconvulsive therapy versus algorithm-based pharmacological treatment. *American Journal of Psychiatry, 172*, 41–51.

Schooler, N. R., Keith, S. J., Severe, J. B., Matthews, S. M., Bellack, A. S., Glick, I. D., … Jacobs, M. (1997). Relapse and rehospitalization during maintenance treatment of schizophrenia: The effects of dose reduction and family treatment. *Archives of General Psychiatry, 54*, 453–463.

Schreiber, L. R., Odlaug, B. L., & Grant, J. E. (2013). The overlap between binge eating disorder and substance use disorders: Diagnosis and neurobiology. *Journal of Behavioral Addictions, 2*, 191–198.

Schuckit, M. A. (2014). Recognition and management of withdrawal delirium (delirium tremens). *New England Journal of Medicine, 371*, 2109–2113.

Schultz, R.T., Grelott, D.J., Klin, A., Levitan, E., Cantey & G. Gore, J.T. (2001). *An fMRI study of face recognition, facial expression detection, and social judgment in autism spectrum disorders*. International Meeting for Autism Research, San Diego, CA.

Schultz, S. K., Hoth, A., & Buckwalter, K. (2004). Anxiety and impaired social function in the elderly. *Annals of Clinical Psychiatry, 16*, 47–51.

Schuurmans, J., Comijs, H., Beekman, A., Beurs, E. D., Deeg, D., Emmelkamp, P., & Dyck, R. V. (2005). The outcome of anxiety disorders in older people at 6-year follow-up: Results from the Longitudinal Aging Study Amsterdam. *Acta Psychiatrica Scandinavica, 111*, 420–428.

Schuurmans, J., Comijs, H., Emmelkamp, P. M., Gundy, C. M., Weijnen, I., Van Den Hout, M., & Van Dyck, R. (2006). A randomized, controlled trial of the effectiveness of cognitive–behavioral therapy and sertraline versus a waitlist control group for anxiety disorders in older adults. *The American Journal of Geriatric Psychiatry, 14*, 255–263.

Schwartz, C. E., Wright, C. I., Shin, L. M., Kagan, J., & Rauch, S. L. (2003). Inhibited and uninhibited infants "grown up": Adult amygdalar response to novelty. *Science, 300* (5627), 1952–1953.

Scott, C. L. (2010). Competency to stand trial and the insanity defense. In R. I. Simon & L. H. Gold (Eds.), *The American psychiatric publishing textbook of forensic psychiatry* (2nd ed., pp. 337–371). Washington, DC: American Psychiatric Publishing, Inc.

Scott, J., Paykel, E., Morriss, R., Bentall, R., Kinderman, P., Johnson, T., … Hayhurst, H. (2006). Cognitive-behavioural therapy for severe and recurrent bipolar disorders: Randomised controlled trial. *The British Journal of Psychiatry, 88*, 313–320.

Scull, A. (2004). The insanity of place. *History of Psychiatry, 15*(60 Pt 4), 417–436.

Seal, K. H., Bertenthal, D., Miner, C. R., Sen, S., & Marmar, C. (2007). Bringing the war back home—Mental health disorders among 103, 788 US veterans returning from Iraq and Afghanistan seen at Department of Veterans Affairs facilities. *Archives of Internal Medicine, 167*, 476–482.

Sechrest, L., & Coan, J. (2002). Preparing psychologists to prescribe. *Journal of Clinical Psychology, 58*, 649–658.

Sedlak, A. J., & Broadhurst, D. D. (1996). *Executive summary for the Third National Incidence Study of Child Abuse and Neglect*. Retrieved from https://www.ncjrs.gov/App/Publications/abstract.aspx?ID=166288

Seeman, P. (2015). Parkinson's disease treatment may cause impulse-control disorder via dopamine D3 receptors. *Synapse, 69*, 183–189.

Seifert, S. M., Schaechter, J. L., Hershorin, E. R., & Lipshultz, S. E. (2011). Health effects of energy drinks on children, adolescents, and young adults. *Pediatrics, 127*, 511–528.

Seignourel, P. J., Kunik, M. E., Snow, L., Wilson, N., & Stanley, M. (2008). Anxiety in dementia: A critical review. *Clinical Psychology Review, 28*, 1071–1082.

Seligman, M. (1975). *Helplessness: On depression, development, and death*. San Francisco: W. H. Freeman.

Selling, L. S. (1940). *Men against madness*. New York: Greenberg.

Semans, J. H. (1956). Premature ejaculation: A new approach. *Southern Medical Journal, 353–358.*

Sergeant, J. A., Geurts, H., & Oosterlaan, J. (2002). How specific is a deficit of executive functioning for attention-deficit/hyperactivity disorder? *Behavioural Brain Research, 130*, 3–28.

Seto, M. C. (2001). The value of phallometry in the assessment of male sex offenders. *Journal of Forensic Psychology Practice, 1*, 65–75.

Severus, E., Taylor, M. J., Sauer, C., Pfennig, A., Ritter, P., Bauer, M., & Geddes, J. R. (2014). Lithium for prevention of mood episodes in bipolar disorders: Systematic review and meta-analysis. *International Journal of Bipolar Disorders, 2*, 15.

Shaffer, D. (1996). A participant's observations: Preparing DSM-IV. *Canadian Journal of Psychiatry. Revue canadienne de psychiatrie, 41*, 325–329.

Shaffer, D., Gould, M. S., Fisher, P., Trautman, P., Moreau, D., Kleinman, M., & Flory, M. (1996). Psychiatric diagnosis in child and adolescent suicide. *Archives of General Psychiatry, 53*, 339–348.

Shah, S. G., Klumpp, H., Angstadt, M., Nathan, P. J., & Phan, K. L. (2009). Amygdala and insula response to emotional images in patients with generalized social anxiety disorders. *Journal of Psychiatry and Neuroscience, 34*, 296–302.

Shanmugham, B., Karp, J., Drayer, R., Reynolds, C. F., & Alexopoulos, G. (2005). Evidence-based pharmacologic interventions for geriatric depression. *Psychiatric Clinics of North America, 28*, 821–835.

Shannon, M. P., Lonigan, C. J., Finch, A.J., Jr., & Taylor, C. M. (1994). Children exposed to disaster: I. Epidemiology of post-traumatic symptoms and symptom profiles. *Journal of the American Academy of Child and Adolescent Psychiatry, 33*, 80–93.

Shapiro, J. R., Berkman, N. D., Brownley, K. A., Sedway, J. A., Lohr, K. N., & Bulik, C. M. (2007). Bulimia nervosa treatment: A systematic review of randomized controlled trials. *International Journal of Eating Disorders, 40*, 321–336.

Sharma, B. R. (2007). Gender identity disorder and its medico-legal considerations. *Medicine, Science, and the Law, 47*, 31–40.

Sharma, M. P., & Manjula, M. (2013). Behavioural and psychological management of somatic symptom disorders: An overview. *International Review of Psychiatry, 25*, 116–124.

Sharp, C., & Fonagy, P. (2015). Practitioner Review: Borderline personality disorder in adolescence—Recent conceptualization, intervention, and implications for clinical practice. *Journal of Child Psychology & Psychiatry, 56*, 1266–1288.

Shaughnessy, K., & Byers, E. S. (2014). Contextualizing cybersex experience: Heterosexually identified men and women's desire for and experiences with cybersex with three types of partners. *Computers in Human Behavior, 32*, 178–185.

Shavers, V. L., Lynch, C. F., & Burmeister, L. F. (2002). Racial differences in factors that influence the willingness to participate in medical research studies. *Annals of Epidemiology, 12*, 248–256.

Shaw, P., Lerch, J., Greenstein, D., Sharp, W., Clasen, L., Evans, A., … Rapoport, J. (2006). Longitudinal mapping of cortical thickness and clinical outcome in children and adolescents with attention-deficit/hyperactivity disorder. *Archives of General Psychiatry, 63*, 540–549.

Shaywitz, S. E., Gruen, J. R., & Shaywitz, B. A. (2007). Management of dyslexia, its rationale, and underlying neurobiology. *Pediatric Clinics of North America, 54*, 609–623.

Sheffield, J. M., Repovs, G., Harms, M. P., Carter, C. S., Gold, J. M., MacDonald, A. W., 3rd, … Barch, D. M. (2015). Evidence for accelerated decline of functional brain network efficiency in schizophrenia. *Schizophrenia Bulletin*, sbv148.

Sheikh, A. (2006). Why are ethnic minorities under-represented in US research studies? *PLOS Medicine, 3*, e49.

Sheikh, J. I., & Yesavage, J. A. (1986). Geriatric Depression Scale (GDS): Recent evidence and development of a shorter version. *Clinical Gerontologist, 5*, 165–173.

Sher, K. (2005). Towards a cognitive theory of substance use and dependence. In R.W. Wiers. & A.W. Stacy (Eds.), *Handbook of implicit cognition and addiction*. New York: Guilford Press.

Sheridan, M. S. (2003). The deceit continues: An updated literature review of Munchausen Syndrome by Proxy. *Child Abuse & Neglect, 27*, 431–451.

Sherman, C. (2005). Dopamine enhancement underlies a toluene behavioral effect. *NIDA Notes, 19*, 4–5.

Sherman, S. L., Allen, E. G., Bean, L. H., & Freeman, S. B. (2007). Epidemiology of Down syndrome. *Mental Retardation and Developmental Disabilities, 13*, 221–227.

Shiffman, S., Hickcox, M., Paty, J., Gnys, M., Kassel, J., & Richards, T. (1997). The abstinence violation effect following smoking lapses and temptations. *Cognitive Therapy and Research, 21*, 497–523.

Shimada-Sugimoto, M., Otowa, T., Miyagawa, T., Khor, S. S., Kashiwase, K., Sugaya, N., … Sasaki, T. (2015). Immune-related pathways including *HLA-DRB1*(*)13:02 are associated with panic disorder. *Brain, Behavior, and Immunity, 46*, 96–103.

Shin, L. M., Wright, C. I., Cannistraro, P. A., Wedig, M. M., McMullin, K., Martis, B., … Rauch, S. L. (2005). A functional magnetic resonance imaging study of amygdala and medial prefrontal cortex responses to overtly presented fearful faces in posttraumatic stress disorder. *Archives of General Psychiatry, 62*, 273–281.

Shinozaki, G., & Potash, J. B. (2014). New developments in the genetics of bipolar disorder. *Current Psychiatry Reports, 16*, 493.

Shifren, J. L., Braunstein, G. D., Simon, J. A., Casson, P. R., Buster, J. E., Redmond, G. P., ... Caramelli, K. E. (2000). Transdermal testosterone treatment in women with impaired sexual function after oophorectomy. *New England Journal of Medicine, 343*, 682–688.

Shumer, D. E., & Spack, N. P. (2013). Current management of gender identity disorder in childhood and adolescence: Guidelines, barriers, and areas of controversy. *Current Opinions in Endocrinology, Diabetes, and Obesity, 20*, 69–73.

Shuttleworth-Edwards, A. B., Kemp, R. D., Rust, A. L., Muirhead, J. G., Hartman, N. P., & Radloff, S. E. (2004). Cross-cultural effects on IQ test performance: A review and preliminary normative indications on WAIS-III test performance. *Journal of Clinical and Experimental Neuropsychology, 26*, 903–920.

Sibley, M. H., Kuriyan, A. B., Evans, S. W., Waxmonsky, J. G., & Smith, B. H. (2014). Pharmacological and psychosocial treatments for adolescents with ADHD: An updated systematic review of the literature. *Clinical Psychology Review, 34*, 218–232.

Siegel, S., Baptista, M., Kim, J., McDonald, R., & Weise-Kelly, L. (2000). Pavlovian psychopharmacology: The associative basis of tolerance. *Experimental and Clinical Psychopharmacology, 8*, 276–329.

Siever, L. J., Koenigsberg, H. W., Harvey, P., Mitropoulou, V., Laruelle, M., Abi-Dargham, A., ... Buchsbaum, M. (2002). Cognitive and brain function in schizotypal personality disorder. *Schizophrenia Research, 54*, 157–167.

Sigerist, H. E. (1943). *Civilization and disease*. Ithaca, NY: Cornell University Press.

Sijbrandij, M., Olff, M., Reitsma, J. B., Carlier, I. V., & Gersons, B. P. (2006). Emotional or educational debriefing after psychological trauma. Randomised controlled trial. *The British Journal of Psychiatry, 189*, 150–155.

Silagy, C., Lancaster, T., Stead, L., Mant, D., & Fowler, G. (2004). Nicotine replacement therapy for smoking cessation. *Cochrane Database Systematic Reviews, 3*, CD000146.

Silber, M. H., Ancoli-Israel, S., Bonnet, M. H., Chokroverty, S., Grigg-Damberger, M. M., Hirshkowitz, M., ... Penzel, T. (2007). The visual scoring of sleep in adults. *Journal of Clinical Sleep Medicine, 3*, 121–131.

Silove, D., Alanso, J., Bromet, E., Gruber, M., Sampson, N., Scott, K., ... Kessler, R. C. (2015). Pediatric-onset and adult-onset separation anxiety disorder across countries in the World Mental Health Survey. *American Journal of Psychiatry, 172*, 647–656.

Silva, A. C., de Oliveira Ribeiro, N. P., de Mello Schier, A. R., Pereira, V. M., Vilarim, M. M., Pessoa, T. M., ... Nardi, A. E. (2014). Caffeine and suicide: A systematic review. *CNS & Neurological Disorders—Drug Targets, 13*, 937–944.

Silveira, J. M., & Seeman, M. V. (1995). Shared psychotic disorder: A critical review of the literature. *Canadian Journal of Psychiatry, 40*, 389–395.

Silverman, J. M., Smith, C. J., Marin, D. B., Mohs, R. C., & Propper, C. B. (2003). Familial patterns of risk in very late-onset Alzheimer disease. *Archives of General Psychiatry, 60*, 190–197.

Simansky, K. J. (2005). NIH symposium series: Ingestive mechanisms in obesity, substance abuse and mental disorders. *Physiology & Behavior, 86*, 1–4.

Simeon, D., Guralnik, O., Knutelska, M., Hollander, E., & Schmeidler, J. (2001). Hypothalamic-pituitary-adrenal axis dysregulation in depersonalization disorder. *Neuropsychopharmacology, 25*, 793–795.

Simeon, D., Guralnik, O., Schmeidler, J., Sirof, B., & Knutelska, M. (2001). The role of childhood interpersonal trauma in depersonalization disorder. *American Journal of Psychiatry, 158*, 1027–1033.

Simeon, D., Knutelska, M., Nelson, D., & Guralnik, O. (2003). Feeling unreal: A depersonalization disorder update of 117 cases. *Journal of Clinical Psychiatry, 64*, 990–997.

Simon, G. E., VonKorff, M., Piccinelli, M., Fullerton, C., & Ormel, J. (1999). An international study of the relation between somatic symptoms and depression. *New England Journal of Medicine, 341*, 1329–1335.

Simoni-Wastila, L. (2000). The use of abusable prescription drugs: The role of gender. *Journal of Women's Health & Gender-Based Medicine, 9*, 289–297.

Simoni-Wastila, L., Ritter, G., & Strickler, G. (2004). Gender and other factors associated with nonmedical use of abusable prescription drugs. *Substance Use & Misuse, 39*, 1–23.

Simpson, D., Joe, G., Rowan–Szal, G., & Greener, J. (1997). Drug abuse treatment process components that improve retention. *Journal of Substance Abuse Treatment, 14*, 565–572.

Simpson, H. B., Foa, E. B., Liebowitz, M. R., Huppert, J. D., Cahill, S., Maher, M. J., ... Williams, M. T. (2013). Cognitive-behavioral therapy vs risperidone for augmenting serotonin reuptake inhibitors in obsessive-compulsive disorder: A randomized clinical trial. *JAMA Psychiatry, 70*, 1190–1199.

Sinadinovic, K., Berman, A. H., Hasson, D., & Wennberg, P. (2010). Internet-based assessment and self-monitoring of problematic alcohol and drug use. *Addictive Behaviors, 35*, 464–470.

Singh, S. P., & Lee, A. S. (1997). Conversion disorders in Nottingham: Alive, but not kicking. *Journal of Psychosomatic Research, 43*, 425–430.

Sitzer, D., Twamley, E., & Jeste, D. (2006). Cognitive training in Alzheimer's disease: A meta-analysis of the literature. *Acta Psychiatrica Scandinavica, 114*, 75–90.

Sivec, H. J., & Lynn, S. J. (1995). Dissociative and neuropsychological symptoms: The question of differential diagnosis. *Clinical Psychology Review, 15*, 297–316.

Sjögren Fugl-Meyer, K., & Fugl-Meyer, A. R. (2002). Sexual disabilities are not singularities. *International Journal of Impotence Research, 14*, 487–493.

Skeem J. L., S., C., Odgers, C., Mulvey, E. P., Gardner, W., & Lidz, C. (2006). Psychiatric symptoms and community violence among high-risk patients: A test of the relationship at the weekly level. *Journal of Consulting and Clinical Psychology, 74*, 967–979.

Skinner, B. F. (1953). *Science and human behavior*. New York: Free Press.

Skodol, A. E., Oldham, J. M., & Gallaher, P. E. (1999). Axis II comorbidity of substance use disorders among patients referred for treatment of personality disorders. *American Journal of Psychiatry, 56*, 733–738.

Slagboom, P. E., & Meulenbelt, I. (2002). Organisation of the human genome and our tools for identifying disease genes. *Biological Psychology, 61*, 11–31.

Smink, F. R., van Hoeken, D., & Hoek, H. W. (2012). Epidemiology of eating disorders: Incidence, prevalence and mortality rates. *Current Psychiatry Reports, 14*, 406–414.

Smink, F. R., van Hoeken, D., & Hoek, H. W. (2013). Epidemiology, course, and outcome of eating disorders. *Current Opinion in Psychiatry, 26*, 543–548.

Smink, F. R., van Hoeken, D., Oldehinkel, A. J., & Hoek, H. W. (2014). Prevalence and severity of DSM-5 eating disorders in a community cohort of adolescents. *International Journal of Eating Disorders, 47*, 610–619.

Smith, B. H., Waschbusch, D. A., Willoughby, M. T., & Evans, S. (2000). The efficacy, safety, and practicality of treatments for adolescents with attention-deficit/hyperactivity disorder (ADHD). *Clinical Child and Family Psychology Review, 3*, 243–267.

Smith, D. E., Marcus, M. D., Lewis, C. E., Fitzgibbon, M., & Schreiner, P. (1998). Prevalence of binge eating disorder, obesity, and depression in a biracial cohort of young adults. *Annals of Behavioral Medicine, 20*, 227–232.

Smith, Y. L., van Goozen, S. H., & Cohen-Kettenis, P. T. (2001). Adolescents with gender identity disorder who were accepted or rejected for sex reassignment surgery: A prospective follow-up study. *Journal of the American Academy of Child and Adolescent Psychiatry, 40*, 472–481.

Smith, Y. L., van Goozen, S. H., Kuiper, A. J., & Cohen-Kettenis, P. T. (2005). Sex reassignment: Outcomes and predictors of treatment for adolescent and adult transsexuals. *Psychological Medicine, 40*, 472–481.

Smith-Bell, M., & Winslade, W. J. (1994). Privacy, confidentiality, and privilege in psychotherapeutic relationships. *American Journal of Orthopsychiatry, 64*, 180–193.

Snorrason, I., Belleau, E. L., & Woods, D. W. (2012). How related are hair pulling disorder (trichotillomania) and skin picking disorder? A review of evidence for comorbidity, similarities and shared etiology. *Clinical Psychology Review, 32*, 618–629.

Sobell, M., & Sobell, L. (1973). Alcoholics treated by individualized behavior therapy: One year treatment outcomes. *Behavior Research and Therapy, 11*, 599–618.

Sobell, M., & Sobell, L. (1978). *Behavioral treatment of alcohol problems: Individualized therapy and controlled drinking*. New York: Plenum Press.

Sobell, M., & Sobell, L. (1995). Controlled drinking after 25 years: How important was the great debate? *Addiction, 90*, 1149–1153.

Sobin, C., Blundell, M., & Karayiorgou, M. (2000). Phenotypic differences in early-and late-onset obsessive-compulsive disorder. *Comprehensive Psychiatry, 41*, 373–379.

Sokolowski, M., Wasserman, J., & Wasserman, D. (2014). Genome-wide association studies of suicidal behaviors: A review. *European Neuropsychopharmacology, 24*, 1567–1577.

Sollman, M. J., Ranseen, J. D., & Berry, D. T. R. (2010). Detection of feigned ADHD in college students. *Psychological Assessment, 22*, 225–335.

Somashekar, B., Jainer, A., & Wuntakal, B. (2013). Psychopharmacotherapy of somatic symptoms disorders. *International Review of Psychiatry, 25*, 107–115.

Song, Y., Shiraishi, Y., & Nakamura, J. (2001). Digitalis intoxication misdiagnosed as depression-revisited [letter]. *Psychosomatics, 42*, 369–370.

Southern, S. (2008). Treatment of compulsive cybersex behavior. *Psychiatric Clinics of North America, 31*, 697–712.

Soykan, I., Chen, J., Kendall, B., & McCallum, R. W. (1997). The rumination syndrome: Clinical and manometric profile, therapy, and long-term outcome. *Digestive Diseases and Sciences, 42*, 1866–1872.

Spanos, N. P. (1994). Multiple identity enactments and multiple personality disorder: A sociocognitive perspective. *Psychological Bulletin, 116*, 143–165.

Sparks, A., McDonald, S., Lino, B., O'Donnell, M., & Green, M. J. (2010). Social cognition, empathy, and functional outcome in schizophrenia. *Schizophrenia Research, 22*, 172–178.

Spencer, T., Biederman, J., & Wilens, T. (2004). Stimulant treatment of adult attention-deficit/hyperactivity disorder. *Psychiatric Clinics of North America, 27*, 361–372.

Spencer, T. J., Biederman, J., & Mick, E. (2007). Attention-deficit/hyperactivity disorder: Diagnosis, lifespan, comorbidities, and neurobiology. *Ambulatory Pediatrics, 7*, 73–81.

Spriggs, M. (2006). Canaries in the mines: Children, risk, non-therapeutic research, and justice. *Journal of Medical Ethics, 30*, 176–181.

Springer, M. V., McIntosh, A. R., Winocur, G., & Grady, C. L. (2005). The relation between brain activity during memory tasks and years of education in young and older adults. *Neuropsychology, 19*, 181–192.

Sripada, C. S., Kessler, D., & Angstadt, M. (2014). Lag in maturation of the brain's intrinsic functional architecture in attention-deficit/hyperactivity disorder. *Proceedings of the National Academy of Sciences, 111*, 14259–14264.

Stafford, J., & Lynn, S. J. (2002). Cultural scripts, memories of childhood abuse, and multiple identities: A study of role-played enactments. *Journal of Clinical and Experimental Hypnosis, 50*, 67–85.

Stafford, K. P., & Wygant, D. B. (2005). The role of competency to stand trial in mental health courts. *Behavioral Sciences and the Law, 23*, 245–258.

Stafford, M. R., Mayo-Wilson, E., Loucas, C. E., James, A., Hollis, C., Birchwood, M., & Kendall, T. (2015). Efficacy and safety of pharmacological and psychological interventions for the treatment of psychosis and schizophrenia in children, adolescents, and young adults: A systematic review and meta-analysis. *PLOS ONE, 10*, e0117166.

Stambor, Z. (2006). Psychology's prescribing pioneers. *APA Monitor on Psychology, 37*, 30.

Stanford, J. L., Feng, Z., Hamilton, A. S., Gilliland, F. D., Stephenson, R. A., Eley, J. W., ... Potosky, A.L. (2000). Urinary and sexual function after radical prostatectomy for clinically localized prostate cancer: The Prostate Cancer Outcomes Study. *Journal of the American Medical Association, 283*, 354–360.

Stanley, M. A., Wilson, N., Shrestha, S., Amspoker, A. B., Armento, M., Cummings, J. P., ... Kunik, M. E. (in press). Calmer life: A culturally tailored intervention for anxiety in underserved older adults. *American Journal of Geriatric Psychiatry*.

Stanley, M. A., Roberts, R. E., Bourland, S. L., & Novy, D. M. (2001). Anxiety disorders among older primary care patients. *Journal of Clinical Geropsychology, 7*, 105–116.

Stanley, M. A., Veazey, C., Hopko, D., Diefenbach, G., & Kunik, M. E. (2005). Anxiety and depression in chronic obstructive pulmonary disease: A new intervention and case report. *Cognitive and Behavioral Practice, 12*, 424–436.

Stanley, M. A., Wilson, N. L., Amspoker, A. B., Kraus-Schuman, C., Wagener, P. D., Calleo, J. S., ... Williams, S. (2014). Lay providers can deliver effective cognitive behavior therapy for older adults with generalized anxiety disorder: A randomized trial. *Depression and Anxiety, 31*, 391–401.

Starcervic, V. (2015). Hypochondriasis: Treatment options for a diagnostic quagmire. *Australasian Psychiatry, 23*, 369–373.

Starkstein, S. E., Mizrahi, R., & Power, B. D. (2008). Depression in Alzheimer's disease: Phenomenology, clinical correlates and treatment. *International Review of Psychiatry, 20*, 382–388.

Statland, B. E., & Demas, T. J. (1980). Serum caffeine half-lives. Healthy subjects vs. patients having alcoholic hepatic disease. *American Journal of Clinical Pathology, 73*, 390–393.

Steadman, H., & Braff, J. (1983). Defendants not guilty by reason of insanity. In J. M. H. Steadman (Ed.), *Mentally disordered offenders: Perspectives from law and social science.* New York: Plenum.

Steckler, T., & Risbrough, V. (2012). Pharmacological treatment of PTSD—Established and new approaches. *Neuropharmacology, 62*, 617–627.

Steenkamp, M. M., Litz, B. T., Hoge, C. W., & Marmar, C. R. (2015). Psychotherapy for military-related PTSD: A review of randomized clinical trials. *Journal of the American Medical Association, 314*, 489–500.

Steffens, B. A., & Rennie, R. L. (2006). The traumatic nature of disclosure for wives of sexual addicts. *Sexual Addiction and Compulsivity, 13*, 247–267.

Steiger, H., Gauvin, L., Israel, M., Kin, N., Young, S., & Roussin, J. (2004). Serotonin function, personality-trait variations, and childhood abuse in women with bulimia-spectrum eating disorders. *Journal of Clinical Psychiatry, 65*, 830–837.

Steiger, H., Joober, R., Israël, M., Young, S., Ng Ying Kin, N., Gauvin, L., Bruce, K. R., Joncas, J., & Torkaman-Zehi, A. (2005). The *5HTTLPR* polymorphism, psychopathological symptoms, and platelet paroxetine binding in bulimic syndromes. *International Journal of Eating Disorders, 37*, 57–60.

Stein, D. J., & Hugo, F. J. (2004). Neuropsychiatric aspects of anxiety disorders. In S.C. Yudofsky & R.E. Hales. (Eds.), *Essentials of neuropsychiatry and clinical neurosciences* (pp. 1049–1068). Washington, DC: American Psychiatric Association.

Stein, D. J., Fineberg, N. A., Bienvenu, O. J., Denys, D., Lochner, C., Nestadt, G., … Phillips, K. A. (2010). Should OCD be classified as an anxiety disorder in DSM-V? *Depression and Anxiety, 27*, 495–506.

Stein, M. B., Koverola, C., Hanna, C., Torchia, M. G., & McClarty, B. (1997). Hippocampal volume in women victimized by childhood sexual abuse. *Psychological Medicine, 27*, 951–959.

Stein, M. B., Roy-Byrne, P. P., Craske, M. G., Bystritsky, A., Sullivan, G., Pyne, J. M., … Sherbourne, C. D. (2005). Functional impact and health utility of anxiety disorders in primary care outpatients. *Medical Care, 43*, 1164–1170.

Stein, S., Chalhoub, N., & Hodes, M. (1998). Very early-onset bulimia nervosa: Report of two cases. *International Journal of Eating Disorders, 24*, 323–327.

Steinberg, M., Cicchetti, D., Buchanan, J., Hall, P., & Rounsaville, B. (1993). Clinical assessment of dissociative symptoms and disorders: The Structured Interview for DSM-IV Dissociative Disorders (SCID-D). *Dissociation: Progress in the Dissociative Disorder, 61*, 108–120.

Steinhausen, H. C., & Jensen, C. M. (2015). Time trends in lifetime incidence rates of first-time diagnosed anorexia nervosa and bulimia nervosa across 16 years in a Danish nationwide psychiatric registry study. *International Journal of Eating Disorders, 48*, 845–850.

Steketee, G., & Barlow, D. H. (2002). Obsessive compulsive disorder. In D. H. Barlow (Ed.), *Anxiety and its disorders: The nature and treatment of anxiety and panic* (2nd ed., pp. 516–550). New York: Guilford Press.

Steketee, G., & Frost, R. (2010). *Stuff: Compulsive hoarding and the meaning of things*. New York, NY: Houghton Mifflin Harcourt.

Steketee, G., Frost, R. O., Tolin, D. F., Rasmussen, J., & Brown, T. A. (2010). Waitlist-controlled trial of cognitive behavior therapy for hoarding disorder. *Depression and Anxiety, 27*, 476–484.

Steketee, G., Kelley, A. A., Wernick, J. A., Muroff, J., Frost, R. O., & Tolin, D. F. (2015). Familial patterns of hoarding symptoms. *Depression and Anxiety, 32*, 728–736.

Stemberger, R. T., Turner, S. M., Beidel, D. C., & Calhoun, K. S. (1995). Social phobia: An analysis of possible developmental factors. *Journal of Abnormal Psychology, 104*, 526–531.

Stewart, S. E., Yu, D., Scharf, J. M., Neale, B. M., Fagerness, J. A., Mathews, C. A., … Osiecki, L. (2013). Genome-wide association study of obsessive-compulsive disorder. *Molecular Psychiatry, 18*, 788–798.

Stice, E., Agras, W., & Hammer, L. (1999). Risk factors for the emergence of childhood eating disturbances: A five-year prospective study. *International Journal of Eating Disorders, 25*, 375–387.

Stice, E., Marti, C. N., & Rohde, P. (2013). Prevalence, incidence, impairment, and course of the proposed DSM-5 eating disorder diagnoses in an 8-year prospective community study of young women. *Journal of Abnormal Psychology, 122*, 445–457.

Stice, E., & Shaw, H. E. (2002). Role of body dissatisfaction in the onset and maintenance of eating pathology: A synthesis of research findings. *Journal of Psychosomatic Research, 53*, 985–993.

Stiegler, L. N. (2005). Understanding pica behavior: A review for clinical and education professionals. *Focus on Autism and Other Developmental Disabilities, 20*, 27–38.

Stinson, F. S., Dawson, D. A., Goldstein, R. B., Chou, S. P., Huang, B., Smith, S. M., … Grant, B. F. (2008). Prevalence, correlates, disability, and comorbidity of DSM-IV narcissistic personality disorder: results from the wave 2 national epidemiologic survey on alcohol and related conditions. *The Journal of Clinical Psychiatry, 69*, 1033.

Stinson F. S., Dawson, D. A., Chou, S. P., Smith, S., Goldstein, R. B., Ruan, W. J., & Grant, B. F. (2007). The epidemiology of DSM-IV specific phobia in the USA: Results from the National Epidemiological Survey on alcohol and related conditions. *Psychological Medicine, 37*, 1047–1059.

Stoffers, J., Vollm, B. A., Rucker, G., Timmer, A., Huband, N., & Lieb, K. (2010). Pharmacological interventions for borderline personality disorder. *Cochrane Database of Systematic Reviews, 6*, CD005653.

Stoffers, J. M., Vollm, B. A., Rucker, G., Timmer, A., Huband, N., & Lieb, K. (2012). Psychological therapies for people with borderline personality disorder. *Cochrane Database of Systematic Reviews, 8*, CD005652.

Stoops, W. W., & Rush, C. R. (2013). Agonist replacement for stimulant dependence: A review of clinical research. *Current Pharmaceutical Design, 19, 7026*.

Storch, E. A., Larson, M. J., Merlo, L. J., Keeley, M. L., Jacob, M. L., Geffken, G. R., … Goodman, W. K. (2008). Comorbidity of pediatric obsessive-compulsive disorder and anxiety disorders: Impact on symptom severity and impairment. *Journal of Psychopathology and Behavioral Assessment, 30*, 111–120.

Strakowski, S. M., McElroy, S. L., Keck, P. E., Jr., & West, S. A. (1996). Racial influence on diagnosis in psychotic mania. *Journal of Affective Disorders, 39*, 157–162.

Strauss, C., Hale, L., & Stobie, B. (2015). A meta-analytic review of the relationship between family accommodation and OCD symptom severity. *Journal of Anxiety Disorders, 33*, 95–102.

Strawn, J. R., Wehry, A. M., DelBello, M. P., Rynn, M. A., & Strakowski, S. (2012). Establishing the neurobiologic basis of treatment in children and adolescents with generalized anxiety disorder. *Depression and Anxiety, 29*, 328–339.

Striefel, S. (2001). Ethical research issues: Going beyond the Declaration of Helsinki. *Applied Psychophysiology and Biofeedback, 26*, 39–59.

Striegel-Moore, R. H., Cachelin, F. M., Dohm, F. A., Pike, K. M., Wilfley, D. E., & Fairburn, C. G. (2001). Comparison of binge eating disorder and bulimia nervosa in a community sample. *International Journal of Eating Disorders 29*, 157–165.

Striegel-Moore, R. H., Dohm, F., Kraemer, H., Taylor, C., Daniels, S., Crawford, P., & Schreiber, G. (2003). Eating disorders in white and black women. *American Journal of Psychiatry, 160*, 1326–1331.

Striegel-Moore, R. H., Fairburn, C. G., Wilfley, D. E., Pike, K. M., Dohm, F. A., & Kraemer, H. C. (2005). Toward an understanding of risk factors for binge-eating disorder in black and white women: A community-based case-control study. *Psychological Medicine, 35*, 907–917.

Striegel-Moore, R. H., & Bulik, C. M. (2007). Risk factors for eating disorders. *American Psychologist*, 181–198.

Striegel-Moore, R. H., Rosselli, F., Holtzman, N., Dierker, L., Becker, A. E., & Swaney, G. (2011). Behavioral symptoms of eating disorders in Native Americans: Results from the ADD Health Survey Wave III. *International Journal of Eating Disorders, 44*, 561–566.

Striegel-Moore, R. H., Silberstein, L. R., & Rodin, J. (1986). Toward an understanding of risk factors for bulimia. *American Psychologist, 41*, 246–263.

Strober, M., Freeman, R., Lampert, C., Diamond, J., & Kaye, W. (2000). Controlled family study of anorexia nervosa and bulimia nervosa: Evidence of shared liability and transmission of partial syndromes. *American Journal of Psychiatry, 157*, 393–401.

Stromme, P., & Magnus, P. (2000). Correlations between socioeconomic status, IQ and aetiology in mental retardation: A population-based study in Norwegian children. *Social Psychiatry and Psychiatric Epidemiology, 35*, 12–18.

Strug, L. J., Suresh, R., Fyer, A. J., Talati, A., Adams, P. B., Li, W., … Weissman, M. M. (2010). Panic disorder is associated with the serotonin transporter gene (*SLC6A4*) but not the promoter region (5-*HTTLPR*). *Molecular Psychiatry, 15*, 166–176.

Stuart, S. (1995). Treatment of postpartum depression with interpersonal psychotherapy. *Archives of General Psychiatry, 52*, 75–76.

Studer, L. H., & Aylwin, A. S. (2006). Pedophilia: The problem with diagnosis and limitations of CBT in treatment. *Medical Hypotheses, 67*, 774–781.

Sturgess, J. E., Ting, A. K. R. A., Podbielski, D., Sellings, L. H., Chen, J. F., & van der Kooy, D. (2010). Adenosine A1 and A2A receptors are not upstream of caffeine's dopamine D2 receptor-dependent aversive effects and dopamine-independent rewarding effects. *European Journal of Neuroscience, 32*, 143–154.

Subramaniam, M., Abdin, E., Vaingankar, J. A., & Chong, S. A. (2012). Obsessive-compulsive disorder: Prevalence, correlates, help-seeking, and quality of life in a multiracial Asian population. *Social Psychiatry and Psychiatric Epidemiology, 47*, 2035–2043.

Substance Abuse and Mental Health Services Administration. (2003). *Results from the 2002 National Survey on Drug Use and Health: National findings*. Rockville, MD.

Substance Abuse and Mental Health Services Administration. (2006). *Results from the 2006 National Survey on Drug Use and Health: National findings*. Rockville, MD.

Substance Abuse and Mental Health Services Administration. (2007). Mental health services administration. *Results from the 2011 National Survey on Drug Use and Health: Summary of National Findings*.

Substance Abuse and Mental Health Services Administration. (2014). *Results from the 2013 National Survey on Drug Use and Health: Summary of national findings*. Rockville, MD.

Sue, S. (1999). Science, ethnicity and bias. *American Psychologist, 54*, 1070–1077.

Suhr, J.A., Hammers, D., Dobbins-Buckland, K., Zimak, E., & Hughes, C. (2008). The relationship of malingering test failure to self-reported symptoms and neuropsychological findings in adults referred for ADHD evaluation. *Archives of Clinical Neuropsychology, 23*, 512–530.

Sullivan, P., Joyce, P., & Mulder, R. (1994). Borderline personality disorder in major depression. *Journal of Nervous and Mental Disease, 182*, 508–516.

Sullivan, P. (2012). Don't give up on GWAS. *Molecular Psychiatry, 17*, 2–3.

Sullivan, P. F. (1995). Mortality in anorexia nervosa. *American Journal of Psychiatry, 152*, 1073–1074.

Sullivan, P. F., Bulik, C. M., Fear, J. L., & Pickering, A. (1998). Outcome of anorexia nervosa. *American Journal of Psychiatry, 155*, 939–946.

Sullivan, P. F., & Kendler, K. S. (1999). The genetic epidemiology of smoking. *Nicotine and Tobacco Research, 1*(2 Suppl), S51–S57; discussion S69–S70.

Sullivan, P. F., Neale, M. C., & Kendler, K. S. (2000). Genetic epidemiology of major depression: Review and meta-analysis. *American Journal of Psychiatry, 157*, 1552–1562.

Sullivan, P. F., Kendler, K. S., & Neale, M. C. (2003). Schizophrenia as a complex trait: Evidence from a meta-analysis of twin studies. *Archives of General Psychiatry, 60*, 1187–1192.

Sullivan, P. F. (2008). Schizophrenia genetics: The search for a hard lead. *Current Opinions in Psychiatry, 21*, 157–160.

Sullivan, P. F. (2015). Genetics of disease: Associations with depression. *Nature, 523*(7562), 539–540.

Summerfeldt, L. J., & Antony, M. M. (2002). Structured and semistructured diagnostic interviews. In M. M. Antony & D. H. Barlow (Eds.), *Handbook of assessment and treatment planning for psychological disorders* (pp. 3–37). New York: Guilford Press.

Sumter, S. R., Bokhorst, C. L., & Westenberg, P. M. (2009). Social fears during adolescence: Is there an increase in distress and avoidance? *Journal of Anxiety Disorders, 23*, 897–903.

Sundaram, S., Harman, J. S., & Cook, R. L. (2014). Maternal morbidities and postpartum depression: An analysis using the 2007 and 2008 Pregnancy Risk Assessment Monitoring System. *Womens Health Issues, 24*, 3381–3388.

Sundaram, S. K., Chugani, H. T., & Chugani, D. C. (2005). Positron emission tomography methods with potential for increased understanding of mental retardation and developmental disabilities. *Mental Retardation and Developmental Disabilities Research Reviews, 11*, 325–330.

Sussman, S. (1998). The first asylums in Canada: A response to neglectful community care and current trends. *Canadian Journal of Psychiatry, 43*, 260–264.

Sutherland, A. J., & Rodin, G. M. (1990). Factitious disorders in a general hospital setting: Clinical features and a review of the literature. *Psychosomatics, 31*, 391–399.

Suzuki, L. A., Ponterotto, J. G., & Meller, P. J. (2001). *Handbook of multicultural assessment (clinical, psychological, and educational applications)* (2nd ed.). San Francisco: Jossey-Bass.

Swanson, J. W., Swartz, M. S., Van Dorn, R. A., Elbogen, E. B., Wagner, R., Rosenheck, R. A., … Lieberman, J. A. (2006). A national study of violent behavior in persons with schizophrenia. *Archives of General Psychiatry, 63*, 490–499.

Swanson, J. W., & Swartz, M. S. (2014). Why the evidence for outpatient commitment is good enough. *Psychiatric Services, 65*, 808–811.

Swanson, S. A. (2011). Prevalence and correlates of eating disorders in adolescents. Results from the national comorbidity survey replication adolescent supplement. *Archives in General Psychiatry, 68*, 714–723.

Swartz, C. (2001). Misdiagnosis of schizophrenia for a patient with epilepsy (letter). *Psychiatric Services, 52*, 109.

Swartz, M., Blazer, D., George, L., & Winfield, I. (1990). Estimating the prevalence of borderline personality disorder in the community. *Journal of Personality Disorders, 4*, 257–272.

Swartz, M., Landerman, R., George, L., Blazer, D., & Escobar, J. (1991). Somatization disorder. In L. N. Robins, & D. Regier (Eds.), *Psychiatric disorders in America* (pp. 220–257). New York: Free Press.

Swartz. M.S. & Monahan, J. (2001) Special section on involuntary outpatient commitment: Introduction. *Psychiatric Services, 52*, 323–324.

Swartz, M. S., Swanson, J. W., Wagner, H. R., Burns, B. J., Hiday, V. A., & Borum, R. (1999). Can involuntary outpatient commitment reduce hospital recidivism? Findings from a randomized trial with severely mentally ill individuals. *American Journal of Psychiatry, 156*, 1968–1975.

Swerdlow, N. (2001). Obsessive-compulsive disorder and tic syndromes. *Medical Clinics of North America, 85*, 735–755.

Swinbourne, J., Hunt, C., Abbott, M., Russell, J., St Clare, T., & Touyz, S. (2012). The comorbidity between eating disorders and anxiety disorders: Prevalence in an eating disorder sample and anxiety disorder sample. *Australian & New Zealand Journal of Psychiatry, 46*, 118–131.

Switzer, W. M., Jia, H., Hohn, O., Zheng, H., Tang, S., Shankar, A., … Heneine, W. (2010). Absence of evidence of xenotropic murine leukemia virus-related virus infection in persons with chronic fatigue syndrome and healthy controls in the United States. *Retrovirology, 7*, 57.

Symonds, C. S., Taylor, S., Tippens, V., & Turkington, D. (2006). Violent self-harm in schizophrenia. *Suicide and Life-Threatening Behavior, 36*, 44–49.

Symonds, T., Roblin, D., Hart, K., & Althof, S. (2003). How does premature ejaculation impact a man's life? *Journal of Sex & Marital Therapy, 29*, 361–370.

Szmukler, G., Brown, S., Parsons, V., & Darby, A. (1985). Premature loss of bone in chronic anorexia nervosa. *British Medical Journal, 290*, 26–27.

Taher, N. S. (2007). Self-concept and masculinity/femininity among normal male individuals and males with gender identity disorder. *Social Behavior and Personality, 35*, 469–478.

Tait, R., & Hulse, G. (2003). A systematic review of the effectiveness of brief interventions with substance using adolescents by type of drug. *Drug and Alcohol Review, 22*, 337–346.

Talbott, J. A. (2004). Care of the chronically mentally ill—Still a national disgrace. *Psychiatric Services, 55*, 1116–1117.

Tan, S. Y., & Yeow, M. E. (2003). Paracelsus (1493–1541): The man who dared. *Singapore Medical Journal, 44*, 5–7.

Tan, S. Y., & Yeow, M. E. (2004). Philippe Pinel (1745–1826): Liberator of the insane. *Singapore Medical Journal, 45*, 410–412.

Tanielian T, & Jaycox, L.H. (2008). *Invisible wounds of war: Psychosocial and cognitive injuries, their consequences, and services to assist recovery*. Santa Monica, CA: RAND Corporation.

Tanofsky-Kraff, M., Cohen, M. L., Yanovski, S. Z., Cox, C., Theim, K. R., Keil, M., … Yanovski, J. A. (2006). A prospective study of psychological predictors of body fat gain among children at high risk for adult obesity. *Pediatrics, 117*, 1203–1209.

Tanofsky-Kraff, M., Wilfley, D. E., Young, J. F., Mufson, L., Yanovski, S. Z., Glasofer, D. R., & Salaita, C. G. (2007). Preventing excessive weight gain in adolescents: Interpersonal psychotherapy for binge eating. *Obesity (Silver Spring), 15*, 1345–1355.

Tanofsky-Kraff, M., Bulik, C. M., Marcus, M. D., Striegel, R. H., Wilfley, D. E., Wonderlich, S. A., & Hudson, J. I. (2013). Binge eating disorder: The next generation of research. *International Journal of Eating Disorders, 46*, 193–207.

Tanofsky-Kraff, M., McDuffie, J. R., Yanovski, S. Z., Kozlosky, M., Schvey, N. A., Shomaker, L. B., … Yanovski, J. A. (2009). Laboratory assessment of the food intake of children and adolescents with loss of control eating. *The American Journal of Clinical Nutrition, 89*, 738–745.

Tanofsky-Kraff, M., Yanovski, S. Z., Schvey, N. A., Olsen, C. H., Gustafson, J., & Yanovski, J. A. (2009). A prospective study of loss of control eating for body weight gain in children at high risk for adult obesity. *International Journal of Eating Disorders, 42*, 26–30.

Tarrier, N., Haddock, G., Lewis, S., Drake, R., & Gregg, L. (2006). Suicide behavior over 18 months in recent onset schizophrenic patients: The effects of CBT. *Schizophrenia Research, 83*, 15–27.

Tarsy, D., & Baldessarini, R. J. (2006). Epidemiology of tardive dyskinesia: Is risk declining with modern antipsychotics? *Movement Disorders, 21*, 589–598.

Tarter, R., Vanyukov, M., & Kirisci, L. (2006). Predictors of marijuana use in adolescents before and after licit drug use: Examination of the gateway hypothesis. *American Journal of Psychiatry, 163*, 2134–2140.

Tarter, R. E., Hegadus, A. M., Alterman, A. I., & Katz-Garris, L. (1983). Cognitive capacities of juvenile, violent, nonviolent, and sexual offenders. *Journal of Nervous and Mental Disease, 171*, 564–567.

Taylor, B. (2006). Vaccines and the changing epidemiology of autism. *Child: Care Health and Development, 32*, S11–S19.

Taylor S. (2011). Etiology of obsessions and compulsions: A meta-analysis and narrative review of twin studies. *Clinical Psychology Review, 31*, 1361–1372.

Taylor, J. J., Neitzke, D. J., Khouri, G., Borckardt, J. J., Acierno, R., Tuerk, P. W., … George, M. S. (2014). A pilot study to investigate the induction and manipulation of learned helplessness in healthy adults. *Psychiatry Research, 219*, 631–637.

Taylor, L. E., Swerdfeger, A. L., & Eslick, G. D. (2014). Vaccines are not associated with autism: An evidence-based meta-analysis of case-control and cohort studies. *Vaccines, 32*, 3623–3629.

Taylor, M. J., Freemantle, N., Geddes, J. R., & Bhagwagar, Z. (2006). Early onset of selective serotonin reuptake inhibitor antidepressant action: Systematic review and meta-analysis. *Archives of General Psychiatry, 63*, 1217–1223.

Taylor, S. (1995). Anxiety sensitivity: Theoretical perspectives and recent findings. *Behaviour Research and Therapy, 33*, 243–258.

Taylor, S., & Asmundson, G. J. (2004). *Treating health anxiety: A cognitive-behavioral approach*. New York: The Guilford Press.

Teipel, S. J., Alexander, G. E., Schapiro, M. B., Moller, H. J., Rapoport, S. I., & Hampel, H. (2004). Age-related cortical grey matter reductions in non-demented Down's syndrome adults determined by MRI with voxel-based morphometry. *Brain, 127*, 811–824.

Tempelman, T. L., & Stinnett, R. D. (1991). Patterns of sexual arousal and history in a "normal" sample of young men. *Archives of Sexual Behavior, 20*, 137–150.

Teng, E. J., Woods, D. W., & Twohig, M. P. (2006). Habit reversal as a treatment for chronic skin picking A pilot investigation. *Behavior Modification, 30*, 411–422.

ter Kuile, M. M., van Lankveld, J. J., de Groot, E., Melles, R., Neffs, J., & Zandbergen, M. (2007). Cognitive-behavioral therapy for women with lifelong vaginismus: Process and prognostic factors. *Behaviour Research and Therapy, 45*, 359–373.

Teri, L., Gibbons, L. E., McCurry, S. M., Logsdon, R. G., Buchner, D. M., Barlow, W. E., … Larson, E. B. (2003). Exercise plus behavioral management in patients with Alzheimer disease: A randomized controlled trial. *Journal of the American Medical Association, 290*, 2015–2022.

Terman, M., & Terman, J. S. (2005). Light therapy for seasonal and nonseasonal depression: Efficacy, protocol, safety, and side effects. *CNS Spectrums, 10*, 647–663; quiz 672.

Tevyaw, T., & Monti, P. (2004). Motivational enhancement and other brief interventions for adolescent substance abuse: Foundations, applications and evaluations. *Addiction, 99*, 63–75.

Thase, M. E., & Kupfer, D. J. (1996). Recent developments in the pharmacotherapy of mood disorders. *Journal of Consulting and Clinical Psychology, 64*, 646–659.

Thase, M. E., & Friedman, E. S. (1999). Is psychotherapy an effective treatment for melancholia and other severe depressive states? *Journal of Affective Disorders, 54*, 1–19.

Theis, W., & Bleiler, L. (2013). Alzheimer's Association; 2013 Alzheimer's disease facts and figures. *Alzheimer's & Dementia, 9*, 208–245.

Thomason, J. W., Shintani, A., Peterson, J. F., Pun, B. T., Jackson, J. C., & Ely, E. W. (2005). Intensive care unit delirium is an independent predictor of longer hospital stay: A prospective analysis of 261 non-ventilated patients. *Critical Care, 9*, R375.

Thompson, C. M., & Durrani, A. J. (2007). An increasing need for early detection of body dysmorphic disorder by all specialties. *Journal of the Royal Society of Medicine, 100*, 61–62.

Thompson, E. A., & Eggert, L. L. (1999). Using the suicide risk screen to identify suicidal adolescents among potential high school dropouts. *Journal of the American Academy of Child & Adolescent Psychiatry, 38*, 1506–1514.

Thompson, E. A., Eggert, L. L., & Herting, J. R. (2000). Mediating effects of an indicated prevention program for reducing youth depression and suicide risk behaviors. *Suicide and Life Threatening Behavior, 30*, 252–271.

Thonon, B., Pletinx, A., Grandjean, A., & Billieux, J. (2016). The effects of a documentary film about schizophrenia on cognitive, affective, and behavioural aspects of stigmatisation. *Journal of Behaviour Therapy and Experimental Psychiatry, 50*, 196–200.

Thornton, L. M., Watson, H., Jangmo, A., Welch, E., Wiklund, C., von Hausswolff-Juhlin, Y., … Bulik, C. M. (Submitted). Binge-eating disorder in the Swedish National Registers: Somatic comorbidity.

Thorsen, A. L., van den Heuvel, O. A., Hansen, B., & Kvale, G. (2015). Neuroimaging of psychotherapy for obsessive– compulsive disorder: A systematic review. *Psychiatry Research: Neuroimaging, 233*, 306–313.

Thys, E., Sabbe, B., & De Hert, M. (2014). Creativity and psychopathology: A systematic review. *Psychopathology, 47*, 141–147.

Tiefer, L. (2001). A new view of women's sexual problems. Why new? *Journal of Sex Research, 38*, 89–96.

Tienari, P., Wynne, L. C., Sorri, A., Lahti, I., Laksy, K., Morning, J., … Wahlberg, K. E. (2004). Genotype–environment interaction in schizophrenia-spectrum disorder. *British Journal of Psychiatry, 184*, 216–222.

Tiggemann, M., & Pickering, A. S. (1996). Role of television in adolescent women's body dissatisfaction and drive for thinness. *International Journal of Eating Disorders, 20*, 199–203.

Tirupati, S. N., Padmavati, R., Thara, R., & McCreadie, R. G. (2006). Psycho-pathology in never-treated schizophrenia. *Comprehensive Psychiatry, 47*, 1–6.

Toftdahl, N. G., Nordentoft, M., & Hjorthoj, C. (2016). Prevalence of substance use disorders in psychiatric patients: A nationwide Danish population-based study. *Social Psychiatry and Psychiatric Epidemiology, 51*, 129–140.

Tolin, D. F., Robison, J. T., Gaztambide, S., & Blank, K. (2005). Anxiety disorders in older Puerto Rican primary care patients. *The American Journal of Geriatric Psychiatry, 13*, 150–156.

Tolin, D. F., Robison, J. T., Gaztambide, S., Horowitz, S., & Blank, K. (2007). Ataques de nervios and psychiatric disorders in older Puerto Rican primary care patients. *Journal of Cross-Cultural Psychology, 38*, 659–669.

Tolman, D. L., & Diamond, L. M. (2001). Desegregating sexuality research: Cultural and biological perspectives on gender and desire. *Annual Review of Sex Research, 12*, 33–74.

Torgersen, S. (1983). Genetic factors in anxiety disorders. *Archives of General Psychiatry, 40*, 1085–1089.

Torgersen, S., Kringlen, E., & Cramer, V. (2001). The prevalence of personality disorders in a community sample. *Archives of General Psychiatry, 58*, 590–596.

Torgersen, S., Myers, J., Reichborn-Kjennerud, T., Roysamb, E., Kubarych, T. S., & Kendler, K. S. (2012). The heritability of Cluster B personality disorders assessed both by personal interview and questionnaire. *Journal of Personality Disorders, 26*, 848–866.

Touyz, S., Le Grange, D., Lacey, H., Hay, P., Smith, R., Maguire, S., … Crosby, R. D. (2013). Treating severe and enduring anorexia nervosa: A randomized controlled trial. *Psychological Medicine, 43*, 2501–2511.

Tozzi, F., Thornton, L. M., Klump, K. L., Fichter, M. M., Halmi, K. A., Kaplan, A. S., … Kaye, W. H. (2005). Symptom fluctuation in eating disorders: Correlates of diagnostic crossover. *American Journal of Psychiatry, 162*, 732–740.

Trace, S. E., Thornton, L. M., Root, T. L., Mazzeo, S. E., Lichtenstein, P., Pedersen, N. L., & Bulik, C. M. (2012). Effects of reducing the frequency and duration criteria for binge eating on lifetime prevalence of bulimia nervosa and binge eating disorder: Implications for DSM-5. *International Journal of Eating Disorders, 45*, 531–536.

Trials of war criminals before the Nuremberg Military Tribunals under Control Council Law No. 10. (October 1946–April 1949). U.S. Government Printing Office. Washington, DC.

Trivedi, M. H. (1995). Functional neuroanatomy of obsessive-compulsive disorder. *The Journal of Clinical Psychiatry, 57*, 26–35.

Troxel, W. M., Buysse, D. J., Monk, T. H., Begley, A., & Hall, M. (2010). Does social support differentially affect sleep in older adults with versus without insomnia? *Journal of Psychosomatic Research, 69*, 459–466.

Trudel, G., Marchand, A., Ravart, M., Aubin, S., Turgeon, L., & Fortier, P. (2001). The effect of a cognitive-behavioral group treatment program on hypoactive sexual desire in women. *Sexual and Relationship Therapy, 61*, 145–164.

Trull, T. J., Sher, K. J., Minks-Brown, C., Durbin, J., & Burr, R. (2000). Borderline personality disorder and substance use disorders: A review and integration. *Clinical Psychology Review, 20*, 235–253.

Trull, T. J., Jahng, S., Tomko, R. L., Wood, P. K., & Sher, K. J. (2010). Revised NESARC personality disorder diagnoses: Gender, prevalence, and comorbidity with substance dependence disorders. *Journal of Personality Disorders, 24*, 412–426.

Trzaskowski, M., Eley, T. C., Davis, O. S. P., Doherty, S. J., Hanscombe, K. B., Meaburn, E. L., … Plomin, R. (2013). First genome-wide association study on anxiety-related behaviours in childhood. *PLOS ONE, 8*, e58676.

Trzepacz, P. T., Meagher, D. J., & Wise, M. G. (2002). Neuropsychiatric aspects of delirum. In R. E. Hales & S. C. Yudofsky (Eds.), *The American psychiatric publishing textbook of neuropsychiatry and clinical neurosciences* (4th ed., pp. 525–564). Washington, DC: American Psychiatric Publishing, Inc.

Tsai, J. L., Butcher, J. N., Muñoz, R. F., & Vitousek, K. (2001). Culture, ethnicity, and psychopathology. In P. B. Sutker & H. E. Adams (Eds.), *Comprehensive handbook of psychopathology* (3rd ed.). New York: Kluwer Academic/ Plenum Publishers.

Tseng, W. S. (2003). *Clinician's guide to cultural psychiatry*. San Diego, CA: Academic Press.

Tsoi, Y. F., & Kok, L. P. (1995). Mental disorders in Singapore. In T. Y. Lin W.S. Tseng,& E. K. Yeh (Eds.), *Chinese societies and mental health* (pp. 266–278). Hong Kong: Oxford University Press.

Tsuang, D. W., & Bird, T. D. (2004). Genetics of dementia. *Comprehensive Text Book of Geriatric Psychiatry*, 39–84.

Tsuang, M. T., Stone, W. S., & Faraone, S. V. (2000). Toward reformulating the diagnosis of schizophrenia. *American Journal of Psychiatry, 157*, 1041–1050.

Tucker, B. T., Woods, D. W., Flessner, C. A., Franklin, S. A., & Franklin, M. E. (2011). The skin picking impact project: Phenomenology, interference, and treatment utilization of pathological skin picking in a population-based sample. *Journal of Anxiety Disorders, 25*, 88–95.

Tükel, R., Ertekin, E., Batmaz, S., Alyanak, F., Sözen, A., Aslantaş, B., … Özyıldırım, İ. (2005). Influence of age of onset on clinical features in obsessive-compulsive disorder. *Depression and Anxiety, 21*, 112–117.

Turner, H., & Bryant-Waugh, R. (2003). Eating disorders not otherwise specified (EDNOS): Profiles of clients presenting at a community eating disorders service. *European Eating Disorders Review, 12*, 18–26.

Turner, S. M., Beidel, D. C., & Townsley, R. M. (1992). Social phobia: A comparison of specific and generalized subtypes and avoidant personality disorder. *Journal of Abnormal Psychology, 101*, 326–331.

Turner, S. M., & Beidel, D. C. (2003). The enriching experience. In J. D. Robinson & L. C. James (Eds.), *Diversity in human interactions* (pp. 195–205). New York: Oxford University Press.

Tusa, A. L., & Burgholzer, J. A. (2013). Came to believe: Spirituality as a mechanism of change in alcoholics anonymous: A review of the literature from 1992 to 2012. *Journal of Addictions Nursing, 24*, 237–246.

Twohig, M. P., Abramowitz, J. A., Bluett, E. J., Fabricant, L., Jacoby, R. J., Morrison, K. L., … Smith, B. (2015). Exposure therapy for OCD from an acceptance and commitment therapy (ACT) framework. *Journal of Obsessive-Compulsive and Related Disorders, 6*, 167–173.

Tyndale, R. F., Zhu, A. Z., George, T. P., Cinciripini, P., Hawk Jr, L. W., Schnoll, R. A., … PGRN-PNAT Research Group. (2015). Lack of Associations of CHRNA5-A3-B4 Genetic Variants with Smoking Cessation Treatment Outcomes in Caucasian Smokers despite Associations with Baseline Smoking. *PLOS ONE, 10*(5), e0128109.

Tyron, W. W. (1998). Behavioral observation. In A. S. Bellack & M. Herson (Eds.), *Behavioral assessment: A practical handbook* (pp. 79 103). Boston: Allyn & Bacon.

Tzschentke, T. M. (2007). Measuring reward with the conditioned place preference (CPP) paradigm: Update of the last decade. *Addiction Biology, 12*(3–4), 227–462.

Uebel, H., Albrecht, B., Kirov, R., Heise, A., Dopfner, M., Joseph Freisleder, F., … Ose, C. (2010). What can actigraphy add to the concept of labschool design in clinical trials? *Current Pharmaceutical Design, 16*, 2434–2442.

Uhde, T. W., & Singareddy, R. (2002). *Biological research in anxiety disorders. Psychiatry as a neuroscience*. New York: John Wiley and Sons.

UK ECT Review Group. (2003). Efficacy and safety of electroconvulsive therapy in depressive disorders: A systematic review and meta-analysis. *Lancet, 361*, 799–808.

Unützer, J., Katon, W., Callahan, C. M., Williams Jr., J. W., Hunkeler, E., Harpole, L., … Lin, E. H. (2002). Collaborative care management of late-life depression in the primary care setting: A randomized controlled trial. *Journal of the American Medical Association, 288*, 2836–2845.

Upadhyaya, H., & Deas, D. (2008). Pharmacological interventions for adolescent substance use disorders. In Y. Kaminar. & O. Bukstein. (Eds.), *Adolescent substance abuse: Psychiatric comorbidity and high-risk behaviors* (pp. 145–161). New York: Routledge/Taylor & Francis Group.

U.S. Department of Health and Human Services. (2014). *The health consequences of smoking—50 years of progress: A report of the Surgeon General.* Atlanta, GA.

U.S. Department of Health and Human Services. (2014a) *Major depression among adolescents.* Retrieved from http://www.nimh.nih.gov/health/statistics/prevalence/major- depression-among-adolescents.shtml.

U.S. Surgeon General's Report. (1988). *The health consequences of smoking: Nicotine addiction*. Washington, DC.

Vajani, M., Annest, J. L., Crosby, A. E., Alexander, J. D., & Millet, L. M. (2007). Nonfatal and fatal self-harm injuries among children aged 10–14 years—United States and Oregon, 2001–2003. *Suicide & Life Threatening Behavior, 37*, 493–506.

Valdovinos, M. G. (2007). Brief review of current research in FXS: Implications for treatment with psychotropic medication. *Research in Developmental Disabilities, 28*, 539–545.

Van Citters, A. D., Pratt, S. I., Bartels, S. J., & Jeste, D. V. (2005). Evidence-based review of pharmacologic and nonpharmacologic treatments for older adults with schizophrenia. *Psychiatric Clinics of North America, 28*, 913–939.

Van den Eynde, F., Suda, M., Broadbent, H., Guillaume, S., Van den Eynde, M., Steiger, H., … Schmidt, U. (2012). Structural magnetic resonance imaging in eating disorders: A systematic review of voxel-based morphometry studies. *European Eating Disorders Review, 20*, 94–105.

van den Wiel, N., Matthys, W., Cohen-Kettenis, P. C., & van Engeland, H. (2002). Effective treatments of school-aged conduct disordered children: Recommendations for changing clinical and research practices. *European Child & Adolescent Psychiatry, 11*, 79–84.

van Dijk, M., Benninga, M. A., Grootenhuis, M., Nieuwenhuizen, A. M., & Last, B. F. (2007). Chronic childhood constipation: A review of the literature and the introduction of a protocolized behavioral intervention program. *Patient Education and Counseling, 67*, 63–77.

Van Duijl, M., Cardeña, E., & Jong, J. (2005). The validity of DSM-IV dissociative disorders categories in southwest Uganda. *Transcultural Psychiatry, 42*, 219–241.

Van Gerpen, M. W., Johnson, J. E., & Winstead, D. K. (1999). Mania in the geriatric patient population: A review of the literature. *American Journal of Geriatric Psychiatry, 7*, 188–202.

Van Hout, H. P., Beekman, A. T., De Beurs, E., Comijs, H., Van Marwijk, H., De Haan, M., … Deeg, D. J. (2004). Anxiety and the risk of death in older men and women. *The British Journal of Psychiatry, 185*, 399–404.

Van Houtem, C. M., Laine, M. L., Boomsma, D. I., Ligthart, L., van Wijk, A. J., & De Jongh, A. (2013). A review and meta-analysis of the heritability of specific phobia subtypes and corresponding fears. *Journal of Anxiety Disorders, 27*, 379–388.

van Kuyck, K., Gérard, N., Van Laere, K., Casteels, C., Pieters, G., Gabriëls, L., & Nuttin, B. (2009). Towards a neurocircuitry in anorexia nervosa: Evidence from functional neuroimaging studies. *Journal of Psychiatric Research, 43*, 1133–1145.

van Loo, H. M., Cai, T., Gruber, M. J., Li, J., de Jonge, P., Petukhova, M., … Kessler, R. C. (2014). Major depressive disorder subtypes to predict long-term course. *Depression & Anxiety, 31*, 765–777.

van Melle, J. P., de Jonge, P., Spijkerman, T. A., Tijssen, J. G., Ormel, J., van Veldhuisen, D. J., … van den Berg, M. P. (2004). Prognostic association of depression following myocardial infarction with mortality and cardiovascular events: A meta-analysis. *Psychosomatic Medicine, 66*, 814–822.

Van Meter, A. R., Youngstrom, E. A., & Findling, R. L. (2012). Cyclothymic disorder: A critical review. *Clinical Psychology Review, 32*, 229–243.

van Os, J., Linscott, R.J., Myin-Germeys, I., Delespaul, P., & Krabbendam, L. (2009). A systematic review and meta-analysis of the psychosis continuum: Evidence for a psychosis proneness-persistence-impairment model of psychotic disorder. *Psychological Medicine, 39*, 179–195.

Van Ryzin, M. J., Fosco, G. M., & Dishion, T. J. (2012). Family and peer predictors of substance use from early adolescence to early adulthood: An 11-year prospective analysis. *Addictive Behaviors, 37*, 1314–1324.

van Son, G. E., van Hoeken, D., Bartelds, A. I., van Furth, E. F., & Hoek. H. W. (2006). Urbanisation and the incidence of eating disorders. *British Journal of Psychiatry, 189*, 562–563.

VanBuskirk, K. A., & Wetherell, J. L. (2014). Motivational interviewing with primary care populations: A systematic review and meta-analysis. *Journal of Behavioral Medicine, 37*, 768–780.

Vandenberg, B. (1993). Fears of normal and retarded children. *Psychological Reports, 72*, 473–474.

Vasey, P. L., & Bartlett, N. H. (2007). What can the Samoan Fa'afafine teach us about the Western concept of gender identity disorder in childhood? *Perspectives in Biology and Medicine, 50*, 481–490.

Velicer, W., Redding, C., & Sun, X. (2007). Demographic variables, smoking variables, and outcome across five studies. *Health Psychology, 26*, 278–287.

Velligan, D., Bow-Thomas, C. C., Mahurin, R. D., Miller, A. L., & Halgunseth, L. C. (2000). Do specific neurocognitive deficits predict specific domains of community function in schizophrenia? *Journal of Nervous and Mental Disease, 188*, 518–524.

Verheul, R., & Widiger, T. A. (2004). A meta-analysis of the prevalence and usage of the personality disorder not otherwise specified (PDNOS) *Journal of Personality Disorders, 18*, 309–319.

Verheul, R., Bartak, A., & Widiger, T. (2007). Prevalence and construct validity of personality disorder not otherwise specified (PDNOS). *Journal of Personality Disorders, 21*, 359–370.

Verma, S., & Gallagher, R. M. (2000). Evaluating and treating co-morbid pain and depression. *International Review of Psychiatry, 12*, 103–114.

Vermetten, E., Schmahl, C., Lindner, S., Loewenstein, R. J., & Bremner, J. D. (2006). Hippocampal and amygdala volumes in dissociative identity disorder. *American Journal of Psychiatry, 163*, 630–636.

Verplanken, B., Friborg, O., Wang, C. E., Trafimow, D., & Woolf, K. (2007). Mental habits: Metacognitive reflection on negative self-thinking. *Journal of Personality and Social Psychology, 92*, 526–554.

Verrico, C. D., Haile, C. N., Newton, T. F., Kosten, T. R., & De La Garza, R., 2nd. (2013). Pharmacotherapeutics for substance-use disorders: A focus on dopaminergic medications. *Expert Opinion on Investigational Drugs, 22*, 1549–1568.

Vidal, C. N., Rapoport, J. L., Hayashi, K. M., Geafa, J. A., Sui, Y., McLemore, L. E., … Gogtay, N. (2006). Dynamically spreading frontal and cingulated deficits mapped in adolescents with schizophrenia. *Archives of General Psychiatry, 63*, 25–34.

Vilarim, M. M., Rocha Araujo, D. M., & Nardi, A. E. (2011). Caffeine challenge test and panic disorder: A systematic literature review. *Expert Review of Neurotherapeutics, 11*, 1185–1195.

Vincent, M., & Pickering, M. R. (1988). Multiple personality disorder in childhood. *Canadian Journal of Psychiatry, 33*, 524–529.

Vita, A., De Peri, L., Silenzi, C., & Dieci, M. (2006). Brain morphology in first-episode schizophrenia: A meta-analysis of quantitative magnetic resonance imaging studies. *Schizophrenia Research, 82*, 75–88.

Vita, A., De Peri, L., Deste, G., & Sacchetti, E. (2012). Progressive loss of cortical gray matter in schizophrenia: A meta-analysis and meta-regression of longitudinal MRI studies. *Translational Psychiatry, 2*, e190.

Vitiello, B., Lazzaretto, D., Yershova, K., Abikoff, H., Paykina, N., McCracken, J. T., … Riddle, M.A. (2015). Pharmacotherapy of the Preschool ADHD Treatment Study (PATS) children growing up. *Journal of the American Academy of Child and Adolescent Psychiatry, 54*, 550–556.

Volkmar, F. R., & Wiesner, L. A. (2009). *A practical guide to autism*. Hoboken, NJ: John Wiley and Sons.

Volkow, N. D., & Baler, R. D. (2014). Addiction science: Uncovering neurobiological complexity. *Neuropharmacology, 76 Pt B*, 235–249.

Von Krafft-Ebing, R., & McCorn, W.A. (1900). The etiology of progressive paralysis. *American Journal of Insanity, 61*, 645–668.

Warburton, D. (2005). Biological aging and the etiology of aneuploidy. *Cytogenetic Genome Research, 111*, 266–272.

Wade, T., Martin, N. G., Neale, M. C., Tiggemann, M., Treloar, S. A., Bucholz, K. K., … Heath, A. C. (1999). The structure of genetic and environmental risk factors for three measures of disordered eating. *Psychological Medicine, 29*, 925–934.

Wade, T. D., Bulik, C. M., Neale, M., & Kendler, K. S. (2000). Anorexia nervosa and major depression: Shared genetic and environmental risk factors. *American Journal of Psychiatry, 157*, 469–471.

Wade, T. D., Tiggemann, M., Bulik, C. M., Fairburn, C. G., Wray, N. R., & Martin, N. G. (2008). Shared temperament risk factors for anorexia nervosa: A twin study. *Psychosomatic Medicine, 70*, 239–244.

Wadsworth, M. E., & Achenbach, T. M. (2005). Exploring the link between low socioeconomic status and psychopathology: Testing two mechanisms of the social causation hypothesis. *Journal of Consulting and Clinical Psychology, 73*, 1146–1153.

Wagner, A., Greer, P., Bailer, U., Frank, G., Henry, S., Putnam, K., … Kaye, W. H. (2006). Normal brain tissue volumes after long-term recovery in anorexia and bulimia nervosa. *Biological Psychiatry, 59*, 291–293.

Wagner, M. K. (2002). The high cost of prescription privileges. *Journal of Clinical Psychology, 58*, 677–680.

Wakefield, A. J. (1999). MMR vaccinations and autism. *Lancet, 354*, 949–950.

Wakschlag, L. S., Tolan, P. H., & Leventhal, B. L. (2010). Research review: "Ain't misbehaving": Towards a developmentally-specified nosology for preschool disruptive behavior. *The Journal of Child Psychology and Psychiatry, 51*, 3–22.

Waldinger, M. D. (2002). The neurobiological approach to premature ejaculation. *Journal of Urology, 168*, 2359–2367.

Waldman, I. D., Tackett, J. L., Van Hulle, C. A., Applegate, B, Pardini, D., Frick, P. J., & Lahey, B. B. (2011). Child and adolescent conduct disorder substantially shares genetic influences with three socioemotional dispositions. *Journal of Abnormal Psychology, 120*, 57–70.

Walker, E. F., Savoie, T., & Davis, D. (1994). Neuromotor precursors of schizophrenia. *Schizophrenia Bulletin, 20*, 441–451.

Walker, W. O. J., & Johnson, C. P. (2006). Mental retardation: Overview and diagnosis. *Pediatrics in Review, 27*, 204–212.

Wallach, J. (1994). Laboratory diagnosis of factitious disorders. *Archives of Internal Medicine, 154*, 1690–1696.

Waller, J., Kaufman, M., & Deutsch, F. (1940). Anorexia nervosa: A psychosomatic entity. *Psychosomatic Medicine, 11*, 3–16.

Wallien, M. S. C., & Cohen-Kettenis, P. T. (2008). Psychosexual outcome of gender-dysphoric children. *Journal of the American Academy of Child and Adolescent Psychiatry, 47*, 1413–1423.

Walsh, E., Moran, P., Scott, C., McKenzie, K., Burns, T., Creed, F., … Fahy, T. (2003). Prevalence of violent victimisation in severe mental illness. *British Journal of Psychiatry, 183*, 233–238.

Walters, G. (2000). Behavioral self-control training for problem drinkers: A meta-analysis of randomized control studies. *Behavior Therapy, 31*, 135–149.

Wang, A., Peterson, G., & Morphey, L. (2007). Who is more important for early adolescents' developmental choices? Peers or parents? *Marriage & Family Review, 42*, 95–122.

Wang, G. J., Geliebter, A., Volkow, N. D., Telang, F. W., Logan, J., Jayne, M. C., … Fowler, J. S. (2011). Enhanced striatal dopamine release during food stimulation in binge eating disorder. *Obesity (Silver Spring), 19*, 1601–1608.

Wang, K., Zhang, H., Bloss, C. S., Duvvuri, V., Kaye, W., Schork, N. J., … Price Foundation Collaborative Group (2011). A genome-wide association study on common SNPs and rare CNVs in anorexia nervosa. *Molecular Psychiatry, 16*, 949–959.

Wang, M., Perova, Z., Arenkiel, B. R., & Li, B. (2014). Synaptic modifications in the medial prefrontal cortex in susceptibility and resilience to stress. *Journal of Neuroscience, 34*, 7485–7492.

Wang, P. S., Berglund, P., Olfson, M., Pincus, H. A., Wells, K. B., & Kessler, R. C. (2005). Failure and delay in initial treatment contact after first onset of mental disorders in the National Comorbidity Survey Replication. *Archives of General Psychiatry, 62*, 603–613.

Wani, A., Trevino, K., Marnell, P., & Husain, M. M. (2013). Advances in brain stimulation for depression. *Annals of Clinical Psychiatry, 25*, 217–224.

Ward, T., & Hudson, S. (1996). Relapse prevention: A critical analysis. *Sexual Abuse: A Journal of Research and Treatment, 8*, 177–200.

Warheit, G., Langer, L., Zimmerman, R., & Biafora, F. (1993). Prevalence of bulimic behaviors and bulimia among a sample of the general population. *American Journal of Epidemiology, 137*, 569–576.

Warshaw, M. G., Dolan, R. T., & Keller, M. B. (2000). Suicidal behavior in patients with current or past panic disorder: Five years of prospective data from the Harvard/Brown Anxiety Research Program. *American Journal of Psychiatry, 157*, 1876–1878.

Wasserman, D., Hoven, C. W., Wasserman, C., Wall, M., Eisenberg, R., Hadlaczky, G., … Carli, V. (2015). School-based suicide prevention programmes: The SEYLE cluster-randomised, controlled trial. *Lancet, 385*(9977), 1536–1544.

Watson, D. (2005). Rethinking the mood and anxiety disorders: A quantitative hierarchical model for DSM-V. *Journal of Abnormal Psychology, 114*, 522.

Watson, H. J., & Bulik, C. M. (2013). Update on the treatment of anorexia nervosa: Review of clinical trials, practice guidelines and emerging interventions. *Psychological Medicine, 43*, 2477–2500.

Watson, J. B., & Rayner, R. (1920). Conditioned emotional reactions. *Journal of Experimental Psychology, 3*, 1–14.

Watson, T. L., Bowers, W. A., & Andersen, A. E. (2000). Involuntary treatment of eating disorders. *American Journal of Psychiatry, 157*, 1806–1810.

Weber, H., Scholz, C. J., Jacob, C. P., Heupel, J., Kittel-Schneider, S., Erhardt, A., … Reif, A. (2014). SPOCK3, a risk gene for adult ADHD and personality disorders. *European Archives in Psychiatry and Clinical Neuroscience, 264*, 409–421.

Weber, J., Coverdale, J., & Kunik, M. (2004). Delirium: Current trends in prevention and treatment. *Internal Medicine Journal, 34*, 115–121.

Webster-Stratton, C., Kolpacoff, M., & Hollinsworth, T. (1988). Self-administered videotape therapy for families with conduct-problem children: Comparison with two cost-effective treatments and a control group. *Journal of Consulting and Clinical Psychology, 56*, 558–566.

Wechsler, D. (1939). *The measurement of adult intelligence* (1st ed.). Baltimore: Waverly Press.

Wechsler, D. (2008). *Wechsler Adult Intelligence Scale: Administration and scoring manual*. San Antonio: Psychological Corporation.

Weck, F., Gropalis, M., Hiller, W., & Bleichhardt, G. (2014). Effectiveness of cognitive-behavioral group therapy for paitents with hypochondriasis (health anxiety). *Journal of Anxiety Disorders, 30*, 1–7.

Weck, F., Neng, J.M.B., Schwind, J., & Höfling, V. (2015). Exposure therapy changes dysfunctional evaluations of somatic symptoms in patients with hypochondriasis (health anxiety). A randomized controlled trial. *Journal of Anxiety Disorders, 34*, 1–7.

Weck, F., Neng, J. M., Richtberg, S., Jakob, M., & Stangier, U. (2015). Cognitive therapy versus exposure therapy for hypochondriasis (health anxiety): A randomized controlled trial. *Journal of Consulting and Clinical Psychology, 83*, 665–676.

Weijmar Schultz, W. C. M., & Van de Wiel, H. B. M. (2005). Vaginismus. In R. Balon & R. T. Segraves (Ed.), *Handbook of sexual dysfunction* (pp. 43–65). Boca Raton, FL: Taylor and Francis.

Weimer, K., Gulewitsch, M. D., Schlarb, A. A., Schwille-Kiuntke, J., Klosterhalfen, S., & Enck, P. (2013). Placebo effects in children: A review. *Pediatric Research, 74*, 96–102.

Weiner, E., & McKay, D. (2012). A preliminary evaluation of repeated exposure for depersonalization and derealisation. *Behavior Modification, 37*, 226–242.

Weiner, S. K. (2003). First person account: Living with the delusions and effects of schizophrenia. *Schizophrenia Bulletin, 29*, 877–879.

Weintraub, D., & Katz, I. R. (2005). Pharmacologic interventions for psychosis and agitation in neurodegenerative diseases: Evidence about efficacy and safety. *Psychiatric Clinics of North America, 28*, 941–983.

Weiss, L. A., Shen, Y., Korn, J. M., Arking, D. E., Miller, D. T., Fossdal, R., … Platt, O. S. (2008). Association between microdeletion and microduplication at 16p11.2 and autism. *New England Journal of Medicine, 358*, 667–675.

Weissman, M. M., Bland, R., Joyce, P. R., Newman, S., Wells, J. E., & Wittchen, H. U. (1993). Sex differences in rates of depression: Cross-national perspectives. *Journal of Affective Disorders, 29*, 77–84.

Weissman, M. M. (1994). Psychotherapy in the maintenance treatment of depression. *British Journal of Psychiatry, 26*, 42–50.

Weissman, M. M., Bland, R. C., Canino, G. J., Faravelli, C., Greenwald, S., Hwu, H. G., … Yeh, E. K. (1996). Cross-national epidemiology of major depression and bipolar disorder. *Journal of the American Medical Association, 276*, 293–299.

Weissman, M. M., Wolk, S., Goldstein, R. B., Moreau, D., Adams, P., Greenwald, S., … Wickramaratne, P. (1999). Depressed adolescents grown up. *Journal of the American Medical Association, 281*, 1707–1713.

Weisz, J. R. (1990). Cultural-familial mental retardation: A developmental perspective on cognitive performance and "helpless" behavior. In R. M. Hodapp, J. A. Burack & E. Zigler (Ed.), *Issues in the developmental approach to mental retardation* (pp. 137–168). New York: Cambridge University Press.

Welch, E., Jangmo, A., Thornton, L. M., Norring, C., von Hausswolff-Juhlin, Y., Herman, B. K., … Bulik, C. M. (2016). Treatment-seeking patients with binge-eating disorder in the Swedish national registers: clinical course and psychiatric comorbidity. *BMC Psychiatry, 16*, 1.

Weller, E., Weller, R., & Fristad, M. (1995). Bipolar diagnosis in children: Misdiagnosis, underdiagnosis, and future directions. *Journal of the American Academy of Child & Adolescent Psychiatry, 24*, 709–714.

Wellings, K., Field, J., Johnson, A. M., & Wadsworth, J. (1994). *Sexual behavior in Britain: The National Survey of sexual attitudes and lifestyles*. Harmondsworth, England: Penguin.

Welsh, R. S. (2003). Prescription privileges: Pro or con. *Clinical Psychology: Science and Practice, 10*, 371–372.

West, J. R., & Blake, C. A. (2005). Fetal alcohol syndrome: An assessment of the field. *Experimental Biology and Medicine, 230*, 354–356.

Westen, D. (1998). Implicit cognition, affect, and motivation: The end of a century-long debate. In R. Bornstein & J. Masling (Ed.), *Empirical studies of unconscious processes*. Washington, DC: American Psychological Association.

Westen, D., & Arkowitz–Westen, L. (1998). Limitations of axis II in diagnosing personality pathology in clinical practice. *American Journal of Psychiatry, 155*, 1767–1771.

Westermeyer, J., & Boedicker, A. (2000). Course, severity, and treatment of substance abuse among women versus men. *American Journal of Drug Alcohol Abuse, 26*, 523–535.

Westermeyer, J., Khawaja, I. S., Freerks, M., Sutherland, R. J., Engle, K., Johnson, D., … Hurwitz, T. (2010). Quality of sleep in patients with posttraumatic stress disorder. *Psychiatry (Edgmont), 7*, 21–27.

Wetherell, J. L., Afari, N., Ayers, C., Stoddard, J. A., Ruberg, J., Sorrell, J. T., & Patterson, T. L. (2011). Acceptance and commitment therapy for generalized anxiety disorder in older adults: A preliminary report. *Behavior Therapy, 42*, 127–134.

Wetherell, J. L., Kaplan, R. M., Kallenberg, G., Dresselhaus, T. R., Sieber, W. J., & Lang, A. J. (2004). Mental health treatment preferences of older and younger primary care patients. *The International Journal of Psychiatry in Medicine, 34*, 219–233.

Wetherell, J. L., Liu, L., Patterson, T. L., Afari, N., Ayers, C. R., Thorp, S. R., … Sorrell, J. T. (2011). Acceptance and commitment therapy for generalized anxiety disorder in older adults: A preliminary report. *Behavior Therapy, 42*, 127–134.

Wetherell, J. L., Petkus, A. J., McChesney, K., Stein, M. B., Judd, P. H., Rockwell, E., … Patterson, T. L. (2009). Older adults are less accurate than younger adults at identifying symptoms of anxiety and depression. *The Journal of Nervous and Mental Disease, 197*, 623–626.

Wetherell, J. L., Petkus, A. J., Thorp, S. R., Stein, M. B., Chavira, D. A., Campbell-Sills, L., … Sullivan, G. (2013). Age differences in treatment response to a collaborative care intervention for anxiety disorders. *The British Journal of Psychiatry, 203*, 65–72.

Weyers, S., Elaut, E., De Sutter, P., Gerris, J., T'Sjoen, G., Heylens, G., … Verstraelen, H. (2009). Long-term assessment of the physical, mental, and sexual health among transsexual women. *Journal of Sexual Medicine, 6*, 752–760.

Whaley, A. L. (1998). Cross-cultural perspective on paranoia: A focus on the Black American experience. *Psychiatric Quarterly, 69*, 325–343.

Wheaton, M. G., Berman, N. C., Fabricant, L. E., & Abramowitz, J. S. (2013). Differences in obsessive-compulsive symptoms and obsessive beliefs: A comparison between African Americans, Asian Americans, Latino Americans, and European Americans. *Cognitive Behaviour Therapy, 42*, 9–20.

Wheeler, J., George, W., & Marlatt, G. (2006). Relapse prevention for sexual offenders: Considerations for the "abstinence violation effect." *Sexual Abuse, 18*, 233–248.

White, F., & Wolf, M. (1991). The biological bases of drug tolerance and dependence. In J.A. Pratt. (Ed.), *The biological bases of drug tolerance and dependence.* (pp. 153–197). London: Academic Press.

White, S.W., Koenig, K., & Scahill, L. (2007). Social skills development intervention in children with autism spectrum disorders: A review of the intervention research. *Journal of Autism and Related Disorders, 37*, 1858–1868.

White, S. W., Kreiser, N. L., & Lerner, M. D. (2014). Autism spectrum disorders. In C. A. Alfano & D. C. Beidel (Ed.), *Comprehensive evidence-based interventions for children and adolescents* (pp. 213–229). New York: Wiley.

Whitehead, W. E., Crowell, M. D., Heller, B. R., Robinson, J. C., Schuster, M. M., & Horn, S. (1994). Modeling and reinforcement of the sick role during childhood predicts adult illness behavior. *Psychosomatic Medicine, 56*, 541–550.

Wichers, M., Geschwind, N., van Os, J., & Peeters, F. (2010). Scars in depression: Is a conceptual shift necessary to solve the problem. *Psychological Medicine, 40*, 359–365.

Widiger, T. A. (1992). Generalized social phobia versus avoidant personality disorder: A commentary on three studies. *Journal of Abnormal Psychology, 101*, 340–343.

Widiger, T. A., & Lowe, J. R. (2008). A dimensional model of personality disorder: Proposal for DSM-V. *Psychiatric Clinics of North America, 31*, 363–378.

Widiger, T. A., & Samuel, D. B. (2005). Diagnostic categories or dimensions? A question for the Diagnostic and statistical manual of mental disorders. *Journal of Abnormal Psychology, 114*, 494–504.

Wieland, J., Van Den Brink, A., & Zitman, F. G. (2015). The prevalence of personality disorders in psychiatric outpatients with borderline intellectual functioning: Comparison with outpatients from regular mental health care and outpatients with mild intellectual disabilities. *Nordic Journal of Psychiatry, 69*, 599–604.

Wiesjahn, M., Jung, E., Kremser, J. D., Rief, W., & Lincoln, T. M. (2016). The potential of continuum versus biogenetic beliefs in reducing stigmatization against persons with schizophrenia: An experimental study. *Journal of Behaviour Therapy and Experimental Psychiatry, 50*, 231–237.

Wilens, T. E., Biederman, J., Brown, S., Tanguay, S., Monuteaux, M. C., Blake, C., & Spencer, T. J. (2002). Psychiatric comorbidity and functioning in clinically referred preschool children and school-age youths with ADHD. *Journal of the American Academy of Child and Adolescent Psychiatry, 41*, 262–268.

Wilfley, D. E., Agras, W. S., Telch, C. F., Rossiter, E. M., Schneider, J. A., Cole, A. G., … Raeburn, S. D. (1993). Group cognitive-behavioral therapy and group interpersonal psychotherapy for the nonpurging bulimic individual: A controlled comparison. *Journal of Consulting and Clinical Psychology, 61*, 296–305.

Willcutt, E. G., Doyle, A. E., Nigg, J. T., Faraone, S. V., & Pennington, B. F. (2005). Validity of the executive function theory of attention-deficit/hyperactivity disorder: A meta-analytic review. *Biological Psychiatry, 57*, 1336–1346.

Williams, M. T., Domanico, J., Marques, L., Leblanc, N. J., & Turkheimer, E. (2012). Barriers to treatment among African Americans with obsessive-compulsive disorder. *Journal of Anxiety Disorders, 26*, 555–563.

Wilson, M. (1993). DSM-III and the transformation of American psychiatry: A history. *American Journal of Psychiatry, 150*, 399.

Wines, D. (1997). Exploring the applicability of criteria for substance dependence to sexual addiction. *Sexual Addiction & Compulsivity, 4*, 195–220.

Winkler, J. A., Christianson, E., Lichtenstein, M. B., Hansen, N. B., Bilenberg, N., & Stoving, R. K. (2014). Quality of life in eating disorders: A meta-analysis. *Psychiatry Research, 219*, 1–9.

Witkiewitz, K., & Marlatt, G. (2006). Overview of harm reduction treatments for alcohol problems. *International Journal of Drug Policy, 17*, 285–294.

Wittchen, H.-U., Kessler, R. C., Beesdo, K., Krause, P., & Hoyer, J. G. (2002). Generalized anxiety and depression in primary care: Prevalence, recognition, and management. *Journal of Clinical Psychiatry, 63*, 24–34.

Wittchen, H. U., Zhao, S., Kessler, R. C., & Eaton, W. W. (1994). DSM-III-R generalized anxiety disorder in the National Comorbidity Survey. *Archives of General Psychiatry, 51*, 355–364.

Wittchen, H. U., Nelson, C. B., & Lachner, G. (1998). Prevalence of mental disorders and psychosocial impairments in adolescents and young adults. *Psychological Medicine, 28*, 109–126.

Wittchen, H. U., Stein, M. B., & Kessler, R. C. (1999). Social fears and social phobia in a community sample of adolescents and young adults: Prevalence, risk factors and co-morbidity. *Psychological Medicine, 29*, 309–323.

Wittchen, H. U., & Hoyer, J. (2001). Generalized anxiety disorder: Nature and course. *Journal of Clinical Psychiatry, 62*, 15–19; discussion 20–11.

Wobrock, T., Guse, B., Cordes, J., Wolwer, W., Winterer, G., Gaebel, W., … Hasan, A. (2015). Left prefrontal high-frequency repetitive transcranial magnetic stimulation for the treatment of schizophrenia with predominant negative symptoms: A sham-controlled, randomized multicenter trial. *Biological Psychiatry, 77*, 979–988.

Wolitzky-Taylor, K. B., Castriotta, N., Lenze, E. J., Stanley, M. A., & Craske, M. G. (2010). Anxiety disorders in older adults: A comprehensive review. *Depression and Anxiety, 27*, 190–211.

Wolpe, J. (1958). *Psychotherapy by reciprocal inhibition.* Stanford, CA: Stanford University Press.

Wolraich,M.L., Hannah, J.N., Baumgartel, A., & Feurer, J.D. (1998). Examinaton of DSM-IV criteria for attention deficit/hyperactivity disorder in a county-wide sample. *Journal of Developmental and Behavioral Pediatrics: 19*, 162–168.

Wong, N. W., Beidel, D. C., & Spitalnick, J. (2014). The feasibility and acceptability of virtual environments in the treatment of childhood social anxiety disorder. *Journal of Clinical Child and Adolescent Psychology, 43*, 63–73.

Woo, E. (2000, February 18). Dr. Martin Orne: Hypnosis expert detected Hillside Strangler ruse. *Los Angeles Times*, p. A28.

Wood, J. M. (2006). The controversy over Exner's Comprehensive System for the Rorschach: The critics speak. *The Independent Practitioner*. Retrieved from http://www.division42.org/MembersArea/IPfiles/Spring06/practitioner/rorschach.php

Wood, J. M., Garb, H. N., Nezworski, M. T., Lilienfeld, S. O., & Duke, M. C. (2015). A second look at the validity of widely used Rorschach indices: Comment on Mihura, Meyer, Dumitrascu, and Bombel (2013). *Psychological Bulletin, 141*, 250–260.

Woods, D. W., & Houghton, D. C. (2014). Diagnosis, evaluation, and management of trichotillomania. *Psychiatric Clinics of North America, 37*, 301–317.

Woods, D. W., & Houghton, D. C. (2015). Evidence-based psychosocial treatments for pediatric body-focused repetitive behavior disorders. *Journal of Clinical Child & Adolescent Psychology*, 1–14.

Woodside, D. B., Garfinkel, P. E., Lin, E., Goering, P., Kaplan, A. S., Goldbloom, D. S., & Kennedy, S. H. (2001). Comparisons of men with full or partial eating disorders, men without eating disorders, and women with eating disorders in the community. *American Journal of Psychiatry, 158*, 570–574.

Woodward, A. T., Taylor, R. J., Bullard, K. M., Aranda, M. P., Lincoln, K. D., & Chatters, L. M. (2012). Prevalence of lifetime DSM-IV affective disorders among older African Americans, Black Caribbeans, Latinos, Asians and non-Hispanic white people. *International Journal of Geriatric Psychiatry, 27*, 816–827.

Woody, G. E. (2014). Antagonist models for treating persons with substance use disorders. *Current Psychiatry Reports, 16*, 489.

Woolfenden, S. R., Williams, K., & Peat, J. K. (2002). Family and parenting interventions for conduct disorder and delinquency: A meta-analysis of randomised controlled trials. *Archives of Disease in Childhood, 86*, 251–256.

Wootton, B. M. (2016). Remote cognitive-behavior therapy for obsessive-compulsive symptoms: A meta-analysis. *Clinical Psychology Review, 43*, 103–113.

World Health Organization. *Depression.* Retrieved from http://www.who.int/mental_health/management/depression/definition/en/

World Health Organization. (1975). *Declaration of Helsinki.* Retrieved from http://history.nih.gov/research/downloads/helsinki.pdf

World Health Organization (Ed.). (1992). *International statistical classification of diseases and related health problems, Tenth Revision.* Geneva: Author.

World Health Organization. (2007). International classification of disease. Retrieved from http://www.who.int/classifications/icd/en/

World Health World Health Organization. (2011). *WHO report on the global tobacco epidemic, 2011.* Geneva: World Health Organization.

World Health World Health Organization. (2014). *Preventing suicide: A global imperative.* Geneva: World Health Organization.

Wright, J. C., Rabe-Hesketh, S., Woodruff, P. W., David, A. S., Murray, R. M., & Bullmore, E. T. (2000). Meta-analysis of regional brain volumes in schizophrenia. *American Journal of Psychiatry, 157*, 16–25.

Wright, P., Takei, N., Murray, R. M., & Sham, P. C. (1999). Seasonality, prenatal influenza exposure, and schizophrenia. In E. S. Susser, A.S. Brown, & J. M. Gorman (Eds.), *Prenatal exposures in schizophrenia* (pp. 89–112). Washington, DC: American Psychiatric Press.

Wu, E. Q., Birnbaum, H. G., Shi, L., Ball, D. E., Kessler, R. C., Moulis, M., & Aggarwal, J. (2005). The economic burden of schizophrenia in the United States in 2002. *Journal of Clinical Psychiatry, 66*, 1122–1129.

Wu, L.-T., & Blazer, D. G. (2011). Illicit and nonmedical drug use among older adults: A review. *Journal of Aging and Health, 23*, 481–504.

Wu, L.-T., & Blazer, D. G. (2014). Substance use disorders and psychiatric comorbidity in mid and later life: A review. *International Journal of Epidemiology, 43*, 304–317.

Wykes, T., Hayward, P., Thomas, N., Green, N., Surguladze, S., Fannon, D., & Landau, S. (2005). What are the effects of group cognitive behaviour therapy for voices? A randomized trial. *Schizophrenia Research, 77*, 201–210.

Yamada, K., Watanabe, K., Nemoto, N., Fujita, H., Chikaraishi, C., Yamauchi, K., … Kanba, S. (2006). Prediction of medication noncompliance in outpatients with schizophrenia: 2-year follow-up study. *Psychiatry Research, 141*, 61–69.

Yamamoto, T., Yoshizawa, K., Kubo, S., Emoto, Y., Hara, K., Waters, B., … Ikematsu, K. (2015). Autopsy report for a caffeine intoxication case and review of the current literature. *Journal of Toxicologic Pathology, 28*, 33–36.

Yap, P. M. (1967). Classification of the culture-bound reactive syndromes. *Australia and New Zealand Journal of Psychiatry, 1*, 172–179.

Yehuda, R. (2002). Current concepts: Posttraumatic stress disorder. *New England Journal of Medicine, 346*, 108–114.

Yorbik, O., Birmaher, B., Axelson, D., Williamson, D. E., & Ryan, N. D. (2004). Clinical characteristics of depressive symptoms in children and adolescents with major depressive disorder. *Journal of Clinical Psychiatry, 65*, 1654–1659.

Young, L. J., & Wang, Z. (2004). The neurobiology of pair bonding. *Nature Neuroscience, 7*, 1048–1054.

Young, R. C. (2005). Evidence-based pharmacological treatment of geriatric bipolar disorder. *Psychiatric Clinics of North America, 28*, 837–869.

Yuen, E. K., Herbert, J. D., Forman, E. M., Goetter, E. M., Comer, R., & Bradley, J. C. (2013). Treatment of social anxiety disorder using online virtual environments in second life. *Behavior Therapy, 44*, 51–61.

Yule, W., Bolton, D., Udwin, O., Boyle, S., O'Ryan, D., & Nurrish, J. (2000). The long-term psychological effects of a disaster experienced in adolescence: I: The incidence and course of PTSD. *Journal of Child Psychology & Psychiatry, 41*, 503–511.

Yurgelun-Todd, D. A., & Ross, A. J. (2006). Functional magnetic resonance imaging studies in bipolar disorder. *CNS Spectrums, 11*, 287–297.

Zahid, M. A., & Ohaeri, J. U. (2010). Relationship of family caregiver burden with quality of care and psychopathology in a sample of Arab subjects with schizophrenia. *BMC Psychiatry, 10*, 71.

Zahl, D. L., & Hawton, K. (2004). Repetition of deliberate self-harm and subsequent suicide risk: Long-term follow-up study of 11,583 patients. *British Journal of Psychiatry, 185*, 70–75.

Zanarini, M. C., Gunderson, J. G., Marino, M. F., Schwartz, E. O., & Frankenburg, F. R. (1989). Childhood experiences of borderline patients. *Comprehensive Psychiatry, 30*, 18–25.

Zanarini, M. C., Frankenburg, F. R., Hennen, J., & Silk, K. R. (2003). The longitudinal course of borderline psychopathology: 6-year prospective follow-up of the phenomenology of borderline personality disorder. *American Journal of Psychiatry, 160*, 274–283.

Zanni, G. R., & Stavis, P. F. (2007). The effectiveness and ethical justification of psychiatric outpatient commitment. *The American Journal of Bioethics, 7*, 31–41.

Zhang, W., Ross, J., & Davidson, J. R. (2004). Social anxiety disorder in callers to the Anxiety Disorders Association of America. *Depression and Anxiety, 20*, 101–106.

Zhang, W., Deng, W., Yao, L., Xiao, Y., Li, F., Liu, J.,... Gong, Q. (2015). Brain structural abnormalities in a group of never-medicated patients with long-term schizophrenia. *American Journal of Psychiatry, 172*, 995–1003.

Zhang, X., Norton, J., Carriere, I., Ritchie, K., Chaudieu, I., & Ancelin, M. L. (2015). Risk factors for late-onset generalized anxiety disorder: Results from a 12-year prospective cohort (the ESPRIT study). *Translational Psychiatry, 5*, e536.

Zhou, J. N., Hofman, M. A., Gooren, L. J., & Swaab, D. F. (1995). A sex difference in the human brain and its relation to transsexuality. *Nature, 378*, 68–70.

Zhou, X., Hetrick, S. E., Cuijpers, P., Qin, B., Barth, J., Whittington, C. J., ... Xie, P. (2015). Comparative efficacy and acceptability of psychotherapies for depression in children and adolescents: A systematic review and network meta-analysis. *World Psychiatry, 14*, 207–222.

Zipfel, S., Giel, K. E., Bulik C. M., Hay, P., & Schmidt, U. (2015). Anorexia nervosa: Aetiology, assessment, and treatment. *Lancet Psychiatry, 2*, 1099–1111.

Zirpolo, K. (as told to Debbie Nathan) (2005, October 30). A long delayed apology from one of the accusers in the notorious McMartin Pre-school molestation case. *Los Angeles Times*. http://articles.latimes.com/2005/oct/30/magazine/tm-mcmartin44

Zoccolotti, P., & Friedmann, N. (2010). From dyslexia to dyslexias, from dysgraphia to dysgraphias, from a cause to causes: A look at current research on developmental and dysgraphia. *Cortex: A Journal Devoted to the Study of the Nervous System and Behavior, 46*, 1211–1215.

Zohar, A. H., & Felz, L. (2001). Ritualistic behavior in young children. *Journal of Abnormal Child Psychology, 29*, 121–128.

Zucker, K. J. (2004). Gender identity development and issues. *Child and Adolescent Psychiatric Clinics of North America, 13*, 551–568.

Zucker, K. J. (2008). On the "natural history" of gender identity disorder in children. *Journal of the American Academy of Child and Adolescent Psychiatry, 47*, 1361–1363.

Zucker, N., Ferriter, C., Best, S., & Brantley, A. (2005). Group parent training: A novel approach for the treatment of eating disorders. *Eating Disorders: The Journal of Treatment and Prevention, 13*, 391–405.

Zucker, N., Copeland, W., Franz, L., Carpenter, K., Keeling, L., Angold, A., & Egger, H. (2015). Psychological and psychosocial impairment in preschoolers with selective eating. *Pediatrics, 136*, e582–e590.

Zuo, L., Tan, Y., Zhang, X., Wang, X., Krystal, J., Tabakoff, B., ... Luo, X. (2015). A new genomewide association meta-analysis of alcohol dependence. *Alcoholism: Clinical and Experimental Research, 39*, 1388–1395.

Credits

Photo Credits

Chapter 1 **page 1**: (woman) Image Source/Getty Images; (solder) iStockphoto/Thinkstock; **page 4**: **(left)** epa european pressphoto agency b.v./Alamy Stock Photo; **(center)** WENN Ltd/Alamy Stock Photo; **(right)** Sueddeutsche Zeitung Photo/Alamy Stock Photo; **page 6**: PacificCoastNews/Newsco; **page 12**: Paul Bevitt/Alamy Stock Photo; **page 13**: bilwissedition Ltd. & Co. KG/Alamy Stock Photo; **page 14**: Portrait of Avicenna (c.992-1037), lithography by F Perez (litho), Spanish School, (19th century)/Museo Real Academia de Medicina, Madrid, Spain/Index/The Bridgeman Art Library; **page 16**: Charles Ciccione/Photo Researchers, Inc.; **page 17**: Photo Researchers, Inc/Alamy Stock Photo; **page 18**: Akademie/Alamy Stock Photo; **page 21**: Photo Researchers, Inc/Alamy Stock Photo; **page 22**: George Rinhart/Corbis/Getty Images; **page 22**: Feng Yu/Shutterstock; **page 29**: Joe Wrinn/Time & Life Pictures/Getty Images; **page 30**: Science Source; **page 32**: Volt Collection/Shutterstock; **page 33**: Jessica Brandi Lifland/Newscom; **page 34**: Thinkstock

Chapter 2 **page 38**: (pencil) John Madden/iStockphoto (stickers) tarras79/iStockphoto; (cups) micropic/iStockphoto; (clipboard) Robyn Mackenzie/iStockphoto; **page 49**: **(left)** Katrina Brown/Shutterstock; **(right)** Fotolia; **page 53**: National Geographic Creative/Alamy Stock Photo; **page 57**: Donn Dughi/Bride Lane Library/Popperfoto/Getty Images; **page 62**: **(top)**Kenneth Wiedemann/Getty Images; **(bottom)** Getty Images; **page 63**: James Steidl/Shutterstock; **page 65**: Monkey Business Images/Shutterstock; **page 66**: Rawpixel/Fotolia; **page 68**: Ben Edwards/Getty Images;

Chapter 3 **page 75**: (puzzle) Greg Nicholas/iStockphoto; (woman) Christopher Robbins/Getty Images; (red bow) Elena Schweitzer/Shutterstock; (house key) Zentilia/Shutterstock; (house key) Zentilia/Shutterstock; **page 78**: Brian Maudsley/Shutterstock; **page 81**: David Livingston/Getty Images; **page 84**: Svyatoslav Lypynskyy/Fotolia; **page 85**: Mangostock/Shutterstock; **page 89**: Wright, Kathleen M., et al., 2005. Structured Clinical Interview Guide for Psychological Screening Programs at Post-Deployment. RESEARCH REPORT #2005-001. US Army Medical Research Unit-Europe, Walter Reed Army Institute of Research; **page 99**: Hero Images Inc./Alamy Stock Photo; **page 103**: Phanie/Alamy Stock Photo; **page 107**: Pearson Education/PH College: **page 109**: Darren1/Stockimo/Alamy Stock Photo

Chapter 4 **page 114**: (chemist) Andres/Shutterstock; (test tubes) Africa Studios/Shutterstock; **page 122**: Bryant Jayme/Shutterstock; **page 127**: Pavel L Photo and Video/Shutterstock; **page 130**: Hero Images Inc./Alamy Stock Photo; **page 132**: Ross D. Franklin/AP Images; **page 136**: Dieter Spears/Getty Images; **page 140**: Dan Lampariello/Reuters; **page 143**: Blend Images/Alamy Stock Photo; **page 144**: Jae C. Hong/AP Images; **page 157**: Erika Schultz/Seattle Times/MCT/Newscom;

Chapter 5 **page 161**: (notepads) Efekt.net/Getty Images; (paper stacks) Efekt.net/Getty Images; **page 166**: Karen H. Ilagan/Shutterstock; **page 169**: Palmer Kane LLC/Shutterstock; **page 171**: **(left)** Tom Watson/NY Daily News/Getty Images; **(right)** Bettmann/Getty Images; **(bottom)** MichaelXuereb.com/Alamy Stock Photo; **page 173**: Rex Features/AP Images; **page 175**: Anonymous; **page 177**: Darko Vrcan/123RF; **page 193**: Courtesy of Suzanne Mouton Odum; Jupiterimages/Creatas/Getty Images

Chapter 6 **page 197**: (stethoscope)Caspar Benson/Getty Images; (surgical equipment) Krechet/Shutterstock; (pills)Heather Laing/iStockphoto; (syringe) Roman Sigaev/iStockphoto; **page 200**: Collection Bourgeron/Bridgeman Images; **page 207**: Shutterstock; **page 212**: Ambrophoto/Shutterstock; **page 213**: (cell phone frame) Fotolia; (screenshot of app) Courtesy of the National Center for Telehealth & Technology/Department of Defense **page 216**: Newscom; **page 219**: Fotolia; **page 226**: epa european pressphoto agency b.v./Alamy Stock Photo

Chapter 7 **page 229**: (raindrops) Vectoria/Shutterstock; (eyelashes/earphones) ICHIRO/Getty Images; **page 234**: Gary B/Alamy Stock Photo; **page 235**: Shutterstock; **page 239**: Tab62/Fotolia; **page 243**: WENN Ltd/Alamy Stock Photo; **page 246**: Ilike/fotolia; **page 250**: **(top)** akg-images/Newscom; **(bottom)** Jim Corwin/Getty Images; **page 253**: Rene Burri/Magnum Photos, Inc.; **page 255**: Paul Sakuma/AP Images; **page 260**: Getty Images; **page 263**: Wavebreak Media Ltd/Alamy Stock Photo; **page 271**: Will McIntyre/Science Source; **page 272**: BSIP SA/Alamy Stock Photo;

Chapter 8 page (knife and fork) Ethan Boisvert/Shutterstock; (tape measure) Siede Preis/Getty Images; (profile) Image Source/Getty Images; **page 278**: (bottom left) AF archive/Alamy Stock Photo; (bottom right) epa european pressphoto agency b.v./Alamy Stock Photo; (top, left) Sydney Alford/Alamy Stock Photo; (top, right) Interfoto/Alamy Stock Photo; **page 280**: Getty Images; **page 283**: AP Images; **page 287**: Marka/Alamy Stock Photo; **page 288**: Interfoto/Alamy Stock Photo; **page 290**: Larry Busacca/Getty Images for HSBC; **page 302**: Voisin/Phanie/SuperStock; **page 303**: Josh Jennings; **page 306**: Paintings/Shutterstock; **page 308**: Neilson Barnard/Getty Images; **page 309**: Frédéric Cirou/PhotoAlto/AGE Fotostock;

Chapter 9 **page 320**: (candy hearts) Zee/Alamy; (candy hearts) D. Hurst/Alamy; (Hershey kiss) skodonnell/iStockphoto; (silhouette) Mode Images Limited/Alamy; **page 323**: Keystone Pictures USA/Alamy Stock Photo; **page 324**: Bettman/Contributor/Getty Images; **page 326**: **(left)** Max Frost/Fotolia; **(right)** Aqnus/Fotolia; **page 330**: Daniel Zuchnik/Contributor/Getty Images; **page 332**: **(top)** Everett Collection Historical/Alamy Stock Photo; **(bottom)** Larry Busacca/Getty Images for Glamour; **page 333**: © Maciej Dakowicz/Alamy Stock Photo; **page 350**: Courtesy of vagismus.com

Chapter 10 **page 364**: (corks) Ray Torino/Shutterstock; (wine rings) Thomas Northcut/Getty Images; (jacks) C Squared Studios/Getty Images; (toy cars) Stas Vulkanov/Shutterstock; **page 366**: Kzenon/Fotolia; **page 372**: **(top)** Incamerastock/Alamy Stock Photo; **(bottom)** Vitor costa/Shutterstock; **page 374**: Carla Gottgens/Bloomberg/Getty Images; **page 376**: **(left)** Martin M Rotker/Photo Researchers/Getty Images; **(right)** Martin M Rotker/Science Source/Getty Images; **page 377**: Rick's Photography/Shutterstock; **page 384**: Jeffrey Zalesny/Fotolia; **page 387**: PA Images MATT DUNHAM/AP/Press Association Images; **page 388**: **(left)** Science Photo Library/Shutterstock; **(right)** Science Source; **page 390**: Gopal Chitrakar/Reuters; **page 397**: Life Boat/Getty Images; **page 399**: Shutterstock; **page 404**: John Boykin/PhotoEdit, Inc.; **page 406**: Shutterstock

Chapter 11 **page 412**: (television) Koksharov Dmitry/Shutterstock; (radio) Gino Crescoli/Getty Images; (eye) Getty Images; (newspaper) David Freund/Gerry Images; **page 414**: Gideon Mendel/Getty Images; **page 417**: PhotoAlto Agency RF Collections/Getty Images; **page 419**: Photo Researchers, Inc./Science Source; **page 420**: Damian Dovarganes/AP Images; **page 423**: Fotolia; **page 427**: Dan Atkin/Alamy Stock Photo; **page 429**: Richard Carson/Corbis; **page 434**: Joshua Rainey/Fotolia; **page 440**: Kablonk/SuperStock; **page 442**: Ted Streshinsky/Corbis; **page 443**: Monty Rakusen/Cultura/Getty Images; **page 445**: Ozgurdonmaz/E+/Getty Images;

Chapter 12 **page 448**: Compassionate Eye Foundation/Siri Stafford/Getty Images; **page 450**: WavebreakmediaMicro/Fotolia; **page 454**: Everett Collection; **page 458**: Chris Whitehead/Getty Images; **page 460**: Mark Elias/AP Images; **page 469**: **(left)** Ilya Andriyanov/Shutterstock; **(right)** Glow Images; **page 471**: RosalreneBetancourt 1/Alamy Stock Photo; **page 476**: Gelpi JM/Shutterstock; **page 477**: Wong Sze Fei/Fotolia; **page 478**: Mixa/Glow Images; **page 480**: **(bottom)** Superstock; **(top)** Guy Cali/Glow Images; **page 483**: Dr. Marsha Linehan

Chapter 13 **page 486**: (gift tag) Sudhir Karnataki/iStockphoto; (socks and shoes) C Squared Studios/Getty Images; (shirt) Ocean/Corbis; **page 490**: Angela Hampton/Alamy; **page 492**: BSIP SA/Alamy Stock Photo; **page 504**: Nancy Kaszerman/Newscom; **page 512**: Yves Gellie/Corbis; **page 518**: Alamy; **page 522**: Gibson/Newscom

Chapter 14 **page 525**: (newspaper stack) Magicoven/Shutterstock; (businessman) Estudio Maia/Shutterstock; (baby cot) Photomak/Shutterstock; (vintage TV) Tungphoto/Shutterstock; (stethoscope) Michael Giannaccio/Shutterstock; **page 528**: Alamy; **page 530**: **(bottom)** Shutterstock; **(top)** Tom Foxall/Fotolia; **page 535**: Alamy; **page 544**: **(left)** Vinicius Tupinamba/Fotolia; (center) bst2012/Fotolia; **(right)** Savannah1969/Fotolia; **page 547**: Photo Researchers, Inc.; **page 555**: Vinicius Tupinamba/Fotolia; **page 556**: A. Pakieka/Photo Researchers, Inc.; **page 557**: Jeff Moreland/Newscom; **page 559**: WitthayaP/Shutterstock

Chapter 15 **page 564**: Sashkin/Shutterstock; **page 568**: Jerry Cooke/Photo Researchers, Inc.; **page 569**: Ted Foxx/Alamy; **page 572**: AFP/Staff/Getty Images; **page 575**: Douglas C Pizac/AP Images; **page 576**: AP Images; **page 578**: AP Images; **page 579**: Rob/Fotolia; **page 582**: Alina Solovyova-Vincent/Getty Images; **page 590**: National Archives and Records Administration

Text Credits

page 109: Reprinted with Permission from the Diagnostic and Statistical Manual of Mental Disorders, Fifth Edition, (Copyright 2013). American Psychiatric Association; **page 178**: Data from Grant, Jon E., and Marc N. Potenza. "Gender-Related Differences in Individuals Seeking Treatment for Kleptomania." CNS Spectrums. U.S. National Library of Medicine, Mar. 2008. Web. 12 Aug. 2016.; **page 264**: Lilienfeld, S., et al. (2009). Psychology: From inquiry to understanding. Allyn & Bacon. Copyright 2009. Reprinted by permission of Pearson Education; **page 413**: Weiner, S.K. (2003). First person account: Living with delusions and effects of schizophrenia. Schizophrenia Bulletin, 29, 877–879. Copyright 2007, Oxford University Press and the Maryland Psychiatric Research Center (MPRC). **page 460**: http://www.criminalprofiling.com/Psychiatric-Testimony-of-Jeffrey-Dahmer_s115.html; **page 527**: http://www.aoa.gov/Aging_Statistics/future_growth/future_growth.aspx#age/U.S. Department Of Health And Human Services; **page 533**: Conwell, Y, Van Orden, K, & Caine, E.D., 2011, Suicide in older adults. Psychiatric Clinics of North America, 34 (2): 451–468. FIG1 http://www.sciencedirect.com/science/article/pii/S0193953X11000207; **page 565**: Radford, B. [managing editor]. Skeptical Inquirer. Copyright © 2001 by the Committee for the Scientific Investigation of Claims of the Paranormal.

Name Index

Subject Index

D

E

F

G

H

N

O